49th Power Sources Conference 2023

Fort Washington, Maryland, USA
27 - 29 June 2023

ISBN: 979-8-3313-0301-3

Printed from e-media with permission by:

Curran Associates, Inc.
57 Morehouse Lane
Red Hook, NY 12571

CURRAN ASSOCIATES INC. proceedings.com

Some format issues inherent in the e-media version may also appear in this print version.

Palisades Convention Management
729 7th Avenue, Suite 1402A
New York, NY 10019-6991

Phone: (212) 460-9700

www.pcm411.com

Additional copies of this publication are available from:

Curran Associates, Inc.
57 Morehouse Lane
Red Hook, NY 12571 USA
Phone: 845-758-0400
Fax: 845-758-2633
Email: curran@proceedings.com
Web: www.proceedings.com

49th POWER SOURCES CONFERENCE

• June 27-29, 2023, Gaylord National Resort & Convention Center, Fort Washington, MD, USA

Welcome to the Power Sources Conference 2023

Welcome!
We are pleased to welcome you to the 49th Power Sources Conference at the Gaylord National Resort & Convention Center in Fort Washington, MD. Our last gathering was in 2018 and we are looking forward to seeing everyone again. This conference was started in 1947 in Fort Monmouth, NJ, and has been managed and produced by General Technical Services and Palisades Convention Management continuously since 1994. This year's meeting will focus on advanced energy storage and power generation technologies (largely, but not exclusively, electrochemical), which are of interest to the DoD, other Government agencies, and the civilian marketplace. As usual, the orientation will be toward advancements in power sources, renewable energy power generation, advanced materials and processes including safety, quality control, testing mechanisms, and power management. In addition, contributions to prototype development, manufacturing technology, device and systems engineering, and economic and environmental considerations will be presented. This year's technical program reflects continued strong interest in high-energy high-power batteries, fuel cells, and other power generation technologies for man portable power, mobile ground vehicles, sea, and aerospace applications. We are certain that you will also enjoy the exhibits and networking opportunities in our convenient National Capital Region setting.

Enjoy the Conference!

~ 49th Power Sources Conference Committee

49th POWER SOURCES CONFERENCE

• **June 27-29, 2023, Gaylord National Resort & Convention Center Fort Washington, MD, USA**

Table of Contents

Ballroom
10:20AM–
12:00 PM

2-1: DEVELOPMENT OF HIGH POWER/HIGH ENERGY DENSITY LITHIUM OXYHALIDE RESERVE BATTERY ~ Paper Unavailable
Hasan Gocmez, *Kutahya Dumlupınar University*
A. Karabatak, *PILTEK Energy System Ltd. Co*
Yener Yesilirmak, *TUBITAK-SAGE*
Anil Alkan, *TUBITAK-SAGE*
Volkan Kalender, *TUBITAK-SAGE*

2-2: Micro-Reserve Battery ~ Paper Unavailable
John Hondred, *Cornerstone Research Group*
Brian Henslee, *Cornerstone Research Group*
Frank Zalar, *Cornerstone Research Group*
Becc Browning, *Cornerstone Research Group*

2-3: Glass Ampoule Analysis Capability Transition...13
Kevin M. O'Connor Jr, *U.S. Army Combat Capabilities Development Command Armaments Center*
Timothy Holmquist, *Southwest Research Institute*
Sidney Chocron, *Southwest Research Institute*
Art Nicholls, *Southwest Research Institute*

2-4: High Power Li/CF_x-MnO_2 Hybrid Technology...16
Mario Destephen, *EaglePicher Technologies, LLC*
Gary Schmidt, *EaglePicher Technologies, LLC*
Ernest Ndzebet, *EaglePicher Technologies, LLC*
David Darch, *EaglePicher Technologies, LLC*

2-5: High Energy Primary Technology Development...19
David Darch, *EaglePicher Technologies, LLC*
Mario Destephen, *EaglePicher Technologies, LLC*
Ernest Ndzebet, *EaglePicher Technologies, LLC*

Session 3: Advanced Materials & Processes I

Chair: Lauren Morris, *U.S. Army CCDC Armaments Center*
Co-Chair: Thomas Jiang

Monday
6/26/2023
Riverview
Ballroom 5
10:20AM–
12:00 PM

3-1: High-Purity, CO_2-Derived Multiwall Carbon Nanotube Formulations for Realizing High-Energy and High-Power Lithium-Ion Cells...23
David L. Wood, III, *SkyNano, LLC*
Anna Douglas, *SkyNano, LLC*

3-2: Integrated Micro-Supercapacitors via Laser Induced Graphene from Photoresist ~ Paper Unavailable
John Hondred, *Cornerstone Research Group*
Rebecca Browning, *Cornerstone Research Group*
Suprem Das, *Kansas State University*

3-3: Direct Battery Electrolyte Heating and Temperature Maintenance at Low Temperatures...27
Jahangir Rastegar, *Omnitek Partners, LLC*

3-4: Novel Si Anode and High Ni NCM Cathode for High Energy Applications...31
Jun Wang, *EaglePicher Technologies, LLC*
Felix Guzman, *EaglePicher Technologies, LLC*
Sean Su, *EaglePicher Technologies, LLC*
Arthur Dobley, *EaglePicher Technologies, LLC*
Karthik Ramaswami, *EaglePicher Technologies, LLC*
Frank Puglia, *EaglePicher Technologies, LLC*

3-5: Mission Engineering applications for Battery System Maintainability ~ Paper Unavailable
Badruddin Pirani, *NSWC Crane*

Session 4: Battery Safety / Quality / Testing II

Chair: Giuseppe Di Bennedetto, *U.S. Army DEVCOM Armaments Center*
Co-Chair: Clinton Winchester, *NSWC - Carderock*

Monday
6/26/2023
Riverview Ballroom 1-2-2
1:20–3:00 PM

Session 5: Fuel Cells, Fuel Processing & Storage I

Chair: Kevin Centeck, *U.S. Army CCDC Ground Vehicle Power & Mobility*
Co-Chair: Deryn Chu

Monday
6/26/2023
Eastern Shore 2 Ballroom
1:20–3:00 PM

Ryan H. DeBlock, *U.S. Naval Research Laboratory*
Jeffrey W. Long, *U.S. Naval Research Laboratory*

Session 6: Advanced Materials & Processes II

Chair: Jeffrey Read, *U.S. Army Research Laboratory*

Monday 6/26/2023 Riverview Ballroom 5 1:20–3:00 PM

Session 7: Battery Safety / Quality / Testing III

Chair: Mark Tisher, *U.S. Naval Surface Warfare Center*

Monday 6/26/2023 Riverview Ballroom 1-2-2 3:20–5:00 PM

Session 8: Fuel Cells, Fuel Processing & Storage II

Chair: Terry DuBois, *U.S. Army CCDC C5ISR*
Co-Chair: Ian Jakupca, *NASA*

Monday 6/26/2023 Eastern Shore 2 Ballroom

3:20–5:00 PM

8-1: **JP-8 Fuel Cell Powered Electric Vehicle and Generator...103**
Saurabh A. Vilekar, *Precision Combustion, Inc.*
Christian Junaedi, *Precision Combustion, Inc.*
Tim LaBreche, *Precision Combustion, Inc.*
Subir Roychoudhury, *Precision Combustion, Inc.*
Kevin Centeck, *U.S. Army Combat Capabilities Development Command (DEVCOM) Ground Vehicle Systems Center (GVSC)*

8-2: **Solid Oxide Fuel Cell Manufacture by Computationally Driven Aerosol Jet Printing...105**
Aaron Bain, *Tennessee Tech University*
Rory Roberts, *Tennessee Tech University*
Thomas Jenkins, *UES, Inc.*
Qiuhong Zhang, *University of Dayton Research Institute*
Bang Tsao, *University of Dayton Research Institute*
L. Jay Deiner, *City University of New York*
Joseph Fellner, *U.S. Air Force Research Laboratory*
Douglas Dudis, *U.S. Air Force Research Laboratory*

8-3: **Spatially Resolving Heterogenous Chemistry on SOFC electrodes with Operando Optical Methods ~ Paper Unavailable**
Elias D. Pomeroy, *U.S. Naval Research Laboratory*
William A. Maza, *U.S. Naval Research Laboratory*
Daniel A. Steinhurst, *Nova Research Inc.*
Jeffrey C. Owrutsky, *U.S. Naval Research Laboratory*
Robert A. Walker, *Montana State University*

8-4: **Power and Energy for Small Unmanned Aerial Systems...109**
Deryn Chu, *U.S. Army Research Laboratory*

8-5: **Fuel Cell Power Sources for the Dismounted Soldier ~ Paper Unavailable**
Shailesh Shah, *U.S. Army DEVCOM C5ISR*
Kevin Chu, *U.S. Army PEO Soldier - Project Manager Integrated Visual Augmentation System*
Richard Scenna, *U.S. Army DEVCOM C5ISR Center*
Dave Schimmel, *U.S. Army PEO Soldier - Project Manager Integrated Visual Augmentation System*

8-6: **Purification of windshield wiper fluid for fuel cell applications ~ Paper Unavailable**
Richard Scenna, *U.S. Army Devcom C5ISR*

Session 9: Advanced Materials & Processes III

Chair: Corey Love, *U.S. Naval Research Laboratory*

Monday
6/26/2023
Riverview
Ballroom 5
3:20–5:00 PM

9-1: **Powder Bed Fusion of Nontoxic Copper(I) Sulfide Thermoelectric Materials for Energy Harvesting...113**
Raden Gustinvil, *University of Miami*
Giuseppe L. Di Benedetto, *U.S. Army Combat Capabilities Development Command Armaments Center*
Donald Skelton, *U.S. Army Combat Capabilities Development Command Armaments Center*
Samuel Stuart, *U.S. Navy Naval Surface Warfare Center*
Emrah Celik, *University of Miami*

9-2: **Decentralized Energy Generation and Environmental Impact Reduction via Perovskite Solar Cells...117**
Lissette Rodríguez-Cabañas, *U.S. Army Futures Command, Combat Capabilities Development Command (DEVCOM)*
Calvin Duong, *U.S. Army Futures Command, Combat Capabilities Development Command (DEVCOM)*
Bradley Stanley, *U.S. Army Futures Command, Combat Capabilities Development Command (DEVCOM)*
Andre Slonopas, *U.S. Army Futures Command, Combat Capabilities Development Command (DEVCOM)*

9-3: **Hydrogen-fueled Power Generator using Nanogalvanic Aluminum Alloy to Produce Hydrogen...122**
Girish Srinivas, *TDA Research, Inc.*
Brady Clapsaddle, *TDA Research, Inc.*
Joe Fredrickson, *TDA Research, Inc.*

Session 10: Battery Safety / Quality / Testing IV

Tuesday
6/27/2023
Riverview Ballroom
1-2-2
8:20–10:00 AM

Session 11: Fuel Cells, Fuel Processing & Storage III

Tuesday
6/27/2023
Eastern Shore 2 Ballroom
8:20–10:00 AM

Session 12: Secondary Lithium Batteries / Li-Ion Batteries I

Co-Chair: Jeffrey Read, *U.S. Army Research Laboratory*

Tuesday
6/27/2023
Riverview
Ballroom 5
8:20–10:00 AM

Poster Session

Tuesday
6/27/2023
Riverview
Ballroom

Session 13: Molten Salt Batteries - Primary & Secondary I

Chair: Patrick Taylor, *U.S. Army CCDC Aviation and Missile Center*
Co-Chair: Sam Stuart, *NSWC*

Tuesday 6/27/2023 Riverview Ballroom 1-2-2 1:30–3:10 PM

Session 14: Customer

Chair: Homeshwar Lalbahadur, *U.S. Army DEVCOM Armaments Center*
Co-Chair: Stanley Rodrigues, *AFRL Wright Patterson*

Tuesday 6/27/2023 Eastern Shore 2 Ballroom 1:30–3:10 PM

Session 15: Secondary Lithium Batteries / Li-Ion Batteries II

Chair: Julianne Douglas, *U.S. Army CCDC C5ISR*

Tuesday 6/27/2023 Riverview Ballroom 5 1:30–3:10 PM

Session 16: Battery Safety / Quality / Testing V

Tuesday
6/27/2023
Riverview Ballroom 1-2-2
3:30–5:30 PM

Session 17: Powering The Force I

Tuesday
6/27/2023
Eastern

Shore 2 Ballroom 3:30–5:30 PM

Session 18: Secondary Lithium Batteries / Li-Ion Batteries III

Tuesday 6/27/2023 Riverview Ballroom 5 3:30–5:30 PM

Session 19: Molten Salt Batteries - Primary & Secondary II

Chair: Richard Dratler, *U.S. Army DEVCOM Armaments Center*
Co-Chair: Adrian Parker, *NSWC Crane*

Wendsday 6/28/2023 Riverview Ballroom 1-2-2 8:30–10:10 AM

Session 20: Powering The Force II

Wendsday 6/28/2023 Eastern Shore 2 Ballroom 8:30–10:10 AM

Session 21: Secondary Lithium Batteries / Li-Ion Batteries IV

Wendsday 6/28/2023 Riverview Ballroom 5 8:30–10:10 AM

Session 22: Molten Salt Batteries - Primary & Secondary III

Chair: Sean Rayman , *USAF/AFMC*

Wendsday 6/28/2023 Riverview Ballroom 1-2-2 10:30 AM –12:10 PM

Session 25: Aqueous Batteries

Chair: Charles Patrissi, *NUWC*

Wendsday 6/28/2023 Riverview Ballroom 1-2-2 1:40–3:20 PM

Session 26: Special Session

Wendsday 6/28/2023 Eastern Shore 2 Ballroom 1:40–3:20 PM

Session 27: Battery Electrolytes & Interfaces II

Chair: Matthew Limpert, *U.S. Army CCDC C5ISR*

Wendsday
6/28/2023
Riverview
Ballroom 5
1:40–3:20 PM

Improved Safety Lithium-ion Chemistry Development

Owen Crowther, Logan Wittmaier, Alex Raney, Mario Destephen and James Bond
R&D
EaglePicher Technologies
Joplin, MO, 64801
owen.crowther@eaglepicher.com / 1-417-208-1787

Abstract

Safer Lithium-ion (Li-ion) chemistries and batteries are needed to support various new high-energy and power applications. Li-ion batteries under abuse conditions can undergo thermal runaway, leading to a battery fire. EaglePicher Technologies has developed a reduced flammability (RF) electrolyte that increases cell safety while maintaining cell performance, including high rate and cold temperature discharge conditions. Cell safety and performance were demonstrated for the RF electrolyte using 26650 cells with a lithium iron phosphate (LFP) cathode and 18650 cells with lithium nickel manganese cobalt oxide (NMC111). Both the LFP 26650 and NMC111 18650 demonstrated improved safety with the RF electrolyte compared to the control cells that use a standard Li-ion carbonate-based electrolyte for the overcharge, overheating and external short tests. 7P2S representative aircraft battery modules subjected to overheating and external short tests did not catch fire when using LFP 26650s with the RF electrolyte. Preliminary results of the RF electrolyte with high Ni (Ni>80%) cathodes will also be presented be highlighted.

Keywords

lithium ion; safety; reduced flammability electrolyte; post suppressant materials

Introduction

Lithium-ion batteries (LIBs) are the most common energy source in many everyday applications such as portable electronics, zero-emission vehicles and renewable energy storage. The global production of LIBs increased one order of magnitude during the 2010s and is expected to do so again in the 2020s. Performance, cost, supply chain stability and safety are current challenges that battery manufacturers are seeking to improve through R&D efforts. Mission-critical defense applications in extreme and harsh environments further require even safer LIBs. This paper focuses on methods to improve the safety of LIBs.

The energy density of mass-produced commercial off the shelf (COTS) Lithium-ion cells has increased threefold from 264 Wh L^{-1} of the 18650s introduced by Sony in 1991 to 760 Wh L^{-1} of the 21700s used today in the Tesla Model 3. This substantial increase of energy in the same volume can lead to dramatic safety events when its release is not controlled. Battery fires have been widely reported by the media and are generally caused by manufacturing defects or misuse. Battery fires are caused by thermal runaway. Thermal runaway occurs when the temperature inside a cell reaches the point that causes an unwanted chemical reaction that produces heat, which propagates further chemical reactions that create more heat eventually causing the cell to deform, vent and in the worst cases fire.

Li-ion batteries are especially prone to thermal runaway events due to their flammable electrolyte. The need for many safety measures could be eliminated by moving to a fully nonflammable electrolyte. However, a nonflammable electrolyte has yet to be commercialized due to difficulties in manufacturing or poor electrochemical performance. For example, attempts to build completely solid cells based on ceramic conducting materials have failed due to the low conductivity of the electrolyte and high interfacial resistance between the electrolyte and electrodes.

This paper will discuss the challenges in incorporating a reduced flammability electrolyte into a Li-ion cell. Cell and module-level electrochemical and safety performance of various Li-ion chemistries using a RF electrolyte will be compared to that of cells with a conventional electrolyte. Finally, additional methods to improve battery safety at the module and pack level will be highlighted.

Reduced Flammability Electrolyte

This paper focused on the inclusion of a RF additive that worked by scavenging free radicals that lead to continuous combustion. Generally, RF additives improve cell safety at the cost of high-rate and cold-temperature performance. The RF additive demonstrated in this work does not suffer from these issues. Additionally, the additive may have improved safety and cycling performance by affecting the solid electrolyte interphase (SEI) composition and uniformity. Finally, the RF electrolyte exhibits a decreased vapor pressure compared to common Li-ion electrolytes.

Figure 1 compares the heat generation using differential scanning calorimetry (DSC) of a RF and a conventional electrolyte used as a baseline (BL). The onset of heat generation is delayed by the RF electrolyte. The total magnitude of heat generated is also decreased by the RF electrolyte.

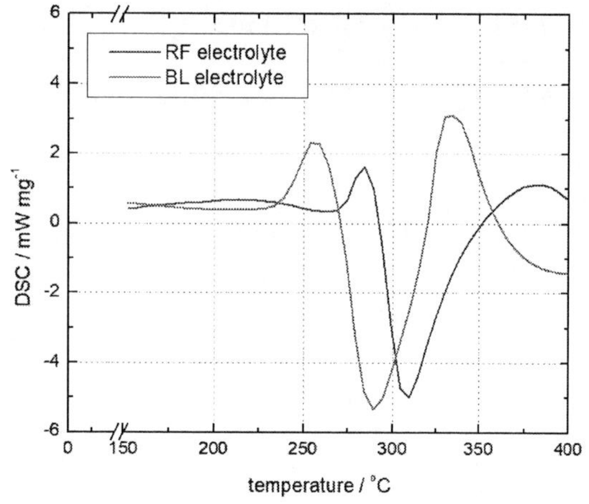

Figure 1. Effect of RF additive on heat generation for electrolytes.

Figure 2 shows the RF electrolyte has no effect on the discharge energy of this same chemistry over the wide temperature range of −20 to 50 °C. The discharge energy is actually improved by 25% at −30 °C most likely due to a thinner, more conductive SEI. Figure 3 shows that the RF electrolyte has no effect on the discharge capacity of 26650 cylindrical cells with a graphite anode and LFP cathode to an 8C rate.

The cells with RF electrolyte all passed the overcharge, overheating and external short circuit tests. Cells without the RF electrolyte often caught fire. 18650s with graphite and NCM111 also demonstrated these same results. The summary of these test are not shown due to space constraints.

Module Level Safety Improvement

The LFP 26650s were then incorporated into a 7P2S module as shown at the top of figure 4. This module is representative of an aircraft battery. The modules, with and without the RF electrolyte, were then subjected to the High-Temperature Test per the S9310-AQ-SAF-01 standard.

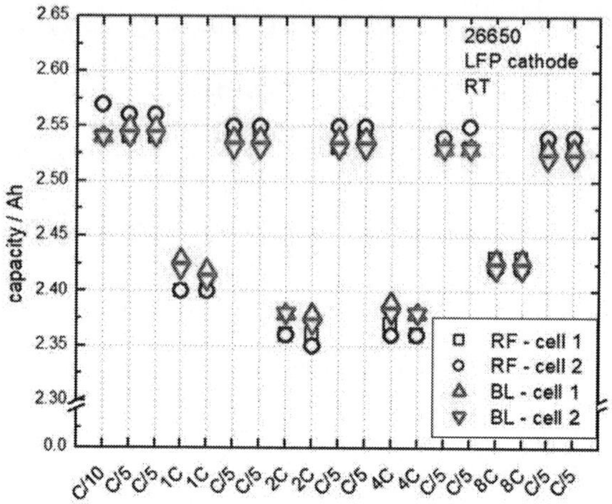

Figure 3. Effect of RF electrolyte on discharge capacity of LFP 26650s at various rates.

The module was heated at a rate of 10 to 20 °C per minute in the presence of a spark emitter. The voltage and temperature profiles of the modules during this test are shown in figure 5. The module with the RF electrolyte-containing cells demonstrated a lower maximum of 200 °C compared to over 300 °C for the BL module. The RF electrolyte also delayed the onset of the module voltage decrease by 20 minutes. The bottom left picture in figure 4 shows the BL module. There is evidence of fire and 13 out of 14 cells vented. The bottom right picture of figure 4 shows the RF module where there is no evidence of fire and only 7 out of 14 cells vented. This demonstrates that safer cells will lead to slower propagation of events between cells and pack thermal runaway.

RF electrolyte with high Ni cathodes

Many new applications require higher energies that cannot be delivered with LFP or NCM111. NMC with Ni content over 70 percent can deliver >25% more energy on an active material basis. However, it is generally considered less safe due to the higher capacity and voltage, as well as the chemical structure.

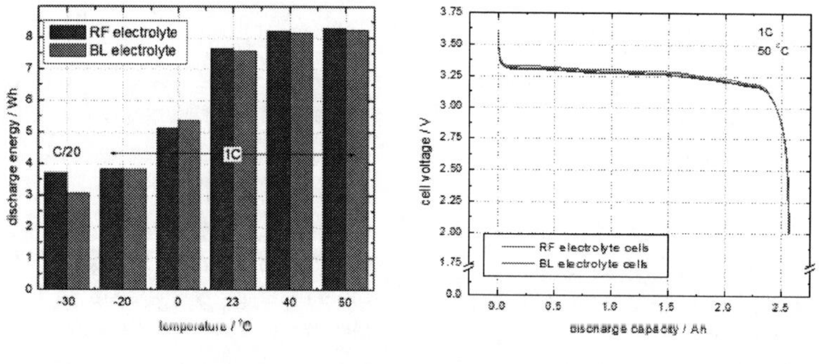

Figure 2. Effect of RF electrolyte on discharge energy of LFP 26650s at various temperatures (left). Discharge curve comparison of LFP 26650s using RF or BL electrolyte.

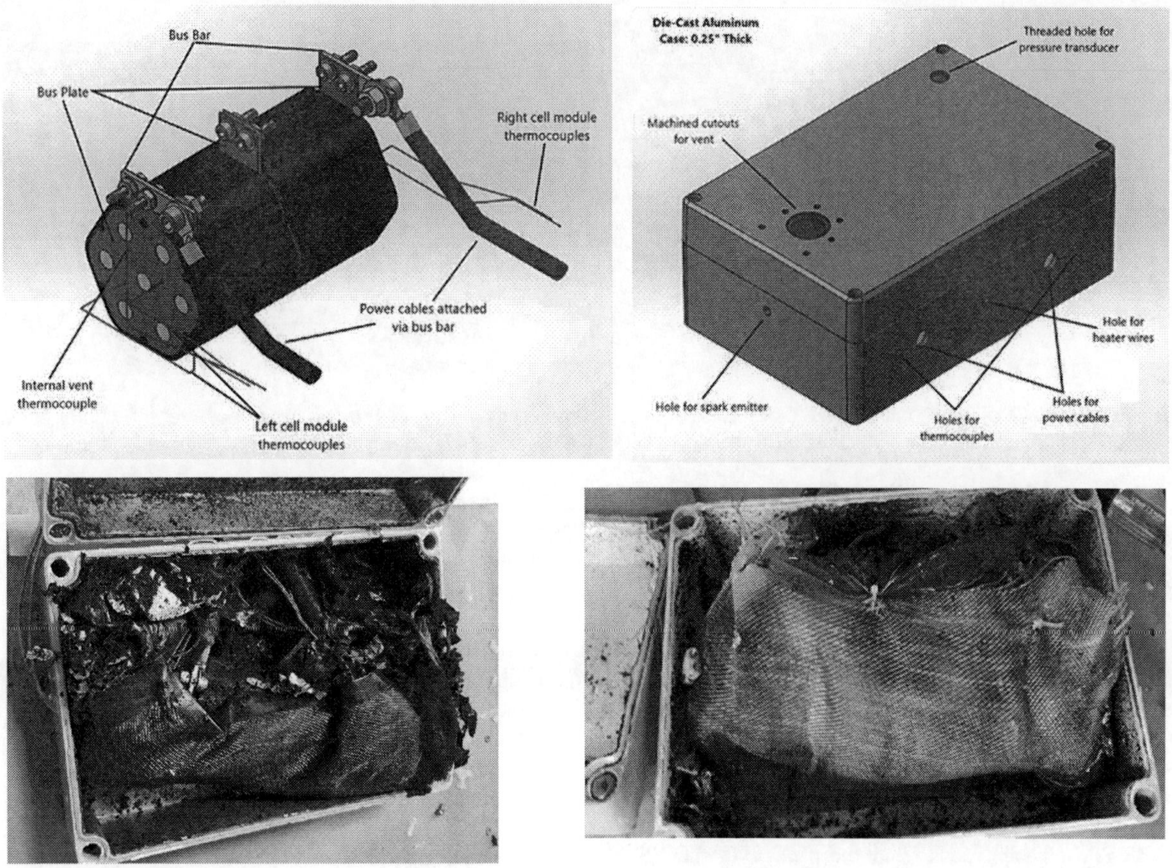

Figure 4. Design drawing of the High-Temperature Test fixture of 7P2S module (top). Picture of the module after the test (bottom)

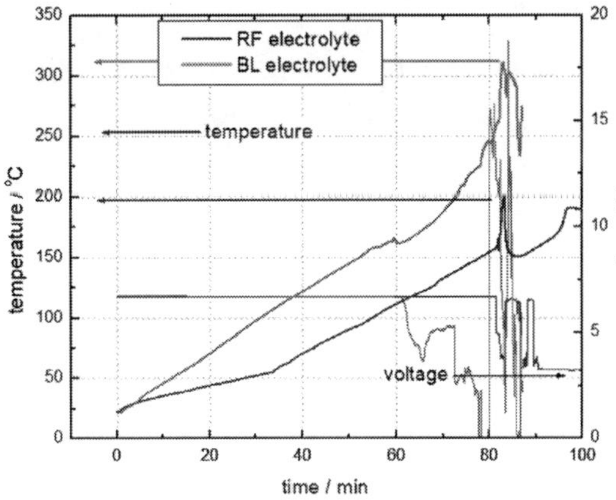

Figure 5. Effect of RF electrolyte on temperature and voltage response of a 7P2S LFP 26650 module during the High-Temperature Test

Initial compatibility of the RF electrolyte with this high Ni cathode is demonstrated by the capacity retention during cycling of 10 Ah pouch cell data in figure 6. The cells with the RF electrolyte demonstrate similar performance to at least 500 cycles. The safety performance of this chemistry will be presented at the conference.

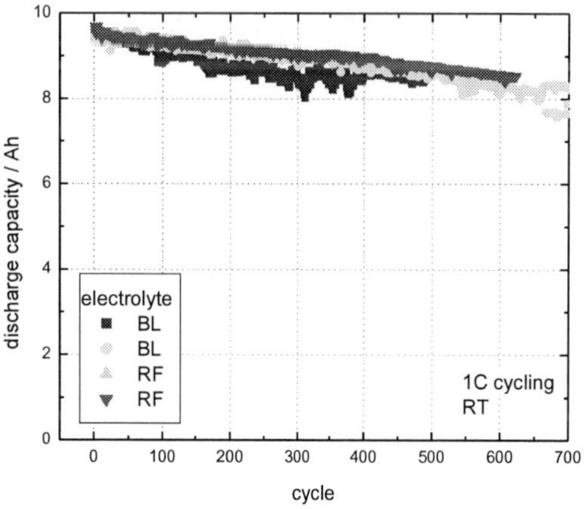

Figure 6. Cycling behavior of RF electrolyte with high Ni cathode.

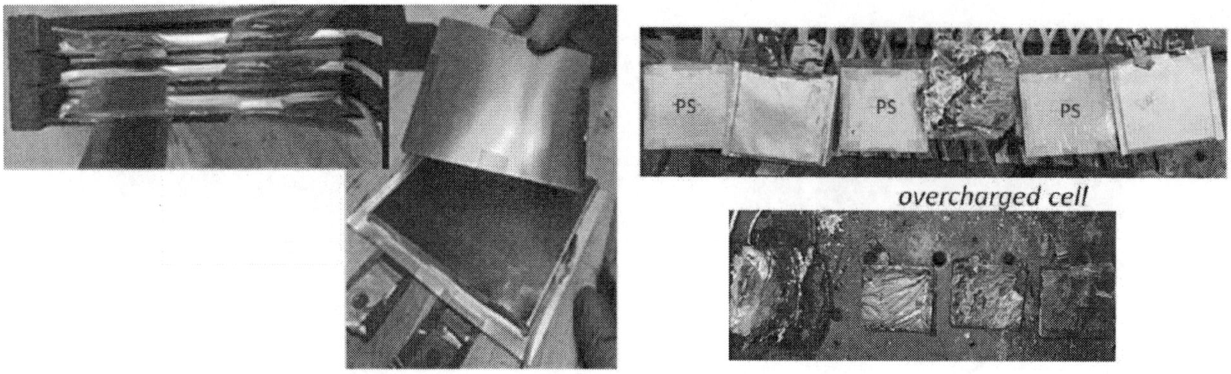

Figure 7. Schematic of 3 cell packs used to demonstrate the PS materials (left). Cells remaining intact after the center cell was forced into thermal runaway in the pack with PS materials (right top). Adjacent cells were completely destroyed in three cell pack without PS materials (right bottom).

Post Suppressant Materials

The RF electrolyte demonstrates improved cell and module safety as part of cell chemistry. Post Suppressant (PS) materials improve pack safety by mitigating propagation between cells after a thermal event has started. Figure 7 shows two different three 10 Ah pouch cell modules. One pack just contained the cells and the other pack had PS materials separating the cells. In each pack, the middle cell was forced into thermal runaway via overcharge. The adjacent cells were destroyed in the pack with no PS materials. The adjacent cells from the pack with the PS materials were able to discharge after the thermal runaway event. This test shows the merits of PS materials and this will be discussed in more detail at the conference.

Conclusions

The RF electrolyte demonstrates improved cell and module safety as part of cell chemistry in LFP as well as NMC cells. Post Suppressant (PS) materials mitigate propagation in a thermal event. Greater details on both topics will be presented at the conference.

Acknowledgments

The authors wish to thank funding received from the FAA and ONR that supported this work.

Advances on High Safety and Longevity Lithium-ion Batteries

Trevor Grant, Elmira Memarzadeh, Raj DasGupta
Electrovaya Inc.
6688 Kitimat Road, Mississauga, ON L5N 1P8, Canada
tgrant@electrovaya.com

Abstract

The rollout of electric vehicles over the past five years has been hindered by recalls due to battery fire incidents and unreliable performance. While fire safety is a critical concern in passenger vehicles, the potential damage of fires is drastically compounded in vehicles which hold many passengers, carry out critical functions, or operate in the vicinity of large capital assets. This paper details Electrovaya's recent developments for its Infinity lithium-ion platform in achieving exceptional battery safety and reliability. Electrovaya's batteries currently leverage key safety technologies across the cell, pack, and battery management system designs. The resulting battery systems show remarkable stability for a high-capacity NMC battery when subject to extreme thermal fluctuation, mechanical shock, and electrical abuse. Infinity cells have also been shown to exhibit outstanding longevity for NMC chemistry, reaching beyond 9000 cycles under 1C cycling conditions. These results demonstrate how Electrovaya's Infinity technology gives superior performance over conventional lithium-ion battery solutions and is exceptionally well-suited for demanding applications where longevity and fire safety are critical metrics.

Keywords

Lithium ion battery; battery safety; ceramic; separator; cycle life

Introduction

Today, battery fires as a result of thermal runaway remain the most critical failure mode of lithium-ion packs in electric vehicle (EV) and stationary energy storage (BESS) applications. As the total number of battery systems in commercial use continue to grow and many applications have been in deployment for over 5 years, the importance of battery safety has become increasing apparent from cases where battery systems have catastrophically failed, or widespread battery replacements have been required. As the number of batteries in operation continues to grow and new types of vehicles are electrified, a greater priority to battery safety and longevity will be necessary to realize a successful electrification transition.

Thermal runaway in lithium-ion batteries can be broadly characterized as a feedback loop of heat-generating events within a battery causing a rapid rise in temperature. If the heat generation is not able to be stopped or dissipated, the thermal runaway process will culminate in a violent fire as the internal energy of the battery is uncontrollably released and components of the battery combust or thermally decompose.[1] In a battery pack made from many individual cells, a thermal runaway event in a single cell may propagate to quickly ignite the entire pack producing a self-sustaining fire that is exceptionally difficult to extinguish unless the system can be cooled and maintained at stable temperature to prevent re-initiation of the thermal runaway process.[2]

The heat required to accelerate a thermal runaway event may be generated by an internal short circuit within a battery cell as a result of direct electrical contact of anode and cathode. Maintaining integrity of the battery separator, responsible for providing electrical insulation between the anode and cathode, is critical to preventing short circuit events. Failure of the separator through mechanical abuse (crushing, bending, penetration), electrical abuse (over charge, over discharge), thermal abuse (rapid charge/discharge, elevated ambient temperature, thermal shock), and manufacturing defects (electrode misalignment, structural defects) may all lead to short circuit events subsequent thermal runaway of the cell.[3]

Conventional battery separators made from polyolefin (PO) materials (i.e. polyethylene and/or polypropylene) provide poor resistance to the propagation of localized internal short circuit events, which may easily produce enough heat to cause shrinkage of the separator resulting in an exponential increase in the severity of the short. PO-based separators begin to soften and lose structural stability above ~100 °C and melt above 135 °C (polyethylene) or 160 °C (polypropylene). Separators formed from layered PO-based materials and ceramic coatings (e.g. alumina) may work to increase the separator's resistance to thermal runaway, however these techniques do not sufficiently mitigate the risk of thermal failure which can remain a limiting factor for instigating thermal runaway below 200 °C.[4] This paper will review results of Electrovaya's deployment and testing of full ceramic composite separators in commercial battery cells and packs, showing exceptional thermal stability while using high capacity Lithium-Nickel-Manganese-Cobalt-Oxide (NMC) cathode chemistry. Additionally, recently collected cycle life testing reveals industry-leading cycling performance for NMC-based cells.

Battery Safety

The building block of Electrovaya's infinity platform battery products is the 'EV-44' cell; an NMC-based lithium-ion cell incorporating a full ceramic composite separator. The ceramic composite separator is an integral cell-level safety to greatly reduce the likelihood and severity of a battery fire

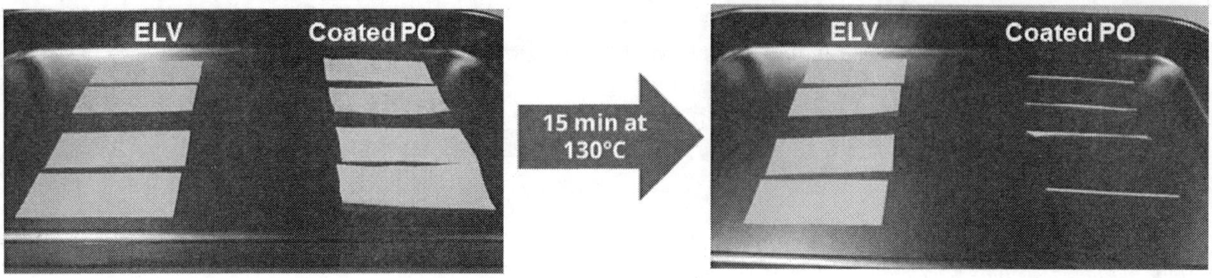

Figure 1. Thermal stability and shrinkage resistance of a full ceramic composite separator (ELV) vs a conventional ceramic coated PO separator (Coated PO).

due to superior thermal stability. Figure 1 demonstrates thermal stability of a full ceramic composite separator in comparison to a ceramic coated PO separator at 130 °C. It can be seen that the dimensional stability of the PO-based separator is critically lost as the base PO material undergoes a melting transition. In contrast, the structural integrity of a fully embedded ceramic composite separator is completely maintained with penetration of the ceramic material through the full depth of the separator film.

The significance of this improved thermal resistance on the cell safety is most appropriately demonstrated through a nail penetration test. In this test, an electrically conductive nail (O.D = 2.5 mm) is used to fully puncture a fully charged NMC-Graphite cell to simulate an internal short circuit. When employing a conventional PO-based polymer separator, the heat generated in the immediate vicinity of the short circuit event is sufficient to cause shrinkage of the separator and exponentially increase the shorted current pathway. In this case the cell fails catastrophically, characterized by rapid cell discharge, venting of the cell (excessive gas generation), and jet flames from ignition of the flammable liquid electrolyte (Figure 2A). Alternatively for a cell employing a full ceramic separator the short is not propagated and remains localized to the point of penetration (Figure 2B). Cell failure in this case is non-catastrophic, with no fire or significant loss of liquid electrolyte weight (< 10% weight loss), and no bulging of the cell pouch. This is an exceptional result for a cell containing NMC-based cathodes, which are known to be more susceptible to aggressive thermal runaway in comparison to other common cell chemistries (i.e. lithium-ion-phosphate, LFP) due to the lower onset temperature and more highly exothermic thermal decomposition reaction of NMC.[5] These tests exemplify the impact of component design on the overall safety of a lithium-ion cell.

Despite efforts at the cell level, the probability of thermal runaway can never be eliminated due to the inherently high potential energy stored within modern lithium-ion batteries. It is therefore critical to consider propagation risks of cell fire across a battery pack to mitigate the severity of an internal cell failure leading to thermal runaway. Electrovaya has recently completed third-party abuse testing of its commercial battery pack through Underwriters Laboratories (UL) safety certification. Among other tests as a part of UL2580 certification (testing standard for batteries for use in electric vehicles), Electrovaya's NMC-based packs successfully passed internal fire propagation abuse testing as a testament to the cell- and pack-level safety design. Figure 3 shows an Electrovaya battery after completing a fire propagation test wherein a single cell in a fully charged battery pack was forcibly ignited. During the test, the cell fire was fully contained within the sub-module holding the faulty cell and no flames exited the battery enclosure. The exterior batter connections and battery case remain intact and undamaged (Figure 3A). Additionally, the battery management system of the pack remained fully intact

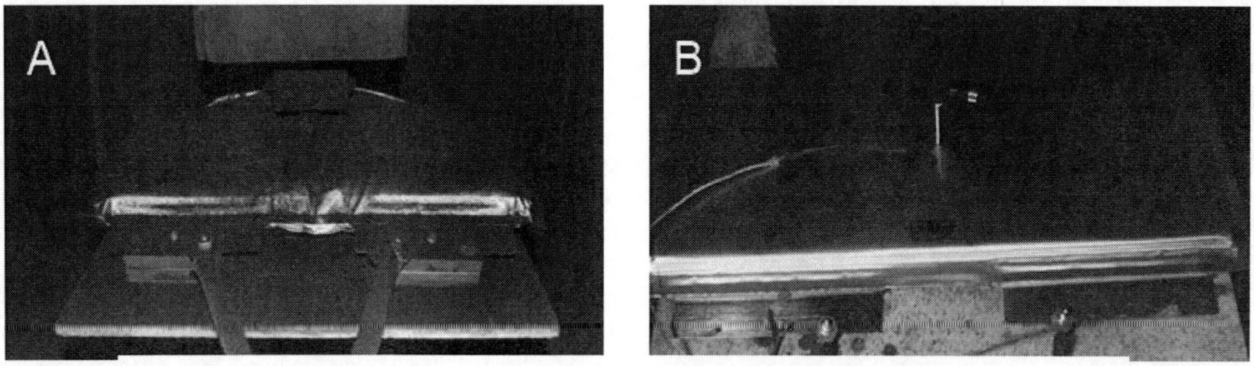

Figure 2. Nail penetration results form a fully charged NMC|Graphite cell having (A) a conventional PO separator, and (B) a full ceramic composite separator.

Figure 3. An Electrovaya 24V battery pack shown after fire propagating testing in which a single cell was forcibly ignited, depicting (A) unscathed battery enclosure and external connections, (B) intact battery management system, and (C) no fire propagation between adjacent modules.

(Figure 3B). Internal investigation of the faulted pack revealed that heat generated by the internal fire was not sufficient to induce separator shrinkage to cells in adjacent modules and no cells in adjacent sub-modules were ignited (Figure 3C).

Battery Longevity

Batteries for typical passenger EVs and other low-use applications may demand only one charge cycle per week under regular operation. In these cases, a battery cycle life of 1000 – 2000 cycles will allow for sufficient capacity retention through the lifetime of the vehicle or application. However, certain applications operating in demanding or continuous use conditions (i.e. busses, materials handling vehicles, autonomous vehicles, stationary energy storage systems, and others) may demand 1 or more full charge cycle per day in standard use. Conventional lithium-ion battery employed in these applications will almost certainly require a costly full battery system replacement through the vehicle or application lifetime as the battery performance becomes insufficient due to degradation.

Electrovaya has developed a commercial lithium-ion cell with industry-leading cycle life through nearly a decade of experience employing full ceramic separators in commercial lithium-ion batteries. Optimization of the cell assembly process, electrolyte composition, electrode chemistry, and other factors have enabled an NMC-based cell with exceptional longevity. Figure 2 shows ongoing long-term data of Electrovaya lithium-ion cells collected from over 2 years of cycle life testing at various state-of-charge (SOC) windows. Leveraging key cell chemistry and design elements along a full ceramic composite separator, Electrovaya cells have been proven to achieve remarkable cycle life beyond 9000 cycles for a relatively high energy density NMC cell, which is over twice the longevity observed from conventional off-the-shelf lithium-ion battery chemistries.[6]

For a given electric vehicle or stationary storage application, it is critical that the total cost of ownership over the battery lifetime is considered. Lithium-ion batteries designed to meet conventional applications (i.e. consumer electronics and passenger EVs) are not necessarily suited for many emerging battery use cases. Load cycle requirements (charge rates, discharge cycles per day) and operating conditions (ambient temperature, heat dissipation, potential mechanical abuse) need to be taken into when selecting a cell or module

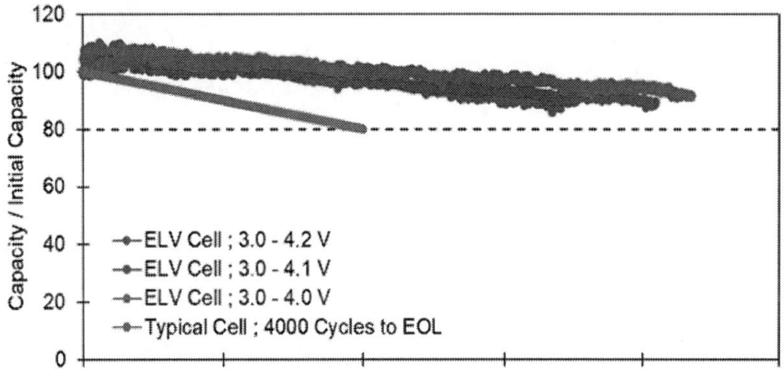

Figure 4. Long-term charge/discharge cycling results for Electrovaya cells at 100% SOC (blue), 90% SOC (red) and 80% SOC (green). Data collected at 25 ± 2°C, 1C current rate. A theoretical cell with a lifetime of 4000 cycles to 80% original capacity is shown for reference (grey)

to enable a successful long-term electrification solution. Electrovaya batteries are designed to excel through the entire lifetime of even the most demanding lithium-ion applications. Two decades of technology development and implementation gives superior performance over conventional lithium-ion battery solutions, and a lithium-ion battery which is exceptionally well-suited for critical use cases where longevity and fire safety are critical metrics.

References

1. X. Feng, M. Ouyang, X. Liu, L. Lu, Y. Xia, and X. He, "Thermal runaway mechanism of lithium ion battery for electric vehicles: A review" Energy Storge Materials, vol. 10, pp. 246-267, 2018

2. P. Sun, R. Bisschop, H. Niu,and X. Huang, "A Review of Battery Fires in Electric Vehicles" Fire Technol, vol. 56, pp. 1361–1410, 2020

3. E. Wang, H. Wu, C. Chiu, and P. Chou, "The Effect of Battery Separator Properties on Thermal Ramp, Overcharge and Short Circuiting of Rechargeable Li-Ion Batteries" J. Electrochem. Soc., vol. 166, no. 2, pp. A125, 2019

4. J. Choi, and P. J. Kim, "A roadmap of battery separator development: Past and future" Current Opinion in Electrochemistry, vol. 3, pp. 100858, 2022

5. S. Ohneseit, P. Finster, C. Floras, N. Lubenau, N. Uhlmann, H.J. Seifert, and C. Ziebert, "Thermal and Mechanical Safety Assessment of Type 21700 Lithium-Ion Batteries with NMC, NCA and LFP Cathodes–Investigation of Cell Abuse by Means of Accelerating Rate Calorimetry (ARC)" Batteries vol. 9, no. 5, pp. 237, 2023

6. Y. Preger, H.M. Barkholtz, A. Fresquez, D.L. Campbell, B.W. Juba, J. Romàn-Kustas, S.R. Ferreira, and B. Chalamala, "Degradation of Commercial Lithium-Ion Cells as a Function of Chemistry and Cycling Conditions" J. Electrochem. Soc., vol. 164, no. 12, pp. 120532, 2020

Commercial and Consumer Battery Fire Trends-Learning from Mistakes of Others

Michael D. Eskra, Paula K. Ralston and Rodney LaFollette
Eskra Technical Products, Inc.
Saukville, WI, USA, 53080

Abstract
Batteries are everywhere in our daily lives. Most battery-powered devices aid to make our daily lives more convenient. However, there are daily occurrences of batteries causing damage to structures and bodily harm to users. End users demand more and more portable power, and the battery industry has responded. Unfortunately, at the same time, the overall quality of the industry as a whole has significantly decreased. The result is that failures are more catastrophic, with higher loss of property and life. The push to go more electric and be off grid has created unanticipated failures that require investigation. This paper will discuss the most common failure modes we have been identifying in the consumer space and how the occurrence could have been mitigated.

Introduction
In the past 25 years lithium-ion battery technology has grown in market share, energy and power density. This has provided end users with capabilities that would have been considered impossible just 20 years ago in power tools, cell phones and vehicles. The battery powered devices have become ubiquitous in modern society. Unfortunately, these high energy and power devices can also cause substantial damage including fire and explosion resulting in large financial losses and bodily harm.

Many of these instances of failure undergo analysis to determine probable cause of failure. These analyses can take place years after the incident has occurred and with little known history of use prior to the occurrence.

When the origin of the incident can be identified a study of the remains of the artifact is undertaken. In the case of battery cells, a CT scan is typically included along with physical examination and at times destructive analysis of the artifact. Electrical testing of an exemplar is performed in an effort to eliminate the possible reasons for failure. It has been our experience that the majority of the failures that are occurring are not related to poor original cell manufacturing but poor battery pack and cell management.

Low Voltage Operation of Lithium Ion
Thermal runaway in lithium-ion (Li-ion) cells can be induced by several factors, including manufacturing defects, exposure to very high external temperatures, or mechanical abuse or damage. The safety of (Li-ion) cells also depends in part on the way they are used. This is particularly true if cells are operated outside of the safe potential range. Overcharge (charging a cell at excessively high potential or significantly beyond the rated cell capacity; mAhr) is known to damage cells and/or create safety hazards. Over discharge (discharge of a cell below the minimum safe value or beyond the rated cell capacity) can also degrade Li-ion cells and cause unsafe conditions.

Over discharge of cells can be prevented using proper control circuits on individual cells, that stop discharge when the cell potential reaches the minimum (cutoff) potential. If multiple cells are connected in series without monitoring and control of individual cells, there is a risk of overdischarging weaker cells. In addition, operating cells at very high rates during either charge or discharge, such as during high current pulses, can temporarily cause the local potentials values adjacent to the electrode surfaces, to be either too high or too low. This is especially true for cells or batteries that are operated at very low temperatures. Over discharge can also take place after the discharge is shut off by the control circuit (for having reached the minimum cutoff potential), if a trickle discharge current is used to operate the Battery Management control circuit. Internal self-discharge of discharged cells allowed to sit at open circuit for extended time can also be over discharged.

Li-ion cells rarely fail directly due to over discharge; rather they fail in subsequent charging. There are physical and chemical changes to the cell, particularly the negative electrode, that make normal healthy recharging of the cell difficult or impossible. This report contains a survey of reported studies of the effects of over discharge on Li-ion cells, particularly with respect to safety. Before that some evidence of gas evolution in the cells from the over discharged cells from fires will be briefly presented.

Long term storage of over discharge cells will usually show bulging at the bottom of their containers upon recharging. This type of swelling is caused by the significant rise of internal cell pressure due to gas evolution, rather than damage from a fire external to the cells. As will be shown in this report, over discharge of a Li-ion cell leads to gas evolution. (This is in contrast to healthy cells undergoing fire attack which will cause bulging of the negative end from thermal decomposition of electrolyte and separator). In a pouch cell this is mainly manifest in increased cell thickness (due to the buildup of additional gaseous species). In a more constrained cell configuration, such as a spirally-wound 18650 cell (housed in a sealed steel can), the presence of evolved gases is manifest in an increase in internal pressure, and possibly in bulging of the cell can.

To further illustrate the buildup of pressure, we use the well-known ideal gas law,

$$P = \frac{nRT}{V}$$

Where P is the pressure, n is the number of moles of the gas, R is the Universal Gas Constant, T is the temperature, and V is the volume of the gas (which is essentially constant inside of the cell). Pressure increases with temperature, and it increases with the number of moles of gas. The cell when first fabricated contains a small amount of gas. As gas is evolved, the number of moles of gas goes up quickly[1]. The number of moles can go from an equivalent of 1 to 18 during over discharge. It does not take a great deal of gas evolution to increase the pressure to several times its initial value; pressures of several tens of psi are easily achieved. As the cell is recharged it is not uncommon for T to go from 20 to 60. Most 18650 Li-ion cells have a built-in pressure relief valve, to vent gas when the pressure reaches a threshold value (such as 140 psi). Still, poorly constructed cells can have a non-functioning relief valve, or a container that can bulge before the pressure reaches the threshold for venting gas. The net effect is that P can increase substantially and would cause distortion of the flat bottom of the 18650 prior to venting of the cells that have been over discharged and subsequently recharged without an immediate thermal event. The probability of a delayed shorting event after charging is increased.

As pointed out in many studies, high levels of over discharge can result in Cu dissolution and then re-deposition in either on the negative electrode, positive electrode or in the separator. This can cause the formation of internal shorts, via Cu dendritic growths. The growth of Cu dendrites is possible after a single over discharge, especially if subsequently charged aggressively.

Changes in the SEI layer invariably took place due to over discharging. In some cases, the SEI layer can disintegrate, raising the increased possibility of catastrophic cell failure during subsequent charging. In other situations, it is made more resistive, due to incorporation of either copper of other species such as hydrogen or growth. Thicker SEI layers of course causes higher internal cell resistance. Cu deposition is the most important result of over discharge, that affects the health or composition of the SEI layer on the negative electrode surface.

All over discharged cells showed evidence of gas buildup in cells. The composition of the gases varied from study to study, but the fact that gas evolution took place is established.

These two factors (Cu dissolution/precipitation and alteration of the SEI layer) are the principal safety concerns for over discharged Li-ion cells. Care should therefore be taken to prevent over discharge for maximum battery safety.

Battery Pack Battery Management System

Lithium-ion chemistry requires the addition of a Battery Management System (BMS). These systems would benefit all battery chemistries if they were implemented. ETP has found that the majority of the BMS prevent overcharge of lithium-ion battery cells. ETP has also found that many of the BMS are not programmed properly to detect failing cells on discharge, to prevent over discharge, to prevent zero or low cells to be recharged; creating instability and possible thermal runaway.

[1] It does not matter what type of gas molecules are involved; one mole of hydrogen gas, the lightest gas known, leads to the same pressure as much heavier gases, such as oxygen, nitrogen or water vapor (at the same temperature, and in the same volume).

The typical low end BMS will have 30+ registers that can help protect a battery pack. Higher end BMS may have more than 60 registers. The typical battery packs that are sold to the consumer, such as laptops, power tools etc, have 5 of those registers activated. These registers are typically called GG files or gas gauge files. As the name implies, the first 5 registers provide information to the computer so that the user knows how much run time they have remaining while on battery power. The computer also uses a 2 wire communication system called SMBus. This system allows the computer to communicate with its components, including the battery. It could prevent poor quality batteries from being operated in the computer, or could be used communicate with the battery to assist in detecting a failing cell. Sadly, in many computers the SMBus is not activated as it relates to the battery. Instead, the computer will charge anything connected in the battery bay whether it is a healthy battery or a battery that has been sitting discharged for several years.

Testing of Exemplars to Determine BMS Settings

Unfortunately, OEM's do not want to provide their GG file settings to those investigating a fire involving their products. To obtain the data required a few simple electrical tests are performed. The battery pack is wired to record pack and individual cell voltage. If possible, connections will be made to determine if any communication is occurring between the battery and device. The unit is charged and discharged with the voltages and currents recorded. This provides the baseline. Many times this test will show that the exemplar is defective out of the box. Next a cell or cell pair is connected to a 10 to 20 ohm resistor. The cycle test is repeated. The resistor will make the cell behave like it has an internal short and each cycle the cell will run down further and not be fully recharged. The good BMS that is set up properly will detect the failing cell. The cell is allowed to stand after device shut down for increasing duration to determine if the battery will be recharged by the charging station as the voltage is stepped down from 1.0, 0.5, 0.0, -0.5 volts. It is not unusual that the product may reverse a cell in this test. The BMS should be set up to detect the failure.

Some power tools will stop operating as the battery hits the lower cut off. If the trigger is pulled again a lower cut off voltage occurs. Holding the tool trigger down allows the battery pack to further discharge resulting in reversal of one or more cells in the battery pack.

The plots below are of a 40-volt battery pack on a name brand tool from 2018. The sequence of the plots after run down and three trigger pulls. What can be seen is that there was already some weakness in the battery pack with mismatched cells. No resistor needed to be added for this test because the exemplar battery pack already showed a major defect. Each time the trigger was pulled the weakest battery cell was driven lower until it reversed. At this point SEI and copper dissolution and plating has occurred and the cell is severely damaged.

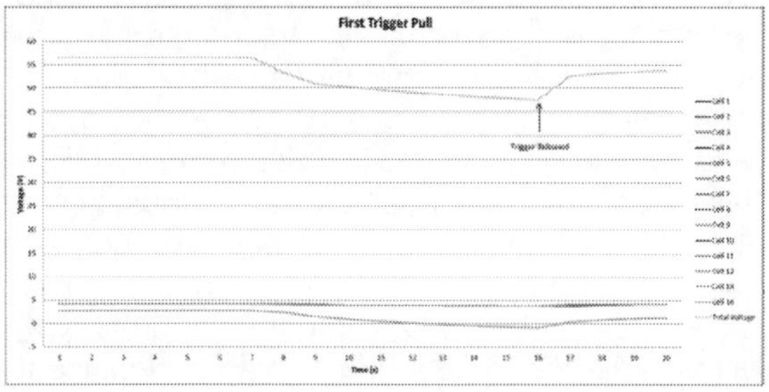

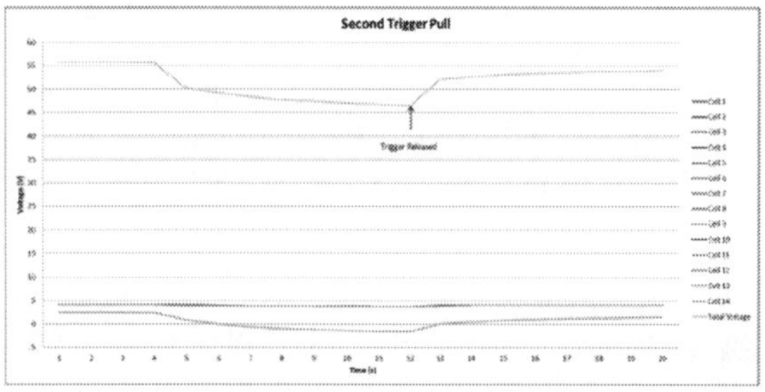

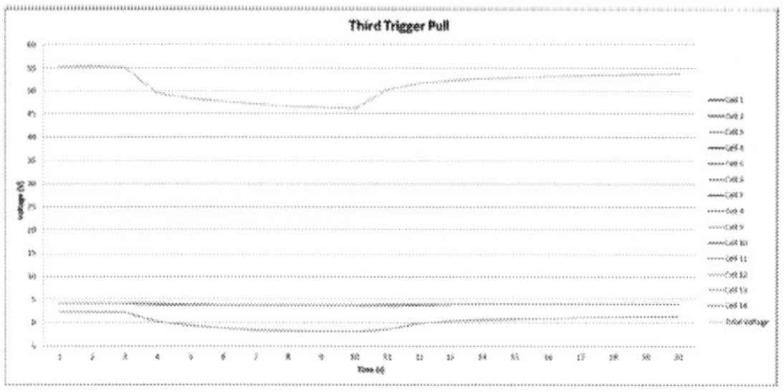

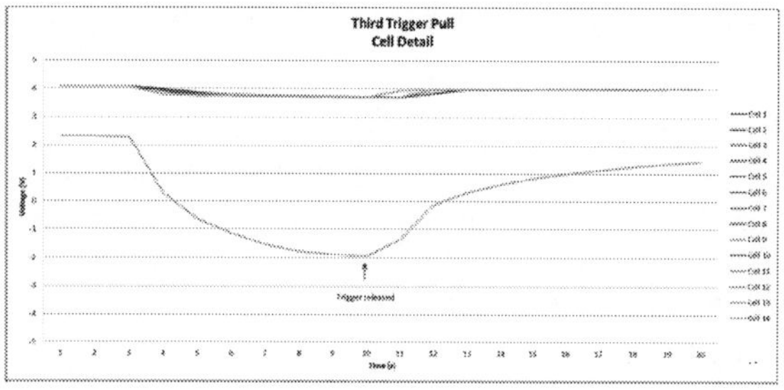

Sadly after this abuse the battery pack was placed on the charger and the charger recharged the battery.

Zero volt recharge capability is in many products both brand name and knock offs. The manufactures believe that with the requirement to ship at low state of charge the capability needs to be enabled so that the customers do not get a dead on delivery product. Unfortunately, it can make a soft shorted or otherwise poor quality cell into a dangerous bomb. ETP has experienced many first charge product fires from a cross section of industry. More importantly, zero volt recharge is seen late in life to play a significant role in catastrophic failures. Whether it is an old MP3 player that is sitting in desk drawer or old toy such as a hoverboard in a closet, or old laptop computer slid under a desk for a year or two, someday someone will decide to plug it in and see if the missing file or maybe to play with it. It might not work immediately or ever, but they leave it on charge in hopes of getting one last shot at it. Unfortunately, the lithium-ion battery chemistry has some very nasty low voltage characteristics occurring. The Solid Electrolyte Interface (SEI) degrades, copper from the anode goes into solution, decrepitation of the anode active material and the cathode can occur. Then when placed on charge even worse reactions occur. The damaged SEI layer attaches to some healthy electrode surface while the are where it fell from the graphitic anode attempts to grow a new SEI with gas generation as a by-product. The copper may have plated on the cathode is not being driven back through the separator and is plated on the graphite potentially growing a dendrite back through the separator and shorting. This does not always result in a fire that burns the house or factory down but it might.

Summary

Lithium-ion batteries are not the most powerful batteries manufactured but they are powerful enough and are widely used enough that they need to be handled properly and respected for the damage they can do. The authors have seen single lithium ion battery cells severe legs, hands and cause substantial bodily injury. They have seen them level 14 acre buildings and farms. The larger systems have generated enough gas to throw fire fighters over 75 feet, and they have caused enough damage that government officials suspected a mortar attack.

Contact Information:

Mike Eskra 262-707-5855
MikeEskra@aol.com
Paula Ralston 203-417-5526
paula.eskratechnical@gmail.com
Dr. Rodney LaFollette 801-376-8615
RMLaFollette@aol.com

Glass Ampoule Analysis Capability Transition

Kevin M. O'Connor Jr
U.S. Army Combat Capabilities Development Command Armaments Center
Picatinny Arsenal, NJ, USA, 07806
kevin.m.oconnor60.civ@army.mil, 973-724-4227

Timothy Holmquist, Sidney Chocron, and Art Nicholls
Southwest Research Institute ®
5353 Wayzata Boulevard Suite 607, Minneapolis, MN, USA, 55416
sidney.chocron@swri.org, 210-522-3698

(U) Abstract: (U) *The U.S. Army Combat Capability Development Command – Armament Center (DEVCOM-AC) is developing an accurate method to perform the analysis and evaluation of glass ampoule designs, with the goal of transitioning this capability to industry partners who develop liquid reserve batteries. The government has partnered with several members of the glass ampoule community as well as modeling subject matter experts to pursue this effort. The project, which is a continuation of work previously started at DEVCOM-AC, leverages mature government created technologies such as the Elastic-Plastic Impact Computations (EPIC) software as a tool for finite element modeling and simulation. The overall mission of this project is to reduce the number of iteration cycles required to develop and troubleshoot glass ampoule designs by improving upon the industry's current design methodology. This is being accomplished through custom material model creation, simulation models, and the characterization of ampoule geometry parameters. The results of all these points will be discussed.*

(U) Keywords: Modeling & Simulation; Liquid Reserve Battery; Ampoule; Glass; Compression Testing; Computational Study; Fracture, Impact; EPIC.

(U) Introduction

(U) Munition power source technologies are a continual source of concern by the Joint Fuzing Community. Fuzing power source performance requirements necessitating higher power density, longer run times, faster rise times, higher reliability, faster component availability, and reduced cost. These have not until very recently been addressed with adequate attention to overcome the technological roadblocks to enable advancement necessary to meet the rapid expansion in programmatic requirements.

(U) Previously, U.S. Army DEVCOM Armaments Center began exploring accurate methods to model glass ampoule fracture behavior to assist industrial partners in reducing the number of iteration cycles required to develop and troubleshoot ampoules used in liquid reserve batteries. The ampoules, which contain the electrolyte solution prior to activation, are a large source of battery performance variability, a long lead item, and currently designed using a design-test-iterate development methodology [2].

(U) The focus of this effort is for government fuze subject matter experts to transition software and modeling & simulation knowledge to industry so that industry can effectively develop enhancements to their liquid reserve battery technologies.

(U) At the conclusion of the project, the team will understand the best practices to analyze glass ampoule behavior using government developed Elastic-Plastic Impact Computations (EPIC) finite element software, transition of EPIC software and DoD HPC access, and capability development within DEVCOM Armaments Center to support the use of EPIC by industry for these specific battery analyses.

(U) The purpose of this paper is to highlight the various stages of the project for a better understanding of how the team will reach the project goals.

(U) Technology Maturity

(U) In this project the government has brought together several advanced technologies to provide high-value and much sought after capabilities that have proven to be elusive to date. The mature technologies leveraged by this effort include EPIC finite element software [1], EPIC Variable User Material (VUMAT) models made available in ABAQUS CAE, and ampoule manufacturing expertise developed by industry partners. Industry partners have invested in and developed the industrial know-how to produce glass ampoules for countless liquid reserve battery configurations over the years. Developing this new capability will reduce the number of cycles required to identify an effective glass ampoule solution for any application. This reduction will aid industry in providing faster and cheaper design solutions to the government.

(U) Glass Material Testing at SwRI

(U) The project partnered with Southwest Research Institute (SwRI) who has a depth of knowledge and experience using compression testing to extract the necessary parameters to create material models for the

EPIC software. For this effort, triaxial compression tests were performed on cylindrical specimens provided by two government contractors. Both contractors are involved in producing glass ampoules using their specific form of borosilicate glass and have partnered with the government on this project. Both contractors provided tempered un-tempered glass cylinders to SwRI for this testing. The idea being that the two glass variants will show the effects of residual stresses from the thermal glass forming process.

(U) All the experiments used SwRI's unique high-pressure testing vessel, and a schematic is presented in Figure 1. The cylindrical glass specimen is placed between two alumina anvils and a thin polymeric membrane is placed around the specimen extending over the alumina anvils protecting the specimen from the confining fluid. Rubber O-rings are used to compress the membrane onto the piston and load cell preventing fluid infiltration. The results are recorded at specimen failure and include the fluid pressure, axial stress, hydrostatic pressure, P, and the von Mises equivalent stress [3].

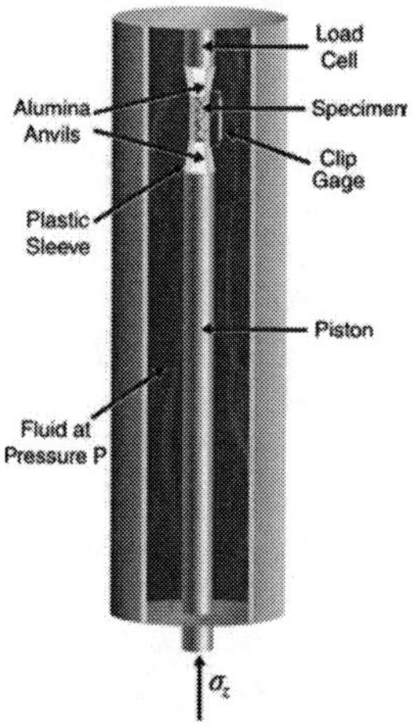

(U) Figure 1. Southwest Research Institute's High-Pressure Testing Vessel [3].

(U) SwRI completed the glass cylinder testing for both contractors and provided a report of the results to the government. Specific results of this glass material testing are not provided in this paper to protect the intellectual property of the contractors. The results of these tests do indicate the necessary parameters of glass material to generate material models in EPIC that are good representation for both contractors. SwRI has further discussed the implementation of the glass material models for use with the EPIC software.

(U) Computational Parametric Study with SwRI

(U) An additional effort of the contracted SwRI effort was to perform EPIC computations of glass ampoules subjected to various impact conditions and orientations. This effort was completed between the government and SwRI members. Since this conceptual effort was performed in parallel with the glass material testing, all computations were completed using the existing borosilicate glass model available in the EPIC software.

(U) A critical design requirement of the ampoule is to survive five-foot drop tests but always break under gun launch conditions that activate the battery. It is time consuming and expensive to experimentally evaluate all the different design concepts that are proposed, but accurate and efficient computations can provide valuable insight into these concepts, identifying the most promising designs and eliminating the ones with issues. The parametric study provides some demonstrations of how computations can be used to help design and evaluate glass ampoules and activation concepts.

(U) One glass ampoule activation concept has been modeled for survivability in a gun launch environment. Only the ampoule model itself, filled with water, is shown here. Several gun launch accelerations were evaluated by changing the initial slope of the applied velocity-time history response. Figures 2 and 3 present the glass ampoule damage when the activation subsystem is subjected to various accelerations. Glass damage occurs in all four loading conditions with only a very small amount resulting from the lower acceleration loads [4].

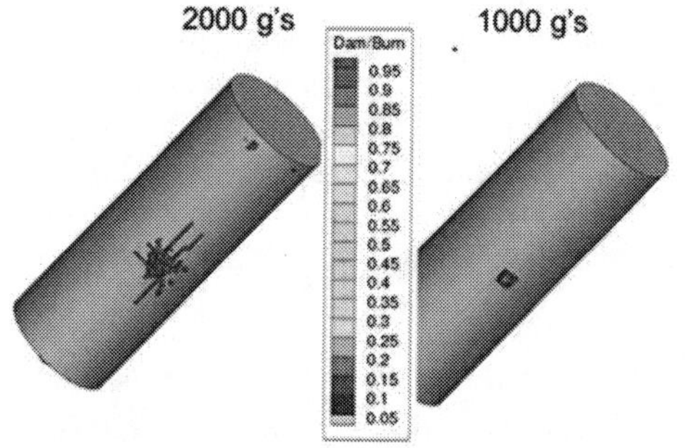

(U) Figure 2. Sample Glass Ampoule damage computation in gun launch conditions [4].

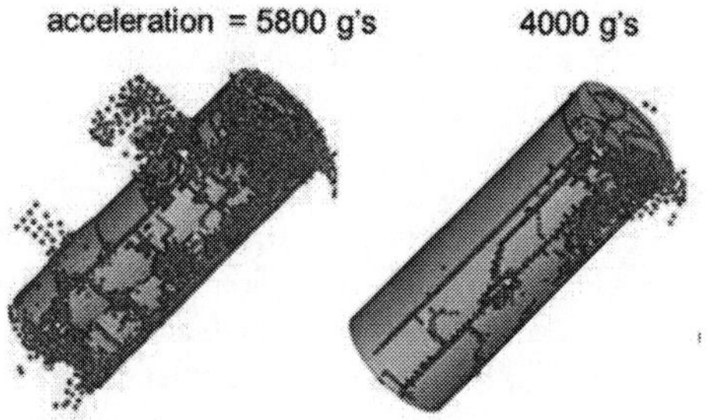

(U) Figure 3. Sample Glass Ampoule damage computation in higher gun launch conditions [4].

(U) Additional activation concepts and ampoule battery package designs were modeled for this contracted effort but are not presented here to protect contractor intellectual property. The effects of changing ampoule geometric and material parameters were also completed in collaboration with SwRI and government.

(U) EPIC Software Transition & Modeling with Industry Partners

(U) Ongoing efforts between the government team and industry partners include the modeling of battery package assemblies with the EPIC software, leveraging the glass models developed by SwRI previously. Working with Army Research Laboratory, a copy of EPIC 2021 Lite has been provided to the industry partners which they can use indefinitely. The explicit dynamics code implements a user defined 'projectile' hitting the 'target' in, among other applications, high velocity impacts. Thus, the government and industry team can model the ampoule and battery packages in drop and gun launch environments to determine ampoule survivability and breakability. Figure 4 shows a sample ampoule, isolated from the assembly, breaking under launch.

(U) Industry partners are sharing battery configurations that support active government programs and are modeling these assemblies with realistic accelerations. The software allows the teams to upload custom designed geometries and assemblies. Current efforts include variations to the glass breaking features within the battery assembly to determine survivability of the glass. This collaboration is not only transitioning the government's knowledge of the EPIC software to industry, but also supporting government programs that will be using these ampoules. Again, no images or specifics about these models are shared here to protect contractor intellectual property.

(U) Figure 4. Isolated view of glass ampoule breaking at specific time after loading is applied.

(U) Utilization of the DoD HPC

(U) Modeling 3-dimensional battery assemblies can be very time and processor consuming, and so the government has assisted contractors in accessing DoD High Performance Computing (HPC) resources. These high-level computing resources are available for routine use by the government research and development community. Extending use to the government contractors allows collaboration through sharing models and results on the HPC servers. In addition, it takes the burden of running these time-intensive analysis jobs away from the individual contractor's computer and use the servers instead. Contractors are actively using these resources to support this effort and will have access to the servers after the project ends, thus allowing industry to continue analyzing ampoule and batteries in the future.

(U) Project Path Forward

(U) As the project is nearing its end, the government and contractor teams are working to continue modeling ampoule battery assemblies. The contractor teams are working on modeling additional battery packages. Results of this project effort will be included in reports from industry as well as government.

(U) Project Transition Potential

(U) Programs relying on such power sources would be immediately affected by an increase of effective and efficient ampoule analysis. This will reduce the number of iteration cycles required to deliver analyzed and effective glass ampoule design. Target joint service programs have been identified and are being pursued [5].

(U) Acknowledgements

(U)The author wishes to thank members of DEVCOM Armaments Center Fuze Division and Analysis Division, Army Research Laboratory, Air Force Research Laboratory, Southwest Research Institute, and liquid reserve battery industry partners for their roles and support with this project.

(U) References

1. (U) Johnson, G. R., (1977). EPIC-3 A Computer Program for Elastic-Plastic Impact Calculations in 3 Dimensions. *BRL Final Contractor Report No. 343.* https://apps.dtic.mil/sti/pdfs/ADA043281.pdf
2. (U) O'Connor, K., Jr., (2019). Glass Ampoule Analysis Capability Transition. *6.3 White Paper for the Joint Fuze Technology Program.*
3. (U) Chocron, S., Anderson, C. E., Dannemann, K. A., & Nicholls, A. E. (2012). Pressure Effects on the Compressive Response of Confined Intact and Damaged Soda-Lime Glass. *Experimental Mechanics, 53*(1), 77–89. https://doi.org/10.1007/s11340-012-9632-2
4. (U) Holmquist, T. Chocron, S, & Nicholls, A. E. (2022). Borosilicate Glass Testing and Glass Ampoule Modeling. *Defense Technical Information Center.*
5. (U) O'Connor, K., Jr., (2022). P20-G3-A6-013 Glass Ampoule Analysis Capability Transition. *Joint Enhanced Munitions Technology Program 2022 Fall Review Meeting*

High Rate Li/CF_x-MnO_2 Hybrid Technology

Mario Destephen, Gary Schmidt, Ernest Ndzebet and David Darch

EaglePicher Technologies, LLC
1215 West "C" Street
Joplin, Missouri 64801
Phone: (417) 623-8000 Fax: (417) 625-1142

Contact Author: Mario Destephen
Email: Mario.destephen@eaglepicher.com

Abstract: *EaglePicher Technologies has developed a hybrid Li/MnO_2-CFx technology capable of delivering high energy at high discharge rates and very low temperatures. Performance of the hybrid chemistry has been validated at up to 4C discharge rates and at temperatures between -55°C and 60°C. These cells deliver a nominal specific energy of >400 Wh/Kg at room temperature, which is >50% above current Li-ion cells. In addition to the advantage in specific energy, the Li/MnO_2-CFx hybrid technology offers advantages in shelf-life and maintenance costs (no need for re-charge prior to use) over Li-ion batteries.*

This technology is suitable for applications requiring a combination of high power and high energy such as single use UAVs and hypersonic applications. This presentation will provide a general overview of recent developments on the hybrid technology at EaglePicher. In addition, testing results from our pouch cells, 2/3A cells and corresponding battery packs will be discussed.

Keywords: carbon fluoride; manganese dioxide; battery.

Introduction

Lithium/Carbon fluoride (Li/CF_x) is an attractive primary power source, because of its high specific energy, low self-discharge (less than 1% per year), excellent thermal stability, wide operating temperature range (-40 to 85°C), and improved abuse tolerance over other lithium systems. However, the obstacles that prevent a wider market penetration of Li/CF_x chemistry are its initial voltage delay at low temperature, thermal management issue at high discharge rates, and its material cost. Several approaches have been used to address these issues, including a partial substitution of CF_x by manganese dioxide to form hybrid cathode [1-2]. Using web-coating process similar to that in lithium-ion battery production, EPT has developed CF_x-MnO_2 hybrid cathode, which not only maintains all the favorable advantages of Li/CF_x but also provides the highest specific energy and excellent performance in wide temperature range as compared to other lithium primary chemistries.

This paper provides a general overview of recent developments on hybrid chemistry technology at EaglePicher Technologies, and discusses results from our work on pouch cells, cylindrical cells and corresponding batteries packs.

Experimental

The materials and cathode process were described previously [3-5]. Carbon fluoride (CF_x) and electrolytic manganese dioxide (MnO_2) used in this work were commercially-available materials. The hybrid cathodes were processed using EPT's advanced web coating equipment similar to that used in lithium-ion technology. The cathode composition and formulation were optimized to achieve high electrode density with enhanced rate capability.

Results and Discussion

EPT has developed a high-power and high-rate lithium primary cell technology that includes a web-coated CF_x/MnO_2 hybrid cathode and proprietary electrolyte formulations through extensive efforts over the last several years. The addition of MnO_2 in the cathode reduces the heat generation, eliminates voltage delay, and lowers the overall cathode material cost. The web coating process enables thinner cathodes with improved rate capability. The choice of carbon type used as the conducting additive and its distribution within the cathode structure, as well as an optimized cathode porosity further enhance the cell rate capability. In order to extend the operating temperature of the Li/CF_x-MnO_2 hybrid cell without sacrificing the rate capability, an electrolyte with low viscosity, low melting-point solvents and optimal lithium salt concentration was developed. This hybrid technology has been evaluated in both cylindrical and prismatic cells configurations. In this paper, we will discuss the performance of the hybrid Li/CF_x-MnO_2 pouch and cylindrical cells for high-rate applications in an extended temperature range.

High-Rate Hybrid Pouch Cell Development

Pouch cells with this hybrid chemistry were developed to maximize cell discharge rate capability, while maintaining the high energy density. The advantages for pouch cells include flexibility in size design, high specific energy, and inexpensive packaging material compared to hard case cells. The pouch cell format also offers improved packaging efficiency for prismatic battery packs. The historic limitations for pouch cells include leakage and swelling due to gassing and CF_x electrode expansion during discharge [6]. Among these limitations, the major challenge for hybrid pouch cells is cell swelling due to the well-known swelling behavior of the CF_x cathodes during discharge; the higher the amount of CF_x in the hybrid cathode, the higher the extent of swelling tends to be. The swelling will not only affect the battery integrity, but also will negatively impact the battery discharge performance in the pouch cell format. These limitations can be addressed through optimization of the electrolyte formulation, the choice of suitable CF_x materials, pouch material selection, and pouch sealing techniques. Figure 1 shows a picture of the first generation high-rate hybrid pouch cell (LCF-136) developed at EaglePicher.

Figure 1. Li/CFx-MnO_2 Pouch Cell

The chemistry and design of the EaglePicher pouch cells were optimized by selecting the proper cathode active material, cathode composition, carbon conductive additives, and binder. Also, for the active materials, the ratio of the amount of MnO_2 to CF_x was optimized in terms of its effect on swelling, heat generation, and energy density requirement for the high-rate battery. The cathode loading was optimized according to the process capability, energy density, and power requirements for the battery. Cathode porosity was also optimized based on its effects on cathode swelling and energy density requirement for the battery.

Performance of the LCF-136 pouch cell was validated at up to a 2C rate for a wide range of temperatures. Figure 2 illustrates the performance of pouch cells at different rates at -40°C. In the figure, it is demonstrated that the cells exhibit a good rate capability at -40°C, delivering 85 to 95% discharge efficiency. Another characteristic of the curves is that the higher the rate, the higher the cell discharge efficiency at -40°C. This is explained by the heat effect of the battery. The higher discharge rate will generate greater amounts of heat, making the battery discharge at a warmer temperature, thus working at a higher voltage, and delivering higher capacity and energy [7].

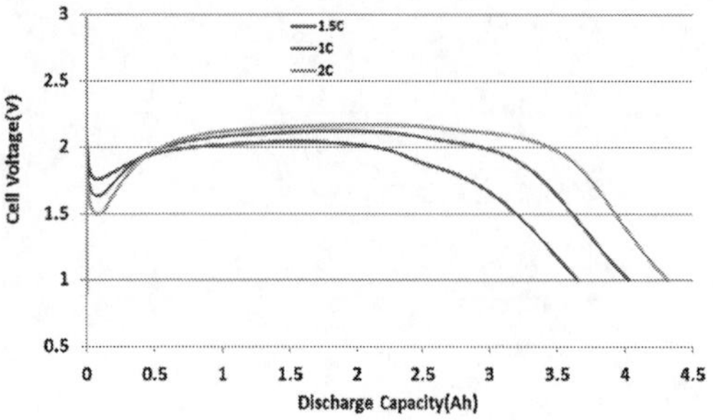

Figure 2. LCF-136 Rate Capability at -40°C

A manufacturing line for the LCF-136 has been installed and is in operation at our Joplin facility. The cells and battery packs have been fully qualified for different applications.

In recent years, Eaglepicher has developed a second generation high rate pouch cell (LCF-145) with increased rate capability for more demanding applications. Performance of the LCF-145 cell has been validated up to a 7C rate for a wide range of temperatures. Figure 3 shows the discharge curves of pouch cells at 20W rate (~3C rate) at various temperatures. As can be seen in the figure, the LCF-145 cells show a high discharge efficiency over the -40°C to 60°C temperature range.

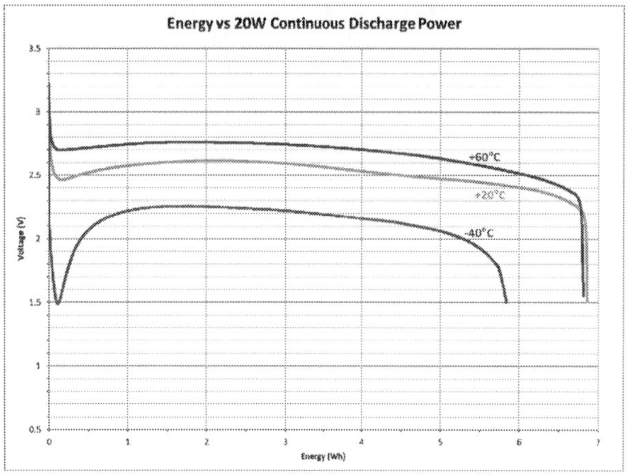

Figure 3. Discharge Performance of LCF-145 Pouch Cell at Various Temperatures

Figure 4 shows the performance of single LCF-145 pouch cells (in a 3-cell pack) under a simulated UAV profile. The discharge profile includes a 7C discharge rate during take-off and a 2C discharge rate during cruise discharge. It can be seen in the figure that the cell demonstrated the power capability required for this type of application. Several battery packs have recently been developed for different applications including UAVs.

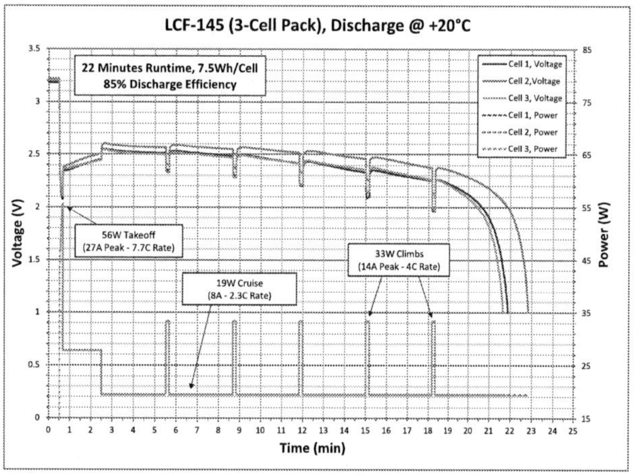

Figure 4. Performance of a LCF-145 pouch cell under a simulated UAV discharge profile

Small cylindrical cells (2/3A and 1/3A cells) have also been recently developed/qualified for hypersonic applications using the high rate hybrid chemistry. Table 1 shows the performance parameters of Eaglepicher's current high rate cylindrical cells and pouch cell products.

Table 1. Eaglepicher's High Rate Products

Product #	LCF-136	LCF-136HR	LCF-145	LCF-144	LCF-314
Electrochemistry	Li/CF_x-MnO_2	Li/CF_x-MnO_2	Li/CF_x-MnO_2	Li/CF_x-MnO_2	Li/CF_x-MnO_2
Form Factor	Prismatic Pouch	Prismatic Pouch	Prismatic Pouch	Cylindrical (2/3A Size)	Cylindrical (1/3A Size)
Exterior Construction	Aluminum-Polymer Laminate	Aluminum-Polymer Laminate	Aluminum-Polymer Laminate	Nickel-Plated Steel	Nickel-Plated Steel
Nominal Voltage (V)	2.6	2.6	2.6	2.6	2.6
Mass (g)	29.5	29.5	24.0	15.5	11.3
Dimensions (mm)	56.5 (H) x 50.0 (W) x 6.5 (T)	58.0 (H) x 49.8 (W) x 6.5 (T)	58.0 (H) x 49.8 (W) x 5.2 (T)	16.5 (Ø) x 32.0 (H)	16.5 (Ø) x 19.0 (H)
Storage Temperatures (°C)	-40°C to +85°C	-40°C to +85°C	-40°C to +85°C	-40°C to +85°C	-40°C to +85°C
Operating Temperatures (°C)	-40°C to +60°C	-40°C to +60°C	-40°C to +60°C	-40°C to +80°C	-40°C to +80°C
Capacity/Energy (Ah/Wh)	4.9Ah / 12.5Wh	4.9Ah / 12.5Wh	3.5Ah / 9Wh	1.4Ah / 3.7Wh	0.8Ah / 2.0Wh
Specific Energy (Wh/kg)	420	420	375	240	180
Energy Density (Wh/L)	680	660	615	540	490
Specific Power* (W/kg)	1800	2400	3000	1700	1200
Power Density* (W/L)	2800	3800	4800	3300	3500

In conclusion, EaglePicher has made great progress in developing a Li/CF_x-MnO_2 hybrid technology, which offers a combination of power and energy for military and space applications requiring high rate capability and long service life in an extended operating temperature range from -40 to 60°C. The hybrid chemistry pouch cells provide an opportunity to develop lightweight, compact, and versatile batteries to address industry needs and requirements.

Acknowledgements

This material is released to the public domain in accordance with ITAR 22 CFR 120.34.

References

1. Marple, J. W., "Performance characteristics of Li/MnO_2-CFx hybrid cathode jellyroll cells" *Journal of Powers Sources*, vol. 19, pp.325-335, 1987.
2. Leger, V. Z., "Non aqueous cell having a MnO_2/polycarbon fluoride cathode," US patent 4327166, April 1982.
3. Zhang, D., E. Ndzebet, and M. Yang, "Advanced Battery Chemistry for Portable Power," *Proceeding of the 44th Power Sources Conference*, Las Vegas, Nevada, 14-17 June 2010.
4. Destephen, M., D. Zhang, H. Bang, J. Wang, U. Viswanathan, and E. Ndzebet, "Advanced Hybrid Battery Chemistry for Portable Power," *Proceeding of the 45th Power Sources Conference*, Las Vegas, Nevada, 11-14 June 2012.
5. Destephen, M., D. Zhang, H. Bang, and E. Ndzebet, "Advanced Li/CFx-MnO2 Hybrid Technology Development," *The 46th Power Sources Conference*, Orlando, Florida, June 9-12, 2014.
6. Read, J., D. Foster, J. Wolfenstine, and S. Zhang, "Microcalorimetry of Li/CFx Cells and Discharge Mechanism", *www.arl.army.mil/arlreports/2009/ARL-TR-5043.pdf*, 2009.
7. Destephen, M, Listerud, E, Ndzebet, E, Zhang, D "Advanced Li-CFx Technologies for Space Applications," AIAA Propulsion and Energy Forum, Atlanta, Georgia, July 10-12, 2017

High Energy Primary Technology Development

David Darch, Mario Destephen, Ernest Ndzebet
EaglePicher Technologies, LLC
1216 W C St, Joplin, MO 64801

Abstract

This paper covers EaglePicher Technologies, LLC (EPT) high energy primary technology. The lithium carbon-monofluoride (Li/CF_x) D-cell is a proven option for high-energy, low maintenance applications. EPT web-coated Li/CF_x -MnO_2 hybrid chemistry in multiple cell formats is used in applications with a focus on portable power. The primary Conformal Wearable Battery (CWB) is an advanced solution to the United States Army's request for a light-weight, flexible source of power that can be carried by an individual without significant burden.

Introduction

From an understanding of fundamental chemistries, to improvements in specific cell formats, to pioneering developments in battery assemblies, EPT has been pushing the limits of battery technology to help meet the industry's growing need for energy. The three topics reviewed represent EPT's push to further refine high-demand, mission-critical products.

Li/ CF_x D-Cell

Overview

LCF-514, also known as the pure CF_x D-cell, is a high-energy cell designed to maximize the life of far-reaching applications such as remote environmental sensors or deep-space missions. These typically feature low-rate discharges and are weight sensitive, so the LCF-514 cell was developed to specifically target these criteria.

Development

The D-Cell was specifically designed to provide a very high energy solution at lower rates. To facilitate this, laser-welded aluminum headers and cans were selected over the traditional steel used with this cell format.

Discharges between 50mA and 250mA yield a capacity of around ~20Ah with this chemistry, where discharges from 750mA to 2A and have resulted in ~17.8Ah. For 50mA discharges, the efficiency of this cell produces a specific energy of approximately 750Wh/kg. Figure 6 displays some example discharge curves at room temperature.

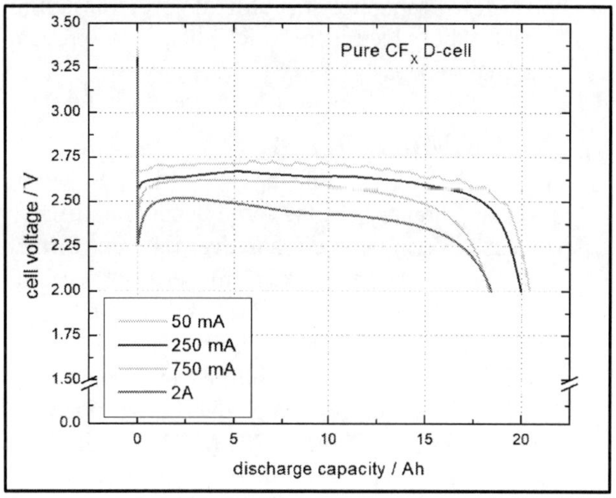

Fig. 6 LCF-514 Discharge Performance at Varying Rates

Li/ CF_x MnO_2 Chemistry

Overview

Lithium carbon-monofluoride electrolytic manganese dioxide, or Li/ CF_x-MnO_2 for short, is a primary battery chemistry with clear advantages over its industry counterparts in regards to weight efficiency, minimal self-discharge, allowable operating temperature, and abuse tolerance.

Drawbacks of the Li/CF_x root chemistry, such as low temperature voltage delay, thermal management in high-rate discharge cases, and material cost are aided with the implementation of electrolytic manganese dioxide (EMD). Performance of the high-energy hybrid chemistry has been validated at up to 1.5C rate and at temperatures ranging -50°C to 85°C.

Both the carbon monofluoride (CF_x) and EMD used in the hybrid-chemistry products discussed in this paper are commercially available resources.
EMD's lower material cost enables an increased affordability in addition to performance benefits. Cathodes processed using the hybrid chemistry were generated using EPT's web-coating process, which is similar to that used to produce lithium-ion cathodes. The specific composition of material was formulated to maximize electrode density without compromising rate capability. This unique combination of cathode materials maximizes energy while enabling high-rate discharges.
To ensure the safety of these high-energy products, shut-down separator was utilized in the design to isolate the electrodes which helps to prevent thermal runaway.

Li/ CF_xMnO_2 D-Cell

Cylindrical cells utilizing the Li/ CF_x-MnO_2 hybrid chemistry see the same benefits and flaws that the pouch cells do, however inherent format differences alter the results in performance and swelling. The targets for this cell was to boast twice the capacity and specific energy of the Li/SO_2 cell. Figure 3 highlights this goal being achieved without the voltage delay intrinsic to the pure CF_x cells. The Li/ CF_x-MnO_2 hybrid cells delivered 15.5Ah, more than double the ~7.5Ah yielded by the Li-SO_2 cell.

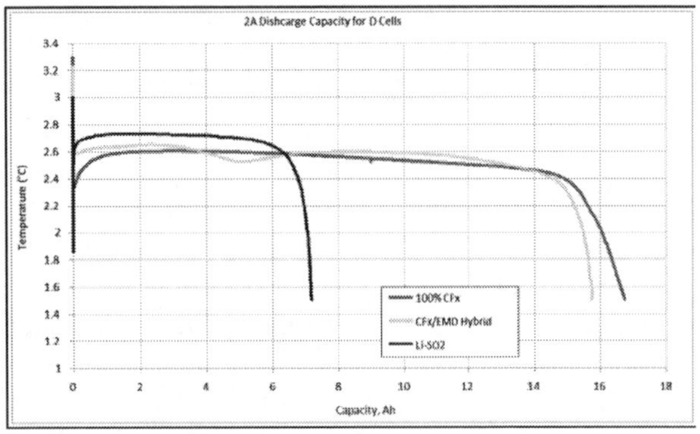

Fig. 3 D-Cell Performance at 2A Continuous, Room-Temperature Discharge

The application demanded full rate capability across a wide range of operational temperatures. This was a consideration during the refinement of the cathode, but also the optimization of electrolyte formulation. The results of that effort culminated in a cell that can deliver 13Ah while under a 2A discharge current in a -40°C environment. Performance at low temperature is displayed in figure 4.

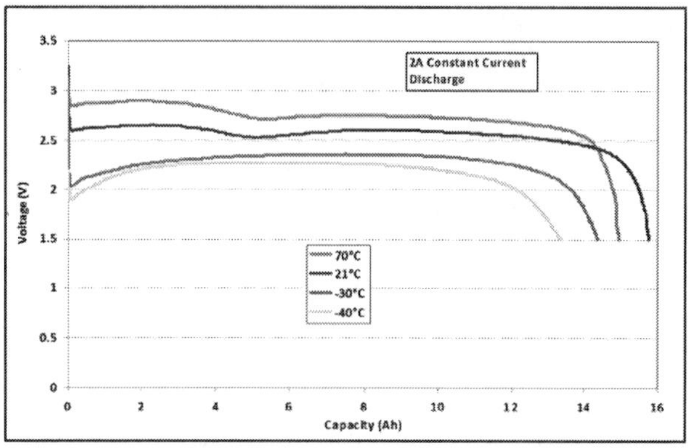

Fig. 4 D-Cell Performance at 2A, Continuous, -40°C Discharge

BA-5790 Battery Performance

The hybrid D-size cell was incorporated into the BA-5790 battery for evaluation. In addition to the advantages in capacity and specific energy, the hybrid chemistry provides significant reduction in heat generation during discharge compared to the pure CF_x chemistry. A specifically designed battery case was developed to increase heat conduction to the exterior of the battery.

Figure 5 shows the discharge performance at 2A of the Li/CF_x-MnO_2 hybrid battery. As can be seen, the hybrid cell delivered 16.0Ah above 20.0V and without voltage delay. This is twice the capacity of Li/SO_2.

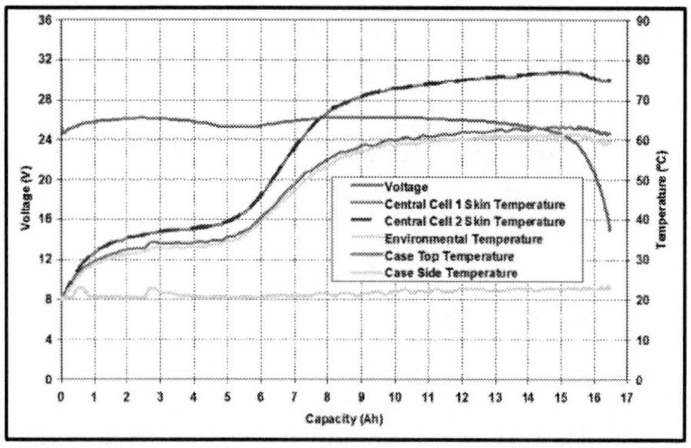

Figure 5. Discharge performance of hybrid battery at 2A

Pouch Cells

EaglePicher's pouch-cell technology benefits weight-sensitive applications by using a light packaging material and an easily packaged design. The pouch format emphasizes energy-density at the cost of physical deformation during discharge. A well-known property of CF_x is that it swells as a result of the reduction-oxidation reaction that occurs when the cell is under a load. The swelling of the CF_x negatively impacts the discharge performance of pouch cells and can deform battery cases.

To overcome the negative effects of the pouch cell and the inherent downsides to the active materials, the proper selection of the grade of the active materials needed to be investigated. Also, conductive carbon additives and carefully selected binder agent had to be chosen for use in the final product. Optimization of the material ratios was a critical effort to lower the impact of swelling, mitigate heat generation during discharge, and maximize energy density. EPT's effort on the selection of cathode loading and porosity aided in the proper balance of energy density, rate capability, and swelling. The fruit of all these efforts is evident below in figure 1 (Composition B).

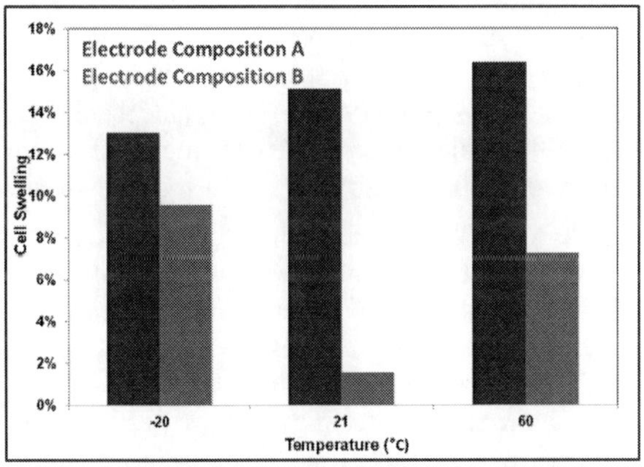

Fig. 1 Electrode Composition vs Swelling at Varied Temperatures

Performance of the hybrid pouch cell (LCF-134) was validated at up to 1.5C rate for a wide range of temperatures. As can be seen in Figure 2, the pouch cells were able to deliver high efficiency from -40ºC to 60°C.

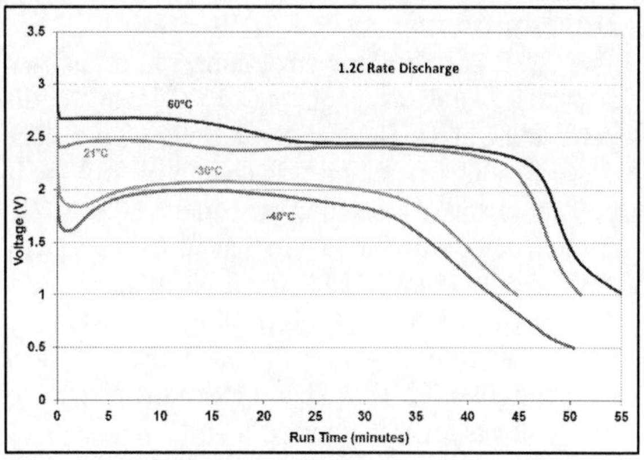

Figure 2. Discharge performance of the LCF-134

The Conformal Wearable Battery (MAP-9553)

Battery Description

The Conformal Wearable Battery (CWB) is a power-supply unit designed to provide accessible energy to soldiers on the high-tech, modern battlefield. The 24-cell, 15V CWB pack encases the Li/ CF_x-MnO_2 hybrid technology in a flexible, hermetically sealed container. With a footprint of 19.5cm x 22.1cm flat, only 2cm thick, and weighing in around 940 grams, the CWB is a designed to impose minimal burden to the wearer. External features to the battery include a state-of-charge indicator (SOCI), a complete-discharge device (CDD), and a GlenAir electrical connector. Figure 7 shows the primary conformal battery (MAP-9553).

Fig. 7 Conformal Wearable Battery

Development

The CWB has been proven at temperatures as low as -20°C and as high as 55°C while still performing at a high level. For baseline, a constant power, room temperature discharge of 20W will pull about 250Wh. Soaking the battery at -20°C for 4 hours before discharging in that temperature will pull about 194Wh and incite a battery skin temperature of only 5°C. Repeating this test at the 55°C condition yields 260Wh and a skin temperature of 72°C. An example of the discharge behavior is shown in figure 8.

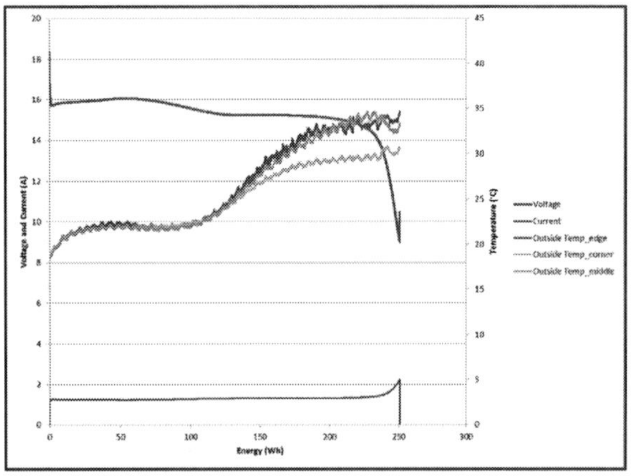

Fig. 8 CWB Discharge 20W Performance at 20°C

The battery is designed to survive the conditions of the battlefield. Subsequently, extensive abuse tests were performed on the system. Army-specified bullet penetration testing featuring 7.62mm rounds did not compromise the functionality of the battery. Visual results of the test can be seen in figure 9.

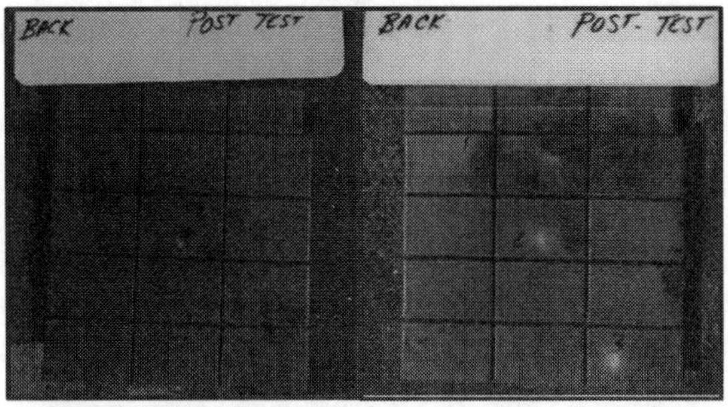

Fig. 9 CWB Bullet Penetration Test Samples

The battery survived impact testing, conformability testing, mechanical shock, random vibration, and transit drop testing. Multiple batteries were run through all of the tests mentioned in this section, with the exception of bullet penetration, and still performed. As a testament to the remarkable resiliency of this technology, one battery that went through this rigorous testing (including 5 impact cycles when only 3 were required) still delivered about 240Wh at a 20W constant power discharge without exceeding an internal temperature of 45°C. This battery also saw multiple 1-minute long, 20W discharges between tests to evaluate potential damage at each stage, which should be considered when appraising its capacitive ability.

Conclusion

EaglePicher Technologies offers an array of high-energy solutions to meet the needs of any situation.

The Li/CF_x D-Cell (EPT's LCF-514) is specially optimized towards extending the service life for single-use technology. With an extreme focus on energy, this cell offers exceptionally long life for critical applications. In pouch cells, cylindrical cells, or other formats (i.e. prismatic), the Li/CF_x-MnO_2 hybrid chemistry provides a high energy solution capable of performing safely in a wide array of temperatures. It is designed to create a long-lasting, no-maintenance solution. The BA-5790 vessel for the hybrid D-Cell displays the battery-level performance capabilities of the Li/CF_x-MnO_2 primary chemistry. The battery is currently finalizing first article testing (FAT), with plans for deliverable batteries to be built this year.

EaglePicher's primary, conformal wearable battery (CWB) is flexible, weighs less than 1.0kg, and will deliver 250Wh at room temperature and over 190Wh at -20°C. It has a very robust design with numerous safety features that has passed bullet penetration testing, impact testing, and numerous other safety tests. This was proven when U.S. Amy field-testing was performed on the MAP-9553 and only one battery was need for a 72-hour mission with energy still in reserve after the mission was completed.

The energy made available by EaglePicher products continues to serve commercial and defense customers safely and reliably, making them a must-have solution for demanding, mission-critical, applications.

High-Purity, CO_2-Derived Multiwall Carbon Nanotube Formulations for Realizing High-Energy and High-Power Lithium-Ion Cells

David L. Wood, III and Anna Douglas
SkyNano, LLC, 4028 Papermill Drive NW, Suite 3, Knoxville, TN
david.wood@skynanotechnologies.com / 1-505-699-5271

Abstract

Multiwall carbon nanotubes (MWCNTs) generated from permanent CO_2 capture, utilization, and sequestration (CCUS) are discussed in the context of advanced conductive additives for lithium-ion battery (LIB) electrodes. An electrochemical molten carbonate electrolysis process is employed to generate the MWCNTs (30-50 nm diameter), and a high-efficiency (95%) thermochemical CO_2 uptake is used to regenerate the lithium carbonate electrolyte for new tube growth. The MWCNTs are then post-processed to remove excess electrolyte, purified to remove metal catalyst, and pre-dispersed in solvent (water or N-methylpyrrolidone) before making the final electrode dispersions. LIB cathode performance data with $LiNi_{0.6}Mn_{0.2}Co_{0.2}O_2$ (NMC 622) is discussed along with Si/graphite anode formulations for realizing simultaneous energy and power density increases. These cathode formulations contain only 10-26% substitution of the baseline conductive carbon black with MWCNTs, which corresponds to 0.50-0.62 wt% MWCNTs in the final electrode coating. The substantial capacity increases for the improved cathodes within the 1-3C discharge range are highlighted, and plans for boosting Si/graphite anode performance with 30 wt% Si and 1.0-2.5 wt% MWCNTs are introduced.

Key Words

Lithium-ion batteries; multiwall carbon nanotube (MWCNT) additives; high power density; extreme fast charging; molten carbonate electrolysis; CO_2 capture, utilization, and sequestration (CCUS)

Introduction

SkyNano, LLC is a domestic woman-owned small business that produces ***low cost***, high-purity multiwall carbon nanotubes (MWCNTs) from CO_2 pollution via molten carbonate electrolysis and thermochemical electrolyte regeneration with atmospheric or point-source-capture CO_2.[1-4] This carbon negative technology enables SkyNano to produce MWCNTs at about 1/10th the cost of state-of-the-art chemical vapor deposition methods. SkyNano battery grade MWCNTs have high CNT purity, high C content (99.90-99.95%), tunable diameter within the range of 10-100 nm, and typical aspect ratios between 100-200. SkyNano's CO_2-derived MWCNTs are well-poised to supplement or replace state-of-the-art carbon black conductive additives in lithium-ion battery (LIB) applications for improved performance that meets the demands of today's warfighter.

These CO_2-derived MWCNTs have been demonstrated to substantially improve high discharge-rate cathode $LiNi_{0.6}Mn_{0.2}Co_{0.2}O_2$ (NMC 622) performance in lithium-ion battery (LIB) pouch cells produced at the DOE Battery Manufacturing R&D Facility (BMF) at Oak Ridge National Laboratory (ORNL) when 10% of the carbon black conductive additive was replace with SkyNano MWCNTs. Increases of 21% at 2C, 62% at 3C and 52% at 5C in discharge capacity were observed over the control cathode with no MWCNTs. For warfighters in the field, this advancement means: 1) higher energy at higher discharge rates (higher peak power density); or 2) increased usage per charge for a given discharge rate, which will improve communication ability, device performance in the field, unmanned ariel vehicle / unmanned underwater vehicle (UAV/UUV) mission duration and maneuverability, and military base grid independence.

Results and Discussion

In these prior efforts to integrate our CNTs into LIBs, we studied the partial replacement of state-of-the-art carbon black (CB) with our CNTs in NMC622 cathodes, a material commonly used in EV and other high energy batteries. Industrially relevant slot-die-coated electrodes were fabricated using a Frontier Industrial Technology Dynacoat pilot slot-die coating line to best mimic commercial processing. **Table 1** below shows the three cathode formulations that were studied. The anode used was the ORNL BMF standard Superior Graphite SLC 1520T material at an active material loading of 92 wt%, a CB loading of 2 wt%, and a PVDF binder loading of 6 wt%. The 95-wt% NMC 622 slurry (formulation "F8") needed to be thickened substantially from 46% solids to 65% solids during the mixing protocol to achieve a viscosity that would allow for slot-die coating, which subsequently taught us *another value proposition of using CNTs as a partial replacement of CB – less solvent use in electrode fabrication*. Single layer pouch cells were

Table 1. NMC622 cathode compositions with SkyNano MWCNTs partially substituted for carbon black.

Formulation	CNT (%)	CB (%)	Total C (wt%)	NMC 622 (wt%)	PVDF (wt%)	Slurry Solids Loading (wt%)
Control 2	0	100	4	91	5	46
F7	10	90	4	91	5	46
F8	26	74	2.4	95	2.6	60

constructed (five replicates for each cell configuration) using these three coatings, which had an average rated capacity of 134 ± 10 mAh. **Figure 1** shows the rate capability data ***normalized to total cathode mass*** for these cell groups, and it is seen that both CNT formulations (F7 and F8) outperform the Control 2 at all discharge rates above 0.5C (below 0.5C all cells perform comparably). The scaled F7 pouch cells performed better than their half coin cell counterparts and significantly outperformed Control 2 (***20.5%, 62.7%, and 46.7% capacity improvements at 2C, 3C, and 5C discharge rates, respectively), showing that only a small amount of CNTs is required to realize large improvements in cathode rate capability***. When examining the performance of the 95-wt% NMC622 formulation (F8) in Figure 1, it is seen that no further improvement in performance was realized over that of the 91-wt% NMC622 one (F7) on a total cathode mass basis except at the low C rates (high energy conditions). Once the discharge rate was increased above 1C, the C/binder network established with the lower mass fractions became performance limiting and electronic conductivity limitations were reached at the higher discharge rates. ***This result demonstrates the need for a fully optimized CNT dispersion network that will be critical for ultra-high active-material loadings of 95-97 wt%, and helps to motivate the proposed tasks in this scope of work.*** **Figure 1** also shows the power densities obtained from the rate capability study. The 91-wt% formulation significantly increased the power density magnitude over Control 2 for the 2-5C discharge rates; however, performance limitations of the 95-wt% formulation are evident here, and underscore the remaining critical challenges related to CNT dispersion optimization for enabling higher active material loadings.

The pouch cells tested for rate capability (discussed above) were immediately subjected to accelerated degradation testing by cycling them at 1C/-2C for 1000 cycles. The capacity retention profiles for Control 2 (91 wt% NMC 622 with no CNTs), formulation F7 (91 wt% NMC 622 with 0.4 wt% CNTs), and formulation F8 (95 wt% NMC 622 with 0.63 wt% CNTs) are shown in **Figure 2** through 500 cycles. The associated capacity results were normalized to the **total cathode mass** for a direct comparison between the 91-wt% (F7) and 95-wt% (F8) NMC 622 cathodes. It is seen that the capacity retention of all cells retained 80% of their initial 1C/-2C capacity over the 500 cycles. However, the capacity magnitudes where substantially higher after 500 cycles for both formulations with SkyNano CNTs (13% improvement), and the error bars (2σ standard deviation) were smaller. Also seen in Figure 2 (lower plot) is the performance of a larger 266-mAh cell with the 91-wt% NMC 622 formulation (F7) subjected to the Department of Energy Vehicle Technologies Office (DOE VTO) extreme fast charging (XFC) 6C/

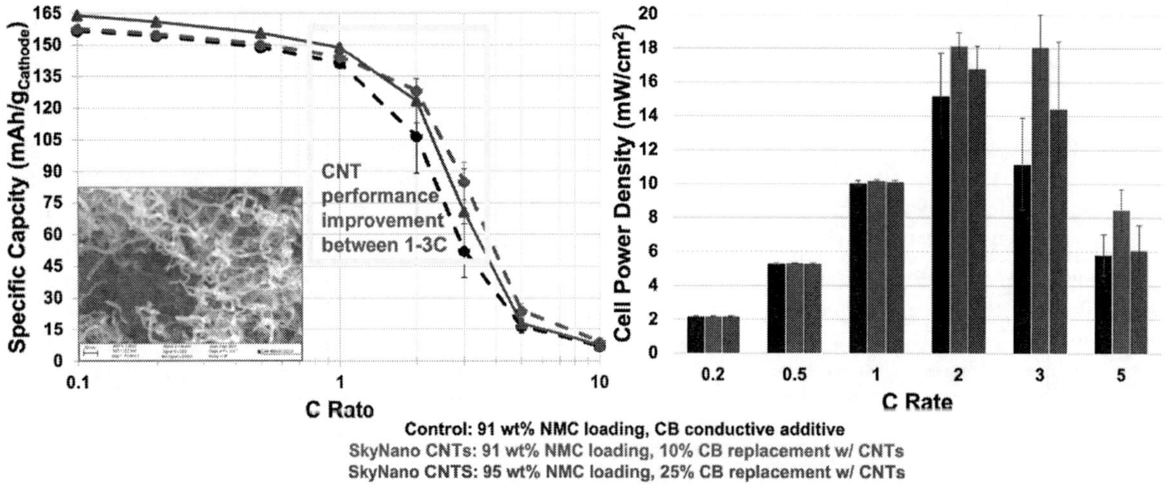

Figure 1. Rate capability (left) and power density (right) of pouch cells enabled with SkyNano CNTs

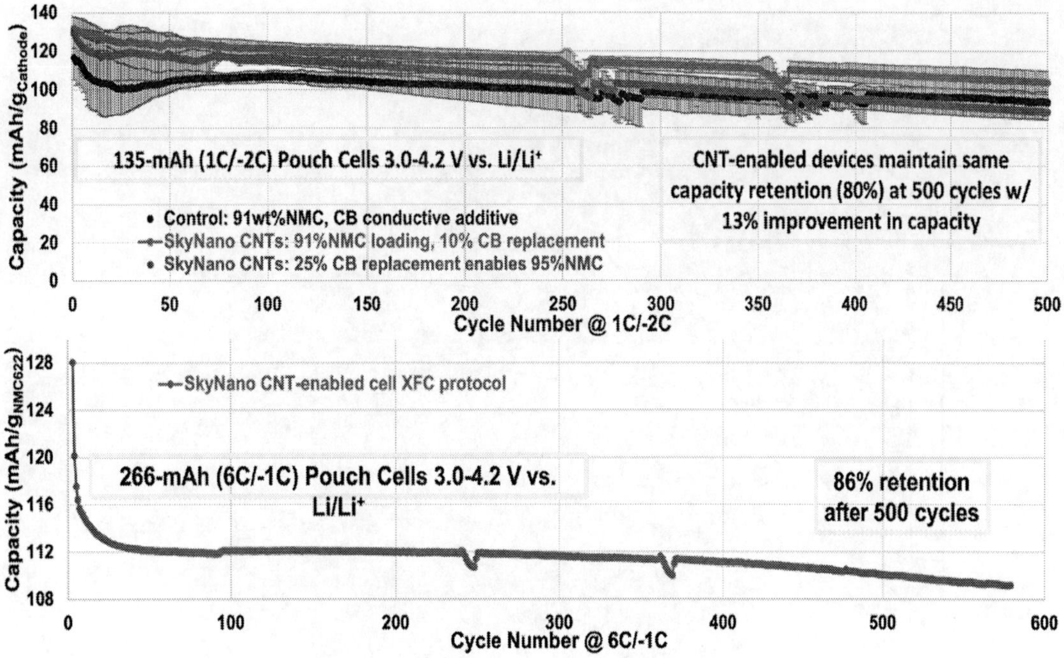

Figure 2. Cycling data of pouch cells enabled with SkyNano CNTs

-1C protocol. It was observed that the XFC cell performed extremely well under these conditions showing 72% of rated capacity (formation capacity at 0.05C) at the onset of cycling, which leveled off at 88% capacity retention after 80 6C/-1C cycles and retained its capacity well at 86% after 500 cycles.

Nanoscale integration of low-cost, electrochemically manufactured MWCNTs into highly loaded, Si based anodes is a major focus of SkyNano's LIB R&D, but there is a great deal of front-end research that needs to occur to create a sub-micron network of spherical primary Si/SiO nanoparticles and MWCNTs in a finished electrode coating. In addition, a network of this type is highly beneficial to Si mechanical and surface chemical stability during long-term cycling (at 4C/-1C) by establishing a scaffold-type structure of individual MWCNTs that encases individual Si/SiO secondary particles. SkyNano MWCNTs have unique surface chemistry compared to conventionally produced materials via chemical vapor deposition (CVD) using methane or ethylene carbon sources, which will be exploited to achieve this anode microstructure with individually dispersed MWCNTs among Si/SiO and carbon black (CB) aggregates. Two control anode compositions will be used, which are 30:55:2.5:4.5:8 and 30:55:1:6:8 compositions of Si/graphite/MWCNT/CB/LiPAA. The VTO Si Anode

Consortium baseline materials will be used with SkyNano MWCNTs such as MSE Supplies 150-nm Si/SiO, Superior Graphite SLC 1520T, Denka CB, LiPAA for aqueous colloids, and polyimide for NMP colloids (see Figure 3 for schematic of desired anode microstructure).

Current obstacles for MWCNT integration into advanced batteries are that cost is too high (4-10 times higher than carbon black), the physical properties (diameter, length, and wall thickness) have not been optimized for high-rate performance (i.e., 2C discharge and 4C charge rates), and CNT co-dispersion with Si nanoparticles is difficult. The latter will feature 30 wt% Si anodes, which is equal to the VTO Si Anode Consortium target loading. Enabling the widespread commercialization of high-energy, advanced batteries with low cost for transportation electrification, renewable energy storage, and portable electronics will result in substantially reduced CO_2 emissions, increased mobility, and ubiquitous opportunity for connectivity for the modern warfighter and the U.S. military in general. In addition, SkyNano produces its MWCNTs through the consumption of ambient or flowing CO_2 streams, which will contribute to slowing the increase in CO_2 emissions and ultimately reducing the current atmospheric content of 421 ppm. MWCNTs provide many commercial advantages in advanced batteries: 1) using thicker, higher-energy electrodes by minimizing electronic conductivity losses; 2) higher power density (i.e., higher capacity at high discharge rates); 3) integrating structured electrode architectures; 4) higher loadings of Si at the anode by forming a more mechanically

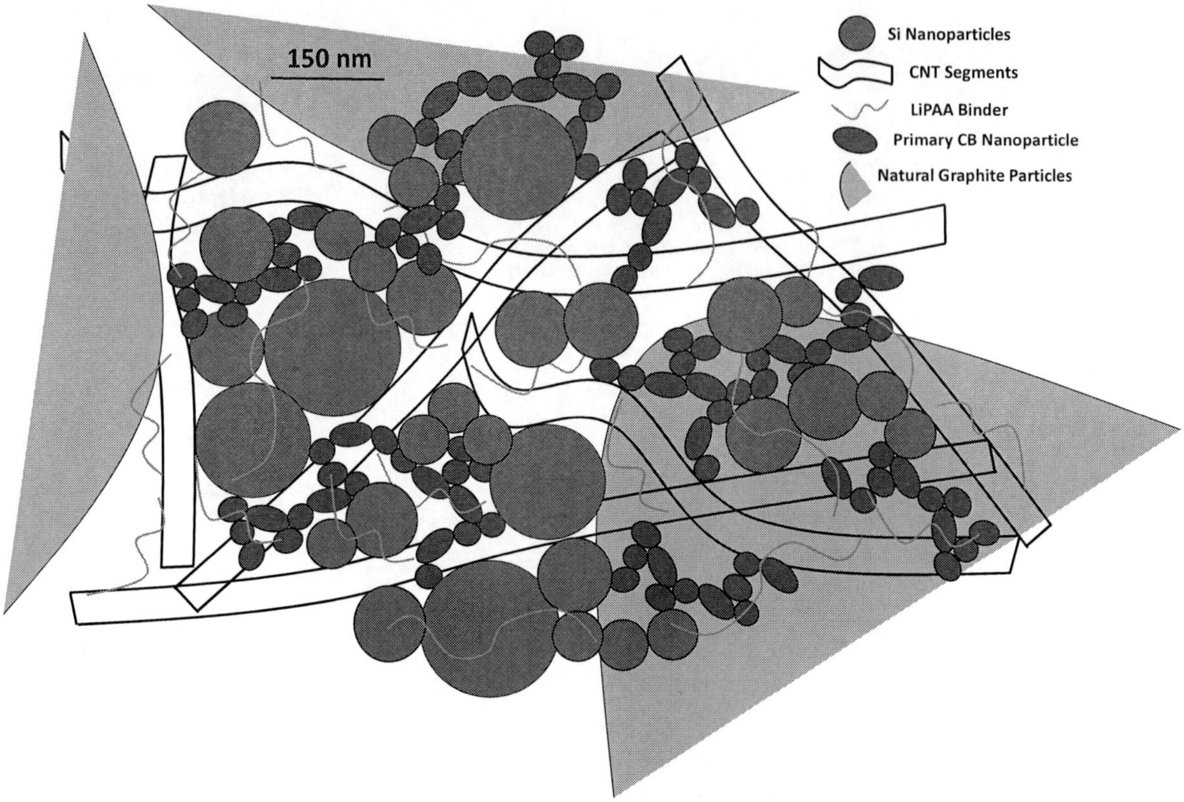

Figure 3. Schematic (to scale) of proposed Si-C anode nanoscale architecture with example composition of 40:40:5:5:10 Si/graphite/MWCNT/CB/LiPAA enabled by micro-dispersion of MWCNTs where Si nanoparticles are encased in a monodispersed MWCNT network.

stable composite with graphite during electrochemical cycling; and 5) faster charging rates approaching 4-6C. In addition, SkyNano MWCNTs at scale will be much less expensive than those produced using the high-vacuum conditions of chemical vapor deposition (CVD), and the material properties may be tailored for the type of electrode of interest. The electrode designs discussed here rely on the use of conventional electrolytes, widely available active materials, and conventional electrode manufacturing approaches and require no capital expenditures to integrate into current manufacturing lines.

Acknowledgements
The authors would like to thank the U.S. Department of Energy Small Business Innovation Research / Small Business Technology Transfer (SBIR/STTR) Program Office and the U.S. Department of the Air Force SBIR Program for funding this R&D. We would also like to thank Oak Ridge National Laboratory for producing the NMC 622 cathode coatings, assembling the pouch cells, and evaluating the electrochemical performance of the cells. Finally, we would like to thank our U.S. Space Force program manager Daniel Romm and his team for helpful discussions and guidance with data interpretation.

References
1. S. Licht, A. Douglas, J. W. Ren, R. Carter, M. Lefler, and C. L. Pint, Carbon Nanotubes Produced from Ambient Carbon Dioxide for Environmentally Sustainable Lithium-Ion and Sodium-Ion Battery Anodes, *ACS Central Science*, **2**, 162-168 (2016).
2. A. Douglas, N. Muralidharan, R. Carter, and C. L. Pint, Sustainable Capture and Conversion of Carbon Dioxide into Valuable Multiwalled Carbon Nanotubes Using Metal Scrap Materials, *ACS Sustainable Chemistry & Engineering*, **5**, 7104-7110 (2017).
3. A. Douglas, R. Carter, N. Muralidharan, L. Oakes, and C. L. Pint, Iron Catalyzed Growth of Crystalline Multi-Walled Carbon Nanotubes from Ambient Carbon Dioxide Mediated by Molten Carbonates, *Carbon*, **116**, 572-578 (2017).
4. A. Douglas, R. Carter, M. Y. Li, and C. L. Pint, Toward Small-Diameter Carbon Nanotubes Synthesized from Captured Carbon Dioxide: Critical Role of Catalyst Coarsening, *ACS Applied Materials & Interfaces*, **10**, 19010-19018 (2018).

Direct Battery Electrolyte Heating and Temperature Maintenance at Low Temperatures

Jahangir Rastegar
Omnitek Partners, LLC,
85 Air Park Drive, Unit 3, Ronkonkoma, New York 11779
j.rastegar@omnitekpartners.com / 1-631-665-4008

Abstract

In this paper, the development of a novel technology for direct and rapid heating of battery electrolyte at low temperatures and maintaining the battery temperature at its optimal performance level is presented. The technology has been extensively tested on a wide range of primary and secondary batteries at temperatures as low as -60°C without causing any damage to the batteries and without interfering with the operation of chargers and existing electronic controls such as the Battery Management System (BMS). The technology is applicable to almost all primary and secondary batteries, such as Lithium-ion, Lithium-polymer, NiMH and lead-acid batteries. The technology is also applicable to super-capacitors and has been used to rapidly charge and heat super-capacitors at temperatures as low as -54°C without any damage.

Keywords

Rechargeable Battery Heating; Lead Acid Battery Heating; Lithium-Ion Battery Heating; Lithium-Polymer Battery Heating; Supercapacitor Heating; Battery Low Temperature Performance Enhancement; Low Temperature Charging of Batteries.

Introduction

The performance of batteries is significantly reduced at low temperatures. This is the case for both primary and rechargeable batteries. In addition, current lithium-ion and Lithium-polymer battery technology does not allow battery charging at temperatures below 0°C and charging at temperatures below their optimal level has been shown to reduce battery life.

Current solutions that try to address cold weather effects on batteries include heating the exterior of the battery by integrating "heaters" into the battery compartment or using heating blankets or pads, or recently by embedding heating elements inside batteries.

Omnitek has developed a novel patented technology [1] for direct and rapid heating of battery electrolyte at low temperatures and maintaining the battery temperature at its optimal performance level. The technology has been extensively tested on a wide range of primary and secondary batteries at temperatures as low as -60°C without causing any damage to the batteries and without interfering with the operation of chargers and existing electronic controls such as the Battery Management System (BMS). The technology is applicable to almost all primary and secondary batteries, such as Lithium-ion, Lithium-polymer, NiMH and lead-acid batteries. The technology is also applicable to super-capacitors and has been used to rapidly heat and charge super-capacitors.

The developed highly innovative technology is based on in-depth studies that were carried out by our scientists of the highly nonlinear dynamic behavior of the battery electrolyte components when subjected to a high-frequency electric field. Based on the results of these studies, a patented technology has been developed that uses high-frequency AC (symmetric with no DC component) current to heat any battery electrolyte directly and uniformly at temperatures that are as low as -60°C. In this direct electrolyte heating technology, the applied high-frequency currents are in general in the range of 50-120 KHz for Lithium-ion and Lithium-Polymer and 20-60 KHz for Lead-Acid batteries, and 1-2 MHz for super capacitors.

The developed electrolyte heating unit is externally powered at very low temperatures at which the battery is unable to provide a significant amount of power. Once the battery can provide enough power, the battery temperature may be raised to its optimal level and maintained at that level by power from the battery itself. The battery may be fully charged or discharged. The battery may be charged while being heated.

The developed electrolyte heating units are inherently highly efficient and safe and do not interfere with battery safety and protection circuits (e.g., various BMS used in Li-ion battery packs). The following are some of the main characteristics of the developed technology:

- It requires no modification to the battery and super-capacitor.
- The basic physics of the process and extensive tests clearly show no damage to the battery and super-capacitor and their safety and protection circuits.
- The battery pack protection electronic units, such as those for Lithium-ion and Lithium-polymer batteries, can be modified to ensure self-powered continuous high-performance operation at low temperatures.
- The battery electrolyte and super-capacitor is directly and uniformly heated, therefore bringing a very cold battery to its optimal operating temperature very rapidly and minimizing heat loss from the battery.
- Direct electrolyte heating requires significantly less electrical energy than external heating.
- Standard sized Lithium-ion or polymer batteries can be used instead of thin and flat battery stack packaging that are used to accelerate external heating via heating blankets or the like.
- Unlike heating elements provided inside the battery, no local hot spots are generated inside the battery while heating at low environmental temperatures.
- By ensuring battery charging and usage at their optimal temperatures, the battery life cycle can be significantly increased.
- The technology is simple to implement and low-cost.

High-Frequency Battery Electrolyte Heating

The basic operation of a battery may be approximately modeled with the equivalent (lumped) circuit shown in Fig. 1. The temperature and frequency dependence of the elements used to model the battery electrolyte component of the battery is critical for describing high-frequency AC current electrolyte heating technology. In this model, the resistor R_e represents the electrical resistance against electrons from freely moving in conductive materials, i.e., electrodes, and wirings, etc. The equivalent resistor R_i and L_i represent the temperature and frequency (f) dependent resistance to free movement of ions and their resistance to acceleration due to their

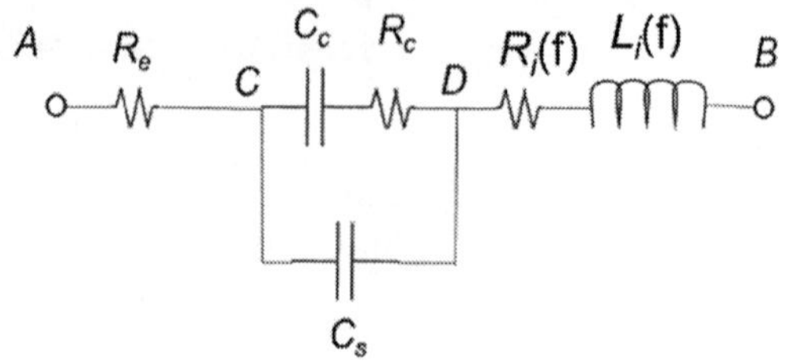

Figure 1: Equivalent lumped circuit model of a battery.

mass, charge interactions, etc. The capacitor C_s is the surface capacitance, which can store electric field energy between electrodes. The resistor R_c and capacitor C_c represent the electrical-chemical mechanism of the battery in which C_c is intended to indicate the electrical energy that is stored as chemical energy during the battery charging and that can be discharged during battery discharging, and R_c indicates the equivalent resistance to discharging current.

As an example, the operation of a Li-ion battery, as modeled in Fig. 1, may then be described as follows. If an AC current with high enough frequency is applied to the battery, due to the low impedance of the capacitor C_s, there will be no significant voltage drop across the capacitor and the circuit effectively behaves as if the capacitor C_s were shorted and the applied high-frequency AC current essentially passes through the resistors R_e and R_i and inductor L_i. Any residual current passing through the R_c and C_c branch would not damage the battery due to its high-frequency and zero DC component.

The resistance R_e is usually very small in batteries and would generate negligible amount of heat. However, at any given temperature, the frequency dependent R_i(f), which is shown below to increase rapidly with increased frequency of the applied current, generates heat in the battery electrolyte at a rate that is proportional to the square of the applied RMS current. It is also noted that since the electrical-chemical components of the battery are effectively bypassed, the applied high AC current and related voltage can be higher than those rated for the battery without causing any damage.

High-Frequency Circuit Model for Direct Battery Electrolyte Heating

A first order electric circuit model must include a frequency dependent "resistive" heating element and an inductive component accounting for the phase shift between the driving AC voltage applied to the battery terminals and the AC current flowing through the electrolyte. One such electric circuit model is illustrated in Fig. 2. The model includes a non-frequency dependent resistor R_o, and a frequency dependent inductive reactance X(f) and a frequency dependent resistor R(f). The battery impedance Z(f) is therefore given by

$$Z(f) = R(f) + j\,X(f) \qquad (1)$$

Using the first order approximation, R(f) and X(f) is expressed as,

$$R(f) = [P_0 + P_1 f] \text{ and } X(f) = P_2 f \qquad (2)$$

where f is the frequency in Hz, P_0 is the resistance in mΩ at f=0, and P_1 and P_2 are constant coefficients to be determined experimentally.

The applied high frequency voltage v(t) and current i(t) to the battery, Fig. 2, are given by

$$v(t)=V_0\cos(2\pi ft+\Theta_v) \text{ and } i(t)=I_0\cos(2\pi ft+\Theta_i) \qquad (3)$$

where V_o and θ_v are the amplitude and phase angle of the voltage and I_o and θ_i are the amplitude and phase angle of the current waves, respectively. The DC voltage term corresponding to the battery voltage is excluded from the equation. Using phasor notation, the battery "impedance" Z(f) is expressed in terms of its magnitude and phase.

$$|Z(f)| = \sqrt{R^2(f)+X^2(f)} = \sqrt{(P_o+P_1f)^2+(P_2f)^2} \qquad (4)$$

$$\Phi(f)[deg] = \frac{180}{\pi}\tan^{-1}\left[\frac{X(f)}{R(f)}\right] = \frac{180}{\pi}\tan^{-1}\left[\frac{P_2f}{(P_o+P_1f)}\right] \qquad (5)$$

Equation (4) or equation (5) can be used to experimentally obtain the unknown coefficients P_0, P_1 and P_2, through a non-linear least squares curve fitting technique. The process of obtaining these parameters for any battery is described below.

During heating, the RMS current I, flowing through the frequency dependent "resistor" R(f) of the battery generates heat due to the absorbed power $I^2R(f)$. It should be noted that R(f) is fictitious and is used to describe the first order heating effect due to the oscillatory motion of the ions in the electrolyte and the electrolyte medium resistance to the motions, and interactions between the ions. The absorbed power, indicated as P(f, I), can then be expressed as

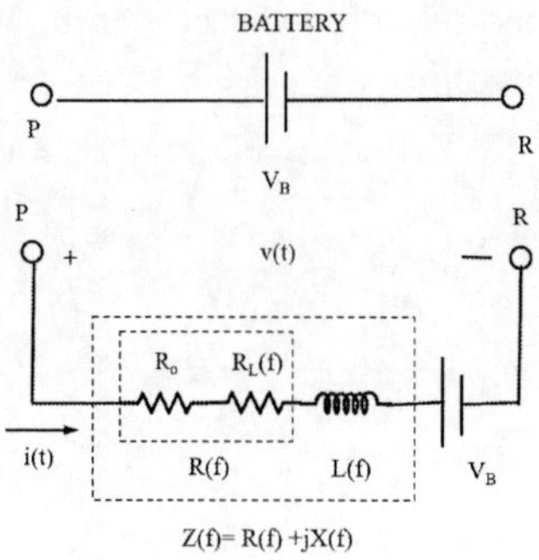

Figure 2: Circuit model for high frequency battery heating.

$$P(f,I) = I^2R(f) = I^2\,[\,P_0+P_1f\,]\,x10^{-3} \quad [W] \qquad (6)$$

This absorbed power raises the temperature of the battery based on its mass m (kg), specific heat capacity C_p ($J.kg^{-1}.{}^oC^{-1}$) and duration t(s). The increase in temperature ΔT (°C) is thereby given by

$$\Delta T=P(f,I)t/C_p m \qquad (7)$$

The battery heating rate HR (°C/s) is then described by equation (8), where $\beta = m\,C_p$.

$$HR(f,I) = \frac{\Delta T}{t} = \frac{1}{\beta}I^2[P_o+P_1f] \quad [{}^oC/s] \qquad (8)$$

Validation of the High-Frequency Circuit Model for Heating

The high-frequency circuit model for battery heating of Fig. 2 and the derived heating rate equation (8) were validated using a Li-ion battery model RCR123A. This is a 3.7 V (800 mAh) cylindrical cell, which is 17 mm in diameter and 34.5 mm in length.

The frequency response of the test battery at room temperature (20°C) was characterized over a range of frequencies from 1 kHz to 100 kHz by driving the battery with a low amplitude AC sinusoidal current signal. The measured voltage and current data across the frequency sweep were then used to determine the amplitude ratio of the voltage and current, which is plotted in Fig. 3 (left). The phase angle (leading) between the voltage and current waveforms, Fig. 3 (right), was extracted directly from voltage and current waveforms.

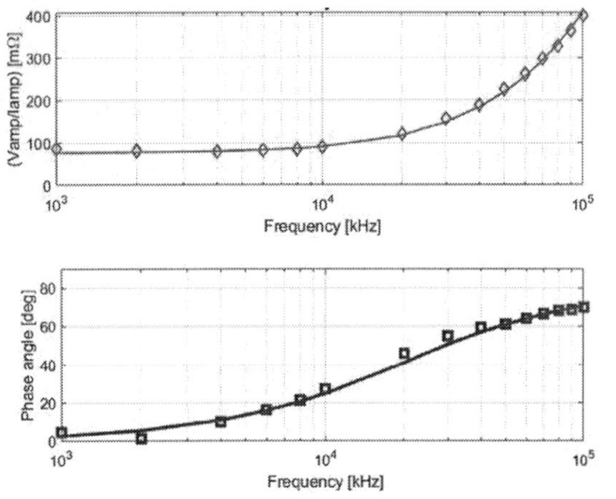

Figure 3: Frequency response of the RCR123 Li-ion battery.

As can be seen in the plots of Fig. 3, as the frequency is increased, the phase shift is increased and approaches 90 degrees, which means that the battery is exhibiting the characteristics of an equivalent non-ideal inductive element. This is exactly the behavior predicted by equations (4) and (5), which include an equivalent frequency dependent heating element R(f) and an ideal reactive inductance X(f) (=2πfL).

The unknown model coefficients P_0 and P_1, equation (2), are then determined by fitting to R(f) data and coefficient P_2 is obtained by fitting to X(f) data as P_0=77.5 mΩ, P_1=5.863x10^{-4} mΩ/Hz and P_2=3.9x10^{-3} mΩ/Hz for the tested battery.

The frequency and current dependent heating rate equation (8) is obtained for the tested RCR123 Li-ion battery using the above model coefficients and the given battery mass and specific heat capacity of m=0.018 kg and C_p =800 J/(kg°C), respectively, and the calculated $\beta = m\ C_p$= 13.4J. $°C^{-1}$, as

$$HR(f,I)=6.95\times10^{-5}[77.5+0.586\times10^{-3}]I^2\ °C/s \quad (9)$$

where f is in Hz and I is the RMS current in A.

The measured heating rate of Fig. 4 confirms the above predicted rate and its increase with frequency. The heating rate data (symbols) and the heating rate calculated from the model (solid line), equation (9), are shown in the plot of Fig. 5. The measured data is observed to show very good agreement with the predicted heating rate described by the model.

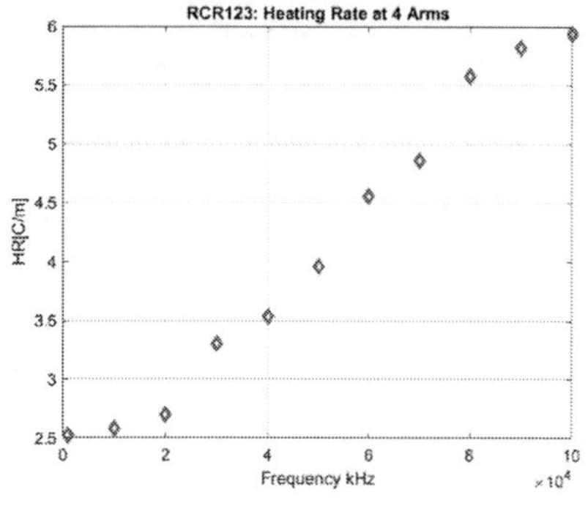

Figure 4

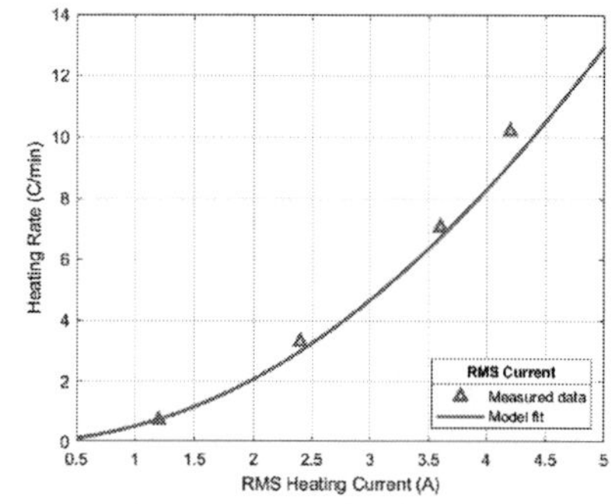

Figure 5

Conclusions

The developed high frequency current battery heating technology is shown to be used for rapid heating of battery electrolyte at low temperatures and maintaining the battery temperature at its optimal performance in low temperature environments. The technology has been extensively tested on a wide range of batteries at temperatures as low as -60°C without causing any damage to the batteries and without interfering with the operation of chargers and existing electronic controls such as the Battery Management System (BMS). The technology is developed based on the experimentally verified model of the behavior of battery electrolyte when subjected to high frequency AC current.

References

1. U. S. Patent Numbers 10,063,076; 10,855,085; 11,183,713; 11,211,810; and 11,211,809 and several U. S. and foreign patents pending.

Novel Si Anode and High Ni NCM Cathode for High Energy Applications

Jun Wang, Felix Guzman, Sean Su, Arthur Dobley, Karthik Ramaswami and Frank Puglia
Research and Development
EaglePicher Technologies
2000 S. County Trail
East Greenwich, RI 02818
jun.wang@eaglepicher.com /1-401-715-0355

Abstract

Rechargeable Li-ion batteries play an increasingly critical role to enable energy mobility and support various new high energy and power applications. However, commercial Li-ion batteries based on intercalation chemistry are approaching the expected specific energy plateau around 300 Wh/kg, beyond which new active materials are very likely needed. To overcome this limitation, an engineered Si/carbon composite with reversible capacity >1900 mAh/g was sourced and evaluated to benchmark against a graphite/SiOx control on the anode side. The graphite/SiOx system has a reversible capacity of over 630 mAh/g. Preliminary tests, based on single layered pouch cells, demonstrated comparable first coulombic efficiency and cell capacity between them. However, the engineered Si/carbon outperformed the graphite/SiOx in long-term cycle life by a significant margin of 50%. Separately, single-crystal nickel cobalt manganese oxide (NCM) with 80% nickel content and cobalt free nickel manganese aluminum oxide (NMA) with 90+% nickel were tested to assess rate performance and cyclability. Combining the Si/carbon anode and high nickel oxide cathode, perspective of the next generation cell design that can reach 350 Wh/kg is provided.

Keywords

Si anode; NCM cathode; Li-ion batteries; high energy.

Introduction

Lithium-ion chemistry based rechargeable batteries continue to gain widespread adoption in many applications since its inception in the 1990s by Sony Corporation [1-2], which was built with lithium cobalt oxide ($LiCoO_2$) cathode and carbonaceous anode. Early commercial demonstration of both energy and life by Li-ion batteries prompts more research and development effort globally to search for new battery materials which operate on reversible intercalation principles [3-4]. This technology push leads to the invention of a wide variety of advanced cathode materials including lithium iron phosphate ($LiFePO_4$), nickel cobalt aluminum oxide (NCA), nickel cobalt manganese oxides (NCM) and graphitic carbon anodes like artificial and natural graphites, mesocarbon microbeads (MCMB), hard and soft carbons, silicon and SiOx [5-8]. Consequently, cell level energy density continued to progress fairly well by incorporating high-capacity active materials, from around 100 Wh/kg initially to 300 Wh/kg and beyond nowadays [9]. Li-ion batteries powered vehicles, a transportation game-changer once viewed as impractical, which finally became a reality and legitimate replacement of combustion engine powered incumbents [10]. However, the needs to address range anxiety and battery charging time continue to challenge battery manufactures even when the cell energy density records keep getting smashed in a matter of days. Some key technological drivers behind this fast-paced Li-ion battery landscape are high nickel (≥80 %) mixed metal oxides, lithium (Li) rich and manganese rich layered cathodes, Li doped SiOx, and high capacity engineered Si anodes [7, 8]. Integration of afore-mentioned battery materials into new designs and products is expected to further raise cell energy density to higher levels thereby pave the way for high energy applications [11].

Commercial demands for Li-ion batteries will continue to drive the trend in battery development and manufacturing, but this also presents opportunities for defense, space and aviation industries to evaluate and adopt some off-the-shelf solutions. Against this background, we selectively sourced a few novel battery materials including single crystal NCM 811, cobalt free NMA cathode and a high capacity engineered silicon/carbon composite. We designed these materials into EaglePicher's Li-ion battery platform technology and benchmarked against internal control to assess the feasibility of leveraging those commercial grades for cells, targeting 300 Wh/Kg or higher specific energy. A few conclusions were drawn based on preliminary cell assembly process and performance testing data.

Experimental Section

Materials: New materials involved in this study were sourced from U.S. domestic battery materials suppliers. The cathode raw materials consist of a single-crystal (SC NCM 811) with D_{50} around 2.5 µm and a cobalt-free NMA with > 90 % nickel. The anode is a highly engineered silicon/carbon composite material with D_{50} around 8.5 µm. Control materials used in this study are commercial grade NCM 811 cathode and SiOx/graphite composite anode. All materials were inspected against material certificate of analysis (COA) and used as-received without further purification.

Electrode fabrication: Cathode and anode electrodes with single sided coating were prepared following EaglePicher's standard R&D scale mixing and coating procedures. A batch with prescribed amounts of active material was blended with conductive carbon, followed by the introduction of binder solution, and solvent. A homogenous slurry was obtained after mixing up to 2000 rpm for 5~10 minutes by a THINKY mixer. The slurry was then coated on thin aluminum (Al) cathode or copper (Cu) anode foils using a doctor blade thin film applicator, and dried at 100°C (212°F) to remove liquid. The resulting electrodes were further pressed to obtain desired electrode thickness and porosity.

Cell assembly: CR2032 coin cells were made for cathode and anode half-cell testing, respectively and Li metal foil of 100 μm thick was used as counter electrode. Single layer pouch (SLP) cells with 70 mm (height) x 55 mm (width) were assembled for full cell performance evaluation. A common poly olefin separator of 16 μm (Celgard, H2512), and an organic carbonates-based electrolyte containing 1.0 M lithium hexafluorophosphate ($LiPF_6$) and other additives were used to build and activate both coin and SLP cells.

Cell testing: Both coin and SLP cells were formed prior to subsequent rate and cycle life tests, detailed formation and performance testing procedures are outlined in Table 1. Coin cells were tested without compression, whereas SLP cells were under 10 psi compression during the course of formation and testing. An Arbin tester with 48 channels was used and all cells were placed in an incubator with temperature controlled at 25±2°C.

Table 1. Cell formation and testing procedures

Step	Cell	Voltage range	Description
Formation	Cathode half cell	4.3-3.0V	CCCV, +C/10, -C/10
	Anode half cell	1.5-0.05V	CCCV, +C/10, -C/10
	SLP	4.2-2.5V	CCCV, +C/10, -C/10
Rate capability	Half cell	4.2-2.5V (cathode)	CCCV, various discharge rates
	Full cell	4.2-2.5V (anode)	
Cycle life	Both SLPs	4.2-2.5V	CCCV, +C/2, -C/2

Results and Discussion

Electrochemical properties of the engineered silicon/carbon composite were investigated to gain insight into specific reversible capacity, as shown in Figure 1. The first discharge capacity (FDC) of the engineered silicon/carbon composite was 1968 mAh/g, significantly higher than that of the control SiOx at 1382 mAh/g. Interestingly, the first charge capacity (FCC) of the engineered silicon/carbon composite was also proportionally higher than that of the control, resulting in a high first coulombic efficiency (FCE) for both materials at about 88% to 91%. It is worth mentioning that such high coulombic efficiency for silicon anode is rare and quite attractive, as it offers a viable path to reach higher cell capacity and energy.

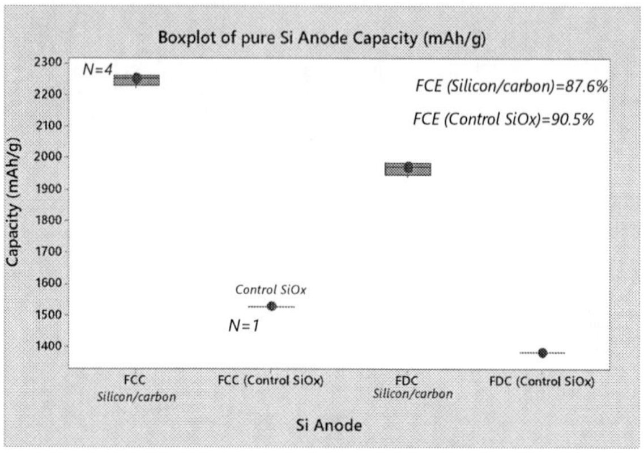

Figure 1 The first charge and discharge capacity comparison of Si anode half-cells

Discharge rate capability of the engineered silicon/carbon was also fairly comparable to the control, as illustrated in Figure 2. The engineered silicon/carbon was mixed with a control graphite which was used for the SiOx control group. SLP cells at 95 mAh with anode specific capacity of 630 mAh/g were assembled to evaluate rate performance. These cells were charged at C/5 constant current to 4.2V, followed by a taper charge to C/10 current cutoff. Under various discharge rates ranging from C/5 up to 3C, both materials exhibited similar discharge capacity. Since both electrodes were prepared using the same recipe, identical coat weight target and press density thus porosity, the rate capability revealed in Figure 2, could be mainly dedicated by the active material. It is therefore reasonable to conclude that the high-capacity engineered silicon should deliver similar rate performance to that of the control.

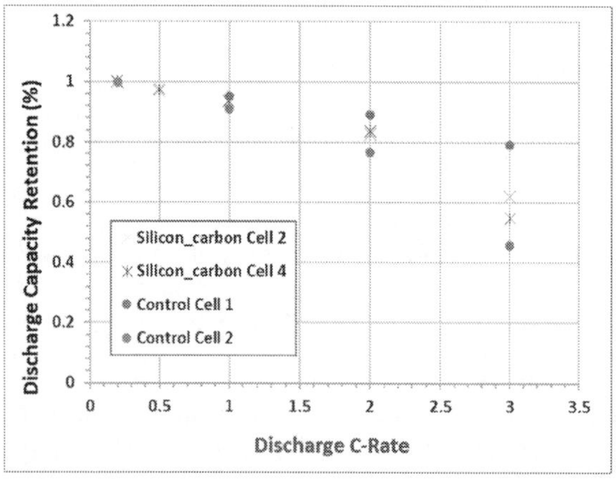

Figure 2 Rate capability comparison of Si anode SLP cells

Long-term cycling stability is always a concern for silicon-based anodes, especially for those with high specific capacities [12]. To assess this critical performance metric, SLP cells, similar to those for rate capability test, were built by pairing a common control cathode with the engineered silicon/carbon blended with graphite and SiOx/graphite control anodes, respectively. According to Figure 3, the silicon/carbon composite based SLPs displayed noticeably better capacity retention than the control group, maintaining >83% after 300 cycles. One of the better performing silicon/carbon SLPs approached 600 cycles with 85% capacity retention. Based on the capacity decay trajectory, it could potentially reach 800 cycles to end-of-life (EOL) barring any catastrophic failure modes. This result is quite appealing for high-energy cells, as high specific capacity anodes enable thinner anodes, thus fast charge capability without sacrificing cell energy [13-14].

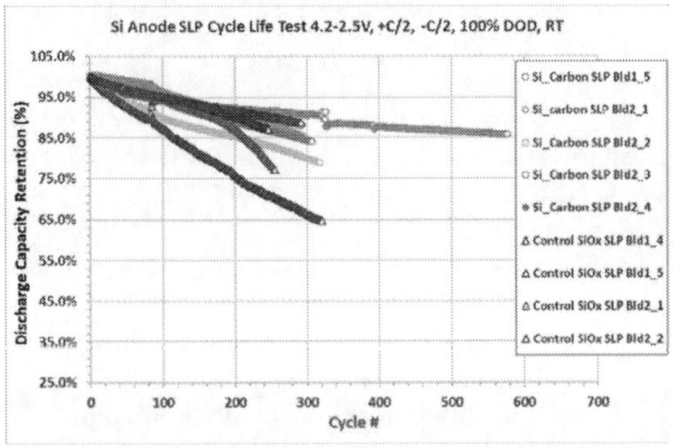

Figure 3 Cycle life of novel silicon/carbon anode vs. control SiOx

Cathode half-cell comparison between SC NCM 811 and control NCM 811 is shown in Figure 4. Average FDC of the SC NCM 811 is about 214 mAh/g, approximately 10 mAh/g higher than that of the control group. Statistically, the range and standard deviation for both groups are quite similar, but sample size of the control group is slightly larger. The first coulombic efficiency (FCE) for the SC NCM 811 is about 87.9% on average, lower than that of the control group of 90.7%. The difference is mainly due to cathode active materials, mostly related to exact nickel content with minor influence from particle morphology since the control group is a conventional polycrystal cathode with secondary particle aggregates around 20 μm, nearly 10 times larger than that of the SC NCM 811.

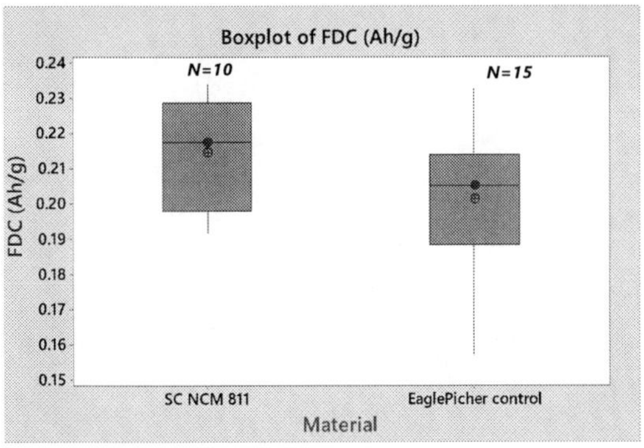

Figure 4. First discharge capacity comparison of cathode half-cells

Compared to the polycrystal counterparts, a main drawback for SC cathode materials is rate capacity owing to the single crystal nature, thus larger primary particle size. However, as shown in Figure 5, this is surprisingly not the case for SC NCM 811, which demonstrated quite comparable discharge rate capacity on par with the control group up to 10C, with rapid capacity reduction beyond 2C discharge rate and down to 40~50% capacity at 4C for both materials.

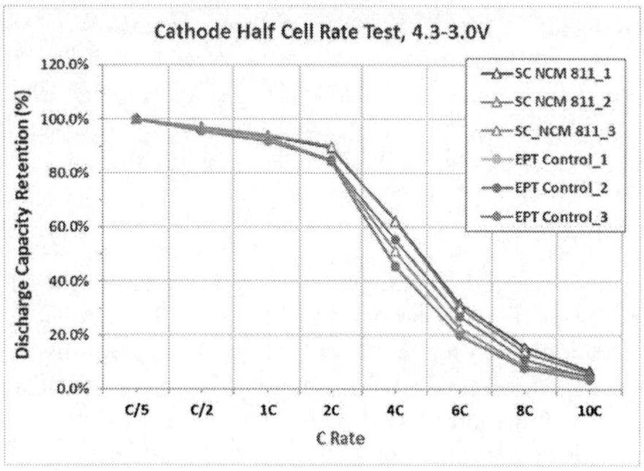

Figure 5 Rate capability comparison of cathode half-cells

SLP cells with reversible capacity around 95 mAh were built to further evaluate the SC NCM 811 cathode in a full cell paired with control SiOx/graphite composite anode. An average FCE of 87.8% was observed, quite close to the control group of 88.0%, this implies that the SC NCM 811 cathode is comparable to the polycrystal control cathode in meeting cell capacity and energy design metrics. Post formation cells were also tested to assess long-term cyclability, as illustrated in Figure 6. Preliminary cycle-life data shows that cells built with the SC NCM 811cathode fade quicker than control cells in the first 50 cycles, however it is premature to draw any conclusions as more cycle numbers are likely needed.

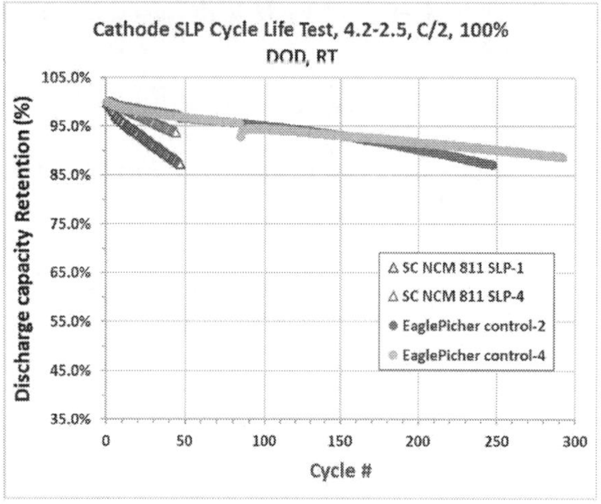

Figure 6 Cycle life of SC NCM 811 vs. control

In addition to the SC NCM 811 cathode, a cobalt-free NMA cathode was being evaluated following exactly the same screening protocol. This NMA material contains >90% nickel and is capable of delivering 230 mAh/g reversible capacity and long-term cycle life. Experiments are currently underway to confirm those claims using cells fabricated by EaglePicher.

Our aforementioned high-energy control chemistry demonstrated 300 Wh/kg specific energy in a pouch cell with over 10 Ah cell capacity. More effort is also being undertaken to reach 350 Wh/kg and beyond. With the addition of high-capacity active materials such as the silicon/carbon composite anode, SC NCM 811 and >90% nickel NMA, we can potentially obtain 350 Wh/kg specific energy based on cell modeling and energy predication.

Conclusions

Novel silicon/carbon compote and single-crystal NCM 811 and NMA cathode materials were evaluated for high-energy applications, they demonstrated comparable performances against control chemistry including coulombic efficiency and rate capability. The silicon/carbon composite out-performed control in long-term cycling. Those materials are expected to enable high cell specific energy at 350 Wh/kg and beyond.

Acknowledgements

This study is supported by an EaglePicher internal research and development (IRAD) project focusing on high-energy battery technologies. The authors wish to thank our strategic partners for providing the raw materials used in this study and critical feedback in materials handling procedures.

References

1. T.B. Reddy (ed.), *Linden's handbook of Batteries 4th Edition*. pp. 26.1-26.4, McGraw-Hill, 2010.

2. M. S. Whittingham. Lithium Batteries and Cathode Materials. *Chem. Rev.,* 104, 4271-4301, 2004.

3. F.J. Gunter and N. Wassiliadis, Stat of the Art of Lithium Ion Pouch Cells in Automotive Applications: Cell Teardown and Characterization. *J. Electrochem. Soc.,* 169, 030515, 2022.

4. M. S. Whittingham, Electrical Energy Storage and Intercalation Chemistry. *Science*, Vol 192, 4244, 1126-27, 1976.

5. J. B. Goodenough and K.S. Park, The Li-Ion Rechargeable Battery: A Perspective. *J. Am. Chem. Soc.*, Vol. 135, No. 4, 1167-1176, 2013.

6. J. T. Frith, M. J. Lacey and U. Ulissi, A non-academic perspective on the future of Lithium-based batteries. *Nat. Commun.*, 14, 420, pp. 1-17, 2023.

7. A. Manthiram, A reflection on lithium-ion battery cathode chemistry. *Nat. Commun.*, 11, 1550, pp.1-9, 2020.

8. M. N. Obrovac and V. L. Chevrier, Alloy Negative Electrodes for Li-Ion Batteries. *Chem. Rev.* 114, 11444-11502, 2014.

9. Q. Li, Y. Yang, X.Q. Yu and H. Li, A 700W·h·Kg^{-1} Rechargeable Pouch Type Lithium Batteries. *Chinese Phys. Lett.*, Vol 40, No. 4, 48201-48206, 2023.

10. Li-Bridge Industry Report: *Building a Robust and Resilient U.S. Lithium Battery Supply Chain.* www.anl.gov/access/reference/libridge-industry-report

11. M. J. Lain, J. Brandon and E. Kendrick, Design Strategies for High Power vs. High Energy Lithium Ion Cells. *Batteries*, Vol 5, No. 4, 64, 2019.

12. Y. Jin, B. Zhu, Z. Lu, N. Liu and J. Zhu, Challenges and Recent Progress in the Development of Si Anodes for Lithium-Ion Battery. *Adv. Energy. Mater.*, 7, pp. 1700715-1700732, 2017.

13. Z. Yang, S. E. Trask, X. Wu and B. J. Ingram, Effect of Si Content on Extreme Fast Charging Behavior in Silicon-Graphite Composite Anodes. *Batteries*, Vol 9, No.2, 138, 2023.

14. M. Weiss, R. Ruess, J. Kasnatscheew, *et. al.*, Fast Charging of Lithium-Ion Batteries: A Review of Materials Aspects. *Adv. Energy. Mater.,* 11, pp. 2101126-2101163, 2021.

Evaluation of Lithium-ion Batteries Following a Single Thermal Insult

Gordon H. Waller[1], Rachel E. Carter[1], Patrick J. West[2], Corey T. Love[1]
[1] Chemistry Division
[2] ASEE Post-doctoral Fellow
U.S. Naval Research Laboratory
Washington, DC 20375 USA

Abstract: *Lithium-ion batteries were subjected to temperatures above the manufacturer specifications in a single "thermal insult" to explore the lasting impacts of these one-time mild abuse events. After the thermal insult, galvanostatic cycling and electrochemical impedance spectroscopy were used to determine impacts on the cell capacity and impedance. Isothermal Battery Calorimetry (IBC) was used to observe changes in heat generation during cycling, while Accelerating Rate Calorimetry (ARC) was used to evaluate the thermal runaway behavior of the cells. The results in this study indicated that commercial-off-the-shelf 18650 are extremely robust to the test conditions explored in this study, and no significant impacts to cell performance or safety were observed. However, current-interrupt-device (CID) activation was observed with sufficiently high temperatures and exposure durations.*

Keywords: Lithium-ion batteries; battery safety; thermal abuse; isothermal battery calorimetry; accelerating rate calorimetry

Introduction

Lithium-ion batteries (LIB) typically have a manufacturer recommended temperature range of 0 °C to 60 °C depending on operation. Electrochemical cycling at the extreme ends of this temperature range is known to result in accelerated capacity fade and impedance rise for most LIB [1]. Heating cells well above the recommended upper temperature limit is a common method to evaluate the safety of lithium-ion batteries. Above some critical temperature, LIB undergo a series of exothermic reactions leading to rapid self-heating, referred to as thermal runaway [2]. Exothermic reactions in LIB begin with decomposition of the solid electrolyte interphase (SEI) layer on the anode at temperatures in the range of 60-80 °C, or just above the manufacturer recommended upper limit [2] [3]. However, temperatures above 120 °C are typically needed before self-heating can no longer be mitigated through passive heat rejection and cell failure occurs. Observed LIB failures depend on chemistry, cell design, and state-of-charge but can range from relatively benign such as the activation of an internal safety device or venting electrolyte vapors to highly energetic ejections of flaming debris [4]. Aging effects by cycling or storing cells near the manufacturer recommended upper temperature limit have been evaluated previously and generally result in a higher observed onset temperatures for thermal runaway due to growth of the SEI, however reported results vary with cathode chemistry [5] [6].

The implications of exposing LIBs to temperature ranges above manufacturer recommend limits but below the onset of self-sustain thermal runway (60 °C to 120 °C) have not been broadly studied. Moreover, an important scenario to consider is a large LIB pack containing many cells wherein one or more, but not all, of the cells have undergone thermal runaway. Propagating thermal runaway can occur due to the failure of a single cell, however brief exposures of adjacent cells to temperatures well above the manufacturer recommended limit without propagating failure is also a possibility.

Experimental

High energy (3.4 Ah, 250 Wh/kg, 700 Wh/L, NCM811 cathode and graphite/silicon composite anode) 18650 LIBs were cycled to two different states of charge (SOC) of 30% and 100% before being subjected to thermal insult at temperatures of 80 °C, 90 °C and 100 °C, for durations of 20 minutes, 100 minutes, and 24 hours. Exposure duration was defined as the time above the desired exposure temperature, with a duration of 20 minutes previously reported as the time required to reach a near-equilibrium temperature condition between the surface and center of an 18650 exposed to a temperature step [7]. A thermal ramp rate of approximately 2 °C $min.^{-1}$ was utilized in every test. The skin-temperature and open circuit voltage (OCV) of each cell were monitored during every thermal insult test, and each test condition was repeated at least in triplicate. Prior to the thermal insult, the capacity of each cell was measured by a C/5 (680 mA) charge and discharge cycle between a voltage range of 2.5 V and 4.2 V using a Maccor battery cycler. A constant voltage hold at 4.2 V was imposed during charging until the charging current decayed to <C/20 (170 mA). After the thermal insult, cells were discharged at a rate of C/5 to determine capacity lost during thermal insult, and then cycled at a C/5 rate to evaluate impacts on capacity retention. Electrochemical impedance spectroscopy (EIS) was collected on each cell at 30% SOC and 25 °C before and after thermal insult using a potentiostat and frequency response analyzer (PARSTAT MC Multichannel Potentiostat). Impedance change was interpreted as the increase in total impedance represented by a low-frequency intercept in a Nyquist plot, occurring at approximately 1-2 Hz. Heat generated during C/5 cycling was evaluated before and after thermal insult using isothermal battery calorimetry with an isothermal temperature of 30 °C (THT IBC-C). Thermal runaway behavior of as-received and post-thermal insult cells were evaluated using accelerating rate calorimetry (THT ARC-

ES) in "heat-wait-seek" mode, using a step size of 5 °C, wait time of 5 minutes, and seek time of 20 minutes. Exothermic behavior was defined as a self-heating rate of >0.02 °C/min, while thermal runaway was defined as a self-heating rate of >5 °C/min. All ARC measurement were conducted with cells at 100% SOC except for cells in which Current Interrupt Device (CID) activation had occurred, in which cells were somewhat below 100% due to self-discharge occurring during the thermal insult experiment.

Results

An example of cell open circuit voltage (OCV) and temperature measured using a surface-mounted thermocouple during a thermal insult experiment is shown in **Figure 1.** Cell voltage (solid lines) were observed to first increase with temperature and then began decreasing for the duration of the thermal insult. Two of three cells shown in Figure 1 experienced a rapid voltage drop prior to the end of the thermal insult, which is attributed to CID activation. Exposure to 80 °C for any duration did not result in CID activation, while 2 out of 3 cells exposed to 90 °C for 24-hours experienced CID activation. Additionally, for the cells exposed to 100 °C, CID occurred in 2 out 6 cells and 3 out of 3 cells after 100 minutes and 24 hours, respectively.

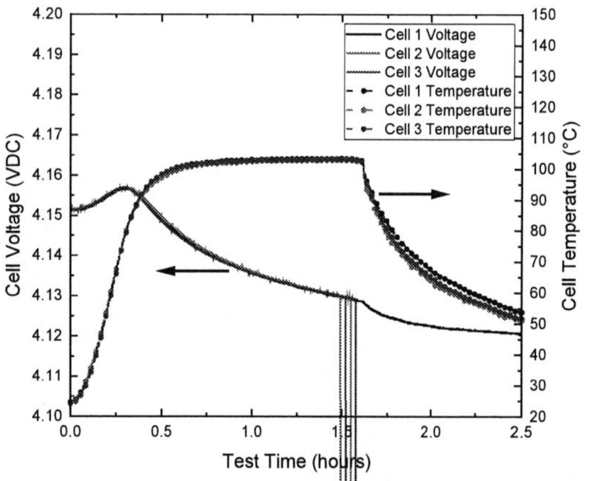

Figure 1. Open circuit voltage (OCV) and skin temperature of 100% SOC cells exposed to 100 °C thermal insult for 100 minutes.

Irreversible capacity loss after the thermal insult was found to correlate most strongly with exposure duration, as shown in **Figure 2.** Observed irreversible capacity loss was generally very mild and on the order of a few percent of the originally measured capacity, with the exception of cells where CID activation was observed and prevented charge and discharge cycling to measure capacity. Temperature was also seen to have a mild effect, with capacity loss generally increasing with temperature. For cells exposed to 90 °C and 100 °C for 100 minutes, increasing SOC from 30% to 100% slightly increased irreversible capacity loss and led to CID activation for some of the cells exposed at 100% SOC.

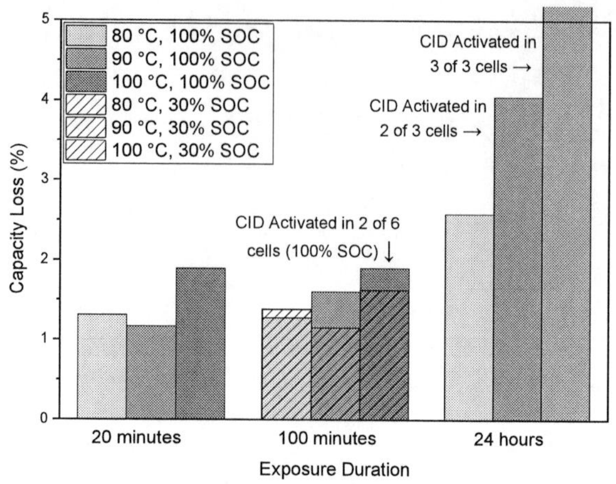

Figure 2. Irreversible capacity loss after thermal insult measured as average C/5 capacity before and after thermal insult.

Representative Nyquist plots displaying real (Zre) and imaginary (Zim) components of AC impedance measured by EIS (**Figure 3)** show the characteristic depressed semi-circle and semi-infinite diffusion tail expected for lithium-ion batteries. Milder thermal insult conditions, notably those with only 20-minute durations or an exposure temperature of 80 °C, resulted in a decrease in total electrochemical impedance based on the low-frequency intercept of the Nyquist plot.

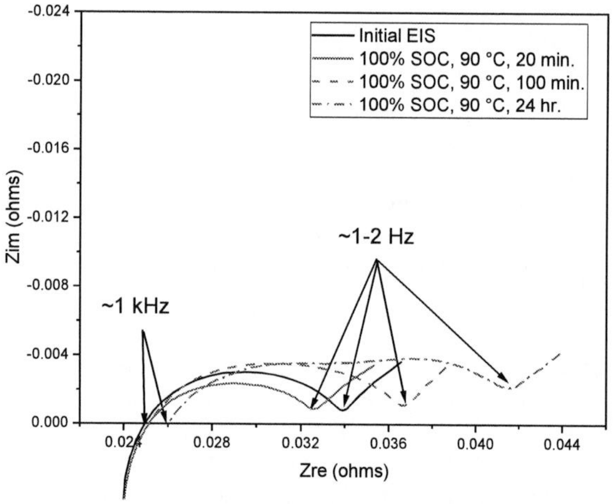

Figure 3. Nyquist plots displaying representative AC impedance for cells before and after thermal insult, collected at 30% SOC and 25 °C.

A summary of AC impedance changes after thermal insult is shown **Figure 4** and followed a similar trend to irreversible capacity loss, with the greatest changes observed for 24-hour exposure durations. The starting AC impedance of the cells used in this study was approximately 35±1 mΩ, meaning the observed increase in impedance was on the order of 6 mΩ.

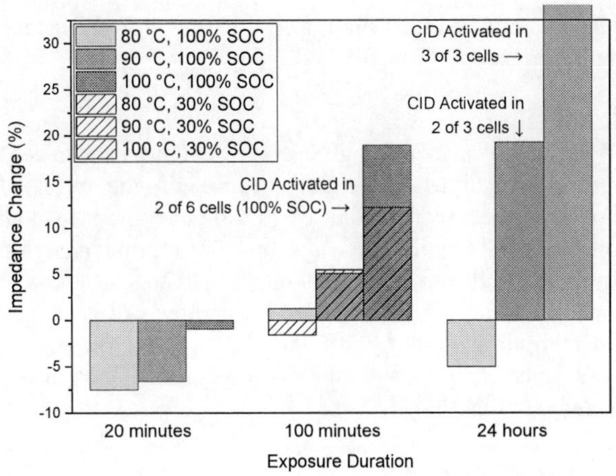

Figure 4. AC impedance change after thermal insult measured at 30% SOC and 25 °C.

Differential capacity plots were derived from C/5 cycling data to observe changes in the electrochemical behavior of cells before and after the thermal insult experiment. As shown in **Figure 5**, slight changes in the four main peaks observed during cell charging are seen, with the magnitude of these shifts increasing at the highest temperatures and longest duration exposures. Like with impedance and capacity measurements, evaluation of cells subjected to 100 °C for 24 hours was not possible due to CID activation.

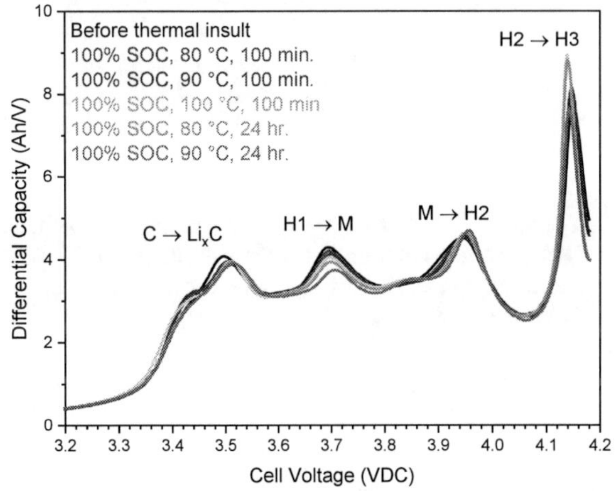

Figure 5. Differential capacity (dQ/dV) vs. voltage for cells before and after thermal insult.

The observed peaks are assigned to structural changes in the graphite/Si anode and NCM811 cathode, specifically the lithiation of graphite to form Li_xC occurring at ~3.5V, followed by crystallographic unit cell transformations in the NCM811 cathode assigned to hexagonal to monoclinic (H1→M), monoclinic to hexagonal (M→H2), and hexagonal to hexagonal (H2→H3) transformations, occurring at ~3.7 V, ~3.95 V, and ~4.15 V, respectively [8]. Analogous peaks are also observed during discharge but are not shown in Figure 5 for clarity. Shifting of the dQ/dV peaks indicates irreversible structural damage occurring in both the anode and cathode materials, with decreasing peak intensity correlating to a loss in electrochemically active electrode materials and shifting peak potentials to higher potentials on charge indicating an increased electrochemical overpotential. The formation of new low-intensity peaks, notably occurring between the H1→M and M→H2 cathode active material structural transitions also suggests that new electrochemically active phases have been produced.

Heat flow of cells before and after thermal insult is shown in **Figure 6** during a C/5 charge and discharge cycle starting from 0% SOC. Heat flow is seen to vary as a function of SOC, and the general appearance of the heat flow during charge and discharge are different despite the use of an identical current. A slight shift along the X-axis (test time in hours) is observed for cells exposed to the most abusive thermal insult conditions, which is related to the lower capacity of these cells due to the irreversible capacity loss described in Figure 2. Total heat produced for all cells was comparable and was approximately 330 mJ during charge and 250 mJ during discharge regardless of thermal insult condition.

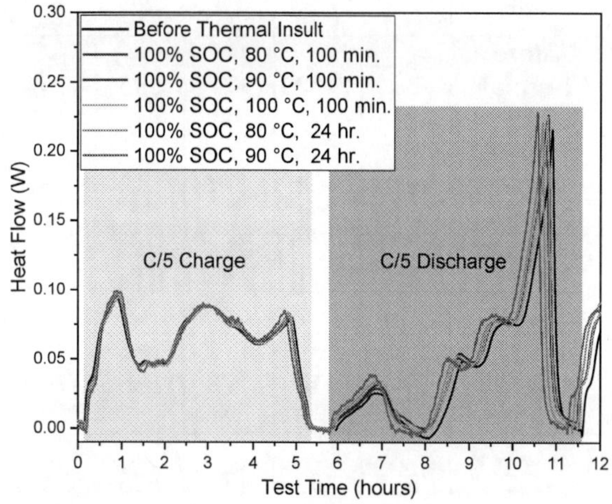

Figure 6. Heat flow during C/5 (680 mA) charge and discharge cycle for cells before and after thermal insult.

Accelerating rate calorimetry testing was conducted on as received and post thermal insult cells to evaluate changes in thermal runaway behavior. As seen in **Figure 7**, the onset of rapid-self heating and maximum self-heating rate for all cells was similar. Critical temperatures associated with the onset of exothermic reactions (defined as the temperature at which a self-heating rate of >0.02 °C/min was first observed), venting (observed as a negative heating rate and slight temperature drop), thermal runaway (defined as the temperature at which self-heating exceeds 5 °C/min), and maximum temperature are shown in **Table 1**. Mass loss expressed as a percentage of the original cell mass is also provided.

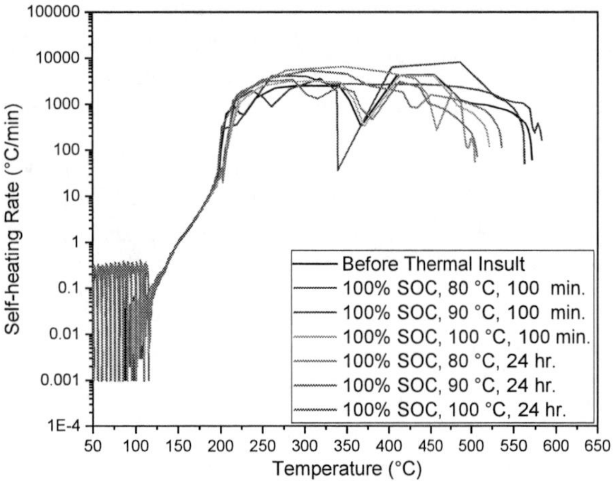

Figure 7. Self-heating rate vs. temperature for Accelerating Rate Calorimetry (ARC) testing of cells before and after thermal insult.

Table 1. Critical temperatures and mass loss observed during Accelerating Rate Calorimetry (ARC) experiments before and after thermal insult.

Cell	T_{Exo} (°C)	T_{vent} (°C)	T_{TR} (°C)	T_{MAX} (°C)	Δ mass
Before Thermal Insult	88	112	177	585	-74%
100%SOC 80 °C 100 min.	91	108	177	618	-76%
100%SOC 90 °C 100 min.	93	111	175	614	-72%
100%SOC 100 °C 100 min.	94	110	178	535	-76%
100%SOC 80 °C 24 hr.	96	109	176	505	-71%
100%SOC 90 °C 24 hr.	106	112	176	494	-77%
100%SOC 100 °C 24 hr.	110	110	177	522	-73%

As seen in Figure 7, temperatures recorded for the onset of thermal runaway (T_{TR}) are very similar, as were temperatures recorded for cell venting (T_{vent}), maximum temperature (T_{MAX}), and mass loss. However, the onset of exothermic reactions (T_{EXO}) was observed to increase with increasing temperature and duration of the thermal abuse experiment. This behavior is interpreted as evidence that the thermal insult experiments exceeded the threshold to begin these same exothermic reactions, however as shown in all the data collected, this did not lead to a significant lasting impact on cell performance and safety.

Conclusions

Commercially available high-energy 18650 lithium-ion cells were subjected to temperatures exceeding the onset of exothermic behavior. In some cases, CID activation led to an "open circuit" failure state which prevented further analysis, however for all surviving cells only mild capacity loss and impedance rise were observed. Measurements of heat flow and thermal stability by IBC and ARC also indicate that these cells are robust to the "thermal insult" conditions explored in this study.

Acknowledgements

Funding for this effort was provided by NAVSEA.

References

[1] D. Ren, H. Hsu, R. Li, X. Feng, D. Guo, X. Han, L. Lu, X. He, S. Gao, J. Hou, Y. Li, Y. Wang and M. Ouyang, "A comparative investigation of aging effects on thermal runaway behavior of lithium-ion batteries," *eTransportation,* no. 100034, 2019.

[2] D. Doughty and P. Roth, "Thermal runaway caused fire and explosion of lithium ion battery," *The Electrochemical Society Interface,* 2012.

[3] T. Bandhauer, S. Garimella and T. Fuller, "A Critical Review of Thermal Issues in Lithium-ion Batteries," *Journal of The Electrochemical Society,* vol. 158, no. 3, pp. R1-R25, 2011.

[4] Q. Wang, P. Ping, X. Zhao, G. Chu, J. Sun and C. Chen, "Thermal runaway caused fire and explosion of lithium ion battery," *Journal of Power Sources,* vol. 208, pp. 210-224, 2012.

[5] Y. Preger, L. Torres-Castro, T. Rauhala and J. Jeevarajan, "Perspective—On the Safety of Aged Lithium-Ion Batteries," *Journal of the Electrochemical Society,* vol. 169, no. 030507, 2022.

[6] C. Geisbauer, K. Wohrl, C. Mittman and H. Schweiger, "Review—Review of Safety Aspects of Calendar Aged Lithium Ion Batteries," *Journal of the Electrochemical Society,* vol. 167, no. 090523, 2020.

[7] N. Spinner, K. Hinnant, R. Mazurick, A. Brandon, S. Rose-Pehrrson and S. Tuttle, "Novel 18650 lithium-ion battery surrogate cell design with anisotropic thermophysical properties for studying failure events," *Journal of Power Sources,* vol. 312, pp. 1-11, 2016.

[8] P. West, C. Quilty, Z. Wang, S. Ehrlich, L. J. C. Ma, D. Fischer, X. K. A. Tong, E. Takeuchi, A. Marschilok, K. Takeuchi and D. Bock, "Degradation in Ni-Rich LiNi1–x–yMnxCoyO2/Graphite Batteries: Impact of Charge Voltage and Ni Content," *Journal of Physical Chemistry C,* vol. 127, no. 15, pp. 7054-7070, 2023.

The Effect of the Heat Transfer Coefficient on Li-ion Battery Failure

Jacob Faulkner[1], Wenhua H. Zhu[1], Paul Dimick[2], Kylie Minor[2], & Bruce J. Tatarchuk[1]

[1] Department of Chemical Engineering,
Auburn University
Auburn, AL, USA, 36849
jzf0072@auburn.edu

[2] Intramicron, Inc.
368 Industry Dr.
Auburn, AL, USA, 36831

Abstract

Transferring heat away from a Li-ion battery under stress could prevent a failure event from ever occurring. As a Li-ion battery starts to retain heat, self-heating reactions begin to occur inside the battery. Once the battery heats to its thermal runaway onset temperature, failure is practically unstoppable. In an inert-adiabatic reactor setup, a failing battery has the capability to produce about 5 kJ/Wh of thermal energy in a very short time period [1]. It is necessary to implement a cooling structure if these batteries are to be used in tightly packed battery packs. This cooling structure must be able to prevent failure propagation and compensate for heat generated during anticipated cycling. A cooling structure with an overall heat transfer coefficient (HTC) of at least 24 W m^{-2} K^{-1} could have the ability to keep a battery from undergoing thermal runaway. This is due to the heat transferred away from the battery outweighing the heat evolved during self-heating reactions. HTC's of 300 and 1000 W m^{-2} K^{-1} are able to prevent failure from heating rates of 0.41 °C/s and 2.26 °C/s, respectively. The 1000 W m^{-2} K^{-1} HTC allows for the stopping of thermal runaway once thermal runaway has been initiated. Knowing how Li-ion batteries interact with a cooling structure is important for battery pack design considerations.

Keywords

Heat transfer modeling; isokinetic modeling; thermal runaway; microfibrous metal mesh; phase change materials.

Introduction

Li-ion batteries under thermal stress are prone to catastrophic failure [1]–[4]. This includes cycling batteries at high charge/discharge rates which is done during pulse power applications. Putting Li-ion batteries under these charge/discharge rates also creates a thermal stress on the battery due to the resistive heating within the battery. If sufficient heating occurs, the battery will reach its thermal runaway (TR) onset temperature where stopping TR is impractical. Before this onset temperature is achieved, self-heating reactions occur within the battery [3,5]. Self-heating reactions aid in bringing the battery to its TR onset temperature. Therefore, it is imperative to dissipate heat from the battery canister.

There are multiple methods for removing heat from Li-ion batteries and they mainly depend on the battery application. Some methods include liquid cooling [6], air cooling [7], or cold plates. Intramicron uses a cooling structure with active and passive cooling capabilities [8]. The passive cooling includes a porous microfibrous mesh (MFM) with a void fraction of 0.88. This MFM is created by sintering metal fibers to one another to create better solid-solid joint contact. This increases the thermal conductivity of the MFM. To fill the void space, a phase change material (PCM) is melted into the void space. The PCM is then solidified to create an MFM-PCM matrix. The MFM acts as the thermal diffuser, and the PCM acts as the thermal sink. Active cooling is provided by flowing cooling water through the passive cooling structure.

If a cooling structure proves to be ineffective, the battery will release a large amount of energy. This amount of energy depends on the kinetics of the reactions and the interaction between the battery and the cooling structure. This paper will study the interactions between a battery under thermal stress and its cooling structure.

Model

A kinetic model is composed of reaction kinetics coupled with an energy balance. The kinetic model is performed in COMSOL 6.1 as a zero-dimensional model. The focus of this paper will be the energy balance between the battery and its surroundings. All the reaction kinetics/energy balance information comes from [9]. These reactions can be seen in Table 1.

Table 1. Reaction Kinetics for Li-ion Battery Failure [9].

$$\frac{dx_c}{dt} = -A_c x_c \exp\left(\frac{-E_c}{k_b T}\right)$$

$$\frac{dx_a}{dt} = -A_a x_a \exp\left(\frac{-E_a}{k_b T}\right)$$

$$\frac{dx_s}{dt} = -A_s x_s \exp\left(\frac{-z}{z_o}\frac{-E_s}{k_b T}\right)$$

$$\frac{d\theta_e}{dt} = -A_e \theta_e \exp\left(\frac{-E_e}{k_b T}\right)$$

$$\frac{dz}{dt} = A_a x_s \exp\left(\frac{-z}{z_o}\frac{-E_s}{k_b T}\right)$$

$$\frac{dSoC}{dt} = -A_{ec} x_a (1 - x_c) \exp\left(\frac{-E_{ec}}{k_b T}\right) + \left(\frac{dx_c}{dt} - \frac{dx_a}{dt}\right) SoC$$

x_c is the fraction of lithium remaining in the cathode, x_a is the fraction of lithium in the anode, x_s is the fraction of lithium within the solid electrolyte interface (SEI), θ_e is the fraction of electrolyte in the liquid phase, z is the thickness of the SEI layer, and SOC is the state of charge of the battery. The reaction kinetic data for each reaction (E_i and A_i) is fitted by [9] from tests done by [2] on a 1.5 Ah Nickel

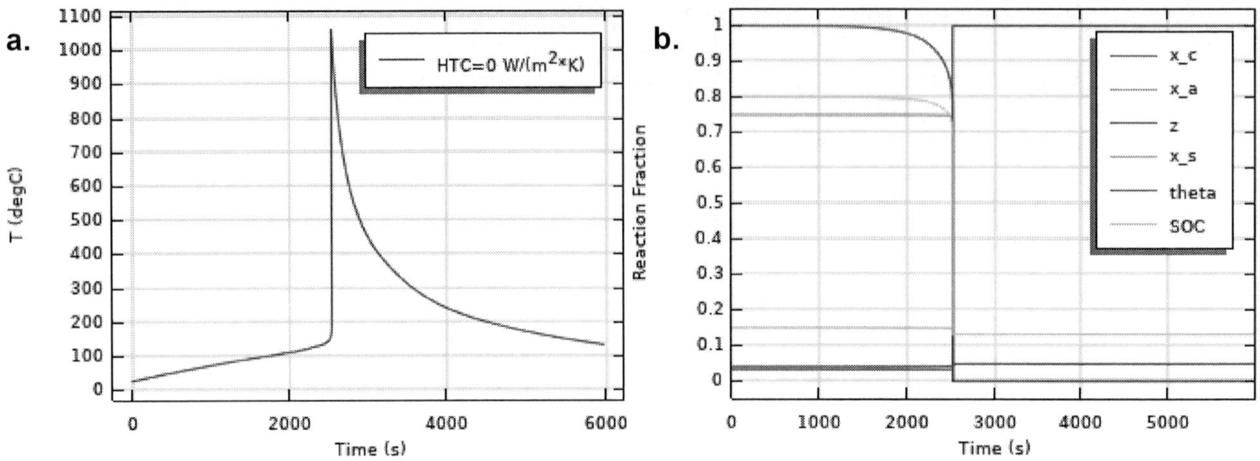

Figure 1. Adiabatic Failure of 1.5 Ah NMC Battery. a) Temperature Profile b) Reaction Fraction Profile.

Manganese Cobalt (NMC) cell. Initial conditions are also provided in [9].

The energy balance that [9] uses is shown in Equation 1:

$$V_{cell}\rho_{jr}c_{p,jr}\frac{\partial T}{\partial t} = -Ah_{conv}(T - T_{amb}) - A\varepsilon\sigma(T^4 - T_{amb}^4) + \sum_i \dot{Q}_i \quad (1)$$

where V_{cell} is the volume of the battery cell in m^3, ρ_{jr} is the density of the jelly roll in kg/m^3, $c_{p,jr}$ is the specific heat capacity of the jelly roll in J kg^{-1} K^{-1}, A is the surface area of the battery exposed to the cooling environment, in m^2, h_{conv} is the heat transfer coefficient (HTC) that corresponds to natural convection occurring outside of the failing cell, in W m^{-2} K^{-1}, T_{amb} is the ambient temperature surrounding the failing battery, in K, ε is the surface emissivity, unitless, and σ is the Stefan-Boltzmann constant, in W m^{-2} K^{-4}. The summation term on the far right considers the energy introduced by the degradation reactions, boiling, and heaters.

$$\sum_i \dot{Q}_i = \dot{Q}_{rxn} + \dot{Q}_{boil} + \dot{Q}_{ej} + \dot{Q}_{heater} \quad (2)$$

$\dot{Q}_{rxn}$ is the heat produced by TR reactions, $\dot{Q}_{boil}$ is the heat removed by the boiling of electrolyte, $\dot{Q}_{ej}$ is the energy removed by the ejecta leaving the battery canister, and $\dot{Q}_{heater}$ is the energy provided by the heater to the battery canister to induce failure. The parameter that this study is interested in is the h_{conv} term.

Methods

A simulated electric heater is used to force the modeled battery into thermal runaway. This heater term is represented by $\dot{Q}_{heater}$ in the energy balance (Equation 2). The heater stays on during the simulation until self-heating is observed. Under normal heater operating conditions, the battery temperature increases at 0.036 ºC/s. In this case, self-heating is defined as any temperature increase above 0.036 ºC/s. Once self-heating is observed, the heater is turned off, and the HTC is applied to the energy balance. The HTC is parameterized to determine the minimum required HTC to keep TR from occurring once self-heating is observed. The same method can be applied when considering the HTC necessary for stopping TR once the onset temperature is achieved.

Results and Discussion

First, the failure of the battery must be understood at adiabatic-like conditions. This will be the baseline for all other calculations. In the adiabatic failure kinetic model, the heater initially changes battery surface temperature at 0.036 °C/s. The battery experiences initial self-heating at 102-103 °C because this is when the temperature change deviates from its steady state value of 0.036 °C/s. The model represents this initial self-heating as an electrochemical heat source because SOC is the first reaction fraction to change in the reaction profile in Figure 1b [9]. Furthermore, this initial heating is partially diminished by the endothermic boiling of the electrolyte because θ_e is also changing during the initial self-heating of the battery. The TR onset temperature is hard to define, but it is usually based on the amount of temperature change occurring within the battery [2]. In this case, the onset temperature is set at around 165 °C where the temperature change of the battery surface is greater than or equal to 2 °C/s. Figure 1b shows that all the reactions are proceeding to a significant extent. This should be kept in mind when considering the reaction profiles in the applied HTC models. It is evident that TR occurred within the battery because it reaches a max temperature of about 1050 °C. A failure of this magnitude is dangerous to battery surroundings, especially in the case where batteries are tightly packed.

With this understanding of adiabatic failure, it is necessary to cool batteries to keep them from failing. This is where the HTC comes into consideration. An overall HTC of 24 W m^{-2} K^{-1} is able to keep the self-heating reactions from driving

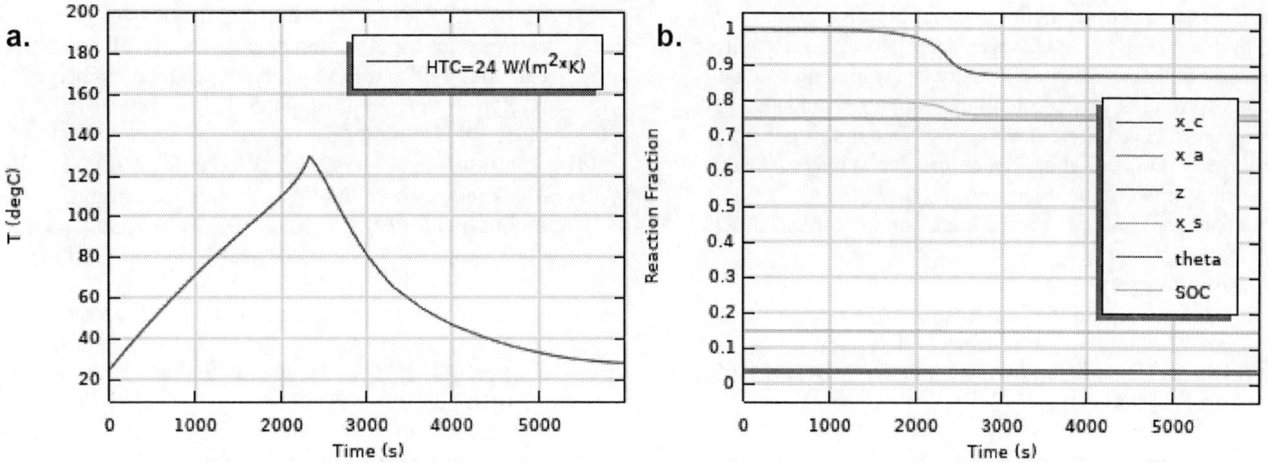

Figure 2. Non-Adiabatic Failure Scenario (24 W m^{-2} K^{-1}) a) Temperature Profile b) Reaction Fraction Profile.

the battery to TR. This HTC is applied once the battery is self-heating at almost triple the original heater rate, 0.1 °C/s. The battery surface temperature is 129 °C when the HTC is applied to the kinetic model. Notice in Figure 2b that the exothermic reactions do not go to completion, but they are halted by the dissipation of heat from the battery canister. Heat is dissipated from the battery canister faster than the electrochemical reactions can produce heat. The other HTC scenarios will undergo similar reaction profiles, so they will not be provided in this document.

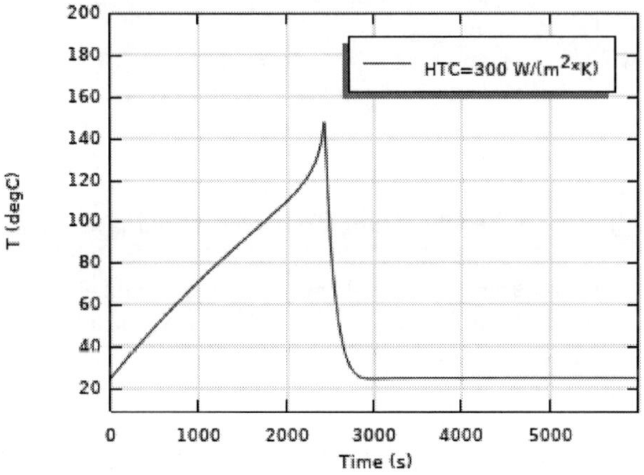

Figure 3. Non-Adiabatic Failure Scenario (300 W m^{-2} K^{-1}).

Figure 3 shows that applying a 300 W m^{-2} K^{-1} HTC allows for the battery surface to be heated to 147 °C without experiencing TR. A temperature change of 0.41 °C/s is able to be overcome by this HTC. Reaction progression will also be limited by the applied HTC.

Applying a 1000 W m^{-2} K^{-1} allows for the TR onset temperature to be reached without proceeding to failure. The maximum temperature change of the battery is 2.26 °C/s at 169 °C. However, the HTC can supply sufficient cooling to the battery. Figure 4 demonstrates the cooling of the battery under these circumstances. This may seem impractical when it comes to cooling capabilities, but this compares to the upper limits of forced convection of air, gases, and vapors [10]. This cooling scenario allows for a greater extent of reaction without allowing the battery to experience TR.

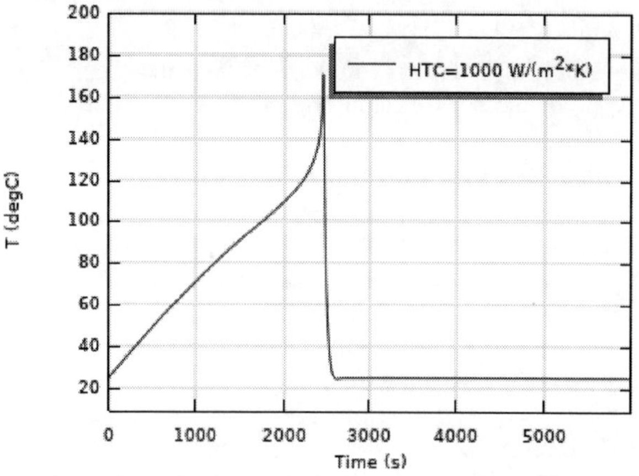

Figure 4. Non-Adiabatic Failure Scenario (1000 W m^{-2} K^{-1}).

Future Work

This work has provided the general methodology for interfacing cooling structure technology with battery kinetic modeling. If the overall heat transfer coefficient of the desired cooling structure is known, then the ability to push battery performance can be determined. This means that batteries can be cycled at higher charge and discharge rates without fear of thermal stress being the initiator of TR. With the Intramicron developed cooling structure, the overall heat transfer coefficient can be observed experimentally and applied to the kinetic model to determine how hot the battery can get without undergoing TR from thermal stress. . Li-ion battery failure varies not only from cell chemistry to cell chemistry, but it varies between cells of the same chemistry and even the same batch. Therefore, it is imperative that batteries are tested within their respective cooling structures before operation. Doing this will help validate the modeling effort and further ensure safe cycling of Li-ion batteries.

The HTC's discussed in this paper apply for a 1.5 Ah cylindrical NMC cell; however, a similar methodology can be used for other battery chemistries provided the kinetic data is provided. Different failure methods should also be considered. The failure method described in this paper is thermally initiated failure not failure due to internal short circuit or other failure mechanisms. Other failure mechanisms could require different cooling capabilities.

Acknowledgements

The authors would like to thank the Office of Naval Research for funding our research and development efforts. Work is done under Navy Contract N6449819D4025, Task Order 1 N6449819F4256.

Conclusions

A lumped kinetic model provides the ability for batteries to communicate with battery cooling structures. This study shows that as a HTC is applied to a Li-ion battery under thermal stress, heat is taken away from the battery to keep the battery from reaching TR. TR is prevented at multiple self-heating rates:

1. Applying a HTC of 24 W m^{-2} K^{-1} once a self-heating rate of 0.1 °C/s is observed quenches TR.
2. Applying a HTC of 300 W m^{-2} K^{-1} in a more pronounced self-heating region of 0.41 °C/s quenches TR.
3. Applying a HTC of 1000 W m^{-2} K^{-1} once the TR onset temperature has been achieved at a self-heating rate of 2.26 °C/s quenches TR.

With effective cooling structures applied to Li-ion batteries, batteries can be pushed to their operating limits. This means that batteries can be cycled faster and can operate under pulse power applications.

References

[1] NASA, NREL, and Electrochemical Innovation Lab, "Battery Failure Databank." NASA, NREL, Electrochemical Innovation Lab, Oct. 2020. [Online]. Available: https://www.nrel.gov/transportation/battery-failure.html

[2] A. W. Golubkov *et al.*, "Thermal-runaway experiments on consumer Li-ion batteries with metal-oxide and olivin-type cathodes," *RSC Adv.*, vol. 4, no. 7, pp. 3633–3642, 2014, doi: 10.1039/C3RA45748F.

[3] A. W. Golubkov *et al.*, "Thermal runaway of commercial 18650 Li-ion batteries with LFP and NCA cathodes – impact of state of charge and overcharge," *RSC Adv.*, vol. 5, no. 70, pp. 57171–57186, 2015, doi: 10.1039/C5RA05897J.

[4] F. Larsson, P. Andersson, P. Blomqvist, and B.-E. Mellander, "Toxic fluoride gas emissions from lithium-ion battery fires," *Sci. Rep.*, vol. 7, no. 1, Art. no. 1, Aug. 2017, doi: 10.1038/s41598-017-09784-z.

[5] Q. Wang, B. Mao, S. I. Stoliarov, and J. Sun, "A review of lithium ion battery failure mechanisms and fire prevention strategies," *Prog. Energy Combust. Sci.*, vol. 73, pp. 95–131, Jul. 2019, doi: 10.1016/j.pecs.2019.03.002.

[6] Y. Ding, H. Ji, M. Wei, and R. Liu, "Effect of liquid cooling system structure on lithium-ion battery pack temperature fields," *Int. J. Heat Mass Transf.*, vol. 183, p. 122178, Feb. 2022, doi: 10.1016/j.ijheatmasstransfer.2021.122178.

[7] P. T. Coman, E. C. Darcy, and R. E. White, "Simplified Thermal Runaway Model for Assisting the Design of a Novel Safe Li-Ion Battery Pack," *J. Electrochem. Soc.*, vol. 169, no. 4, p. 040516, Apr. 2022, doi: 10.1149/1945-7111/ac62bd.

[8] W. Zhu, Y. Hongyun, P. Dimick, and B. Tatarchuk, "A Metal Microfibrous Enhanced Cooling Structure for Heat Rejection and Temperature Control of High Power Mid-Form Li-ion Battery Packs," presented at the 48th Power Sources Conference, Denver, Colorado, Jun. 11, 2018.

[9] P. T. Coman, S. Rayman, and R. E. White, "A lumped model of venting during thermal runaway in a cylindrical Lithium Cobalt Oxide lithium-ion cell," *J. Power Sources*, vol. 307, pp. 56–62, Mar. 2016, doi: 10.1016/j.jpowsour.2015.12.088.

[10] C. J. Geankoplis, *Transport processes and separation process principles*, Fifth edition. in Prentice Hall international series in the physical and chemical engineering sciences. Boston, MA: Prentice Hall, 2018.

Designs to Mitigate Thermal Runaway Propagation for Cells Packaged for Transportation

Tapesh Joshi and Judith A. Jeevarajan

Electrochemical Safety Research Institute (ESRI)
UL Research Institutes
5000 Gulf Fwy, UHTB, Bldg 4, Rm 230A, Houston, TX 77204
judy.jeevarajan@ul.org

Abstract

Lithium-ion cells may go into failure and thermal runaway due to off-nominal abuse conditions or defects. Incidents during transportation of batteries are causes of major concern due to the hazards from failure. The severity of hazards is magnified when thermal runaway from a single cell is propagated to other cells in a package. Interstitial separation between cells can be effective in preventing the propagation of thermal runaway from a single cell failure to other cells in a shipping package. Materials from different manufacturers were studied to evaluate the efficacy in preventing the propagation of thermal runaway at different state of charge (SOC). Block type material was effective in preventing further propagation of thermal runaway even in the fully charged conditions while other materials also were effective in preventing propagation of single cells at 33 % SOC. Conduction through the tabs resulted in worse outcomes at 33 % SOC for 25P electrically conducted configurations compared to single cells. Design considerations for testing to define the test end conditions and packaging requirements to allow pressure release through venting are also presented.

Keywords

battery safety; thermal runaway; propagation; mitigation; transportation

Introduction

The demand for lithium-ion batteries continues to rise to meet growing needs for powering personal devices to electric vehicles and energy storage systems. Shipment of li-ion cells and batteries is inevitable since these are manufactured in different parts of the world and shipped to end users. This provides safety challenges during shipping to the end-users if proper precautions are not taken. Mechanical, electrical, or environmental hazards occurring in a single cell could lead the cell into thermal runaway and, in worst cases, propagate to neighboring cells in a package or a battery[1]. Hazards such as gas and electrolyte leakage, elevated temperature, fire, and deflagration are possible during thermal runway in lithium-ion batteries[2]. Transportation guidelines and restrictions based on state of charge (SOC) are in place for transporting batteries. Despite transportation guidelines in place, there have been incidents leading to damages resulting from battery failures during shipping[3].

Effective test methods to study the propagation behavior and hazards for batteries in configurations used for shipments can inform improved design requirements for enhancing safety. Additionally, considerations for barrier materials and cell spacing are imperative in mitigating the propagation of thermal runaway. The current study focused on developing test methods and analyzed the effectiveness of several barrier materials to prevent thermal runaway propagation and contain it within the shipping container.

Experimental method and configuration

Commercial 18650 format lithium-ion cells were tested as 25 single cells (unconnected) and 25P electrically connected 5X5 configurations in shipping boxes (4.25" x 4.25" x 3.125") as shown in Figure 1. The center cell was heated using a 40W tape heater with a target heating rate of 10 °C/min until the trigger cell went into thermal runaway or reached 200 °C. Cells were placed inside corrugated packaging box and tested at 100 % and 33 % state of charge (SOC) to test the worst-case scenario and maximum allowable SOC for shipping, respectively. Interstitial materials from different manufacturers were used to separate the cells from neighboring cells. Materials having different properties were tested in addition to a baseline case with air separation of 2 mm between cells. Testing was also conducted with secondary shipping packages resembling available shipping methods.

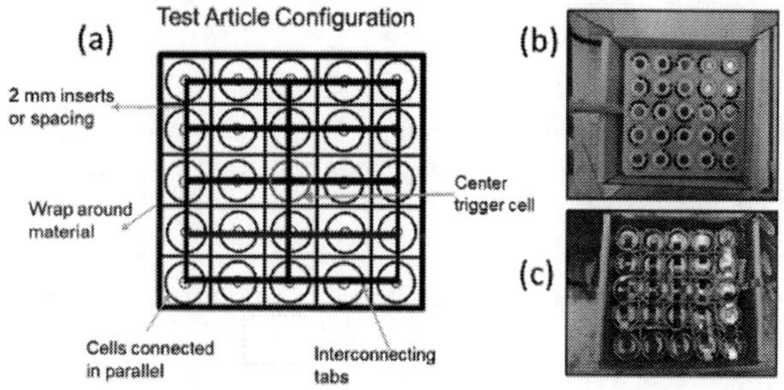

Figure 1. (a) Test article configuration showing the arrangements of 25 cells with trigger cell at the center of the configuration with inserts around each cell, (b) block-type phase change material and (c) combination of tubes and insert materials to separate 25P electrically connected cells in a shipping package.

Results and Discussion

Thermal runaway propagation at different SOC and test configurations and the effectiveness of the interstitial materials in mitigating these hazards are summarized in Table 1. For different materials, the expected trends of increasing hazards with increase in cell SOC were observed[2].

Baseline: Single cells separated by packaging paper inserts and 25P electrically connected cells separated by 2mm air were tested at 33 % SOC as baseline tests. Thermal runaway in the trigger cell was followed by no subsequent propagation for single cell configuration with no fire or charring on the outside of the packaging box. For the 25P electrically connected configuration, full propagation of thermal runaway with fire was observed as the worst-case scenario.

Manufacturers A, C, G: Interstitial materials were ineffective in preventing cell-to-cell thermal runaway propagation from the trigger cell to the neighboring cells. In all tests with materials as interstitial separators, full propagation of thermal runaway with fire occurred at 100 % SOC. Fire following the trigger cell thermal runaway and immediate propagation of the thermal runaway to all of the cells in the package was observed, as seen in Figure 2 for material from manufacturer G. Ejection of the jelly roll and sidewall rupture were also evident.

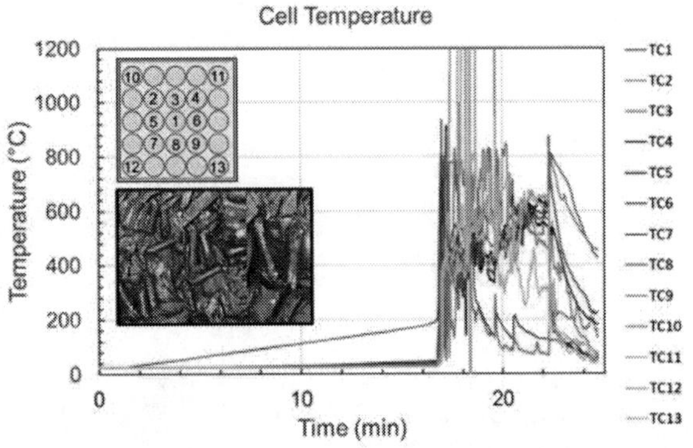

Figure 2. Cell temperatures and thermocouple layout for 100 % SOC test with interstitial material from manufacturer G. Inset shows post-test cell pictures with sidewall rupture.

At 33 % SOC for single cells and 25P electrically connected tests, the propagation of thermal runaway from the trigger cell to neighboring cells were prevented. The trigger cell went into thermal runaway and charring around the trigger cell location along with electrolyte leak was observed.

Manufacturer B: Structural support and the heat dissipation provided by the block material were effective in preventing further propagation of thermal runaway. Tests with and without an ejecta-control pouch placed on the top of the cell yielded no propagation of thermal runaway from the trigger cell to the neighboring cells. The pouch captured ejecta released from the trigger cell (inset Figure 3). For all 100 % SOC tests, the cells maintained pre-test voltage after the completion of the tests.

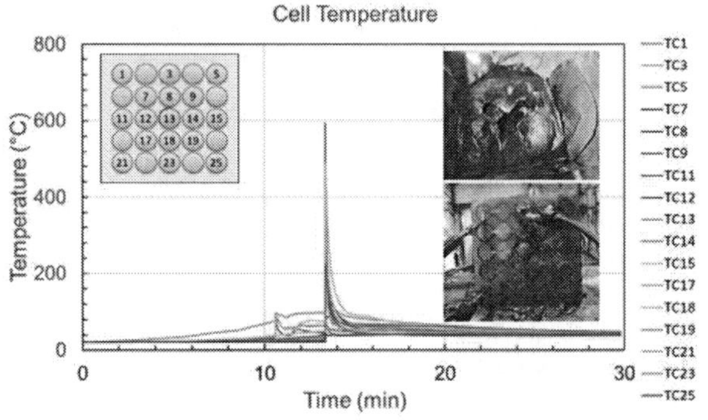

Figure 3. Cell temperatures and thermocouple layout for 100 % SOC 25P connected test with block material from manufacturer B.

Tests at 33 % SOC with the block material prevented full propagation of thermal runway from trigger cell to all of the cells in the package. For single cells test, there was no propagation from the trigger cell to the neighboring cells. Thermal runaway on the trigger cell was followed by the ejection of the jelly roll and fire, but no further thermal runway was observed. In case of 25P connected test, heavy gas and electrolyte release was observed. Although full propagation was prevented, some of the neighboring cells went into thermal runaway.

Manufacturer D, H: Interstitial materials configured in interlocking grid-pattern from manufacturers D and H showed volume expansion during tests, but the propagation of thermal runaway and fire was not mitigated. The materials charred and burned lacking structural support. Full propagation of thermal runaway with ejected contents and sidewall rupture was observed.

Single cell tests as barrier between the cells prevented full propagation of thermal runaway in case of single cell, however, full propagation of thermal runaway occurred in 25P electrically connected case. Heavy gas and electrolyte release was observed for 25P electrically connected test and the conduction through the tabs led to worse outcome compared to the single cell configuration.

Secondary containers: Inherently safe packaging design with mitigation materials that can prevent the propagation of thermal runaway from cell-to-cell in cases of off-nominal abuse and incidents are ideal. In transportation, secondary containers that can withstand cell failures and contain the ejecta, fire, and heat within the package are desired. Tests with three such packaging designs highlighted successful packaging design and failure modes.

Table 1. List of materials, SOC and configurations for the different tests and propagation outcomes.

Manufacturer	Medium	SOC/Configuration	Propagation
Baseline	Interlocking paper insert	33 % (single)	N
Baseline	Air	33 % (25P)	Full
A	Interlocking separator	100 % (25P)	Full
B	Block	100 % (single)	N
B	Block	100 % (25P)	N
B	Block	33 % (single)	N
B	Block	33 % (25P)	Partial
C	Interlocking separator	100 % (25P)	Full
C	Tubes	100 % (25P)	Full
C	Interlocking separator+ tubes	100 % (25P)	Full
C	Tubes	33 % (single)	N
C	Tubes	33 % (25P)	N
D	Interlocking separator-2mm	100 % (25P)	Full
D	Interlocking separator-4mm	100 % (25P)	Full
D	Interlocking separator-2mm	33 % (single)	N
D	Interlocking separator-2mm	33 % (25P)	Full
D	Interlocking separator-4mm	33 % (single)	N
D	Interlocking separator-4mm	33 % (25P)	Full
D	Interlocking separator	33 % (single)	N
E	Interlocking paper insert (Secondary box)	100 % (single)	N
F	Cell sleeves, separators (Secondary box)	100 % (25P)	Full
G	Interlocking separator-2mm	100 % (25P)	Full
G	Interlocking separator-4mm	100 % (25P)	Full
G	Interlocking separator-2mm	33 % (single)	N
G	Interlocking separator-2mm	33 % (25P)	N
H	Interlocking separator	100 % (25P)	Full
I	Silica granules (Secondary box)	100 % (25P)	Full
I	Silica granules	33 % (single)	N
H	Silica granules	33 % (25P)	Full

Thermal runaway propagation and hazards were mitigated for manufacturer E. For manufacturer F, delayed thermal event after more than 5.5 hours since the beginning of the test was noted (Figure 4a). The dangers of delayed propagation of thermal runaway and the need to design test completion criteria to account for stranded energy and to ensure safety of personnel and equipment is highlighted from this test. In Figure 4b, the secondary package from manufacturer I did not contain pressure relief vents for releasing excess gas build-up within the container. As gases accumulated after cell failures due to thermal runaway in the package, deflagration and fire resulted in the package.

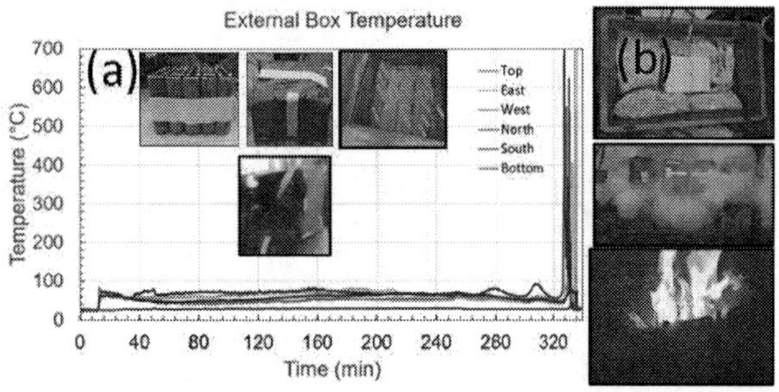

Figure 4. (a) External box temperature showing delayed thermal event within the box. Inset shows test article preparation and placement within secondary container and fire at the end of the test. (b) Pictures showing placement of test article within the secondary container and pressurized gas release and fire due to a lack of venting mechanism in the secondary box.

Table 2 lists the material properties of the interstitial materials used in the tests. These properties were shared by the manufacturers and the missing property values were not reported or shared.

Table 2. List of material properties for interstitial materials used in the tests.

Materials	Thermal Conductivity (W/m.K)	Phase Transition Temperature
Manufacturer A (Kaowool)	0.06 (260 °C) 0.12 (538 °C)	-
Manufacturer B Block/Mold	0.65	122 °C
Pouch	0.74 (xy plane)	95-110 °C(Thermal Dissipation – 1600 -2000 J/g)
Manufacturer C Flexible Mica Tubes	0.04 (22 °C); 0.15 (816 °C)	-
Flexible Flame Barrier	0.2 (200 °C); 0.35 (400 °C)	-
Manufacturer D Intumescent cell separators	0.54	Expansion Temp: 200 °C
Intumescent flat sheets	0.54	Expansion Temp: 200 °C
Manufacturer G	0.024 (0 °C) 0.054 (600 °C)	-
Manufacturer I	0.06 (20 °C)	-

Conclusions

Mitigation materials from different manufacturers were tested to study the efficacy in preventing the propagation of thermal runaway to neighboring cells in a shipping package configuration. Interstitial material with a block/ mold design that provided structural support to the cells and effectively dissipated excess heat prevented thermal runaway propagation for worst-case scenario at 100 % SOC. Single cell configurations tests with materials from all manufacturers were tolerant to abuse and prevented propagation of thermal runaway and fire at 33 % SOC. For 25P electrically connected configuration at 33 % SOC, tab-conduction contributed to worse outcomes including full propagation for some manufacturers. For tests including secondary containers, manufacturer E was effective in preventing propagation while the other manufacturers underwent full propagation with fire. Because of the nature of the hazards present, a combination of fire retardation, insulation, and heat dissipation is desired to effectively prevent the propagation of thermal runaway.

Acknowledgements

Internal research funds from UL Research Institutes (ULRI) were used for this test program and is gratefully acknowledged. The safety tests were carried out at the Energy Systems Test Area (ESTA) at NASA - Johnson Space Center (JSC) and the support of Dereck Lenoir and the team of technicians is acknowledged. Material manufacturers are acknowledged for working with the testing team to provide materials in desired configurations.

References

1.Jeevarajan, J. A.; Joshi, T.; Parhizi, M.; Rauhala, T.; Juarez-Robles, D., Battery Hazards for Large Energy Storage Systems. *ACS Energy Letters* **2022,** *7* (8), 2725-2733.

2.Joshi, T.; Azam, S.; Lopez, C.; Kinyon, S.; Jeevarajan, J., Safety of Lithium-Ion Cells and Batteries at Different States-of-Charge. *Journal of The Electrochemical Society* **2020,** *167* (14), 140547.

3.Kapp, E. A.; Wroth, D. S.; Chapin, J. T., Analysis of Thermal Runaway Incidents Involving Lithium Batteries in U.S. Commercial Aviation. *Transportation Research Record* **2020,** *2674* (11), 584-592.

A Three-Dimensional Thermal Resistance Network Model for Thermal Runaway in Lithium-Ion Batteries

Mohammad Parhizi[1], Jason Ostanek[2], Judith Jeevarajan[1]

1 – Electrochemical Safety Research Institutes
UL Research Institutes
5000 Gulf Fwy, UHTB, Bldg. 4, Rm 138, TX, USA, 77204
Mohammad.Parhizi@ul.org

2 – School of Engineering Technology
Purdue University
401 N. Grant Street, West Lafayette, IN 47907

Abstract

Lithium-ion (Li-ion) batteries have been used widely for various applications, including consumer electronics, electric vehicles, grid storage systems, and military and space applications. However, despite their superior electrochemical characteristics, Li-ion batteries are prone to thermal runaway under certain off-nominal conditions. Under these conditions, Li-ion cells generate excessive amounts of gas and heat, resulting in the venting of flammable gases out of the cell, and causing a potential fire hazard. Modeling and simulation of thermal runaway in Li-ion cells can provide insights into the safe operating limits, help provide guidelines for safer pack/module designs and assist in post-failure diagnostics and analysis. However, modeling thermal runaway in Li-ion cells and batteries is extremely complex due to the multi-physics phenomena involved and the highly nonlinear equations describing them. Thus, systematically reduced-order models are required for specific applications, particularly for scaling up the modeling framework or where a series of simulations must be run. One challenge with reduced-order models is the loss of modeling fidelity that comes with dimensional reduction or simplification of the physical processes. This work presents a series of case studies using a thermal resistance network and lumped mass framework with superior usability that allows creation of complex networks to track heat transfer in all three directions. Due to its simplicity and computational efficiency, the present model can be used for model calibration and parameter estimation (thermophysical properties and kinetic parameters), cell-to-cell variability and statistical analysis, and extending thermal abuse modeling to large battery systems. This presentation will provide examples of some of these practical applications mentioned above and highlights the importance of capturing three-dimensional effects in a thermal resistance network and lumped mass framework.

Keywords
Lithium-Ion Battey, Thermal Runaway, Modeling & Simulation, Thermal Network Model

Introduction

Despite significant advances towards electrification and design improvement of Lithium-ion (Li-ion) batteries, thermal runaway and potential fire hazards are still unsolved issues associated with Li-ion batteries. Consequently, extensive research on thermal runaway has been carried out experimentally and incorporating modeling and simulation techniques. Various modeling frameworks, including lumped capacitance [1], 1-D [2], 2-D axisymmetric [3], and 3-D [4] models, have been used to simulate thermal runaway at the cell level and battery packs. Moreover, a wide range of numerical models with different levels of complexity, from simplified thermal network models [5] up to Computational Fluid Dynamics (CFD-based) models accounting for fluid flow [3] and combustion [6], are available in the literature.

In general, high-fidelity thermal runaway models are extremely complex and computationally expensive due to the highly nonlinear equations describing the multi-physics phenomena involved, a large number of mesh elements, and the small time-step size required for convergence [7]. Reduced-order models, on the other hand, may suffer inaccuracies that come with dimensional reduction or over-simplification of the physical processes. However, reduced-order models are required for scaling up the modeling framework, model calibration, and sensitivity analysis. Thus, a reduced-order model capable of reconstructing the 3-D geometry without many elements is desirable. Current simplified models are primarily based on the concept of lumped mass, which ignores the directional heat transfer entirely. This results in ignoring spatial temperature gradients, lack of capability to account for local phenomena, and limiting the boundary conditions used.

This work develops a 3-D thermal resistance network with excellent versatility, allowing heat transfer calculations in all three dimensions using complex thermal networks and allowing expandability to the module-level. A systematic investigation varying the spatial resolution is conducted and the implications on parameter identification are presented.

Single Cell Thermal Abuse Experiment

The test case considered for the thermal modeling and parameter identification analysis was based on a single 18650 Li-ion cell thermal abuse experiment. The cell was placed in a closed volume chamber, sitting upright on a ceramic tile as shown in Figure 1(a). An axial fan was placed near the top of the chamber to encourage mixing and a baffle was used to protect the fan from ejecta and debris.

The cell was driven to thermal runaway by an external heater having dimensions 25 mm x 25 mm and placed at the midline of the cell, shown in Figure 1(b). The heating power was controlled to maintain a constant 9 °C/min rate of temperature increase. The surface of the cell was instrumented with an array of thermocouples at various axial and circumferential locations, as shown in Figure 1(b) and listed in Table 1. Thermocouple signals were recorded at 1Hz sampling frequency.

Table 1. Thermocouple designations and positions.

Designation	X (mm)	Y (mm)	Z (mm)
TC1	0	32.5	9
TC2	9	32.5	0
TC3	0	32.5	-9
TC2U2	9	55	0
TC4U2	-9	55	0
TC2L2	9	10	0
TC4L2	-9	10	0

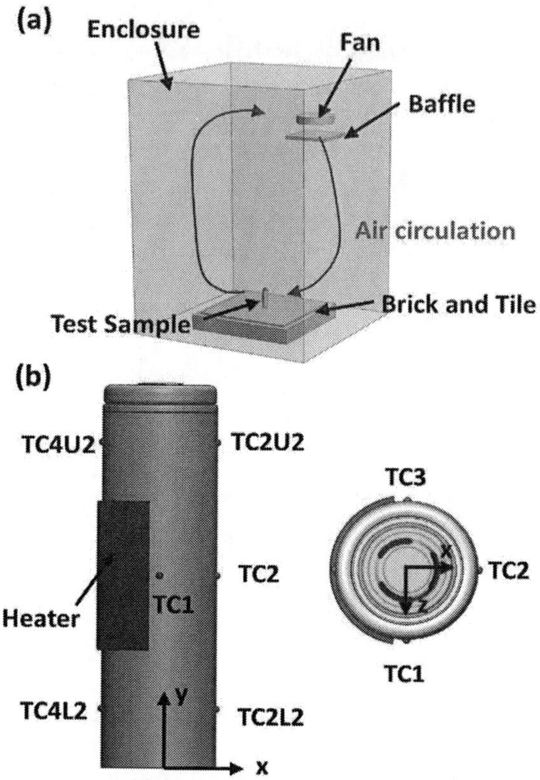

Figure 1. Schematic of experimental apparatus for thermal abuse testing (a) and schematic of instrumented test sample (b).

Model Framework

The present investigation considers the effect of spatial resolution on parameter identification when using a thermal resistance and lumped mass modeling framework. The thermal model was created using GT-SUITE v2022 for its useability and flexibility in developing system-level models.

A schematic of the modeling approach is shown in Figure 2(a). The 18650 cell is split into two sections: the header and the cell body. The header is modeled as a single, homogeneous, and isotropic material and assigned thermophysical properties of steel. The cell body is modeled as a single, homogeneous material with cylindrical-anisotropic thermal conductivity. The sides and top of the cell were assigned a constant heat transfer coefficient of h = 16 W·m^{-2}·K^{-1} from the air circulation in the enclosure. The bottom of the cell was assigned h_{tile} = 150 W·m^{-2}·K^{-1} representing the combined heat conduction to the tile below the cell and subsequent convection to the air in the enclosure. The initial cell temperature was T_0 = 13.9 °C and the ambient temperature in the enclosure was T_∞ = 16.5 °C.

Table 2. Spatial discretization schemes for the cell body.

Designation (number of thermal masses)	Discretization (number of thermal resistances)
1TM	1 radial 0 circumferential 2 axial
5TM	3 radial 8 circumferential 2 axial
13TM	7 radial 8 circumferential 2 axial
21TM	11 radial 8 circumferential 2 axial

The cell body was discretized with varying levels of spatial resolution, as shown in Figure 2(b) and Table 2. The model designated "1TM" uses a single thermal mass element, resolves radial conduction with one thermal resistance, and resolves axial conduction with two thermal resistances. The model designated "5TM" uses five thermal masses to capture heat conduction in the circumferential direction and to increase spatial resolution in the radial direction from one to three thermal resistances. The model designated "13TM" increases the spatial resolution to seven thermal resistances in the radial direction and "21TM" further increases the resolution to 11 thermal resistances in the radial direction.

Each thermal mass element in GT-SUITE consists of a thermal node (lumped body) and one or more thermal resistances to allow heat conduction to/from the thermal node. A source heat rate is applied to each thermal mass within the cell body to account for the heat generated from exothermic decomposition reactions. A four-reaction thermal abuse model was used, including reactions for SEI-decomposition, anode-electrolyte reaction, cathode-electrolyte reaction, and electrolyte decomposition [9].

Thermophysical parameter identification was conducted using the optimization tool within GT-SUITE v2022. Table 3 lists the thermophysical parameters, initial values, and allowable range for parameter identification. The accelerated genetic algorithm within GT-SUITE was used for parameter identification.

Table 3. Thermophysical parameter identification.

Parameter	Initial Value	Range
Radial thermal conductivity (k_r)	1 W·m^{-1}·K^{-1}	0.1 to 50 W·m^{-1}·K^{-1}
Circumferential thermal conductivity (k_θ)	20 W·m^{-1}·K^{-1}	0.1 to 50 W·m^{-1}·K^{-1}
Axial thermal conductivity (k_θ)	20 W·m^{-1}·K^{-1}	0.1 to 50 W·m^{-1}·K^{-1}
Specific Heat Capacity (C_p)	1200 J·kg^{-1}·K^{-1}	800 to 2000 J·kg^{-1}·K^{-1}
Emissivity (ε)	0.8	0.5 to 1.0

Results and Discussion

The thermophysical properties, listed in Table 3, were identified by conducting the non-linear optimization routine over the time range, t = 0 to 1000 s. The identified radial thermal conductivity is shown in Figure 3(a), the identified circumferential and axial thermal conductivity are shown in Figure 3(b), the identified specific heat capacity is shown in Figure 3(c), and the identified surface emissivity is shown in Figure 3(f). The identified parameters show convergence toward expected values as the number of thermal masses increases. For 21TM, the identified parameters were: k_r = 0.43 W·m^{-1}·K^{-1}, k_θ = 18.55 W·m^{-1}·K^{-1}, k_a = 18.69 W·m^{-1}·K^{-1}, C_p = 1168 J·kg^{-1}·K^{-1}, and ε = 0.79.

The identified parameters were then transferred from each 3-D thermal resistance model (TM1, TM5, TM13, TM21) to a high-resolution finite volume model (19 x 10^3 volumes, second order spatial discretization, second order implicit time integration). The finite volume had identical geometry, initial conditions, boundary conditions, and material properties as the GT-SUITE optimization model. The experimental and simulated temperatures are compared in Figure 4(a) for 1TM, Figure 4(b) for 5TM, Figure 4(c) for 13 TM, and Figure 4(d) for 21TM. The relatively high radial conductivity identified with the 1TM model resulted in a smaller temperature gradient than the experimental data shown, in Figure 3(a). The 1TM model parameters resulted in an RMSE of 9.6 °C. The lower radial conductivity identified by the 5TM model resulted in a temperature gradient more similar to the experimental data, but the RMSE of 11.4 °C was unimproved relative to the 1TM model. The RMSE of the 5TM model was driven by TC1 and TC3, shown in Figure 1(b), which are directly adjacent to the edge of the heater. Though the 5TM model has increased spatial resolution relative to the 1TM model, the 5TM is still relatively coarse. The heat dissipated by the heater was distributed into the large control volumes and the response of TC1 and TC3 in the model were dampened relative to the experiments, leading to an error in the identified thermophysical properties. The same trend continued for 13TM with RMSE of 11.2 °C and 21TM with RMSE of 10.0 °C. The 21TM model is recommended for thermophysical parameter identification and further improvements may be realized by capturing the temperature gradient between the heater and adjacent thermocouples (TC1 and TC3), through increasing spatial resolution in the circumferential direction.

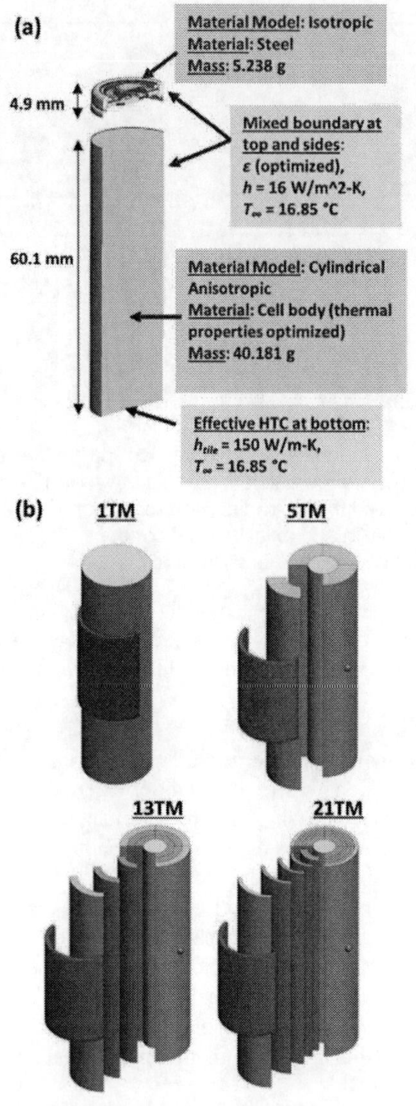

Figure 2. Schematic of geometry, material models, and boundary conditions of numerical model (a) and schematics of four spatial discretization schemes for the cell body (b).

After identifying the thermophysical parameters, each model was used to simulate the full thermal runaway event. Figure 5 compares the temperature of TC2 vs time for each model and experimental data. The 1TM model clearly enters thermal runaway prior to the other models. This implies that

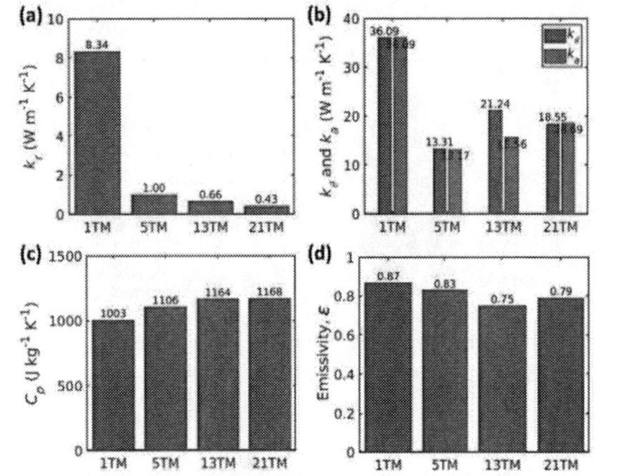

Figure 3. Identified thermophysical properties for 3-D thermal resistance network models of varying degrees of spatial resolution: radial thermal conductivity (a), circumferential and axial thermal conductivity (b), specific heat capacity (c), and emissivity (d).

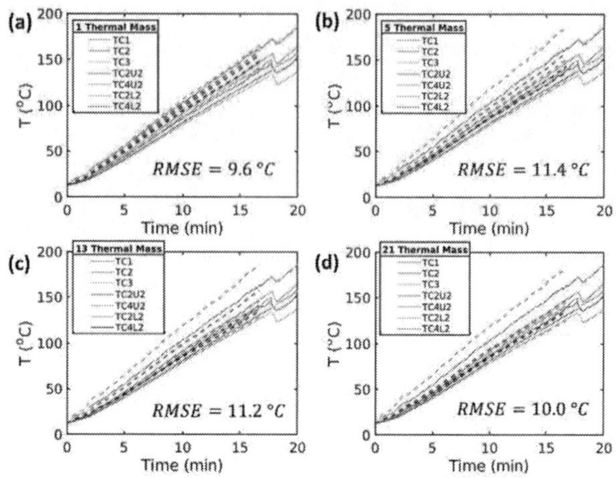

Figure 4. Comparison of high-resolution finite volume simulations (dashed) and experimental temperature vs. time (solid) using parameters identified from the 3-D thermal resistance model: 1TM (a), 5TM (b), 13TM (c), and 21TM (d).

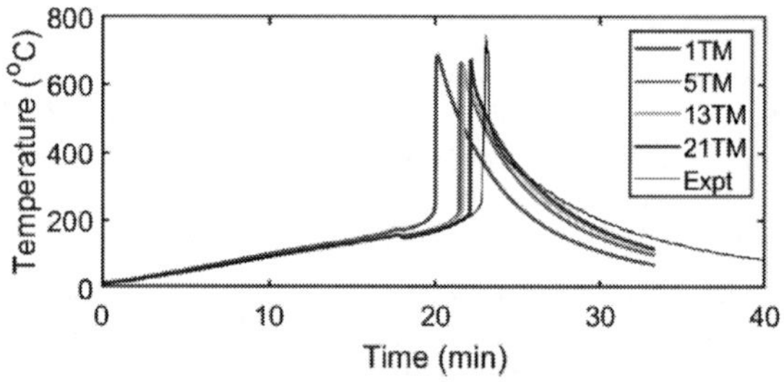

Figure 5. Temperature of TC2 vs. time for each thermal resistance network model and experimental data.

use of low dimensional models for kinetic parameter identification may produce erroneous results when scaled to high resolution finite volume or finite element models.

Conclusions

A 3-D thermal resistance network with varying degrees of spatial resolution was used to model external heating and thermal abuse of a single, 18650 format cell. The GT-SUITE framework was used due to its built-in optimization tool and scalability to module-level studies. In this work, the built-in optimization tool was used to identify thermophysical and kinetic parameters of decomposition reactions. Parameter identification depends strongly on spatial resolution of the thermal resistance network. Using too few thermal mass elements, particularly in the radial direction, results in errors in thermophysical and kinetic parameters.

References

1. J. K. Ostanek, W. Li, P. P. Mukherjee, K. Crompton, and C. Hacker, "Simulating onset and evolution of thermal runaway in Li-ion cells using a coupled thermal and venting model," *Applied Energy,* vol. 268, 2020.
2. T. Hatchard, D. MacNeil, A. Basu, and J. Dahn, "Thermal model of cylindrical and prismatic lithium-ion cells," *Journal of The Electrochemical Society,* vol. 148, no. 7, p. A755, 2001.
3. J. Kim, A. Mallarapu, D. P. Finegan, and S. Santhanagopalan, "Modeling cell venting and gas-phase reactions in 18650 lithium ion batteries during thermal runaway," *Journal of Power Sources,* vol. 489, 2021.
4. D. Mishra, P. Zhao, and A. Jain, "Thermal Runaway Propagation in Li-ion Battery Packs Due to Combustion of Vent Gases," *Journal of The Electrochemical Society,* vol. 169, no. 10, p. 100520, 2022.
5. Z. Jiang, Z. Qu, J. Zhang, and Z. Rao, "Rapid prediction method for thermal runaway propagation in battery pack based on lumped thermal resistance network and electric circuit analogy," *Applied Energy,* vol. 268, 2020.
6. D. Kong, G. Wang, P. Ping, and J. Wen, "A coupled conjugate heat transfer and CFD model for the thermal runaway evolution and jet fire of 18650 lithium-ion battery under thermal abuse," *E-transportation,* vol. 12, 2022.
7. M. Parhizi, A. Jain, G. Kilaz, and J. K. Ostanek, "Accelerating the numerical solution of thermal runaway in Li-ion batteries," *Journal of Power Sources,* vol. 538, 2022.
8. G. Wang *et al.*, "Modeling venting behavior of lithium-ion batteries during thermal runaway propagation by coupling CFD and thermal resistance network," *Applied Energy,* vol. 334, 2023.
9. Kim et al., "A three-dimensional thermal abuse model for lithium-ion cells," *Journal of Power Sources*, vol. 170, 2007.

Lithium Ion Battery Failures and the Formation of Thermite Reactions

Rodney LaFollette and Michael D. Eskra

Eskra Technical Products, Inc.
Saukville, WI 53080

Abstract

It is often observed that some runaway Li-ion cells with layered cathode materials, become much hotter internally than existing thermal runaway models predict, Further, metals originally in the positive active material (such as Co, Ni, and Mn) are often found in cells whose temperatures became very high. It has been postulated that the formation of metals can be attributed to reduction of rock salt species (MO, where M is the metal), or the reaction of lithiated active material ($LiMO_2$) with CO_2. We propose an alternate explanation for formation of metals, that also results in very high cell temperatures, namely thermite reactions between the Al positive electrode current collector, and the positive active material. These reactions are highly exothermic, in contrast with the reactions of MO and $LiMO_2$ mentioned. In this paper the chemistry of thermite reactions is presented. Incorporating thermite reactions in runaway models will likely improve temperature prediction of Li-ion cells in thermal runaway.

Introduction

Numerous mathematical models have been developed to better understand thermal and chemical process that take place, including those involved in thermal runaway in troubled Li-ion cells (1,2,3,4,5,6,7,8). These models include chemical and thermal effects of solid-electrolyte interface (SEI) decomposition; reactions between the exposed anode and the electrolyte; melting of the polymer-based separator; reactions between the cathode material and electrolyte, and electrolyte evaporation.

Evidence from autopsied runaway cells often show that internal temperatures probably exceeded those predicted from such models. It is our view that in models that deal with very high temperature reactions, inclusion of thermite reactions would allow more accuratele predict of cell temperatures. Thermite reactions take place at elevated temperatures (usually > 300 C). A thermite reaction is similar to a typical redox type reaction, involving a metal and an oxide of a different metal. The basic reaction is

$$M^1 + M_y^2 O_x \rightarrow M^1 O_x + yM^2 \qquad (1)$$

Where M^1 and M^2 are dissimilar metals. Thermite reactions can be highly exothermic. In the case of Li-ion cells, we consider that the most common thermite reaction would take place between an aluminum current collector and the positive metal oxide active material. In principle though, it could also involve reaction of other metals in the cell, such as the copper foil current collector used in most negative electrodes. In this paper reaction between Al and the positive active material will be considered.

The standard accepted processes that take place in thermal runaway of Li-ion cells, are first presented, as a context for later discussion of thermite reactions. For the most part thermal runaway models treat the following sequence (1). **Initial heating** takes place, due to either external heat or internally generated heat usually from an internal short. This is the initiation of temperature rise in the cell.

A solvent-electrolyte layer (SEI) layer exists on the surface of the negative active material. **SEI decomposition** begins at around 85 - 135 C. The metastable species $(CH_2OCO_2Li)_2$ reacts, according to

$$(CH_2OCO_2Li)_2 \rightarrow Li_2CO_3 + C_2H_2 + CO_2 + 0.5O_2$$

$$2Li + (CH_2OCO_2Li)_2 \rightarrow 2Li_2CO_3 + C_2H_2 \qquad (2)$$

The above reactions are mildly exothermic (-20 kJ/mol C). The C_2H_2 and O_2 that are generated can later react in additional exothermic reactions.

The **separator melts** at 130 – 150 C, depending on its composition. While this is an endothermic process, it often leads to internal shorting from softening of the polymer, which accelerates heat generation.

Oxidation of the polymer separator also can take place, depending on the availability of oxygen or other reducing species. Separators are usually a composite of polymers such as polyethylene and polypropylene. For polyethylene, the reactions are

$$[C_2H_4]_n + 3O_2 \rightarrow 2H_2O + 2CO_2$$

$$[C_2H_4]_n + 2O_2 \rightarrow 2H_2O + 2CO \qquad (3)$$

with heats of reaction of -44.6 and -31.1 kJ/g polymer, respectively. These reactions also lead to a pressure increase in volume-constrained cells. Oxidation of the separator usually competes with oxidation of the electrolyte solvent(s). The presence of reductants such as O_2 or CO will determine the oxidation rate.

At 165 – 220 C, the (exposed) **anode reacts with the electrolyte solvent**. Most electrolytes use mixed solvents. Ethylene carbonate (EC) is often chosen to model the effective electrolyte reactions (9). The EC reactions are

$$C_3H_4O_3 + Li^+ + e^- \rightarrow 0.5(CH_2OCO_2Li)_2 + C_2H_4$$

$$C_3H_4O_3 + Li \rightarrow Li_2CO_3 + C_2H_4 \qquad (4)$$

these reactions are exothermic (-28 – 114 kJ/mol C).

In cells using layered cathode active materials, **decomposition of the active material** begins at 180 – 200 C. There are many different reactions of a layered material ($LiMO_2$). Shurtz and Hewson (9) have provided an accounting of the various reactions, which are of the form

$$LiMO_2 \rightarrow \begin{array}{l} LiMn_2O_4 \\ MO_2 \\ MO \\ M_3O_4 \end{array} + O_2 \qquad (5)$$

The above reactions are characteristic of most layered oxides (where M = Co, Ni, Mn, Al). Exception are found with Ni and Al, where not all of the reactions take place.

Shurtz and Newson used the following notation for the most important degradation reactions (Equations 5):

$$\begin{array}{lll} R1: 2MO_2 & \rightarrow 2MO & + O_2 \\ R2: 3MO_2 & \rightarrow M_3O_4 & + O_2 \\ R3: 2M_3O_4 & \rightarrow 6MO & + O_2 \\ R4: LiMO_2 + MO_2 & \rightarrow LiM_2O_4 & \\ R5: 3LiM_2O_4 & \rightarrow 3LiMO_2 + M_3O_4 + O_2 & \\ R6: 2LiM_2O_4 & \rightarrow 2LiMO_2 + 2MO + O_2 & (6) \end{array}$$

R1 is an overall reaction, and does not likely occur directly; rather it is the result of several successive reactions (9).

Shurtz and Hewson do not include reactions involving M_2O_3. There are a number of models that do include it (10). It is likely an intermediate in the formation of spinel species (M_3O_4) from MO_2.

The heats of reaction for Reactions R1 – R5 are given in Table 1. It should be noted that Reactions 3 and 5 are always endothermic, and in the case of Reaction 3, strongly so. Reaction 4 is always exothermic.

Table 1. Heats of Reactions for Metal Layered Oxides.

		ΔH_R	kJ/molar basis		
Reaction	1	2	3	4	5
molar basis	MO_2	MO_2	M_3O_4	LiM_2O_4	$LiMn_2O_4$
Co	47.7	-20.6	205.1	-73.9	53.3
Ni	-3.2	NA	NA	-29.9	NA
Mn	134.8	58.5	228.9	-22.2	80.7
Al	467.8	18.4	1348.2	-73	91.4

There are two important assumptions of in the thermodynamic development of Shurtz and Hewson, both of which appear to be quite reasonable. The first is that partially discharged positive active material (Li_xMO_2) is treated as a solution of two separate phases,

$$Li_xMO_2 \rightarrow xLiMO_2 + (1-x)MO_2 \qquad (7)$$

The other is that mixed metal oxides (NCA, NMC, etc.) can be treated as an ideal mixture of the individual metal oxides. As an example, $LiNi_{0.8}Co_{0.15}Al_{0.05}O_2$ would be

$$LiNi_{0.8}Co_{0.15}Al_{0.05}O_2 = 0.8LiNiO_2 + 0.15LiCoO_2 + 0.05LiAlO_2 \qquad (8)$$

The outgrowth of this latter assumption is that thermodynamic properties (such as heats of reaction) of mixed metal oxides can be treated as the sum of the contributions of the single metal materials. These authors compared their predictions of properties for several mixed metal oxides to measured values, and found agreement to be quite good. This powerful assumption allows modelers to perform calculations for mixed metal layered oxides where thermodynamic properties are not available.

Oxidation of electrolyte solvents usually takes place as cathode degradation begins. This is due to the availability of oxygen which is a byproduct of these reactions. Table 2 shows heats of oxidation for three common electrolyte solvents, EC, propylene carbonate (PC), and dimethyl carbonate (DMC), full and partial oxidation,

Table 2. Heats of Reaction for Solvent Oxidation.

Reaction	ΔH_R (kJ/mol O_2)
EC: $C_3H_4O_3 + 2.5O_2 \rightarrow 2H_2O + 3CO_2$	-472.2
PC: $C_4H_6O_3 + 4\ O_2 \rightarrow 3H_2O + 4CO_2$	-454.3
DMC: $C_3H_6O_3 + 3\ O_2 \rightarrow 3H_2O + 3CO_2$	-476.4
EC: $C_3H_4O_3 + 1.5O_2 \rightarrow 2H_2O + 3CO$	-86.0
PC: $C_4H_6O_3 + 2\ O_2 \rightarrow 3H_2O + 4CO$	-110.9
DMC: $C_3H_6O_3 + 1.5O_2 \rightarrow 3H_2O + 3CO$	-11.6

Full oxidation of solvents is highly exothermic. Their oxidation results not only in increased temperatures, but pressure rise due to generation of CO_2 and CO. Many reactions are possible beyond those shown in Table 2 (11).

There are other thermal runaway reactions that are often considered in runaway models. One is the interaction of the electrolyte salt (often $LiPF_6$). Another is reaction involving the electrolyte binder (usually polyvinylidene fluoride; PVDF). Both of these reactions release HF, which participates in and enables other runaway processes.

Thermite Reactions. Shurtz and Hewson observed that on occasion metal products (initially present in the cathode material), have been found in autopsied runaway cells (9). They postulate that the reduction of the active material to metals, is the result of either reduction of MO to form the metal and oxygen, or the reaction of $LiMO_2$ with CO_2, to form Li_2CO_3, metal and gaseous oxygen. They note that both of these processes are highly endothermic.

We propose that it is quite reasonable that metal formation is due to thermite reactions, which are exothermic. In these reactions no gaseous oxygen is formed; rather oxygen removed from the metal oxide, shows up in reaction products such as Al_2O_3.

A thermite reaction is essentially a redox-type reaction between a pure metal and the oxide of another metal (see Reaction 1). The initially pure metal is oxidized, and the metal in the initial oxide is reduced. In our present interest (runaway Li-ion cells), we confine discussion of thermite reactions largely to Al and the layered metal oxides.

There have been a number of reports of thermite reactions in Li-ion cells or related conditions. Jiaxing et al. (10) performed DSC/TGA experiments with MnO_2, with and without Al present. They determined that the degradation reaction is not a simple redox reaction, but involves reduction of MnO_2, resulting in oxygen loss and formation of Mn_2O_3 and Mn_3O_4. They found that when stoichiometric amounts of Al were present (inert atmosphere), reaction products included Al_2O_3, but no Al. Exothermic peaks in the DSC/TGA data, with Al present, could explain by thermite reactions. There was also metallic Mn present in reaction products. Thermite reactions of both Mn_3O_4 and MnO_2 with Al are highly exothermic, and more than compensated for the endothermic formation of Mn_2O_3 and Mn_3O_4, as well as melting of Al metal. Thermite reactions take place in parallel with the decomposition reactions of MnO_2 (in the absence of Al).

Inouye and Mukai also studied various cathode materials (NCA, NMC, $LiCoO_2$) using DSC/TGA. They also examined the heating behavior of full cells, including electrodes, electrolyte (EC/DEC, 1 M $LiPF_6$), both with and without current collectors. They observed many exotherms typical of the reactions with the materials described. Cells with Al current collectors though showed a very strong exotherm as the temperature approached 480 C, not present when no Al was not in the cell. Unfortunately, their instruments did not go above 480 C. Even so, their measured peak (which they state could only be due to a thermite reaction), was as large or larger than the exotherms observed when no Al was present. They calculated that had the instrument worked through a higher temperatures, the energy released would have been ~ 3200 J/g active material (compared to 1116 J/g and 1792 J/g for the two large exothermic peaks).

Wu et al. did DSC/TGA (and other) analysis of NMC 811, with and without Al (12). They also observed exothermic peaks with Al, that they attributed to thermite reactions.

Wu et al. also did XRD measurements of material at different placed in the electrode thickness. They found that in general the extent of their "thermite-type" reaction was limited by the available contact with Al, as the thermite products were largely limited to the Al/active material interface at the back of the electrodes.

It is normal to consider the delithiated material (MO_2; see Reaction 7) as participating in a thermite reaction, as it is less stable than the lithiated species ($LiMO_2$). Possible reactions are

$$\begin{aligned} &T1:\ 3\,MO + 2Al \rightarrow 3M + Al_2O_3 \\ &T2:\ 3\,M_3O_4 + 8Al \rightarrow 9M + 4Al_2O_3 \\ &T3:\ M_2O_3 + 2Al \rightarrow 2M + Al_2O_3 \\ &T4:\ 3\,MO_2 + 4Al \rightarrow 3M + 2Al_2O_3 \end{aligned} \qquad (9)$$

Calculated heats of reaction are shown in

Table 3. The reactions are highly exothermic. Table 4 shows the change in Gibbs free energy. Contrasting the heat of reaction with the Gibbs free energy, one can see that there is only a small difference between the two. Since G = H – TS, it can be deduced that the enthalpy term is dominant, and reactions are not hindered by the entropy change.

Table 3. Heats of Thermite Reactions, Positive Electrode.

	ΔH (kJ/mole MO_x)			
Reaction	T1	T2	T3	T4
Co	-320.8	-1324.2	-1098.2	-1117.1
Ni	-318.0	-1275.2	-1186.2	-881.0
Mn	-173.7	-846.5	-718.8	-597.0
Fe	-286.5	-1113.4	-850.2	

Table 4. Gibbs Free Energy of Thermite Reactions, Positive Electrode.

	ΔG (kJ/mole MO_x)			
Reaction	T1	T2	T3	T4
Co	-313.2	-1314.7	-1004.8	
Ni	-315.7			
Mn	-164.5	-826.5	-701.1	-589.7
Fe	-276.0	-1058.1	-838.8	

Thermite reactions can only proceed if Al comes into intimate contact with the metal oxides found in the positive electrode. This is not necessarily a given, as molten Al is quite mobile within a cell experiencing runaway. However, when the materials do meet, release of large amounts of energy can raise the internal cell temperatures beyond those predicted from "normal" runaway reactions.

The presence of metals in autopsy results of runaway cell has been presented as possible evidence of the reduction of metal oxides (MO, $LiMO_2$), to produce metal and gaseous oxygen, in endothermic reactions. We feel it is more likely that the presence of metals (originally in the cathode active material) are due to thermite reactions

Thermite reactions compete with other active material degradation reactions. To illustrate this the degradation steps proposed by Shurtz and Hewson will be described for $LiCoO_2$ (9). The partially discharged active material ($LixCoO_2$) is present as two comingled phases as posited earlier (Figure 1). The less stable delithiated species (CoO_2) reacts to form the spinel species, Co_3O_4, which in turn (and eventually) will form the rock salt CoO. Oxygen is produced in these reactions. The lithiated species ($LiCoO_2$), though more stable, can react with CO_2 if available in the cell. The reaction would produce the delithiated CoO_2, along with the rock salt and Li_2CO_3. The Co_2O_3 species might appear in the normal (non-thermite) degradation process, as an intermediate species in the reduction of CoO_2 to form the spinel species (Co_3O_4).

Figure 2 shows the same processes with consideration for thermite reactions. At every stage of degradation, a thermite reaction potentially competes with the non-thermite reaction. In fact, there is an extra possible thermite reaction not matched with a comparable non-thermite reaction, namely the reduction of the CoO to Co.

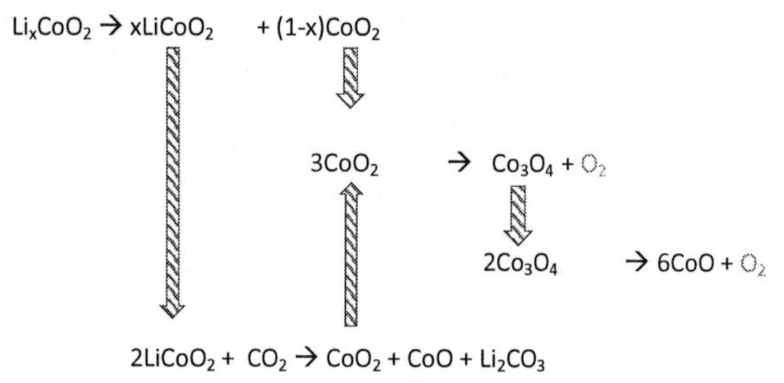

Figure 1. $LiCoO_2$ Degradation Based on Thermodynamic Analysis of Shurtz and Hewson (9).

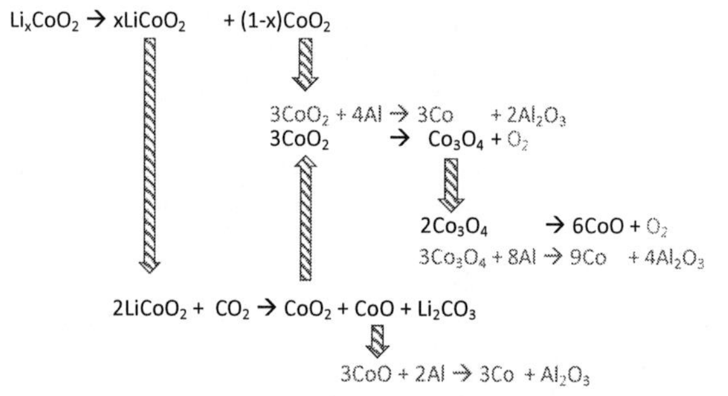

Figure 2. $LiCoO_2$ Degradation Processes with Thermite Reactions Considered. Thermite Reactions in Red.

Thermite reactions start to take place at higher temperatures. This could play a role in determining which of the reaction in Figure 2 are favored, and the fraction of the degradation processes due to thermite reactions. The very rapid temperature rise in many runaway cells could allow thermite reactions to compete successfully.

Observations and Conclusions

Anecdotal experiences of many researchers after autopsies of runaway Li-ion, have led many to believe that thermite reactions not only take place but are an important contributor to the heat generation within the cell. Support for this is provided by several studies using DSC and TGA. In these studies, exotherms where observed, along with mass loss measurements, whose only plausible explanation would be thermite reactions. Those exotherms did not take place when Al was not present. The formation of metallic species originally in the cathode active material, provided further evidence of thermite reactions.

Thermite reactions depend on intimate contact between Al and the cathode material. Experience has shown that Al can move within a cell as the temperature rises. Still, accurate predictions of cell temperatures can require consideration of this important class of reactions, so that model predictions can more closely reflect physical reality.

References

1 Spotnitz, R., Franklin, J., "Abuse Behavior of High-Power, Lithium-ion Cells," Journal of Power Sources, **113**, p. 81 (2003).

2 Hatchard, T., MacNeil, D., Basu, A., Dahn, J., "Thermal Model of Cylindrical and Prismatic Lithium-ion Cells," Journal of the Electrochemical Society, **148**, p. A755 (2001).

3 Hatchard, T., MacNeil, D., Basu, A., Dahn, J., "Thermal Model of Cylindrical and Prismatic Lithium-ion Cells," Journal of the Electrochemical Society, **148**, p. A755 (2001).

4 Chen, S., Wan, C., Wang, Y., "Thermal Analysis of Lithium-ion Batteries," Journal of Power Sources, **140**, p. 111 (2005).

5 Kim, G., Pesaran, A., Spotnitz, R., "A Three-Dimensional Thermal Abuse Model for Lithium-ion Cells, Journal of Power Sources, **170**, p. 476 (2007).

6 Lopez, C., Jeevarajan, J., Mukherjee, P., "Characterization of Lithium-ion Battery Thermal Abuse Behavior Using Experimental and Computational Analysis," Journal of the Electrochemical Society, **162**, p. A2163 (2015).

7 Muller, R., Cygan, R., Deng, J., Frischknecht, A., Hewson, J., Kanouff, M., Larson, R., Moffat, H., Tenney, C., Schultz, P., Wagner, G., "Modeling Thermal Abuse in Transportation Batteries," Sandia National Laboratory Report SAND2012-7812 (2012).

8 Lin, C., Cui, C., Xu, X., "Lithium-ion Battery Electro-thermal Model and Its Application in the Numerical Simulation of Short Circuit Experiment," World Electric Vehicle Journal, **6**, p. 0603 (2013).

9 Shurtz, R., Hewson, J., "Review – Materials Science Predictions of Thermal Runaway in Layered Metal-Oxide Cathodes: A Review of Thermodynamics" Journal of the Electrochemical Society. **167 p.** 090543 (2020).

10 Jiaxing, S., Tao, G., Wen, D., Yiming, M., Xiang, F., Hao, W., "Study on Thermal Chemical Reaction of Al/MnO_2 Thermite," *2018 IOP Conf. Series: Earth and Environmental Science,* **186** 012046 (2018).

11 Abraham, D., Roth, E., Kostecki, R., McCarthy, K., MacLaren, S., Doughty, D., "Diagnostic Examination of Thermally Abused High-Power Lithium-Ion Cells," Journal of Power Sources, **161**, p. 648 (2006).

12 Wu, C., Wu, Y., Feng, X., Wang, H., Zhang, F., Chen, S., LI, B., Deng, T., Ouyang, M., "Ultra-High Temperature Reaction Mechanism of $LiNi_{0.8}Co_{0.1}Mn_{0.1}O_2$ Electrode, Journal of Energy Storage, **52**, p. 104870 (2022).

Optimizing Hydrogen Storage for Military Vehicle Applications

Benjamin Paczkowski
Fuel Cell Technologies
US Army DEVCOM Ground Vehicle Systems Center
Warren, MI, 48397
benjamin.v.paczkowski.civ@army.mil

Abstract

As the Army begins to explore the electrification of its ground vehicle fleet, several technologies are of interest to help clear the large hurdle presented by vehicles' energy needs. Hydrogen fuel cells have potential as a solution to this problem but there are many challenges that need to be addressed, such as hydrogen storage. Siemens LMS Amesim was used to simulate the performance of several wheeled and tracked vehicles in order to evaluate several hydrogen storage methods and materials to determine if they are suitable for military ground vehicle use. Several technologies were found to perform better than the state of the art compressed gas storage, exemplifying that advanced hydrogen storage could enable the electrification of the heaviest ground vehicles in the Army's fleet.

Keywords

Hydrogen; hydrogen storage; fuel cells; fuel processing and storage; modeling and simulation

Introduction

The Army has identified climate change as a significant threat, increasing the difficulty of the Army's core mission. In order to face the threat posed by climate change, the Army has planned several lines of effort including the fielding of fully electric tactical vehicles by 2050 [1]. A technology of interest that has the potential to mitigate these issues while maintaining vehicle performance is hydrogen fuel cells. However, hydrogen is not without its difficulties, namely poor volumetric energy density at ambient conditions. Many hydrogen storage methods have been studied over the past decade, but there has not been an in-depth study on how certain methods would fit into military vehicle applications.

Hydrogen is of military interest due to the quieter and cooler operation compared to internal combustion engines. Proton exchange membrane (PEM) fuel cells, a common fuel cell type used in automotive applications, operate at around 80°C [2]. This is a significantly lower temperature than diesel engines typically used in military vehicles, reducing the thermal signature immensely. PEM fuel cells also operate very quietly due to a lack of moving parts. Advantageous as it may be, hydrogen is not without flaws. In the gas phase, it has a very poor energy density. Storing hydrogen as a compressed gas requires lightweight but difficult to package cylindrical pressure vessels usually constructed from expensive carbon fiber. There are several technologies that have been developed to store hydrogen in a more effective way. Most of these have been investigated in passenger vehicle applications, not heavy-duty applications that would be more relevant to military vehicles.

Scope

A select group of vehicles and hydrogen storage methods and materials were investigated for this analysis. The vehicles included are the M1280 Joint Light Tactical Vehicle (JLTV), M1085 Long Wheelbase Medium Tactical Vehicle (LWB MTV), M1075 Palletized Load System (PLS), M113 armored personnel carrier, Mobile Protected Firepower prototype (MPF), and M88 Recovery Vehicle. These vehicles were selected for a variety of weight ranges for both wheeled and tracked vehicles. The weights range from the 10,000 kg class to above 50,000 kg in roughly 10,000 kg steps to provide a broad range of data.

The hydrogen storage methods and materials included in this analysis are 350 and 700 bar compressed gaseous hydrogen, liquid hydrogen, cryo-compressed hydrogen (CcH_2), aluminum hydride (alane), magnesium nanoparticles encapsulated in reduced graphene oxide (rGO-Mg), metal organic framework 5 (MOF 5), and methylcyclohexane (MCH)/toluene liquid organic hydrogen carrier (LOHC).

A fuel cell hybridized with a battery is used as a "drop in" replacement for the engine. A simple hybrid control strategy is used to control if the power comes from the fuel cell or the battery. For each simulation, the strategy was set to sustain the charge of the battery to maximize the usage of the fuel cell, also known as charge sustaining. Regenerative braking was also simulated to recapture some of the vehicle's energy while braking.

Assumptions and Methodology

The vehicle model was made using Siemens LMS Amesim. The core of the model was the road load equation. For each vehicle, a one-dimensional model was built that accounted for the speed, grade, rolling resistance, cooling load, drag, and fuel consumption. For ease of analysis, vehicles are assumed to be weight neutral after the conversion to a fuel cell powertrain. The model includes performance characteristics for an 80 kW fuel cell stack, which is scaled in integer steps depending on vehicle power requirements, as some vehicles require more than 80 kW. The polarization and fuel consumption curves are used to calculate the amount of hydrogen consumed at any point in time. This fuel consumption is output and compared to the hydrogen storage material properties.

The material properties of the hydrogen storage technologies of interest were compiled from literature sources and physical property databases. Fluid flow and heat transfer models were used to calculate the flow rate and thermal loading requirements for the gaseous and cryogenic storage systems. Both heat transfer and kinetic models were used to determine the reaction rate and heater energy needed for the material-based hydrogen storage technologies.

Results and Discussion

Vehicle parameters including weight, frontal area, drag coefficient, and rolling resistance were input into the Amesim model. The first simulation was run to determine how much hydrogen is required onboard each vehicle to meet the required range in Table 1. Vehicle speed was set to a constant value, described in Table 1, on a 0% grade paved road 10 miles long.

Vehicle	Speed (mph)	Economy (mi/kg)	Required Range (mi)	Required H_2 Storage (kg)
M1280	35	23.2	300	12.9
M1085	35	10.6	300	28.4
M1075	35	6.7	300	44.7
M113	25	3.8	300	78
MPF	25	3.3	300	91
M88	20	0.88	280	318.9

Table 1: Hydrogen storage capacity simulation results.

As expected, the amount of hydrogen required onboard increases with vehicle weight. Lighter vehicles achieve better fuel economy and utilize less power, requiring less fuel to meet the range target. There is also a noticeable increase in power and fuel needs for tracked vehicles compared to wheeled vehicles. This could be due to the varying frontal area, as the tracked vehicles have a much more box-like profile than the wheeled vehicles, and the increased rolling resistance of the track. The required amount of hydrogen stored on board the vehicle is used in later calculations to determine several storage system parameters, such as overall mass, volume, and heater power requirements.

In addition to the flat 10 mile simulation, two courses were simulated: Munson, a primary road with a single hill, and Churchville, and aggressive cross country course. The profiles are based on courses at Army Testing and Evaluation Command (ATEC). These courses were simulated to find the maximum hydrogen consumption rate at the fuel cell, which is a metric that is used to determine if a storage technology is appropriate for use in the vehicles modeled.

Hydrogen consumption over the courses followed the same trend seen in the flat simulation with the heavier vehicles exhibiting higher peak hydrogen consumption than the lighter vehicles. The highest peak hydrogen demand for all vehicles was seen on the off road course. Consumption ranged from 1.4 grams per second (g/s) for the M1280 to 11.8 g/s for the M88.

Based on the results of the first simulation, the mass of each system for each vehicle was calculated. The required amount of hydrogen was divided by the gravimetric capacity of the system to provide the overall system mass, shown in Table 2.

There are several interesting trends to note. The first is that the heaviest storage technology is 700 bar compressed gas.

Method	M1280	M1085	M1075	M113	MPF	M88
350 bar	239	526	828	1444	1685	5906
700 bar	307	676	1064	1857	2167	7593
Liquid	163	359	566	987	1152	4037
CcH2	117	258	406	709	827	2899
rGO-Mg	198	437	688	1200	1400	4906
Alane	128	281	443	772	901	3157
MOF-5	165	364	573	1000	1167	4088
MCH	208	458	721	1258	1468	5144

Table 2: The mass of the hydrogen storage system for each vehicle in kilograms.

Even with material advances, the sheer amount of carbon fiber required to safely store such high pressure hydrogen is still significant. High safety margins are required and long service life is expected, driving the need for bulky systems. A potential compromise is 350 bar compressed hydrogen, which requires less material due to the lower pressure. However, the loss of capacity due to the lower pressure while remaining the second heaviest system make its use difficult to justify.

On the other hand, cryo-compressed hydrogen (CcH_2) is consistently the lightest weight storage method. CcH_2 involves the storage of hydrogen at cryogenic temperatures and elevated pressures, usually around 60 K or below and 500 bar [3]. Storing the hydrogen at elevated pressures significantly reduces the boil-off of hydrogen compared to liquid [4]. Boil-off is the release of hydrogen from the ullage (gaseous layer above the liquid) to maintain operating pressure in the vessel as hydrogen boils due to external heat input. Storing the hydrogen in a compressed state at cryogenic temperatures reduces the frequency of hydrogen gas purges because the system is designed to handle pressure. This is not the case with conventional liquid storage, which is designed to hold an unpressurized cryogenic liquid. The increased density of hydrogen in its liquid state allows for significantly more to be stored onboard while the low pressure operation requires less material than compressed gas. There is a requirement for insulation and heat exchangers, which slightly increase the weight compared to CcH_2. There is one significant drawback with liquid hydrogen storage: boil-off. If a vehicle sits dormant for an extended period, the potential exists to lose a significant amount of hydrogen to boil-off, reducing the ability for vehicles to be ready for use at a moment's notice. The release of hydrogen from vehicles also introduces a challenge in storing the vehicles when not in use. The vehicles will need to be stored in a well-ventilated area that will not allow for the accumulation of hydrogen due to the wide flammability range of the gas [5].

Another concern that is applicable to both liquid and CcH2 is the energy cost of liquefaction. Hydrogen has a very low boiling point of 22 K, requiring significant energy to reach. About 40% of the higher heating value of hydrogen is required to liquefy hydrogen with current technologies [6]. This energy cost is not borne by the vehicle but rather an external cost paid at the or before the fueling point, so there is no impact in range due to this energy requirement. This is a significant area for improvement and there are some technologies being developed to reduce the energy input for hydrogen liquefaction, such as magnetocaloric liquefaction [7].

Of the less conventional hydrogen storage materials, alane has the lowest weight followed by MOF-5. Both are slightly heavier than CcH_2, yet significantly lighter than both compressed gas systems. This is encouraging, as alane is a stable hydrogen storage medium that can allow for long-term storage of vehicles. The drawback for alane is that it is a single use material, much like a primary battery. The hydrogen can be easily released from the material onboard a vehicle by heating, but it cannot be easily recharged onboard a vehicle due to thermodynamic constraints [9]. In order to refill the vehicles with alane, solid block(s) will need to be unloaded and reloaded, which could become a time consuming process. Depending on the vehicle, significant amounts of alane are required, ranging from 100 kg to over 1,500 kg. Smaller amounts could be man-lifted onto the vehicle by several people, but larger amounts will require material handling equipment, which is concerning.

For the materials requiring heat to release the hydrogen (rGO-Mg, alane, MOF-5, and MCH), the energy required to heat the materials to a sufficient temperature to release the hydrogen was calculated. The energy required was then compared to the lower heating value of hydrogen to determine the percentage of hydrogen stored within the material used for the purpose of heating the material. MOF 5 utilizes only 0.6% of the hydrogen stored, while alane uses 1.4%, rGO-Mg uses 5.6%, and MCH uses 6.97%. In each case, the range of the vehicle will be impacted by this requirement because the percentage of hydrogen listed above will be utilized to heat the material rather than propel the vehicle, effectively reducing the amount of hydrogen stored in the system. To account for this, the amount of hydrogen stored on board will need to be increased. This leads to a recursive relationship, as increasing the amount of hydrogen stored will increase the mass of the system and therefore the vehicle, potentially requiring more fuel to meet the required range. This impact will be critical to understand as research into alternative propulsion continues.

The kinetics of the material-based hydrogen storage materials was investigated by modeling the kinetic performance of each material using models found in the literature. Each model was compared to the peak flow rate found in earlier vehicle modeling to determine if the material is suitable for each vehicle. Both rGO-Mg and MOF-5 were found to release hydrogen at a rate that meets the needs of each vehicle. MOF-5 was also able to uptake hydrogen at the same or higher rate than current technology, 60 g/s, while rGO-Mg was unable to maintain that flow for anything other than the two largest vehicles due to kinetic limitations. Alane did not immediately release hydrogen at the desired flow rate. There was a lag between 10 to 30 seconds, depending on the vehicle, consistent with the induction period observed by Graetz et al where hydrogen release is slower at low levels of fractional decomposition [8]. A lag in hydrogen release is not a desirable trait, but the model demonstrates that the required flow rates are met within a relatively short period of time. There are potential engineering strategies that can be used to compensate for the delayed time to full flow.

The model validates that MCH can be dehydrogenated at a fast enough rate to provide hydrogen to each vehicle under the most demanding conditions. The rate is controlled by the amount of catalyst in the system, which can be a significant factor for the system weight. This weight penalty varies between 5 and 19 percent of the mass of liquid needed to meet the required range. Like the energy requirements for the heater, the added mass of the catalyst will reduce the gravimetric density of the overall system, from 6.2 weight percent to between 5.2 and 5.9 weight percent. This still surpasses 700 bar compressed hydrogen but reduces the margin for any other components required to support the system, such as the reactor vessel. MCH may also require hydrogen purification after the dehydrogenation step, as the hydrogen may not meet the purity standards for fuel cell use.

Modeling also validated the performance of both the gaseous and cryogenic hydrogen systems. Pipe flow, heat transfer, and vaporization were modeled. All the systems saw no excessive pressure drops or flow restrictions when filling the vehicles with hydrogen or while providing hydrogen to the fuel cell.

Conclusion

This analysis has demonstrated that there are several technologies that can potentially outperform 700 bar compressed gas hydrogen storage, the current state of the art, when applied to military vehicles. When optimized for mass, volume, and ability to sustain the maximum flow of hydrogen in demanding conditions, it was found that cryo-compressed hydrogen provides the best performance. Compared with 700 bar compressed hydrogen, cryo-compressed hydrogen can store 160% of the hydrogen per unit weight and 300% more hydrogen per liter. The use of cryo-compressed hydrogen in the place of 700 bar compressed gas has the potential to reduce the cost of the storage vessel by reducing the amount of carbon fiber needed [4]. Cryo-compressed hydrogen can be refilled at a similar speed to current fuels, maintaining current readiness levels.

Several other technologies are worth investigation and have the potential to be future hydrogen storage methods for military ground vehicles. MOF 5 has incredibly fast kinetics and higher gravimetric and volumetric storage densities than compressed hydrogen gas. If the gravimetric density can be maintained near room temperature, MOF 5 systems could be less complex than both compressed gas and cryo-compressed while providing similar performance. Alane is also of interest due to its high gravimetric and volumetric hydrogen densities, however there may be challenges with loading and unloading large amounts of the material onto vehicles. This lends it towards smaller vehicle use, where less material is needed.

The simulations also found that rGO-Mg and MCH are potentially unsuitable for military ground vehicle application. Both rGO-Mg and MCH require 5% or more of the energy of the stored hydrogen to be released. There is a challenge with rGO-Mg meeting the filling time requirements for the vehicles. The smaller vehicles are unable to uptake hydrogen at a rate near the current state of the art. MCH also requires a catalyst, which reduces the gravimetric storage capacity compared to the other technologies. There is a chance the hydrogen coming from the MCH dehydrogenation reactor does not meet the purity requirements for hydrogen vehicles, requiring a purification step that will also add mass and volume to the system. The added challenge of storing two liquids onboard with an MCH system reduces its attractiveness. The toluene product from the dehydrogenation reaction will need to be stored onboard to be reprocessed offboard for future use. This added complexity is not present in the two leading technologies.

As military vehicles embrace electrification and its many benefits, this analysis shows that hydrogen fuel cells and advanced hydrogen storage technologies can play a role in future ground vehicle applications. While storing hydrogen as a compressed gas is the current state of the art, other technologies are quickly advancing and show potential to outperform it. Based on the encouraging results of the simulations performed, continued research into the applications of cryo-compressed hydrogen, MOF 5, and alane for military ground vehicle applications is recommended.

Acknowledgements

The author would like to acknowledge Andrew Wiegand for his help in developing the vehicle model and his excellent guidance while undertaking this project.

References

[1] J. Zhang, T. Fisher, P. Ramachandran, J. Gore and I. Mudawar, "A Review of Heat Transfer Issues in Hydrogen Storage Technologies," *Journal of Heat Transfer,* pp. 1391-1399, 2005.

[2] "Army Climate Strategy," 2022.

[3] K. Kunze and O. Kircher, "Cryo-compressed Hydrogen Storage," in *Cryogenic Cluster Day*, Oxford, 2012.

[4] R. Ahluwalia, D. Papadias, J.-K. Peng and H. Roh, "System Level Analysis of Hydrogen Storage Options," in *2019 Annual Merit Review and Peer Evaluation Meeting*, Washington, D.C., 2019.

[5] "Lower and Upper Explosive Limits for Flammable Gases and Vapors (LEL/UEL)," [Online]. Available: https://www.mathesongas.com/pdfs/products/Lower-(LEL)-&-Upper-(UEL)-Explosive-Limits-.pdf. [Accessed 9 March 2020].

[6] J. Milliken, J. Petrovic and W. Podolski, "Hydrogen Storage Issues for Automotive Fuel Cells," in *International Workshop on Hydrogen in Materials and Vacuum Systems*, Newport News, 2002.

[7] J. Holladay, "MagnetoCaloric Hydrogen Liquefaction," in *Department of Energy Annual Merit Review*, Washington, D.C., 2019.

[8] J. Graetz, J. Reilly, V. Yartys, J. Maehlen, B. Bulychev, V. Antonov, B. Tarasov and I. Gabis, "Aluminum hydride as a hydrogen and energy storage material: Past, present and future," *Journal of Alloys and Compounds,* vol. 509, no. S2, pp. S517-S528, 2010.

Lightweight Hydrogen Fuel Cells for Unmanned Aircraft and Small Unit Power

Kevin R. Cronin[1], Benjamin D. Gould[2], Richard O. Stroman[1], Yannick Garsany[3], Andrew J. Dellechiaie[3], Joseph A. Rodgers[4]

[1]Chemistry Div., [4]Tactical Electronic Warfare Div.,
U.S. Naval Research Laboratory, Washington, DC 20375 USA
[2]Hydrogen and Fuel Cell Technologies Office, Department of Energy, Forrestal Building, Washington, DC 20585
[3]Excet, Inc., Springfield, VA 20150 USA
kevin.cronin@nrl.navy.mil

Abstract:

The Naval Research Laboratory (NRL) has used decades of fuel cell research to create a Navy-owned hydrogen fuel cell prototype for Unmanned Air vehicles (UAVs). During development, a parallel opportunity to apply the hydrogen fuel cell system for small unit power (H-SUP) was identified. The resultant H-SUP prototype offers a low signature solution for electric power production, up to 1.2 kW continuous power, in a ruggedized package. Beyond the advantages of increased specific energy and decreased detectability, H-SUP establishes that fuel cells can be used interchangeably for both organic UAVs and for small unit power in the USMC context of expeditionary advanced base operations (EABO).

Keywords: Hydrogen; fuel cell; unmanned; UAV; expeditionary energy; small unit power; generator

Introduction

The DoD has a critical need for Unmanned Air Vehicles (UAVs) with increased power and endurance. For Group 2 and light Group 3 aircraft in particular, batteries have insufficient specific energy and heavy fuel engines are both inefficient and expensive from a total cost of ownership perspective [1, 2] Hydrogen fuel cells can fill this gap to enable important new capabilities, but there are presently no U.S. vendors of a 1-3 kW hydrogen fuel cell suitable for military use. The Naval Research Laboratory (NRL) has applied decades of fuel cell research to making a Navy-owned hydrogen fuel cell prototype for UAVs. Through an Office of the Secretary of Defense Manufacturing Science and Technology Program (OSD MSTP), this lightweight fuel cell has gone from a laboratory prototype to a Technology Readiness Level (TRL) 7 and Manufacturing Readiness Level (MRL) 7 product. Transition of this fuel cell is now underway via an integration effort led by the Naval Air Warfare Center Aircraft Division (NAWCAD) and sponsored by Naval Aviation Operational Energy (NAOE), with the first adopter being a Group 2 UAV called "Stalker". The Stalker UAV is the Intelligence, Surveillance, and Reconnaissance (ISR) workhorse of the Marine Corps. During development, a parallel opportunity to apply the hydrogen fuel cell system for small unit power (H-SUP) was identified and sponsored by the Office of Naval Research (ONR). The resulting H-SUP prototype provides a low signature solution for electric power generation, at up to 1.2 kW continuous power, in a ruggedized package. Aside from the benefits of improved specific energy and lower detectability, H-SUP proves that fuel cells may be utilized interchangeably for both organic UAVs and small unit power in the USMC context of expeditionary advanced base operations (EABO). This paper describes NRL's development and demonstration of this lightweight hydrogen fuel cell.

Fuel Cell System Development

There are numerous advantages to electric propulsion relative to internal combustion engines (ICE) for group 2 (under 55 lbs.) tactical UAVs, including near silent operation, reduced vibrations, reduced thermal signature, reduced maintenance, and instant starting [1]. High energy density batteries have historically been the primary power source for electric UAVs, but the DoD desires longer endurance flight times than batteries can offer [2]. Hydrogen fuel cells are a good alternative to batteries because of the high specific energy of hydrogen and high efficiency of electrochemical energy conversion. Because of this capability gap that fuel cells fill, and because of the lack of domestic commercial offerings suitable for military use, NRL developed its own lightweight Proton Exchange Membrane Fuel Cell (PEMFC) system (US Provisional Application No. 62/423,975) [3].

It is well understood that PEMFC systems convert hydrogen and oxygen electrochemically into electricity, heat and water. In the case of NRL's design, the PEMFC operates at relatively low temperatures, from 50°C – 80°C, and uses a supporting system of pumps, motors, sensors, actuators and controls, known as the Balance of Plant (BoP), to maintain optimal operation. Some distinguishing features of this BoP include a liquid cooling system for heat rejection, a closed cathode design with a passive exchange humidifier for membrane humidification, and an air compressor to deliver oxygen from the ambient air to the cathode (Fig 1. Top).

Furthermore, NRL's lightweight PEMFC borrowed techniques from the automotive fuel cell industry and scaled them down to realize best in class performance. These techniques include:

- Hydro-formed stainless steel bipolar plates for minimizing weight

- Liquid cooling with an ethylene glycol-based coolant for a wide window of ambient operating conditions
- Individual cell voltage monitoring for fuel cell state of health analysis and advanced control
- Material selection rated for 5000 hours of operation

NRL demonstrated a functional laboratory prototype of this fuel cell system in 2020, and subsequently executed a maturation effort to improve its manufacturability. As part of the maturation effort, NRL partnered with Northwest UAV (NWUAV), a small American UAV engine manufacturer (Fig 1. Bottom). Through this partnership, the following improvements were made to the original NRL design:

- More robust and maintainable system controls, including the use of industry standards such as CANBus communication
- Improved state of health monitoring with prototype subsystems replaced by manufacturable ones.
- Fewer fabrication and assembly steps with greater process control
- System layout and packaging improvements to decrease weight and volume, and increase serviceability with simple hand tools
- Component selection to reduce cost and supply chain risk

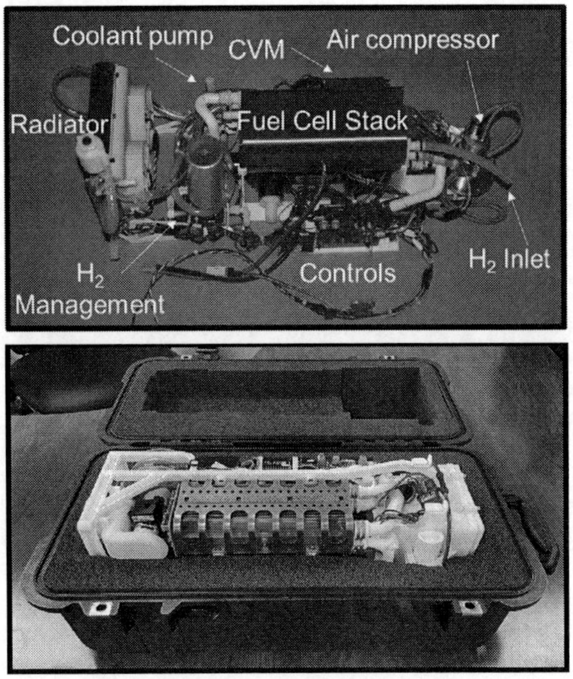

Figure 1. Top: NRL prototype PEMFC. Bottom: NWUAV Manufactured NRL PEMFC.

In addition, a fuel cell production facility at NWUAV was built, with better processes, tooling, and assembly methods [4].

The matured NRL lightweight PEMFC has high nominal specific power at 400 W/kg, and a nominal net power output of 1500 W. At no load, the nominal fuel cell system voltage is approximately 45 V, and at full load the nominal fuel cell system voltage is 26 V.

UAV Application

Upon reaching sufficient TRL and MRL, the NRL PEMFC was sought for integration into a UAV. To integrate into existing UAV electrical architectures, a 1280 W DC/DC converter was implemented to regulate the variable fuel cell voltage to a constant 28 V output.

Most other PEMFC systems of this power class are air cooled, open cathode architectures which are highly sensitive to ambient operating conditions and may not be well suited to operating in austere environments [5-6]. The NRL fuel cell system is designed to support UAV operations in a wide range of ambient conditions.

Because of its high specific power and robust operating envelope, NAWCAD and NRL integrated the lightweight PEMFC system into the Stalker UAV as part of a NAOE program to improve the Stalker's operational capabilities [7].

Figure 2. Front: NRL PEMFC, Rear: Hydrogen Stalker UAV

To date, fuel cell systems built by NWUAV have flown the Stalker UAV several times in flights that demonstrated the operational advantages the NRL PEMFC brings, including greatly improving upon the endurance of the battery version of the Stalker (Fig. 2). This integration effort was particularly significant because the Stalker is a fielded platform that is currently used as an ISR asset by the Marine Corps and Special Forces [8]. The success with the Hydrogen Stalker program has proven that the NRL lightweight PEMFC system is sufficiently capable and mature for military use and transition.

Small Unit Power Application

During the Stalker integration effort, an additional application for the NRL lightweight PEMFC was identified. Many of the advantages of using fuel cells over ICEs to power UAVs also apply to expeditionary power generators. The PEMFC was adapted to provide ground power to expeditionary small units, resulting in a prototype system called "Hydrogen – Small Unit Power" (H-SUP).

USMC Expeditionary units currently rely on power sources such as generators and ground vehicles that have significant audible and thermal signatures and therefore make them vulnerable [9]. Units executing EABO will require improved signature management to avoid detection. Solutions such as batteries and solar panels have the advantage of silent operation, but they suffer from limitations such as low energy density and visible signature. The H-SUP solves this capability gap by repackaging the NRL PEMFC system in a ruggedized case such that it can be used for small unit power with greater energy density than batteries (Fig. 3).

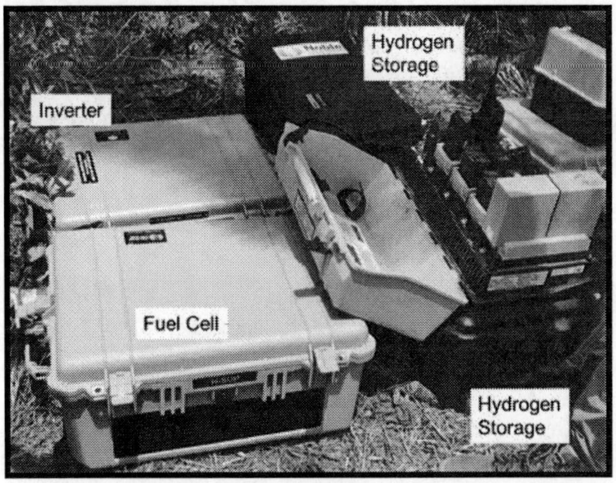

Figure 3. Hydrogen Small Unit Power Prototype

The advantages of H-SUP over the incumbent engine technology are numerous: decreased signature (thermal and acoustic), reduced maintenance burden, lighter weight, and greater modularity. The decreased signature is important for silent watch capabilities in contested environments. Additionally, fuel cells are self-heating with zero emissions and zero self-discharge, so they can supply waste heat to help batteries operate in arctic climates, and hydrogen fuel can be cached for long durations. Furthermore, H-SUP demonstrates that the NRL PEMFC system can be an interoperable power source that supports both UAV and ground power applications.

This interoperability supports the USMC vision of EABO by providing greater operational reach, increasing flexibility to meet changing needs, and simplifying the equipment set that must be transported to and, then supported, at remote locations.

Demonstration

The high energy density of H-SUP can be used to reduce the weight burden and re-supply needs of units, or to supply them with more energy to support energy-intensive loads. This concept was explored at the Technology Operational Experimentation Exercise (TOEE) 22.

At TOEE (Marine Corps Base Camp Lejeune, August 2022), active-duty Marines were trained to operate the H-SUP, and then used it independently to power real USMC payloads for days during Mission Essential Training evolutions [10]. The primary use case for the H-SUP at TOEE was to provide power to the Combat Operations Center for the headquarters element of a rifle company, powering loads like battery chargers and laptops. Previously, the Marines would charge their radio batteries with a charger mounted in a Joint Light Tactical Vehicle (JLTV). To prevent the vehicle battery from dying when they did this, they would turn on the engine and let the vehicle idle, which is inefficient, loud, and has a large thermal signature. That process was repeated hourly throughout the mission to keep the batteries fully charged. With the H-SUP they were able to charge batteries continuously without turning on the JLTV, which not only reduced the Marines' detectability, but also improved their readiness, as they were able to sleep through the night.

The H-SUP was also demonstrated at Marine Corps Base Quantico, Virginia in March 2023 [11]. The concept of operation (CONOP) demonstrated at Quantico involved powering a Network On The Move (NOTM) system with the H-SUP. The NOTM is a fielded communications payload used by the USMC to establish secure networking capabilities in theatre [12]. In this case, the NOTM was mounted to a JLTV which is representative of the typical implementation.

Figure 4. H-SUP powering NOTM

The NOTM would typically be powered by the JLTV battery and the vehicle would idle to keep the battery charged. Not only is the running vehicle highly detectable due to the audible and thermal signatures of the engine, but idling for extended periods accelerates engine degradation, leading to premature maintenance events.

The H-SUP powered the NOTM in two different configurations (Fig. 4), through an auxiliary power input, and by tying into the vehicle's electrical system via the NATO slave port on the front bumper. In both cases the vehicle remained off, decreasing detectability and preventing unnecessary wear and tear on the engine. In the latter case, the H-SUP also provided power to the vehicle electronics, such as cabin lights, headlights, and center console display.

Conclusions

NRL developed a lightweight hydrogen fuel cell system and matured it with a commercial partner to achieve a TRL 7, MRL 7 product. This fuel cell system has utility both in UAV applications and in small unit power due to its high specific energy and low signature. Furthermore, the same fuel cell can be used interchangeably for UAV and ground power applications, enabling a wide range of CONOPs for expeditionary units aligned with EABO.

Next Steps

The Naval Research Laboratory will continue to improve the performance of the fuel cell system across the entire vertical of research and development: from materials selection and fundamental research to implementation of advanced control algorithms and component selection at the system level. As NRL continues to support the transition of the Hydrogen Stalker, other targets for transition will be identified and pursued, such as multi-day UAVs, Group 3 UAVs, and other unmanned vehicle platforms: surface, undersea and ground.

Other existing efforts include building out the H-SUP ecosystem with both larger and smaller systems all based on the same NRL fuel cell technology, and will continue to incorporate warfighter experimentation and feedback early and often to ensure valuable systems are developed.

Acknowledgements

The authors thank the Office of Naval Research for supporting the underlying fuel cell research and initial H-SUP development, the Office of the Secretary of Defense Manufacturing Science and Technology program for supporting the maturation of the fuel cell system, NAWCAD and NAOE for the integration with the Stalker UAV and the USMC Expeditionary Energy Office for supporting further H-SUP development.

References

1. K. Swider-Lyons, R. Stroman, et al., *Hydrogen Fuel Cell Propulsion for Long Endurance Small UAVs*, AIAA Centennial of Naval Aviation Forum "100 Years of Achievement and Progress", Aviation Technology, Integration, and Operations (ATIO) Conf., (2011).
2. K. Swider-Lyons, R. Stroman, J. Rodgers, B. Gould, J. Mackrell, M. Schuette, and G. Page, *Hydrogen Fuel Cells for Small Unmanned Air Vehicles, ECS Transactions*, 64 (3) 963-972 (2014).
3. *Notice of Availability of Fuel Cell System Software for Licensing*, TechLink News Article, 2 March 2022.
4. *Northwest UAV Hosts Grand Opening Event for Their Hydrogen Fuel Cell Manufacturing Center*, Northwest UAV Press Release, 26 July 2021
5. T. Fabian, J.D. Posner, et al., *The role of ambient conditions on the performance of a planar, air-breathing hydrogen PEM fuel cell*, Journal of Power Sources, (2006)
6. R. Atkinson, M. Hazard, et al., *An Open-Cathode Fuel Cell for Atmospheric Flight*, Journal of The Electrochemical Society (2016)
7. *Exhibit Brochure*, Pentagon Energy Expo, “Hydrogen Stalker”, pp 23, (2022).
8. Stalker VXE 30 Product Card (https://www.lockheedmartin.com/en-us/products/stalker.html)
9. USMC Mobile Power Portfolio (https://www.marcorsyscom.marines.mil/Portfolios/Logistics-Combat-Element-Systems/Engineer-Systems/Power-Team/Mobile-Power/)
10. W. Duffie, *The Cutting Edge: ONR Sponsors Technology Experimentation at Camp Lejeune*, Navy.mil News Article, (2022).
11. *Manufacturing Science and Technology Program Hosts Joint-Service Hydrogen Demonstration Event at Marine Corps Base Quantico*, OSD ManTech News Article, 5 May 2023
12. M. Gonzales, *Mobile Satellite System Reduces Communication Gaps, Increases Naval Interoperability,* MARCORSYSCOM News Article, 14 December 2021

Scalable Hydrogen Storage and Transport Systems

Stephen Johnston, Chris Kondogiani, Anthony Lancione
Noble Gas Systems
Novi, Michigan USA 48375
info@noblegassys.com / 1-248-607-0890

Abstract

Advances in conformable tank technology have resulted in opportunities to harness and deploy hydrogen energy in a variety of operational environments. Various use cases are described, and the benefits of these unique storage systems in vehicular, stationary, and bulk storage applications are illustrated. The impressive scalability of conformable hydrogen tank production is also explained, as it relates to the cost effective and broad application of these storage systems.

Keywords

Hydrogen; Containers; Conformable Tanks; Compressed Gas; Hydrogen Transport; Type 3; Type 4; HGV2; Bulk Storage

Introduction

As the demand for clean and sustainable energy sources continues to rise, scalable hydrogen storage and transport systems play a crucial role in facilitating the widespread adoption of hydrogen as an alternative fuel. This white paper aims to highlight the benefits of scalable systems for high-pressure hydrogen storage in transportation and usage, focusing on advantages to end-users and the production process.

Hydrogen Storage and Transport System Types

Traditional Storage Systems: Storage and transport of hydrogen has traditionally been accomplished in three ways: (1) compressed and/or cryogenic storage of liquid hydrogen (LH2), which is most applicable for the transport of large quantities of hydrogen, but within a limited timeframe; (2) compressed hydrogen gas (CH2), which involves the storage at high pressures, typically 250 – 700 bar in cylindrical containers made of metal (Type 1), hoop reinforced metal (Type 2), fully reinforced metal (Type 3), and fully reinforced plastic liners (Type 4); and (3) lower pressure, chemical storage such as in ammonia (NH_3) or with metal hydrides.

Conformable Tanks: Conformable tanks, a type of scalable system, offer increased storage capacity and design flexibility. They optimize space utilization within ships and vehicles and enable efficient integration without compromising safety or performance. These types of tanks were envisioned as a way to store high pressure gasses, beginning with patent 3,432,060 for a tubular pressure vessel, filed in 1965 by John James Crowley.[1]

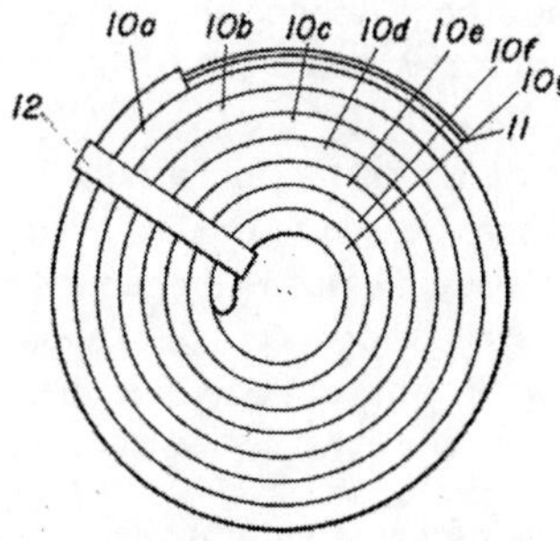

Figure 1. Image from J.J. Crowley patent.

More recently, with the advent of improved materials and manufacturing methods, these types of conformable tanks have been refined and developed to provide viable alternatives to more traditional methods. Additionally, existing regulatory standards, such as CSA / ANSI HGV2:2021 (HGV2)[2] have defined a pathway for certification for these tanks for use on hydrogen powered vehicles and transport systems. A few types of conformable tanks are addressed by this standard, as defined below:

Tank Arrays: Tank arrays consist of multiple smaller cylinders strategically arranged within a vehicle or storage system. This arrangement allows hydrogen to be stored in non-cylindrical shapes, which may be easier to package than a single large cylinder. The topology of these systems is similar to the racks used to deliver industrial gas cylinders in quantities like eight or 16.

Serpentine-Style Containers: Serpentine-style containers feature a multi-segment construction that maximizes the use of available space. These containers offer increased storage capacity without compromising vehicle design or performance. The serpentine configuration minimizes wasted space, improving the overall efficiency of the hydrogen storage system. These tanks are made up of multiple interconnected segments typically contained inside a protective shell. Segments of different lengths and quantity can be used to fill a given space, even if it is irregular. An additional benefit to these systems is the elimination of connections between the segments, which reduces potential leak paths and reduces the weight and complexity of the storage system.

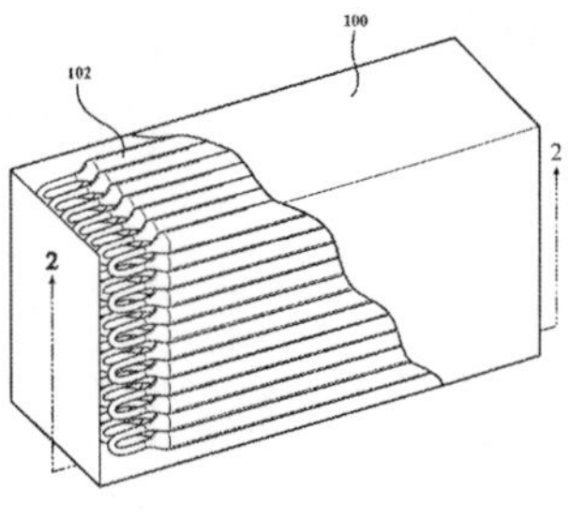

Figure 2. Image from Kondogiani and Donoughe patent 9,850,852 showing serpentine style conformable tank.[3]

Use Cases for Conformable Tanks

Because it is lighter, easier to produce, and contains more specific energy than batteries, hydrogen has many potential applications across a wide spectrum of applications. While the following list is not exhaustive, it does illustrate how conformable tanks can enhance these attributes.

Portable Applications: Conformable tanks enable the production of purpose-built, small, lightweight systems for portable applications. Because they can be made to fit inside existing containers, the convenience of storage and transport is enhanced. These systems can be used to power remote generators, either with internal combustion engines or silently operating fuel cells.

Because hydrogen is easy to produce from water using electrolysis, an entire remote production and storage facility for hydrogen can be deployed to eliminate the need for the transport of fuel to remote locations.

This system is also lighter weight and exhibits a shorter refilling time, leading to more uptime compared to the long recharge cycles of batteries.

Mobility Applications: Because of their ability to increase the storage capacity of hydrogen within irregular spaces, mobile platforms including ground vehicles, aerial systems, underwater vehicles, and aerospace applications benefit from the application of conformable tanks.

Using hydrogen in mobility applications can be superior to batteries because of the ability to store more onboard energy. In 2022, Lockheed Martin announced that it had successfully flown an unmanned drone over 39 hours using a hydrogen fuel cell,[4] which is a significant multiple of what is achievable using a battery powered counterpart. Larger vehicles, from cars to heavy duty trucks, airplanes, and cargo ships can all benefit from the ability to carry more energy and refuel faster.

In these cases, because compressed hydrogen takes up more space than liquid fuels, conformable tanks can be employed to minimize the additional space required.

Bulk Storage and Transport: As hydrogen applications begin to come online, it will be necessary to store and move large quantities of compressed hydrogen from sources of production to intermediate users and end customers.

Current systems of transport, such as cryogenic containers for liquified hydrogen, and pipelines will need to be supplemented by additional compressed gas storage to meet the needs of users across a diverse range of geographies and with a variety of demand profiles. The benefits of lightweight, space-efficient conformable tanks are ideal for those applications requiring large quantities of compressed hydrogen at maximum storage efficiency and flexibility to reduce the number of containers and shipments.

Benefits to End Users

Increased Storage Capacity: Scalable hydrogen storage and transport systems allow for higher hydrogen storage capacity compared to traditional cylinders. These systems can be customized and expanded to fit various vehicle designs, maximizing the use of available space, and enabling longer driving ranges. Compared to a single large cylindrical volume, the ability to take up more of the available space is enhanced using smaller, modular vessels or segments.

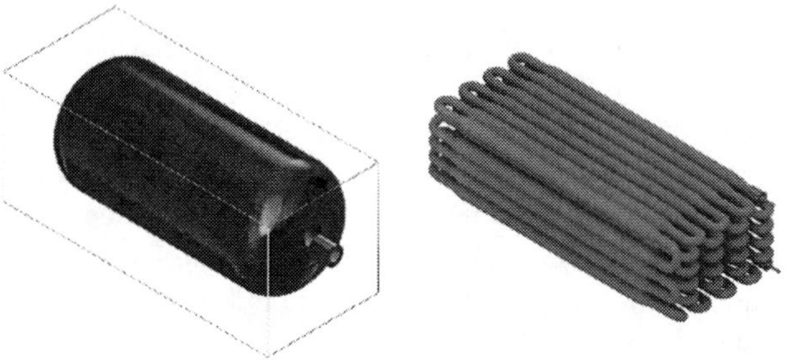

Figure 3. Conformable tank increasing storage within a rectangular volume.

Enhanced Safety: Scalable systems incorporate advanced safety features, such as integrated pressure relief systems and impact-resistant materials. These advancements minimize the risk of leakage or rupture, ensuring the safety of both end-users and hydrogen-powered vehicles. Additionally, the fact that the gas volume is separated into multiple segments, whether they be interconnected or not, provides a natural attenuation for the energy released by a tank failure.

Improved Efficiency: The lightweight construction of scalable systems reduces the overall weight of the storage system, leading to improved vehicle efficiency, extended driving range, and increased payload capacity. Additionally, the reduction in weight translates to lower energy consumption during transportation, making scalable systems more energy-efficient overall.

Design Flexibility: Scalable systems offer design flexibility, allowing for customization and integration into various vehicle types. These systems can be adapted to fit the available space without compromising vehicle functionality or aesthetics, reducing the cost of adapting existing platforms to enable the use of hydrogen fuel.

Scalable Production Process Benefits

Cost Efficiency: The manufacturing process of scalable hydrogen storage and transport systems offers cost advantages over traditional cylinders. A significant cost driver is associated with the tooling required to make each unique size of cylinder liner, and tooling cost grows with increasing cylinder size. For larger cylinders with lower expected production volumes, these costs are amortized over fewer units, making them even more costly to produce.

In contrast, using smaller, modular tanks reduces total tooling costs, and increases the production volume associated with any particular vessel size. In the case of serpentine-style conformable tanks, the length of each segment can also be varied, meaning that a single set of tools can produce an infinite number of tank designs. The tank design framework shifts from a discussion of smaller vs. larger tanks to less vs. more tank.

Tank Certification: Production designs must be certified to an applicable standard, such as HGV2, prior to full production. Design qualification tests must be repeated for tank designs that vary from each other (e.g. vessel length, diameter, reinforcement material, etc.) beyond a small operating window. However, using the same vessel construction to make repeated or conformable systems allows the same certification to apply to a wide variety of shapes and sizes. While some system tests, like the drop test, for example, may need to be repeated for each tank design, most of the vessel-specific tests still apply. Because tank certification is a costly and time-consuming process, this feature can significantly reduce the cost and the time to market for implementing new designs.

Production Efficiency: Scalable systems can be manufactured using automated processes, resulting in increased production efficiency and reduced labor costs. The flexibility in design and production processes facilitates seamless integration into assembly lines, streamlining production and enhancing overall manufacturing productivity.

Distributed Manufacturing: The low cost of production equipment enables multiple smaller production sites that are located near customers and demand centers. This reduces the burden of supply chain costs and logistics, improving responsiveness to customers.

Economic Benefits

Materials Supply: As with many lightweight components, particularly in aerospace and high-performance automotive applications, the reinforcement of Type 3 and 4 tanks are typically constructed with carbon fiber. As the demand for these tanks increases, tank manufacturers will become significant consumers of this difficult to produce material, which will increase costs, and result in significant capital expenditures to increase capacity. Conformable tanks can be produced with a wider variety of materials, many of which do not compete with the construction of lightweight components in other industries.

Recyclability and Circularity: Because the fiber used in the construction of composite reinforced tanks is embedded in epoxy, it is not easily reused or recycled. As a result, much of the tank ends up in a land fill at the end of its life. Alternative construction, such as dry fiber application used in some conformable tanks enables the different materials to be separated. So, these types of tanks enable recycling and reuse of the constituent components, resulting in a significantly higher circularity index, and a lower waste footprint.

Production Scale: The future demand for hydrogen storage tanks is significant, particularly when automotive and aviation applications are forecasted to rise significantly in the late 2020's and early 2030's. Meanwhile, the lack of significant infrastructure, high cost of hydrogen production, and limited number of applications means the current market is small. This means that current tank prices are a burden to the adoption and growth of early adopters. By the nature of the production of conformable tanks, the same equipment can be used to produce a wide variety of tanks at a reasonable cost. As a result, many small markets can be served economically, as demand growth increases.

Just as the production methods and modularity of these systems enable economic production at low part volumes, they also enable small and large capacity systems to be produced at proportional costs. As described above, the cost of tooling and equipment for large tanks is disproportionately high, which causes them to be relatively more expensive. However, making large containers from many small containers, especially conformable tanks, means that the cost of the system varies more linearly with the capacity.

Transitional Infrastructure: Compared with liquid fuels, current hydrogen infrastructure is limited. Although significant public funding is beginning to emerge, building the vast gas storage and transportation networks required to enable widespread hydrogen usage will be costly and slow. Alternatively, using intermodal storage containers to move hydrogen from production to fueling sites, through existing networks of shipping, rail, and trucking, can happen relatively quickly and with require much less investment.

While hydrogen production and demand centers are developing, it may be difficult to predict the most advantageous locations. The risk of wasted infrastructure investment means that sites and pipelines must be carefully studied and planned. Alternatively, mobile storage containers for compressed hydrogen gas, enable fueling sites to be quickly built and operationalized. If the chosen site turns out to not be an ideal location, the facility can just as easily be moved to one of higher value.

This same mechanism can be used to serve temporary, remote, underserved, or peak demand locations that could not otherwise justify the establishment of permanent infrastructure. The ability to easily and cost effectively adjust the size, working pressure, and shape of the containers also makes it possible to optimize the development of ideal hydrogen storage and delivery mechanisms.

Conclusion

Scalable hydrogen storage and transport systems offer a wide range of benefits for high-pressure hydrogen storage, transportation, and usage. From increased storage capacity and enhanced safety to improved efficiency and design flexibility, these systems provide significant advantages to end-users. The production process also benefits from cost efficiency, scalability, and production efficiency. By considering various scalable system types, such as conformable tanks, tank arrays, and serpentine-style containers, the hydrogen industry can revolutionize storage and transportation, accelerating the adoption of hydrogen as a clean and sustainable energy source in various sectors.

Acknowledgements

The authors wish to acknowledge the funding received through the National Science Foundation (NSF), including Phase I SBIR award number 2051253 and Phase II award number 2223187, which has helped to support the development of Noble Gas' lightweight conformable tanks. The authors wish to thank the organizers and partners of PortXL, the world port accelerator, based in Rotterdam, The Netherlands, who introduced new opportunities for bulk storage and transportation in the maritime market. Finally, the authors wish to thank the defense, aviation, and mobility customers of Noble Gas, who have continued to support the advancement of conformable storage technology.

References

1. Crowley J, inventor; Therapeutic Research Corp Ltd, assignee. Tubular pressure vessel. United States patent US 3,432,060. 1969 Mar 11.
2. Canadian Standards Association, American National Standards Institute; Compressed hydrogen vehicle containers; CSA / ANSI HGV2:2021. 2021 Jan.
3. Kondogiani C, Donoughe M, inventors; Noble Gas Systems Inc, assignee. Compressed gas capture and recovery system. United States patent US 9,850,852. 2017 Dec 26.
4. https://news.lockheedmartin.com/2022-04-11-Lockheed-Martin-Stalker-VXE-UAS-Completes-World-Record-39-Hour-Flight

Modeling Hydrogen Generation from Hydroreactive Chemical Hydrides

Michael Hook[1,2], Michael Janik[2], Ali Borhan[2], and Martin Klanchar[1]

[1]The Pennsylvania State University
Applied Research Laboratory
P.O. Box 30, Mailstop 9630J
State College, PA 16804

[2]The Pennsylvania State University
Department of Chemical Engineering
205 Chemical and Biomedical Engineering Building
University Park, PA 16802

Contact Author (Klanchar) Email: i60@arl.psu.edu

Abstract
Experimental and modeling results are presented that characterize the hydrogen (H_2) generation process when a lithium hydride (LiH) or lithium aluminum hydride ($LiAlH_4$) solid shape or powder is fully immersed in water. The reaction itself is fast, but what truly controls the rate of H_2 generation is the mass transfer of reactants and products to and from the hydride solid-water interface. Primary accomplishments of this study were demonstration of how variables such as surface area, temperature, pressure, product solubility, and water quality affect the rate of H_2 generation, and, with the help of experimental data, development of a mathematical model, based on mass and energy balances for a reacting system.

Keywords
Hydrogen generation reactions; Dense hydrogen storage; Lithium hydrides; Reaction modeling.

Introduction
Hydroreactive materials, including LiH and $LiAlH_4$, offer a hydrogen-dense and fast-reacting method of generating a high-purity pressurized hydrogen (H_2) supply when contacted with water. They have particular application for fueling a polymer electrolyte membrane (PEM) fuel cell [1] in remote locations by drawing on a local water source. The hydride materials under study are stable, lightweight, and transportable in a backpack. Additionally, their reaction products are easily removed from a batch-type vessel, allowing for quick refueling.

Reaction Mechanism and Chemistry
The two hydrides of interest for this study react exothermically with water as follows to generate H_2:

$$LiH(s) + H_2O(l) \rightarrow LiOH(aq) + H_2(g) + heat \quad (1)$$

$$2LiAlH_4(s) + 5H_2O(l) \rightarrow Al_2O_3(s) + 2LiOH(aq) + 8H_2(g) + heat \quad (2)$$

The reaction itself is very fast, however, the actual rate of H_2 generation is governed by the mass transfer of reactants and products to and from the hydride solid surface, for example, the movement of hydroxides/oxides and H_2 away from the reacting surface, against the incoming flow of fresh water.

The reaction process is depicted in Figure 1. The concept shows bulk solid hydride and water phases, with a reaction and mass transfer zone in between. Near the interface, fresh water reactant must migrate through a counter current flow of H_2 gas plus hydroxide as it dissolves into the bulk water phase. It is this exchange of materials that governs the rate of reaction, including the net rate of H_2 generation, and consumption of hydride.

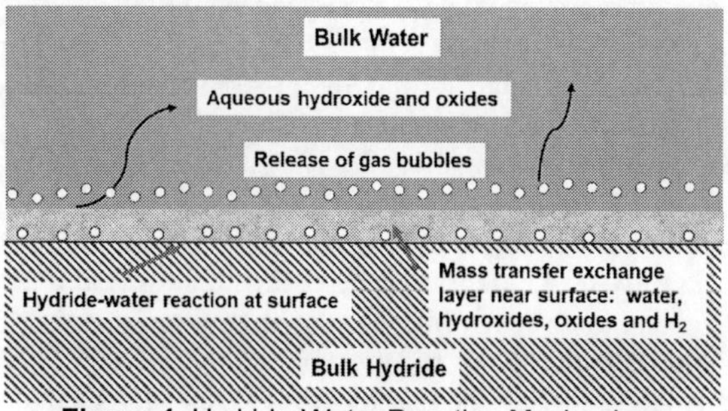

Figure 1. Hydride-Water Reaction Mechanism.

As is typical with this type of multiphase surface reaction with mass transfer, a number of variables including surface area, temperature, pressure, reaction kinetics, and water quality control the H_2 generation rate.

For many fueling applications, it is desired to generate H_2 either at a defined rate, or as rapidly as possible. And usually high purity and conversion efficiency are essential. Thus it is important to understand, and account for how all the variables mentioned above affect the desired production and quality of H_2.

Experimental
This investigation focused on the H_2-generating reaction of solid LiH and $LiAlH_4$ pellets and powder while fully immersed in water. An experimental system was designed and built (Figure 2) for collection of data over a range of variables. The variables studied in this particular report include:

- Hydride material in the form of both solid cylindrical pellets and 100 μm powder.
- Initial water temperature.
- Water volume.
- Fresh vs. salt water (seawater).
- Vessel pressure (maintained constant during experiments).
- Reaction rate of single vs. multiple pellets.

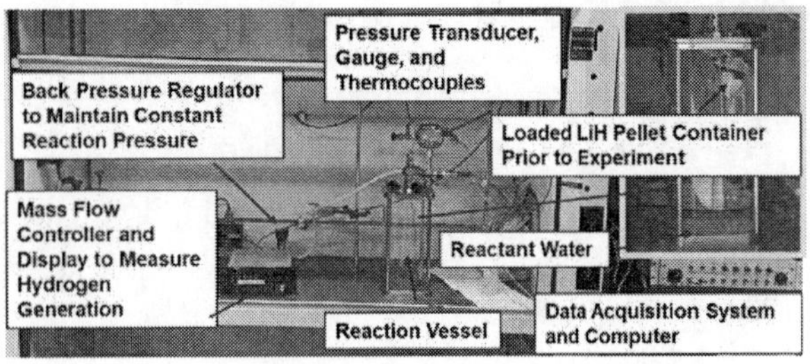

Figure 2. Experimental System for Collecting Hydride Hydrogen Generation Data.

The LiH was obtained from Albemarle Corporation in the form of 97%, < 100 μm powder. Solid pellets were pressed from the powder into 25 mm x 5 mm discs at near fusion density. Each pellet contained nominally 1.74 g LiH, capable of producing 0.44 g or 5.35 standard liters of H_2.

The $LiAlH_4$ was sourced from Sigma-Aldrich as 95%, 10 mm x 6 mm pellets, weighing approximately 0.5 g and theoretically producing 0.11 g or 1.39 standard liters of H_2.

Experiments were typically conducted batch-wise in a large excess of water (800 ml). The hydride sample was initially held above the water, while the vessel interior headspace was maintained at a defined pressure with a pure H_2 atmosphere. To start the reaction process, the weighted hydride container was released into the water, where it quickly sank to the bottom. As the hydride began reacting, H_2 bubbled through the water and into headspace, exiting the vessel and passing through the back pressure regulator and the mass flow meter. The back pressure regulator maintained a near constant system pressure throughout the duration of the reaction. Recorded data included hydrogen flow rate, vessel pressure, bulk water temperature, and temperature inside the hydride container. Experiments were typically designed to investigate one particular variable, while holding other variables constant.

Mathematical Model Development

A primary goal of this work was to develop a reaction model as a means of predicting H_2 generation according to the variables mentioned above. Some general data and knowledge about the reaction process were known, but additional data from experimental testing were needed to create a useful model.

The mathematical model for predicting hydrogen generation was developed from fundamental equations that characterize conservation of mass and energy for a reacting system. In all equations, the subscripts 'w' and 'p' denote a property of water or the hydride pellet respectively, while infinity (∞) represents a location in the bulk surroundings sufficiently far from the reaction to be unaffected by any change. Initial values, represented with a '0' subscript are taken at 20 °C.

The time varying mass balance for a reacting system shown by equation 3, relates the effective volume of water interacting with the system, V_w, surrounding the surface reaction that takes places as water reaches the pellet.

$$V_w \frac{dC}{dt} = k_0 e^{\frac{-E_a}{R}\left(\frac{1}{T}-\frac{1}{T_\infty}\right)} A_p (C_{sat} - C) \qquad (3)$$

C(t) represents the concentration of the product lithium hydroxide (M), k_0 is the initial mass transfer coefficient (m/s), E_a is the activation energy (J/mol) of the reaction, R is the ideal gas constant (8.314 J mol^{-1} K^{-1}), T(t) is the temperature at the reaction site (K), and $A_p(t)$ is the surface area available for reaction.

The corresponding energy balance, equation 4, gains terms from the heat of reaction, ΔH, and heat transfer around the reaction through a lumped heat transfer coefficient, h, that accounts for conduction and induced convection. C_p and ρ_p are the specific heat capacity (J kg^{-1} K^{-1}) and density (kg m^{-3}) of the hydride pellet.

$$\rho_p\, C_p\, V_p \frac{dT}{dt} = -\Delta H\, k_0 e^{\frac{-E_a}{R}\left(\frac{1}{T}-\frac{1}{T_\infty}\right)} A_p (C_{sat} - C) - hA_p(T - T_\infty) \qquad (4)$$

For these equations, the rate of reaction is modeled by the Arrhenius equation ($k = A\, e^{-\frac{Ea}{RT}}$) with rate constant units of length per time. The equation for ΔH(t) is taken from a correlation of electrolytic solutions as used by Leckey, et al. [2].

$$\Delta H = 4.18\,(-4900 + 18.8\,(C/\rho_w)^{0.5}(T - 298)) \qquad (5)$$

Additional parameters arise from the time-dependence of C_{sat} and h. Due do the expected nature of an initial ramp up in C_{sat} and convection, both functions are approximated in the form shown by equation 6.

$$X = X_0\, Tanh\left({}^{t}/_{t_x}\right) \qquad (6)$$

Time parameters t_{eq} and t_0 are used respectively to capture the ramp up of C_{sat} and h some time into the reaction.

Concentration of the metal-hydroxide product is taken to be at saturation level at the surface due to the fast nature of the reaction in comparison to the time scale of diffusion. In order to account for reduction in pellet size as the extent of reaction rises, the simplifying assumption was made that all parts of the hydride pellet react equally so pellet surface area, A_p, is able to be directly related to the pellet geometry through an additional conservation of mass equation.

With all other physical properties defined, the remaining six unknown variables needed to solve concentration and temperature profiles for a reaction of given chemical hydride size and dimensions are: V_w, the initial mass transfer coefficient (k_0), the activation energy (E_a), the maximum heat transfer coefficient (h_0), and the time parameters t_{eq} and t_0.

Results and Discussion

Effect of Initial Bath Temperature

Figure 3 shows the H_2 generation of single LiH pellets in fresh water over the temperature range of 16.7-40.0 °C, as system pressure is held constant at 221 kPa.

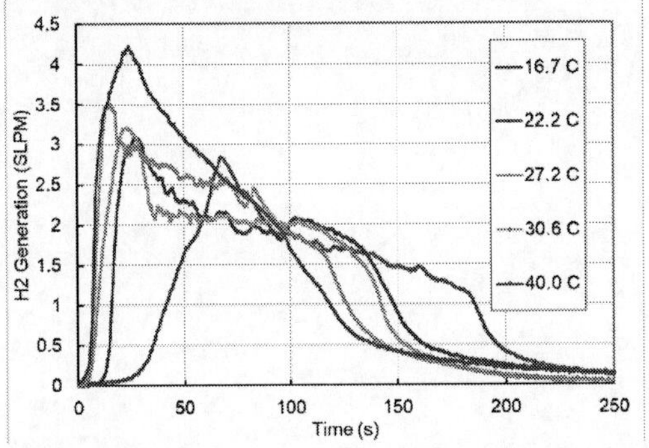

Figure 3. H_2 Generation for a Single Pellet at Various Initial Bath Temperatures.

As predicted by the Arrhenius equation, the rate constant – and thus H_2 generation rate – are strong functions of temperature. Peak rates generally increase with temperature while the time for complete reaction decreases. Integration of the generation data shows >95% conversion for all temperatures. Typically the heat of reaction increased the bulk water temperature about 2.2 °C over the course of the reaction.

Effect of Total Surface Area

Experiments were conducted to investigate the linearity of hydrogen generation as LiH pellet count – and surface area – was doubled and quadrupled. Figure 4 shows H_2 generation per pellet for experiments consisting of 1, 2, and 4 pellets at similar initial ambient temperature.

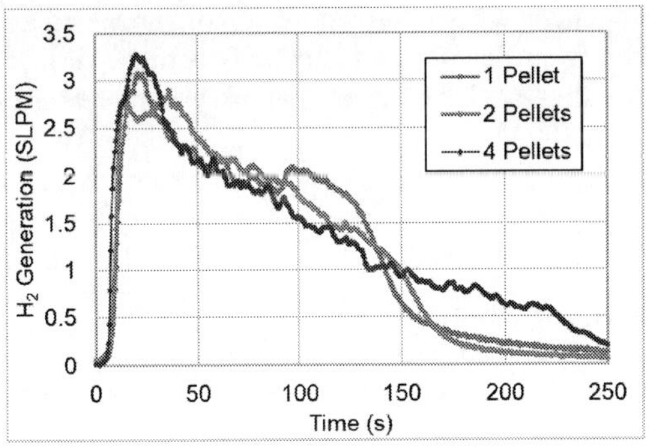

Figure 4. H_2 Generation per Pellet for Systems Containing 1, 2, and 4 Pellets at 221 kPa.

For this experimental system, the near overlay of data plots shows that the pellets react independently, despite the presence of other reacting pellets nearby. At least for systems consisting of 1-4 pellets, there appears to be sufficient and identical LiH-water contact such that H_2 generation is a linear function of total surface area.

Effect of Pressure

While most experiments with LiH were conducted at 221 kPa, a few were done at 386 kPa in order to investigate the effect of pressure, at least over a narrow range. Figure 5 overlays H_2 generation data from experiments at each pressure using 4 pellets.

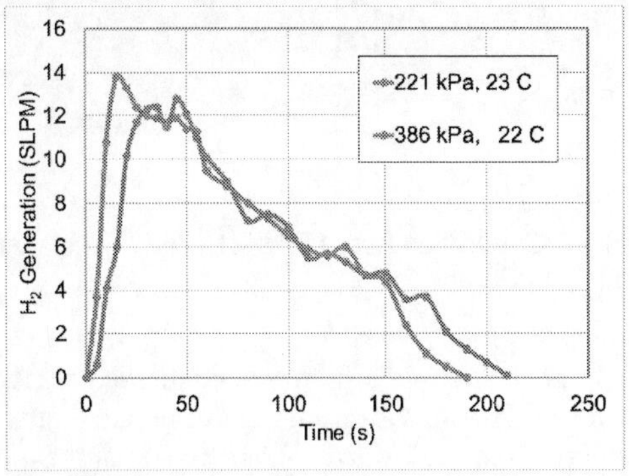

Figure 5. Comparison of H_2 Generation at 221 and 386 kPa for a 4 Pellet System.

The generation plots show little difference between the two pressures. The slight initial delay at 386 kPa is likely due to mechanical lag from the back pressure regulator.

Effect of Water Salinity – LiH and $LiAlH_4$

LiH experiments with 1 pellet were done in both fresh water and salt water (Instant Ocean mixed to simulate typical seawater). Figure 6 overlays data from each, which shows very similar generation curves.

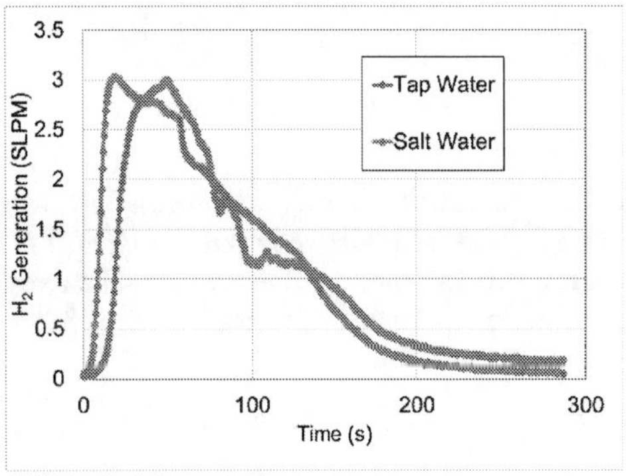

Figure 6. H_2 Generation from 1 LiH Pellet in Fresh and Salt Water at 221 kPa and 27 °C.

Thus, the salt ion concentration in seawater appears to have no effect on the LiH reaction mechanism.

However, the presence of dissolved salt for the $LiAlH_4$ – water reaction appears to alter H_2 generation. Figure 7 compares $LiAlH_4$ experiments from both fresh and salt water. In the case of salt water, generation slows and fluctuates as compared to the bell-like curve from fresh water. Additional experiments with multiple $LiAlH_4$ pellets confirmed this result. It appears a solid, likely insoluble product forms near the reacting surface that impedes/blocks the normal transfer of water and/or release of H_2 from the surface. This result plus product examination/identification will be investigated in future work.

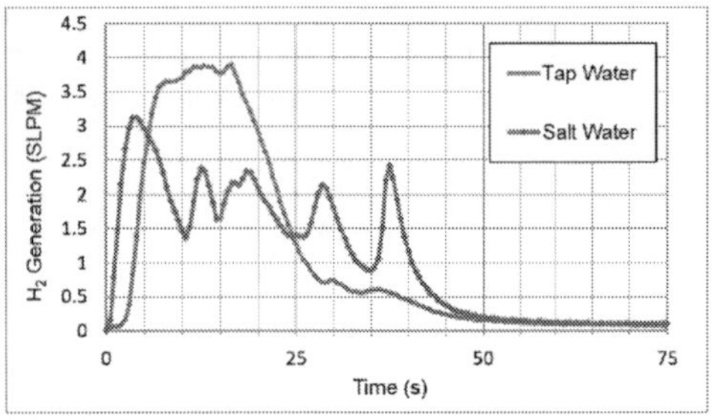

Figure 7. H_2 Generation from 1 $LiAlH_4$ Pellet in Fresh and Salt Water at 221 kPa and 25 °C.

Experiments with LiH Powder

Hydrogen generation data from the submerged reaction of monolayer LiH powder over a range of temperatures were used to derive required kinetic parameters k_0 and E_a for the mathematical model. The data, plotted in Figure 8, show the immediate generation of H_2 followed by a quick decay to zero within 5 seconds.

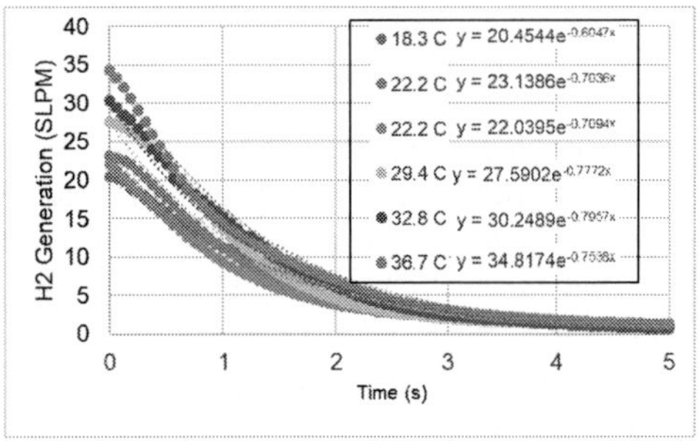

Figure 8. H_2 Generation from a Small Quantity of LiH Power Over a Range of Temperatures.

Exponential fits of the data in combination with the Arrhenius equation led to derivation of E_a = 8680 J/mol and an average k_0 = 0.133 mm/s at T = 293 K. The derived E_a compares well to a previously reported value of 8360 J/mol [2].

Mathematical Model Development and Parameter Definitions

Data from the single pellet reactions were used along with the kinetic parameters found from powder reactions to fit the remaining parameters with the model. The governing equations were solved numerically within Mathematica and a nonlinear model fit was performed to minimize residuals created by manipulating V_w, h_0, t_0, and t_{eq} when compared with the experimental data. The dimensional model prediction is plotted alongside the data used for fitting in Figure 9.

The unknown parameters from equations 3 and 4 for the Figure 9 model fit were determined as follows:

- **E_a = 8680 J/mol** (Activation energy)
- **k_0 = 0.133 mm/s** (Initial surface reaction rate constant)
- **V_w = 29.4 ml** (Effective water volume)
- **h_0 = 141 J/(s m^2 K)** (Initial heat transfer coefficient)
- **t_0 = 17.6 s** (Heat transfer coefficient time parameter)
- **t_{eq} = 9.0 s** (Saturation concentration time parameter)

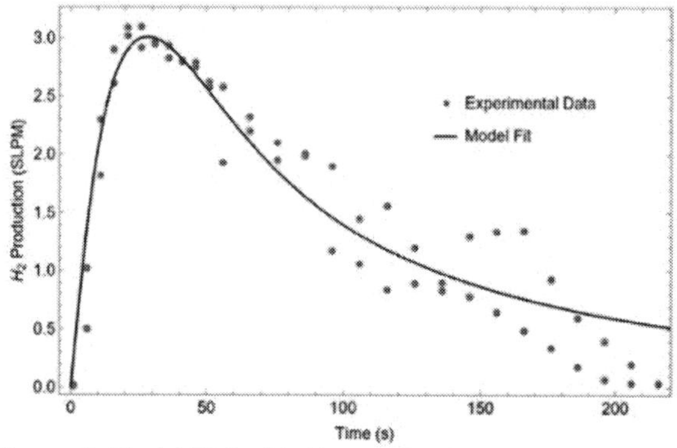

Figure 9. Model Fit for H_2 Generation for 1 LiH Pellet at 221 kPa and 20 °C Initial Temperature.

Discussion and Conclusions

This report presents only a portion of the collected experimental data and analysis accomplished to date. The authors intend to continue model development, including derivation of a dimensionless model that can be applied to a range of reactions and initial conditions.

Primary findings reported here include:

- LiH and $LiAlH_4$ are both H_2 dense solids that react very quickly and to completion when submerged in fresh water. The LiH reaction is unaffected in salt water, but the $LiAlH_4$ reaction is suppressed.
- Reaction rate increases with initial water temperature.
- H_2 generation is a linear function of surface area when there is sufficient water contact/flow to the surface.
- Reaction rate is not dependent on system pressure up to about 400 kPa.
- The reaction can be accurately modeled via mass and energy balance equations for time-varying, reacting systems, with identification of key model variables.

Acknowledgements

This work was funded via the 2021-2022 Collaborative Defense Research Seed Grant Program between Penn State's Applied Research Laboratory (ARL) and College of Engineering. In addition, Michael Hook, Penn State Chemical Engineering undergraduate, was supported by the Schreyer Honors College and ARL's Distinguished Research Undergraduate Program (DURP).

References

1. https://www.energy.gov/eere/articles/4-ways-fuel-cells-power-us-military
2. Leckey, J.H., Nulf, L.E., and Kirkpatrick, J.R., "Reaction of Lithium Hydride with Water," *Langmuir*, 12 (26), 6361-6367, 1996.

Saving Pt-Catalyzed PEM Fuel Cells from CO Poisoning by Getting COPROX to Work!

Debra R. Rolison,[1,] Travis G. Novak,[1] Paul A. DeSario,[1,*] Todd H. Brintlinger,[2] Ryan H. DeBlock,[1] and Jeffrey W. Long[1]*

[1] Surface Chemistry Branch, U.S. Naval Research Laboratory, Washington, D.C. 20375, United States

[2] Materials & Sensors Branch, U.S. Naval Research Laboratory, Washington, D.C. 20375, United States

*Corresponding Authors: debra.rolison@nrl.navy.mil; paul.desario@nrl.navy.mil

Abstract: We design ultraporous metal nanoparticle–modified oxide aerogels as architected platforms that impose size comparability of the networked, covalently bonded oxide nanoparticles (NPs) and the catalytic NPs supported thereon. This arrangement permits a degree of physical and chemical interfacial intimacy uncommon in heterogeneous catalysis. We find that such high contact intimacy for photodeposited copper nanoparticles on reducing oxide aerogels such as ceria stabilizes Cu in its more catalytically active, low-valent (0 or +1) state, even poising sufficient Cu(0) in the supported particle for plasmonic character to persist even under oxidizing conditions. We previously evaluated the selectivity and activity of this architected catalyst and a related aerogel, $Cu/Gd_xCe_{1-x}O_2$, for preferential oxidation of CO (COPROX) in H_2 feedstreams, finding that $Cu/Gd_xCe_{1-x}O_2$ outperformed Cu/CeO_2 when H_2 and H_2O were present in the feedstream. Here, we explore a series of $Cu/Gd_xCe_{1-x}O_2$ aerogels and evaluate their performance for dry CO oxidation. The surface area of the aerogels increases as Gd content increases, explaining the improved performance of $Cu/Gd_xCe_{1-x}O_2$ under humid COPROX conditions where transport is known to be a limiting factor, but catalytic activity towards CO oxidation decreases under dry conditions. These results reflect an important trade-off between improved transport but reduced fundamental redox capacity with Gd substitution into CeO_2 aerogels.

Keywords: Catalysis, aerogel, oxygen vacancy, oxidation, mesoporous

Introduction

Transition metals supported on or embedded in a CeO_2 support provide exceptional catalytic properties for many reactions relevant for fuels production/purification and environmental remediation, including preferential oxidation of CO (COPROX), water–gas shift (WGS), CO_2 hydrogenation, and NO_x reduction.[1] An aerogel expression of CeO_2 provides an excellent platform for catalysis because this morphology provides a high-surface area and an interconnected pore network, exposes abundant active sites, and maximizes interfacial intimacy between the metal and oxide support.

Oxygen vacancies (O_{vac}) in the CeO_2 play an important role in many oxidation reactions, often serving as defect sites for adsorption and activation of reactant species, e.g., adsorbed H_2O on CeO_2 dissociates at oxygen vacancies to form surface hydroxyls.[2] Activation of the reactants is not always the rate-limiting step; DFT calculations reveal an inverse relationship between the activity of CeO_2 for WGS and its oxygen-vacancy density.[3] In cases where metal cations with <4+ valency are substituted into the CeO_2 lattice to generate additional oxygen vacancies, the catalyst morphology may be affected, making it difficult to deconvolve the effects.

In this work we assess the impact of Gd-substitution on oxygen-vacancy concentration and CeO_2 aerogel morphology. We evaluate the CO oxidation activity of Gd(III)-substituted and native CeO_2 aerogels after photodepositing 5 wt% Cu on the aerogel network. We find that as the Gd content increases in $Gd_xCe_{1-x}O_2$, so does the surface area of the aerogel and its oxygen-vacancy concentration. However, the intrinsic activity of $Cu/Gd_xCe_{1-x}O_2$ for CO oxidation decreases.

Results and Discussion

Aerogels were synthesized using a previously reported sol–gel method.[4–7] For CeO_2, 2.39 g of $CeCl_3 \cdot 7H_2O$ was dissolved in 10 g of anhydrous methanol, followed by adding 6 g of propylene oxide, vigorously stirring for 20 min, then leaving the sol to gel overnight. For Gd(III)-substituted CeO_2 (GCO) aerogels, 5, 10, and 20 mol% of $GdCl_3 \cdot 6H_2O$ were substituted for corresponding amounts of $CeCl_3 \cdot 7H_2O$ to form gels designated 5GCO, 10GCO, and 20GCO, respectively. The wet gels were rinsed several times in isopropanol, then acetone, then supercritically dried in CO_2. For CO oxidation testing, 5 wt% Cu was photodeposited by mixing 200 mg of ground aerogel with 38 mg of $Cu(NO_3)_2 \cdot H_2O$, adjusting the dispersion pH to 9.5±0.1 with NaOH, and irradiating for 48 h using a 500 W Xe arc lamp. This protocol yields well-dispersed, aerogel-supported nanoparticulate Cu in which the Cu is stabilized primarily in its low-valent ($Cu^{0/1+}$) state. The wetting/drying steps necessary to photodeposit Cu from aqueous media does not affect the morphology of the calcined aerogel.[5,7]

Figure 1 summarizes the impact of Gd(III) substitution on CeO_2 morphology, as measured by Brunauer–Emmett–Teller (BET) surface area. After being supercritically dried, all CeO_2 and GCO aerogels show essentially identical surface areas, between 299.6 and 302.8 m^2/g, differences well within typical experimental error. The Gd precursor itself is highly amenable to gel formation, previously reported to form monolithic Gd_2O_3 aerogels with high surface area through a similar synthesis route,[8] so it does not adversely affect surface area.

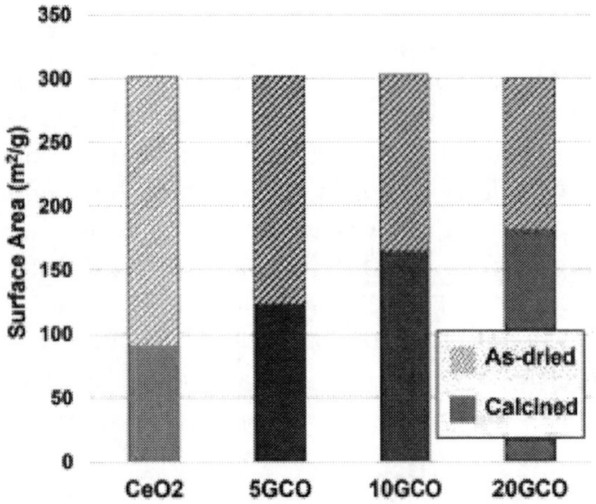

Figure 1 | BET surface area of dried (shaded) and 500 °C-calcined (solid) aerogels.

As Gd content increases, the aerogels retain more surface area after calcination at 500 °C (Figure 1). All aerogels inevitably lose surface area during calcination as crystallite growth reduces porosity, but Gd substitution slows crystallite growth in CeO_2.[9] As a result, the surface area of 20GCO (181.6 m^2/g) is nearly double that of the native CeO_2 aerogel (91.1 m^2/g).

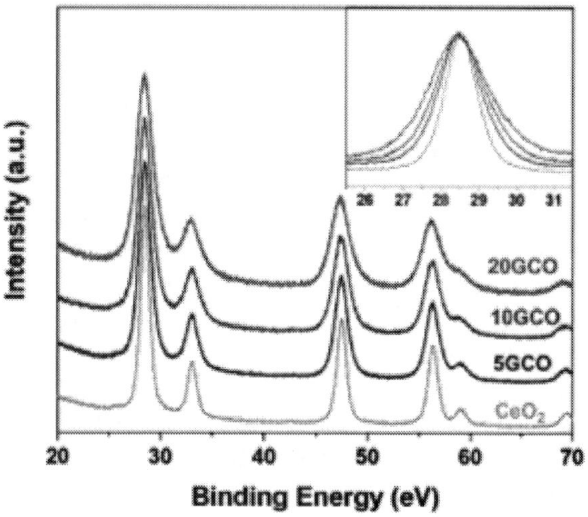

Figure 2 | XRD patterns of CeO_2 and GCO aerogels, with inset showing broadening of the ⟨111⟩ peak as the mol% of Gd(II) substituted into CeO_2 aerogel increases.

Changes to the crystallite size upon Gd-substitution are corroborated by X-ray diffraction (XRD) analysis (Figure 2). All diffraction peaks correspond to the CeO_2 fluorite structure, indicating that even at 20 mol%, Gd does not form a discrete Gd_2O_3 phase. Increasing Gd content results in peak broadening (Figure 2, inset), a product of smaller crystallite size and/or lattice strain as Gd(III) substitutes in Ce(IV) sites. Crystallite size, estimated using the Scherrer equation, decreases from 8.9 nm in CeO_2 aerogel to 4.9 nm in 20GCO. The primary ⟨111⟩ peak also slightly shifts; the calculated lattice spacing expands from 3.132 Å for CeO_2 to 3.138 Å for 20GCO.

We use X-ray photoelectron spectroscopy (XPS) to probe the changes in chemical states between different compositions of aerogels (Figure 3). In the O1s region, the lower binding energy peak (O_a) is assigned to lattice oxygen in stoichiometric CeO_2, while the higher binding

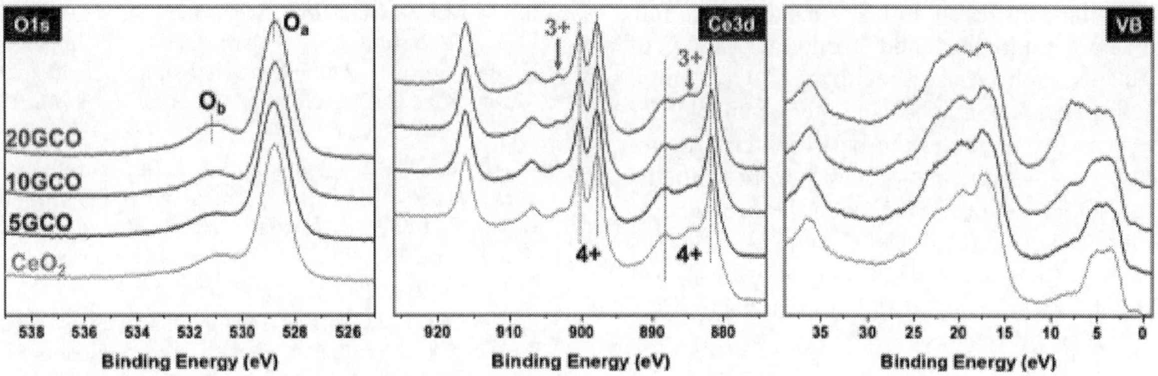

Figure 3 | XPS of the O1s, Ce3d, and VB regions of CeO_2 and GCO aerogels.

energy peak (O_b) originates from O or OH coordinated with Ce^{3+}.[10] The intensity of the O_b peak increases with increasing Gd mol%, and the presence of increased oxygen vacancies is also evident in the slight increase in Ce^{3+} peaks in the Ce3d region. The valence band (VB) region further confirms the presence of Gd by the appearance of a progressively bigger shoulder at ~9 eV as Gd content increases, a binding energy characteristic of a Gd–O chemical state.[11]

We then photodeposited 5 wt% Cu over the four aerogel supports and evaluated their performance for the CO oxidation reaction. Oxidation of CO is often used as a benchmark reaction and is generally thought to proceed via the Mars van Krevelen (MvK) mechanism, where adsorbed CO is oxidized by a lattice oxygen, and the resulting oxygen vacancy is healed to restart the catalytic cycle.[12] For the active site to turnover, it is not the presence of oxygen vacancies prior to CO exposure that is beneficial, but rather the ability of the CeO_2 to cycle between 3+/4+ states as vacancies are generated and healed. A persistent oxygen vacancy – i.e., one that does not heal in the presence of oxygen – should adversely affect catalysis if the MvK mechanism is dominant.

Although 5Cu/CeO_2 and 5Cu/5GCO show similar CO oxidation light-off curves (Figure 4), the impact of fixed vacancies becomes more pronounced at higher Gd loading. 5Cu/20GCO, which has the highest oxygen vacancy content, is by far the least active aerogel across the measured temperature range. The activity of 5Cu/10GCO decreases at lower temperatures, but eventually reaches approximately the same activity of 5Cu/CeO_2 at 150 °C. It is possible that as conversion percentages become higher, the greater surface area of 10GCO is better able to ease kinetic limitations. Alternatively, a non–MvK mechanism, such as one invoking Cu–Ce dual-site adsorption,[13] may become favorable at higher temperatures. Overall, these results indicate that the increased surface area and oxygen-vacancy concentration induced by Gd(III)-substitution do not positively impact low-temperature CO oxidation.

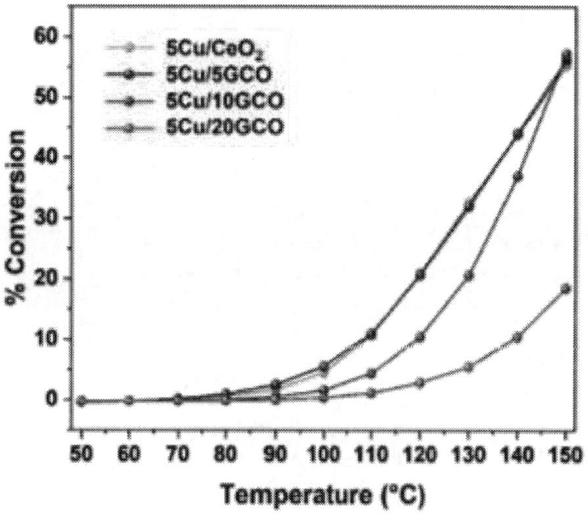

Figure 4 | CO oxidation light-off curves for 5 wt.% Cu photodeposited over CeO_2 and GCO aerogel supports.

Summary

We demonstrate a tradeoff between the surface area/oxygen vacancy concentration and CO oxidation performance when Gd(III) is substituted into the lattice of CeO_2 aerogels. The results hold important implications for catalyst design, where the specific reaction limitations should be considered. In reactions that have few transport limitations and facile activation of reactants, such as the case with dry CO oxidation, maximizing the number of sites available for 3+/4+ redox promotes the best low-temperature activity. However, our previous work with the COPROX reaction finds that in the presence of water, Gd-substituted CeO_2 aerogel, with its greater surface area and ability to activate H_2O at oxygen vacancy sites, affords superior activity.[5]

Acknowledgments

This work was supported by the Office of Naval Research. T.G.N. and R.H.D. were NRL-NRC postdoctoral associates from 2020–2023.

References

1. Konsolakis, M. The Role of Copper–Ceria Interactions in Catalysis Science: Recent Theoretical and Experimental Advances. *Appl. Catal. B* **2016**, *198*, 49–66.

2. Yang, Z.; Wang, Q.; Wei, S.; Ma, D.; Sun, Q. The Effect of Environment on the Reaction of Water on the Ceria(111) Surface: A DFT+U Study. *J. Phys. Chem. C* **2010**, *114*, 14891–14899.

3. Vecchietti, J.; Bonivardi, A.; Xu, W.; Stacchiola, D.; Delgado, J.J.; Calatayud, M.; Collins, S.E. Understanding the Role of Oxygen Vacancies in the Water Gas Shift Reaction on Ceria-Supported Platinum Catalysts. *ACS Catal.* **2014**, *4*, 2088–2096.

4. Novak, T.G.; DeSario, P.A.; Johannes, M.D.; Brintlinger, T.H.; DeBlock, R.H.; Long, J.W.; Chervin, C.N.; Stroud, R.M.; Rolison, D.R. CeO_2 Aerogel-Induced Resilience of Catalytic $Ni(OH)_2$ under Oxidizing Conditions. *Chem. Mater.* **2022**, *34*, 5644–5653.

5. Novak, T.G.; DeSario, P.A.; Brintlinger, T.H.; DeBlock, R.H.; Long, J.W.; Rolison, D.R. Cu/CeO_2 and Cu/Gd-Substituted CeO_2 Aerogels as Active, Selective, and Stable COPROX Catalysts. *ACS Sustain. Chem. Eng.* **2023**, *11*, 2853–2860.

6. Novak, T.G.; Balow, R.B.; Buck, M.R.; Rolison, D.R.; DeSario, P.A. Dark and UV-Enhanced Degradation of Dimethyl Methylphosphonate on Mesoporous CeO_2 Aerogels. *ACS Appl. Nano Mater.* **2023**, *6*, 3075–3084.

7. Pitman, C.L.; Pennington, A.M.; Brintlinger, T.H.; Barlow, D.E.; Esparraguera, L.F.; Stroud, R.M.; Pietron, J.J.; DeSario, P.A.; Rolison, D.R. Stabilization of Reduced Copper on Ceria Aerogels for CO Oxidation. *Nanoscale Adv.* **2020**, *2*, 4547–4556.

8. Zhang, H.D.; Li, B.; Zheng, Q.X.; Jiang, M.H.; Tao, X.T. Synthesis and Characterization of Monolithic Gd_2O_3 Aerogels. *J. Non-Cryst. Solids* **2008**, *354*, 4089–4093.

9. Inaba, H.; Nakajima, T.; Tagawa, H. Sintering Behaviors of Ceria and Gadolinia-Doped Ceria. *Solid State Ionics* **1998**, *106*, 263–268.

10. Sohn, H.; Celik, G.; Gunduz, S.; Dogu, D.; Zhang, S.; Shan, J.; Tao, F.F.; Ozkan, U.S. Oxygen Mobility in Pre-Reduced Nano- and Macro-Ceria with Co Loading: An AP-XPS, In-Situ DRIFTS and TPR Study. *Catal. Lett.* **2017**, *147*, 2863–2876.

11. Zatsepin, D.A.; Boukhvalov, D.W.; Zatsepin, A.F.; Kuznetsova, Y.A.; Mashkovtsev, M.A.; Rychkov, V.N.; Shur, V.Y.; Esin, A.A.; Kurmaev, E.Z. Electronic Structure, Charge Transfer, and Intrinsic Luminescence of Gadolinium Oxide Nanoparticles: Experiment and Theory. *Appl. Surf. Sci.* **2018**, *436*, 697–707.

12. Sun, Y.; Li, C.; Djerdj, I.; Khalid, O.; Cop, P.; Sann, J.; Weber, T.; Werner, S.; Turke, K.; Guo, Y.; Smarsly, B.M.; Over, H. Oxygen Storage Capacity versus Catalytic Activity of Ceria–Zirconia Solid Solutions in CO and HCl Oxidation. *Catal. Sci. Technol.* **2019**, *9*, 2163–2172.

13. Ji, W.; Chen, X.; Li, Q.; Lin, K.; Deng, J.; Xing, X. Insights into CO Oxidation in Cu/CeO_2 Catalysts: O_2 Activation at the Dual-Interfacial Sites. *Eur. J. Inorg. Chem.* **2023**, *26*, e202200656.

Dry Processed, Layered, Flexible Lithium-Ion Manufacturing Process

Michael D. Eskra
Rodney LaFollette
Paula K. Ralston
Eskra Technical Products, Inc.
Saukville, WI, USA, 53080

Abstract

The dry PVDF electrode process, developed under a DLA BATTNET project, provides improved electrical performance compared to solvent-based electrodes. The process allows multiple electrode layers, tailoring active material particle size. Conductive additives and polymer loadings can provide significant improvements in life, power and cell capacity. This paper will briefly go over the ETP process and explore the improvements that a controlled tailored anode and cathode electrode system can provide. Performance of commercial solvent cast electrodes will be compared with that of single coat dry process electrodes, then multi-layered electrode technology will be evaluated while defining the improvements that occur in high performance battery cells.

Keywords: Lithium-ion; layered separator, low-cost lithium-ion manufacturing; just-in-time manufacturing; solventless; solvent free; lithium-ion manufacturing; dry process; batteries.

Introduction

From 2012 to 2015, ETP worked under a DLA BATTNET Project. ETP Inc. was tasked to develop an electrode manufacturing process for Lithium-Ion batteries, which would enable just-in-time capability and small order delivery for the Defense Community. Under the STP task ETP was to demonstrate a pre commercial pilot process for a totally dry, solvent free manufacture of electrodes (Figure 1). It turned out that an important ancillary benefit of the ETP solvent-free process was that production costs were lowered substantially. Additionally, the process allows fabrication of electrodes with multiple layers, each of which can have their own composition. This can lead to performance enhancements in cells using dry-processed electrodes.

Concept

The ETP process is based upon the concept of a charged fluidized bed, depositing onto a grounded electrode current collector. The electrodes materials (active materials, additives and polymer binder) are suspended in a fluidized bed, charged electrostatically (10s of kV), and then sprayed onto a heated and grounded metal foil current collector. The loose deposit is then calendered to a desired thickness and porosity. The deposition/calendering stages can be repeated multiple times to achieve the desired thickness and capacity, and if desired, apply layers with differing properties (porosity, composition, etc.).

The process reduces initial capitalization costs by 50%, while providing an ongoing cost savings of greater than 30%. The cost of manufacturing is lowered as the process allows for the total elimination of solvents, slurry preparation, drying and solvent recovery. Facility costs are lowered as the method requires a much smaller footprint compared to conventional manufacturing techniques.

The same binder and active materials used in conventional lithium-ion batteries are used in the ETP solvent-free manufacturing of electrodes, leaving no issues with non-compatible components being added to the cell to limit life or hinder performance.

Figure 1. Pre-Production Manufacturing Line.

This line has successfully produced both cathodes and anodes for lithium-ion batteries. It has also been used for bipolar lead acid batteries and several lithium primary chemistries. Performance of test cells has been at or better than the level of commercially made electrodes.

The ETP process can be effectively used with all common active materials and particle sizes for both cathodes and anodes. It has also demonstrated the ability to spray ceramic separator layers on the surface of electrodes, eliminating the need for a discrete component separator.

Description of the Process

The dry process consists of multiple stations where the active material is applied on either a single or dual sided onto the current collector (Figure 2). The stations can be reduced or increased to accomplish the design of the electrode with thicknesses ranging from the width of individual active material particles to much greater thicknesses (> 0.1 cm). The electrode thickness is built up in a single pass through the roll to roll process.

Active materials, binders and conductive carbons are dry blended and applied in an electrostatic spray. Each successive layer is added to the preceding layers. Calendering can be performed between layers or after final coating. A schematic of a single sided coating is shown on the left sides of Figure 3 and Figure 4. An electrode prior to calendering is shown in Figure 5.

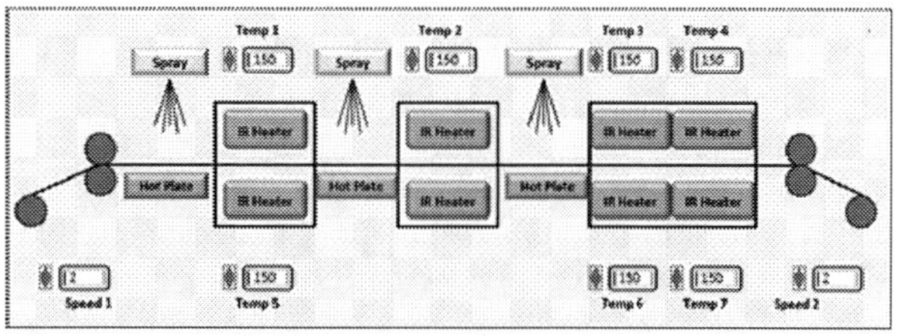

Figure 2. ETP Dry Process Flow Schematic.

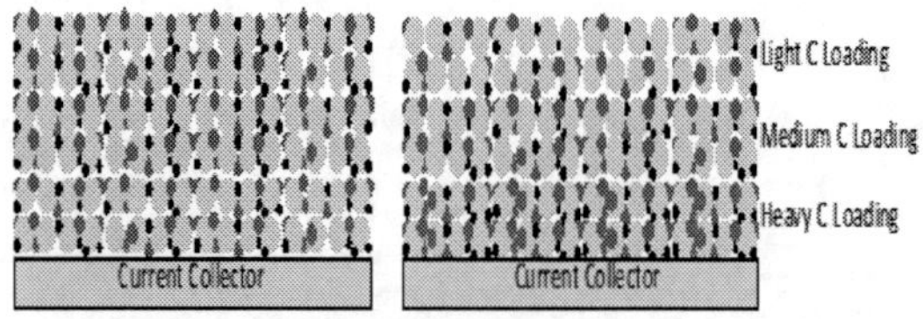

Figure 3. Depiction of Electrodes with Uniform Composition (Left) and with Layers of Variable Composition (Right).

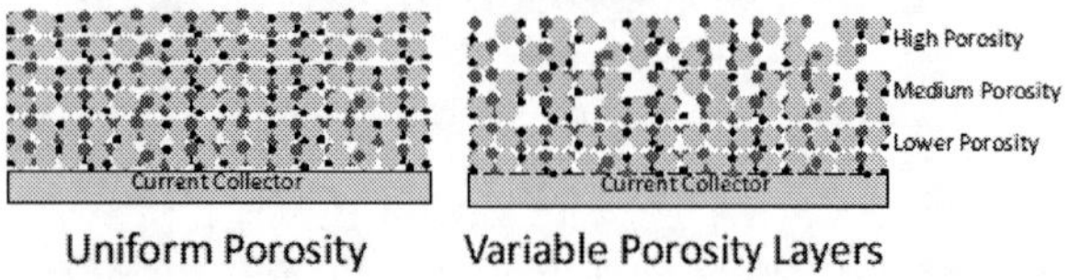

Figure 4. Depiction of Electrodes with Single Layer and Multiple Layers with Variable Porosity.

The temperatures are controlled such that the PVDF polymer does not flow. It is the intent to keep the polymer out of the pores of the active material so as not to fill them with polymer. This has shown to provide substantially higher rate capability compared with solvent cast electrodes.

Keeping the active materials dry enables the ability to start and stop the machine, or change over active materials or continuous runs hindered only by the changing of the foils.

Figure 5. Electrode Before Calendering.

Dry blending is quicker and more cost effective than solvent blending. The finished electrodes are dry as they exit the process and can be slit or cut and built into cells immediately. This lowers the amount of work in process inventory along with lowering the probability of damage to WIP due to further handling and storage.

ETP is presently in the process of switching over to an alternative spraying system. The existing Wagner systems demonstrated uniform coating and strip coating capabilities but they were not as effective at patch coating capability. The lag of active material internal to the coating gun made precision start and stops difficult to manage. The Wagner equipment did provide a working demonstration of the capabilities of uniform very thin to thick capability and may be used on dedicated high volume manufacturing lines. Even they demonstrated that micron control could be achieved with uniform powder feed.

The advantage of the existing dry powder delivery system is that the equipment and in particular the nozzles are very low cost and can be designed and built using 3-D modeling. The tips wear very slowly and have a great deal of flexibility.

ETP typically increases the level of polymer and conductive carbons on the base layer. This improves adhesion of the active materials to the foil. The second and subsequent layers can be thicker with less polymer percentages. The layers can also be tailored to optimize performance as will be discussed in the next section.

ETP has been developing a sprayed ceramic separator. This allows a lower amount of polymer to be used in the separator. This has been shown to provide an improved safety separator. The ceramic separator collapses as thermal runaway begins with the PVDF liquifying and entering the pores of the ceramic. This limits ion transport to allow a slower failure.

Th existing prototype machine (Figure 1) can handle 8" wide foil and can coat up to 40 feet per minute spraying wo sides.

Multi-Layer Capability

ETP's solvent-free electrode fabrication process has the capability of applying the electrode in multiple layers with multiple compositions. This powerful aspect of the process allows battery manufacturers to optimize the electrode for improved performance, especially in applications requiring high power and energy output.

The standard industrial practice at present is to make electrodes by mixing the electrode constituents in powder form (active materials, carbon additives, polymer binder) in an organic liquid which dissolves the binder, and then coating the slurry onto metal foil current collectors. After drying and compressing, the electrode usually has fairly even composition throughout the electrode thickness.

An even distribution of materials through the electrode thickness though is often not ideal. For example, the current flowing through the solid electrode material is highest at the back of the electrode, so the conductive carbon content would be ideally higher at the back of the electrode.

This is easily accomplished using ETP's solvent-free process. Several layers are sprayed onto the current collector, each with a different composition. The bottom layer would have higher carbon content, to reduce voltage drop during high power operation. In contrast, the single-layer (solvent-cast) electrode will have a more uniform carbon content profile. The carbon content at the front of the electrode is the same as that at the bottom, where higher carbon content is most needed.

Figure 3 shows schematically how this might take place. On the left is a single layer electrode. On the right is one with three different layers, with increasing carbon content nearer the current collector.

Other performance variables can also be affected by using layers of differing compositions. For example, porosity can also be changed from one layer to another. Higher porosity reduces the resistance caused by current flow through the electrolyte. In some cases (for example at lower temperatures), the electrolyte resistance can reduce cell voltage. The porosity at the front of the electrode could be increased, where electrolyte current flow is highest. This would improve overall cell performance. Figure 4 illustrates the multi-porosity layers concept.

The powerful design flexibility offered by ETP's solvent-free process extends to the use of different or mixed active materials and carbon powders of differing sizes (depicted in the figures by the grey and black spheres of differing sizes). All in all, use of the ETP process allows quantum upgrading of Li-ion cell design and performance.

An additional advantage of the ETP process is the improvement in distribution of the binder throughout the electrode structure. Presently the binder precipitates preferentially toward the back of the electrode, due to the nature of the evaporation process. This is not necessarily an advantage. Improved binder distribution can be accomplished by elimination of the solvent used in the casting process. Instead, the binder levels, and the location of the binder, can be controlled, further improving electrode and cell performance. Figure 6 shows a 2.8 C discharge of an LTO anode-limited cell, where both electrodes were made using the ETP solvent-free process. Comparison with cells made with solvent-cast electrodes of comparable loadings, show performance is at least equivalent.

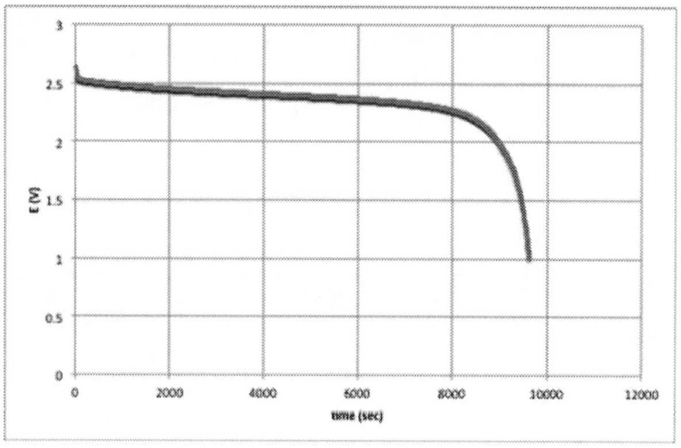

Figure 6. LTO Anode-Limited Cells with and Initial Specific Capacity of 0.485 mAh/cm^2

Solid State Battery Processing

Solid state batteries show significant promise but seem to be suffering from interfacial resistance between the electrolyte and the active material. ETP has recently begun an internal project to use dry process solid state electrolyte and active materials. Again, ETP has chosen to process the materials completely dry and use a modified spray coating process to make composite electrode/separators. This has required elevated temperatures to enable the manufacture of quality electrodes along with operation inside of a glove box. It is our plan to move this process to a dry room in the future.

Summary

The cost and time advantages of the use of the dry fabrication process developed by ETP are well-established. Perhaps overlooked have been significant performance advantages, which can be achieved by applying multiple electrode layers with different properties. Additionally, depositing a ceramic-polymer separator on the surface of electrodes greatly improves electrode alignment and safety.

Finally, at the present time much effort is being expended to find ways to effectively fabricate all solid-state lithium-ion cells. It is widely believed that solid electrolyte cells cannot be made effectively when a solvent-casting manufacturing approach is used to make electrodes. The use of the ETP dry process avoids the problems of using a solvent-based process, which include a residual and resistive film that remains on the surface of the solid electrolyte.

Contact Information:

Mike Eskra 262-707-5855
MikeEskra@aol.com
Paula Ralston 203-417-5526
paula.eskratechnical@gmail.com
Dr. Rodney LaFollette 801-376-8615
RMLaFollette@aol.com

High Power, High Energy, High Safety Cell Technologies

Ionel Stefan
Amprius Technologies, Inc.
1180 Page Avenue
Fremont, CA, USA, 94538
ionel@amprius.com / 1-510-512-5484

Abstract

Amprius is continually improving its pure silicon anode with nanowire structure that has enabled lithium-ion batteries with energy density and specific energy performance exceeding current state of the art graphite cells by 50-100%, depending on cell size and form factor. The rooted nanowire structure has very good mechanical stability, electrical conductivity, and connectivity, and allows material expansion within the structure, extending the cycle life to hundreds of cycles. Amprius cells have shown that silicon anode-based batteries can reach 1,300 Wh/L and 500 Wh/Kg while maintaining a cycle life compatible with aerospace, military, and other high-end applications. Moreover, the open nanowire structure enables cells to function at high rates of charge and discharge without overheating, achieving 1000 W/kg power density in cells with over 400 Wh/kg specific energy density. Recent cell design optimizations have substantially improved resilience to thermal runaway conditions, such as internal short circuit and nail penetration.

Keywords

silicon anode; lithium-ion; batteries; energy density; specific energy; power; aerospace; wearable batteries; drones.

Introduction

Amprius is a Li-ion cell manufacturer with silicon anode and related technologies that enables an increase in energy density of over 50% compared to cells containing graphite anodes. Amprius' main technology, a highly engineered silicon structure made of 100% silicon, enables Li-ion cells with specific energies reaching 500 Wh/kg and energy densities of over 1300 Wh/L. The technology thus provides a significant step forward in lithium-ion battery development, roughly equivalent to the entire improvement over the last two decades with graphite anodes.

Amprius' silicon nanowire anode is unique in the industry because it is the only anode that is made of pure silicon (i.e., no binders, conductive carbons, or other inactive materials) and physically rooted in (i.e., grown from) the current collector foil, which confers unprecedented mechanical stability to the anode structure. The growth-rooted low tortuosity structure is optimal for high power (fast charge/discharge) performance due to very good electrical connectivity between the active anode material and the foil and an open, short pore structure. This combination of properties led to the development of cells that are not only energy dense (Wh/kg and Wh/L) but also power dense (W/kg and W/L), capable of fast charge (minutes instead of hours) and high-power delivery.

Amprius cells are used in unmanned drone applications, such as high-altitude pseudo satellites, unmanned and manned flying drones and vehicles. Amprius cells have also been integrated for a demonstration in conformal wearable batteries (CWB). The CWB battery, developed in collaboration with Inventus Power with C5ISR funding, has demonstrated a doubling of energy stored in the same volume and mass as the graphite cell model, achieving a specific energy above 300 Wh/kg and capacities of more than 300 Wh. To meet the MIL-PRF-32383/4X specifications, the CWB cell safety was improved in order to survive mechanical abuse, which includes crushing, impact (bowling ball test), and nail penetration, by developing additional safety cell components, such as non-flammable and flame-retardant gel polymer electrolytes for silicon anode cells.

The silicon nanowire technology, currently in low volume manufacturing of about 400 kWh annually, will scale to MWh capacity in 2023, and to hundreds of MWh by 2025. This capacity will be enough to support many aerospace and defense applications as well as to demonstrate competitive manufacturing costs at scale, further enabling investment for GWh capacities for electric mobility (electric vehicles and electric flight), replacing graphite-based cells with energy dense storage solutions in most applications, with game changing impact on energy storage weight and endurance. The technology relies entirely on a domestic supply chain, with silane, the silicon precursor available in large quantities, made in the USA.

Technical Description

Structure and Properties: The silicon nanowire structure, shown in Figure 1, includes a metallically conductive nanowire core, metallurgically connected to the current collector. This robust connection is essential in creating and maintaining a stable electrical connection and mechanical structure at the electrode level. Each silicon wire is directly connected and does not need to rely on particle-to-particle contacts for conductivity. Since this connection is very robust compared to connections between particles created by electrode calendaring and binders, the silicon material remains in electrical contact, i.e., electrochemically active, over the entire cycle life of the cell. The fast loss of electrical connectivity and changes in mechanical structure that plague the majority of other silicon technologies are virtually non-existent in the rooted silicon nanowire anodes. Moreover, this significant stability is achieved in a structure that is virtually 100% silicon, without any binder or conductive additive to dilute its active material content.

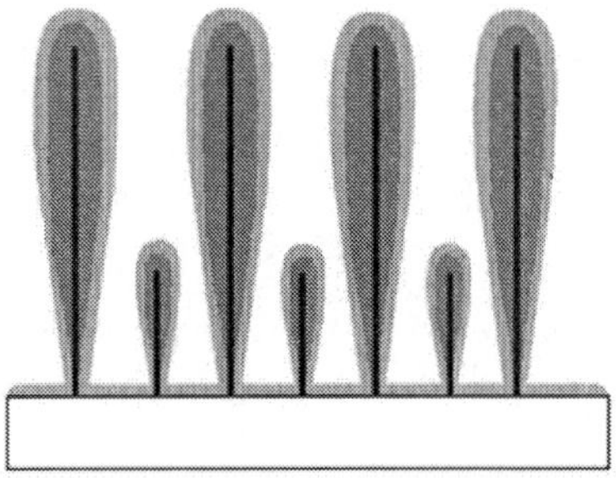

Figure 1. Amprius' growth rooted silicon nanowire structure

The silicon nanowire has a tapered shape, with a much lower thickness toward the root, where it connects to the current collector. This shape is essential in reducing the mechanical stress at the interface during lithiation/delithiation cycles. When silicon films or particles are coated on foils as thin as those used currently in lithium ion cells, e.g. 6-12 μm in thickness, upon lithiation the foils are stretched and that leads to wrinkles, ripples and foil ripping. In the case of silicon nanowire electrodes, the minimum contact surface between the root of the silicon wire and foil eliminates mechanical stress in the foil during cell cycling.

A second feature of Amprius' silicon nanowire material is its nanostructure. The internal porosity and amorphous structure accommodate and dissipate some of the mechanical stress induced in the material during lithiation/delithiation processes. Since these processes start from the silicon/electrolyte interface, they occur mostly radially, and the stress and material expansion are of the same geometry. The silicon nanowire structure can accommodate a large amount of lithium without significant radial expansion. Even at full lithiation, the axial expansion, which is responsible for the cell expansion, is less than 25%, resulting in less than 10% cell thickness increase. This allows electrode loadings (mAh/cm^2) that are significantly higher (approaching 100% increase) than conventional graphite electrodes.

Because the nanowires, which work as electron conduction paths, are attached to the current collector, the structure does not rely on particle-to-particle contact for electronic conductivity and is able to achieve high conductivity, energy and power. This structure difference is shown in Figure 2, where the difference in the ionic and electronic conductive paths are indicated by arrows. Both paths are short and straight in the nanowire anode case, making the structure ideal for high power applications. Combined, these properties result in superior results to particle type graphite, silicon, or lithium metal anodes, exceeding them both in energy density and power capability, including fast charge capability and low temperature operation.

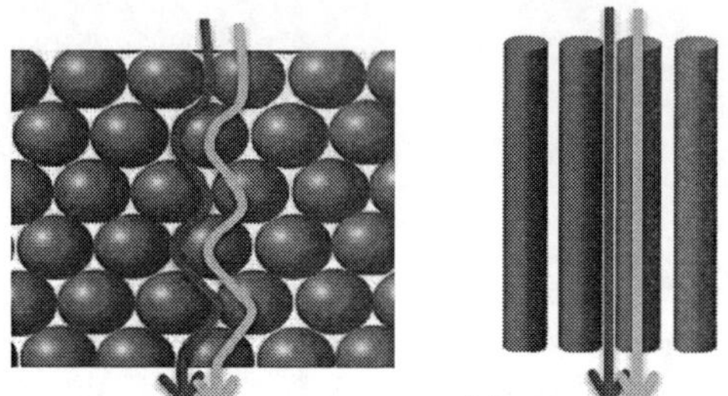

Figure 2. Electronic and ionic conductivity paths in silicon nanowire anode (b) are shorter and straight compared to the tortuous paths in graphite anodes (a

The nanowire material structure also enables a relatively high 94% first coulombic efficiency in half cells and 90% coulombic efficiency in full cells with LCO cathode. These values are competitive with graphite materials and reduce or eliminate the need for prelithiation steps that compensate for the first cycle loss in the cell fabrication. A typical first cycle at a 0.05C rate of a silicon nanowire electrode is shown in Figure 3.

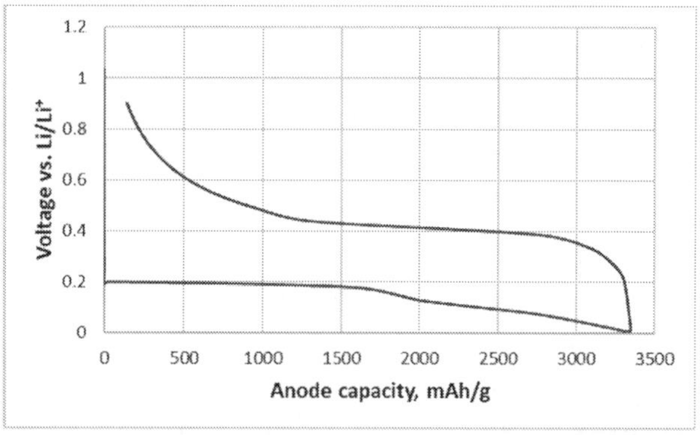

Figure 3. Silicon nanowire voltage profile in half cell, lithiated to 10mV vs. Li/Li+ electrode and delithiated to 0.9V at a 0.05C rate

Energy and Power Density: As described in the previous section, the silicon nanowire anode has intrinsically high-power capability. The Ragone plot in Figure 4 shows the energy and power application range of three silicon nanowire cell types that were developed by matching silicon nanowire anode with different cathode structures. With high loading cathodes, the specific energy reaches over 450 Wh/kg, but has a relatively narrow power range. This platform is used in applications that need operation times of many hours, such as day/night cycles or long mission applications. A porosity optimized high loading structure resulted in cells with a specific energy of over 400 Wh/kg and specific power of 1000 W/kg. This power-and-energy platform is used in long endurance drones and eVTOL applications where target endurance exceeds one hour.

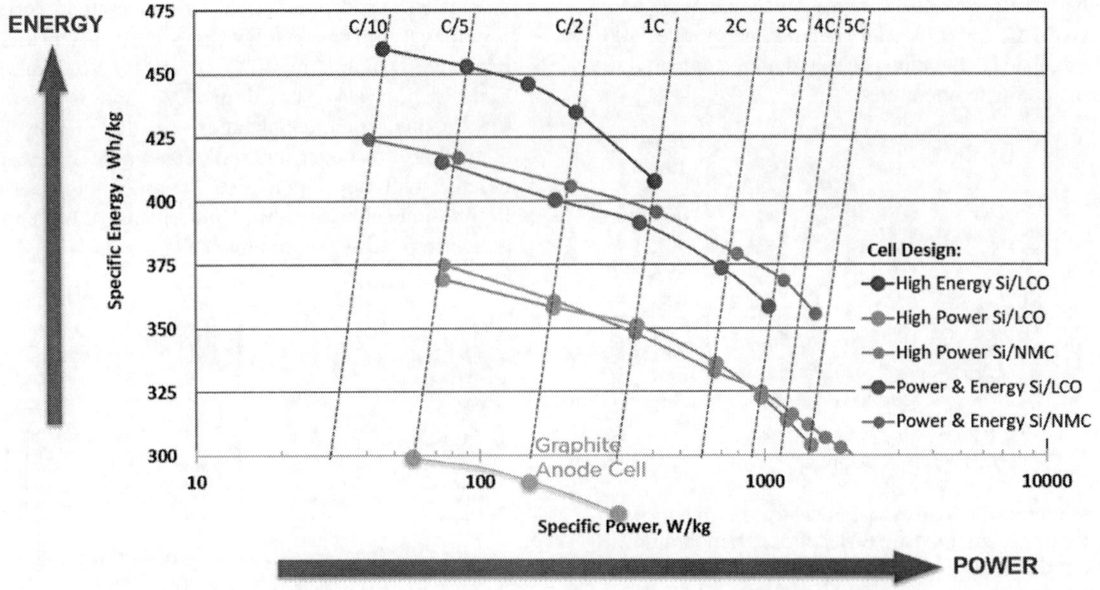

Figure 4. Amprius has developed three power-energy platforms by matching silicon nanowire anode with Lithium Cobalt Oxide (LCO) and Nickel Manganese Cobalt (NMC) cathodes with different loadings.

When matched with a high-power, thin cathode, the cells still have over 350 Wh/kg specific energy and can support 3000 W/kg of continuous power load. This power platform is used for applications that require very high specific power, such as load carrying power drones, and typically doubles the running times compared to graphite cells. In most high-power applications, the limits are usually the cell body temperature and the thermal management of the battery.

Cycle Life: The silicon nanowire anodes can cycle for hundreds of cycles in full cells due to limited swell at the material and cell level, and stable material and electrode structure. The stability of the material and partial utilization of the theoretical capacity of silicon also limits lithium consumption for SEI repair and, thus, extends the cycle life to numbers approaching those of graphite cells. In real applications, when cells are not fully discharged, cycle life exceeds 1000 cycles (Figure 5).

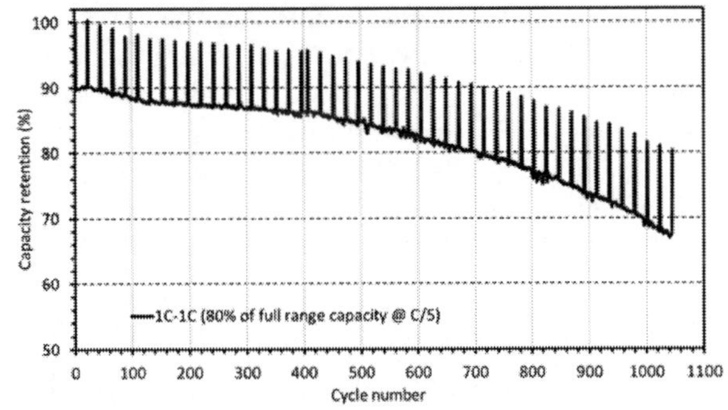

Figure 5. 1C/-1C cycling with 80% depth of discharge and +0.2C/-0.2C capacity check every 20 cycles.

Extreme Fast Charge: As shown in Figure 2, the silicon nanowire anode has a low diffusion distance (thin electrode), low tortuosity structure (straight pores), and short electric path to current collector (all silicon is "metallurgically" connected to the foil). These properties have led to cells products that have demonstrated 5-minute charge (Extreme Fast Charge, XFC) capability in cells with 360 Wh/kg specific energy (see Figure 6). Thus, additional capabilities that are only possible with silicon anode are available for deployment.

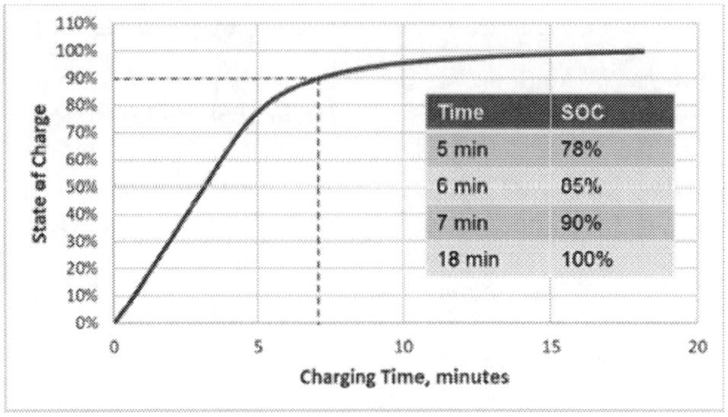

Figure 6. 1C/-1C cycling with 80% depth of discharge and +0.2C/-0.2C capacity check every 20 cycles.

Low Temperature: Silicon also has intrinsically better capability at low temperatures, due to its slightly higher operating voltage than graphite. For example, Amprius cells operate down to -30°C without low temperature optimized electrolytes and can operate even at -50°C with low freezing point electrolyte formulations. Similarly, the high temperature limit can be tailored by electrolyte formulation to meet targets. Cell data shown in Figure 7 indicates that about 80% of the energy available at 20°C is available at -20°C, for cells with specific energy over 400 Wh/kg. This capacity retention is about double compared to graphite cells at low temperatures.

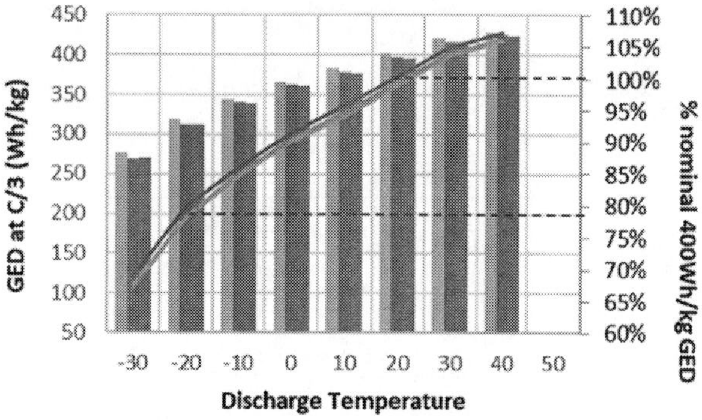

Figure 7. Amprius' 400 Wh/kg silicon cells perform very well at low temperatures, retaining 80% of room temperature performance at -20°C. The figure shows the retained specific energy of three cells between -30°C and 50°C).

Safety: Silicon nanowire cells developed in the last few years were successfully tested in multiple abuse and safety evaluation conditions, including electrical, mechanical, and thermal factors. For example, 5.4Ah pouch cells with silicon nanowire anode and LCO cathode were certified to pass the tests required for air cargo shipping, according to UN 38.3 specifications. Amprius has developed a gel polymer electrolyte formulation that insulates penetrating objects, such as nails, preventing thermal runaway. Separately, silicon nanowire cells passed other abuse and safety tests, including hot box at 130°C and overcharge by 150% charge capacity. These results suggest that there is little argument to support the assumption that silicon materials are inherently less safe than graphite anodes.

Products: Amprius has developed cells in multiple sizes, from 200mAh capacity for wearable applications to 45Ah for electric vehicles. Cells of 5.4Ah capacity were built into battery packs for drone applications by primary defense contractors, setting records of endurance in multi-rotor flight. In smaller form factors, Amprius is currently performing on a contract with Army's RCCTO office to develop a battery for the nano-UAS drones and has demonstrated an increase in flight endurance of over 60%. Pouch cells can be customized in different form factors with relative ease, and Amprius has experience in prototyping and developing such cells. Moreover, the silicon chemistry platform can be used as developed or with small optimization changes in multiple cell form factors. The cell pictures shown in Figure 8 illustrate the variety of designs in different cell form factors and stages of production.

Manufacturing: The complete set of manufacturing processes was integrated by 2016 into a continuous roll-to-roll pilot scale anode fabrication line. Two pilot lines and associated cell production are operated currently in Fremont, California, with expansion to a ten times larger capacity available in 2023. A 500MWh manufacturing scale project also started in 2023 and is the next step toward the commercialization of the silicon nanowire technology for larger markets. Customers in aerospace and defense will be able to use Amprius' high-performance lithium-ion cells to the full requirements of these markets at prices competitive to graphite cells.

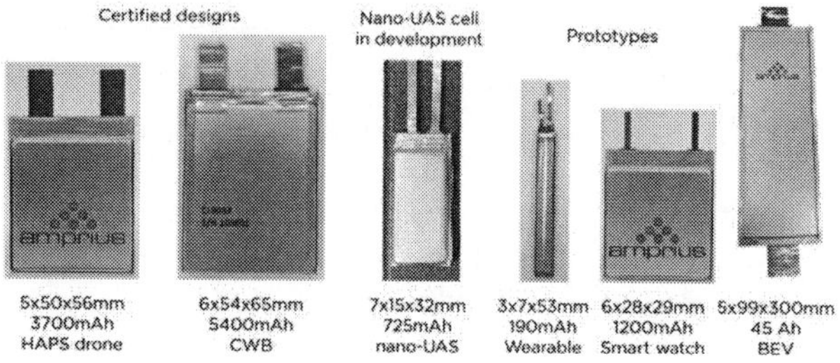

Figure 8. Multiple designs were developed with Amprius' silicon anode chemistry.

Summary and Conclusions

Silicon is recognized as one of the most promising materials for next generation lithium-ion battery anode to replace the conventional carbon-based anode due to its high theoretical capacity, similar discharge potential and reliable operation safety. However, in most silicon material structures and compositions, the critical drawback of huge volume expansion upon lithiation causes series of adverse consequences, leading to very poor cyclic stability.

The rooted silicon nanowire structure developed by Amprius has largely mitigated the drawbacks that afflict other silicon materials and has led to the development of lithium-ion pouch cells with energy and power performance significantly above those of commercial state of the art graphite anode cells, in most cases by 50-100% improvement. Moreover, the cycle life of these cells is closing in on graphite cell performance, already meeting the requirements of a variety of markets. Some of the silicon nanowire cell products have already been qualified for applications, including safety and abuse tolerance validation. In general, the development of the first silicon nanowire products has shown that the safety and abuse tolerance of silicon nanowire cells can be as good or better than that of similar graphite cells. It is expected that, in parallel with an increase in manufacturing capability and capacity, the application scope of silicon nanowire cells will expand from premium and mission critical markets to consumer and commercial application in the next few years.

Acknowledgements

Amprius wishes to acknowledge the funding received from US Army (W56KGU-18-C-0025/STEP-EGS), DOE (EE0010224) and USABC (DE-EE0006250).

The Quest for a Better Battery Model

John B. Olson
Jolson Technologies LLC
Boulder, CO 80305
john@jolsontechnologies.com

Abstract

Batteries are a key component of the smart grid also described as the internet of things (IoT). The military has a decidedly greater need for digital information on not only batteries but all key components of its military equipment. It is not surprising that these demands for increased high fidelity battery information might be benefitted by using artificial intelligence algorithms.

Jolson Technologies is developing battery models based on neural networks that provide two key metrics, namely a state of charge (SOC, fuel gauge) and a state of health (SOH, life gauge). We will show how both these fundamental values are dependent on the determination of the end of discharge charge capacity. The focus on charge capacity is most important in motive power or cycling applications (EVs and others), where the battery capacity is paramount. Perhaps more generally, we will describe an approach to battery models that is perhaps "anti-Google".

Keywords

battery management; neural network model; artificial intelligence; state of charge; state of health; diagnostic

Introduction

The 'Smart Grid' and 'Internet of Things' are related concepts of creating a better electrical grid with the use of digital communications and control technology. It has many potential benefits including: grid energy efficiency, regulation and cost savings. It is a concept that has been widely embraced by industry, but slow to deploy. Batteries are a key component since they must be connected to an electrical grid for charging and they represent a significant resource of stored electrical power. Accurate models for batteries are a key need for the use of batteries in the smart grid [1, 2].

The military is also involved in developing its version of the smart grid, not only for batteries but for all their military equipment. Since logistics are often the hidden factor that portends the success of military objectives, the motivations are clear.

The smart grid depends on information. What is the information needed from batteries? Certainly, the ability to deliver stored energy and their amounts is key. The need for charging and when are also key. Some of this information involves the user and some of it is based on the state of the battery. It is the battery states rather than user demands that are the focus here.

The state parameters common to all rechargeable batteries are: state of charge (SOC), state of power (SOP) and state of health (SOH). SOC is generally the fuel gauge, most important for cycling applications. SOP is important for applications where power is more important than capacity. An example is hybrid electric applications where the battery is used for surges in electrical demand allowing for a lower power prime mover. SOH is a life gauge which tracks the degradation of the battery as it ages. SOH might have SOC and/or SOP as key metrics depending on the application.

The battery applications are important, since different applications have different ways of operating the batteries. The major battery applications include: engine starting, back-up power, motive power and portable electronics. While there are certainly overlaps in these broad categories, it is the way the batteries are charged that creates the differences in these applications. Motive power applications are also known as cycling applications where the battery is discharged, usually followed by a full charge. For back-up power applications, the batteries typically remain on charge (float charge) except for power outages where they are discharged and then recharged back to float charge. Engine starting is a hybrid of these applications, where the first battery task is starting the engine and then the battery is recharged and float charged as long as the vehicle is running. Our focus is on motive or cycling applications where the primary battery parameters are energy and charge capacity. The decline in capacity due to degradation over life is the primary consideration in increasing the accuracy of battery monitors for cycling applications.

We are all told by the technology companies that calculating data in the cloud represents the end goal for IoT applications. Most accept this without question. However, if SOC and SOH can be computed at the battery rather than in the cloud (which really means a remote computer), then the amount of data transmitted can be reduced by 4 orders of magnitude as represented in Figure 1.

Cloud based solutions make sense for some applications, but perhaps not all. While transmitting massive amounts of data is clearly in the interest of the technology companies, for the companies and individuals this transmission of data is an expense that is best minimized. This efficiency is probably more critical in the military.

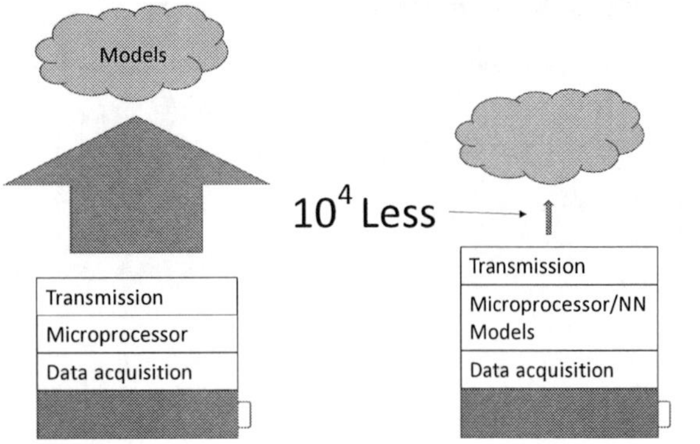

Figure 1. Two scenarios for computing battery data. On the left, all data is transmitted to the cloud where calculations are done. On the right, calculations are done at the battery with NN models thus reducing data transmission by a factor of 10^4.

State of Charge

Most would consider current integration or Ah counting to be the state of the art for determining battery capacity and many might question why improvements are needed. We will first relate an anecdote that most should recognize and then describe the underlying factors.

Most of us have had a cell phone battery go bad. When the phone battery is new the Ah counting works well with the SOC gauge counting down from 100% to low values prior to the phone shutting off. However, after the phone battery has aged, the SOC gauge seems to count down at the same rate as usual, but when reaching a SOC of perhaps 50% the phone shuts down. This scenario continues with the SOC increasing at the point of shut down until we replace the battery or phone. This is a failure of the Ah counting SOC model. After the battery capacity degrades significantly, the gauges yield no real information for when the phone will shut off. Ideally, we want a SOC gauge that goes from 100% to near 0% and then shuts down, at any time over the battery life. After some capacity loss, this will also make the 'count-down' go faster which will again be accurate to the condition of the battery and useful information to the user.

Ah counting will only determine the Ah discharged (and does so with excellent accuracy), but to determine the SOC you also need to know the full discharge capacity. This is shown by the equation for SOC

$$SOC = (1 - AhD / AhCap) * 100 \quad (1)$$

where AhD is the Ah discharged determined by Ah counting and AhCap is the battery capacity in Ah. As mentioned, the AhCap can change over life due to degradation but can also change from discharge to discharge and with temperature and Peukert effects (changing capacity with discharge rate). In other words, it normally has some variation.

So for the cell phone anecdote, the programmed AhCap was set to the new battery capacity. When new, the battery capacity matched the programmed AhCap and the SOC gauge worked well. However, after the battery aged and the battery capacity declined we have the phone shutting off at a higher SOC. For example, at a 50% loss of capacity the battery shuts off at 50% SOC, an error of 50%.

If the programmed AhCap is changed over life to match the actual battery capacity, the SOC gauge will work ideally. So what is needed is a way to measure or calculate the AhCap. The difficulty of this simple task is demonstrated by the lack of commonly available accurate SOC and SOH battery monitors.

AhCap is certainly easy to determine if we discharge the battery fully, and record the AhD at the end of discharge. However, doing this every cycle is a constraint that would be unacceptable to users and in some applications like hybrids, never attained. This means that the AhCap must be determined prior to the end of discharge, a demand that requires accurate prediction of the future.

The easiest next step of improvement would be to implement a changing AhCap over life. For an application that has a static use profile, this is possible and has been used to 'fix' the problem in sophisticated systems (like EVs). But most battery applications don't have a static use profile, in reality far from it. So a better battery SOC monitor is needed.

State of Health

The SOH metric can be defined in many ways, but capacity decline and/or power decline (internal resistance increase) are the most applicable. For motive applications, the SOH can simply be based on the battery capacity, as shown in this equation for SOH

$$SOH = (1 - (AhCap - AhE) / (AhN - AhE)) * 100 \quad (2)$$

where AhCap is still the battery capacity in Ah, AhN is the Ah capacity of a new battery (a constant) and AhE is the end of life Ah capacity. For SOH, the required metric is the same value required for SOC, namely the AhCap.

So the AhCap is the single most important parameter in the determination of both SOC and SOH, buts its determination remains elusive.

We have been working on using neural network (NN) models to advance the state of the art in battery modeling. NN models are one of the first and most widely used techniques that have become known as artificial intelligence. They are a member of learning or trained algorithms which use data to create the models. Once created, the result is just one multiple input equation ideal for performing repetitive calculations on large data sets. The ability to calculate large data sets, which is common knowledge, is based on the models' fast calculation abilities. But they can also be used on small data sets generated in a time series, as is the case with battery data. In addition, due to the low calculation overhead required, the model code can easily fit in the programming space of any battery specific integrated circuit with an integrated microprocessor.

At a fundamental level, NN models are trained by minimizing the total errors (difference between model results and the 'answers' of the training data). Better models have lower average errors than poor models. In effect, the models are pattern recognizing. The patterns are the correlations in the training data set. For battery modeling, if the training data set represents all the battery states over life, the resulting models will reflect that. These models could be aptly called battery life models. This is quite different from most battery models, which model the battery or component in some singular state.

Our training data is derived from laboratory cycle life data. In operation, the models calculate in real time using input data derived from battery raw data, namely current, voltage and temperature. We typically collect data at 1 s intervals, which is adequate to capture the variability of most battery behavior. Not all this data is used, since we have developed selection criteria for the raw data. However, if we had to transmit all this data to the cloud (assuming 6 inputs and 4 bytes per input) we would transmit over 2 MB of data per battery per day. With NN models we might transmit 200 bytes of data a day. This is a factor of 10,000 in data reduction with no loss in information. This is perhaps the greatest attribute of these models after their accuracy.

Model Validation – Field Test

We will now describe field testing of our modeling technology using VRLA (gel) wheelchair batteries. We worked with a major manufacturer of powered wheelchairs to install data acquisition and model calculations over the life of a set of wheelchair batteries. This data was supplemented with laboratory cycle life data on two additional batteries.

The data acquisition consisted of current, voltage, temperature, Ah depletion (Ah counting) and a Unix time stamp. Data was stored locally on the chair and periodically collected manually. In addition, we performed periodic laboratory testing on the field test batteries to determine their capacity and power over life.

Figure 2 shows the cycle life plot of Ah capacity versus discharge Ah throughput for the field test and two lab cycled batteries. Immediately recognizable is the dramatic difference in Ah throughput for the three batteries. This is an indication, at least for the batteries tested, of the cycle life extension possible with laboratory cycling versus actual field use. The laboratory batteries were cycled with two different charge regimes, differing in the amount of finish charge delivered. Battery B used a charge algorithm analogous to that used normally with the wheelchair and battery A used a more aggressive finish charge. The batteries also differ somewhat in initial capacity likely attributable to manufacturing variations. The combination of significantly different cycle lives and capacities presented a true test for our NN modeling technology.

Figure 3 shows the results of SOC modeling versus measured SOC for the field data batteries. The data consisted

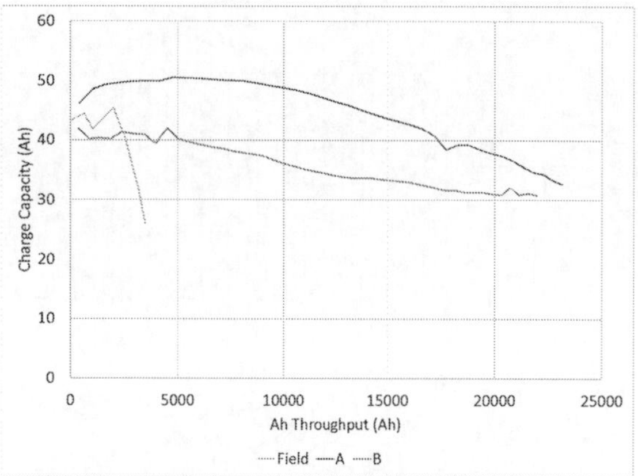

Figure 2. Cycle life profiles for Field test and the two laboratory cycled batteries.

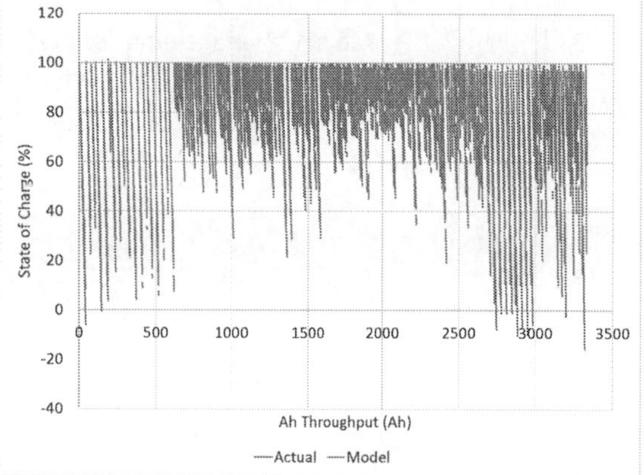

Figure 3. Model results for SOC versus actual values for field test battery.

of both full discharges (user was asked to discharge over several days to end of discharge) and partial discharges reflecting actual use patterns (middle of life).

Figures 4 & 5 show the corresponding results for the laboratory cycled data.

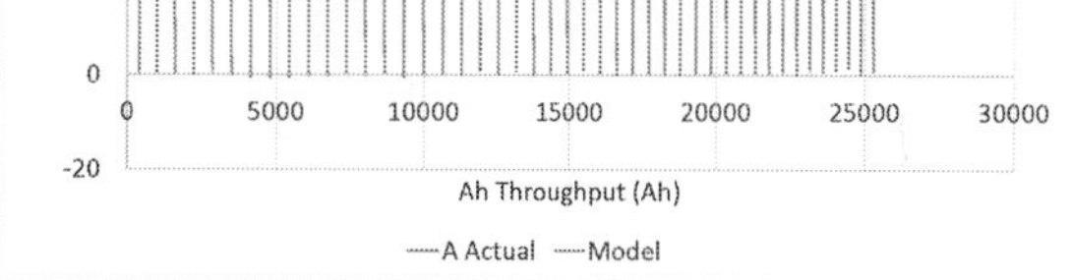

Figure 4. Model results for SOC versus actual values for lab battery A.

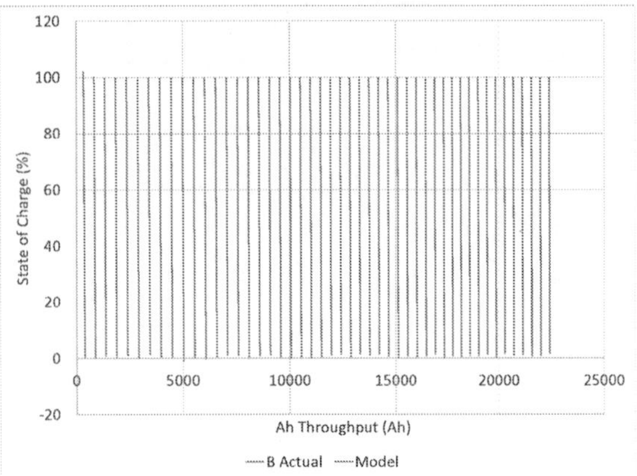

Figure 5. Model results for SOC versus actual values for lab battery B.

Here all discharges were full discharges. The average errors are shown in Table 1. The average errors for all three batteries were similar, at about 5%.

Table 1. Average error for SOC for the three test batteries.

Battery	Average Error (%)
Field	5.1
A	4.1
B	5.3

Figure 6 shows the SOH results plotted versus Ah throughput.

While calculating average error using linear Ah Throughput is possible, it appears the SOH is to a large degree reflecting the AhCap data in Figure 2. The key goal of differentiating the different cycle lives done with the model has been achieved, despite large variations in Ah Throughput and AhCap over the lives of the test batteries.

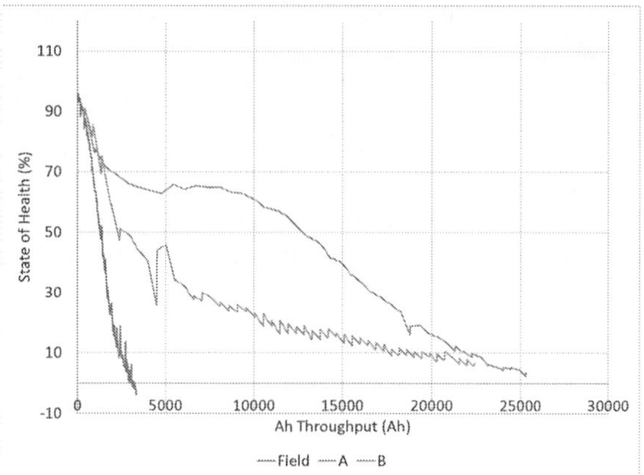

Figure 6. Model results for SOH for the three test batteries.

Acknowledgments

This paper is based upon work fully funded by Jolson Technologies LLC. Any opinions, findings and conclusions or recommendations expressed in this material are those of the author and do not necessarily reflect the views of the US DoD.

References

1. Olson, J., Heinzel, J., "Neural Network Models for Battery Management Systems" *Proceedings of the 46th Power Sources Conference,* Paper #33.4, Orlando, FL, June 9-12, 2014.

2. Olson, J. "Neural Network Models Using Multiple Indicators for State of Charge and State of Health", *Proceedings of the 47th Power Sources Conference,* Paper 22.3, Orlando, FL, June 2016.

ALE Nail-Penetration Safe 2Ah Si Li-ion Prismatic Cell for Conformal Wearable Battery

Linhua Hu, William Michael Hadala JR, and Jiang Fan

American Lithium Energy Corporation
2261 Rutherford Road, Carlsbad, CA 92008
lhhu@americanlithiumenergy.com / 1-760-599-7388

Abstract

ALE has developed a nail-penetration safe and UN38.3 certified 2Ah Li-ion prismatic cell (34 mm wide and 50 mm height and 6.5mm thick) using Si negative electrode for the application in U.S. Army conformal wearable battery (CWB). Compared with same sized commercial graphite cell, ALE's 2Ah Si prismatic cell shows >60% higher capacity. The cells passed not only nail penetration at 100% State of Charge (SOC) but also all UN38.3 tests including altitude simulation, thermal, vibration, shock, external short circuit, impact, overcharge, and forced discharge. The cells also showed good cycle life and demonstrated approximately ~90% capacity retention after 100 cycles at 100% Depth of Discharge (DOD). The results will be discussed with our production schedule and the future improvement road map.

Keywords

Conformal Wearable Battery; CWB; 2Ah Prismatic Si Li-ion Cell; SafeCore, Safety; Penetration; UN38.3; Soldier; Thermal Runaway.

Introduction

The conformal wearable battery, CWB, has become increasingly important for soldiers, particularly in modern warfare, where the use of technology has become more widespread. These wearable batteries provide power to a range of wearable devices used by soldiers, including communication devices, GPS systems, night vision devices, and sensors, among others.

The primary benefit of conformal wearable batteries for soldiers is their lightweight and flexible design. Conformal batteries are lightweight and can be easily integrated into wearable technology, reducing the overall weight burden on the soldiers. Additionally, the flexibility of the battery allows it to conform to the shape of the wearable technology, making it more comfortable to wear and reducing the risk of damage to the battery.

One of the challenges of using conformal wearable batteries in the military is the limited capacity. Conformal batteries have a smaller capacity compared to traditional batteries, which can limit their usefulness in military operations. Soldiers rely heavily on their wearable technology to carry out their duties effectively, and the limited capacity of conformal batteries can lead to devices running out of power quickly, compromising the success of a mission. The current available conformal wearable batteries have energies of 150Wh (8S4P) with nominal capacity 10Ah and nominal voltage 14.8V (reference 1). The single graphite cell capacity is 1.25Ah. Therefore, larger capacity Li-ion cells for CWB are highly demanded.

Safety is another challenge of using conformal wearable batteries in the military. Li-ion cells contain a flammable electrolyte and a highly reactive lithium-based cathode material. If the cell is damaged or exposed to extreme or abuse conditions, such as overcharging, impact, or bullet penetration , nail, puncture, it can result in a thermal runaway reaction, leading to a fire or explosion.

Thermal runaway in single cell level would cause chain reactions and whole battery pack failure, resulting in catastrophic effect in electric vehicles or energy storage devices. It's widely accepted that most cases are caused by mechanical, electrical, or thermal abuses, and all these abuses would cause short circuit in cell, which finally lead to thermal runaway. Figure 1a depicts the temperature change during the three stages from initiate minor internal short circuit to SEI decomposition, separator melting, cathode decomposition, electrolyte oxidation, and finally thermal runaway. The solution of thermal runaway needs to interrupt the internal short and limit the accumulation of Joule heating, and subsequent positive feedback loop reactions.

ALE has developed SafeCore® technology in the assembly of electrodes (figure 1b and 1c), i.e., insert a resistive layer between either two layers of separator and cathode layer, separator and anode layer, cathode layer and cathode current collector, anode layer and anode current collector. In the case of abuse conditions, the short circuit will be interrupted by the decomposition of the resistive layer triggered by the set voltage, current, or temperature. Furthermore, The resistive layer doesn't change the normal cell performance.

ALE has developed a 2Ah Li-ion Si prismatic cell, >60% higher capacity than the current 1.25Ah graphite cell. The cell is nail-penetration safe and passed all UN38.3 tests based on SafeCore® technology for conformal wearable batteries. The width, height, and thickness of the cell is 34mm, 50mm, and 6.5mm, respectively. The active compositions are high nickel NMC for positive electrodes and nano Si for negative electrodes. The specific energy of ALE's 2Ah Si prismatic cell is ~260 Wh/kg.

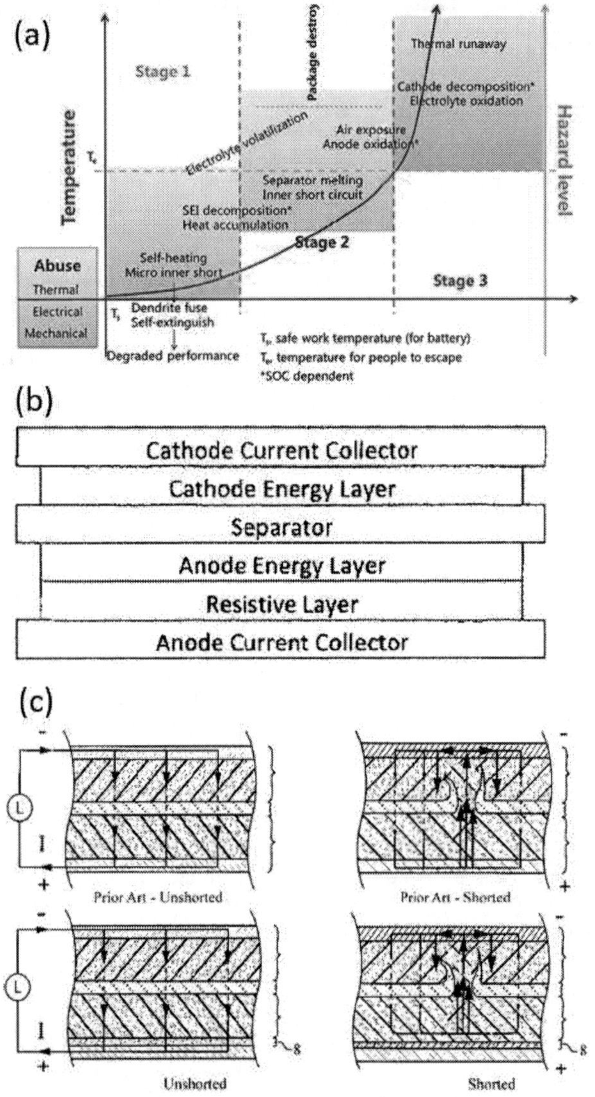

Figure 1. (a) Three stages in battery TR, Ts, safe work temperature (for battery); Te, temperature for people to escape; *SOC dependent, reproduced from reference 2;(b) the cross view of electrode of Li-ion batteries with a resistive layer (c) Four scenario of current flow of film-type Li-ion batteries between unshorted and shorted, and without and with a resistive layer between, reproduced from reference 3.

ALE 2Ah CWB Cell Performance

As shown in Figure 2, ALE 2Ah CWB cells have been evaluated for their cycle life at C/5 rate (0.4A, clamped) and at C/2 rate (1A, no clamp). The capacity of the 1st cycle is 2Ah, and of the 300th cycle is 1.74Ah, thus the capacity retention is 87% at C/5 rate (Figure 3a, 3b). The capacity of the 1st cycle is 1.84Ah, and of the 100th cycle is 1.68Ah, thus the capacity retention is 91.3% at C/2 rate. Therefore, the energy in an 8S4P CWB is 224Wh with nominal capacity 16Ah and nominal voltage 14V.

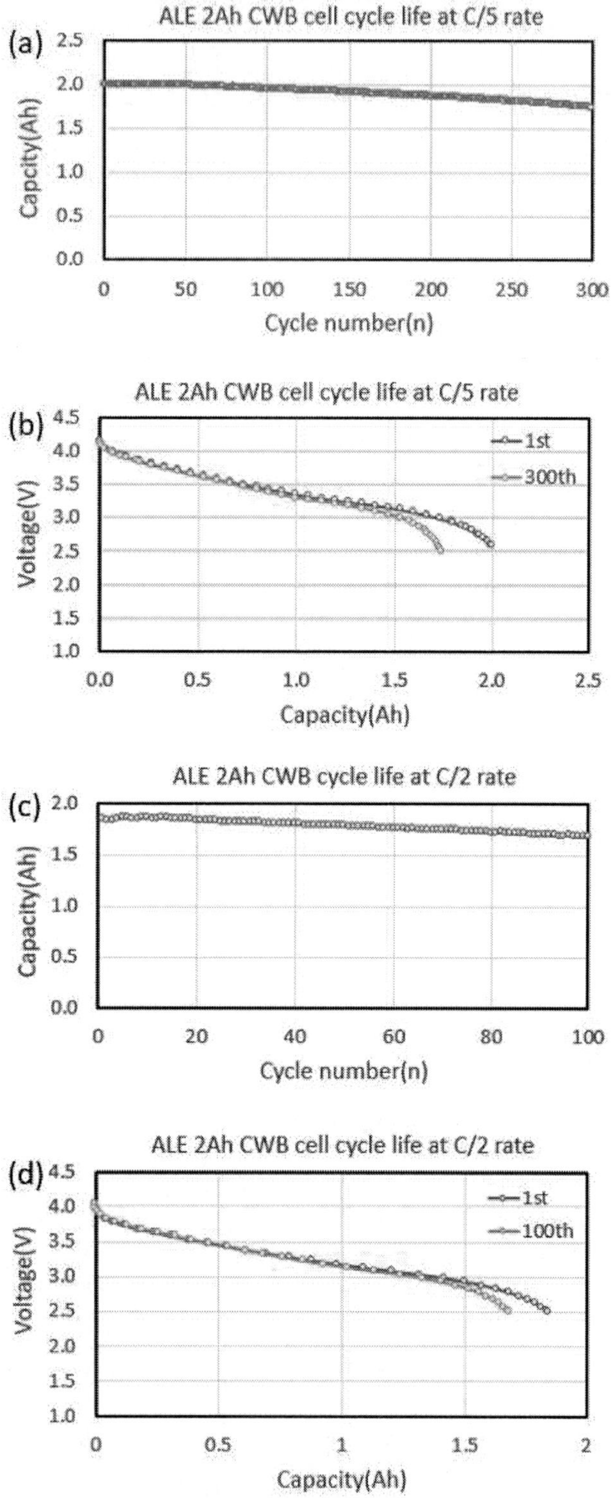

Figure 2. ALE 2Ah CWB cell cycle life (a) discharge capacity at 0.4A vs cycle number profile (b) voltage-capacity at 0.4A profile at different cycle numbers (c) discharge capacity at 1A vs cycle number profile (d) voltage-capacity at 1A profile at different cycle numbers

Nail Penetration

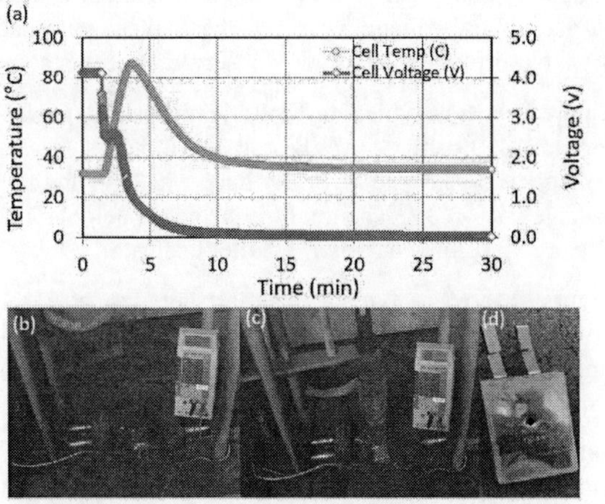

Figure 3. (a) Temperature and voltage observed on 2Ah Li-ion CWB cell during nail test (b) voltage before nail (c) voltage during nail (d) cell image after nail.

Figure 3 shows a typical nail test of 2Ah Li-ion CWB cell. The cell was first put in a chamber, positive and negative tabs were connected to a voltage meter to monitor voltage change, and a thermocouple was attached on the surface of the cell. The cell OCV reading was 4.13V for two-minute rest time before being penetrated by a 3 mm diameter nail for 30 minutes. Figure 3a shows the voltage and temperature change during the test. The voltage drops from 4.13V to 2.5V in the first 3 minutes, and slightly back a while and slowly drops to 0V in the remaining test time. No fire, smoke or explosion was observed.

Mechanical Abuse Test

Figure 4 shows the two different groups that underwent impact tests (T6 in UN38.3), Group A cycled 1 time and group B cycled 25 times. The voltage immediately drops to 0V from 3.4V after impact, with the temperature increasing from room temperature to 50~70 °C. The cells were severely distorted, but no leaks, fire, or explosion was observed. Table 1 summarizes the detailed values for weight and voltage before and after the test.

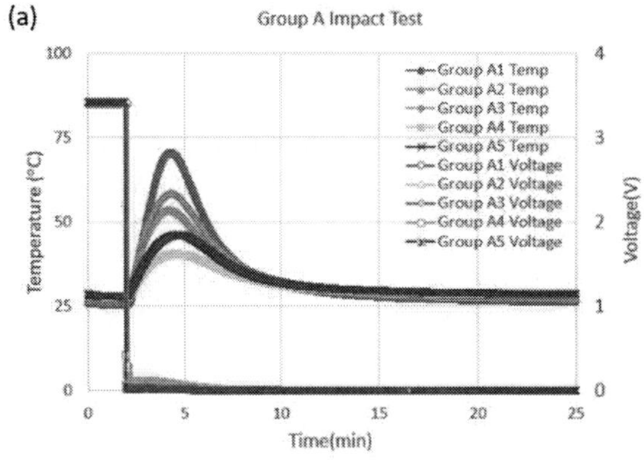

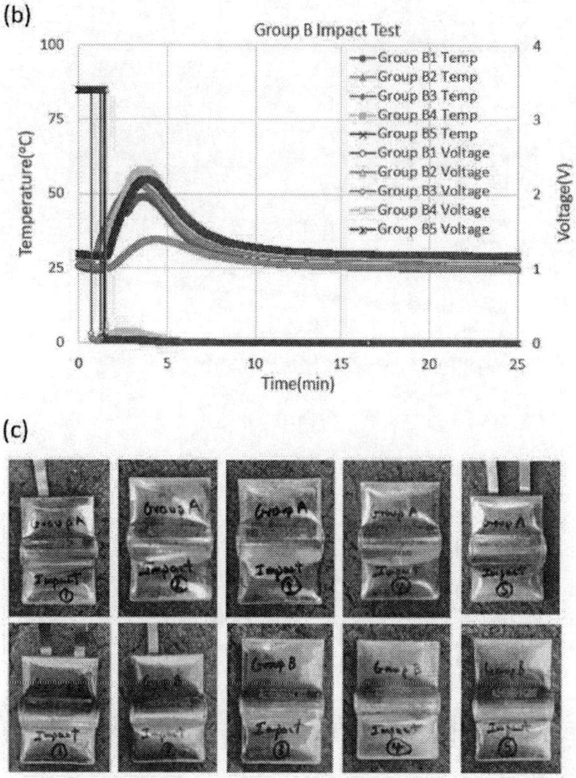

Figure 4. (a) Group A impact test with temperature and voltage recorded (b) group B impact test with temperature and voltage recorded (c) Cell images after impact test

Table 1 Impact test for 10 cells for before test (B.T.) and after test (A.T.)

S/N	A1	A2	A3	A4	A5
Weight B.T.(g)	26.82	26.68	26.92	27.20	26.70
Voltage B.T.(V)	3.406	3.418	3.416	3.410	3.419
Weight A.T.(g)	26.82	26.68	26.92	27.20	26.70
Voltage A.T.(V)	0.006	0.003	0.005	0.002	0.001
Max. Temp. (°C)	70.5	53.6	58.4	40.4	46.2
S/N	B1	B2	B3	B4	B5
Weight B.T.(g)	26.86	26.95	26.92	26.80	26.89
Voltage B.T.(V)	3.415	3.410	3.426	3.423	3.418
Weight A.T.(g)	26.86	26.96	26.92	26.80	26.89
Voltage A. T.(V)	0.003	0.002	0.008	0.007	0.003
Max. Temp. (°C)	49.1	34.8	53.3	58.1	54.9

Electrical Abuse Tests

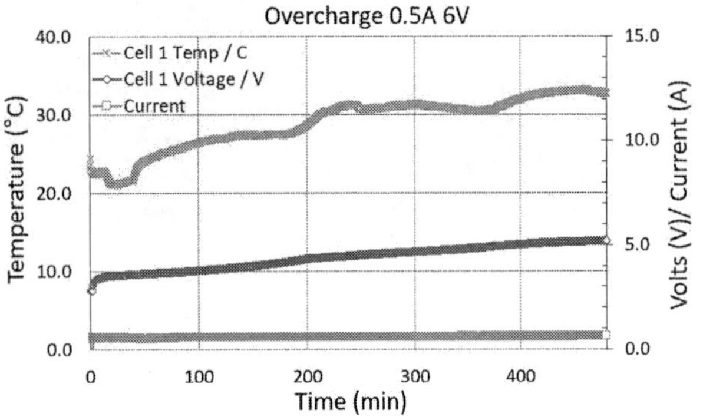

Figure 5. A typical overcharge test at 0.5A 6V for 8 hours

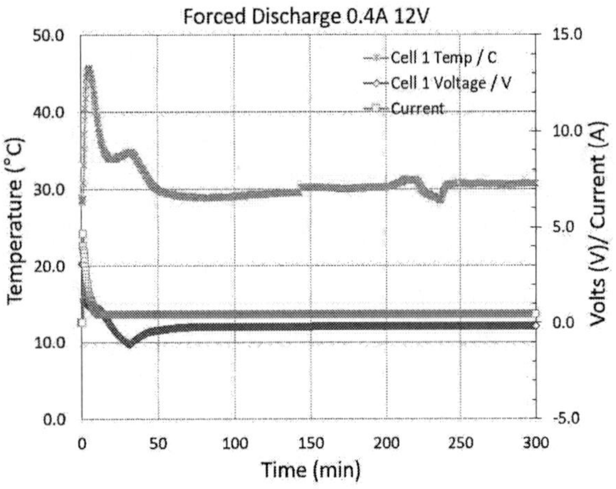

Figure 6. A typical force discharge at 0.4A 12V

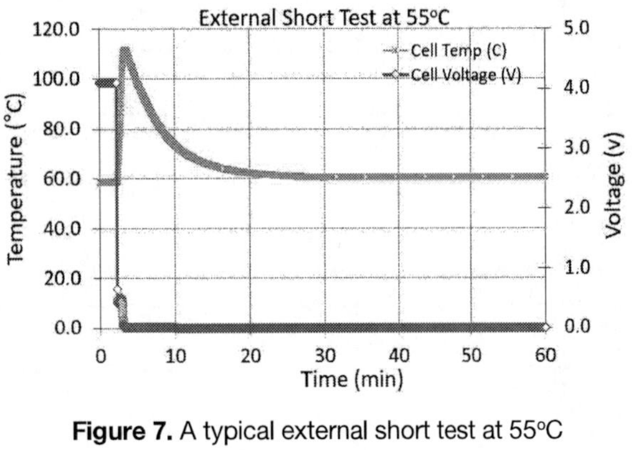

Figure 7. A typical external short test at 55°C

Figure 5 shows a typical overcharge test (T7 in UN 38.3) for 2Ah prismatic CWB cell for 8 hours. The initial voltage was ~3V, and final voltage was 5.2V, the total charge capacity is 4Ah. No fire or explosion was observed after the test.

Figure 6 shows a typical force discharge test (T8 in UN 38.3) for a 2Ah prismatic CWB cell for 6 hours. The initial voltage was ~3V, the lowest voltage was -1V, and the final voltage was -0.2V. The total discharge capacity is 2Ah. No fire or explosion was observed after the test.

Figure 7 shows a typical external short test at 55°C. The voltage fast drops to 0V after external short with the immediate temperature increase up to 110 °C. No fire or explosion was observed after the test.

Other abuse tests T1-T5, altitude simulation, thermal, vibration, shock, external short circuit, have been tested in different cells and packs by Bren-Tronics, Inc. They all passed UN 38.3 tests.

In summary, 2Ah prismatic Si Li-ion cells have been developed for CWB, with high safety passing nail penetration, and certified with all UN 38.3 tests for safe transport. Although the energy density has been increased to ~260Wh/kg, it still needs to be improved at least 25%, ~325Wh/kg, i.e., 2.5Ah in the same cell size. This will require extremely stable positive electrodes or materials, or the non-flammable electrolyte which might suppress the decomposition of high nickel compounds at fully charged state and subsequent thermal runaway.

Acknowledgements

The authors gratefully acknowledge lab tests from Bren-Tronics, Inc. and thank Steven Chew, David Shoemaker, Julianne Douglas for research guidance and helpful discussion.

References

1. https://www.c5isr.ccdc.army.mil/news_and_media/Conformal_Wearable_Battery/
2. Wu, X., Song K., Zhang X., et al. "Safety Issues in Lithium-Ion Batteries: Materials and Cell Design", *Frontiers in Energy Research*, Vol 7, Article 65, pp. 1-17, 2019.
3. Fan, J., Wu, D. "Rechargeable Battery with Resistive Layer for Enhanced Safety". *US patent*, 10,020,545 B2, pp.1-30, 2018.
4. "UN Recommendations on the Transport of Dangerous Goods", *Manual of Test and Criteria*, 7th Revised Edition. United Nations, New York and Geneva, pp. 415-434, 2019.

Testing of Commercially Available USB-Rechargeable Single-Cell Batteries to Inform Military Applications

Calvin Y. Duong
C5ISR Center
U.S. Army Combat Capabilities Development Command
Aberdeen Proving Ground, MD, USA, 21005
calvin.y.duong.civ@army.mil

Abstract

Single-cell batteries that can be recharged through a Universal Serial Bus (USB) connector are commercially available in the same form factors as AA, CR123, 18650, and 21700 cells. Forty brands of these batteries were purchased and studied to inform development of a militarized version, known as the Operational Single-Cell for Accessory Readiness (OSCAR) battery for increased safety, reduced weight burden, and simpler logistics compared to loose cells. This paper presents the results of cycle testing and other observations about the batteries, such as USB connector location, overcurrent protection, overdischarge protection, and identical designs. No destructive testing was performed. Due to page limitations, only the AA batteries will be discussed in this paper.

Keywords

USB; rechargeable; single cell; batteries; cycle testing

Introduction

For military applications, switching to rechargeable batteries would simplify logistics because the same batteries could be recharged and reused, unlike primary cells which need to be constantly resupplied after they are used. Discarded primary cells contain a significant amount of energy most of the time, which is a waste of energy. With rechargeables, leftover energy could be stored and used after the next recharge. Loose cells have a safety risk of being short circuited without protection whereas a proper battery would have a battery management system (BMS) to protect itself from faults.

Because of the possible benefits of single-cell rechargeable batteries, a military version is being developed, known as OSCAR. To learn what goals and metrics OSCAR should meet, a market survey was performed. The study specifically focused on USB-rechargeable batteries because of the interoperability and ease of charging that USB enables. Among the metrics studied were energy capacity, USB connector type and position, and state of charge indicator. Further details are described in the next section.

Methods

Commercial off-the-shelf (COTS) batteries were purchased from Amazon and a few other websites in 2021 (Figure 1). As many brands as possible were purchased for this study.

Figure 1. Boxes of some COTS USB-rechargeable single-cell batteries that were purchased for the study.

To automate the cycling of these batteries, a test stand was built. It can simultaneously cycle up to six cylindrical batteries that can be recharged through a USB connector. It consists of:

- One (1) USB hub to charge batteries (Figure 2)
- Six (6) e-loads to discharge batteries (Figure 2)
- Six (6) thermocouples to monitor temperature (Figure 2)
- A box to facilitate cable connections and hold up to six (6) batteries (Figure 3)

Figure 2. Part of the test stand used for this study. Includes the e-loads, USB hub, and thermocouple reader.

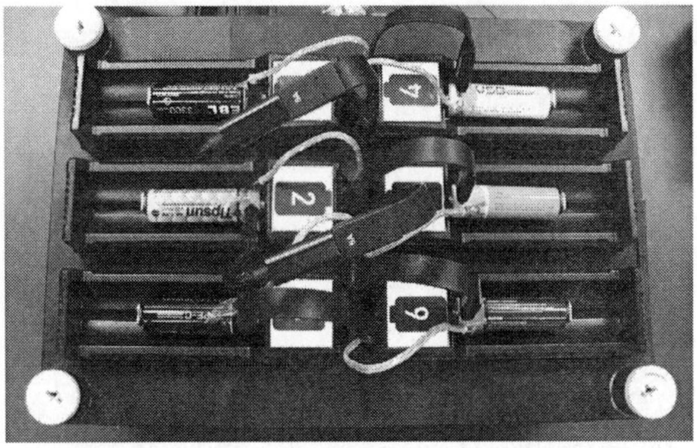

Figure 3. The box that held the batteries that were tested.

Voltage and current are continuously measured through the USB hub and e-loads. Everything is controlled with LabVIEW.

One battery of each brand was cycled with the OSCAR test stand. Primary cells were also discharged for comparison with rechargeable batteries but only for the AA and CR123 sizes.

To go through all brands quickly throughout 2022, each battery was cycled for **up to 10 cycles**. (Primary cells could only be discharged once. Technical difficulties with the OSCAR test stand reduced the planned number of cycles for some brands.) All charges were subject to the battery's battery management system (BMS). That is, 5 V was provided to the batteries, as per the USB standard, while the current was controlled by the BMS. All discharges were at a **constant power of 0.5 W**. The Watt-hour results that are shown in Table 1 are **averaged across all cycles**. There was a five-minute rest period between charges and discharges.

Results

For cycling results, see Table 1 on the next page.

Discussion – Cycling

Energy Capacity: **Almost all batteries have less energy capacity (Wh) than advertised** when discharged at a constant power of 0.5 W. (See all the red or negative signs in the Difference Wh column of Table 1.) Primary cells also had lower capacity than advertised, but their datasheets explained that the capacities were obtained from a constant current discharge of 100 mA [1][2]. The difference in capacities can be explained by the different discharge conditions. For the rechargeable batteries, it is unclear under what conditions they derived the capacities that were advertised.

Rechargeable Capacity vs. Primary Capacity: As of 2022, **COTS USB-rechargeable batteries do not have more energy capacity** for a single discharge **when compared to primary lithium cells of the same form factor**. Only AA and CR123 primary cells were tested. This is important because it is a potential drawback of going from primary cells to rechargeable batteries.

USB Connector: For AA batteries, the USB connector type, location, and orientation combinations are ranked below from highest to lowest energy capacity:

1. Micro-B, side, horizontal
2. Micro-B, top
3. USB-C, side, horizontal
4. Micro-B, side, vertical

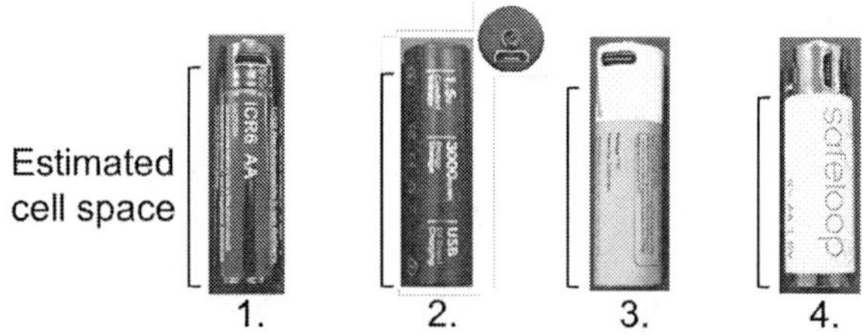

Figure 4. An example of each kind of USB configuration with a bracket drawn to show the estimated space for a cell.

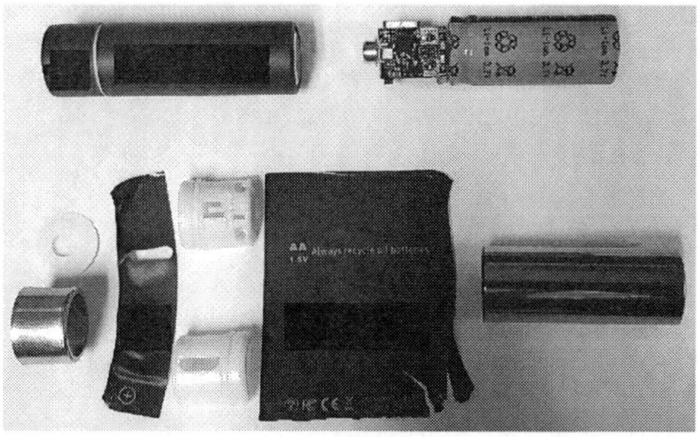

Figure 5. A disassembled Micro-B/side/vertical battery. The cell and PCB at the top-right show how much space the circuitry takes up.

It is thought that the reason for this order is because the USB configuration that takes up the least space in the can provides more space for a bigger cell, resulting in a higher capacity (Figure 4). USB Micro-B receptacles are smaller than USB-C receptacles. This leaves more space on the printed circuit board (PCB) to fit all necessary components without using additional PCBs. Thus, the Micro-B/side/horizontal configuration would allow the most space for a cell. Micro-B/top is a close second. Turning the receptacle at right angle to board would give more room for components on the PCB compared to Micro-B/side/horizontal, but the receptacle would take up more of the can's height. USB-C came in third because a USB-C receptacle takes up almost all of one side of a circular AA-sized PCB. There would need to be multiple PCBs to fit all components, which takes up more height. Finally, Micro-B/side/vertical is the worst because it wastes a lot of space by turning the USB connector and the entire PCB sideways (Figure 5).

Table 1. List of AA batteries purchased, their descriptions, and average energy capacity results from cycling.

Brand	USB			Advertised			Results	
	Type	Location	Orientation	V	Ah	Wh	Actual Wh	Difference Wh
Energizer Ultimate Lithium (L91)	Primary	-	-	1.5	3.50	5.25	4.24	-1.01
Epoch	Micro	Side	Horizontal	1.5	2.30	3.45	3.17	-0.28
CT-Energy	Micro	Side	Horizontal	1.5	2.33	3.50	2.95	-0.55
Keeppower	Micro	Side	Horizontal	1.5	2.26	3.39	2.86	-0.53
Nitecore	Micro	Side	Horizontal	3.6	0.75	2.70	2.80	0.10
Skylaxy	Micro	Top	-	1.5	1.85	2.78	2.58	-0.20
Pownergy	Micro	Top	-	1.5	1.97	2.96	2.57	-0.39
Fenix	Micro	Side	Horizontal	1.5	1.60	2.40	2.57	0.17
EBL	Micro	Side	Horizontal	1.5	2.20	3.30	2.56	-0.74
Tipsun	Micro	Side	Horizontal	1.5	1.30	2.80	2.53	-0.27
Fuvaly	Magnetic	Top	-	1.5	2.00	3.00	2.49	-0.51
AmpTorrent	Micro	Top	-	1.5	1.97	2.96	2.42	-0.54
Naccon	Micro	Side	Horizontal	1.5	1.60	2.40	2.23	-0.17
Bluerise	Type-C	Side	Horizontal	1.5	1.70	2.55	2.21	-0.34
Tinoteen	Type-C	Side	Horizontal	1.5	1.73	2.60	2.11	-0.49
Maxwel	Type-C	Side	Horizontal	1.5	1.73	2.60	2.04	-0.56
JWWYJ	Type-C	Side	Horizontal	1.5	1.70	2.55	2.01	-0.54
Anvow	Type-C	Side	Horizontal	1.5	2.27	3.40	1.96	-1.44
Lankoo	Type-C	Side	Horizontal	1.5	1.73	2.60	1.89	-0.71
Vivitar	Type-C	Side	Horizontal	1.5	1.60	2.40	1.77	-0.63
Uzone	Type-C	Side	Horizontal	1.5	1.73	2.60	1.75	-0.85
Deleepow	Micro	Side	Vertical	1.5	1.87	2.80	1.54	-1.26
Fuvaly	Micro	Side	Vertical	1.5	1.50	2.25	1.40	-0.85
Bump	Micro	Side	Vertical	1.5	1.20	1.80	1.40	-0.40
Sorbo	Type-A Male	Top	-	1.5	1.20	1.80	1.39	-0.41
Safeloop	Micro	Side	Vertical	1.5	1.25	1.88	1.21	-0.67
PaleBlue	Micro	Side	Vertical	1.5	1.56	2.34	1.18	-1.16
Energizer Alkaline Power	Primary	-	-	1.5	1.00	1.50	0.76	-0.74

This is the only USB configuration in which the PCB is not a circular cross-section of the can.

Discussion – Other Observations

No State of Charge Indicators: No batteries (not even larger sizes, such as 18650 or 21700) have a state of charge indicator. They only have indicators to show whether the battery is charging or full. State of charge indicators would allow users to know how much energy is left in the batteries and plan accordingly.

Identical Designs: Based on the type and placement of charging indicator light-emitting diodes (LEDs), it is probable that groups of certain brands share the exact same designs. The only way to be sure would be to take the batteries apart, but most were not disassembled for safety reasons. They are too suspiciously identical to be a coincidence. The implications are unclear. This could mean some brands may be owned by the same parent company, or intellectual property is not well-protected in some other countries.

This is interesting because it reduces the number of unique designs on the market. Out of 26 AA brands, there are just seven types of designs plus three truly unique designs. The most obvious cases of copied designs are shown in Figure 6 through Figure 9. (These pictures are best viewed in color. The captions also describe position based on an hour hand's position on a clock.)

Overcurrent Protection: Batteries had some form of overcurrent protection, but it was not fully effective. With an e-load in constant power mode, the power was increased in 0.1-W steps until the battery's voltage dropped to near zero. This usually happened when the current exceeded 1

A. The current then dropped to around 300 mA, which is still a substantial amount of current.

Figure 6. Though these look like three batteries from the same brand, they are actually three different brands. They all have a red charging LED at the 3:00 position that turns green when fully charged.

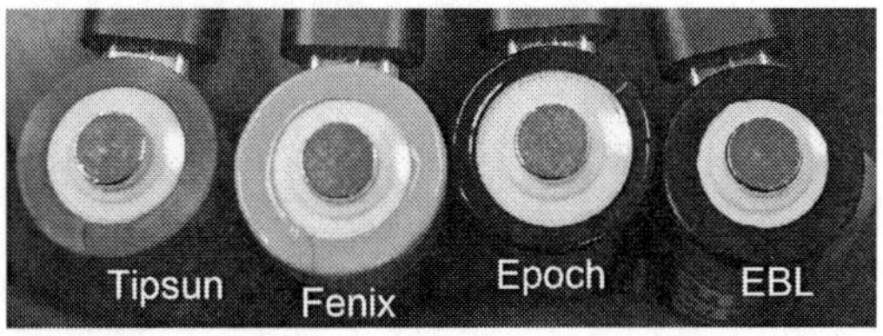

Figure 7. Batteries that have a red LED at 3:00 that turns blue when fully charged. They have the same positive contact material, and the LEDs are half covered with the edge of the label.

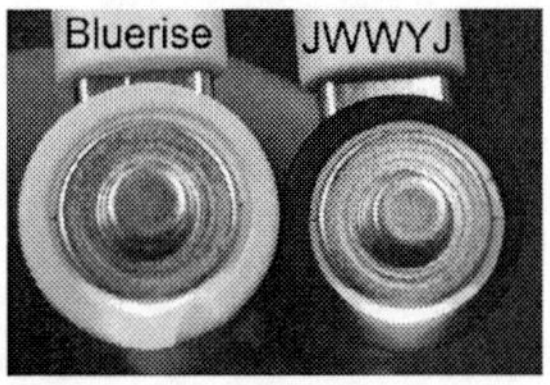

Figure 8. Batteries that have a blinking green LED that shines through a crack at 6:00. The LED remains on when fully charged.

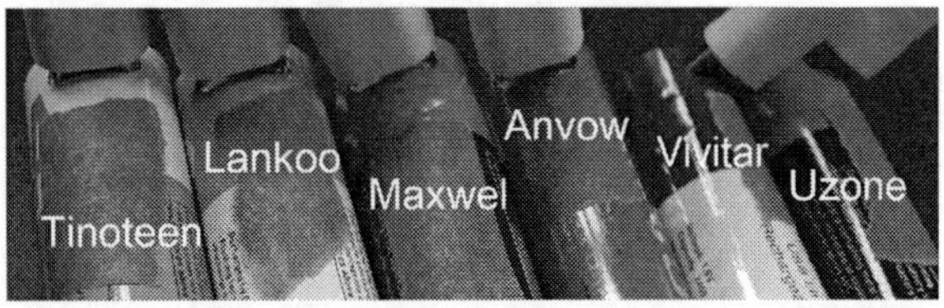

Figure 9. All USB-C batteries had a red LED that blinks through the USB-C connector when charging. The LED stays on when fully charged.

Overdischarge Protection: There were overdischarge problems with some batteries which continued to discharge a significant amount of current even though the voltage was close to zero. Zero voltage is a sign that the battery was trying to disconnect from the load, but it could also be an artifact of the e-load being set to constant power mode. The e-load could have been shorting the battery to draw more current to maintain a power of 0.5 W. Either way, the overdischarge protections do not seem to work for some batteries, as seen in Figure 10, which shows the most extreme case. There was an associated temperature spike from 27°C to 30°C.

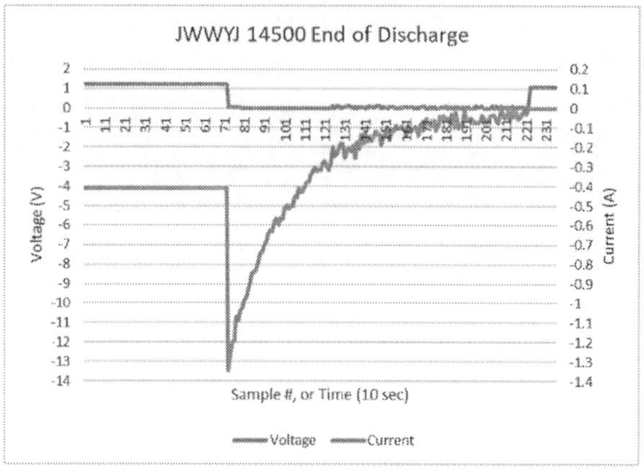

Figure 10. The JWWYJ brand battery at the end of a discharge. The top curve shows the voltage drops to zero. The bottom curve shows the current spikes to 1.4 A (negative because of the chosen convention) and exponentially decays to zero over the next 25 minutes. When the load is turned off, the voltage recovers to 1.1 V.

Caution when Charging and Using Simultaneously: Roughly half of these AA batteries have 5 V across the ends of the battery while charging, which suggests that they are connected directly to the USB connector's V_{BUS} and GND pins. For this reason, the batteries should not be charged while they are being used in a device because the 5 V could break devices that are expecting only 1.5 V.

Conclusion

The COTS USB-rechargeable single-cell batteries generally function as promised. They can all be charged with a standard USB cable and discharged through the anode and cathode as claimed. However, cycle testing revealed that the batteries had lower energy capacities (Watt-hours) than advertised, with five exceptions (only two AA batteries). There are just a few unique designs; multiple brands showed indications of sharing the exact same mechanical and electrical design. The overcurrent protection in the AA batteries functions to some extent by reducing the current and preventing thermal events. For some AA batteries, overdischarge protection is not effective at stopping further current from exiting the battery while it is still connected to a load.

Acknowledgements

The author would like to thank Dr. Nathan Sharpes and intern Sam Floyd for their assistance with this work.

References

1. Energizer L91 Ultimate Lithium datasheet, https://data.energizer.com/pdfs/l91.pdf
2. Energizer LR6 Alkaline Power datasheet, https://data.energizer.com/pdfs/alk-power-aa.pdf

Scale-Up Challenges for Passively Propagation Resistant Batteries: 18650 to 21700

David Petrushenko[1], Eric Darcy[1], Paul Coman[2], and Ralph E. White[2]

[1]NASA Johnson Space Center, Houston, TX 77058
[2]University of South Carolina, Columbia, SC 29208

Abstract

In this study, we present some challenges associated with scaling from 18650 to 21700 batteries while maintaining a passively propagation resistant (PPR) battery architecture. A collaboration between NASA and NAVSEA has achieved PPR battery designs with gravimetric and volumetric energy densities of 166 Wh/kg and 459 Wh/L, respectively. Commercially available 18650 cells were arranged in various electrical topologies to achieve the power requirements for each application. Will those design metrics improve when scaling up with the best commercially available 21700 cell designs? A design, analysis, assembly, and test effort with blast plate composites revealed that the gap for dispersion of the thermal runaway ejecta relied on in 18650 PPR batteries must be increased to allow for sufficient volume when scaling up to a 21700 cell to offer protection between axially stacked battery modules. Furthermore, fractional thermal runaway calorimetry (FTRC) energy yields have shown that the output of high energy cells 21700 cells is 75% more despite an electrochemical energy increase of 50% compared to an 18650 high energy cell design. A thermal analysis model predicts that the interstitial aluminum heat sink webbing thickness, an integral part of the PPR design, would protect the adjacent cells more robustly when increased from 0.5mm to 1mm. Validation by battery PPR testing will be presented.

Keywords: Passive propagation resistance (PPR), lithium-ion, battery, thermal runaway

Introduction

Lithium-ion batteries are critical for storing electrical energy in applications that require high energy and/or power density, such as EVs, grid storage, space vehicles and underwater submersibles. Building and integrating battery packs and modules into battery systems requires rigorous designs and optimization to lower the risk of thermal runaway propagation, provide a uniform pack temperature, absorb shocks or other perturbations, and most importantly, fit within and perform to predetermined operating conditions. Safety is a significant criterion when introducing battery systems into vehicles rated for human use as a single incident, such as a thermal runaway event, can have catastrophic consequences.

Materials and Methods

The objective of the NASA-NAVSEA collaboration effort is to design batteries that can tolerate a single cell thermal runaway event without causing failure to propagate. Four design guidelines were followed:

1. Protecting adjacent cells from possible side wall and/or spin groove breaches of cell undergoing thermal runaway.
2. Provide adequate spacing between cells and an appropriate heat rejection path for the cell undergoing thermal runaway.
3. Individually fuse parallel cells or strings of series cells and prevent bypassing of fuses by conductive ejecta.
4. Protect the adjacent cells from the hot ejecta produced during thermal runaway with appropriate temperature tolerant dissipation gaps.

To achieve a high performance PPR battery, interstitial aluminum heat sinks were utilized between cells as the primary mechanism for dissipating heat generated during thermal runaway. Rapid dissipation of heat away from a failed cell is critical to ensure thermal runaway propagation does not occur in neighboring cells.

Results And Discussion

In 2021, a battery with a 134P-3S electrical topology was designed with commercially available 18650 cells and successfully demonstrated passive propagation resistance. First, a model was utilized to predict cells most vulnerable to propagation during thermal runaway. Twelve cell locations in total were identified for thermal runaway testing. During battery assembly, cells equipped with Internal Short Circuit Devices (ISCD) were installed strategically, following guidance from the thermal modeling. Figure 1 shows a CAD rendering of the “M3” Battery assembly. This design achieved 166 Wh/kg and 459 Wh/L gravimetric and volumetric energy densities, respectively.[1]

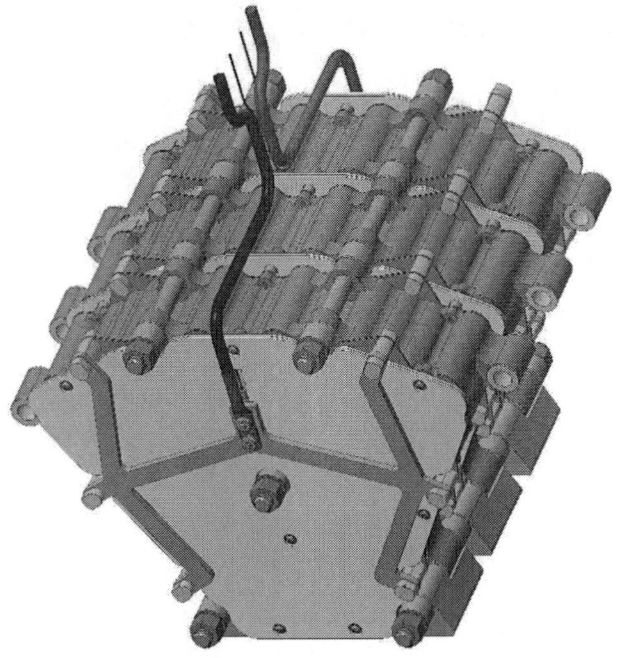

Figure 1: CAD rendering of M3 PPR Battery pack with a 134P-3S electrical topology. This battery successfully demonstrated PPR with 12 individual thermal runaway tests.

The M3 Battery design features an interstitial aluminum webbing thickness of 0.020 inches [~0.5mm] between adjacent cells. The heat sink, designed to match the overall length of the cell, provides the necessary structural support and a heat rejection path in the event of a thermal runaway event. Furthermore, the webbing between cells protects adjacent cells in the event of off-nominal cell failures, such as side wall- and spin-groove ruptures, which may spread hot ejecta to neighboring cells, causing thermal runaway propagation. One out of twelve individual thermal runaway events caused minor pitting in the interstitial aluminum heat sink, demonstrating its robust design.

When combining modules in a battery pack, it is necessary to protect cells in neighboring modules, especially when cells are aligned axially as is the case in the M3 Battery design, with a barrier. This barrier ensures that thermal runaway does not propagate to adjacent modules. A metal-ceramic composite with a 5mm standoff gap, between the cell and barrier, has been tested rigorously and shown to provide sufficient protection in 18650 battery packs. Testing results indicate that a sufficient standoff distance is necessary to allow thermal runaway ejecta to disperse effectively away from adjacent cells.[1] A test setup was conceived to allow cells to be triggered via nail or by heat to determine whether a 5mm standoff gap is sufficient for battery architectures featuring 21700 cell formats. Figure 3 below details the main features of the test apparatus. First, cells are bonded into thin aluminum sleeves, like the procedure used for battery assembly. Simultaneously, blast plate test coupons are prepared by bonding candidate materials to be evaluated onto a rectangular aluminum substrate plate. Nine thermocouples are attached directly onto the back of the aluminum plate in a one-inch array for capturing thermal data. Prior to testing, the cell and blast plate coupon are mounted into the cell chamber and onto the sliding blast plate stage, respectively, followed by adjustment of the sliding stage. The desired standoff distance is achieved adjusting the position of the sliding blast plate stage. Thermal runaway is initiated remotely via nail penetration utilizing the pneumatic actuator or via cartridge heaters installed into the cell chamber.

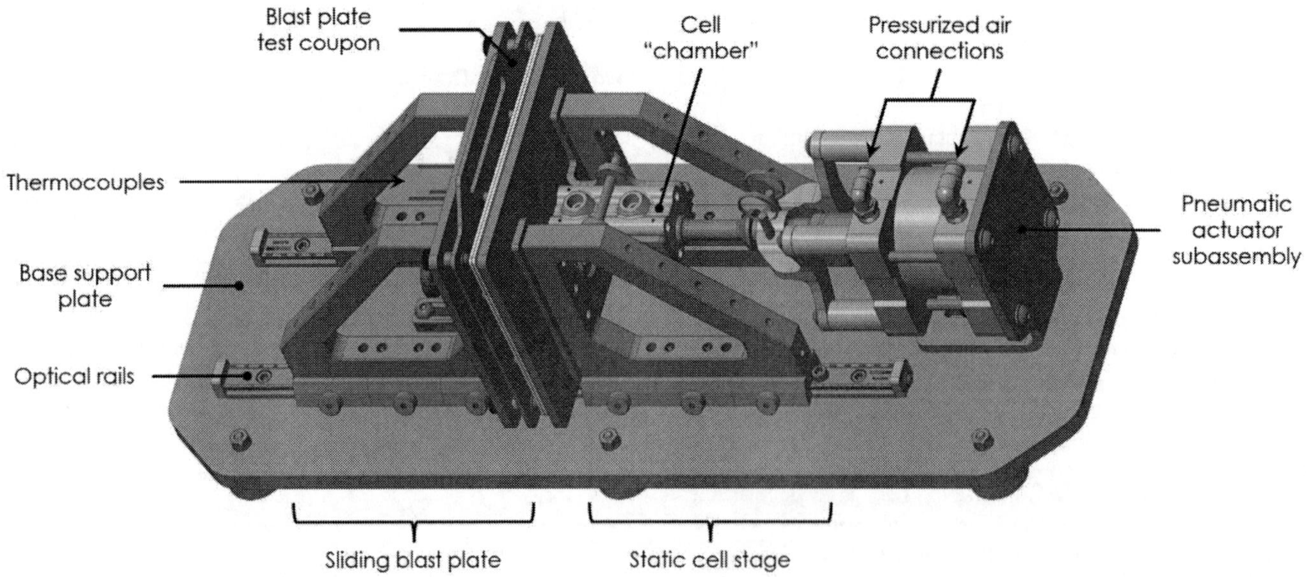

Figure 2: Blast Plate Test Stand (BPTS) designed to evaluate various blast plate materials at a fixed distance from the cell header. Cells are driven into thermal runaway in the cell chamber via axial nail penetration or cartridge heaters.

Several thermal barrier materials were tested including ones manufactured by Morgan Advanced Materials, Zircar, and Oerlikon. The purpose of these materials is to protect a 1/32 inch [~0.8mm] aluminum substrate plate from perforating by thermal runaway ejecta from the cell. An additional success criterion for a selected standoff distance is to ensure that accumulation of ejecta mounting onto the surface of the blast plate does not touch the trigger or neighboring cells. Tests in which ejecta was observed touching the trigger cell were considered unsuccessful and deemed to have inadequate spacing for dispersion of ejecta. Accumulation of hot ejecta near the adjacent cells may result in thermal abuse and potential failure and potential shorting or discharge of cells.

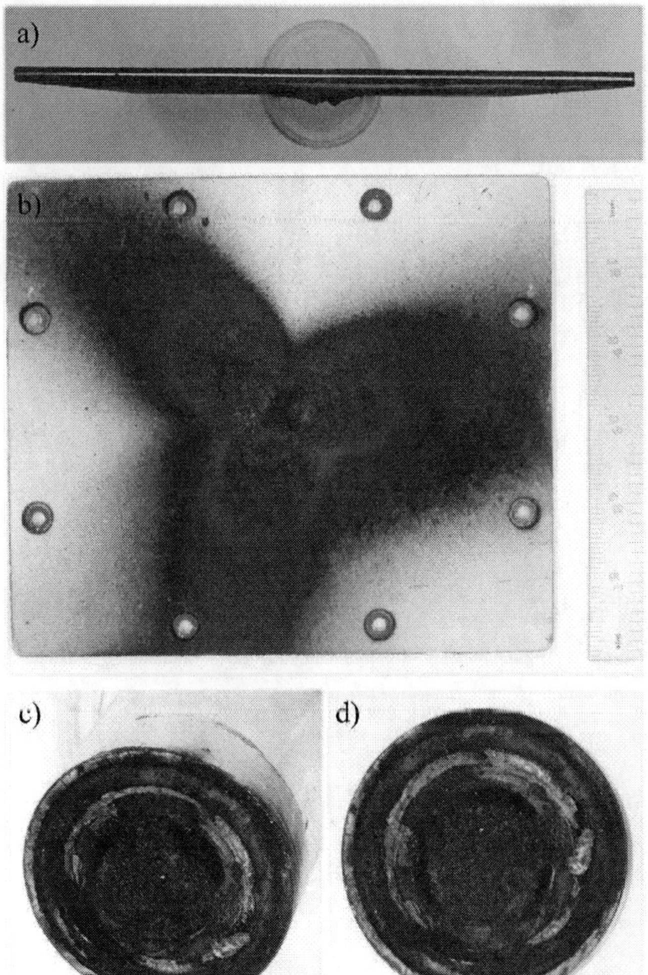

Figure 3: Post-test images of blast plate and cell a) top view of blast plate test coupon after testing with view of ejecta mounting, b) front view of the blast plate showing the uniformity of ejecta dispersion, c) angled view of a Samsung 50S cell following a blast plate test at 8mm standoff distance and d) top view of cell showing the activation of all three vent holes and a nominal failure.

In total, four blast plate materials, three standoff (gap) distances, two cell types and two trigger methods were evaluated. Each test condition (material, gap, cell, and trigger method) was repeated a minimum of six times. Our test result revealed that for two 21700 cell designs (LG INR21700 M52V and Samsung INR21700 50S) triggered via nail penetration, a standoff distance of 8mm is required to provide for adequate ejecta dispersion. Various levels of damage and ablating were observed on the blast plate shielding materials, however, no perforations in the aluminum substrate was observed in any of the tests performed with nail penetration. Figure 3a and b show the top and front views of a blast plate test coupon reinforced with Morgan Advanced Material shielding. This test was performed at an 8mm standoff distance. Note the symmetry of ejecta spread corresponding to the activated vent holes of the Samsung 50S cell shown in Figures 3c and d.

A series of heater confirmation runs were performed at 8mm which resulted in severe bending and some perforation of the blast plate test coupons. Thermal energy added to the cells to initiate thermal runaway causes a much more kinetically energetic output. Since our design objective is to prevent cell propagation, the thermal trigger is likely an over test and therefore not representative of a defect induced field failure thermal runaway event. However, the test results were informative of the potential damage that a battery system may sustain if propagation does occur; successive cell failures are more severe than the defect that induced the initial thermal runaway event. Subsequent testing with ISCD implanted 21700 trigger cells will be performed with our selected barrier composite material and standoff distance to simulate a field failure and verify the barrier's ability to protect adjacent cells. Cells with implanted ISCD require a thermal activation temperature just above 60°C to active; significantly less thermal energy compared to a normal cell.

Fractional Thermal Runaway Calorimetry (FTRC) testing of the newest 21700 cell designs has revealed that the total thermal runaway energy output can be as much as 75% higher than the incumbent 18650 Molicel M35A despite only providing 50% more electrochemical energy. The plot in Figure 4 provides a comparison of overall and cell body energy releases for three cells: Molicel INR18650 M35A, Samsung INR21700 50S and LG INR21700 M52V with various activation mechanisms including heat trigger, ISCD heater trigger and nail penetration. Our thermal analysis predicts that increasing the thickness of the interstitial aluminum webbing between cells from 0.020 inches [~0.5mm] to 0.040 inches [~1.0mm] will reduce the maximum temperature of the adjacent cells by 15°C with our maximum calorimetric output for a 21700-cell determined by FTRC.[3]

The results of PPR tests and with 19-cell subscale batteries will be presented along with analysis anchored by the thermal runaway test results.

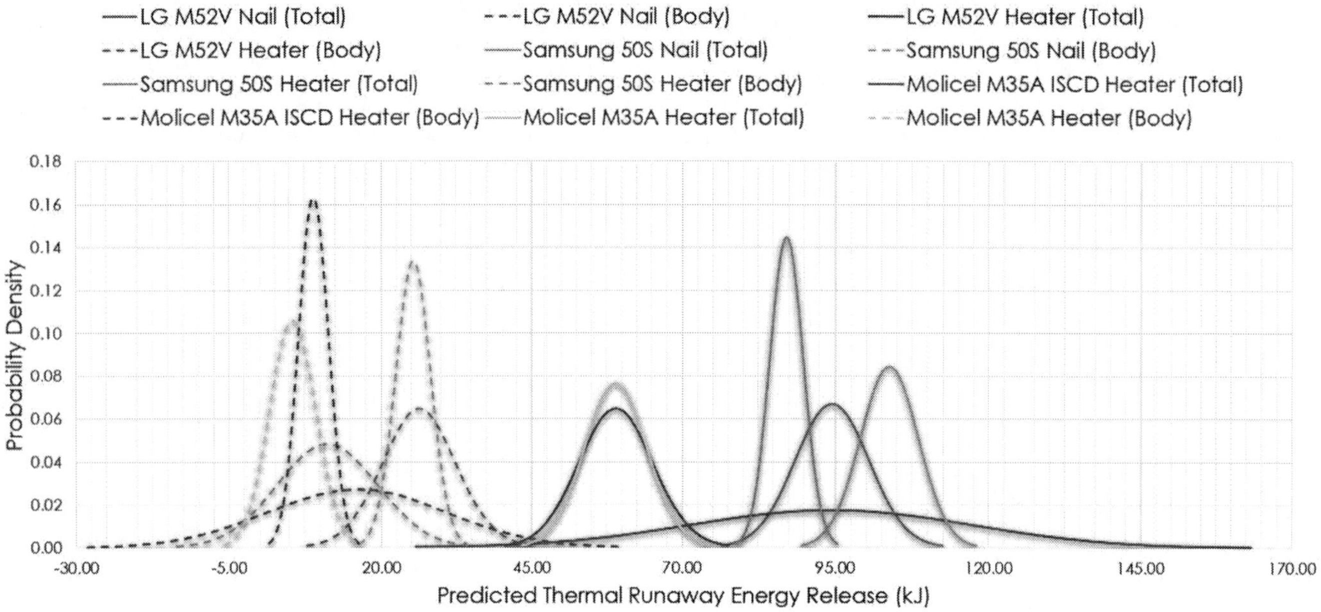

Figure 4: Energy yields of three select cells: Molicel INR18650 M35A, Samsung INR21700 50S and LG INR21700 M52V for selected trigger mechanisms. Overall and cell body energies are plotted as a function of trigger and cell type.

Conclusion

This study is part of a broader collaborative effort between NASA and NAVSEA with the primary objective of designing passively propagation resistant batteries for application in human-rated vehicles. We present challenges associated with up-scaling lithium-ion PPR battery architectures from 18650 to 21700 cell formats, namely the results from a blast plate testing campaign as well as preliminary PPR testing results form subscale batteries. These results will be used to inform future designs of full-scale PPR battery architectures featuring 21700 cells.

Acknowledgements

The authors would like to acknowledge and thank NASA Johnson Space Center, the US Navy's Naval Underwater Warfare Center (NUWC) Newport Division and the US Navy's Naval Surface Warfare Center (NSWC) Crane and Carderock Divisions for their collaboration and ongoing support. We would also like to acknowledge Jesus Trillo (NASA Johnson Space Center) for testing support and test data processing.

References

[1] Petrushenko, D., Coman, P., Trillo, J., Darst, J., White, R., Darcy, E., Moyar, J., Izzo, J., Adams, T., and Fontaine, J., "M3 PPR Battery Development," *NASA Aerospace Battery Workshop*, Huntsville, AL, 2022.

[2] Trillo, J., Petrushenko, D., and Darcy, E., "Li-ion Sidewall Rupture Characterization with 3 Battery Designs" NASA Aerospace Battery Workshop, Huntsville, AL, 2022.

[3] Coman, P., White, R., Darcy, E., Petrushenko, D., Darst, J., and Trillo, J., "Thermal Analysis Projections for Scale Up From 18650 to 21700", NASA Aerospace Battery Workshop, Huntsville, AL, 2022.

Improved Methods for Soft Short Detection in Li-ion Cells

And Automated Cell Screening

By Eric Darcy/NASA-JSC

William Walker/KULR

NASA's standard method for screening Li-ion with soft shorts has been to measure their OCV after resting at room temperature for at least 1 year as received after fabrication. Recent comparison tests with ΔOCV methods at 30% and 0% SoC over 3-6 month periods indicate that they are more discriminatory than the 1-year method. Separately a rapid (1 week) high resolution OCV method with tight temperature control was found to also be more discriminatory than the 1-year wait method. Tear downs of cells with outlying ΔOCVs are being examined for separator bridging defects to validate the method. Incorporating these methods into an automated cell screening process will be presented.

Despite extensive quality improvements in the world-wide Li-ion cell manufacturing process since 1991 along with standardize cell screening prior to release of the cells by the manufacturer, catastrophic field failures are still occurring along with major product recalls. Many of these safety incidents in the field originate due to an internal short defect that was not detectable with current techniques at the point of manufacture due to its latency. These incidents have been found to occur with cells from nearly all manufacturers, even from the most experienced, reputable, and highest volume suppliers.

With the expansion and contraction of the electrode jellyroll or stack inside Li-ion cells, latent conductive defects between anode and cathode can potentially grow from soft shorts to hard internal shorts. This was demonstrated experimentally with strategically implanted Ni particles in cells and reported by Barnett at the 2012 Power Sources Conference.[1] Such experimental cells with their implanted particle behaved normally through initial cycling and several failed catastrophically into thermal runaway with many cycles.

NASA and NAVSEA have a centralized the process of procuring, validating, screening, and distributing commercial cylindrical 18650 cell designs to its programs. Two high energy and two high power cell designs were selected after a series of performance, quality, and safety tests and establish channels for procuring these with chain of custody evidence from the manufacturer. The designs are listed in Table 1.

Figure 1 show a plot of the OCV of 1000 M35A cells at the as received SOC and > 1 year old. Note that about 5% of the cells are about 5mV higher than the mean at 3.4990V mostly likely set at slightly higher SOC by the manufacturer. This causes a wider than expected standard deviation and only 2 cells breach the -3 sigma threshold with the 1 year method. The ΔOCV method with the same cells at the same state of charge over 6 months is shown in Figure 2 yields a mostly uniform distribution and detects the same 2 plus 4 more cells breaching the -3 sigma threshold. Figure 3 shows the ΔOCV method at 0% SoC on half of the same 1000 cells. Here the cells were given 2 months to stabilize after the full discharge and the ΔOCV was measured at end of months 2 and 3. This detects 5 outliers out of 500 cells of which 3 were detected by the other methods.

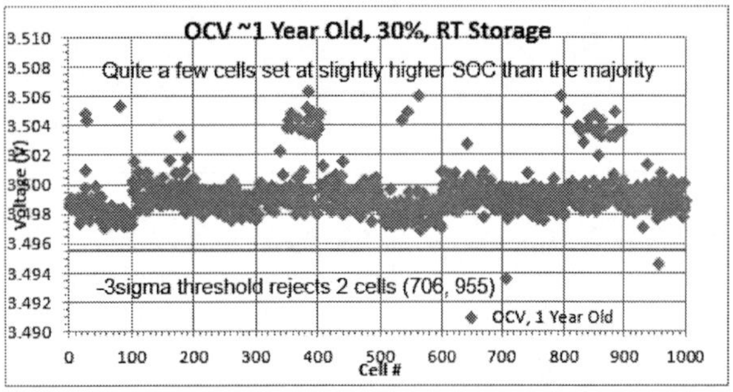

Figure 1. Cell OCVs at 1 year after their date of manufacture in as received 30% SOC.

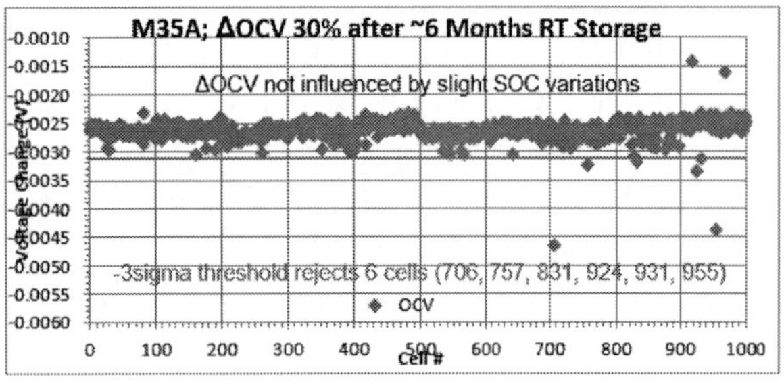

Figure 2. Calculated ΔOCV at 30% SOC about 6 months apart using the same cells as in Figure 1.

Table 1. Attributes of Cell Designs in NASA-NAVSEA Cell Reserve

Item	Cell Model	Cap (Ah)	Wh/kg	Wh/L	ACR (mΩ)	DCR (mΩ)
1	LG INR18650 M36	3.4	270	710	23.9	29.8
2	Molicel INR18650-M35A	3.5	277	725	24.4	32.5
3	Samsung INR18650-30Q	3	207	528	12.4	9.2
4	Molicel INR18650-P28B	2.75	202	510	9.2	22.3

Cell tear downs are planned for the ΔOCV rejects to look for bridging defects across the separator, similar to those found for the outliers of the 1-year method.[2] Overall, the ΔOCV methods at the as received and 0% SoC are more discriminatory than the wait 1-year method. Note that an instrument is in development by CAMX Power and is capable of rapidly (~1 week) grading the microvolts of self-discharge rates of cells against a known good cell from the same lot. It also has been shown to be superior to the wait 1-year method.[3] This will be reported on separately at this conference.

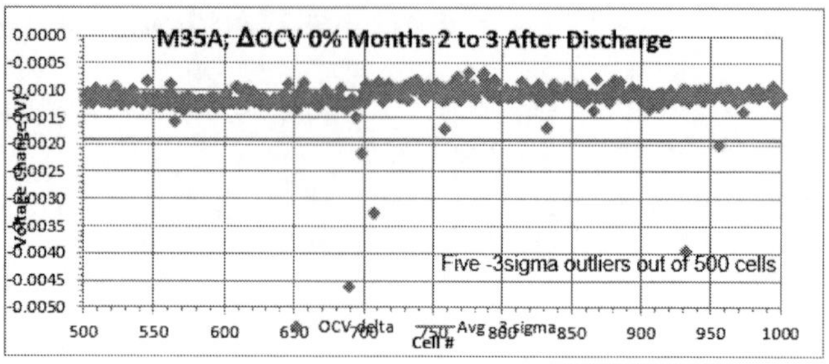

Figure 3. Only half of the cells, discharged to 0% SoC with ΔOCV taken at end of months 2 and 3.

Battery cell safety is of utmost importance in the development and production of lithium-ion batteries. To ensure that these batteries are safe, it is critical to subject the battery cells to rigorous testing, such as EP-WI-037. This technical paper explores the reasons for subjecting battery cells to EP-WI-037, which includes various tests such as OCV, self-discharge, ΔOCV, visual inspection, mass, dimensions, DCIR, and capacity. These tests help identify various defects such as separator bridging defects, seal corrosion, defects in can wall or header, insufficient or too much electrolyte, bulged bottom, and matching performance in cells that populate a battery. By identifying these defects early on, it is possible to prevent potential safety hazards and ensure that the battery performs optimally throughout its service life.

KULR Technology Group has developed an automated and comprehensive screening process for lithium-ion battery cells intended for use in manned space applications, adhering to NASA's EP-WI-37B testing standard. This standard ensures the safety and reliability of these cells in space conditions, where failure or poor performance could have catastrophic consequences. This screening process is critical to ensuring the safety and reliability of battery products.

KULR's automated screening process begins with vision cameras that extract the unique manufacturer ID and date of manufacture, and a laser engraver that cuts the sleeve without damaging the cell body. Vision inspections are performed, and the length and diameter of each cell are measured twice, with the system only keeping the highest and lowest values. A custom-designed SCADA system manages the machine operation, collects data, performs mean and standard deviation calculations, and generates data reports. KULR also uses a custom-designed SQL database to securely house all collected data.

The cells are then subjected to the advanced Chroma process, involving several tests to ensure safety and reliability. The Chroma system can test batches of 576 cells simultaneously, with 18-bit analog-to-digital conversion resolution and 9 units with 64 channels each. The cells undergo continuity checks, OCV measurements, charging and discharging to calculate charge and discharge capacity, and measure DCIR. KULR's screening process selects only high-quality cells, ensuring optimal performance and safety.

When all the tests are complete the SCADA system pulls the necessary data from the database and performs the Mean and Standard Deviation calculations. The system analyzes the results of the calculations and rejects cells with measurements that lie outside of three standard deviations. All of the data is saved, and reports can be generated for every batch of cells processed.

KULR's Automated Cell Screening System can process cells without human handling, under strict quality control to ensure temperature and humidity requirements are maintained. The system assigns a unique KULR ID electronically to all cells and sequences them in series for data tracking integrity. The system uses a sophisticated laser cutting process to cut cell sleeves without impacting cell can surfaces, and an array of cameras and rotating turntable for visual inspection of cells. Cells are optically measured for length and diameter and then electronically tested in nine identical systems. After electronic testing, cells are charged to 10% SOC and packed in closed cell egg crate boxes holding 100 cells. The KULR system achieves all requirements for NASA flight certification and can process 5000+ cells a week, eliminating nearly all operator handling potential damage due to human interaction. KULR can perform both the 1 year and 6-month delta OCV methods mentioned previously in its process. The most important aspect of the KULR Automated Cell Screening System is it's calibrated and its controlled repeatability in each step ensures a high level of accuracy and consistency.

The ΔOCV screens at "as received" or discharge states-of-charge are superior to the single measurement method after 1-year of storage, but this requires additional OCV measurements. This is burden is reduced by automated screening.

KULR's commitment to safety is paramount in its product and battery pack design. Ensuring that battery cells meet the highest safety standards through the EP-WI-037 testing procedures is critical to KULR's goal of delivering cutting-edge battery technology that delivers high performance and unparalleled safety.

References

1. Barnett, B. et. al., *Power Sources Conference*, Las Vegas, NV, 2012
2. Darcy, E. and Weintritt, J., *NASA Aerospace Battery Workshop*, Huntsville, AL, 2013
3. Darcy, E., Adams, T., Strangways, B., and McCoy, C., NASA Aerospace Battery Workshop, Huntsville, AL, 2022.

JP-8 Fuel Cell Powered Electric Vehicle and Generator

Authors: Saurabh A. Vilekar[a], Christian Junaedi[a], Tim LaBreche[a], Subir Roychoudhury[a], Kevin Centeck[b]

[a]Precision Combustion, Inc., 410 Sackett Point Rd., North Haven, CT 06473

[b]U.S. Army Combat Capabilities Development Command (DEVCOM) Ground Vehicle Systems Center (GVSC), 6501 E. 11 Mile Rd., Detroit Arsenal, MI 48397

sroychoudhury@precision-combustion.com / 203-287-3700 ext. 267

Abstract

This paper summarizes development and demonstration of a JP-8-fueled Fuel-Cell Electric-Vehicle that offers silent-mobility, silent-watch, and export-power as well as a JP-8-fueled Fuel-Cell Generator – both developed with DoD support. The core design consists of a Solid Oxide Fuel Cell (SOFC), balance of plant components, an onboard multi-fuel reformer, and an integrated sulfur trap for processing JP-8. It does not require on-board hydrogen storage. In this paper, the results from evaluation of the 1-kW and 10-kW SOFC prototype systems will be presented. This will include system performance, transient and steady state data, thermal cycling data, power conditioning, and packaging constraints. The advanced SOFC generator combines multiple innovations. This paper will also highlight the system characteristics relating to sulfur cleanup, water balance, and stack performance. We will discuss performance metrics with respect to objectives and thresholds for system fielding, which include start-up, shutdown, user interface, and maintenance requirements.

Keywords

Solid oxide fuel cells (SOFC); JP-8; electric vehicle; generator; silent; MIL-SPEC power; Battery hybridized; high efficiency; low-carbon.

Introduction

JP-8 fueled power generators that can operate silently, with low thermal signature and much more efficiently than conventional generators not only offer expanded capabilities for the DoD but also reduce carbon footprint. The sulfur in JP-8 has been a hurdle for developing practical solutions. The system design developed for the present applications uses a sulfur filter capable of operating with JP-8 containing up to 3000 ppm sulfur. Field operation also requires robustness to exacting environmental conditions and use.

Precision Combustion, Inc. (PCI) has developed standalone Solid Oxide Fuel Cell (SOFC)-based power generation systems (with F-24/JP-8, Sasol IPK, etc.). The systems include fuel reformer, sulfur cleanup, power electronics, water recovery, start/tail-gas burners, heat exchangers, balance of plant components, controls, and packaging. Systems have been developed for various applications and platforms. Electrochemical power generation, without moving parts, is a potential disruptive development.

Electric Vehicle

The prototype was fueled with MIL-SPEC JP-8 and can potentially be operated with other logistic fuels. This 10-kW onboard system included all components required for standalone operation. It was hybridized with a rechargeable battery for startup, peak loads, and load following. Water neutrality and silent operation (i.e., ~60 dBA at 1-meter) was confirmed. The power produced was sufficient for vehicle propulsion and export power. Both 28-32 VDC and 110 VAC for charging batteries and supporting external load demands (for off-grid vehicle charging) were available onboard. Initial off-road demonstrations were conducted at PCI and Detroit Arsenal.

A photograph of the battery hybridized SOFC vehicle prototype delivered to the US ARMY DEVCOM GVSC is shown in Figure 1. A semi-autonomous, off-road vehicle, Squad Multipurpose Equipment Transport (SMET), was chosen for this demonstration. It is designed to lighten infantry soldier load by carrying an array of supplies and gear. It was developed by General Dynamics Land Systems (GDLS). The original vehicle was used as a mule for the prototype developed at PCI. The original vehicle only had a rechargeable battery which required charging from an external power source. PCI's prototype does not require external charging during operation, was designed for 10 kWe export power, and is fueled by F-24/JP-8. It is analogous to a plug-in hybrid, but without the range anxiety.

Figure 1. F-24/JP-8 fueled, electric SMET prototype developed at PCI with US ARMY DEVCOM GVSC support. It is self-charging and provides 10-kWe export power.

Generator

A 1-kW JP-8-fueled Fuel-Cell Generator prototype was also demonstrated (Figure 2). It was suitable for quiet, portable micro-grid compatible operation for stationary and auxiliary power units. It offers improved combat capabilities and meets the single-fuel forward concept. The prototype was successfully demonstrated with field communication equipment. Stable operation over 1,500 hours and over 20 start stop cycles was demonstrated. Designs targeted for MIL-SPEC compliance, improved system weight and efficiency are being advanced.

Figure 2. 1.2 kW JP-8/Diesel fueled SOFC generator prototype developed with USTRANSCOM support.

System Performance

The EV produced up to 10 kWe of variable/continuous electrical power. The generated power was used to charge onboard batteries, power external components (i.e., user load), and support BOP requirements. During vehicle operation, rapid transient demands (e.g., acceleration and turning) were managed via battery hybridization. Instantaneous demands to 15 kWe, necessary to execute vehicle maneuvers, were seamlessly provided by the battery/fuel cell hybrid setup. Vehicle demonstrations (stationary and mobile) were completed at PCI facilities as well as at Detroit Arsenal and Camp Grayling. The 1.2 kW SOFC generator was demonstrated for the US Transportation command at MacDill AF base in Tampa. Ability to power communication equipment was confirmed. Thermodynamic considerations were used to direct system optimization via CHEMCAD process simulation software. It was used to identify components specifications and achieve high system efficiency via effective thermal and flow balancing.

The power conditioning system was developed to provide output control (maintain required voltage range and power quality to the electrical loads), charge management of hybridized batteries, and fuel cell stack protection from overload, current surge, ripple, and load distortion. This feature not only allowed hybridization with MIL-SPEC rechargeable batteries but also included flexibility for microgrid integration and direct battery charging. Battery hybridization for load balancing and maintaining power quality required development of custom algorithms and hardware for matching load and fuel cell transients.

Effectively packaging within the SMET vehicle of the fuel reformer, sulfur filter, fuel cell, and associated components to account for efficient flow, thermal integration, and space claim management was critical towards meeting form factor requirements. This includes separation of hot and cold zone components, designing for shock, vibration and environmental conditions, resistance to electrical interference, and manufacturability. Multiple iterations were performed to optimize the packaging. Finite Element Analysis of the primary components was completed to determine the structural strength and requirements for the enclosure frame and supporting hardware and vibration testing to meet the packaging requirements. This analysis was used to identify the required materials of construction and thickness to support the components, sub-systems, and the complete fuel cell system and source vibration isolators, tailored for the SMET vehicle.

Conclusions

An F-24/JP-8 fueled, fuel cell based, electric-semi-autonomous vehicle was developed and successfully demonstrated. It was able to achieve strategic benefits of silent-watch, silent-mobility, and MIL-SPEC quality export-power with standard logistic fuels. This was the first demonstration of a long-envisioned goal and highlighted the potential of using a "solid state" power generation technology for a range of DoD applications, including auxiliary power, propulsion, unmanned platforms, portable generators, sensors, etc. This advance has also generated considerable commercial interest and non-military applications are being advanced as well. Transition to fielded applications will require significant work to address manufacturing and operational requirements. Importantly, MIL-SPEC requirements, cost optimization, weight and size reduction, fast start, long-term durability, etc. are required for widespread implementation.

Acknowledgements

We are grateful to the US Army and Air Force for supporting the development of these prototypes. Any opinions, findings, and conclusions or recommendations expressed in this paper are those of the authors and do not necessarily reflect the views of the DoD. The authors are also grateful to the technical and engineering support groups at PCI, GVSC, and TRANSCOM.

Solid Oxide Fuel Cell Manufacture by Computationally Driven Aerosol Jet Printing

Aaron Bain, Rory Roberts
Department of Mechanical Engineering,
Tennessee Tech University
Cookeville, TN 38505
atbain@tntech.edu

Thomas Jenkins
UES, Inc.
Materials and Processes Division
Dayton, Ohio 45432

Qiuhong Zhang, Bang Tsao
University of Dayton Research Institute
Dayton, Ohio 45469

L. Jay Deiner
Department of Chemistry
City Tech, City University of New York
Brooklyn, NY 11202

Joseph Fellner
Air Force Research Laboratory
Aerospace Systems Directorate
Wright Patterson Air Force Base, OH 45433
joseph.fellner@us.af.mil

Douglas Dudis
Air Force Research Laboratory
Materials & Manufacturing Directorate
Wright Patterson Air Force Base, OH 45433

Abstract: *An innovative printing method, computationally driven aerosol jet deposition (AJP), has been successfully utilized for the manufacture of solid oxide fuel cells (SOFC). A model revealed that a functionally graded anode can simultaneously enhance SOFC performance and durability by decreasing the polarization resistance and thermal expansion coefficient mismatch. The layer-by-layer nature of aerosol jet deposition allowed functional grading in a single electrode processing step without adding manufacturing time. The process is scalable from lab to stack size.*

Keywords: solid oxide fuel cells; genetic algorithm; additive manufacturing; aerosol jet printing; functionally graded materials; thermal stresses; composites.

Introduction

Aerosol jet printing is an additive manufacturing method that enables deposition of functional inks comprised of colloidally dispersed metals, ceramics, or organics[1]. AJP permits structural control over the mesoscopic to macroscopic length scales. X-Y resolution is on the order of 10 microns and thickness resolution is on the order of the average particle size in the ink. AJP can also enable functional grading of materials (FGM) through simultaneous deposition of varying proportions of disparate materials. In the context of electrochemical energy storage devices, 3D printing has been used to fabricate electrodes and electrolytes not possible through conventional methods [2], [3]. AJP is appealing for manufacturing because of its ability to achieve high resolution electrode designs including tuned thickness, porosity, and composition, in a single processing step. An AJP M3D printer (Mesoscale Materials Deposition, Optomec Inc.) with a dual pneumatic atomizer is depicted in Figure 1. The independent atomizers allow material mixing during the printing process, as inks are blended in the deposition head.

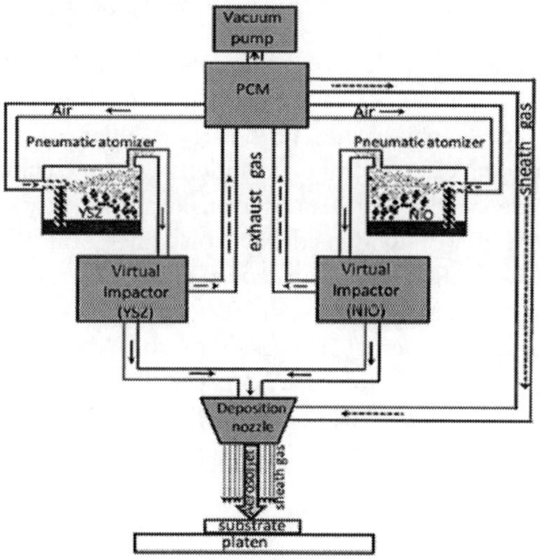

Figure 1. Schematic of Optomec AJP M3D Printer. Reproduced with permission from Elsevier [4].

Figure 2 depicts the process of printing full-size 100 cm^2 SOFC electrodes on an electrolyte substrate. The AJP method could be scaled to yet larger sizes by utilizing wider spray nozzles. Figure 3 displays a SEM image of an SOFC with printed anode, barrier layer, and cathode. Layer thickness resolution was ~ 1 micron.

Figure 2. Depiction of 100 cm^2 cathode on electrolyte support.

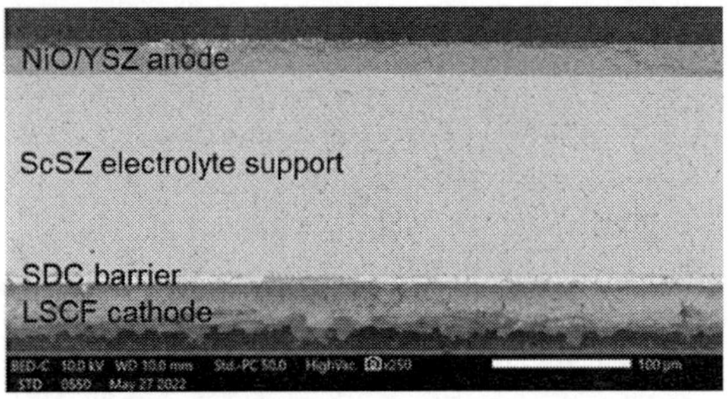

Figure 3. Cross-sectional SEM of AJ-Printed electrolyte-supported SOFC button cell

Design Methodology

Rational FGM SOFC Design via Computation

To guide the design of printed solid oxide cells, a computational model of a SOFC electrode has been created to predict the polarization resistance and thermal stresses present under operating conditions. The volumetric electrode is reduced to a one-dimensional boundary value problem (BVP) to numerically solve the local Butler-Volmer kinetics and percolating electronic and ionic conduction. The BVP is solved through finite difference collocation via the bvp5c algorithm within Matlab with a relative tolerance enforced at 1e-5. This algorithm uses the four stage Lobatto IIIa formula which is fifth order accurate within the boundary value range. To address the polarization resistance, maximal local value of overpotential, η (V), is used as scoring criterion of resistance for a printed electrode design under consideration. The model also addresses the thermal stresses that arise due to the mismatch of the respective layers' thermal expansion coefficients which can lead to delamination in SOFCs [5]. Functionally graded materials (FGMs) represent a technique to eliminate discrete layers. The dependence of in-plane normal thermal stresses on the concavity of FGM profiles is shown in Figure 4. Local material properties are calculated through rules of mixtures introduced by Nemat-Alla [6] and are here applied to SOFC layer materials. The maximal absolute value of normal stress is a second scoring criterion for electrode designs.

(a)

(b)

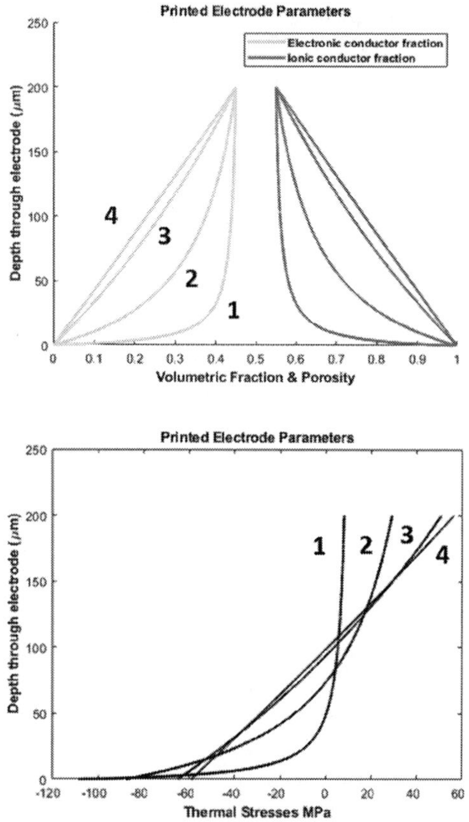

Figure 4. (a) SOFC Ni (electronic cond.) -YSZ (ionic cond.) electrode compositional grading profiles (0 µm= electrolyte) (b) Corresponding thermal stresses predicted

A genetic algorithm (GA), NSGA-II, is used to breed individual electrode designs. Microstructural parameters such as composite local phase fraction, mean grain size, grain size variance, porosity, and compositional profile concavity are considered as design variables. An example of a Pareto front produced by the optimization of a 30 µm thick Ni-YSZ anode is shown in Figure 5. Individual A, a noninferior solution and near-optimal compromise of objectives, had a mean YSZ grain size of 0.43 µm, Ni grain size of 0.41 µm, and porosity of 40%. The convergence of phase grain sizes under maximal performance is explained in [7]. The range of allowable grain sizes based on preprocessing available for commercial powders was set at 0.4-1.0 µm. It is predicted that the functionally graded Ni/YSZ anode with second-order profile would result in an overpotential reduction of the half-cell from 0.19 V to 0.14 V at a current density of 1.0 A/cm^2 and a thermal stress reduction from 76 MPa to 48 MPa as shown in Figure 6 compared to a homogeneous electrode. Both electrodes have a composition of Ni:YSZ 36:64 by percent solid volume at the current collector.

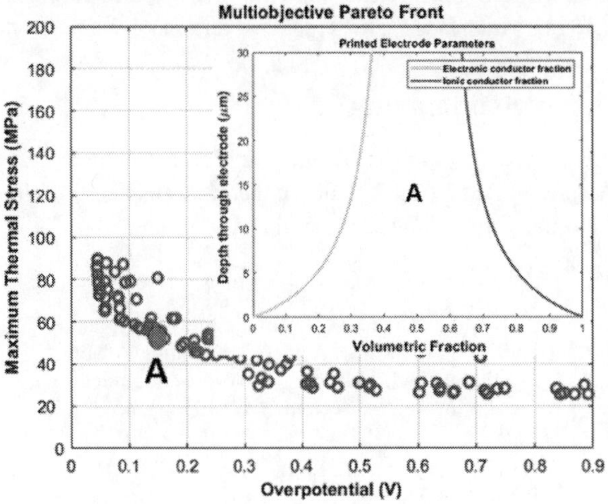

Figure 5. Pareto front of final generation of Ni-YSZ anode individuals with compositional grading profile inlay of individual "A" (Ni: green; YSZ: red)

(a)

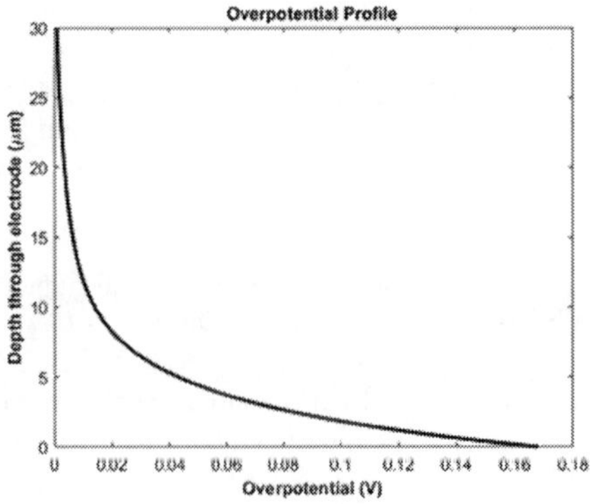

(b)

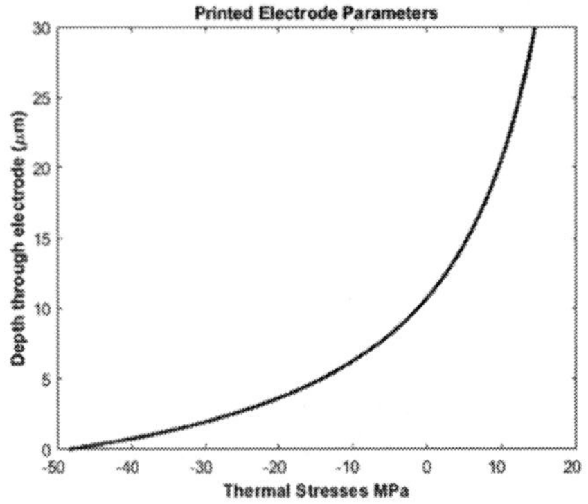

Figure 6. (a) Individual "A" Profile of Overpotential (b) Individual "A" Profile of Thermal Stresses

Functionally Graded Button Cell Printing

To achieve a functional graded anode structure, commercial NiO and YSZ powders (FC Materials) were colloidally dispersed to form jet printable inks. A suitably printable ink would have stably dispersed sub-micron particles, a room temperature viscosity < 40 mPas, and a low vapor pressure solvent [8]. Relative to other drop on demand techniques like inkjet printing, AJP can deposit inks with a solids loading range of 20 – 40 wt. %. The ink formulations for the printed SOFC anode included components present in traditional tape casting recipes, such as an ethyl cellulose binder for green strength, and plasticizers like benzyl butyl phthalate, polyalkylene glycol, and polyvinyl butyral. Ink stability was provided by a phosphate ester dispersant and enhanced by viscosity tuning with the polymeric binder and plasticizers. The ceramic loading was above 35 wt.%. Using this ink, a linearized grading profile was deposited via AJP as a first order approximation of the more complex quadratic profile "A". The linear profile has a lower predicted absolute maximum normal stress of 31 MPa compared to 48 MPa of the quadratic profile. The atomic weight percent of Ni and YSZ in the printed layer was assessed by EDX (Figure 7). Micron scale functional grading of the Ni/YSZ anode was achieved.

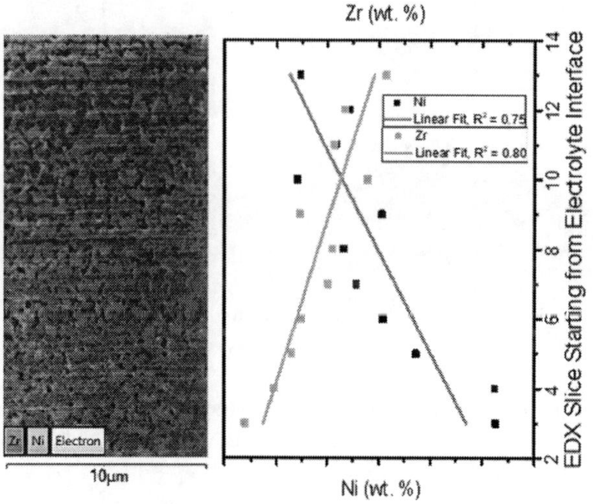

Figure 7. Overlay of EDX and SEM Image of Compositionally Graded Anode

Stack Scale SOFC Printing Verification

To demonstrate the scalability of the AJP process, full size 10 cm x 10 cm electrolyte supported SOFCs with homogeneous composition electrodes were printed. AJP was used to deposit a ~ 20 micron thick Ni/YSZ anode, ~20 micron thick LSCF cathode, and ~5 micron thick barrier layer of SDC. Even with compositionally homogeneous electrodes, precise control over layer thicknesses and the creation of seamless conformal interfaces may increase AJ printed cell performance over screen-printing or dip-coating methods.

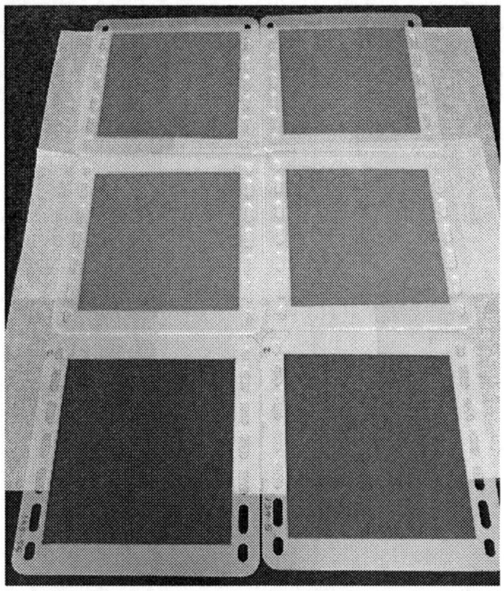

Figure 8. Finished 10 cm x 10 cm Printed SOFCs (upper two rows NiO-YSZ anode face up, lowest row LSCF cathode face up)

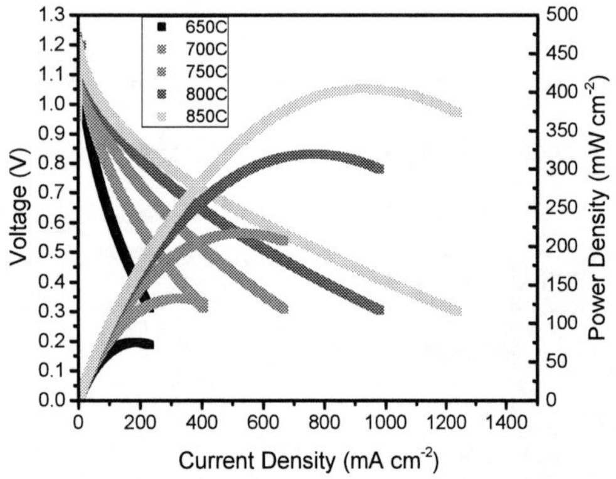

Figure 9. Electrochemical performance of AJ printed electrolyte-supported SOFC. Testing was performed in H_2(48 sccm)/air (150 sccm).

The electrochemical performance of AJ printed button cells using the same materials as the stack cells show a performance competitive with commercial cells despite commercial cells being tested at fuel/oxidant fluxes approximately an order of magnitude greater than the AJ printed cells [9].

Conclusions

Aerosol jet deposition provides fine geometric control of electrical and electrochemical components from the microscale to macroscale. Applied to SOFCs, both homogeneous and functionally graded cell layers benefit from this level of manufacturing precision. Enhancements in electrochemical performance are still being verified experimentally, while the ability to provide gradation at material interfaces to reduce stresses has been demonstrated.

Acknowledgements

This work was funded by the Air Force Research Lab (Award #FA8650-19-2-9300) under the auspices of the Seedlings for Disruptive Capabilities Program.

References

[1] N. J. Wilkinson, M. A. A. Smith, R. W. Kay, and R. A. Harris, "A Review of Aerosol Jet Printing-A Non-Traditional Hybrid Process for Micro-Manufacturing," *Int. J. Adv. Manuf. Technol.*, vol. 105, pp. 4599–4619, 2019.

[2] L. J. Deiner and T. L. Reitz, "Inkjet and Aerosol Jet Printing of Electrochemical Devices for Energy Conversion and Storage," *Adv. Eng. Mater.*, vol. 19, no. 7, 2017.

[3] A. M. Sukeshini, P. Gardner, T. Jenkins, T. L. Reitz, and R. M. Miller, "Aerosol Jet Printing and Microstructure of SOFC Electrolyte and Cathode Layers," *ECS Trans.*, vol. 35, no. 1, pp. 2151–2160, 2011.

[4] A. M. Sukeshini, F. Meisenkothen, P. Gardner, and T. L. Reitz, "Aerosol Jet Printing of Functionally Graded SOFC Anode Interlayer and Microstructural Investigation by Low Voltage Scanning Electron Microscopy," *J. Power Sources*, vol. 224, pp. 295–303, 2013.

[5] M. Peksen, "Numerical thermomechanical modelling of solid oxide fuel cells," *Prog. Energy Combust. Sci.*, vol. 48, pp. 1–20, 2015, doi: 10.1016/j.pecs.2014.12.001.

[6] M. Nemat-Alla, "Reduction of thermal stresses by developing two-dimensional functionally graded materials," *Int. J. Solids Struct.*, vol. 40, no. 26, pp. 7339–7356, 2003, doi: 10.1016/j.ijsolstr.2003.08.017.

[7] A. M. Gokhale, S. Zhang, and M. Liu, "A stochastic geometry based model for total triple phase boundary length in composite cathodes for solid oxide fuel cells," *J. Power Sources*, vol. 194, no. 1, pp. 303–312, 2009, doi: 10.1016/j.jpowsour.2009.05.012.

[8] "Aerosol Jet Materials FAQs," 2017. https://optomec.com/wp-content/uploads/2014/04/AJ_MATERIALS_FAQs-Web0417.pdf.

[9] M. Seabaugh, "NextCell versus NextCell-HP:Comparing Performance Data," 2017. https://fuelcellmaterials.com/nextcell-versus-nextcell-hp-comparing-performance-data/.

Power and Energy for Small Unmanned Aerial Systems

Deryn Chu,
U.S. Army Combat Capabilities Development Command
Army Research Laboratory,
2800 Powder Mill Rd., Adelphi, MD 20783-1107
Deryn.d.chu.civ@army.mil

Abstract
Small unmanned aerial systems have great potential for many different applications. However, one of the major technical challenges encountered by small unmanned aerial systems today is working endurance, which is directly limited by fuselage space capacity for the on-board battery. This restricts the endurance, range, and nature of the functions which may be performed by the small unmanned aerial systems. Developing and implementing a high energy density and high-power density alternative power system is critical for these small unmanned autonomous systems. This work is studies alternative power and energy systems for small unmanned aerial systems.

Keywords
Unmanned Aerial System, Li-ion Battery, Li-Polymer Battery, Thin Film Solar Cell, Polymer Electrolyte Membrane Fuel Cell, Solid Oxide Fuel Cell.

Introduction
Unmanned aerial systems (UASs) have been used by many forces worldwide and were rapidly adopted during the Global War on Terror. Their development enabled the users to operate more effectively, efficiently, and safely in different working environments. However, state of the art battery technology is ill-suited for present and future mission requirements. For example, Li-polymer batteries provide less than 2 hours of flight time for similar small UAS platforms. This restricts the endurance, range, and nature of the functions which may be performed by the UASs. Therefore, it is critical to develop and implement alternative power systems for these small UASs. The other key drawbacks are the weight and size of the small UAS, which restrict the mounting of larger payloads or extra batteries. The objective of this study is to further investigate the viability of power and energy for small UASs extending flight endurance.

Results and Discussions
Several energy storage and power generation technologies were explored to maximize energy stored on-board and to achieve long endurance performance. This study focused on extending the endurance of small UASs, which are considered in the Group I (less than 20 and Group II (less than 50lbs) category [1].

I. Battery:

Fig 1. Battery powered a RQ-11 Raven (top) and RQ-20 Puma (bottom) systems.

A battery is an electrochemical energy storage device that stories energy at the electrodes. Currently, most of the small UASs are powered by either lithium-ion (Li-Ion) or lithium polymer (Li-Po) batteries. However, the flight endurance is usually limited between 60 to 90 minutes before requiring a forced recovery to replace depleted batteries. Lithium polymer batteries are becoming more popular for commercial and military UAS application due to their lower weight and greatly increased cycle life. However, lithium polymer batteries have a greater cycle life degradation rate than that of lithium-ion batteries. For storage purposes, lithium polymer batteries can be stored for one or two months without significant degradation in its state of charge, whereas other batteries will lose a significant amount of their charge during similar storage conditions. For long-term storage, it is highly recommended that the battery be stored at 40% of its full charge. A relevant example is the battery used for providing propulsion power on-board a small UAS. It is highly desirable to have an energy source that offers both high energy density and power density to sustain UAS flight extensive endurance missions. Several other common batteries that can be considered for small UAS applications are sodium-sulfur batteries and lithium-sulfur batteries. It is also important to develop fast charging batteries for future applications. Lithium batteries have degradation issues at high temperatures and serious degradation occurs when the cell is discharged below two volts. Additionally, when overcharged, they will experience capacity loss or thermal runaway. Figure 1 shows battery powered Raven (top) and Puma (bottom) small unmanned aerial systems [2-3].

II. Thin-Film-Solar-Cells:

A solar cell is a simple semiconductor device that converts light into electric energy. Some important characteristics of solar cells include that cell output voltage constant with the varying sunlight intensity and is independent of cell size, and decreases at a rate of 2mV/C as temperature rises. On the other hand, cell current is relatively stable at high temperature and is directly proportional to sunlight intensity and cell-size. Therefore, to obtain a high output power, solar panels need to be operated at lower temperatures with multiple large sized cells connected individually. The additional power provided by solar cells to sUAS with electrically powered propulsion systems will increase UAS flight endurance and flight time and will give users with added field surveillance capabilities. The idea is to hybridize the use of a thin-film-solar-cell with a lithium battery to power small UAS. A hybrid battery/thin-film-solar cell system would extend Raven or Puma flight endurance and has been studied by the Air Force Research Laboratory (AFRL) for the last two decades [4-5]. The AFRL partnered with UES, Inc. and Microlink Devices, Inc., to integrate a new lightweight, flexible, high-efficiency solar panel onto a small, unmanned aircraft system (UAS) platform (Fig.2). This would allow a Raven/Puma to be powered by a solar cell during the day and use its rechargeable battery for night operation. This approach needs Raven/Puma that incorporate larger wing surface area would benefit from this approach due to the increase in output power, along with better lift capability. Also, a DC-DC converter would be required allow for the solar cells to recharge the battery. This provides a desired output voltage and delivers maximum power from the thin film solar cells to the battery and load. Although promising, the thin film solar cell efficiency needs to be improved or using a high efficiency triple junction solar cell is needed for this application. However, using solar cells is highly dependent on the sun, and thus intermittent and difficult to predict, so a battery must still be used be to meet the UAS power demand.

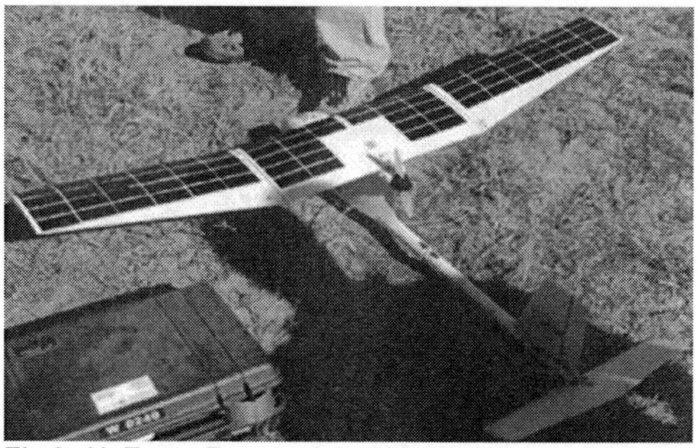

Fig 2. Air Force Research Laboratory partnership with UES, Inc. and Microlink Devices, Inc., has integrated new lightweight, flexible, high-efficiency solar panels onto a small, unmanned aircraft system (UAS) platform [4-5].

III. Fuel Cell:

A fuel cell produces electricity from an external fuel supply as opposed to the limited internal energy storage capacity of a battery. In simple terms, a fuel cell is an electrochemical device that converts hydrogen fuel directly into electricity, water, and heat without combustion. A fuel cell will continue to operate for as long as the externally stored fuels are supplied. Considerable attention has also been paid to the type of fuel cell that would be best suited for small UAS applications. The main fuel cells discussed in here are H_2 based polymer electrolyte membrane fuel cell (PEMFC) and solid oxide fuel cell (SOFC). PEMFC and SOFC are the most mature fuel cell technologies which could be suitable to use for UAS applications.

Department of Energy (DoE) has supported numerous H_2 based PEMFC programs due to their potential to become practical power generators for use in commercial applications, especially for electric vehicles. Several research and development programs designed to develop and demonstrate an H_2 based PEMFC systems for extending Puma flight endurance were supported by the Department of Defense's SBIR program around 2010 [6-7]. However, the issue for PEMFCs are they typically require a high purity hydrogen (99.99%). While hydrogen itself has a tremendous gravimetric energy density (energy/mass), it has an exceptionally low volumetric energy density (energy/volume). This means such systems are either too large for small

UAS or require a heavy high pressures H_2 storage tank. Further, the transport and storage of hydrogen is extremely difficult for practical applications. In this regard, SOFCs have a significant advantage over PEMFCs. SOFCs have much greater fuel flexibility due to higher operational temperatures. The other advantage of SOFCs is that the high operational temperatures produce waste heat, which can be used for endothermic reforming reactions. The challenges for SOFCs lies in finding materials which have both the necessary performance and stability (thermal and mechanical) to operate at high temperatures (~800°C).

Defense Advanced Research Project Agency (DARPA) and Army Research Laboratory (ARL) had jointed development on a propane fueled solid oxide fuel cell (SOFC) system to power the small UAS [8]. Since a robust and rigorous SOFC system is needed for this special application, a tubular SOFC stack design was chosen. The SOFC was hybridized with a high power density Li-polymer battery to power the small UAS; this system is shown in Fig 3. A block diagram for fuel cell and battery hybrid power system is shown in Fig. 4. Initial power flows from the battery to start the fuel cell. After the fuel cell reaches normal operation and provides power with battery, the UAS takes off and begins its mission. The fuel cell recharges the battery during the UAS's cruise flight.

In partnership with Adaptive Materials Inc., Army Research Laboratory completed an evaluation of a 300W propane fueled ground SOFC system for its performance and thermal cyclic durability. The system performance and thermal cyclic durability met the performance expectation.

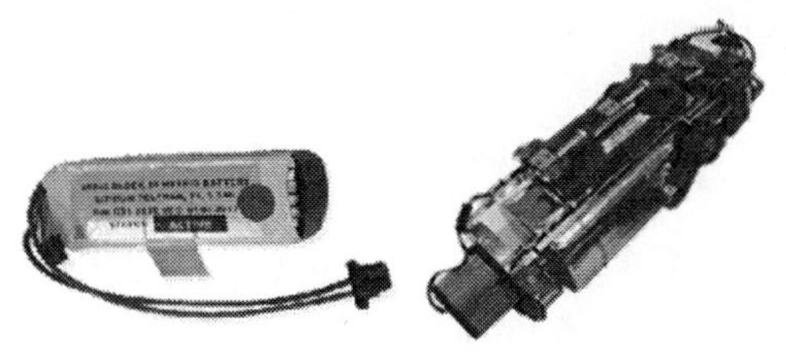

Fig. 3. SOFC/Li-polymer battery hybrid power system to power small UAS. Left photo is a lithium polymer battery and right photo is a solid oxide fuel cell.

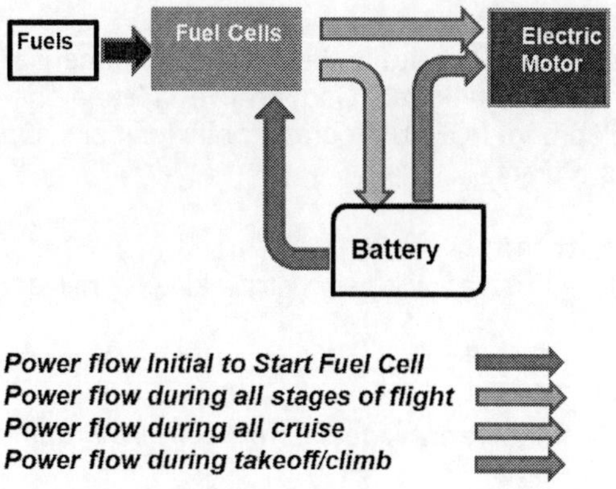

Fig. 4 A general block diagram of the fuel cell with battery hybrid power system.

Summary:

The battery is an energy storage system, and its energy capacity is a function of its battery size. Currently, the energy density of Li-ion or Li-polymer batteries are a limiting factor for UAS flight time. Although there is no great solution, SOFCs are currently used by the military as a power and energy solution to power UASs. High energy density batteries need to be developed for a long endurance UAS mission. Thin-film-solar-cell conversion efficiency is not high enough to power a small UAS, but better than 30% high efficiency triple junction solar cell may be a possible solution to power small UAS. PEMFCs are a viable technical solution to power portable electronic and equipment systems, but the effective use of PEMFCs in the practical applications would be a logistical problem since they require a safe, high-energy density, transportable, reliable source of hydrogen sources. Solid oxide fuel cells provide a fuel flexible advantage but need to be improved thermal cyclic durability. With respect to a UAS application, the fuel cell system power density is an extremely important figure of merit.

A fuel cell with a battery hybrid power system is the best power system to power small UAS for a long endurance and long-range missions. Fuel cells will offer lighter, more energetic power sources than are currently available, will extend mission time, reduce weight, and decrease the logistical burden associated with batteries. Batteries will offer high power density for UAS during take-off and climb. Some of the remaining challenges are meeting the size, space, and weight constraints for fuel storage on-board these small UASs. Understanding the performance characteristics of power system is clearly important for realizing the optimum cost/weight/volume/performance ratios.

Acknowledgments
The author would like to thank the Department of the Army's International Cooperative Research and Development (ICRD) program for its financial support of this project.

References:

1. https://en.wikipedia.org/wiki/U.S._military_UAS_groups
2. https://en.wikipedia.org/wiki/AeroVironment_RQ-11_Raven
3. https://en.wikipedia.org/wiki/AeroVironment_RQ-20_Puma
4. https://www.uasvision.com/2012/11/21/us-air-force-research-lab-incorporates-solar-cell-technology-into-small-unmanned-aircraft-systems/
5. https://www.wpafb.af.mil/News/Article-Display/Article/399512/afrl-incorporates-solar-cell-technology-into-small-unmanned-aircraft-systems/
6. https://newatlas.com/aerovironment-puma-hybrid-fuel-cell-uav-flight-record/8948/
7. https://www.upi.com/Defense-News/2007/11/29/Protonex-announces-fuel-cells-success/34921196350321/
8. https://en.wikipedia.org/wiki/Lockheed_Martin_Stalker.

Powder Bed Fusion of Nontoxic Copper(I) Sulfide Thermoelectric Materials for Energy Harvesting

Raden Gustinvil[1], Giuseppe L. Di Benedetto[2], Donald Skelton[2], Samuel Stuart[3], and Emrah Celik[1]

[1]Mechanical and Aerospace Engineering Department University of Miami Coral Gables, FL, USA, 33146

[2]U.S. Army Combat Capabilities Development Command Armaments Center, Picatinny Arsenal, NJ 07806, USA

[3]U.S. Navy Naval Surface Warfare Center, Crane Division, IN 47522, USA

Contact Author Email: e.celik.miami.edu

Abstract

Copper(I) sulfide (Cu_2S) has gained significant appeal as a thermoelectric material recently, since it is an earth-abundant, nontoxic material with high conversion efficiency in the middle-high temperature range (>650 K). Melting-based manufacturing of copper(I) sulfide, however, leads to the sulfur deficiency and dramatic reduction of its thermoelectric performance. In this study, we present the use of powder bed fusion (PBF) additive manufacturing technology to fabricate $Cu_{2-x}S$ samples with high thermoelectric performance for the first time. PBF allows enhanced designed freedom and the following sulfur infusion postprocessing reverts the impaired thermoelectric properties back to its original state. Thermoelectric characterization of the fabricated specimens indicated a p-type material with peak electrical conductivity of 115 Scm^{-1} at 650 K, Seebeck coefficient of 182 μVK^{-1} at 775 K, and a power factor of 0.34 $mWm^{-1}K^{-2}$ at 775 K. This is the first report of $Cu_{2-x}S$ fabricated using this additive manufacturing methodology and with high thermoelectric performance. This work demonstrates the importance of the sulfur infusion postprocessing to revert the lost sulfur thus enhancing the energy conversion efficiency. Fabrication of environmentally friendly thermoelectric materials with extended design freedom and at high conversion efficiency has the potential to greatly impact the thermoelectric industry with novel energy harvesting applications and lowered manufacturing costs.

Keywords

Powder bed fusion; Copper(I) sulfide; 3D printing; Thermoelectrics; Sulfur infusion

Introduction

The direct and thermodynamically reversible conversion of heat energy into electrical energy and vice versa is commonly referred to as thermoelectricity [1]. Thermoelectric (TE) materials use this phenomenon in thermoelectric generators (TEG) to improve energy efficiency in a variety of systems by recapturing surplus heat that would otherwise be wasted to the environment. To measure the performance of various thermoelectric materials, the dimensionless figure of merit, *ZT*, is used:

$$ZT = \frac{\sigma S^2}{\kappa} T$$

where σ is the electrical conductivity, S is the Seebeck coefficient, κ is the thermal conductivity and T is the absolute temperature in Kelvin.

The thermoelectric phenomenon has garnered significant scientific interest since the 1950s [2]. The most common and widely known materials for commercial thermoelectric applications being from the chalcogen family specifically: bismuth telluride (Bi_2Te_3) [3, 4] and lead telluride (PbTe) [5, 6] as they have been reported to have a *ZT* value around one in low to medium range temperature settings. Although these are currently the most used TE materials for commercial applications, these materials are highly toxic and expensive. Copper-based chalcogenides, specifically copper sulfides, address these issues. Copper sulfides are an earth abundant, non-toxic, and compositionally versatile class of materials with a high *ZT* level [7].

Copper(I) sulfide (Cu_2S), often known as chalcocite, has three different crystal phases. Monoclinic *P21/c* crystal structure of γ-Cu_2S below 370 K, hexagonal β-Cu_2S between 370 and 700 K, and cubic α-Cu_2S phase above 700 K (. With reported values of a maximum ZT of 1.7 at 1000 K for bulk solids [8], copper(I) sulfide has previously been shown to be an effective substitute as a thermoelectric material. However, it has one of the more complicated phase diagrams of any metal sulfide, making it challenging to synthesis with stoichiometric precision [9] throughout the full composition range. The stoichiometry and thermoelectric characteristics of Cu_2S are strongly connected. Under the correct circumstances, the mobility of copper ions can increase copper surface migration above the superionic phase transition temperature (~350 K), which influences the conversion efficiency. This can be reduced by either reducing the operating current or adding a grain-boundary designed microstructure. Consequently, permitting the transport of electrons and holes while obstructing the transit of ions [10].

Traditional TE leg fabrication involves powder synthesis, sintering or ingot pressing, leg dicing, metallization, and interconnect fabrication [11]. There are fundamental limitations, however, to thermoelectric systems preventing their integration into modern society including low conversion efficiency and this complex multistep fabrication process. The procedure is time consuming, costly, and limited to simple planar geometric structures. Three-dimensional (3D) printing technologies offer a transformative potential for manufacturing the next generation of TE systems by overcoming these challenges. Various additive manufacturing (AM) technologies have been previously implemented for the fabrication of TE materials including fused filament fabrication [12], stereolithography [13], and powder bed fusion [14]. Powder bed fusion (PBF), also known as selective laser sintering/melting, is an additive manufacturing process that allows for the generation of complex parts by selectively solidifying layers of powder material on top of each other by means of a high-power laser. In the build chamber, a thin layer of powder typically 40-60 microns [15] is spread across the print bed and the laser is directed onto specific regions to fuse the powder together. Afterwards, the platform is moved down a predetermined distance where the entire process is repeated until the final part is complete. Polymers [16], metals [17], and ceramics [18] have been fabricated using this technology. The only report work of additively manufactured $Cu_{2-x}S$ was accomplished using a pseudo 3D printing paste extrusion technique with a maximum ZT of 0.63 at 966 K [19]. In this work we present the first successfully demonstrated use of a commercial PBF printer (EOS M100) with a modified recoater blade capable of processing irregularly shaped Cu_2S powder feedstock.

Methodology

Sample Fabrication: Commercial copper(I) sulfide (Cu_2S) powder (American Elements, 99.995%) was sieved using a vibratory sieve shaker (Gilson, Lewis Center, OH) to a particle size distribution of ~20 – 45 μm. The PBF process was conducted using an EOS M100 (EOS, Krailling, Munich) with a customized vibratory recoater blade as shown in Figure 1. The machine is equipped with a 200 W Yb fiber laser with a focus spot size of 40 μm. Samples were printed in various geometries with a layer height of 20 microns on a stainless-steel ⌀100 mm substrate.

Sulfur Infusion Postprocessing: Due to the high energy input from the laser, sulfur in the alloy volatilizes, causing the sample to become sulfur deficient. After the sintering process, copper precipitates can be observed within the cross section of the sample. This decreases the sample's thermoelectric performance. Postprocessing was applied to infuse sulfur back into the specimens and enhance thermoelectric properties. The sintered specimens were heated at 1073 K, well below the sintering temperature of copper(I) sulfide, for 2 hours with sulfur powder (99.5%, Alfa Aesar) in the vacuum sealed furnace and purged with argon gas to diffuse the lost sulfur back into the system. For post-processing, five percent of the total mass of the sample in sulfur was utilized.

Compositional Characterization: Scanning electron microscopy (SEM) was conducted on as-is and post-processed samples with images taken on the Zeiss Gemini Field Emission SEM (Germany). Sputter coating was not required due to the conductive nature of the samples.

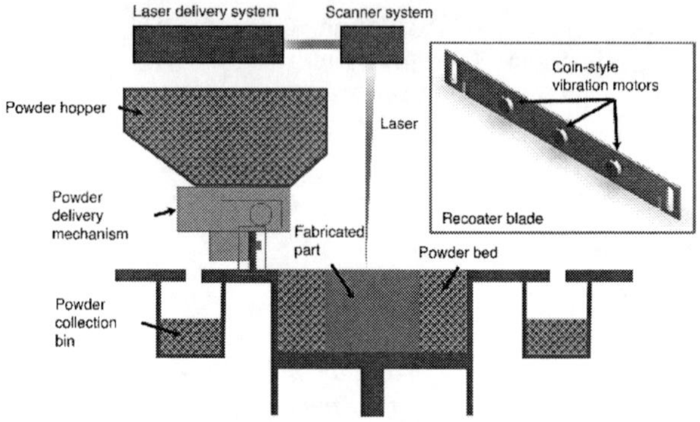

Figure 1: Schematic overview of PBF process

Thermoelectric Characterization: Electrical conductivity and Seebeck coefficient were measured using the Linseis LSR-3 system (Linseis, Germany). Electrical conductivity was calculated using the measured resistivity of the sample via the four-point probe method with a current of 10 mA being applied through the upper and lower electrodes at the time of measurement. The voltage was recorded in the middle of the sample by two (2) affixed thermocouples. Seebeck coefficient measurements were conducted using an upper and lower heater maintaining a constant thermal gradient of 30 K. The voltage and temperature differential were recorded using the same platinum-coated thermocouples spaced approximately three (3) mm apart. All measurements were performed from room temperature to 774 K in 25 K intervals with a heating rate of 10 $Kmin^{-1}$. Properties were probed three (3) times at each temperature point with a dwell time of one (1) minute in-between each consecutive measurement. Density (ρ) of the 3D-printed samples were measured using a density determination kit (Ohaus, Parsippany, NJ) based on the Archimedes' principle. For the thermoelectric characterization, sample dimensions were required to have a minimum thickness of two (2) mm, a height of seven (7) mm and a width of four (4) mm.

Parameter Optimization: Prior to fabricating thermoelectric specimens, optimal printing parameters must be obtained for the Cu_2S powder in the EOS M100 machine. The energy density given by the equation:

$$E = \frac{P}{vht}$$

where P is the laser power (W), v is the scan speed (mms^{-1}), t is the layer height (mm), and h is the hatch distance (mm) needed to be identified. These parameters can be optimized by conducting a single line test varying the laser power and scan speed while visually identifying the appropriate melt pool width. Laser speed was assessed from 25 – 175 W in 25 W increments while scan speed was tested from 200 – 1600 mms^{-1} in 200 mms^{-1} increments as shown in Figure 2. The laser parameters chosen were 30W, 400 mms^{-1}, and a hatch distance of 0.07 mm and layer thickness of 0.02 mm giving a volumetric energy density of 53.57 Jmm^{-3}.

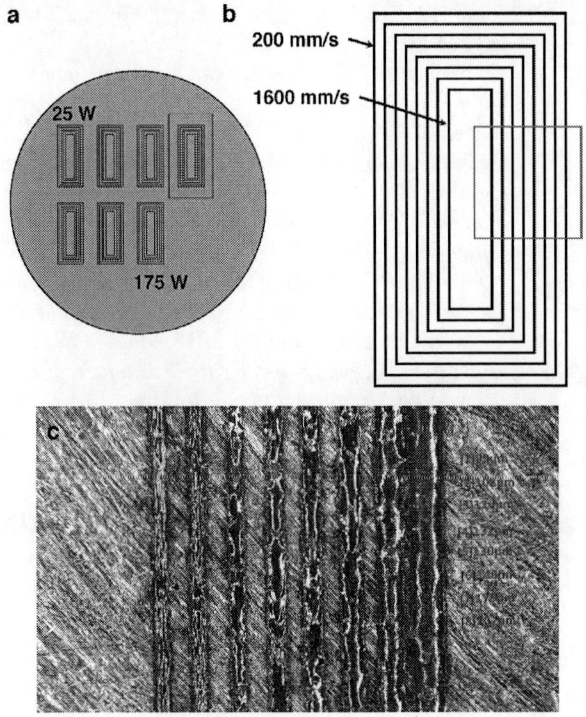

Figure 2: Single line test conducted with a single layer of Cu_2S powder. a) Arrangement of test on print substrate. b) Layout of scan lines. c) Melt pool width analysis conducted using FIJI

Results

Morphological Analysis: Using the obtained parameters, samples were fabricated in various complex geometries with a total of 100 layers yielding an approximate height of two (2) mm. As shown in Figure 3, these features would otherwise be difficult to fabricate using traditional manufacturing methodologies. Samples were found to be highly dense with a density of 5.422 ± 0.291 gcm^{-3} after post processing. No separation of the subsequent layers was present in the cross section of the sample indicating full melting of each layer was achieved. The internal defects in Figure 3d can be attributed to gas entrapment [ref] due to the rapid solidification during the PBF process.

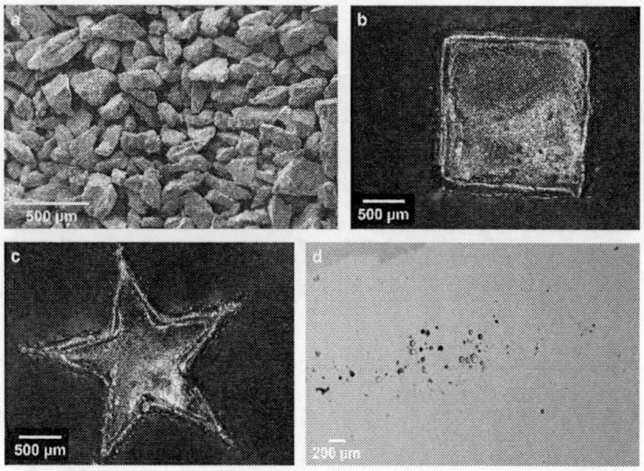

Figure 3: a) Cu_2S feedstock powder. b-c) Samples fabricated in the EOS M100 in various geometries. d) SEM of a polished cross section of the post processed sample.

Thermoelectric Characterization: Figure 4 displays the electrical conductivity, Seebeck coefficient and power factor of the as-is and sulfur infused samples. Electrical conductivity (displayed in log scale) ranged from 35 to 115 Scm^{-1} for post processed samples and from 0.02 to 4 Scm^{-1} for as printed samples. Seebeck coefficient varied from 76 to X 182 μVK^{-1} for post process samples and -736 to 416 μVK^{-1} for as printed samples. Between 370 – 700 K the cause for printed samples acting as a n-type could be due the increased mobility of copper ions and the excess electrons associated with it.

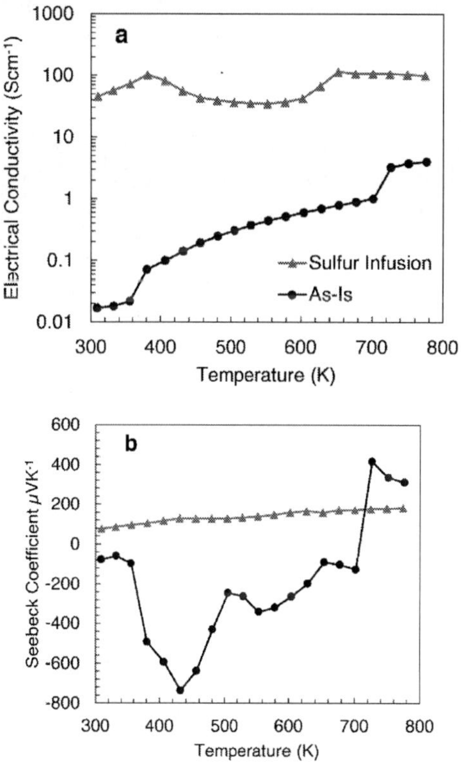

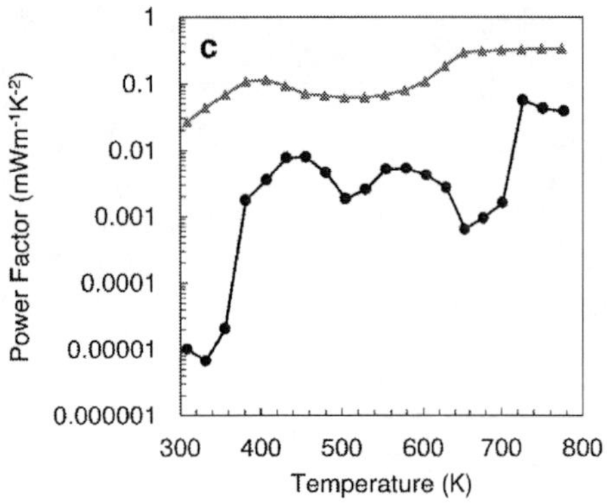

Figure 4: Thermoelectric properties of PBF fabricated $Cu_{2-x}S$ samples: a) electrical conductivity, b) Seebeck coefficient, and c) power factor.

The effect of transitioning from copper-rich to sulfur-rich material can be so dramatic that the power factor increases two orders of magnitude as reported here.

Conclusion

The work presented here exhibits the first successful use of a commercial PBF system to produce $Cu_{2-x}S$ samples using irregularly shaped powder. Using a sulfur infusion post processing method, samples' stoichiometry transition from copper rich to sulfur rich marked by a significant increase in thermoelectric properties. Post processed samples demonstrated a peak electrical conductivity of 115 Scm^{-1} at 650 K, Seebeck coefficient of 182 μVK^{-1} at 775 K. Leading to a power factor of 0.34 $mWm^{-1}K^{-2}$ at 775 K, the highest reported for $Cu_{2-x}S$ bulk samples made using this AM methodology.

Acknowledgements

This work is supported by the U.S. Army Combat Capabilities Development Command Armaments Center under the Project Number DOTC-19-01-INIT0903.

References

1. Twaha, S., et al., *A comprehensive review of thermoelectric technology: Materials, applications, modelling and performance improvement.* Renewable and Sustainable Energy Reviews, 2016. **65**: p. 698-726.
2. Beretta, D., et al., *Thermoelectrics: From history, a window to the future.* Materials Science and Engineering: R: Reports, 2019. **138**.
3. Goldsmid, H.J., *Bismuth Telluride and Its Alloys as Materials for Thermoelectric Generation.* Materials, 2014. **7**(4): p. 2577-2592.
4. Poudel, B., et al., *High-thermoelectric performance of nanostructured bismuth antimony telluride bulk alloys.* Science, 2008. **320**(5876): p. 634-638.
5. Dughaish, Z.H., *Lead telluride as a thermoelectric material for thermoelectric power generation.* Physica B-Condensed Matter, 2002. **322**(1-2): p. 205-223.
6. LaLonde, A.D., et al., *Lead telluride alloy thermoelectrics.* Materials Today, 2011. **14**(11): p. 526-532.
7. Liu, W.D., et al., *Promising and Eco-Friendly Cu2 X-Based Thermoelectric Materials: Progress and Applications.* Adv Mater, 2020. **32**(8): p. e1905703.
8. He, Y., et al., *High thermoelectric performance in non-toxic earth-abundant copper sulfide.* Adv Mater, 2014. **26**(23): p. 3974-8.
9. Dennler, G., et al., *Are Binary Copper Sulfides/Selenides Really New and Promising Thermoelectric Materials?* Advanced Energy Materials, 2014. **4**(9).
10. Qiu, P., et al., *Suppression of atom motion and metal deposition in mixed ionic electronic conductors.* Nat Commun, 2018. **9**(1): p. 2910.
11. Zhang, H., et al., *Laser additive manufacturing of powdered bismuth telluride.* Journal of Materials Research, 2018. **33**(23): p. 4031-4039.
12. Oztan, C., et al., *Additive manufacturing of thermoelectric materials via fused filament fabrication.* Applied Materials Today, 2019. **15**: p. 77-82.
13. Orrill, M. and S. LeBlanc, *Printed thermoelectric materials and devices: Fabrication techniques, advantages, and challenges.* Journal of Applied Polymer Science, 2017. **134**(3).
14. Thimont, Y., et al., *Thermoelectric Higher Manganese Silicide: Synthetized, sintered and shaped simultaneously by selective laser sintering/Melting additive manufacturing technique.* Materials Letters, 2018. **214**: p. 236-239.
15. Vock, S., et al., *Powders for powder bed fusion: a review.* Progress in Additive Manufacturing, 2019. **4**(4): p. 383-397.
16. Chatham, C.A., T.E. Long, and C.B. Williams, *A review of the process physics and material screening methods for polymer powder bed fusion additive manufacturing.* Progress in Polymer Science, 2019. **93**: p. 68-95.
17. Oliveira, J.P., A.D. LaLonde, and J. Ma, *Processing parameters in laser powder bed fusion metal additive manufacturing.* Materials & Design, 2020. **193**.
18. Florio, K., et al., *Process characterization and analysis of ceramic powder bed fusion.* International Journal of Advanced Manufacturing Technology, 2021. **117**(7-8): p. 2105-2116.
19. Burton, M.R., et al., *Earth abundant, non-toxic, 3D printed Cu2−xS with high thermoelectric figure of merit.* Journal of Materials Chemistry A, 2019. **7**(44): p. 25586-25592.

Decentralized Energy Generation and Environmental Impact Reduction via Perovskite Solar Cells

Lissette Rodríguez-Cabañas
U.S. Army Futures Command, Combat Capabilities Development Command (DEVCOM), C5ISR Center
APG, MD 21005

Calvin Duong
U.S. Army Futures Command, Combat Capabilities Development Command (DEVCOM), C5ISR Center
APG, MD 21005

Bradley Stanley
U.S. Army Futures Command, Combat Capabilities Development Command (DEVCOM), C5ISR Center
APG, MD 21005

Andre Slonopas
U.S. Army Futures Command, Combat Capabilities Development Command (DEVCOM), C5ISR Center
APG, MD 21005

Abstract

Perovskite solar cells (PSC's), and metal-halide variants specifically, continue to be some of the most researched and promising materials for the low-cost energy generation among other applications. Metal-halide perovskites, possess the highly desirable direct band-gap and highly tunable band structures. Furthermore, organic nature of the materials greatly simplifies the deposition of the materials and thus makes them good candidates across a broad range of applications. PSC's consistently demonstrate Power Conversion Efficiencies (PCE's) above 24% through a low temperature simplified deposition that reduces the overall device cost by over 30%. As technology advances the energy consumption increases and Perovskites are key in reducing those operational costs. This paper also focuses on the CO_2 generation and the environmental impact reduction associated with the technology. Successful stabilization of perovskites, in thermal, hydro, and oxygen environments, will enable PSC's to be scaled for applications in multiple markets.

Keywords: perovskite solar cells, stability, semiconductors, radiation

Introduction

Energy remains the most crucial commodity among established and emerging economies. Despite supply chain disruptions energy consumption across all markets continues to grow exponentially [1]. More recently the demand for decentralized sustainable energy sources increased dramatically [2]. Solar energy harvesting has the potential to fill the gap of the energy generation due to the stable, predictable, and continuous supply of solar radiation. Annual solar irradiance is estimated to be nearly 1,361 W/m^2 in the upper atmosphere which equates to over 170,000 TW of power and over 1 zettajoule of energy [3]. This volume of energy is nearly unfathomable, abundant, steady, and even at 20% Power Conversion Efficiency (PCE) of a conventional solar device is orders of magnitude above current global consumption. Furthermore, solar energy is evenly distributed across the globe, with solar irradiation exceeding 1,600 kWh/m^2 between North and South latitudes of 45° [4]. Thus, an enormous opportunity exists to harvest energy locally, reduce energy transportation inefficiencies, and provide sustainable energy to established and emerging markets.

While a variety of semiconducting materials are available for solar energy harvesting, in recent years perovskites emerged as the most promising and novel class of materials for this application. Perovskite materials in general, and methylammonium lead iodide ($MAPbI_3$) chemistries in particular, demonstrate favorable opto-electronic characteristics for such applications [5, 6]. Hybrid versions of the perovskite materials consist of inorganic-organic, ABX_3, stoichiometries, where the A & B cations and X anions are interchangeable [7]. This interchangeability within the chemical structure of the material enables a highly tunable material that can be optimized for a broad range of applications. Furthermore, both cations and anions can be substituted with materials that possess highly ameliorable, environmentally friendly among other favorable properties besides being readily available.

It has been demonstrated that the perovskite materials can be synthesized via a variety of scalable low-cost methodologies that include spin/spray coating, inkjet printing, chemical bath, chemical vapor among other prevalent techniques [8, 9, 10]. The variety of deposition techniques further broadens the range of chemical constituents that can be leveraged in A & B locations of the structure. Success of various depositions methods has been demonstrated by various research groups with perovskite minimodules of 49 cm^2 reaching PCE's of 24% [11, 12]. Given the recent success in the maturation of perovskite materials, numerous groups began exploring the scalability of the materials for eventual penetration of the market.

Given the recent successes of these materials, Perovskites are becoming a desired material for multiple applications including the reduction of CO_2 footprint. These materials, however, are unable to penetrate the markets due to their instabilities under thermal and humid conditions [13, 14].

The low activation energy of the anions induces ion migration under light thermal stresses [15]. Migration of the anions leaves a vacancy within the X location of the perovskite structure, hence generating defects and inducing exciton recombination rates. Given the hygroscopic and hydrophilic nature of the materials, materials have been shown to degrade even under low humidity conditions [16]. Thermal and humid stabilities need to be addressed prior to large scale applications of the materials. Perovskites, however, need to be stabilized and ruggedized for a broad range of austere conditions before they can be widely utilized.

Perovskite Solar Cell

PSC Structures

Unlike their inorganic counterparts, perovskite solar cells (PSC's) consist of three layers, i.e. perovskite material (active layer) is sandwiched between electron- and hole-transporting layers, ETL and HTL respectively. This basic design is analogous to the n-i-p and p-i-n structures of the traditional solar cells, *Figure 1 (a)*. Given the ABX_3 structure of the materials, perovskites band structure is highly malleable and tunable. Given this tunability, a broad range of ETLs and HTL's can be applied to the materials and band structure can be aligned to maximize electron extraction. Sn has been one of the most explored substitutes for the Pb position within the structure, Sn changes the morphological and band structures of the material, but also provides an opportunity for lead free perovskite solar cell in the future, *Figure 1 (b).*

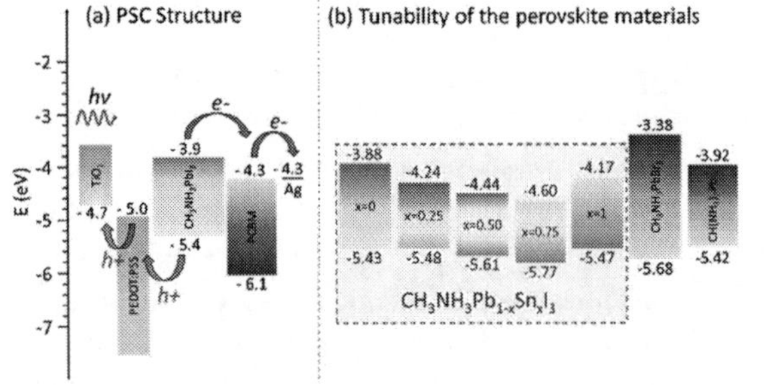

Figure 1. (a) Typical PSC structure.
(b) Tunability of the perovskite materials based on the B location cation replacement.

Materials such as fullerene C_{60}, various fullerene derivatives such as [6,6]-phenyl C_{61} butyric acid methyl ester (PCBM), bathocuproine (BCP), CdS, have all been explored as possible ETLs for the PSC. A broad range of materials for HTLs has also been explored to include poly(3,4-ethylene dioxythiophene):polystyrene sulfonic acid (PEDOT:PSS), NiO, and Poly(N,N'-bis-4-butylphenyl-N,N'-bisphenyl)benzidine (polyTPD), tert-butylpyridine (TBP), 2,2′,7,7′-tetrakis-(N,N-di-4-methoxyphenylamino)-9,9′-spirobifluorene (spiro-MeOTAD), poly[bis(4-phenyl)(2,4,6- trimethylphenyl) amine] (PTAA). Thus it is possible to select stoichiometries with various band-structures that can be optimized for performance under various conditions [17].

Another benefit of the tunability of the perovskite solar structure is the ability to use multiple Transparent Conducting Oxides (TCO's) on either the electron- or hole-extracting layer side. This enables a broader range of deposition techniques where the more stable layers can be deposited earlier in the process. As an example the PEDOT:PSS is often leveraged as an HTL in the PSC. PEDOT:PSS is also known to be highly hydrophobic and thus provides an additional layer of protection against humidity for the functional material, *Figure 2 (a)*. Phase line mapping of the perovskite performance with PEDOT:PSS HTL and various fullerene based ETLs is shown to change significantly based on the stoichiometries of the materials, *Figure 2 (b)*. Hence, conditions must exist where the chemical compositions of the materials are such that enable optimized performance of PSC's.

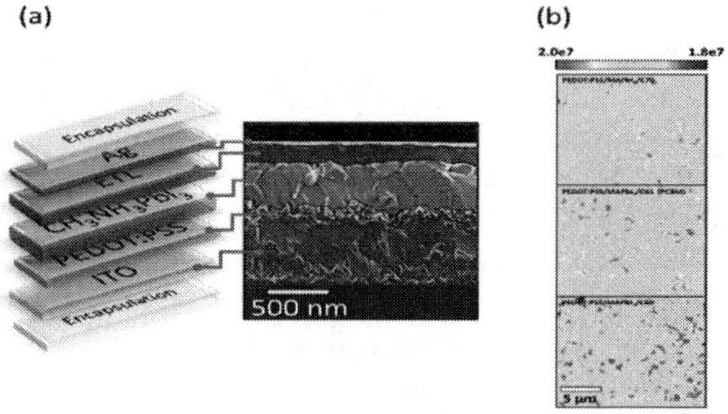

Figure 2. (a) Inverted PSC device configuration with PEDOT:PSS and its associated SEM image **(b)** forward and backward sweeps of the J-V curve comparison for n-i-p and p-i-n PSC structures.

Perovskite Film Degradation

Long term stability continues to plague perovskite materials. This is also the biggest factor that inhibits material deployment and utilization in multiple markets. Humidity has been identified as one of the most detrimental to perovskite performance. Exposure to the environment without the correct encapsulation will rapidly degrade the technology complicating its use. Amine molecules of the materials are known to be hygroscopic and thus absorb humidity from ambient environments which leads to degradation [18]. Since the instability is led by the anion molecules of the materials, similar degradation mechanisms and rates are observed across multiple perovskite stoichiometries.

Materials are found to be hygroscopic because of the amine molecules and hydrophilic in the A & B cation sites. Thus any effective control of degradation must include elimination or segregation of moisture from the materials. Deposition techniques must thus include inert atmosphere encapsulation and multilayer micro-encapsulation. Moisture has been found to prevent solidification of the films during the deposition. Thus, deposition of the materials must also take place in controlled chambers with limited moisture and controlled ambient environment [19].

Several moisture degradation mechanisms have been proposed in the past, most prevalent however is the hydrolysis reaction of the moisture with the film. This forces the amine group to migrate from the cation sites, effectively forcing ion migration and defects, *Figure 3 (a)*. Inorganic components of the materials can delay the migration of ions and help achieve stability of the materials [20]. Ultimate goal of the perovskite based solar cells, however, is to obtain fully organic materials.

Significant degradations are observed in materials that are deposited in 40% RH and further exposed to ambient atmosphere, *Figure 3 (b)*. Power conversion efficiency of materials degrades by over 50% within 10 days, and degrades nearly completely within 20 days. This data further solidifies the need for robust and ruggedized encapsulation and stabilization of the materials. Furthermore, segregation of ambient atmosphere is crucial with micro- and inert-atmosphere encapsulation. Additional approach to stabilization of materials has been through mesoporous interatomic layers [21]. Mesoporous layers have shown to prevent degradation in environments of up to 45% humidity even after 2,000 hours of operations. Despite significant achievements in stabilizing the materials, significant additional achievements are required for further applications.

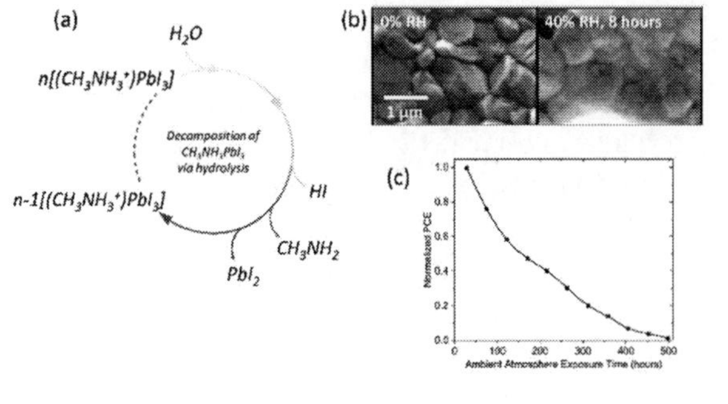

Figure 3. (a) Proposed hydrolysis decomposition of $CH_3NH_3PbI_3$ with the main byproduct of PbI_2. **(b)** SEM images of perovskite films deposited in 0% and 40% RH. **(c)** Normalized PCE of perovskite films exposed to ambient atmosphere.

A novel methodology of chemical vapor deposition (CVD) with inline micro-scale encapsulation with inert atmosphere capture will provide additional stability to the final device. Goal of this effort is to encapsulate inert atmosphere into a final device, which will enable further deleterious elements segregation and stabilize the materials. Although additional deposition steps are required, this methodology is expected to further expand the lifetime of these materials and nudge the technology towards maturation and deployment.

Perovskites have qualities that supersede current technologies such as the absorption of sunlight, ease of manufacturing, lower cost and flexibility. PSC's possess highly tunable opto-electrical properties, *Figure 4 (a)*. Thus, materials can find applications in multi-junctions of various combinations, making them suitable for innumerable applications. Furthermore, these materials exhibit exceptional radiation-induced photocurrent, *Figure 4 (b)*. Organic components of the perovskites, however, decay under thermal exposure above ~380K, thus cooling needs to be introduced at temperatures above these temperatures. Perovskites also undergo phase changes at 330K and 160K transitioning from cubic to tetragonal to orthorhombic phases respectively.

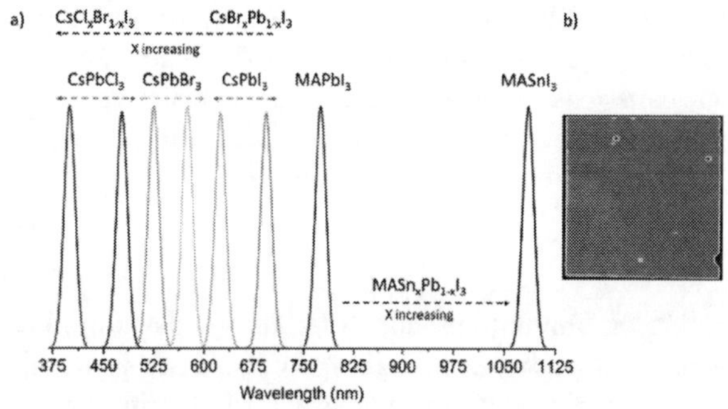

Figure 4. (a) Opto-electrical tunability of ABX_3 perovskite materials. **(b)** Radiation induced photocurrent in perovskite cells.

Temperature ranges can vary greatly, the Perovskite material will have the ability to undergo all three phase changes. While optimal performance of the materials is observed in orthorhombic phase, maintaining temperature of the materials below 380K will be crucial to prevent degradation.

Anion migration under thermal stresses also plays a role in generating defects and leaving to degradation. Activation energy for anions has been reported to be between 0.37 and 0.50 eV [22]. This low activation energy results in a significant portion of the anions to leave their sites, thus degrading the morphology of the materials and generating recombination sites. Ion migration has been mitigated via functionalized and engineered ionic fluids, control of the nucleation during deposition, and gradual crystallization of materials. 2- and 3-dimensional perovskites with varying quantum-well depths have also been explored to stabilize anions and prevent material degradation.

Material stability continues to be one of the most pursued research efforts in the field of perovskites. Preliminary data demonstrates that no 'silver-bullet' exists to resolve the stability issues. Thus, a combination of stabilization methodologies needs to be explored in order to achieve significant results.

Conclusion

Perovskites are an emerging class of hybrid materials that have enormous potential. While perovskites have applications well beyond energy harvesting, material applications for energy generation would be of great interest and impact. Application of these materials for energy harvesting will bring significant impact in reducing energy reliance on traditional fuel based sources and reduce the overall CO_2 footprint. Despite their promising nature and performance, perovskites still suffer from stability which needs to be addressed before wider acceptance. Extensive work is done to ensure that the stability of the materials is obtained thermal, humid, and ambient atmospheric environments. Additional stability is pursued via packaging and inert atmosphere encapsulation. CO_2 emissions to the atmosphere are the major cause for global warming and worldwide environmental disasters. Hence the potential for energy generation via resilient, cost-effective, and sustainable energy source is of great interest.

Having the ability to produce a technology that would be economically accessible, rugged, diverse, sustainable, and effective in reducing carbon footprint will be critical in the years to come..

References

[1] C. Chen, M. Pinar and T. Stengos, "Renewable energy consumption and economic growth nexus: evidence from a threshold model," *Energy Policy,* vol. 139, p. 111295, 2020.

[2] M. Blondeel, M. J. Bradshaw, G. Bridge and C. Kuzemko, "The geopolitics of energy system transformation: A review," *Geography Compass,* vol. 15, no. 7, 2021.

[3] M. Wild, "The global energy balance as represented in CMIP6 climate models," *Climate Dynamics,* vol. 55, pp. 553-577, 2020.

[4] A. Slonopas, L. Rodriguez-Cabanas, C. Duong, D. Baker, V. Parameshwaran and B. Stanley, "Low-cost perovskite materials for decentralized energy generation and Department of Defense environmental impact reduction," *SPIE Organic Photonics + Electronics: Organic, Hybrid, and Perovskite Photovoltaics XXIII,* vol. 12209, 2022.

[5] M. K. Nazeeruddin and G. Grancini, "Dimensional tailoring of hybrid perovskites for photovoltaics," *Nature Reviews Materials,* vol. 4, pp. 4-22, 2019.

[6] A. Slonopas, H. Ryan and P. Norris, "Ultrahigh energy density CH3NH3PbI3 perovskite based supercapacitor with fast discharge," *Electrochimica Acta,* vol. 307, pp. 334-340, 2019.

[7] J. Teuscher, A. Ulianov, O. Müntener, M. Gratzel and N. Tetreault, "Control and study of the stoichiometry in evaporated perovskite solar cells," *ChemSusChem,* vol. 8, no. 22, pp. 3847-3852, 2015.

[8] A. Slonopas, B. Kaur and P. Norris, "Role of the colossal frequency and temperature dependent dielectric constant in the performance of the organo-metallic tri-halide perovskites," *Applied Physics Letters,* vol. 110, no. 22, p. 222905, 2017.

[9] I. A. Howard, T. Abzieher, I. M. Hossain, H. Eggers, F. Schackmar, S. Ternes, B. S. Richards, U. Lemmer and U. W. Paetzold, "Coated and Printed Perovskites for Photovoltaic Applications," *Advanced Materials,* vol. 31, no. 26, p. 1806702, 2019.

[10] Z. Li, P. Li, G. Chen, Y. Cheng, X. Pi, X. Yu, D. Yang, L. Han, Y. Zhang and Y. Song, "Ink engineering of inkjet printing perovskite," *ACS Applied Material Interfaces,* vol. 12, no. 35, p. 39082–39091, 2020.

[11] Z. Song, C. L. McElvany, A. B. Phillips, I. Celik, P. W. Krantz, S. C. Watthage, G. K. Liyanage, D. Apul and M. J. Heben, "A technoeconomic analysis of perovskite solar module manufacturing with low-cost materials and techniques," *Energy & Environmental Science,* vol. 10, pp. 1297-1305, 2017.

[12] A. Roy, B. Ding, M. Khalid, M. Alzahrani, Y. Ding, A. A. Tahir, S. Sundaram, S. Kinge, A. M. Asiri, A. Slonopas, P. J. Dyson, M. K. Nazeeruddin and T. K. Mallick, "Certified high-efficiency ''large-area'' perovskite solar module for Fresnel lens-based concentrated photovoltaics," *iScience,* vol. 26, p. 106079, 2023.

[13] S. Ruan, M. A. Surmiak, Y. Ruan, D. P. McMeekin, H. Ebendorff-Heidepriem and Y.-B. Cheng, "Light

induced degradation in mixed-halide perovskites," *Journal of Materials Chemistry C,* vol. 7, no. 30, pp. 9326-9334, 2019.

[14] J. Yang, B. D. Siempelkamp, D. Liu and T. L. Kelly, "Investigation of CH3NH3PbI3 degradation rates and mechanisms in controlled humidity environments using in situ techniques," *ACS Nano,* vol. 9, no. 2, p. 1955–1963, 2015.

[15] P. Vashishtha and J. E. Halpert, "Field-driven ion migration and color instability in red-emitting mixed halide perovskite nanocrystal light-emitting diodes," *Chemistry of Materials,* vol. 29, no. 14, p. 5965–5973, 2017.

[16] A. Bouich, J. Mari-Guaita, F. Baig, Y. H. Khattak, B. Mari Soucase and P. Palacios, "Investigation of the surface coating, humidity degradation, and recovery of perovskite film phase for solar-cell applications," *Nanomaterials,* vol. 12, no. 17, p. 3027, 2022.

[17] H. S. Jung and N.-G. Park, "Perovskite solar cells: from materials to devices," *Small,* vol. 11, no. 1, pp. 10-25, 2014.

[18] C. Fu, Z. Gu, Y. Tang, Q. Xiao, S. Zhang, Y. Zhang and Y. Song, "From structural design to functional construction: amine molecules in high-performance formamidinium-based perovskite solar cells," *Angewandte Chemie,* vol. 61, no. 19, 2022.

[19] J. A. Christians, P. A. Miranda Herrera and P. V. Kamat, "Transformation of the excited state and photovoltaic efficiency of CH3NH3PbI3 perovskite upon controlled exposure to humidified air," *Journal of American Chemical Society,* vol. 137, no. 4, p. 1530–1538, 2015.

[20] D. Li, P. Liao, X. Shai, W. Huang, S. Liu, H. Li, Y. Shen and M. Wang, "Recent progress on stability issues of organic–inorganic hybrid lead perovskite-based solar cells," *RSC Advances,* vol. 6, no. 92, pp. 89356-89366, 2016.

[21] C. Worsley, D. Raptis, S. Meroni, A. Doolin, R. Garcia-Rodriguez, M. Davies and T. Watson, "γ-Valerolactone: a nontoxic green solvent for highly stable printed mesoporous perovskite solar cells," *Energy Technology,* vol. 9, no. 7, p. 2100312, 2021.

[22] S. R. Pering and P. J. Cameron, "The effect of multiple ion substitutions on halide ion migration in perovskite solar cells," *Materials Advances,* pp. 7918-7924, 20223.

Hydrogen-fueled Power Generator using Nanogalvanic Aluminum Alloy to Produce Hydrogen

Girish Srinivas*, Brady Clapsaddle, Joe Fredrickson, Jackson Brandstaetter, Jeff Martin
TDA Research, Inc.
Wheat Ridge, Colorado, U.S.A., 80033
gsrinivas@tda.com / 1-303-422-7819

Abstract

Hydrogen gas (H_2) has many benefits as an alternative energy source, including environmental and energy supply benefits. Hydrogen can be used to produce electricity in fuel cells and hydrogen internal combustion engines. Producing H_2 at the point-of-need is especially attractive, as storing and transporting pressurized tanks of hydrogen is hazardous due to the high pressure and flammability of the gas involved. There are several solids that can produce H_2 when reacted with water that have far higher energy densities than hydrocarbon-based fuels and are safer to transport than pressurized hydrogen. One material is a novel nanogalvanic aluminum alloy developed by the Army that has the highest volumetric energy density of any solid hydrogen fuel. However, equipment for safely generating hydrogen from fuels at the point-of-need does not exist. To realize the potential of solid hydrogen fuels, hazardous, pressurized fuel tanks must be eliminated and replaced with an on-demand hydrogen generation capability at the point-of-need. TDA has developed a novel, portable, 900-Watt power generator that relies on hydrogen gas produced from the chemical reaction of the alloy and water to produce hydrogen as power is needed from the generator. The DC generator is portable, does not require high pressure sources of hydrogen, and only produces hydrogen as it is needed at the point of operation. The power generator is ideal for operating portable electronics (laptops, mobile phones, etc.) and charging batteries.

Keywords

Alternative Energy, Aluminum, Clean Energy, Fuel Cell, Gas generation, Hydrogen, Portable, Power Source

Introduction

The use of hydrogen to fuel power sources in mobile Military operations is very attractive as a replacement for hydrocarbon fuels. Producing hydrogen (H_2) at remote, mobile Military installations, however, can be difficult. Several solid chemical compounds exist that produce H_2 when reacted with water, including hydrides and metals, to name a few, but these compounds are difficult to transport and react violently and can ignite when they react with water.

Aluminum (Al) metal, in contrast, is easily handled, has a favorable H_2 production reaction with water and is controllable. However, *pure* Al contains a passivating oxide layer that is extremely stable in water, preventing the reaction of the underlying metal from forming hydrogen. As a result, pure aluminum will only produce hydrogen in water at high pH's (> 9) that first dissolve the passivating oxide layer, thus alkali solutions containing caustic, strong bases during reaction are required for full H_2 recovery from Reaction 1. Disposal and/or storage of this waste stream is

$$\text{Reaction 1. } Al + 3H_2O = Al(OH)_3 + 1.5\ H_2(g)$$
$$\Delta H \approx 100\text{kcal/mol}$$

not practical for mobile Military operations.

Recently, researchers at the Army Research Laboratory (ARL) have developed a novel, nanogalvanic aluminum alloy powder (Al-alloy; Figure 1) that can produce hydrogen upon direct contact with water without the oxide-passivation that typically hinders Al/water reactions during H_2 production (Figure 1). The novel Al-alloy has the fastest H_2 generation rate ever reported for an Al-water based H_2-production reaction, and 100% of the hydrogen yield is obtained within 3 minutes.[1]

Figure 1. ARL's nanogalvanic aluminum powder. *Upper left*: powder. *Upper right*: water-powder reaction producing H_2. *Bottom*: SEM of the powder. *Bottom right*: TDA's pelletized Al-alloy powder (1/4" pellets).

While having great potential as a new power source for Military and commercial applications, ARL's powder suffers from the same problem as all solid H_2 producing fuels; *equipment for safely generating H_2 gas from solid fuels at the point-of-need does not exist.* To solve this problem, TDA Research, Inc. (TDA), has been developing a first of its kind, point-of-use hydrogen gas production system that is integrated with a PEM fuel cell in a portable power generator. The power generator uses pellets made from the ARL's nanogalvanic aluminum powder to generate hydrogen gas in a water-filled reactor in a design based on previous gas generators built at TDA.[2] The hydrogen produced *via* Reaction 1 is directly fed to a fuel cell and converted to power. The novel, hydrogen-powered generator currently produces enough hydrogen (~0.7 g/min.) for *c.a.* 1 kW of power and is designed to run continuously for 4 hours before refilling with Al-alloy pellets. Most importantly, the generation of the hydrogen gas that fuels the generator is self-regulating; hydrogen is produced *on-demand* as power is drawn from the generator and will stop once no power is needed. Currently, TDA's gas production system is integrated with the power generator (Figure 2) and is 4.5 ft^3, ~40 lbs., and has 12/24 V DC and 120 V AC output.

Design and Fabrication

The hydrogen-fueled power generator is a self-contained machine consisting of 2 independent subsystems: the hydrogen production reactor, and the electrical energy generation/storage system.

Figure 2. Design rendering of TDA's hydrogen-fueled portable power generator. The gas production unit with a spherical reactor is located at the front of the generator, and the fuel cell and power outputs are housed in the casing. An aluminum frame protects the generator.

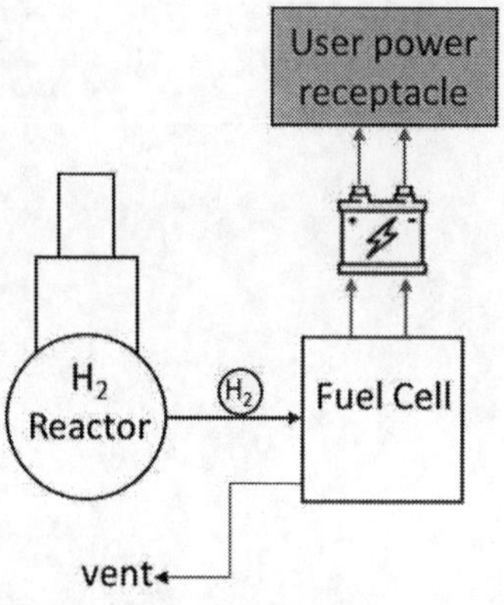

Figure 3. Schematic for TDA's H_2-fueled power generator.

The Hydrogen Production Reactor. The hydrogen production reactor is composed of a pellet dosing mechanism and a water reactor. The pellet dosing mechanism is a simple feeding mechanism that feeds Al-alloy "fuel" pellets into the water-containing reactor until an operable pressure (~30 psi) is obtained. The dosing mechanism provides Al-alloy to the reactor when hydrogen is demanded by the fuel cell to produce electricity. When power is needed, Al-alloy is fed to the water reactor, where it reacts with water to produce hydrogen for the fuel cell, which then produces electricity. When the power from the generator is no longer required, the Al-alloy dosing mechanism shuts down and halts hydrogen production *via* an electronically controlled feedback loop. In this manner, hydrogen is only produced as power is needed, and no fuel is wasted while power is not being drawn from the generator (compare this to a hydrocarbon-fueled generator that still idles when no power is being drawn).

A major part of the hydrogen production reactor is heat management, as the hydrogen production reaction (Reaction 1) is very exothermic. Removing the heat from the system is important in order to ensure that Rection 1 remains controlled and does not affect the reaction kinetics of hydrogen generation. Therefore, a custom heat removal system has been integrated into the reactor to ensure that the system does not exceed an operating temperature of 80-100 °C.

Energy Generation and Storage System. When power is demanded from the generator, hydrogen gas is fed to an on-board fuel cell, which produces direct current (DC) electricity that can be used directly, or be stored in a battery. When large loads are demanded from the system, the battery will take stress off the fuel cell when large current spikes are demanded and will allow the power generator to deliver continuous electricity if the hydrogen generation system fails to produce sufficient hydrogen for short periods of time.

Figure 3 Shows a schematic for the power generation system. To fabricate the hydrogen-fueled power generator, we have used a combination of off-the-shelf (OTS) parts and electronics, as well as custom-built parts, and the entire generator was built in TDA's machine and electronics shop.

Figure 4. TDA's 900-Watt, on-demand H_2 fueled power generator.

The current hydrogen-fueled power generator with the hydrogen production reactor and the energy production/storage system can be seen in Figure 4.

The specifications of our current 900-Watt, H_2-fueled power generator are summarized in Table 1 and compared to a gasoline-powered generator with a similar power output. TDA's 900 W generator is built to run continuously for four hours using 3.3 lbs. (1.5 kg or 0.6 L) of Al-alloy pellets before needing to be refilled with pelletized fuel and water. A hydrocarbon (gasoline) fueled generator needs 1.5 gallons (9 lbs. or 6 L) of fuel to produce the same amount of electricity. Our H_2/fuel cell system weighs 40 lbs., while a 1.2 kW gas-fueled power generator weighs ~58 lbs. with no fuel (45% more). TDA's H_2-fueled power generator produces *no carbon emissions*, compared ~8 lbs. of CO_2 for the 1.2 kW gasoline power generator (EPA, 2022).[3] Further, unlike a standard gasoline generator, TDA's generator system can stay turned-on for long periods of time without wasting any fuel should the power demand drop to zero, since the fuel cell stops consuming (and producing) hydrogen when the output current drops to zero. In contrast, a hydrocarbon fueled generator continues to consume fuel as it idles, even if there is no current draw.

Table 1. Specifications for TDA's H_2-fueled power generator vs. a commercial gasoline powered generator.

Specification	Fuel	
	H_2 (TDA)	Gasoline
Size	4.5 ft^3	2.5 ft^3
Weight	40 lbs.	58 lbs.
Power output	900 W	1,200 W
Fuel (wt)	3.3 lbs	9 lbs.
Fuel (vol.)	0.6 L	5.7 L
Water	2 liters	--
Operation time	4 hours	5 hours
Noise	45 dB	65-75 dB

Operation

TDA demonstrated its hydrogen fueled power generation system system: an H_2 gas generator with H_2 produced from Reaction 1 and electricity generation in a PEM fuel cell. The entire system self-regulates to meet the H_2 demand required by the electrical load placed on the fuel cell. A custom-designed hydrogen gas regulation and flow system was implemented between the H_2 reactor and the fuel cell in order to ensure that H_2 was provided to the fuel cell at a flow rate of 200 mL/minute, resulting in the production of ~2.6 A of current and a voltage of 0.7 V. (Note, in actual practice, the flow rate can be much higher depending on the power demand; the system is designed to be self-regulating to produce and supply the fuel cell with the amount of hydrogen needed to keep up with the power demand.) The H_2 flow rate and reactor pressure, as well as the current and voltage of the fuel cell during operation are shown in Figure 5. In our test, changing the current draw from the fuel did not affect the delivery of hydrogen to the cell, which operated independently of the fuel cell and continued to provide steady H_2 flow to the fuel cell. Finally, the fuel cell was also operated using pure hydrogen from a pressurized cylinder of H_2 gas (Figure 5 top; dashed lines). When hydrogen from the cylinder was supplied at 200 mL/minute, the fuel cell produced identical power, thus demonstrating that there is no difference between the hydrogen produced chemically in our generator and pure H_2 from a high-pressure gas cylinder.

Conclusions

TDA has developed a first of its kind hydrogen fueled power generator. The generator is designed to be portable, produce hydrogen on-demand and at the point of use, and mitigates many of the hazards associated with transporting pressurized hydrogen tanks. The key to on-demand hydrogen generation is the use of a novel, aluminum alloy powder produced by the Army Research Laboratory that reacts with water to produce hydrogen gas. The power generator prototype is designed to operate for four hours using 3.3 lbs. of Al-alloy and two liters of water. The power generator produces no carbon emissions and does not consume fuel when power is not needed from the generator.

Acknowledgements

Funding for this work was provided by Army SBIR Contract W911QX-21-C-0012. The authors would like to thank Drs. Anit Giri and Christopher Haines at the Army Research Lab (ARL) for supplying Al-alloy powders for this work.

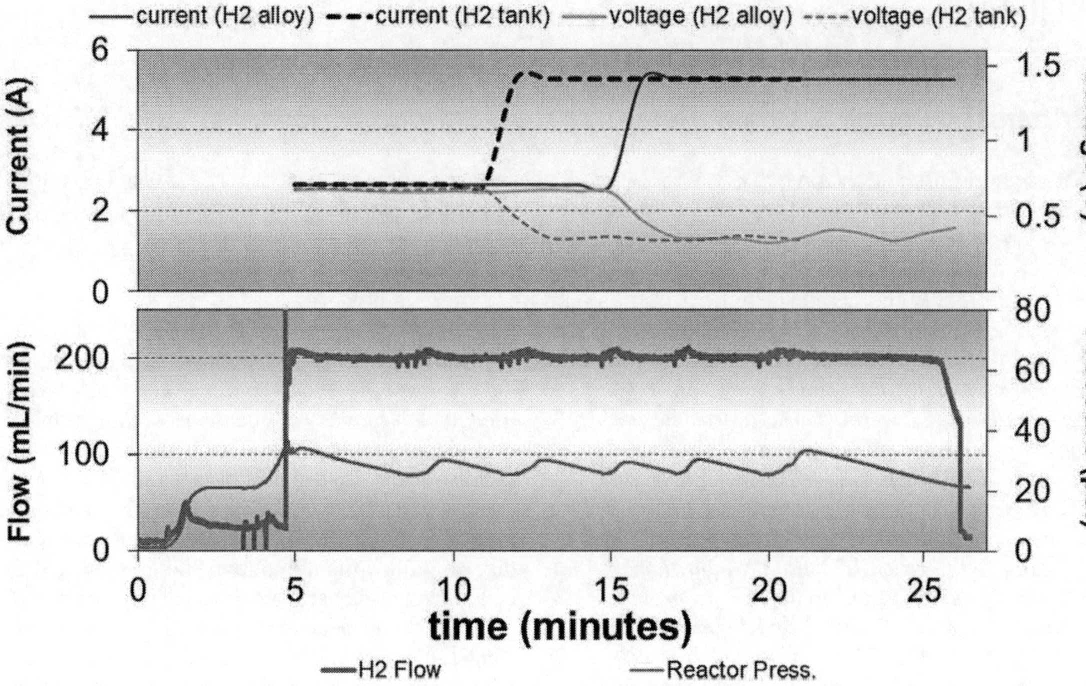

Figure 5. Hydrogen production reactor pressure and hydrogen flowrate with concurrent fuel cell current and voltage vs. time for operation of TDA's power generation system. The fuel cell was operated with a hydrogen flow of 200 mL/minute using both hydrogen produced from Reaction 1 (Al-alloy; solid lines) and from a pressurized tank of H_2 gas (dashed lines). For the chemically produced hydrogen run, the generator was allowed to "start-up" (*i.e.*, pressurize to its operating pressure of ~30 psi) before the fuel cell was started at 5 minutes. For the chemically generated hydrogen run, current draw from the fuel cell was increased at ~15 minutes to demonstrate the continued operation of the H_2 generator as power demand was increased.

References

1. Giri, A.K.; Roberts, A.J.; Hornbuckle, B.C.; Grendahl, S.M.; Darling, K.A. (2021) "Aluminum Based Nanogalvanic Compositions Useful for Generating Hydrogen Gas and Low Temperature Processing Thereof," U.S. Patent 11,198,923 B2, Dec. 14, 2021,

2. Clapsaddle B., Fredrickson J., Bell, W., Martin J., Haanstad T. (2019) "Humidity Tolerant Carbon Dioxide Generator for Arthropod Trap and Method of Using Same," U.S. Patent 10,420,345 B2, September 24, 2019.

3. EPA (2022) "Greenhouse Gas Emissions from a Typical Passenger Vehicle," U.S. Environmental Protection Agency, updated June 30, 2022; available at https://www.epa.gov/greenvehicles/greenhouse-gas-emissions-typical-passenger-vehicle#burning.

High-Energy Dense Power Sources for Low-Power Operation in Extreme Temperature Environments

Tom E. Adams[1,2], Darrell S. Cheu[2], Peter Cabauy[4], Shripad T. Revankar[2], and Vilas G. Pol[3]

[1] Power and Energy Division
Naval Surface Warfare Center, Crane Division
Crane, IN, USA, 47522

[2] School of Nuclear Engineering
[3] School of Chemical Engineering
Purdue University
West Lafayette, IN, USA, 47907

[4] City Labs, Inc.
Miami, FL, USA, 33186

Contact Author Email / Phone: thomas.e.adams7.civ@us.navy.mil / 1-440-897-6801

Abstract

Radioisotope power sources are being realized in many compelling applications that were deemed unfeasible due to limitations of batteries in temperature, chemical instability, irreversible losses, and electrolyte leakage. Betavoltaics are a rapidly maturing technology that can provide continuous milliwatt to nanowatt power for decades. City Labs' NRC general licensed Nanotritium™ betavoltaic has been demonstrated to be safe, to provide continuous power for over 15 years, and to operate in extreme temperature (-55°C to 150°C) without permanent energy loss or damage, and is available for purchase. Though the technology not a new concept, betavoltaics were discovered in the 1950's, which led to the development of photovoltaics. The development peaked in mid-1970 by Larry Olsen with the Betacel and successfully demonstrated in over pacemaker implants. The growth of the technology has been minimal and sporadic due to lithium battery technology, until recent advancements have materialized in ultra-low power electronics and low-power applications for extreme environments. The Defense Science Board have identified Betavoltaics as a disruptive technology that DOD and NASA should pursue, and now, the technology is being developed for a few applications. Recent work in material development, experiments, modeling, designs, tritium thermoelectrics, and proposed advances will be presented and discussed along with an overview of current projects and improved capabilities. With the development of a lithium-ion battery by Dr. Vilas Pol at Purdue University that can charge and discharge at -100°C, results from a hybrid design with a betavoltaic will be presented. Experimental and modeling will be extended towards commercial and non-commercial applications with near-term advancements and developments to continue the momentum on betavoltaic research.

Keywords

Extreme temperature operation; decadal operating life; solid-state; hybrid battery; NRC General License; tritium; sensor power.

Introduction

Radiation interaction with materials can have beneficial uses, such as in betavoltaic cells, a type of radioisotope power source where the kinetic energy is converted into electricity. Though not a new concept, research and development has been minimal for many years due to limited low-power applications, rapid semi-conductor degradation, limited availability and high cost of suitable radioisotopes, and public perception. Novel and compelling need-based applications are emerging in the military, intelligence, commercial, and medical markets that can utilize the diminutive energy produced from such cells. Present-day sensors, medical implants and electronic devices make betavoltaics an attractive alternative to electrochemical batteries enabling applications to perform for much longer periods in extreme temperatures. Betavoltaics can operate in excess of 10 years over temperatures ranging from -55°C to 150°C.[1] Because the technology is far from mature, many challenges and issues remain to be solved to increase energy density, reduce cost, and make it easier to use. Radioisotopes are used safely in many common applications such as watch dials, gun sights, smoke detectors and exit signs as shown in Figure 1.

Figure 1. Examples of use of radioisotopes

Requirements of the Nuclear Regulatory Commission (NRC) for product licensure often delay development until a sealed source device registry (SSDR) is granted, but recently companies have been working with the NRC and state regulatory bodies to obtain the necessary licensure for distribution of betavoltaic products.

Background

The first betavoltaic battery was developed in 1953 at RCA by Rappaport using strontium-90 (^{90}Sr) but degraded rapidly due to the high beta energy.[2] Others continued research using promethium-147 (^{147}Pm) but were only able to achieve <1% efficiency.[3,4] The most promising development was led by Larry Olsen at the Donald W. Douglas Laboratories in *ca.* 1974 on the Betacel pacemaker battery which exhibited a 4% efficiency using ^{147}Pm and silicon p-n junctions.[5,6] Over 285 patients received Betacel pacemakers, 60 patients inside the United

States. German and U.S. medical institutions were seriously considering the Betacel for wider use but lithium batteries quickly entered the picture and were selected for pacemakers instead.[7] Most advancements in the last 16 years concentrated on designs using tritium with City Labs leading the development by successfully producing NanoTritium™ betavoltaics in 2008 (Figure 2) that are still operating. The betavoltaic design was granted a NRC General License for manufacture and sales within the U.S.

Figure 2. City Labs' NanoTritium™ betavoltaics.

Theory of Operation: Electricity is produced similar to a photovoltaic using the kinetic energy of the beta particles. The basic concept of operation is shown in Figure 3. Beta particles enter the p-n junction and collide with atoms creating electron-hole pairs (EHPs) as they slow down. A 5.7 keV particle, average energy of a tritium beta particle, creates over 1000 EHPs. A portion of the kinetic energy is lost to the lattice. According to the Klein formula, the average kinetic energy required to create an electron-hole pair of energy equal to the semiconductor band gap (E_g) is 2.8 E_g + 0.5 eV while during the conversion process, 1.8 E_g eV and 0.5 eV are lost by emission of acoustic and optical phonons, respectively.[1,8] The voltage developed in a betavoltaic is directly related to the quality of the semiconductor and its band-gap energy.[9]

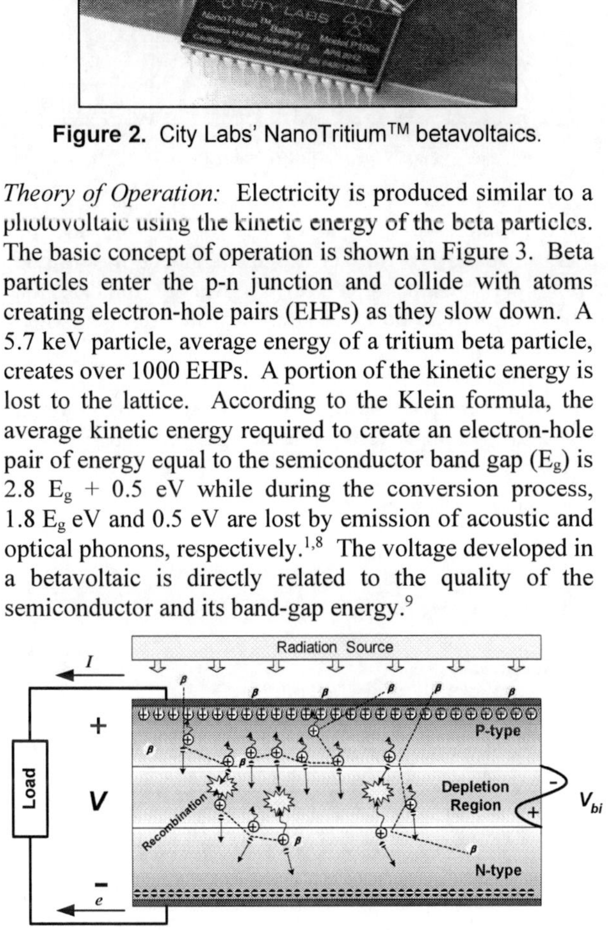

Figure 3. Overview of a betavoltaic cell.

Radioisotope Source: Beta emitting radioisotopes are selected over alpha and gamma emitting ones due to their relatively low mass and short lifetimes. Alpha particles, monoenergetic in the MeV range, have a mass 8,000 times greater than a beta particle immediately damages even the hardest semiconductor materials. Gamma rays are high energy photons (MeV) that travel long distances and difficult to efficiently shield.[10] The most important attributes of beta emitters are the maximum beta energy, decay half-life ($T_{1/2}$), and specific activity (Curies/gram). The high beta energy from ^{90}Sr and krypton-85 (^{85}Kr) exceeds the minimum dislocation energy of 300 - 400 keV for most semiconductor materials which damages the semiconductor and creates Bremsstrahlung.[11] The 25-day half-life of phosphorus-33 (^{33}P) loses 99% of its beginning of life energy (BOL) in 9 months. Therefore, three potential beta emitter candidates are listed in Table 1 with tritium (^{3}H) being the most attractive due to its availability and low cost; readily available from Ontario Power in Canada and is least expensive at $3.00/Curie (Ci). Russia is the only provider of ^{147}Pm and ^{63}Ni, which are costly at >$5000/Ci in present day values.[12] Reprocessing in the U.S. would greatly increase the availability.

Table 1. Potential Beta Emitting Radioisotopes.

Isotope	$T_{1/2}$ (yr)	E_{AVG} (keV)	E_{max} (keV)	Ci/g	W/g	$/Ci
^{3}H	12.33	5.7	18.5	9,664	0.33	$3.5
^{63}Ni	100.1	17.1	67	59	0.006	$5k
^{147}Pm	2.6	65	220	600	0.22	* >$5k

* *start-up cost is $10M and limited to 200 Ci/year (~$2M/year)*

Designs invoking tritium stored as a tritide demonstrated many practical difficulties in the loading and retention of tritium. Models using MC-SET (Monte Carlo Simulation of Electron Trajectories in solids) were developed to predict surface beta flux for storage materials. Models have been recently developed Monte Carlo N-Particle (MCNP) to continue modeling on other substrate materials such as lithium.

Temperature Performance Results

Betavoltaics were evaluated under temperature from -30°C to 70°C. Current-voltage (I-V) curves were acquired by stepping the applied voltage from 1.00 V to -0.10 V in steps of 1 mV while measuring the current. Figure 4 shows I-V curves from cold to hot, where the open-circuit voltage, V_{oc}, decreased from 0.95V to 0.65V while the short-circuit current (I_{sc}) increased from 82 to 86 nA.

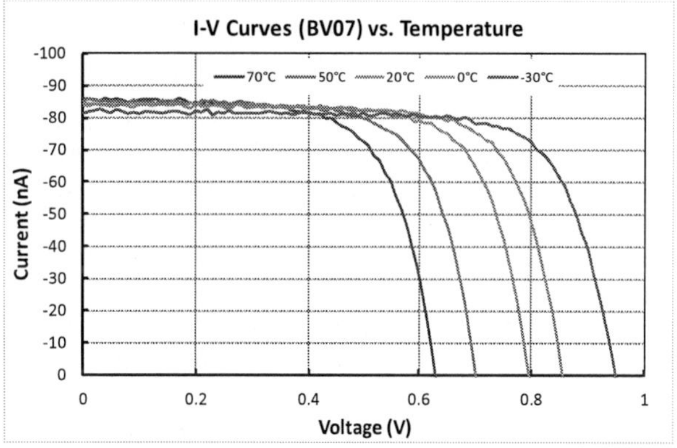

Figure 4. I-V curves of BV07 at -30°C to 70°C

Advances in Higher Power Density

Thinner P-N Semiconductor Substrates: With NASA and Department of Air Force (DAF) driving higher power mission requirements, City Labs has developed process to reduce the thickness of the p-n semiconductor substrate thickness from 625 µm in early P100a devices to <10 µm in new devices (Figure 5). Since tritium betas only travel up to 2 µm, p-in substrates as thin as 5 µm would be sufficient and allow for more betavoltaic layers in a package. Presently, it is possible to stack 50 cells in the NRC general licensed SSD package. The Power Density Roadmap in Figure 6 shows that it is possible to achieve 1 mW/cm^3 or higher.

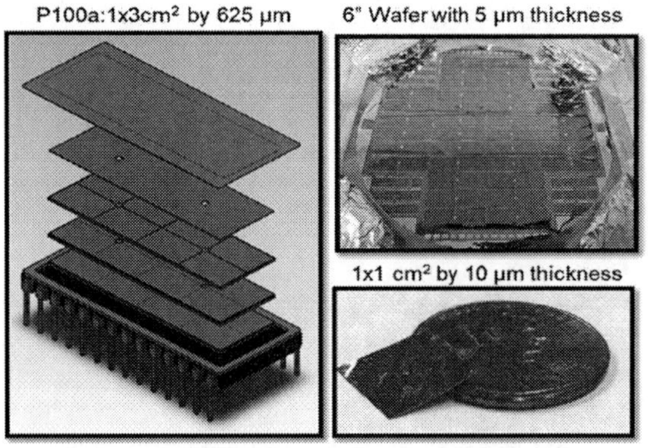

Figure 5. Progression of Thin P-N Substrates

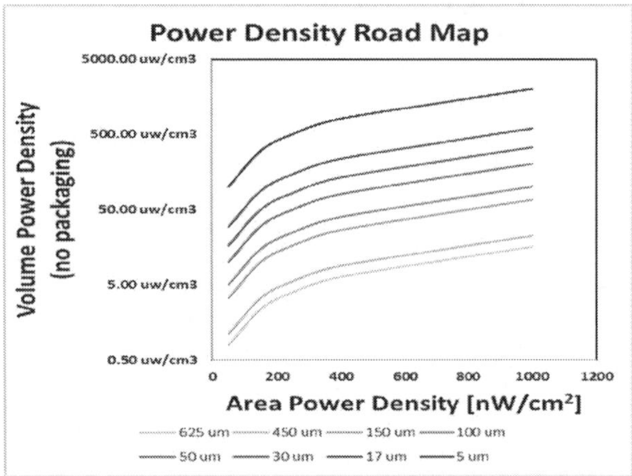

Figure 6. Projected power for Model P200 betavoltaic

Advances in Tritium Source Manufacturing: City Labs has moved into a new facility to establish a state-of-the-art tritium filling capability. The Tritium Filling Rig shown in Figure 7 can handle up to 2.0 MPa (20 bar) of tritium pressures, and temperatures up to 600°C in order to load current hydride materials and new alloys. The tritium capacity of 10g (10 kCi) that can be expanded. The loading process can be automated for production or performed manually to investigate new materials. A new tritium filling vessel was designed to handle the filling rig temperatures and pressures while maintaining an inert atmosphere before extracting loaded films in a glovebox. The combination of the tritium filling rig and vessels provides the only domestic commercial capability to load materials with tritium under high pressure, high temperature, and high activity.

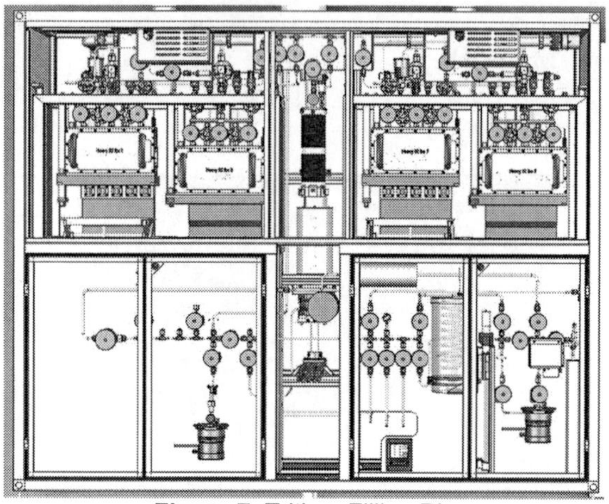

Figure 7. Tritium Filling Rig

Higher Beta Energy Sources: Improvements are being made to increase the tritium density and increase the energy yield from the surface facing the p-n substrate. Preliminary results at Purdue University indicate that lithium films can be loaded safely with hydrogen which would yield higher surface energy as shown in Figure 8. Further development is needed to understand the hydrogen retention behavior. Newer materials such as light-weight high entropy alloys (HEAs) are being investigated.

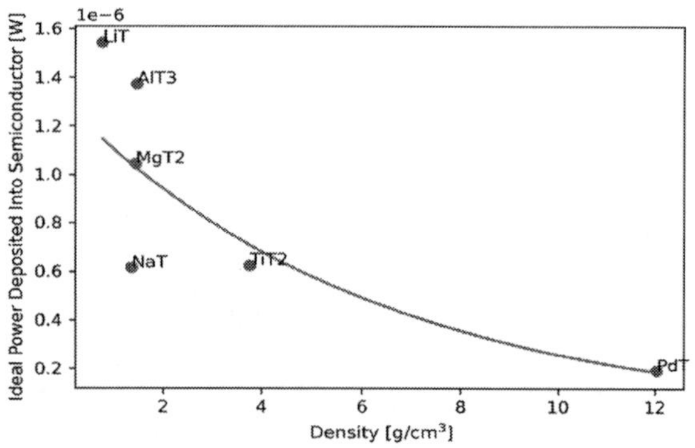

Figure 8. Progression in Tritium Source Substrate

Tritium Thermoelectric Generator (TTG): A novel tritium powered radioisotope thermoelectric generator (RTG) is advancing through two recent research efforts. Prototypes shown in have been developed with deuterium using simulations to estimate the heat power tritium would deliver and project electrical output power.

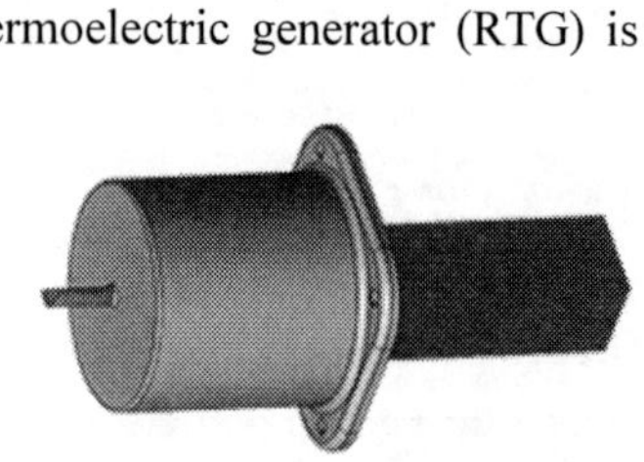

Figure 9. TTG prototype, Patent Pending

There is a point where the tritium-based RTG (TTG) becomes a better potential solution than a betavoltaic. The breakpoint shown Figure 10 occurs at 20 mW (2g or ^{3}H).

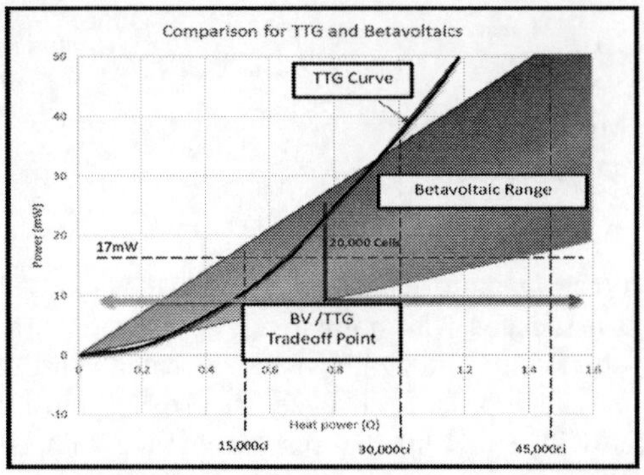

Figure 10. TTG comparison with Betavoltaics

The effects of self-shielding in a TTG are less significant than in a betavoltaic and TTGs more cost-effective in tritium quantities greater than 1-2g. With tritium capable of generating ~0.34 W/g of thermal power, TTGs may present cost and regulatory benefits over traditional RTGs.

Extreme Low Temperature Hybrid Design: Purdue is developing a hybrid battery consisting of a betavoltaic and lithium-ion battery for operation in Arctic and space that can operate below -100°C. To test at temperatures down to -175°C, the Extreme Low Temperature System (ELTS) using liquid nitrogen was developed. The ELTS was validated by cycling a novel lithium-ion cell which received a Guinness World Record for Coldest Operating Battery.[13] The test system is currently being modified for a hybrid betavoltaic and lithium-ion battery demonstration.

Conclusions

Tritium powered devices are a safe enabling technology for DOD, NASA, other government agencies, and commercial applications. Though direct replacement of tritium betavoltaics and RTGs are not straight-forward, work is being done to develop hybrid designs to allow for burst power in extreme temperature environments. Purdue University continues its research in enhancing hydrogen storage quantities in new materials assessing and hydrogen loading system. Purdue is also developing hybrid power sources with their novel lithium-ion battery technology to demonstrate performance at extreme temperatures and beyond. City Labs is leading the development and realization of radioisotope power sources in their betavoltaic and RTG designs.

- Available Supply of Tritium: Department of Energy, National Nuclear Security Administration and Canada Ontario Power Generation
- NRC Licensure: SSDR General, Specific License, Custom Devices
- Transport Regulations: Exempt, Type A, and Type B Packages and Shipment
- Generally Licensed Production & Manufacturing Facility: Achieved Industry's 1st and Only
- City Labs' betavoltaic products not subject to ITAR: 2013 Commodities jurisdiction letter revealed that Models P100a-c and Model p200a-b are not ITAR restricted
- Facility Security Clearance: Achieved Opens Contract Opportunities & Bids on Classified Contracts; Non-active presently

Acknowledgements

National Heart, Lung, and Blood Institute (NHLBI) grant 1R43HL145950-01, NASA contract 80NSSC19C0178, and Office of Naval Research Grant N000142112070.

References

1. Olsen, L.C., P. Cabauy, and B.J. Elkind, Betavoltaic power sources. Physics Today, 2012. 65(12): p. 35-38.

2. Rappaport, P., The electron-voltaic effect in pn junctions induced by beta-particle bombardment. Physical Review, 1954. 93(1): p. 246.

3. Flicker, H., J.J. Loferski, and T.S. Elleman, Construction of a promethium-147 atomic battery. IEEE Transactions on Electron Devices, 1964. 11(1): p. 2-8.

4. Manasse, F.K., J.J. Pinajian, and A.N. Tse, Schottky barrier betavoltaic battery. IEEE Trans. Nucl. Sci, 1976. 23(1).

5. Olsen, L., Betavoltaic energy conversion. Energy Conversion, v. 13, no. 4, pp. 117-127, 1973. 13(4).

6. Olsen, L. Advanced betavoltaic power sources. 1974.

7. R. Franco, M.L.S. Benefits and Risks of Promethium Battery-Powered Pacemakers. in Advances in Pacemaker Technology. 1974. Erlagen Springer-Verlag.

8. P. Bhattacharya, Semiconductor Optoelectronic Devices, 2nd Ed. Prentice-Hall Inc., 1996.

9. Adams, T. E., 2014. "Hydrogen Loading System Development and Evaluation of Tritiated Substrates to Optimize Performance In Tritium Based Betavoltaics." Dissertation, Purdue University.

10. Adams, T. E., 2011. "A Study of Palladium Thin-Films for Radioisotope Storage in Betavoltaic Power Sources Design." Thesis, Purdue University.

11. Santos, I., Marques, L. A., Pelaz, L., and Lopez, P., "Molecular dynamics study of damage generation mechanisms in silicon at the low energy regime,"pp. 37-40.

12. Bower, Kenneth E, Barbanel, Yuri A., Shreter, Yuri G., and Bohnert, George W., Polymers, Phosphors, and Voltaics for Radioisotope Microbatteries, CRC Press, Boca Rotan (2002).

13. Kim, S., Zhang, Y., Wang, H., Pol, V. Enabling Extreme Low-Temperature Battery Cycling with Niobium Tungsten Oxides Electrode and Tailored Electrolytes, in release process

CAMX Power Technologies for Battery-Integrated Internal Short Circuit Detection

Christopher H. McCoy
CAMX Power LLC
35 Hartwell Avenue, Lexington MA 02421
mccoy.chris@camxpower.com

Abstract: *We present recent advancements in CAMX Power technologies for sensitive, early detection of incipient internal short circuits in cells of lithium-ion batteries. Results demonstrating high-sensitivity detection performance in complete battery system demonstrators are reported for both our Universal Detection Technology (UDT) and Real-time Detection Technology (RDT). We further present results for UDT implemented as a stand-alone, portable diagnostic instrument for scanning batteries for the presence of internal shorts.*

Keywords: lithium-ion; internal short circuit; battery safety; early detection.

Introduction

The superior energy and power on both a weight and volume basis of lithium-ion (Li-ion) battery technology has made this chemistry the clear choice for a number of DoD applications. However, utilization of this high-performance battery chemistry has been limited by safety concerns. Under certain triggers, Li-ion cells can experience thermal runaway, i.e., a rapid increase in cell temperature accompanied by venting, vent-with-flame, ejection of cell parts, fire and explosion. Internal short circuits (most typically attributable to metal contaminants in the cell) are the most commonly identified mechanism by which such battery failure events occur in the field. Internal short circuits causing failures in the field typically develop after some period of normal cell operation and service and occur in cells that passed all manufacturing safety and quality control screening. In many DoD operational scenarios, it is important to minimize the likelihood of these failures and maximize safety and reliability of fielded Li-ion systems. Doing so requires effective management of the threat posed by internal shorts. As internal short-induced battery failures can occur after months or even years of battery service life, there is need for technologies that can detect internal shorts as early as possible before they pose an imminent threat to the safety of the battery and surrounding assets, and while opportunities to productively intervene to avert internal short-induced catastrophic failure are still available.

Challenges of detecting internal shorts: Detecting an internal short with enough sensitivity to deliver early warning of a fault condition, requires that certain hurdles be overcome. When a short first appears, it is small in magnitude, high in resistance and draws little current, with its electrical signature being heavily masked by much higher currents associated with normal cell operation. Further, a minor short (e.g., 1000 ohms) has essentially negligible impact on cell impedance characteristics (e.g., 1ppm at 1kHz on a cell with 1 mΩ internal resistance) unless impedance data are acquired at very low frequencies with accompanying lengthy acquisition times (e.g., hours or longer depending on cell characteristics). The default approach for detection of internal shorts is to monitor cell voltage over a sufficiently long period of time that voltage loss due to self-discharge through the internal short can be identified and adequately quantified (doing so requires that the cell is at rest and fully equilibrated). This engineering perspective, coupled with actual laboratory trials, led us to look for other means to achieve the sensitivity and rapid detection necessary for in-pack safety monitoring. In doing so, we identified reliable electrical signals that are obtained only when internal shorts are present in a cell. This knowledge has been utilized in the development of two distinct, non-invasive and chemistry-agnostic technologies for sensitive early detection of internal shorts in Li-ion (or other) batteries before the shorts pose a thermal runaway threat. These technologies are based on extensive research into the underlying electrochemistry governing internal shorts, and on experience gained through safety audits of failures of Li-ion batteries in the field. They comprise hardware and software developed specifically to acquire and interpret the specific electrical markers we have identified that indicate that internal shorts exist in a cell and deliver warning signals proportional to short severity. These technologies provide early warning of incipient internal shorts that may lead to unsafe conditions in a battery and can be implemented either independently of, or integrated with, the battery management electronics employed in Li-ion battery packs.

Characteristics of internal shorts: We have been studying the nature and underlying electrochemistry of particle-induced internal shorts in lithium-ion cells for a number of years. Figure 1 depicts, in a generic manner, evolution of a fault that progresses to cell failure - thermal runaway, often accompanied by release of significant heat, sparks, flame, particulate matter, toxic and hot flammable gases: stage 3 in Figure 1. This heat release can drive neighboring cells to failure (stage 4) in a process known as *cascading* or *propagation* and, in the worst case, can progress to a large-scale fire or equipment damage, presenting catastrophic hazards to surrounding assets and to personnel. The evolution of a fault progressing to cell failure, as depicted in Figure 1, can be viewed in terms of four stages. First, the fault initiates. This fault could be the very first point of formation of, for example, an internal short resulting from Foreign Object Debris (FOD). In stage 1 the fault grows in severity until reaching stage 2 where the fault has become "critical" in that it is severe enough to trigger a thermal runaway. In stage 3, the cell exhibits thermal runaway, which may then result in cascading/propagation of the failure to adjacent cells (stage 4) and, potentially, the rest of the battery in a worst-case incident. The greatest opportunity to manage a fault in a cell, and avoid a catastrophic failure of even one cell, is present when the fault is detected at or near the point of initiation, where the fault is still small and harmless. Later detection (i.e., the longer one waits) increases risks. For example, waiting until a first cell actually fails at stage 3 (smoke, flame, etc.,), may not allow sufficient opportunity for productive intervention to avoid widespread violent failure.

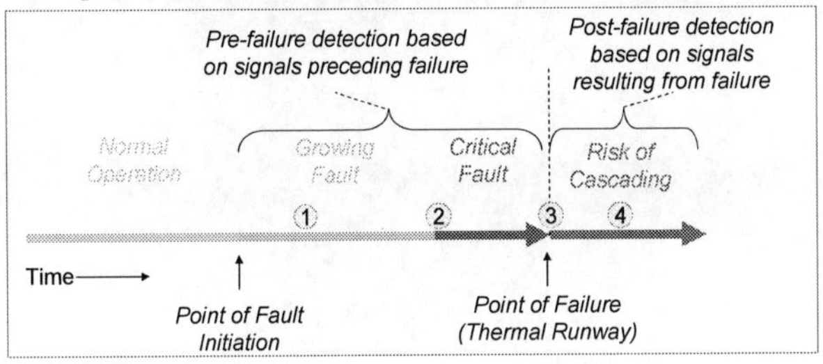

Figure 1. Representation of the timeline of a single-cell failure (thermal runaway) with subsequent risk of cascading of failure to other cells. CAMX Power technologies support pre-failure detection of faults in cells, i.e., stage 1, identifying a fault well before any cell gets "close" to thermal runaway, providing more time to implement preventive actions to suppress cascading of thermal runaway.

We have created well over 1000 particle-induced shorts in our laboratories under a variety of conditions using methodologies we have developed to reproduce particle-induced internal short-based cell failures. From this body of work, we have found that internal shorts typically progress through several phases, initiating as very minor cell faults of high resistance (thousands of ohms or more), growing slowly for a period of time, followed by a period of more rapid growth, sometimes abruptly, to higher severity (or runaway). Aspects of this pattern of short development are seen in the data shown in Figure 2. We believe that internal short detection capability must be of sufficient sensitivity to identify shorts *before* they grow severe enough to trigger thermal runaway and while productive intervention to avoid catastrophic cell failure is still possible. It must also be recognized that internal shorts not severe enough to trigger a thermal runaway event can still critically compromise battery performance and reliability, leading to sudden unexpected loss of battery function which could be unacceptable in mission-critical applications.

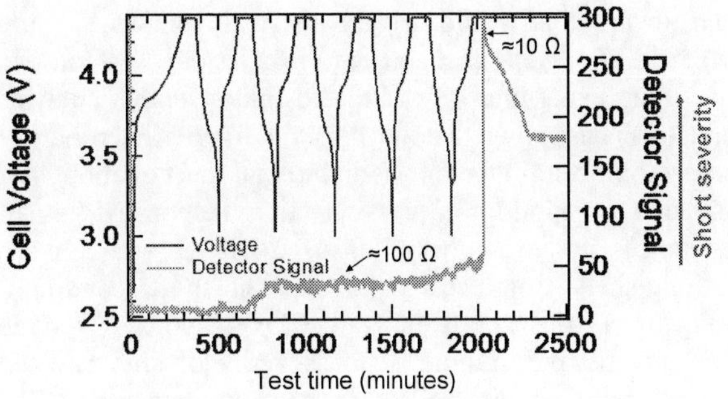

Figure 2. Cell voltage and output from our detection technology for a short created in a Li-ion cell by implantation of a metal particle. The detection signal (lower trace) shows the short initiate in the second cycle, grow to a moderate level (~ 100 Ω) for several cycles, and then abruptly spike to more dangerous levels (~ 10 Ω) in cycle six.

We have developed two distinct technologies for battery-integrated monitoring of lithium-ion energy storage systems for the presence of internal short circuits: the Universal Detection Technology (UDT), so-named because of its applicability to batteries of any cell configuration, and the Real-time Detection Technology (RDT), which provides real-time monitoring for internal shorts whether the battery is at rest or actively cycling. Both technologies have been demonstrated for a wide range of lithium-ion chemistry variants, are functional over a wide range of temperature (tested from -30°C to +55 °C to-date), and are sensitive enough to detect internal shorts at least three orders of magnitude weaker in severity than the levels needed to trigger a thermal runaway, irrespective of the shorts' root cause. Attributes of UDT and RDT include:

- *Universal Detection Technology (UDT)*
  - Minimally disruptive to battery design, easily integrated with BMS.
  - Can utilize existing voltage-sense wiring (no changes in the pack).
  - Performs monitoring diagnostic while battery is at rest.
- *Real-time Detection Technology (RDT)*
  - Real-time monitoring including under complex current profiles and at rest.
  - Delivers detailed state-of-health monitoring for the battery.
  - Utilizes a network of sensors placed at certain strategic points in the battery.

The following sections present results for UDT and RDT demonstrating performance and sensitivity, and recent hardware advances that implement the technologies in compact form-factors for direct integration into battery systems.

UDT: Detection performance, implementation in a Full Battery Demonstrator, as a stand-alone diagnostic instrument, and in a compact module for all UDT applications.

The Universal Detection Technology (UDT) executes electrical diagnostics on Li-ion battery systems while the battery is at-rest (i.e., no charge or discharge processes occurring) to scan for the presence of internal short circuits. The high detection sensitivity of UDT is demonstrated by the data, presented in Figure 3, for detection trials carried out on a 2.6Ah 18650 cell. Detection sensitivities to 20,000Ω - an internal short more than four orders of magnitude weaker than levels that could trigger thermal runaway – are achieved. For reference, prior work in our laboratories (including experimentally validated finite element analysis modeling) has shown that the threshold for thermal runaway in an 18650 cell (in free air) is an internal short of about 4Ω. As seen in Figure 3, raw detection responses for all resistances tested – from 50 to 20,000Ω - are well-distinguished from scans for the no-short condition. Analysis metrics applied to raw UDT responses provide semi-quantitative grading of the severity of any detected internal short circuits and are used in implemented UDT systems to trigger alerts of potentially unsafe conditions.

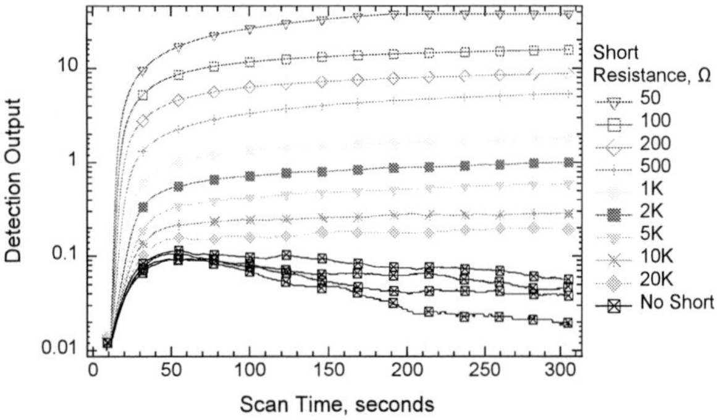

Figure 3. UDT Scans for a 2.6Ah 18650-format cell.

We have now implemented and demonstrated UDT monitoring for internal shorts in a variety of battery configurations including a "Full Battery Demonstrator" in which UDT was integrated into a 28V (7S), 25Ah battery built-to-specification for a DoD application. When performing a diagnostic scan on the battery, the UDT system scans each of the seven 25Ah cell blocks of the 7S battery in sequence. Figure 4 shows detection trial results for the Full Battery Demonstrator for one of the 25Ah cell blocks scanned with five scans at each test resistance, demonstrating consistent, reproducible UDT responses. Internal shorts of 3000Ω - three orders of magnitude weaker than levels that could trigger a runaway- in a single cell of the 60+ cell battery are easily detected.

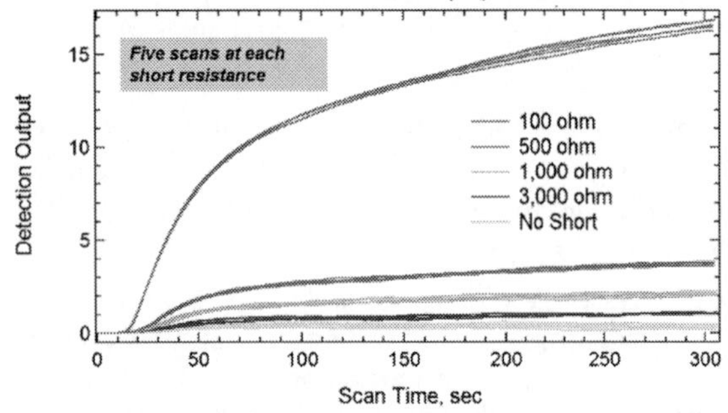

Figure 4. Scan results for a UDT-Equipped Full Battery Demonstrator.

Our present standard UDT system configuration is designed to accommodate batteries of up to eight cells/cell groups in series. Using a modular implementation directly analogous to that practiced in battery management system design, UDT monitoring can be configured for batteries of arbitrary stack size to >1000V.

Another application area for UDT in which we have made significant advancements implements UDT as a stand-alone diagnostic instrument for laboratory or field assessment of batteries for internal shorts. A number of such UDT-based instruments have been constructed to date, including units delivered to a DoD customer and units used both in-house and for remote on-site evaluations of Li-ion cells and batteries. A photograph of a UDT diagnostic instrument kit is shown in Figure 5. The kit includes the USB-powered UDT diagnostic instrument (right) and a connection harness (left).

Figure 5. Stand-alone UDT-based diagnostic kit.

UDT implementations share a common "detection engine" core that carries out the UDT electrical interrogation to scan for internal shorts. To broadly support implementation of UDT in different applications, we are implementing this UDT detection engine as a compact, surface-mount module (Figure 6) that provides core electronics common to essentially any UDT application.

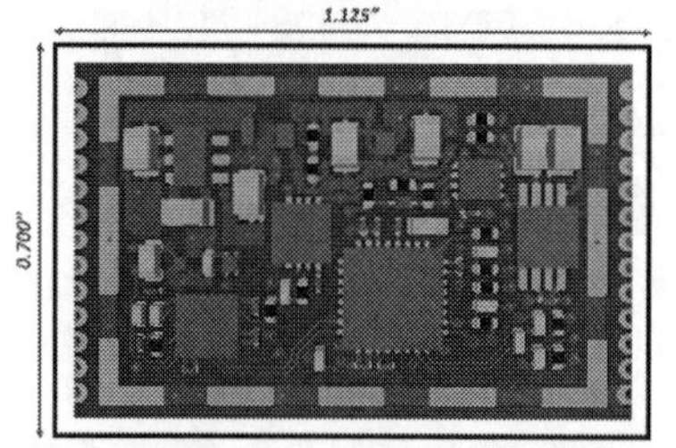

Figure 6. UDT Core module circuit board.

This UDT Core module will be qualified for, and demonstration in, DoD battery applications with the objective of full integration for safety monitoring of the associated Li-ion systems.

RDT: Capabilities and 300-cell battery implementation

The Real-time Detection Technology (RDT) continuously monitors Li-ion batteries for the presence of internal short circuits using proprietary hardware and algorithms and a sensor network within the battery. RDT monitoring is able to discern electrical signatures that are markers for internal shorts irrespective of battery state – whether the battery is at rest, charging, or delivering power – and irrespective of the underlying cause of the short. An example of detection of an internal short in an actively cycling battery is shown in Figure 7. During this test, the battery was subjected to an automotive drive cycle test protocol and a load resistance was placed across one cell of the battery as a safe, quantitative surrogate for an internal short. As seen in the top graph of Figure 7, standard BMS cell voltage sensing data contains no indication of the presence of the internal short but, as shown in the bottom graph, the RDT system immediately detects the presence of the short even against a background of a complex waveform of rapidly changing charge and discharge currents.

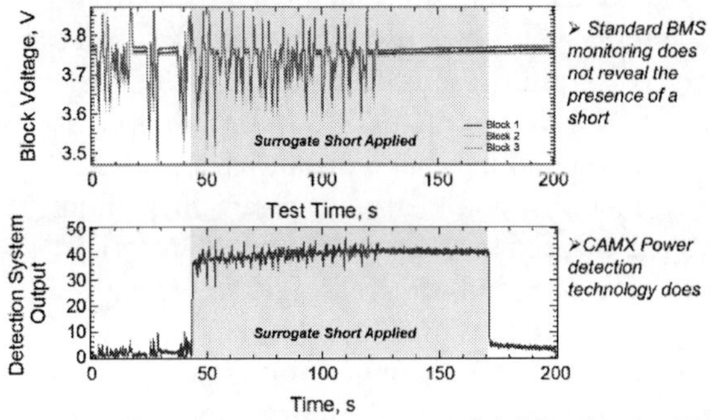

Figure 7. Test data showing successful detection by RDT of an internal short, invisible to the Battery Management System, under a demanding automotive drive cycle test protocol with rapid, high currents charge/discharge swings.

Figure 8 shows a recently implemented RDT-equipped 300-cell Full Battery Demonstrator. Figure 9 shows detection during discharge of a 100Ω internal short (load resistance as surrogate) with the battery actively cycling.

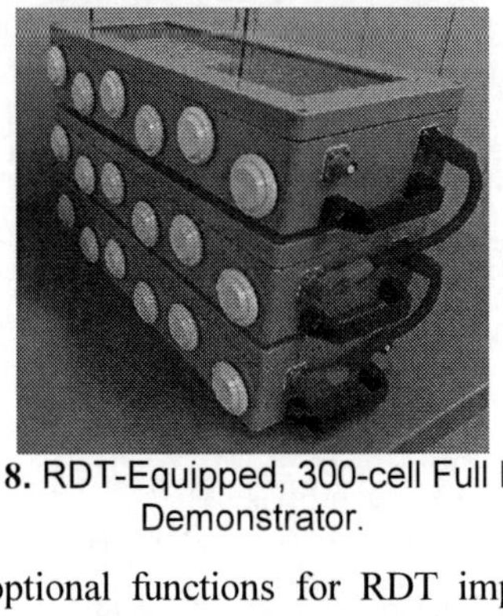

Figure 8. RDT-Equipped, 300-cell Full Battery Demonstrator.

Additional optional functions for RDT implementations include use of already-acquired RDT sensing data to provide detailed, cell-level battery state-of-health metrics, and with addition of an appropriate cut-off device comprehensive battery management functionality. RDT monitoring can also detect single-cell fail-open events within a battery.

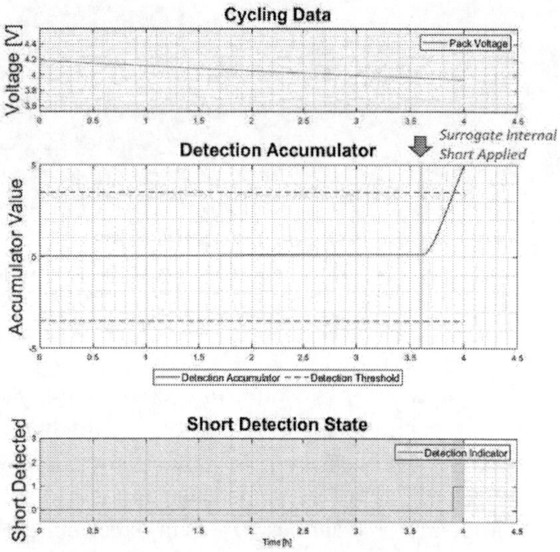

Figure 9. RDT detection of a 100-ohm internal short for one cell in the actively cycling 300-cell battery. A detection warning (level 1, 2 or 3) results when the associated detection threshold is crossed in the detection accumulator of the RDT algorithm system.

To support design and implementation of RDT, we have developed a small, surface-mount module that provides all RDT functions and components exclusive of the battery-specific RDT sensor network. This 1.2”x1.2” unit is shown in Figure 10.

Figure 10. (Left) RDT Core unit circuit board (1.2’ x1.2”). (Right) With protective cover fitted.

In conclusion, we have significantly advanced the TRL of both UDT and RDT, with UDT nearing readiness for fielding in DoD battery systems. We have developed compact, small form-factor implementations of both technologies which can be made available in the form of evaluation kits to support the design process for integration into battery systems and can be made in quantity for incorporation into a wide range of Li-ion applications.

Acknowledgements

We gratefully acknowledge the Department of Energy, Missile Defense Agency, and the United States Navy for partial support of this work. The author gratefully acknowledges the many staff of CAMX Power who have contributed to the development and advancement of these technologies over a number of years.

Laboratory-Based X-Ray Absorption Spectroscopy as a New Research Tool for Battery-Relevant Materials and Beyond

Ryan H. DeBlock,[1] *Hunter O. Ford,*[2] *Michelle D. Johannes,*[3] *Debra R. Rolison,*[1] *Rachel E. Carter,*[1] *and Jeffrey W. Long*[1*]
[1]Code 6170, Surface Chemistry Branch, Naval Research Laboratory, Washington, DC, 20375
[2]National Research Council Postdoctoral Associate, Naval Research Laboratory, Washington, DC, 20375
[3]Code 6390, Center for Computational Materials Science, Naval Research Laboratory, Washington, DC 20375
Email: ryan.deblock@nrl.navy.mil

Abstract: X-ray absorption spectroscopy (XAS) is a powerful technique for investigating the local electronic and structural characteristics of a wide range of complex materials, including many compositions that are used in electrochemical energy storage and conversion applications. Recent advances in bench-scale instrumentation have brought XAS from synchrotron facilities to the local research laboratory, making this technique more accessible for everyday use. The Naval Research Laboratory (NRL) recently procured a commercially available XAS unit, which has since been used to analyze a large number of procured and NRL-developed materials. In this paper, we describe XAS investigations focused on the established battery cathode material, $LiFePO_4$, in the form of powder-composite electrodes from a commercial vendor. We demonstrate that the laboratory-based XAS unit is capable of generating high-quality XANES data, even for transmission measurements through a fully packaged pouch-cell battery under electrochemically controlled state-of-charge. Shifts at the Fe K-edge are consistent with prior XANES analyses of $LiFePO_4$ collected at synchrotron-based spectrometers, showing that laboratory-based XAS is a viable alternative.

Keywords: X-ray absorption spectroscopy, XANES, EXAFS, lithium-ion batteries

Introduction

X-ray absorption spectroscopy provides fundamental insights on structure, mechanisms, and stability in such research fields as catalysis and energy storage.[1,2] A typical X-ray absorption spectrum contains element-specific information in two distinct energy windows. In the vicinity of the absorption edge, X-ray Absorption Near-Edge Spectroscopy (XANES) yields information on elemental oxidation state and electronic structure. Beyond the absorption edge, Extended X-ray Absorption Fine Structure (EXAFS) data provide such structural information as coordination number, bond distances, and atomic arrangement. In contrast with X-ray diffraction, XAS can be used to analyze disordered materials, which are becoming increasingly relevant for energy science. While one turns to X-ray photoelectron spectroscopy to measure surface-sited element-specific information under ultrahigh vacuum, XAS probes the bulk material and can operate at ambient conditions or even in an in situ mode.

The collection of XAS data historically required the use of synchrotron-based photon sources to achieve necessary flux and energy specificity, limiting researcher access to this characterization tool. But now, laboratory-scale XAS units are available, enabled by contemporary advances in X-ray optics and design. The general layout of such an instrument (Figure 1) uses a polychromatic X-ray source that is first sent to a spherically bent crystal analyzer (SBCA). The now-monochromatic X-ray passes through the sample after which detectors collect signals in transmission mode (fluorescence detection is also possible). The X-ray source, SBCA, sample, and detector all lie upon a Rowland-circle geometry that allows such operation, a configuration based on designs from Seidler et al.[3–5]

The NRL Advanced Electrochemical Materials section recently installed a commercial XAS system that is capable of collecting measurements

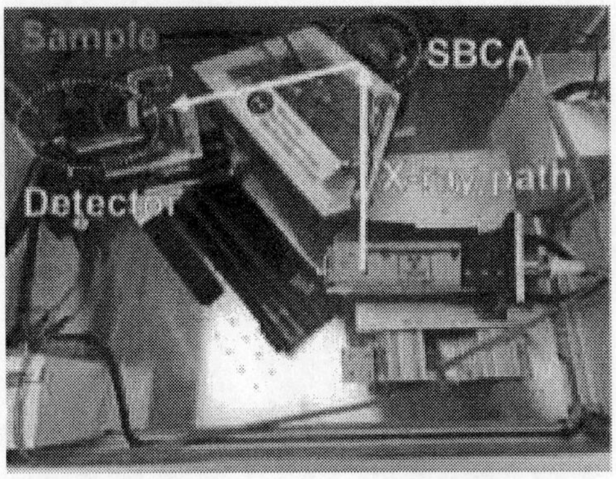

Figure 1. Interior configuration of a laboratory-scale X-ray absorption spectrometer.

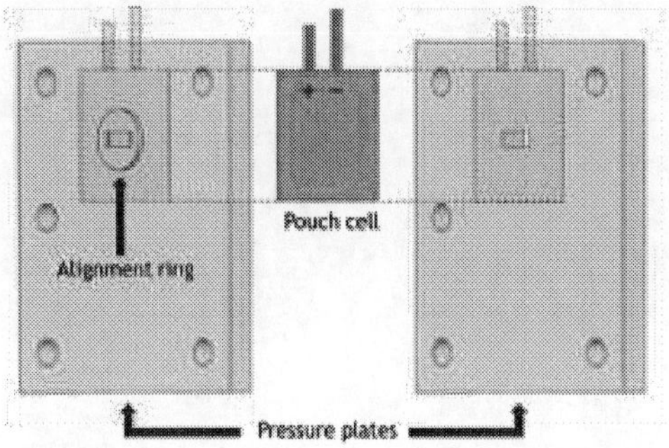

Figure 2. Schematic of a custom-made acrylic pouch cell holder for in situ electrochemical measurements.

spanning the energy range from 5–18 keV. This energy range includes K-edge excitations for the first-row transition metals, elements critical for materials used in electrochemical energy storage and catalysis.

Using this laboratory X-ray absorption spectrometer, we analyze battery-relevant materials in a variety of form factors, including pressed-powder pellets, thin films, and device-ready electrodes, the latter of which may also be interrogated in situ when incorporated into functional pouch cells. As a demonstration of these in situ XAS capabilities, we interrogate a $LiFePO_4$ cathode in a packaged battery, using shifts in the Fe K-edge absorption to track changing Fe oxidation state as the cell is charged.

Results and Discussion

Lithium-ion battery pouch cells suitable for XAS measurements are constructed using powder-composite electrodes on metal foils: $LiFePO_4$ on aluminum (sourced from Oak Ridge National Laboratory) as the cathode and graphite on copper (MTI Corp.) as the anode. Nickel tabs welded to the respective foils provide electrical contact to the outside of the cell. Electrodes (~7 cm^2) are physically separated with a layer of Celgard 2500 soaked with electrolyte [1 M $LiPF_6$ in ethylene carbonate:diethyl carbonate (1:1)]. Pouches are heat sealed under mild vacuum and then mounted between custom-designed acrylic plates (Figure 2) that provide pressure on the cell and maintain alignment within the X-ray beam path.

Iron K-edge XANES measurements are collected using an in-lab X-ray absorption spectrometer (easyXAFS300) with a 1.2 kW X-ray tube operating at 30 kV and 12 mA. An SBCA of Si ⟨110⟩ is used to control X-ray energy at a step size of 0.2 eV and a dwell time of 10 s per point. To improve the signal-to-noise ratio, three consecutive scans are run at each state-of-charge (0, 25, 50, 75, and 100%). Spectra are analyzed using ATHENA software contained within the Demeter system for analyzing XAS data.[6]

Because the photon flux of laboratory-based XAS is orders of magnitude lower than at a synchrotron, the total absorption of all sample components in the beam must be carefully considered. Prior to XAS analysis of the fully packaged pouch cell, we measured the X-ray transmission of the $LiFePO_4$ cathode and then additional layers of the pouch cell and holder (Figure 3), expressed as intensity at the X-ray detector. Even transmitting X-rays through both electrodes and packaging material, detector counts are in the 60–80 kCount range. The thick acrylic used to construct the cell holder is a significant X-ray absorber, thus we cut slit-shaped apertures (5×13 mm) to accommodate beam transmission. With the fully packaged cell plus cell holder, detector counts remain healthy at ~30–40 kCounts, sufficient for recording high-resolution spectra.

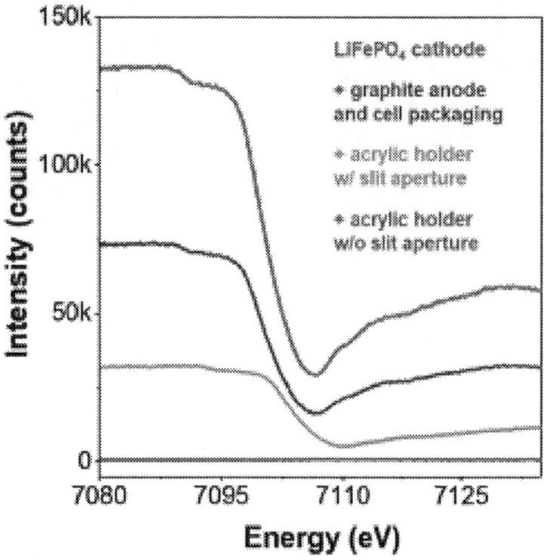

Figure 3. X-ray transmission through various combinations of pouch cell and holder components in the energy window coincident with the Fe K-edge absorption.

Prior to XAS measurements, cells are galvanically cycled three times at C/10 (300 μA) from 2.5 to 4 V, ending in the discharged state. This step is performed to precondition the cell and ensure that the expected capacity (9.5 mAh) is achieved. The discharged cell is then charged in increments of 25% capacity at 300 μA with each charge step followed by relaxation at open circuit for 2.5 h, during which time XAS data are collected (Figure 4).

Upon charging, iron sites in $LiFePO_4$ oxidize from Fe^{2+} to Fe^{3+}, accompanied by removal of Li^+ for charge compensation. Prior reports from synchrotron-based XANES measurements[7,8] show that oxidation of $LiFePO_4$ shifts the Fe K-edge positive and alters the shape of the white line. We observe similar results in Fe K-edge behavior at comparable energy resolution during in situ analysis of our pouch cells using the laboratory-based X-ray absorption spectrometer (Figure 5). The analysis of the extended fine structure is underway for comparison to DFT computation.

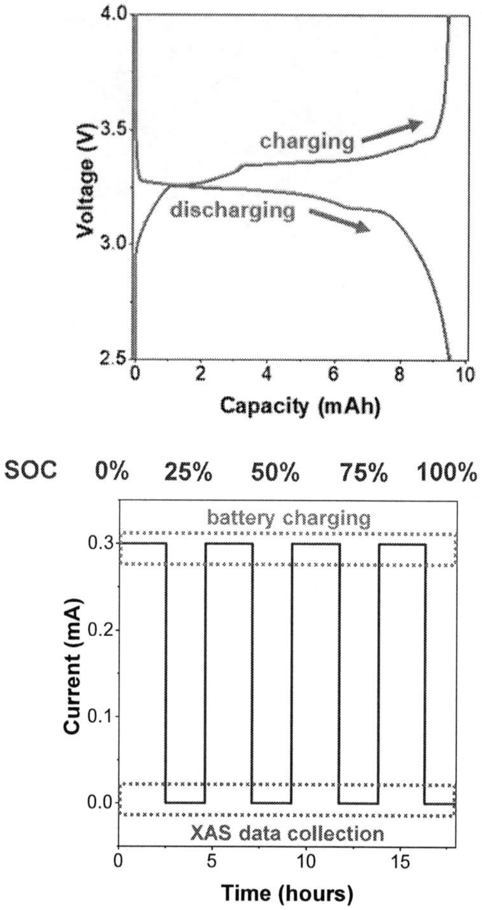

Figure 4. Electrochemical conditions for XAS data collection on a pouch cell: (top) Charge/discharge pre-conditioning; (bottom) charge profile and operation scheme.

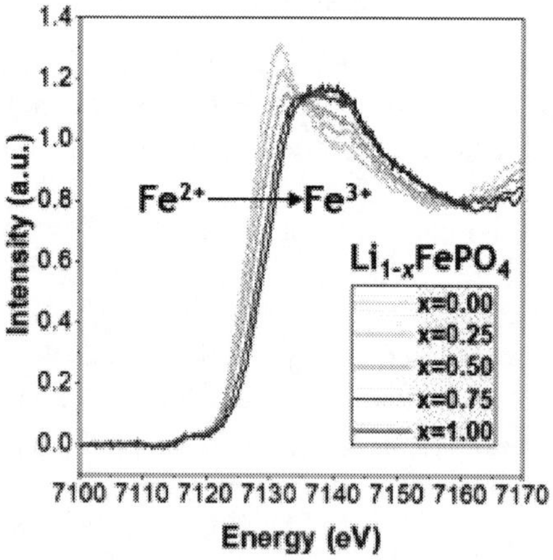

Figure 5. Iron K-edge XANES of a lithium-ion battery pouch cell containing $LiFePO_4$ as a function of state of charge (SOC).

Conclusion

In-lab X-ray absorption spectroscopy at the NRL enables facile, walk-up XANES and EXAFS measurements of a functional battery cell. We can now routinely observe the oxidation state of and local environment in energy-relevant materials without the need for synchrotron beam time and expense. We expect these new capabilities will expand fundamental understanding in such fields as electrochemical energy storage and catalysis.

Acknowledgements

This work was supported by the US Office of Naval Research (Award #N0001420WX01405). R.H.D. was an NRL-NRC Postdoctoral Associate (2020–2023).

References

1. J. Singh, C. Lamberti, and J.A. van Bokhoven. Advanced X-Ray Absorption and Emission Spectroscopy: In Situ Catalytic Studies. *Chem. Soc. Rev.*, **2010**, *12*, 4754.
2. Q. Gu, J.A. Kimpton, H.E.A. Brand, Z. Wang, and S. Chou. Solving Key Challenges in Battery Research Using in situ Synchrotron and Neutron Techniques. *Adv. Energy Mater.*, **2017**, *7*, 1602831.
3. G.T. Seidler, D.R. Mortenson, A.J. Remesnik, J.I. Pacold, N.A. Ball, N. Barry, M. Styczinski, and O.R. Holden. A Laboratory-Based Hard X-Ray Monochromator for High-Resolution X-Ray Emission Spectroscopy and X-Ray Absorption Near Edge Structure Measurements. *Rev. Sci. Instrum.*, **2014**, *85*, 113906.
4. D.R. Mortenson, G.T. Seidler, A.S. Ditter, and P. Glatzel. Benchtop Nonresonant X-Ray Emission Spectroscopy: Coming Soon to Laboratories and XAS Beamlines Near You? *J. Phys.: Cong. Ser.*, **2016**, *712*, 012036.
5. E.P. Jahrman, W.M. Holden, A.S. Ditter, D.R. Mortenson, G.T. Seidler. T.T. Fister, S.A. Kozimor, L.F.J. Piper, J. Rana, N.C. Hyatt, and M.C. Stennett. An Improved Laboratory-Based X-Ray Absorption Fine Structure and X-Ray Emission Spectrometer for Analytical Applications in Materials Chemistry Research. *Rev. Sci. Instrum.*, **2019**, *90*, 024106.
6. B. Ravel and M. Newville. ATHENA, ARTEMIS, HEPHAESTUS: Data Analysis for X-Ray Absorption Spectroscopy Using IFEFFIT. *J. Synchrotron Rad.*, **2005**, *12*, 537.
7. C.T. Love, A. Korovina, C.J. Patridge, K.E. Swider-Lyons, M.E. Twigg, and D.E. Ramaker. Review of $LiFePO_4$ Phase Transition Mechanisms and New Observations from X-ray Absorption Spectroscopy. *J. Electrochem. Soc.*, **2013**, *160*, A3153.
8. S. Pongha, B. Seekoaon, W. Limphirat, P. Kidhunthod, S. Srilomsak, Y.-M. Chiang, and N. Meethong. XANES Investigation of Dynamic Phase Transition in Olivine Cathode for Li-Ion Batteries. *Adv. Energy Mater.*, **2015**, *5*, 1500663.

Using Rapid Impedance Measurements for Cell Screening and Qualification

Jon P. Christophersen
Dynexus Technology
Troy, ID 83871, USA
jon.christophersen@dynexustech.com / 1-208-521-2537

Abstract

The inline Rapid Impedance Spectroscopy (iRIS) system enables multispectral AC impedance measurements during a battery screening and qualification process. A set of single-cell packs were screened using standard metrics such as voltage, capacity, pulse resistance, and self-discharge. From the batch of qualified cells, 120 packs were subjected to 5-s iRIS measurements. The captured impedance spectra revealed two distinct groups, with 20 packs having a smaller mid-frequency semicircle compared to the rest. An aging study is presently underway to evaluate pack degradation as a function of cycling. The first set of tests consists of mild abuse conditions (denting and dropping). The packs with smaller impedance spectra show higher capacities and lower pulse resistances through 860 cycles.

Keywords

Screening; qualification; rapid; impedance spectroscopy.

Introduction

Energy storage demand is continuing to increase for multiple industries, including consumer electronics, automotive, and telecommunications. As a result, several new gigafactories are being planned in the US and abroad [1]. However, increased battery utilization also comes with an increased risk of catastrophic failure during operation. A critical step towards mitigating field failures is cell screening and only qualifying the batteries that fall within specific acceptance criteria. Multiple screening tests can be conducted at several locations to ensure faulty cells are removed before integrating batteries into a field-deployed application. Initial screenings can be very extensive and require multiple hours or days to evaluate charge retention and/or discharge capacity. Other screening applications can also include safety considerations such as the battery response to abuse conditions [2]. Once the manufacturer ships cells to the battery assembler, they will likely be screened again (sometimes using extensive methods [2], other times with quick checks such as open-circuit voltage) to properly qualify cells and, where feasible, match them for module and/or pack assembly. The screening process must also be repeated when certifying batteries in second use applications.

Electrochemical impedance spectroscopy (EIS) provides unique insights into battery chemical, physical, and structural attributes as a function of time and use [3-4]. However, a standard EIS measurement can take minutes to hours depending on system settings, making it impractical as an in-situ sensor for rapid decision-making processes. Thus, inline EIS research has generally focused on single frequencies or a subset of targeted frequencies. The data acquired from the targeted frequencies have been used for various predictive applications such as safety/stability [5], and state-of-charge (SOC) or state-of-health (SOH) estimations [4].

Dynexus Technology has developed a fast EIS method known as inline Rapid Impedance Spectroscopy (iRIS) that can yield broadband measurements within seconds [6]. The iRIS system is also scalable so that it can be used to monitor battery characteristics from inception to recycling. High-voltage systems (50V and a 100+V prototype) have been developed for end-of-line assessment and/or battery second-use applications. High-resolution iRIS systems have been developed for battery cell assembly, screening, qualification, and matching applications.

A consumer electronics (CE) Fortune 500 company is presently evaluating an iRIS-based screening and qualification process for their batteries in collaboration with Dynexus. The batteries sent to Dynexus had been fully qualified for product use based on the specific CE company requirements and metrics. The first qualification stage was at the cell level. Screening tests at the manufacturer site included open circuit voltage (OCV), alternating current internal resistance (ACIR), a full discharge capacity, and a self-discharge test. The cells that met the acceptance criteria were sent to the pack assembler where battery management "gas gauges" were connected. The single-cell packs were then subjected to a second round of qualification testing using the same metrics plus an additional direct-current internal resistance (DCIR) measurement. The packs that met the acceptance criteria were sent to the CE customer for integration into their devices. Thus, extensive qualification testing was conducted over several hours at two different locations to ensure consistent, repeatable cells were delivered to the end user.

Dynexus received 120 fully qualified single-cell packs for iRIS screening. Upon receipt, each pack was subjected to a 5-s iRIS measurement using galvanostatic excitation at 470 mA_{RMS} with 14 frequencies over a range of 0.2 to 1638.4 Hz. The iRIS measurement was conducted through the gas gauge terminals (i.e., through the battery management electronics and not directly on the cell tabs). Figure 1 shows the impedance spectra for all 120 packs; the data have been normalized by the pack weight per the customer's request.

For this cell screening, lower frequencies were not considered to ensure rapid measurements (i.e., mass transport effects were not considered), but the mid-frequency semicircle was clearly defined. Results from the 5-s iRIS screen revealed two distinct groups of packs; 20 of the packs (shown in red) had a smaller mid-frequency semicircle compared to the other 100 packs (shown in blue).

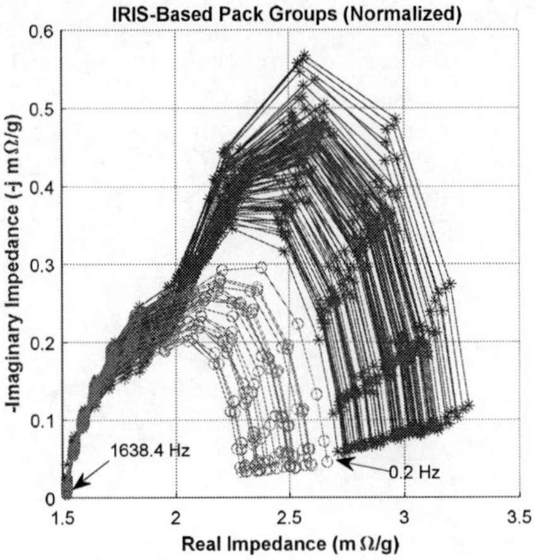

Figure 1. Screening results from 120 qualified packs.

Experimental

To determine the long-term effects of the observed differences in Figure 1 (i.e., how SOH is affected between the two groups), the packs have been assigned to an aging matrix. The full test matrix consists of standard cycle-life aging at 25, 55, and 5°C and some abuse conditions. The abuse conditions include high-temperature, high SOC calendar aging and some mild damage scenarios such as cell bending and dropping. The test conditions include packs from both groups. The first stage of aging at 25°C with packs damaged by bending and dropping is presently underway. There are 10 packs in each condition, three of which are from the smaller iRIS impedance group.

Characterization and reference testing consisted of a DCIR pulse every 10% SOC with 0.2C-rate discharges down to each 10% increment. IRIS measurements were then conducted at full discharge, 50% SOC, and full charge. For this aging study, a broader frequency range from 12.5 mHz to 1638.4 Hz was used (i.e., an 80-s measurement with 18 frequencies at 470 mA_{RMS}) to fully capture mass transport effects at lower frequencies.

Pack aging was initiated with eight discharge cycles at a 1C-rate, followed by two discharges at a 0.2 C-rate. The penultimate cycle was used to measure the discharge capacity; the final cycle included a DCIR pulse sequence every 10% SOC increment down to full discharge based on the measured capacity. Following these initial 10 cycles, the packs were removed from the thermal chamber and subjected to abuse. Ten packs were placed on an angled jig. When pressure was applied, the bottom portion of the pack was bent by the jig. The other ten packs were gently affixed to a piece of foam core and connected to vacuum cups at a 4-ft height. Once the suction was released, the packs were dropped, resulting in damage to the bottom right corner.

After damage, the packs were placed back in thermal chambers and reconnected to the tester for continued cycling at 25°C. Reference tests were conducted every 50 cycles. Within each cycle set, 48 discharges were at a 1C-rate, and the other two were at a 0.2C-rate. The final cycle included the DCIR pulse sequence as part of the reference test.

Results

Discharge Capacity: To date, the packs have completed 860 cycles. Figure 2 shows the discharge capacity for the packs subjected to bend damage normalized by the overall maximum measured capacity. The three packs with smaller mid-frequency semicircles are shown in red lines; they consistently have higher discharge capacities compared with the other seven packs. The same is generally true for the packs subjected to drop failure, as shown in Figure 3. These results suggest that the packs with smaller impedance spectra should have longer cycle-life capability.

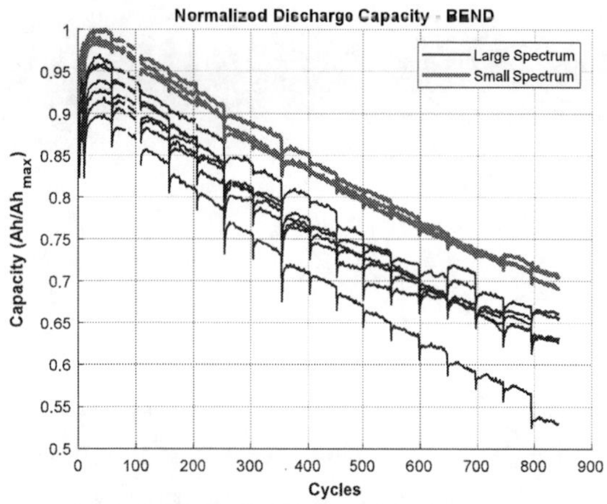

Figure 2. Discharge capacity for the BEND packs (1C rate).

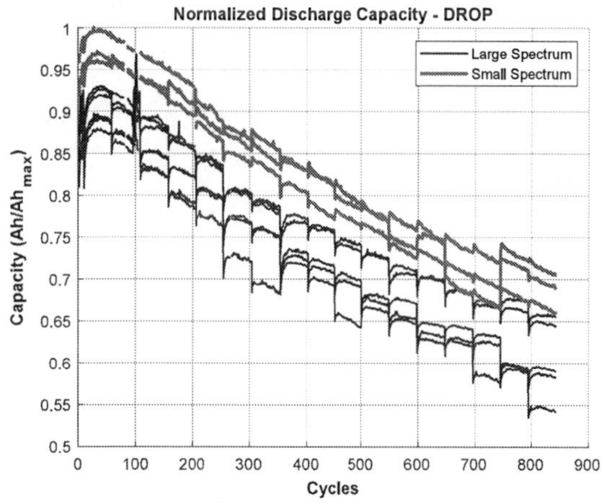

Figure 3. Discharge capacity for the DROP packs (1C rate).

The periodic drops observed in Figures 2 and 3 correspond with the reference tests every 50 cycles, in which the packs are subjected to a DCIR sequence and iRIS measurements. When cycling resumes at a 1C rate, the discharge capacity requires a few cycles to stabilize again. The packs with the smaller mid-frequency impedances generally have lower capacity drops at these intervals, indicating faster stabilization times.

DCIR Pulse Resistance: Every 50th cycle, the packs were subjected to a DCIR pulse test sequence at every 10% SOC condition. Figures 4 and 5 show the DCIR pulse resistance normalized by the overall minimum calculated resistance over 860 cycles at 100% SOC for the bend and drop packs, respectively. In all cases, the pulse resistance is lower for the packs that have smaller impedance spectra. This observation is true for each 10% SOC condition, but is the most pronounced at 100% SOC. These results suggest that the packs with smaller impedances have a better overall SOH condition as a function of age.

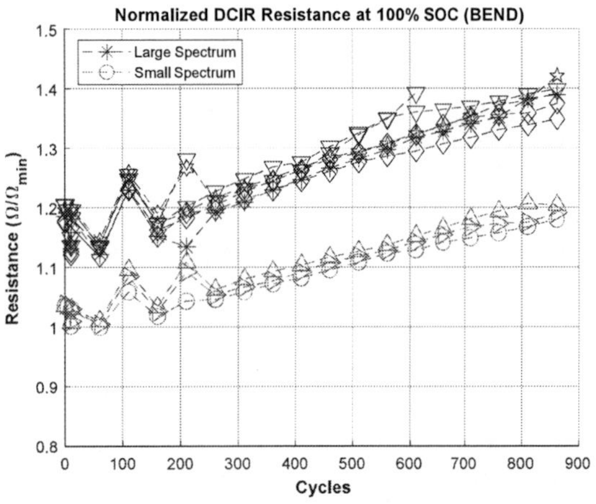

Figure 4. DCIR at 100% SOC for the BEND packs.

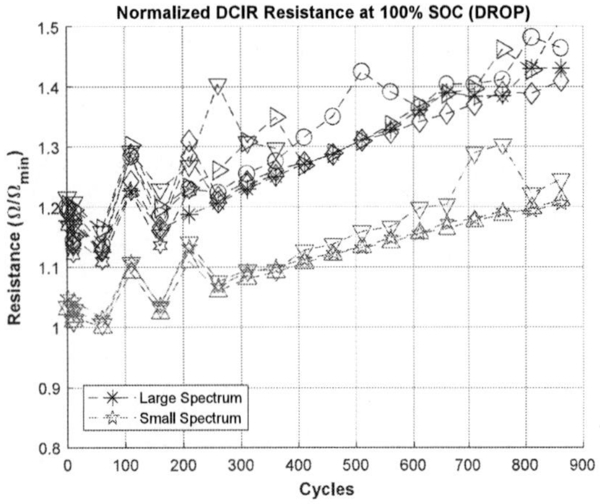

Figure 5. DCIR at 100% SOC for the DROP packs.

IRIS Measurements: As part of the reference test, iRIS measurements were also conducted at full discharge, 50% SOC, and full charge. Figure 6 shows representative impedance spectra (normalized by the pack weight) for a large and small charge transfer resistance group after 860 cycles for the bend packs (the spectra are similar for the drop packs as well). With an 80-s measurement, the impedance spectra now include a good representation of the low-frequency Warburg tail (on the right side of the spectrum). As shown, the observed differences between spectra from Figure 1 are still present out to 860 cycles.

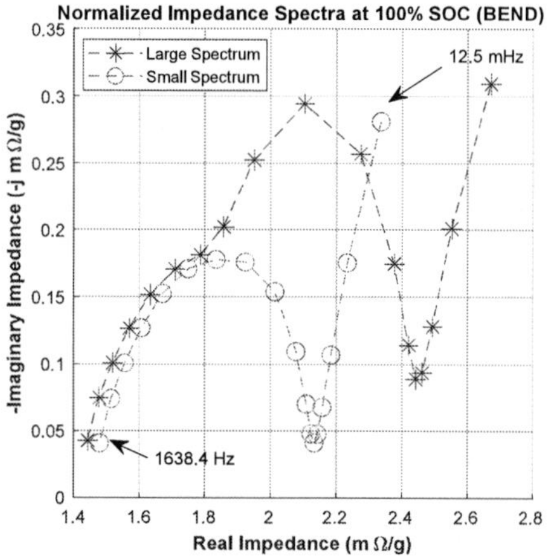

Figure 6. Representative impedance spectra after 860 cycles for the BEND packs.

The impedance spectra were modeled using the apparent equivalent circuit in Figure 7, which is based on a distribution of relaxation times (DRT) analysis [7]. It consists of an ohmic resistance (Ro) in series with an inductor and three parallel RC circuits representing the cell tabs and current collectors (R1), effects from the solid electrolyte interphase (SEI) with R2, and the charge transfer resistance (R3). Diffusion is modeled with a Warburg element (W). From the model fit, the growth in the mid-frequency semicircle is primarily dominated by R2 (i.e., SEI resistance growth). Figures 8 and 9 show the SEI resistance (normalized by the overall minimum resistance) for the bend and drop packs, respectively, over 860 cycles. As with the DCIR results, the smaller group (shown in red) consistently had lower overall SEI resistances during aging. These results also indicate a stronger SOH condition for these packs.

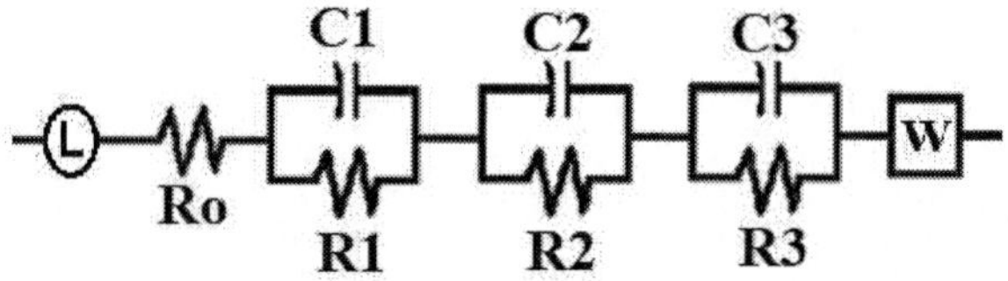

Figure 7. Equivalent circuit model for the packs.

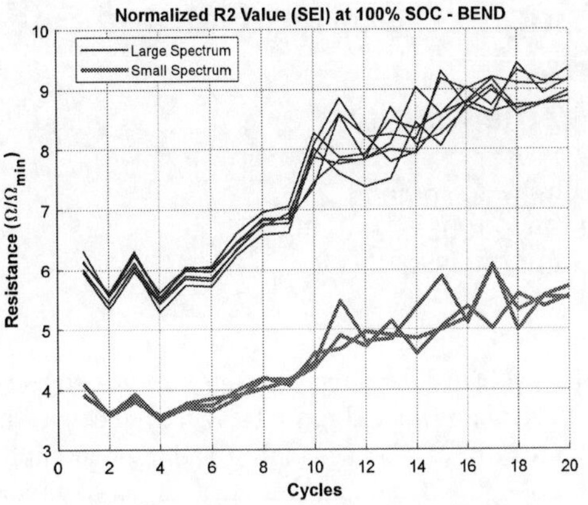

Figure 8. R2 value for BEND packs.

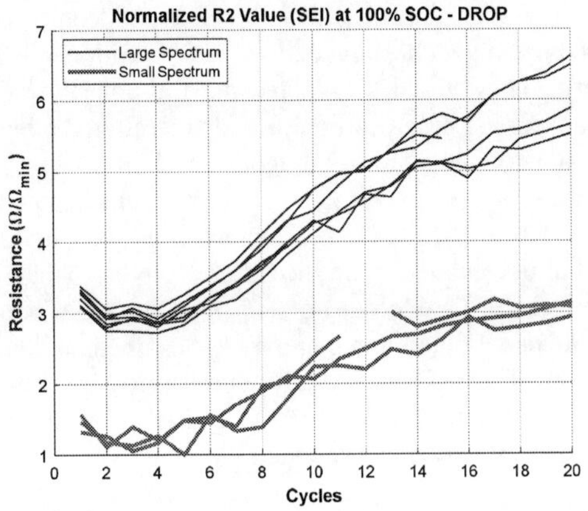

Figure 9. R2 value for DROP packs.

Discussion

The cells were manufactured in March 2021 and assembled into single-cell packs in April 2021. Within that initial month of battery life, the standard screening metrics (e.g., capacity and DCIR resistance) did not reveal any obvious difference between the packs. Pack cycling at Dynexus was initiated in October 2022 (i.e., a year and a half later, in which the packs were placed in cold storage). After this extended rest period, there was a clear distinction between the packs based on both capacity (Figures 2 and 3) and DCIR (Figures 4 and 5). However, calendar aging for an extensive period is not a practical solution for battery screening.

By way of contrast, the initial 5-s iRIS measurements were conducted at Dynexus in May 2021 (i.e., one month after the standard screening was completed). It immediately revealed a difference between pack groups which has remained through 860 cycles (see Figure 6). Additionally, equivalent circuit modeling of the impedance spectra can help provide some explanations for the differences. In this case, the packs with the lower mid-frequency semicircles primarily show lower resistances in the SEI layer (i.e., R2 in Figure 7), as demonstrated by Figures 8 and 9. Lower SEI resistances indicate reduced electrolyte consumption which can come from better cell construction in the manufacturing process and/or a more stable SEI development in the formation process. Thus, cell manufacturing quality control is critical for improved battery SOH and extended cycle-life capability. This study demonstrates that iRIS-based impedance measurements could be used as an effective screening tool for cell qualification.

Conclusion

A set of 120 consumer electronics single-cell packs were subjected to 5-s iRIS measurements to evaluate an alternative screening process. The batteries had been extensively screened and qualified using standard metrics such as discharge capacity and DCIR. These metrics did not reveal any obvious differences between the packs, but the iRIS measurements identified two distinct groups of packs; 20 had a smaller charge transfer resistance compared to the other 100. The packs have been assigned to a test matrix; mild abuse testing is presently under way. One set of packs was bent and the other was dropped from a 4-ft height. The packs having smaller impedance spectra generally show higher capacities and lower DCIR resistances through 860 cycles. These results indicate that the packs with smaller impedances may have extended cycle life, improved SOH, and better charge retention during extended calendar aging. Equivalent circuit modeling of the impedance spectra has indicated that the primary difference between the two pack groups is the resistance growth in the SEI layer, which is developed during the manufacturing and formation process. Cycle life aging for the mild abuse conditions will be completed soon, and then the groups cycling at different temperatures will be initiated for continued performance evaluation between the two groups of single-cell packs.

References

1. https://www.greencarcongress.com/2022/05/20220521-benchmark.html, accessed April 28, 2023
2. Jeevarajan, J., and Winchester, C. S., "Battery Safety Qualifications for Human Ratings," Electrochem. Soc. Interface, 21, pp. 51-55, 2012.
3. Schweiger, H. et. al., "Comparison of Several Methods for Determining the Internal Resistance of Lithium Ion Cells," *Sensors*,10, pp. 5604-5625, 2010.
4. Huang, W., and Qahouq, J. A. A., "An Online Battery Impedance Measurement Method Using DC–DC Power Converter Control," *IEEE Trans. Ind. Electron.*, vol. 61, no. 11, pp. 5987-5995, 2014.
5. Love, C. T., and K. Swider-Lyons, "Battery Health Monitoring System and Method," US 9,465,077 B2, October 2016.
6. Christophersen, J. et. al., "Long-Term Validation of Rapid Impedance Spectrum Measurements as a Battery State-of-Health Assessment Technique," *SAE Int. J. Alt. Power*, vol. 2, no. 1, pp. 146-155, 2013.
7. Schmidt, J. P. et. al., "The distribution of relaxation times as basis for generalized time-domain models for Li-ion batteries," *Journal of Power Sources*, 221, pp. 70-77, 2013.

Synthesis of a Copper Zinc Oxide Catalyst using Pre-Coated Gamma Phase Alumina Supports

Richard Scenna, Terry Dubois, Mathew Limpert
C5ISR Center
U.S. Army Combat Capabilities Development Command
Aberdeen Proving Ground, MD, USA, 21005
Richard.m.scenna.civ@army.mil / 443-395-4384

Abstract

As part of the effort to operate a fuel cell with windshield wiper fluid, the need to study steam reforming catalyst deactivation became apparent. However, there wasn't enough information about commercial grade catalysts to be able to conduct a complete study, so an effort was made to develop our own methanol steam reforming catalyst which will be used to evaluate the effects of contaminants. Typically, research grade catalysts are most commonly created and evaluate in a powdered form, and in more limited cases the catalyst powder is wash coated onto a support structure. However, in this work an alpha phase support (pellet) was precoated with a high surface area gamma phase alumina powder, then the catalyst was applied. This approach allows for the catalyst to be evaluated under a more realistic conditions, while maintaining consistency offered by the precoated support. The catalyst was evaluated at reactor temperatures between 224 and 367°C. The fuel feed was a fixed molar steam to carbon ratio of 1.23 and a volumetric flow rate of 1 ml per minute. The catalyst performed well achieving ~56% conversion as low as 224°C and achieving full conversion at ~300°C, which is consistent with literature. Carbon monoxide selectivity ranged from 0.73% at 224°C and increased to 36.94% at 367°C. This work seeks to show how the base line catalyst was developed and its performance under realistic conditions.

Keywords

Use Methanol; Steam Reforming; Catalyst; Copper Zinc Oxide

Introduction

The goal of this work is to develop a basic methanol steam reforming catalyst which can be used to evaluate the effects of contaminates found in windshield wiper fluid. Methanol steam reforming is an endothermic reaction between methanol and water to produce carbon dioxide and hydrogen.

$$CH_3OH + H_2O => CO_2 + H_2$$

Methanol steam reforming has been an active research area for a past 40 years. Typically, research grade catalysts are most commonly created and evaluate in a powdered form, and in more limited cases the catalyst powder are wash-coated onto a support structure.

Argell [1] evaluated the effects of supports on a copper zinc oxide catalyst in powdered form. He achieved conversion at temperatures of 325°C. The catalyst had a molar copper to zinc ratio of 0.8:1. He found that the addition of zirconium oxide improved a catalyst resistance to redox cycles. Cecilia Mateos-Pedrero et al [2] evaluated how surface area and polarity of the support effected reformate composition. They achieved 97.7% conversion at 300°C with a WHSV = 0.95 hr^{-1}. They found that increasing the polarity ratio of ZnO carriers increased carbon dioxide selectivity. Cheng et al[3] evaluated the effects of magnesium doping of a copper zinc oxide catalyst at WHSV = 3.84 hr^{-1} using a powdered catalyst. He found 3-5% mg content improved hydrogen yields but decreased carbon dioxide selectivity. Chen used a molar copper to zinc ratio of 1:1. Jones et al [4] studied the influence of alumina nano particles methanol steam reforming. The reference catalyst preformed the best. It achieved full conversion at 283°C at LHSV at 2088 hr^{-1}. They used a molar copper to zinc ratio of 1:1.

Test Bed

A test stand was developed to evaluate catalysts. This test stand, shown in Figure 1 (without insulation), was built using existing components. The approach used to develop this test stand was based on a previous effort. The premixed reactants (methanol/water) are held in a 250ml flask with silicon stopper. A HPLC pump is used to draw the fuel/water mixture (S/C=1.23@ 1mlpm) from the tank and inject it into a vaporizer.

The vaporizer consisted of a cartridge heater (300W) nested inside a tube, filled with $1/8^{th}$ inch dimeter stainless steel (304) ball bearings. The ball bearing served to increase the heat transfer area. The fuel water mixture temperature is directly measured after the vaporizer before being injected into the reactor.

Following vaporization, the reactants then flow into the heated reactor/ catalyst bed where they are converted into hydrogen and carbon dioxide. The tubular reactor is wrapped in 2ft off heat tape (300W). The catalyst (3.1mm pellets) are held in place with 1.5" of glass wool at either end of the reactor. The tubular reactor had an inner diameter of 0.68" and a length of 4". A thermocouple is placed inside the reactor, down the middle to provide catalyst bed temperatures. The 10 grams of catalyst were loaded into the reactor. The fuel was preheated to the same temperature as the reactor. Under the conditions tested the reactor had a weight hourly space velocity of 5.19 hr^{-1}.

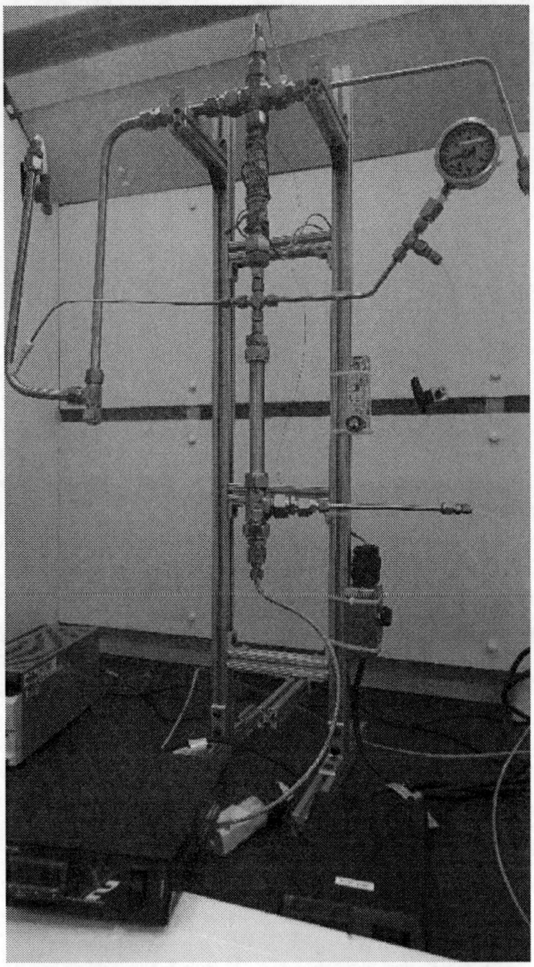

Figure 1. Test stand shown without insulation

The gasses are then cooled in a micro chiller before a sample is being processed in an online gas chromatograph (GC) Inficon Micro Fusion GC equipped with four channels. The condenser removes any potential water which would damage the capillary columns. It was configured with the refinery gas package, allowing detection of fixed gasses and hydrocarbon up to hexanes.

Process

An alumina coated pellets was selected as a support, as this material is compatible with the incipient wetness technique and provides excellent surface area as a catalyst support. The support had a high surface area of $247m^2/g$ and a total pore volume of 1.12 cm^3/g. The average diameter was 3.1mm. The baseline catalyst was chosen as copper nitrate and zinc nitrate were dissolved in distilled water. Based on literature a molar ratio of one part copper to one part zinc was chosen. The solution had a molarity of 1.61 mol/L. The support was then placed in a beaker and the dissolved catalyst was dripped in. The mixture was then coated onto the pellets through incept wetness. The coated alumina supports were then dried for 12 hours at 110°C, followed by calcination for an additional 12 hours at 350°C. Figure 2 show the catalyst after calcination.

The catalyst was loaded into the reactor and reduced. The catalyst was then reduced within the reactor, with 5.19% hydrogen and a balance of argon at 250°C at a flow rate of 0.1slpm for a period of 2 hrs. Following this the catalyst was allowed to cool to room temperature. After its reduced, the catalyst will turn black.

Figure 2. Catalyst prior to reduction

However, if the catalyst is exposed to oxygen for an extended period of time the catalyst begins to oxidize and will need to be reduced again. In typical applications, this is not an issue as the system typically remains sealed or limits the availability of oxygen to come into contact with the catalysts. To protect the catalyst at the end of every test all ports are sealed at the end of the experiment to prevent oxidation of the catalyst.

Results

The catalyst was evaluated at 1 mlpm of methanol water mixtures (59%$_{weight}$ methanol) at reactor temperatures of 224 to 367°C. The maximum temperature was restricted to prevent catalyst sintering. The catalyst performed well as shown in Fig. 2. It was able to achieve full conversion between 280-300°C.This is typical for the copper zinc oxide catalysts [1, 4] and indicates it will be a good representative baseline catalyst. The catalyst exhibited high hydrogen (73.8-76.8%) and carbon dioxide concentrations (16.5-23.0%), with low concentrations of carbon monoxide (0.0-9.6%). Higher temperatures suppressed hydrogen concentrations and promoted less favorable conditions (higher carbon monoxide formation. This is believed to be either the result high temperatures promoting reverse water gas shift reaction or promotion of methanol cracking. Decreasing hydrogen concentrations and carbon dioxide concentrations, and increasing carbon monoxide concentrations support either assertion, as seen in Figure 3.

$$H_2 + CO_2 => CO + H_2O$$

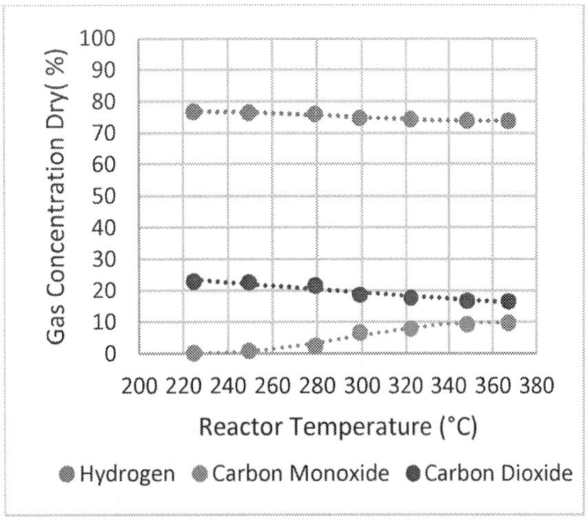

Figure 3. Reformate concentrations at reactor temperatures of 224-367°C and a molar S/C ratio of 1.23

Figure 4 shows reforming efficiency and fuel conversion. Reforming efficiency is defined as the ratio of the energy content of the hydrogen (based on LHV) to the energy content of methanol (based on LHV) minus the enthalpy for steam reforming. Conversion is defined as the ratio of molar flow rates of carbon monoxide and carbon dioxide to the molar flow rate of methanol.

$$Conversion = \frac{Molar\ flowrate\ CO + CO_2}{Molar\ flow\ rate\ of\ CH_3OH}$$

$$Reforming\ Effiency = \frac{LHV\ (H_2)}{LHV\ CH_3OH - Heat\ SR}$$

Reforming efficiency ranged from low 60% to a high of 96.2% at 300°C, which is typical for this catalyst. The catalyst performed well achieving ~56% conversion as low as 224°C and achieving full conversion at ~300°C, which is consistent with literature. As expected, higher reactor temperatures promoted greater conversion as a result of increased kinetic activity, which improved efficiency up until 300°C or full conversion. At reactor temperatures exceeding 300°C, the reforming efficiency decreased. This was a result of the decreasing hydrogen content, which was believed to be a result of the reverse water gas shift or the promotion of methanol cracking.

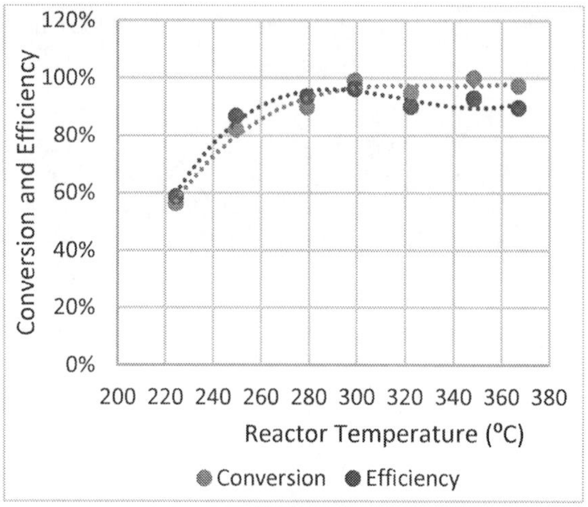

Figure 4. Conversion and efficiency at reactor temperatures of 224-367°C and a molar S/C ratio of 1.23

Low temperatures favored higher selectivity towards carbon dioxide. At reactor temperatures of 224°C-249°C the carbon dioxide selectivity was greater than 94%. Increasing reactor temperature beyond this caused selectivity to rapidly drop, as more carbon monoxide formed. At full conversion (Reactor temperature of 300°C) carbon monoxide carbon dioxide selectivity was 73%. At reactor temperatures exceeding 348°C-367°C selectivity stabilized only varying between 63-64%. The change in selectivity at temperature above 300°C is believed to be a result of increased active in the reverse water gas shift reaction.

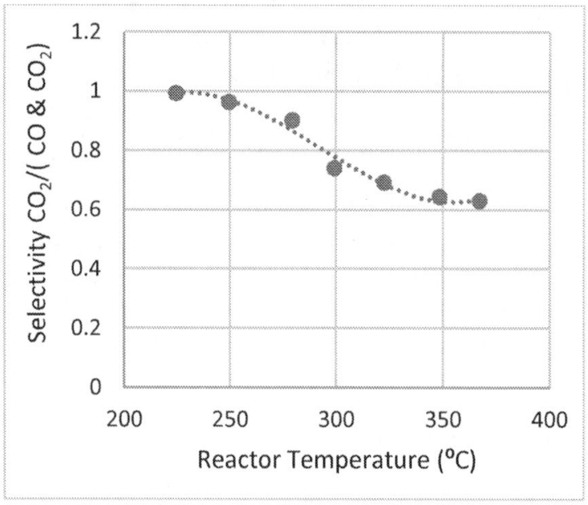

Figure 5. Carbon dioxide selectivity at reactor temperatures of 224-367°C and a molar S/C ratio of 1.23

Conclusion

This approach demonstrated comparable efficiency to conventional methanol steam reforming catalyst, indicating that it will be a good surrogate for future work focusing on contamination. Full conversion was achieved at reactor temperatures 280-300°C, which was comparable to what was identified in literature. This also indicated that using the precoated support showed no adverse effects in reformate catalyst.

At full conversion, the reformate consisted of 74.7% hydrogen, 18.7% carbon dioxide and 6.6% carbon monoxide. Reforming efficiency achieved 96.2%. In a real system a water gas shift reactor would have also been included to reduce carbon monoxide concentrations. This should be sufficient for evaluating the effects of contaminants on methanol steam reforming.

At temperatures exceeding 300ºC there was a degradation in performance. It is believed that this could be the result of the reverse water gas shift or the promotion of methanol cracking over methanol steam reforming. As reactor temperature increased beyond 300°C the hydrogen and carbon dioxide concentrations, along with an increase in carbon monoxide concentrations. This could support either assertion.

References

1. J Agrell, H Birgersson, M Boutonnet, I Melián-Cabrera, R.M Navarro, J.L.G Fierro, "Production of hydrogen from methanol over Cu/ZnO catalysts promoted by ZrO2 and Al2O3", Journal of Catalysis, Volume 219, Issue 2, 2003, Pages 389-403
2. Cecilia Mateos-Pedrero, Hugo Silva, David A. Pacheco Tanaka, Simona Liguori, Adolfo Iulianelli, Angelo Basile, Adelio Mendes, "CuO/ZnO catalysts for methanol steam reforming: The role of the support polarity ratio and surface area", Applied Catalysis B: Environmental, Volumes 174–175, 2015, Pages 67-76
3. Zaizhe Cheng, Wenqiang Zhou, Guojun Lan, Xiucheng Sun, Xiaolong Wang, Chuan Jiang, Ying Li, "High-performance Cu/ZnO/Al_2O_3 catalysts for methanol steam reforming with enhanced Cu-ZnO synergy effect via magnesium assisted strategy", Journal of Energy Chemistry, Volume 63, 2021, Pages 550-557
4. Samuel D. Jones, Luke M. Neal, Helena E. Hagelin-Weaver, "Steam reforming of methanol using Cu-ZnO catalysts supported on nanoparticle alumina", Applied Catalysis B: Environmental, Volume 84, Issues 3–4, 2008, Pages 631-642

1D Borophosphates for Use as Electrolyte Membranes in Solid Acid Fuel Cells

J. August Ridenour[1], Brian L. Chaloux[1], Michelle D. Johannes[2], Matthew T. Finn[1], Heonjune Ryou[2], Albert Epshteyn[1]
[1] Chemistry Division, [2] Materials Science and Technology Division
US Naval Research Laboratory
4555 Overlook Ave, SW, Washington, DC 20375
brian.chaloux@nrl.navy.mil

Abstract

We investigate the proton conduction, thermal stability, and viability of the borophosphate compounds sodium borophosphate (NaBOB, $Na_5[BOB(PO_4)_3]$) and ammonium borophosphate (NH_4BOB, $(NH_4)_3H_2[BOB(PO_4)_3]$) for use as solid polyelectrolytes in intermediate temperature solid acid fuel cells. Bulk synthesis methods are presented for laboratory scale (> 5 g) batch preparation of each borophosphate. Electrochemical impedance spectroscopy (EIS) was utilized to determine the ionic conductivities of NH_4BOB and NaBOB as a function of temperature; conductivities under dry N_2 flow reach 2 μS cm^{-1} and 0.9 μS cm^{-1} at 200 °C, respectively. Although NH_4BOB displays higher ionic conductivity, thermal gravimetric analyses (TGA) show much higher thermal stability in NaBOB, which remains unperturbed to 600+ °C. The thermal stability of NaBOB was also assessed under reducing atmosphere (1 atm H_2), exhibiting no reductive mass loss up to at least 400 °C. *Ab initio* molecular dynamics (MD) simulations help elucidate the mechanism of ionic conduction in these borophosphates, showing that free H^+ mobility is coupled to the gyrational mobility of the polyanionic borophosphate chains.

Keywords

borophosphate; proton conductor; fuel cell

Introduction

Over the past few decades, solid acid fuel cells (SAFCs) have been investigated as alternatives to polymer exchange membrane (PEMFCs) and solid oxide (SOFCs) fuel cells with the promise of enabling fuel cell device operation at 'intermediate' temperatures.[1-3] Operating at intermediate temperatures – between 100 and 450 °C – allows for improved water management, heat rejection, and catalytic activity, yet avoids the expensive high-temperature refractory materials required in SOFCs.[1, 4, 5] At these temperatures, polymer-electrolyte membrane (PEM) electrolytes that require water for proton conduction, dry out and can no longer be used. Also, SOFC ceramic oxide electrolytes are not able to operate in this relatively low temperature regime since they rely on high temperature mobility of the oxide anion, which has a high activation energy for motion. Achieving high efficiency fuel cell operation at intermediate temperatures thus necessitates the development of *proton* conducting solid materials sufficient thermal stability that are compatible with hydrogen under operating conditions.

Solid acids are a subset of protic, crystalline materials, such as $CsHSO_4$ and CsH_2PO_4, that bear labile protons in the solid state. The aforementioned $CsHSO_4$ and CsH_2PO_4 have been investigated as solid polyelectrolytes in SAFCs for over 20 years.[6-8] These solids exhibit a 'superprotonic' phase transition at elevated temperature wherein the protic anion becomes rotationally disordered, causing a solid-solid transition to a new phase that exhibits several orders of magnitude increase in proton mobility.[9] Of these materials, CsH_2PO_4 (cesium dihydrogen phosphate, CDP) has emerged as a primary contender for SAFCs due to its high proton conductivity above 225 °C and its good stability in a reducing environment;[8, 10, 11] however, CDP is thermodynamically unstable above this superprotonic transition, slowly dehydrating to inert pyro- and polyphosphates unless hydrated with a constant flow of humidified (p_{H_2O} ~ 0.3 atm) gas.[8]

To circumvent material shortfalls and push the upper operating temperature limit of solid acid membrane materials, we continue to investigate a broad class of solid acid compounds characterized by one-dimensional (1D) polyanionic chains. Boro*sulfates* – chemical formula $X[B(SO_4)_2]$ – are 1D polyanions containing alternating SO_4 and BO_4 tetrahedra with interstitial cations (X = NH_4, K, etc.). In general, these materials are thermally stable above 250 °C even without humidification, allowing the elimination of cumbersome humidification systems.[4, 12] Herein, we discuss a related class of 1D solid acids that substitute sulfate with the more thermally and reductively robust phosphate anion: boro*phosphates*. The ammonium and sodium borophosphate variants (NH_4BOB and NaBOB, respectively) are investigated as potential solid polyelectrolyte membrane materials by analyzing their ionic conductivity, as well as thermal and chemical stability. *Ab initio* molecular dynamics (MD) computational simulations illustrate the functional similarity of borosulfates and borophosphates[4, 12]: that temperature dependent gyrational mobility of the 1D chains facilitates proton hopping, with both material types exhibiting quite high proton mobility.

Experimental

Ammonium- and sodium-bearing borophosphates were synthesized in a low temperature flux reaction using ionic liquids (e.g., 1-butyl-3-methylimidazolium bromide, BMIM-Br) in a Teflon-lined stainless steel autoclave by heating the reactants without active mixing at 100–250 °C for 1–7 days. The solid white products were washed sequentially with glacial acetic acid, isopropanol, and diethyl ether to remove residual ionic liquid and unreacted starting materials.

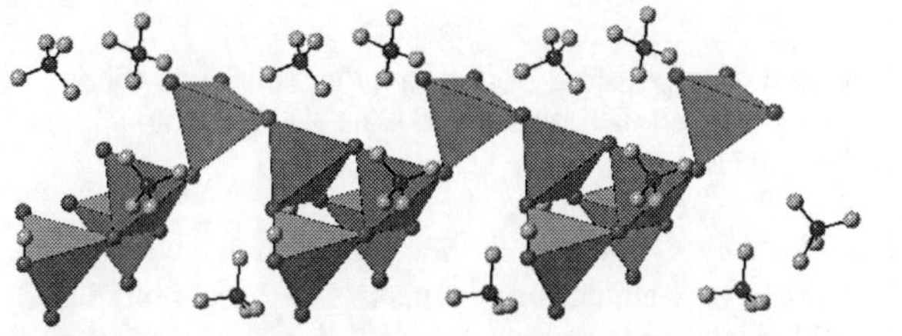

Figure 1. Structure of NH_4BOB. Orange and grey polyhedra represent PO_4 and BO_4 units, while red, blue, and white spheres represent oxygen, nitrogen, and hydrogen atoms, respectively. NaBOB exhibits the same polyanion structure.

Single crystal X-ray diffraction was utilized to determine the novel crystal structure of NH_4BOB, $(NH_4)_3[BOB(PO_4)(PO_3OH)_2]$, using a MiTeGen MicroMount™ and reflections collected with 0.5° ω scans on a Bruker D8 Quest diffractometer equipped with a Photon II detector using Mo Kα (λ = 0.71073 Å) radiation at 100(2) K. The data were integrated, absorption corrected, solved (intrinsic phasing), and refined with SAINT, SADABS, ShelXT, and SHELX2018-1, respectively, all within the APEX III software suite.[13-17] The crystal structure was illustrated (**Figure 1**) with CrystalMaker.[18] Thermal stabilities were assessed using thermogravimetric analysis (TGA, Netzch Jupiter system) at a 10 K min^{-1} scan rate under an argon atmosphere. A custom gas pressure thermogravimetric analysis instrument was used to investigate thermal decomposition under reducing conditions (800 torr H_2) and results were compared to decomposition under inert atmosphere for a qualitative assessment of reductive chemical stability.

Disc-shaped pellets (100–200 mg, 300–700 µm thick) were pressed in a 12.7 mm tungsten carbide die between Carver press platens (≈240 MPa, 200 °C for 16 h) for electrochemical impedance spectroscopy (EIS) analysis of ionic conductivity. Bulk density of the pellets was determined using a digital micrometer to measure thickness and an analytical balance for mass. Scanning electron microscopy (SEM) was performed on a Quattro environmental SEM at 20 kV to acquire images of NaBOB post-consolidation to qualitatively assess the degree of consolidation and porosity of the pellet. Ionic conductivity was determined by performing EIS on pellets sandwiched between gold-coated (50 nm by sputtering), porous, powder-sintered steel electrodes using a Gamry Reference 3000 potentiostat applying 100 mV AC over a frequency range of 1 MHz to 1 Hz. The sample-electrode assembly was mounted in a machined aluminum cell allowing for precise heating (±0.1 °C) with cartridge heaters and dry nitrogen to be flowed over both sides of the sample. Raw impedance spectra were fit with a modified Randles circuit and conductivities were estimated from the calculated electrolyte resistance and measured dimensions of each sample.

To assess proton diffusivity, we used ab-initio molecular dynamics (AIMD) to model the dynamics of 2×2×2 supercells of NH_4BOB and NaBOB (containing 32 total $[BOB(PO_4)_3]^{5-}$ repeat units) with 1–4 excess H^+ per supercell (charge balanced with a uniform negative background). Each cell at each proton concentration was fully relaxed at T=0, with a very high energy cutoff of 670 eV to ensure accurate stresses for lattice relaxation. An NRL-developed AIMD formulation[19] was used to simulate the cells at 900K over 16 ps with a 0.5 fs time step; input forces and energies were imported from the Vienna Ab Initio Simulation Program (VASP)[20] using the Perdew Burke Ernzerhof (PBE) approximation to the exchange correlation functional.[21]

Discussion

The 'BOB' borophosphates are so named because of their characteristic bridging boron–oxygen–boron linkages along the backbone of the 1D polyanions. There exist three known BOBs, which are isostructural (but not isomorphous) in that the chemical composition and connectivity of the chain are identical, and only the charge balancing cations (NH_4^+, Na^+, and Rb^+) and unit cell vary.[22, 23] The NH^+ variant ($(NH_4)_3H_2[BOB(PO_4)_3]$, NH_4BOB) is a novel compound (**Figure 1**) that can be synthesized in high isolated yield (70–90%) in the same manner as the Na^+ and Rb^+ variants using a novel process involving a low-temperature ionic liquid reaction, instead of the high temperature, molten-salt fluxes reported in prior literature.[22, 23] Under inert atmosphere, NH_4BOB and NaBOB are thermally stable up to 250 °C and 600 °C, respectively. In a reducing environment (800 mmHg H_2), as would be experienced in an operating fuel cell,

Figure 2. SEM image of a consolidated pellet of NaBOB showing sintering of grains.

NH_4BOB loses significant mass below 200 °C, possibly through condensation and loss of H_2O. In NaBOB, which lacks intrinsic protons, negligible thermal decomposition was observed under H_2 up to at least 450 °C.

Disc-shaped monolithic pellets were made by pressing small amounts of NH_4BOB / NaBOB powder in a 12.7 mm diameter tungsten carbide die press while heating to 100 °C. On average, consolidation of the pellets was >90 % comparing volumetric pellet density to the density of a single crystal. SEM imaging (**Figure 2**) shows the deformation of individual crystallites in a NaBOB pellet and minimal retained porosity. To determine ionic conductivity, EIS was conducted on pellets after heating under flowing, dry N_2 to give approximately anhydrous conditions. Overall, NH_4BOB exhibits slightly (~2x) higher ionic conductivity than NaBOB across the range of temperatures investigated (**Figure 3**), which may be due to the presence of intrinsic protic sites on the NH_4BOB backbone. Although the performance of NaBOB is slightly lower than NH_4BOB at comparable temperatures, its higher thermal stability allows for greater operational temperatures. The ionic conductivity of NH_4BOB at 205 °C was measured to be 2.2 μS cm^{-1}, whereas conductivity of NaBOB at 310 °C reached 7.5 μS cm^{-1}.

Since these borophosphates are 1D chains, their mechanism of proton conduction is fundamentally dissimilar to the 'superprotonic' mobility observed in 0D solid acid electrolytes materials such as CDP. In separate studies on borosulfates,[4, 12] temperature dependent gyrational mobility of the chains wash shown to allow efficient proton hopping pathways along and between chains as the sulfate oxygens move closer together. Molecular dynamics simulations of single crystal derived structural data for NH_4BOB and NaBOB show a similar mechanism for 1D borophosphates; AIMD at 900K shows phosphate gyrational mobility facilitating the movement of extrinsic protons throughout the bulk of these materials.

Conclusion

A class of one-dimensional borophosphates has been shown to be thermally and chemically stable under conditions relevant to intermediate temperature solid acid fuel cells (SAFC). These compounds, particularly sodium borophosphate (NaBOB), represent a group of 1D polyelectrolytes having ionic conductivity and thermal properties well-suited for advanced SAFC technologies.

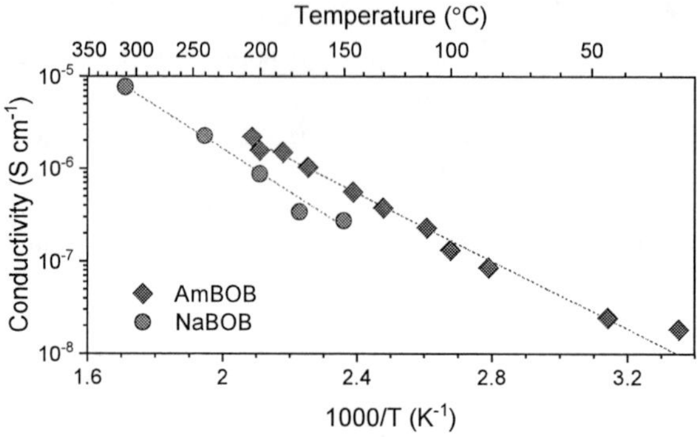

Figure 3. Temperature-dependent ionic conductivity of NH_4BOB (green diamonds) and NaBOB (magenta circles) under dry N_2.

Modest ionic conductivities (2–8 μS cm^{-1}) at elevated temperatures are driven by gyrational motion of the 1D chains, as highlighted by ab initio molecular dynamics simulations, lowering the energy barrier for proton hopping along and between chains. This provides high mobility to the existing free protons in the system, while the relatively low observed conductivities are driven by a lack to carriers and therefore low carrier concentrations. Efforts are currently underway to investigate these materials in hydrogen fuel cell systems as well as to modify the electrolyte by cation doping to improve proton conductivity and pellet consolidation.

Acknowledgements

This material is based upon work supported by the Office of Naval Research through the U.S. Naval Research Laboratory. Dr. J. August Ridenour thanks the National Research Council for administering his postdoctoral fellowship.

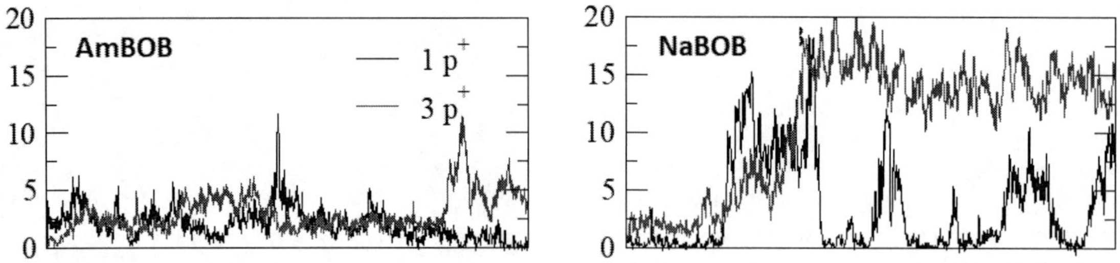

Figure 4. Average mean squared displacements (in $Å^2$) of excess H^+ in NH_4BOB (left) and NaBOB (right) tracked over 16 ps at 900K with 1 (black trace) or 3 (blue trace) H^+ per 2×2×2 supercell.

References

1. Mohammad, N.; Mohamad, A. B.; Kadhum, A. A. H.; Loh, K. S., *Journal of Power Sources* **2016,** *322*, 77-92.
2. Ndubuisi, A.; Abouali, S.; Singh, L.; Thangadurai, C., *J. Mater. Chem. A* **2021,** *10*, 2196-2227.
3. Parekh, A., *Front. Energy Res.* **2022,** *10*, 956132.
4. Ward, M. D.; Chaloux, B. L.; Johannes, M. D.; Epshteyn, A., *Adv. Mater.* **2020,** *32* (42), 2003667.
5. Murthi, V. S.; Urian, C.; Mukerjee, S., *J. Phys. Chem. B* **2004,** *108* (30), 11011-11023.
6. Haile, S. M., *Nature* **2001,** *410*, 910-913.
7. Haile, S. M., *MaterialsToday* **2003,** *6* (3), 24-29.
8. Boysen, D. A.; Uda, T.; Chisholm, C. R. I.; Haile, S. M., *Science* **2004,** *303*, 68-70.
9. Chisholm, C. R. I.; Merle, R. B.; Boysen, D. A.; Haile, S. M., *Chem. Mater.* **2002,** *14* (9), 3889-3893.
10. Haile, S. M.; Chisholm, C. R. I.; Sasaki, K.; Boysen, D. A.; Uda, T., *Faraday Discussions* **2007,** *134*, 17-34.
11. Chisholm, C. R. I.; Haile, S. M., *Chem. Mater.* **2007,** *19* (2), 270-279.
12. Chaloux, B. L.; Ridenour, J. A.; Johannes, M. D.; Epshteyn, A., *Advanced Energy and Sustainability Research* **2022,** *3* (8).
13. SAINT, B. A. I. M., Wisconsin, USA, **2013**.
14. APEX III, B. A. I. M., Wisconsin, USA, **2013**.
15. Sheldrick, G. M., *Acta Crystallogr.* **2008,** *A64*, 112-122.
16. Sheldrick, G. M., *Acta Crystallogr.* **2015,** *C71* (1), 3-8.
17. Krause, L.; Herbst-Irmer, R.; Sheldrick, G. M.; Stalke, D., *J. Appl. Crystallogr* **2015,** *48* (1), 3-10.
18. *CrystalMaker®: a crystal and molecular structure program for Mac and Windows*, CrystalMaker Software, Ltd: Oxford, England.
19. Perdew, J. P.; Burke, K.; Ernzerhof, M., *Phys. Rev. Lett.* **1996,** *77* (18), 3865-3868.
20. Bernstein, N.; Johannes, M. D.; Hoang, K., *Phys. Rev. Lett.* **2012,** *109* (20).
21. Kresse, G.; Hafner, J., *Phys. Rev. B* **1993,** *47* (1), 558-561.
22. Ewald, B.; Prots, Y.; Menezes, P.; Natarajan, S.; Zhang, H.; Kniep, R., *Inorg. Chem.* **2005,** *44* (18), 6431-6438.
23. Hauf, C.; Friedrich, T.; Kniep, R., *Z. Kristallogr.* **1995,** *210*, 446.

CO_2 Electrochemical Reduction to C1 Compounds

Deryn Chu [(1)], Jiangtian Li [(1) (2)], Terry DuBois [(3)], Annika Benson [(4)], Tristan Weaver [(4)], and Dr. Enoch Nagelli [(4)]

[(1)] U. S. Army Combat Capability Development Command
Army Research Laboratory, 2800 Powder Mill Rd., Adelphi, MD 20783
[(2)] Oak Ridge Associated Universities (ORAU)
[(3)] U. S. Army Combat Capability Development Command, C5ISR Center, 6631 Cyber Street, Aberdeen Proving Ground, MD 21005
[(4)] Department of Chemistry & Life Science
United States Military Academy, West Point, NY
deryn.d.chu.civ@army.mil

Abstract
The development of renewable energy source is one of the most significant scientific challenges facing the world. In CO_2 reduction, its thermodynamic nature, coupled with the large activation energy associated with the multi-electron and multi-proton reduction, makes the conversion of CO_2 a grant challenge. The electrochemical reduction reaction pathway for CO_2 to C-1 chemical fuels is complicated. The electrochemical reactions for conversion of CO_2 on Cu and a fluorine-doped tin oxide (SnO_2:F, FTO) Sn electrodes surface to C1 chemical compounds are performed. This research proposes to characterize and understand electrochemical reduction of CO_2 and H_2O to C1 compounds on Cu and FTO electrode surfaces. The goal of this work is to study the feasibility of an electrochemical device to chemically synthesize fuels.

Key Words: Electrochemical Reduction, CO_2 Electrochemical Reduction, and Hydrogen Evolution.

Introduction

Sunlight is the most abundant renewable energy source and has intrinsic potential in meeting future global energy demand. Converting solar energy to chemical energy stored as chemical fuels has received enormous attention world-wide due to the renewable fuel generation and benefit to the environment. Solar fuels are the chemicals such as hydrogen and small organic hydrocarbon compounds that store the chemical energy converted from the solar energy. Since Fujishima and Honda reported water splitting with a titanium dioxide-based photo-electrochemical cell (PEC) in 1972 [1], photo-electrochemical water splitting with photoactive semiconductors has been extensively studied, especially under sponsorships from the U. S. Department of Energy Programs and the National Science Foundation Programs [2]. Hydrogen is an attractive clean fuel for general purpose. However, hydrogen storage and transportation are challenging for practical applications. From a practical point view, high energy density liquid fuels are more favor due to their easy transportation and storage. Compared to hydrogen, carbon-based fuels have high volumetric energy density and easy integration into the present infrastructure. Figure 1 shows an ideal diagram for CO_2 reduction to high energy density liquid fuels.

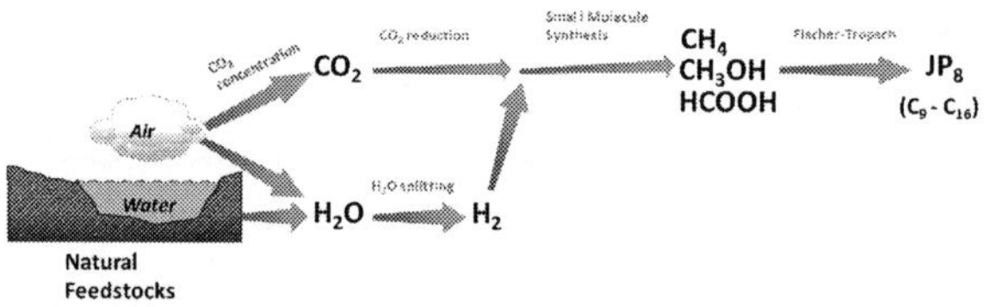

Figure 1: The schematic diagram is a renewable energy from CO_2 to liquid fuels.

Converting water and carbon dioxide into C1 hydrocarbon fuels is an important route for renewable energy development. Four different technical approaches have been reported in literature to synthesize C-1 hydrocarbon fuels from CO_2 with water: (1) conventional chemical catalytic technology, (2) biocatalysts enzyme technology [3], (3) photo-electrochemical technology [4-6], and (4) electrochemical technology [7-9].

This study focuses on converting water and CO_2 to C1 chemical fuels through an electrochemical reaction pathway. The thermodynamic nature of the CO_2 reduction reaction, coupled with the large activation energy associated with the multi-electron and multi-proton reduction, makes it a great challenge. Dr. Thomas Jaramillo at Stanford University has observed a total of 16 different CO_2 reduction products (C_1-C_3) from a polycrystalline copper electrode [7-9]. This research is to evaluate catalysts (such as Cu and Sn) for the electrochemical reduction of CO_2 and H_2O to C1 hydrocarbon fuels, aiming to study feasibility for an electrochemical device for chemically synthesize fuels.

Experimental:

The experiments were carried out with a Cu electrode or FTO/Sn glass electrode in a conventional electrochemical glass cell with three separate compartments for the working, counter, and reference electrodes. A platinized platinum gauze was used as the counter electrode. A saturated calomel electrode (SCE) saturated with KCl was used as the reference electrode. The reference electrode was connected to the main compartment (working electrode) via a luggin capillary that acts to minimize the IR drop and to prevent Cl^- ion reacting with working electrode. The counter electrode was connected to main compartment (working electrode) via a fine glass filter to separate reaction products generation from counter electrode to working electrode compartment. A Pine instrument potentiostat was employed for all electrochemical experiments. All potentials reported here are referred to SCE.

High purity potassium bicarbonate ($KHCO_3$) was procured from Sigma Chemical Company. 0.5 M $KHCO_3$ solution was prepared by solving $KHCO_3$ in distilled water. The 0.5 M $KHCO_3$ electrolyte was saturated with ultrapure CO_2 (99.99%, Airgas, USA) by bubbling for at least 30 minutes before performing CO_2 electrochemical reduction. Continuous CO_2 flow was maintained over the tested electrolyte during the experiment. Chronoamperometry and Cyclic voltammetry techniques were used for experiments. Cyclic voltammetry technique was performed to obtain the electrochemical potentials vs. electrochemical current response for CO_2 electrochemical reaction (reactant adsorption/reduction and products desorption) at the Cu and FTO/Sn (Fluorene Doped Tin Oxide) electrodes. Chronoamperometry is the current-time transient following a potential step and used to study the CO_2 electrochemical reaction at the Cu and FTO electrodes. In this study, the potential was set up to step from -0.2V (vs. SCE) to a potential at which the CO_2 electrochemical reduction occurs potentials.

Products Analysis:

The analysis of gas products from the electrochemical reduction of CO_2 was analyzed on an SRI Gas Chromatography (GC) -Flame Ionization and Thermal Conductivity Detectors (GC-FID&TCD) (SRI, GC 8610). Liquid phase products were analyzed by nuclear magnetic resonance (NMR).

Results and Discussion:

There have two electrochemical reduction reactions at cathodic sweep direction for CO_2 saturated 0.5M $KHCO_3$ electrolyte: CO_2 reduction reaction ($CO_2 + m(H^+ + e^-) \rightarrow C_xH_yO_z + nH_2O$) and H_2 evolution reaction ($2H^+ + 2e^- \rightarrow H_2$). Two reactions compete dependent on applied potentials. Table I shows theoretical thermodynamic electrochemical reduction potentials (E^0) for CO_2 to various products through two or multi-electron and multi-proton reduction reactions. The CO_2 potentials are calculated for aqueous solutions at pH=7.

Table I. Theoretical thermodynamic electrochemical reduction potentials (E^0) for CO_2 to various products through two or multielectron reduction reactions. n represents the involved electron numbers for the corresponding reactions.

Water Splitting:	n	E^0
$2H^+ + 2e^- \rightarrow H_2$	2	E^o= 0.00V
$H_2O \rightarrow ½ O_2 + H_2$	2	E^o= 1.23V
CO_2 Electrochemical Reaction		
$CO_2 + 2H^+ + 2e^- \rightarrow CO + H_2O$	2	E^o= -0.53V
$CO_2 + 2H^+ + 2e^- \rightarrow HCOOH$	2	E^o= -0.61V
$CO_2 + 4H^+ + 4e^- \rightarrow HCHO + H_2O$	4	E^o= -0.48V
$CO_2 + 6H^+ + 6e^- \rightarrow CH_3OH + H_2O$	6	E^o= -0.38V
$CO_2 + 8H^+ + 8e^- \rightarrow CH_4 + 2H_2O$	8	E^o= -0.24V
$CO_2 + 12H^+ + 12e^- \rightleftharpoons C_2H_4 + H_2O$	12	E^o= 0.079V

Figure 2 compares cyclic voltammetry (CV) for Cu electrode in 0.5M $KHCO_3$ electrolyte saturated with Argon (Ar) (curve A) and CO_2 (curve B), respectively. To get a real transient CV curve for a Cu electrode by suppressing H_2 reduction reaction, the sweep potential range was limited between -0.2V to -0.8V vs. SCE. Curve A shows a well-defined CV for a bare Cu electrode. Three small reduction peaks (~-0.25V, ~-0.375 and ~-0.65V) at the cathodic scan direction have been attributed to CuO, Cu_2O or Cu_4O_3 reduction reactions. To the best of our knowledge, this is the first time to have a CV curve for a Cu electrode in this potential range since Cu surface is too unstable and easily being oxidized to get a well-define Cu CV curve. Curve B shows the CO_2 electrochemical reduction reaction on Cu electrode in CO_2 saturated 0.5M $KHCO_3$. The cathodic peak at ~-0.6V obviously indicates the CO_2 electrochemical reduction. A close comparison for curves A and B current scale, CO_2 reduction current is almost 5 time less than that of Ar saturated electrolyte. This is probably attributed to the strong adsorption of CO_2 reduction product (such as CO) on Cu surface, poisoning Cu electrode and therefore blocking the Cu activity available surface.

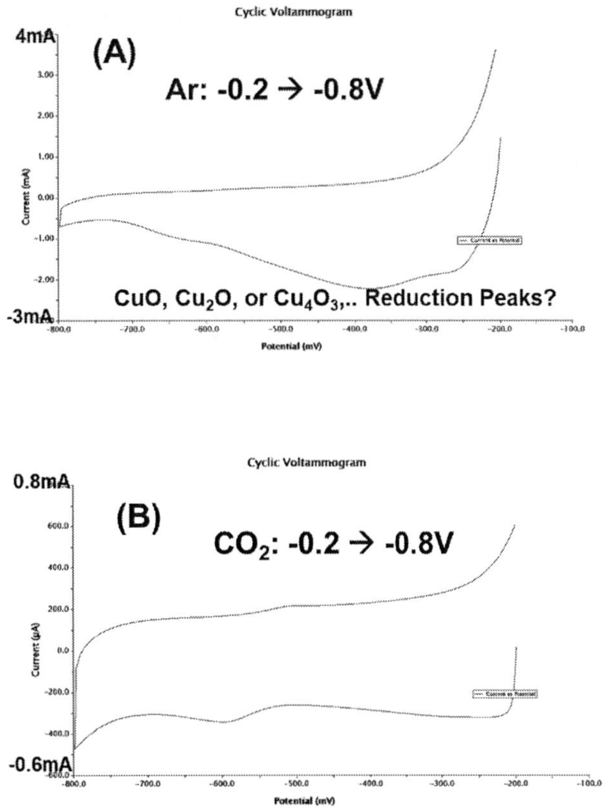

Fig. 2 Cyclic voltammetry for a Cu electrode in 0.5M $KHCO_3$ saturared with Ar (A) and CO_2 (B), Scan rate: 50mv/s, Potential from -0.2 V to -0.8V.

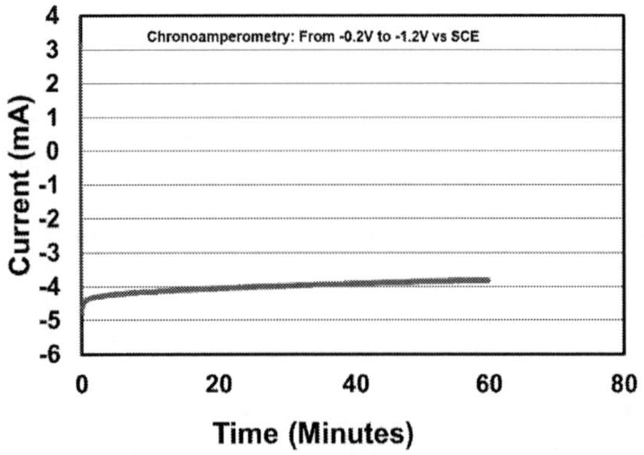

Fig. 3 Chronoamperometry experiment for a Cu electrode in 0.5M $KHCO_3$ saturared with CO_2, Potential Step from -0.2 V to -1.2V vs SCE.

Figure 3 shows a chronoamperometry experiment for for a Cu electrode in 0.5M KHCO3 saturared with CO_2, Potential Step from -0.2 V to -1.2V vs SCE.

Table 2 tabulates the products of CO_2 reduction on a Cu electrode at different potentials. The results are based on GC analysis of gas products and NMR analysis of liquid phase product (HCOOH). The Chronoamperometry experiment results for CO_2 reduction to CO agreed well with the cyclic voltammetry experiment results.

Table II. CO_2 reduction reaction on Cu electrode generates various products at different potentials vs SCE.

Cu	H_2	CO	CH_4	C_2H_4	C_2H_2	$HCOO^-$	CH_3OH
-0.65V		V					
-0.8V		V					
-1.0V	V	V					
-1.2V	V	V					
-1.4V	V	V	V	V	V		
-1.6V	V	V	V	V	V	V (trace)	
-1.8V	V	V	V	V	V	V (trace)	

Figure 4 compares cyclic voltammetry curves for a FTO electrode in 0.5M $KHCO_3$ electrolyte saturated with Argon (Ar) (curve A) and CO_2 (curve B), respectively. The potential was scanned between -0.2V to -0.6V vs. SCE. The cathodic/anodic peak couple in curve (A) is related to Sn (II) and Sn (IV) redox reaction. The reaction is reversible. Curve (B) shows the CO_2 electrochemical reduction on FTO electrode. The CO_2 reduction starts at -0.3V and reaches a plateau at -0.5V vs SCE, respectively. A comparison of current scale for curves A and B, CO_2 reduction current is almost 10 time larger than that of Ar saturated electrolyte. As shown in Table 3, only H_2 and CO reaction products have been detected for the FTO/Sn electrode, even the electrode potential reaching -2.0V vs SCE, indicative of high CO_2 reduction selectivity on FTO electrode.

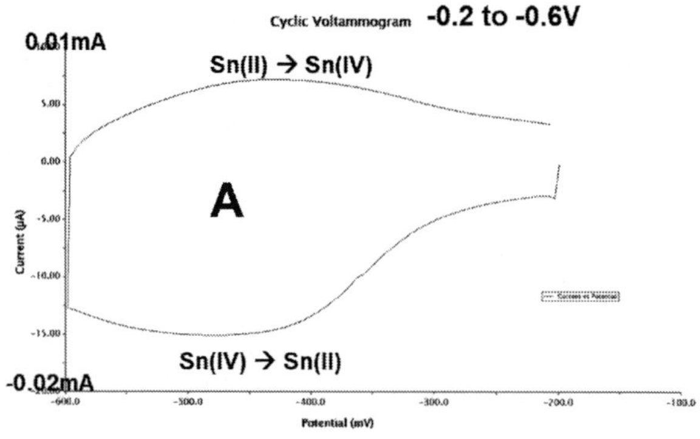

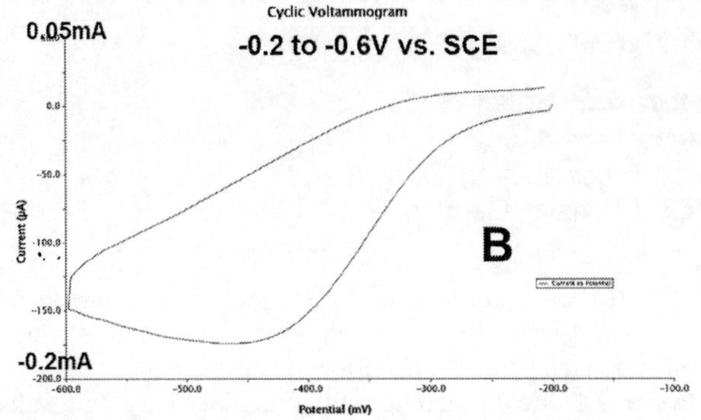

Fig. 4 Cyclic voltammetry for a FTO electrode in 0.5M $KHCO_3$ saturated with Ar (A) and CO_2 (B), scan rate: 50mv/s, potential from -0.2 V to -0.6V.

Table III. CO_2 reduction reaction at FTO/Sn electrode only generates H_2 and CO products at different potentials vs SCE. The Gas phase products from GC analysis.

FTO	H_2	CO	CH_4	C_2H_4	C_2H_6	CH_3OH	
-0.65V		V					
-0.8V		V					
-1.0V	V	V					
-1.2V	V	V					
-1.4V	V	V					
-1.6V	V	V					
-2.0V	V	V					

Summary

We performed the electrochemical CO_2 reductions on Cu and FTO/Sn electrodes and compared the products by varying the applied potentials. Based on the electrochemical experimental results from this study, we have a couple of preliminary conclusions. Cu electrode is unstable and easily oxidized to Cu oxides in the electrolyte, whereas Sn surface is very stable under CO_2 electrochemical reduction conditions. CO is the only gas product at -0.65 & -0.8V vs SCE, for CO_2 electrochemical reduction on both Cu and Sn electrodes. The CO adsorption on Cu surface is strong, while weak on Sn surface. Observed CO product concentration is high at the initial electrochemical reaction and then decreases with increasing time for experiment on Cu. CO generation rate is constant at the Sn surface. H_2 generation reaction stars from potential ~ -1.0V vs SCE. At higher potentials > -1.4V vs SCE, H_2, CO, CH_4 and C_2H_4 are products for CO_2 electrochemical reduction reaction on Cu.

Electrochemical reaction can convert CO_2 with water to C1 hydrocarbon compounds. However, the thermodynamic potential for hydrogen generation reaction is more favorable than that of CO_2 electrochemical reduction. The electrochemical device for CO_2 reduction suffers from low stability and efficiency, preventing them to become a practical application. There are also grand challenges with the separation and collection of liquid hydrocarbon products. Developing multi-functional catalysts or selective surface catalysts for the simultaneous carbon dioxide and water chemical conversion to syngas is pivotal for further research and development efforts. Continued improvements in efficiency, durability, and cost are still needed for practical applications.

References:

1. A. Fujishima and K. Honda, Nature, 238 (1972), 37-38.
2. Oscar Khaselev and John A. Turner, Science, 280 (1998), 425-427
3. Stefanie Schlager and Niyazi S. Sariciftci, Energy Technology, 5 (2017), 812-821.
4. Bocarsly, A. B.; Gibson, Q. D.; Morris, A. J.; L'Esperance, R. P.; Detweiler, Z. M.; Lakkaraju, P. S.; Zeitler, E. L.; Shaw, T. W., ACS Catalysis 2012, 2 (8), 1684-1692.
5. Morris, A. J.; McGibbon, R. T.; Bocarsly, A. B., Chemsuschem 2011, 4 (2), 191-196.
6. Cole, E. B.; Lakkaraju, P. S.; Rampulla, D. M.; Morris, A. J.; Abelev, E.; Bocarsly, A. B., Journal of the American Chemical Society 2010, 132 (33), 11539-11551.
7. K. Kuhl, E.R. Cave, D.N. Abram, T.F. Jaramillo, Energy & Environmental Science, 5 (2012), 7050-7059.
8. D. Koshy, S. Chen, D. Un Lee, M.B. Stevens, A. Abdellah, S. Dull, G. Chen, D. Nordlund, A. Gallo, C. Hahn, D.C. Higgins, Z. Bao, T.F. Jaramillo, Angewandte, (2020). DOI: 10.1002/ange.201912857
9. L.Wang, D.C. Higgins, Y. Ji, C.G. Morales-Guio, K. Chan, C. Hahn, T.F. Jaramillo, Proceedings of the National Academy of Sciences, (2020).

Investigation of Load-Temperature Balancing of the Operation of Commercial HT-PEMFC Stacks with Reformed Logistic Fuels

Carsten Cremers, Stefan Bürger
Division for Applied Electrochemistry
Fraunhofer Institute for Chemical Technology (ICT)
Joseph-von-Fraunhofer-Str. 7, 76327 Pfinztal, Germany

Abstract: Fuel cells can be a relevant to address low signature power generation demands in military operations. The requirement to operate on logistic fuels is a significant obstacle in achieving this goal. Fuel cells operating at higher temperatures are known to be less prone to poisoning by impurities like CO and H_2S. High temperature polymer electrolyte fuel cells operating at 160 – 180 °C offer sufficient resistance against such impurities avoiding other issues arising from still higher operating temperatures of solid oxide fuel cells. Military power sources often need to operate at low partial load. As the operation of fuel cells at reduced load increases the conversion efficiency, less rejected heat is available to maintain the stack operation temperature. To evaluate this operating condition test were performed on commercial Serenergy S165L-35 stacks analysing the heat rejection at different loads and temperatures. It was found that for reduced loads the stack temperature needs to be reduced to temperatures as low as 135 °C. Still a stable operation with pure hydrogen as well as with surrogate reformate was possible.

In total the results proved that low level part load operation of HT-PEMFC is viable not providing obstacles for a military use. In the systems design the water management of the fuel gas processing needs careful attention.

Keywords: fuel cell; HT-PEMFC; logistic fuels; partial load

Introduction

Fuel cells can continuously provide electric power by conversion of several different fuels. As this happens with low noise and IR signatures, fuel cells are an interesting alternative for military application requiring low signatures and needing long operating times which cannot be covered by batteries easily. If logistic fuels are used, the fuel stream resulting from the down stream fuel processing will contain CO and may contain H_2S. Both substances act as poison for the fuel cell electrode. Thereby the strength of the effect depends on the operating temperature. As was shown [1–3], high temperature polymer electrolyte fuel cells operating at 160 – 180 °C offer sufficient resistance against such impurities avoiding other issues arising from still higher operating temperatures of solid oxide fuel cells. A second prerequisite to the use of fuel cells as military power source is now the ability to operate at low partial load conditions, as military power sources are usually over dimensioned. Part load operation of fuel cells increases their expected lifetime and efficiency and thus decreases more than linearly the available rejected heat. This leads to the questions at which operation temperatures HT-PEMFC can function at reduced load and if a stable operation still is possible. Here the results of an experimental investigation of these questions are presented.

Experimental set-up

Experiments were carried out on commercial HT-PEMFC stacks S165L-35 by Serenergy, Aalborg (DK). These stacks have a geometrical cell area of 165 cm^2 and 35 cells. The rated power with steam reformed methanol is 1.5 kW @ 400 mA cm^2. The stack was tested in a Greenlight FCATS G40 test rig specially designed for the test of HT-PEMFC in combination with online mixed surrogate reformate. Cooling as well as heating of the stack if required are performed with a closed Triethyleneglycol cycle. The control of the stack temperature is done by regulating the coolant outlet temperature by varying the coolant inlet temperature and the coolant flow. The heat performance of the stack can thus be calculated from the temperature difference between coolant inlet and coolant outlet using the following equation:

$$P_{therm} = \left(T_{cool_{in}} - T_{cool_{out}}\right) \cdot \frac{dm_{cool}}{dt} \cdot cp_{cool} \quad (1)$$

Hereby negative values indicate heat rejection from the stack whereas positive values indicate heat delivery to the stack. A value of zero signifies, that the stack temperature is maintained without heat exchange via the coolant circuit. In a series of test P_{therm} was measured as function of load with the coolant outlet temperature set-to different values. This was used to determine the operating temperature range. Subsequently this temperature range was also used for test with surrogate reformed NATO-F34 (JP-8).

Results

In a first tests the effect of different stack operating temperatures on the stack performance was evaluated. It was found that a larger reduction of the stack temperature will reduce the achievable performance but that a minor reduction by 5 K has not a significant influence.

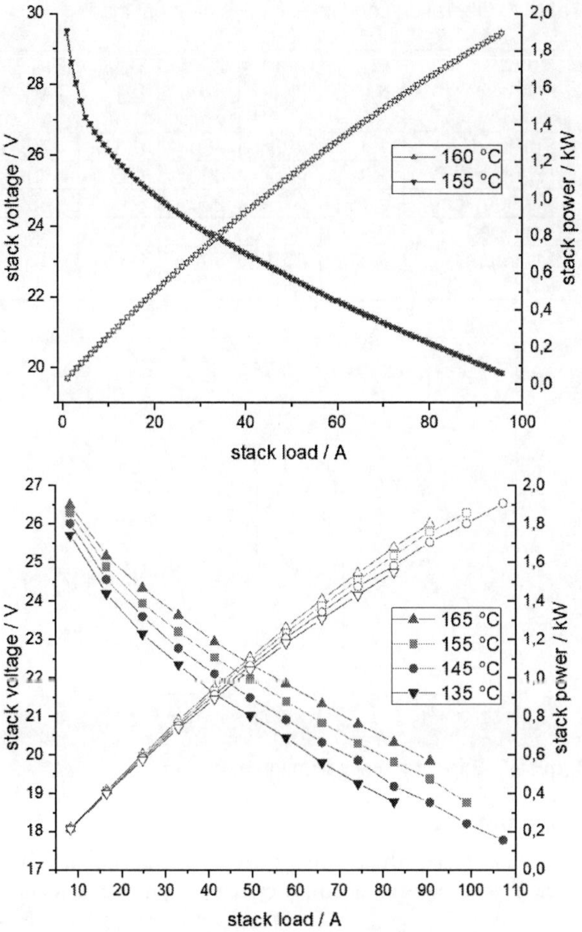

Figure 1. Effect of a reduction of the stack temperature by 5 K (upper) and by 30 K in 10 K steps (lower).

For the iV-curves in figure 1, the temperature of the stack, i.e. the temperature of the coolant outlet was maintained at the listed constant value. As the reject heat varies with the load, this requires that the cooling adjust itself to the load by reducing coolant inlet temperature. This can be seen in figure 2.

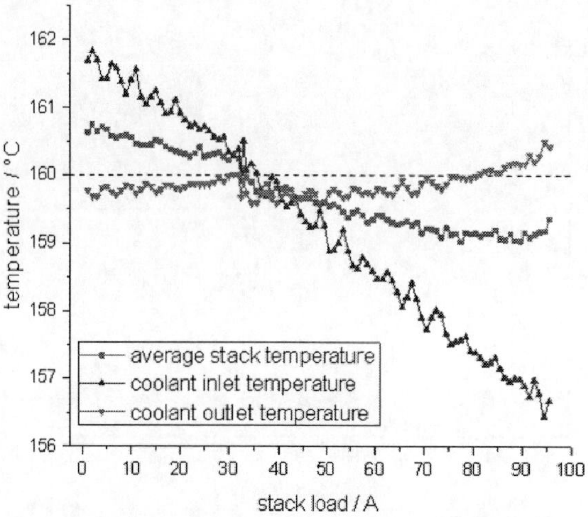

Figure 2. Load dependents of coolant in, coolant out and average stack temperature for a coolant out set value of 160 °C

The difference between coolant inlet and outlet temperature indicates the heat exchange via the cooling circuit with positive values signifying a heat-up take by the stack. As can be seen in figure 3 at a stack temperature of 160 °C this I the case until about 40 A load.

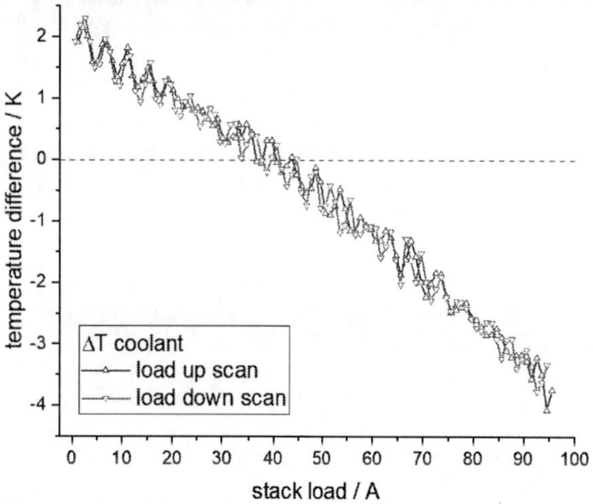

Figure 3. Load dependence of the difference between coolant inlet and outlet temperature for a set value of 160 °C

If the stack temperature is reduced, the load up to which a heating of the stack is required reduces as well (cf. Figure 4)

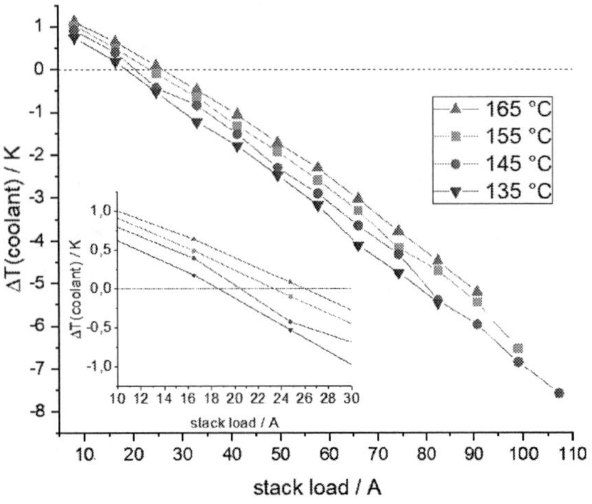

Figure 4. Load dependence of the difference between coolant inlet and outlet temperature for a set values between 135 °C and 165 °C

At low loads the stack should therefore preferably be operated at a reduced temperature. As the operating temperature also influences the tolerance against fuel impurities it was investigated if operation at reduced temperature with surrogate reformed NATO F34 fuel (JP-8) is possible. For that the stack was operated with a surrogate reformate with a dry gas composition of 55 vol.% H_2, 0.5 vol.% CO, 5 ppm$_v$ H_2S balance N_2 and a dew point of 55 °C. The iV-curves in figure 5 reveal that at high load the standard operating conditions with $\lambda_A = 1.4$ and an operating temperature of 165 °C are not sufficient to meet the target of achieving 90 % of the rated power of 1.5 kW for operation with steam reformed methanol. To accomplish this either the anode stoichiometry or the operating temperature needs to be increased. At low loads the raise of operating temperature to 175 °C has no effect.

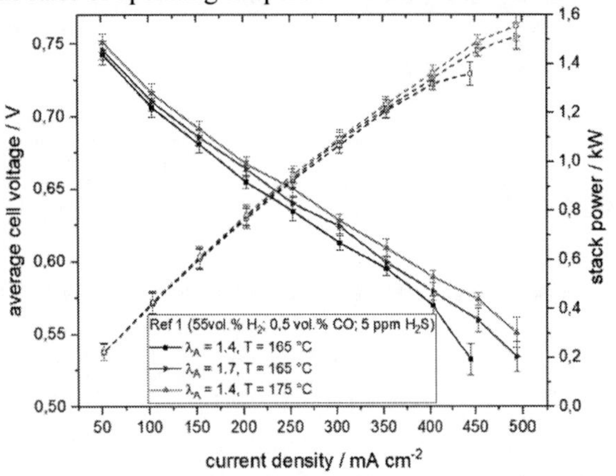

Figure 5. iV curves fo operation with surrogate reformate

Therefore, it was tested if at such low loads also a reduction of the operation temperature is possible. As can be seen in table 1 and figure 6 that can be confirmed.

Table 1. Operation conditions for five different loads

Point	P_{el} [kW]	load [%]	i [mA cm^{-2}]	U_{cell} [V]	T_{op} [°C]
Full load	1.4	100	400	0.61	175
High load	1.07	76.7	300	0.62	165
Medium load	0.762	54.5	200	0.66	165
Low load	0.404	28.9	100	0.70	155
Minimum load	0.211	15.1	50	0.73	155

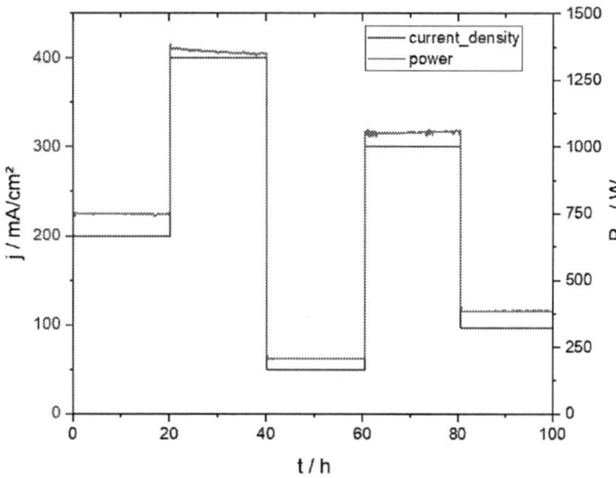

Figure 6. Experimental validation of load point

Conclusions

Due to increased efficiency the rejected thermal power of the stack at low loads is much lower. This requires a reduction of the operating temperature. Tests with surrogate NATO-F34 containing CO and H_2S have shown, that at low loads operation at temperatures as low as 135 °C is possible even with that fuel.

References

[1] T.J. Schmidt, J. Baurmeister, Durability and reliability in high-temperature reformed hydrogen PEFCs, ECS Transactions 3 (2006) 861–869. https://doi.org/10.1149/1.2356204.

[2] C. Cremers, M.S. Rau, A. Niedergesass, K. Pinkwart, J. Tubke, Effect of Model Fuel Impurities for Reformed Jet Fuels on the Hydrogen Oxidation at Platinum Based Catalyst under HT-PEMFC Conditions, ECS Trans. 75 (2016) 919–929. https://doi.org/10.1149/07514.0919ecst.

[3] C. Cremers, M.S. Rau, A. Niedergesäß, F. Jung, K. Pinkwart, J. Tübke, High Temperature Polymer Electrolyte Fuel Cell Developments for the Mobile Power Generation from Logistic (Liquid) Fuels, in: Proceedings of the 47th Power Sources Conference, Orlando, FL, USA, 2016, 17-4

Pyrolysis of Conductive 2D Coordination Polymers for Use as Solid Acid Fuel Cell Electrode Materials

J. August Ridenour[1], William A. Maza[1], Olga Baturina[1], Bethany Hudak[2], Hannah Ashberry[3], Brian L. Chaloux[1], Matthew T. Finn[1], Albert Epshteyn[1]

[1] Chemistry Division, US Naval Research Lab, 4555 Overlook Ave, SW, Washington, D.C., 20375

[2] Materials Science and Technology Division. US Naval Research Laboratory, 4555 Overlook Ave, SW, Washington, D.C., 20375

[3] Former NRC Postdoctoral Fellow, Chemistry Division, US Naval Research Lab, 4555 Overlook Ave, SW, Washington, D.C. 20375

Abstract

There is continued interest in the development of next-generation hydrogen-based energy systems that have greater power output, energy density, reliability, and lower costs. Solid acid fuel cells (SAFCs), which use solid acid electrolyte membranes and operate at intermediate temperatures (150–450 °C), have the potential to address those technological targets.[1, 2] However, due to challenges arising from having a solid electrolyte, SAFC electrodes underperform as compared to those used for polymer electrolyte fuel cells (PEMFCs), and development of new materials is needed to tackle challenges associated with producing high electrochemically active surface area (ECSA) electrodes for solid-state architectures in SAFCs. Based on the requisite desirable properties, metal-organic coordination polymers[3] are attractive precursor compounds for producing new SAFC electrode materials; specifically due to existing porosity for gas diffusion, catalytically-active metal nodes, and a tunable carbon framework that can be made to become more electrically conductive via pyrolysis. Here we investigate metal-organic hybrid precursor materials modified *via* pyrolysis under vacuum to create metal-doped graphitized materials in pursuit of highly electrically conductive and porous carbonaceous materials with embedded metal nanoparticles. We submit these results as an important step toward producing more robust SAFC electrode materials.

Introduction

Intermediate temperature fuel cell technologies which enable operation in the temperature range of 100–450 °C offer the possibility of improvements over other fuel cell systems, such as polymer electrolyte fuel cells (PEMFCs), or solid oxide fuel cells (SOFCs).[4, 5] Higher operational temperatures as compared to PEMFCs can provide multiple fuel cell system benefits including improved water management, heat rejection, and possibly provide additional benefits such as ability to use non-precious metal catalysts, as well as reducing catalyst susceptibility to poisoning. Bulky humidification systems may be eliminated with improved proton mobility kinetics, alternative proton mobility pathways (*i.e.* non-water), and elimination of need for active humidification.[6, 7] Further, intermediate temperature systems operating in the 100-450 °C range can be constructed from standard engineering materials without the use of expensive refractory components.[6, 8, 9] One type of intermediate temperature fuel cell systems, solid acid fuel cells (SAFCs), utilize a highly protonated solid-form acid as the electrolyte membrane.[1, 2] Due to the lack of liquid/gel proton electrolytes in these systems, SAFC electrodes suffer from lower electrochemical surface area and therefore lower power output. New approaches in nanoscopically textured/architected electrode design are needed to produce higher electrochemically active surface areas (ECSAs) for SAFC-specific requirements stemming from electrolyte compatibility considerations.

The fundamental requirements of viable electrode materials include reasonable electrical conductivity, porosity for gas infiltration, maximized number of accessible catalytic sites, and stability under fuel cell operating conditions; yet materials that exhibit all characteristics at appropriate levels for SAFC operation are few and noteworthy.[12-14] Metal-organic-based hybrid materials, particularly those with multi-dimensional architectures, may fill many of these attribute niches.[15, 16] Pyrolytic post-modification of such hybrid precursors can then improve chemical and thermal stability, as well as electrical conductivity, through graphitization of organics to access beneficial architectures and/or generate catalytic sites.[17-19] As such, we have investigated the modification of the highly conductive metal-hexaaminotriphenylene (HATP) coordination polymers[20, 21] toward performance improvement *via* post-synthetic pyrolysis. Initial investigations found that anaerobic thermal decomposition of Ni_3HATP_2 produces nanoparticles (NPs), with modest size control afforded by pyrolysis temperature while confined in a C-based matrix. In search of a more appropriate electrode material, a novel Pt-HATP precursor was synthesized using methodology similar to that of Ni_3HATP_2, yet producing a significantly different crystalline material. Pyrolysis experiments with the Pt-HATP demonstrated similar reductive decomposition accompanied by graphitization of the organic linkers and the formation of size-controllable Pt NPs with significantly greater size control over the Ni system. Electrochemical experiments to investigate the Pt-HATP activity for ORR catalysis using rotating disk electrode (RDE) methods are presented.

Synthesis, Pyrolysis, and Characterization

All precursor materials discussed herein were synthesized in a process modified from the original $Ni_3(HITP)_2$ investigation by Dincă, *et al.*[20, 21] A metal salt and the 2,3,6,7,10,11-hexaaminetriphenylene (HATP) ligand were combined in an aqueous ammonia solution and left stirring overnight while heated to 65 °C. A black solid suspension was then filtered, washed, and dried. This black solid, as the metal-organic precursor material, was then pyrolyzed at 600 °C in a tube furnace at 50 mtorr under dynamic vacuum.

High angle annular dark field (HAADF) imaging and *in situ* pyrolysis were done to investigate the pyrolytic formation of nanoparticles with a scanning transmission electron microscope (Nion UltraSTEM-X 200 STEM, 60 kV, 10^{-9} Torr) equipped with a Protochips E-chip heating TEM grid. Samples were drop-cast with EtOH onto the grid, fully dried, and upon insertion into the instrument heated *in situ* to 500 °C in 50 °C steps and from 500 °C to 1200 °C in 100 °C steps, with a nearly instantaneous rate of heating at 1000 °C/ms. Thermogravimetric analysis and differential scanning calorimetry (TGA/DSC) were conducted on both the Ni-HATP and the Pt-HATP materials to investigate inert atmosphere thermal decomposition.

For electrochemical analyses, an ink was prepared by dispersing 8 mg of the pyrolyzed catalyst in 2 mL of inking solution (20 mL of H_2O, 80 mL of IPA, and 0.4 mL of 5 wt. % Nafion ionomer solution (Ion Power, Liquion 1100)). The catalyst suspension was homogenized by ultrasound, stirred overnight, then sonicated again prior to drop-casting 10 and 20 μL droplets on the surface of a 5 mm mirror-polished and clean glassy carbon electrode. The same procedure was used for both the 40 wt. % Pt/VC and the 38 wt. % Pt nanoparticles embedded in the pyrolyzed Pt-HATP material, respectively. Cyclic voltammetry (CV) and polarization curves were collected in a 125 mL commercial 3-electrode electrochemical cell filled with 0.1 M $HClO_4$ solution, using a Autolab μ-III potentiostat (Metrohm). Spiral Pt wire and Ag/AgCl served as a counter and reference electrodes, respectively. The electrolyte solution was purged with UHP N_2 or O_2 prior to collecting CV and polarization curves, and bubbling was maintained throughout the electrochemical measurements. Prior to collecting polarization curves, the catalyst was activated by running 120 CV curves at 200 mV s^{-1} between -0.35 and 1.15 V. The ECSAs were calculated from hydrogen desorption regions on CV curves as described previously[22] and kinetic currents were extracted from total ORR currents using a previously reported and established procedure.[22]

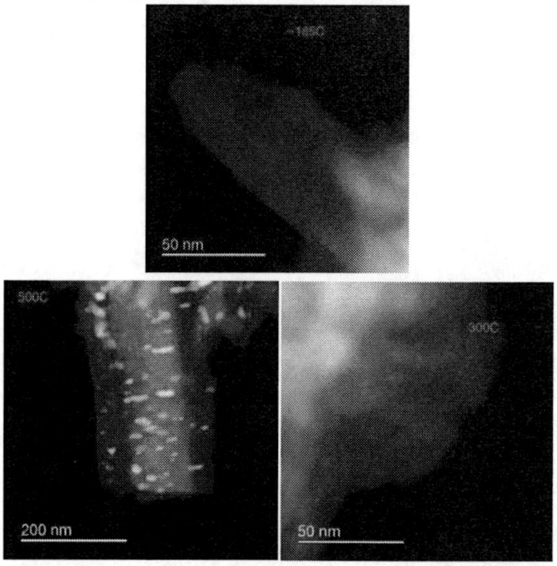

Figure 1. HAADF images of $Ni_3(HITP)_2$. Left) Crystalline domains show 1.8 nm pores. Middle) In regions of high crystallinity, thermal decomposition facilitates formation of rod-shaped Ni nanoparticles along the pores of the coordination polymer. Right) Elongated nickel nanoparticles grow as the temperature increases.

Discussion

As its most fundamental function, a fuel cell electrode must be sufficiently electrically conductive. Our search for suitable SAFC electrode materials began with the metal-organic coordination polymer, $M_3(HATP)_2$, known for high intrinsic bulk electrical conductivity, as reported by Dincă, *et al.*[20] Unmodified $M_3(HATP)_2$ (where M = Ni^2, Cu^{2+}, or Co^{2+}) materials have been shown to exhibit conductivities comparable to common amorphous carbon substrates (1 to 10 S/cm^{-1} range) and some were also found to exhibit significant internal surface areas (*e.g.* ~281.0 m^2/g for $Co_3(HATP)_2$).[23] This transition metal-HATP material system provides an attractive starting point to further improve conductivity and stability of the proposed electrode material *via* pyrolysis.

To facilitate the synthesis and characterization of our proposed Pt-HATP material, the previously reported $Ni_3(HATP)_2$ [20, 24] was synthesized as confirmed *via* HAADF-TEM imaging (**Fig. 1**). Rod-like crystalline domains of $Ni_3(HATP)_2$ show pore sizes on par with published data (~1.8 nm).[21] Heating this material to 300 °C during TEM imaging forms Ni NPs smaller than 5 nm (**Fig. 1**). Interestingly, in regions of high crystallinity, elongated rod-like Ni NPs are formed along the pores of the coordination polymer, providing a proxy visualization of the original material pore structure. As treatment temperatures are increased, further NP growth occurs yielding Ni particles of lengths between 5 and 25 nm.

The Pt-HATP precursor synthesis was conducted under similar conditions as for $Ni_3(HATP)_2$, although the dark brown solid product is of an unknown structure. Pt-HATP behaves

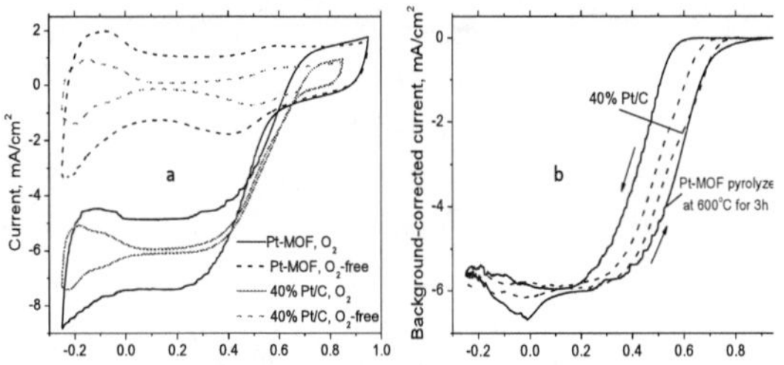

Figure 3. (a) CV and ORR polarization curves of thin films of 38 wt% Pt-HATP and 40 wt% Pt/C catalysts (0.1M $HClO_4$, 20 mV/s, 1600 rpm); (b) ORR corrected for current in O_2-free environment. Pt loading: 153.2 and 81.6 $\mu g_{Pt}/cm^2$ for Pt-HATP and Pt/C, respectively.

similarly during pyrolysis, with decomposition at the same temperature. Spheroidal Pt NPs of sizes significantly smaller than 5 nm are observed at 300 °C and grow to 3-5 nm by 500 °C (**Fig. 2**). Pt NP distribution *density* varies significantly, although the Pt NP *size* distribution is narrow at specific pyrolysis temperatures (**Fig. 2**). This likely stems from a much more stable structure of the material that likely is the result of tetrahedral binding around the Pt, as opposed to the square planar arrangement for the Ni structure; although at this point this is just conjecture. Unlike the $Ni_3(HATP)_3$ material, the Pt NPs in the pyrolyzed material are crystalline, remain small over a wide temperature range (**Fig. 2**), and only grow to sizes larger than 25 nm above 1000 °C.

Bulk precursor Pt-HATP pyrolyzed '*ex situ*' in a tube furnace under vacuum shows similar Pt NP growth, according to HAADF imaging. Homogenously sized spherical NPs form at 300 °C, and continue growing as temperature increases, as shown by evidence of NP ripening within the 300 °C to 600 °C temperature range (**Fig. 2**).

CV and polarization curves (**Fig. 3**) were measured on thin films of the 38 wt. % Pt-HATP sample that had been pyrolyzed at 300 °C and a 40 wt. % Pt/C standard. Both CV curves have well-pronounced hydrogen (-0.25 <E< 0.08V) and oxygen adsorption/desorption regions. The hydrogen region is featureless for Pt-HATP as compared to Pt/VC, possibly due to smaller sized Pt NPs (2.5 nm vs 5 nm for Pt/C). When comparing the Pt-HATP sample versus the Pt/C control, the adsorption of OH groups from water activation occurs at the same potential of *ca* 0.55V, while the reduction of surface

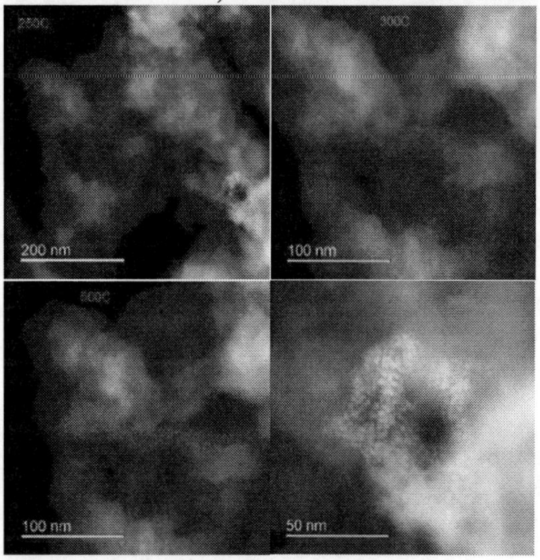

Figure 2. HAADF images of Pt-HATP at several temperatures showing evolution of Pt NP during *in situ* pyrolysis. Top. left) 250 °C; Top. right) 300 °C, decomposition temperature, Pt NPs begin to form; Bot. left) 500 °C; Bot. right) Area of high Pt NP density.

oxide occurs at a more negative potential of 0.4V for Pt-HATP compared to 0.5V for Pt/C; again possibly due to the smaller size of Pt. Interestingly, the Pt-HATP CV curve has higher currents in the double layer region, located between hydrogen and oxygen adsorption/desorption regions, which are attributed to electrical double layer charging currents, leading to distortion of the ORR polarization curves. The ORR curves (**Fig. 3**) have a plateau at -6 mA/cm^2 in the diffusion-limited region for the Pt/C catalyst corresponding to a 4e$^-$ ORR pathway. At potentials more negative than 0.06V, however, the plateau is affected by currents in the hydrogen adsorption/desorption region and is even more pronounced for the Pt-HATP catalyst. In the region occurring under mixed kinetic-diffusion control (0.3 V<E<0.68 V), ORR currents on Pt/C catalyst are more negative than those on Pt-HATP at a given potential, which may indicate higher activity of Pt-HATP. Considering the high contribution of capacitive currents into the ORR currents for Pt-HATP catalysts, we calculated ORR currents corrected for the currents measured in O_2-free environment (**Fig. 3**). Both polarization curves have a more traditional shape, with clearly separated cathodic and anodic scans. In the diffusion-limited region, both are centered around -6 mA/cm^2, which indicates a 4 e- pathway for both catalysts (rotation rate; 1600 rpm). In the mixed kinetic-diffusion region, the hysteresis between the cathodic and anodic sweeps is more pronounced for Pt-HATP,

Table 1. ECSA, area- and mass-specific activities for Pt-HATP and Pt/C for ORR at 0.65V in 0.1M $HClO_4$: 20

	Pt load, $\mu g_{Pt}/cm^2$	Specific activity, Mass - A/mg_{Pt}
38 wt% Pt-HATP	153.2	0.011
40 wt% Pt/C	81.6	0.022
	ECSA, m^2/g_{Pt}	Specific activity, Area - $\mu A/cm^2_{Pt}$
38 wt% Pt-HATP	22.0	48.6
40 wt% Pt/C	49.8	45

which agrees with higher capacitive currents observed for this catalyst. To compare area- and mass-specific activities of the two catalysts, the ECSAs and kinetic currents were calculated at a potential of 0.65 V. The results are presented in **Table 1**. Unexpectedly, the ECSA for the Pt-HATP catalyst is more than a factor of 2 lower than that of commercial Pt/C. One possible reason for that may be lower utilization of 2.5 nm Pt NPs in the framework due to incomplete electrical connectivity with all Pt NPs, or porosity occlusions. The area-specific activities are close, indicating that there is potential for improvement of the Pt-HATP catalyst.

Conclusions

In situ in vacuo pyrolysis in TEM captures the appearance of small Pt NPs (2 to 5 nm) at low temperatures and provides a mechanistic link between thermal degradation of the amine of the HATP ligand and reduction of coordinated Pt^{2+}. Ripening occurs as the pyrolysis temperature increases, providing a range of Pt NPs sizes from 2 nm to several hundred. The pyrolyzed Pt-HATP material represents an interesting pyrolytic approach to generating size-controlled platinum nanoparticles within a carbonized framework. This method produces materials with modest ORR activity in acidic media, with potential for future engineered improvements. Ultimately, this novel Pt-HATP electrocatalyst demonstrates promising ORR activity, yet greater Pt utilization is needed to improve overall performance. Efforts to increase effective catalytic surface area are currently underway, as are experiments utilizing pyrolyzed Pt-HATP as an electrode in a PEM fuel cell.

References

1. Haile, S. M.; Chisholm, C. R. I.; Sasaki, K.; Boysen, D. A.; Uda, T., *Faraday Discussions* **2007,** *134*, 17-34.
2. Boysen, D. A.; Uda, T.; Chisholm, C. R. I.; Haile, S. M., *Science* **2004,** *303*, 68-70.
3. Xie, L. S.; Skorupskii, G.; Dinca, M., *Chem. Rev.* **2020,** *120* (16), 8536-8580.
4. Lee, S.-Y.; Ogawa, A.; Kanno, M.; Nakamoto, H.; Tasuda, T.; Watanabe, M., *J. Am. Chem. Soc.* **2010,** *132*, 9764-9773.
5. Azad, A. K.; Abdalla, A. M.; Afif, A.; Azad, A.; Afroze, S.; Idris, A. C.; Park, J.-Y.; Saqib, M.; Radenahmad, N.; Hossain, S.; Elius, I. B.; Al-Mamun, M.; Zaini, J.; Al-Hinai, A.; Reza, M. S.; Irvine, J. T. S., *Scientific Reports* **2021,** *11* (1), 19382.
6. Ward, M. D.; Chaloux, B. L.; Johannes, M. D.; Epshteyn, A., *Adv. Mater.* **2020,** *32* (42), 2003667.
7. Chaloux, B. L.; Ridenour, J. A.; Johannes, M. D.; Epshteyn, A., *Adv. Energy Sustainibility Res.* **2022,** *3*, 2200029.
8. Ormerod, R. M., *Chem. Soc. Rev.* **2003,** *32*, 17-28.
9. Haile, S. M., *MaterialsToday* **2003,** *6* (3), 24-29.
10. Baturina, O. A.; Aubuchon, S. R.; Wynne, K. J., *Chem. Mater.* **2006,** *18* (6), 1498-1504.
11. Joo, S. H.; Park, J. Y.; Tsung, C.-K.; Yamada, Y.; Yang, P.; Somorjai, G. A., *Nature Materials* **2009,** *8*, 126-131.
12. Uda, T.; Haile, S. M., *Electrochem. Solid-State Lett.* **2005,** *8* (5), A245-A246.
13. Varga, A.; Brunelli, N. A.; Louie, M. W.; Giapis, K. P.; Haile, S. H., *J. Mater. Chem.* **2010,** *20* (30), 6309-6315.
14. Papandrew, A. B.; Crisholm, C. R. I.; Elgammal, R. A.; Özer, M. M.; Zecevic, S. K., *Chem. Mater.* **2011,** *23* (7), 1659-1667.
15. Zheng, W.; Lee, L. Y. S., *ACS Energy LEtt* **2021,** *6* (8), 2838-2843.
16. Sulaiman, M. R.; Gupta, R. K., In *Nanotechnology in Fuel Cells*, Song, H.; Nguyen, T. A.; Yasin, G., Eds. Elsevier Inc.: 2022; pp 173-199.
17. Wang, Y.; Wang, J.; Wei, D.; Li, M., *ACS Appl. Mater. Interfaces* **2019,** *11* (39), 35755-35763.
18. Mukherjee, S.; Hou, S.; Watzele, S. A.; Garlyyev, B.; Li, W.; Bandarenka, A. S.; Fischer, R. A., *ChemElectroChem* **2021,** *9* (7), e202101476.
19. Zou, L.; Hou, C.-C.; Liu, Z.; Pang, H.; Xu, Q., *J. Am. Chem. Soc.* **2018,** *140* (45), 15393-15401.
20. Sheberla, D.; Sun, L.; Blood-Forsythe, M. A.; Er, S.; Wade, C. R.; Brozek, C. K.; Aspuru-Guzik, A.; Dincă, M., High *J. Am. Chem. Soc.* **2014,** *136* (25), 8859-8862.
21. Chen, T.; Dou, J.-H.; L, Y.; Sun, C.; Libretto, N. J.; Skorupskii, G.; Miller, J. T.; Dincă, M., *J. Am. Chem. Soc.* **2020,** *142* (28), 12367-12373.
22. Baturina, O. A.; Garsany, Y.; Zega, T. J.; Stroud, R. M.; Schull, T.; Swider-Lyons, K. E., *J. Electrochem. Soc.* **2008,** *155* (12), B1314-B1321.
23. Xing, D.; Wang, Y.; Zhou, P.; Liu, Y.; Wang, Z.; Wang, P.; Zheng, Z.; Cheng, H.; Dai, Y.; Huang, B., *Applied Catalysis B: Environmental* **2020,** *278*, 119295.
24. Miner, E. M.; Fukushima, T.; Sheberla, D.; Sun, L.; Surendranath, Y.; Dincă, M., *Nature Communications* **2016,** *7*, 10942.

Advance Anode Chemistry for High Energy Li-ion Cell

Hyun Joo Bang, Anson Yang, Alexandre Ndedi, Dennis Perng and Mario Destephen
Research and Development
EaglePicher Technologies, LLC
C&Porter Street, Joplin, MO 64801
Email: Hyun.Bang@eaglepicher.com / 1-417-623-8000

Abstract: *The incorporation of silicon base anode chemistries has been expected to be a viable and most feasible approach to achieve demanding higher energy requirements due to the high specific capacity of silicon anode material. Several technical challenges still impede the high degree of utilization of silicon material in products. Poor cycling and initial capacity loss are typical drawbacks of silicon material, mostly resulting from mechanical swelling and electrochemical instability of silicon material during continuous cycling.*
Research and development efforts at EaglePicher have focused on implementing silicon-based anodes and high-specific cathodes for high-energy lithium-ion cells. The technical efforts were focused on selecting appropriate binder materials and the optimal composition of the anode for the high degree of silicon content in the anode, more than 20%, and the development of optimal electrode processing conditions to overcome its inherent drawbacks. A selection of binder and binder content optimization proved critical to reducing silicon anode material's structural instability for better cycling performance. Also, it was found that the incorporation of pre-lithiated silicon material improves overall performance.

Keywords: Li-ion battery; high energy density; silicon carbon anode; high power capability;

Introduction

In the past few years, EaglePicher Technologies (hereinafter: EPT) has developed a lithium-ion cell that has a high energy density of 300Wh/kg. As part of the technical effort to develop high-energy lithium-ion (Li-ion) cells, EPT intends to develop a chemistry and cell design for high-energy lithium-ion cells to be used in the existing Li-ion cell production line, established through the award of the Title III Lithium Ion Battery Production for Military Applications (LIMA) project in 2013 and completed in 2017. Several applications can be supported by EPT's Li-ion cell production line, which is an automated production line for high-volume production.

Technical efforts for high-energy-density lithium-ion (Li-ion) cell development are to incorporate a high-specific capacity cathode with silicon-carbon composite anode for a wide spectrum of applications [1] and [2]. The incorporation of silicon-carbon composite anode chemistry requires the reliable design of cells and electrode chemistry to be suitable for reliable performance as well as high power capability [3].

Scope of Development

The technical objectives of high-energy Li-ion cell development are to achieve more than 300Wh.kg-1 of high energy density and power capability. Considering silicon carbon anode chemistry was selected to achieve high energy density, cycling performance, and cell life are key technical aspects to confirm. The major technical tasks are: 1) identifying the core design to meet the needs, 2) determining the optimal anode composition, with a particular focus on binder selection, 3) optimizing electrode processing, and 4) determining the appropriate electrolyte composition for silicon anodes to maximize their stability and power. Two different sizes of cells are developed to support overall technical demands. Table 1 summarizes the detailed information on the two cells.

Table 1. Summary of cells developed at EPT

Cell Model No.	SLC-202	SLC-203
Capacity nominal	2.3 Ah	13Ah
Specific Energy density	240 Wh/kg	300Wh/kg
Tested Max continuous C-Rates	Up to 8C	Up to 8C
Max Pulse rate	12C-rate	8 C-rate
Operation temperature	-30°C~50°C	-30°C~50°C
Cell Dimension, W x H x T (mm)	50 x 57 x 7	115 x101 x 7
Packaging Material	Polymer Coated Aluminum	Polymer Coated Aluminum
Target Applications	UAV, Portable Power, etc.	UAV, eVTOL Portable Power, etc.

Cell and chemistry development

Objectives of cell and chemistry development were to meet the following goals 1) high energy density with high power capability, 2) flexibility to customize cell performance for optimal power and energy relationship 3) compatibility to incorporate next-generation chemistry higher specific capacity cathode and high content of silicon material in anode 4) enhancing safety.

SLC-202 cells (2.3Ah pouch cell)

SLC-202 is designed to provide high power capability with relatively high energy density which can be operated in a wider temperature range of -30°C to 50°C as shown in Table 2. A picture of SLC-202 cell is shown in Figure 1.

Table 2 Specification of SLC 202 cell

Part Number	SLC-202
Nominal Capacity @ C/5	2.3Ah
Nominal Energy @ C/5	8.2Wh
Specific Energy @ C/5	240 Wh.kg-1
Max. Pulse Current	>10 C-rate, 23A
Dimensions	50.0 x 56.0 x 7 mm
Operation Temperature	-20°C to 50°C
Nominal Voltage	3.55V
Cycle life	> 500 cycles
Anode	SiO-Carbon composite
Cathode	High Ni content NMC
Separator	Shutdown separator

Figure 1. Picture of SLC-202 cell (2.3Ah)

Performance of SLC-202 Cell

To ensure that the developed SLC-202 cell performs as designed, its performance was evaluated by testing its rate and power capabilities using constant current discharge and constant power discharge techniques, across various levels of current and power. SLC-202 cells delivered 2.0 Ah at 8C-rate constant current discharge, 88% of their nominal capacity obtained at C/5 discharge, as shown in Figure 2(a).

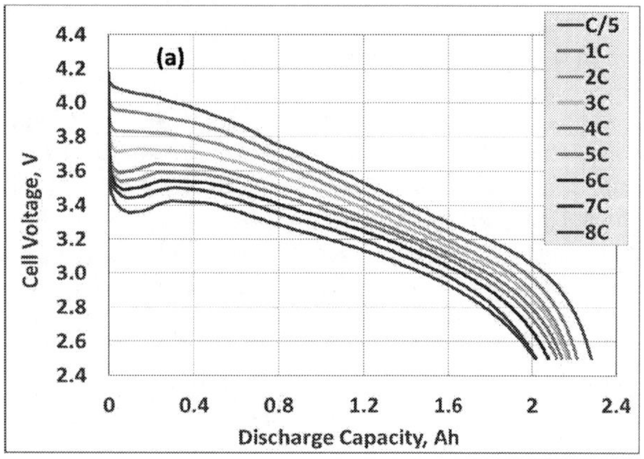

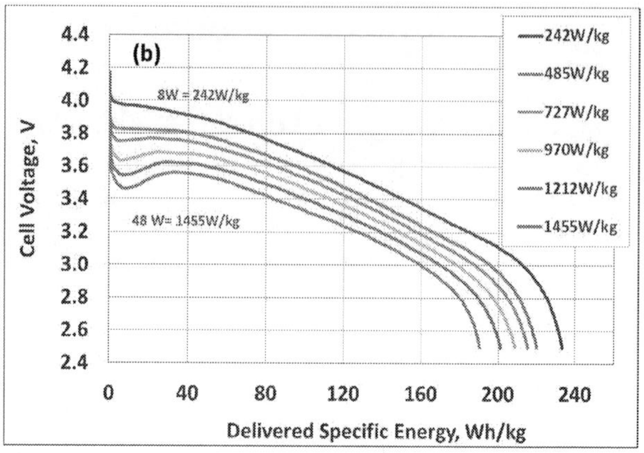

Figure 2. Rate and Power capability of SLC-202 cells, a) tested at various constant discharge currents and b) tested with various constant power rates; in the voltage range of 2.5V-4.2V and at 20°C

Figure 2(b) demonstrates the consistent power discharge test performed on SLC-202. The results indicate that the cell can deliver 233Wh/kg at a constant power discharge of 242W/kg, and still maintain an energy density of 190 Wh/kg at a constant power discharge of 1455 W/kg.

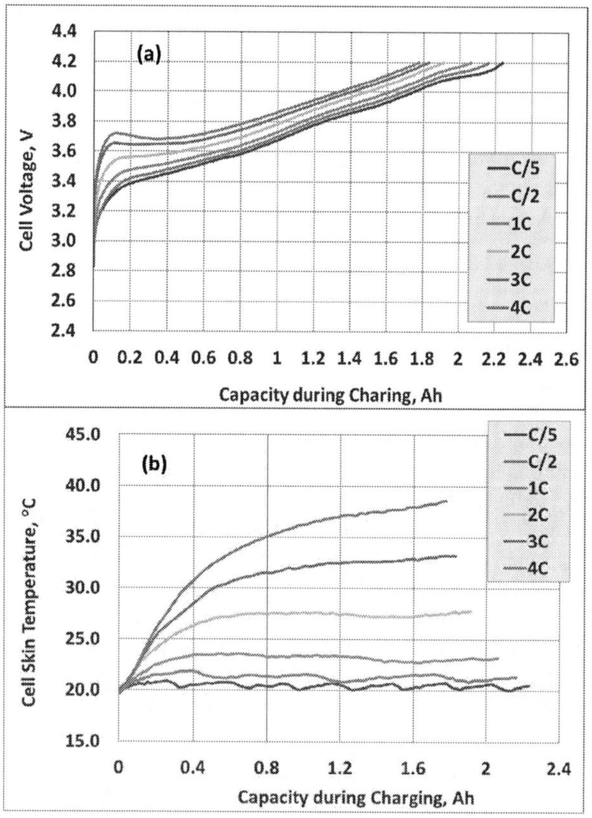

Figure 3. Fast charging capability of SLC-202 cell (a) charge capacity at various charging currents without trickle charge, b) cell temperature response at each charging current

Figure 3(a) displays the charge capacity at varying charging rates without constant voltage charge. At C/5 charging rate, the capacity reached 2.23Ah, which is 97% of the cell's nominal capacity, but it declines as the charging rate increases. Even at 4C-rate charging, a capacity of 1.77Ah was still achieved, representing 77% of SLC-202 cell nominal capacity.

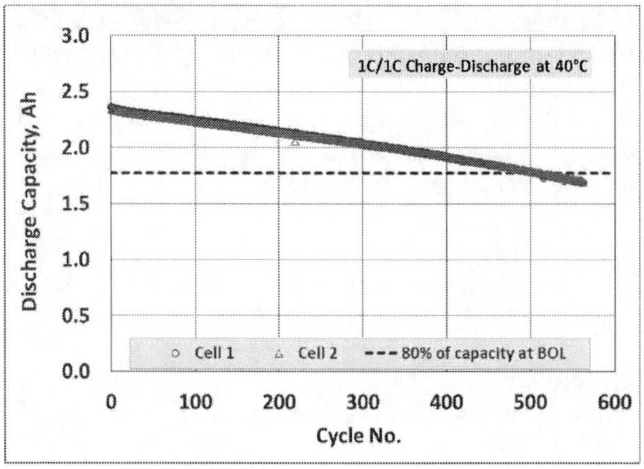

Figure 4. Cycling Performance of three SLC-202 cell 40 °C and 1C-rate charge/1C-rate discharge in the voltage range of 2.5V-4.2V

Figure 4 shows the cycling performance of two of SLC-202 cells. The test was performed by cycling them at 1C-rate charge and followed by 1C-rate discharge until their discharge capacity reached 80% of the capacity at the beginning of life (BOL). The cells were able to maintain a discharge capacity above 80% of the BOL capacity for 500 cycles, as shown in Figure 4.

SLC-203 cell (13Ah) for high-power application

The technical goal for SLC-203 cell development is to achieve an energy density of 300Wh/kg and to provide high power capability for a wide spectrum of applications. Table 4 shows a preliminary specification of the current SLC-203 under development.

Table 4 Specification of SLC-203 Cell

Part Number	SLC-203
Nominal Capacity @ C/5	13 Ah
Nominal Energy @ C/5	45 Wh
Specific Energy @ C/10	300 Wh.kg-1
Max. Pulse Current	8C (104A)
Dimensions	115 x 101 x 7.0 mm
Operation Temperature	-20°C to 50°C
Nominal Voltage	3.55V
Cycle life	> 500 cycles
Anode	SiO-Carbon composite
Cathode	High Ni content NMC
Separator	Shutdown separator

Figure 5. Picture of 13Ah SLC203 cell

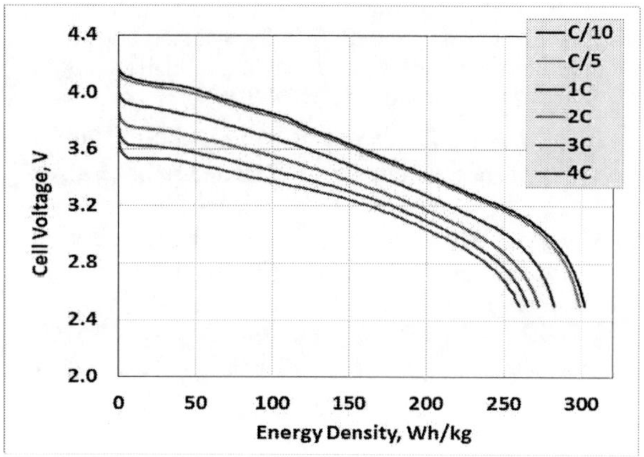

Figure 6. Discharge curves of SLC 203 cells tested at different C-rate to estimate specific energy density; 1C current is 13A, the voltage range of 2.5V-4.2V at room temperature

Figure 6 shows several discharge curves performed at different levels of discharge current to estimate the specific energy density of the developed SLC-203 cells. SLC-203 cells delivered 300Wh/kg (13Ah) at C/10 and 299 Wh/kg at C/5-rate. SLC-203 cell still delivered more than 250Wh/kg at 4C-rate discharge in the same voltage range. The test results of SLC203 were summarized in Table 5.

Table 5 Summary of the energy density of SLC-203 cell discharged at different C-rate

Discharge rate and current, A	Discharge current, A (Continuous)	Specific energy density, Wh/kg
C/10 rate	1.3A	302 Wh/kg
C/5 rate	2.6A	299 Wh/kg
1C rate	13A	282 Wh/kg
2C rate	26A	273 Wh/kg
3C rate	39A	265 Wh/kg
4C rate	52A	259 Wh/kg

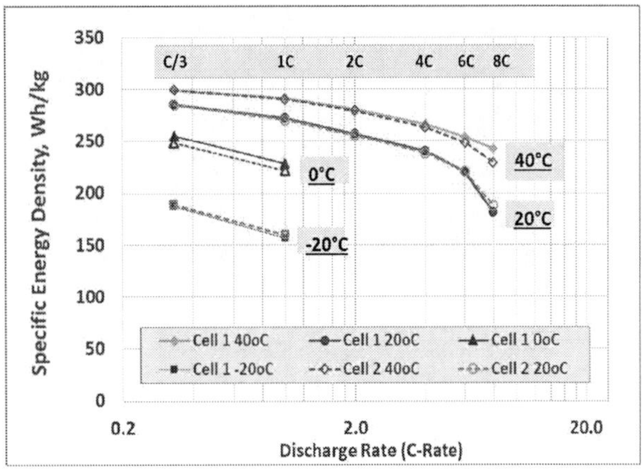

Figure 7 Performance of SLC-203 cell tested at various temperatures and various current levels. In the voltage range of 2.5V-4.2V

In Figure 7, specific energy densities of SLC-203 are displayed for various temperatures and current levels (C-rates). The cell achieved a specific energy density of 300Wh/kg at C/3-rate and 40°C. Even at C/3-rate to 8C-rate at 40°C, SLC-203 cells still maintained a high specific energy density.

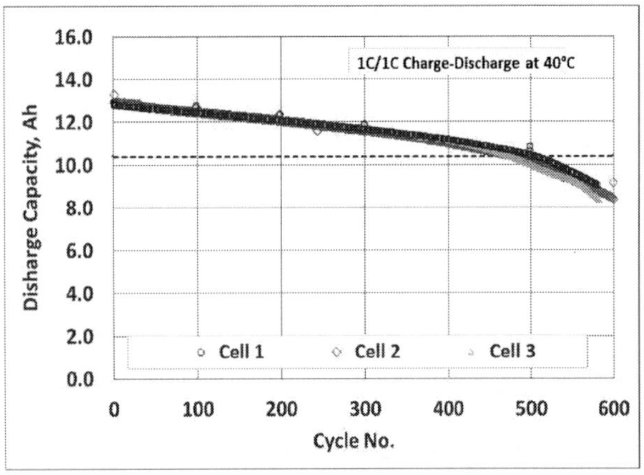

Figure 8. Cycling Performance of three SLC-202 cell 40 °C and 1C-rate charge/1C-rate discharge in the voltage range of 2.5V-4.2V

The cycling performance of several SLC-203 cells cycled at 40°C is displayed in Figure 8. These cells were designed to have an initial discharge capacity (or BOL energy) of around 13Ah. A cycling test was conducted until the discharge cell capacity reached 80% of the BOL capacity. Figure 8 shows that the tested cells maintained a discharge capacity above 80% of the BOL capacity for 500 cycles.

Summary

EPT has been developing next-generation lithium-ion chemistry and the cells by utilizing high specific cathode material and silicon-carbon-based anode material.

The Li-ion cells that have been developed at EPT are currently available in two sizes: 2.3Ah for SLC-202 cells and 13Ah for SLC-203 cells. Both cells have a high energy density and can discharge at up to 8C rate continuously. The SLC-202 cell can also discharge at a constant power of 1450W/kg.

SLC-202 and SLC-203 show good cycling performance at a temperature of 40°C. These cells were designed with an initial discharge capacity of 2.3Ah and 13Ah. A cycling test was conducted until the discharge cell capacity reached 80% of the initial capacity. It was observed that the cells maintained a discharge capacity above 80% of the initial capacity for 500 cycles.

Acknowledgment

"This material is released to the public domain by ITAR 22 CFR 120.34."

References

1. Bloom, I., S.A. Jones, V.S. Battaglia, G.L. Henriksen, J.P. Chrsitophersen, R.B. Wright, C.D. Ho, J.R.Belt, and C.G. Motloch, "Effect of cathode composition on capacity fade, impedance rise", *Journal Power Sources* vol. 124, pp. 538-550, 2003.
2. Jung, Y. S., K.T. Lee, and S.M. Oh, "Si-carbon core-shell composite anode in lithium secondary battery", *Electrochimica Acta* vol. 52, pp. 7061-7067, 2007.
3. Asenbauer, J., T. Eisenmann, M. Kuenzel, A. Kazzazi, Z. Chen, and D. Bresser, "The success story of graphite as a lithium-ion anode material – fundamentals, remaining challenges, and recent developments including silicon (oxide) composites", *Sustainable Energy & Fuels* vol. 4, pp. 5363-5870, 2020.

Silicon-Nanowire Anode Battery Assessment and Comparison to Li-Ion

Patricia H. Smith*, Michele J. Cervenak, Kimberly R. Garvin

Naval Surface Warfare Center- Carderock Division
9500 MacArthur Blvd., West Bethesda, MD 20817-5700
Patricia.h.smith1.civ@us.navy.mil

Abstract

Silicon is considered a viable substitute for graphitic carbon as an electrode in lithium-ion batteries. It has a theoretical capacity ten times that of graphite however there are issues regarding extreme volume change during cycling leading to reduced cycle and calendar life. Amprius Technologies has developed a novel silicon nanowire architecture that attempts to mitigate this problem. This study sought to assess the silicon nanowire battery capability under a variety of test conditions.

Keywords

Lithium-ion battery; silicon anode; rechargeable battery

Introduction

Over the last 15 years, lithium ion (Li-ion) batteries have become the established leader in energy and power densities for electronic devices. The BB-2590, with an energy density of 186 Wh/kg (278 Wh/L) and composed of 18650-type cells, is the military's standard rechargeable Li-ion battery. Developed in the 1980's, Li-ion is nearing its theoretical limits in energy. Today's cells already have twice the gravimetric energy density (~250 Wh/Kg) of the first commercial versions sold by Sony in 1991 and they cost ten times less.[1] Only modest improvements are expected in future years. Therefore, new electrode materials and novel power source device architectures will be necessary if the military chooses to use advanced electronics and weapon systems that require ever increasing power and energy.

One approach to obtain energy densities that are beyond present Li-ion battery capabilities is to replace the layered graphitic anode with silicon (Si). While the specific capacity of graphite (372 mAh/g) is higher than present cathodes materials, it has a relatively low density of 2.25 g/cm^3 that limits capacity to 837 mAh/cm^3. Si however, exhibits one of the highest theoretical specific and volumetric capacities (4,200 mAh/g and 9,782 mAh/cm^3) of the various anode materials investigated. In addition, it has a low electrode potential (~0.3 V versus the Li/Li$^+$ electrode). Anodes using Si allow the battery to be designed using a thinner, lighter electrode than the present graphite electrode. As a consequence, both battery gravimetric and volumetric energy densities are increased.

Experimental

Prototype cells utilizing Si nanowires as anodes were obtained from Amprius Technologies. The high-energy cells referred to as CL-0009 were designed for high altitude drones, targeting the highest energy density for a cycle life of at least 100 cycles. The cells were of laminate aluminum foil pouch cell construction and used a lithium cobalt oxide cathode and a proprietary electrolyte consisting of $LiPF_6$, ethylene carbonate and ethyl methyl carbonate. The supplier's specifications noted a cell voltage range of 2.75 V to 4.39 V, a nominal voltage of 3.60 V and a nominal capacity of 3.7 ampere hour (Ah). The dimensions of the cells were approximately 57 mm high, 49 mm wide and 4.75 mm thick. The weight was approximately 33.4 g.

Lithium-ion cells were obtained from Samsung for comparison purposes. The cells (INR18650-35E) are of 18650 configuration, a nominal capacity of 3500 mAh and a nominal voltage of 3.6 V. The cells consist of a graphite anode and a lithiated nickel manganese cobalt oxide cathode. The voltage range is 4.2 V to 2.65 V and they are capable of a continuous 8 A discharge rate.[2] The diameter of the cell is 18.75 mm and the length is 65.25 mm. The cell typically weighs 47.63 g.

A MACCOR 4000 Battery Cycler was used for galvanostatic cycling tests. Unless noted, cells were evaluated using a constant-current/constant-voltage (CC-CV) protocol. In this procedure, the cell is charged at a current to a pre-determined voltage followed by holding the cell at that voltage until the current declines below a specified current or for 1 hour. A Tenney Environmental Chamber was used to control cell temperature during testing. Cells were allowed to equilibrate at temperature for at least 4 hours.

Results

A comparison of cell specific energy density of the silicon pouch-cell design and the 18650 cylindrical-cell design is shown in Figure 1. Both Amprius and Samsung cells were cycled to the voltage endpoints (2.75 V to 4.39 V, 2.65 V to 4.2 V respectively) recommended by the manufacturer at the 5-hour (C/5) charge/discharge rate and 25°C. The silicon pouch-cell delivered approximately 120 cycles with a specific energy density at mid-point averaging 51% higher than the 18650 cell. Cells showed evidence of gassing during these experiments suggesting decomposition of the electrolyte. Discussions with Amprius later revealed that lowering the upper voltage cutoff to 4.25 V would minimize gassing and extend cycle life although at the expense of specific energy.

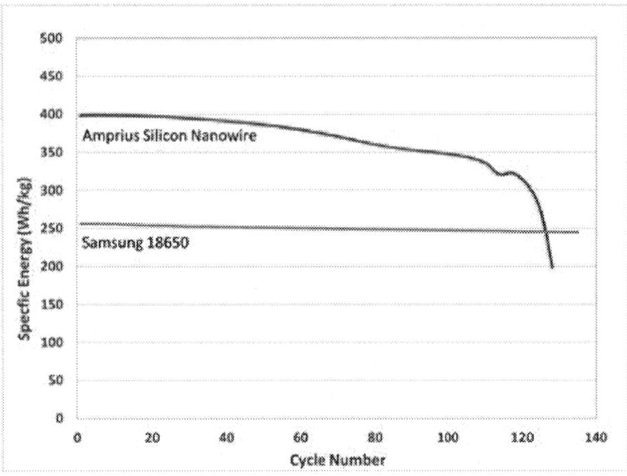

Figure 1. Gravimetric energy density comparisons of an Amprius pouch cell and a Samsung 18650 cell. Both cells were charged and discharged at 25 °C and the C/5 rate.

Battery investigators evaluating new technologies often charge and discharge cells at the same temperature to minimize the time to conduct experiments. Although informative, the data does not necessarily represent real-world scenarios when batteries are used in the field at sub-ambient temperatures. Most military users recognize that batteries charge more efficiently near 20°C and consequently avoid charging at or below 0°C. To gain a better assessment of the silicon nanowire cell under more realistic military conditions, one group of cells was cycled using the more typical method (0°C for both charge and discharge) and another group cycled using the following test procedure: (1) equilibrate cell at 0°C for 8 hours, (2) discharged at 0°C (C/5 rate) to 2.75 V, (3) equilibrate cell at 25°C hours for 8 hours, (4) charge at 25°C (C/5 rate) to 4.39 V, then (5) trickle charge at 4.39 V until either the current falls to 0.075A or 1 hour has passed. Cells charged at 25°C delivered over 30% more cycles than cells charged at 0°C (Figure 15). A subset of the study was to investigate the effect of cell compression on electrochemical performance. Figure 2 shows the applying 30 psi pressure to the cell may be beneficial especially when cycling at low temperatures. We speculate that applying pressure forces the active electrode materials to be in intimate contact with each other and with the current collector and therefore extends cycle life.

STATEMENT A Approved for public release; distribution is unlimited.

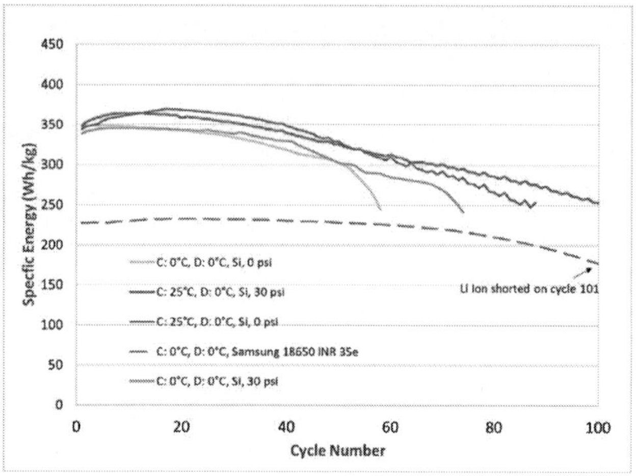

Figure 2. Effect of charging temperature and compression on specific energy density and cycle life of Amprius cells discharged at 0°C. Dash line denotes performance of Li-ion 18650 (3.5 Ah Samsung INR) cell cycled at 0°C and C/5 rate.

Summary

Silicon nanowire prototype cells (3.7 Ah) were evaluated to determine their potential value for Navy and Marine Corps applications. Cells were cycled under the supplier's recommended "high-energy" test procedures. The silicon anode cells displayed approximately 40% greater specific energy than the graphite-anode (18650) cells (100th cycle). Despite this promising feature however, the Amprius prototype cells charged to 4.39 V displayed limited cycle life. To realize the full potential of this technology, the upper limit of the charging voltage should be reevaluated and/or improved electrolytes and protective anode coatings should be considered.

Acknowledgements

Funding for this investigation was provided by the Office of Naval Research. The Vehicle Technologies Office of the Department of Energy was instrumental in allowing the US Navy access to this emerging technology in the early days of its development.

References

1. M.S. Ziegler, J.E. Trancik, Re-examining Rates of Lithium-ion Battery Technology Improvement and Cost Decline, Energy Environ Sci. 2021,14,1635.
2. Samsung SDI data sheet for model INR18650-35E, January 1, 2016.

Increasing the Ionic Conductivity of Alkali Carbonphosphonitride Thermosets through Plasticization and Formulation

Andrew P. Purdy[1], Daniel M. Fragiadakis[1], Hunter O. Ford[2], Mark O Bovee[2], Christopher A. Klug[1], Brian L. Chaloux[1], and Megan B. Sassin[1]

[1]Chemistry Division Code 6100, Naval Research Laboratory, Washington DC 20375
[2]NRC Postdoctoral Associate, Chemistry Division Code 6100, Naval Research Laboratory, Washington DC 20375
andrew.purdy@nrl.navy.mil / 1-202-404-7444

Abstract

Alkali dicyanamide ($AN(CN)_2$, A = Li, Na, K, Rb, Cs) reacts with phosphorus cyanide ($P(CN)_3$) in a 2:1 or greater mole ratio in any anhydrous non-protic mutual solvent to form a resin. We will report our systematic efforts to increase alkali ion conductivity by introducing small amounts of non-volatile poly(oxoethylene) based plasticizers, and by copolymerizing the resin with other cyano monomers to increase the alkali concentration. We also mixed highly conductive ceramic powders such as LLZO with the resins to use as binders to prepare a composite. Additionally, combustibility was tested to determine how much plasticizer can be added without compromising the inherent non-flammability of the thermoset materials.

Keywords
Ionic conductor; Lithium; Sodium; Plasticizer; Cyano; Flammability; Thermoset

Introduction

The reaction of phosphorus cyanide $P(CN)_3$ with alkali (Li, Na, K, etc) dicyanamides or other related cyano compounds in any mutual non-protic solvent results in a thermosettable resin which has ionic conductivity, forms adherent films on glass and some metals.[1-2] While still solvated, conductivity of the Li-P-C-N solid at 25 °C can be as high as 10^{7} S/cm, but on thermal treatment, the C≡N groups polymerize,[1-3] along with other processes, resulting in an amorphous dark red solid. Full cure, to where the solid state NMR is unchanging, requires >2h at 250-275 °C. Once cured, the polymeric material is non-flammable. Such a liquid processable electrolyte could be useful for metal-ion batteries, but the ionic conductivity of the fully cured material at $10^{-13} - 10^{-11}$ S/cm at 300K - far too low to be a practical electrolyte. To improve the conductivity we are exploring plasticization of the cured resin, increasing the alkali ion concentration, variation of the organic solvent used, and using the resin as a binder/filler for more conductive materials [12].

Experimental

The syntheses of $P(CN)_3$ and $LiN(CN)_2$ were described previously. [1-4] Pyridine, tetramethylurea (TMU), and 1,3-dimethyl-2-imidazolidinone (DMIZ) were dried with 3 Å molecular sieves, and acetonitrile (MeCN), 1,2-dimethoxyethane (DME), and sulfolane were vacuum distilled from suitable drying agent (e.g., P_2O_5, Na–benzophenone ketyl) before bringing into an inert atmosphere drybox. Lithium Lanthanum Zirconium Oxide (LLZO) powder was obtained from MSE supplies. Polyethylene glycol dimethyl ether 500 (PEG 500 dimethyl ether), DMIZ, TMU, and $NaN(CN)_2$ were obtained from Sigma-Aldrich and the other solvents from Fisher Scientific. The PEG 500 dimethyl ether was dried by heating the liquid under dynamic vacuum to 200 °C in an oil bath for 16 hours under dynamic vacuum and the resulting anhydrous, light orange oil was kept under argon. All reagents were stored and all reactions were conducted in an argon filled drybox. Samples were cured on a temperature controlled hotplate before being removed for *ex situ* analysis. Reactions between $P(CN)_3$ and $AN(CN)_2$ (A=Li, Na) were conducted in standard 20 mL glass scintillation vials with ~0.1 g $P(CN)_3$ and the appropriate mole ratio of other reactants in 2-4 g of the anhydrous solvent and were allowed to react in the vial for a day before application onto the substrate. Reactions in DME, unlike other solvents, produced a dense, deeply colored secondary liquid phase ('goo') that was separated from the colorless supernatant and redissolved in acetonitrile prior to application. Circles of Pallflex® tissue quartz (from VWR) were punched out and heated at 900 °C under vacuum to remove surface moisture and hydroxyl groups prior to infiltration with liquid resin. LLZO powder was pressed into pellets for infiltration with resin or mixed with resin and cured on a metal coupon.

Complex dielectric permittivity (from 10^{6} to 10^{-2} Hz) was measured by dielectric relaxation spectroscopy (DRS) via a Novocontrol Alpha analyzer, under vacuum in a cryostat (Cryo Industries Model 1899-350).

For measurement of conductivity by impedance spectroscopy (EIS) in coin cell configuration, each side of a A-P-C-N electrolyte infiltrated in Pallflex® fiber paper was treated with 10 µL of dry diglyme. The swelled electrolytes were placed between two tin blocking electrodes and sealed within 2032 type coin cells with spacer and wave spring.

The voltage stability windows of Li-P-C-N electrolytes were similarly assessed using asymmetrical coin cells with one tin and one Li metal electrode. With the tin metal electrode taken as the working electrode, linear sweep voltammetry was used to assess the electrochemical stability window. In a typical experiment, the sample was held at 150 °C while the voltage was swept in the positive direction starting from open circuit voltage (OCV) at a scan rate of 10 mV/s until a sharp rise in current was observed. The same experiment was repeated with a fresh electrolyte sample in the negative direction to assess the reductive stability.

Results

The most successful methods of achieving A-P-C-N electrolyte with good top and bottom electrode contacts was found to be: a) depositing films on 0.75 " x 0.75" x .125" thick copper plates with a Sn foil top electrode melted on, and b) repeatedly impregnating silica fiber paper with liquid resin and curing on a hotplate. Efforts to produce composites of our resins and LLZO are still in progress. We know from prior work [1-2] that the reaction between $LiN(CN)_2$ and $P(CN)_3$ consumes 2 eq of the dicyanamide per mole of $P(CN)_3$, any excess dicyanamide remains unreacted, and some of the solvent participates in the likely radical reaction that incorporate it into the product. Furthermore, the excess dicyanamide will trimerize or polymerize at elevated temperatures,[4-9] and these species are undoubtedly present in material cured above 250 °C.

Samples were prepared with excess $LiN(CN)_2$ or LiCN to increase the mobile Li^+ ion concentration and their behavior compared to pressed pellets of $LiN(CN)_2$ that were thermally trimerized/polymerized [4], and data is displayed in Figure 1. Addition of 0.7 eq of LiCN to Li-P-C-N (turquoise right-facing triangles) showed little improvement in conductivity, similar to a sample incorporating double the amount of $LiN(CN)_2$ (pale green left-facing triangles). However, adding a large excess of LiCN (2 eq) produced a dramatic (3 order-of-magnitude) increase in conductivity (blue upright triangles). This material was prepared in pyridine because of the much higher solubility of LiCN in that solvent compared to DMIZ, and these conductivities are only slightly lower than pressed sintered pellets of trimerized/polymerized $LiN(CN)_2$ (black squares and red circles). Sodium dicyanamide is quite soluble in DMIZ, and Na-P-C-N materials were prepared in this solvent both with and without addition of PEG-500 plasticizer. Even without added plasticizer, the Na-P-C-N materials are about 2 orders of magnitude more conductive (orange diamonds) than the equivalent Li variety, and the addition of about 35 wt % plasticizer increased the conductivity nearly 100-fold (periwinkle down-facing triangles). Samples of Li-P-C-N containing PEG-500 (brown points) had only negligible improvements in conductivity. In most cases the activation energies are about 35 J/mol-K, but the upward curve in the lines for the pellets shows an unusual non-linear dependence of E_a on temperature.

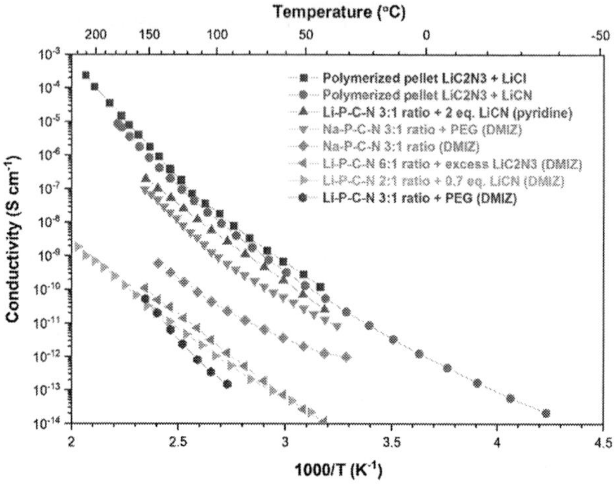

Figure 1. DRS conductivity data on cured A-P-C-N materials impregnated in silica fiber paper. Black squares and red circles show data typical for a pressed pellet (without fiber paper support) of polymerized LiC_2N_3 containing other Li salts: 36 mol% LiCN (red circles) or 34 mol% LiCl (black squares), respectively.

Electrochemical impedance spectroscopy (EIS) was conducted to assess the impact of diglyme plasticization on ionic conductivity. For two different electrolyte formulations shown above, the 6:1 $LiN(CN)_2$:$P(CN)_3$ material (blue upright triangles) and 3:1 $LiN(CN)_2$:$P(CN)_3$ + 2 eq LiCN (pale green left-facing triangles), the room temperature ionic conductivities with added diglyme plasticizer increased to 1 x 10^{-7} S/cm, and 6 x 10^{-8} S/cm respectively. The large conductivity improvement likely stems from the ability of the plasticizer to facilitate ion dissociation (leading to more charge carriers) and assist in vehicular ion transport (leading to enhanced ion mobility).

Solid state ^{13}C (MAS) NMR spectra show that the carbon-containing moieties in Na-P-C-N materials are similar regardless of whether PEG plasticizer is included in the reaction. Peaks ascribed to the Na-P-C-N backbone show up around +120 ppm (cyano species) and +165 ppm (triazine/heptazine moieties). A peak at +71 ppm corresponds to the PEG backbone carbons. The two peaks at +33 ppm and +48 ppm, arise from either residual DMIZ (methyl groups) trapped in the thermoset of from reaction of the starting materials with DMIZ, incorporating it into the final product.

In order to assess the voltage stability of the Li-P-C-N materials linear sweep voltammetry was used to assess the electrochemical stability window for the formulations. The 6:1 LiN(CN)2:$P(CN)_3$ material is quite stable over a window of -2 V to about 5 V vs Li/Li^+, while the 3:1 $LiN(CN)_2$:$P(CN)_3$ + 2 eq LiCN sample has a fairly quick onset of degradation current exceeding 1 μA below -1 V and above 3 V vs Li/Li^+. The lower voltage stability window of the 3:1 $LiN(CN)_2$:$P(CN)_3$ + 2 eq LiCN sample may be attributed to the excess LiCN, indicating the addition of LiCN may pose a potential tradeoff between enhanced conductivity (in the dry state) and decreased voltage window. $LiBF_3CN$ was reported to have some degradation under reductive conditions [11].

Discussion

It is clear from the results that both increasing the alkali ion concentration and adding organic plasticizers have a positive effect on the ionic conductivity, but the level of improvement is still insufficient. While addition of diglyme has a dramatic effect, that is probably from the coordination of Li^+ ions with a small molecule, and that is not compatible with the goal of a non-flammable solid electrolyte. The higher conductivity for the Na-P-C-N system is intriguing, and justifies an examination of the entire alkali series, which is presently underway. Ceramic materials with high alkali ion conductivities are known [10], but are not solvent processable. Efforts to prepare composites of A-P-C-N resins and LLZO are still in progress.

Acknowledgements

We thank the Office of Naval Research for financial support.

References

[1] A. P. Purdy, W. A. Maza, B. L. Chaloux, J. P. Yesinowski, M. G. Lanetti, K. N. McPherson, A. Epshteyn *Journal of Solid State Chemistry* **305**, 122649 (2022).

[2] A. Epshteyn, A. P. Purdy, B. L. Chaloux *US Patent* 10,510,458 B2 , issued Dec 17, 2019.

[3] B.L. Chaloux, B.L. Yonke, A.P. Purdy, J.P. Yesinowski, E.R. Glaser, A. Epshteyn, *Chem. Mater.* **27**, 4507–4510 (2015).

[4] A.P. Purdy, E. Houser, C.F. George, *Polyhedron* **16**(20), 3671–3679 (1997).

[5] C. A. Klug, D. M. Fragiadakis, A. P. Purdy, *MRS Advances* 7(21), 433-437 (2022).

[6] E. Irran, B. Jurgens, W. Schnick *Chem. Eur. J.* 7(24), 5272-5381 (2001)

[7] B. Jurgens, W. Milius, P. Morys, W. Schnick *Z. Anorg. Allg. Chem.* **624**, 91-97 (1998)

[8] O. Reckeweg, F. J. DiSalvo, A. Schulz, B. Blaschkowski, S. Jagiella, T.] *Z. Anorg. Allg. Chem.* **640**(5), 851–855 (2014)

[9] O. Reckeweg, R. H. Wakabayashi, F. J. DiSalvo, A. Schulz, C. Schneck, T. Schleid *Z. Naturforsch.* **70**(6)b: 365–372 (2015)

[10] A. Das, S. Sahu, M. Mohapatra, S. Verma, A. J. Bhattacharyya, S. Basu *Materials Today Energy* **29** (2022) 101118

[11] O. B. Chae, V. A. K. Adiraju, B. L. Lucht *J. Electrochem. Soc.* **169** 110506 (2022)

[12] A. P. Purdy, D. M. Fragiadakis, C. A. Klug, B. L. Chaloux, H. O. Ford, M. O. Bovee, M. B. Sassin *MRS Advances* (2023). https://doi.org/10.1557/s43580-023-00550-0

Multifunctional Electrolyte Additive for Alkaline Electrolytes in Zinc Batteries

Akash Kota[1], Alex Karpinski[2], and Emily Dickens[1]
[1]Octet Scientific Inc., 7100 Euclid Avenue, Cleveland, OH, USA, 44103
[2]EaglePicher Technologies, 2000 S County Trail, East Greenwich, RI, USA, 02818
Contact Author Email: akash.kota@octetsci.com

Abstract

Rechargeable alkaline Zn metal batteries are emerging as promising candidates for stationary energy storage systems due to the intrinsic safety of aqueous electrolytes and appealing advantages of Zn metal anodes. However, the practical applications of Zn metal batteries are limited because of the poor reversibility of the zinc anode caused by the unstable electrolyte-anode interface. In this work we demonstrate the use of benzyltrimethylammonium hydroxide (BTMAH) as an electrolyte additive for high concentration alkaline electrolytes to suppress the Zn dendrites. The efficacy of BTMAH at different concentrations in aqueous electrolytes containing 8 M potassium hydroxide (KOH) and 0.1-0.2 M zinc oxide (ZnO) is investigated using electrochemical methods. It has been observed that BTMAH at 2% concentration is an effective electrolyte additive for suppressing dendritic growth during Zn electrodeposition.

Keywords

Zinc metal batteries; dendrite suppression; electrolyte additive; zinc electrodeposition; aqueous electrolyte

Introduction

Energy storage systems based on rechargeable zinc electrodes are potential candidates to fulfill the need for stationary and high discharge rate applications. Owing to its unique merits, including high theoretical capacity of 820 mAh/g, nontoxicity, easy availability, and low processing cost, zinc has been widely used as anode material in many alkaline batteries such as Zn-MnO_2, Zn-Ag_2O, Zn-NiO, and Zn-air batteries. In a zinc metal battery typically, zinc powder is used as the active material in anode and concentrated alkaline solutions are used as electrolyte. However, the practical applications of Zn metal batteries are limited because of the poor reversibility of the zinc anode caused by the unstable electrolyte-anode interface. Zn metal is thermodynamically unstable in aqueous electrolytes. During the charging, deposition of zinc-active material is a non-homogeneous process which results in uneven electric field distribution on the electrode/electrolyte interface. The uneven distribution of zinc on the electrode surface provokes dendritic diffusion-controlled deposition, which promotes zinc corrosion. In addition, zinc dendrites can easily detach from the electrode surface and lowers the zinc consumption rate. Dendrite growth may also cause a short-circuit over time. These detrimental processes will result in the loss of capacity retention and cycle life of battery in the long term.

To improve the stability of zinc anode, it is significantly important to suppress the dendrite growth. In the past, some functional materials including nano-$CaCO_3$, polyvinylidene fluoride (PVDF), and montmorillonite [1-3] have been reported as coatings on a Zn anode to regulate uniform Zn^{2+} flux, thus suppressing the dendrite growth. However, the traditional protective layers not only increase the interfacial resistance but are also easily pulverized during continuous cycling. As an alternative, in this work we demonstrate the use of benzyltrimethylammonium hydroxide (BTMAH) [2] as an electrolyte additive for high concentration alkaline electrolytes to suppress the Zn dendrites. The efficacy of BTMAH at different concentrations in aqueous electrolytes containing 8 M potassium hydroxide (KOH) and 0.1-0.2 M zinc oxide (ZnO) is investigated using different electrochemical methods such as chronoamperometry, potentiodynamic polarization, and electrochemical impedance spectroscopy.

Experimental

Materials: Aqueous electrolytes containing 8 M potassium hydroxide (KOH, Thermo Scientific) and 0.2 M zinc oxide (ZnO, Alfa Aesar) are used to perform Zn electrodeposition. Benzyltrimethylammonium hydroxide (BTMAH, TCI) is used as an electrolyte additive. The structure of BTMAH is shown in Figure 1.

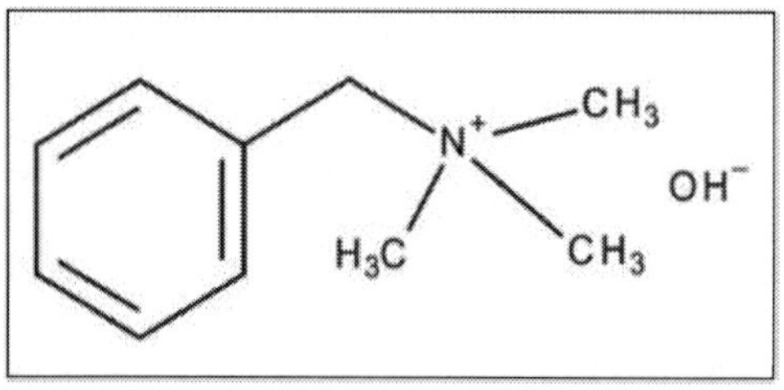

Figure 1. Molecular structure of BTMAH additive.

All electrolytes are prepared using analytical-grade reagents and deionized (DI) water.

Prior to testing, all the electrolytes are sparged using industrial grade nitrogen for 45 mins.

Methods: Zinc dendrite growth tests are performed using an electrochemical cell in a three-electrode configuration. The base electrolyte has 8 M KOH and 0.2 M ZnO. Experiments are performed either in the absence of BTMAH or in the presence of 0.1-2% BTMAH. A 1 mm diameter Zn wire (99.95% purity, Thermo Scientific), coated with AquaMend underwater repair epoxy is used as the working electrode (WE) for dendrite growth and polarization tests. Prior to each experiment the tip of epoxy coated zinc wire WEs are sanded with 1000 grit sandpaper, then polished with 5 μm alumina slurry (Aztron Technologies) on a terry cloth polishing pad (Grainger). A Hg/HgO electrode filled with 4.24 M KOH is used as the reference electrode (RE, $E_{Hg/HgO} = +0.098$ V vs SHE). A 0.5 mm diameter platinum wire (Sigma-Aldrich) is used as the counter electrode. A USB digital microscope camera is used to capture the images of electrodeposited zinc on the glassy carbon electrode. All electrochemical measurements are performed with BioLogic SP-300 potentiostat at room temperature.

Effect of BTMAH During Zinc Electrodeposition

To characterize the effect of BTMAH on zinc dendrite suppression, chronoamperometry tests are performed. Zinc electrodeposition is initiated by applying a constant potential (-1.6 V vs Hg/HgO (4.24 M KOH)) to the zinc wire WE. Two electrolytes are investigated: an additive-free control electrolyte, and electrolyte containing 2% BTMAH. The chronoamperometry curves are shown in Figure 2.

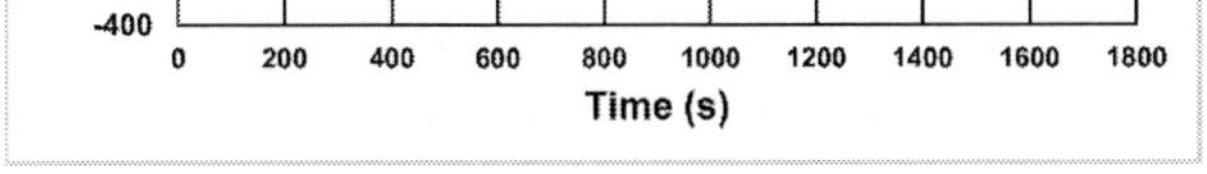

Figure 2. Chronoamperometry curves during zinc electrodeposition at -1.6 V vs Hg/HgO with and without BTMAH additive.

After 1800 seconds of zinc deposition at -1.6 V, digital microscopy confirms needle-like dendrites (Figure 3(a)) on the zinc wire electrode when using the 'no additive' control electrolyte. In the presence of BTMAH additive in the electrolyte, zinc dendrite formation is completely suppressed (Figure (3(b)).

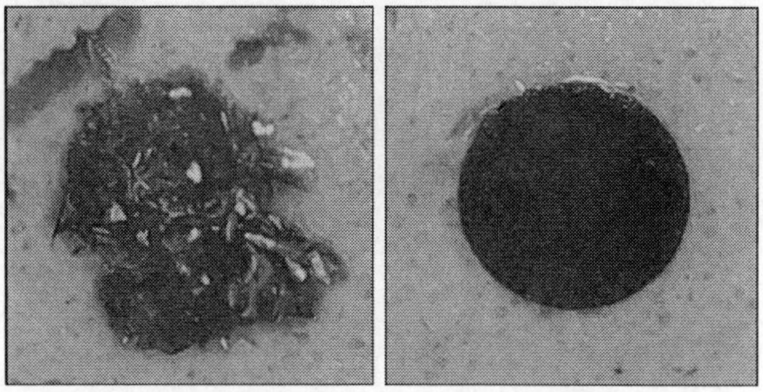

(a) (b)

Figure 3. Microscopic image of zinc wire WE which shows **(a)** needle-like dendrites when using the base electrolyte, and **(b)** complete suppression of zinc dendrites when using 2% BTMAH additive in the base electrolyte.

The chronoamperometry curves in Figure 2 represent the evolution of the electroactive surface as dendrites grow on the WE. In the additive-free case ('red' curve), a substantial increase in the surface area due to dendrites is noted. However, in the presence of BTMAH ('green' curve), after 1000 seconds the current reaches at a time-invariant values of ~25 μA corresponding to a current density of ~3.125 mA/cm^2. The time-invariant current implies no evolution of surface area and thus no dendrite formation in the presence of BTMAH, which is consistent with the digital microscopy data shown in Figure 3(b). Therefore, it can be concluded that BTMAH suppresses dendrites formation when the WE undergo zinc electrodeposition near its diffusion limit. These results indicate that by preventing the evolution of electroactive surface BTMAH additive can inhibit zinc electrochemical corrosion, which can be verified from polarization tests.

Effect of BTMAH on the Polarization Behavior of Zinc

To obtain the polarization curves, potentiodynamic Tafel scans are performed. The control electrolyte has 8 M KOH and 0.1 M ZnO. Experiments are performed on four electrolytes: an additive free control electrolyte, and electrolyte containing 0.1%, 1% and 2% BTMAH additive. The polarization behaviors of zinc in the alkaline electrolyte with and without BTMAH additive is shown in Figure 4. The corrosion inhibition efficiency of BTMAH additive is given as

$$\eta_p = \frac{i_{corr} - i'_{corr}}{i_{corr}}, \quad (1)$$

where, i_{corr} and i'_{corr} are the corrosion current densities of zinc with and without BTMAH additive in the electrolyte.

Table 1. Electrochemical corrosion parameters of zinc in 8 M KOH solution in the absence and in the presence of BTMAH at different concentrations.

Additives	Control	0.1% BTMAH	1% BTMAH	2% BTMAH
E_{corr} (V)	-1.428	-1.392	-1.389	-1.393
i_{corr} ($\mu A/cm^2$)	2081	238	239	219
η_p (%)	-	88.6	88.5	89.5
ΔE_{corr} (mV)	-	36	39	35

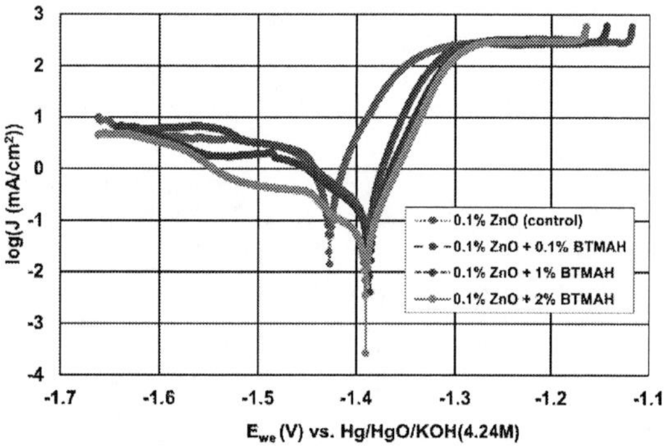

Figure 4. Tafel plot from potentiodynamic polarization curves of zinc in 8 M KOH solution with and without BTMAH additive obtained at a scan rate of 1mV/s.

The electrochemical corrosion parameters obtained from Figure 4 are listed in Table 1.

As shown in Figure 4 and summarized in Table 1, the control electrolyte (8 M KOH + 0.1% ZnO) has an E_{corr} of -1.428 V vs Hg/HgO/KOH (4.24 M). Compared with the corrosion potential of zinc in the control electrolyte, the corrosion potential becomes more positive in the presence of BTMAH additive. From Table 1, it can be observed that the presence of BTMAH additive at different concentrations in the electrolyte lead to an anodic shift of the corrosion potential with respect to the control electrolyte. This confirms that BTMAH additive can inhibit zinc electrochemical corrosion mainly by suppressing the anodic reaction, namely zinc dendrite suppression.

Effect of BTMAH on the Ionic Conductivity of the Electrolyte

Electrochemical impedance spectroscopy (EIS) tests are performed to study the effect of BTMAH concentration on the ionic conductivity of the electrolyte. The ionic conductivity is obtained for the control electrolyte (8 M KOH + 0.1% ZnO) and electrolyte containing 2% BTMAH additive. To perform the EIS experiment, electrolyte under test is loaded into a CR2032 coin cell with stainless steel (SS) electrodes [5]. The area of SS electrodes is 2.85 cm^2. A 25 μm thick polypropylene (PP) sheet is used as the separator. The coin cell components are assembled in the following order: SS electrode, 100 μl electrolyte, separator, and SS electrode. The prepared coin cell is connected to a BioLogic SP-300 potentiostat and EIS data is obtained in the frequency range of 0.1 Hz to 1 MHz at an applied alternating current (AC) potential of 10 mV. The EIS plot of electrolyte with 2% BTMAH is shown in Figure 5. The real (Z'_{real}) and imaginary (Z''_{img}) impedances are plotted on the x and y axes, respectively. The x-intercept on the plot is taken as the electrolyte resistance (R_{ele}) from which the ionic conductivity (σ) is calculated as

$$\sigma = \frac{t}{R_{ele} \times A}, \quad (2)$$

where, t is the thickness of the separator and A is the area of the SS electrode.

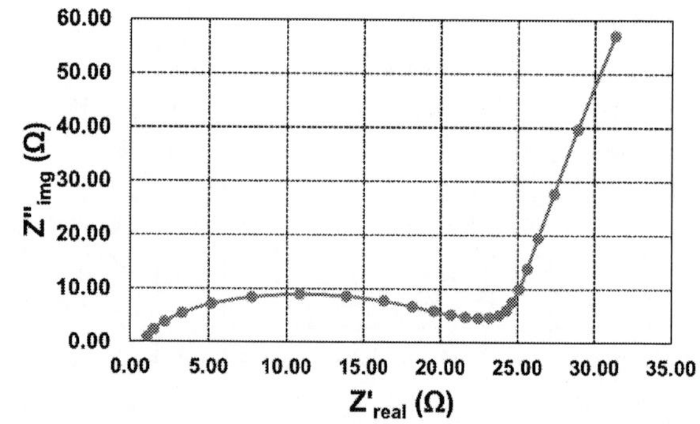

Figure 5. EIS plot of electrolyte with 2% BTMAH additive.

From Figure 5, it can be observed that the resistance of the electrolyte containing 2% BTMAH additive is found out to be 1.08 Ω. Using (2) the ionic conductivity can be calculated as 8.12×10^{-4} (S/cm). Similarly, the electrolyte resistance and ionic conductivity of the control electrolyte can be calculated as 0.42 Ω and 2.09×10^{-3} (S/cm), respectively. The effect of 2% BTMAH additive on the ionic conductivity of the electrolyte is shown in Figure 6.

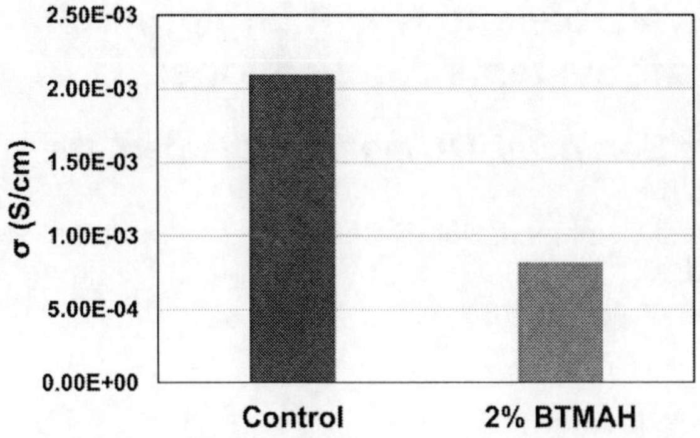

Figure 6. Plot comparing the ionic conductivities of the control electrolyte and the electrolyte containing 2% BTMAH additive.

From Figure 6 it can be observed that the ionic conductivity value of the electrolyte with 2% BTMAH additive is an order magnitude low compared with that of the control electrolyte. The decrease in the ionic conductivity suggests that BTMAH additive can suppress the dendrites by slowing down the kinetics of Zn^{+2} ions in the electrolyte during the electrodeposition process.

Conclusion

In this work, we demonstrate the use of BTMAH as an electrolyte additive in aqueous electrolytes containing 8 M KOH and 0.1-0.2 M ZnO. From the chronoamperometry tests it can be concluded that during zinc electrodeposition complete suppression of dendrites is noticed in electrolytes containing 2% BTMAH. The potentiodynamic polarization tests reveal that the electrochemical corrosion inhibition efficiency of BTMAH additive remains approximately the same at 89% within the concentration range of 0.1-2%. EIS tests reveal that the ionic conductivity of the electrolyte with 2% BTMAH is lower than that of the control electrolyte by an order magnitude. This behavior suggests that the BTMAH additive can regulate the Zn^{+2} ions by slowing down the Zn^{+2} kinetics to enable smooth plating of zinc during electrodeposition process.

References

1. Kang, L.; Cui, M.; He, Y.; Jiang, F.; Gao, Y.; Luo, H.; Liu, J.; Liang, W.; Zhi, C. Nanoporous CaCO3 Coatings Enabled Uniform Zn Stripping/Plating for Long-Life Zinc Rechargeable Aqueous Batteries. *Adv. Energy Mater.* **2018**, 8, 1801090.

2. Yan, H.; Li, S.; Nan, Y.; Yang, S.; Li, B. Ultrafast Zinc-Ion-Conductor Interface toward High-Rate and Stable Zinc Metal Batteries. *Adv. Energy Mater.* **2021**, 11, 2100186.

3. Wang, Y.; Tian, C.; Zhang, D.; Zhao, B.; Wang, Y.; Liu, M. Design of Inorganic-Organic Hydrophobic Coating on Zn Anode Realizes Highly Reversible and Dendrite-Free Zn-Ion Batteries. *Energy Technol.* **2023**, 11, 2201216.

4. Liu, X.; Bolton, O.; Akolkar, R. Experimental and Modeling Studies of the Hysteresis Behavior and Dendrite Suppression Efficacy of an Electrolyte Additive in Zinc Electrodeposition. *J. Electrochem. Soc.* **2019**, 166, D583.

5. Kota, A.; Wung, L.; Vallurupalli, K.; Gogia, A.; Neidhard-Doll, A.; and Chodavarapu, V. Highly Flexible Stencil Printed Alkaline Ag_2O-Zn Battery for Body Conformal Electronics. *Batteries*, **2022**, 8, 74.

Comparative Testing of Commercially Available and Novel Lithium Cell Technologies for Unmanned Aircraft Systems Applications

Dr. Robert Emmett, Michael Clarkson, Dr. Elyse Baroncini, Dr. Matthew Limpert, Dr. Ashley Ruth

U.S. Army Combat Capabilities Development Command, C5ISR Center
Aberdeen Proving Ground, MD, 21005
Corresponding author: elyse.a.baroncini.civ@army.mil

Abstract

Unmanned Aircraft Systems (UAS) encompass a variety of air vehicles with different sizes, shapes, propulsion systems, launch methods, and power systems depending on the application. Certain UAS require batteries that can provide both high power for launch and high energy for endurance. In this work, commercially available rechargeable lithium ion cells used in air vehicles were evaluated for electrochemical performance and compared to novel rechargeable lithium ion technologies to assess the state of commercial technology and provide recommendations for improved power and energy capabilities for UAS.

Commercial-off-the-shelf (COTS) cylindrical 18650 cells and pouch cells from two vendors were obtained and were evaluated according to respective specification sheets. Novel lithium ion technologies from three vendors were also evaluated for comparison. Additional testing of high discharge currents and low operating temperatures was performed to push the technologies to their boundaries for assessment of applicability in consideration of more extreme military conditions. Most cells were able to meet power requirements of current UAS, however, the novel technologies were able to provide more well-rounded performance: one vendor's cells provided increased energy density in addition to high power capability whereas another vendor's cells provided improved performance at low temperature in addition to high power capability. A third vendor was able to demonstrate increased flight time. Anonymized comparative data plots will be presented.

This work establishes a baseline of performance evaluation of commercially available lithium ion cells for UAS applications and assesses the performance advantages offered by more novel cell technologies. For all applications, cell electrochemical performance advantages and non-technical considerations, such as cost, must be balanced between COTS and novel developmental cells.

Keywords

Unmanned aircraft systems; UAS; lithium ion; batteries.

Introduction

Development of high power density and high energy density lithium ion cells have enabled UAS with increased range, electronic loads, and weight. As UAS technology advances, the power loads required from the propulsion and electronic units increases, requiring batteries with improved capabilities. High power density is required for the elevated power load that occurs during takeoff, landing, and electronic pulses, and high energy density is required for extended range and loitering capabilities. Additionally, cold temperature resilience is a key characteristic of these batteries because of altitude at which UAS can operate. Therefore, focus on chemistry design that maintains high energy density capability at low temperatures is paramount for effectiveness. Safety can be addressed through battery management systems and cell architecture. These priorities are essential to UAS development and to increasing overall UAS capabilities.

Results

Cylindrical Cell Comparison: Commercially available cylindrical 18650 rechargeable lithium ion cells from Vendor 1 were evaluated for comparison against novel cylindrical 18650 rechargeable lithium ion cells from Vendor 2. Vendor 1 cells are known for use in commercial drone applications. Technology from Vendor 2 contained anode with >25% silicon and advanced electrolyte materials to improve accessible voltage range, energy density, as well as safety.

Vendor 1 cells were tested in accordance with manufacturer's specifications. The cells displayed relatively high rate capabilities, achieving approximately 65% nominal capacity at approximately 6.5C rate, though this capacity retention was lower than reported by the manufacturer. As depicted in manufacturer's specifications, the cell skin temperature at these high rates did increase to above 80°C.

Vendor 2 cells yielded energy densities almost 50% higher than Vendor 1 cells at low (<C/5) discharge rates, but comparable at 1C discharge rates. Vendor 1 cells demonstrated better rate capabilities, see Figure 1.

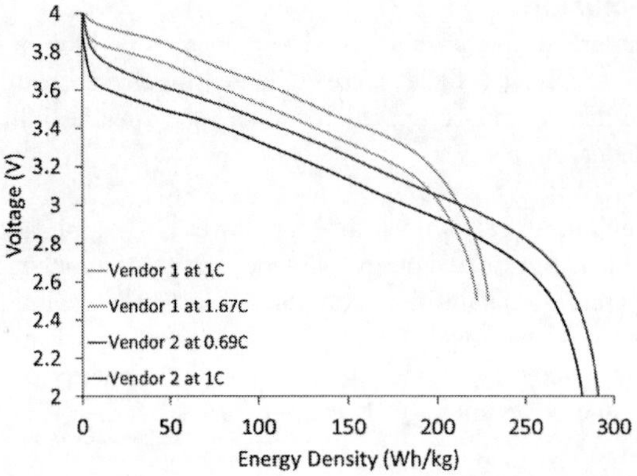

Figure 1. Vendor 1 cells demonstrated better rate capability but Vendor 2 cells achieved higher energy densities.

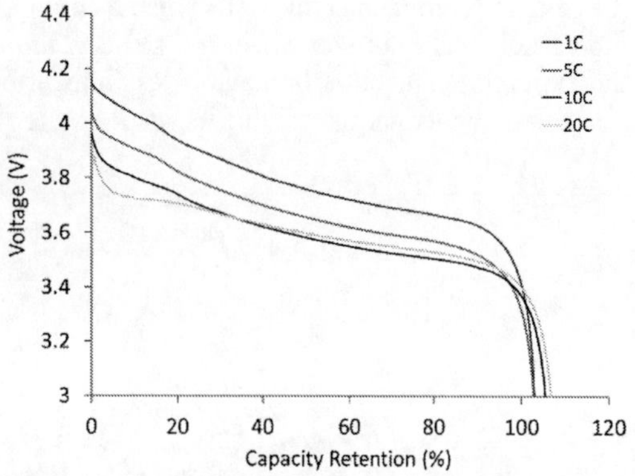

Figure 3. Rate capability of Vendor 3 cells at 1C, 5C, 10C, 20C rate. Capacity retention in percent relative to nominal capacity.

Temperature testing of Vendor 2 cells revealed greater than 80% capacity retention at -20°C and greater than 60% capacity retention at -40°C, whereas Vendor 1 cells were only rated for discharge down to -20°C, see Figure 2.

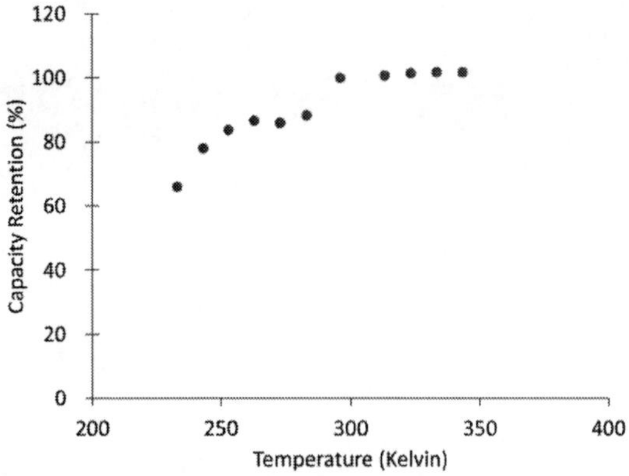

Figure 2. Vendor 2 cells retained surprising capacity retention across wide temperature ranges. Capacity retention in percent relative to nominal capacity.

Vendor 2 cells were only tested to 50 cycles due to the low manufacturing readiness level of the Vendor 2 cells compared to commercially available Vendor 1 cells.

Pouch Cell Comparison: Commercially available rechargeable lithium ion pouch cells from Vendor 3, known for use in commercial drone applications, were tested and evaluated to verify manufacturer's listed specifications. Pouch cells of similar capacity containing advanced lithium metal anode and enabling electrolyte formulations from Vendor 4 were evaluated for high power and high energy capabilities. Commercially available lithium polymer (LiPo) pouch cells of similar capacity were also tested to provide comparison.

Vendor 3 cells were able to achieve relatively high discharge current rates (tested up to 20C) with no impact on capacity, see Figure 3.

As shown in the Ragone plot in Figure 4, though Vendor 4 cells were marketed as a high power variant, Vendor 3 cells had better power capabilities. Vendor 4 cells, with advanced anode material, displayed improved energy densities compared to Vendor 3 and Vendor 5 cells.

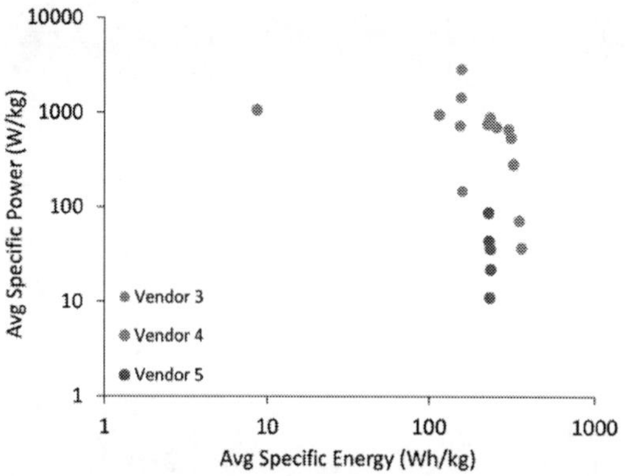

Figure 4. Ragone plot of pouch cells of similar capacity. Plot of Vendor 3 cell data is not complete due to limitations in testing capabilities at the time of testing. Plot of Vendor 5 cell data is not complete due to resource limitations. However, the tradeoff and comparison of energy and power densities are evident.

Additional Pouch Cell Testing: An alternative Vendor 6 was selected to improve the performance of an existing carried UAS system. Cells were manufactured according to the volume and weight requirements using advanced anode technology in order to increase capacity. Cells were subjected to testing across a wide temperature range to ensure suitability.

As seen in Figure 5, Vendor 6 cell discharge curves demonstrated cold temperature limitations due to cutoff voltage. A wider voltage range would have accommodated the cold temperature voltage drop with more capacity remaining within the cells at cutoff. Importantly, the capacity of cells at room temperature was twice as high as the incumbent cell (data not shown) in the same volume making the extreme temperature limitations less impactful given the extension under normal conditions.

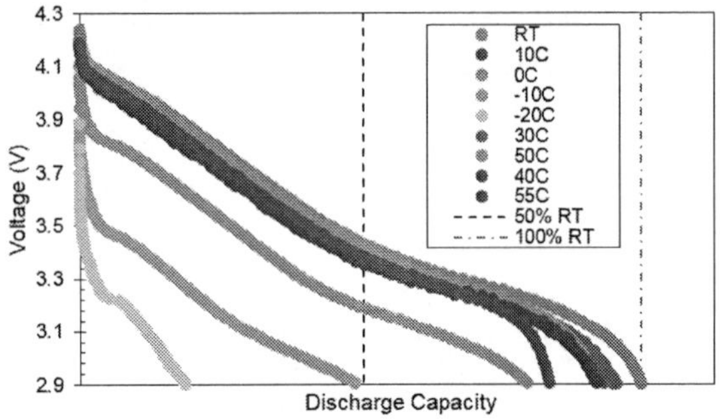

Figure 5. Performance of Vendor 6 cells over a wide temperature range. X axis shows discharge capacity retention relative to nominal capacity.

Conclusions

Commercial off the shelf (COTS) rechargeable lithium ion cells used in air vehicles were evaluated for electrochemical performance and compared to novel rechargeable lithium ion technologies.

Novel lithium cells touted for high power UAS applications provided expanded energy densities, and in some cases, temperature capabilities compared to COTS solutions. However, these novel chemistries still require improvements in power density and rate capability to offer an energy-power combination technology alternative for UAS.

Acknowledgements

The authors would like to thank Ronald Thompson, Daniel Berka, Sergio Mancilla, Michael Szabad, and David Shoemaker for their assistance.

The Small Tactical Universal Battery Series – Helping To Solve Modern Tactical Power Challenges

Mike Stein, Chris Whetstone, Vivek Patel
EXO Charge Division
Xentris Wireless
Addison, IL USA 60101
mike.stein@xentriswireless.com, chris.whetstone@xentriswireless.com, vivek.patel@xentriswireless.com
1-800-458-2820

Abstract
Today's Soldiers use a multitude of tactical electronic devices for operations – including some COTS devices adapted for military use. Many of these tactical electronics devices rely on different or unique types of batteries for power. This has created an undue 'battery burden' on the Soldier, and logistical complexity for the military. The Small Tactical Universal Battery (STUB) addresses all of these issues and brings the latest power technology to the field as well. Delivering unequaled levels of power interoperability, commonality, flexibility, and standardization, the STUB is the next-generation of mission-ready tactical power.

Keywords
STUB; Military Batteries; Tactical Power; C5ISR; USB; USB-C; USB PD; USB PPS; USB-IF; Army Modernization

Introduction
The modern Warfighter relies upon numerous electronic devices to operate as an integrated platform in a wider network that delivers unmatched operational performance. However, this technologically-enabled capability presents some very real operational energy challenges.

For the dismounted Warfighter this typically means having to carry numerous spare batteries of multiple types in order to have enough power for a 72-hour operational period – as different devices have to use different types of batteries matched to the power requirements of that device, and some devices with the same power profile nonetheless use batteries with a different mechanical or electrical interface than others.

The Tactical Power Challenge
This lack of power source interoperability has placed a heavy burden on our Soldiers, often amounting to 20-40 lbs. or more of spare batteries being carried. This often also contributes to a total individual operational load of well over 100 lbs. Needless to say, this erodes both physical and cognitive performance, with also degrades readiness, operational performance, and lethality.

The illustration that follows shows how the ever-growing need for tactical power has put an increasing burden on the Warfighter (and the operational issues this can lead to). This "battery burden" however, has also led to increased program cost, logistical complexity, and supply chain vulnerability.

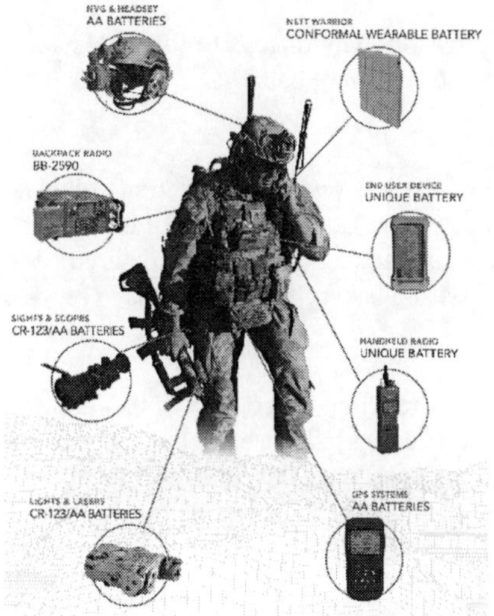

Figure 1. Illustration of the various types of batteries needed to power typical dismounted tactical electronic devices.

As the US Army began numerous modernization initiatives in recent years, it became clear that the power demands of new tactical electronics systems would require even more spare batteries to be carried by the Soldier. Using data from the US Army's Command, Control, Communications, Computers, Cyber, Intelligence, Surveillance and Reconnaissance Center (C5ISR) power team, the graph below shows that we are already past the point of needing more than double the amount of operational energy required by the Nett Warrior system- and will need even more as time goes on.

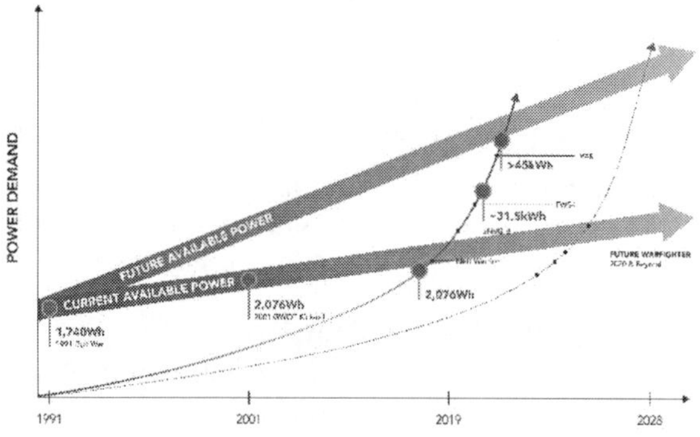

Figure 2. Illustration showing the total Wh / kWh of energy required by a typical infantry squad for a 72-hour operation.

Scoping the Challenge(s)

Although not shown on the previous graph, the Army's solicitation for Next-Generation Squad Weapon (NGSW) specifications included the requirement for future incorporation of a powered rail system with a common power source mounted on or attached to the weapon. This requirement was due to the next-generation aiming and targeting systems intended for the NGSW weapons and highlighted the importance (and urgency) of devoting efforts towards creating standardized families of batteries for tactical electronics.

Now, there are valid reasons why different military devices have traditionally needed different batteries:

1. Output Voltage
    a. Different devices operate at different voltages – ranging from 3.3-21V – and cell chemistry, cell configuration, and power requirements dictate what a battery's output needs to be
2. Form Factor
    a. A device's required energy drives the number and type of cells used in a battery, which it turn shapes a battery's size, weight, and form – as to human factors such as ergonomics
3. Connection Interface
    a. Several commonly used military batteries are similar in size, weight, and energy capacity but are not interchangeable as they have different electrical and mechanical connections
4. COTS Compatibility
    a. Military electronics equipment traditionally isn't interoperable with commercial devices – as there hasn't been a need to COTS-compatibility, military equipment also needs to meet more rigorous standards of robustness

In studies from 2018-2019, the C5ISR team also identified what they saw as three fundamental human factors design criteria for a family of portable / handheld device batteries:

1. Must have a common interface
2. Keep a constant 2D cross section
3. Expand in 3rd dimension to increase capacity

However, the team also established that the lack of a common battery/cell voltage would limit interoperability even more than a common form or mechanical interface.

USB Provides a Path Forward

USB protocols are defined by USB Implementers Forum (USB-IF) - the group of companies that has developed, certified, and shepherded the USB standard over the years, and now counts more than 700 companies in its membership.

USB protocols have come a long way since the initial standard was launched in 1996 to standardize the connection of peripherals to personal computers. It is fact no exaggeration to say that mobile USB devices have now totally transformed the way that consumers and businesses utilize communications and information technology.

Mobile technologies are also transforming operations in the tactical environment. Operators are relying more and more on the power of mobile solutions to make informed decisions that impact mission success. One example of this is the Nett Warrior (NW) system which uses a secured, COTS mobile device running the Android Team Awareness Kit (ATAK) app to enhance operational capabilities.

While mobile platforms have proven to be a force multiplier for our Warfighter, the power and equipment needed to support these devices has resulted not only in an increase to the Soldier's combat load but also adds a new layer of complexity.

In response to that challenge, the Army developed the Conformal Wearable Battery (CWB). This ergonomic power source was originally developed in 2008 and was a significant step forward in supporting the need for a wearable power solution. Referring back to Figure 2, we can see however that only 10 years after its introduction, the CWB was already becoming over-stretched in delivering the amount of power needed by the modern Warfighter.

Built on a culture of innovation, Xentris Wireless has been working with leaders in the commercial mobile device industry to solve the same challenges faced by the military – how to provide power, more efficiently, with less weight and bulk, for new mobile products with more advanced features.

Features like Wi-Fi, GPS, Bluetooth, sensors, video, social media apps, etc. are all commonly found in modern-day mobile phones – and have enabled the mobile data-enable lifestyle that we take for granted. However, these applications also heavily use the processor, as do hardware features such as color LCD screens, and they all draws significant amount of power - especially if they are used at the same time.

With the evolution of the 5G network and advances in data speeds, today's mobile devices consume more and more power. But because 5G deployment is also limited in its coverage, the constant switching between the 5G and 4G networks also has a significant impact on battery life.

Referring again to Figure 2, the Army is also experiencing the fact that increasing device features and capabilities dramatically increases power consumption. Another inescapable fact is that although the Army has fielded devices with USB technology incorporated, they are based on protocols and standards that are now obsolete and don't deliver the full capabilities and benefits that the Army needs.

USB power capabilities have dramatically improved over the past 13 years. USB Power Delivery (PD) 3.0 introduced in 2019 has the capability to charge devices at 100 watts. But it's not just about raw power, power also needs to be managed and delivered at the right rate for more efficiency and faster charging times - both the charger and the device need to be able to communicate the maximum they are capable of or else they will default to a lower charging rate. This continual source / sink communication is what happens with USB PD and Programmable Power Supply (PPS).

PPS allows for stepwise changes in current and voltage – decreasing the conversion loss during charging, and thereby ensuring that charging is more efficient. Due to more efficient charging, less heat is produced - which increases a battery's lifespan, and decreases thermal radiation (i.e., heat signature). USB PD together with Programmable Power Supply (PPS) also enables devices to fast-charge over a USB connection.

USB PD brings other benefits, too. The direction of power is not fixed, so you charge a device and at the same time charge the battery pack itself. Knowing the importance of such adaptive fast-charging solutions, Xentris Wireless was the first mobile device company to develop and receive certification for a USB PD device.

As we noted earlier, Soldiers are equipped with a variety of devices that have different voltage requirements (see Figure 1). This is one of the main reasons why Soldiers are therefore burdened with different types of batteries for different devices. In the commercial world however, as the multi-voltage capabilities of USB PD have expanded, Xentris Wireless has developed high capacity, fast-charging solutions that handle everything from 5-volt smartphones and tablets to 20-volt laptops. Radios that require 14-volts can also be supported USB PD and PPS.

The final piece of the USB puzzle was the development of the USB Type-C / USB-C connector. USB-C is designed to replace all previous types with a single reversible connector that can be used to transmit power, data, video, and audio signals with quantum leaps forward in capability.

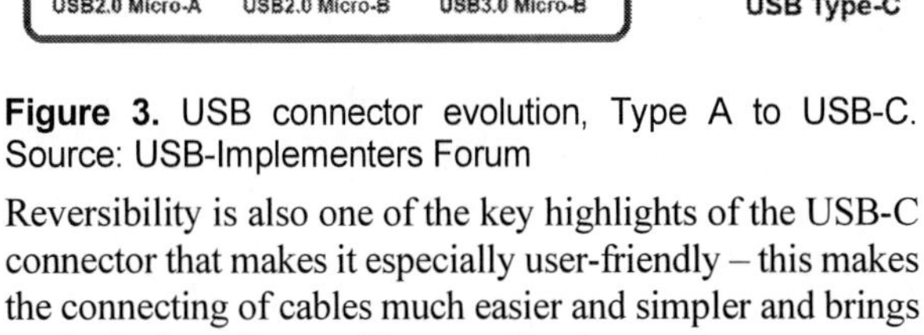

Figure 3. USB connector evolution, Type A to USB-C. Source: USB-Implementers Forum

Reversibility is also one of the key highlights of the USB-C connector that makes it especially user-friendly – this makes the connecting of cables much easier and simpler and brings particular benefits to military applications.

With a view to all the capabilities and benefits that modern USB technologies can deliver, Army DEVCOM's C5ISR center approached Xentris Wireless with a project to explore the feasibility of incorporating the USB Power Delivery (USB PD) standard for military batteries into the existing Battery Management System (BMS) circuitry. The project would demonstrate how this function could allow battery packs of different configurations to be interoperable across multiple devices by managing the delivery of different voltages as required.

The USB PD BMS concept was successfully demonstrated, and this became the nexus for the development of what became known as the Small Tactical Universal Battery (STUB) series. At its core, the STUB was intended become a standard, USB-enabled, centralized power source that supports different voltages to eliminate the need for multiple types of spare batteries.

The advantages aren't just technical though. Even more importantly, a standard family of improved, adaptive, dismounted power sources would have the benefits of reducing the Soldier's battery burden – while improving operational capabilities and Soldier lethality – and also simplify the Army's logistics tail. Leveraging commercial technologies and components would additionally provide overall program cost savings through standardization and economies of scale.

Figure 4. The US Army's Battery Standardization vision / road map, as defined in 2020 by the C5ISR team. Source: Dr. Nathan Sharpes, C5ISR Team, DEVCOM Power Division

The STUB Is Born

In July 2020 the Small Tactical Universal Battery (STUB) program was kicked off, and the EXO Charge division of Xentris Wireless began working on the STUB series with a C5ISR team led by Dr. Nathan L. Sharpes.

The STUB series supports adaptive power requirements across multiple device platforms and features a standard interface that allows Soldiers to swap STUBs between devices - eliminating the need for device-specific batteries.

Applications for the STUB series include HF/UHF radios, GPS systems, night vision devices, satellite communication systems, surveillance systems and sensors, ranging and targeting systems, mine detectors and more.

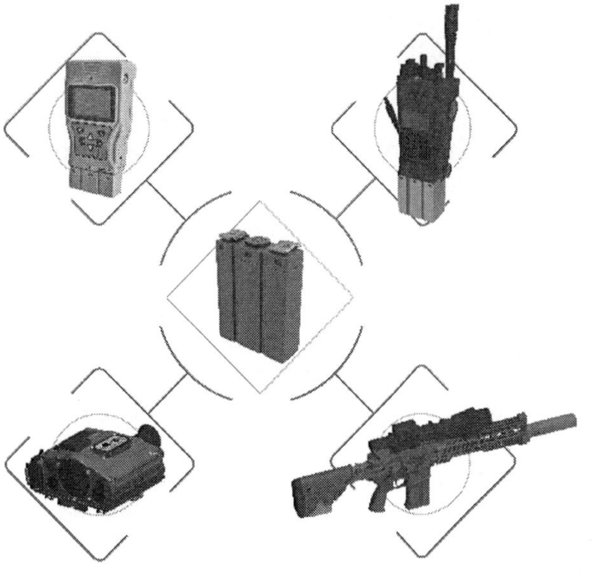

Figure 5. The Small Tactical Universal Battery (STUB) series is intended to become the interoperable power source for all handheld equipment in the DoD.

With eight different size/capacity options, as well as multiple different attachment methods, all with the same standard connection interface, the STUB delivers unprecedented levels of interoperability for maximum operational flexibility and capability.

Figure 6. The eight different sizes of the Small Tactical Universal Battery (STUB) series – in both single cell-stack and double cell-stack configurations.

The STUB series features rechargeable Lithium-Ion battery packs in 1-cell (1S1P) through 8-cell (4S2P) configuration, with a capacity of 3.5 Ah (xS1P) or 7Ah (xS2P). The STUB series features USB PD (Power Delivery) interface and PPS (Programmable Power Supply) output interface, with VBus and GND output terminals as well as a CC (Communication Channel) terminal – as well as reversible, bi-directional, multi-voltage, power delivery through its USB-C connector. The available output voltage through PD interface is 5V, 9V, 12V, 15V and 20V. The available output voltage through 1S1P PPS interface is 3.3V and 11V. Maximum discharge current depends on output voltage and battery pack configuration and can be as low as 750 mA or as high as 5A.

STUBs are charged using the USB PD interface. A charging voltage is applied to the PD connection interface using a USB Type-C cable in order to charge, and any USB PD compliant charger can be used to execute fast charging. STUB packs can also be charged using contact terminals (VBus and GND), and adapters for the standard Army chargers (ABC & UBC) are currently in development.

For added practicality and user-friendliness, each STUB model incorporates a unique 'double-tap' feature that enables users to check the battery's State-of-Charge via LED indicators on the top of the battery. This double-tap feature also activates the built-in Power Transfer feature that enables a STUB to transfer its energy to another STUB through a USB-C cable.

Figure 7. An illustration showcasing the 'double-tap' feature for checking the state-of-charge, as well as activating the STUB-to-STUB power transfer feature.

The STUB series is now USB-IF certified, is successfully going through MIL-PRF qualification, and has already been certified to MIL-STD-810H and -461G, UN 38.3 and IP68 standards. Delivering unequaled levels of interoperability, commonality, flexibility, and standardization, the STUB family is ready to become the ideal mission-ready power source for next generation tactical electronics.

References

1. Dr. Clifford Cook, "Supporting the Dismounted Soldier with Advanced Tactical Power Solutions," Future Soldier Technology Conference, June 2022.
2. Dr. Nathan L. Sharpes, "History of the Small Tactical Universal Battery (STUB) Family," Presentation, March 2022.

Development of High Energy Density Lithium-Oxygen Reserve Batteries with Integrated Chemical Oxygen Generation

Javier Alvaré
Wasatch Ionics LLC
Salt Lake City, UT 84093
javier@wasatchionics.com
Dr. Jay Rastegar
Omnitek Partners LLC
85 Air Park Drive-Unit 3
Ronkonkoma, NY 11779
j.rastegar@omnitekpartners.com

Abstract

Some smart munitions require that reserve batteries operate multiple days after activation in a low power sleep mode, while providing multiple high-power pulses. This operational profile requires batteries with energy and power densities beyond the limits of the current liquid reserve batteries. Therefore, there is an urgent need to find the next generation of high energy density reserve battery systems that can meet these operational targets. Wasatch Ionics and Omnitek Partners, in collaboration with Brigham Young University, are developing the next generation reserve batteries based on high energy density lithium-oxygen chemistry with integrated chemical oxygen generation (COG). Lithium-oxygen batteries offer the highest known theoretical energy density of all existing lithium metal batteries. Our novel high surface area/high mesopore volume fraction oxygen cathode electrode maximizes discharge capacity by providing a large storage capacity for lithium peroxide, while enhancing oxygen diffusion and electrolyte wetting. The use of internally generated high pure oxygen enables the fabrication of a self-contained and hermetically sealed battery design, therefore, eliminating the adverse effects of moisture, nitrogen, and carbon dioxide, which are present in batteries, where oxygen is sourced from air. The result of this innovation is a novel oxygen activated reserve battery that is expected to deliver a 10-fold increase in energy density, as compared today's lithium thionyl chloride liquid reserve batteries. The main objective of the research work is to demonstrate the technical feasibility of our Li-O2 reserve battery technology by fabricating and testing functional prototypes that can meet the energy density requirements of the application. The implementation of our novel primary reserve high energy density Li-O2 batteries offers multiple advantages that address the limitations of today's lithium thionyl chloride liquid reserve batteries. The resulting product will be the development of a new type of reserve battery with significantly higher energy density, faster activation time, and lower cost than the existing liquid reserve batteries. As part of this effort, we are also developing metal-oxygen batteries with stored compressed oxygen that can be used as reserve and primary batteries.

Keywords
Reserve batteries; lithium-oxygen batteries; oxygen chemical generation; on-demand activation/deactivation.

Introduction

Single use reserve batteries for military applications range from ordinance guidance systems to torpedoes, smart ammunition, mines, sonobuoys, unattended ground sensors, UAVs, artillery fuses, and many others [1]. These types of batteries must be able to operate in the harshest outdoor environments over a wide temperature range (-55°C to 125°C); they must be ready on very short notice with activation times of less than 100 ms; and must have extremely long shelf lives (>20 years). Thermal batteries and liquid reserve batteries have generally filled these requirements. However, while the military systems are becoming more sophisticated and miniaturized, the reserve battery technologies used to power them have remained essentially unchanged for decades. Traditional primary liquid reserve batteries rely on the lithium thionyl chloride ($Li-SOCl_2$) chemistry. In these types of batteries, thionyl chloride ($SOCl_2$) serves both as the cathode active material and the electrolyte. The battery is activated when the liquid electrolyte enters in contact with the lithium metal anode. Although $Li-SOCl_2$ batteries have an impressive theoretical energy density of 1,470 Wh/kg, high operating voltage (>3V), and decent discharge rate capability, practical reserve configurations can only deliver a small fraction of this value. This is mainly caused by the need to store the toxic and corrosive thionyl chloride liquid electrolyte, separately from the rest of the battery, inside a bulky liquid ampoule that needs to be ruptured during the activation step.

The new Bottom Attach munitions for the Close Terrain-Shaping Obstacles (CTSO) program, currently under development by the Army, requires that reserve batteries operate 30 days after activation in a low power sleep mode, while providing multiple high-power pulses. This operational profile requires batteries with energy and power densities beyond the limits of the current reserve batteries. Therefore, the Army has an urgent need to find the next generation of high energy density reserve battery systems that can meet these operational targets.

After decades of basic and applied research efforts dedicated to the development of rechargeable lithium-oxygen batteries (LOBs), they have become one of the most promising lithium metal chemistries. In their simplest configuration LOBs consist of an active porous carbon electrode, as the cathode material, a lithium metal anode with a separator, and an organic electrolyte in between (Figure 1). During the discharge process, lithium metal in the anode is oxidized to lithium ions (Li^+), which migrate through the liquid electrolyte and across the separator to the carbon cathode electrode. At the same time, oxygen accepts electrons from the external electrical circuit, and it combines with Li^+ to form the solid discharge products (mostly lithium peroxide, Li_2O_2) on the active sites of the porous cathode carbon electrode. During the battery charging step, the electrochemical process is reversed, and lithium peroxide is converted back to lithium metal and oxygen gas. The oxidation of lithium to lithium peroxide is a two electron exchange reaction. The underlying electrochemical reactions are:

Anode Reaction: $2\ Li \leftrightarrow 2\ Li^+ + 2e^-$
Cathode Reaction: $2\ Li^+ + O_2 + 2e^- \leftrightarrow Li_2O_2$
Overall: $2\ Li + O_2 \leftrightarrow Li_2O_2$ (E_{OCV}=2.96 V vs. Li/Li^+)

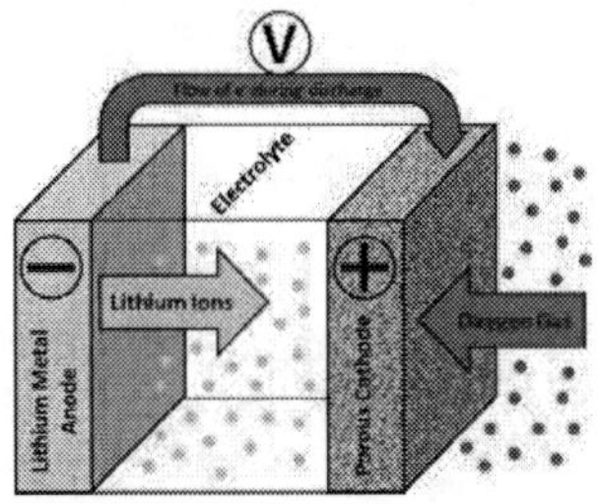

Figure 1. $Li\text{-}O_2$ battery

Although, the thermodynamic open cell voltage (OCV) of 2.96V is comparably low to other lithium battery chemistries, such as lithium-ion or lithium thionyl chloride, lithium-oxygen has the highest theoretical specific mass and volumetric energy densities of all the lithium batteries.

Despite the considerable energy density advantage, LOBs also face several challenges, derived mainly from the solid and insulative discharge product (Li_2O_2), the sluggish oxygen reduction reaction (ORR) and oxygen evolution reaction (OER) kinetics, and the strong oxidative environment encountered during the charging step. These issues result in: (1) poor rate capacity due to clogging and deactivation of the active cathode electrode sites, (2) a large overpotential (>1V) during charging, which results in low coulombic efficiency, and (3) low cycling life.

In the last decade, there has been significant progress in the formulation of new porous cathode electrode materials that maximize the solid Li_2O_2 storage capacity. In addition, the incorporation of novel ORR and OER catalysts into the oxygen cathode structure, and the use of solid-state electrolytes, has substantially reduced the charge overpotential and improved the cycling ability of the batteries.

Our Innovation

Wasatch Ionics and Omnitek Partners have been working on the development of the next-generation reserve batteries based on high-energy-density lithium-oxygen chemistry with integrated chemical oxygen generation (COG).

Our novel high surface area/high mesopore volume fraction oxygen cathode electrode maximizes battery discharge capacity by providing a very large storage capacity for lithium peroxide (Li_2O_2), while enhancing oxygen diffusion and liquid electrolyte wetting. The use of internally generated high-purity oxygen enables a self-contained and hermetically sealed battery design, therefore, eliminating the adverse effects of moisture, nitrogen, and carbon dioxide, which are present in batteries where oxygen is sourced from air. The result of this innovation is a reserve battery that delivers a significant improvement in energy density, as compared to all of today's commercial lithium thionyl chloride liquid reserve batteries. Figure 2 compares the actual energy and power

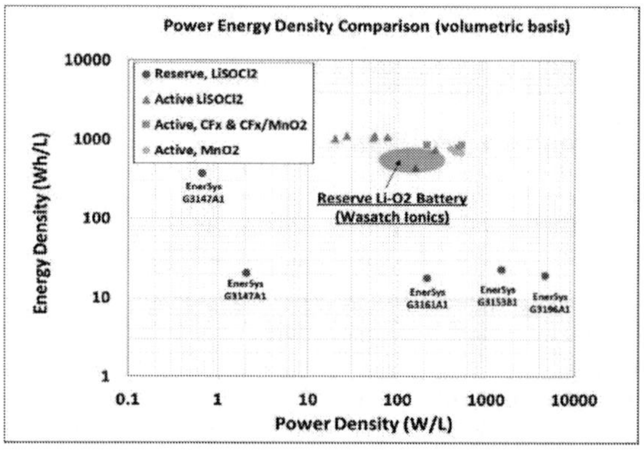

Figure 2. Comparison of energy density (Wh/l) vs. power density (W/L) for commercial lithium thionyl chloride, CFx, and MnO_2 liquid reserve and active batteries vs. Wasatch Ionic's O_2 activated reserved Li-O2 battery with integrated chemical oxygen generation.

densities of our reserve O_2-activated LOB, with integrated chemical oxygen generation, against several existing commercial liquid reserve and active batteries. The improvement is very significant when compared to commercial liquid reserve lithium thionyl chloride batteries, and it can even match the energy density performance of active CFx and $LiSOCl_2$ batteries.

Chemical Generation of High Pure Oxygen

An alkaline metal chlorate-based chemical oxygen generation (COG) system is integrated inside the reserve LOB to supply high-purity pressurized oxygen to the battery during discharge. The battery can remain inactive for many years, and then be quickly activated on-demand by this generation capability. COG by thermal decomposition of alkali metal chlorates and perchlorates is a mature and safe technology used for emergency oxygen supply in mines, submarines, and airplanes. The many advantages of COG include:

1. **Supply of pure oxygen without battery damaging contaminants.** Traditional lithium-air batteries suffer from deactivation and poor electrochemical efficiency caused by the presence of air contaminants. The lithium metal anode reacts very energetically with water and nitrogen, and CO_2 can interfere with the formation of a stable protective solid electrolyte interface layer (SEI) on the anode surface. By comparison, thermal decomposition of chlorates generates a very pure stream of oxygen gas, free of those contaminants.
2. **On-demand generation of pressurized oxygen.** The rate of oxygen generation by the thermal decomposition of chlorates is independent of the oxygen pressure [10]. Hence, oxygen can be pressurized inside the battery casing without affecting its rate of production. The use of oxygen chlorate candles is a much more efficient long-term O_2 storage method since the reactants occupy less volume (for any oxygen pressure less than 4000 psi). The method also prevents undesirable leaks or safety issues derived from long-term storage of high-pressure oxygen.
3. **Fast activation and preheating of the battery active material.** As opposed to the standard liquid reserve batteries, wherein the release of an externally stored liquid electrolyte activates the battery, metal-oxygen batteries are activated by the diffusion of oxygen gas into the porous cathode electrode. In a reserve LOB, the liquid electrolyte is added to the battery during assembly. This ensures that the electrolyte is already uniformly distributed and wetted by all the porous surfaces within the battery by the time of activation. It is well known that gases diffuse much faster than liquids. Therefore, reserve LOBs can be activated much faster than liquid reserve batteries. Another advantage of LOBs with integrated chemical oxygen generation is that the produced oxygen will be above ambient temperature due to the heat released during the thermal decomposition of the chlorates. As a result, the gas can help to quickly preheat the battery. This is a key advantage for reserve batteries that need to be stored and/or are operated in very cold environments and activated very quickly.

On-Demand Reserve Battery Activation/Deactivation

Currently available reserve batteries cannot be turned off or deactivated once they have been activated. However, to extend their operational time, it is highly desirable that reserve batteries can be partially or completely deactivated in times of low power or no-power periods, and similarly be reactivated to their full power capacity when the external power requirements increase. Figure 3 illustrates a conceptual design of a LOB, with integrated chemical oxygen generation, that can be activated and deactivated on demand. Driven by a prescribed acceleration profile, an inertial igniter initiates the first COG unit, which fills the gas storage compartment with oxygen. A normally closed O_2 flow control valve allows enough oxygen to flow into the battery's core to activate the LOB, which can now power the device and operate a linear solenoid to actuate the oxygen flow control valve from that point on. The flow control valve would open when more oxygen is required by the LOB to keep supplying electric power to the external load, or close to deactivate the battery in no-power periods. Additional COG units can be added to the reserve battery to increase the amount of oxygen. These additional COG units can be activated on demand by powering an electrical initiator. Alternatively, or in combination, the reserve

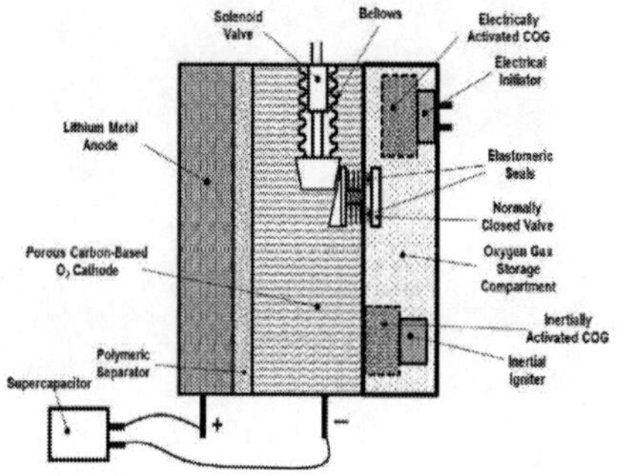

Figure 3. Conceptual design of a LOB with integrated chemical oxygen generation that can be activated and deactivated on demand.

battery can also be fitted with a supercapacitor that is charged from the LOB. The energy stored in the supercapacitor can be used, for instance, to provide high power pulses to external loads. In summary, our concept provides a lot of flexibility in terms of how the reserve battery can be used, while it significantly extends the on-line operational time.

Acknowledgements

Wasatch Ionics and Omnitek Partners wish to acknowledge the US Army for their funding and support.

References

[1] S. Jacobs, "Choosing Battery-Powered Options for Single-Use Military Applications," Tadiran Batteries, 30 January 2018. [Online]. Available: https://www.designworldonline.com/choosing-battery-powered-options-for-single-use-military-applications/. [Accessed 10 August 2020].

[2] W. H. Schechter, R. R. Miller, R. M. Bovard and C. B. Jackson, "Chlorate candles as a source of

oxygen," *Industrial and Engineering Chemistry,* vol. 42, no. 11, pp. 2348-2353, 1950.

[3] W. M. Haynes, CRC Handbook of Chemistry and Physics, 91st ed., 2010.

[4] A. Kondori, M. Esmaeilirad, A. M. Harzandi, R. Amine, R. Shahbazian-Yassar and P. C. Redfern, "A Room Tempeature Rechargeable Li2O-based Lithium-Air Battery Enabled by a Solid Electrolyte," *Science,* vol. 379, pp. 499-505, 2023.

MagLev Fly Wheel Energy Storage System

Dr. Herbert Hess, Brian Peterson, Sebastian Garcia
Department of Electrical & Computer Engineering
University of Idaho, Fly Wheel Energy Storage Research Group
Moscow, Idaho, USA, 83843
garc8660@vandals.uidaho.edu / 1-208-885-4341

Abstract

This sample file was produced for use by authors of convention, symposium, and conference publications. Authors are encouraged and requested to use this template to produce their final submission for the electronic and print publications. Kindly follow this sample file so that the publication will have the same or very similar formatting throughout and provide attendees with a good source of venue documentation. Advanced warfighting technologies increasingly rely on a stable supply of electrical power for effective control of the battlespace. While flywheels as a means of energy storage is not a new concept, emerging technologies are making them viable again. High temperature superconductors supported by magnets facilitate the near-frictionless interaction between two surfaces, creating the opportunity for a shaftless flywheel, storing energy in the form of a rotating mass with new, low levels of energy losses. We have designed and built a 20 kg fly wheel that forms the rotor of an "inside-out" field regulated reluctance motor topology. The rotor has neither physical nor electrical contact with the rest of the machine. A Halback array of magnets support a configuration of high temperature superconductors for passive stabilization in the vertical axis. Two sets of optical sensors and magnetic actuators provide horizontal position control and stabilization of roll and pitch. Field regulation enables flexible, resilient torque control of yaw. Experimental results confirm levitation of a 20 kg shaftless fly wheel rotor in this manner. We have precise position sensing for horizontal stabilization. We have created and simulated appropriate field regulated reluctance machine models of the shaftless flywheel motor, verifying appropriate modulation strategies. At a target rotational speed of 3600rpm, the flywheel stores approximately 224 kJ (kilo-Joules) of stored rotating kinetic energy. With much reduced energy losses from incumbent flywheel technologies, this shaftless reluctance machine can hold much of its energy for several days. The paper will contain experimental results to support the above stated shaftless reluctance machine performance descriptions.

Keywords

Electrical Power; Flywheel; Superconducting Magnets; Near-Frictionless; Shaftless;

Introduction

This paper briefly describes some of the functional sensor and actuator subsystem hardware testing for our flywheel energy storage system. The block diagrams describe ideal sensor and actuator behavior. The simulation facilitates critical evaluation of candidate signal processing (e.g., sampling, filtering, response time, etc.) in the context of the energy storage system. The MATLAB Simulink simulation(s) are extended to Simulink Real-Time hardware-in-the-loop testing with physical sensors and actuators, enabling verification of modeling assumptions and limitations.

The electrical current actuator is mathematically modeled using H-bridge PWM current control [23]. While the theory is well established, the limitations and non-idealities of the physical current actuator subsystem need to be well understood prior to integration into the FESS.

The electrical current sensor is well defined in the mathematical model and is based on the manufacturers' data for the actual hardware. The current sensors' ratiometric output sensitivity to the current sensors' 5V supply voltage warrants careful selection of a 5V power source. This is an example of a small but important hardware implementation detail only observed during physical hardware testing.

The position or displacement sensor is also well defined in the mathematical model and is based on the manufacturers' data for the actual hardware. The physical hardware testing was notably consistent with the mathematical model and MATLAB Simulink simulations.

For all three sensors and actuators subsystems, the physical interface is described and documented for integration into the flywheel energy storage system.

The rotary absolute encoder is used in the UI FESS. The rotary encoder interface did not work initially. However, troubleshooting steps were taken to get to the root cause and this problem has since been solved. After root cause was identified and sufficiently addressed, the Renishaw Resolute™ rotary absolute encoder system block diagram was functional on the bench.

Having the UI FESS rotor assembly supported magnetically by a Halbach magnet array is a major component of this protects end goal. An intermediate development step specifically pertaining to the rotor assembly's support along its axis of rotation, the z-axis, is further explained in this paper.

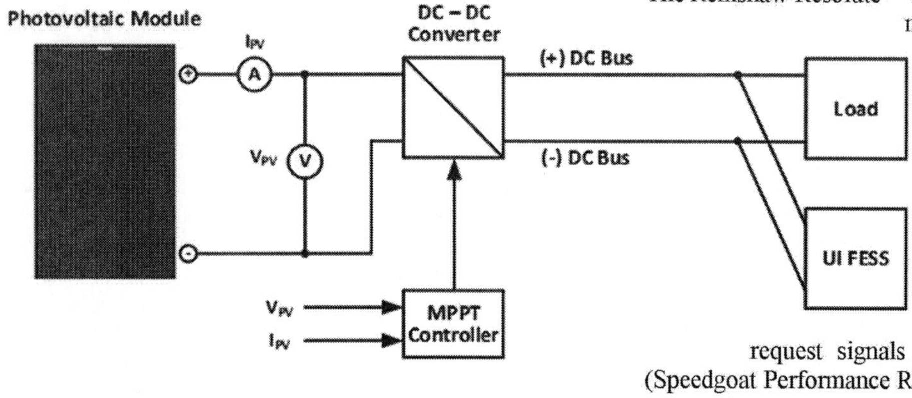

Figure 1 UI FESS Functional Block Diagram

Active Magnetic Bearing

In order to control all six degrees of freedom on the flywheel, a single-axis active-magnetic-bearing (AMB) academic test fixture was created to help develop, test, and improve the AMB control software and hardware used for the University of Idaho (UI) Flywheel Energy Storage System (FESS). The single-axis AMB academic test fixture serves as an intermediate step before the design and implementation of the more complex Field Regulated Reluctance Machine (FRRM) AMB and stabilization AMB in the UI FESS.

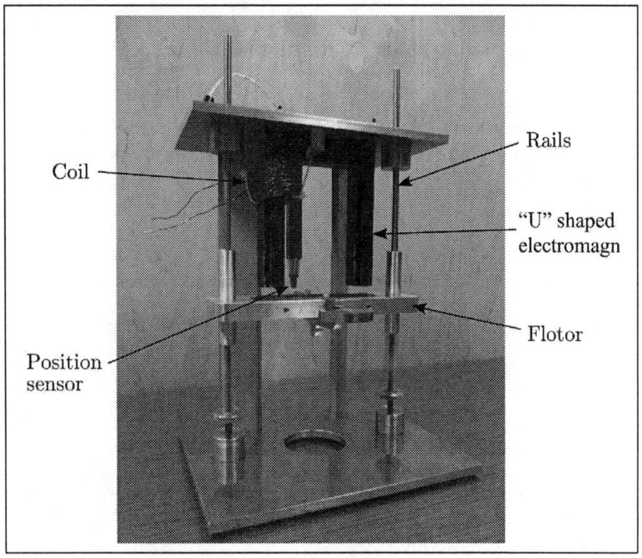

Figure 2 AMB Academic Test Fixture

The single-axis AMB academic test fixture has a "U" shaped electromagnet. The coil consists of 150 turns of 18 AWG solid core copper wire coated with a thin layer of enamel insulation. The floater is free to translate up and down along the vertical axis. The iron core of the electromagnet is M36 electrical steel (μr = 1616).

Rotary Absolute Encoder

The Renishaw Resolute™ rotary absolute encoder system is not used in the single-axis active-magnetic-bearing (AMB) academic test fixture. But this rotary encoder system is used in the University of Idaho (UI) Flywheel Energy Storage System (FESS) as shown in Figure 2. The Resolute encoder calculates rotational position on demand. The readhead receives a series of request signals from the host control system (Speedgoat Performance Real Time Target Machine). Each time it receives a request, the readhead determines rotational position by two independent methods: 1) decoding a single image without any information from previous positions, and 2) linear extrapolation from the two most recent rotational position readings, assuming constant velocity. Once the two rotational position methods have been calculated, the encoder decides which position to output and whether to set the error flag. If the position calculated by the two methods agree within ±15 μm (half a scale period) of one another, then the encoder outputs the position from method 1 and sets an internal counter to zero.

Figure 3 Rotary Encoder Test Fixture

If the positions disagree, then the encoder outputs the position from method two and increments the internal counter. If the internal counter ever exceeds four, then the readhead sets the error flag. The readhead makes sure that there is never more than 75 μs between images by capturing extra images between requests if necessary. For a system requesting position every ≤ 75 μs, the time between outputting the first incorrect position and raising the error flag is five times the request interval. For a slower system

requesting position at 500 μs intervals, this time will be 500 μs as the readhead will have processed six further images between each pair of requests to make sure that the time between images never exceeds 75 μs. In both cases, the time between outputting incorrect position and raising the error flag is sufficiently short that appropriate action can be taken in response to the error flag before the incorrect rotational position data can influence the control system.

Mechanical Development-Air Bearing Fixture

Having the machine's rotor supported magnetically by a Halbach magnet array (as shown in Figure 1.3) is a major component of this protects end goal. The first approach to achieving this was an all-up test where the array of superconducting magnets was brought down to their operating temperature (approximately −320°F) and an attempt was made at "hovering" the rotor. However, this type of machine has 6 degrees of freedom and properly controlling all of them at once (though one degree is passively controlled) requires more learned information about its inherent physical and electrical characteristics.

Consequently, a staged approach (specifically pertaining to the rotor's support along its axis of rotation, the z-axis) has been adopted and the following chapter will outline key aspects of the mechanical design that facilitate this staging approach. As an intermediary step for eventually working up to using the Halbach magnet array of superconductors, an air bearing will provide the passive support along the rotor's axis of rotation (z-axis) for incremental development testing stages. Part of the motivation for using an air bearing is to partially reduce the degrees of freedom that need to be controlled. This allows for more focused tuning of the coil energizing sequence as well as the active magnet bearing (AMB).

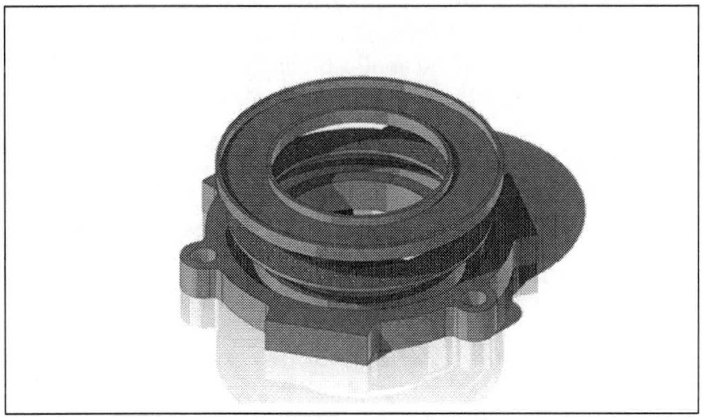

Figure 4 Final Assembly of Rotor Air Bearing

There is a channel in which the "cap" on the bottom of the rotor will ride through which also has physical guard rails, thereby assisting in the AMB's responsibility to correct for roll and pitch of the rotor assembly.

Conclusions

The research presented herein establishes the feasibility of the AMB control software and hardware for the University of Idaho (UI) Flywheel Energy Storage System (FESS). A single-axis active-magnetic-bearing (AMB) academic test fixture was used to test the sensor and actuator subsystems.

The current sensors' digital signal was observed to be noisy. Reducing the analog bandwidth of the current sensor, i.e., reducing the cut-off frequency of the analog low-pass-filter of the current sensor analog output signal reduced the observed measurement noise.

Acknowledgements

We would like to thank the outstanding support of NASA and the Pacific Northwest Transportation Consortium for providing the necessary funding to continue moving this project throughout its stages of development through to its eventual completion. Additionally, we would also like to thank the support of our friends and colleagues in the University of Idaho's Electrical and Computer Engineering Department.

Overview of MIL-STD-3071 – Tactical Microgrid Standard

Frank W Bohn
U.S. Army Combat Capabilities Development Command, C5ISR Center
APG, MD
Frank.W.Bohn.civ@army.mil

Abstract

MIL-STD-3071, or the Tactical Microgrid Standard (TMS), is a data and communication standard for power devices to maximize interoperability between power solutions from various vendors. The TMS implements a data model for each type of power device that allows participants on the microgrid to know the type of device and associated capabilities. TMS also implements the role of Microgrid Controllers (MC) and Microgrid Dashboard (MD). The MC collects the real time data from the various power devices and acts as a supervisory controller to optimize the power devices in terms of fuel efficiency or resiliency. The MD provides the ability to display all the real time data to the user in one location.

The TMS will open the possibility for the latest and greatest power technologies to integrate with existing power technologies and create more efficient, adaptable, and resilient power.

As of January 2023, the TMS has been approved as a Military Standard, MIL-STD-3071. The TMS was developed by U.S. Army Combat Capabilities Development Command C5ISR Center, U.S. Army Corps of Engineers Engineer Research and Development Center (ERDC), MIT Lincoln Labs, and is owned and maintained by U.S. Army PEO Combat Support and Combat Service Support (CS & CSS). Future procurement of power devices may require TMS compliance to ensure interoperability.

C5ISR Center is developing a suite of tools to assist in the development of TMS complaint devices to include a TMS Topic Monitor and TMS Simulator.

This paper will present a high-level overview of the standard, what tactical power solutions it may enable, and what tools are being developed to assist TMS developers.

Keywords

Tactical Microgrid Standard; TMS; Microgrid; Military Standard; Military; MIL-STD-3071; Communication; Control; Interoperability;

TMS Overview

The Tactical Microgrid Standard (TMS) supports robust power for the Warfighter by standardizing the communications and controls architecture across mobile electric power systems. TMS enables monitoring and management of tactical power devices through the establishment of communication protocols, messaging patterns, and data models and in turn can provide more resilient, adaptable, and efficient power for the Warfighter. Additionally, the TMS allows for an opens systems approach to microgrids, providing a diverse and open ecosystem to enable future power systems to easily integrate into existing microgrids.

The TMS was developed by U.S. Army Combat Capabilities Development Command C5ISR Center, U.S. Army Corps of Engineers Engineer Research and Development Center (ERDC), MIT Lincoln Labs, and is owned and maintained by U.S. Army PEO Combat Support and Combat Service Support (CS & CSS).

The TMS was ratified and approved by the Defense Standardization Program in January 2023 as MIL-STD-3071 and is now an official standard to be used in Department of Defense acquisitions.

Although developed for the tactical space, the TMS has applications for all services and in all environments to include air crafts, ships, unmanned vehicles, space assets, and installations. Additionally, the TMS has applications outside of the Military for commercial and other state and federal applications. Efforts to utilize the TMS are already undergoing in many of these areas.

Where to find the standard

The TMS, MIL-STD-3071, can be found online on the Acquisition Streamlining and Standardizing Information System (ASSIST) at quicksearch.dla.mil and searching for document number 3071.

What TMS is and what it is not

At its core, TMS is a document that defines the communication and control interface requirements between power components and enables the development of Tactical Microgrids. Ultimately, the intent for the TMS is to provide a framework for power system vendors to develop the intelligent control of microgrids to allow for optimization for resiliency, efficiency, adaptability, and to ensure adequate power quality and electrical stability.

For instance, although the TMS does standardize the communications and data model for a Microgrid Controller (MC), the standard does not provide an actual implementation of an MC, nor does it provide control theory or specific electrical performance requirements that a microgrid needs to meet. Instead, a controls vendor would utilize their expertise in power physics and control theory and develop a MC that complies with the TMS. The combination of the vendors expertise and the standard would result in a TMS compliant MC that can control and optimize power devices.

Benefits of TMS

The main benefit of the TMS is that it enables interoperability for power systems, allowing for vendor agnostic and plug and play solutions. The TMS provides an ecosystem where power systems from any vendor can communicate and optimize This interoperability that is enabled by TMS will allow ease of procurement for the defense acquisition community.

Secondary benefits from the application of the TMS are that it will provide resilient, adaptable, and efficient power networks.

Resilient: Enabling TMS microgrids allows for redundancy of power assets so in the case of equipment failure there are other resources to immediately provide power and more available to come online.

Adaptable: Microgrids can be setup and reconfigured based on mission needs. Units operating their own microgrid can come together to further optimize their power systems and separate when needed.

Efficient: TMS Microgrids can enable the resiliency required while reducing the number of running generators to reduce fuel usage. Additionally, TMS Microgrids can utilize energy storage and alternative energy sources to further increase the energy efficiency.

The addition of resilient, adaptable, and efficient microgrids will have profound impacts on Warfighting applications and allow the Warfighters to increase mobility and adaptability while decreasing reliance on the logistics trail.

Technical Overview

To create a standard set of data, the data is structured as a "topic". A topic defines a group of closely related data and is published and subscribed to by different devices on the microgrid based on the Device Role (further described below). Each topic has one or more data type that specifies the data to transfer and what how the data should be structured. Additionally, each topic has timing specified for when the data is transferred. The timing at which the topics are published is based on the variability of the data. Highly variable data such as power measurements are included in topics that are updated up to 100ms, while other data that changes infrequently or not at all are included in topics that are published on change or at discovery.

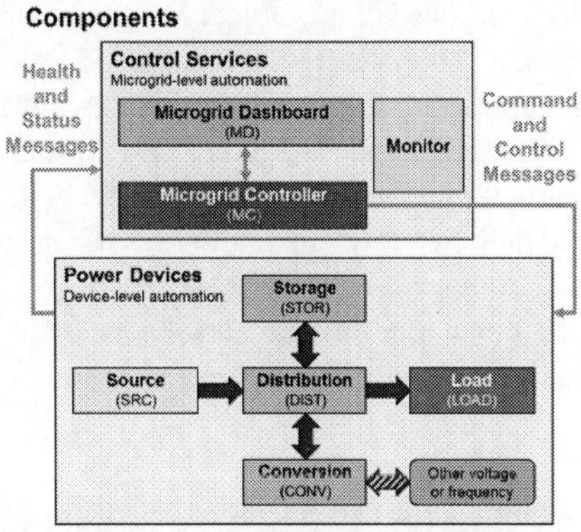

Figure 1. TMS Device Roles

Figure 1 shows the various device roles that are established in the TMS. The TMS established five Power Device Roles:

- Source (SRC) - a device that provides power to the microgrid (generator, solar panels, wind turbines).
- Distribution (DIST) – a device that connects other power devices together and may have metering and switching capabilities.
- Load (LOAD) - a device that consumes power.
- Conversion (CONV) - a device that modifies power to a different frequency or voltage (inverters, rectifiers, transformers).
- Storage (STOR) - a device to store energy and provide it back to microgrid when needed (batteries, flywheels).

Additionally, the TMS establishes three Control Device Roles:

- Microgrid Controller (MC) - a device which coordinates and dispatches power devices across the microgrid.
- Microgrid Dashboard (MD) - a device that provides a user interface and depicts the health and status of the microgrid, while also allowing the user to provide control requests.
- Monitor (MON) - a device used for passive monitoring of the microgrid.

The TMS specified which topics each Power and Control Device needs to publish and subscribe to. A power device will publish topics related to its capabilities and its real time power metrics while subscribing to various control topics to allow for instructions to adjust its performance. A MC will subscribe to most topics and utilize the data to determine an optimization strategy and publish control request topics.

The TMS makes use of the Object Model Group Data Distribution Service (OMG DDS) standard to provide the communication middleware which includes the network logic and creates the publisher and subscriber architecture. OMG DDS also provide a cyber security plug in, DDS Security, that allows for end-to-end encryption of the data and certified participants. In the future, additional requirements may be included in the TMS standard for additional cyber protections.

Compliance

Procurements of military power systems will likely need to comply with the TMS, MIL-STD-3071. Efforts are currently under way to stand up a testing capability that will allow the government to verify compliance and should be completed at the end of 2023. Additionally, a subset of the capability may be released to government contractors which will allow initial checks for compliance via a software tool called the Compliance Checker.

A separate compliance document has been written that outline the test procedures that need to be performed to verify compliance to the standard. That document can be made available to government contractors.

Tools

Developer Tools have been and are being developed to assist with the development of TMS compliant devices.

TMS Monitor - This tool provides several basic functions needed for verifying interoperability and communication patterns with TMS devices. It can be used for: 1) Verifying connectivity to a specific set of TMS devices; 2) Displaying published data in both tabular and graphical formats; 3) Record captured data to disk in JSON format; 4) Visually inspect message content. The topic monitor is similar in nature to a network packet inspector, such as Wireshark, and is just one tool that can be used for data capture, analysis, or monitoring purposes.

TMS Simulator – This tool can simulate any TMS device role to include a microgrid controller. This tool can provide insight to a developer by allowing them to see the data flows for a fully implemented TMS device. Additionally, the tool can be used to send requests from an MC to a real implemented TMS device to perform end to end testing of that device.

TMS Compliance Checker – This tool can be used to perform initial checks for validation and verification of a TMS device. The tool is not intended to be an authoritative source for compliance but instead provide a general indication that the TMS implementation in on the right track. The tool only covers a subset of the tests prescribed in the compliance document.

Governance and Industry Participation

PEO CS&CSS is standing up a governance process for the TMS for long term support of the standard. It is clear that the standard will need to be a living document and be updated as issues or limitations are identified, and as new technologies are developed that require new capabilities. The updating process will allow for government and industry participation in the development of the proposed updates to ensure that any updates to the standard are properly prepared and reviewed before inclusion in the official standard.

Conclusion

The TMS, MIL-STD-3071, is officially approved and is ready to usher in a new ecosystem that is required for innovation for tactical power solutions. The interoperability between power components from different vendors facilitate streamlined procurement and will bring resiliency, adaptability, and efficiency to tactical, air, sea, space, installation, and commercial microgrids alike.

Acknowledgements

The TMS Team would like to thank the Office of Secretary of Defense, Operational Energy – Innovation Office and the U.S. Army PEO Combat Support and Combat Service Support (CS & CSS) for supporting the Tactical Microgrid Standard since its infancy. The TMS Team would also like to acknowledge the critical technical contributions made by the U.S. Army Corps of Engineers Engineer Research and Development Center (ERDC), MIT Lincoln Labs, the U.S. Army Combat Capabilities Development Command (DEVCOM) C5ISR Center, and Parsons Corporation. Lastly, the TMS Team would like to thank those industry partners who have been partners and provided impactful reviews at various stages through the development of the standard.

References

1. "MIL-STD-3071, Tactical Microgrid Communications and Control." ASSIST, US Army Communications Electronics Command, Jan. 2023.
2. About the DDS Security Specification Version 1.1, https://www.omg.org/spec/DDS-SECURITY/.

High-Volume Cobalt Disulfide Thermal Battery Production

Carl Schousboe[1], Mark Hart[1], Peter Jacobelli[2]
[1]EnerSys Advanced Systems Inc., 5430 70th Ave N, Pinellas Park, FL 33781
[2]EnerSys Advanced Systems Inc., 104 Rock Rd, Horsham, PA 19044
frederik.schousboe@eas.enersys.com / 1-727-520-1393

Abstract

Molten salt batteries, referred to herein as thermal batteries, serve a critical role in providing on-demand electrical power for a wide array of defense applications. Although the manufacture and certification of thermal batteries remain a complex, arduous endeavor, the long storage life, and incredible power density of thermal batteries position them as the power source of choice in myriad systems. The introduction of an improved cathode material, Cobalt Disulfide (CoS_2), has extended the performance regime of thermal batteries and given rise to an even greater number of use cases. However, the structure of the improved cathode material has presented several manufacturing challenges that hindered adoption for many high-volume production applications. In the current work, several advances are outlined that have allowed the continued on-time delivery of high-volume thermal battery production employing the novel CoS_2 catholyte material. By providing a tailored particle size distribution, continuous pellet manufacturing techniques, and semi-automated assembly equipment, EnerSys Advanced Systems Inc. (EAS) has demonstrated the ability and capacity to serve high-volume production requirements using the superior CoS_2 electrochemical solution.

Keywords

Thermal batteries; high-volume production; Cobalt Disulfide; cathode; electrochemical cell

Introduction

Thermal batteries serve as a critical power source for the operation of a wide array of defense systems, including Air-to-Air/Air-to-Ground weapons systems, Gun-Launched Artillery systems, and several advanced applications within the Ballistic Missile Defense System.

Beginning in the late 1990s, implementation of cutting-edge CoS_2 cathode technology has allowed the use of thermal batteries in otherwise unsuitable applications [1]. Owing to its increased electronic conductivity and thermal stability at elevated temperatures, thermal batteries produced with CoS_2 technology have demonstrated an ability to serve mission profiles with increased discharge rates and longer mission life requirements, while minimizing the size and weight impacts of the power storage solution [2].

While CoS_2 cathode material has provided a meaningful advancement in thermal battery capabilities, the material structure itself presents unique manufacturing challenges, which have here-to-fore hindered the large-scale deployment of this advanced cathode material in high-volume thermal battery manufacturing.

Purpose:

The purpose of the current work has been to demonstrate a step change in process capability across multiple production facilities, allowing for sustained high-rate delivery of thermal batteries produced with CoS_2 cathode material.

Methods:

The success of the current work has been made possible by three technological advancements: Tailored Powder Processing, Continuous Cathode Pellet Production, and Semi-Automated Assembly.

Tailored Powder Processing: By pursuing vertical integration of CoS_2 production, EAS has developed the capability to synthesize a material with tailored particle size distribution that retains preferential activation dynamics, while improving powder flow and enabling enhanced pellet pressing techniques. Furthermore, integrated cathode powder production has positioned EAS to increase throughput in support of industry demand by evolving right-sized batch processing and deploying dedicated synthesis and characterization equipment.

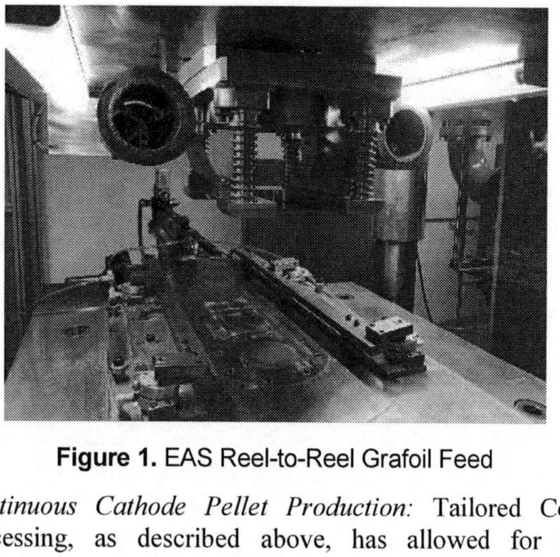

Figure 1. EAS Reel-to-Reel Grafoil Feed

Continuous Cathode Pellet Production: Tailored CoS_2 processing, as described above, has allowed for the deployment of enhanced pellet production techniques, namely automated cavity fill. As a complement to automated cavity fill, EAS has developed and implemented mechanized reel-to-reel grafoil feed systems as well as automated pellet inspection techniques to allow for continuous cathode pellet production. Such a system is shown in Figure 1, above. The combined system enhancements have increased throughput two-fold, while also increasing labor efficiency by a factor of four, by removing the need for additional handling, as demonstrated in Figure 2, below.

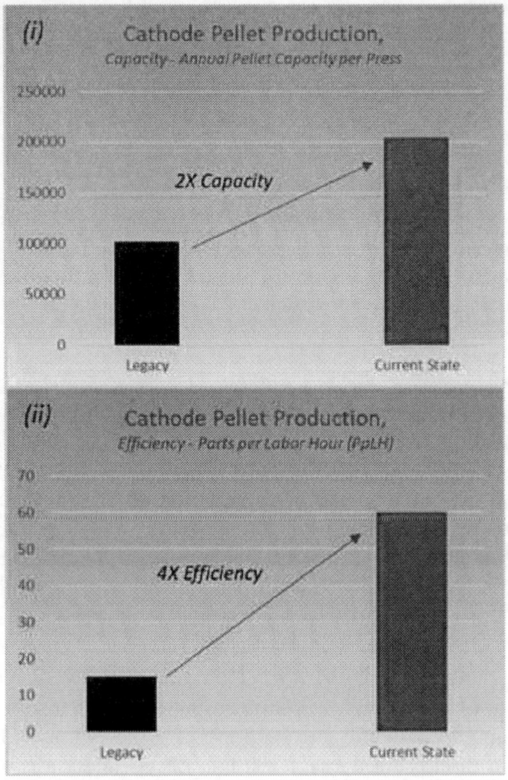

Figure 2. EAS Continuous Cathode Pellet Production, *(i)* Capacity Increase, *(ii)* Efficiency Increase

Semi-Automated Assembly: Two final key elements of the high-volume manufacturing capability established by EAS has been the development and implementation of semi-automated stack and wrap assembly equipment. These critical elements of the production process have enabled consistent production levels and reduced process variation by providing for: Recipe Controlled Stacking Order, 100% Visual Stack Inspection, and Error-Proof (Poka-Yoke) Tooling Design. Figure 3 shows the automated stacking system equipment.

Conclusions:

Thermal batteries employing advanced **CoS_2** cathode materials continue to provide enhanced performance in demanding applications. EAS has developed enhanced synthesis and manufacturing techniques to overcome inherent fabrication challenges stemming from the specific material structure. Advances related to Tailored Powder Processing, Continuous Cathode Production, and Semi-Automated Assembly have allowed EAS to meet large-scale customer demands. These advances have provided additional industrial capacity to deliver high-performing thermal batteries and allowed for consecutive years of on-time delivery of over 15,000 large format CoS_2 thermal batteries, manufactured across two production facilities.

References

1. Guidotti, R A., "Thermal Batteries: A Technology Review and Future Directions" SAND-95-1313C. Sandia National Lab (SNL-NM), Albuquerque, NM (United States), 1995.
2. Wesolowski, Daniel Edward, and Papenguth, Hans W., "Study of Cell Performance in Long-Life Thermal Battery Design Space" SAND2010-0082C. Sandia National Lab (SNL-NM), Albuquerque, NM (United States), 2010.

Figure 3: EAS Semi-Automated Stack Assembly Equipment

High-Power Density Thermal Batteries for Space and Defense Applications

Eric Scherzberg
Advanced Thermal Batteries, Inc.
1231 Independence Way
Westminster, MD 21074
Eric.Scherzberg@atb-inc.com / 1-443-821-7929

Abstract

The ASB Group's LAN anode has been utilized for thermal batteries used in space and defense applications requiring high power density. The battery design provides a higher cell voltage, lower impedance and single flat voltage plateau compared to conventional lithium alloy anodes. Results are demonstrated in differing applications with consideration for practical application.

Keywords

Molten Salt Battery; Thermal Battery Power Density; LAN Anode

Introduction

Due to their maturity, reliability, and high-power densities, thermal batteries used in "one shot" systems are well known within the defense industry. They require no charging, no heating, no logistic constraints for transportation/storage, and no dedicated ground installation. Thermal batteries provide the highest power densities of any reserve battery technology and are unaffected by environmental conditions such as pressure, temperature, humidity, etc. They can be used in sets of several batteries connected in parallel or series thus providing modularity. Thermal batteries can be activated before the launch and safely sit during the no-load "idle time" in the minutes leading up to the high-power discharge. With such a proven record, thermal batteries are a great solution to support growing needs within the space and defense industry.

The use of LAN anodes for thermal batteries has been demonstrated in prior applications within the defense industry. LAN consists of a pure lithium anode, mechanically immobilized to allow practical implementation without the need to alloy the lithium with another material. Due to the inherent performance characteristics of LAN anodes, it has been used in applications requiring high power output within a relatively small battery volume.

Design Considerations

Current Density: Thermal batteries typically operate at steady state current densities of 1A/cm2, with short duration high current pulses of 10A/cm2 for durations in the hundreds of milliseconds. Practical implementation for satisfying high current requirements requires an increased battery volume, with a goal of increasing voltage and cell surface area. The primary means of addressing this is through increasing the cell diameter and thus the battery diameter, as well as increasing the battery length to accommodate parallel cell stacks or increased voltage. This can be challenging due to size and weight constraints experienced in aerospace applications as well as maximum allowed voltages for the system electronics. Use of the LAN anode provides an alternative to these constraints.

Voltage Profile: The LAN anode has the operating voltage of pure lithium. The voltage under discharge offers a relatively flat voltage plateau compared to the lithium alloys used broadly in thermal batteries. The single voltage plateau allows a higher operating voltage and thus higher power output during the entire battery discharge. Unlike lithium silicone alloy anodes, the consumption of all lithium during the discharge without subsequent lower voltage plateaus results in a safer battery design without excess and unusable electrochemical capacity. This becomes increasingly important when high current is being sourced which generates additional heat within the battery cells. In addition to high power output, the single voltage plateau provides a greater ability to remain within the required operating voltage during high current draw and the subsequent reduction in voltage due to cell impedance. Figure 1 provides comparison of lithium silicone, lithium aluminum, and LAN anodes for a cell of the same total capacity.

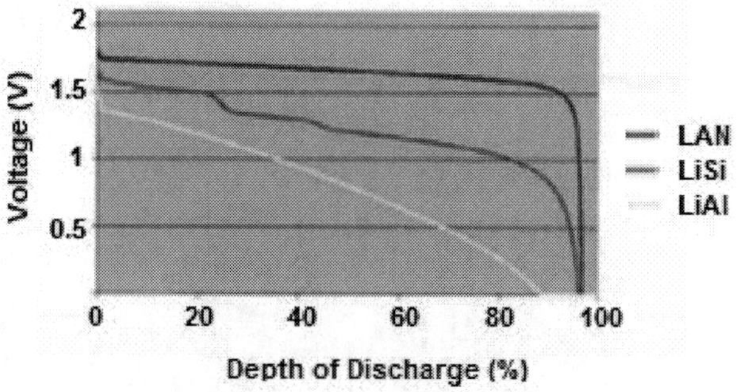

Figure 1. Cell Voltage Comparison

Cell Impedance: The internal resistance of a LAN anode is very low, in fact lower than in alloy anodes. Additionally, it is almost constant during discharge, since there is always liquid lithium which can react at the surface of the electrolyte separator layer. This is necessary during high current draws when the voltage is still required to be within the required operating voltage limits.

Temperature Considerations: By design, the lithium in the LAN anode is molten when in the operating state, but mechanically constrained to prevent it from leaving the confinement of the cell. Because the lithium is always and intentionally molten, it does not have the same risk of thermal runaway as lithium alloy anodes where the alloy can be broken down releasing lithium to escape from the cell. During high current discharge, the cell temperature will increase due to resistive heating. In small batteries with short operating times this increase in temperature may not be significant due to heat dissipation, however it becomes increasingly important in larger batteries with longer operating times. In these applications the heat is retained within the cells due to the inherent thermal mass, as well as the thermal insulation used to retain heat for longer operating life. The LAN anode's ability to tolerate increased temperatures without significant degradation in performance nor risk for thermal runaway makes it ideal for such uses

Conductors: Transmission of the high current from the battery requires special consideration. Battery size must be sufficient to fit the required number of internal leads between the cell stack and glass to metal sealed terminals in the header. Similarly, the header must have sufficient space for terminals and connections that may be larger than a typical battery. External connections that are welded or mechanically clamped are preferred as opposed to soldered to mitigate risk of the solder melting due to current induced temperature rise.

Battery Application A

A battery was developed and tested for an emergency power application requiring a very high current draw sustained for between 4 to 5 seconds. The maximum allowed voltage was 60V. The battery design consisted of a single cell stack of 28 cells in series. The overall battery size was 3.60 inches in diameter by 4.15 inches in length utilizing a stainless steel container. The LAN anode was paired with all lithium ternary electrolyte and iron disulfide cathode.

Figure 2. Thermal Battery A Configuration

Batteries were tested at operational temperatures of -40°C and 71°C. The battery is activated into an open circuit condition for up to 10 seconds followed by up to 16kW in the hot battery and 12kW in the cold battery for 4-5 seconds. Following the high current application, a bleed down current was applied until the capacity was depleted at approximately 300 seconds. In both cases the batteries supported the required load and continue to perform nominally after the high current. The load applied results in a constant current draw of up to 9.5A/cm^2 and a power density of more than 23 W/cm^3. Due to the activation mechanism used for the battery tested at -40°C, the battery was activated just before data recording started, not capturing the initial voltage rise.

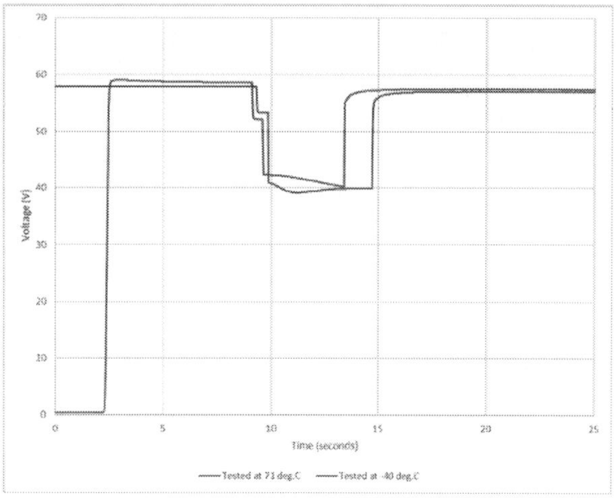

Figure 3. Thermal Battery A High Power Discharge

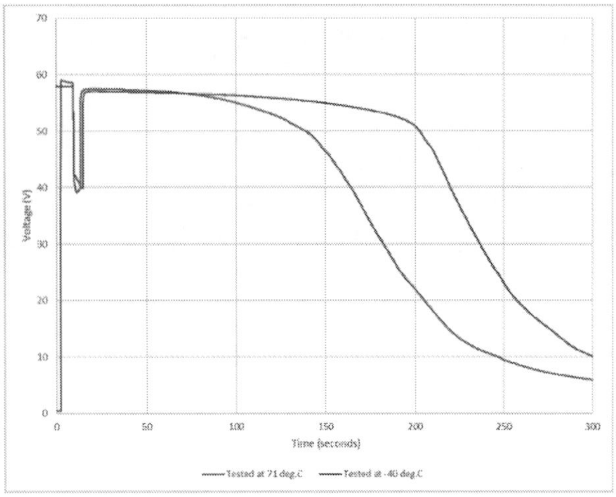

Figure .4 Thermal Battery A Complete Discharge

In addition to testing under normal system conditions, abuse tests were performed. One battery was preconditioned to 71°C and discharged using a high rate condition simulating the device continually drawing the peak power expected, with the load applied immediately upon battery activation. A second battery was tested after preconditioning to 71°C and activating into an open circuit condition. Both batteries remained intact with no abnormal conditions experienced. Upon completion of the tests, post-fire disassembly confirmed that the battery cells remained in nominal condition with no indication of degradation or thermal runaway.

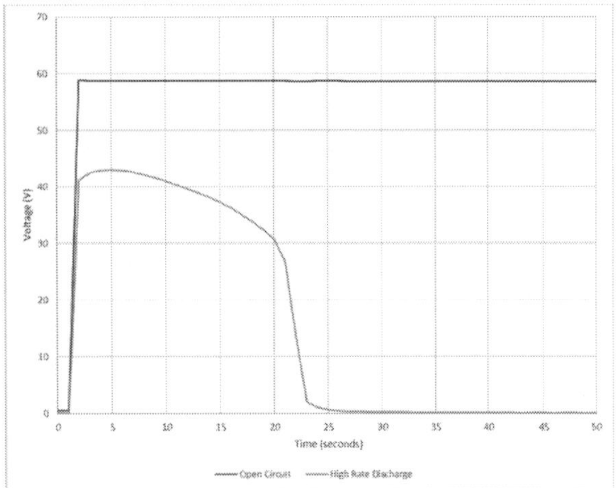

Figure 5. Thermal Battery A Abuse Testing – 50 Seconds

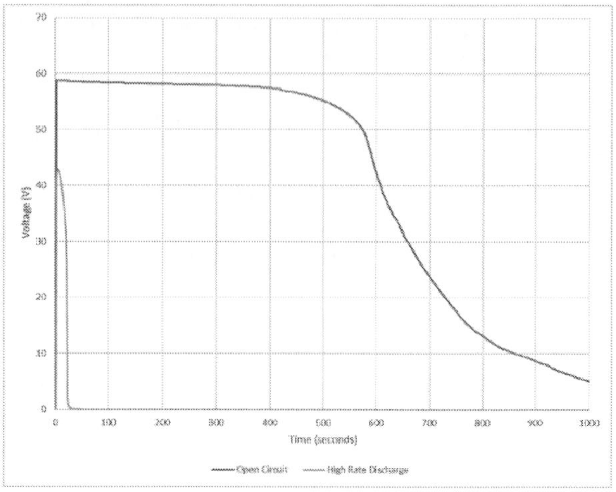

Figure 6. Thermal Battery A Abuse Testing – 1,000 Seconds

Battery Application B

A battery was developed and tested for an application that required a long operating life consisting mostly of a no load condition, but included high current pulses applied periodically through the discharge. The maximum allowed voltage was 200V. The battery design consisted of a single cell stack of 95 cells in series. The overall battery size was 3.00 inches in diameter by 8.7 inches in length utilizing a stainless steel container. The LAN anode was paired with a binary ternary electrolyte and iron disulfide cathode.

Figure 6. Thermal Battery B Configuration

Batteries were tested at room temperature. The battery is activated into an open circuit condition, with pulses of up to 16kW applied for 0.50 seconds each. The battery is able to support the high pulse load for over to 1000 seconds without significant change in voltage under pulses. Due to the use of the LAN anode, the battery remained stable during the discharge with no signs of thermal runaway or degradation of the cell stack. The load applied results in a pulsed current draw of up to 3.5A/cm^2 and a power density of more than 15 W/cm^3.

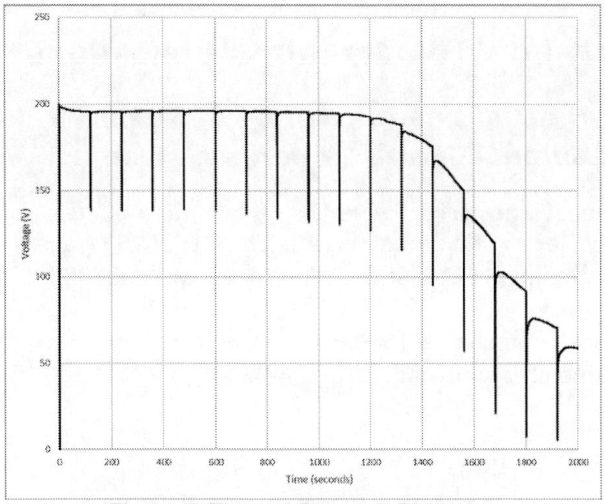

Figure 7. Thermal Battery B Discharge

Potential Applications

Development and testing work has demonstrated the use of thermal batteries using the LAN anode in applications requiring high current draw and power density across a range of conditions including constant and pulse loading Long operating time including low or no current draw is also tolerable. The unique set of performance characteristics allows for use in systems where high power is required in conjunction with the typical benefits of a thermal battery. Potential applications include emergency power, directed energy, charging capacitor banks, and decoy power.

High Power Reserve Battery for Extremely Low Temperature Applications

Lin-Shu Du[1], Art Driedger[1], William J. Epply[1], Kevin Vriarte[1], Jeffrey A. Swank[2], Giuseppe L. Di Benedetto[3], Richard Dratler[3], Lauren A. Morris[3], Andrew G. Warne[3]***

[1] MaxPower, Inc., 141 Christopher Lane, Harleysville, PA 19438
[2] U.S. Army Combat Capabilities Development Command Army Research Laboratory, Adelphi, MD 20783 (retired)
[3] U.S. Army Combat Capabilities Development Command Armaments Center, Picatinny Arsenal, NJ 07806

*Point of Contact (MaxPower, Inc.): ls.du@maxpowerinc.com / 215-256-4575 ext. 115
**Point of Contact (U.S. Army): andrew.g.warne.civ@army.mil / 973-724-6894

Abstract

Medium caliber fuze power source applications require high power density, extremely fast activation times, low temperature operation, and small form factors. The currently used lithium thionyl chloride system exhibits increased viscosity in cold environments, which results in decreased activation speed as compared to higher temperatures. To investigate alternative systems that can meet rise-time requirements across the temperature range, the U.S. Army and MaxPower, Inc. have renewed ammonia reserve battery technologies. Originally retired based on short run time and relatively low load voltage, liquid ammonia-based batteries are the ideal solution for medium caliber fuze applications where long run time is not required. An ammonia-based electrolyte is capable of meeting both temperature and rise time requirements due to its valuable intrinsic properties: strong solvation (high power), low freezing point (low temperature operation), and low viscosity while maintaining high vapor pressure (fast activation). Historically, the ammonia battery has demonstrated rapid activation (reaching 10 ms) in application temperatures from +160 °F to -65 °F (+71.1 °C to -53.9 °C). Dynamic forces that aid cell wetting during activation are assisted by the high vapor pressure of the system's liquid ammonia electrolyte. MaxPower, Inc.'s research exceeds previous limitations of the ammonia battery. In this presentation, various cathode fabrication processes and key parameters will be discussed. Additionally, MaxPower, Inc. has identified two cathode candidates that provide higher load voltages than the conventional ammonia battery cathode. Lastly, a 3V lithium-containing ammonia battery has been demonstrated for the first time. Strategies to improve the compatibility between ammonia and the lithium-based anode will be discussed.

Keywords

Liquid ammonia battery; lithium ammonia battery; reserve battery; high power battery; extremely low temperature operation

Introduction

There exists an area of improvement with low temperature activation of medium caliber fuze power sources. The typical lithium thionyl chloride system has high viscosity in cold environments which slows the activation process. This creates an opportunity for an alternative solution that can improve rise time across a large temperature range. To address this challenge, MaxPower is proposing the reintroduction of the ammonia reserve battery. This battery has a history in reserve battery applications where it demonstrated rapid activation at temperatures from +160 °F to as low as -65 °F (+71.1 °C to -53.9 °C).[1] Ammonia reserve batteries first made their debut in 1947 and saw continued use through the 1960s until being supplanted by lithium primary systems. Lithium primary batteries became the system of choice due to higher energy densities and lower electrolyte vapor pressures. However, some applications such as medium caliber munitions may have a need for extremely fast activation, high power densities, and low temperature operation; the requirements of which lithium and thermal batteries cannot fully meet. Liquid ammonia-based batteries are the perfect solution for medium caliber and other fuze applications that do not require long operation time but require fast activation time and high power, especially at low operating temperatures. Using ammonia as the electrolyte solvent yields significant benefits due to its valuable intrinsic properties, such as low viscosities with high vapor pressures (fast activation), strong solvation ability (high power) and low freezing point (low temperature operation). Furthermore, reduced dynamic forces that normally aid cell wetting during activation are also driving the need for cells that utilize a high vapor pressure electrolyte, such as ammonia.

High Voltage Cathode Materials

MaxPower has rejuvenated the ammonia battery chemistry that was developed by Honeywell more than 55 years ago. A new cathode chemistry has been further developed to increase load voltages. MaxPower has discovered two new patent pending cathode materials that perform better (higher load voltages; See Figure 1) than the meta-dinitrobenzene (m-DNB) cathode used by Honeywell for mass production.[2] MaxPower developed cathodes that help to provide outstanding rate performance. Figure 2 shows that one of the cathodes can handle current density of 150 mA/cm^2 with load voltages above 2V at ambient temperature. The significant voltage decay is shown when discharged at 150 mA/cm^2. The performance can be further improved by using a high salt concentration electrolyte (HSCE), indicating the decay is due to concentration polarization.

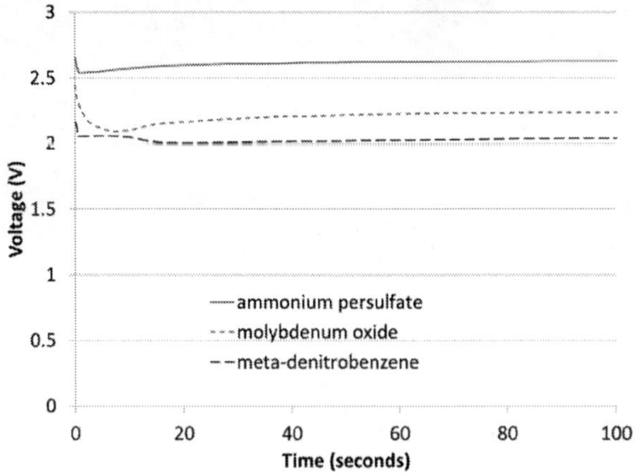

Figure 1: Discharge time vs. voltage for Mg ammonium batteries with MaxPower developed cathode materials and the baseline cathode material discharged at 10 mA/cm^2 at -49 F (-45 °C).

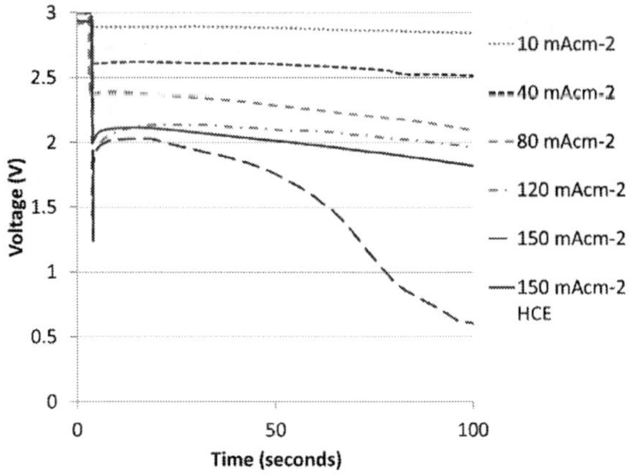

Figure 2: Discharge time (first 100 seconds) vs. voltage for MaxPower's Mg ammonia battery discharged at 10 to 150 mA/cm^2 at ambient temperature.

Electrolyte enabling Lithium Ammonia Batteries

MaxPower has also successfully demonstrated for the first time that lithium metal can be used as the anode in the ammonia battery to further increase the load voltage. Magnesium is known to be the only metal among alkali and alkali earth metals that is stable in ammonia and is therefore the choice of anode in the ammonia battery. When in contact with ammonia, lithium metal forms lithium ion and solvated electron (so-called lithium blue; see Figure 3a) which is very reactive and can immediately react with cathodes and sometimes could lead to explosion. MaxPower has successfully developed a patent pending high concentration electrolyte (HCE) that can inhibit the formation of lithium blue (see Figure 3b) and successfully demonstrate the lithium-based ammonia cell with much improved load voltages.[3]

Figure 4 shows the discharge profile of a Li-based ammonia cell at 40 mA/cm^2 at ambient temperature. The load voltage reaches 3V with the lithium-based cells having 30 ms of rise time.

Figure 3: Images of (a) Li reacts in ammonia at -108 °F (-78 °C), forming Li blue and (b) Li is stabilized in a saturated ammonia electrolyte.

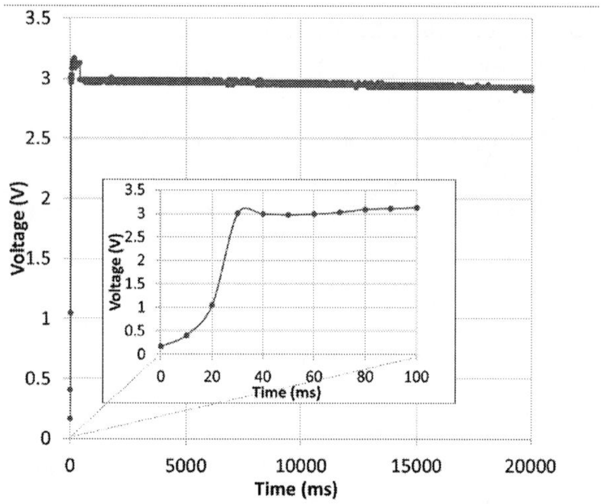

Figure 4: Discharge profile at room temperature at 40 mA/cm^2 of a Li based liquid ammonia cell. The inserted plot is the discharge profile during the first 100 ms.

Anode Stabilization

Besides using HCE to stabilize the lithium anode and to enable the high voltage lithium-based ammonia battery, MaxPower has additionally developed patent pending lithium alloying based anode materials that can be used along with the electrolyte having lower salt concentration.[4] The cell voltage when using Li alloy is comparable to that when using lithium metal. Strategically, enabling the use of lower salt concentrations can provide faster rise time due to the relatively lower electrolyte viscosity especially at extremely low temperatures.

Battery Design

A 3-cell battery with a cell diameter of 18mm and length of 35mm. The battery design is shown in Figure 5 where the cell holder design concept has been proposed to provide easy cell assembly and minimize intercell leakage. The 3-cell Mg-based ammonia battery shows good performance at room temperature as well as at -40 ºF (-40 ºC) (Figure 6). The rise time at -40 ºF (-40 ºC) is 20 ms (see inserted figure in Figure 6).

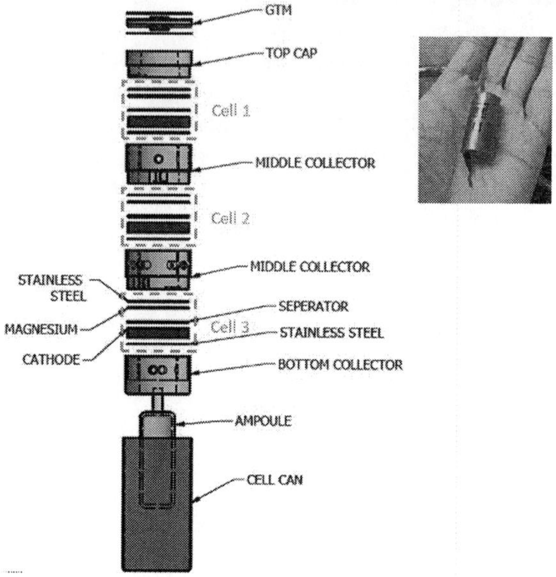

Figure 5: MaxPower developed 3-cell Mg ammonia battery with the cell holder design.

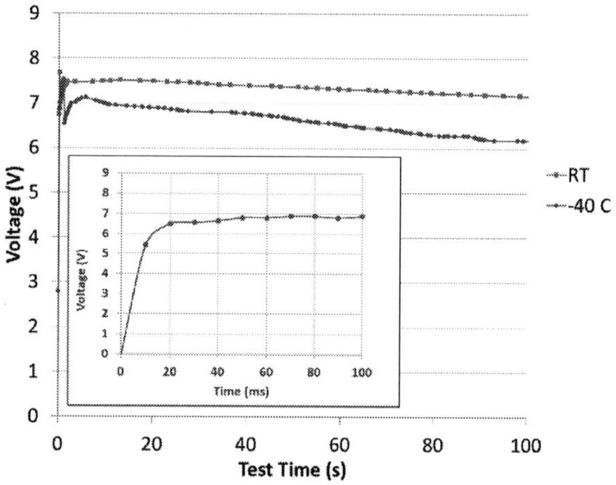

Figure 6: Discharge time (first 100 seconds) vs. voltage for MaxPower developed Mg-based 3-cell battery, discharged at 40 mA at room temperature (RT) and -40 °F (-40 °C). Inserted figure shows the voltage response at -40 °F (-40 °C).

Conclusion

The liquid ammonia battery provides high power and fast response time (rise time) at low temperatures and therefore can meet the needs for the medium caliber reserve battery applications. MaxPower has developed high voltage cathodes that are ~0.5 V higher than the baseline m-DNB cathode. The cathode can operate at exceedingly high current densities (150 mA/cm^2). In addition, MaxPower has demonstrated, for the first time, a stable 3V lithium-based ammonia battery via the use of high salt concentration electrolyte and alloy anodes to improve the electrolyte and anode compatibility.

Acknowledgements

This research was funded and supported by U.S. Army DEVCOM Armaments Center and under the NJIT index (997039 2018-2019) and Army SBIR (W911QX-18-P-0158, 2018-2019; W911QX-20-C-0018, 2020-2022).

Reference

1. W.C. Spindler "Ammonia Batteries", U.S. Naval Ordnance Laboratory, 1965.
2. L.-S. Du, N. Aulicino, A. Driedger, J. Pastore, G.L. Di Benedetto and J. Swank, "High Voltage Cathode Materials for Non-aqueous Ammonia Based Primary and Reserve Batteries", US Patent US 20220328848A1.
3. L.-S. Du, J. Pastore, N. Aulicino, A. Driedger, G.L. Di Benedetto and J. Swank, "Non-aqueous Ammonia Electrolytes for Lithium Anode Based Primary and Reserve Batteries", US Patent Application # 17/300,843.
4. L.-S. Du, A. Driedger, C. Shen, K. Vriarte, W. J. Eppley, B. Hayes-Oberst, G.L. Di Benedetto and J. Swank, "Lithium Alloy Based Anode for Non-aqueous Ammonia Primary and Reserve Batteries", US Patent Application # 17/803,259.

Coupled Thermal-Electrochemical Full Battery Modeling of LiSi/FeS_2 Batteries

Tyler G. Voskuilen*, Harry K. Moffat, Nathan W. Porter, Scott A. Roberts
Sandia National Laboratories, PO Box 5800, MS 0828, Albuquerque, NM, 87185-0828
*Corresponding Author: tvoskui@sandia.gov, (505) 845-0390

Abstract: *Modeling a full thermal battery stack provides physical insights about axial cell variations that occur during start up, load variations, and freeze-out regimes that are not immediately apparent from single-cell models. In addition, a full battery model enables simulation of the electrical behavior of multi-tap batteries in combination with more complex thermal boundary conditions. A thermal model of a full battery can predict axial temperature variations in the battery, but the electrical performance of a multi-tap battery with a temperature gradient cannot be readily predicted by a single-cell model alone.*

Our prior work focused on development of a coupled multi-physics model for a single cell of a thermal battery [1] and simplification of that model to reduce computational cost [2]. In this work, we extend this approach to a two-dimensional full stack LiSi/FeS_2 thermal battery and focus on aspects of the full battery that are not predicted by the single-cell model. Since the batteries freeze from the outside in, the full battery model allows prediction of different lifetimes from different tap locations and can better simulate the battery performance under loads near the end of its life. We also demonstrate that the model can capture the effects of Joule heating and electrochemical reaction heating, which produces load-dependent spatially non-uniform effects that change the predicted battery lifetime. Sensitivity of the model predictions to model inputs was quantified using Sobol' indices, allowing relative effects of the various model inputs on predicted quantities to be compared.

Keywords: thermal battery; primary lithium cell; molten salt electrolyte; iron disulfide; computational modeling

Introduction

Our prior work on multi-physics modeling of thermally activated batteries has focused on single-cell models to keep computational times tractable and provide model validation against single-cell experimental data [1,3,4]. These efforts have been successful in terms of producing a model capturing a rich set of physical processes, including heat transfer, electrochemical reactions, ion and species transport, porous flow, capillary effects, phase change, and mechanical deformation. The model reductions applied in [1] have brought the computational cost of the model down enough to extend the model to full battery stacks of multiple cells.

In this work, we present a coupled modeling approach for a full battery, including multiple taps, thermal insulation, the ignition train, and the battery can. To make the model tractable, we separate the electrochemical stack from the thermal solve, which allows the use of different meshes for different physics with independent resolution requirements. We show that this model provides a substantial savings in computational cost while maintaining accuracy of key quantities of interest (QoIs) for a demonstration full battery.

The coupled modeling approach is demonstrated using an open-source battery [5]. Additionally, a sensitivity study was conducted on a structurally similar proprietary battery design using the same computational approach described in this work. Both electrical and thermal parameters are sampled simultaneously. This sensitivity study allows the exploration of the parameter space, demonstration of model robustness for different parameter inputs, and identification of important model parameters.

Methods

In this section, we briefly describe the full physics model and then outline the different approaches and unique challenges associated with extending the single cell model to a full battery.

Model: Many of the details of the current model have been described in our prior publications so we will focus on adaptations needed to extend the model to a full battery [1]. As shown in Figure 1, the model is separated into two domains–an electrochemical domain and a thermal domain. The energy equation is solved in the thermal domain and solid electrical conduction, species and ion transport in the molten electrolyte, electrochemical reactions, and porous flow of electrolyte are solved for in the electrical domain.

There is a two-way coupling between the two domains, with the thermal domain supplying temperature for the electrical domain, and the electrical domain providing a Joule heating energy source for the thermal domain. At each time step, the thermal domain is solved using the lagged Joule heating source, then the

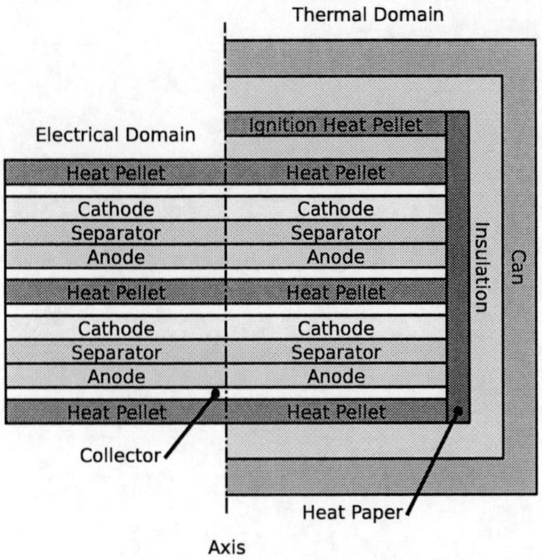

Figure 1. The two-dimensional axisymmetric simulation domains for a two-cell full-battery simulation (not to scale).

temperature field is interpolated into the electrical domain and the transport equations in the electrical domain are solved, then finally the updated Joule heating source is transferred back to the thermal domain.

The computational cost of the electrochemical domain is significantly higher than the thermal domain due to the larger number of equations, the expensive chemistry model evaluations, and the greater number of nonlinear iterations required to converge the more nonlinear set of equations. However, after the initial battery activation the electrochemical stack behavior is close to one-dimensional in the axial direction, while the thermal problem is largely radial through the insulation (except for the battery ends). For this reason, we can use a radially coarse mesh (10 elements) for the electrical domain while still using a radially finer mesh (100 elements) for the thermal domain to resolve the radial heat pellet burn progression and losses in the radial direction at later times. This approach provides considerable computational cost savings for a full battery, and allows better parallel load balancing for the electrical solve work than using a single domain.

Heat Pellet Ignition: The actual battery ignition is initiated at the center of the ignition heat pellet at the top of the stack (see Figure 1). This burns out to several discrete heat paper strips which burn down the length of the battery igniting the heat pellets in the stack. In this model, we do not model the heat paper burn, but instead initialize the level set field on all heat pellets to appropriately account for the heat paper burn speed.

The initial level set field (ϕ) in the ignition heat pellet

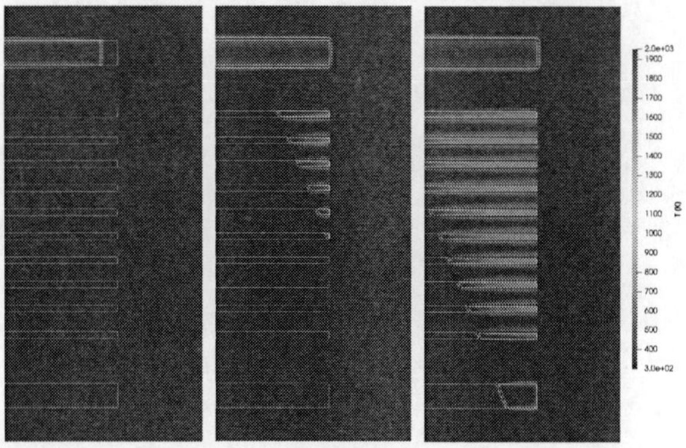

Figure 2. Simulated burn progression from ignition heat pellet down the stack to the remaining heat pellets. White lines show heat pellet locations and black lines show the position of the level set burn (and associated energy source).

is equal to the radius (r) since its burn initiates at the center and burns outward. On the remaining heat pellets, the level set field is initialized as

$$\phi = |z_{ign} - z|\frac{V_{pellet}}{V_{paper}} - r \tag{1}$$

where z_{ign} is the axial position of the ignition heat pellet, V_{pellet} is the burn speed of the heat pellet, and V_{paper} is the burn speed of the heat paper. This provides a realistic ignition timeline for the heat pellets without requiring resolution of the heat paper. Since the heat paper strips are not wrapped around the entire battery, accurately modeling them in a two-dimensional model would require additional adjustments to energy output and thermal properties.

The result of this initialization is a conical-shaped initial level set field that moves across the non-ignition heat pellets as shown in Figure 2.

Simulation Setup: The demonstration battery used for the simulations in this work is a 9-cell battery [5]. Electrical boundary conditions were applied at four collectors to provide a negative voltage tap (-2V), a 0V tap, and two positive voltage taps (nominally 4V and 14V, using 2 and 8 cells respectively). The time varying electrical load shown in Figure 3 was applied to all taps except the 0V tap, which used a fixed voltage boundary condition. After 1 second, the two positive taps have a steady high load, followed by a series of pulses over a lower base load. After the pulses end, the load is kept constant until the battery freezes out.

The exterior surface of the battery was set to a convective boundary condition to ambient temperature (300 K).

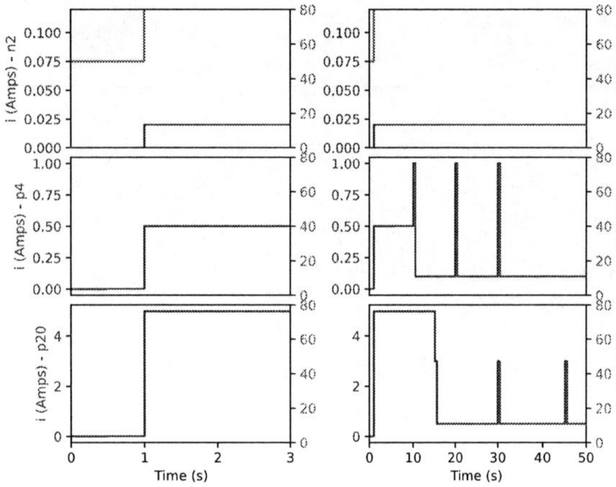

Figure 3. Battery loads (combination resistance and current loads) for all three battery taps. Loads are constant after 50 seconds. Current loads are in blue and resistive loads in red.

Sensitivity Studies: Sensitivity studies are an important part of model development which explore the parameter-to-QoI relationship. In the current study, we sample 55 parameters (both electrical and thermal) using Latin Hypercube Sampling (LHS), which is a method for efficiently and evenly sampling a high-dimensional space (for more details, see [6, 7]). Sensitivity results are summarized using Sobol' indices, which range between zero and one and measure the fraction of total QoI variance that can be attributed to the uncertainty in each parameter. For brevity, we refer the reader to [8, 9] for more details on Sobol' Indices. All parameters are sampled uniformly to avoid biasing the sensitivity results.

Results

The model described in the prior section was run from heat pellet initiation to freeze-out (the time where any cell is more than 90% re-solidified). To test the effect of the decoupling approach where the electrical domain uses a coarser mesh, the simulation was run in two configurations: one with a coarser electrical mesh (10 radial elements in the electrical mesh and 100 radial elements in the thermal mesh) and one with identical meshes (both using 100 radial elements). The effect on run-time of this change was substantial, with the different-mesh configuration taking 5.8x less time to complete the simulation on the same number of MPI ranks.

Voltage Predictions: The predicted voltage from all three taps is shown in Figure 4 for both mesh configurations.

The effect of multiple taps is visible in the 14 V tap trace at 10 and 20 seconds, when the current pulse on the 4 V tap causes a drop in the voltage supplied at the

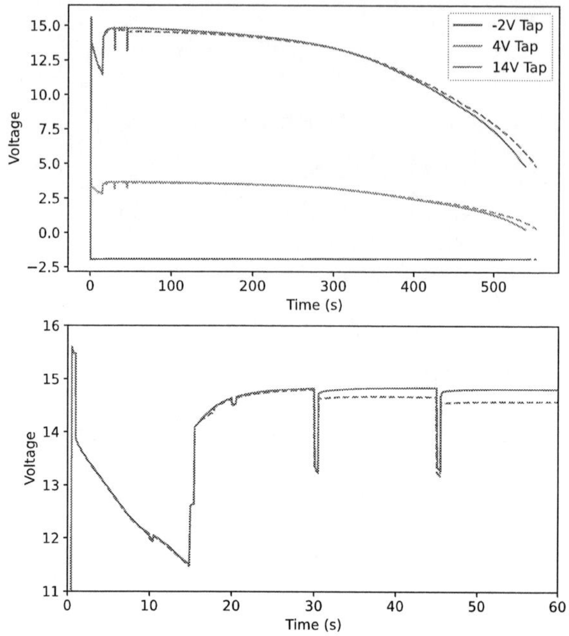

Figure 4. Predicted voltage vs. time with a coarser electrical mesh (solid lines) and identical meshes (dashed lines) showing performance under load and the relative effect of using a coarser electrical mesh.

14 V tap. The behavior with the different mesh configurations is nearly indistinguishable at early times, but there is a small difference in polarization loss in the 30 to 200 second range.

Some of the relevant quantities of interest (QOIs) from the full battery simulation are the rise time (defined here as time for the 14 V tap to reach 10 V), voltages at various times, and the freeze-out time (the time when any cell is more than 90% re-solidified). A comparison of how these QOIs change with the two mesh configurations is shown in Table 1.

Table 1. Change in quantities of interest from using dissimilar meshes (R10) vs the same mesh (R100)

QOI	R100	R10	Change
Rise Time (s)	0.457	0.455	0.44 %
V(10.2s)	11.967	11.987	0.17 %
V(25.0s)	14.756	14.781	0.17 %
V(60.0s)	14.576	14.809	1.60 %
V(200s)	14.190	14.281	0.64 %
Freeze (s)	553.45	539.49	2.52 %

Table 2. Main Sobol' Indices for simulation scalar responses (highlighted cells indicate $S > 0.10$)

Parameter	$T_{max,cath}$	$T_{max,ano}$	Rise Time	V_{max}
$V_{heatpellet}$	0.06	0.09	0.82	0.03
$k_{insulator}$	0.01	0.06	0.00	0.08
$k_{blanket}$	0.00	0.02	0.01	0.02
$C_{p,heatpellet}$	0.24	0.21	0.00	0.25
$C_{p,collector}$	0.17	0.13	0.00	0.27
$k_{cathode}$	0.35	0.02	0.00	0.03
$C_{p,insulator}$	0.07	0.03	0.00	0.03
$C_{p,anode}$	0.00	0.04	0.00	0.15
k_{anode}	0.01	0.30	0.00	0.00

Sensitivity Study: The Sobol' indicies for the various input parameters for select QOIs are shown in Table 2 (for a different battery). The most important input parameter for rise time prediction is the heat pellet burn speed ($V_{heatpellet}$). Other quantities, such as the maximum anode or cathode temperature, have a strong dependence on thermal properties (conductivity, k and specific heat, C_p). The predicted maximum voltage is sensitive to the specific heat of the stack components, likely through the temperature-dependence of the open-circuit voltage. These parameters, along with an uncertainty analysis, can help define which properties have the highest impact on predictions and which may require more detailed measurements.

Summary & Conclusions

In this work we presented a method for reducing the computational cost of a full-battery coupled thermal-electrical model using different mesh discretizations for different transport equations. We demonstrate that this approach provides greater than 5x reduction in computational cost while preserving accuracy of key quantities of interest.

We also developed a model sensitivity workflow to calculate Sobol' indices for a full-battery model to help quantify which model inputs have the largest impact on predicted quantities. This approach can be extended to include a large number of inputs and quantities of interest, and can be used to define where property measurements will provide the highest impact to the accuracy of the model predictions.

Acknowledgments

The authors gratefully acknowledge funding from the Joint Department of Defense/Department of Energy Munitions Technology Development Program. Sandia National Laboratories is a multi-mission laboratory managed and operated by National Technology and Engineering Solutions of Sandia, LLC., a wholly owned subsidiary of Honeywell International, Inc., for the U.S. Department of Energy's National Nuclear Security Administration under contract DE-NA0003525. The views expressed in this article do not necessarily represent the views of the U.S. Department of Energy or the United States Government. Unclassified Unlimited Release.

References

1. Voskuilen, T., H. Moffat, B. Schroeder, and S. Roberts. "Multi-fidelity electrochemical modeling of thermally activated battery cells." *Journal of Power Sources*, vol. 488, p. 229469, 2021.

2. Voskuilen, T., C. Jove-Colon, H. Moffat, B. Schroeder, B. Trembacki, and S. Roberts. "Multi-Physics Cost and Complexity Reduction Strategies for Modeling Thermally Activated Batteries." Proceedings of the 48th Power Sources Conference, 2018.

3. Voskuilen, T., J. Hewson, H. Moffat, and S. Roberts. "Multi-Physics, Multi-Plateua Reaction Model for LiSi/FeS_2 Batteries." Proceedings of the 47th Power Sources Conference, 2016.

4. Roberts, S. A., K. N. Long, J. R. Clausen, M. R. Martinez, E. S. Piekos, and A. M. Grillet. "Towards a Coupled Multiphysics Model of Molten Salt Battery Mechanics." Proceedings of the 46th Power Sources Conference, 2014.

5. Krieger, F. C. and M. Ding. "Heat Transfer in the LCCM Thermal Reserve Battery." Army research laboratory report ARL-TR-4843, 2009.

6. McKay, M. D., R. J. Beckman, and W. J. Conover. "A Comparison of Three Methods for Selecting Values of Input Variables in the Analysis of Output from a Computer Code." *Technometrics*, vol. 21, no. 2, pp. 239–245, 1979.

7. Swiler, L. P. and G. D. Wyss. "A User's Guide to Sandia's Latin Hypercube Sampling Software: LHS UNIX Library/Standalone Version." Tech. Rep. SAND2004-2439, Sandia National Laboratories, 2004.

8. Sobol', I. M. "Global Sensitivity Indices for Nonlinear Mathematical Models and their Monte Carlo estimates." *Mathematics and Computers in Simulation*, vol. 55, no. 1, pp. 271–280, 2001.

9. Li, C. and S. Mahadevan. "An Efficient Modularized Sample-Based Method to Estimate the First-Order Sobol' Index." *Reliability Engineering and System Safety*, vol. 153, pp. 110–121, 2016.

Development of a Cloud-Based Tool for Predicting Thermal Battery Performance: TABS v6

*Scott A. Roberts**, Adam V. Baca, Sylvain R. Bernard, Wesley A. Brooks, Ashley C. Fate, Emily Heintzelman, Edward S. Piekos, Tyler G. Voskuilen**

Sandia National Laboratories, PO Box 5800, MS 0836, Albuquerque, NM, 87185-0828

*Corresponding Author: sarober@sandia.gov, (505) 844-7957

Abstract: *Predicting the thermal and electrical performance of a thermal battery using computer simulations has the potential to save significant time and cost in the battery development process. However, traditional battery models can have a high barrier to adoption, often limited to those with significant expertise in computational modeling. We have previously developed the Thermally Activated Battery Simulator (TABS) [1] as a user interface to wrap around models for thermal performance and single-cell electrochemical performance. This capability has enabled battery designers at Sandia and in the US Department of Defense to predict battery thermal performance and reduce design cycles. However, the barriers to adoption of the legacy TABS simulation were still significant.*

In a companion talk, we present a new, advanced model that couples thermal and electrochemical performance at a full thermal battery scale [2]. Because of this significant increase in predictive capability — and simultaneously the computational expense required to solve it — we took the opportunity to re-develop TABS as a modern, cloud-based web application with a significantly improved user experience. We performed in-depth user experience research, tightly coupled with the consistent design of a new user interface and implementation using modern web technologies. By using cloud computing technologies, we moved the computational expense off the user's desktop and onto shared computing resources, allowing the user to focus on battery design and performance.

In this paper, we detail the development of version 6 of TABS. We discuss lessons learned from previous TABS deployments and from user experience research. We also demonstrate its ability to allow users to intuitively study the impact of battery design changes on performance while accurately simulating the electrical performance of complex battery designs.

Keywords: thermal battery; computational modeling

Introduction

Version 5 of TABS [1] has gained wide adoption amongst the thermal battery design and analysis community, including at Sandia National Laboratories and the U.S. Department of Defense laboratories. However, this previous version had focused on two analysis scenarios - thermal analysis of full thermal batteries and electrochemical analysis of single cells. With the development of a full battery coupled thermal and electrochemical model [2], we must now consider the deployment of this novel capability to our users.

The previous version of TABS suffered from a number of barriers to even wider adoption. First is its reliance on the Linux operating system. While Sandia could deploy the software to Windows computer in virtual machine environment, this is less than ideal for a majority of our potential users. Secondly, while the user interface (UI) was fairly intuitive (especially when compared to building the simulation manually), it still required extensive training to learn its effective use.

TABS development process

TABS version 6 (v6) is developed from the ground up as a cloud-hosted web application to provide thermal and electrochemical modeling capabilities for full thermal batteries to our user base. Its development principles and technologies are outlined below.

User experience research: The goal of TABS v6 is to provide an updated user interface and incorporate improved functionality to positively impact the user experience. To achieve our goal, the TABS team needed a foundational understanding of the users and their needs rooted in user research. Users were identified as existing and prospective users (people who "should" be using the tool but are not) to identify: what is working well in the existing tool; opportunities for improvement; barriers to adoption; and gaps between user expectations of the new tool capability and design.

The foundational research helped identify five distinct use cases for the tool. Use cases help us understand the types of engineering question categories users are attempting to answer. This understanding leads to better system design because the team intentionally, and explicitly, targets satisfying the identified use cases. For example, "Ad-Hoc Curiosities" was identified as a use case where users wanted to be exploratory — they wanted to investigate engineering questions as a means to building more informed research inquiries; "we don't know what we don't know." Additionally, the foundational research helped define specific user types and their respective design drivers. We can consider the needs of each user type as the team works to design a tool to meet specific user needs. For example, a "Novice User" wants to "be empowered to investigate a whole manner of engineering questions." To accomplish this driver, TABS v6 needs to provide; a clean, simple UI; an easily accessible tool; the ability to progress through standard and non-standard workflows; enable the user to answer their questions without tool subject matter expertise (SME) intervention; help grow the user's expertise through exploration and access to support materials. When we understand 'why' behind user's needs, we build better systems to meet those needs.

User interface design: The user research directs the UI design; once the user data is collected and user needs are understood, ideation and system design occur. During the initial design concept, key stakeholders are included to help ensure design concepts meet both user and customer requirements. Design concepts, presented as low- and high-fidelity mockups (figs. 1a and 1b), are presented to users as tangible hypotheses the research team looks to invalidate. Understanding how the design concept(s) fail to meet user needs allows for evolution of the design. The research team also focuses on task accomplishment — users are provided with tasks they should be able to accomplish if the system is designed correctly to meet their needs and expectations. This research method is called *usability testing.* During usability testing, if users are unable to successfully accomplish tasks, researchers identify patterns and findings as "usability issues." New design concepts are created (fig. 1c) to help overcome usability issues and the new concepts are tested with users. The design, test, and refinement process is iterative and requires multiple rounds of feedback elicitation and testing throughout the development lifecycle.

User interface implementation: One of the goals of version 6 of TABS is to modernize the overall user experience while working in the TABS user interface. The UI has been upgraded from a Java Swing application to a Vue.js web application utilizing the Vuetify material design library. Vue.js is a progressive javascript framework built on top of HTML, CSS, and Javascript. It is a reactive, component based framework that also provides a compiler-optimized rendering system. Vuetify is a material design framework that provides a large selection of components that help give the UI a consistent look and feel. In addition, the UI makes use of Chart.js, Three.js, and Trame, for 2D and 3D modeling and results visualization. The UI has a back-end written in Node/Express that utilizes a MongoDB database and also interfaces with the tabs-api Kubernetes orchestrator.

Cloud computing infrastructure: By adopting cloud computing technologies, TABS will easily support on-demand simulation requests from the new web interface, via horizontal scaling. The various codes associated with TABS for backend computing are being containerized and then orchestrated on a Kubernetes cluster. We have developed a RESTful API to help with the management of these containers, allowing any client to submit jobs and retrieve results. Our containers are being developed and hosted on GitLab, leveraging continuous integration pipelines to build updated container images and push them onto our registry. Our Kubernetes deployment pulls these images directly from our registry for the API itself and the simulation codes. The on-demand simulations are ran as Kubernetes jobs. We are also leveraging a Simple Storage Service (S3) instance for an API-based data management solution. Thanks to that approach we are able to share data across the web application, the backend API, and the multiple ad-hoc Kubernetes jobs.

TABS v6

It would be a near-impossible task to fully describe the advancements and features of TABS v6. Instead, in fig. 2 we briefly highlight some of the key innovations and design changes in this upcoming release.

When first entering the tool, users are greeted with a new landing page (fig. 2a) that more intuitively guides users towards their goal. On first use, a panel on the right orients the users to the workflow for building a battery. Templates are available to quickly jump-start simulations with battery designs that they might already be familiar with. Once users have their own projects, they are also presented a searchable, filterable list of their projects for quick access.

The battery design page (fig. 2b) will be familiar to previous users, but with significantly improved graphical layout and an improved 3D to-scale view of the battery (fig. 2c). Because of the addition of electrochemical physics to the model, fig. 2d allows specification of the voltage tap locations within the battery, along with specification of the transient load (current, voltage, or resistance) experienced by that tap.

The materials database experience has been completely revamped. To allow for carefree editing of material properties, upon entering the database editor (fig. 2e), the user is greeted with an orientation as to the hierarchy of material property databases. The reference database of material properties that comes

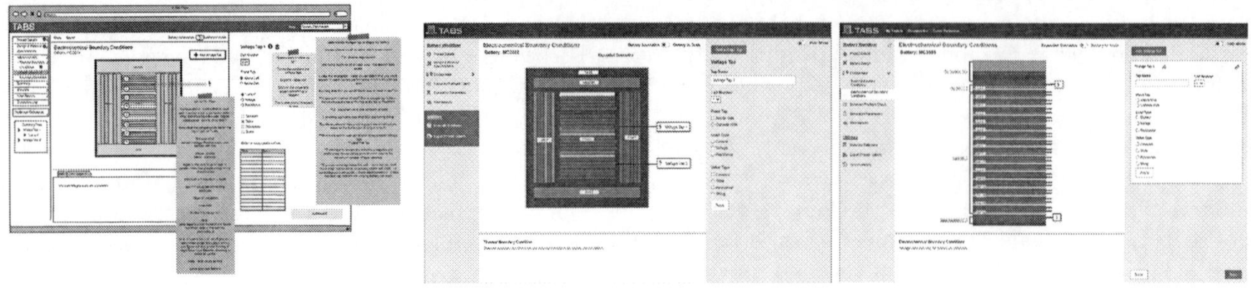

(a) Low fidelity mockup **(b)** First high fidelity mockup **(c)** Second high fidelity mockup

Figure 1. Evolution of electrochemical boundary condition specification feature from low fidelity (a) to high fidelity (b, c) mockups.

with TABS cannot be edited, but users can freely clone those materials and make modifications without fear of messing up other projects. For new materials that show promise, properties can be promoted to the user's personal database for use in other projects (fig. 2f), or shared with the TABS developers for potential inclusion in the reference database. The materials are easily filterable and sortable.

Users have long asked for ways to make (and later compare) tweaks on the same battery design without creating new projects. In TABS v6, we are introducing two new concepts. First is the "design iteration" (fig. 2g), which allows users to start with a baseline battery design and make modifications to it (e.g., change constituent material thicknesses or material properties). Secondly, the user can define multiple "test conditions" for each design (fig. 2h), which includes things like initial battery temperature, external thermal boundary conditions, or loads on each tap. Each of these design iterations and test conditions have their own simulations, and the results can be compared on the same plot (fig. 2k).

Prior to running simulations, a series of pre-checks (fig. 2i) must be conducted to verify the validity of the design and to calculate certain statistics about the battery. The performance simulations themselves are performed simultaneously for all test conditions using secure cloud computing resources.

Finally, we have put significant investment into improving the ability to post-process and visualize the simulation results (fig. 2k). Line plots of key quantities of interest are available, and you can compare simulations for multiple design iterations and test conditions on the same plot, exporting the completed figures for use in reports and presentations. Users can also make multiple plots, customizing the content of each one (fig. 2l). Two-dimensional plots of calculated variables are also available.

Summary

We expect that the advancements in TABS v6 (both in terms of model capability and interface usability) will be strongly desired by the thermal battery design community. We expect to complete development of the first production capability this year, with deployment to licensed users in early 2024.

Acknowledgments

The authors gratefully acknowledge funding from the Joint Department of Defense/Department of Energy Munitions Technology Development Program. Sandia National Laboratories is a multi-mission laboratory managed and operated by National Technology and Engineering Solutions of Sandia, LLC., a wholly owned subsidiary of Honeywell International, Inc., for the U.S. Department of Energy's National Nuclear Security Administration under contract DE-NA0003525. The views expressed in this article do not necessarily represent the views of the U.S. Department of Energy or the United States Government.

References

1. Roberts, S., C. Jove-Colon, H. Moffat, M. Neilsen, E. Piekos, B. Schroeder, B. Trembacki, and T. Voskuilen. "TABS : A Thermal Battery Desktop Design Tool." Proceedings of the 48th Power Sources Conference, 2018.

2. Voskuilen, T. G., H. K. Moffat, N. W. Porter, and S. A. Roberts. "Coupled Thermal-Electrochemical Full Battery Modeling of LiSi/FeS_2 Batteries." In *Proceedings of the 49th Power Sources Conference*, 2023.

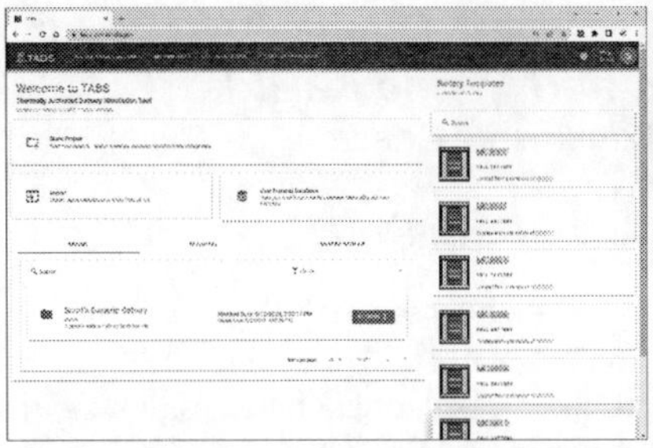

(a) Front landing page showing templates and user projects.

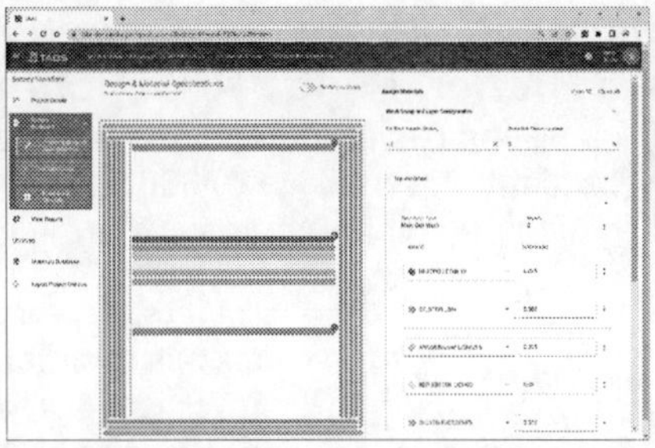

(b) Point-and-click battery design pulling materials from database.

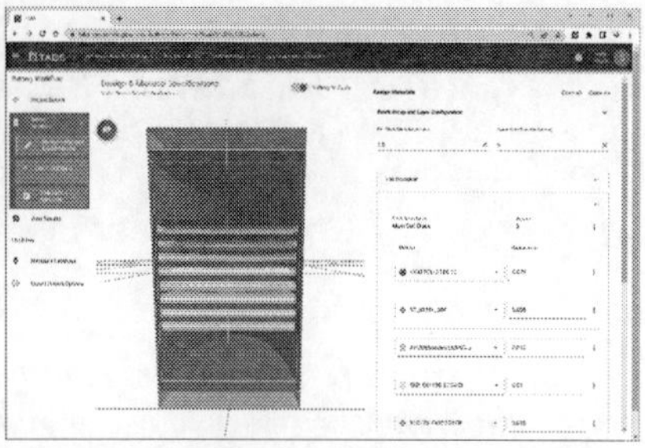

(c) View your battery design to scale in 3D.

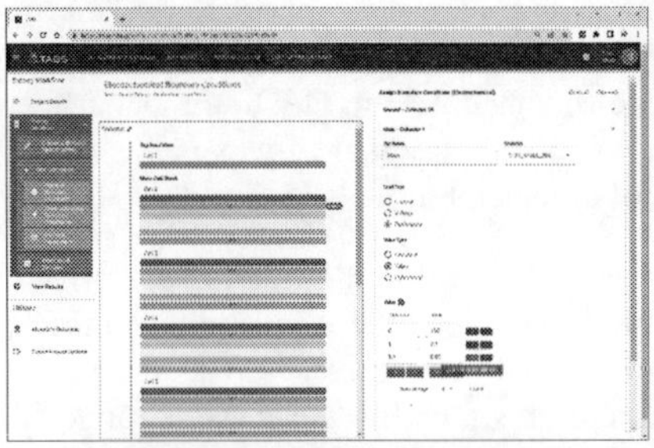

(d) Specification of voltage tap loads.

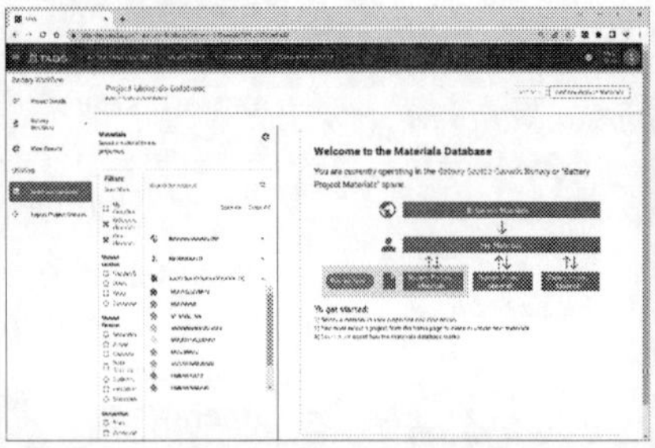

(e) Landing page for the materials database editor, showing the hierarchy of databases.

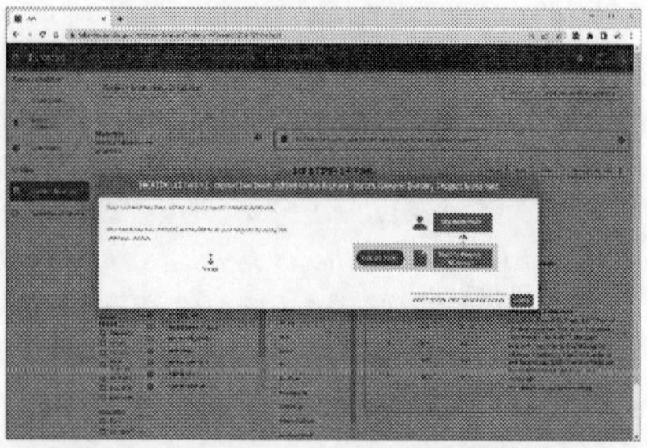

(f) Ability to promote properties to user database after editing.

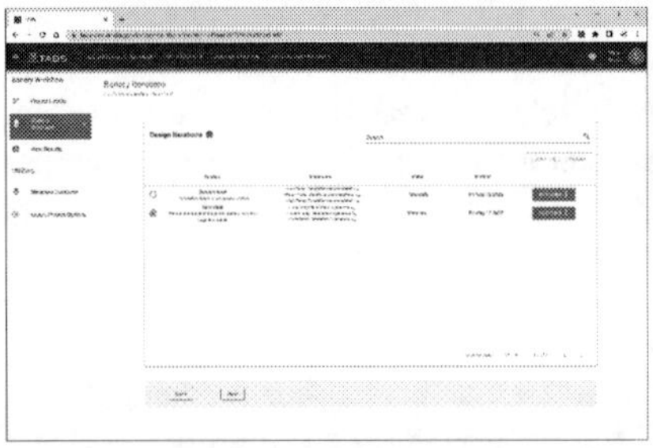

(g) Design iterations, allowing multiple simulations per design.

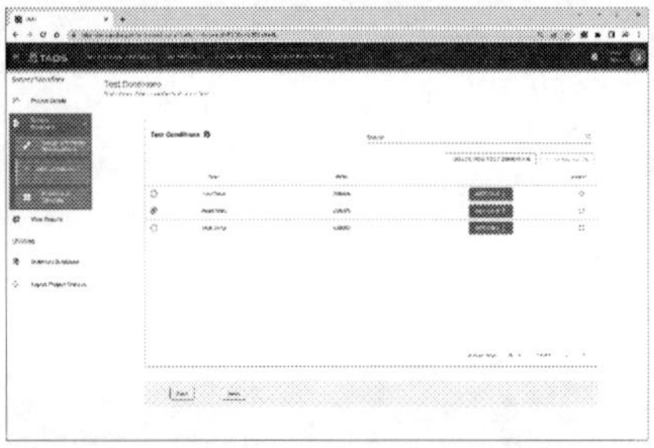

(h) Test conditions, allowing simulating multiple initial temperatures or boundary conditions simultaneously.

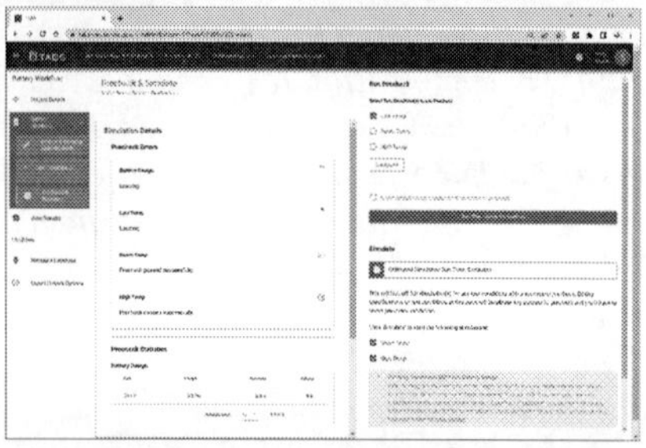

(i) Pre-simulation check calculates key metrics to provide feedback before a full simulation, ensuring it will run well.

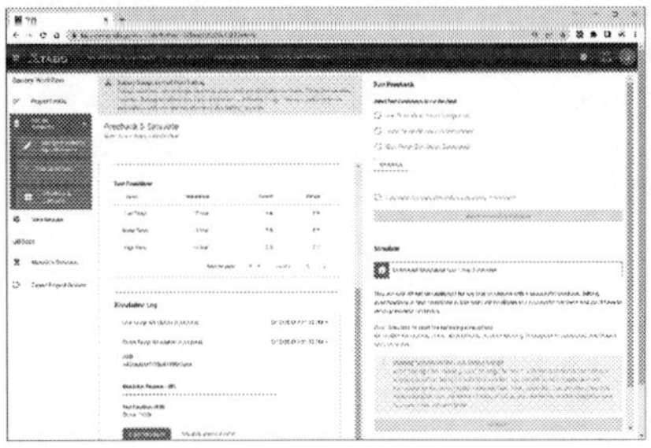

(j) Run simulations using cloud computing resources and monitor progress.

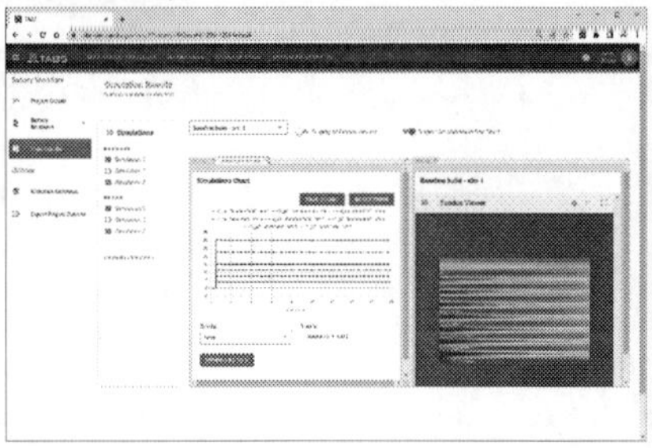

(k) Visualize simulations using line plots and 2D viewer, comparing design iterations and test conditions simultaneously.

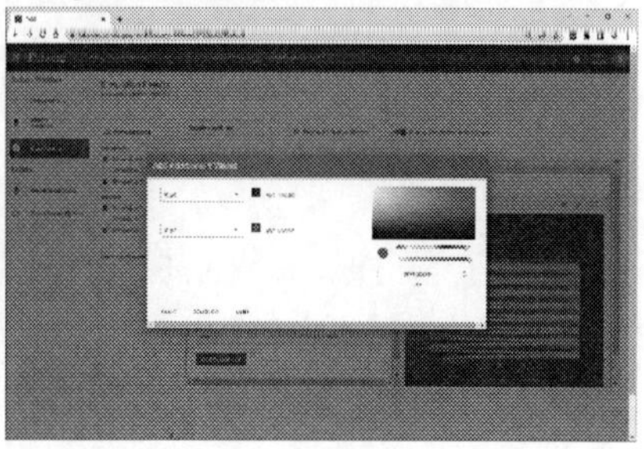

(l) Plots can be customized to choose which color to use for each variable.

Figure 2. Screenshots of the new TABS v6 tool highlighting new elements over previous TABS versions.

Thermal Characterization of Materials for Improved Modeling and Simulation of Thermal Batteries

Giuseppe L. Di Benedetto, Charles W. McMullan, Lauren A. Morris, Daniel P. Schmidt, Aaron M. Stern, Richard Dratler, Peggy A. Sanchez, and Lynne K. Rider

U.S. Army Combat Capabilities Development Command Armaments Center,
Picatinny Arsenal, NJ 07806, USA
Contact Author Email: giuseppe.l.dibenedetto.civ@army.mil / 1-973-724-1977

Abstract

Thermal batteries are the predominant power source for defense munitions systems due to their high-power performance and extreme ruggedness. U.S. Army Combat Capabilities Development Command Armaments Center (DEVCOM-AC) employs modeling and simulation to understand and optimize internal heat distribution to improve thermal battery performance. Sandia National Laboratory's Thermally Activated Battery Simulator (TABS) is a robust software tool set for simulating heat transfer throughout the entire lifetime of a thermal battery; its simulations rely on the use of physical and chemical material properties within the materials database.

In this study, anode, cathode, separator, and insulation materials were characterized experimentally using simultaneous thermal analysis (STA). Temperature-dependent heat capacity, melting temperature, enthalpy of melting, decomposition temperature, etc. were determined by differential scanning calorimetry (DSC) and thermogravimetric analysis (TGA) over the full range of operating temperatures for thermal batteries (25-600 °C). The experimentally determined thermal properties were uploaded into the TABS materials database and simulations attained with the updated material properties were compared to those generated using the legacy database. TABS simulations estimate internal cell stack temperatures for various configurations and heat balances that allow comparison of peak temperature and runtime.

Keywords

thermal properties; thermal battery; molten salt battery; modeling and simulation; thermal analysis

Introduction

Back in 1991, the Deputy Secretary of Defense approved a plan to strengthen the use of modeling and simulation (M&S) across the Department of Defense (DoD) to aid in research and development, test and evaluation, and operation and cost analysis [1]. The initiative has proven to be heavily successful, especially as computing technology has advanced allowing even desktop computers to design and model DoD products [2-3]. Over the years, as M&S tools were validated with test and evaluation, considerable M&S implementation has accelerated research and development and resulted in significant schedule and cost savings [2-3]. In recent years, M&S tools in the commercial sector shifted some focus to modeling power sources, especially with the potential to investigate new chemistries for batteries [4]. However, these M&S investigations focused on commercial battery applications, and, naturally, did not include niche battery applications such as missiles and munitions [4]. Focus on the M&S of missiles and munitions batteries, particularly thermal reserve batteries, also known as molten salt reserve batteries, would not occur until the DoD and Department of Energy (DOE) made considerable investments toward the development of advanced models [5-7].

Thermal reserve battery design and modeling are difficult as their performance is dependent on many intricate material and interfacial parameters [8]. The high operational temperatures with the vast range of environmental temperatures required, as well as the relatively small size of thermal battery cells make it incredibly problematic to accurately study and observe these thermal and electrochemical processes in isolation without high-end characterization equipment and specialized custom test fixtures [8-14]. To overcome these obstacles, multiple efforts have been progressing to develop competing thermal reserve battery design models. The Erigo Technologies led model was funded through several DoD SBIR programs and progressed to establish a code consisting of a 2-D or 3-D finite element thermal model coupled to a user-defined number of 1-D electrochemical models of individual battery cells [6,15]. The model has limitations but has improved through corrective fitting to experimental data [15]. The other major model is a multi-physics simulator called Thermally Activated Battery Simulator (TABS) [16]. TABS was developed and led by Sandia National Laboratories, and partially funded through the DoD/DOE Joint Munitions Program [16]. TABS started as only a thermal model but has progressed to include predictions of electrochemical performance and coupling of the thermal-electrochemical portions for single-cell and full battery simulations [16-17]. Both models allow customized materials databases through the inclusion of accurately measured material and thermal properties.

DEVCOM-AC has adopted TABS v5.1 to understand and optimize thermal reserve battery design and performance. To fully accomplish this adoption, DEVCOM-AC engineers have thermally characterized many thermal reserve battery materials including cathodes, electrolytes, separators, anodes, insulations, and other internal material components, and established an advanced TABS Materials Database [14]. Utilizing the advanced TABS Materials Database, an investigation to model and improve the Low-Cost Competent Munition (LCCM) Battery performance was completed.

Material Characterization

Material Characterization Details: For all internal material research and development investigations, an extensive material characterization strategy is employed to monitor and understand effects of the investigation on the materials and thermal properties of the samples [14]. Complete thermal analysis was performed using a Netzsch STA 449F1 Jupiter 449C (Netzsch Instruments North America, Burlington, MA, USA) thermal analysis system: simultaneous TGA-DSC (thermogravimetric analysis-differential scanning calorimetry) was performed in a silicon carbide (SiC) furnace under Ar with a heating rate of 5 K min^{-1}; heat capacity (Cp) measurements were performed in a platinum (Pt) furnace under Ar with a heating rate of 20 K min^{-1} using sapphire as a reference standard. Data analysis was performed using Proteus Analysis software and Cp was calculated using ASTM 1269.

TABS Material Properties: In order to add new materials to the TABS Materials Database, key material and thermal properties must be accurately measured or retrieved from reliable sources. The key thermal properties are powder density (ρ), pellet density, solidus temperature, peak temperature, liquidus temperature, latent heat of fusion (ΔH_m), heat capacity (Cp), and thermal conductivity (k). The database has the ability to vary the properties based on temperature if information is available. Using the characterization capabilities described earlier, Cp and k were measured as a function of temperature as well as a function of powders or consolidated pellets. Characterization was also conducted for pure compounds and formulated mixtures. The TABS Materials Database has options for M&S with both sets of material and thermal properties. Figure 1 displays an example of measured thermal characterization results. In this case, the measured results are micron FeS_2 and nanostructured FeS_2. The DSC and TGA data were used to determine solidus temperature, peak temperature, and liquidus temperature, while the calculated Cp was recorded as a function of temperature and added accordingly to the TABS Materials Database.

Modeling & Simulation Parameters

Battery Design: The LCCM battery was chosen for the investigation due to its unique design, history, and Government owned technical data package. Figure 2 shows a cross-section of the test setup used by Krieger, et. al [19] when evaluating the performance of the LCCM battery. The large steel case and insulation layers made up the reusable test fixture (RTF). The battery chemistry was assumed to be 95% LiSi/5% electrolye-binder mix for the anode, 65% LiCl-KCl/35% binder for the separator, and 73.5%FeS_2/1.5% Li_2O/25% electrolyte-binder mix for the cathode.

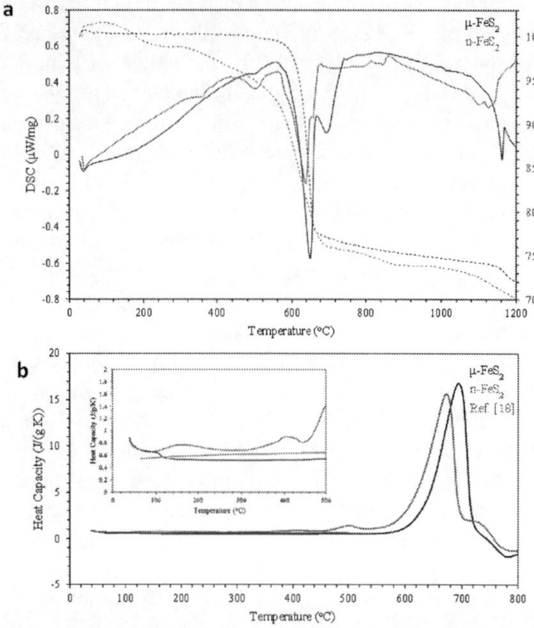

Figure 1: Example measured thermal property data: (a) DSC (solid) and TGA (dashed) of μ-FeS2 and milled n-FeS_2 powders in argon at 5 K min^{-1}, and (b) calculated heat capacity of μ-FeS_2 and n-FeS2 plotted against reference data [18] with inset showing heat capacity data for T < 500 °C (932 °F).

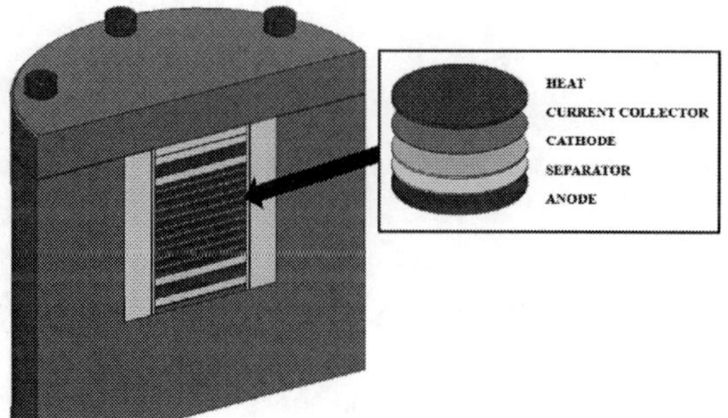

Figure 2: Cross-section drawing of LCCM in RTF assembly with cell component details.

Modeling Parameters: Full battery TABS models utilized radiative and convective boundary conditions for the top, side, and bottom of the battery can. The emissivity of the can material was assumed to be 0.25, and the environmental temperature for discharge was 20°C (68°F). The initial starting temperature of the battery and all of its components was set to either -40°C (-40°F) or +70°C

(+158°F) to evaluate the heat balance of the battery at hot and cold.

Single cell models used the output of the full battery model to define the thermal environment of the cell. There are 9 cells in the LCCM model [19-20], the single cell model used the thermal environment of cell number 5. The system load was assumed to have a load with a constant resistance of 1Ω. Single cell models were only investigated at cold since the model does not include the effects of overheating, so discharge at cold will be the factor limiting performance estimates. The multi-plateau mode for both the anode and cathode were used to improve accuracy.

Modeling & Simulation Results

Full Battery Thermal results: Three versions of the LCCM battery were modeled. V1 was the base configuration, V2 utilized a Fiberfrax based insulation blanket, and V3 used an advanced insulation material. Figure 3 shows the full battery thermal results using the temperature of all nodes of the separator at -40°C (-40°F) to evaluate the thermal lifetime of the battery. The thermal lifetime of this battery configuration is projected to be reduced with the V2 configuration and improved with the V3 configuration.

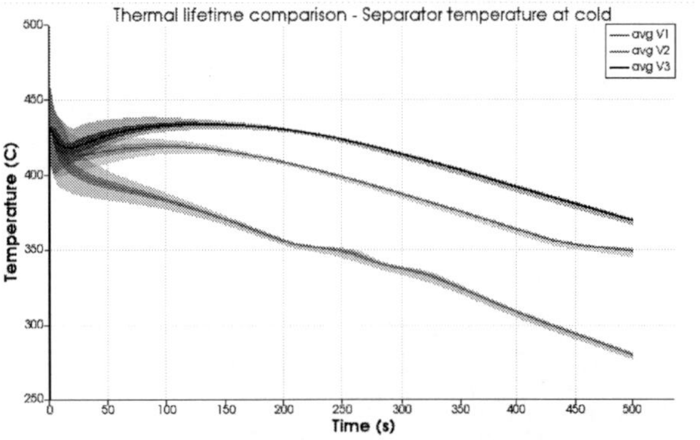

Figure 3: TABS simulations of all battery separator temperature nodes with starting temperature of -40°C (-40°F) to estimate thermal lifetime of the battery.

Figure 4 shows the temperature of all cathode nodes at +70°C (+158°F), which is when it would be most likely to decompose. While the model assumes this is not occurring, the cathode will start to decompose when exposed to these conditions in reality, as it will negatively affect battery performance. The cathode temperatures near activation are all very similar for these three battery configurations, which indicates that the change in configurations is not expected to reduce the performance of discharging the battery at hot with all other parameters held equal. It does not appear that a change in the heat balance of the cell stack is necessary.

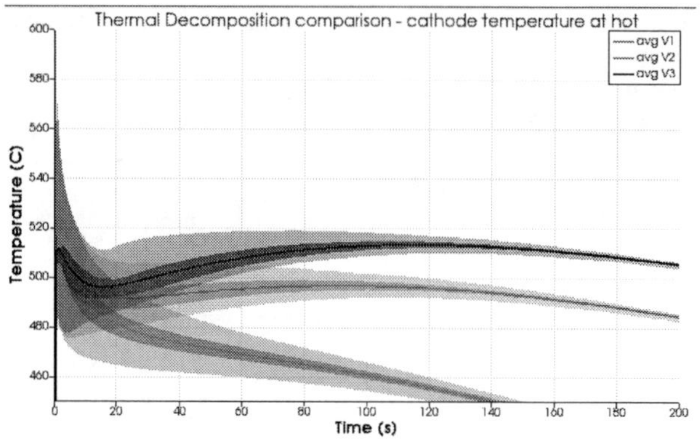

Figure 4: TABS simulations of all battery cathode temperature nodes with starting temperature of 70°C to estimate thermal decomposition.

Single cell modeling allows us to estimate the electrochemical output of a cell with these different thermal profiles. For this study we have multiplied the voltage prediction of the middle cell by the number of cells to estimate the overall performance of the battery. This is likely an optimistic estimation since the middle cell is probably the warmest cell. This is important to keep in mind when comparing to application specific requirements and margin projections, but the trend should still be the same regardless of which cells were utilized in the analysis.

Figure 5 shows these voltage predictions for each of the battery configurations. The runtime to 12V is 112s, 109s, and 137s for V1, V2, and V3 respectively. If you consider the baseline as the worst performer, the advanced insulation is projected to improve runtime by 30% with no additional changes.

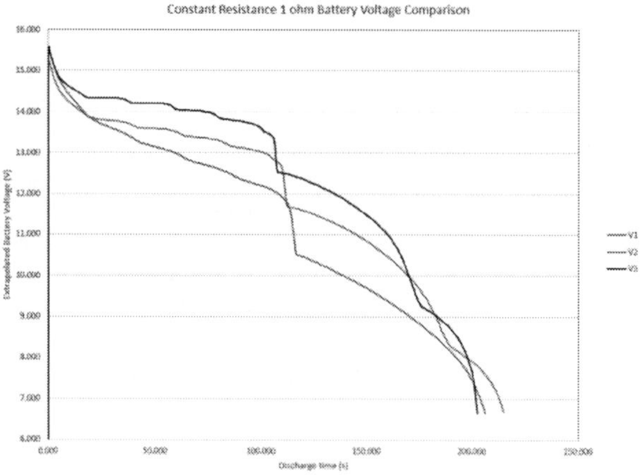

Figure 5: TABS single cell simulations extrapolated to battery performance by multiplying the result by the number of cells.

Conclusion

These simulations describe an approach to evaluating the expected performance of a thermal battery design with various insulation materials. The materials characterization work we have completed allows us to make these estimates of battery performance without even building a battery. While this is not a substitute for actual prototypes, it could be used to focus a more limited set of prototype builds on those designs that are expected to have the most impact.

Acknowledgements

This work is supported by the Power for Advanced Munitions effort on DEVCOM-AC's Fuze and Power Technologies for Munitions program, directly supporting the Army Modernization priority for Long Range Precision Fires (LRPF).

References

1. Piplani, Col. L. K., et. al., "Systems Acquisition Manager's Guide for the use of Models and Simulations," Report of the DSMC 1993-1994 Military Research Fellows, Defense Systems Management College Press, Ft. Belvoir, VA, September 1994.
2. Carter, III, J. R., "A Business Case for Modeling and Simulation," U.S. Army AMRDEC Special Report RD-AS-01-02, September 2001.
3. Oswalt, I., et. al., "Calculating return on investment for U.S. Department of Defense modeling and simulation," Defense A R Journal, vol. 18, no. 2, 2011.
4. Tamilselvi, S., et. al., "A Review of Battery Modeling Techniques," Sustainability, vol. 13, p. 10042, 2021.
5. Ingersoll, D., et. al., "Highly Instrumented Thermal Battery for Thermal Model Validation," Proceedings of the 43rd Power Sources Conference, Philadelphia, PA, 7-10 July, 2008.Grillet,
6. Kenton, M., et. al., "A Comprehensive, Physics-Based Model for Thermal Batteries," Proceedings of the 44th Power Sources Conference, Las Vegas, NV, 14-17 June, 2010.
7. Roberts, S. A., et. al., "Modeling Separator Deformation and Electrolyte Flow in Thermally-Activated Batteries," Proceedings of the 45th Power Sources Conference, pp. 603-606, 2012.
8. Guidotti, R. A., and P. J. Masset, "Thermally activated ("thermal") battery technology: Part I: An overview," Journal of Power Sources, vol. 161, no. 2, pp. 1443-1449, 2006.
9. Masset, P. J., and R. A. Guidotti, "Thermally activated ("thermal") battery technology: Part II. Molten salt electrolytes," Journal of Power Sources, vol. 162, pp. 397-414, 2007.
10. Masset, P. J., and R. A. Guidotti, "Thermally activated ("thermal") battery technology: Part IIIa: FeS_2 cathode material," Journal of Power Sources, vol. 177, pp. 595-609, 2008.
11. Masset, P. J., and R. A. Guidotti, "Thermally activated ("thermal") battery technology: Part IIIb. Sulfur and oxide-based cathode materials," Journal of Power Sources, vol. 178, pp. 456-466, 2008.
12. Guidotti, R. A., and P. J. Masset, "Thermally activated ("thermal") battery technology: Part IV. Anode materials," Journal of Power Sources, vol. 183, pp. 388-398, 2008.
13. A. M., et. al., "High temperature mechanical properties of thermal battery separators," Proceedings of the 44th Power Sources Conference, Las Vegas, NV, 14-17 June, 2010.
14. Di Benedetto, G. L., et. al., "Nanostructuring of Iron Disulfide Cathode Materials for Enhanced Thermal Batteries," J. Electrochem. Soc., vol. 168, no. 4, 046520, 2021.
15. Kenton, M., and D. Bhakta, "Improving Thermal Battery Performance through Model-Based Development and Improved Component Designs," Proceedings of the 48th Power Sources Conference, Denver, CO, 11-14 June, 2018.
16. Roberts, S. A., et. al., "TABS: A Thermal Battery Desktop Design Tool," Proceedings of the 48th Power Sources Conference, Denver, CO, 11-14 June, 2018.
17. Voskuilen, T. G., et. al., "Multi-fidelity electrochemical modeling of thermally activated battery cells," Journal of Power Sources, vol. 488, 229469, 2021.
18. Gronvold, F., and E. F. Westrum, "Heat Capacities of iron disulfides Thermodynamics of marcasite from 5 to 700 K, pyrite from 300 to 780 K, and the transformation of marcasite to pyrite," J. Chem. Thermodyanmics, vol. 8, p. 1039, 1976.
19. Krieger, F. C., and M. Ding, "Heat Transfer in the LCCM Thermal Reserve Battery," Tech. Rep. ARL-TR-4843, Army Research Laboratory, 2009.
20. Krieger, F. C., "Reducing Low Cost Competent Munition (LCCM) Thermal Battery Volumesby Factors of 2 to 3 and Extending LCCM Thermal Lifetimes by Factors of 10 to 20 or More: Part 1," Tech. Rep. ARL-TR-8822, Army Research Laboratory, 2019.
21. Ahrens, J., et. al. "ParaView: An End-User Tool for Large Data Visualization," Tech. Rep. LA-UR-03-1560, Los Alamos National Laboratory, 2005.

Mechanical Characterization of Insulation Materials During Thermal Battery Manufacturing

Laura D. Jacobs, Christopher R. Esquibel, Christine C. Roberts, Henry A. Padilla
Sandia National Laboratories
Albuquerque, NM, USA, 87185-0613
ldjacob@sandia.gov /1-505-844-8521

Abstract

The current study focuses on the material properties of insulation materials during manufacturing of thermal batteries. Manufacturing is characterized by cyclic loading, short stabilization times, and the relatively quick application of loads. Rigidized Fiberfrax, MinK, Zircal, Duraboard, Microtherm and WDS Shape insulation materials are subjected to cyclic loading using comparable closing forces employed in thermal batteries, and stress-strain curves are reported. Insulation stress responses show evidence of both elastic and irrecoverable plastic behavior which are important to understand for specifying insulation thicknesses and closing pressures in thermal battery designs.

Keywords

Insulation; Closing Force; Modeling

Introduction

Porous, ceramic felt-based insulation materials are utilized axially above and below the electrochemical cell stack in thermal batteries. In addition to heat insulation, the materials maintain a compressive stress on the stack that enables proper cell wetting with electrolyte during activation and prevents pellet slip during mechanical environments. Computational performance models using digital engineering tools are increasingly important for achieving shorter design cycles, fewer costly development builds, and more optimized designs. A crucial piece of thermal battery modeling is the mechanical response, however performance models for are hindered by poorly characterized material behavior. The mechanical response of thermal battery insulation materials throughout its lifetime, from manufacturing through deployment and use, is largely unknown, despite their crucial function to ensure thermal performance and mechanical robustness.

Insulation materials that are suitable for inclusion in thermal batteries must have mechanical properties that withstand multiple load and unload cycles characteristic of thermal battery manufacturing, as well as recovery strain properties to allow for sufficient stress to remain on the stack after the battery is fired, the electrolyte melts, and the stack shrinks in height. The ability to maintain pressure on the stack after activation is crucial to the battery being able to operate before and after being subjected mechanical environments, maintaining electrical contact throughout the stack during events, and the closing pressure of the thermal battery must be matched to the thickness of insulation materials in the battery design to achieve a weldable case height.

The mechanical behaviors of insulation that are key to modeling thermal batteries include the elastic modulus, cylic loading hysteresis, recovery strain, and time dependent stress relaxation. Elastic modulus is a common parameter used in modeling. Cylic loading hysteresis is key to understanding the state of the insulation during and after manufacturing. Recovery strain behavior is crucial for modeling what happens in the battery post activation. Stress relaxation is needed to model the stress on the stack for different durations of service life. .

The current study focuses on the material response of insulation materials during manufacturing. Manufacturing is characterized by cyclic loading, short stabilization times, and the relatively quick application of loads. The experiments in this study mimic load profiles during manufacturing.

Experimental Method

Materials: Six insulation materials, either commonly found in thermal batteries or potential candidates for future designs, were selected for investigation.

The materials selected were Fiberfrax stiffened with a rigid binder, Fiberfrax Duraboard, Thermal Ceramics TE-1400 Min-K, WDS Shape, Zircal, and Microtherm.

Sample Preparation: The samples were primarily 1" diameter cylinders that were fabricated using a punch. The Zircal and WDS Shape samples were not conducive to punch fabrication and, instead, were cut into approximate cubeswith a 1" square face. The thickness of the samples was dictated by the thickness of the stock material. The rigidized Fiberfrax was only 0.100" in thickness, so to ensure that the deformations were measurable, 5 samples were stacked vertically to make a 0.5" thick specimen. Dimensions and pictures of the samples can be found in Table 1. After the samples were cut out, they were then dried at 600°C for 2 hours in a dryroom with a maximum dewpoint of -28°C and stored in vacuum sealed bags until testing. The samples were tested in a radially unconfined state, which differs from the radially confined state in actual batteries. They were chosen to be tested in a radially unconfined state to get the material response to create material models.

Table 1. Sample Dimensions

Material	Picture	Dimensions
Duraboard		1" D x 2" H
Fiberfrax		1" D x 0.1" H
Microtherm		1" D x 1.575" H
MinK		1"D x 3"H
WDS Shape		1" x 1" x 2"
Zircal		1" x 1" x 0.5"

Equipment: The experiments were conducted using an ADMET eXpert 2613 Dual Column Table Top Universal Testing System controlled using the MTEST Quattro Controller & Software. The test frame has the specifications shown in Table 2. A 10,000 lb load cell was used to make the force measurements. The ADMET was located in a dryroom with a maximum dewpoint of -28°C to test the materials in their dry state.

An Epsilon Technology Group model 3540-012M-ST deflectometer was used to measure sample deformation. It uses a full bridge arrangement for strain measurement. It has a 12 mm range with => 0.25% linearity of full displacement range (linear up to 30 microns).

Table 2. ADMET Specifications [1]

Characteristic	Specification
Capacity	11,250 lb
Stroke	46 inches
Total Vertical Test Space	52 inches
Speed(max):	20 inches/min

Crush Tests: Crush tests were performed, wherein each sample was loaded at increasing levels until it failed to support the load. The goal of the crush test was to collect information on the yield andfracture strength of the materials to inform test conditions for cyclic load testing.

Cyclic Tests: The goal of the cyclic load test was to mimic the cyclic loading experienced by the insulation material during battery manufacture. The tests were strain controlled using a crosshead velocity of 2 inches/second. Three samples of each material were loaded to a peak force and held at a constant strain for 2 minutes, then unloaded to 10 lbs and held at a constant strain for 2 minutes, twice, followed by being loaded to the peak stress and held at a constant strain for 5 minutes and then unloaded to 10 lbs and held at a constant strain for 1 minute. The peak forces were selected so that the stresses on the samples were both representative of battery closing pressures and below the yield or fracture stress determined in the crush test. The peak stresses for each material can be found in Table 3.

Table 3. Maximum Stress Applied in Cyclic Load Tests

Material	Maximum stress (psi)
Duraboard	250
Fiberfrax	150
Microtherm	150
MinK	150
WDS Shape	100
Zircal	400

Experimental Results

Crush Tests: The primary goal of the crush tests was to investigate the material response and use it to inform the cyclic load tests. Figure 1 shows a wide variety of material behaviors and load magnitudes at failure for the insulation materials.

The Zircal and rigidized Fiberfrax (FF) were the two stiffest materials and could support the greatest stress. Both stiffened as the stress increased. MinK and WDS Shape had very similar mechanical behaviors. They had a linear stress-strain relationship until failure and the lowest failure loads of all the materials. The Min-K maximum loads were lower than observed in-situ. One possible explanation for this is that, in-situ, the material is radially confined. Future testing should include radial confinement. Also, during punch fabrication, some of the material fibers were pulled, causing the samples to be curved rather than straight, and potentially weakening the material. The Microtherm was able to support more load than the WDS Shape and MinK and had an elastoplastic behavior. The Duraboard had a very long crushing phase which is nearly linear elastic prior to stiffening. A possible explanation for this behavior is that an initial densification must occur before the Duraboard supports larger stresses.

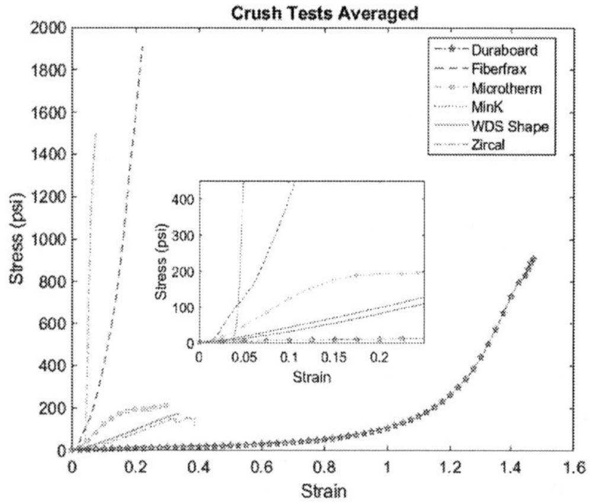

Figure 1. Averaged Stress-Strain Curves from Crush Tests

The cyclic load test maximum stress values were selected to be stresses that are typically found in batteries, but below the stresses where failure was observed. For the Microtherm, the stress was also limited to be lower than the point where the behavior was observed to transition to a plastic deformation. For the Duraboard, the stress was selected to be above the point where the material starts to stiffen.

Cyclic Load Tests: As with the crush tests, it is clear that the different materials span a broad range of behavior on the first cycle of loading. However, on the second and third cycles, the materials behave more similarly to one another. Time domain and stress-strain data both provide insight into the material behavior.

To compare stress-time data across materials, the stresses for were normalized by the maximum stress applied. The holding periods then all begin at the same normalized stress.

As can be seen in Figure 2, Fiberfrax exhibits stress relaxation during the hold after the maximum stress is applied. With each subsequent load and unload cycle, the amount of stress relaxation is reduced. Similar results were found in the other materials (Table 4) MinK and WDS Shape have the least amount of stress relaxation at about 3%. Microtherm and Zircal have about 6% stress relaxation. The Fiberfrax and Duraboard have about 20% stress relaxation in the first cycle and 15% in the later cycles. This is a significant drop in the amount of stress in the insulation materials and needs to be accounted for in the design of thermal batteries.

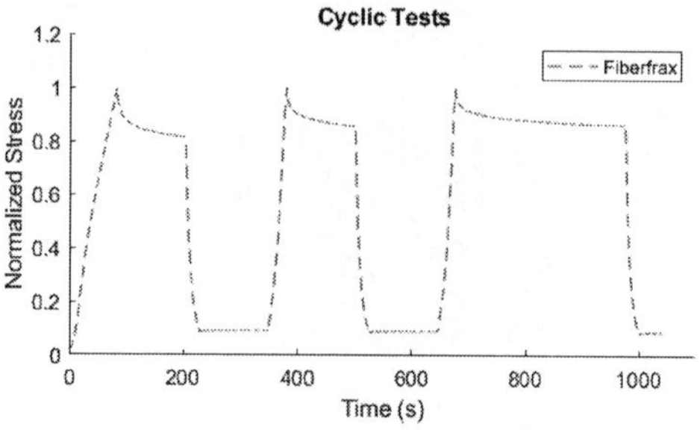

Figure 2. Normalized Stress vs Time During Cyclic Loading

Table 4. Percent Stress Relaxation per Cycle

Cycle	Dura-board	Fiber-frax	Micro-therm	Min-K	WDS Shape	Zircal
1	20.6	18.7	4.9	2.5	4.7	5.3
2	16.6	15.1	3.5	1.2	3.0	3.8
3	16.2	13.6	3.9	1.5	2.8	3.0

The first load and unload cycle for each of the materials, shown in Figure 3, crushed the material resulting in unrecoverable strain. The Duraboard experienced an order of magnitude more strain than the other five materials. The rigidized Fiberfrax and Microtherm had similar behavior in the first load and unload cycle. The MinK and WDS Shape had similar behaviors during the first load and unload cycle.

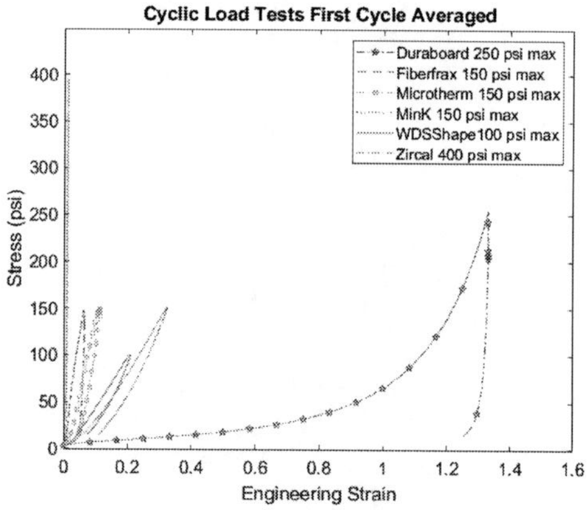

Figure 3. Stress-Strain Curve from the First Load-Unload Cycle

To compare the second and third cycles (Figure 4), the strains at the start of the second cycle were normalized to zero. The second and third load and unload curves produced more consistent behavior because the material went through an initial crushing during the first load. During the second load and unload cycles, the MinK and WDS Shape behaved similarly. They both exhibit more strain than the other materials.

Another parameter of interest for the predictive models is the modulus of elasticity when the materials are being loaded.

The elastic modulus during loading is calculated using the load portions of the stress-strain curves.

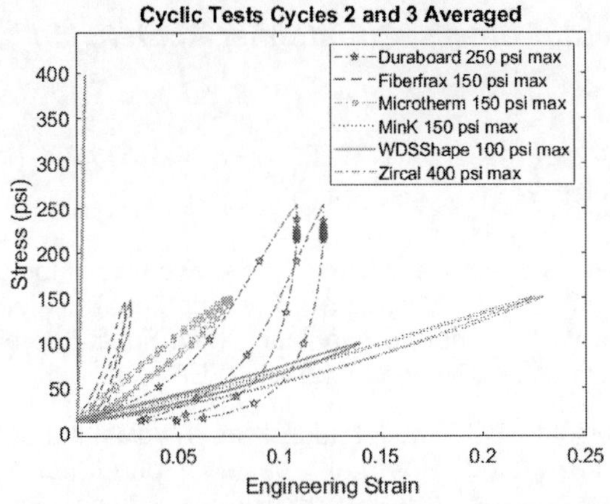

Figure 4. Stress-Strain Curve from the Second and Third Load-Unload Cycles

One of the critical parameters for predictive models is the recovery modulus which allows for predicting the stack force after activation. To determine the recovery stress-strain behavior of each material, the elastic modulus was calculated from the unload portions of the stress-strain curve in the second load cycle. The values for each of the materials are listed in Table 5. It is interesting to note that the moduli for the MinK and WDS Shape are nearly identical.

Table 5. Modulus of Elasticity for Loading and Unloading

Material	Maximum stress (psi)	Loading Elastic Modulus (psi)	Recovery Elastic Modulus (psi)
Duraboard	800	15750	50700
Fiberfrax	650	32020	68060
Microtherm	153	1840	2120
MinK	152	610	700
WDS Shape	100	544	676
Zircal	1000	96460	107430

Conclusions

This study begins the characterization of insulation materials found in thermal batteries. Six insulation materials were tested in representative manufacturing conditions. The materials exhibited a variety of materials properties and behaviors.

The stress-strain behavior of all the materials was different in the first cycle compared to the later cycles, due to an initial, irreversible crushing of the insulation material. The value of the recovery elastic modulus of the later cycles is representative of how the insulation materials would recover after the battery is activated, because in manufacturing the insulation goes through multiple load-unload cycles.

During this study, stress relaxation was observed during the relatively short hold times encountered during manufacturing. Some of the materials experienced as much as a 20% reduction in stress. Characterizing the stress relaxation is crucial for effective modeling of thermal batteries under mechanical loads. Additional studies are currently be performed that build upon the work done by Roberts et al [2] to characterize the stress relaxation over time of the insulation materials from this study in a battery representative atmosphere.

The current study should be expanded to look at multiple maximum stresses to determine if the material parameters are stress dependent. Additionally, tests with radial confinements that are representative of those found in a thermal battery would be useful in characterizing the materials.

Acknowledgements

The authors would like to thank Aaron Melad for his assistance with the ADMET, Marco Inzunza-Ibarra for his assistance with the deflectometer, Alan Harrington and Patrick Benavidez for preparing the test samples, Nicholas Streeter and John Taphouse for providing manufacturing loading information, and Nathaniel Johnson for calculating typical closing pressures on thermal batteries.

References

1. www.admet.com/products/universal-testing-machines/expert-2600/

2. C.C. Roberts et al. Experimental Characterization of Mechanical Deformation and Fluid Transport Within Thermal Battery Constituents, SAND2017-8209, Sandia National Laboratories, 2017

Accelerating Thermal Battery Design with Set-Based Concurrent Engineering

Henry A. Padilla II, Laura D. Jacobs, Edward Piekos, Scott Roberts, Christopher Apblett, Ian Barney
Sandia National Laboratories
Albuquerque, NM, USA, 87185-0613
hapadil@sandia.gov /1-505-844-1625

Abstract

Set-based concurrent engineering (SBCE) methods, applied to thermal battery design, offers the promise of faster, cheaper design cycles when paired with complementary higher fidelity digital engineering tools. Using a limited subset of requirements, a reasonable first order thermal battery design can be optimized using set-based tools, which allows for rapidly exploration of design options before committing to either hardware builds or time intensive higher fidelity simulations. The model is described, with an example given to demonstrate functionality in the areas of mass, volume, thermal behavior and electrochemical performance.

Keywords

Thermal Battery; Design; Modeling

Introduction

Thermal battery development traditionally involves designing a battery to meet electrochemical and thermal requirements, realizing that design, and testing it to determine its mechanical and thermal response. This process, iterated until requirements are met, produces only a single point design and validates that design only to those specific requirements. These design-build-test iterations are very slow and expensive. Impacts can be minimized by only exploring designs similar to existing product and assuming equivalent reliability across similar environments. That approach becomes challenging as requirements evolve beyond those of current products. New tools are needed to rapidly screen larger design spaces for solutions that can meet requirements and determine what is practical in terms of cost, schedule, performance, and reliability.

Set-based concurrent engineering (SBCE) is one way to address these challenges. The commercial software tool *Success Assured* © [1] was chosen to build an SBCE model for design of thermal batteries due to ease of use, included visualization tools which support decision making, the ability to re-use models for multiple designs, and broad applicability during system and component design. Because the SBCE model is complementary to existing 3D finite element simulation capabilities (TABS), these two sets of tools enable informed evaluation across potential design spaces (SBCE) before simulating high fidelity point designs in selected configurations (FEA).

The current SBCE model addresses a typical subset of inter-related thermal battery performance requirements in three broad areas: mechanical envelope (mass and volume), thermal performance (thermal conductivity and temperature during use), and electrochemical performance (state of charge and current density). Mechanical and non-mechanical environments are not currently included. The design of a thermal battery for purposes of the model is assumed to include a cell stack, insulation and a case. A standard cell is composed of a heat pellet, anode, cathode, separator, and two collectors, while the stack is the sum total of all the cells in adjacent proximity (i.e. not separated by insulation). Axial and radial insulation fill the gap between a cell stack and the case, which is modeled as a header, base and thin-walled tube.

Model Description

In this SBCE model, mechanical envelope (ME) requirements are assumed to include only the outer dimensions and mass of the battery. Piece part dimensions and material choices (i.e. density) are the lowest level of decisions to compute these quantities. Volume and mass are computed for each piece part and then summed to create a standard cell, complete stack, and battery using the definitions illustrated in Figure 1. Although density of some parts (e.g. collectors, leads, case material) are dictated directly by the material choice, others like insulation and pellet density are not as straightforward. Insulation density depends on the level of compression applied by a closing force. Cell design requires additional considerations, such as performance characteristics of the heat pellet (handling strength, burn speed, ignition sensitivity) or electrochemical cell operation (anode and cathode wetting, deformation after activation). Theoretically all of these constraints could be modeled as discrete relationships, however historical values for compressed insulation density and pellet density were used for simplification.

Thermal performance within the SBCE model addresses the two most important aspects of thermal battery operation: the initial temperature after activation, and the final temperature at the end of the required activated life. The battery stack is approximated as a lumped mass. This enables an estimate of the average post-activated temperature by calculating the energy balance of a standard cell:

$$T_p = \sqrt{\left(\frac{Cp_b}{Cp_m}\right)^2 + \frac{2}{Cp_m}\left(\frac{q}{M} + \frac{1}{2}Cp_m T_i^2 + Cp_b T_i\right)} - Cp_b/Cp_m, \quad (1)$$

where T_i is the required ambient starting temperature of the battery, q_{hp} is the energy per mass of the heat pellet, m is the mass of the standard cell in the battery, and c_p is the effective specific heat of the battery. Specific heat is assumed to be linear in temperature, defined by a slope (c_{pm}) and intercept (c_{pb}) with unique values depending on whether the battery has a small or large size. The lumped mass approximation implies the use of Newton's Law of Cooling, expressed as the exponential equation:

$$T_f = T_{env} + (T_p - T_{env})e^{-t_f/\tau}, \quad (2)$$

where T_p is the starting temperature from Equation 1, T_{env} is the asymptotic environment temperature (melting temperature of the electrolyte salts), t_f is the elapsed time to the end of the activated life, and τ is a time constant. The time constant in Equation 2 functions similarly to a decay constant in an electrical circuit and controls the rate of thermal decay as the starting temperature cools to the environment temperature. In this case, τ is defined as:

$$\tau = hA/C, \quad (3)$$

where h is a convection coefficient, A is the area through which the heat exchange occurs, and C is the thermal capacitance $(c_p * mass)$. Although h is not straightforward to calculate, the heat loss through the different surfaces of the stack (top, bottom, side) can be treated as thermal resistors acting in parallel, yielding:

$$(hA)^{-1} \propto \frac{L_1}{k_1 A_1} + \frac{L_2}{k_2 A_2} + \cdots \quad (4)$$

where L is the layer thickness, k is its thermal conductivity, and A is the area through which heat exchange occurs. The proportionality constant for Equation 4 was determined empirically by simulating several batteries using the TABS tool with a wide range of sizes and insulation configurations. Comparison of the thermal model (Equations 1 and 2) with TABS simulations demonstrates an agreement that almost always falls within 10%. An example is shown in Figure 2 for a long-life battery. TABS simulation results are shown in blue with ±10% error bars and the set-based formula results are shown in red.

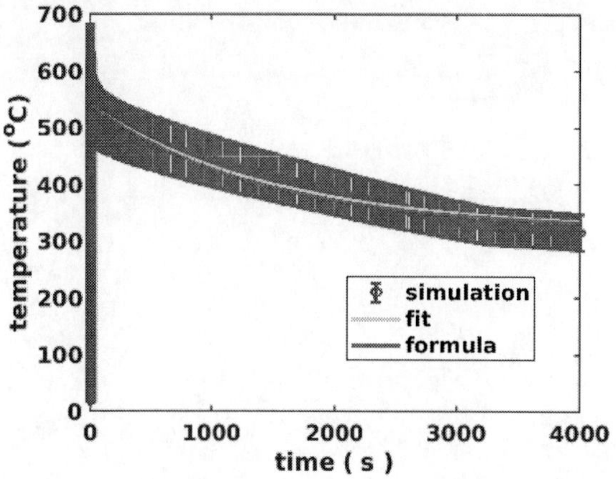

Figure 1. Set-based thermal model comparisons with TABS predictions for a long life thermal battery.

Electrochemical performance is the final part of the SBCE model, building on the decisions and relationships defined in the mechanical envelope and thermal areas. This capability predicts battery voltage given several other known or computed quantities: temperature (from the thermal model), current density (from required loads and cell diameter), duration (from required activated life), and state of charge (SOC) using capacity consumed (required loads and duration). These parameters can adequately define the polarization expected for a given cell chemistry if the discharge curves are known or computed across the entire parameter space. A full factorial design of experiments to obtain this data is not practical, so as an alternative, we have opted to simulate this performance space. This was done using the TABS single cell electrochemical model (LiSi/FeS2 chemistry with a LiCl/KCl electrolyte) calibrated against measured performance data [2, 3, 4]. In this way, several thousand constant current simulations were run across variations of pellet thicknesses, current density, temperature, and state of charge.

These TABS simulations were defined by eight (8) even spaced points between the minimum and maximum values for all parameters except capacity consumed. Since each simulation run yields voltages which could be extracted for an arbitrary number of points in capacity consumed space, twenty (20) values were selected in log space in order to produce predictions for small capacity consumed, and fewer values at larger capacity consumed. Figure 3 shows some of these results, with cell voltage plotted against different parameters.

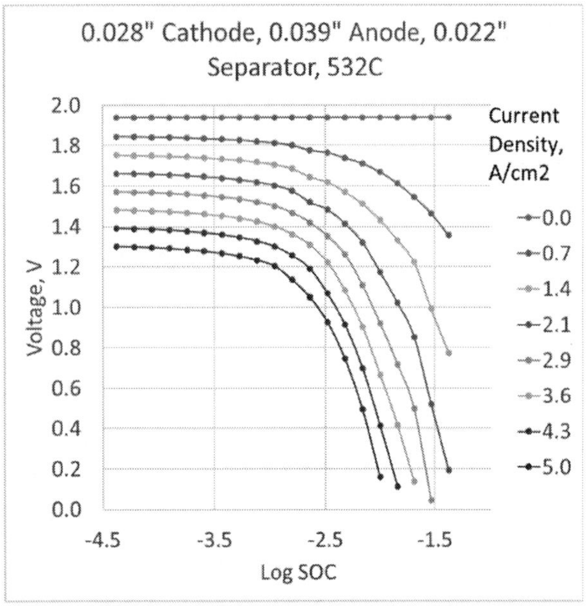

Figure 2. TABS single cell voltage predictions plotted against log(SOC).

Exemplar

The SBCE model is capable of finding the complete set of solutions with all constraints and requirements enforced, but available computational resources can limit the ability to complete those calculations in a reasonable timeframe. Faster results were achieved by breaking the problem into more manageable sub-maps, wherein the solution space is narrowed down by a combination of set-based computation and engineering judgement. Three example design trade spaces are shown in Figure 4. Constraints enforced in these tradeoff charts are that the chemistry of a cell is a LiSi anode/FeS_2 cathode with coulombic capacities, respectively, of 1746 and 1206 $A \cdot s/g$ and a standard LiCl/KCl electrolyte ($T_m = 352°C$). Initial and post-activated temperature are $T_o = 25°C$ and $T_p = 550°C$, insulation is assumed to have a thermal conductivity and density properties 0.025 W/mK and 0.32 g/cc, and the maximum battery diameter is enforced to be no greater than 3 inches.

The capacity – ME tradeoff chart shown in Figure 4a shows that for a given cell diameter of 1.875 inches, a minimum height and mass can be achieved with a margin of 6x the required capacity. This design corresponds to pellet thicknesses (heat, cathode, anode) of 0.035, 0.020, 0.026 inches, respectively for a 15-cell stack. The thermal performance tradeoff chart (Figure 4b) predicts that this design will be above 450°C after an activated life of 4098 seconds, which is at least 100°C above the melting temperature of the electrolyte salts, if the axial and radial insulation thicknesses are set above 0.94 and 0.6 in, respectively. The rightmost boundary indicates a constraint from the maximum battery diameter. The voltage tradeoff chart (Figure 4c) illustrates that a 15-cell stack with this heat balance and cell design will be above 26.5V at the end of life given the predicted final temperatures and a capacity consumed of 97 mA-hr.

Conclusion

Development of this SBCE model required significant costs in time and labor to create the comprehensive model, collect data to populate the model, and identify gaps in knowledge. Completing the ME, thermal, voltage areas required an estimated 1.5 labor-years of work, using 3-5 experts, over the course of ~2 years. Subsequent activities are expected to take less time to implement. These three areas are working well and able to make accurate predictions about existing designs. The model is currently being used to assess new requirements and come up with performance, weight and sizing estimates within a developing project.

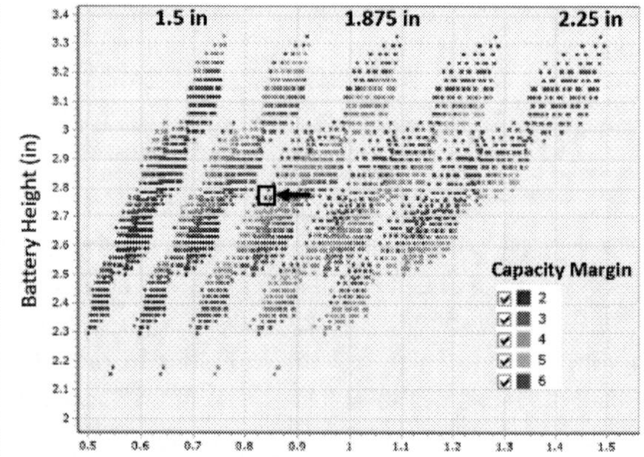

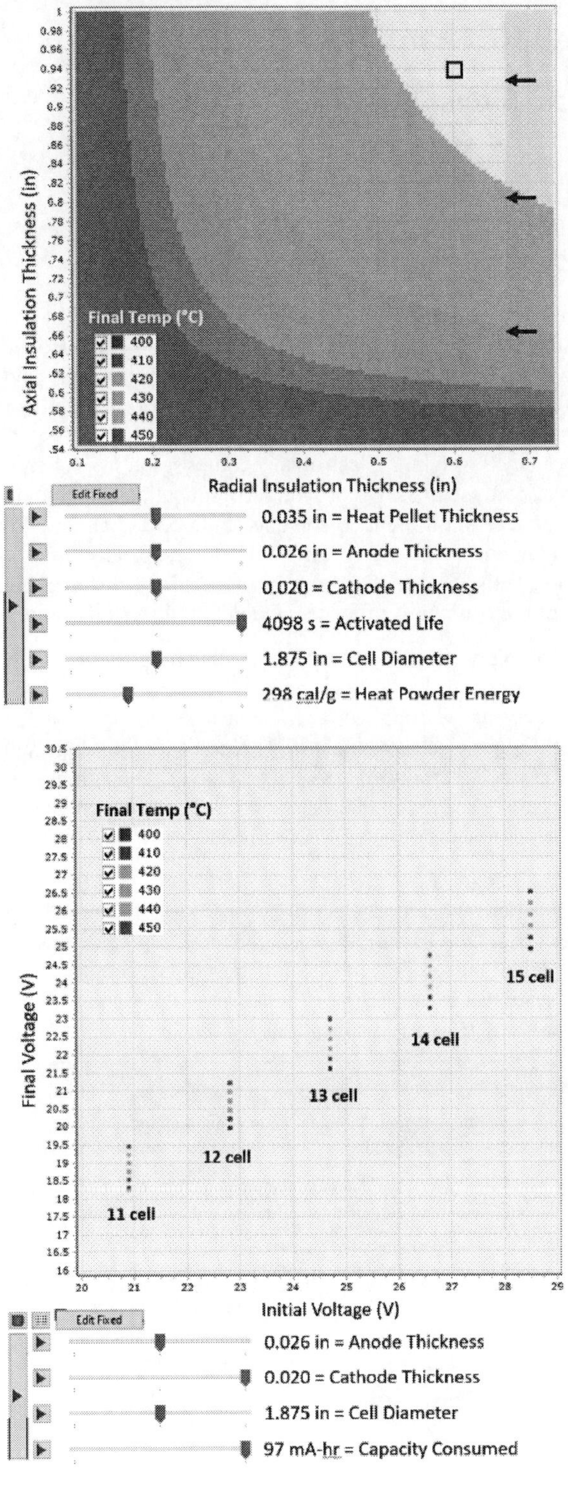

Figure 3. Tradeoff charts for (a) capacity, (b) final temperature and (c) final voltage.

Future developments include relationships for mechanical environments, manufacturing variability and reliability. These improvements will continue to imrove the overall agility of the design process and allow for a faster, more quantitative approach.

Acknowledgements

The authors would like to thank Steven Criel and Vincenzo Castle-Hinojos at Sandia National Laboratories and Kent Harmon and Brian Kennedy at Targeted Convergence Corporation for their assistance in using the set-based tools within *Success Assured* ©.

This article has been authored by an employee of National Technology & Engineering Solutions of Sandia, LLC under Contract No. DE-NA0003525 with the U.S. Department of Energy (DOE). The employee owns all right, title and interest in and to the article and is solely responsible for its contents. The United States Government retains and the publisher, by accepting the article for publication, acknowledges that the United States Government retains a non-exclusive, paid-up, irrevocable, world-wide license to publish or reproduce the published form of this article or allow others to do so, for United States Government purposes. The DOE will provide public access to these results of federally sponsored research in accordance with the DOE Public Access Plan https://www.energy.gov/downloads/doe-public-access-plan. This paper describes objective technical results and analysis. Any subjective views or opinions that might be expressed in the paper do not necessarily represent the views of the U.S. Department of Energy or the United States Government.

References

[1] https://www.targetedconvergence.com.

[2] T. G. Voskuilen, H. K. Moffat, B. B. Schroeder, and S. A. Roberts, "Multi-fidelity electrochemical modeling of thermally activated battery cells," Journal of Power Sources, vol. 488, p. 229469, 2021, doi: 10.1016/j.jpowsour.2021.229469.

[3] T. G. Voskuilen, C. F. Jove-Colon, H. K. Moffat, B. B. Schroeder, B. L. Trembacki, and S. A. Roberts, "Multi-Physics Cost and Complexity Reduction Strategies for Modeling Thermally Activated Batteries," Proceedings of the 48th Power Sources Conference, 2018.

[4] S. A. Roberts et al., "TABS : A Thermal Battery Desktop Design Tool," Proceedings of the 48th Power Sources Conference, 2018.

Blended Electrolyte for Li-Ion Cell R&D and Production

Carl Thoemmes, Tobias Johnson
Koura
3587 Anderson St. #108
Madison, WI 53704
carl.thoemmes@kouraglobal.com | 1-608-467-5626

Abstract

The domestic supply base for liquid blended electrolytes for Li-Ion cell development, and low to medium volume production is currently limited to few options. Current production of Li-Ion cells for U.S. Department of Defense (DoD) applications often relies on electrolyte provided by U.S. foreign entities of concern. To address this market gap, and outstanding DoD production risk, Koura is scaling up a low and medium volume electrolyte facility in Madison, WI. This facility will supply highly flexible and cost-effective domestically blended electrolytes for Li-Ion cell development and production, especially for DoD batteries. The facility will aim to source upstream raw material supply from both domestic sources and free-trade countries.

Keywords

Electrolyte; lithium-ion R&D; blended electrolyte; domestic electrolyte; solvents; salt; additives; electrolyte formulation; electrolyte production; carbonates; electrolyte bottles; electrolyte kegs; $LiPF_6$; lithium hexafluorophosphate.

Introduction

Electrolytes enable Li-ion technology. All traditional Li-Ion cells require an electrolyte to facilitate ion transfer between electrodes (Figure 1) and liquid electrolytes serve that function today in nearly all commercial Li-ion cells. Electrolytes also stabilize the active materials and enable long life cell performance. The electrolyte formulation depends on the active materials and the application requirements (e.g., temperature, life, etc.).

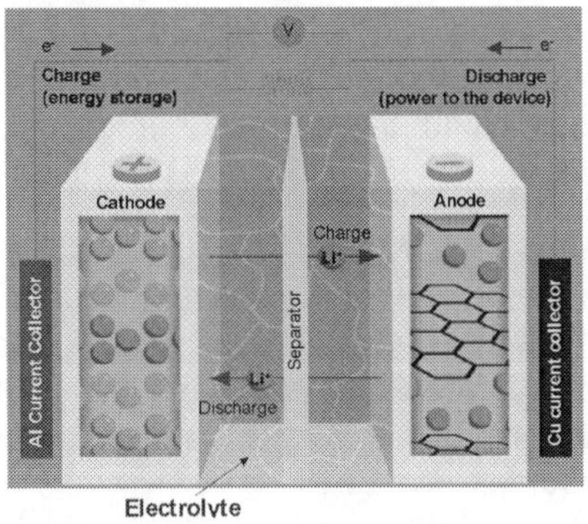

Figure 1: Schematic of a Li-ion cell showing the key components. The electrolyte not only enables transfer of lithium ions between the anode and cathode, but also plays a critical role in stabilizing the active materials and hence dictating cell life.

The composition of the electrolyte is often specified by the battery producer, and blended-to-order by the electrolyte supplier. Electrolytes typically consist of solvents, salts, and additives, carefully blended to a specific formulation, for example: 1.1M $LiPF_6$ in EC:EMC 3:7 vol/vol +1% VC +5% FEC by weight. Electrolyte composition can vary significantly across various target applications, including use of several different co-solvents, cathode and anode film forming additives, and co-salts. This is especially true for Li-ion cells used in DoD applications given the extreme operating conditions often demanded in military missions.

Traditionally, electrolytes for DoD cells produced in the US were supplied by a few non-US electrolyte blenders. However, these suppliers are increasingly focused on the much larger electric vehicle (EV) market forcing domestic Li-ion cell producers serving DoD applications to desperately search for alternate sources. A similar challenge awaits producers of non-EV Li-ion batteries in the US.

Recognizing this business opportunity, Koura has established a blended electrolyte operation (Figure 2) in Wisconsin with the aim of serving the non-EV applications. Our initial customers are Li-ion battery producers for DoD applications. In due course of time, we will expand to serve other non-EV battery applications as well.

Figure 2: Core value propositions for the electrolyte blending operation.

Electrolyte Market Overview

Global Blended Electrolyte Market: Today, most of the blended electrolyte production and consumption occurs in Southeast Asia, logically located close to where most of the Li-ion cell production occurs. As of 2022, the global market for blended electrolytes was approximately 1.1 billion metric tons, generating ~\$19 billion U.S. dollars [1]. This market is expected to continue growing at relatively the same rate as baseline Li-Ion cell production.

Domestic Blended Electrolyte Demand: The demand for blended electrolytes in the U.S. is currently developing in line with the continued announcements of new domestic Li-Ion cell production facilities. While many of these announcements for production capacities are for giga-scale EV battery production, there are several existing and announced production sites that will focus on non-EV applications (see Figure 3).

The existing and announced non-automotive capacity in the United States alone totals ~10GWh per year. Applying the conservative estimate that 700MT of blended electrolyte is required per 1GWh of cell production equates to non-automotive domestic blended electrolyte requirement of approximately 7,000 MT per year.

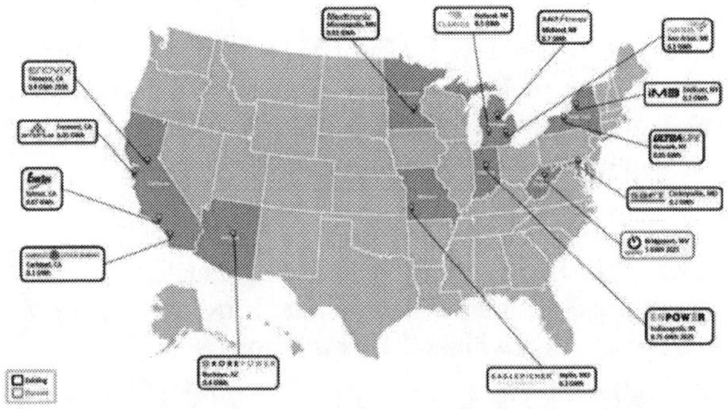

Figure 3: Data from Avicenne Energy shows existing and announced non-automotive domestic cell manufacturing capacity totaling ~10GWh / year.

Domestic Blended Electrolyte Supply Challenges

Existing blended electrolyte suppliers from Korea and Japan have announced plans for significant capacity installation within The United States; however, these facilities are primarily being scoped to support high volume EV battery demands and are not expected to be equipped to service the market demands from cell manufacturers for DoD and industrial applications:

- Automotive manufacturing scale requires supporting high-volume, low mix blended electrolytes and can be delivered to cell manufacturing facilities via rail car.
- DoD and industrial batteries require more varied electrolyte formulations at much lower volumes. For these applications material is to be delivered in bottles, kegs, or IBC totes at the high-end. This low volume market is where the largest supply gap exists domestically.

Koura will maintain inventory of all common commodity electrolyte materials including carbonate co-solvents (EC, PC, FEC, EMC, DEC, DMC, etc.), Ester co-solvents (EP, PP, MA, etc), Lithium salts ($LiPF_6$, LiTFSI, LiFSI, LiBOB, LiDFOB, $LiPO_2F_2$, etc.), and additives (VC, VEC, PS, DTD, AN, SN, HTCN, EGPN, OS3® etc.). This list is not all inclusive and additional electrolyte materials can be sourced as needed for specific customers.

New Domestic Electrolyte Blending Facility

To address the current domestic supply gap, Koura | Silatronix will scale up a new electrolyte blending facility, specifically designed to meet the needs of the non-automotive cell manufacturer volumes. The facility will be centrally located in Madison, WI. Initial production of blended electrolyte has already started, leveraging expertise, capabilities, and facilities at Silatronix (built over a decade of commercializing organosilane electrolyte additives) [3].

Current production assets can support bottle and keg scale, with a production line with larger batch size capability scheduled to come online in late 2023. The production line is being designed to support low-volume and high-mix requirements based on the wide range of specific cell design requirements. The production facility will incorporate new semi-automation techniques designed to reduce labor content and improve end-product quality.

Voice of Customer Feedback

Market Survey Input: Prior to launching the initial phase of the Koura | Silatronix blended electrolyte business, an extensive 'voice of customer' survey was conducted surveying domestic producers of low and medium volume Li-Ion cells, including cells for DoD applications. Feedback noted that lead-times for custom blended electrolytes were highly variable but generally longer than desired. Prices had been increasing, and some suppliers had exited the business entirely. Customers also noted that even though blending could be done domestically, the upstream production of solvents, salt, and additives was and still is dominated by supply from foreign entities of concern.

Voice of Customer Actions: Based on the results of the voice of customer survey, the core value proposition of this new blending facility will be modeled around maintaining four key aspects (Figure 2).

Consistent 4-week or less Lead-time: Customer feedback supported strong desire for lead-time of four weeks or better. This requires stocking a broad range of individual components and designing operations to support blending of materials, performing quality checks, and shipping on a rapid schedule. A key driver in the desire for shorter lead-times is that blended liquid electrolytes, in most cases, have limited shelf-life. Liquid electrolyte that has degraded in quality or picked up moisture can significantly compromise the performance and quality of the Li-Ion cell it is used in.

Domestic Sourcing: While establishing blending operations domestically is an important first step towards building a domestic supply chain, it will be equally important to have the ability to qualify and use domestic raw material supply or at a minimum supply from free trade countries. The current operation is focused on building a raw material supply chain that is both lowest-cost and domestic focused.

A critical component of the electrolyte is the $LiPF_6$ salt, of which 90% of the world's $LiPF_6$ is produced in China today. With support from the US Department of Energy under the Bipartisan Infrastructure Law funding, Koura is establishing the first $LiPF_6$ plant outside of Asia at out industrial complex in St. Gabriel, Louisiana [4]. This plant is expected to be operational in late 2025.

The Wisconsin electrolyte blending facility will use domestically produced $LiPF_6$ from Koura's facility in St. Gabriel, LA when that facility becomes operational.

Competitive Pricing: Competitive pricing will be achieved in several ways. Raw material cost considerations are a significant factor, and optimizing the upstream supply chain is a critical consideration. Operationally, blending production lines are being designed to align to specific batch size targets. Additionally, multiple lines are used in parallel to allow for constant workflow in between line cleaning and formulation changeover. Lines will also be designed to allow for semi-automation of the process, which historically has been quite manual, specifically for low and medium volume production.

High Purity Material: Electrolytes require low water content, low contaminants, and correct blending ratios. We are establishing a quality control process to ensure all these metrics are met with consistency as well as adding special measurement equipment to provide regular quality control monitoring.

Package Size Options and Timing

Blended Electrolyte Packaging: Customer packaging requirements for blended electrolyte fall into four main categories: bottle, keg, drum, and rail. These various package sizes support the progressive stages of a Li-Ion cell from development into production.

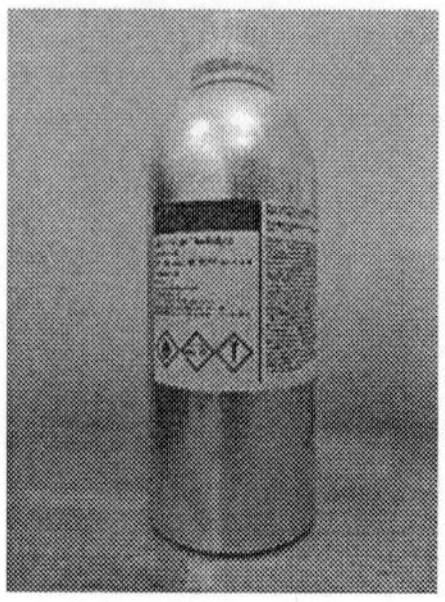

Figure 4: Example of blended electrolyte 1L container.

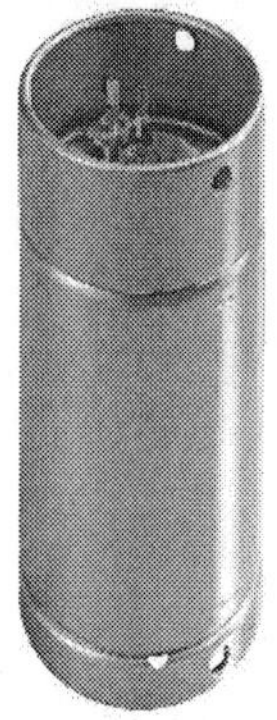

Figure 5 Example of blended electrolyte 16L container.

Bottle Service: Bottles of electrolyte are typically used in the research and development phase of battery cell development (see Figure 44 above). They are also sometimes used for low-volume production. During the development of a Li-Ion cell, several different electrolyte formulations will be tested to optimize cell performance. Small bottles in the 100mL – 1L size range help to facilitate evaluation of several formulations. Koura | Silatronix is currently supporting several customers with bottle service now.

Keg Service: Kegs, approximately 16L in size, are used to facilitate low and medium volume production requirements (see Figure 5 above). These kegs contain up to 20kg of blended electrolyte material and feature quick-connect couplers to facilitate quick and easy interchange of kegs and production plumbing lines. Koura | Silatronix is currently supporting several customers with keg service now.

200L Drums: Between kegs and full-size ISO or intermodal containers, 200L drums will be available starting later this year in conjunction with the installation of a higher-capacity blending line.

ISO Containers: Longer term, planning is underway to support 20,000kg ISO containers as part of a second phase scale-up in 2024. This would potentially enable rail-shipment of large volumes of blended electrolyte.

Material Quality

Quality Control: Quality control of blended liquid electrolytes starts by ensuring that both the input raw materials as well as final product are dry and pure, and blended accurately to customer specifications.

For incoming raw materials, certificates of analysis are reviewed and verified for KF moisture (which must be < 20ppm), purity (GC, HPLC, IC, NMR, ICP), and acid content. Finished goods blended electrolyte are tested for moisture (KF), acid content (titration), and composition by High Performance Liquid Chromatography. Density and weights are all verified as well. The Koura | Silatronix Madison Technology Center has dedicated equipment installed for electrolyte blending QC, including Karl Fischer titrator, Color comparator, Acid Titrator, HPLC, GC-FID/TCD, and GC-MS.

To support a robust quality assurance process, all blended batches produce a hold-back sample, which is kept in storage for a minimum of six-months. In the event a customer reports a potential quality issue, a sample provided by the customer can be returned to the quality assurance lab to be analyzed against the hold-back sample. This process supports identification and validation of any potential quality issues with blended materials.

Shelf-Life and Logistics Considerations

Shelf-Life Considerations: Blended electrolytes have a limited shelf-life. The specific shelf life for various formulations can vary significantly based on the specific materials used.

The physical location of the Koura | Silatronix facility helps to optimize the supply chain and logistics considerations for domestic cell production. By being centrally positioned in the United States, materials from the Madison, WI facility can reach to both coasts of the country in a matter of days vs. imported materials having to travel by sea freight or high-cost air freight.

Transport Considerations: Material being imported by air will be subject to a significant shipping cost penalty. Material being transported by sea freight avoids that cost penalty but incurs a much longer transit time ranging from 6-12 weeks depending on the destination. That additional lead-time puts pressure on cell manufacturers to consume the delivered materials faster as the shelf-life clock has already started counting down on the blended materials.

Potential Improvements: While supporting shorter transit times for materials is key to cell manufacturing operations, we are also keen to drive improvements in the shelf-life of blended electrolytes to provide greater flexibility for customers. One area of current investigation underway at Koura | Silatronix is the application of Silatronix organosilicon electrolyte materials to improve shelf-life stability of blended liquid electrolytes.

Summary

The electrolyte blending being scaled up by Koura | Silatronix in Wisconsin will enable domestic Li-ion cell suppliers to support DoD applications without disruption. The facility is currently supplying up to 20kg drums of electrolytes blended to DoD cell suppliers' specifications. Ongoing expansions will enable production of 200 kg drums of blended electrolytes towards the end of 2023. By the end of 2024, the planned facility expansions will enable the production of ton-size batches of blended electrolytes.

References

1. Pillot, Christophe, and Noel, Oliver, The Rechargeable Battery Market and Main Trends 2022-2030, Threats, challenges and opportunities, International Battery Seminar, p.101, 2023.
2. Pillot, Christophe, and Noel, Oliver, The Rechargeable Battery Market and Main Trends 2022-2030, Threats, challenges and opportunities, International Battery Seminar, p.123, 2023.
3. Receipt of Commercial Orders for OS3 Electrolyte Material, https://silatronix.com/receipt-of-commercial-orders-for-os3-electrolyte-material/
4. DOE BIL Battery FOA-2678 Selectee Fact Sheets (energy.gov)
5. Thielmann Electrolyte Containers for Lithium-Ion Battery Manufacture https://www.thielmann.com/en/products/small-industrial-containers/un-and-dot-hazardous-storage-vessels/drum-for-electrolytes

Future Power Needs in Fuze and Munitions Applications

Giuseppe L. Di Benedetto, Homesh R. Lalbahadur
U.S. Army Combat Capabilities Development Command Armaments Center,
Picatinny Arsenal, NJ 07806, USA
Contact Author Email: giuseppe.l.dibenedetto.civ@army.mil / 1-973-724-1977

Abstract

The U.S. Department of Defense (DoD) has an active tri-service team focused on addressing the need for improved military munitions power solutions. Munitions power have seen little technological advances in an era of great technical growth. These designs and chemistries were developed decades ago and often do not meet the requirements of modern munitions. The increased power demands, extended shelf life and environmental ruggedness of modern weapons represents a unique challenge to the current battery industrial base. With the advent of artificial intelligence (AI), hypersonic and collaborative armaments applications, the additional demand for power is greater than ever.

To meet shelf-life requirements munitions batteries are often designed in a reserve architecture which activate when the munition is fired. These reserve cells remain in an inactive state until power is required. Once activated they need to provide power in a short amount of time and provide this power to the munition throughout its mission. The reserve nature of munitions batteries and the unique environments they are required to survive represent significant design challenges. This is often in direct contrast with commercial primary and secondary battery solutions which are designed to keep costs as low as possible. The DoD also uses power generators to provide on-board munition power.

The Joint Munitions Power Sources Integrated Product Team (JMPS IPT) has become the U.S. Department of Defense's strategic leader in supporting Warfighter needs in munitions power. This team will provide centralized leadership and advocate for the research, development, production, and sustainment of a viable munitions power sources industrial base. Our goal is to leverage manufacturing lessons learned and commercial battery expertise to build better and more cost-effective munitions power solutions. This presentation will provide an overview of the IPT, progress, and power needs for future fuzing and advanced munitions applications.

Keywords

munitions, armaments, munitions power, reserve battery, power generators, fuzing, DoD, JMPS IPT

High-Energy-Density and Low-Cost Lithium-Ion Batteries Using Sulfurized Polyacrylonitrile Cathodes

Donghao Ye and Jim P. Zheng*
[a]Department of Electrical Engineering, State University of New York at Buffalo, Buffalo, NY 14260, USA
*Tel: (716) 645-1194, Fax: (716) 645-3656, Email: jzheng@buffalo.edu

Abstract: The paper presents preliminary results on a novel high-energy lithium-ion-battery (LIB), in which the sulfur-polyacrylonitrile (S-PAN) is cathode material, the micro silicon oxide (SiO_x) is anode material, and pre-lithiation technique is utilized to introduce lithium (Li) into the battery in order to match the electrode capacity and also to compensate for the initial Li loss of SiO_x anode. In this novel battery structure, high sulfur weight ratio in S-PAN is prepared by heat treating sulfur and long chain PAN under inert gas to achieve a specific capacity above 650 mAh/g. The specific capacity of SiO_x is over 700 mAh/g. The specific energy of the new LIB can exceed the current LIBs.

Keywords: Lithium-ion batteries, sulfurized polyacrylonitrile, graphite, silicon/carbon

Introduction

With the global push toward green energy, researchers world-wide are pursuing the development of low-cost, high-energy-density, long-life rechargeable battery technologies to be used in many civilian and military applications. Achievement of a specific energy (e.g. >500 Wh/kg), a cycle life (e.g. >1,000 cycles), and a cost (e.g. < $100/kWh) has become a technical target adopted by many major industrial countries. We have developed a novel approach to fabricate high-specific and low-cost LIBs using sulfurized polyacrylonitrile (S-PAN) as cathode, graphite or silicon-carbon (Si/C) as anode, and pre-lithiation technique to introduce required lithium-ion.

Specific Energy

The ultimate specific energy based on active electrode materials only in a LIB can be expressed as:

$$E = V\left(\frac{1}{c_a} + \frac{1}{c_c}\right)^{-1} \qquad (1)$$

where c_a and c_c are the specific capacities of anode and cathode, respectively; V is the average cell voltage. In amount of cathode materials, we chose $LiNi_{0.33}Co_{0.33}Mn_{0.33}O_2$ (NCM333) having the highest specific capacity of 220 mAh/g as an example [1]. Fig. 1 shows the specific energy of a LIB (blue line) using NCM333 as a function of specific capacity od anode. The average cell voltage of 3.7 V was used. It can be seen that the specific energy is from 525 Wh/kg (c_a=372 mAh/g for graphite), increases to 685 Wh/kg (c_a=1,000 mAh/g for Si-carbon) and 791 Wh/kg (c_a=3,860 mAh/g for Li metal). The specific energy increases 28% when the specific capacity of anode increases 2.7 times (from 372 to 1,000 mAh/g), and increases only 15% when the specific capacity of anode increases another 3.8 times (from 1,000 to 3,860 mAh/g). It is because that the reciprocal of the effective specific capacity of the cell is the sum of reciprocal of the specific capacity of the anode and cathode electrodes as shown in Eq. (1); therefore, among the two electrodes, the electrode with the smaller specific capacity will play a predominating role in determining the final specific energy of the cell. One of the big challenges for developing high-energy LIBs is that so far, a high-capacity cathode material matching the high-capacity metal Li or Si-C anode, has not yet been found. The specific energy formula tells us that when the specific capacity of the cathode electrode and the anode electrode are both large, it will be a more effective way to increase the specific energy of the battery. Looking at the currently known electrode materials in Li system, sulfur and Si-carbon composite become candidates as cathode and anode materials for high-energy batteries.

With developed S-PAN cathode, SiO_x anode, and pre-lithiation techniques, the high specific energy cell can be built. The specific energy based on active materials (cathode, anode, and extra Li source for pre-lithiation) is calculated and shown in Fig. 1 as orange line using the following equation [2].

$$E' = V\left(\frac{1}{c_a} + \frac{1}{c_c} + \frac{1}{c_{Li}}\right)^{-1} \qquad (2)$$

where, c_{Li}=3,860 mAh/g is the specific capacity of Li metal. From Fig. 1, it can be seen that when the specific capacity of anode is less than 1050 mAh/g, the specific energy of conventional LIB is greater than that using S-PAN due to low cell voltage (1.9 V); however, the increase rate of specific energy is greater than that for conventional LIB. When the specific capacity of anode is 1,200 mAh/g, the specific energies are 706 Wh/kg vs. 722 Wh/kg for LIB using NCM and S-PAN cathodes, respectively. From the preliminary simulation results as shown in Fig. 1, we can conclude that using a high-capacity but low-potential S-PAN is more likely to achieve a specific energy exceeding 500 Wh than using any lithium-metal-oxide as a cathode to combine with a high-capacity anode to form a LIB. Although lithium-metal-oxide has a higher potential, the specific capacity is not satisfactory and is much less than that of S-PAN. The highest specific capacity of S-PAN at 900 mAh/g was reported [3].

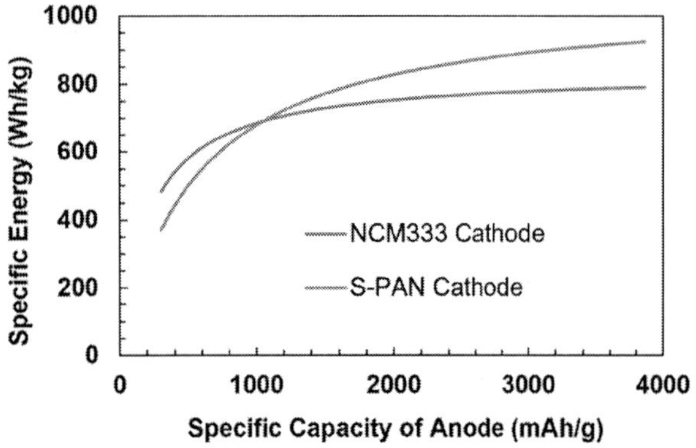

Fig. 1 Specific energy of proposed LIB using S-PAN cathode and LIB using NCM333 cathode based on active materials only including anode, cathode, and Li source for LIB using S-PAN. The specific capacities of 222 and 650 mAh/g are used for NCM333 and S-PAN cathodes, respectively. The cell voltages of 3.7 and 1.9 are used for cells used NCM333 and S-PAN cathodes, respectively.

Experimental

S-PAN was prepared by mixing sulfur (Sigma-Aldrich) and polyacrylonitrile (Sigma-Aldrich) at a weight ratio of 4:1, and then heating the mixture at 350 °C for 3 hours in a nitrogen atmosphere to form the S-PAN composite material, and S-PAN powders were obtained by grinding in a mortar and pestle for 30 minutes.

The cathode was made by mixing 80 wt% S-PAN powders, 10 wt% Super P C65, and 10 wt% styrene-butadiene rubber/carboxymethylcellulose (SBR/CMC) binder, then the mixture was dispersed in water to form the slurry. The well-mixed slurry was cast by using a doctor blade on aluminum foil as current collector. After drying at room temperature, the electrodes were dried again in a vacuum oven at 70 °C for 12 h to remove moisture. Then the cathodes were cut to ½ inch diameter discs. The typical cathode loading was about 8 mg/cm^2.

The anode was made with SiO_x and graphite powders as active materials. the anodes were cut to ½ inch diameter discs and dried at 90 °C in vacuum oven for 12 h. During the assembly of the cell, a 20 µm-thick Li foil is pressed on the surface of the anode or cathode as the pre-lithiation source. The size of Li foil was determined such that the Li capacity was equal to the sum of the capacity of the anode and the irreversible capacity of the cathode during the initial cycle.

The coin cells were assembled in an Argon filled glove box. Three different kinds of coin cells were assembled including 1) Li/S-PAN half-cells, 2) Li/SiO_x-graphite half-cells, and 3) SiO_x-graphite/S-PAN full-cells. In all cells, the separator was Celgard 2400. The electrolyte was LP40 (1 M $LiPF_6$, ethylene carbonate (EC)/diethyl carbonate (DEC)=1:1). After SiO_x-graphite/S-PAN full-cells were assembled, we waited for 270 h for pre-lithiation before any characterization.

The galvanostatic discharge/charge for assembled cells in voltage ranges of 1.0-3.0 V for Li/S-PAN, 0.01-1 V for Li/SiO_x-graphite, and 0.01-3 V for SiO_x-graphite/S-PAN were tested by using a battery tester (Neware).

The electrode morphology, particle size, and elemental mapping were observed by a field emission scanning electron microscopy (FE-SEM) using a Carl Zeiss AURIGA CrossBeam. The elemental mapping was studied with an IXRF energy dispersive X-ray spectrometer (EDS) using a Hitachi S4000.

Results and Discussion

Fig. 2 shows (a) the voltage profile of initial cycle and (b) specific capacity capacities and Coulombic efficiency as a function of cycle number from a Li/S-PAN half-cell. It can be seen that the specific capacity of the 2nd cycle decreased from 789 mAh/g in the 1st cycle to 654 mAh/g, a loss of 20%; however, after the 1st cycle, the decay of the specific capacity of the S-PAN cathode is less than 2% per cycle in the next more than 40 cycles. It can also be seen from Fig. (a) that the potential of the S-PAN cathode in the 1st discharge was about 0.2 V lower than that in the 2nd cycle and could be due to solid electrolyte interface layer formation, S-S and C-S bonds broken [4]. After the 1st cycle, the potential of S-PAN cathode is stable. From Fig. 2(c), the S-PAN cathode capacity exhibits a sharp drop at 1C rate, in sharp contrast to our previous results [5], in which the loading of S-PAN was roughly half and the weight ratio of carbon in the electrode was more than double. However, further studies are needed to understand the most dominant factors limiting S-PAN cathodes.

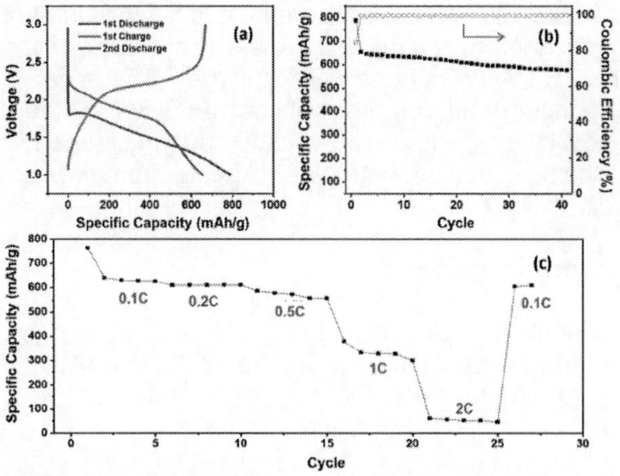

Fig. 2 (a) Voltage profile (b) cycling performance at 0.1C rate, and (c) rate performance of Li/S-PAN cells.

Similar tests were performed on Li/SiOx-graphite half-cells, Fig. 3 shows a comparison of cycling performance of SiO_x-graphite and S-PAN during 1st 40 cycles. Different to the S-PAN cathode, the specific capacity of SiO_x-graphite anode increased from an initial 600 mAh/g to a maximum of 710 mAh/g, about 18% increase. It is believed that is due to an activated process that because low current density could form more irreversible conductive Li_4SiO_4 and Li_2O to increase the electrode Li-ion conductivity [6]. In order to fully activate the SiO_x-graphite anode, during the initial few cycles, the SiO_x-graphite anode needs to be cycled at a low rate, such as less than 0.05C rate. After several cycles, both electrodes have good Coulombic efficiencies. It can be seen from Fig. 3 that the capacity decay rate of anode is faster than that of cathode.

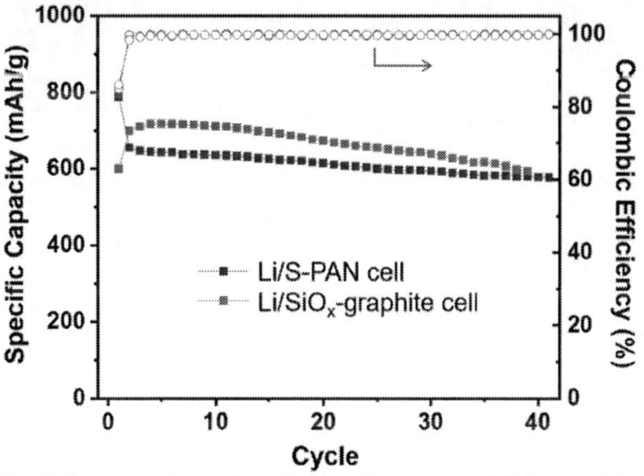

Fig. 3 A comparison of cycling performance of SiO_x-graphite and S-PAN. SiO_x-graphite was cycled at a rate of 0.05C for the first two cycles and then at a rate of 0.1C.

SiO_x-graphite/S-PAN full-cells were assembled with capacities of 6.84 mAh for anode and 8.31 mAh for cathode. The thicknesses of pristine electrodes are 59 µm and 222 µm for anode and cathode, respectively. Both electrode diameter is ½ inch. For SiO_x-graphite/S-PAN cells, the pre-lithiation is essential because neither the anode nor the cathode is pre-doped with Li, so all Li sources only enter the anode or cathode through pre-lithiation, in addition, the pre-lithiation can also canoed and compensate for the initial Li loss of S-PAN cathode and SiO_x-graphite anode.

Fig. 4 shows performance measured from SiO_x-graphite/S-PAN full-cells. From Fig. 1(a), the Coulombic efficiency of the 1st cycle is about 84%. The capacity decayed about 22% during the 1st cycle, then the decay of the cell capacity is about 2.5% per cycle in the next more than 24 cycles as shown in Fig. 4(b). The capacity decay rate of full cell is slightly higher than that of cathode. Fig. 4(c) shows the rate capabilities of the cell from 0.1C to 1C. It can be seen that the capacity drops sharply at the 1C rate, which is consistent with rate performance of S-PAN cathode; therefore, the rate performance of SiO_x-graphite/S-PAN cell was limited by slow cathode response.

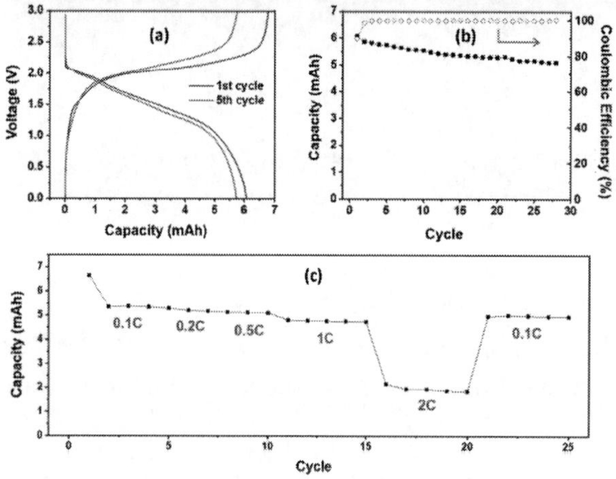

Fig. 4 (a) Voltage profile, (b) cycling performance at 0.1C rate, and (c) rate performance of SiO_x-graphite/S-PAN full-cells. The S-PAN cathode was pre-lithiation before the 1st cycle.

Due to high specific capacities of both electrodes, the volume and porosity of the electrodes may change greatly after being fully lithiated. Fig. 5 shows SEM images of S-PAN cathode surface (a) before and (b) after pre-lithiation. It can be seen that the particle size was significantly increased after pre-lithiation. The thickness of the cathode electrode was measured and found to be expanded from 222 µm to 243 µm, before and after pre-lithiation, an increase of about 9.5%. The porosity of cathode was estimated to be 59% and 49% before and after pre-lithiation, respectively.

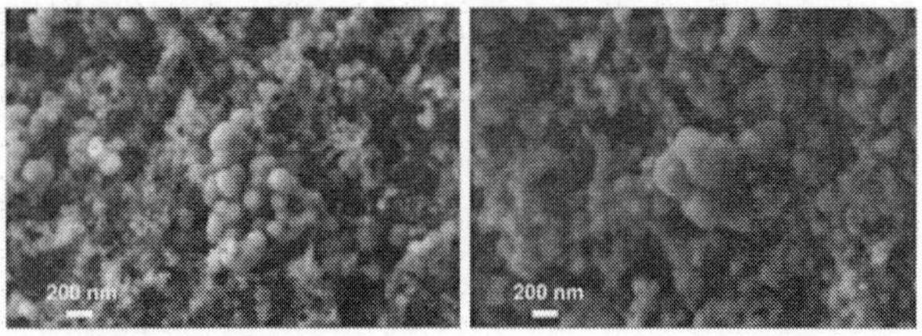

Fig. 5 SEM images of S-PAN cathode surface (a) before and (b) after pre-lithiation.

Fig. 6 shows SEM images of SiO_x-graphite anode surface (a) before and (b) after pre-lithiation. The thickness of the anode electrode was found to be expanded from 59 µm to 112 µm before and after pre-lithiation, an increase of about 90%, which is much greater than that obtained from cathode electrode. Unlike the cathode, the porosity of anode increased from 44% of the pristine electrode to 56% after pre-lithiation. It can also be seen from SEM images, the particle size after pre-lithiation became smaller. This is because after the lithiation, a huge volume expansion occurred, leading to severe structural collapse and fragmentation inside the SiO_x particles.

Fig. 6 SEM images of SiO_x-graphite anode surface (a) before and (b) after pre-lithiation.

Conclusion

Both electrodes in SiO_x-graphite/S-PAN cells are made with low-cost raw materials. In cathode, sulfur is one of the most abundant elements on the Earth and another major material in cathode, PAN is also low in price; in anode, micron-sized SiO_x is commercially available on low-cost that is comparable to graphite. Theoretically, the specific energy of LIB using S-PAN based cathode can be greater than that using Li metal oxide based cathode. We have demonstrated that when sulfur is bonded to macromolecular PAN to form S-PAN, soluble lithium polysulfides are not formed during lithiation; thus, S-PAN exhibits good cycle life and high Coulombic efficiency. However, there are still many challenges to make this new battery comparable to existing LIBs, such as improving the rate capability and cyclability of the S-PAN cathode. The large difference in expansion and compression of the S-PAN cathode and SiO_x-graphite anode volumes during charge and discharge makes battery packaging and modules very difficult.

Acknowledgements

This work is supported by National Science Foundation grant No. 2128488 and NASA ULI Program agreement No. 80NSSC22M0068. Authors would like to thank Dr. Ben Cao and Ting Du at Nanoramic Lab for technical discussions.

References

1. Arup Chakraborty, Sooraj Kunnikuruvan, Sandeep Kumar, Boris Markovsky, Doron Aurbach, Mudit Dixit, and Dan Thomas Major, Layered Cathode Materials for Lithium-Ion Batteries: Review of Computational Studies on $LiNi_{1-x-y}Co_xMn_yO_2$ and $LiNi_{1-x-y}Co_xAl_yO_2$, Chem. Mater. **2020**, 32, 915−952.
2. Liming Jin, Junsheng Zheng, and Jim P. Zheng, Theoretically Quantifying the Effect of Pre-lithiation on Energy Density of Li-ion Batteries, *The Journal of Electrochemical Society*, **2021**, 168, 010532.
3. Huijun Yang, Ahmad Naveed, Qinyu Li, Cheng Guo, Jiahang Chen, Jingyu Lei, Jun Yang, Yanna Nuli, Jiulin Wang, Lithium sulfur batteries with compatible electrolyte both for stable cathode and dendrite-free anode, *Energy Storage Materials*, **2018**, 15, 299-307.
4. Shuya Wei, Lin Ma, Kenville E. Hendrickson, Zhengyuan Tu, and Lynden A. Archer "Metal-sulfur battery cathodes based on PAN–sulfur composites." *Journal of the American Chemical Society*, **2015**, 137, 12143-12152.
5. Chao Shen, Donghao Ye, Liming Jin, Petru Andrei, and Jim P. Zheng, "A simple and scalable pre-lithiation approach for high energy and low cost lithium ion sulfur batteries", *Journal of The Electrochemical Society*, **2020**, 167, 060517.
6. Lee, Jun Kyu, Woo Young Yoon, and Bok Ki Kim. "Kinetics of reaction products of silicon monoxide with controlled amount of Li-ion insertion at various current densities for Li-ion batteries." *Journal of The Electrochemical Society*, **2014**, 161, A927.

Advanced Phosphate Cathodes at SAFT

Jacob Nykaza, Xilin Chen, Thomas A. Greszler
Saft America, Space and Defense Division
107 Beaver Court, Cockeysville, MD 21030
Jacob.Nykaza@saft.com / 1-410-568-0057

Abstract

Saft has successfully applied Li-ion electrochemistry to defense, space, and commercial applications which require very high power and safety. By optimizing both the electrochemical and electro-mechanical cell design, Saft has developed a range of Li-ion products that can deliver over 50 kW/kg of power for a fraction of a second for joint strike fighter or racing application or >250 Wh/kg for applications requiring high energy content. This paper presents research and development efforts of advanced Li-ion electrochemistry at Saft. In particular, advanced phosphates cathodes such as LMFP are developed for PHEV2 and military BB-2590s with high safety and improved electrochemical performance. Furthermore, tavorite structure LVPF chemistries to further improved energy density are under development.

Keywords

High Energy; High Safety; LMFP, LVPF, Solid-State Battery

Introduction

Saft has been manufacturing Li-ion batteries for more than 30 years and is a world leader in providing state-of-the-art Li-ion systems for demanding applications in commercial, defense and space markets. Our products have evolved to match the requirements of the market with a focus on high performance over a wide temperature range, long life, high quality and reliability, and rugged systems that can operate in uncontrolled and abusive environments. Saft continues to improve current Li-ion batteries and develop next-generation energy storage devices. Here, we highlight the results and status of Saft's research and development efforts on safe Li-ion based on phosphate LMFP and LVPF cathodes and beyond Li-ion batteries.

LMFP Cathode Chemistry

Saft has investigated the use of advanced-phosphates such as high voltage olivine structured Lithium Manganese Iron Phosphate ($LiMnFePO_4$; LMFP) as a replacement to traditional Lithium Nickel Manganese Cobalt Oxide ($LiNiMnCoO_2$; NMC) and the lower voltage olivine structured Lithium Iron Phosphate ($LiFePO_4$; LFP) for over 10 years. The higher operating voltage of LMFP, shown in Figure 1, increases the energy density significantly (15-20%) compared to existing LFP chemistry while maintaining LFP's excellent safety, performance, and cost. [1-2]. Along with dramatically improved safety, these advanced phosphate chemistries also have additional benefits compared to NMC materials including constant power throughout discharge, reduced cost and easier supply chain due to no cobalt or nickel as shown in the spider chart in Figure 2.

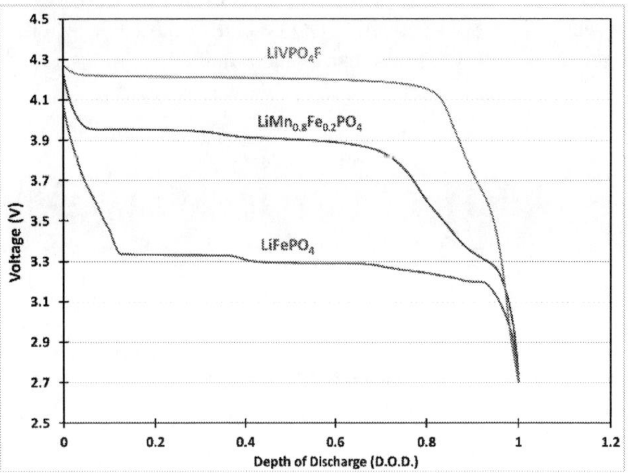

Figure 1. Voltage Profiles of LFP, LMFP, and LVPF

The increased energy and safety make LMFP chemistry attractive to various defense, aerospace, and industrial applications. Examples include military batteries like BB-2590 and CWB or 28V aviation batteries. Drawbacks to commercialize LMFP technology lies in i) poor ionic/electronic conductivity, ii) poor cycle life due in part to distortion of Jahn-Teller active Mn^{3+} ion and transition metal dissolution. Saft has improved the electrochemistry especially in rate capability, cycle life and manufacturing/process quality by optimization of electrode formulation and choice of suitable anode materials. Cells with different form factors (cylindrical, hard case prismatic, and pouch) were assembled and evaluated for different applications. [3]

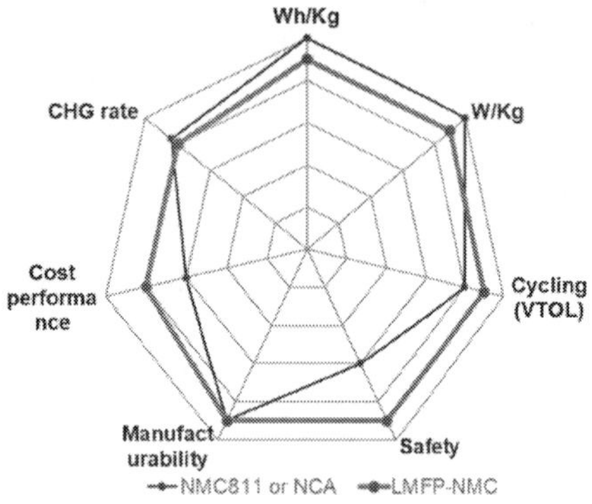

Figure 2. Spider chart comparing NMC811 to LMFP

Figure 3 summaries progress made in a 35 Ah PHEV2 size cell with LMFP cathode for both cycle life and rate capacity. The cells cycle over 3000 cycles at C/2 rate to greater than 80% capacity. The cells also have exceptional rate capability with less than 5% loss at 2C.

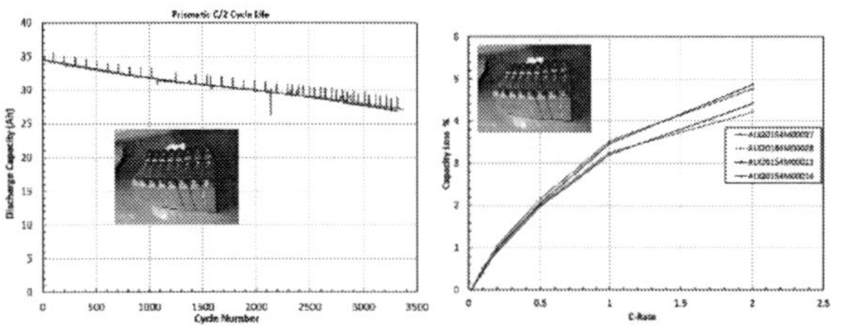

Figure 3. Cycle life and rate capability of 35 Ah PHEV2 cells with LMFP cathode.

As mentioned, the safety of LMFP cathodes is one of the main benefits due to its olivine-structure. Figure 4 reports the nail penetration of two 35 Ah PHEV2 cells. The cells meet the target of no fire, no explosion, and T < 450 °C with a EUCAR 3 and no propagation to neighboring cell in the battery pack.

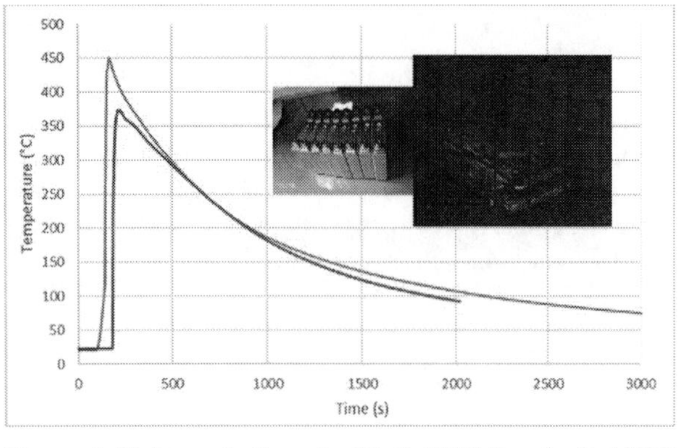

Figure 4. Nail penetration of a 35 Ah PHEV2 cell with LMFP cathode.

Saft has started to use LMFP cathodes for military batteries (i.e., BB-2590s, x6Ts, ect) along with our commercial applications. An ongoing funded program is development of a Solid-State polymer battery for BB-2590 for the Defense Logistic Agency. The program initially focused on high Ni content cathodes but these were determined, even with semi-solid-state electrolyte, to be too reactive in abuse conditions. Saft is committed to the safety of our warfighters and switched to advanced-phosphates in 2022. The program replaced the 24x 18650 commercial cells with 8x custom Saft designed pouch cells as shown in Figure 5.

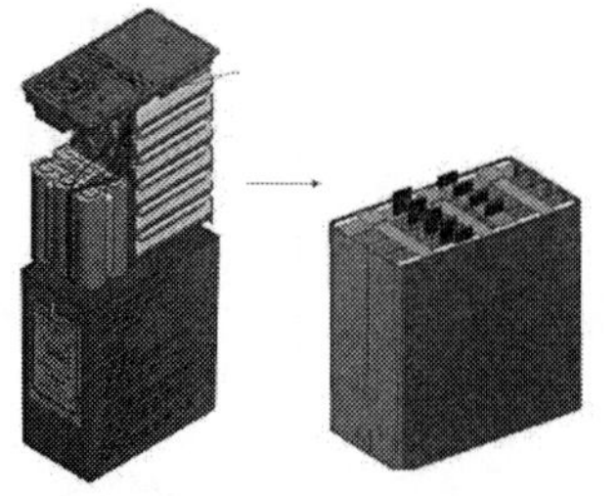

Figure 5. Example of replacing 18650s with pouch cells for a BB-2590

To further increase safety, Saft's in-situ polymerized gel polymer electrolyte was incorporated as shown in Figure 6. This process allows Saft to use traditional Li-ion cell fabrication processes but enables polymer gelation throughout the cell.

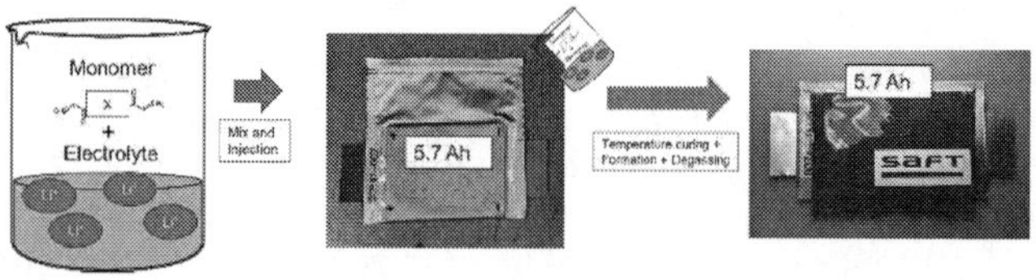

Figure 6. Example of Saft's semi-solid state chemistry design.

The final deliverable cells have an energy density ~205 Wh/kg and meet or exceed all safety requirements of MIL-PRF-32383/3 including overcharge, short circuit, forced discharge, nail penetration, and crush. Specifically, for nail penetration, cells were tested at 4.2 V, 100% state of charge, where a nail was inserted into the cell. The maximum temperature was < 170 °C with no fire/flame upon abuse and <1wt% weight loss resulting on Hazard Level 3. Figure 7 shows the setup and BB-2590 pouch cell after nail penetration tests. A metal oxide-based pouch cell is also shown with a very energetic results.

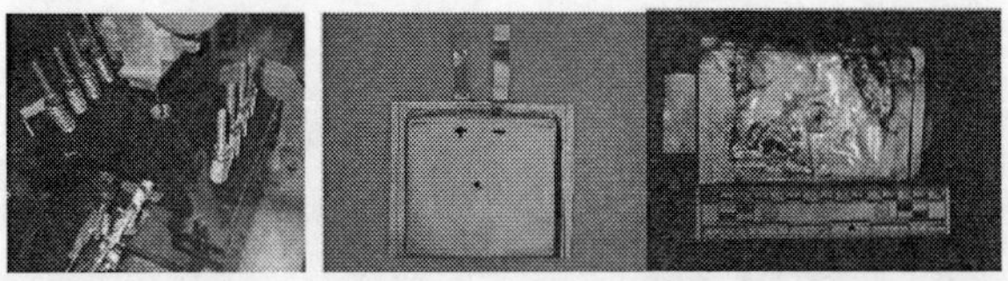

Figure 7. Nail penetration results of SAFT BB-2590 LMFP cell with semi-solid state gel polymer electrolyte (left) compared to an NMC based cell (right)

The cells with the semi-solid state gel polymer electrolyte are on pace to meet or exceed the MIL-PRF specification for cycle life and initial results show an improvement over pure liquid electrolyte as shown in Figure 8.

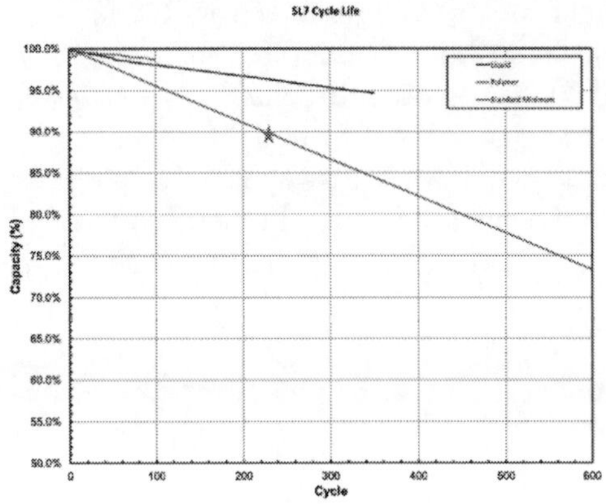

Figure 8. BB-2590 cells on cycle life.

While the program was a success at providing a very safe cell for the BB-2590, there are still areas that need improvement in future work including low temperature performance and increasing the energy density while maintaining the safety.

LVPF Cathode Chemistry

$LiVPO_4F$ is expected to be an intrinsically safer cathode material than other available cathodes such as Lithium Cobalt Oxide (LCO), Nickel Cobalt Aluminum Oxide (NCA), and Nickel Manganese Cobalt Oxide (NMC) because of the presence of PO_4 group (as show in Figure 9) in its tavorite structure, which is similar to lithium iron phosphate. In addition, $LiVPO_4F$ has a higher energy density than $LiFePO_4$ due to the higher lithiation/delithiation potential (4.2V) than that of (3.4V) $LiFePO_4$ as shown in Figure 1. $LiVPO_4F$ is expected to have excellent cycle life like other phosphate cathodes, which may lead to overall lower battery lifetime cost, compared to other chemistries with much shorter life.

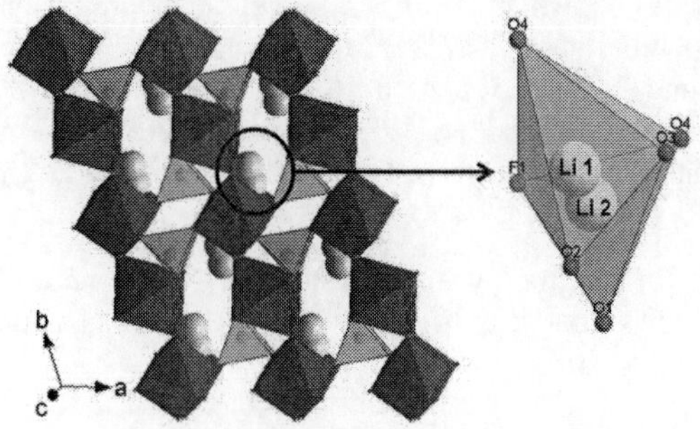

Figure 9. Pictorial representation of the structures of $LiVPO_4F$ with a close-up view of the split lithium position. The vanadium octahedra are shown in blue, phosphate tetrahedra are shown in yellow, and the Li atoms are shown in white.[4]

Saft's preliminary results of $LiVPO_4F$/Graphite cells demonstrated that the cells can deliver comparable energy density, better safety and rate performance than that of NMC/graphite cells. The safety of $LiVPO_4F$/Graphite cells is comparable to lithium iron phosphate chemistry. $LiVPO_4F$ delivers 142mAh/g, 91% of theoretical capacity (155 mAh/g) [5] at 4.2V, corresponding to an energy density of 596Wh/kg (theoretical energy density 651Wh/kg). The achieved energy density of $LiVPO_4F$/Graphite cells is comparable to 608 Wh/kg for LCO and is higher than 577 Wh/kg for NMC111, 574 Wh/kg for NCA, and much higher than 531 Wh/kg for LFP. In addition, the tavorite structure of LVPF overcomes the 1D ion conductivity challenge in other phosphates (i.e. lithium ion phosphate) with olivine structures and thus exhibits high ionic conductivity. [3]

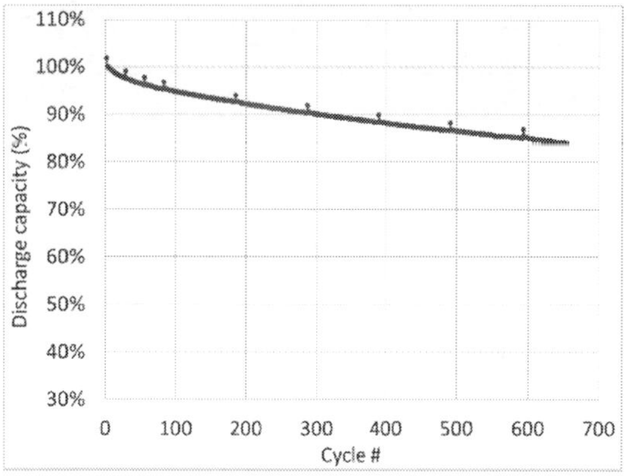

Figure 10. Cycling performance of a 4Ah LVPF/Gr cell

Figure 10 shows the preliminary cycling performance of a 4Ah LVPF/Gr pouch cell, which delivers 84% of initial capacity after 655 cycles. The rate capability of 4Ah LVPF/Graphite pouch cells is tested under different temperatures. The tests were completed for 25 °C, 0 °C and -20 °C. As shown in **Table 1**, the cells delivered a great rate capability at 25 °C, 98% capacity at 1C, 95% capacity at 2C and 74% at 5C. At 0 °C, the cell delivered 84% capacity at 1C and 61% at 2C. At negative 20 °C, the rate capability is still decent at C/2, 63% of capacity at C/10 rate.

In prelimnary abuse tests (i.e., Nail penetration, overcharge, short-circuit), the LVPF/Gr cells achieve EUCAR 2-3 ratings.

Acknowledgements

The LMFP and semi-solid state gel polymer electrolyte was sponsored by the Defense Logistic Agency under Contract Number SP-4701-20-C-0026

The LVPF Research was sponsored by the Army Research Laboratory and was accomplished under Cooperative Agreement Numbers of W911NF-20-2-0284 and W911NF-22-2-0021.

References

1. Zhao, X., An, L., Sun, J., and Liang, G., "LiNiCo0.2Mn0.3O2-LiMn0.6Fe0.4PO4 Mixture with Both Excellent Electrochemical Performance and Low Cost as Cathode Material for Power Lithium Ion Batteries," *J. Electrochem Soc*. Vol. 165(2), pp. A142-A148, 2018
2. Zhang, X., Hou, M., Tamirate, A. G., Zhu, H., Wang, C., and Xia, Y., "Carbon coated nano-sized $LiMn_{0.8}Fe_{0.2}PO_4$ porous microsphere cathode material for Li-ion batteries," *J. Power Sources*, Vol 448, no. 1, pp. 227438, 2020
3. Huang, W., Hu, J., Yang, L., Zhao, W., Wang, Z., Wang, H., Guo, Z., Li, Y., Liu, J., Yang, K., and Pan, F., "Revealing the degradation mechanism of $LiMn_xFe_{1-x}PO_4$ by single particle electrochemistry method," *ACS Applied Mat. & Int.,* vol. 11, no. 1, pp. 957-962, 2019
4. Ellis, B. L., Ramesh, T. N., Davis, L. J. M., Goward, G. and Nazar, L. F., "Structure and Electrochemistry of Two-Electron Redox Couples in Lithium Metal Fluorophosphates Based on the Tavorite Structure", *Chemistry of Materials*, vol. 23, pp. 5138-5148, 2011
5. Barker, J. Saidi, M. Y., Swoyer, J. L. "Electrochemical Insertion Properties of the Novel Lithium Vanadium Fluorophosphate, $LiVPO_4F$," *J. Electrochem. Soc.,* vol. 150, pp. A1394, 2003

Table 1. Rate capability of 4Ah LVPF /Graphite pouch cells

	25°C		0°C		– 20°C	
	Discharge Capacity (Ah)	Discharge (% C/10)	Discharge Capacity (Ah)	Discharge (% C/10)	Discharge Capacity (Ah)	Discharge (% C/10)
C/10	4.20	100%	3.89	93%	3.74	89%
C/2	4.16	99%	3.78	90%	2.66	63%
1C	4.10	98%	3.53	84%	1.46	35%
2C	4.00	95%	2.55	61%	0.16	4%
5C	3.11	74%	0.47	11%	N/A	N/A

Free-Standing Carbon Nanofoam Papers Vapor-Infiltrated with Sulfur as Lithium-Sulfur Battery Cathodes

Matthew J. Lefler,[1] Zachary G. Neale,[1] Rebecca A. Hunt,[2] Jeffrey W. Long,[2] Megan B. Sassin,[2] and Rachel E. Carter[2]

[1]NRL/NRC Postdoctoral Associate,
U.S. Naval Research Laboratory, Washington, D.C. 20375 USA
[2]Chemistry Division, Surface Chemistry Branch (Code 6170),
U.S. Naval Research Laboratory, Washington, D.C. 20375 USA

Abstract: Sulfur-based battery systems offer the potential to achieve high practical energy densities without the need for expensive and exotic material components. However, low electronic conductivity and tendencies toward redox shuttling of soluble polysulfide species in alkali-metal-sulfur systems inhibit the practical capacity of these batteries, which often falls short of achieving the 1675 mAh g^{-1} theoretical specific capacity of sulfur. In addition to the gravimetric aspect of these electrodes, areal and volumetric capacities must be considered for practical applications of such systems. To address these issues, we investigate the use of a highly scalable porous carbon nanofoam paper (CNFP) scaffold that has highly tunable pore size distributions, developed at the U.S. Naval Research Laboratory. A facile vapor deposition technique used to deposit sulfur on these CNFPs ensures that the electrode is binder-free. These sulfur-loaded CNFPs were examined via electrochemical cycling in a Lithium-Sulfur system, and the results of this study have indicated that an equilibrium between the pore size and sulfur mass loading yields the optimal performance of these materials with regards to the mass, areal, and volumetric capacities. Additionally, the CNFP scaffold has been demonstrated to be robust enough that it can function in pouch cell geometries without the need for an aluminum current collector, effectively reducing the amount of materials required for fabrication and overall mass of the cell.

Introduction

Although the past couple decades have seen a dramatic increase in the number of small consumer products powered by Li-ion batteries, many larger items, most notably electric vehicles, remain out-of-budget for the average consumer largely due to the high cost of the material components of the battery systems used to power them. There are three main factors hindering the widespread proliferation of these battery systems: availability of critical materials, expense of those materials, and limitations to the theoretical capacity of certain Li-based systems. Common Li-ion cathodes are composed of materials such as lithium iron phosphate (LFP) or mixed metal oxides that include metals like nickel, manganese, and cobalt (NMC). Though NMC has a higher energy density than LFP, expensive, rare, and geographically localized components like cobalt make forward-thinking consumers wary of placing too much stock in this type of cathode. And while its relative abundance and low cost make LFP seem an attractive substitute, the theoretical capacity of these electrodes is almost half that of NMC electrodes.

An alternative to the intercalation-based energy storage employed by Li-ion batteries is the conversion-based Lithium-Sulfur (Li-S) battery. The simple, widely available, non-toxic, and inexpensive materials used in this system can achieve a theoretical 1675 mAh g^{-1}, approximately an order of magnitude higher than that of LFP. [1] However, "polysulfide shuttling," where soluble polysulfide species dissolve into the electrolyte, effectively diminishes the coulombic efficiency of the cell, thus reducing cycle life and preventing the system from reaching its full capacity. [1] [2] To mitigate this shuttling effect, many studies focus on the material properties of the sulfur host, which is critical to effective performance of the sulfur electrode. Due to their high surface area, low mass, and moderately high conductivity, carbon aerogels or nanofoams serve as effective hosts for the active sulfur material, and it has been shown that sulfur infiltration of these materials followed by formation of a composite electrode with a polymer binder form capable Li-S electrodes. [3] [4]

Here, we demonstrate the unique capabilities of the highly versatile carbon nanofoam paper (CNFP) developed at the U.S. Naval Research Laboratory, which contains a porous carbon aerogel network supported by a robust scaffold of carbon fiber paper, thus enabling the CNFP to act as a free-standing electrode without binders or additives. The pore sizes of the nanofoam are tunable, making CNFPs highly adaptive to system optimization, and they have been proven an effective sulfur host in Li-S battery systems. In this work, we demonstrate that these papers have the potential to be used on a practical level, such that higher voltages and larger format cells are possible with CNFPs.

Experimental details

CNFP fabrication

The CNFPs used in this study were synthesized via a resorcinol-formaldehyde (RF) sol–gel process as previously described [5] [6] that allows for control of the pore size distribution, making these papers highly tunable for different applications. In short, resorcinol and formaldehyde were mixed in a 1:2 part ratio in water with Na_2CO_3 to create the sol precursor. Commercial carbon fiber paper (Lydall, 90 μm thick, 0.2g cm^{-3} density) was soaked in the sol precursor under vacuum, then the paper was aged and heated to ~90°C. The sheets were extracted, dried, and pyrolyzed under argon at 1000°C for 2h at a 1°C/min ramp rate.

The carbon fiber paper scaffold of the CNFPs makes this material robust and easy to work with. Coin cell electrodes can be cut from the CNFPs, or the full sheet can be used for pouch cell geometries. Figure 1a demonstrates both types of CNFP electrode shapes.

Sulfur infiltration

Once the desired electrode geometry was determined and prepared, the CNFP was infiltrated with sulfur using a vapor technique [7] [8]. The electrodes were put into a Teflon infiltration chamber on a 316 stainless steel mesh above a well containing sulfur powder. The chamber was sealed and placed in an oven at 175°C for 2h, then allowed to cool for approx. 30 minutes. The electrodes were massed before and after infiltration to determine sulfur loading.

EDS analysis on a cross section of a sulfur infiltrated CNFP (S@CNFP) electrode shows that the sulfur is deposited evenly throughout the depth of the sample, and that the sulfur preferentially deposits within the carbon nanofoam pores instead of on the larger carbon fiber features.

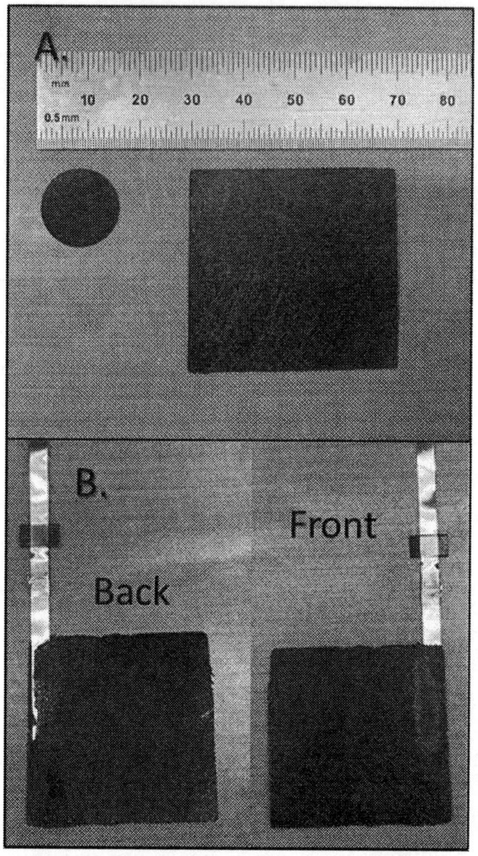

Figure 1. CNFP electrodes in different shapes. (A) The stiff carbon fiber framework allows the CNFP to be cut into different shapes and used for any number of cell geometries. (B) For use in the pouch cell, an aluminum tab can be glued directly to the CNFP without the need for a metal current collector.

Electrochemical testing

Standard 2032 coin cells were fabricated using Hohsen coin cell parts and an automated Hohsen 2032 coin cell crimper for characterization of the S@CNFP electrodes versus a Li metal (MTI) electrode with an Entek Gold separator and 1M LiTFSI and 0.2M $LiNO_3$ in DOL/DME (50/50) electrolyte.

The coin cell assembly does not allow for demonstration of the current-collector-free capabilities of CNFP; however, pouch cells were also fabricated to exhibit the ability of the CNFP host material to act as cathode and current collector simultaneously. Aluminum pouch cell tabs were adhered to a small portion of the CNFP electrode using conductive carbon glue (Fig. 1b). Pouch cells were fabricated using Li metal (MTI) on a copper current collector, an Entek Gold separator, and the S@CNFP electrode with tab. During assembly, the pouch cell was flooded with ~500 μL of electrolyte.

Electrochemical cycling was performed on a ParSTAT multichannel potentiostat PMC1000 under constant current conditions at 0.1C from 1.8 V to 2.6 V for the single pouch cell and 6.0 V to 7.8 V for the coin cells in series.

Results

Ongoing studies will determine the optimal CNPF pore structure for the Li-S system, but preliminary results show that when cycled at a rate of 0.1C, this material can enable stable cycling capacities over 300 mAh g^{-1} with regards to the full electrode. While these data indicate that there is much room for improvement with the system, this cathodic capacity is already greater than the theoretical capacity of NMC (~275 mAh g^{-1}). Additionally, although NMC has the advantage in terms of specific energy because its average discharge voltage is much higher than that of a Li-S cell, one facile method to increase the voltage of a cell and thus improve the Wh kg^{-1} of a system is to place two or more cells in series.

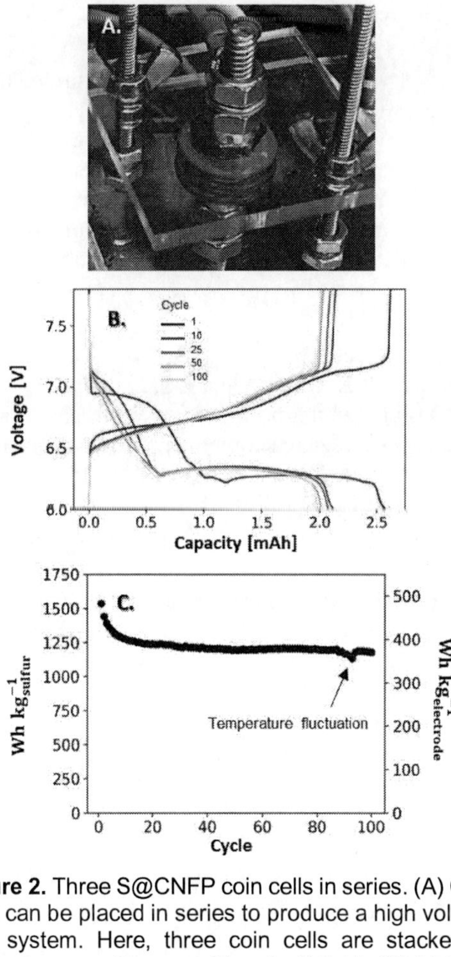

Figure 2. Three S@CNFP coin cells in series. (A) Coin cells can be placed in series to produce a high voltage Li-S system. Here, three coin cells are stacked to generate a system capable of >7.0 V. (B) Voltage profiles at various cycles and (C) cycling capacity are also shown.

Increasing the voltage of the Li-S system was achieved by putting three S@CNFP coin cells in series (shown in Figure 2a), raising the maximum voltage of the system from 2.6 V to >7.0 V. Figure 2 not only shows the cycling stability of the system, where after the first initial capacity loss the capacity remains stable from cycle 10 through cycle 100 (voltage profiles in Fig. 2b), it also shows the remarkable specific energy of the system, which can achieve ~1250 Wh kg^{-1} with respect to sulfur, or almost 400 Wh kg^{-1} when the whole electrode is taken into account (Fig. 2c). This is a much higher gravimetric energy density than the current benchmark for commercial Li-ion technologies, which achieve approximately 240 Wh kg^{-1} with NMC electrodes.

In addition to cell voltage, total capacity of the cell is an important metric to improve. While a modular approach of placing multiple cells in parallel would serve to increase the overall capacity, perhaps a more efficient means of producing a higher capacity

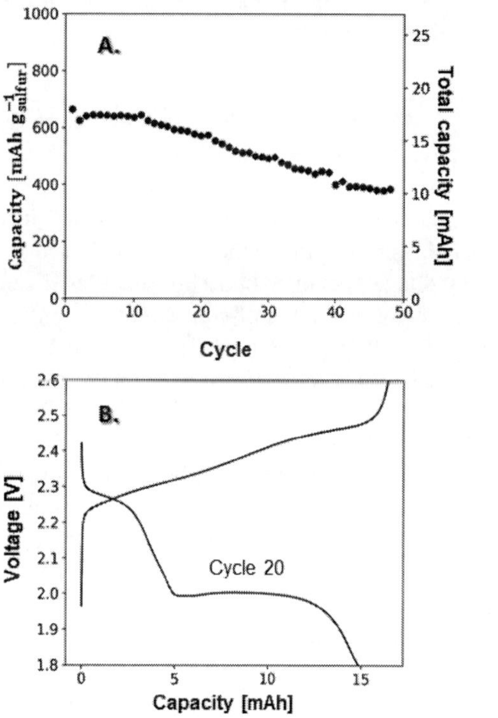

Figure 3. Electrochemical data for a pouch cell fabricated from a full sheet of S@CNFP. No metallic cathodic current collector was used in this cell. (A) Cycling data for ~50 cycles and (B) a representative voltage profile taken from cycle 20 detail the performance of the pouch cell.

Li-S system is simply to increase the size of the S@CNFP electrode. These cathodes were prepared for pouch cells by infiltrating the full CNFP sheet (~16 cm^2) in the same Teflon chamber as the coin cell electrodes. Even though the electrodes are ~10x the area of the coin cell electrodes, this process was simple and effective when scaling up to the larger electrode.

Figure 3a displays the cycling performance of the pouch cell fabricated from the S@CNFP electrode. Though the initial capacity of the pouch cell scaled well with the increase in electrode size (from ~2 mAh for a 1.77 cm^2 coin cell electrode to ~18 mAh for the 16 cm^2 pouch cell electrode), it declined over 50 cycles to approximately half of its initial value. Despite this diminution in performance, the similarity of the charge-discharge profile of this cell (Figure 3b) to a typical Li-S cell establishes the ability of the S@CNFP to function sans current collector. This feature, as well as the lack of binders and conductive additives, are just a few of the more beneficial aspects of the CNFP material, which has been demonstrated to be a capable sulfur host material for Li-S batteries. The material efficiency of CNFPs serves to improve overall gravimetric energy density and reduce the material needs and costs of the cell.

Conclusions

The simplicity of the Li-S system makes it attractive for future batteries, and here we show how sulfur-infiltrated CNFPs can provide high energy systems efficiently and with materials that incur a much lower cost than other Li-based systems. The high voltage system comprised of three coin cells in series serves as a proof-of-concept that the S@CNFP material can provide realistic gravimetric energy densities needed to power large commercial devices. Additionally, the fabrication of a larger capacity pouch cell without a metallic current collector shows the capability to scale both the CNFP material and the integrated Li-S@CNFP system such that it would be a viable, lightweight, and inexpensive option for commercial batteries.

Acknowledgements

The authors thank Dr. Joseph Parker (Office of Naval Research, grant N0001422WX01023) and the U.S. Naval Research Laboratory for financial support of this work. This research was performed while Matthew J. Lefler and Zachary G. Neale held NRC Research Associateship awards at the U.S. Naval Research Laboratory.

References

[1] M. Wang, X. Xia, Y. Zhong, J. Wu, R. Xu, Z. Yao, D. Wang, W. Tang, X. Wang and J. Tu, "Porous Carbon Hosts for Lithium-Sulfur Batteries," *Chemistry - A European Journal,* vol. 25, no. 15, pp. 3710-3725, 2018.

[2] W. Ren, W. Ma, S. Zhang and B. Tang, "Recent Advances in Shuttle Effect Inhibition for Lithium Sulfur Batteries," *Energy Storage Materials,* vol. 23, pp. 707-732, 2019.

[3] M. Nojabee, B. Sievert, M. Schwan, J. Schettler, F. Warth, N. Wagner, B. Milow and K. A. Friedrich, "Ultramicroporous Carbon Aerogels Encapsulating Sulfur as the Cathode for Lithium-Sulfur Batteries," *Journal of Materials Chemistry A,* vol. 9, no. 10, pp. 6508-6519, 2021.

[4] F. Qun, K. Zhang, Z. Zhang, J. Fang, J. Li, Y. Lai and H. Huang, "Graphene/Carbon Aerogel for High Areal Capacity Sulfur Cathode of Li-S Batteries," *Ionics,* vol. 25, no. 10, pp. 4615-4624, 2019.

[5] J. C. Lytle, J. M. Wallace, M. B. Sassin, A. J. Barrow, J. W. Long, J. L. Dysart, C. H. Renninger, M. P. Saunders, N. L. Brandell and D. R. Rolison, "The right kind of interior for multifunctional electrode architectures: carbon nanofoam papers with aperiodic submicrometre pore networks interconnected in 3D," *Energy & Environmental Science,* vol. 4, no. 5, pp. 1912-1925, 2011.

[6] M. B. Sassin, C. P. Hoag, B. T. Willis, N. W. Kicko, D. R. Rolison and J. W. Long, "Designing high-performance electrochemical energy-storage nanoarchitectures to balance rate and capacity," *Nanoscale,* vol. 5, no. 4, pp. 1649-1657, 2013.

[7] R. E. Carter, L. Oakes, N. Muralidharan, A. P. Cohn, A. Douglas and C. L. Pint, "Polysulfide Anchoring Mechanism Revealed by Atomic Layer Deposition of V2O5 and Sulfur-Filled Carbon Nanotubes for Lithium-Sulfur Batteries," *ACS Applied Materials & Interfaces,* vol. 9, no. 8, pp. 7185-7192, 2017.

[8] M. Li, R. E. Carter, A. Douglas, L. Oakes and C. L. Pint, "Sulfur Vapor-Infiltrated 3D Carbon Nanotube Foam for Binder-Free High Areal Capacity Lithium–Sulfur Battery Composite Cathodes," *ACS Nano,* vol. 11, no. 5, pp. 4877-4884, 2017.

Advanced Lithium-Sulfur Batteries Based on Lyten 3D Graphene™

Ratnakumar Bugga, Celina Mikolajczak, Karel Vanheusden, Arjun Mendiratta, Anurag Kumar, Babu Ganguli, Yongtao Meng, Jefferey Bell, Zack Favors, and Dan Cook
Lyten Inc., 145 Baytech Dr., San Jose, CA 95134
kumar.bugga@lyten.com / 1-626-684-2545

Abstract

Li-S batteries promise significant advantages over Li-ion batteries but have been hampered by poor cycle life caused by polysulfide shuttle. Lyten, an advanced materials company, has developed new 3D Graphene™ material with mechanically flexible and electrically conductive framework, and hierarchical porous structure designed for potentially confining sulfur and polysulfides and mitigate polysulfide shuttle. Lyten 3D Graphene™ materials have shown enhanced sulfur utilization in Li-S cells far superior to the commercial nanocarbons, and upon integration with Lyten's new protected Li anodes, advanced electrolytes, and multi-functional separators have resulted in Li-S cells with specific energy comparable to current Li-ion cells (~250 -275 Wh/kg). The cycle life is, however, relatively modest with 300 cycles @ 100% DOD, C/3 in coin cells, and 150 cycles@100% DOD and over one thousand cycles @ 50% DOD in multi-layer pouch cells and 18650 cylindrical cells. There is a steady growth in both these categories enabled by further tuning of 3D graphene and advances in other materials. Preliminary safety tests performed on early prototype cells have yielded surprisingly good results for the Li-S cells containing Li metal anode.

Keywords

Lithium-sulfur cells; 3D graphene; polysulfide shuttle; abuse tolerance; specific energy; high-capacity sulfur cathode; multi-layer pouch cells; 18650 Li-S cells, green technology; abundant and inexpensive raw materials.

Introduction

With the projected need for a large number of Li-ion batteries (LIB) to support rapidly expanding EVs, there are serious challenges from the availability and supply of key materials (e.g., Co and Ni), which are exacerbated by the relentless control of Asian countries on the processing of these critical materials, and their overwhelming dominance in battery manufacturing. It is expected that these issues will impact critical DoD applications that require high energy batteries, making it strategically disadvantageous for the US government. Additionally, the future EVs and DoD applications demand battery technologies with higher specific energy and energy density, beyond the capabilities of LIB. Lithium - sulfur (Li-S) batteries are the leading candidates among the next generation high energy systems to supplement or supplant LIB. Unlike other high energy systems with NMC cathodes, Li-S chemistry has the distinct advantage of being unaffected by the criticality and scarcity of raw materials (e.g., Co, Ni and Mn), and is benefited by a robust supply chain and stable pricing for the key materials. Li- S cells can potentially offer 2-3-fold higher specific energy compared to LIB at significantly lower cost and have better compliance with environmental regulations and a significantly reduced carbon footprint.[1] Despite their numerous advantages, the implementation of Li-S batteries in practice has been impeded by their classic problem of 'polysulfide (PS) shuttle', which is a result of PS dissolution in liquid electrolyte, and is primarily responsible for poor cycle life.[2]

Lyten, an advanced materials company founded in 2015, has developed Lyten 3D Graphene™ (3DG) from methane cracking that has a flexible, electrically conductive framework and a hierarchical porous structure to accommodate high proportions of sulfur. Lyten's patented[3] reactor technology allows fine tuning of key parameters of 3D graphene such as porosity, surface area, conductivity, surface energy etc., to create a novel host for sulfur cathode that can support facile sulfur reduction and potentially sequester polysulfides within the cathode structure through "nano-capture". Figure 1 shows the nano-phase features of Lyten 3D graphene through a SEM image of a 3D graphene-sulfur cathode made with proprietary post-synthesis processing, lithium infusion and finally casting electrodes using industry-standard fabrication methods and equipment.

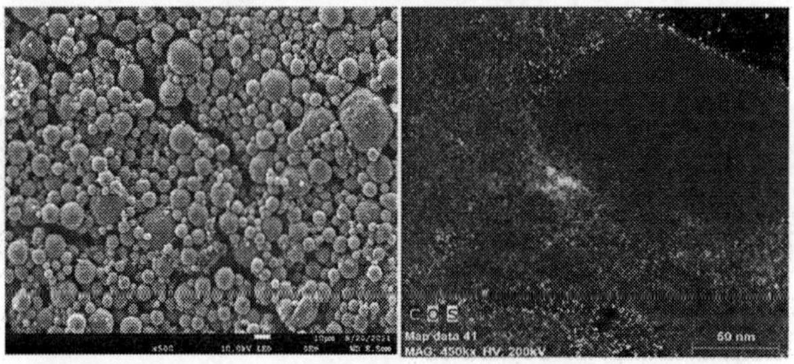

Fig. 1 SEM of Lyten 3D Graphene-sulfur cathode (left) and uniform distribution of sulfur in the cathode from SEM_EDS (right)

Lithium-sulfur chemistry is rather complex not only due to the sulfur cathodes, but due to the challenges from the lithium anode, which include severe morphological changes, dendritic deposition, and continued electrolyte consumption in the form of SEI formation. Lyten's Li-S cell development is thus focused on developing multiple components: i) 3D graphene tuned chemically and for appropriate nano/micro porosity, ii) 3d graphene sulfur composite cathodes with high areal capacity (mAh/cm^2), iii) protected Li anodes for dendrite-free cycling, iv) electrolytes compatible with Li anode and sulfur cathode kinetics, v) multi-functional separators and vi) energy-efficient cell designs, both multi-layer pouch cells and cylindrical 18650 cells.

Tuning of 3D Graphene

The unique morphology, surface characteristics and tunability of Lyten 3D graphene nano carbons have rendered them impressive performance compared to the commercial nano-porous carbons commonly used in Li-S cells (Fig.2).

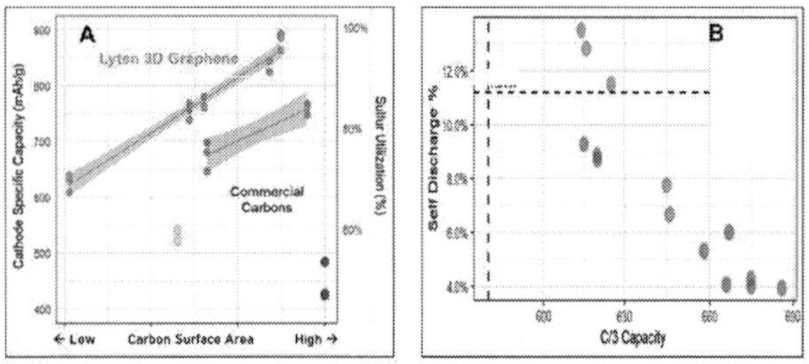

Fig. 2 Superior performance of Lyten 3D graphene-sulfur cathodes compared to the commercial analogs: A) Discharge @ C/20 and B) Self-discharge over one week at 100% State of charge.

As shown in Fig. 2, both sulfur utilization and self-discharge are distinctly superior for Lyten 3D graphenes, with the sulfur utilization improving by 15% and self-discharge decreasing to 30%, compared to the best commercial analog.

Protected Li Anode

Designing a stable Li anode is more challenging in Li-S cells compared to other Li metal batteries due to the adverse effects of polysulfides in forming insulting lithium sulfide films on the anode. Lyten has developed new protected Li anodes incorporating modifications both in the bulk composition and interfacial conditions, which have led to noticeable improvements in the cycle life of Li-S cells. Fig. 3 shows the cycle life of Li-S coin cells with different anodes and high sulfur loading cathodes during 100% DOD cycling at C/3, and the improvement of rate capability with a 3D anode.

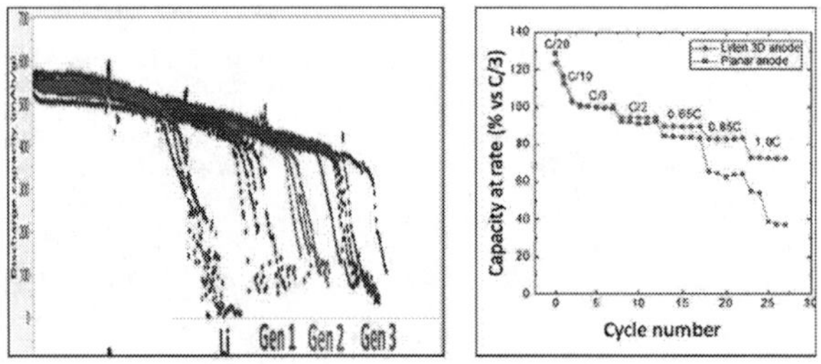

Fig. 3. Various innovative anodes, Gen-1, Gen-2 and Gen -3, displaying progressively increasing cycle life in Li-S coin cell vs. Li anode. The new 3D anode (Right) shows improved high-rate performance (1C)

As shown above, there is progressive improvement in cycle life from Li anode through the various generations of anode, and an improvement in the high-rate performance with our first generation of 3D Li anode.

Advanced Electrolyte

Since sulfur undergoes solid-liquid-solid reaction in our current design with liquid electrolytes, the choice of electrolyte is very crucial not only in achieving adequate stability at the anode, but also to support sulfur reduction kinetics at the moderate to high discharge rates ($\geq$C/3). Another requirement for the electrolyte is that it needs to enable the cells to operate with low electrolyte quantity i.e., electrolyte to sulfur ratio (E/S), which is crucial in realizing high specific energy. Unlike Li-ion cells, electrolyte indeed contributes to ~50% of the cell mass and it is a challenge to bring it down, especially with cathodes with high sulfur-loadings. Lyten has investigated hundreds of binary and ternary formulations with different salts and additives and identified a family of electrolyte formulations that outperform the electrolyte formulations commonly used in the literature. Fig. 4 shows the performance of some of these electrolytes in coin cells with the Li anode, and in pouch cells with Gen-1 or Gen-2 anodes containing low E/S.

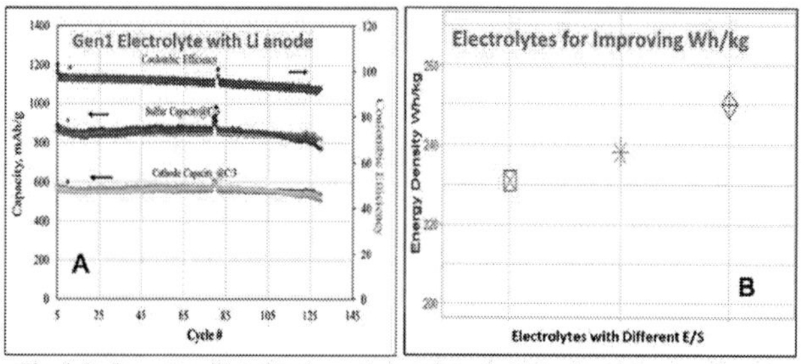

Fig. 4. Performance of Lyten's advanced electrolytes in Li-S cells: A) In coin cells with Li anode, B) In pouch cells enabling low E/S for improving specific energy.

Multi-layer Pouch (MLP) and Cylindrical 18650 Cells

Lyten has developed high-energy cell designs in both cylindrical and pouch format. Two key design parameters to realize high specific energy in a Li-S cell are: i) low E/S and ii) high sulfur loadings (Fig.5)[4], both of which pose challenges for achieving long cycle life.

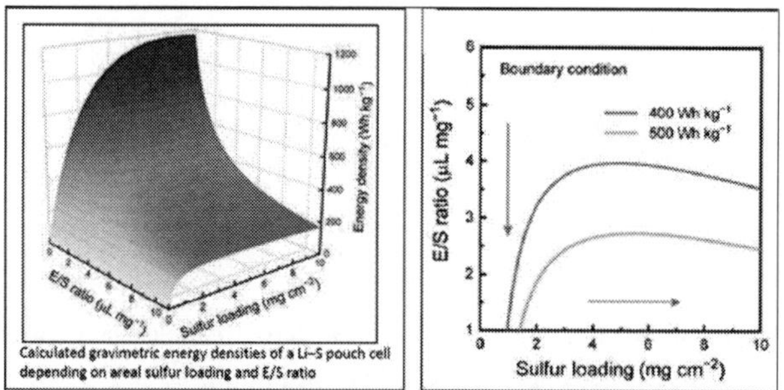

Fig. 5.High specific energy of a Li-S cell dictated by low electrolyte content (E/S) and high sulfur loading (Yang et al., Electrochemical Energy Reviews (2018) 1, 239-293.

Lyten has developed 3D graphene-sulfur cathodes with new binders in smaller proportions, high sulfur loadings and high areal capacities (mAh/g), and high-energy cell designs with minimal excess anode capacity (low N:P ratio) and low quantities of electrolyte (low E/S ratio). These advances have culminated in Lyten Li-S cells with high specific energy (275 Wh/kg), on par with current Li-ion cells. The cycle life in MLP and 18650 cells is currently shorter, at ~150 cycles at 100% DOD, in contrast to the 300 cycles realized in coin cells, and improvements are underway to close this gap.

Partial DOD Cycling

Similar to other battery chemistries, e.g., aqueous Ni rechargeable batteries or LIB, Li-S cells also provide longer cycle life at partials DODs. Partial DOD cycling is adopted in several applications, especially satellites to extend the cycle life and operational life of batteries. Our early version prototype cells that have lower specific energy have demonstrated ~600 cycles at 40% DOD and ~1200 cycles at 20%. We have been able to achieve similar benefit from partial DOD cycling in our recent high-energy cell designs (Fig. 6).

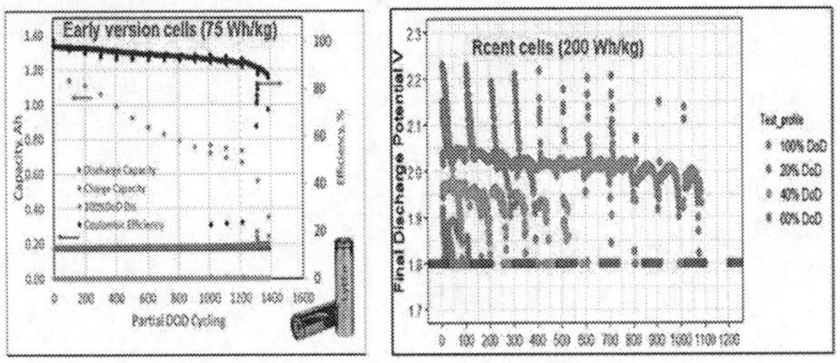

Fig. 6 Cycling of Lyten's early version 18650 Li-S cells at 20% DOD (left) and of recent high energy cells at variuos DODs.

Based on the extrapolation from the Wohler curve between cycle life and DOD, we expect to get >1000 cycles at 50% DOD and >2000 cycles at shallower DOD in our recent high-energy cells.

Safety of Lyten Li-S cells

Another notable advantage of Lyten Li-S cells is their superior abuse tolerance, compared to LIB, during electrical, mechanical, and thermal abuse. Though Li-S cells, like other Li metal batteries, are suspected to be less safe due to metallic Li, the safety of Lyten Li-S (1.5 Ah) multi-layer pouch and 18650 cylindrical cells has been surprisingly good as demonstrated in our preliminary abuse tests: nail penetration simulating internal short, external short, overcharge, over-discharge, and mechanical crush test (Fig. 7, only nail penetration and overcharge are shown).

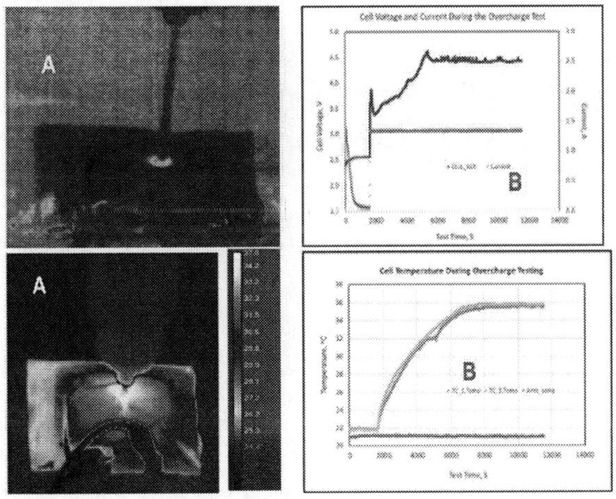

Fig. 7 Safety tests on Lyten Li-S cells (1.5 Ah): A) Nail penetration and B) Overcharge

There is no flame, smoke, charring, rupture, or thermal runaway in any of these abuse tests, underlining the innate safety of Lyten Li-S cells. This behavior is consistent with previous studies in literature. For example, nail penetration tests conducted on Oxis's MLP Li-S cells by Offer et al[4] reveal that the cells could survive nail penetration well, while also maintaining the cell voltage. This is possibly due to the non-conductive reaction products such as Li_2S_2 and Li_2S formed locally at the penetration site during high current events, which insulate the short circuit and allow the cell to behave normally. Alternately the soluble polysulfides formed locally may make the electrolyte viscous, less conducting and limit the reaction. The overcharge tolerance of Li-S is also consistent with the studies by Huang et al.[5] and is attributed to the disproportionation reaction of long-chain lithium polysulfides and the absence of oxygen evolution from the cathode. Fig. 8 summarizes the results of various safety tests performed on MLP and 18650 cells.

Electrical	External Short	Rapid drop to 0V	pouch	1.90 Ah	No damage/fire, T_{max} = 26 °C
			18650	1.03 Ah	No damage/fire, T_{max} = 37 °C
	Over charge	1C Charge until > 200% SoC	pouch	1.87 Ah	No damage/fire, T_{max} = 32 °C
			18650	1.36 Ah	No damage/fire, T_{max} = 93 °C
	Over discharge	1C Discharge	pouch	1.85 Ah	No damage/fire, T_{max} = 26 °C
			18650	1.24 Ah	No damage/fire, T_{max} = 37 °C
Mechanical	Nail Penetration	3 mm Nail puncture at 10 mm s^{-1}	pouch	1.86 Ah	No damage/fire, T_{max} = 35 °C
			18650	1.43 Ah	No damage/fire, T_{max} = 62 °C
	Ball Crush	51 mm Sphere at 2 mm s^{-1}	pouch	1.75 Ah	No damage/fire, T_{max} = 27 °C

Fig. 8. Summary of abuse test results on Li-S MLP/18650 cells.

As shown above, there is no flame, smoke, charring, rupture, or thermal runaway or any damage except for a small rise in temperature, in any of these abuse tests. More recently, thermal runaway tests performed on similar Oxis cells show the absence of runaway behavior during thermal ramp tests even up to 300°C, especially in cells with lean electrolyte.[6] We are planning to perform a full suite of safety testing including ARC (Accelerated Rate Calorimetry) on larger prototype cells (4-5 Ah) to be fabricated in-house.

Prototype Cell Manufacturing

Concurrent with the on-going material and cell development for enhanced performance and safety demonstration, semi-automatic cell assembly lines have been installed and are being commissioned to manufacture prototype cells at a rate of about 100k/y cells of both cylindrical (18650/2170/26650) and pouch cells of 10 Ah. The pilot scale assembly lines have a projected total capacity of 2.4 MWh/y) (Fig. 9).

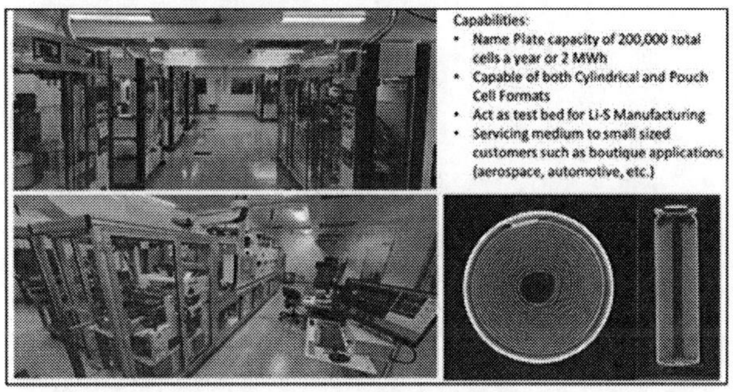

Fig. 9. Pilot lines for assembling MLP (10Ah) and 18650/ 2170/ 26650 cylindrical Li-S cells

Cell fabrication processes of Li-S cells are similar to LIB, and involve the standard processes of electrode coating, electrolyte filling and cell sealing, which allowed us to adopt conventional equipment used for the assembly of LIB cells in our pilot cell assembly lines. Additionally, multiple battery tester units (Maccor and Arbin) with >3000 test channels have been set up for cell formation and cycling.

Lyten's Li-S Roadmap

Subsequent to a successful manufacturing of prototype cells on the in-house pilot scale assembly lines for MLP and cylindrical cells, Lyten is planning to set up a mini-GW plant, which will enable us provide samples to various boutique customers, e.g., aerospace and niche DoD applications, such as drones, UAVs, CubeSats and Smallsats. Lyten plans to infuse their Li-S battery technology into various civilian and commercial applications, which will supplement or drive additional production volumes in domestic markets, as the performance levels match the requirements of these applications. As the technology is matured for large-scale implementation in commercial (EV) and a range of DoD applications, one or two GW factories will be planned within US at strategic locations. Detailed lists of BOM and assured and redundant suppliers are being established for the materials and components. Fig. 10 shows the roadmap, both for technology and production, for Lyten Li-S batteries over the next few years.

Lyten's Li-S technology will alleviate supply chain challenges, sole source dependency concerns, variable procurement practices, and prohibitive costs associated with the current battery technologies. Being a domestic manufacturer, Lyten will be a reliable and robust source of rechargeable batteries, which is critical importance to the US defense industrial base.

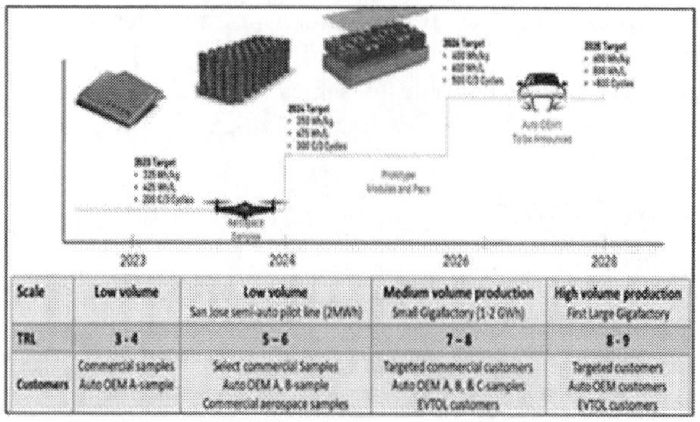

Fig. 10. Lyten Li-S Cell performance and production roadmap

Acknowledgements

The authors acknowledge the US Space Force and DIU for partially funding part of this work.

References

1. Z. Chen et al., *Adv. Mater*. 2022, 2201555.
2. Y. V. Mikhaylik et al., *J. Electrochem. Soc*., 151, A1969-A1976 (2004).
3. Lyten patent "Carbonaceous material for Li-S cells" *US patent* 11309 545 B2, April 19, 2022.
4. I. Hunt et al., *J. Energy Storage*, 2, 25 (2015).
5. X. Huang et al., *J. Energy Storage Materials*, 30, 87 (2020).
6. F. Jiang et al., *Particuology*, 79, pp10-17 (2023).

Lithium Sulfur Pouch Cells with Improved Energy Density for Portable Power Applications

Ernest Ndzebet, Mario Destephen, Logan Wittmaier and Anulekha Haridas
Research and Development
EaglePicher Technologies
1215 West C Street, Joplin, MO 64801
ernest.ndzebet@eaglepicher.com

Abstract: *The Lithium-Sulfur (LiS) battery has been considered one of the most promising rechargeable power sources because of its high theoretical energy density, low cost, and environmentally friendly elemental Sulfur cathode material. However, LiS batteries still suffer from historical limitations that include short cycle life, poor shelf life, and low energy density and rate capability. EaglePicher has developed an electrolyte formulation, high loading cathode, and proprietary Nanoclay separator to address these limitations, demonstrating improved performance in a small 2 Ah pouch cell format. A nominal specific energy greater than 400 Wh/kg at room temperature is projected in a larger 10 Ah pouch cell format. Moreover, early prototypes of the LiS pouch cells passed preliminary safety tests and successfully operated in a wide temperature range. These results prompted EaglePicher to build 28 Volt prototype batteries with an internally developed battery management system (BMS).*

Keywords: Lithium-Sulfur; Nanoclay separators; shelf life; cycle life; intermittent discharge performance

Introduction

There has been increasing demand for secondary batteries with lighter weight and higher capacity for portable power applications. Lithium-Sulfur is a promising chemistry which offers a high theoretical capacity of 1672 mAh/g and theoretical specific energy of 2600 Wh/kg [1]. In addition, Sulfur is cheap and environmentally safe, which makes Lithium-Sulfur an attractive chemistry for next generation batteries beyond Li-ion. There are some challenges associated with this chemistry, however. Sulfur (5x10-30 S/cm) and its final discharge product, Lithium sulfide, are both insulators, requiring a high percentage of Carbon to achieve sufficient cathode conductivity and rate capability [2]. The high carbon content in the cathode can result in LiS cell will low practical energy density.

The discharge of a Lithium-Sulfur battery proceeds in multiple steps. In the first plateau, Sulfur is converted to polysulfides (Li_2S_n, n varies from 3 to 8). In the second plateau these polysulfides are reduced to solids, Li_2S_2 and finally to Li_2S. The polysulfides (Li_2S_n, $3<n<8$) are soluble in electrolyte and can be deposited as Li_2S either on the anode or on the cathode. When deposited on the cathode, the Li_2S clogs the pores over multiple charge/discharge cycles. In addition, there is also volume change due to the differences in the molar volumes of S and Li_2S, which affects the cathode structure. Both of these effects lead to a decrease in capacity over the course of the cycle life.

During charging, the Li_2S on the cathode side is oxidized to higher-order polysulfides, which can migrate and get reduced to lower-order polysulfides as Li_2S deposits on the anode. Thus, the soluble polysulfides can shuttle between cathode and anode causing extended charging times and low coulombic efficiency in the Lithium-Sulfur chemistry. This causes further capacity fading over multiple charge/discharge cycles [3]. In addition, upon storage, Sulfur can dissolve in the electrolyte as a polysulfide via a self-discharge mechanism [4], leading to poor shelf-life performance.

Different approaches, including the use of highly porous Carbon materials to confine Sulfur and polysulfides in the cathode structure, have been attempted to address these issues [5]. In addition, the use of redox-active interlayers consisting of Sulfur impregnated polar ordered mesoporous silica was found effective as a means to increase cell capacity and to protect the anode [6].

With respect to electrolyte, numerous reports exist regarding the choice of solvents in liquid electrolyte, the use of gel electrolytes, and polymer electrolytes to reduce the diffusion of polysulfides towards the anode [7, 8]. In some cases, anode protection from polysulfide deposition has been achieved through the use of electrolyte additives [8]. Indeed, the additive $LiNO_3$ is known to suppress the redox shuttle of the dissolved polysulfides on the Li anode [9]. Although the above-mentioned approaches led to LiS cells with improved rate capability and cycle life, further work is still needed to increase their practical energy density.

This paper details the development of high energy density LiS pouch cells for portable power applications. In this work, a combined approach that includes advanced high loading cathode development, electrolyte formulation, separator development, and in situ anode protection was used to improve the energy density and shelf-life performance of LiS cells. Preliminary safety evaluations of these cells and their performance in a battery configuration were also evaluated.

Experimental

EaglePicher has developed a high energy density LiS pouch cell that includes a web-coated high loading Sulfur cathode consisting of proprietary Carbon materials and separator. This was achieved through extensive development efforts over the last several years. The web coating process enables thinner cathodes with improved rate capability, which contributes to improvements in LiS cell performance. The type of Carbon used as a conducting additive and its distribution within the cathode structure, as well as optimized cathode porosity further enhance the cell rate capability. Carbon and Sulfur were processed in a specified ratio to form a Carbon/Sulfur composite cathode. Our cathode processing is a modified version of the process reported elsewhere [3]. The Carbon/Sulfur composite was mixed with the binder and solvent, and the resulting slurry was coated on an aluminum current collector to form the cathode.

The electrochemical performance of the Lithium-Sulfur cell was evaluated in a stack pouch cell configuration using our proprietary nanoclay/polymer separator, which was made by a solution casting method. Cells were activated with our proprietary electrolyte. The cell performance evaluation was conducted at temperatures ranging from -20°C to 60°C using an Arbin battery cycler. Cycling was between 2.7 V and 1.7 V (vs. Li^+/Li) at a rate of $\geq$0.4 mA/cm^2. Li-S cells undergo more severe self-discharge than more typical LIBs due to polysulfide shuttling. Because of this, the cell shelf-life evaluation was carried out through accelerated aging at 45°C up to one (1) month. Preliminary safety evaluations including nail penetration, overcharge, external short circuit, and crush tests were carried out at room temperature.

The performance improvements observed at the cell level prompted us to build a 28V prototype battery consisting of 14 stack pouch cells in series with an in-house developed BMS. The battery was cycled at similar rates at room temperature.

Results & Discussion

Figure 1 shows the performance of LiS cells discharged at C/8 and room temperature. As can be seen, the cells delivered an average capacity of 1.92 Ah when discharged to 1.7V. They delivered an average specific energy of 213 Wh/kg on the first cycle and 175 Wh/kg on the 30th, as illustrated in Figure 2. It is expected that, with further cell design optimization including higher Sulfur loadings and lower electrolyte amounts, this chemistry can deliver 250 Wh/kg in this 2 Ah pouch format. In a larger 10 Ah pouch cell, a projected nominal specific energy of greater than 400 Wh/kg at room temperature can be achieved.

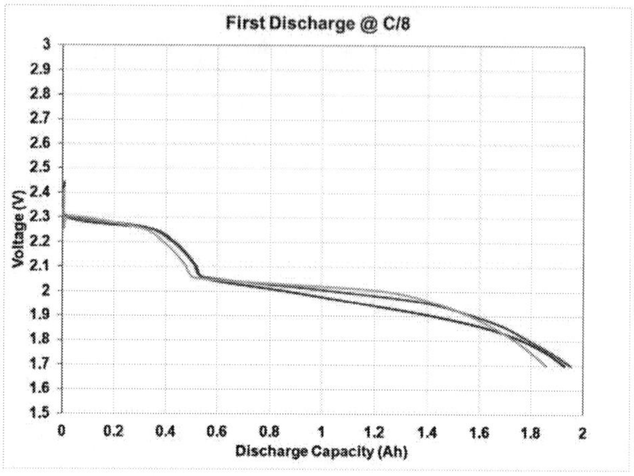

Figure 1. Discharge profile of LiS at room temperature

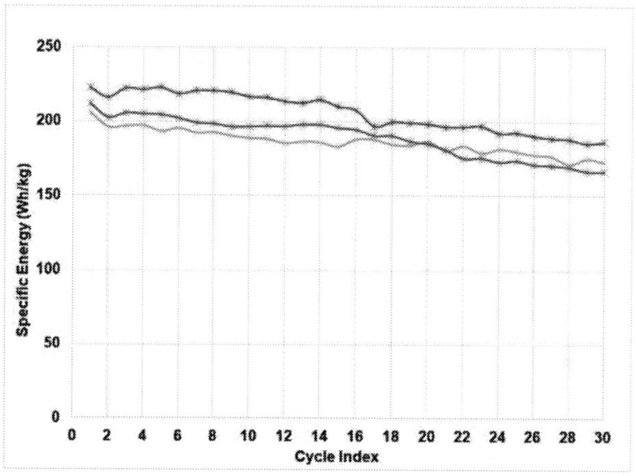

Figure 2. Cycling performance at room temperature

Discharge performance of these cells was also evaluated at temperatures ranging from -20°C to 60°C, illustrated in Figure 3. As can be seen, cells showed initial capacities higher than 750 mAh/g for most of the investigated temperatures, with higher temperatures yielding higher initial capacities. The lowest performance observed was in cells tested at -20°C, which can be attributed to an increase in electrolyte viscosity and slow diffusion of polysulfides in the cathode at low temperatures.

The cycling performance of LiS cells at different discharge rates is shown in Figure 4. As can be seen, high capacity and improved cycle life is observed in cells tested at C/8. When tested at rates higher than C/8, cells showed capacities of 700 mAh/g for 10 cycles, but after 30 cycles this is reduced to 500 mAh/g. Further development work focusing on the use of Carbon nanotubes and new binders in the cathode, anode protection, and electrolyte additives is under way to improve cell rate capability and capacity.

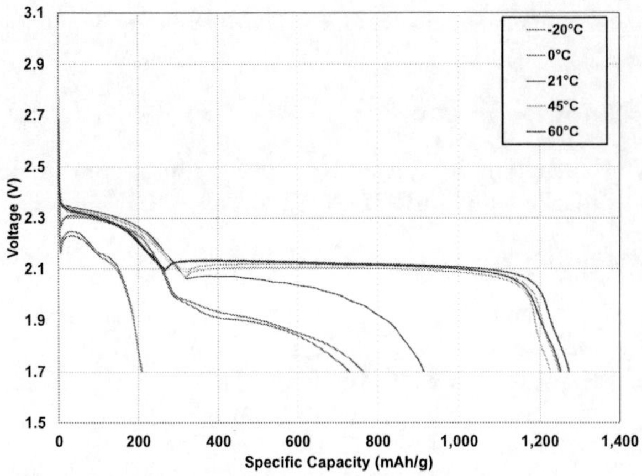

Figure 3. Effect of temperatures on LiS cell performance

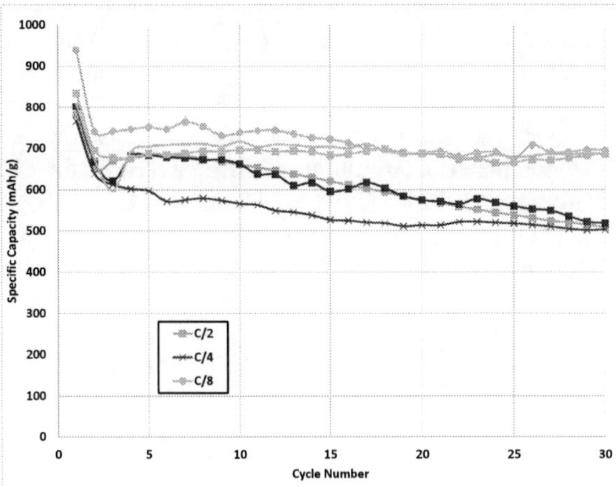

Figure 4. Cycle life performance at different discharge rates

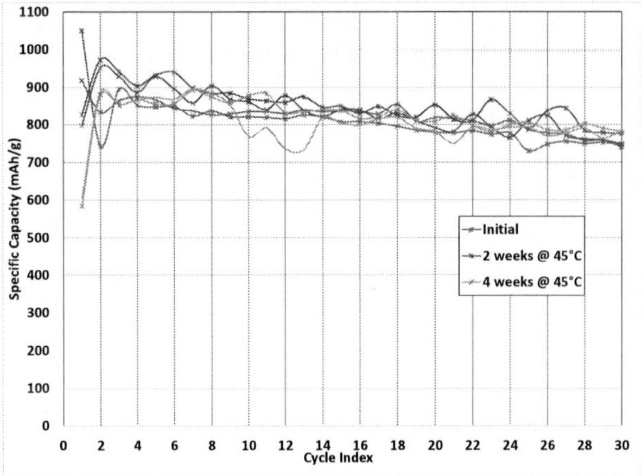

Figure 5. Shelf-life performance of cells after 45C storage

Cells were stored at 45°C for two and four weeks to evaluate their shelf-life performance. Data from fresh cells is provided for comparison. As can be seen in Figure 5, the initial capacity is lower after two weeks and four weeks of storage compared to that of fresh cells, but the capacity recovered after one discharge/charge cycle. Overall, these cells showed good cycle life with minimum capacity loss over 30 cycles after being stored at 45°C.

Initial safety evaluations were conducted on the LiS pouch cell, and the conditions and results of each test are summarized in Table 1. The cells passed each test without producing fire or smoke. These preliminary results are encouraging, but further testing is still needed for a full safety assessment of this cell design.

Table 1. Preliminary Safety Tests of LiS Pouch Cell

Test	Conditions	Observation	Result
Nail Penetration	-Fresh cells at 100% SOC -After 10 cycles at 100% SOC	No smoke or fire	Passed
Over Charge at 1C rate (2A)	-Fresh cells at 100% SOC -After 10 cycles at 100% SOC	No fire, Cell swelled	Passed
External Short-Circuit (1.5mΩ resistance)	Fresh cells at 100% SOC -After 10 cycles at 100% SOC	No fire, Cell swelled	Passed
Crush Test – 13±0.78 kN @ 1.5 cm/s speed	Fresh cells at 100% SOC -After 10 cycles at 100% SOC	No smoke or fire	Passed

As mentioned earlier, the observed cell performance improvements were achieved through cathode processing and design, along with our proprietary electrolyte formulation and functionalized nanoclay separator. This separator has showed improved performance over commercially available separators, as previously reported [11]. The efficacy of the nanoclay separator is believed to be arising from the ability of its positive functional groups to electrostatically bond with the negatively charged polysulfides.

LiS cells with these improvements were built into a battery in a 14S1P configuration with a BMS that was developed in-house. This yielded a battery pack with nominal voltage and capacity of 28V and 2Ah, respectively. The first prototype battery was cycled at the C/8 rate at room temperature, but was stopped after 5 cycles due to a BMS related error. Figure 6 shows this cycling effort. The first cycle shows low capacity, but it increases after subsequent cycles.

The capacity delivered by the battery is lower than the expected 2Ah due to the nature of the implemented BMS and the configuration of the battery. With cells in series, one poor performing cell will greatly affect the performance of the battery overall. Cell balancing in a series string of cells such as this prototype would require additional development work on a more advanced BMS.

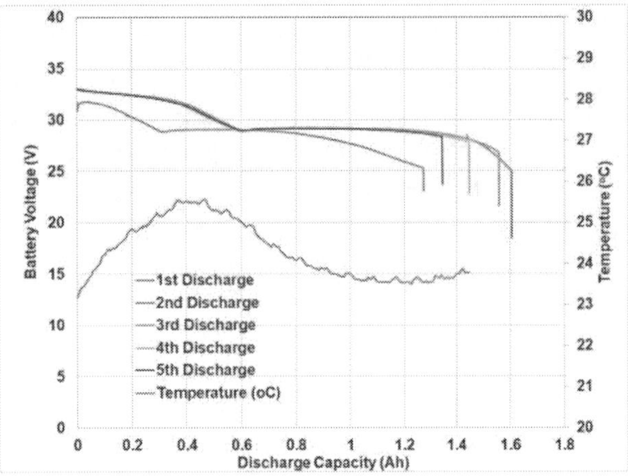

Figure 6. Discharge profile of the prototype battery

A second prototype was made and subjected to more extended cycling, shown in Figure 7. This battery went through more than 30 charge/discharge cycles before testing was stopped. This battery shows lower capacity and higher capacity fade than the individual cells shown earlier, but with a more advanced BMS that can better balance individual cells in the pack, both of these effects can be minimized.

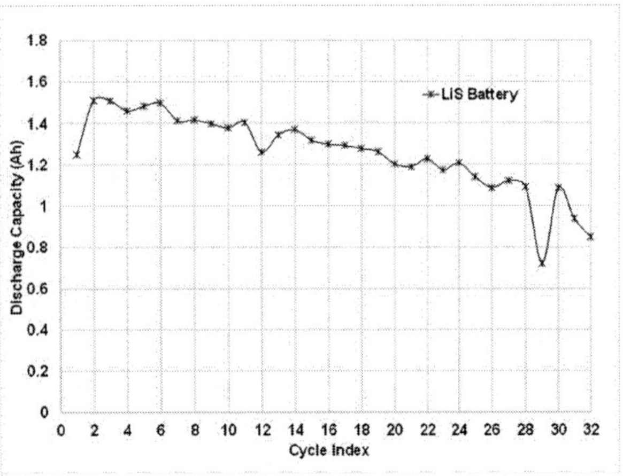

Figure 7. Cycle life of second prototype LiS battery

Conclusion

EaglePicher has developed 2Ah LiS pouch cells with improved discharge, cycle life, and shelf life performance. This was achieved through use of our proprietary electrolyte formulation, high loading cathode, and proprietary nanoclay separator. A nominal specific energy greater than 400 Wh/kg at room temperature is projected in a larger 10Ah pouch cell format. Moreover, early prototypes of the LiS pouch cells passed preliminary safety tests and successfully operated in a wide temperature range. The performance of these cells was evaluated in 28V, 2Ah prototype batteries with an internally developed battery management system (BMS) with encouraging results.

Acknowledgments

This material is released to the public domain in accordance with ITAR 22 CFR 120.11.

References

1. Ji, X. and L.F. nazar, "Advances in Li-S batteries", *J. Materials. Chem.*, vol. 22, pp. 691-714, 2010.
2. Han, J-S., S-S. Choi, S-H. Park and Y-S. Choi, "Positive electrode for Lithium-Sulfur battery", *US Patent*, no, 7147968B2, Dec. 12, 2006.
3. Ji, X., K.T. Lee and L.F. Nazar, "A highly ordered nanostructured Carbon-Sulfur cathode for Lithium-Sulfur batteries", *Nature Materials*, vol. 9, pp. 500-506, 2009.
4. Yamin, H. and E. Peled, "Electrochemistry of a nonaqueous Lithium/Sulfur cell", *J. Power Sources*, vol. 9, pp. 281-287, 1983.
5. Liang, C., N.J. Dudney and J.Y. Howe, "Sulfur-Carbon nanocomposites and their application as cathode materials in Lithium-Sulfur batteries", for *US Patent*, no. 2011/0052998A1, Mar. 3, 2011.
6. Lee, BJ. et al, "Development of high-energy density non-aqueous lithium sulfur batteries via redox-active interlayer strategy", Nat Commun 13, 4629 (2022). https://doi.org/10.1038/s41467-022-31943-8.
7. Chu, M.-Y., L.C. De Jonghe, S.J. Visco and B.D. Katz, "Liquid electrolyte Lithium-Sulfur batteries", *US Patent*, no. 6030720, Feb. 29, 2000.
8. Ryou, M.H. et al, "A gel polymer electrolyte based on initiator-free photopolymerization for Lithium secondary batteries", *Electrochim. Acta*, vol. 60, pp. 23-30, 2012.
9. Aurbach, D., E. Pollak, R. Elazari, G. Salitra, C.S. Kelly, J. Affinito, "On the Surface Chemical Aspects of Very High Energy Density Rechargeable Li-Sulfur Batteries", *J. Electrochem. Soc.*, vol. 156, pp. A694-A702, 2009.
10. Zhang, S.S, Electrochim. Acta Vol. 70, pp.344-348, 2012
11. Janakiraman, U. et al, Power Sources Conf. Vol. 45, 2012

A Standardized Testing Framework for Baselining & Benchmarking Pre-commercial Lithium-ion Cells

Dillon Hayman[2] and Corey Love[1]

[1]Chemistry Division
U.S. Naval Research Laboratory
4555 Overlook Ave SW, Washington, DC 20375
corey.love@nrl.navy.mil

[2]Excet Inc
6225 Brandon Ave #360, Springfield, VA 22150

Abstract: *A testing methodology for unbiasedly benchmarking and comparing emerging and existing battery technologies is presented. Each step of the testing process is described in general terms along with the motivation for the test design. Additional information about the testing procedures can be found in the Naval Research Laboratory Battery Test Manual for Baselining & Benchmarking Pre-commercial Cells[1]. Experimental data produced by following the steps in the testing framework is presented and explored for a few selected procedures. As more cell-types are examined, further revisions and expansions to these methodologies are intended.*

Keywords: battery testing; Lithium-ion batteries; 18650; Sodium-ion batteries; battery characterization; rate study; cycle life; calendar life

Introduction

Modern batteries are available in a wide array of chemistries and form factors. The varied nature of available cell-types creates a diverse energy storage landscape with each set of cell construction parameters exhibiting specific strengths and weaknesses. Generally, the benefits of one cell-type will also come with a set of weaknesses such as an increase in energy density, but a decrease in cycle life. However, in many cases cell performance metrics are more complex to characterize and require a full spectrum of testing to provide a complete description of the technology. Additionally, if the testing framework is not intelligently designed to remove bias towards any cell-type, then comparisons can be difficult to make even with a full-spectrum of tests. Due to these challenges, there is a need for a standardized, rigorous testing framework that can be used to draw unbiased conclusions about advantages and disadvantages of each cell-type. After a neutral profile is created, each unique technology can be applied to a need which matches its performance parameters enabling greater and faster utilization of existing and emerging technologies. Although other high-quality battery testing methodologies exist[2,3,4], most focus on testing procedures specifically catered to electric vehicle applications. In other cases, the testing design is too simplified to be replicated exactly in separate laboratories and battery testing centers. This testing methodology aims to provide a detailed description of testing procedures such that unaffiliated battery testing locations can follow the outlined steps and arrive at the same conclusions. When battery data is easily comparable, benefits of emerging technologies can be quickly identified, even when testing occurs at a different testing center. Additionally, the procedures in this framework are well-suited to characterizing pre-commercial cells for which there are limited rigorous testing methods publicly available. Testing procedures within this framework were inspired by an amalgamation of previous testing methods designed by the United States Advanced Battery Consortium[3], Federal Consortium For Advanced Batteries[2] and Idaho National Laboratory[4] combined with battery research expertise from the Naval Research Laboratory.

Experimental

High energy 18650 lithium-ion and pouch cell sodium-ion cells were tested in this work. Cells were charged and discharged using Maccor Series 4000 and Series 4300 battery cyclers. During all steps of testing, the ambient temperature was controlled to a desired setpoint within a +/- 2°C tolerance. Temperature control was accomplished using Maccor EV chambers and Tenney environmental chambers. 18650 cells were connected to the testers using Maccor 18650 holders and Anderson connections. Pouch cells were connected to the testers via Anderson connectors with the electrode tabs contacted by a screwed down copper bar. Data was collected at an interval of every 2 mV or 30 seconds.

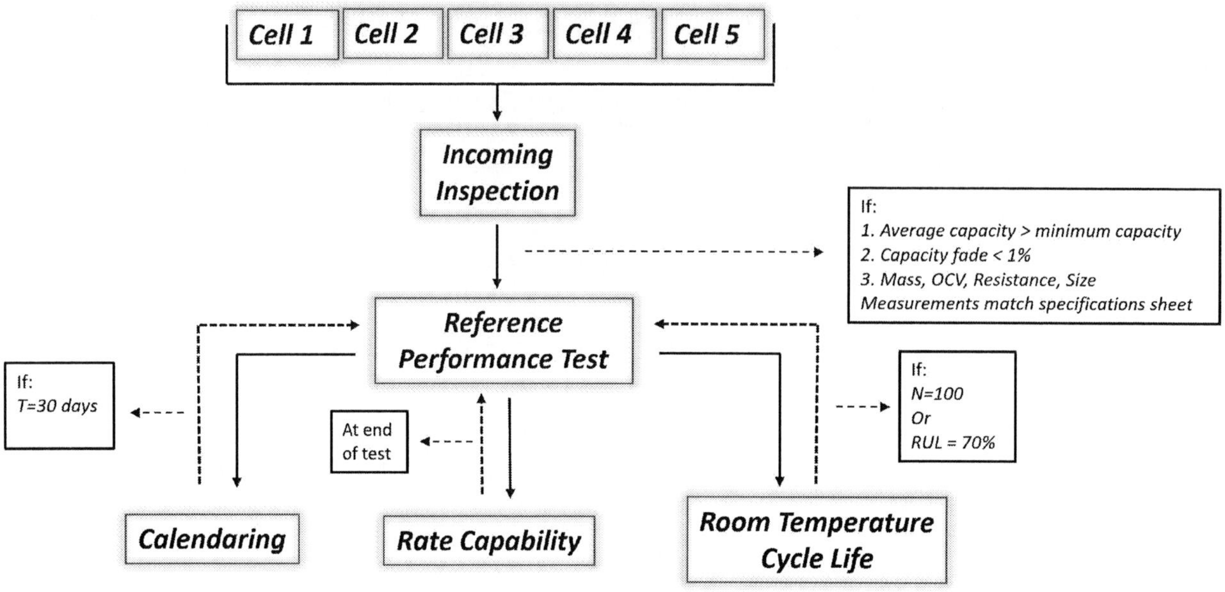

Figure 1. Battery Testing Framework Schematic

Testing Framework

Battery testing generally falls into 3 broad categories: Cycle life, rate capability and calendar life. At the beginning and at regular intervals throughout testing, reference performance tests (RPTs) are conducted to establish a baseline and measure changes in relevant parameters. However, prior to general testing, a set of incoming inspection procedures must be performed to ensure any outliers or damaged cells are removed from the batch before testing. The flow of procedures for a sample of cells is shown in **Figure 1**. In the first phase of the incoming inspection, physical and electrical parameters such as mass, open-circuit voltage (OCV), resistance and cell dimensions are compared with the cell manufacturer's specifications sheet and used to screen out cells if any criteria is not met. After cells pass through the initial set of measurements, 3-10 cycles are performed using cycling parameters from the manufacturer's specification sheet. In general, specifications sheets will contain information about standard cycling voltages and rates for charge and discharge. In cases where cycling information is unavailable, a C/2 charge to the upper voltage limit combined with a C/20 current cut-off can be used in conjunction with a C/5 discharge. Additionally, a one-hour rest should always exist between the charge and discharge. Once a set of 3 cycles records a discharge capacity within +/- 1% for those 3 cycles, cycling is stopped. From those 3 cycles, an average capacity is calculated for each cell which is compared with the rated capacity on the manufacturer's specifications sheet. If a cell cannot achieve stability within 10 cycles or record an average discharge capacity greater than the rated minimum, then the cell is excluded from further study. Following inspections, batches of screened cells are baselined using an initial RPT. After the baseline RPT is completed, the cells can move on to each of the 3 tests. Each test should be conducted using a minimum of 5 cells in each batch. Additionally, a batch of cells used in one test should not be used in another. A minimum of 15 cells is required to complete all tests in this framework. However, greater insights can be elucidated if a higher number of cells are available for testing.

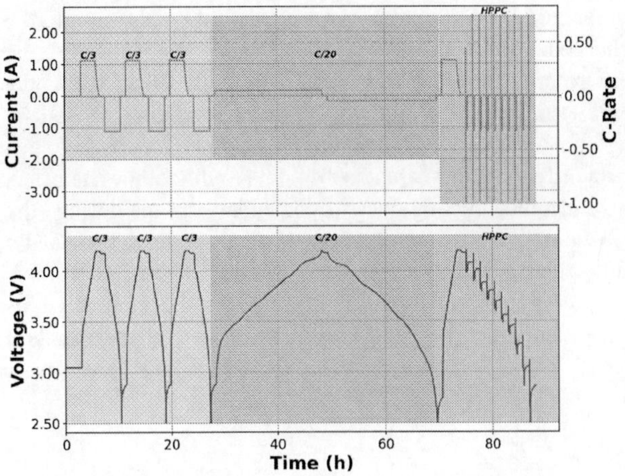

Figure 2. Reference Performance Test Current Profile and Representative Voltage Response

Prior to each test, one RPT should be completed as a baseline. RPTs consist of 3 cycles with a rate of C/3, 1 cycle with a rate of C/20, and 1 set of Hybrid Pulse Power Characterization (HPPC) measurements following a standard charge. A schematic of the current, C-rate and voltage during an RPT is shown in **Figure 2**. Additionally, it is critical that each RPT is performed at 25°C to remove any temperature effects. The initial 3, C/3 cycles serve as a benchmark for comparison of cell cycling behavior under mild conditions. The C/20 slow-cycle characterizes the cell behavior when kinetic limitations are reduced allowing thermodynamic behavior to be more fully explored. Using the unique cell signature from this cycle, incremental capacity analysis (dQ/dV) can be performed and high-fidelity dQ/dV peaks indicative of reactions in the cell can be resolved. Movement, height, and shape of each peak can be used to track and compare degradation pathways throughout testing. In the final cycle, HPPC is used to characterize the charge and discharge resistance of each cell across all states of charge. The HPPC procedure uses a 30-second discharge pulse followed by a 40-second rest and a 10-second charge. The discharge pulse is conducted at a 1C rate, and the charge is performed at a 0.75C rate. After the HPPC profile is completed, cells are discharged 10% of the minimum capacity at a C/3 rate. Each set of measurements is separated by a one-hour rest to allow the cell to equilibrate before another set of measurements is taken. During HPPC, the voltage should be limited to the cell upper voltage limit. In some cases, this may reduce the applied current before the 10-second duration is reached. When this occurs, the resulting resistance calculations should not be utilized due to the strong time dependence of battery resistance measurements. Similarly, incomplete discharge pulses near 0% SOC should not be utilized for comparison. Generally, 10 resistance calculations can be made from a single RPT, but this number will reduce with aging as the minimum voltage is reached more quickly.

Results

The cycle life test evaluates a cell's ability to deliver rated capacity while operating with moderate C-rate and ambient temperature (25°C) over long-term cycling. Cycle life testing provides a description of cell capacity, degradation, and stability over its useful life. Cells are cycled using a constant-current, constant-voltage (CC-CV) profile with a C/3 rate and CV current cut-off as detailed in the manufacturer's specifications sheet. Every 100 cycles, an RPT is performed to measure changes in battery behavior in relation to the baseline. If the cell reaches 70% remaining-useful-life (RUL) as based on the rated

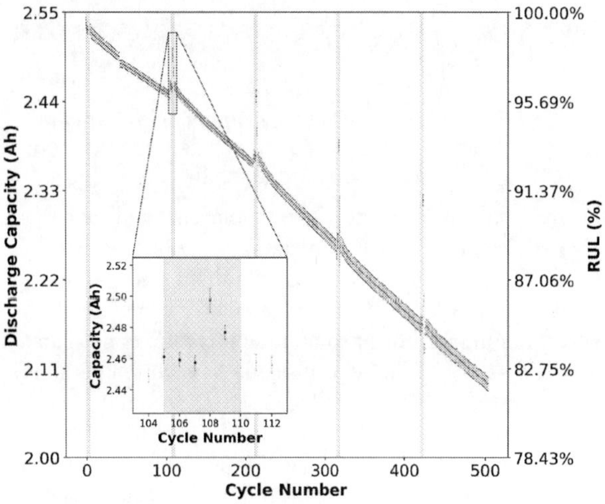

Figure 3. Cycle Life Data from a Batch of 5, Li-ion cells

minimum capacity, cycling is stopped and a final RPT is performed. **Figure 3** shows an ongoing set of room temperature cycle life data from a batch of Li-ion 18650s. The average discharge capacity of the batch is plotted with standard deviation error bars versus cycle number. Each highlighted region indicates where an RPT was performed. In the **Figure 3** inset, an RPT is shown with each cycle's average capacity marked in black. The degree of variability when comparing cell capacities increases over time as clearly exhibited by the rise in standard deviation especially after 200 cycles. Each RPT can be used to elucidate changes in the cell resistance, capacity, and reaction profile as the cells follow different aging paths.

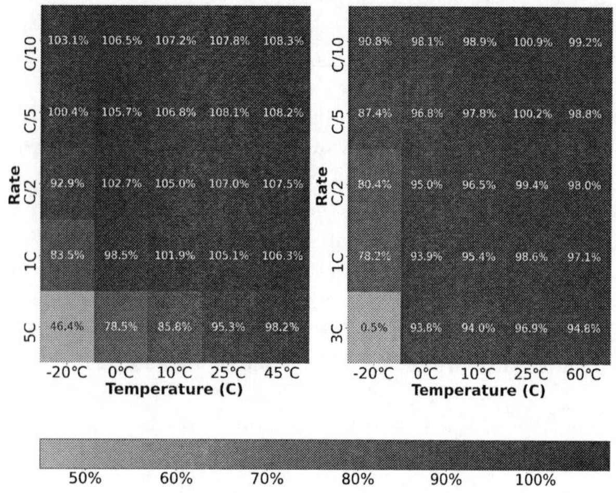

Figure 4. Percentage of Capacity Retention in terms or Rate Capability for a Na-ion pouch cell (left panel) and a Li-ion 18650 (right panel)

The rate capability test assesses current and capacity delivery over a range of temperatures. Cells are tested at 0°C, 10°C and 25°C as well as minimum and maximum temperature as listed on the manufacturer's specifications sheet. If a minimum or maximum temperature is not listed, -20°C and 40°C can be used instead. At each temperature, cells are tested at 5 rates: C/10, C/5, C/2, 1C and max C-rate. The resulting dataset can be visualized in a heatmap as shown in **Figure 4**. Testing cell-types over a range of temperatures and rates enables technologies to be matched with corresponding environments and rate requirements. Darker regions in the heatmap indicate a cycling condition that is favorable for the cell-type. Comparing the lower left region of each plot in **Figure 4** where high C-rate and low temperature coincide, the Na-ion cell (left) exhibits significantly enhanced capacity retention even when cycled under a higher C-rate condition than the Li-ion cell (right). However, the Li-ion cell is rated for cycling at higher temperatures and exhibits a relatively insignificant capacity loss at 60°C except for near max rates.

A third consideration when choosing a battery technology for a particular application is its ability to store over long periods of time without degradation. Shelf life is a critical factor in determining which energy storage device to deploy when use will be intermittent leaving the battery to sit without cycling for months or years. The calendar life test investigates aging phenomena when a cell is stored at ambient temperature (25°C) and 100% State-Of-Charge (SOC) for long periods of time (~6-12 months). After cells are baselined, they are set inside environmental chambers where the temperature remains at 25°C, +/- 2°C. At an interval of ~30 days, the cells are removed and an RPT is conducted. It is worth noting that the cells must be discharged prior to performing the standard RPT procedure. Additionally, afterwards the cells should be charged back to 100% SOC and placed into the environmental chamber again. As with other tests, the RPTs serve as a window into the degradation caused by aging. Additionally, comparisons can be made between cycle life data and calendar life data to de-couple the effect of periodic cycling versus calendar aging during the calendar life test. Completion of all three tests provides a full-spectrum view of the capabilities of each cell-type. Further application-specific testing can be conducted as necessary after the cells are characterized in the standard tests.

Conclusions

Battery testing is a complex, but necessary topic to improve the utilization of emerging battery technologies. Battery data is highly context specific and cannot be interpreted fully without a set of metadata related to the conditions during testing. Without standardizing the conditions surrounding battery experiments, the resulting data can become incomparable with other data leading to a waste in research efforts and funds. A testing framework was presented which attempts to improve upon past testing methodologies from well-known battery organizations by creating a detailed, step-by-step procedure for neutral characterization of dissimilar battery technologies. The use of these procedures can enhance and enable cross-operability of data generated at independent battery testing facilities. Further research is needed to continue the refinement of these methodologies and increasingly provide a more well-rounded approach to characterizing and comparing pre-commercial cells.

Acknowledgements

The authors thank the U.S. Naval Research Laboratory for funding through the Naval Innovative Science and Engineering (NISE) program.

References

1. Battery Test Manual for Baselining & Benchmarking Pre-commercial Cells, Revision 1, NRL/6170/MR--2022/8, September 2021
2. Federal Consortium For Advanced Batteries Battery Test Manual, Revision 1, INL/MIS-21-62073, August 2021
3. USABC Electric Vehicle Battery Test Procedures Manual, Revision 3.1, INL/EXT-15-34184, October 2020
4. J. Christophersen, Battery Test Manual For Electric Vehicles, Revision 3, INL/EXT-15-34184, June 2015

Experimental Study of Battery Parameters and Their Variations During Cycle Aging and State of Charge of a Sealed Lead Acid Battery

Jagmohan Singh[1], Ruben Hidalgo-Leon[2], and Pritpal Singh[1]
[1]Department of Electrical and Computer Engineering
Villanova University
Villanova, Pennsylvania, USA, 19085
{jsingh16,pritpal.singh}@villanova.edu
[2]Centro de Energias Renovables y Alternativas
Escuela Superior Politecnica del Litoral
Guayaquil, Guayas, Ecuador, 90902
rhidalgo@espol.edu.ec

Abstract

Sealed lead acid batteries are widely used for backup power in telecom centers, data centers and for energy storage systems for microgrids. Yet determining the condition of a lead acid battery is still a challenge. We have set out to study how a 12V 200Ah sealed lead acid battery performs when cycle aged. This paper describes the experiments to measure and characterize the battery parameters of a sealed lead acid battery - current, voltage, battery capacity, and DC internal resistance for a fresh battery and two batteries that have undergone deep discharge cycling for 70 cycles and 180 cycles. The results show a steady change in the internal resistance of the battery with cycle aging. Variations of the load voltage as a function of state-of-charge and battery capacity after 70 cycles and 180 cycles are also presented.

Keywords

Sealed lead acid battery; battery characterization; battery parameters; battery aging; State of Charge; State of Health

Introduction

The use of lead acid batteries (LABs) is still very wide in different applications such as microgrids, frequency regulation, electric vehicles, uninterruptible power supplies, among others. Although this battery technology has a low energy density and shorter cycle life compared to other technologies (Nickel-Cadmium, Nickel-Metal Hydride, and Lithium-ion) [1], it has several advantages in terms of cost, ease of use, maintenance, reliability, high rate discharge, safety, among others [2]. In addition, a LAB becomes attractive compared to other technologies because over 90% of its parts can be recycled [3], [4]. LAB technologies include flooded lead-acid batteries, valve-regulated lead acid battery (VRLA), tubular and bipolar batteries [5]. The composition, geometry and internal chemical reactions of a LAB are well known because it typically consists of positive electrodes (porous PbO_2), negative electrodes (porous Pb), plastic separators, and corrosive sulfuric acid as electrolyte [6], [7].

Accurately and precisely measuring parameters of a LAB during cycling is fundamental to determining aging effects, as well as State of Health (SoH), battery degradation, and State of Charge (SoC) of a LAB. At each cycle, the LAB gradually decreases in capacity, increases internal resistance, decreases load efficiency, and increases self-discharge [8]. Merrouche et. al. [9] obtained the SoH of a LAB within the context of a PV application through voltage, current and temperature measurements in experimental charge/discharge tests. Marchildon et al. [10] presented a procedure based on applying two discharge current pulses on a 185Ah-LAB to determine its SoC and SoH. In addition, Fru et al. [11] indicated that LAB batteries with a high SoH have higher energy recovery abilities and relatively small open circuit voltage (OCV) variations. However, when the SoH of a battery is reduced, it has larger OCV variations and lower energy recovery ability.

Some internal processes during LAB cycling: The charging and discharging processes of a LAB cause deterioration of the battery properties. LABs are charged through procedures such as constant current, constant voltage, combined constant current constant voltage [3]. These processes produce a decrease in the battery capacity, an increase in the internal resistance, a reduction in the charging efficiency, and even an increase in the self-discharge [8]. It should be noted that the loss of capacity due to cycling is known as aging, where its main processes on the battery are anodic corrosion, and degradation of active mass, among others [12]. Anodic corrosion is a progressive process that leads to the failure of a LAB, mainly in applications such as vehicles and backup power [13]. DoD during cycling accelerates positive active mass degradation [14]. When exposed to high temperatures added to the heat generation of its cells during cycling, a LAB can considerably affect its performance and cycle life [15]. In addition, other processes that accelerate the degradation of a LAB are over-charging, over-discharging, and storing batteries for long periods in a discharged state [16].

Battery parameters reflect the changes in the battery states and their performance arising from their SoC and with their cycle age. In this paper, we present battery parameters measured during cycle aging of a 12V, 200Ah sealed lead acid battery over 70 and 180 cycles and the corresponding assessed SoH degradation.

Methodology

Battery parameter values are sensitive to the procedures used to obtain the required SoC and cycle-age of the battery. Further, the variations of these parameters, with the SoC and cycle-age of the battery, are exceedingly small as a result of the improved battery designs. Therefore, the following battery characterization procedures (for 12V, 200Ah Sealed Lead Acid Battery), have been carefully specified and adopted for the parameter measurements described in this section. The next procedures are based on the observations and their analysis, of test measurements, during charging and discharging for battery characterization.

Experimental Setup: The following equipment has been used for conducting the experiments / measurements for battery characterization:

1. DC Power Supply – Chroma, Model 62012P-40-120
2. DC electronic load – Chroma, 63205A-150-500
3. 6 Digit Multimeter – Agilent, 34401, 6 ½ Digit Multimeter
4. Charge-discharge software

The setup is shown in Figure 1.

Battery Parameters: The battery parameters selected for measurement are given below:

1. OCV at full charge
2. Battery capacity at three selected levels of its cycle-age.
3. Voltage under load, V_L @ 10-hour rate and its variation with the Depth of Discharge (DoD) up to 80% and the value, V_{Lmin} at this level, for each of the three stages of battery life (cycles) – 0, 70, and 180 cycles.
4. Stabilized battery voltage, $V_{under\ load.stable}$ and its variation with DoD up to 80% during battery discharge @ 10-hour rate.
5. Battery internal DC resistance, R_{int} of fully charged battery of the three selected cycle-age levels of 0, 70, and 180 cycles of the battery.

Characterization Procedures: Characterization procedure to extract battery parameters used the following steps:

1. Fully charge the battery: Charge the battery at constant voltage (CV) - 14.8V, 80A maximum, till the charge current reduces to 1.0 amp. Float charge the battery at 14.0 V, till charge current reduces to 0.2A or charge current begins to rise. The lead resistance for these CV and float charges is to be around 5 mΩ. Stabilize the battery for at least 1 hr. Measure the battery capacity at a C/10 constant current (CC) rate. After a rest period of 15-18 hours of fully charging the battery, start CC discharge of a fully charged battery, at 10 hrs. rate (=20A), till battery terminal voltage, V_L reduces to the End of Discharge Voltage (EODV) (=10.8 V @ 10 hr. rate – as per manufacturer's datasheet). Note the time taken in hours "h".
   - Find the actual battery capacity C_n (=20*h). 10% DoD = C_n/10.
   - Note the minimum battery load voltage @80% DoD, $V_{Lmin.}$
   - Restore battery charge to at least 20% SoC level
2. Plot discharge characteristics - V_L vs DoD @ 10 hr. rate: CC discharge the fully charged battery at C/10 rate for 8 hrs to obtain this plot. Note the value of load voltage, V_L after 8 hrs (for ~80% DoD), and record this value, as V_{Lmin} @C/10.
3. Conduct a Step-Discharge as per procedure below:
   - Discharge the fully charged battery at 10 hr. constant current rate, C/10 (=20A) in steps of 1 hour, for 8 hrs.
   - Measure the battery voltage under load, V_L at the end of each hour and switch off the CC load. Stabilize the battery for 1 hour and measure this corresponding stabilized battery voltage, $V_{under\ load.stable}$
   - Obtain "V_L vs $V_{under\ load.stable}$ @ C/10" plot.

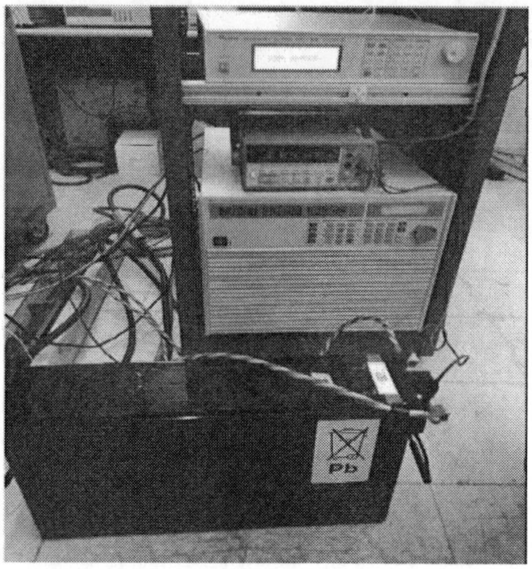

Figure 1. Experimental setup for battery auto cycling and battery characterization.

Experimental Results

Present experiments are being conducted for cycle-aging of the batteries – 24 hours a day, 7 days a week, and battery characterization to generate a battery database for five, 12V, 200 Ah, sealed lead acid batteries that have undergone five stages of their lives. We have made the above measurements for one new battery and for two others, which have undergone 70 and 180 cycles of aging. The results of these measurements are presented next.

1. V_L vs %DoD @ 10-hour discharge rate up to the end of discharge voltage, EODV of the battery.
This experiment provides: Open circuit voltage (fully charged battery) OCV, V_L vs %DoD plot, battery capacity and V_{Lmin} for the battery, at a particular age level. A plot of V_L vs. %DoD for a new battery is shown in Figure 2

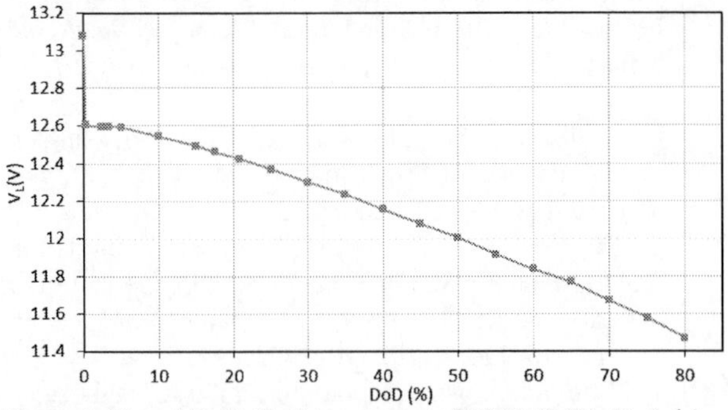

Figure 2. V_L vs %DoD @ 10-hr rate up to EODV=10.8V; V_L (min) = 11.375V; Ah max = 192.953 at EODV=10.8V

2. Step Discharge @ 10-hour CC discharge rate (up to EODV) for a new battery, which provides stabilized battery voltage corresponding to different battery load voltages during the discharge is shown in Figure 3.

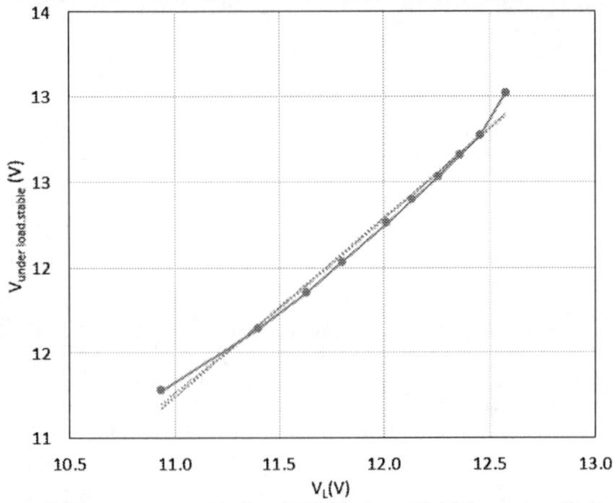

Figure 3. $V_{under\ load.stable}$ vs V_L for a NEW battery @ 10-hour step discharge rate up to EODV=10.8V; V_L = battery voltage during discharge.

3. DC Internal Resistance, R_{int} (DC Load-interruption Method (Load to No-load approach):
R_{int} of a fully charged battery was measured during the CC C/10 step discharge. The stabilized no load voltage, $V_{under\ load.stable}$, after 1 hour of load switch-off also asymptotically reached the measurable OCV of the battery at its fully charged level. This method was further validated by the voltage relaxation technique [17].
Variation of R_{int} with SoC @ C/10 current, for a new battery, 70 cycle age battery, and 180-cycle-age battery are shown in Figure 4.

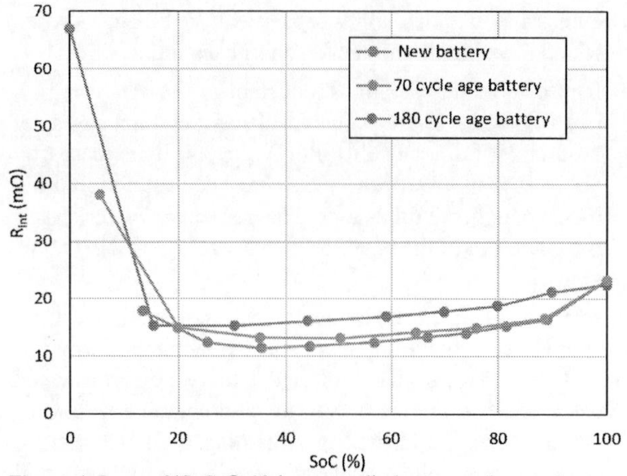

Figure 4. R_{int} vs. %SoC @ 10-hour step discharge rate for new battery, 70 cycle age battery, and 180-cycle-age battery.

Studies with the new, 70 and 180 cycle-age batteries indicate that there is not much difference in their OCV levels at full charge. However, their capacities seriously decrease and R_{int} deterioration below 20% SoC level is much steeper, with higher cycle-ages. For example:

- R_{int} variation with SoC for the 70 -cycles old battery, indicates a steep rise from 15 mΩ to more than 38 mΩ, at below 20% SoC levels to EODV levels.
- R_{int} variation with SoC for the 180-cycles old batteries, indicates a very steep rise from 15 mΩ to 70 mΩ, at below 20% SoC levels to EODV levels.

The measured capacity data, during the continuous and step discharge experiments with 0, 70 and 180 cycle age batteries, have been identified and are given below:

- New battery: continuous discharge: 192.952Ah
- New battery: step discharge: Not available.
- 70 cycle age battery: continuous discharge: 130 Ah
- 70 cycle age battery: step discharge: 124.3333Ah
- 180 cycle battery: continuous discharge: 62.32Ah
- 180 cycle battery: step discharge: 99.31Ah

Discussion

A few salient takeaways during the experiments are given below:

- A very linear reduction in V_L with time has been observed during a constant current discharge, with time till V_{Lmin}.
- Experiment-runs for C/10 continuous- and step- discharge (CC at 10 hrs. rate) indicate that higher Ah capacity maybe expected to be delivered during intermittent discharge as compared to continuous discharge use of the battery.
- While the fresh battery exhibited close to the rated capacity, the battery capacity dropped to almost 2/3 of its original capacity after 70 cycles and to almost 1/3 of its capacity after 180 cycles, when continuously discharged. The battery capacity dropped by about 35% after 70

cycles and to about half its capacity after 180 cycles when tested through intermittent discharge testing.

- Rint of a battery is almost constant in the active region (90-20%SoC) of the battery. It suddenly increases by around 30% for close to EODV levels. It increases by about 10% at lower SoC and is has been found to a little (~12%) higher at full charge. This resistance increases, as the cycle age of the batteries increases (Figure 4).

Conclusions

This paper shows the experimental results of cycling tests on LABs. Here, we have set out to study how the performance of a 12V 200Ah sealed lead acid battery performs when cycle aged. The measurements for ~~and~~ characterization of the LABs were performed by obtaining their parameters, such as current, voltage, battery capacity, and DC internal resistance, for a fresh battery and two batteries that have undergone deep discharge cycling for 70 cycles and 180 cycles. These are the initial results of a deeper study of this technology of an energy storage system.

The battery parameter measurements and generation of the battery data base has been motivated by the potential of the diagnostic information, to not only provide the charge condition of the battery but also its relative ability to perform as per design of the battery. These parameters provide experimentally validated battery characteristics.

So far three batteries have been measured - a fresh one, one that has undergone 70 cycles and one that has been cycled 180 times. Given that the data sheet for these batteries indicate a 400-cycle capability for these batteries under the cycling conditions being used, we plan to make additional measurements at 270 cycles and 360 cycles. This data will be incorporated into a look up table for estimating the SoH of a battery. This should provide an easy way through some simple measurements to estimate the battery's performance.

References

[1] F. Yang *et al.*, "Thorn-like and dendrite lead sulfate as negative electrode materials for enhancing the cycle performance of lead-acid batteries," *J. Energy Storage*, vol. 49, p. 104112, 2022.

[2] K. Vignarooban *et al.*, "State of health determination of sealed lead acid batteries under various operating conditions," *Sustain. Energy Technol. Assessments*, vol. 18, pp. 134–139, 2016.

[3] A. Roy, R. B. Patil, and R. Sen, "The effect of fast charging and equalization on the reliability and cycle life of the lead acid batteries," *J. Energy Storage*, vol. 55, p. 105841, 2022.

[4] S. K. Pradhan and B. Chakraborty, "Substrate materials and novel designs for bipolar lead-acid batteries: A review," *J. Energy Storage*, vol. 32, p. 101764, 2020.

[5] Y. Wang, J. Wu, N. Lin, D. Liu, Z. Liu, and H. Lin, "Enabling stable cycling performance with rice husk silica positive additive in lead-acid battery," *Energy*, vol. 269, p. 126796, 2023.

[6] M. Wang *et al.*, "Pollution-free recycling of lead and sulfur from spent lead-acid batteries via a facile vacuum roasting route," *Green Energy Resour.*, vol. 1, no. 1, p. 100002, 2023.

[7] C. W. Stone *et al.*, "High energy X-ray imaging of heterogeneity in charged and discharged lead-acid battery electrodes," *J. Power Sources*, vol. 557, p. 232538, 2023.

[8] P. Křivík, P. Bača, and J. Kazelle, "Effect of ageing on the impedance of the lead-acid battery," *J. Energy Storage*, vol. 36, p. 102382, 2021.

[9] W. Merrouche *et al.*, "Improved model and simulation tool for dynamic SOH estimation and life prediction of batteries used in PV systems," *Simul. Model. Pract. Theory*, vol. 119, p. 102590, 2022.

[10] J. Marchildon, M. L. Doumbia, and K. Agbossou, "SOC and SOH characterisation of lead acid batteries," in *IECON 2015-41st Annual Conference of the IEEE Industrial Electronics Society*, 2015, pp. 1442–1446.

[11] S. E. Fru, P. Tsafack, and E. Tanyi, "The exploitation of open circuit voltage parameters and energy recovery after discharge, to decipher the state of health of lead acid batteries," *J. Energy Storage*, vol. 44, p. 103477, 2021.

[12] U. S. Kim, C. B. Shin, S. M. Chung, S. T. Kim, and B. W. Cho, "Modeling of the capacity loss of a 12 V automotive lead-acid battery due to ageing and comparison with measurement data," *J. Power Sources*, vol. 190, no. 1, pp. 184–188, 2009.

[13] S. Jiang and Z. Song, "A review on the state of health estimation methods of lead-acid batteries," *J. Power Sources*, vol. 517, p. 230710, 2022.

[14] P. Ruetschi, "Aging mechanisms and service life of lead–acid batteries," *J. Power Sources*, vol. 127, no. 1–2, pp. 33–44, 2004.

[15] A. B. Ansari, V. Esfahanian, and F. Torabi, "Thermal-electrochemical simulation of lead-acid battery using reduced-order model based on proper orthogonal decomposition for real-time monitoring purposes," *J. Energy Storage*, vol. 44, p. 103491, 2021.

[16] J. A. Osara and M. D. Bryant, "Thermodynamics of lead-acid battery degradation: Application of the degradation-entropy generation methodology," *J. Electrochem. Soc.*, vol. 166, no. 16, p. A4188, 2019.

[17] M. S. Sudhan, T. M. Noveske, L. S. Holden, and S. L. Mraz, "Use of AC impedance/conductance and DC resistance for determining the reliability of VRLA battery systems," in *Proceedings of Intelec 93: 15th International Telecommunications Energy Conference*, 1993, vol. 2, pp. 384–391.

CAMX Power High Sensitivity Cell Screening Technology: Recent Advancements and Results from Evaluations of Li-Ion Cell Populations

Christopher H. McCoy
CAMX Power LLC
35 Hartwell Avenue, Lexington MA 02421
mccoy.chris@camxpower.com

Abstract: *CAMX Power has developed an ultra-high sensitivity Cell Screening Technology (CST) that has been demonstrated to rapidly detect anomalous self-discharge in lithium-ion (Li-ion) cells to sensitivities of 10MΩ or greater. CST has been implemented in multiple prototype instrument designs to-date that deliver multi-megaohm detection sensitivity in scans taking just hours versus months or even years to achieve the same sensitivities by typical long-term monitoring of cell Open Circuit Voltage (OCV). The throughput and sensitivity of CST enables efficient, cost-effective acceptance screening of Li-ion cells for self-discharge that would otherwise be impractical from cost and/or calendar time perspectives. We report results demonstrating capabilities of CST and for validation and performance benchmarking for our latest-generation, 100-cell capacity CST prototype instrument. We further present results for screening of populations of thousands of Li-ion cells.*

Keywords: Li-ion; acceptance screening; self-discharge; screening throughput; short detection; cell screening.

Introduction

Acceptance Testing of Li-Ion Cells: Background, Considerations, & Objectives

Acceptance testing of Li-ion cells comprises evaluating incoming cells against protocols and metrics selected and defined by the end-user to verify that the cells they will utilize conform to standards of safety, reliability, and/or performance selected by and controlled by the end user. While cell manufacturers carry out certain quality control testing on the cells they manufacture, the associated test protocols and pass/fail criteria are generally not made available to any but the most significant of their customers. It is only these exceptional, top-level customers that are granted access to quality control practices, procedures, and metrics and may further even have staff embedded in the cell manufacturing facilities as well as foreknowledge and approval authority over any changes to manufacturing and QC processes. For all other end-users of Li-ion cells, however, no such access is available and manufacturer QC is a relatively opaque process as are the specific QC protocols and pass/fail metrics employed, and any changes or modifications to those protocols over time.

The practice of acceptance screening gives the end-user full control of qualification protocols to which cells are subjected and full knowledge of the results of those qualification protocols. One of many key benefits of this level of control and knowledge of incoming cell screening metrics is that the end-user can have advance warning of unexpected changes to cell quality that may indicate cause for concern. Such advance warning, prior to any such cells being assembled into batteries, is a valuable tool to manage safety and reliability of Li-ion energy storage systems and can be of special importance where cells are sourced from third parties, rather than directly from the cell manufacturer, adding a layer of uncertainty regarding cell provenance.

While manufacturers generally test cells against, for example, specifications for minimum available capacity and may also test for basic impedance characteristics (e.g., 1kHz impedance), by far the most time-consuming quality control check – and the most crucial with respect to the safety of the cell - is evaluating cells for anomalous self-discharge. This process attempts to eliminate cells that may be developing internal short-circuits, a primary cause of violent failures of cells in the field, and typically comprises tracking cell Open Circuit Voltage (OCV) over a significant holding period (e.g., 14-days). This OCV tracking process dominates cell manufacturing cycle time and thus represents a significant cost to the manufacturer owing to the equipment, manufacturing floor space, and residence time associated with it. This cost is accepted as part of the cell manufacturing process because of the critical importance of reducing the likelihood that a cell with an incipient internal short circuit will enter service and cause a catastrophic failure (e.g., thermal runaway) in the field. However, OCV change over time is not a particularly sensitive means to measure self-discharge and therefore to achieve reasonable detection sensitivity lengthy hold periods are needed. Accordingly, manufacturers face a fundamental trade-off between the effectiveness of QC for detection of anomalous self-discharge, and the cost and time required by that process. There is a strong cost incentive for manufacturers to minimize the duration of the hold period for OCV monitoring even though it is recognized that the shorter the monitoring period, the lower the sensitivity for detection of anomalous self-discharge/soft shorts in cells. Thus, there are strong economic pressures on cell manufacturers to balance the cost of quality control against sensitivity and effectiveness of that quality control in identifying cells with anomalous self-discharge that may develop internal shorts. These economic pressures only mount further as manufacturers are driven to reduce Li-ion cell production costs.

To provide some perspective on how and why a cell with anomalous self-discharge can still pass manufacturer QC, we present some technical background on the process of testing cells for soft shorts/anomalous self-discharge via cell OCV monitoring over time. The data in Figure 1 shows test results for a set of cells for which OCV was tracked for 14 days. In this test, a set of cells was prepared that included cells with load resistances connected across the cell terminal, as surrogates for internal self-discharge processes, ranging in value from 5000 Ω to 1,000,000 Ω (this technique reproduces, with high electrical fidelity, the equivalent circuit comprised by an internal short forming an electronically conductive path between the positive and negative electrodes of a cell of a given resistance). The cell group also included cells without such surrogates. All cells had previously been screened (OCV monitoring for >6 months) to be free of any anomalous self-discharge. The test sequence we used simulates the protocol cells might see in manufacturer QC in which cells are brought to full charge after initial formation and capacity testing and then held for a period of time to measure level of OCV loss. Our test results illustrate how some levels of cell self-discharge are detectable by OCV tracking for a given period of time while others (of higher resistance) are not. As can be seen from the traces in Figure 1, cell OCV decline for self-discharge test resistances of 100,000 Ω or lower is distinct from the black (no self-discharge) control cells. However, at self-discharge resistances greater than 100,000Ω OCV changes are no longer sufficiently distinguishable from the responses of the normal (no self-discharge/black traces), allowing these cells to pass manufacturer QC despite having elevated self-discharge.

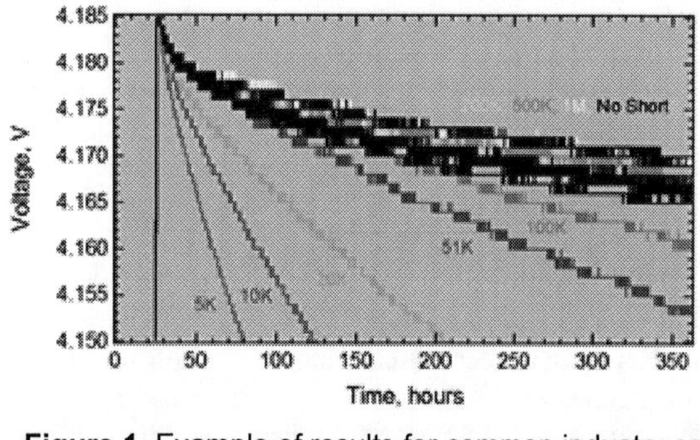

Figure 1. Example of results for common industry cell screening practice of long-term voltage monitoring. 2.6Ah 18650 cells were aged for 14 days after a formation-rate charge (C/20). Steps in the traces arise from the intrinsic resolution limit of the battery test equipment. Black traces show multiple cells with no simulated shorts, while other traces show cells with simulated shorts of the resistances indicated. Shorts from 5000 to 100,000 ohms were distinguishable from short-free cells over the 14-day monitoring period, while higher resistance shorts were not.

It should be noted that this test was conducted with commercially available cells that had already been formed (and screened by the manufacturer) prior to this test. This might, of course, tend to yield a *tighter* distribution in short-free cell voltage decay characteristics than would be expected in a population of newly formed cells (and thus our test may have yielded *higher* sensitivity than might actually be achieved with newly formed cells).

The CAMX Power Cell Screening Technology

The CAMX Power ultra-high sensitivity Cell Screening Technology (CST) employs electrical diagnostics developed specifically to measure and quantify self-discharge in Li-ion cells and to identify cells with anomalous levels of self-discharge (i.e., levels that are greater than normal background self-discharge levels typical for a cell of a given type). CST electrical diagnostics are intrinsically far more sensitive to the presence of internal shorts in cells than long-term monitoring of cell voltage. Figure 2 shows test data demonstrating the sensitivity and performance of our cell screening technology in the rapid detection of anomalous self-discharge even at high resistance levels.

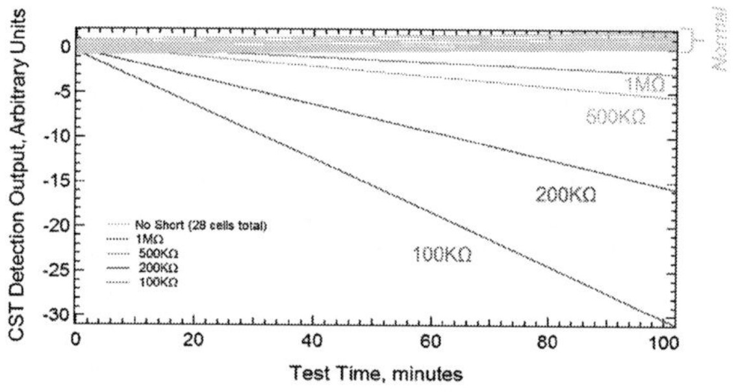

Figure 2. CST response for a group of 32 cells (2.6Ah 18650-format) with calibrated self-discharge levels introduced for four cells (load resistance as surrogates).

Data in Figure 2 shows that a self-discharge resistance of 100KΩ is readily detectable by CST in under an hour versus the many days required via existing industry practice of tracking OCV change over time (as shown in Figure 1).

Characterization of self-discharge resistance by CST is quantitative. Figure 3 shows the linear relationship between CST grade (the slope of the raw CST scan data) and conductance (1/resistance) of the self-discharge/soft-short resistance. Data of the type shown in Figure 3 provides a simple means to establish the quantitative relationship needed to translate CST grade to self-discharge resistance for a given cell type.

Accurate and effective identification of cells with anomalous self-discharge using CST has been extensively verified via independent confirmation using long-term tracking of cell OCVs following testing with CST. Without exception, cells identified by CST as showing elevated self-discharge have shown accelerated drop in OCV over time, confirming the CST findings.

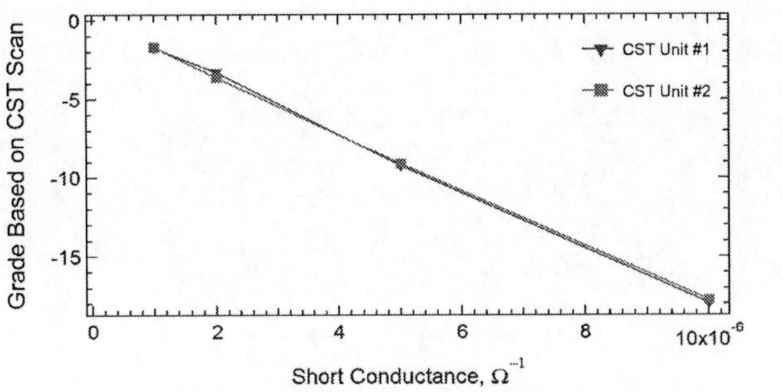

Figure 3. As shown here for two CST instruments tested, CST grade is linearly dependent on self-discharge conductance (1/resistance). Results shown are for self-discharge resistances of 1MΩ, 500KΩ, 200KΩ, and 100KΩ.

We have found that CST can detect and quantify self-discharge levels in excess of 10,000,000 ohms (10MΩ) under appropriate test conditions. We note that to fully realize the benefits of the CST diagnostic methodology, test conditions need to be regulated in certain respects to avoid factors that might cause measurement perturbation and/or drift. These factors include changing cell temperature and recent charge or discharge processes that create non-equilibrium cell conditions.

The ability of CST to identify cells with anomalous self-discharge/soft shorts not identified by manufacture QC is illustrated by the example in Figure 4. Here, CST testing showed that *10% of the cells* had elevated self-discharge. That these cells with elevated self-discharge were not identified by manufacturer QC is perhaps not surprising – in each case the levels of self-discharge were beyond our estimate of the limit of detection for OCV change over a 14-day hold period. This group of cells had been provided to us for construction of a battery module. We note that only cells from the group that passed CST (free of anomalous self-discharge) were utilized to construct that module. Cells that failed CST (elevated self-discharge) were rejected.

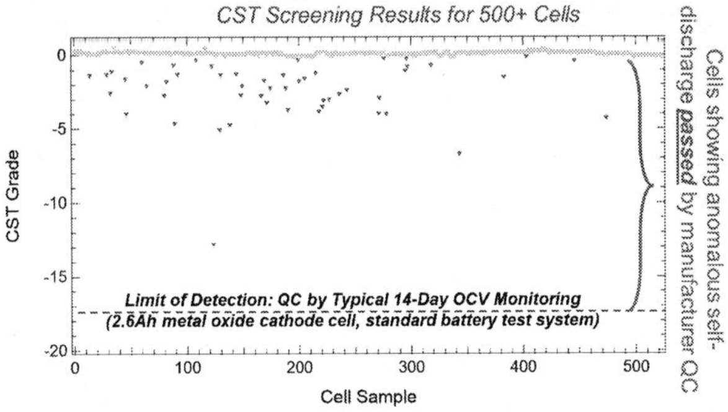

Figure 4. CST results for a group of > 500 commercially-available 18650 cells (leading manufacturer). Anomalous self-discharge was identified in 10% of the cells.

It is not typical in our experience to-date to find that 10% of a cell population has elevated self-discharge levels/soft shorts, so this finding was significant. We have now tested over 45,000 cells to-date using CST for DoD and Government clients. In each lot of cells tested, CST has identified cells with elevated self-discharge levels. Table 1 summarizes CST screening results for nine cell groups we have screened and number of cells failed from each group.

Table 1. CST Test Results for Tested Groups of 18650 Cells.

Cell Group Tested	Total Cells Failed
600 Type A 2.6Ah 18650	59
18,000 Type A 2.6Ah 18650	189
2,400 Type B 3.5Ah 18650	27
2,500 Type C 3.5Ah 18650	18
2,500 Type B 3.5Ah 18650	16
2,500 Type C 3.5Ah 18650	27
5,100 Type B 3.5Ah 18650	23
5,000 Type C 3.5Ah 18650	48
3,000 Type C 3.5Ah 18650	49

All cell types from major global manufacturers. Pass/fail thresholds client-specific but generally 2-3MΩ of elevated self-discharge or > 3 std. dev. from the mean.

It is important to recognize that the presence of elevated self-discharge does not necessarily mean that a cell is unsafe. While there are many uncertainties associated with the appropriate level of concern that should be attributed to anomalous self-discharge in a cell, consideration of the root cause of self-discharge provides an important framework for understanding and evaluating risk. Anomalous self-discharge can be classified into two main categories as a function of the underlying mechanism that produces the self-discharge, as described in Figure 5.

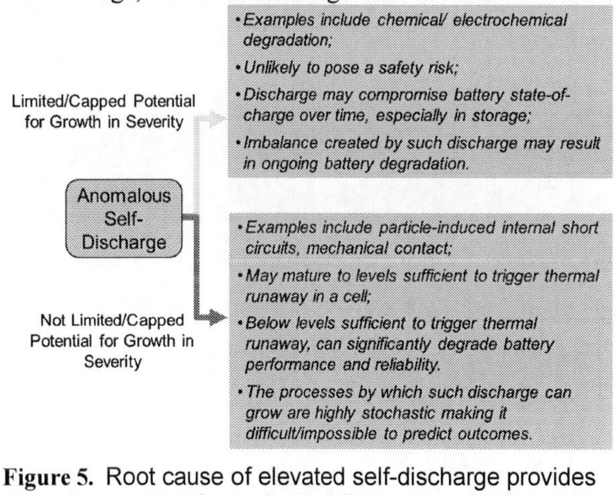

Figure 5. Root cause of elevated self-discharge provides important context for understanding and evaluating risk.

Prototype 100-Cell Capacity CST Instrument: Capabilities and Test Results

Our most recently implemented prototype CST instrument is a 100-cell capacity unit for 18650-format cells. A photograph is shown in Figure 6. The unit is designed to accept cells in the same 10x10 rectangular array configuration in which the cells are typically packaged for shipping. The instrument is powered via USB connection to a computer running the CST graphical user interface which provides all user operation, control, data logging, and CST instrument settings and parameter management functionalities.

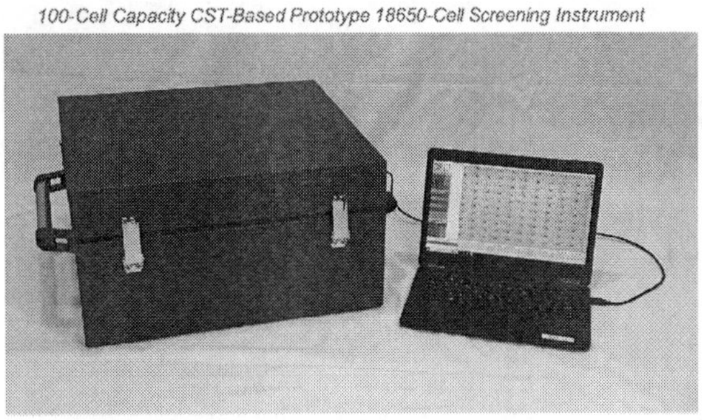

Figure 6. Photograph of our state-of-the-art prototype CST instrument. The laptop in the photograph is running the CST user interface.

Example test results (3.5Ah 18650 cells) using the 100-cell prototype CST instrument are shown in Figure 7. The CST instrument provides a surrogate self-discharge resistance functionality at four of the cell test positions which has been enabled during the test in Figure 7 at the resistance levels shown. This functionality can be used to obtain the cell-specific quantitative calibration data that is used to translate CST grade to self-discharge resistance using the linear relationship between self-discharge conductance and CST grade (as seen in the inset graph in Figure 7).

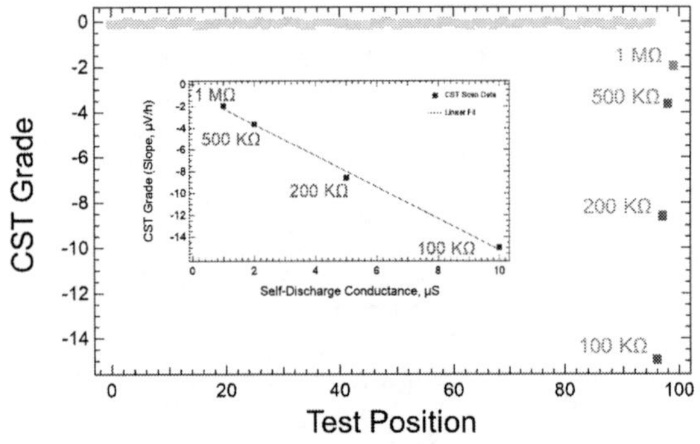

Figure 7. Test results using our 100-cell CST Instrument prototype for 3.5Ah 18650 cells from a major manufacturer. The self-discharge resistance surrogate functionality is enabled for the last four test positions in this run at the resistances noted.

CST can resolve differences in self-discharge between cells well into the multi-megohm range as demonstrated by the test data shown in Figure 8 which includes test resistances to 5MΩ. With respect to the maximum sensitivity that may be achievable using CST, the test data and detection thresholds shown in Figure 9 support achievable sensitivities of 10 MΩ or greater. As the results show, a cell with CST grade at the detection threshold for 10 MΩ is distinguishable and separated from the cluster of normal, anomalous self-discharge free cells (96 samples in total) discharge) and thus 10MΩ would be a detectable level.

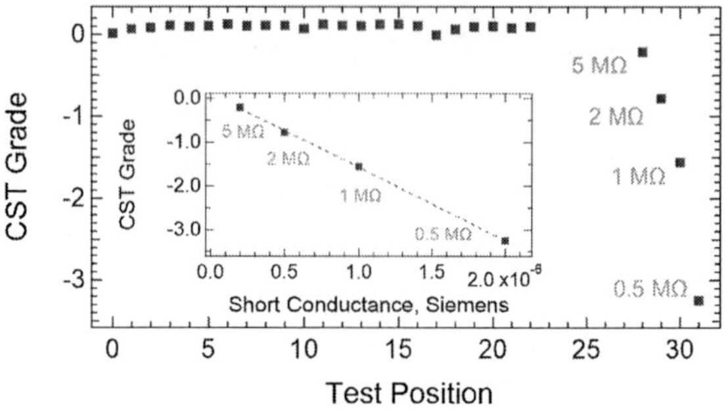

Figure 8. Test results demonstrating the ability of CST to resolve self-discharge resistances tested here to 5MΩ (2.6Ah 18650 cells).

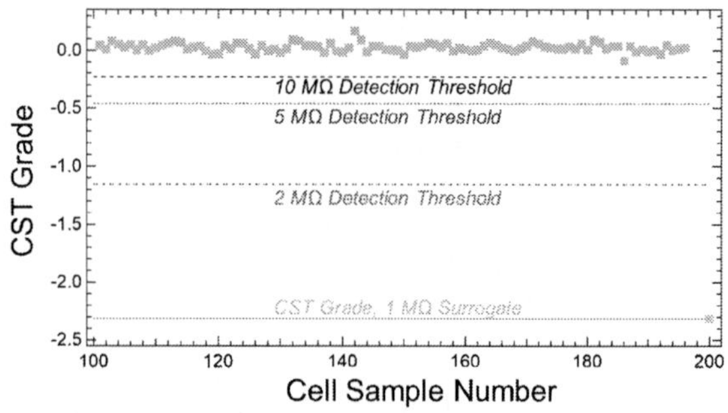

Figure 9. CST test data for 3.5Ah 18650 cells including one cell (bottom right of graph) with a 1 MΩ self-discharge surrogate enabled (load resistance across cell). Resistance detection thresholds were calculated from calibration data establishing the quantitative relationship between CST grade and self-discharge resistance (e.g., as described with respect to Figure 3).

In conclusion, CST delivers rapid, ultra-high sensitivity characterization of self-discharge in Li-ion cells. CST can be utilized for rapid acceptance screening of cells in a small fraction of the time that would be required using typical industry practice of OCV change over an extended holding period. CST discerns self-discharge in the multi-megaohm range in scans taking just hours. These capabilities have been validated and demonstrated in multiple prototypes including our most recently implemented 100-cell capacity prototype instrument, for which results have been presented here.

Acknowledgements

The authors gratefully acknowledge the support of the Defense Logistics Agency, the United States Navy, and the National Aeronautics and Space Administration. The author gratefully acknowledges the many staff of CAMX Power who have contributed to the development and advancement of these technologies over a number of years.

Safety and Performance Testing of Commercially Available Sodium-ion Batteries

Rachel Carter[1], Gordon Waller[1], and Corey T. Love[1]

[1]*Alternative Energy Section (Code 6173), U.S. Naval Research Laboratory, Washington, DC, USA*

ABSTRACT: Sodium-ion batteries (SIBs) have emerged on the global market and are poised to complement the ubiquitous Li-ion battery (LIB). SIBs deliver a lower energy density compared to LIBs but utilize more globally abundant materials and boast a higher degree of safety. The cell safety comes from less reactive cathode materials, lower cell energy density, and, in some cases, less flammable electrolytes. SIBs function much like the LIBs but with larger alkali ions. However, material compatibility distinct from lithium results in a wide range of active and passive materials present in SIBs. The wide range of material components make safety risk assessment difficult. Herein we assess safety of two commercial prototype SIBs; one aqueous and one non-aqueous with accelerating rate calorimetry and electrochemical analysis. The safety and electrochemical stability of these cells are then compared with commercial Li-ion battery chemistries. The aqueous and non-aqueous SIBs utilize aluminum metal foil for both positive and negative current collectors since sodium and aluminum do not alloy. This is a unique feature in comparison to LIBs which require a copper current collector at the negative electrode, preventing low voltage storage, where the copper reduces and dissolves. Therefore, we investigated "de-energized" or 0 V storage of both SIBs. The aqueous proved robust to these excursions, while the non-aqueous exhibited capacity loss but maintained a high degree of safety.

Keywords: Sodium ion battery, Na-ion battery, safety, accelerating rate calorimetry, 0V storage, safety

Introduction

The demand for lithium-ion batteries (LIBs) is steadily increasing and their material supply chain is of growing concern. Sodium-ion batteries (SIBs) operate mechanistically similar to LIBs but deliver lower energy density. In the 2010s, SIB companies were incentivized to address niche needs like grid storage and load leveling. More recently, commercial SIBs have emerged from these companies, boasting safety and high-power capability.

Among commercial LIBs, the cathode type may vary, but the anode and electrolyte differ very little. However, SIBs have different material compatibilities than LIBs and shuttle a larger ion. Therefore, a wider range of active and passive material components are used among the few (<10) SIB companies. For example, anodes may be hard carbon, alloying material, or intercalation materials; electrolytes may be aqueous or non-aqueous. This makes safety and performance generalizations about the chemistry difficult. Here we compare an aqueous and non-aqueous SIB.

Quantitative and qualitative comparisons of failure modes for aqueous and non-aqueous SIBs are assessed with accelerating rate calorimetry. This adiabatic assessment allows for measurement of onset temperature of self-heating behavior, calculation of heat release during thermal runaway, and visual inspection of the failure mode. Using our prior art, we can compare our findings for aqueous and non-aqueous commercial SIBs to commercial LIBs.

Additionally, a benefit of the different material components of SIBs is the use of Al current collectors at both electrodes. Sodium does not alloy with aluminum, like lithium does. LIBs require use of a Cu anode current collector which, prevents 0V storage due to Cu dissolution, which would compromise performance and safety. Therefore, SIBs can be stored in a "de-energized" or 0V state.

Methods

Accelerating rate calorimetry (ARC) was used to characterize thermal stability behavior and assess cell safety[1] (Thermal Hazard Technology, UK). This measurement allows calculation of peak heat rates (W and °C/min), peak temperature, and chemical energy of the electrochemical system (heat of reaction). We employ a heat-wait-seek (HWS) testing methodology whereby a thermocouple instrumented cell is "heated" in 5 °C increments, the chamber "waits" for equilibrium (40 min) and "seeks" for self-heating or heating of the test article any rate beyond a threshold of 0.02 °C/min. If self-heating is not detected the calorimeter continues to the next 5 °C increment.[2] When self-heating is detected, the chamber approximates adiabatic conditions by maintaining the temperature chamber as close to the self-heating rate of the cell as possible. For battery thermal runaway this test is effective and adiabatic except in the regions where cell-venting and peak heat rates are observed. A cell is considered to be in thermal runaway when the heat rate surpasses 5 °C/min. For reference, Li-ion cells often surpass a maximum self-heating rate of 1000 °C/min.[2]

Two commercial Na-ion cell types were assessed: one aqueous (pouch type, 4.3Ah, 1.2-1.8 V) and one non-aqueous (18650, 0.7 Ah, 2-4.2 V). Both cells were tested in a fixtured apparatus which replicates a single cell situated with neighbors and experiencing thermal runaway.

Electrochemical assessment of cell capacity, rate capability and 0 V tolerance were assessed using MACCOR Series 4200 and Series 4000 cyclers. Environmental chambers were used to assess various ambient thermal environments.

Results and Discussion

Heat-wait-seek test of the aqueous cells, which are a large pouch form factor, were completed in the ARC EV. The fixtured aqueous cell (Figure 1 A) experiences voltage loss and venting at about ~100°C, however self-heating is not detected until ~175°C. This is a demonstration of heat rejected into the cell fixture, reducing self-heating. We designed a cell fixture of approximately the same mass as the aqueous cell, ~290 g. This mimics a neighboring cell in a pack.

Accelerating rate calorimetry data for the non-aqueous SIB is given in Figure 1B. After the onset of self-heating, a vent is observed between 110-120 °C. This temperature is similar to the onset of self-heating observed in conventional Li-ion cells, likely due to similar volatile solvents used for the battery electrolyte.[2, 3] These solvents are vented off by a pressure release. After the vent, low self-heating is observed until the components are burned and the samples are cooled down at a safety temperature of 300 °C.

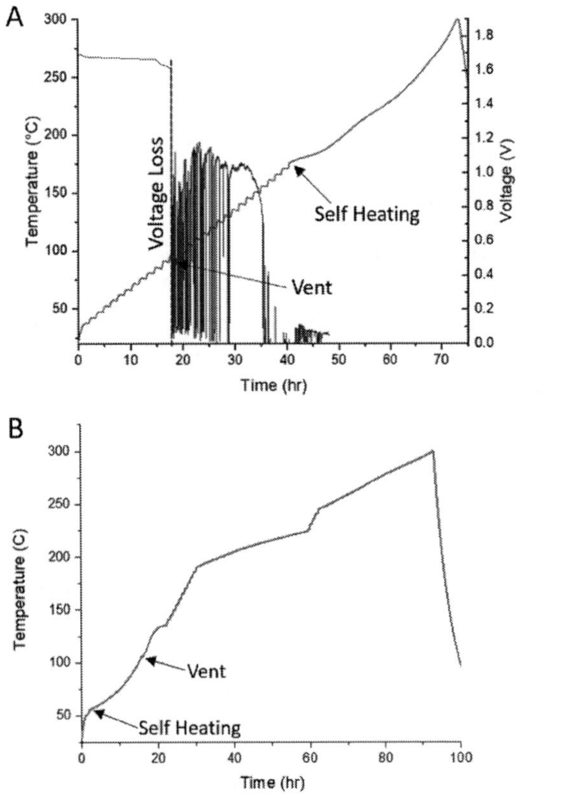

Figure 1- Heat-Wait-Seek ARC measurement of (A) aqueous and (B) non-aqueous SIBs.

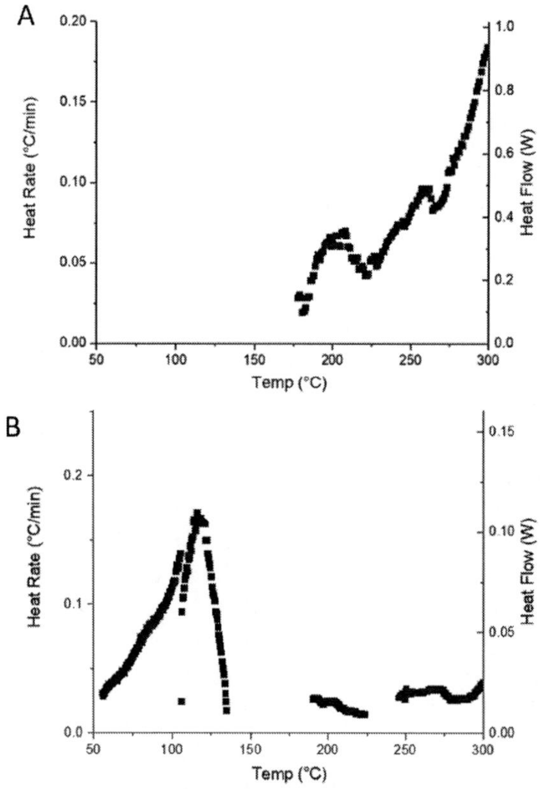

Figure 2- Heat-rate or heat flow measured in self-heating regimes of aqueous (A) and non-aqueous (B) SIBs.

The self-heating regimes of the HWS measurements in Figure 1 are manipulated into heat rate vs. temperature plots, which are often used to compare safety among cells. For the aqueous cell (Figure 2A), self-heating is not observed until ~175 °C and remains minimal (<1 W) in up to the safety temperature of 300°C. However, the non-aqueous cell (Figure 2B) exhibits a notably low onset temperature of ~50 °C, but the heat rates remains low (< 0.2 °C/min and 0.2 W). In practice, this heat would easily dissipate to neighboring cells or packaging when assembled into a pack.

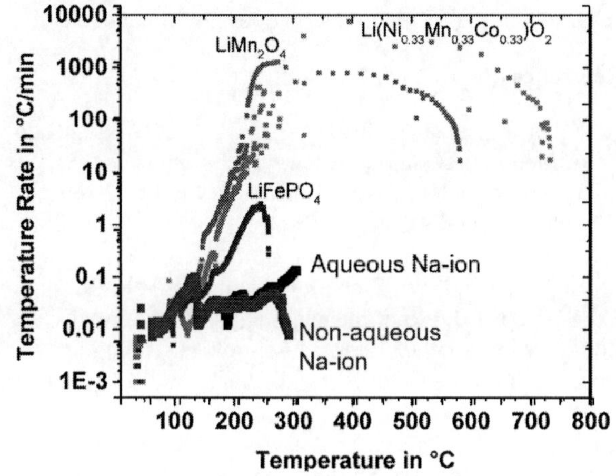

Figure 3- Temperature rate with respect to temperature in self-heating regimes of conventional LIB cells and SIB cells investigated here.

To put our observations on SIBs into context, the SIB heat rates are overlayed with commercial LIB data for various cathodes (Figure 3). Both the aqueous and non-aqueous SIBs have temperature rates far below that of LIBs. A threshold of ~5 °C/min indicates thermal runaway, which is observed for all LIBs but neither SIB.

A notable quality of SIBs is the elimination of the copper current collector, which allows for safe 0 V or 0% SOC storage. Figure 4A shows cell cycling data within the manufactured recommended voltage range (1.2 – 1.8 V) with additional periodic excursions to 0 V, 0% SOC. On the 5th cycle the cell was discharged to 0 V and rested for 5 hours. Minimal degradation was observed over this protocol, even after twenty 0 V excursions for a total of ~100 cycles (Figure 4B).

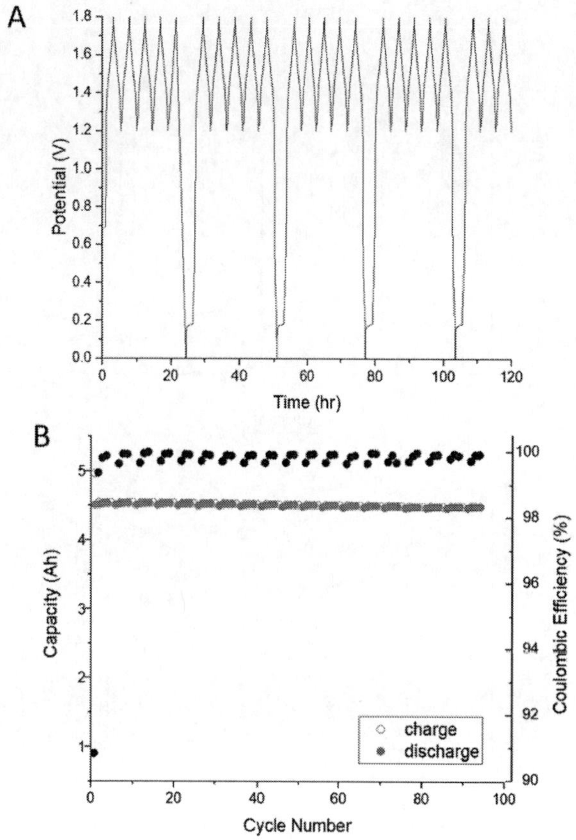

Figure 4- 0V excursions every 5 cycles on aqueous SIB

The 0 V capability of the non-aqueous cells was examined in a similar manner: 4 cycles in the conventional voltage range (2- 4.2V) followed by a 5th cycle with discharge to 0 V and a 5-hour rest (Figure 5A). In contrast to the aqueous cells, the non-aqueous cells exhibited capacity loss after discharging to 0 V. After only six repetitions of this test, 15% capacity loss was observed (Figure 5B), revealing degradation to the cells.

Capacity degradation has been associated with compromised cell safety in LIBs.[4] Therefore, we completed HWS assessment of the non-aqueous cell degraded by 0V excursion. At the same state of charge as the pristine non-aqueous cell from Figure 1B and Figure 2B, the degraded cell demonstrated a similar HWS test response. This indicated that, the capacity loss due to 0 V hold did not translate into compromised safety of the non-aqueous SIB.

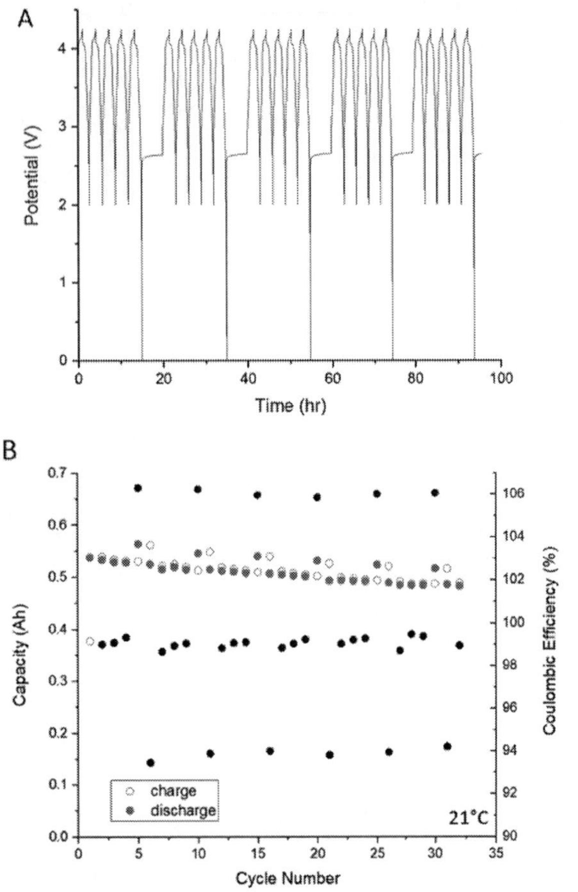

Figure 5-0 V excursions every 5 cycles on non-aqueous SIB

Conclusions

The failure modes of two sodium-ion batteries, one with aqueous electrolyte and one with non-aqueous electrolyte were assessed with accelerating rate calorimetry. Neither cell type exhibited thermal runway or catastrophic failure. Both cells deliver low (<5 W) heat release attributed to material combustion. The aqueous cell delivered the most benign failure, likely since it has a non-flammable electrolyte and low energy density (22 Wh/kg). The aqueous cell is a large pouch cell, allowing seal breaching from electrolyte vaporization at ~100 °C and does not exhibit self-heating until temperatures >150 °C. The peak heat rate during component combustion was 0.18 °/min or 2 W of heat flux.

The non-aqueous cell has a higher energy density (77 Wh/kg) and contains flammable electrolyte. This cell exhibits self-heating at milder temperatures, 55 °C. Cell venting occurs around 100 °C when electrolyte is ejected from the cell leading to a peak heat rate of 0.1 °C/min or 0.12 W.

An advantage of SIBs over LIBs is the ability to store cells in a de-energized state, 0 V or 0% SOC. We examined the influence of 0 V storage on safety and performance for both the aqueous and non-aqueous cells. aqueous cells remained robust to 0 V storage and cycling. No degradation was observed. The non-aqueous cells exhibited capacity fade after 0 V storage, indicating degradation to the cell. However, when subjected to ARC testing the non-aqueous cells degraded by 0 V storage delivered similar failure modes to pristine non-aqueous cells, indicating the degradation does not impact safety.

References

(1) Klein, E. J.; Carter, R.; Love, C. T. Accelerating Rate Calorimetry and Complementary Techniques to Characterize Battery Safety Hazards. *J Vis Exp* **2021**, (175). DOI: 10.3791/60342 From NLM.

(2) Lei, B.; Zhao, W.; Ziebert, C.; Uhlmann, N.; Rohde, M.; Seifert, H. J. Experimental Analysis of Thermal Runaway in 18650 Cylindrical Li-Ion Cells Using an Accelerating Rate Calorimeter. In *Batteries*, 2017; Vol. 3.

(3) Peters, J. F.; Peña Cruz, A.; Weil, M. Exploring the Economic Potential of Sodium-Ion Batteries. *Batteries* **2019**, *5* (1), 10.

(4) Carter, R.; Klein, E. J.; Atkinson, R. W.; Love, C. T. Mechanical collapse as primary degradation mode in mandrel-free 18650 Li-ion cells operated at 0 °C. *Journal of Power Sources* **2019**, *437*, 226820. DOI: https://doi.org/10.1016/j.jpowsour.2019.226820.

Safety Characterization of Flow Battery of Two Chemistries

***Judith A. Jeevarajan*[1]*, Migo Szeman Ng*[1]*, Taina Rauhala*[1] *and Carlos F. Lopez*[2]**

[1]Electrochemical Safety Research Institute (ESRI)
UL Research Institutes, Houston, TX 77204
[2]Stress Engineering Services, Inc., Houston, TX 77041
judy.jeevarajan@ul.org

Abstract

Flow batteries are becoming more common in grid energy storage systems around the world. There are several flow battery chemistries that are being studied and some of the chemistries have been commercialized. Flow batteries consist of liquid electrolytes contained in two tanks or reservoirs. They are aqueous systems and the voltage associated with any single flow battery for the various chemistries used today is less than or equal to 2 V. The quantity of electrolyte used determines the capacity. For stationary grid energy storage applications, where weight and volume are not significant concerns, they are a good candidate, due to their much lower costs compared to other rechargeable battery systems. The performance of flow batteries has been of interest to researchers and the refinement of this property has been in work for quite some time. However, the safety of these systems is not studied widely. Safety standards typically tend to study the flammability of the electrolytes rather than studying the cell or system as a whole. The Electrochemical Safety Research Institute (ESRI) at UL Research Institutes has carried out performance and safety characterization tests on two flow battery chemistries. They are the vanadium system and the zinc-bromine system.

Introduction

Redox flow batteries (RFBs) are currently used in large megawatt- and gigawatt-size grid energy storage systems. They store energy in electrolyte solutions which contain two redox couples that are pumped through the battery cell stack. Different redox couples can be utilized, such as V/V, Zn/Br_2, V/Br_2, S/Br_2, and Fe/Cr which influence the performance metrics of the batteries.[1] The energy stored by RFBs depends on the volume of the electrolytes in the tanks and the power depends on the size of the electrochemical cell stack. The specific energy of RFBs is relatively low compared to e.g., lithium-ion batteries, which generally limits RFBs' applications to stationary systems. The advantages of flow batteries include low cost, high cycle life, design flexibility and tolerance to deep discharges.[2] The factors and components affecting flow battery performance have been extensively studied but not the safety under off-nominal conditions. It is usually assumed that the high heat capacity of the aqueous electrolyte can prevent temperature rise. Moreover, the toxicity of the gases released, or the degradation of the flow battery components has not been widely investigated.

The vanadium redox flow battery (VRFB) is the most widely researched of the different flow battery chemistries and is already in a mature state for grid-level applications.[2, 3] The first VRFB was originally developed by Skyllas-Kazacos and coworkers at the University of New South Wales in Australia. The VRFB consists of two electrolyte reservoirs and a cell stack in which the two electrodes and respective electrolytes are separated from each other by an ion-exchange membrane (Figure 1). A solution of vanadium in a sulfuric acid supporting electrolyte is used in both half-cells, which has the advantage of eliminating the risk of electrolyte cross-contamination.[1] The negative half-cell utilizes the V^{2+}/V^{3+} redox couple and the positive half-cell the VO^{2+}/VO_2^+ couple, yielding a standard cell voltage of 1.26 V at 25 °C through the following reactions:[1]

Positive electrode: $VO^{2+} + H_2O \leftrightarrow VO_2^+ + 2H^+ + e^-$

Negative electrode: $V^{3+} + e^- \leftrightarrow V^{2+}$

Cell reaction: $VO^{2+} + V^{3+} + H_2O \leftrightarrow VO_2^+ + 2H^+ + V^{2+}$

A feature of the VRFB electrolytes is the distinct colors of each of the different vanadium oxidation states, with V(II) being violet, V(III) green, V(IV) blue, and V(V) yellow.[4] This allows visual qualitative state of charge (SOC) determination and enables quantitative determination using spectroscopic measurements.[4]

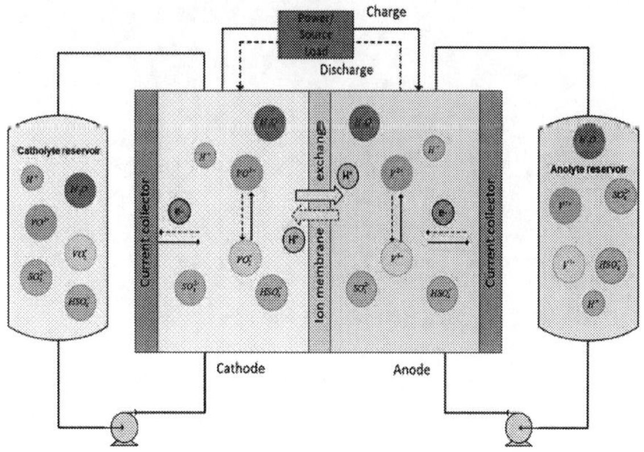

Figure 1. Schematic of a vanadium redox flow battery

Graphitic and carbonaceous materials are used as the electrodes for both the positive and negative half-cells due to their ability to withstand the highly corrosive electrolyte. The energy density of the VRFB system is limited by the solubility of the various vanadium species in the acidic electrolyte within the battery operating temperature range.[1] Therefore, some of the recent VRFB systems utilize a mixed sulfuric acid-hydrochloric acid supporting electrolyte to increase the solubility of the vanadium species, thereby increasing the energy density and reducing issues with precipitation.[1, 5] However, the addition of hydrochloric acid into the electrolyte is associated with a risk of chlorine gas evolution, especially in case the battery is exposed to off-nominal conditions.[6]

Unlike the vanadium RFB system that has four different oxidation states, the zinc-bromine (Zn/Br_2) flow battery involves one solid phase and one liquid phase of active species.[7] The fundamental electrochemical reactions of the Zn/Br_2 RFB can be described as follows:
At the positive electrode:

$$2Br^-_{(aq)} \underset{\text{Discharge}}{\overset{\text{Charge}}{\rightleftarrows}} Br_{2(l)} + 2e^- \qquad (E_0 = +1.09\text{V vs: SHE}) \qquad (1)$$

At the negative electrode:

$$Zn^{2+}_{(aq)} + 2e^- \underset{\text{Discharge}}{\overset{\text{Charge}}{\rightleftarrows}} Zn_{(s)} \qquad (E_0 = -0.76\text{V vs: SHE}) \qquad (2)$$

The overall cell reaction:

$$ZnBr_{2(aq)} \underset{\text{Discharge}}{\overset{\text{Charge}}{\rightleftarrows}} Zn_{(s)} + Br_{2(l)} \qquad (E_{cell} = +1.85\text{V vs: SHE}) \qquad (3)$$

Figure 2 is a schematic of the Zn/Br_2 RFB. During charging, the bromide ions are oxidized to liquid bromine, Br_2 at the positive electrode and the Zn^{2+} is reduced to metallic zinc, Zn^0, at the negative electrode. The opposite reactions occur during the discharging process. The redox reactions occur in the interface of electrolyte and electrode, in which the metallic Zn is electrodeposited on the electrode surface during charging and is dissolved back in the electrolyte during the discharge process.[2]

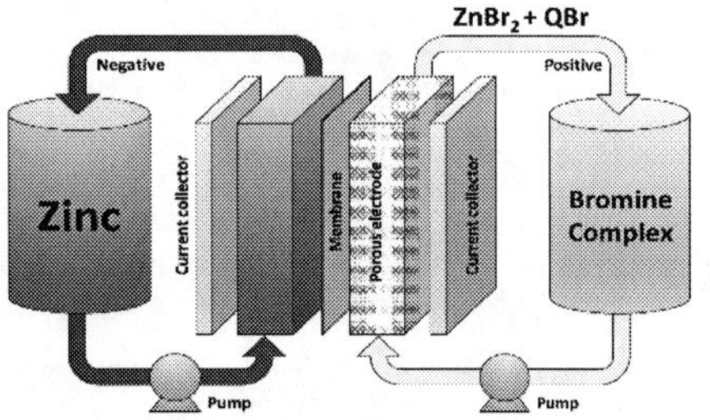

Figure 2. Schematic of the Zn/Br_2 RFB.

The bromine formed is sequestered and prevented from going into the vapor phase with the help of a complexing agent such as *N*-methyl-*N*-ethyl pyrrolidinium bromide (MEP) or *N*-methyl *N*-ethyl morpholinium bromide (MEM).[4–6] Furthermore, due to the higher density of these complex polybromide species, permeation of bromine and bromine aggregation across the ion exchange membrane is impeded.[4] An elevated conductivity in this system is crucial to avoid ohmic losses.[2] In addition, the operating pH range of most Zn/Br_2 commercial systems is between 1–3.5.[6] The narrow pH range is carefully controlled throughout the operation, to avoid the formation of bromate (pH >3), solid zinc oxide (pH >6), as well as prevent hydrogen evolution (pH <1) which can lower the coulombic efficiencies which in turn lower the cyclability of the system.[1, 3]

Experimental

The lab scale vanadium flow battery was built using typical components used for a fuel cell. A photo of the lab scale system is shown in Figure 3.

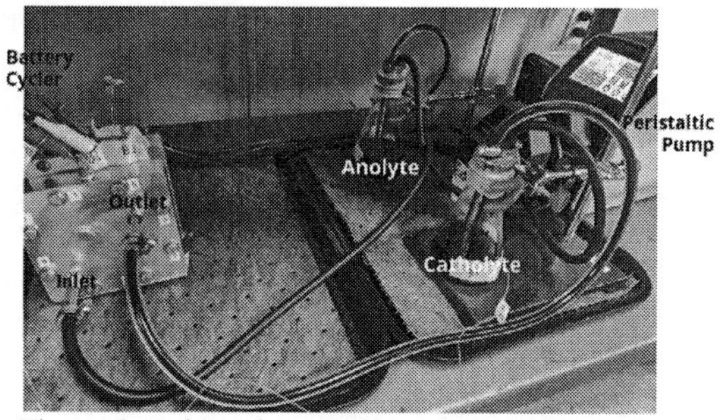

Figure 3. Lab-scale vanadium redox flow battery.

Vanadium sulfate solution (1M $VOSO_4$ and 3M H_2SO_4) was used as the catholyte and anolyte. Since the electrolyte has a charge of 3.5, pre-charge of the catholyte needs to be performed in order to have the relevant oxidation state of V^{5+} for the redox reaction. The catholyte flask had twice the volume of the anolyte during this pre-charge stage. After the cell was charged to 1.7V, half of the volume of the catholyte was removed. The cell consisted of typical acid fuel cell hardware with a triple serpentine flow pattern and an active area of 50 cm^2. The electrode was Sigracell carbon felt with a thickness of 2.5 mm and 90% porosity and a surface area of 0.4 m^2/g. The membrane was Nafion 212 with a thickness of 0.8 micron and a conductivity of 0.1 S/cm. A neoprene rubber gasket of 1/16" thickness was used. The flow rate of the electrolytes was 50 ml/min. The resulting flow battery cell had a voltage of about 1.26 V and a capacity of 2.0 Ah. The cells were cycled between 1.7 V and 0.7 V using a charge and discharge current of ~1 A (20 mA/cm^2).
The off-nominal safety tests carried out were overcharge and overdischarge. For the overcharge test, the flow battery was taken to a full charge of 1.7 V with a 1.0 A current and continued into an overcharge condition for another 6 hours. For the overdischarge test, the flow battery was subjected to a load of 1 A to remove an additional 150% of the original capacity after the cell reached 0 V.
The commercial large-scale zinc/bromine redox flow battery was procured from Redflow Ltd. The battery was a 60 V 200 Ah system. A photo of the test article is shown in Figure 4.

The battery has an integrated module management system (MMS) that provides protection against several off-nominal conditions. The MMS provides protection against overvoltage, undervoltage, overtemperature, and overcurrent (short circuits) and also shuts down in the event of electrolyte leakage and gas evolution. The off-nominal tests on this battery were carried out with the MMS bypassed and connecting directly to the cell terminals in order to subject the module to the off-nominal condition without the MMS interception. This was the only way worst-case results could be determined in the event of an off-nominal condition and failure of MMS protections.

Figure 4. Commercial-scale Zn/Br_2 redox flow battery.

The overcharge was carried out by charging the module with a current of 45 A to a limit of 100 V or for a total capacity of 600 Ah. The overdischarge was carried out initially by taking the battery down to 0 V and then removing 150% of additional capacity. However, the current steadily fell from 30 A to 0.5 A with the voltage going from -3 V to greater than 0 V. The test was therefore carried out by holding it at ~ 500 mV for a period of almost 24 hours. The external short circuit was carried out with a load of 20 mohms for a total of three hours. Voltage, current, and temperatures were monitored during the entire test period. Gas sensors from MSA were used to monitor oxygen, carbon dioxide, hydrogen, and bromine gas.

Results and Discussion

Vanadium Flow Battery

The vanadium lab scale flow battery was subjected to overcharge and overdischarge tests only. The overcharge test resulted in excessive gas production in both the catholyte and anolyte and the graphite plates in the flow battery cell on the side of the cathode showed severe degradation while the anode side appeared very clean, as shown in Figure 5. However, bubbling inside the Erlenmeyer flasks was observed only in the case of the catholyte while the gas production in the anolyte was mainly observed by the presence of significant gas bubble production in the tubes, shown in Figure 6. The voltage and temperature data are shown in Figure 7 for the overcharge test.

The overdischarge test did not result in any significant gas production. The voltage and temperature data for the overdischarge test is shown in Figure 8. No degradation of either of the electrodes or flow channels was observed.

Figure 5. Vanadium flow battery cell showing the electrolyte flow channels on both electrodes.

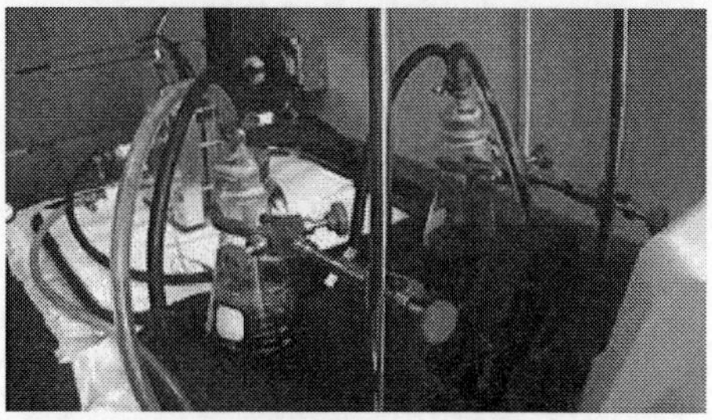

Figure 6. Overcharge test showing bubbling in the catholyte flask.

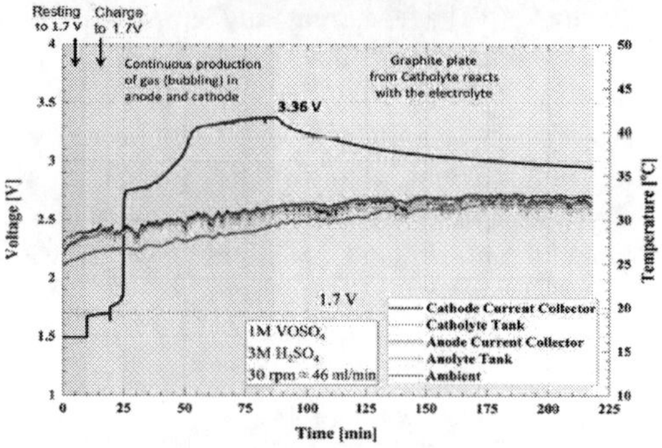

Figure 7. Voltage and temperature plots for the overcharge test of the vanadium system.

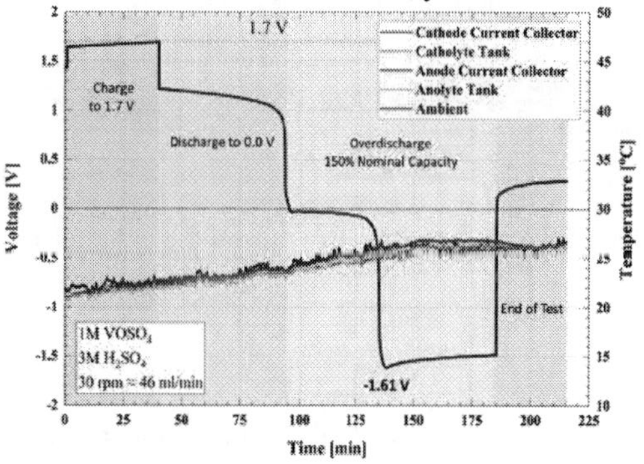

Figure 8. Plot of voltage and temperature for the overdischarge test of the vanadium system.

Zinc – Bromine Flow Battery

The overcharge test of the Zn/Br_2 system caused the release of bromine gas from the electrolyte tank. The measured gas concentration was >5 ppm at 9 inches from the pressure relief vent. A review of the electrochemical equations shows that bromine gas is released during the charge process and the MEP is used to sequester gaseous bromine and keep it in solution. However, when there is excessive bromine gas released, the quantity of MEP in the system is not sufficient for the sequestration causing the gas to be released through the vents. It is not clear if hydrogen gas was evolved since the excess bromine release may have masked any evolved hydrogen gas. A maximum temperature of 83 °C was recorded in the zinc (catholyte) tank. Figure 9 shows the voltage, current, and temperature of the RFB during the overcharge test. The zinc tank displayed a temporary deformation at the end of the overcharge test.

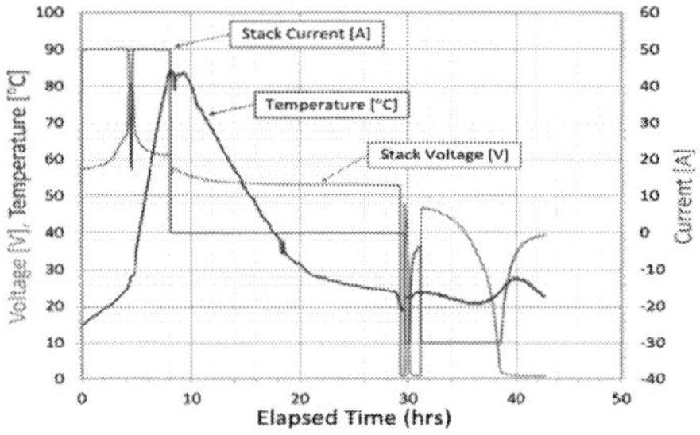

Figure 9. Plots of voltage, current, and temperature for the overcharge test of the Zn/Br_2 RFB.

The overdischarge test did not show any excessive gas production or high temperatures. The external short test caused the voltage of the battery to fall to 0 V before the 3 hour hold and the maximum temperature observed was less than 80 °C, as shown in Figure 10.

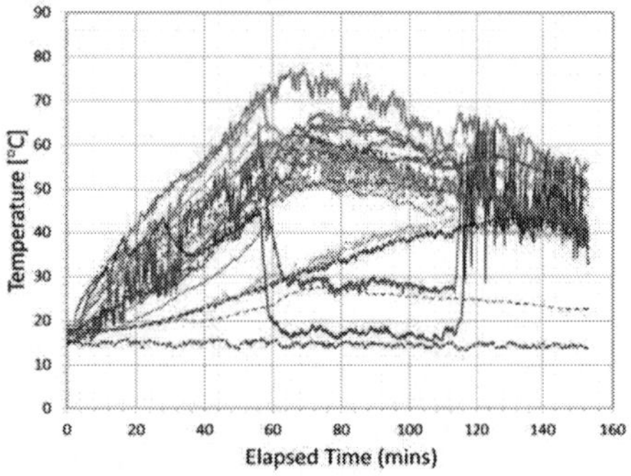

Figure 10. Temperature trends during the external short test.

Conclusions

The two flow battery chemistries studied in this work indicate that a good characterization and understanding of the system as a whole is required to determine the worst-case results of an off-nominal condition. Gas production in both systems indicate that if the controls are not set in the relevant manner, combustible and toxic gases can be released into the environment. The test articles should be tested under off-nominal conditions to fully understand the worst-case behavior before safety limits are set into the module and battery management systems.

Acknowledgment

UL Research Institutes' internal funding was used to carry out the tests. We would like to express our gratitude to Dr. Steve Kinyon at Stress Engineering Services, Inc. and to our former colleague, Dr. Daniel Juarez-Robles who carried out the work on the vanadium lab-scale RFBs. Dr. Byoungchul Kwon is thanked for drawing the schematic of the Zn/Br_2 RFB.

References

1. Tomazic, G.; Skyllas-Kazacos, M., Redox Flow Batteries. In *Electrochemical Energy Storage for Renewable Sources and Grid Balancing*, Moseley, P. T.; Garche, J., Eds. Elsevier: 2015; pp 309-336.
2. Fan, X.; Liu, B.; Liu, J.; Ding, J.; Han, X.; Deng, Y.; Lv, X.; Xie, Y.; Chen, B.; Hu, W.; Zhong, C., Battery Technologies for Grid-Level Large-Scale Electrical Energy Storage. *Transactions of Tianjin University* **2020,** *26* (2), 92-103.
3. DOE Global Energy Storage Database. https://sandia.gov/ess-ssl/gesdb/public/statistics.html (accessed April 10, 2023).
4. Skyllas-Kazacos, M.; Cao, L.; Kazacos, M.; Kausar, N.; Mousa, A., Vanadium Electrolyte Studies for the Vanadium Redox Battery-A Review. *ChemSusChem* **2016,** *9* (13), 1521-43.
5. Li, L.; Kim, S.; Wang, W.; Vijayakumar, M.; Nie, Z.; Chen, B.; Zhang, J.; Xia, G.; Hu, J.; Graff, G.; Liu, J.; Yang, Z., A Stable Vanadium Redox-Flow Battery with High Energy Density for Large-Scale Energy Storage. *Advanced Energy Materials* **2011,** *1* (3), 394-400.
6. Wittman, R. M.; Poirier, C.; Pratt, H. D.; Anderson, T. M.; Preger, Y., Quantification of Chlorine Gas Generation in Mixed-Acid Vanadium Redox Flow Batteries. *ACS Applied Energy Materials* **2023,** *6* (6), 3167-3172.
7. Khor, A.; Leung, P.; Mohamed, M. R.; Flox, C.; Xu, Q.; An, L.; Wills, R. G. A.; Morante, J. R.; Shah, A. A., Review of zinc-based hybrid flow batteries: From fundamentals to applications. *Materials Today Energy* **2018,** *8*, 80-108.
8. Arévalo-Cid, P.; Dias, P.; Mendes, A.; Azevedo, J., Redox flow batteries: a new frontier on energy storage. *Sustainable Energy & Fuels* **2021,** *5* (21), 5366-5419.
9. Sasaki, T.; Tange, K.; Okawa, M.; Suzuki, Y. Zinc-bromine battery. Patent No 4,677,039, 1987.
10. Kim, M.; Yun, D.; Jeon, J., Effect of a bromine complex agent on electrochemical performances of zinc electrodeposition and electrodissolution in Zinc–Bromide flow battery. *Journal of Power Sources* **2019,** *438*.
11. Rajarathnam, G. P.; Vassallo, A. M., Description of the Zn/Br RFB System. In *The Zinc/Bromine Flow Battery: Materials Challenges and Practical Solutions for Technology Advancement*, 1 ed.; Rajarathnam, G. P.; Vassallo, A. M., Eds. Springer Singapore: 2016; pp 11-25.

IPOWER: A Dismounted Warfighter Energy Simulation and Analysis Tool

Richard O. Stroman[1], Christopher Buesser[2], Brian Somes[2], and Jacob Amtmann[2]
[1]Chemistry Division, U.S. Naval Research Laboratory, Washington DC, 20375
[2]Excet Inc., 6225 Brandon Ave Ste 360, Springfield, VA 22150

Abstract: *The US Army and Marine Corps need a way to understand dismounted warfighter energy systems quantitatively to inform acquisitions and doctrine development. The U.S. Naval Research Laboratory (NRL) developed the IPOWER energy simulation tool to satisfy this need with quantitative analysis of dismounted warfighter missions and equipment in realistic environments. IPOWER combines step-wise state integration, nonlinear component models, and climate data with optimization algorithms and a simple user interface. Ease of use is key; it runs as a web app and users interact with it through a browser much like a website. IPOWER is currently distributed as a standalone application, but work is underway to make it widely available within DoD as a cloud service with CAC login.*

Keywords: energy; power; soldier; model; simulation; mission; optimize.

Introduction

Dismounted warfighters face constantly evolving challenges on the battlefield, and one way they meet those challenges is with new, more capable equipment. They rely on program offices, the research and development community, and industry to provide that new equipment. Unfortunately, it often comes with greater complexity and energy consumption. The modern warfighter is more capable, but the energy problem has grown to a point where their performance is hindered by the weight of batteries they must carry and the time they spend on energy management. Furthermore, the need for frequent energy resupply makes warfighters vulnerable to attack. This problem is forcing decision-makers to consider energy in the selection of new equipment and architectures for dismounted warfighters.

In the past, the only sources of energy information available to acquisition offices were rough approximations, anecdotal evidence, and field experiments with many uncontrolled variables. That made it difficult and time consuming (or even impossible) to compare options quantitatively and make decisions confidently. The Intelligent Power Optimization with Environmental Reactivity (IPOWER) simulation tool was developed to inform the acquisition process with fast, rigorous, and quantitative energy analyses.

IPOWER users set up a mission scenario (location and activity timeline), assign equipment to individuals and units, and then run the energy simulation. They can configure equipment models, mission activities, and unit structures based on templates in IPOWER. That flexibility enables them to base their analyses on existing equipment or incorporate hypothetical equipment to answer "what if" questions and guide development priorities. IPOWER provides results in the form of metrics, charts, plots, and other graphics that examine the scenario from different perspectives. Examples include the number of batteries required for the mission, the amount of fuel consumed, and the amount of energy harvested. Results can be exported to a spreadsheet for further analysis.

IPOWER users can simulate different scenarios in the same environment, or the same scenario with different equipment, to make apples-to-apples comparisons with a consistent baseline. IPOWER can help winnow candidate technologies early in the evaluation process and improve the chances that an expensive field-test will identify a winning solution.

Workflow

The simulation process follows five steps: (1) Setup, (2) Mission Definition, (3) Equipment Selection, (4) Unit Assignment, and (5) Results. A different page is dedicated to each step, and the workflow is shown across the top of the page for context. The mission and equipment together form the mission scenario.

Setup: Give the scenario a name and select a location from among from a list stored in the IPOWER database. Typical Model Year (TMY) data for each location is used to estimate the ambient temperature and solar irradiance at 30 min intervals throughout the simulated mission. [1]

Mission Definition: Select among standard activities stored in the IPOWER database to compose timelines that describe what the warfighters are doing and when they do it. Each timeline represents a "mission". Timelines can start on any date or time and have any length, but all the timelines in a simulation must start at the same time and end at the same time. Multiple timelines can be configured, saved, and reloaded. An example is shown in Fig 1.

Equipment Selection: Define the unit structure (e.g. a platoon consisting of four squads) and then assign equipment to individuals and to units. For example, a radio might be assigned to an individual warfighter, or a shared battery charger might be assigned to a squad. Equipment is assigned by creating a blank "system pane" and then choosing equipment from the IPOWER database to populate it. There are two ways to do this. Users can choose a load that always uses the same type of battery, in which case IPOWER will auto-populate the batteries. Alternatively, they can choose a power manager or hub that connects other equipment. In that case, IPOWER creates empty ports and users can choose among a list of compatible equipment to populate the ports. An example of the "System Builder" feature that enables systems to be created and visualized as block diagrams is shown in Fig. 2. At the top of the system

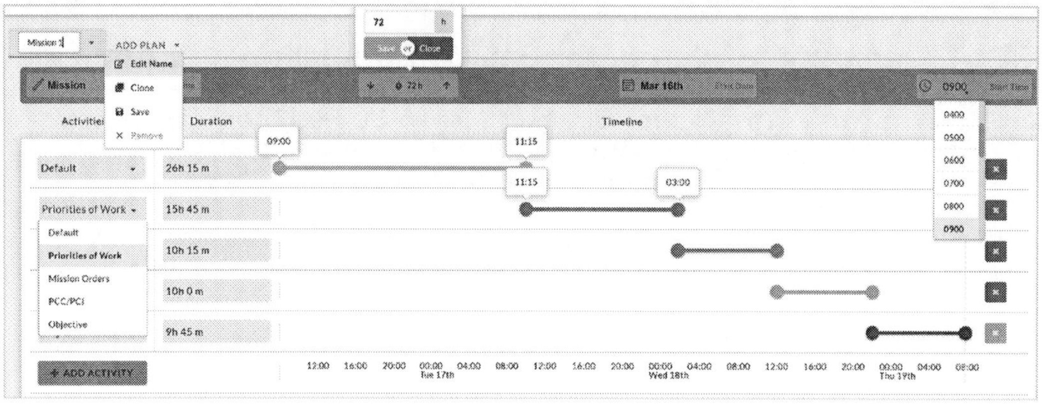

Figure 1. Mission definition step where users define one or more mission timelines using standard activities.

pane, users can define alternative configurations of the system and indicate which configuration is active during each mission activity. Multiple systems can be assigned to an individual warfighter or unit.

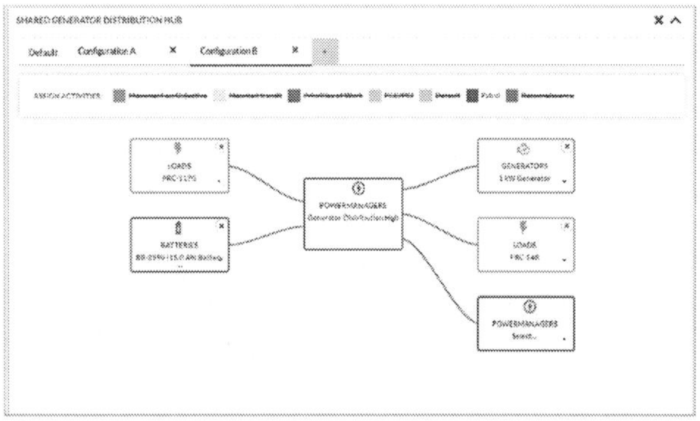

Figure 2. System pane with example system; in this case a power manager connected to a generator, two loads, a battery, and another power manager.

Unit Assignment: Choose which elements of the unit (e.g. squads) execute each mission from the Mission Definition step. IPOWER assumes units executing the same mission are co-located and able to share energy (batteries, fuel, etc.) and share equipment (battery charger, generator, etc.)

Results: Simulation results are communicated through metrics, plots, and charts. A summary is provided at the top of the results page and increasingly detailed results are available as users scroll down. Summary data includes the total amount of energy consumed, energy used to recharge batteries, number of batteries consumed by type, and weight of energy-related equipment needed for the simulated mission. Top-level plots include energy consumption, total energy stored in batteries, and energy harvested as functions of mission time.

There are constraints on the scenarios that can be configured in IPOWER; for example, systems that consume power but have no power source are not allowed. IPOWER checks for such problems during the configuration process, and when it finds one, it displays a descriptive warning with a link to the source of the problem so it can be rectified easily.

The steps in an IPOWER simulation are explained in the IPOWER Step-by-Step guide. [2]

Simulation Process

Fundamentally, IPOWER works by breaking the mission into many time steps, and then solving an energy balance for each system over each time step in sequence from the beginning of the mission to the end. For each time step, the process is:

1. Compute the power required by connected loads.
2. Compute power available from harvesters, generators, fuel cells, and batteries.
3. Balance power. Preferentially draw power from harvesters, generators and fuel cells, and batteries, in that order to satisfy the loads.
4. Update state variables, such as battery state of charge (SOC) and fuel consumed.
5. Advance to next time step

The process is shown in Fig. 3. IPOWER typically runs with a 3 min timestep and takes ~1 sec to complete a 72 h mission simulation for a platoon.

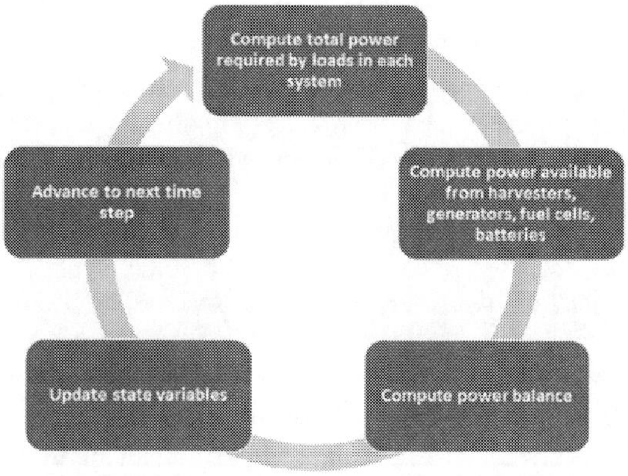

Figure 3. Basic simulation process in IPOWER.

Once a timestep is complete and the state variables have been updated, energy management features are applied for the next step. These energy management features play an important role in making IPOWER simulations realistic.

Battery management is a good example. If a battery is exhausted at the end of a timestep, IPOWER will look for a replacement in the "pool" of batteries carried by the unit. If one is available, then the batteries are swapped. If a battery charger is available, the mission activity allows the use of a battery charger, there is power for the battery charger, and a slot is available, then IPOWER will plug an exhausted battery into the battery charger.

When a battery is needed and none are available, IPOWER creates a new battery and adds it to the total that must have been carried from the beginning of the mission. This simple process yields the minimum number of batteries required to complete the mission. Preferentially drawing power from energy harvesters, generators/fuel cells, and then batteries yields the minimum fuel consumption constrained by the minimum number of batteries.

Structure and User Interface

As a web app, IPOWER consists of a front end that runs in a web browser and a back end that runs behind a server. The front end is predominantly JavaScript with TypeScript, and the back end is written in Go with a Postgres database. Each is containerized to make IPOWER modular and easily deployed. This structure was chosen both because of its flexibility and because it opened the way to a future service implementation.

The IPOWER user interface (UI) was designed in collaboration with a web development company and considered input from users to ensure it is simple and easy to use. Examples are shown in Fig. 4.

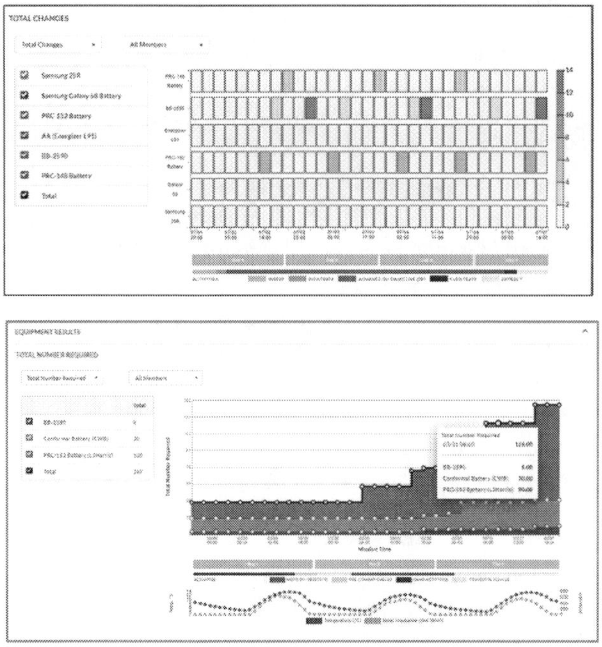

Figure 4. UI examples. A heat map showing when and how many batteries are replaced (top) and a plot of the number of batteries required as a function of mission time (bottom).

It was developed with standard web development tools, such as the React framework, to minimize the learning curve for new users and leverage the intuitive nature of many website features.

The IPOWER UI includes the ease-of-use features that would be expected for any application:

- Missions, equipment models, activities, and scenarios can be saved and later re-loaded.
- Mission timelines and units can be edited, cloned (copied), renamed, and deleted.

Plots on the results page include the mission timeline and estimated environment for context when interpreting the results. Hovering the cursor over plots and charts reveals pop-ups with detailed information. Many plots, including those shown in Fig. 4, include a legend where some curves can be turned off to focus on a specific result.

Equipment Models

IPOWER is delivered with several battery models based on battery characterization studies at NRL, however users are expected to provide the other equipment data relevant to their simulations. The user interface includes an "Admin" section where users can populate models for loads, batteries, energy harvesters, generators, fuel cells, and power managers. Each class of equipment has a series of pages that walk users through the configuration process, and once a model is created, any of the editable parameters can be updated. When a model is changed in the database, and the same model appears in a saved simulation, IPOWER will ask the user if the model parameters in the simulation should be updated to the values in the database.

All equipment models include metadata fields for a name, description, weight, and volume.

Load models can be defined in two ways:

- Define the power consumed during each mission activity.
- Define a set of operating modes and the power consumed in each mode. Define the duty cycle for each mode (fraction of time spent in that mode) for each mission activity.

Modifiers can be applied to change the power consumption of a load based on the ambient temperature or day/night. This feature can be used to configure equipment, such as night vision devices, for which the power consumption differs during day and night.

There are three types of battery model in IPOWER. The simplest is an "energy bucket" model that can be configured using basic information from a manufacturer's specification sheet. It is the least accurate, but simplest to configure. The dynamic battery model applies features of the battery discharge curve and chemistry to estimate more accurately the current and voltage for a given power flow. [3] The most detailed, the equivalent circuit model, uses an empirical equation of state to relate terminal voltage to SOC, temperature, and power flow. The tables underlying the equivalent circuit model are populated at NRL by measuring battery series resistance and open circuit voltage as functions of SOC and temperature. [4] The equivalent circuit model responds to ambient temperature to capture effects such as reduced performance in cold environments.

All three battery models include fields for the minimum and maximum voltage, charging current, charging termination current, and maximum discharge current. These bounds influence the termination of the charge or discharge process, and they limit the power that can be withdrawn. They also influence the constant current/constant voltage charging profile typically used for lithium-ion batteries and simulated in IPOWER.

Solar panels are currently the only energy harvester in IPOWER. They are defined by an active area, efficiency, and temperature coefficient. IPOWER assumes they lay flat on the ground and uses the global horizontal irradiance to estimate the power production at each simulation time step.

Generator and fuel cell models are based on curves relating net power output to fuel consumption rate. The point at 0 W net output captures the idle fuel consumption rate. Parameters for startup energy cost and maximum idle time can be used to capture tradeoffs related to generator underutilization.

Power managers are the most complex equipment in IPOWER. They are defined by a fixed number of ports, the equipment compatible with each port, the directionality (in, out, or bidirectional) of each port, and the efficiency of each port. Power managers can be connected to other power managers to create complex system topologies. An iterative power balance within each time step is applied to systems with multiple power managers to ensure loads are satisfied efficiently.

Analysis Tools

IPOWER includes two tools for analyzing simulations. The comparison tool presents the results from two or more simulations side-by-side with corresponding results fields for easy comparison. The parametric analysis tool (PAT) can be used to vary one parameter in a simulation and then plot results over that range. For example, in a simulation with a battery, the battery capacity can be varied from a lower bound to an upper bound, and the number of batteries required for a mission will be plotted against that range. This tool is useful for understanding tradeoffs and identifying target values. For a goal, such as reducing battery weight by 10%, the PAT can be used to estimate how much radio efficiency and battery capacity would have to increase, and then use those results to pursue the least expensive solution.

Looking Forward

IPOWER is deployed as a standalone application that users run locally, however the IPOWER team is currently working to make it a cloud service. The new service-oriented approach has several benefits:

- It will be accessible from any internet connected computer via CAC login.
- Users can easily share equipment models, missions, and results.
- Organizations can maintain validated and verified models to ensure confidence in results.
- It can be updated and maintained efficiently, like most other software we use every day.

The ability to share and aggregate models and data will likely be the most valuable feature of the IPOWER service. Rather than starting from scratch, users will be able to build on the models and data accumulated by their organization. The service will run in the Air Force's Platform One DEVSECOPS environment. The IPOWER service is expected to become available in late 2023.

IPOWER includes a REST API between the front and back ends that will enable other DoD applications to interact with it if they are properly credentialed. The API is documented as an OpenAPI 3.0 specification. [5]

A new version of IPOWER is ready to be released as the first cloud service. Version 4.4 includes improvements to the user interface and a new feature, called Custom Power Management Logic, with which users can define custom state machines to govern how power managers behave.

Acknowledgements

The authors thank Army PEO Soldier, the Marine Corps Expeditionary Energy Office, the Office of Naval Research, and the Operational Energy Capability Improvement Fund for supporting this work.

References

1. National Solar Radiation Database (NSRDB) at https://nsrdb.nrel.gov, National Renewable Energy Laboratory, 2022.
2. R. O. Stroman, C. J. Busser, B. D. Somes, J. Amtmann, *IPOWER 4.2.0 Step-By-Step Guide,* NRL Memorandum Report, NRL/MR/6170— 2022/1, January 11, 2022.
3. O. Tremblay, L.-A. Dessaint, and A.-I. Dekkiche, "A Generic Battery Model for the Dynamic Simulation of Hybrid Electric Vehicles," in *IEEE Vehicle Power and Propulsion Conference*, Arlington TX, 2007.
4. R. O. Stroman, R. Carter, C. J. Busser, B. D. Somes, J. Amtmann, D. Hayman, *Battery Modeling and Simulation in IPOWER,* NRL Memorandum Report, NRL/6170/MR— 2022/7, September 8, 2022
5. U.S. Naval Research Laboratory, "IPOWER v4.3 Application Programming Interface," Washington DC, 2022.

Warfighter Alternative Energy Study (WAES)

Alexis Moy; Julianne Douglas
U.S. Army AFC DEVCOM C5ISR
alexis.m.moy.civ@army.mil /732-766-3752

Abstract

As we move forward into contested near-peer conflicts, the risks to our power and energy supply chains increases. The tyranny of distance in INDOPACOM increases costs, reaction time, and decreases readiness. Little to no investments/studies have focused on solving these problems for inland or land-based operations in this Area of Responsibility (AOR), which this study seeks to rectify. Due to increasing power demand for Warfighters, it is critical to investigate the future power and energy needs to determine and remedy gaps. This increasing power demand is due to both the deployment of new and novel devices that support Joint All Domain Situational Awareness (JADSA), and future operating concepts in the INDOPACOM theater. The added time with limited to no resupply, increases the need for power and energy for the land-based Warfighter on the move. Additionally, there is no guide for alternative energy or available resources in the AOR, which makes planning and sustainment more difficult. Combining these challenges creates a significant gap that must be addressed to support the deployment of mobile and distributed operations with decreased logistical footprint in contested environments.

This study seeks to determine the most useful ways to leverage our joint investments by modeling the future fight and technology projections to determine the best path forward and influence policy, TTPs and CONOPS to increase readiness for future conflict. The operational impact of alternative energy in INDOPACOM is in JADSA, lethality, survivability, logistics, and mobility of the future force that it enables. Addressing the recommended technology investments and policy changes could mean the difference between lives and wars lost versus won. The right changes and actions need to be identified now and actioned to ensure tactical advantage and survivability to meet wartime production capability needs.

The focus of this study is to 1) determine and leverage resources available within the AOR's regions of interest to create an alternative energy logistics-planning guide; and 2) identify the power and energy gaps and potential solutions by identifying critical alternative energy technologies for investment. These will lead to recommended changes in Concepts of Operations (CONOPs), Tactics, Techniques, and Procedures (TTPs), and policy changes to achieve tactical advantage among joint dismounted forces in INDOPACOM.

This study is aimed at using results from recent and upcoming joint service test events to determine gaps and extrapolate power demands for next generation alternative energy technologies. The energy demands will be for a company or below of dismounted Warfighters and focus on the feasibility of implementing alternative energy in the INDOPACOM region. This study also focuses on looking at what potential types of alternative energy sources can be used to close the gaps that are identified for the future fight. The end state of this project will be a report and briefing on the findings of the study. The report will recommend technologies and policies (CONOPS and TTPs) for the resources, gaps, scenarios, and case studies identified and analyzed during the study. It will also estimate the opportunities for investments in the near-, mid-, and far-term for alternative energy to provide power at the tactical edge.

Keywords

Alternative Energy; INDOPACOM, Power; Energy; Energy Conversion; Tactical Advantage; Energy Availability; Energy Resupply; Area Of Responsibility; Change of Policy

Introduction

As we move forward into contested near-peer conflicts, the risks to our power and energy supply chains increases. The tyranny of distance in INDOPACOM increases costs, reaction time, and decreases readiness. Little to no investments/studies have focused on solving these problems for inland or land-based operations in this Area of Responsibility (AOR), which this study seeks to rectify. Due to increasing power demand for Warfighters, it is critical to investigate the future power and energy needs to determine and remedy the gaps. This increasing power demand is due to both the deployment of new and novel devices that support Joint All Domain Situational Awareness (JADSA), and future operating concepts such as multi-day semi-autonomous / limited resupply operations in the INDOPACOM theater. The added time with limited to no resupply, increases the need for power and energy for the land-based Warfighter on the move. Additionally, due to lack of available resources in the AOR, planning and sustainment is more difficult. Combining these challenges creates a gap that must be addressed to support the deployment of mobile and distributed operations with decreased logistical footprint in contested environments.

Alternative energy for the land-based Warfighter presents opportunities to shift the paradigm and for competition and success on this field of battle. Alternative energy is typically defined as "energy generated in ways that do not deplete natural resources or harm the environment, especially by avoiding the use of fossil fuels and nuclear power." For the purposes of this study, alternative energy encompasses solar, wind, water, kinetic and other energy harvesting, urban energy scavenging, fuel cells, alternative power or fuel generation from readily available fuels, among other technologies. These technologies allow our land-based Warfighters to live off the land between resupplies or using only the supplies they bring with them. The benefits to the joint force are significant and include decreased logistics and maintenance costs, increased readiness, continuity of operations and communications in contested environments, minimal footprint, maintained responsiveness to JADSA, and reduced environmental cleanup after the military leaves a location. This translates to lives saved during land or sea resupply operations.

Approach

This study first assesses the gaps and identify the reference architecture that is used for the study while leveraging prior studies and programs from OECIF, INDOPACOM, SOCOM, and the Joint Services. This includes joint service and commercial technologies and takes information from recent and upcoming joint service tests to use in the gap assessment. Next, the study develops possible scenarios in a future battlefield and select the scenarios that were run for the study. The part also projects the power and energy demand based on incorporating lessons learned from prior OECIF efforts and INDOPACOM-focused programs into the current problem space. The gaps and technology advancement projects will be input into an unclassified version of the scenario using a common software package to determine if and how the technologies can meet the joint forces power and energy demands. Finally, the assessment of the state-of-the-art alternative energy technologies will be done to see what technologies can feasibly close the gaps that were identified and what changes to the TPs/CONOPS/policy is needed to achieve tactical advantage.

The study utilized a common software package model that was developed in a previous OECIF project and has since been improved to input the case studies into and run the different scenarios for this effort to guide our future investment strategy and policy development. Data from joint test events will be used as inputs to the model to gain additional Warfighter feedback on technologies in this scenario. Simultaneously, this study determines, consolidates, and leverages resources available in select regions within INDOPACOM into an alternative energy sustainment guide for logistics planners by leveraging existing databases.

In this instance, the common software package model can rapidly simulate any number of scenarios for an infantry brigade combat team (IBCT) and run the scenarios using a variety of equipment such as different soldier energy sources, power consumers, battery charging behavior and available energy, renewable energy sources, logistics package (LOGPAC) resupply scenarios, and many other variables. Expert analysis and lessons learned, as well as software optimization of the solution sets, can help guide product and CONOPs development without taking years to field and test materiel, only to learn it no longer applies to the current threat scenario.

Results

The output of the common software package model includes the timeline of the input scenario showing energy use during each individual mission activity, periods of battery recharging, and utilization of renewable energy. Analysts will iterate different equipment sets and CONOPs to identify optimal energy usage equipment and behaviors. The written report will discuss why the optimum solution(s) were chosen, and how acquisition and CONOPs can be tailored to achieve the desired outcomes. Outcomes could also affect recharging TTPs based on mission and available technology. Identified solutions will provide analytics-backed guidance to shape technology development and acquisition strategies. This study will utilize a combination of Warfighter feedback from test events, requirements community knowledge, technology subject matter expert analysis, and common software package model products to influence high-level policy and shape the future fight.

Outcomes

This study is aimed at using results from recent and upcoming joint service test events to determine gaps and extrapolate power demands for next generation alternative energy technologies. The energy demands will be for a Company or below of land-based Warfighters and focus on the feasibility of implementing alternative energy in the IDOPACOM region. This study also focuses on looking at what potential types of alternative energy sources can be used to close the gaps that are identified for the future fight. The end state of this project will be a report and briefing on the findings of the study. The report will recommend technologies and policies (CONOPS and TTPs) for the resources, gaps, scenarios, and case studies identified and analyzed during the study. It will also estimate the opportunities for investments in the near, mid and far term for alternative energy to provide power at the tactical edge.

References

1. Douglas J., “FY 2022 OECIF Proposal: Warfighter Alternative Energy Study (WAES)”

Family of Lightweight Logistics Fueled Generators

Timothy LaBreche, Subir Roychoudhury, David Spence
Precision Combustion Inc.
410 Sackett Point Road
North Haven, CT 06473
tlabreche@precision-combustion.com / 1-203-287-3700 ex231

Abstract

Precision Combustion, Inc. (PCI) has developed 7 variants of battery-hybridized lightweight JP-8 generators by utilizing reliable, low-cost, commercial, off-the-shelf (COTS) 4-stroke engines. The fueling system was modified to operate on JP-8/DF-2 via PCI's novel and patented octane-matching approach. Multiple generators from 300W to 5kW output were matured. AC and DC paralleling of multiple generators was demonstrated. Custom power electronics enable simultaneous DC and AC outputs. Logistics packages and TDPs (Technical Data Packages) were developed for scaling and manufacturing the generators.

The 450 W 28VDC generator had a dry-weight of ~17 lbs. and is ruck-packable. The 300W 28VDC Generator included an on board fuel tank and weighed < 20 lbs. The 1kW 28VDC Generator weighed 25 lbs. The 900W AC version weighed 28 lbs., the 1.65kW AC version was Tactical Microgrid Ready, had electromagnet pulse protective features, weighed 72 lbs. and included an 8 hour onboard fuel tank. The 2kW 28VDC generator weighed 55 pounds, and the 5kW 28VDC generator weighed 112 pounds. All generators include electric start, paralleling/microgrid capability, and external fueling capability.

The family of generators enables a range of solutions that can be used alone or combined together for 0.3kW to 10kW. For comparison, the current power sources in this range are the much heavier and larger i.e., the 2 kW MTG (MEP-531A) weighs 124 lbs. while the 3kW TQG (MEP-831A) weighs 304 lbs.

Stable operation with other liquid and gaseous fuels has also been demonstrated for multi-fuel capability. Any COTS spark ignited engine can be suitably adapted. The particular engines used were chosen for reliability, low noise, and availability.

PCI's proven octane-matching approach is inherently superior to other "fogging" approaches for enabling spark ignited (SI) engine operation on JP-8. SI engines require octane numbers of >80 for stable operation and avoiding knock, yet JP-8 has an octane number of only ~20. PCI uses its in-situ and on-demand JP-8 upgrading reactor (the size of a D-cell battery) and an advanced direct fuel injection approach to upgrade the octane and thereby reliably operate SI engines on JP-8 or other liquid and gaseous fuels. No carburetor, special start fluids or starting procedures are required. This also allows attitude independence during operation. The JP-8 upgrading reactor is tolerant to 3000 ppm sulfur (JP-8 spec) and its performance has been proven over 1000's of hours of testing.

Keywords

Portable; Packable; PPG; STEP; TMS; Reforming; Fuel Processing; Power Generator; JP-8; Diesel; APU.

Introduction

Commercial off-the-shelf gasoline engines are inexpensive and meet the weight, size, and power output requirements for the deployed soldier. These engines however run on gasoline, a high octane fuel (octane number 85-100). As a result, these engines cannot operate with JP-8 heavy fuel, whose octane number is in the range of 15-25. Multiple alternative means have been developed to allow operation on JP-8 however they are inherently flawed due to their reliance upon approaches that do not actually overcome the core octane number problem.

PCI's technical approach: From 2018 to 2022 Precision combustion Inc. (PCI) developed 5 custom generators for the U.S. Army and United States Air Force based on the PCI fuel conditioning technology. These generators built upon prior DoD funded projects in which COTs generators were modified with add-on reformer kits.

The octane number of JP-8 fed to the engine was directly increased to the 80+ range, suitable for operation of SI engines via "Octane Matching". The JP-8 is instantaneously (order of milliseconds) converted to high octane fuel, immediately prior to injection into the combustion chamber via an extremely compact (D-cell battery size), octane-boosting reactor. PCI's underlying CPOX reactor breakthrough has been advanced in collaboration with both automotive and DoD support. Details of each system requirements and specifications are shown below.

Program Goals

PPG: Platoon Power Generation (PPG) is a 28 Volt (V) Direct Current (DC), tactical, quiet, power generation system. The PPG is soldier borne, fitting in a standard ruck sack, with the capability to provide 900 Watts (W) from 2 x (450W) 16.7 pound generators.

The PPG generator was developed to provide up to 72 hours of power for the small unit level, including networked communication devices in austere environments without requiring resupply. The PPG was designed to be the platoon's primary energy producing source for recharging during missions in austere environments where power resupply is limited or non-existent. The PPG was designed to support the Universal Battery Charger (UBC) and Squad Power Manager (SPM).

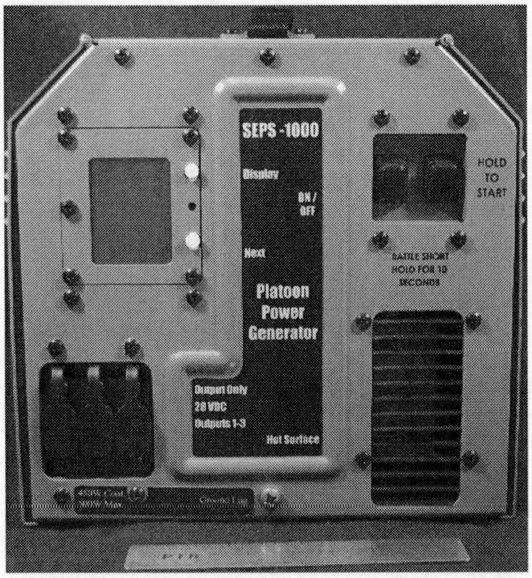

Figure 1. Platoon Power Generator. Scale in foreground is 6 inches wide. 28VDC (450W / 500W Peak).

STEP: The Small Tactical Electric Power (STEP) generator was developed to meet the mission requirements currently met by legacy 2 kW Military Tactical Generator (MTG) and 3 kW Tactical Quiet Generator (TQG). With advances in Tactical Network capabilities and technology supporting enhanced situational awareness the need for lightweight, mobile, scalable power generation is growing. The project focused on maturing the technology and reliability of lightweight generator sets. The sets were capable of paralleling and maintaining Ground Fault Circuit Interrupter (GFCI) protection while connected in parallel.

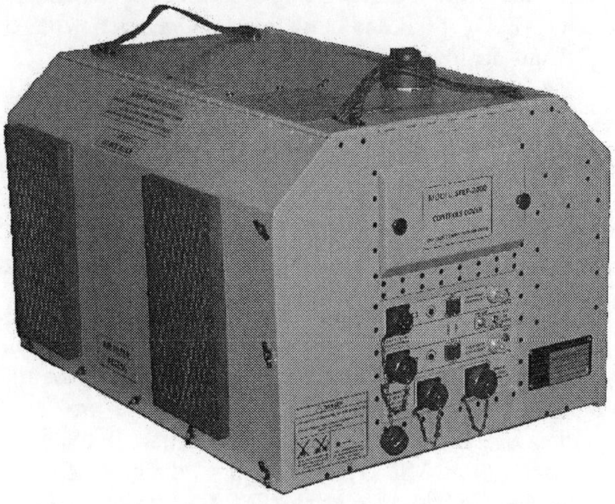

Figure 2. Small Tactical Electric Power Generator 1.65kW / 120VAC / 2kW Peak.

AFRL 1kW, 2kW, 5kW: Existing modified commercial Off-The-Shelf (COTS) 1kW, 2kW and 5kW "flex fuel" generators often require significant user attention. During operation, particularly at part loads, the generator does not run hot enough to completely burn diesel fuel causing the remaining fuel to seep into the oil reservoir, causing it to fill to the point which triggers the generators' safety auto shut

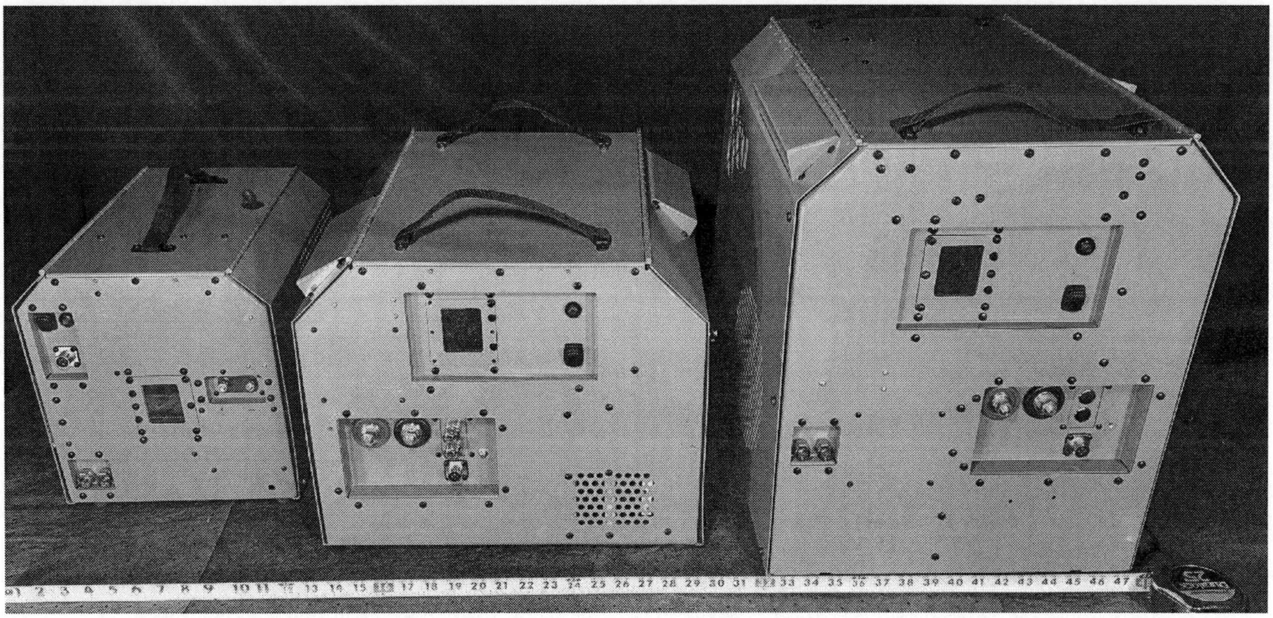

Figure 3. 28VDC Generators Developed for Air Force Research Laboratory. Left to Right - 1kW, 2kW, 5kW.

off. The oil and diesel fuel mixture must be drained to a safe level to allow the generator to continue operation. In some cases the oil may have to be changed frequently, (<1- hour) intervals.

In response to the challenge, PCI developed Lightweight multi-fuel generators based on COTS spark ignited engines that operate without oil dilution and risk of engine damage for HQ AFSOC/SGR and other Special Operations Unit or DoD Units deployed to austere locations.

This family of generators are among, if not the, lightest 1kW, 2kW and 5kW logistics fueled flex fueled generators in existence. The generators weigh 5kW – 112 Pounds, 2kW - 55 pounds, 1kW – 25 pounds. For comparison, the 2kW MEP-501A 28VDC generator weighs more than 138 pounds, 26 pounds more than the 5kW generator developed in this program.

Logistics Packages: Logistics work products were provided based on requirements of each program. Not all programs required every work product. These products included: Electronic Technical Manual (ETM) in accordance with MIL-STD-40051-2. Failure Modes, Effects, and Criticality Analysis (FMECA). Maintenance Analysis in accordance with Army Regulation 750-1 to analyze maintenance support functions necessary for the system, and operator and maintenance tasks. Level of Repair Analysis (LORA) for the system in order to determine repair level decisions. Maintenance Allocation Chart (MAC) in accordance with MIL-STD 400051-2C and DA PAM 750-8. Program of Instruction (POI) including a Training Support Package (TSP) for Operator and Maintainer levels.

Common Principle of Operation

PCI's Fuel conditioning Module (FCM) for each system is based on the concept of converting any spark ignited commercial off the shelf (COTS) gasoline engine or generator to run on low octane, heavy distillate fuels such as JP8 or diesel. Over the course of each program, a solution was developed to meet the power specification by changing a small number of components on the engine and control variables. This makes the technology relatively engine agnostic over a wide range of power levels.

In order to operate the balance of plant components during startup of the FCM a system battery is required. The battery needed to be robust enough to manage operation of these components, while also being lightweight and power dense. In the case of the PPG and STEP generators an Army Standard BB2590 battery was used. For the AFRL generators a commercial $LiFePO_4$ battery was used. Once

Table 1. 450W – 5kW Generator Specifications

	PPG 450W	AFRL 1kW	STEP	AFRL 2kW	AFRL 5kW
Power	450W 28VDC 500W Peak	1kW 28VDC	1.65kW 120VAC 2kW Peak *TMS Ready	2kW 28VDC	4.3kW 28VDC 5kW Peak
Fuel at rated load	9.9 hours/gallon F24/JP8	5.4 hours/gallon F24/JP8	3.8 hours/gallon F24/JP8	3.1 hours/gallon F24/JP8	1.4 hours/gallon F24/JP8
Weight	16.7 Pounds	25 Pounds	73 pounds **	55 pounds	112 pounds
Dimensions	9x11x10 inches	12x13x11 inches	15x24x18 inches	13x16x16 inches	20x19x16 inches
Volume	0.57 ft^3	0.9 ft^3	3.7 ft^3	2.1 ft^3	3.2 ft^3
Status	30 Units completed	Prototype	15 Units completed	Prototype	Prototype
Testing	Independent testing performed by 3rd parties and ATC	PCI Internal Power Quality, Efficiency and Transient Testing	Independent testing performed by 3rd parties and ATC	PCI Internal Power Quality, Efficiency and Transient Testing	PCI Internal Power Quality, Efficiency and Transient Testing
Noise	Max 70.7 dB @ 23 feet	<70 dB @ 23 feet	Maximum 72 dB @ 23 feet	<72 dB @ 23 feet	<72 dB @ 23 feet
Start	Fully Automatic - Electric <5 minutes				
Fuels	F24, JP8, Jet A, Kerosene, Gasoline				
Features	External Tank. With Dry Break Disconnects. HMI with status, and operator prompts. Remote Start. Parallel Operation.		Internal or External Tank, HMI with status, and operator prompts. TMS & Remote Start	External Tank. With Dry Break Disconnects. HMI with status, and operator prompts. Remote Start. Parallel Operation.	
Additional STEP Features	*Tactical Microgrid Gateway developed and evaluated. **includes internal tank, BB2590 Starting Battery, TMG interface, automatic paralleling inverter, HEMP Protective features. Additional capabilities: N+1 operation-up to 15 generators may be connected in single phase 2W configuration. Non-N+1 operation: Generators may be connected in single phase 3W (120v/240V) and 3 phase 4W.				

the system was operating, the control and power electronics recharge the battery and monitor battery state of charge.

The primary requirements with respect to control and power electronics were to provide high fidelity fuel conditioner operation and reliable integration with the engine to properly meter fuel at steady state and transient conditions. The power electronics were implemented to provide reliable AC and DC power as well as providing power management between the balance of plant components and the rechargeable battery.

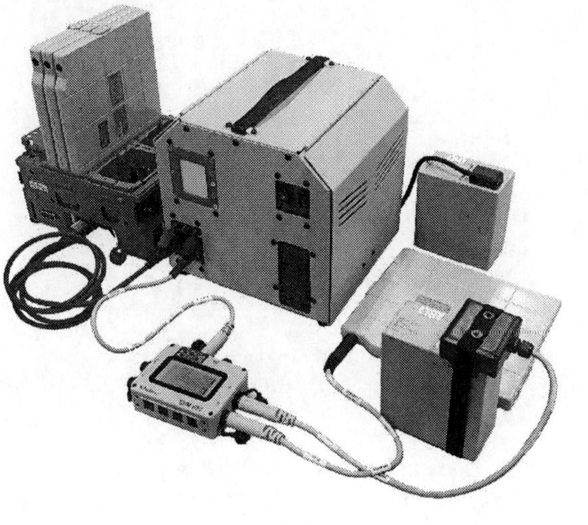

Figure 4. Complete PPG System including Generator, UBC, and SPM.

Common Generator Features

- Contains a two-button HMI for easy operational interfacing
- Integrated starter generator that allows for push button electric start of the power system
- Contains a hybridized DC/DC converter (both DC & AC generators) designed to regulate voltage and protect from overload and short circuits by automatically interrupting power to the output or inverter. Once the short circuit or overload is removed, output is restored. If the overload condition persists power will be interrupted and restored after the user presses "Reset" on the HMI.
- Simple starting controls. 2-position rocker control switch and a momentary start/reset button enable easy starting, stopping, and resetting the system.
- Contains internal fans that provide fresh air to the fuel conditioner and aid in cooling the electronics, engine, and fuel system during operation and after shutdown
- Contains a fuel conditioner designed to allow for conventional spark ignition engines to operate on low octane fuels such as JP8, F24 and Diesel

External Fuel Source: Each generator connects to an external fuel source of any size using two lines for supply and return. Flexible fuel bladders with fuel capacity of 3 L (0.8 Gallons), 6 L (1.6 Gallons) and 20 L (5.3 Gallons) have been tested.

Conclusions

The feasibility of converting lightweight spark ignited gasoline engines without any internal engine modification, and operating on distillate fuels (i.e. diesel and JP-8), in addition to gasoline has been demonstrated in multiple generators ranging in power from <500W to 5kW. Two designs were produced in low volume initial production and delivered for electrical, environmental and endurance testing. Three additional unique prototypes 1kW, 2kW, 5kW were delivered for evaluation. The generators were capable of starting and operating in varied weather and temperatures, maintaining speed and voltage during load transitions.

Acknowledgements

Precision Combustion Inc. wants to acknowledge the funding received from DoD that enabled these systems to be developed. Project Manager Expeditionary Energy & Sustainment Systems (PM E2S2), Product Manager Mobile Electric Power Systems (PdM MEPS) and the Air Force Research Lab (Wright Patterson).

We also acknowledge the prior support that enabled the core FCM technology from the DoD (CERDEC, Picatinny Arsenal, and WPAFB). Any opinions, findings, and conclusions or recommendations expressed in this paper are those of the authors and do not necessarily reflect the views of the DoD and DOE.

Development of 3 and 15 Ah Rechargeable Lithium Pouch Cells

Owen Crowther
R&D
EaglePicher Technologies
Joplin, MO, 64801
owen.crowther@eaglepicher.com / 1-417-208-1787

Abstract

Commercially available Li-ion batteries using graphite or graphite-silicon blended anodes are currently approaching a cell level specific energy of 350 Wh kg^{-1}. This paper will overview the technologies developed for a 3 Ah pouch cell with a specific energy above 400 Wh kg^{-1}. Several areas will be highlighted that resulted result in improved cell performance such as increasing the tab size, optimizing the electrolyte type and amount, and introducing excess lithium metal into the anode. The cell delivers ~425 Wh kg^{-1} at low rate and >300 Wh kg^{-1} at 6.6C. Finally, the initial prototype performance of a 15 Ah rechargeable lithium pouch cell with a specific energy >500 Wh kg^{-1} will be highlighted.

Keywords

battery; lithium anode; lithium metal; rechargeable; high energy

Introduction

Lithium metal is an ideal negative electrode material because it is the lightest metal and very electronegative (−3.04 V vs the standard hydrogen electrode). These properties lead to a battery that demonstrates extremely high specific energy and energy density. The chemistries that use lithium metal as the anode in figure 1 have the highest practical specific energies at the cell level.

All attempts to commercialize rechargeable lithium metal batteries since they were first proposed in the early 1970s have failed due to poor cycling and safety performance caused by rough Li deposits formed on the negative electrode during cell charging. These deposits are often referred to as mossy lithium and in the worst-case dendrites. Though the exact cause of mossy and dendritic lithium is unknown, it is most likely related to the solid electrolyte interphase (SEI). The SEI is a passivating layer that forms on lithium metal when in contact with nonaqueous electrolyte because most organic solvents are not thermodynamically stable at lithium's low potential. The SEI prevents further reduction of electrolyte components allowing for cell operation. The SEI impacts most areas of battery performance, including power density, cycle efficiency and life, and safety.

The mossy lithium has a very high surface area which leads to additional SEI formation that consumes active lithium. This lowers the cycle coulombic efficiency leading to poor

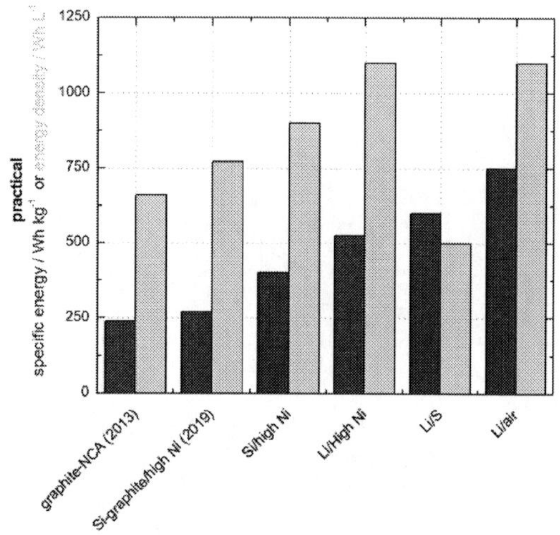

Figure 1. Comparison of practical cell-level specific energy and energy density for different lithium battery chemistries.

cycle life. Furthermore, lithium deposits can become electrically isolated from the anode. Electrically isolated lithium deposits are referred to as "dead lithium" and can no longer be discharged leading to lower capacities and poor cycle life. Dendritic lithium deposits have branch-like morphology. The dendrites will continue to grow as the cell cycles and can eventually transverse the separator to the cathode forming a hard short. This will lead to cell thermal runaway and typically explosion. The cells described in this paper fail before any internal short causes an explosion.

Despite the poor cycle life and potential safety hazard, the lithium metal anode is considered the "holy grail" of lithium battery chemistries due to its extremely high specific energy and energy density. One potential application for this chemistry of interest to these proceedings is military unmanned aerial vehicles which often do not fly more than 50 missions. A cycle life of ~100 cycles above 300 Wh kg^{-1} would enable longer times for these missions.

Anodeless cell design

One possible way to build a cell with a lithium metal anode is to replace a conventional lithium-ion graphite or graphite and silicon composite anode that is web-coated onto copper foil with lithium metal. This design would have active

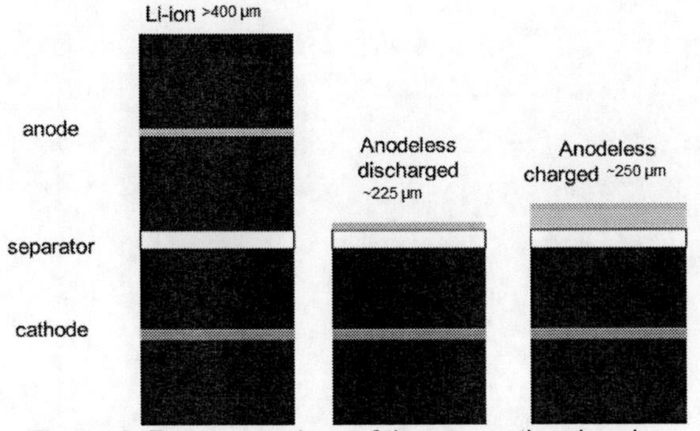

Figure 2. Representations of the conventional and anodeless cell designs.

lithium in both the anode and cathode. This excess lithium would lead to better cycle life but only a modest specific energy increase over SOA Li-ion cells. Candidate cathodes that do not contain lithium like MnO_2 and metal fluorides (e.g. CuF_2, FeF_3, etc.) have poor reversibility leading to extremely low cycle life. Others with good reversibility like V_2O_5 have low specific capacity. Finally, cathodes like sulfur and air are several years away from commercialization despite the widespread academic and industry interest.

Another possible cell configuration would be to build a cell with just copper foil as the anode. The lithium metal anode is plated out onto the copper foil during the first charge. This cell configuration, shown in figure 2m has no excess lithium leading to the highest energy densities. However, the lack of excess lithium leads to relatively low cycle life. Other advantages of this design are the need for only one webcoated electrode, no lithium metal, quick formation and the possibility to ship in the uncharged state.

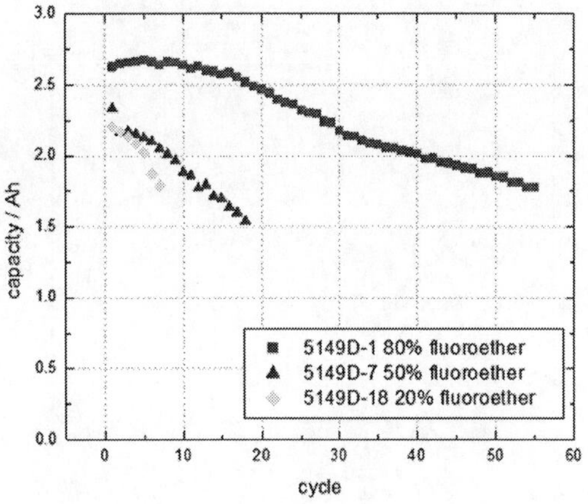

Figure 4. Effect of fluorether content on cell cycling performance.

Figure 3 shows the initial cycles of a cell with an anodeless design using a conventional Li-ion electrolyte. The cell delivers 2.2 Ah which is a 22% capacity improvement on the same cell design with graphite. The cell's thickness when charged is also 44% less than the graphite design. This leads to a large improvement in energy density. The pictures clearly show lithium deposits on the anode but the optical microscope images show the morphology is very grainy. Alternate electrolytes were explored to improve this morphology leading to better cycle life. A commercially available fluoroether was found to stabilize the cycling to >50 cycles when used at >80% solvent composition. This data is shown in figure 4. All data presented in the next section uses the anodeless cell design with a fluoroether based electrolyte.

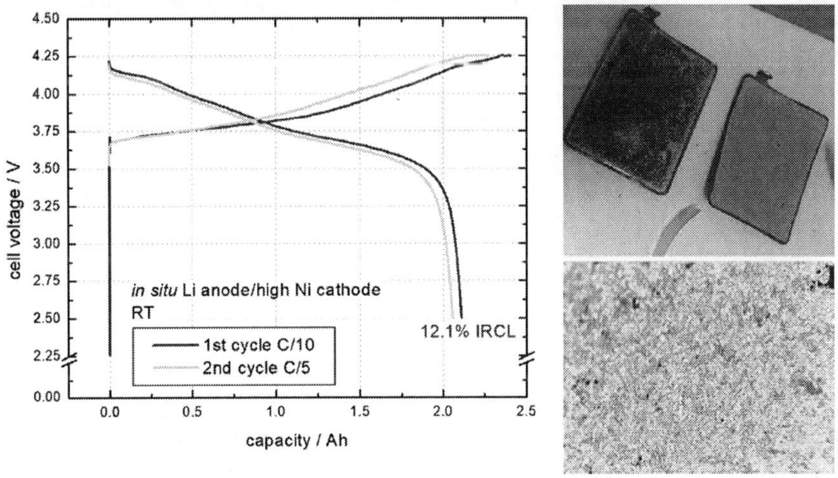

Figure 3. Pathfinder performance formation cycles of an anode less cell (left). Picture (top right) and optical microscope image (bottom right) of lithium plated on copper after 10 cycles.

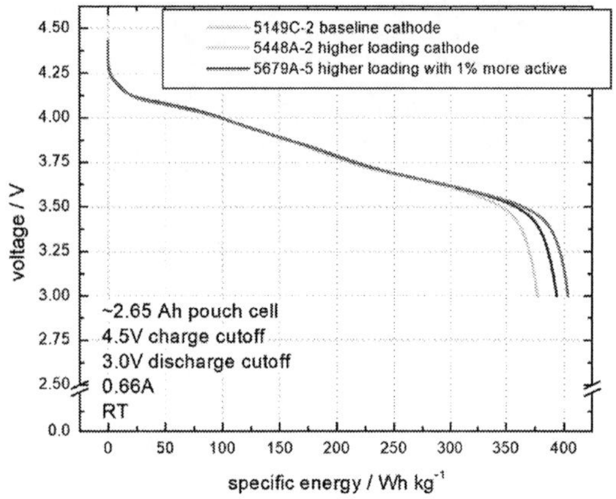

Figure 5. Cathode development for EaglePicher's anodeless lithium metal cell.

Anodeless Performance Data

The project this cell was developed on required a cell level specific energy >400 Wh kg^{-1}. More cathode active material must be added to this cell design to increase the capacity of the cell. This can be accomplished by increasing the cathode area (i.e. adding more cathode plates in a stacked pouch cell design), increasing the electrode loading and/or increasing the active percentage in a cathode formulation. All three methods were used for this project. Figure 5 shows the cell level specific energy was increased from 375 to 405 Wh kg^{-1} by increasing the loading and active percentage.

The rate capability of the cell is shown in figure 6. The cell has an excellent rate capability for an energy cell delivering >300 Wh kg^{-1} at a 6.6C continuous rate. The cell also was able to do >1 min 30A pulses. The rate capability is generally limited by the anode in a Li-ion cell. Since the discharge reaction for Li metal is a one electron oxidation it is very fast compared to a deintercalation process.

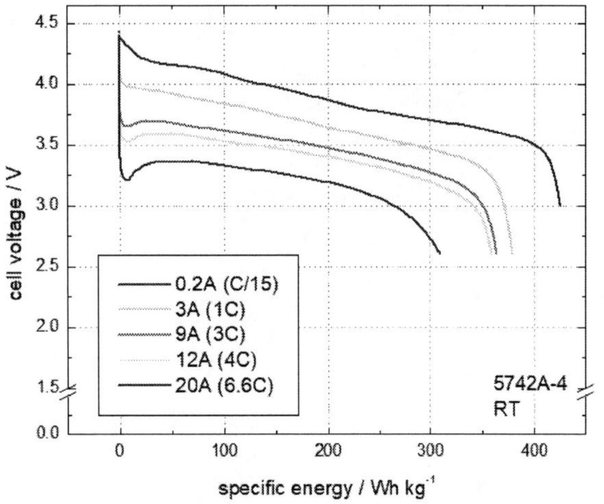

Figure 6. Rate capability of EaglePicher's anodeless lithium metal cell.

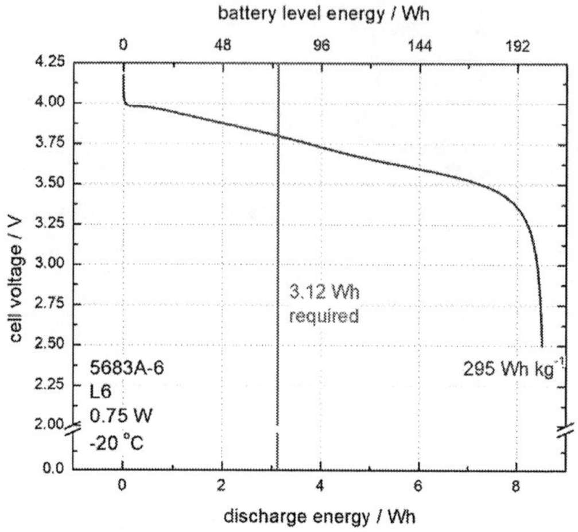

Figure 7. Cold discharge of anodeless lithium metal cell.

The cell was also able to discharge over a wide temperature range of −20 to +55 °C. Figure 7 shows the cell is able to deliver almost three times the required energy of the L6 Cold Discharge test in MIL-PRF-32383/4.

Figure 8 shows the cycle life of the cell. The cell is able to deliver 50-60 cycles consistently before its capacity retention <80%. New electrolytes and the addition of Li metal are being investigated to improve this cycle life. These will be discussed in the presentation.

Conclusions

EaglePicher has developed a 3Ah rechargeable lithium metal cell with the anodeless cell design. The cell delivers >400 Wh kg−1 at a C/4 rate with excellent rate capability of 6.6C continuous. The cell is able to be discharged over a wide temperature range of −20 to +55 °C. Current efforts are underway to improve the cycle life to >125 cycles. Cell modeling shows specific energy >500 Wh kg^{-1} is possible at larger cell form factors.

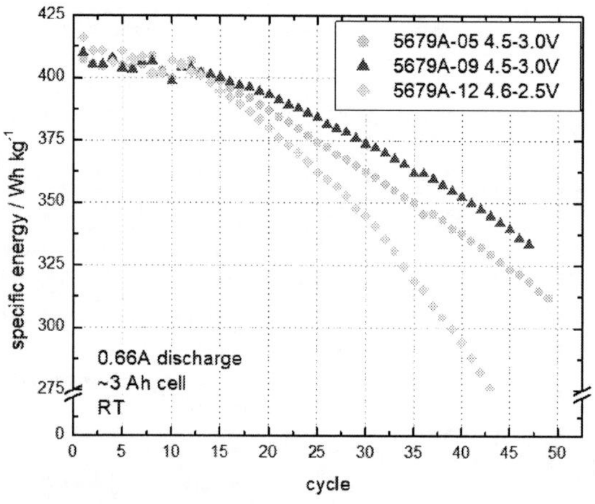

Figure 8. Cycle life of anodeless lithium metal cell.

All Solid State Battery with Glass Electrolyte and High Energy Density

William Rauch, Adrian Grant and Lazbourne Allie
Johnson Energy Storage
275 Decatur Street, Atlanta, GA, 30312 USA
brauch@johnsonenergystorage.com

Abstract

Solid state batteries hold the promise of higher energy density and increased safety over today's lithium ion batteries and many companies are competing to define the technology. High energy is achieved by enabling a lithium metal anode in lieu of graphite, decreasing the weight and volume at a cell level. A process has been developed at a lab scale which has the ability to create high surface contact between a glass electrolyte and the active cathode material. Further, this process allows the simultaneous creation of the separator layer integral to the electrolyte in the cathode structure. Glasses are being optimized for the desired battery profiles and process compatibility. They are in a family of glasses best characterized as Oxy-Sulfides. These glasses limit the instabilities known with Argyrodite and similar sulfide electrolytes while maintaining conductivities in the 10^{-3} S/cm range. Further, the process completes the cell structure as a continuous glass with no porosity or grain boundaries for dendrite path formation. The surface is conducive to long cycle life of the lithium anode.

Keywords

Battery: Solid State: Solid Electrolyte: Glass: Lithium Metal: Safety

Introduction

Lithium ion batteries have become ubiquitous throughout society due to their ever increasing energy density, cycle life and performance. It is noted however, that lithium ion is quickly approaching thcorctical limits that do not fully satisfy the needs of the future. With concerns of global warming driving the need to limit the use of fossil fuels, batteries have come to the forefront for solving issues with mobility and energy storage for grid stability. Solid state batteries offer a new generation of batteries that can increase safety, enhance energy density and provide a durable solution to today's energy needs.

Current lithium ion batteries have three shortcomings that need addressing in order to meet expectations of the future. One of the largest issues is safety. Lithium ion batteries use an electrolyte that is highly flammable. This is what is required to provide sufficient conductivity of lithium ions while being stable over a wide voltage range. The flammability is exaggerated by the low boiling point and volatility of these liquids. As batteries increase in size, the concern over this hazard grows as well.

Secondly, the demand for more energy in applications, the size and weight of the batteries must grow. Lithium ion batteries are fast approaching theoretical limits of volumetric and gravimetric efficiency. The desire for automobiles with longer range between charges meets space limitations. This is even more pronounced when one envisions electrification of aircraft where energy per weight is critical. This limitation in lithium ion may prevent viable electric aviation.

And finally, there is cost. While lithium ion batteries have dropped more than 10 fold in cost to manufacture in the past decade, they are displacing fossil fuel engines that have a century of engineering to bring costs under control. Of note here in particular is that while batteries are now reaching cost competitive levels for displacement of fossil fuels, any enhancements in safety and energy density cannot raise the price relative to the energy stored.

Most in the research community agree that a non-flammable electrolyte is a starting point for all advanced batteries. As batteries join the automotive environment, actuaries are summing the cost of the electric vehicle with the risk they may pose if a vehicle bursts into flames or is the cause of injury. Long efforts too eliminate flammability from liquid electrolytes have led to compromises in performance, particularly at lower temperatures, and battery life. Solid electrolytes can limit safety hazards in two ways. Firstly, by providing a solid barrier to short circuiting between the anode and cathode which produces local heating and secondly by limiting the potential to boil the electrolyte into a flammable vapor.

Many researchers and several start-up companies are investigating a range of solid electrolyte options to add safety to batteries while maintaining general performance metrics of batteries made with liquid electrolytes. Development parameters of interest often focus around the rate at which lithium can move through the electrolyte as that is its primary purpose. Lithium ion batteries typically use a liquid electrolyte that ranges for 5 to 20 milli-siemens. This can be a challenging value to achieve in solids as the mechanism for ionic motion is much more constrained. But with careful engineering of materials, some polymers, ceramics, and glasses can approach these values.

The solution to the second issue of energy density follows directly behind the use of a solid electrolyte. Early batteries (ca 1980) relying on lithium ions for charge transport directly used lithium metal as the anode. This led to an early generation of batteries in personal electronics that were prone to electrical shorting. The direct use of lithium metal can allow the growth of lithium on the anode in poor structure. Lithium would plate to the anode current collector in non-dense structure and in particular could form growths, known as dendrites, that could cross from the anode to the cathode, shoring the cells. These dendrites led to the use of intercalation anodes such as graphite to give the lithium a home on the anode side of the cell and limit dendrites. The upside was safety, but the downside was a substantial loss of energy density.

With the advent of solid electrolytes, it is believed that lithium metal anodes will again be employed to gain back lost energy density. Plated lithium metal as an anode, stores almost 10 times the energy in the same space as graphite. This can lead to cells that have twice the specific energy (Wh/l) and also twice the energy density (Wh/kg) as today's lithium ion batteries. Solid electrolytes are seen to prevent dendrite growth as they are a solid barrier to lithium metal within the cell.

Polymer electrolytes have been practically used for many years in various forms. Many polymer batteries struggle with performance at low temperatures and scientists often create polymer gels to enhance the conductivity to counter this effect. Polymers will likely move towards the market first due to the ease of using polymers in manufacturing. Polymers can both create a solid separator film and integrate into the cathode structure where the lithium ions are stored. But polymer electrolytes may not fully address safety concerns as their strength may not be able to withstand the driving force of dendrite growth.

Ceramic electrolytes offer another potential for a solid electrolyte. The ceramics (defined here as crystalline metal oxides) discovered thus far require high temperature processing to produce and has that "grandma's china" tendency to fracture. Given that solid electrolytes are in reality, performing two functions, the transport of lithium within the cell and the electrical separation of the anode from the cathode, they must be integrated into a cell for both purposes. Most work to integrate ceramic solid electrolytes into battery structures has limited the ceramic to a solid thin film between the cell halves and must then use a more flexible electrolyte to reach into the depths of the cathode for general transport. The use of ceramic powders within the cathode structure has generally failed due to the poor pathways provided between pressed hard particles.

Sulfide electrolytes, typified by the Argyrodite materials with the base formula Li_6PS_5Cl have been developed due to their high conductivity that approaches that of liquid electrolytes. Known issues with this chemistry is the instability of these compounds in moisture and their reactivity within the battery cell environment. Cells are constructed using the material as a powder and pressing together to create contacts between the particles. The softer nature of the material can make for some compelling results. This does not produce a solid barrier layer and the lack of electrochemical stability means that it cannot at this time be readily used with a lithium metal anode. In this case, the larger safety picture is addressed because the material possesses lower flammability than liquid electrolytes, but the potential for shorting may still exist in that it does not prevent dendrite propagation. Finally, without the ability to utilize a lithium anode, the gains in energy density promised are not realized.

Finally, we get to glass electrolytes. Conduction of various ions through glass has been studied for more than 50 years. Glass in this case is defined as an inorganic, amorphous material that transitions from an immobile solid, to a flowable glass phase and finally to a molten liquid with increasing temperature. Glasses most typically studied are oxide glasses where the network is formed with specific metal oxides such as SiO_2, B_2O_3 and P_2O_5. The literature through the years shows a maximum limitation in oxide glasses to about 0.01 milli-siemens in conductivity, or about 4 orders of magnitude lower than liquid electrolytes. Recently, glasses have been discovered which replace some of the Oxygen with Sulfur within the structure. With full replacement, the materials fall into the Sulfide class of materials with the Argyrodites. With sulfide glasses high levels of conductivity are achieved but suffer the same issues of electrochemical instability with lithium. Being that we are now working with glasses, structures are more fluid and the potential to mix Oxides and Sulfides into the same glass network becomes possible. These glasses, termed "oxy-sulfides".

Glass electrolytes allow flexibility in designing chemistry to make engineering trade offs in various properties. As noted, sulfide networks are characterized by high conductivity but low electrochemical stability relative to oxides. Johnson Energy Storage has been working alongside Professor Steve Martin of Iowa State University who has been exploring ion conducting glasses for over 40 years. To this unique area of chemistry, we bring in a new dimension in processing that does not limit the material to a sheet of separator or to packed particles. We have discovered that glass offers flexibility in battery construction that allows a single glass electrolyte to be formed as part of the separator as well as integrated into the interparticle space between the active cathode material making for continuous ion pathways throughout the cell.

Methodology

Johnson Energy Storage produces and investigates its own proprietary glass formulations, and the results here focus on glasses which are best termed as oxy-sulfide glasses. Batch materials suitable for production of the desired chemistry are heated to melt point in a controlled atmosphere environment. These melts are then subsequently quenched to form solid sheets for basic electrochemical testing.

Samples of the glass are then utilized in cell construction in combination with a porous cathode structure to form full battery cells. The cells produced have a seed layer of lithium metal evaporated onto the surface to complete the desired cell configuration for testing (Figure 1). Cells are charged and discharged using a Maccor battery cycler to evaluate various aspects of the battery performance.

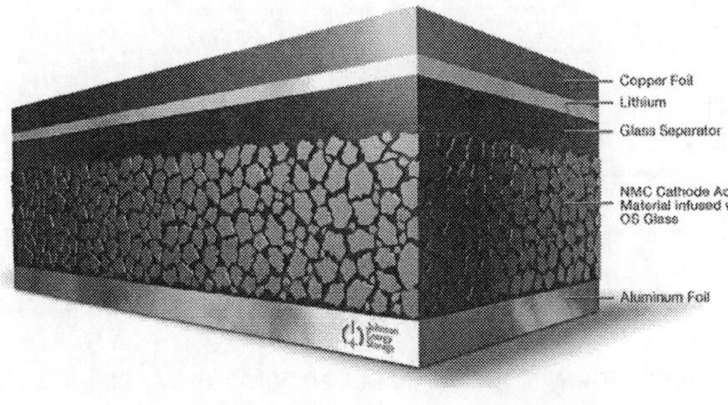

Figure 1: Illustration of the cell configuration utilized by Johnson Energy Storage.

Battery performance is compared and correlated to the specific microstructure as determined through Scanning Electron Microscope imaging. Primary details of interest include thickness of the separator layer, relative ratio of cathode active material to electrolyte within the cathode region and the depth of fill of the glass into the cathode structure. Many of these features are linked to primary glass properties such as glass transition temperature (Tg), and crystallization temperature (Tc)

Results

Within this program, numerous compositions of oxide and oxy-sulfide glass have been produced to investigate critical properties relevant to solid state battery applications. Figure 2 illustrates the conductivity of broad classes of electrolyte materials and includes typical values observed for potential glass electrolytes. Conductivity is inversely proportional to the internal resistance of the cell and controls the ultimate rate of charge and discharge, losses in efficiency and defines at some level, the necessary operational temperature for a battery. The figure indicates the potential for oxy-sulfide glasses to replace liquid electrolyte system. With the superior conductivity of liquid based electrolytes as the benchmark, there is a need to minimize other contributors to resistance during cell construction in order to match the performance of lithium ion batteries.

Herein lies the reason why thoughtful cell construction is critical. Is solids, ions conduct based on their concentration and mobility within the material structure. Discontinuities in the material, such as grain boundaries, particle to particle transfer or passing from one conductive material to another adds substantial resistance that is not part of the scientific measurement of conductivity. Secondly, the function of the solid electrolyte as a separator is to prevent electronic conduction between the anode and cathode while allowing ions to pass freely. The separator needs only to be thick enough to block electronic leakage and is ideally in the small micron range. This design parameter relies on a difference in lithium ion conduction and electron conduction that is greater than 4 orders of magnitude. With 5 orders of magnitude separation seen in the oxy-sulfide glasses, the separator layer can be as thin as 10 microns.

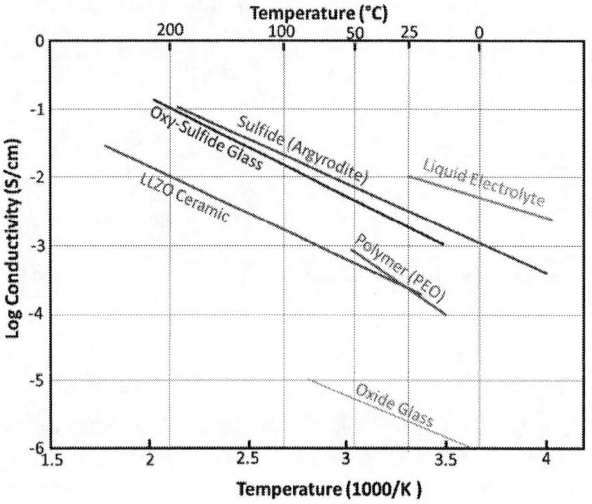

Figure 2: General range of conductivities for the broad classes of potential solid electrolytes.

The image below, Figure 3, shows the structure developed in laboratory sample cells. The layers shown from top to bottom include 2 microns of lithium, 22 microns of glass separator, on a 48 micron cathode. The glass electrolyte penetrates deep into the cathode in the observed structure allowing lithium stored throughout the structure to be accessed and utilized to store energy.

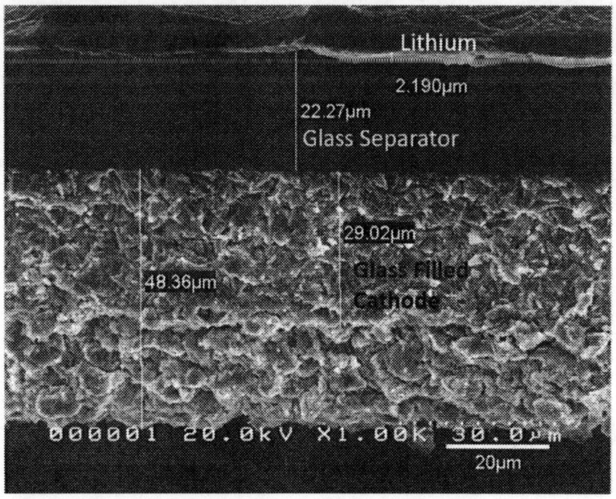

Figure 3: Cross Section image of the cell layers in a glass electrolyte based solid state battery.

The cathode preferred for this solid state battery construction uses $Li(NiMnCo)O_2$ (811) which can be used up to 4.6 volts versus a lithium anode. Below (Figure 4) is a plot from a staircase potential voltammetry test showing the stability of the glass electrolyte with capability of withstanding voltages in excess of the anticipated cell potential.

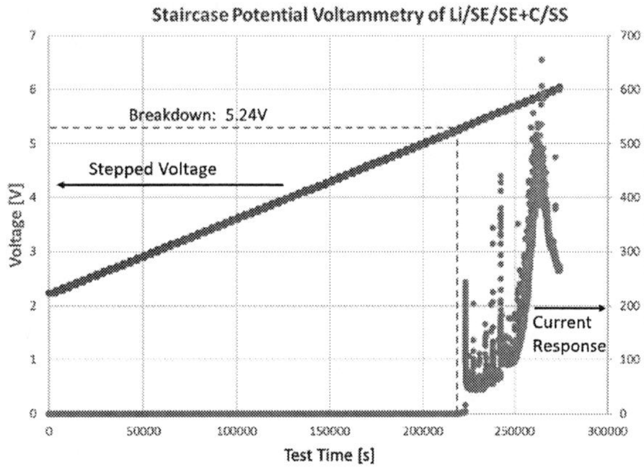

Figure 4: Staircase potential voltammetry for a cell in the configuration Li|OSglass|OSglasss-C|StainlessSteel.

A small laboratory cell constructed using the above mentioned techniques and materials underwent basic battery testing, cycling initially at C/20 rate for 2 cycles and then at a rate of C/4. Battery tests were performed in a glove box at ambient temperature in an unpackaged state. The cycling curves (V and I versus time) and charge-discharge capacity plots are shown in Figures 5 and 6 respectively. While this cell is small and has low capacity it shows the stability of the materials and construction techniques in a true solid state battery. This cell shows 28 stable cycles as of publication and is continuing to cycle with high efficiency.

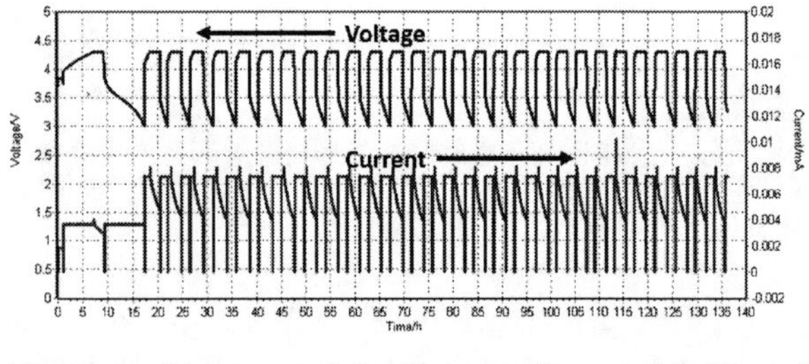

Figure 5: Voltage and Current plots for a solid state cell constructed using an oxy-sulfide glass electrolyte as Aluminum|NMC-OSglass|OSglass|Lithium|Copper.

The potential energy density was calculated based on practical configurations using the current construction techniques. Through the course of experimentation, it has been discovered that full theoretical capacity of the chosen cathode material can be utilized in the battery so long as the glass electrolyte extends throughout the cathode structure. Figure 7 below was generated assuming aluminum cathode current collector of 10 microns, cathode with 60% active material loading at the plotted thickness, a 10 micron glass separator, 2 microns of seed lithium and 10 microns of copper anode current collector. Energy density is compelling at cathode thicknesses above 40 microns.

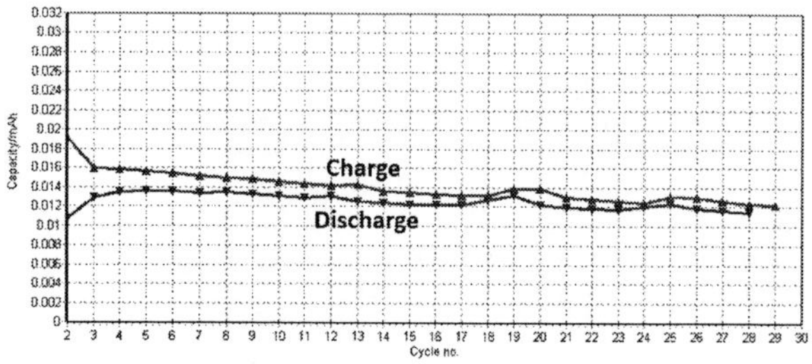

Figure 6: Charge/Discharge capacity for above cell

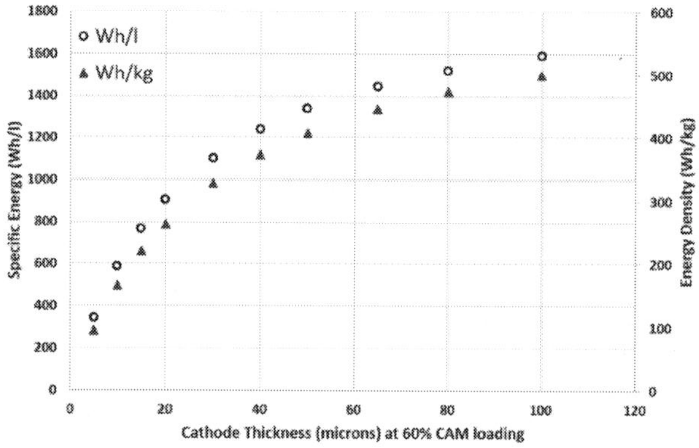

Figure 7: Calculated energy density at a cell level for solid state batteries utilizing glass electrolyte and the noted cathode thickness.

Conclusions

Johnson Energy Storage has demonstrated the capability to utilize highly conductive glass electrolytes in the Oxy-Sulfide range to build a solid state lithium battery. This battery has the capability to operate safely in a wide temperature range from -20 °C to over 100 °C. The glass has good voltage stability and can be used with a lithium anode which will enable high energy density. Specific energy in excess of 1400 Wh/l and energy density of over 400 Wh/kg are predicted at the cell level.

Acknowledgements

The work presented here is currently funded internally but JES is always looking for strategic partners with vision.

Phthalocyanine-based Hybrid Catalyst for Rechargeable Lithium-Oxygen Batteries

Padmakar Kichambare[1], Stanley Rodrigues[2], David Firsich[3], William A. Feld[3], Perla B. Balbuena[4] and Lawrence Scanlon[2]

[1]UES Inc., 4401 Dayton-Xenia Road, Dayton, OH 45432

[2]Air Force Research Laboratory, Aerospace Systems Directorate

Wright-Patterson Air Force Base, OH 45433

[3] Department of Chemistry, Wright State University, Dayton, OH 45433

[4] Department of Chemical Engineering, Texas A & M University, College Station, TX 77843

Padmakar.Kichambare.1.ctr@US.AF.MIL

Abstract: *A mixture of tetrabutylammonium lithium phthalocyanine (TBA-LiPc) and dilithium phthalocyanine (Li_2Pc)) functions as a soluble bifunctional catalyst in tetraethylene glycol dimethyl ether (TEGDME) for a rechargeable lithium-oxygen cell. Cyclic voltammetry (CV) measurements of the hybrid catalyst in TEGDME show highly symmetrical and reversible peaks at 2.54 V and 3.22 V vs Li/Li^+, corresponding to the reduction of the peroxide and oxidation of Li_2O_2, respectively. Density functional theory (DFT) calculation shows that the oxygen complex with the LiPc anion is already in the superoxide state since the oxygen-oxygen bond length is 1.32 Å. Once reduction takes place it goes into the peroxide state, forming lithium peroxide. A Cell with graphene nanosheets (GNSs) coated onto a hierarchical porous carbons (HPC) cathode was discharged to 2V in an oxygen atmosphere, delivering an initial capacity of 20448 $mAh/g_{(carbon)}$. Long-term cycling of cells with GNSs coated HPC cathodes at a fixed capacity of 1200 $mAh/g_{(carbon)}$ in oxygen and dry air (relative humidity < 0.01% at room temperature) is in progress. Cells have completed 295 and 284 cycles in oxygen and dry-air, respectively.*

Keywords: lithium-air battery; oxygen reduction; oxygen evolution; tetraethylene glycol dimethyl ether; tetra-butyl ammonium lithium phthalocyanine.

Introduction

A lithium-oxygen battery is attractive due to its very large theoretical energy density [1]. The cell operates on a simple chemical reaction between lithium ions and oxygen radicals. Significant efforts have been made to use stable electrolytes and solid-state catalysts decorated on oxygen electrodes to improve the cycling stability and electro-catalytic activity for the oxygen reduction reaction (ORR) and oxygen evolution reaction (OER) [2]. Among various non-aqueous solvents, TEGDME is a promising electrolyte and among catalysts, phthalocyanine based derivatives are also attracting interest as non-precious catalysts. High discharge capacity was reported when Li_2Pc was employed as cathode catalyst [3]. In other work [4], a solution-phase bifunctional iron phthalocyanine (FePc) catalyst dissolved in TEGDME and dimethyl sulfoxide (DMSO) electrolyte was employed. The FePc catalyst acts as a molecular shuttle of $(O_2)^-$ between the surface of carbon cathode and insulator Li_2O_2, product of discharge. Recently transition metal phthalocyanines were used as solution phase redox mediators in rechargeable lithium-oxygen batteries [5]. It is reported that redox mediation for the Mn, Co, and Ni configuration is better than Fe and Cu configuration.

In continuation of our work [6], we report here the use of GNSs coated HPC as an oxygen cathode with a mixture of two moles of TBA-LiPc and one mole of a Li_2Pc as soluble hybrid catalyst in TEGDME electrolyte. TEGDME was selected due to its electrochemical stability over a wide a potential window and good oxygen solubility (4.43 mM/cm^3) [7]. To lower the over-potential, LiI was used as redox mediator. During the charge, LiI is oxidized at the cathode and oxidized form of redox mediator then chemically reacts with Li_2O_2 and suppress the charge voltage [8].

Experimental Details

Synthesis of HPC was carried using zinc oxide nanoparticles as a hard template. This HPC powder was used to fabricate the oxygen cathode. Lithium bis(fluorosulfonyl)imide (LiFSI) (Sigma-Aldrich) was dried overnight under vacuum at 120 °C, prior to use. Li_2Pc was purchased (Signa-Aldrich) and purified into acetone by crystallization process. TBA-LiPc catalyst was synthesized and purified. Both catalysts were vacuum dried at 110 °C before use. Electrolyte was prepared by mixing 1.5 M LiFSI, 50 % v/v (0.2 M Li_2Pc and 0.4M TBA-LiPc), 0.4 M LiI, and 3 wt. % FEC (fluoroethylene carbonate) (Sigma-Aldrich) into a mixture of TEGDME (Sigma-Aldrich) and TTE (1,1,2,2 – tetrafluoroethyl- 2,2,3,3-tetrafluoro propyl ether) (Sigma-Aldrich) with a ratio of 8:2 (v/v). CV measurements were performed in a standard three-electrode cell configuration using electrolyte solution of LIFSI and hybrid catalyst in TEGDME at 25 °C with a scan rate of 5 $mVSec^{-1}$. Graphite rod was used as working electrode. Platinum foil was used as the counter and reference electrode. All potentials were measured with respect to standard Pt electrode and converted to Li|Li^+ reference scale. The electrolyte solution was purged with argon to remove any dissolved oxygen. The electrolyte was then saturated with oxygen prior to the CV measurements.

To fabricate the oxygen cathode, HPC powder was mixed and dispersed in N-methyl-2-pyrrolidone (NMP) using sonication for 90 min. This process was carried to load cathode material in the open voids of nickel foam that is used as a current collector. 0.1 wt.% GNSs in NMP was drop casted on HPC deposited nickel foam. Subsequently, specimen was dried overnight at 120 °C, under vacuum. Cells with 1.2 cm^2 active area were fabricated using a Swagelok type cell in a dry room. Nickel foam with GNSs coated HPC was used as working cathode, lithium metal as anode and a glass fiber (Whatman, GF-A) separator soaked with soluble hybrid catalyst (mixture of two moles of TBA-LiPc and one mole of Li_2Pc) in the electrolyte 1.5 M LiFSI, 3 wt.% FEC, 0.4 M LiI in TEGDME-TTE. Cells were discharged and charged with a constant current of 50 μA at 25 °C. Galvanostatic charge-discharge measurements of the specimens were conducted using a computer controlled VersaSTAT 4 (Princeton Applied Research) electrochemical workstation.

Results and Discussion

The morphology of cathode examined under SEM reveals a porous architecture with interconnected pore channels. Nitrogen adsorption–desorption isotherm measurements were carried out at 77 K. The Brunauer-Emmett-Teller (BET) surface area of HPC was found to be 1533 m^2/g with a porosity of 47%. The pore size distribution indicates a wide variation from 2 nm to 137 nm. A remarkable nitrogen uptake above the relative pressure ratio of 0.40 was observed in the BET isotherm and is due to condensation of nitrogen in the HPC matrix. Such high porosity facilitates oxygen transport, diffusion of electrolyte in the cathode matrix and helps to improve cell capacity. The electro-catalytic ability of hybrid catalyst in oxygen saturated electrolyte was evaluated by CV. Cyclic voltammogram (Fig. 1) shows highly symmetrical and reversible ORR and OER peaks at 2.5 V and 3.22 V, respectively with the current peak amplitude of ~0.125 mA/cm^2 for ORR and OER. The ORR peak corresponds to peroxide formation and OER peak for oxidation of Li_2O_2. The cyclic voltammogram shows no evidence of superoxide oxidation but only lithium peroxide oxidation at 3.2 V. The peak separation of the cathodic (2.5 V) and anodic potential (3.2 V) is found to be 700 mV. The CV study indicates that the oxygen reduction in the presence of hybrid catalyst is reversible. Theoretical calculations have

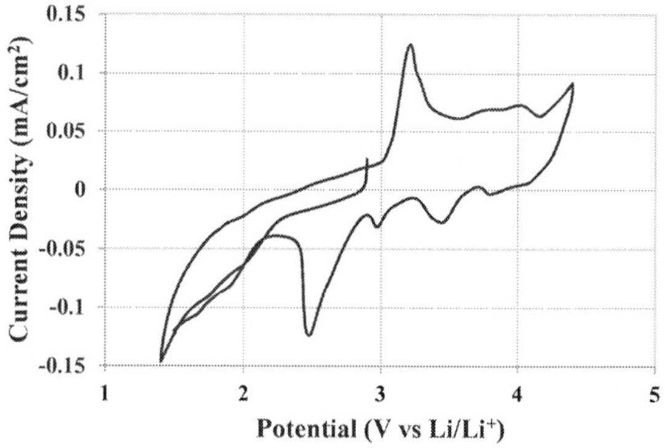

Figure 1. Cyclic voltammogram of (TBA-LiPc-Li_2Pc) as a hybrid catalyst in oxygen saturated electrolyte with a scan rate of 5 mV/sec at room temperature.

shown that the site for oxygen interaction when using TBA-LiPc as the catalyst is located with the lithium-ion in the center of lithium-phthalocyanine anion [6]. With the hybrid catalyst, it is proposed that the Li-Pc anion acts as the main site for oxygen complex formation. The oxygen complex formed in the superoxide state, prior to electrochemical reduction, is due to the electrostatic interaction between oxygen and the lithium-ion resulting in an elongation of the oxygen-oxygen bond (1.32 Å). It is this type of complex that is involved in the reduction of oxygen to peroxides and subsequent re-oxidation to oxygen.

To understand the mechanism of interaction of oxygen with the phthalocyanine, the density functional theory (DFT) was used to investigate the behavior of molecular oxygen near a TBA cation and a LiPc anion. Fig 2 shows the interaction of oxygen in the triplet state with the lithium-ion in the center of the LiPc anion. The resulting complex shows that there is an increase in the oxygen-oxygen bond length to a value of 1.32 Å when compared to a bond length of 1.2 Å for a gas phase oxygen molecule in the triplet state. This bond elongation resembles that of O_2 molecule adsorbing on a Pt_2 cluster forming a triplet superoxol state. The 1.32 Å bond length is also consistent with the superoxo bond length in lithium superoxide (LiO_2). Correspondingly, upon complex formation, there is a transfer of charge. For the triplet state, the charges of the O atoms are -0.39 and -0.32e while the charge on the Li atom is 0.64e. The charge transfer and O_2 reduction is driven by the P_C anion acting as a catalyst. The long cycle

Figure 2. TBA-LiPc interacting with oxygen with spin multiplicity of 3. Geometry was optimized from the MO5-2X functional. Color code: Oxygen atoms are in red, lithium in purple, nitrogen in blue, carbon in grey and hydrogen in white.

times observed in our investigation of the lithium-air battery when using the hybrid catalyst might stem from the fact that the singlet oxygen is complexed and thus unavailable to participate in the electrolyte decomposition process.

Based on the high surface area with the porous structure of HPC and the electro-catalytic activity of the hybrid catalyst towards oxygen reduction and evolution, the electrochemical performance of hybrid catalyst in TEGDME electrolyte was evaluated in the potential range 2 – 4.3 V in oxygen atmosphere. Two lithium-oxygen cells were assembled, one cell with a cathode composed of only HPC and another cell with GNSs coated HPC. The cells with and without GNSs delivered the initial discharge cell capacity of 20450 $mAh/g_{(carbon)}$ and 14760 $mAh/g_{(carbon)}$, respectively at discharge current of 50 μA in oxygen atmosphere (Fig 3). In our previous work [6], the high capacity of 14264 $mAh/g_{(carbon)}$ s also observed upon deep discharge when using 2mM TBA-LiPc as the catalyst. The source of the extra capacity for the cell with GNSs coated HPC cathode (Fig 3) is associated with graphene and is still being investigated. Hu *et al* reported that a graphene-modified $LiFePO_4$ cathode in Li-ion battery exhibited specific capacity of 208 mAh/g, which is beyond the theoretical capacity of 170 mAh/g [9]. The excess capacity is attributed to the reversible reduction-oxidation reactions between the lithium ions of the electrolyte and the exfoliated graphene flakes. The main feature of electrochemical reduction of oxygen is exhibited as the flat discharge voltage profile from 2.75 to 2.65 V. The cell polarization value (ΔV) between discharge and charge cycles with and without graphene was ~ 1.45 V. ΔV was selected at the mid-point of discharge and charge cell capacity profiles. High capacity of both the cells in Fig 3 is due to the solution phase reaction involving hybrid catalyst, thereby avoiding reaction products build up on the cathode that shuts down the reaction for oxygen reduction and evolution.

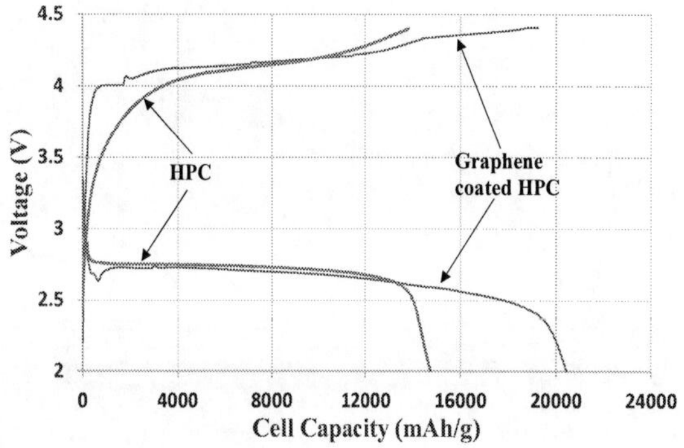

Figure 3. Deep discharge-charge profiles of cells with and without GNSs coated HPC in TEGDME electrolyte in oxygen atmosphere at 25 °C.

Fig 4 shows the long-term cycling stability of a lithium-oxygen cell with GNSs coated HPC cathode in pure oxygen with shallow depth of discharge. Cell was discharged and charged with a constant current of 50 μA for a fixed duration of 11 hours. The cell was operated in the potential range of 2.5 V to 4.2 V.

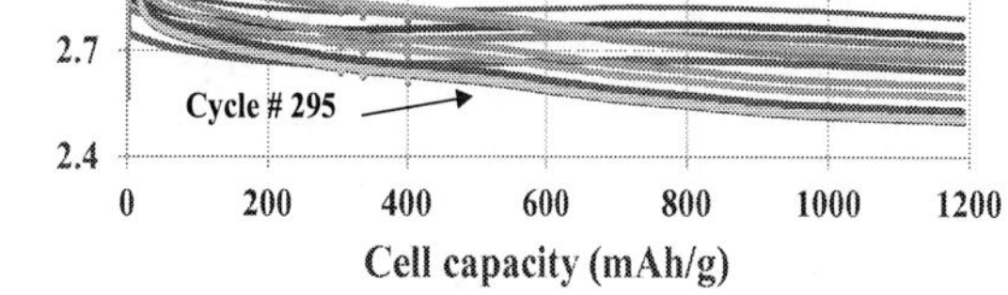

Figure 4. Cycling performance of cell with GNSs coated HPC cathode in TEGDME electrolyte in oxygen atmosphere at 25 °C.

The cell exhibits good cycle performance for 295 cycles with stable reversible capacity of 1190 mAh/$g_{(carbon)}$ in the presence of hybrid catalyst. The cell has an average coulombic efficiency of 97% with ΔV between 1st discharge and 1st charge is 0.81 V. The long cycle life is due to superior electrocatalytic activity of the hybrid catalyst that helps the solution phase formation and oxidation of Li_2O_2.

Fig 5 shows the cycling behavior of a lithium-air cell with GNSs coated HPC cathode where the source of oxygen is from air inside a dry room. The relative humidity of the air is 0.01 %. The cell was discharged and charged using a constant current of 50 μA for 11 hours (0.55 mAh). The cell was operated in the potential range of 2.4 V (in dry air)

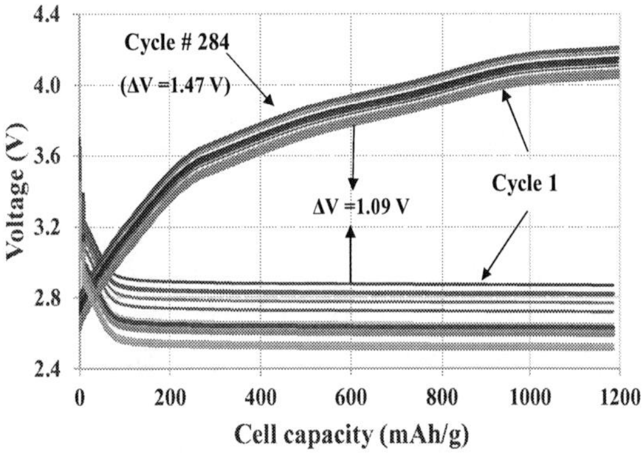

Figure 5. Cycling performance of cell with GNSs coated HPC cathode in TEGDME electrolyte in dry-air atmosphere at 25 °C.

to 4.2 V. The cell exhibits good cycle performance for 284 cycles with stable reversible capacity of 1190 mAh/$g_{(carbon)}$. The cell has an average coulombic efficiency of 97% with ΔV between 1st discharge and 1st charge is 1.01 V. There is a gradual increase in ΔV. At the end of end of 200th cycle, ΔV increased to 1.47 V. The increase in ΔV may be due to the increased thickness of the SEI layer on the lithium metal anode.

Conclusion

In conclusion, CV study demonstrates the significance of a mixture of TBA-LiPc and Li_2Pc as bifunctional catalyst in TEGDME. The catalyst plays a key role in promoting a solution phase process for reversible formation and oxidation of the peroxide anion in a low-donor-number solvent. Long-term cycling of lithium-oxygen / lithium-air cells coupled with theoretical calculations strongly suggests the importance of oxygen complexation with the LiPc anion as the first step in reduction of molecular oxygen when using a low-donor-number solvent. It is through this interaction that a long cycle life of over 280 cycles is possible and provides valuable insight of the factors affecting rechargeability of lithium-air cells.

Acknowledgements

This research was supported by the Air Force Research Laboratory, Wright-Patterson Air Force Base, Ohio.

References:

1. Kwak, W.-J., R. Sharon, C. Xia, H. Kim, L.R. Johnson, P.G. Bruce, L.F. Nazar, Y.K. Sun, A.A. Frimer, M. Noked, S.A. Freunberger, and D. Aurbach, "Lithium-Oxygen Batteries and Related Systems: Potential, Status, and Future", *Chem. Rev*, vol. 120, pp. 6626-6683, 2020.

.2. Shao, Y., S. Park., J. Xiao, J.-G. Zhang, Y. Wang, and J. Liu, "Electrocatalysts for Nonaqueous Lithium-Air Batteries: Status, Challenges, and Perspective", *ACS Catal.,*. vol. 2, pp. 844-857, 2012.

3. Selvaraj, C., N. Munichandraiah, and L.G. Scanlon, "Dilithium Phthalocyanine as a catalyst for Oxygen Reduction in Non-Aqueous Li-O_2 Cells", *J. Porphyrin Phthalocyanines.,* vol. **16**, pp. 255-259, 2012.

4. Sun, D., Y. Shen, W. Zhang, L. Yu, Z. Yi, W. Yin, D. Wang, Y. Huang, J. Wang, D. Wang, and J.B. Goodenough, "A Solution-Phase Bifunctional Catalyst for Lithium-Oxygen Batteries", *J. Am. Chem. Soc.,* vol. **136**, pp. 8941-8946, 2014.

5. Mandal, S., R.N. Samajdar, S. Parida, S. Mishra, and A.J. Bhattacharyya "Transition Metal Phthalocyanines as Redox Mediators in Li-O2 Batteries: A Combined Experimental and Theoretical Study of the Influence of 3d Electrons in Redox Mediation", *ACS Appl. Mater. Interfaces,* vol. **14**, pp. 26714-26723, 2022.

6. Kichambare, P., S. Rodrigues, K. Hankins, P.B. Balbuena, W.A. Feld, and L. Scanlon, "Phthalocyanine as Catalyst for Rechargeable Lithium-Oxygen Batteries", *J. Porphyrin Phthalocyanines.,* vol. **26**, pp. 308-315, 2022.

7. Laoire, C.O., S. Mukerjee, K.M. Abraham, E.J. Plichta, and M.A. Hendrickson, "Influence of Nonaqueous Solvents on the Electrochemistry of Oxygen in the Rechargeable Lithium-Air Battery", *J. Phys..Chem. C.,* vol. **114**, pp. 9178-9186, 2010.

8. Bi, X., J. Li, M. Dahbi, J. Alami, K. Amine, and J. Lu, "Understanding the role of Lithium Iodide in Lithium-Oxygen Batteries", *Adv. Mater.,* vol. **34**, pp. 2106148, 2022.

9. Hu, L.-H., F.-Y. Wu, C.-T. Lin, A.N. Khlobystov, and L.-J. Li, "Graphene-modified $LiFePO_4$ cathode for lithium-ion battery beyond theoretical capacity", *Nature Comm.,* vol. **4**:1687, pp. 1-7, 2013.

EnerSys CWB Prismatic Cell Characteristics and Development Strategy

Hiroshi Nakahara
Quallion R&D Group
EnerSys Advanced Systems
12744 San Fernando Road, Suite 03-100, Sylmar, CA 91342, U.S.A.
Hiroshi.nakahara@eas.enersys.com / 818-833-2000

Abstract

Quallion, a subsidiary of EnerSys Advanced Systems (EAS), has developed a 063450 prismatic lithium-ion cell (6mm^t x 34mm^w x 50mm^h) for conformable wearable battery (CWB) to establish U.S. domestic battery cell supply. EAS's pilot manufacturing line has been set up in Sylmar, California. EAS is trying to establish a domestic supply chain of cell mechanical hardware as well to secure the above cell manufacturing. In this paper, the status of CWB cell development and the characteristics of CWB cells is introduced. Key development items to increase energy density is discussed as well.

Keywords

Lithium-ion cell; Conformable wearable battery; CWB, Prismatic cell; High energy density; Supply chain; Domestic manufacturing

Introduction

Over the past several years Lithium-ion cell technology has been in high demand especially for electric vehicle application lately due to its high weight specific energy density. As a result, lithium-ion cell manufacturing demand has increased significantly with for large-sized prismatic and cylindrical for EV power sources . These cells are being commoditized because of EV market potential volume. In contrast, the production volume ratio of the lithium-ion cells available is relatively small or unique aspect ratio in prismatic shape for each application has become smaller than decades ago. These small volume cells are not getting needed attention to establish supply chain of not only cell by itself but also mechanical components due to cost effectiveness in cell manufacturing. As a result, the small prismatic cell production is localized more in Asia.

EAS has been developing small prismatic cells for US-domestic demands and establishing a cell production line to meet the expected volumes. EAS is also setting up the domestic supply chain for the mechanical components and is one of important key items to support domestic cell manufacturing. Pilot manufacturing line for 063450 cell (6.0mm^t x 34mm^w x 50mm^h) has been established, and 653450 cell (6.5mm^t x 34mm^w x 50mm^h) is in planning phases to be added as another product line.

1.35 Ah lithium-ion cell in 063450 cell format has been developed. This cell has successfully passed the nail penetration test which is one of the more challenging safety requirements for this cell. EAS has been focused on increasing the energy density of the prismatic cell. The balanced chemistry design is not determined between performances in higher energy density and safety. In this paper, the characteristics of EAS prismatic cell for CWB and the prototyped high energy density cell are introduced.

EAS Prismatic Cell Characteristics

The developed 063450 prismatic cell (Fig. 1) demonstrated 1.35Ah, 3.6V nominal voltage 216Wh/kg). The cell was prototyped domestically in U.S.A. Table 1 summarizes the cell characteristics. This cell is designed with NCA cathode and graphite anode. The cell passed nail penetration test which is one of critical requirements. Fig. 2 shows the typical discharge curve for 063450 cell (1.35Ah).

Fig. 1 Photograph of EAS's 063450 prismatic lithium-ion cell

Table 1 EAS 063450 Cell Characteristics

	Existing Chemistry (NCA)	Advanced Chemistry (NMC811)
Discharge Capacity (Ah)	1.35	2.3
Cell Weight (g)	22.5	28.5
Weight Energy Density (Wh/kg)	216	303
Abuse Test (Nail Penetration)	Pass	Need Improvement
Cell Safety Devices	Safety Valve, (Internal Fuse available)	Safety Valve, (Internal Fuse available)

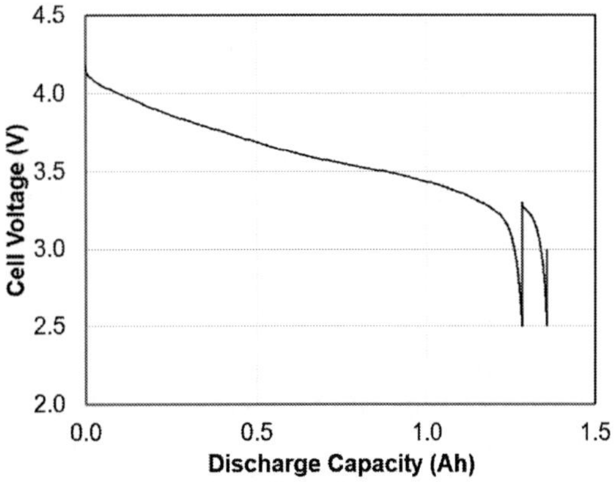

Fig. 2 Discharge curve of 063450 cell with EAS's existing chemistry

Furthermore, 653450 prismatic cell hardware (6.5mm^{t} x 34mm^{w} x 50mm^{h}) was designed to increase discharge capacity from the existing 063450 prismatic cell (1.35Ah, 216Wh/kg) to 1.75Ah (248Wh/kg) with the reengineered electrode design with NCA / graphite chemistry

EAS has been evaluating the chemistry design to observe the balances between energy density and safety. 063450 cell with NCA cathode and Si-graphite mixed anode has been prototyped to push the energy density to the edge with the current available technology. Fig. 3 shows discharge curve for one of prototype-cell configuration designed with 1.85Ah (255Wh/kg). Fig. 4 shows the discharge curves of NCA/Si-graphite cell at various discharge rate between C/20 ~ 1C at room temperature.

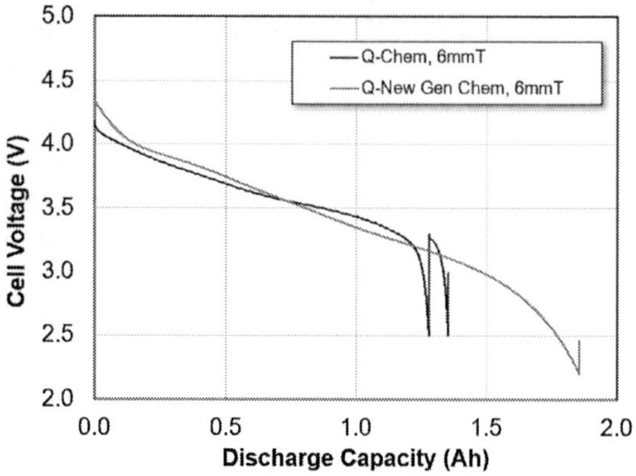

Fig. 3 Discharge curve of 063450 cell with EAS's existing chemistry (NCA/graphite; black line) and new chemistry (NCA/Si-graphite; purple line)

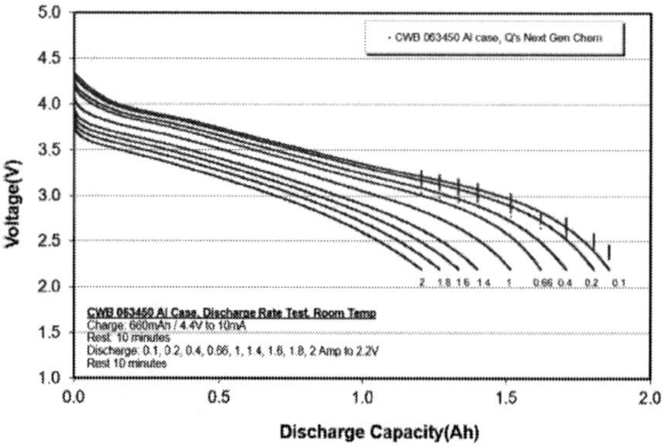

Fig. 4 Discharge curves of 063450 cell at various discharge rate with EAS's new chemistry

The prototype cell demonstrated 2.5Ah, 3.6V nominal voltage (355Wh/kg) shown in Fig. 5 while the safety improvement is still in process. The goal of development is to obtain 653450 prismatic cell with 2.5Ah (350Wh/kg) with passing nail penetration test. The utilized chemistry is NMC cathode and Si anode. Another key development is to suppress cell thickness increase under long term usage of the cell. EAS has developed the advanced electrolyte to help the suppression of swelling. EAS owns and operates the cathode material manufacturing facility for NCA. NMC cathode manufacturing capability can be added to this facility to support material supply chain. This addition helps to establish the vertically integrated manufacturing from electrode active material to CWB prismatic cell.

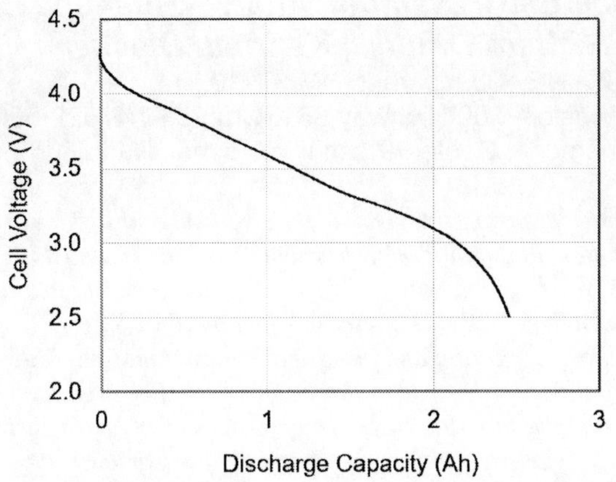

Fig. 5 Discharge curves of 350Wh/kg-class 063450 cell at various discharge rate with EAS's new chemistry

At last, EAS is trying to establish secure supply chain of not only chemicals but also mechanical components such as cell case and cover assembly. EAS has developed plans and designed the manufacturing of critical mechanical components to support these prismatic cell productions in U.S.A.

Summary

EAS has developed lithium-ion 063450 1.35Ah cell for CWB application. The developed cell has passed nail penetration test meeting one of the most challenging safety performance requirements. EAS is trying to increase energy density without losing safety performance. High energy cell up to 2.5Ah, 350Wh/kg were prototyped during the cell development. However, these cells have not met the safety requirements yet. EAS is optimizing the material designs of electrolyte and separator membrane to pass the safety requirements at higher energy density. In parallel, EAS is planning to set up higher volume production with secure domestic supply chain of materials and components.

Development of Magnesium Oxide (MgO) Binder for Thermal Batteries

Viswanath Krishnamoorthy[1], David Smith[1], Nathan Berg[1], Samuel Stuart[2], Giuseppe L. Di Benedetto[3], Lauren Morris[3], Aaron Stern[3], Richard Dratler[3], Kenneth Blecker[3]
[1]Qynergy Corporation, 8601 Paseo Alameda NE, Albuquerque NM 87113
[2]U.S. Navy Naval Surface Warfare Center (NSWC) Crane Division, 300 Highway 361, Crane, IN 47522-5001
[3]U.S. Army Combat Capabilities Development Command Armaments Center, Picatinny Arsenal, NJ 07806-5000

Abstract: *Thermal batteries (TBs) are primary reserve batteries that employ inorganic salt electrolytes. These electrolytes are non-conductive solids at ambient temperatures. Pyrotechnic materials are used to provide sufficient thermal energy to melt the electrolytes and activate the cell. TBs are used in variety of Department of Defense applications including missiles and munitions. The fundamental unit cell of a thermal battery consists of an anode and cathode separated by a binder material infused with the salt electrolyte. The binder material provides structural support and separates the anode and cathode for the molten, liquid electrolyte when the battery is activated. The key performance characteristic of the binder material is the ability to provide reliable structural support while maximizing the electrolyte binding characteristics to minimize the required binder volume. Without an adequate performing material, the gap between the anode and cathode could not be maintained resulting in a voltage noise, localized heating, or an intracell short. The two highest performing binder materials commercially produced were Maglite S and Marinco OL, both of which were discontinued by their manufacturers more than 20 years ago due to economic reasons. No documentation of the precursor or manufacturing processes used was ever made available to allow the products to be recreated. Subsequently, TB manufacturers have been using the dwindling stockpile and/or developed stop-gap non-optimal (lower performing) but adequate solutions to meet military need. These binders have suffered from process instability and intermittent failures and the government has spent millions in an attempt to accommodate the lack of reliability. Qynergy, in order to stabilize the supply chain of critical TB materials, has developed a magnesium oxide (MgO) binder material ("GoMax") for the binary LiCl:KCl electrolyte that outperforms the existing binder materials used in the industry. Qynergy has scientifically engineered the material in such a way that it can now be produced from several suppliers of precursors, thus mitigating supply chain risk. Qynergy's GoMax MgO will both secure the supply chain for current thermal battery manufacturing and lead to performance enhancements in the TB applications space. The mechanism and powder properties driving the binder's performance have been studied. This understanding allows for optimization and control of the binder material properties to specific thermal battery applications, as well as enabled the scaled production achieved under the Office of the Secretary of Defense (OSD) Manufacturing Science and Technology Program (MSTP). In this paper the link between salient powder properties such as pore volume and surface area as a function of binder performance will be presented. Multiple precursor sources were evaluated as potential suppliers for MgO binder production. Powder characterization and performance test data from MgO produced using one of these sources will be presented and compared to Maglite S. The powders were characterized using laser scattering, and mercury porosimetry. Performance was evaluated using deformation tests.*

Keywords: thermal batteries; magnesium oxide; binder; separator; deformation; pore volume; particle size.

Introduction

Thermal batteries are constructed as stacks of bipolar electrochemical cells; each cell consisting of an anode, a separator, a cathode, and a heat pellet (Figure1). The pellets are composed of different pressed powder mixes. The separators contain MgO as a binder to keep the molten electrolyte in place after the battery is activated. As produced, the pellets are dry, solid, and inert. The cell stack is contained in a stainless steel can and covered with a header containing terminals for electrical connections. The can and cover are placed under pressure (the stacking or closure force) and then hermetically sealed by welding.

The mechanical properties of the separator pellet are extremely important for proper operation of thermal batteries. Excessive deformation of the pellet while the electrolyte is molten can result in voltage noise, localized heating due to a high-resistance shunt path, and worst case, intracell shorting. Insufficient deformation can result in poor wetting of the electrodes resulting in high electrical resistance at the separator-anode and separator-cathode interface. Consequently, a nominal deformation of 15% to 30% has been empirically determined to be ideal, [1] with 20% as an optimal target [2]. With halide electrolytes a reduction in density of 20-25% going from solid to liquid phase is typical. For this study the LiCl-KCl eutectic electrolyte is utilized as it has been well described in literature, is commonly used in thermal batteries, and has the lowest solid and liquid densities; ρ_s of 2.02 g/cm^3 and ρ_l of 1.59 g/cm^3.[2] Although the separator pellet is processed with the electrolyte in solid form the electrolyte density in the liquid form determines the volume of electrolyte that must be retained by the MgO binder during battery operation. The properties of the MgO binder material such as pore volume etc. then dictate the optimum volume fractions of electrolyte and binder.

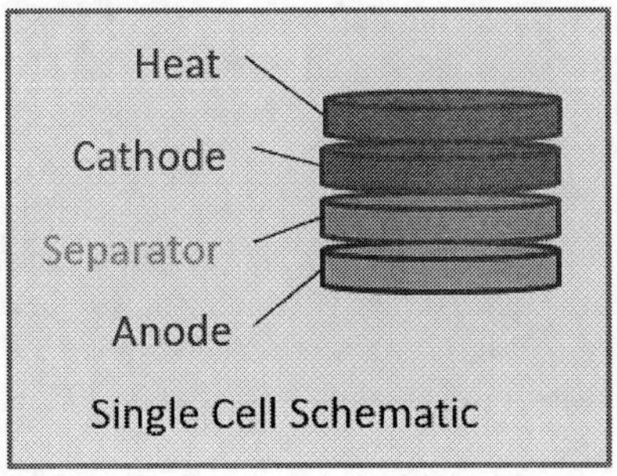

Figure 1. Schematic of Thermal Battery Single Cell Stack

Select physical and chemical properties of MgO materials were evaluated by Sandia National Laboratories (SNL) in the mid-1990s for correlation to deformation performance including purity, surface area, particle size distribution, morphology, and pore-size distribution. In the referenced study, particle and pore size distributions appeared to affect deformation performance. Also, among the materials studied, Maglite-S was the only one with a bi-modal particle size distribution and a smaller particle size which they theorized provided better performance. Maglite-S also had slightly larger pore diameters than other materials. They attributed the binder performance to the ability of the molten electrolyte to penetrate these pores. [1]

Maglite-S MgO powder manufactured by the Calgon Company was used as the standard binder material for over 30 years throughout the industry, however production of the material was discontinued by the manufacturer for economic reasons [4]. Other MgO materials were screened by SNL to identify and qualify a substitute material [4]. After several years' effort, a substitute material, Marinco OL was successfully qualified, but that manufacturer also decided to discontinue production shortly after the material was qualified [4]. Since that time efforts have been underway to produce MgO specifically for thermal battery applications [4]. Given the performance of Maglite-S these efforts have primarily focused on attempting to reproduce similar particle size distribution and pore volume [4].

Qynergy has been developing MgO binders for thermal battery applications since 2012, and has evaluated multiple precursor formulations, sources, and processing conditions. An MgO binder has been developed called GoMax that has been thoroughly characterized with the LiCl-KCl binary eutectic, and the deformation performance correlated with the particle characteristics. The performance and characteristics were compared to Maglite-S material evaluated under identical conditions. In the case of Maglite-S the deformation performance correlated with the available pore volume of the binder and the total volume of electrolyte that must be retained in the melt state. The deformation performance of GoMax, however, exceeded the predicted value based on available pore volume. Therefore, a secondary mechanism must be contributing to electrolyte retention. GoMax has a significantly larger active surface area than Maglite-S. The improved binding performance is attributed to the active surface interacting/holding the molten electrolyte. The degree of surface activity can be controlled by processing conditions and precursor selection.

In this study, deformation performance of Maglite-S and GoMax is compared to demonstrate this mechanism by varying the ratio of electrolyte (LiCl-KCl eutectic) and binder in mixes processed and tested under identical conditions.

Methods and Materials

GoMax was prepared by continuous calcination of precursor in a rotary furnace. The resultant MgO was collected in a dry air environment in an O-ring sealed container which was then moved to storage in a dry air purged glove box. Samples of GoMax and Maglite-S were analyzed using laser scattering and Hg porosimetry for particle size distribution and pore volume, respectively.

Preparation of the electrolyte salts, EB mixes, and deformation testing closely followed a procedure described in literature [3]. All handling and processing of materials was performed in dry air purged glove boxes with nominal dew points of -80 °C (-112 °F) or less.

Reagent-grade halide salts of LiCl and KCl were used in the preparation of the binary electrolyte. A ratio of 45 weight percent (w/o) LiCl 55 w/o KCl was used to produce an electrolyte with a melting point of 352 °C (665.6 °F). The appropriate amount of salts were blended in a Turbula mixer and fused at 650 °C (1202 °F) for 3 hours. After quenching in an Inconel tray the electrolyte was ground to 100 mesh using a Fitzmill.

Prior to blending with electrolyte, the MgO was baked at 600 °C (1112 °F) for 4 hours to ensure complete moisture removal as well as decompose any hydroxides or carbonates that may have formed during storage. EB mixes were prepared by blending the electrolyte and binder at ratios of 65:35, 70:30, 75:25, and 80:20. The mixtures were fused at 400 °C (752 °F) for 16 hours. Mixes were then ground to 80 mesh prior to pelletizing into separators for deformation testing.

3.1 cm diameter separator pellets were pressed to 70% of theoretical density with a final thickness of 1.5 mm.

Heated thickness deformation analysis was performed to evaluate the effectiveness of the separator. Separator pellets were secured between mica sheets and stack thickness recorded prior to testing. The pellet was compressed at 14 psi and 500 °C (932 °F) in an argon glove box using Qynergy's heated deformation tester (shown in Figure 2). The final thickness reading was taken after 30 seconds (at which point the thickness was stabilized in response to the compaction force). Final percent (%) thickness deformation was then calculated. A minimum of three separator pellets were tested for each EB mix ratio to ensure uniformity.

Figure 2. Qynergy Heated Thickness Deformation Tester

Results

Particle size distributions for Maglite-S and GoMax are compared in Figure 3 and shows the overall larger particle size of GoMax (~2x). When interpreting cumulative pore volume and surface area characteristics using Hg intrusion porosimetry it is necessary to differentiate between interparticle porosity and intraparticle void space. In this evaluation pore diameters larger than 25% of the median particle size determined via laser scattering were considered intra-particle pores and, therefore, excluded. This is shown graphically in Figure 4.

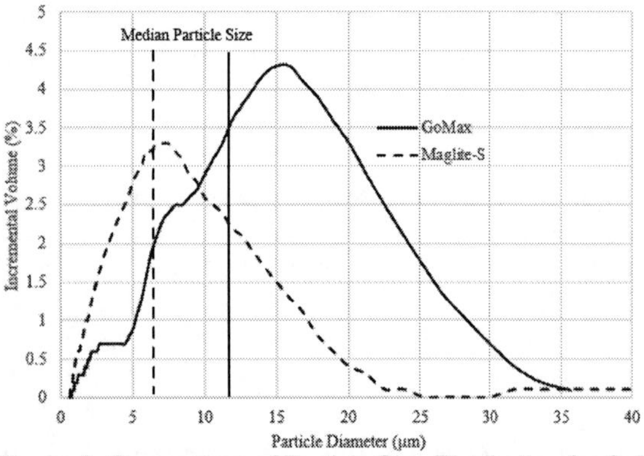

Figure 3. Comparison of Particle Size Distribution for GoMax and Maglite-S

Figure 5 shows the cumulative pore volume and pore area distributions for GoMax and Maglite-S and shows that Maglite-S has greater overall pore volume while GoMax has significantly higher pore area due primarily to the contribution of extremely small diameter surface porosity. Values for median particle size, pore volume and pore area are summarized in Table 1 which shows the 2x larger median particle size, slightly reduced pore volume and nearly 4x greater pore area of GoMax versus Maglite-S.

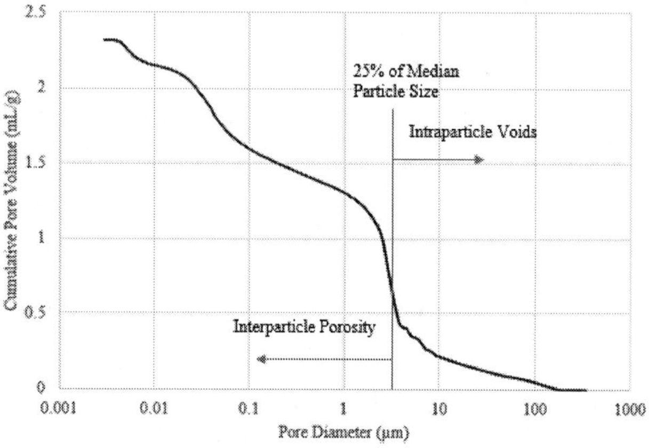

Figure 4. Pores Larger Than 25% of Median Particle Size are Excluded from Total Pore Volume and Area Calculation

Table 1. Summary of Particle Size, Pore Volume, and Pore Area

Sample	Particle Size (µm)	Pore Volume (mL/g)	Pore Area (m^2/g)
	x̃	Σ	Σ
GoMax	11.98	1.561	191.179
Maglite-S	6.056	1.733	48.701

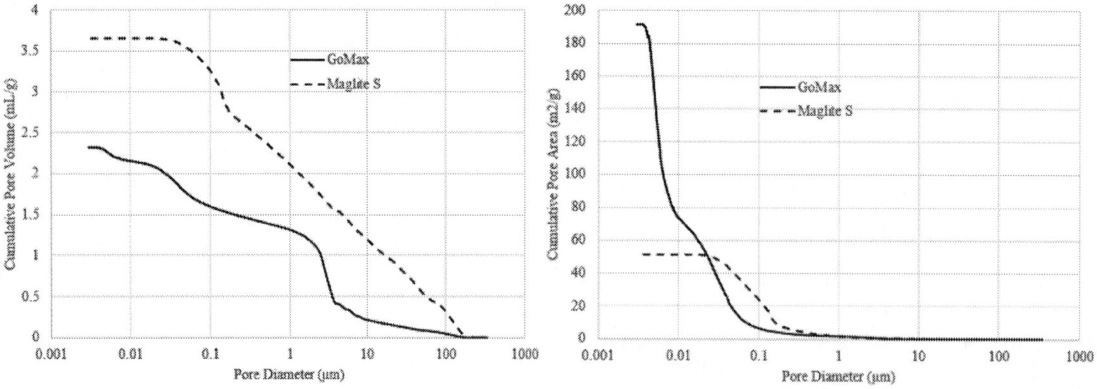

Figure 5. Cumulative Pore Volume (Left) and Cumulative Pore Area (Right) Distributions for GoMax versus Maglite-S

Based on a ρ_l of 1.59 g/cm^3 total required pore volume in mL/g was calculated for EB-mix ratios ranging from 65:35 to 80:20 and is shown in Table 2 along with the % thickness deformation results. Figure 6 graphically shows the comparison of % thickness deformation versus theoretically required pore volume. From Figure 6 it is apparent that deformation performance for Maglite-S correlates well with total pore volume, while GoMax deformation remains low well beyond the predicted threshold.

Table 2. Heated Thickness Deformation Test Results

EB Mix Ratio:	65/35	70/30	75/25	80/20
Maglite-S (1.733 mL/g)	14.60%	22.00%	37.60%	71.10%
GoMax (1.561 mL/g)	9.20%	12.30%	28.60%	79.50%
Required Pore Volume (mL/g) (ρ_l 1.59 g/cm^3)	1.161	1.458	1.875	2.500

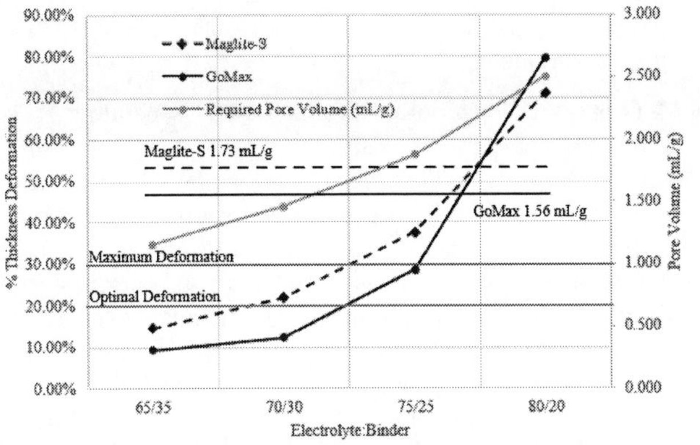

Figure 6. Comparison of Thickness Deformation and Required Pore Volume

Conclusions

Binding characteristics of MgO have been attributed to molten electrolyte being retained in the pores only. Varying pore volume and pore area and evaluating deformation performance with a range of electrolyte to binder ratios indicates that pore volume alone is not entirely responsible for immobilization of electrolyte when high surface activity MgO is evaluated (as in GoMax). These high surface active MgO materials continue to perform better in deformation testing even when the quantity of liquid electrolyte exceeds the available pore volume. When liquid electrolyte exceeds pore volume in a non-surface active or low surface area MgO deformation performance is dramatically reduced. Surface activity is a property that can be modulated via MgO processing conditions and provides a second parameter that can be controlled to optimize binder performance. Qynergy has developed scaled processes for manufacturing production quantities of GoMax MgO binder materials.

Acknowledgements

This work was supported by the Office of the Secretary of Defense (OSD) Manufacturing Science and Technology Program (MSTP) and received a Defense Manufacturing Technology Achievement Award (DMTAA) in the Supply Chain Project Category at DMC 2022.

References

1. Guidotti, Ronald A., and W. Reinhardt. Characterization of MgO powders for use in thermal batteries. No. SAND-90-2104. Sandia National Lab. (SNL-NM), Albuquerque, NM (United States), 1996.
2. Masset, Patrick, Serge Schoeffert, Jean-Yves Poinso, and Jean-Claude Poignet. "Retained molten salt electrolytes in thermal batteries." Journal of power sources 139, no. 1-2 (2005): 356-365.
3. Guidotti, Ronald A., Frederick W. Reinhardt, and Edward V. Thomas. Deformation study of separator pellets for thermal batteries. No. SAND-90-2318. Sandia National Lab.(SNL-NM), Albuquerque, NM (United States), 1995.
4. Papenguth, Hans W., Martin B. Nemer, Christine C. Roberts, Robert C. Moore, and Timothy J. Boyle. "Historical Production of Maglite S and the Development of New Magnesium-Oxide Binder for Thermal Batteries." Proceedings of the 48th Power Sources Conference, SAND2018-4481C, 2018.

Synthetic Production of Tunable Magnesium Oxide for Thermal Batteries: Drag and Drop

Aoife Celoria[1]; Wish Krishnamoorthy[2]; Brittany Urban[1]; Nathan Berg[2]
[1]EnerSys Advanced Systems Inc., 5430 70th Ave N, Pinellas Park, FL 33781
T: 512-856-4607, Email: aoife.celoria@eas.enersys.com
[2]Qynergy, 6201 Pan American Fwy NE Suite A, Albuquerque, NM 87109
T: 505-890-6887, Email: wish@qynergy.com

Abstract

Magnesium oxide (MgO) is a critical binder material in the manufacture of thermal batteries, owing to its stability and ability to immobilize molten electrolyte. Established supply chains can cease production and new sources must be evaluated at great expense in terms of time and revenue. To ensure the supply of this critical material, Qynergy has developed an MgO binder material ("GoMax") for electrolytes. The new MgO binder material is scientifically engineered in such a way that it can be produced from multiple precursors, thus mitigating supply chain risk. The purpose of this work is to demonstrate the benefit of such production from synthetic precursors, as well as the ability to tune the morphological properties to 'drag and drop' the as-synthesized MgO into current separator design without disrupting pellet production or battery performance. In the current work, two forms of the Qynergy GoMax MgO are characterized with electrolyte salt mixtures made in-house by EnerSys Advanced Systems Inc. (EAS) to demonstrate the tunability of the synthesized materials and common morphologies with the currently used material. Tests include morphological characterization of GoMax and Electrolyte/Binder (EB) mix using different iterations of GoMax. EAS and Qynergy have demonstrated common physical characteristics of GoMax and current binder used in our thermal batteries.

Keywords

Thermal batteries; magnesium oxide; binder; separator; particle size distribution; morphology; single cell.

Introduction

Thermal batteries are primary reserve power sources. They are single use, dormant at room temperature and activated on demand. They are primarily used in military applications owing to several attractive characteristics including >20-year shelf life, high rate capability, wide operating temperature range, and little/no self-discharge. The technology has been well-studied and characterized over time owing to such defense applications [1, 2]. The batteries are comprised of primary components: the electrochemical cell which includes the anode, cathode, and EB mix, also known as the separator, and the heat source which ignites upon activation, causing the electrolyte in the separator to heat to a molten state, thus activating the battery through ionic transfer. Figure 1 outlines the structure and sequence of activation of a thermal battery.

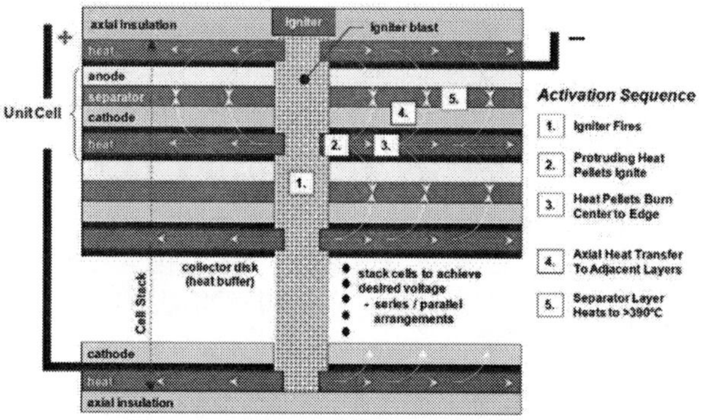

Figure 1: Thermal battery schematic with activation and operation sequence.

MgO is a vital material in thermal battery separators; it is thermally stable, inert, and electrically non-conducting material [3]. It provides physical separation between the anode and the cathode to prevent cell shorting, as well as binding molten electrolyte to prevent leakage. The morphology of MgO is also critical to its performance. Numerous grades are commercially available in large quantities, but not all will function effectively in thermal battery separators. Important properties include purity, powder flow, deformation, and binding characteristics. Current commercial manufacture is not directed towards thermal battery applications and quality control in this environment is not a priority for suppliers. Previous supply chains for qualified MgO have ceased production and new sources had to be evaluated at great expense in terms of time and cost. Thermal battery manufacturers have little control over the quality and future supply of purchased MgO.

MgO synthesis from widely available precursors would allow for vertical integration and strict quality control of this vital material. The goal at Qynergy has been to synthesize MgO materials from widely available precursors to retain or improve powder flow, pellet strength, and binding capability. The MgO synthesis process permits highly tunable material that can be tailored towards a specific electrolyte. In this work, EAS has partnered with Qynergy to evaluate such MgO with electrolyte currently used in commercial thermal batteries developed and manufactured by EAS. The physical characteristics of two iterations of GoMax MgO and EAS electrolyte have been evaluated to establish whether it is possible to 'drag and drop' one of these iterations into EAS's current separator powder. EAS matches characteristics of currently used MgO with the new

GoMax MgO in an attempt to retain the physical and chemical properties of separator in terms of powder flow, particle size distribution, morphology, and electrochemical performance.

Methods and Materials

The importance of evaluating material properties for the MgO separator component has been outlined. Subsequently, several methods of physical and chemical evaluation are employed in this work to evaluate GoMax in EAS's EB mix.

Two iterations of GoMax MgO were evaluated in this study, hereafter referred to as GoMax A and GoMax B. Upon receipt, both materials were tested for moisture using the Karl Fisher Titration method. As received, GoMax A and GoMax B were also evaluated for particle size distribution (www. Microtrac.com).

To further evaluate GoMax A and GoMax B the material was combined with EAS electrolyte to form two EB mixes, hereafter referred to as Separator A (using GoMax A) and Separator B (using GoMax B). The methods of this material synthesis as well as the nature of the EAS electrolyte are proprietary. Upon synthesis, Separator A and Separator B were evaluated for physical and chemical properties. The morphology of the EB mixes was examined using Morphologi G3 (www. Malvern.com) and compared with current EAS separator. Tap density of both EB mixes was also evaluated. Chemical characteristics of Separator A and Separator B were explored using Differential Scanning Calorimetry (DSC). Finally, electrochemical cell analysis was performed on a single cell setup for Separators A and B.

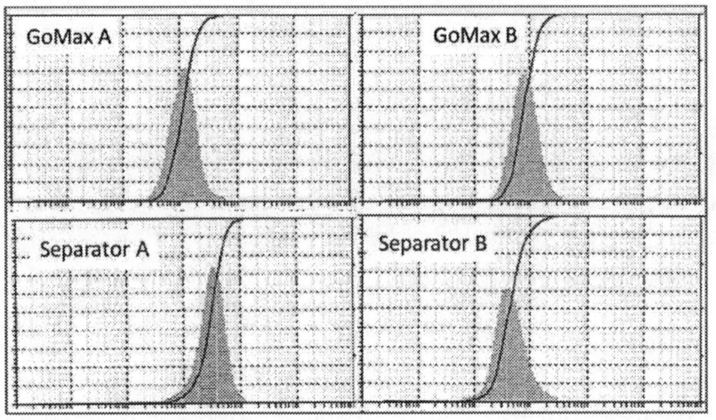

Figure 2: Particle size distribution for GoMax A, GoMax B, Separator A, and Separator B.

Results

In this work, two forms of GoMax MgO are evaluated. MgO was inspected upon arrival for water content and conformed to requirements. Particle size distribution was examined on GoMax MgO alone as well as the resulting EB mix. Figure 2 outlines the particle size distribution for four materials: GoMax A, GoMax B, Separator A, and Separator B. The particle size distribution is relatively narrow, which is a good indication of favorable powder flow.

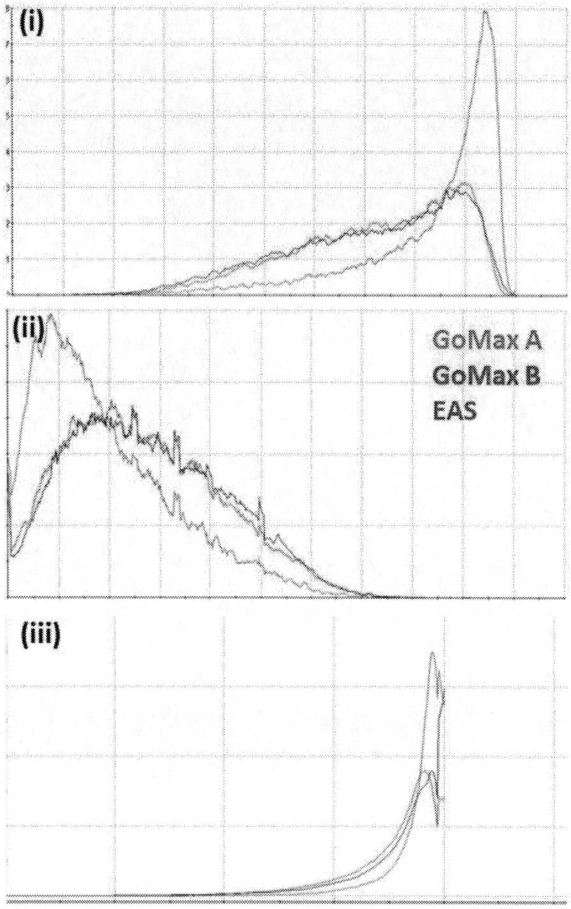

Figure 3: Morphology data for Circularity (i), Elongation (ii), and Convexity (iii) of GoMax A (green), GoMax B (red), and current EAS MgO (blue).

The morphology of the EB mix is also a good indication of pellet manufacturability, as well as performance of the material during battery actuation. Figure 3 outlines a comparison of GoMax A, GoMax B, and EAS MgO for circularity, elongation, and convexity. It is particularly interesting to note that the particle size and shape characteristics of GoMax B agree well with EAS MgO, which may be used to predict ease of manufacture with the new MgO material as well as operational behavior. Separator A and Separator B were also examined with Morphologi G3. Figure 4 outlines a comparison of circularity, elongation, and convexity for each material. It is noteworthy that for the fused separator material, EAS separator is in better agreement with Separator A (utilizing GoMax A), which demonstrates that process reactions play a large part in separator design.

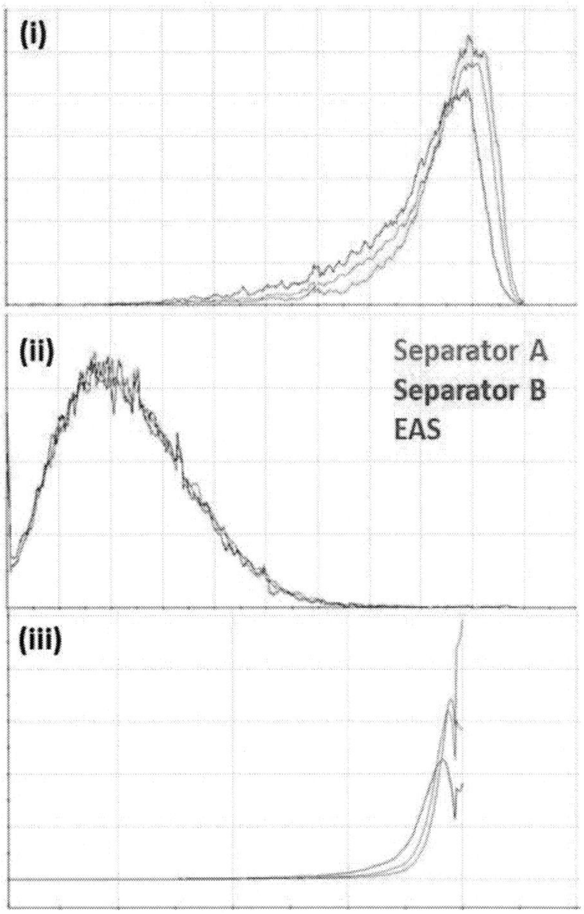

Figure 4: Morphology data for Circularity (i), Elongation (ii), and Convexity (iii) of Separator A (green), Separator B (red), and current EAS EB (blue).

The Hausner ratio of powders is a good indicator of powder flow in manufacturing. Table 1 outlines the Hausner ratio for Separator A and Separator B.

Material	Hausner Ratio
Separator A	1.44
Separator B	1.40

Table 1: Hausner Ratio for Separator A and Separator B.

While the values deviate somewhat from the 'ideal 1.1' value, it should be noted that for pellet manufacture, it is important to find a compromise between powder flow and ease of pellet pressing, as the two can sometimes be inversely proportional. Therefore, while a powder may flow well according to this ratio, it may be difficult to form a rugged pellet with the same material.

The chemical properties of Separator A and Separator B were evaluated with DSC, which outlines melting point and heat of fusion. These parameters allow us to inspect the performance of the material at temperature to ensure that the separator functions in a manner that is cohesive with the temperature of operation. It is noteworthy that both mixes display a very clean profile which is an indication of the purity of the GoMax MgO for both iterations examined (A and B). This allows for more predictable behavior and greater quality control of separator materials.

Upon completion of Separator A and Separator B powder evaluation, each material was pressed into pellets and formed into a cell with anode and cathode pellets to probe behavior under heat and pressure at open circuit voltage (OCV). A predefined operating temperature and pressure were applied to a single cell each of Separator A and Separator B and the resulting voltage output at OCV was observed. Figure 5 outlines the curves for each cell at OCV over several minutes. The consistency of the output voltage upon melting of the electrolyte is clear and demonstrates the viability of GoMax MgO as a binder material in thermal batteries.

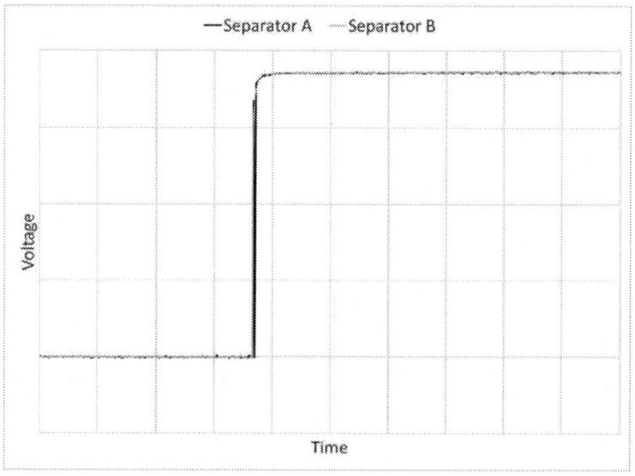

Figure 5: Single cell tests on Separator A and B at open circuit voltage.

Next steps in this study must include examination of deformation and leakage of these pellets. This will help to evaluate the behavior of the new EB mix material in an operating thermal battery.

Conclusions

Synthesis of MgO from widely available precursors is very attractive in thermal battery manufacturing with respect to quality control and vertical integration. In this work EAS demonstrated initial testing of Qynergy GoMax MgO in EAS EB mix. Physical and morphological studies demonstrated that GoMax can be tailored to fit a particular electrolyte mix owing to the tunability of the synthesis process. GoMax EB mixes exhibited comparable electrochemical behavior to currently used materials which may allow us to 'drag and drop' this material into existing separator pellets without the necessity of modification of the manufacturing process.Further testing and examination will provide an enhanced understanding of this material and its viability in thermal batteries.

References

1. Guidotti, Ronald A., masset, Partick.
   Thermally activated ("thermal") battery technology.
   Part I: An overview.
   J. Power Sources, 161 (2006) 1443 – 1449.
2. Masset, Patrick, Guidotti, Ronald A.,
   Thermal activated (thermal) battery technology
   Part II. Molten salt electrolytes.
   J. Power Sources 164 (2007) 397-414
3. Guidotti, Ronald A., and W. Reinhardt.
   Characterization of MgO powders for use in thermal batteries. No. SAND-90-2104. Sandia National Lab. (SNL-NM), Albuquerque, NM (United States), 1996

Analytical Exploration of Iron Disulfide Performance in Molten Salt Batteries

Noah B. Schorr*, Teal Harbour, Martin B. Nemer, Hans W. Papenguth, Samantha Reyes, and John H. Taphouse
Sandia National Laboratories
Albuquerque, NM, USA
nschorr@sandia.gov

Abstract

Molten salt batteries play a vital role as a long shelf-life power source in a variety of single use defense applications. In this work we focus on the performance of iron disulfide as an active cathode material for molten salt batteries that operate at ~500°C and identifying the properties of the material that influence performance. Various iron disulfide powders are investigated, with particles ranging from ~5 – 100 μm in size. A suite of analytical techniques has been used to determine physical and chemical properties of the iron disulfide particles. Using this information, we contrast the discharge performance of single cell molten salt tests. To better correlate properties from the electrochemical data with other analytical data, all cells tested are cathode capacity limited, eliminating anode contributions to recorded voltage transitions. Three discharge profiles are also applied to each iron disulfide investigated to probe multiple aspects of the relationship between physical properties and electrochemical performance. This work advances our understanding of iron disulfide as a cathode material for molten salt batteries and ultimately will assist in the selection of material based on desired performance.

Keywords

Iron disulfide; molten salt battery; single cell; electrochemistry; particle size; morphology.

Introduction

Batteries that use a molten salt electrolyte are ideal for single use devices that require minimal discharge during storage and access to high current densities when activated. In this work we explore iron disulfide as the cathode material in molten salt batteries (MSB). Specifically, six FeS_2 materials are analyzed using a suite of analytical techniques and electrochemical evaluations. In single cells the FeS_2 was discharged versus a lithium-silicon alloy anode with a LiCl-KCl mixture serving as the electrolyte. While pyrite is a known material for MSBs, often only a single source of the dichalcogenide is examined under different conditions or a single commercial-off-the-shelf product is compared to a synthetic material. By conducting experiments with a variety of FeS_2 powders we ascertain which physical and chemical properties are most important to the MSB discharge performance.

Experimental

Pyrite was procured from five different sources, with two powders acquired from a single vendor. All powders were processed in a moisture free dry room. For single cell experiments the pyrite powders were combined in a 75:25 wt% ratio with a premixed electrolyte-binder of MgO and LiCl-KCl. The FeS_2 was not processed in any fashion before mixing. The FeS_2 powder mixture was then pressed into 1" diameter cathode pellets. An oversized MgO based pellet with eutectic electrolyte was used as the separator and the cell was completed with an oversized $Li_{13}Si_4$ anode (both 1.25" diameter). The FeS_2 pellets had a theoretical capacity of 1418 As (394 mAh), for the full conversion of FeS_2 to Fe and Li_2S and the anode 1723 As (478 mAh) for the $Li_{13}Si_4$ to Li_7Si_3 transition.

All electrochemical tests were performed in an Ar filled glovebox with O_2 and $H_2O < 1$ ppm. Assembled single cells were placed between platens heated to 500 °C. Three different profiles done in triplicate, unless otherwise noted, were performed on each of the six FeS_2 materials. The first test was a discharge at a 1 C rate, where C rates are defined by the first transition capacity of the FeS_2 (1206 As/g). Second, cells were held at 500°C for 1 hr before discharging at 1 C. Third, a constant areal current density of 50 mA/cm^2 was applied along with series of four pulses lasting for 5 s with a 10 s return to 50 mA/cm^2 between pulses. Each pulse series included four pulses of increasing magnitude (125, 250, 500, 625 mA/cm^2; 0.6334, 1.2668, 2.5334, 3.1669 A).

Results and Discussion

To focus on the FeS_2 properties the MSB single cells were designed to be cathode limited in capacity. This was done to ensure the alloy transition of the anode would not cause a change in cell voltage during the discharge. Borrowing a technique that is commonplace in Li-ion battery research, we undersized the FeS_2 pellet compared to the separator and anode. To ensure this geometry manipulation would produce reliable and reproducible results a 1.25" diameter cathode of the same composition was tested. As seen in Figure 1 the 1" FeS_2 pellet outperformed the 1.25" pellet in capacity utilization and in discharge voltage. Due to the favorable performance of the 1" diameter cathode when compared in

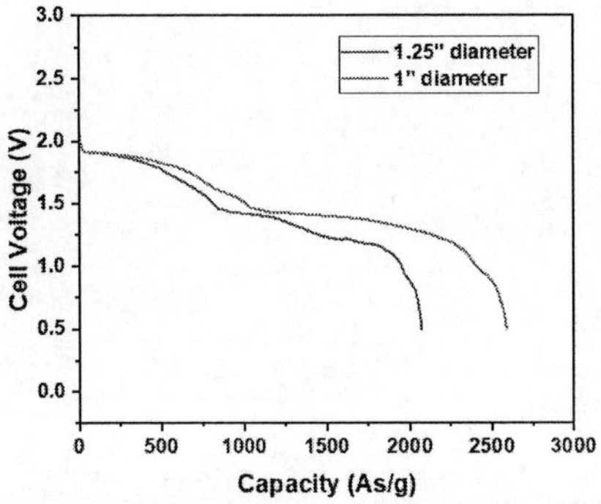

Figure 1. Constant current 1 C discharge comparison of two different sized FeS_2 pellets. Cathodes were fabricated using the same source of FeS_2.

triplicate for each size (not shown) we moved forward with this size pellet for all subsequent electrochemical tests.

The six different FeS_2 powders investigated all performed differently when discharged at a constant current (Figure 2A). When discriminating performance of the cells, four voltage regimes were chosen to quantify capacity; > 1.92 V (transient voltage and capacity), 1.8 – 1.5 V (high voltage), 1.5 – 0.5 V (first transition $FeS_2 \rightarrow Li_3Fe_2S_4$), 0.5 V (voltage cutoff, total capacity). These regions are marked in Figure 2B. In Table 1 the capacities of the various regions of the discharge are given for each sample.

The same constant current discharge profile was then used on the six different materials but with a 1 hr open circuit voltage (OCV) hold before sourcing a current. The capacity values from this discharge profile are recorded in Table 2. Except in sample 2, every capacity has decreased after the heating during the 1 hr OCV. This is unsurprising given the known phenomenon of self-discharge in FeS_2 based MSBs.[1] The largest percent change of capacity loss due to heating was in the transient regime. Represented in Figure 3A, in cells heated for 1 hr essentially no transient capacity was produced. This tracked with a similar trend of a decrease in

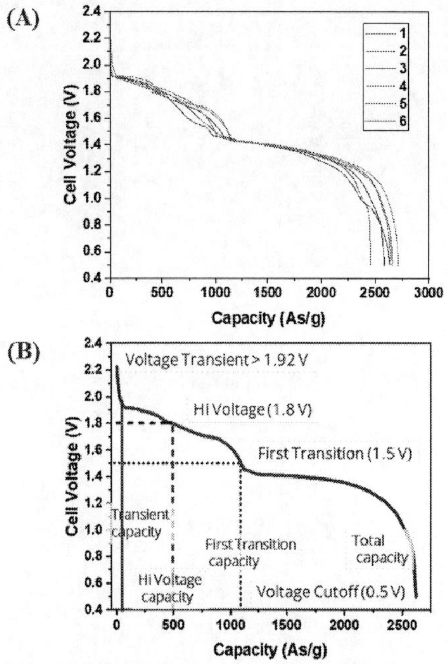

Figure 2. (A) Constant current 1 C discharge comparison six different FeS_2 cathodes. **(B)** Voltage cutoffs and the associated capacity regimes used to analyze the MSB discharge curves.

maximum voltage produced by the cell under load. A decrease in maximum voltage and loss of transient capacity indicates impurities or iron phases reacted at an elevated temperature. It should be noted that only sample 5, with the highest voltage and transient capacity, showed any contaminants (Zn, As, Cu, Al) above 1000 ppm when analyzed by elemental analysis. The consistent maximum voltage from each sample after the preheat indicates a stabilization of the FeS_2 polarization with a lower potential phase.

Ideally an FeS_2 cathode would not lose any capacity upon reaching the operating temperature of the MSB, but most

Table 1. Utilized capacity (As/g) of cells at different voltage regimes from a constant current 1 C discharge.

Sample	Transient Capacity (>1.92 V)	+/-	Hi Voltage (1.8 V)	+/-	First Transition (1.5 V)	+/-	Total Capacity (0.5 V)	+/-
1	23.8	2.2	480	30	1062	15	2560	53
2	16.74	0.44	474	24	994	68	2514	140
3	34.9	4.4	523	49	995	45	2560	89
4	9.9	2.8	455	25	1159	39	2684	42
5	69.6	1.7	577	6	1019	22	2512	52
6	24.03	0.52	425	25	1122	10	2699	11

Table 2. Utilized capacity (As/g) of cells that underwent 1 hr at 500°C before discharging at a 1 C rate.

Sample	Transient Capacity (>1.92 V)	+/-	Hi Voltage (1.8 V)	+/-	First Transition (1.5 V)	+/-	Total Capacity (0.5 V)	+/-
1	0.16895	0.00043	371	42	874	29	2510	14
2	0.1599	0.0079	481	25	953	53	2602	39
3	0.16886	0.00012	389	30	812	37	2393	58
4	0.085	0.029	352	16	851	7	2319	118
5	0.95	0.39	354	5	750	18	2378	35
6	0.173	0.020	332	56	935	12	2610	30

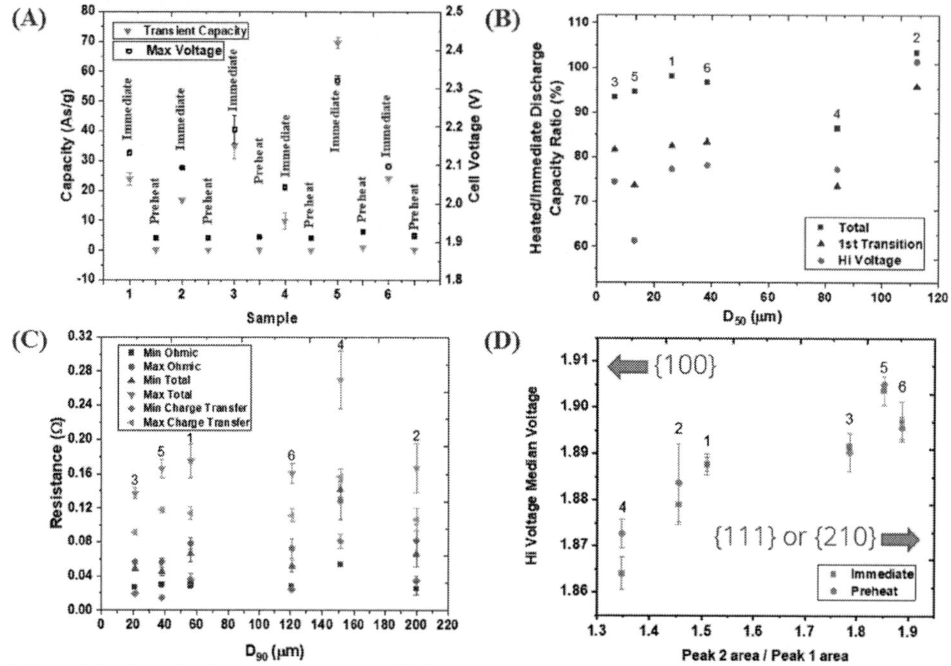

Figure 3. (A) Plot of the transient capacity above 1.92 V and the maximum cell voltage during an applied load. Each sample has four associated points, the two above the sample number are from the immediate constant current discharge and the points to the right are from the preheat discharges. **(B)** Scatter of the capacity ratio of the preheat discharge to immediate discharge compared against the average FeS_2 particle size in microns. **(C).** Resistance values of samples plotted versus the D_{90} particle size in microns. **(D)** Plot of the high voltage median voltage versus the peak area ratio (A_g/E_g).

electrodes suffer from active material loss. Figure 3B shows the capacity ratio of the heated and immediately discharged cells vs average particle size, where a larger percentage indicates less capacity loss from the 1 hr OCV hold at 500°C. capacity. However, sample 2 retained above 95% of these capacities. This led sample 2 to have the best high voltage capacity after preheating, even though it ranked fourth in this category when immediately discharged. Most materials preform similarly, losing 75-85% of the high voltage and first transition.

When comparing the capacity retention ratio, as seen in Figure 3B, a clear trend did not emerge with particle size. Sample 2, which had the best retention, has the largest average particle size but sample 4, which has the second largest average particle size did not have a better retention than smaller FeS_2 samples 3, 1, or 6. Powders with larger particles having better retention would be expected due to the increase in temperature of degradation observed in thermogravimetric analysis (not shown).

In pristine cells the six FeS_2 samples were discharged using a pulse protocol to acquire information about the cell resistance. The minimum and maximum calculated resistance values for the six samples is shown in Figure 3C. By comparing against the D_{90} particle size none of the resistance values follow a particular trend. Samples 6 and 2 show similar resistance values to powders containing largest particles which are less than half the size. Sample 4 had the highest resistance of any sample, indicating that there is not a direct correlation between the largest particle size and resistance or there are unique properties of samples 2 and 6.

Raman spectroscopy is a valuable tool to look at polarizable bonds in materials. Pyrite is known to have active vibrational modes including the sulfur bend (E_g) and sulfur stretch (A_g).[2] demonstrated that the ratio of these two peaks correlated with the predominant exposed Miller index faces of particles in the FeS_2 powder. Reference 3 showed that crystals irradiated by a normal incident laser a peak ratio closer to 1 indicated an exposed {100} faces and values of 1.8 and 2.1 were collected for {111} and {210}. When this ratio was calculated for the six samples the strongest trend emerged when compared to the high voltage median voltage (Figure 3D). The samples with lower average voltage values have lower ratios. This includes sample 4 with the lowest peak ratio, indicating an exposed {100} faces, and lowest median high voltage. The exposed crystal orientation only impacting the high voltage regime makes intuitive sense since as the exposed FeS_2 reacts first leaving the remaining particle to discharge without a preferred directionality.

The lack of correlation between electrochemical and particle size, thermal, and structural analysis is an unexpected result. The general absence of trends in the data presented above, when examined exclusively, implies another factor or certain combination of factors is controlling the FeS_2 discharge behavior. Images of the six samples were taken with a scanning electron microscope (SEM) to identify particle morphology (Figure 4). While samples 1, 3, 4, and

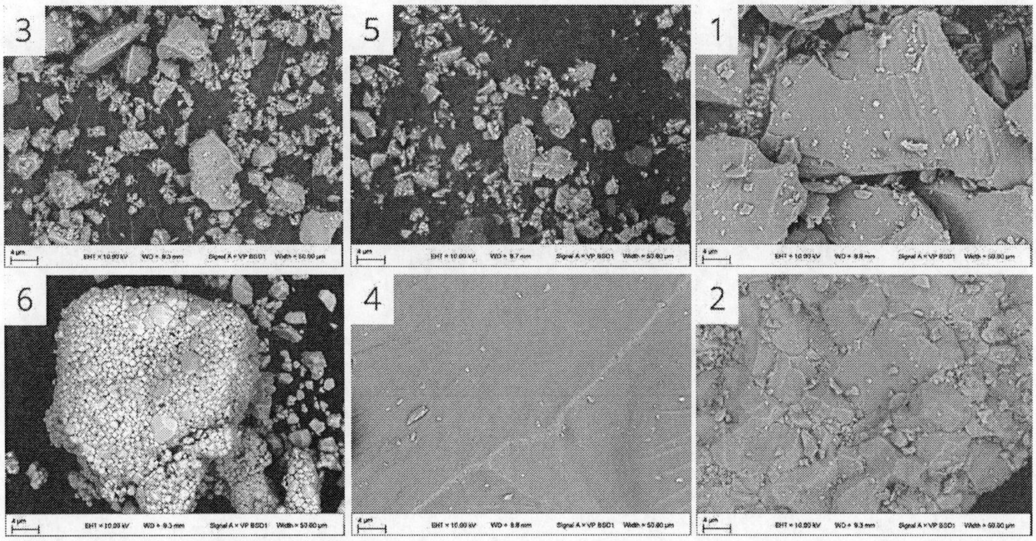

Figure 4. SEM images of the six FeS_2 powders shown in increasing average particle size (left to right). All images were taken under the same magnification, scale bar is 4 μm.

5 share the similar appearance of a broken-up crystal, samples 2 and 6 display different surface morphologies. Sample 6 appears to have the highest surface area and the particles are agglomerates of smaller FeS_2 structures. Sample 2 has a rougher surface than samples 1, 3, 4, and 5. The greater surface area of samples 6 and 2 is likely the reason why these samples have resistance values closer to the smaller particles. The larger particle size and high surface area characteristics could also play an essential role in sample 2 and 6, which have the largest high voltage and first transition capacities retentions after heating at 500°C for 1hr. SEM characterization of particles enables discrimination between vendors' products not achievable through more quantitative methods.

Conclusion

Six different FeS_2 powders were investigated for use as the active material in molten salt battery cathodes. Single cells were discharged using three current profiles to evaluate the electrochemical performance of the various pyrites. The voltage, capacity, and resistance taken from these tests were compared to chemical and physical analyses of the powders. Some trends emerged, but no single chemical or physical feature of the FeS_2 powders could fully explain the cell discharge performance. However, when using particle size and surface structure metrics, the voltage and capacity retention are rationalized.

Acknowledgements

Sandia National Laboratories is a multimission laboratory managed and operated by National Technology & Engineering Solutions of Sandia, LLC, a wholly owned subsidiary of Honeywell International Inc., for the U.S. Department of Energy's National Nuclear Security Administration under contract DE-NA0003525. This paper describes objective technical results and analysis. Any subjective views or opinions that might be expressed in the paper do not necessarily represent the views of the U.S. Department of Energy or the United States Government.

This article has been authored by an employee of National Technology & Engineering Solutions of Sandia, LLC under Contract No. DE-NA0003525 with the U.S. Department of Energy (DOE). The employee owns all right, title and interest in and to the article and is solely responsible for its contents. The United States Government retains and the publisher, by accepting the article for publication, acknowledges that the United States Government retains a non-exclusive, paid-up, irrevocable, world-wide license to publish or reproduce the published form of this article or allow others to do so, for United States Government purposes. The DOE will provide public access to these results of federally sponsored research in accordance with the DOE Public Access Plan https://www.energy.gov/downloads/doe-public-access-plan.

The authors wish to thank Linda Johnson, Alan Harrington, Bertha Montoya, and Martin Salazar for technical input.

References

1. Masset, P.J., Guidotti, R.A., "Thermal activated ("thermal") battery technology Part IIIa: FeS_2 cathode material" J Power Sources, vol. 177, pp. 595-609, 2008.
2. Vogt, H., Chattopadhyay, T., Stoltz, H.J., "Complete First-order Raman Spectra of the Pyrite Structure Compounds FeS_2, MnS_2, and SiP_2," J. Phys. Chem Solids, vol. 44, no. 9, pp 869-873, 1983.
3. Bryant, R.N., Pasteris, J.D., Fike, D.A., "Variability in the Raman Spectrum of Unpolished Growth and Fracture Surfaces of Pyrite Due to Laser Heating and Crystal Orientation," Applied Spectroscopy, vol. 72(1), pp. 37-47, 201

Enhanced Performance in Thermal Batteries Containing Nanostructured Cathode Materials

Lauren A. Morris[1*], Giuseppe L. Di Benedetto[1], David B. Swanson[2], Brian D. Wightman[2], Charles W. McMullan[1], Richard Dratler[1], Aaron Stern[1]

[1] U.S. Army Combat Capabilities Development Command Armaments Center, Picatinny Arsenal, NJ 07806
[2] EnerSys Advanced Systems, Inc., 104 Rock Road, Horsham, PA 19044.

*Contact Author Email: lauren.a.morris17.civ@army.mil / 973-724-1946

Abstract

The U.S. Army is developing advanced munitions systems that require higher power and larger current densities than what can be supplied by commercially available thermal batteries. Nanoscale materials have properties which differ significantly from their conventional counterparts due to their high specific surface area (SSA) and increased reaction rates. Incorporating nanomaterials into otherwise legacy power sources has the potential to provide the necessary performance improvements, such as higher voltages at increased current densities. Particle size reduction via high energy milling (HEM) is one way to shift the primary particle size of a material into the nanoscale. Brittle materials such as iron disulfide, FeS_2, mill quite readily and so very high SSA is attainable, and with very little contamination.

Previously, U.S. Army Combat Capabilities Development Command Armaments Center (DEVCOM-AC) and EnerSys Advanced Systems, Inc. jointly reported on an optimized, high SSA, nanostructured FeS_2 for thermal battery manufacturing synthesized via HEM. In that work, performance improvements were realized using nanostructured FeS_2 at the single cell level. In this study, full lithium primary reserve multi-cell batteries were built with nanostructured catholyte made from nanoscale FeS_2, as well as with standard catholyte, and blends thereof. The battery prototypes were built with different thermal balances and end-heating configurations and the electrochemical performance was characterized during discharge testing and polarization type scans. It was determined that full prototype batteries built with the nanostructured FeS_2 have higher voltage performance and higher current handling capacity than the legacy batteries. However, data from the electrochemical testing of the different end heat configurations indicates that a fully optimized thermal balance for the nanostructured cathode material has not yet been fully achieved.

Keywords

nanomaterials, thermal battery, molten salt battery, cathode, nanoscale, iron disulfide, polarization, milling

Introduction

The thermal battery is the chosen power source for many critical defense weapons systems due to its long shelf life and high power density. The defense industry continues to produce more sophisticated munitions and longer-range weapons systems, which has triggered a high demand signal for advanced thermal batteries that can provide higher voltages and longer run times as compared to the current commercial, off-the-shelf batteries.

New material solutions are being investigated to design and develop thermal batteries with superior performance that will meet future munition power requirements. One such solution is the use of nanostructured and nanoscale cathode materials as a direct replacement for conventional cathodes. Recently, the use of nanoscale iron disulfide (n-FeS_2) has been reported by many research groups. Improved performance and nanomaterial properties were reported including increased total power density, increased run time, and increased robustness of electrode pellets, all attributed to the ultra-small particle size (<100 nm) of the FeS_2 [1]. Additionally, single cell thermal battery (SCTB) testing demonstrated higher maximum cell voltages and longer run time using n-FeS_2 (< 100 nm) in place of standard micron-sized FeS_2 (μ-FeS_2) [2]. While n-FeS_2 has been synthesized by chemical hydrothermal synthesis [3,4], high energy ball milling [2,5,6] has been employed more recently. Previously, our group has reported scale up of high energy ball milling, fully characterized the chemical and physical properties of n-FeS_2 and demonstrated performance benefits of using n-FeS_2 in place of μ-FeS_2 in single cell thermal battery testing [2]. In this study, we explore the use of high energy milled n-FeS_2 as a replacement for standard μ-FeS_2 in full scale battery prototypes, using the commercial G3190B2 battery as a model system.

Experimental

Cathode Preparation and Characterization

High energy ball milling was used to synthesize n-FeS_2 from commercially available micron-sized powder using previously reported milling conditions [2]. All powders were stored in an inert argon environment with less than 10 ppm oxygen and water. Catholyte powders were produced using micron and nanoscale FeS_2 as previously reported [2,6]. The resultant micron and nanostructured catholyte powders were pressed into micron cathode (μ-cathode) and nano cathode (n-cathode) pellets, respectively. In this study we also investigated cathodes synthesized from blends of the micron and nano FeS_2. Synthesis of the blended cathode pellets was identical except that the micron and nano FeS_2 powders were blended using resonant acoustic mixing prior to being mixed with the electrolyte. The blends of micron:nano that were investigated were 100/0, 75/25, 50/50, 25/75, and 0/100 by weight and are referred to herein as Blends A, B, C, D, and E, respectively.

The synthesized nanoscale FeS_2 powder properties were characterized using a variety of techniques. X-ray diffraction (XRD) was performed using a Rigaku Ultima with Cu-Kα source with MDI Jade software. Chemical analysis was performed using inductively coupled plasma optical emission spectroscopy (ICP-OES) and ASTM D1353 to determine Fe and S content by weight. The Barret-Emmet-Teller (B.E.T.) method for surface area analysis and particle size derivation was done using a Quantachrome Nova 4000e. Scanning Electron Microscopy (SEM) was performed using a Zeiss Supra V40 using in-lens and backscatter detectors at 15 kV. Particle size analysis was performed using a Horiba LA-950V2 to determine the d10, d50, and d90 on a volume basis.

Battery Design and Testing

Single cell thermal battery (SCTB) testing was performed as previously reported [2]. A constant 350 mAh discharge was applied to the cell for the entire discharge time with a 7 A by 500 ms pulse occurring every 60 seconds. Finally, full prototype batteries were built using micron and nano cathodes and blends thereof at EnerSys using their commercial thermal battery production line and standard methods. The anode and separator pellet chemistry, size, and compaction force were maintained consistent with the standard G3190B2 battery. Three different battery build groups and a total of 124 batteries were produced. Batteries were soaked to three temperatures: cold [-45 °F (-42.8 °C)], ambient, and hot [+160 °F (+71.1 °C)] and tested.

Results and Discussion

Cathode Preparation and Characterization

Six kilograms of high energy ball milled FeS_2 was synthesized from micron powder and analyzed; its properties were characteristic of those previously reported and are summarized in Table 1. The empirical formula was within the acceptable limit ($FeS_{2.129}$ – $FeS_{1.882}$); however, ICP analysis revealed an increase in the acid soluble iron (free iron) content in the milled powder as compared to the unmilled powder.

Table 1: Properties of micron and nano iron disulfide.

		μ-FeS_2	**n-FeS_2**
Empirical Formula		$FeS_{2.014}$	$FeS_{2.040}$
Acid Soluble (Fe_2O_3)	(%)	0.03	3.41
Specific Surface Area	(m^2/g)	0.512	19.561
BET Equivalent Diameter	(nm)	2493	65.0
Crystallite Size	(nm)	> 500	50.8

SEM images of cathode pellets synthesized from blends of micron and nano FeS_2 powders are shown in Figure 1 and illustrate that smaller length scales of mixing among the catholyte constituents exist with increased n-FeS_2 content.

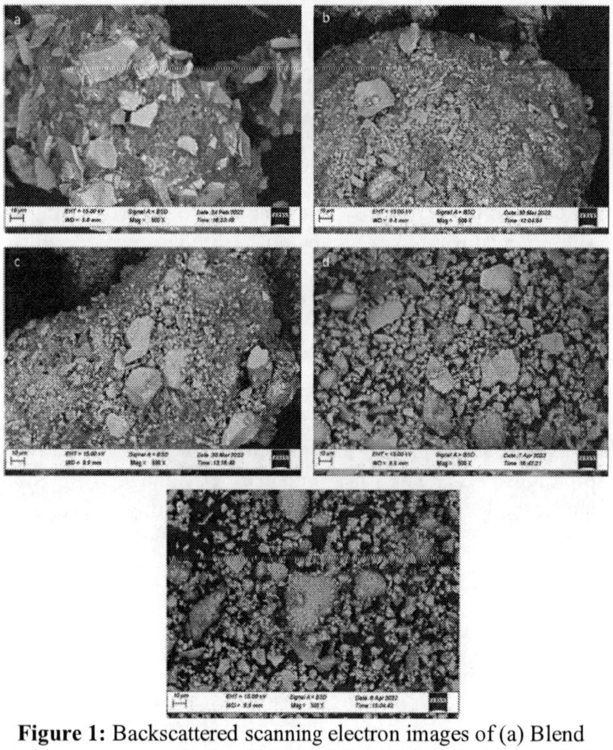

Figure 1: Backscattered scanning electron images of (a) Blend A/100% μ-FeS_2 catholyte, (b) Blend B, (c) Blend C, (d) Blend D, and (e) Blend E/100% n-FeS_2 catholyte powders.

Battery Design and Testing

Cathode, separator, and anode cells were prepared with Blends A-E cathodes and subjected to single cell capacity testing. The average cell voltage with respect to time is plotted in Figure 2. The Blend E/100% n-FeS_2 cell had the highest initial cell voltage, performed best under the pulse loads in the capacity test, and maintained the highest voltage under the background load for the first 6 minutes of discharge. Blends A and D performed best and second best, respectively, in the capacity tests under background load out to 14 minutes of discharge. Blends A, D, and E were therefore down selected for full battery builds in Battery Group 1.

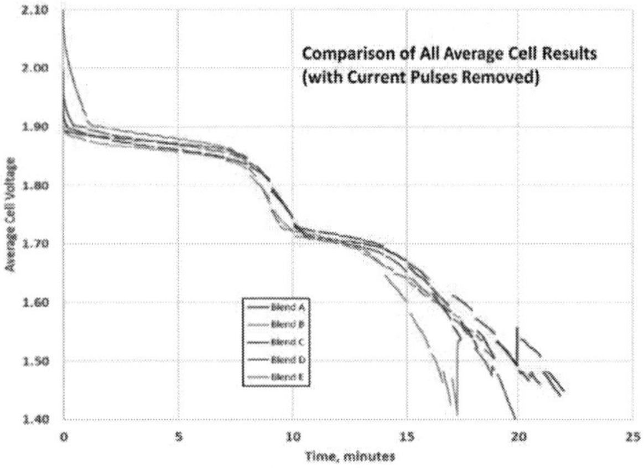

Figure 2: SCTB discharge testing of cells made of Blends A, B, C, D, and E with a 350 mAh background load current and a 500 ms 7A pulse every 60 seconds at 500 °C platen temperature.

A total of 36 Group 1 batteries were built (12 each of Blends A, D, and E) with identical cell stack configuration and pellet weights. Group 1 batteries were tested using a combined constant current and pulse discharge profile until the battery dropped to 1.5 V or 10 pulse cycles were achieved. Battery testing revealed that the batteries made with Blend A performed best at ambient and hot temperatures, while Blend E batteries performed best at cold temperature. Blend E batteries also demonstrated slightly better power capability than Blend A and D batteries. Ambient battery test data from Group 1 batteries is shown in Figure 3. The performance advantages of the nanocathode demonstrated in SCTB testing were not realized at the full battery level in Group 1 batteries.

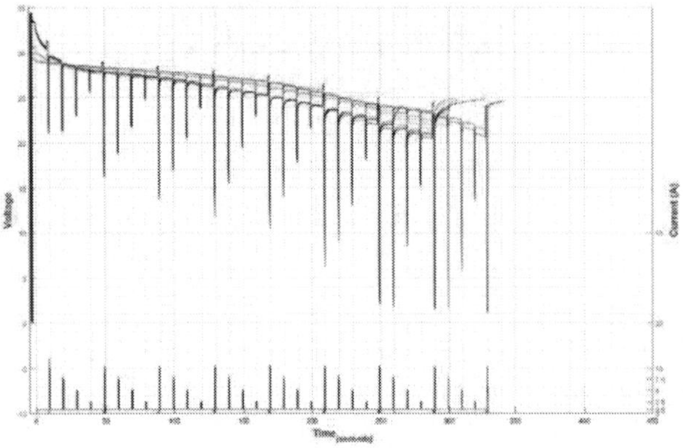

Figure 3: Voltage and current battery test data for batteries built with Blend A/100% μ-FeS_2 (red), Blend D (teal), and Blend E/100% n-FeS_2 (blue) cathodes.

It was hypothesized that the nanocathode may require design changes within the battery to maximize its capacity. A second group of batteries (Battery Group 2) was designed and built using only 100% $nFeS_2$. DEVCOM AC used a multi-physics simulator called Thermally Activated Battery Simulator (TABS) [7] to explore design changes and simulate predicted performance of batteries built with the nanocathode. Initial thermochemical simulations in TABS indicated that the nanocathode pellets may be overheating and so design options were explored which may lower the internal temperature of the molten nanocathode. A promising design, "Army V8" was identified which utilized an optimized end heat configuration that minimized local overheating of the ends of the cell stack. Simulations demonstrated that the optimized end heat configuration may protect the nanocathode pellets located near the end heat from instantaneous overheating when the battery is activated. A second potential design that was explored used a lower heat balance that was designed to run ten degrees lower (-10 °C) than the standard design.

A total of four (4) battery designs (48 batteries) were tested in Battery Group 2, all containing 100% nanocatholyte: Group 2.1 was built using the standard design, same as Battery Group 1, Blend E (control); Group 2.2 was built using the Army V8 design; Group 2.3 was built using the standard design but with lower heat balance; and Group 2.4 was built using the Army V8 design and lower heat balance. Twelve of each battery design were made and tested at cold [-45 °F (-42.8 °C)], ambient, and hot [+160 °F (+71.1 °C)]. The batteries built with the higher heat balance (Groups 2.1 and 2.2) performed best overall in run time and pulse performance at all temperatures. Batteries built with the Army V8 design configuration resulted in more consistent discharge performance and significantly reduced battery to battery performance variations.

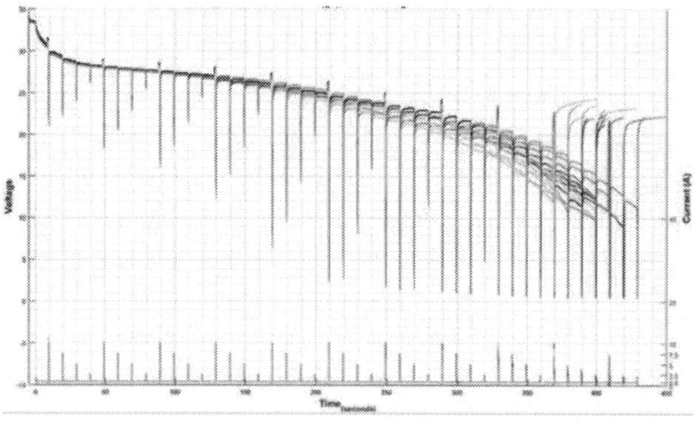

Figure 4: Voltage and current battery test data for batteries built with Group 2.1 (red), 2.2 (purple), 2.3 (cyan), and 2.4 (green) modified designs.

Finally, 40 batteries were built for Group 3 testing. Group 3.1 consisted of 24 batteries built with the Army V8 configuration and 100% nanocatholyte (same as Group 2.2) and Group 3.2 consisted of 12 batteries built with 100% micron catholyte and the Army V8 configuration. All batteries were tested with the same load profile at cold [-45 °F (-42.8 °C)], ambient, and hot [+160 °F (+71.1 °C) temperatures. Results from the battery testing indicated that the Army V8 design normalized the heating within the batteries in both Groups 3.1 and 3.2 and no evidence of overheating was observed. The Group 3.1 batteries performed best overall at the extreme cold temperature during background load and with high current pulses. The Group 3.1 (nanocatholyte) batteries consistently showed higher voltage response early in life at all temperatures as compared to the Group 3.2 (micron catholyte) batteries, but that response diminished 30-40 s into discharge. The Group 3.2 batteries outperformed the Group 3.1 batteries at ambient and hot temperatures for overall run time and voltage under the high current pulse load profile. The battery test results at ambient temperature are shown in Figure 5.

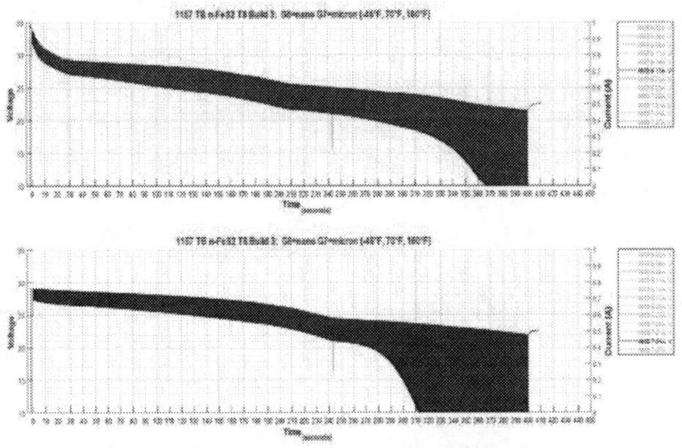

Figure 5: Voltage battery test data for Group 3.1 (top), and Group 3.2 (bottom) batteries built with the Army V8 configuration and 100% nano and 100% micron catholyte, respectively.

In all test cases explored here, batteries built with the nanocatholyte experienced higher initial cell voltage at the beginning of life. It remains unclear if this higher initial voltage is the result of the high specific surface area of the nanocathode material or if it is due to excess iron. Chemical analysis results shown in Table 1 reveal that high energy milling induces minor chemical changes in the FeS_2 cathode material, including an increased amount of excess acid soluble iron. If the high voltage is due to increased excess iron, then there would be a corresponding drop in cell/battery capacity as well, which is observed in many of the nano batteries tested in this effort (see Figures 3 and 5). Further optimization of the high energy milling process could minimize the formation of excess iron and should be explored in future studies.

Conclusion

The batteries built with 100 % n-FeS_2 perform better than the batteries built with 100 % μ-FeS_2 at cold temperature; however, at ambient and high temperature the batteries built with μ-FeS_2 perform best. There is no observed performance advantage in blending the n-FeS_2 and μ-FeS_2. An optimized cell stack design for the n-FeS_2 was necessary and was driven by M&S using TABS. No nano cathode decomposition was observed using the optimized Army V8 cell stack design which utilized an optimized end heat configuration. The nano batteries built with the Army V8 design performed better than the standard design and outperformed micron batteries built with the same configuration at extreme cold temperatures; but, the micron batteries performed better than the nano at ambient and extreme hot temperatures. The work discussed here comes closer to achieving performance improvements demonstrated for the n-FeS_2 previously in SCTB testing in full scale batteries and demonstrates a clear performance enhancement using n-FeS_2 for applications in extreme cold environments. However, more work should be done to further optimize cell stacking and n-FeS_2 chemistry to maximize nano cathode performance in a full battery.

Acknowledgements

This work is supported by the Power for Advanced Munitions effort on DEVCOM-AC's Fuze and Power Technologies for Munitions program.

References

1. Au, M., Y. Lei, and T. Yadav, "Thermal Batteries Made with Nanostructured Material," *NASA Tech Briefs*, vol. 23, no. 4, pp. 28-29, April 1999.
2. Morris, L.A., Di Benedetto, G.L., Swanson, D., Wightman, B., et.al, "Advanced Nanostructuring and Enhanced Performance of Thermal Battery Cathode Materials," *Proceedings of the 48th Power Sources Conference*, pp.476-479, 2018.
3. Guidotti, R. A., F. W. Reinhardt, J. Dai, and D. E. Reisner, "Preparation and Characterization of Synthetic Pyrite for Thermal-Battery Cathodes," *Proceedings of 40th Power Sources Conference*, p. 339, 2002.
4. Guidotti, R. A., P. J. Nigrey, F. W. Reinhardt, and J. G. Odinek, "Evaluation of Nanoparticulate Metal Disulfides in Thermal Batteries," *Proceedings of 40th Power Sources Conference*, p. 250, 2002.
5. Au, M., "Nanostructured Thermal Batteries with High Power Density," *Journal of Power Sources*, vol. 115, pp. 360-366, 2003.
6. Di Benedetto, G. L., R. Carpenter, D. Swanson, and B. Wightman, "Enhanced Nanostructuring of Iron Disulfide for Thermal Battery Cathode Materials," *Proceedings of 46th Power Sources Conference*, pp. 469-472, 2014.
7. Roberts, S.A., et.al., "TABS: A Thermal Battery Desktop Design Tool," *Proceedings of the 48th Power Sources Conference*, Denver, CO, 11-14 June, 2018.

High Voltage Cathode Battery Development

[1]Nathan V. Moss, [1]Jim J. Ferraro and [2]Joe Edington
[1] EaglePicher Technologies, 1215 West C Street Joplin, MO 64801
[2]CFD Research Corporation, 701 McMillian Way NW, Suite D, Huntsville, AL 35806
Contact Author Email: nathan.moss@eaglepicher.com

Abstract

As with any power source, the pressure to provide more energy in a smaller package is just as real in thermal batteries. Improvements in insulation materials and additives have greatly influenced the state of the art. However, greater gains will need to come from a fundamental transformation in the basic electrochemistry used. Since CFD Research Company's roll out of the High Voltage Cathode EaglePicher has been moving toward using the material in batteries. This paper presents the results of the battery development effort to produce two production ready designs using the High Voltage Cathode with the associated electrolyte. These results include inertial activation tests as well as discharge into power loads at temperature extremes.

Keywords

Thermal Batteries: high voltage cathode; power load; HVC

Introduction

For many years, molten salt batteries have mainly been developed and manufactured around lithium or lithium alloy anodes with iron disulfide or cobalt disulfide cathodes. While these systems were great improvements to the state of the art when they came about, increased demands for even more power in smaller packages has found them wanting. The ever-increasing prevalence of programs requiring power loads, as opposed to resistive or current loads, can be especially difficult as electrochemical discharge reduces voltage which, in turn, increases the current demand to sustain the same power. Taken another way: in aggressively sized batteries space is valuable and has to be used judiciously.

One of the best solutions to this vicious loop is to be able to increase the voltage in each cell. The resulting space saved from the reduced number of cells can be used to increase the electrochemical capacity. CFD Research Corporation's High Voltage Cathode (HVC) provides one such solution [1] with a baseline of 2.6 volts per cell is a significant improvement over the 1.85 volts of FeS_2 cell. The height of the cell stacks in a battery can be reduced by 30% thereby increasing the capacity which gives the batteries a longer operating life. Successful single cell tests with current loads are a great start. Power loads in batteries tested at temperature extremes is the next logical step.

Starting Out

It was generally accepted that this Li (Alloy)/HVC couple would not to be an interchangeable replacement for the Li(Alloy)/Iron Disulfide system. Results would need to be interpreted in the light of a potential new paradigm.

As this was also the first time the HVC and associated electrolyte were blended at EaglePicher instead of CFD Research Corporation, the development goals also included demonstrating manufacturability by producing batch sizes capable of supporting low rate initial production (LRIP) battery production and demonstrating flow and fill capability for all materials on automated presses at EaglePicher.

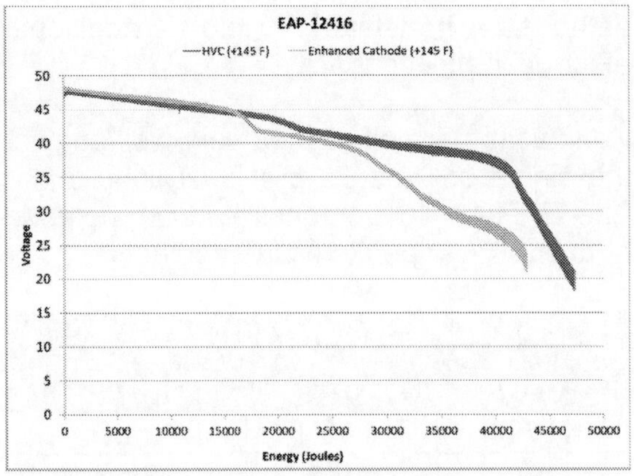

Figure 1: EAP-12416 high temperature tests of HVC compared to the Enhanced Cathode.

Design Approach

EaglePicher sought to develop two batteries, the electric igniter activated EAP-12416 and the inertial igniter activated SAP-12417. The EAP-12416 uses EaglePicher's EP-250-1 electric igniter where the SAP-12417 utilizes the EP-1205 inertial igniter to provide battery activation upon application of a prescribed shock pulse. In either case, the igniter fires through a center hole directly igniting the heat pellets.

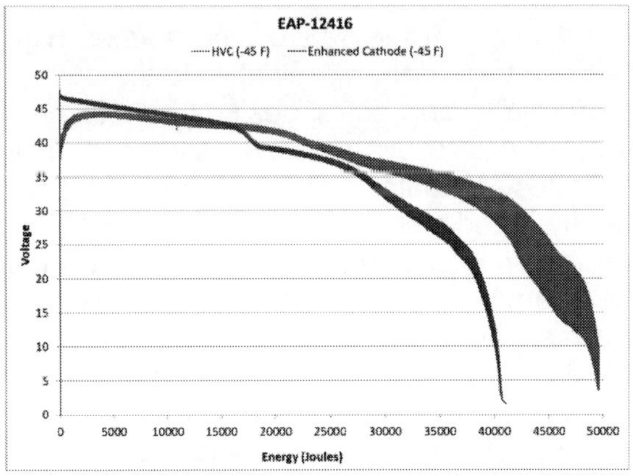

Figure 2: EAP-12416 low temperature tests of HVC compared to the Enhanced Cathode.

Both batteries are identically sized with additional volume allowed outside the SAP-12417 header to accommodate the length of the inertial igniter. Although tested to different load profiles, these batteries require essentially the same electrochemical capacity. While both loads are power loads they differ slightly in the application. The EAP-12416 is tested with power pulses at a 50% duty cycle applied on top of a power base load. The load for the SAP-12417 is several increasing constant power loads.

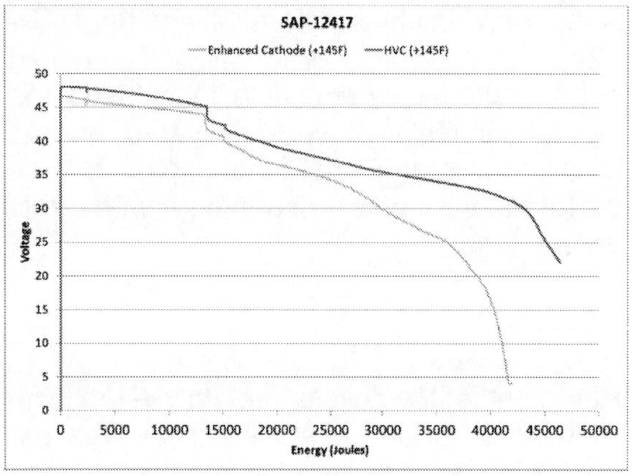

Figure 3: SAP-12417 high temperature tests of HVC compared to the Enhanced Cathode.

Initial development included a parallel path for both batteries that utilized EaglePicher's enhanced Iron Disulfide cathode with additives [2]. Eventually, this alternate design was no longer pursued in favor of the HVC designs that exhibited much better performance by supporting the required load with a higher voltage for a longer duration.

Having similar performance lifetimes, the same insulation arrangements were used on both batteries. This was also facilitated by both batteries as well as both electro-chemistries using the same cell size.

Development

Performance testing of each prototype occurred after sufficient temperature conditioning at the temperature extremes of -45°F to +145°F. Two high voltage-stable electrolytes have been developed and demonstrated by CFD Research: a high rate, all-lithium salt electrolyte, and a lower melting electrolyte to extend operating life and improve rise times for batteries using high voltage cathode materials. Both of these electrolyte formulations were tested. However, the all-lithium formulation was found to provide the best results. Alternately, the design advantages of the lower melting electrolyte were not found to be necessary to meet the desired lifetime in the required size.

After a few initial test iterations of the SAP-12417 in an electrically activated configuration the remaining tests used the inertial igniter and were activated on the shock tower at EaglePicher. No adverse performance , was observed with this advancement.

Results

At the end of the development cycle the High Voltage Cathode electrochemistry was the only path to provide the required power within the required volume. As can be seen in the voltage versus discharge energy plots (see Figures 1-4), initial voltage plots for both the High Voltage and Enhanced cathodes are nearly identical. The difference, however, is at around 20,000 Joules of discharge the HVC design maintains greater voltage. This is a direct result of the space savings of the high voltage

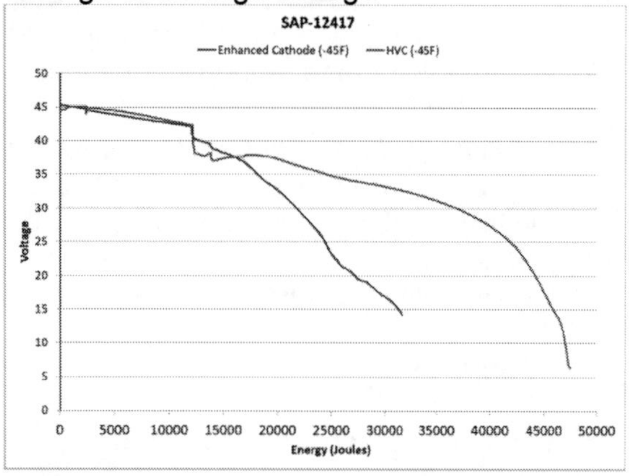

Figure 4: SAP-12417 low temperature tests of HVC compared to the Enhanced Cathode.

cathode translated into additional electrochemical capacity.

Peak volts per cell aligned very well against the single cell results previously published. The EAP-12416 demonstrated an increase of over 30% in peak volts per cell.

EAP-12416		
Cathode	**Temp**	**Volts/Cell**
HVC	+145°F	2.66
HVC	-45°F	2.53
Enhanced	+145°F	1.96
Enhanced	-45°F	1.91

Similarly, the SAP-12417 showed slightly better increases of 33%-44% at the low and high temperatures, respectively.

SAP-12417		
Cathode	**Temp**	**Volts/Cell**
HVC	+145°F	2.67
HVC	-45°F	2.51
Enhanced	+145°F	1.85
Enhanced	-45°F	1.89

Safety

In advance of the S9310 test regimen high temperature open circuit tests were performed on both designs in fixtures indicative of a tactical next assembly. The voltages of both units peaked and then gently rolled off without experiencing cell to cell shorting seen in thermal runaway events with complete voltage decay occurring in just over an hour (reference Figures 5 and 6). Maximum case temperature of both designs remained below 150 °C. This type of uneventful roll off is not typical of thermal batteries in general and especially not the case in aggressively sized batteries like the EAP-12416 and SAP-12417, but has been experienced with the High Voltage Cathode.

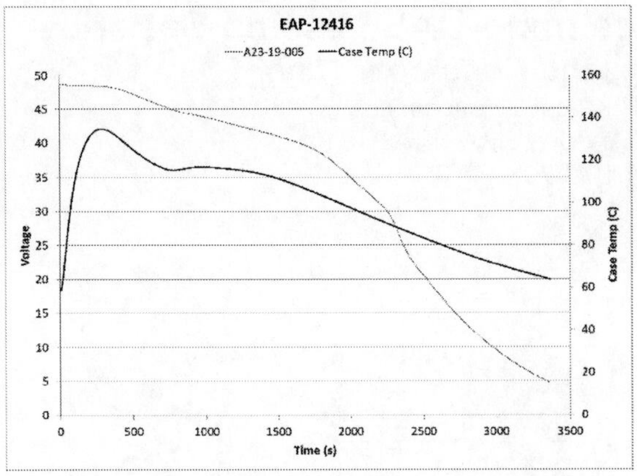

Figure 5: EAP-12416 tested open circuit with case temperature.

Next Steps

At the time of this writing both the EAP-12416 and the SAP-12417 are undergoing a sequence of non-operating and operating environmental tests.

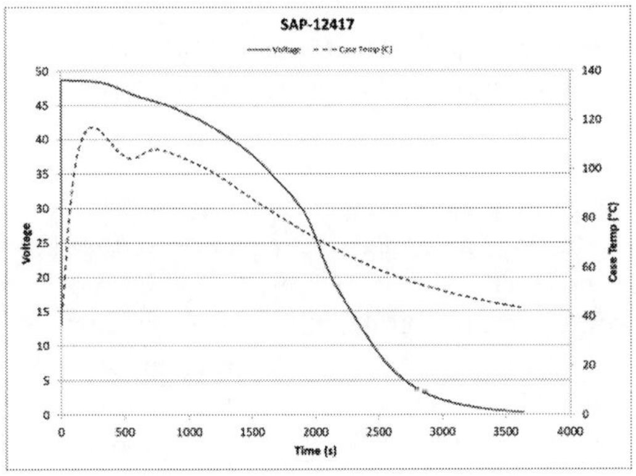

Figure 6: SAP-12417 tested open circuit with case temperature.

Also, the authors intend to revisit some of the initial larger battery HVC experiments incorporating the discoveries from the current effort.

Currently, plans are being made to construct a full rate production scale facility to produce the High Voltage Cathode and the corresponding electrolyte at EaglePicher.

Conclusion

CFD Research Corporation's High Voltage Cathode is demonstrating the capability to be a solution to greater energy densities in thermal batteries. Greater voltage per cell yields an opportunity for smaller batteries, greater energy densities or, perhaps, some combination of the two.

Acknowledgements

This work was performed in support of U.S. Army Contract W15QKN-20-F-0248

References

[1] Edington, J. *et al. Novel Materials for High Voltage Thermal Batteries* 48th Power Sources Conference, Paper 25-1, 2018.

[2] Swift, G. *et al.* (2014). *Thermal Battery Cathode Materials Containing Nickel Disulfide and Batteries Including Same* (U.S. Patent No. 8,652,674 B2). U.S. Patent and Trademark Office

Rapid Development of High Endurance nano-UAS Mission Batteries

James Pander, Devon Shedden, and Christopher Lang
Imperia Batteries, a division of Physical Sciences Inc.,
20 New England Business Center, Andover, MA USA 01810
jpander@psicorp.com / 1-978-738-2257

Abstract
Physical Sciences Inc. (PSI)'s Imperia Batteries division developed and demonstrated a high energy density Li-ion battery with a silicon nano-wire anode targeted for nano-unmanned aerial systems (nUAS). This included development of the cell design to address the size, weight, and energy requirements of nUAS vehicles, scale-up of the chemical vapor deposition (CVD) process to produce anode active material for the effort, a thorough screening of cathode materials to find one that meets the performance requirements, cell production, thorough electrochemical validation, and delivery of 20 prototype cells to the customer.

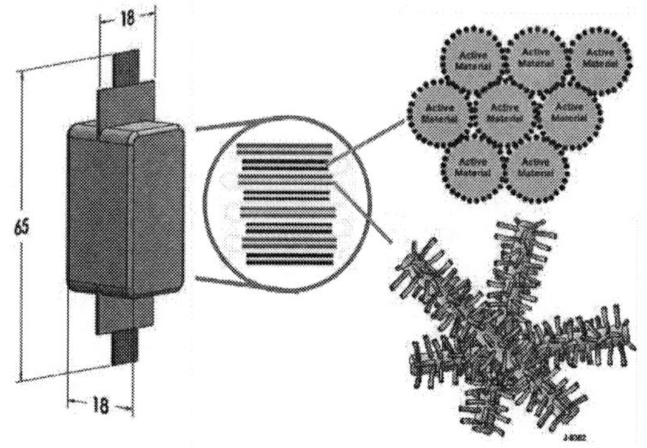

Figure 1. Schematic design of Imperia's nUAS cell design with equivalent length, width, and height to an 18650. Pop-outs illustrate the component cathode and anode technologies employed to improve energy density over commercial solutions.

Key Words
Silicon anode; high energy density; nano-UAS; nano-UAV; 18650

Introduction and Prior Work
In order to improve mission duration and flight time of nano-unmanned aerial systems (nUAS) and maximize soldier field effectiveness, it is necessary to develop high energy density battery technologies. To that end Physical Sciences Inc's Imperia Batteries® division developed a high energy density battery solution targeted for nUAS applications. The initial form factor for the battery was determined to fit within the length, width, and height of a standard 18650 cell so that one-to-one comparisons to commercial cells could be straightforwardly made. Figure 1 demonstrates an initial conceptual cell design, as well as the component technologies that enabled the improved energy density of the system at such a small form-factor.

In order to improve cell level energy density, Imperia leveraged patented cathode and anode technologies, as well as a larger-scale baseline UAS cell and battery design. Imperia Batteries® has designed and produced 185 Wh UN certified Mission Batteries for use in military small-Unmanned Aerial System (sUAS).[5] The Mission Battery was developed and delivered in <12 months and improves vehicle endurance over consumer-off-the-shelf (COTS) solutions by 100%.[1] Utilizing this current product as a design baseline, Imperia resized the cell and incorporated supporting technologies to improve vehicle endurance in nano-UAS vehicles. On the cathode side, Imperia's high active (HA) coating technology enables the design of a battery that delivers the required energy and power density by maximizing the active content in the electrodes.[2,3] This technology minimizes the required electrode thicknesses, reducing the electrolyte required and maximizing rate performance by decreasing ion transport distances. The HA coating was applied to commercial high energy cathode materials, enabling an increase in energy density of the cells by 10-12% while requiring less cathode material.[2,3] On the anode side, Imperia employs a patented composite silicon anode material that is formed by growing silicon whiskers on a commercially carbon substrate.[3,4] This Si anode material has been demonstrated to have a tailorable reversible capacity >1200 mAh/g-composite. Imperia has developed custom electrolyte blends and formation procedures that enable high energy designs with good cycle life.[4,5]

Prototype Cell Design and Build
To increase the cell capacity and energy, a high energy cathode material was used. Imperia screened a number of commercial high capacity cathode

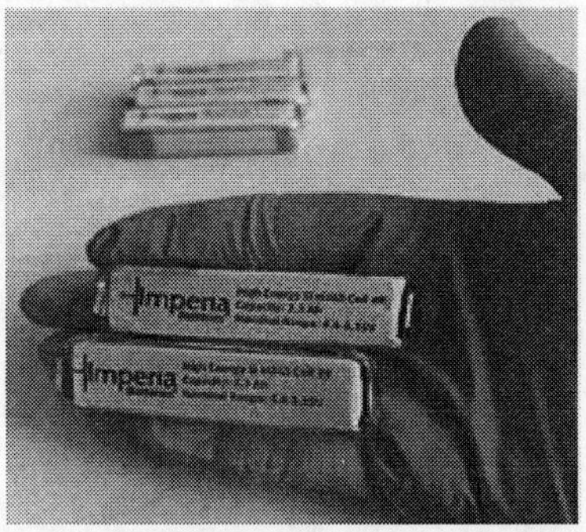

Figure 2. nUAS Cells achieving >300 Wh/kg. Cell weight <31 grams with equivalent size (LxWxH) to 18650 battery.

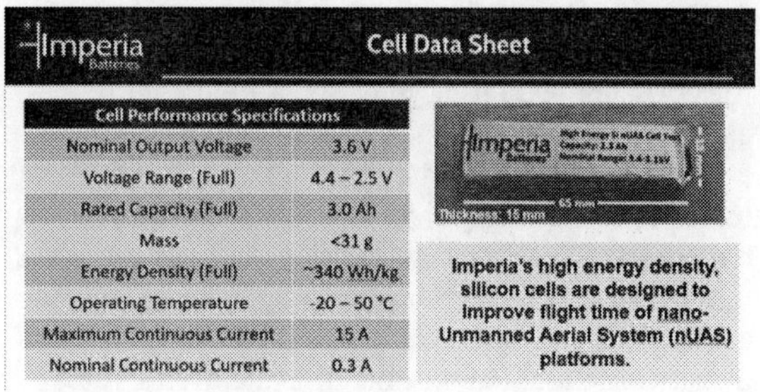

Imperia Batteries — Cell Data Sheet

Cell Performance Specifications	
Nominal Output Voltage	3.6 V
Voltage Range (Full)	4.4 – 2.5 V
Rated Capacity (Full)	3.0 Ah
Mass	<31 g
Energy Density (Full)	~340 Wh/kg
Operating Temperature	-20 – 50 °C
Maximum Continuous Current	15 A
Nominal Continuous Current	0.3 A

Figure 3. Cell Specifications for Imperia's high energy density Si nUAS cell.

materials against the performance targets (energy density, cycle life, rate performance, temperature performance, etc.). Imperia's HA coating was applied to the selected commercial NCM 811 material. Imperia has previously demonstrated that the HA cathode coating supports an increase in the active percent of the cathode material, allowing for thinner electrodes and higher energy densities.[2,3] The initial slurry consisted of 99% HA coated active material and a solids loading >80%.[2,3] The slurries were cast onto an aluminum current collector, and the cast thickness was controlled by a doctor blade for R&D cells and an automated slot-die coating machine for deliverable cells. The electrodes were dried under vacuum at 100 °C overnight. After drying, the electrodes were calendared to a final density of >3.5 g/cc and punched to the target electrode shape.

Imperia's patented silicon composite material is produced through a CVD reaction where silicon is grown off of a graphite-based precursor.[4,5] The precursor uses nanoparticles that are adhered to a graphite surface by mechanical mixing. During the CVD process the precursor interacts with gaseous silane forming a liquid eutectic to grow solid nanowhiskers on the graphite substrate.[4,5] The formation of whiskers improves the performance of the silicon anode due to the single crystal direction growth of the whisker and the direct connection path to a conductive current collector. The nanoparticle size defines the width of the whiskers and the population of nanoparticles on the graphite surface define the packing density of the whiskers.[4,5] To ensure that the anode material produces a sufficiently smooth slurry, the material produced by CVD was mechanically sieved. Anode electrode rolls were prepared by casting using a slurry consisting of 85 wt% silicon composite material. The slurry was cast onto a copper current collector with the cast thickness controlled by a doctor blade. Prior to use, the electrodes were dried under vacuum at 100 °C overnight and then punched to the target electrode shape.

Pouch cells were produced by manually stacking electrodes in alternating cathode/anode pairs between a commercial Celgard separator material. The woven electrode stacks were welded together using ultra-sonic welding to the external terminals. The cells were then heat sealed in an aluminized Mylar pouch material which was pre-formed to accommodate the thickness of the electrode stack. Cells were initialized by the introduction of electrolyte to the cell, followed by vacuum diffusion cycles to ensure thorough wetting.

A limited number of prototype cells was produced and delivered for evaluation, with examples shown in Figure 2 and a summary of cell specifications shown in Figure 3. Cells provide 10.4 Wh (3.0 Ah) when fully discharged. Cells were characterized for size, mass, and energy density.

Performance Results and Discussion

When discharged at a standard C/10 rate from 4.4 V to 2.5 V, Imperia's nUAS cells provide *ca.* 10.4 Wh and 3.0 Ah, corresponding to an energy density of 337 Wh/kg (Figure 4).

The ability of the cell to support high current discharges (i.e. high power operation) is important for UAS applications. Typically, as higher currents are drawn from a cell, the capacity (and therefore energy) that is delivered by the battery is reduced due to due to increasingly challenging ion transport conditions. This effect can be seen very clearly in the initial voltage drop when increasingly larger currents are applied. It is not sufficient to raise the energy density baseline if at the operational currents very little capacity is retained. Therefore, to improve vehicle flight times, rate/power performance must also be considered.

Figure 5 shows discharge curves for Imperia's nUAS cell discharged between 4.4 V and 2.0 V at various rates between C/10 to 5C. For the target 3 Ah cell, a 5C rate corresponds to a current draw of 15 A, which is the target maximum current draw. As expected, as the current increases, the voltage drops due to cell resistance, lowering the capacity retention of the cell for a given lower voltage cutoff. At a 1C rate (a full discharge in 1 hour), the cell retains approximately 75% of the baseline capacity, whereas at 5C only 20% of the baseline capacity is retained. Dependent on the shutoff voltage for the vehicle, decreasing the lower voltage limit can allow for additional capacity to be utilized at high currents.

In order to provide reliability and expand mission capabilities, the ability to utilize nUAS cells across a range of hot and cold temperatures is of interest. Discharge capacity at elevated temperature matched or exceeded the room temperature performance without noticeable generation of gas. At cold temperatures, discharge capacity was decreased due

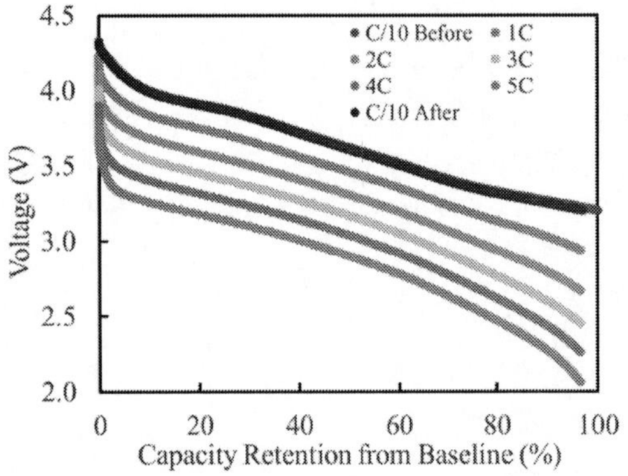

Figure 5. Discharge curves for an HA NCM811/Si composite cell at rates between C/10 and 5C. The minimum cutoff voltage is set to 2.0 V and the cutoff capacity is set to 95% of the baseline.

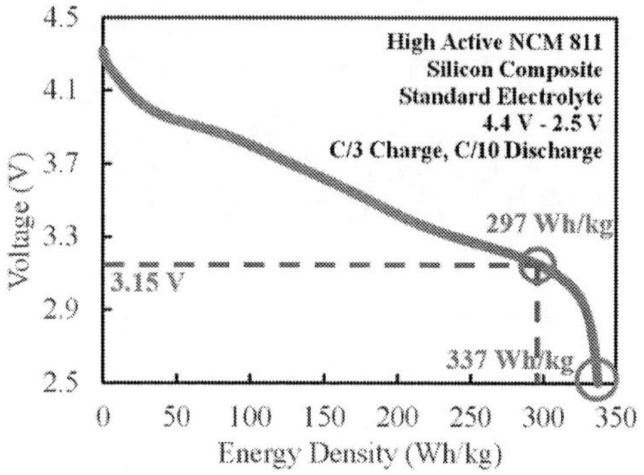

Figure 4. Full discharge of prototype cell from 4.4 V to 2.5 V at a rate of C/10. An energy density of 337 Wh/kg was obtained for the full discharge, with 297 Wh/kg obtained between 4.4 V and 3.15V.

to the increased cell resistance. At -20 °C, cells provided ca. 60% capacity retention during discharge at 1C with a lower voltage limit of 2.0 V to account for the overpotential caused by the extreme temperature.

To demonstrate the cells' capability to alternate between extreme temperatures, cells were cycled continuously while the ambient temperature was adjusted. The results of this experiment are summarized in Figure 6. The cell first underwent 3 baseline cycles at room temperature where no fade was observed. The cell then underwent 3 cycles where the charge was performed at room temperature and the discharge was performed at 0 °C, with a 1 hour thermal soak between each step to ensure the temperature equalized. At 0 °C, approximately 67% of the initial capacity was retained when discharged

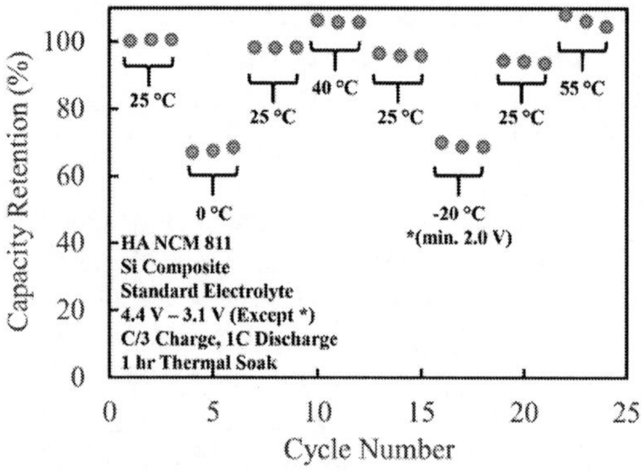

Figure 6. Alternating room temperature and operational temperature cycling of a nUAS cell between 4.4 V and 3.1 V.

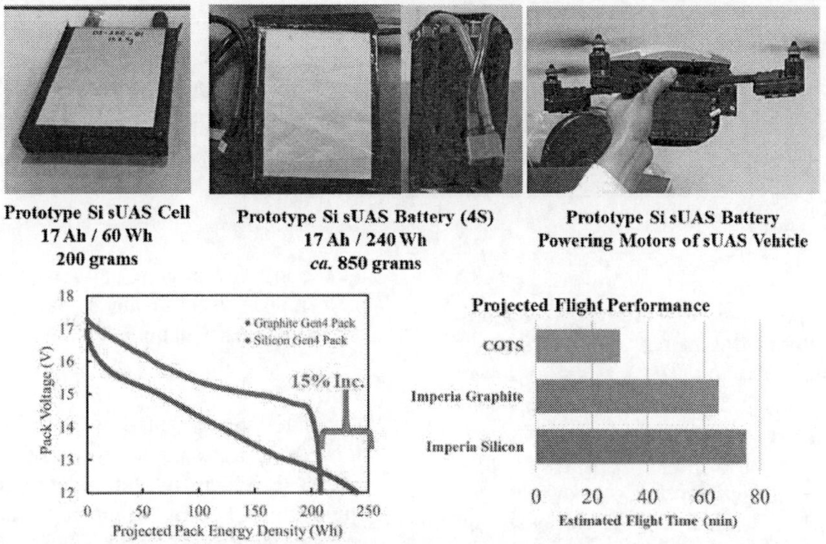

Figure 7. (top, left) Scaled-up version of NCM 811/Si battery to sUAS relevant sizes (top, center) 4S battery pack made from the scaled-up cells (top, right) Prototype battery pack powering sUAS vehicle. (bottom, left) projected energy density improvement over graphite solution (bottom, right) projected flight time improvements for sUAS vehicle.

from 4.4 V to 3.1 V. When the cell returned to cycling at 25 °C, approximately 98% of the initial capacity was retained. The process was repeated at 40 °C, where the cell performance was approximately 6% higher than the baseline. For the cycling at -20 °C, the lower voltage limit was decreased to 2.0 V to accommodate the overpotential associated with the extreme temperature. Between 4.4 V and 2.0 V at -20 °C, the cell delivered approximately 69% of the initial capacity. Finally, at 55 °C, approximately 6-8% energy above the baseline was observed; however, more cycle-to-cycle fade was observed than at other temperatures. Optimizations to the electrolyte formulation during future design iterations is expected to help to stabilize both high and low temperature operation.

In order to further demonstrate the core cell design and component technologies, Imperia scaled the cell design from the 3 Ah, 18650 equivalent cell size for nUAS to a size suitable for sUAS vehicles. The sUAS cell design chosen was the Mission Battery that was used as the baseline for the cell design. The silicon cell was designed to be the same mass as the baseline graphite cell (200 grams), resulting in an increased capacity compared to the baseline cell (17 Ah vs. 13 Ah). These cells were formed using the same procedure as the nUAS cells and then connected into a 4S battery pack (17 Ah, 240 Wh). This battery was demonstrated in-vehicle (Figure 7). Energy density and flight time were estimated to be at least 15% higher than the baseline graphite design. These rapid prototyping efforts demonstrate the efficacy of these technologies for improving energy density for UAS batteries. Moving forward, work focused on optimization of electrolyte composition and formation procedure will help to improve long term performance (cycle life, temperature stability, storage life) and processing/production optimization will help to ensure consistency and quality of solutions for these applications.

References

1. C.M. Lang, P.D. Moran, and K.J. Rosina, "Construction of High Energy Density Batteries (DOE Phase II SBIR)," *2017 DOE Merit Review*, Washington, DC. June 7, 2017.
2. C.M. Lang, P.D. Moran, and K.J. Rosina, "Construction of High Energy Density Batteries (DOE Phase II SBIR)," *2017 DOE Merit Review*, Washington, DC. June 7, 2017.
3. C.M. Lang, "Conductive Coatings for Active Electrochemical Materials," US Patent Application 2016/0072123 A1 (Sept 8, 2014).
4. C. M. Lang, P. D. Moran, and J.A. Vega, "Efforts to Construct High Energy Density Cells using PSI's Silicon Whisker and Carbon Nanofiber Composite Anode," *Next Generation Batteries*, San Diego, CA, November 12, 2013.
5. C.M. Lang, K.J. Rosina, and P.D. Moran, "Development of a Nonflammable Electrolyte for Li-Ion Batteries," 47th Power Sources Conference, Orlando, FL, June 13, 2016.

Lithium-Ion Battery/Lithium-Ion Capacitor Hybrid Energy Storage Device in UUV Applications

Kyle G. Waterman, Raymond B. Sepe Jr., Andrew Vose
Electro Standards Laboratories
36 Western Industrial Dr., Cranston, RI 02921
kwaterman@lab.electrostandards.com / 1-401-943-1164

Abstract

The technique of pairing a battery and supercapacitor has been accomplished electronically through the development of a hybrid power management unit. The device uses power electronics, closed loop control, and power management algorithms to facilitate the combination of an energy dense battery and a power dense super capacitor. The combination has been demonstrated to significantly improve battery performance in pulsed power applications in terms of energy density, peak power capability, battery lifetime, and total energy delivered over the lifetime of the paired battery. The approach is applied to an unmanned underwater vehicle (UUV) through station keeping and obstacle avoidance applications which experience pulsed loading under these conditions. The hybrid UUV battery shows regulated operation within a defined envelope using the supercapacitor element to support the peak pulse requirements of the thrusters used to maneuver the UUV. Operation of the UUV battery in this manner projects to provide improved performance over the battery lifetime with higher endurance and dynamic response for the UUV.

Keywords

Supercapacitor; Battery; Hybrid; Power; Energy; Power Management; Lithium Ion; Autonomous Vehicles; Underwater Unmanned Vehicles; UUV; Marine; Pulse Power; Marine Energy; Power At Sea

Introduction

The work presented expands on previous results detailing the hybrid power unit [1]. The unit features a lithium-ion battery/lithium-ion capacitor system directed at managing bidirectional pulsed power that improves battery performance. For primary type batteries, pulse power loads draw down voltage proportional to the internal impedance reducing energy availability. During pulsed voltage drawdown, the minimum voltage is reached before the battery's energy is depleted in terms of state of charge. This is due to the fundamental property of batteries as being an energy dense storage device with relatively high impedance. Pairing the battery with a low impedance power dense device such as a lithium-ion capacitor in support of load pulsing allows the battery to operate at a lower constant power and deliver a greater portion of its energy. ESL has developed a hybrid power system consisting of a power dense supercapacitor and power electronics along with management circuitry and algorithms to facilitate hybrid operation. The system pairs with energy sources whose performance degrades under pulsed loading or are current limited in a particular application.

Motivation

Meassured performance of the hybrid power management unit demonstrates the motivation for pursuing hybrid power system development and integration into a wide range of applications. Figure 1 compares a standard BA5790 battery system (blue) and hybrid system (red) pairing a BA5790 with a 1000F hybrid system for primary type batteries. A SATCOM load defined as 1 minute @ 100W, 9 minutes @ 12W is applied to each system. The resulting energy densities achieved by each system are shown in Table 1. There is an 83% improvement in effective energy density when utilizing the hybrid technology For the BA5790 battery system. Note the voltage drawdown is significantly reduced under hybrid control.

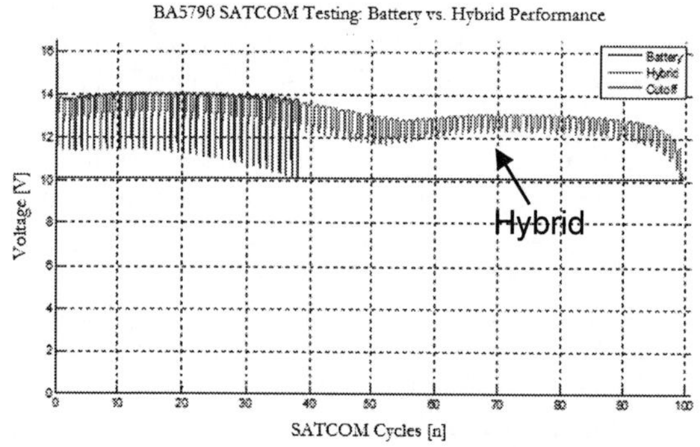

Figure 1: Primary SATCOM Performance: Battery System vs. Hybrid System

Table I: Primary Battery System Performance vs. Primary Hybrid System Performance

Primary System SATCOM Performance		
System	SATCOM Cycles	Energy Density
BA5790	38	113.44 Wh/kg
BA5790 + Hybrid	99	207.71 Wh/kg
Improvement	~160%	~83%

For secondary type batteries, a similar demonstration was conducted with cell equivalent testing, the result is provided in Figure 2. A cell equivalent SATCOM pulsed profile was applied to an INR18650MJ1 rechargeable cell assuming a battery approach (blue) and to another INR18650MJ1 cell assuming a hybrid approach (red) which operates the battery at a low constant current. The result is two points of improvement providing greater overall energy delivery from the hybrid approach. The hybrid approach showed greater single cycle capacity delivery as well as greater cycle life. The single cycle capacity improvement, measured by the difference in capacity retention each cycle, averaged ~10% until 375 cycles where the battery approach cell failed below the 80% capacity cutoff. The total cycle life of the hybrid approach was extended beyond 1100 cycles an improvement of 193%. The results are summarized in Table II.

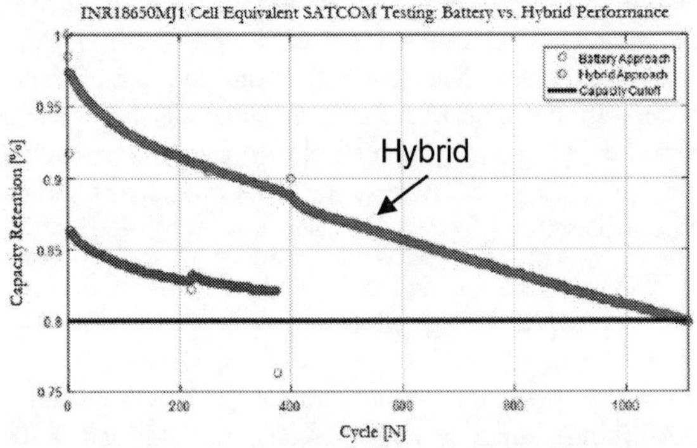

Figure 2: Secondary SATCOM Performance: Battery Approach vs. Hybrid Approach

Table II: SATCOM Performance: Secondary Battery System vs. Secondary Hybrid System

Secondary System SATCOM Performance (Cell Equivalent Testing)		
System	Avg Cycle Capacity	Cycles
INR18650MJ1	83.3%	375
INR18650MJ1+Hybrid	92.2%	1100
Improvement	~10%	~193%

Hybrid Architecture and Operation

Hybridization of a battery or energy dense device is achieved according to Figure 3. An energy dense storage device such as a lithium-ion battery is connected to a hybrid bus. Connected to the hybrid bus in parallel is a power dense device such as a supercapacitor. Between the supercapacitor and the physical bus connection are power electronics which facilitate the interfacing while also actuating closed loop control of the power system. The hybrid power management unit based on this hybrid architecture automatically fuses the benefits of energy dense devices and power dense devices.

Figure 4 captures the basic operating principle of the hybrid power system. The top plot shows the system currents, the middle plot shows the load and battery voltages, and the bottom plot shows the supercapacitor voltage. Negative batter current is out of the battery, negative load current is into the load and the hybrid regulates battery current to maximum of one amp. The sequence follows: 1. The battery supports the baseline load and recharges the supercapacitor, 2. The load pulses beyond the battery operating envelope and the supercapacitor discharges to support the difference, 3. The load becomes regenerative beyond the operating envelope of the battery and the supercapacitor absorbs the difference, 4. The baseline regenerative load falls within the battery operating envelope and the supercapacitor provides the difference to charge the battery. The plots demonstrate the basic operating states of the hybrid system. The system sinks and sources power capable of handling power pulses in either direction. Maintaining the battery to operate within a defined envelope is key to providing the energy performance improvement.

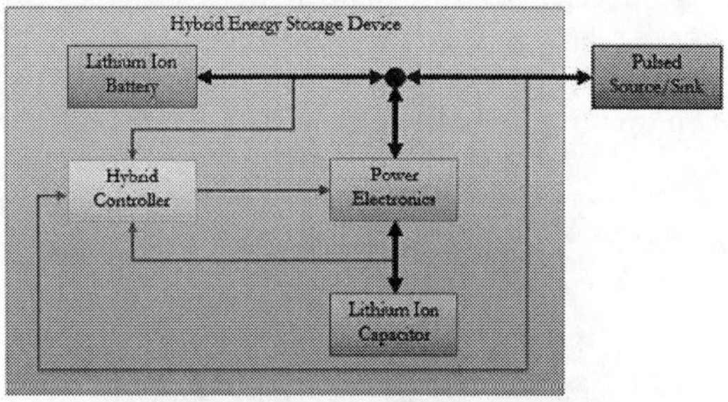

Figure 3: Hybridization Architecture

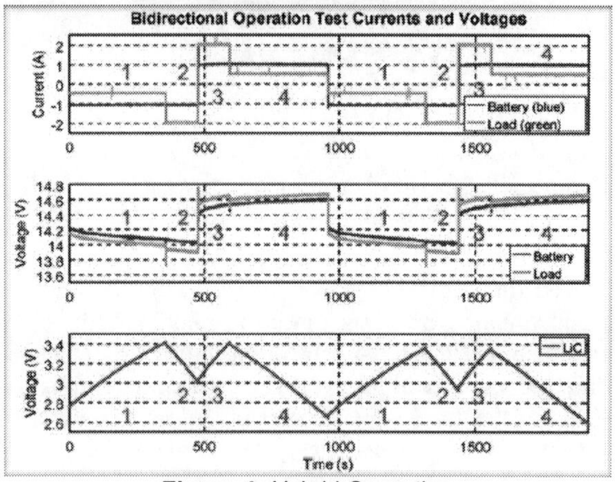

Figure 4: Hybrid Operation

Unmanned Underwater Vehicle Integration

Unmanned underwater vehicles (UUV) are suitable for hybridization as evidenced by their operation. The UUV power source experiences pulsed loading from a variety of sources including propulsion, positioning, actuation of robotic armatures, and various payload technologies such as communications. Advances in UUV controls and geometry are being made to improve mission performance but often do not account for the resultant electrical stress degradation of the battery [2]. This work focuses specifically on hybridizing the operation of the thrusters used to maintain station and depth. Rough conditions, underwater currents, stiction lifting off a muddy sea floor, and obstacles create the need to provide pulsed power to the vehicle's thrusters.

The test platform used to demonstrate hybridization was a Blue Robotics BlueROV2, a flexible UUV development platform. For this work, the power to the four vertical thrusters is disconnected from the main battery and connected to the hybrid system contained within the cylindrical watertight enclosure located in the payload area. The hybrid power system consisted of a BB2557/U lithium-ion rechargeable battery and ESL's hybrid power management unit comprised of ESL power management circuit board and a 1500F lithium-ion supercapacitor (LiC) as shown in Figure 5. Its dimensions are approximately 4.9"X4.3"X1.4". The prototype unit was not optimized for this application but was sufficient for testing. The power management circuity board contains power electronics for interfacing the battery and supercapacitor, closed loop power electronics control, and processing power for intelligent power management algorithms.

Figure 5: ESL Hybrid Power Management Board and Lithium-Ion Supercapacitor

The pairing of the power management unit and the battery is achieved through cabling that forms the hybrid bus. To integrate into the UUV, the power distribution of the UUV is modified such that the supply for the thrusters is connected to the load interface of the hybrid bus. Communications and power exit the tube via penetrators in the end cap. Figure 6 shows the fully integrated UUV. The vertical thrusters are located on each corner at the top of the vehicle. The hybrid power management unit is contained within the watertight acrylic enclosure fixed to the payload frame as the bottom of the UUV.

Figure 6: Hybridized UUV

Hybrid UUV Testing

The hybrid system used in testing was sized to accommodate pulsing on the order of 100W to 200W for durations under 1 minute. The hybrid power management circuit board contains on board measurement conditioning, data logging and storage capabilities for post processing and analysis, ideal for testing in the field and limiting cabling. The UUV system of ROV type is controlled remotely through the connected tether. The hybrid system is evaluated under station keeping and obstacle avoidance test cases.

Station Keeping: Station keeping refers to the ability of the UUV to maintain a particular orientation at depth and is important for performing various tasks such as underwater maintenance. To maintain position, the UUV is required to quickly respond to disturbances through the use of vehicle thrusters. In this experiment, a wave tank is used to generate a periodic disturbance. The vehicle thrusters must provide a pulsed profile to quickly regulate positional errors induced by the waves.

The UUV was commanded to maintain a 20cm depth at level orientation while being subjected to a 7cm wave with a roughly 1 second period. Figure 7 (top) shows the results from station keeping testing. The power flow between the battery (blue), supercapacitor (green), and the load (red) is captured in the data. The load is the sum of the four vertical thruster power requirements. Power pulsing due to the periodic wave disturbance were observed to peak around 150W for a duration on the order of milliseconds. Negative power indicates discharging of the battery and supercapacitor and utilization by the load. A positive power indicates charging of the battery and supercapacitor and regeneration by the load. The battery operating envelope for this application was defined to be between +/- 25W. The battery is allowed to operate anywhere within this envelope and is capped once the limit is reached. The difference in power required by the load is then provided by the supercapacitor.

The station keeping power cycle includes a power pulse towards 150W, the battery discharge is limited to 25W by the hybrid power management unit control, the supercapacitor provides the 125W difference plus some additional power to offset losses due to power conversion efficiencies. The pulsed load returns towards baseline as the wave disturbance subsides. As the load power draw falls within the battery operating envelope the difference is then used to restore charge to the supercapacitor in anticipation of future pulsing. Note just before 27s and 28s the battery is seen sinking power as the load becomes regenerative demonstrating the bidirectional capabilities of the hybrid system.

Obstacle Avoidance: The second experiment evaluated the hybridized thrusters assuming a nonperiodic pulsing profile such as would occur in obstacle avoidance operation. In this

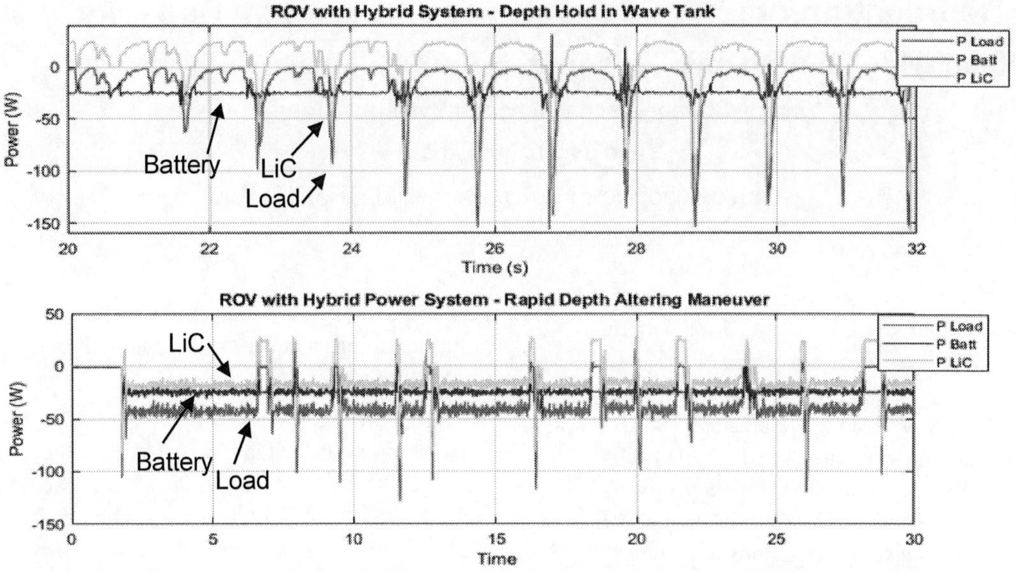

Figure 7: Hybrid UUV Testing: Station Keeping (top), Obstacle Avoidance (Bottom)

situation the UUV was aggressively commanded to change depth with random magnitude and pattern. The resulting waveforms are shown in Figure 7 (bottom).

The load profile (red) shows a baseline load around 45W with discharge pulsing around 100W magnitude and periods where the load rests around 0W. The supercapacitor profile (green) is shown to provide the difference between the load requirement and the battery discharge limit during pulsing. During periods where the load falls below the baseline towards zero, the battery then provides power to the supercapacitor to restore charge. The battery profile (blue) shows operation within a +/-25W envelope indicating the hybrid controller is tightly regulating battery operation. Operation within the envelope provides performance improvement via single cycle life and total cycle life as demonstrated in the above sections.

Conclusion

The hybrid system demonstrated the ability to limit battery operation to within a predefined current envelope to ensure that the battery operates within its highest efficiency operating region. The energy device and power device must be sized according to the application's peak power and duration requirements. The hybrid architecture is effective when seeking to minimize weight and volume while improving endurance and dynamic performance such as the UUV. To achieve minimal form factor, power density and energy density must be achieved simultaneously. The hybrid architecture addresses this through integration of a power dense device in the supercapacitor and an energy dense device in the battery made interoperable through use of the hybrid power management board.

Future Development

Future work in the UUV area includes integrated learning algorithms for adaptability in the field. Dynamic battery operating envelopes based on measured performance and environmental conditions can further enhance performance. Dynamic hybrid state based on load usage looks to adapt the hybrid unit autonomously to perform optimally in both sourcing and sinking applications. This would allow the UUV's to incorporate more aggressive optimal control algorithms to handle a wide range of sea and mission conditions without degrading its batteries. In addition, scalability in terms of power and energy are being explored to address higher and lower power applications.

Acknowledgements

We would like to thank the Army for continued support in our hybrid power systems research.

References

1.Smith, P. H., Sepe Jr. R. B., Waterman, K. G., and Myron, L. J., "Development and analysis of a lithium carbon monofluoride battery-lithium ion capacitor hybrid system for high pulse-power application," Journal of Power Sources, vol. 327, pp. 495-506, Sep. 2016.

2. Saad, M., et al. ,"Modeling and simulation of electric propulsion system for UUVs to observer variations in drag and motor's power against operational and design parameters using MATLAB," IBCAST, 533-536, Jan. 2020.

Degradation of Li-ion Cells Beyond 80% Initial Capacity

Reed Wittman, Armando Fresquez, Babu Chalamala, Yuliya Preger

Energy Storage Technology and Systems Group,

Sandia National Labs

Albuquerque, New Mexico, Bernalillo, 87102

rwittm@sandia.gov

Abstract

To better understand the true useful life of Li-ion batteries for various applications, we have been conducting a systematic cycling study of 18650 format cells. Lithium Iron Phosphate (LFP), Nickel Manganese Cobalt Oxide (NMC) and Nickel Cobalt Aluminum Oxide (NCA) cells have been systemically cycled to below 80% capacity. We find that cells have significant useful life beyond 80% and their useful life is dictated by conditions of cycling. We find that for each chemistry, state of charge range has the most impact while discharge rate and temperature show a mixed trend depending on chemistry. New trends in capacity fade of NMC and NCA cells cycled at different C-rates and NCA cells cycled at different temperatures arise post 80%. Finally knee point formation does not always occur in cells and its occurrence does not correlate to one parameter of cycling but instead is dependent on all the cycling conditions experienced by the battery.

Keywords

Li-ion Battery; Post 80%; Long Term Cycling.

Introduction

Selecting and operating Li-ion batteries currently involves significant uncertainty. Variations in positive electrode chemistry change ideal cycling conditions. Changes in ideal conditions are not well mapped. Also, the useful life of different cell chemistries for different applications is unknown. Public cycling studies traditionally stop at 80% capacity. A metric for electric vehicles may not be valid for grid applications with different energy and power requirements.

We aim to address this gap with a multi-year cycling study of 18650 commercial Li-ion cells containing three different positive electrode chemistries: Lithium Iron Phosphate (LFP), Nickel Manganese Cobalt Oxide (NMC) and Nickel Cobalt Aluminum Oxide (NCA). Cycling was conducted at varied temperatures, state of charge (SOC) range, and discharge rates.

First, cells were cycled to 80% capacity. Analysis of cell performance for this stage of cycling was conducted by Preger et al.[1] The full data sets from that part of the study can be found at battery archive.[2] Cells of interest were then disassembled and subject to materials characterization to understand the underlying causes of degradation.

The remaining cells are now cycling to 40% of initial capacity. 64 of the original 82 cells are still cycling after six years. 3 NMC and 3 NCA cells have reached the final EOL of 40%. No LFP cells have reached EOL, and half remain above 80% capacity. Each cell chemistry has shown significant ability to operate post 80% capacity. Average energy throughputs for each chemistry range from 1.4 to 6.8 kWh. Trends that existed before 80% capacity become more pronounced. New trends in capacity fade rates are observed as well. Finally, we analyze the occurrence of knee points. We find that their occurrence is dependent on chemistry and conditions of cycling.

Methods

Full experimental details can be found in Preger et al.[1]

Tested Batteries: The following commercial 18650 cells were examined: LFP from A123 Systems (Part #APR18650M1A, 1.1 Ah), NCA from Panasonic (Part #NCR18650B, 3.2 Ah), and NMC from LG Chem (Part #18650HG2, 3 Ah). The three batteries were selected because they included common electrode formulations.

Cycling Equipment: Cycle aging was done with Arbin SCTS and Arbin high-precision (Model: LBT21084) battery testing systems. Individual cells were tested in 18650 battery holders from Memory Protection Devices. The holders were connected to the Arbin with 18-gauge wire. During cycling, the cells were placed in SPX Tenney Model T10C-1.5 environmental chambers. A K- or T-type thermocouple monitored the cell skin temperature.

Cycle Aging Protocol: Each round of cycling consisted of an initial capacity check, cycling at the designated conditions, and a final capacity check. Capacity checks consisted of three charge/discharge cycles from 0%–100% SOC at protocol for all cells studied. A round of cycling for each cell varied from 125 to 1000 cycles. This value depended on the rate of degradation at the specific

Table 1: Conditions of Cycling

DOD, Temperature, Discharge Rate*			
40-60%, 25°C, 0.5C	0-100%, 15°C, 1C	0-100%, 15°C, 2C	40-60%, 25°C, 3C
20-80%, 25°C, 0.5C	0-100%, 25°C, 1C	0-100%, 25°C, 2C	20-80%, 25°C, 3C
0-100%, 25°C, 0.5C	0-100%, 35°C, 1C	0-100%, 35°C, 2C	0-100%, 25°C, 3C

*0.5C charge rate for all

test conditions. The cycle count for a round was halved if a cell experienced over 5% capacity loss in the previous round. Study Conditions Table I shows the combinations of cycling conditions examined. The nominal capacities of the cells were used as references for calculating C-rates. All cells were charged at a rate of 0.5C, per manufacturer guidance. NCA cells were not discharged at 3C as the 9 A required for this is outside of manufacturer specifications.

Results and Discussion

Overview of Results: Overview of Results: To date our study indicates that NMC, NCA and LFP cells have significant useful life post 80% capacity. Table 2 shows the status of cells cycling below 80% capacity for each chemistry. While 3 NMC and NCA cells have reached an EOL of 40% capacity, no LFP cells have reached EOL. Currently only half the LFP cells are below 80% capacity. Figure 1 shows the capacity retention of cells as a function of equivalent full cycles (EFC). Post 80% NMC, NCA and LFP cells have averaged 685, 486 and 392 EFCs respectively. NMC, NCA and LFP cells currently have a respective mean capacity retention of 63%, 60% and 74%. This has allowed the cells to discharge 6.8, 4.9 and 1.4 kWhr of energy after passing 80% capacity.

Table 2: Summary of cell performance post 80% capacity by cell chemistry. *Half of the LFP cells are still above 80%

Chemistry	# of Cells Below 80%	# of Cells at EOL	Mean + EFC Post80% to date	Mean Energy Discharged Post80% to date	Mean Capacity of Post80% Cells
NMC	19	3	685 +/- 306	6.8 +/- 3 kWhr	63%
NCA	13	3	486 +/- 286	4.9 +/- 2.8 kWhr	60%
LFP	* 15	0	392 +/- 291	1.4 +/- 0.9 kWhr	74%

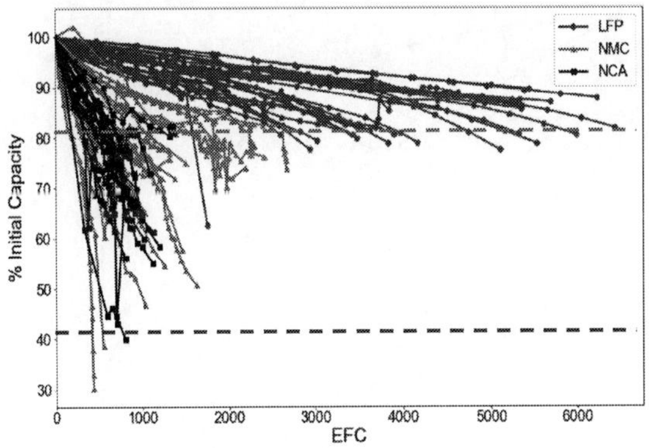

Figure 1: Cycling data for all cells in the study since the start of the study.

The cell capacity fade shows significant dependence on the conditions of cycling. We observe this in Figure 1, where there is significant variance in capacity fade rates within each chemistry studied. This is better quantified when looking at Table II which shows the standard deviation for the mean EFC and discharged energy post 80% capacity. This large standard deviation is most pronounced in the NMC cells, which have a standard deviation of approximately 50% of the mean totals for both EFC and energy discharge data.

Developing Trends in Capacity Fade: Figure 2 shows capacity fade for each chemistry as a function of State of Charge (SOC) range, ambient temperature, and discharge rate. The most significant factor in degradation rate for each chemistry pre-80% capacity was the SOC range it was cycled at. As the SOC range increased, the capacity fade rate increased for all the cells studied. Temperature showed a mixed trend based on the cell chemistry. Only the LFP cells showed a significant trend associated with discharge rate.

For all cells the impact of SOC range becomes more significant post 80% capacity. NCA cells appear particularly affected by SOC range. The 0-100% cell reached EOL by 800 EFC, while by 1,000 EFCs the 20-80% cells are near 65% capacity. The 40-60% cells remain in a linear degradation regime near 80% capacity at ~1300 EFCs. NCA cells reached 80% capacity within ~400EFC of each other, however currently there is ~600EFC separating the lowest and highest capacity cell. NMC and LFP cells follow a similar trend but in a less dramatic fashion.

NMC cell's preference towards higher temperature cycling is more pronounced below 80% capacity. The cells reached 80% capacity with approximately 500EFC between the low and high temperature cells. The 15oC cell reached EOL at ~550 EFC, while the 25oC cells are all below 70% in a range of 1100 to 1300 EFC and the 35oC cell is at ~75% capacity at around 1400 EFC. This data suggests that the higher temperature cells may achieve an order of magnitude higher through put by EOL.

New Trends in Capacity Fade: Post 80% capacity, new trends have emerged in the data for the cycling of NMC and NCA cells with different discharge rates and NCA cells at different temperatures.

The NCA cells showed the new discharge rate trend most prominently, with the 0.5C cell at EOL around 600EFC and the rest of the NCA cells exhibiting a varied capacity above 60% at 1200EFC. For the NMC and NCA cells, increased degradation at lower discharge rates may correlate to time spent at high SOCs. We may be seeing both calendar and cycling aging acting on the cell. Further study is needed to understand how degradation occurs.

Below 80% capacity, NCA cells show slower capacity fade at lower temperatures than NCA cells cycled at higher temperatures. Currently the 35oC NCA cells are below 60% capacity near 800EFC. The 25 and 15oC cells do not reach 60% capacity until at least 1100EFC. This shows that high temperature degradation needs to build before it impacts an NCA cell's external performance.

Knee Points: A notable conclusion of our study is that so called knee points do not always occur. Knee points are where batteries transition from a linear degradation rate to an exponential degradation rate. Figure 3 shows examples of different degradation trends in Li-ion batteries. The superlinear degradation curve shows linear degradation until ~400 cycles, after which the degradation rate becomes increasingly rapid. This is an example of a knee in battery degradation. Knees have long been a topic of concern as they can cause the rapid loss of functionality in batteries [3, 4].

We find that the occurrence of knee points is dependent on the conditions of cycling and the cell chemistry. Figure 4 shows selected NMC cells that have not displayed a knee and cells that have shown a knee. The behavior of these cells to form or not form knees does not appear to have a clear trend. The cells that clearly experienced knees operate at a variety of temperatures, discharge rates and SOC ranges, without a clear common factor in their cycling performance. Likewise, the cells that have not

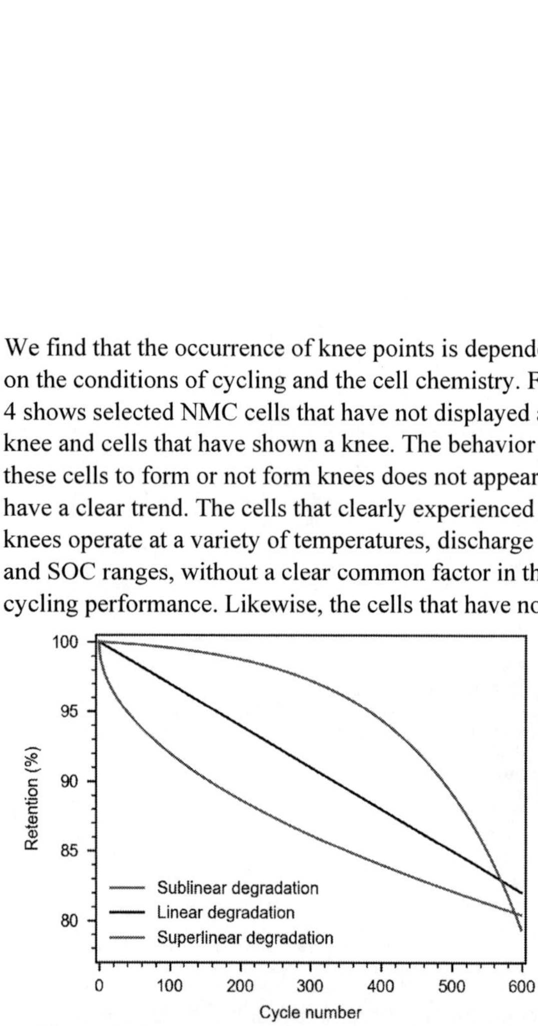

Figure 3: Schematic of three Li-ion battery aging trajectories, sublinear, linear, and superlinear ("knees"). Reprinted from Attia et al. JECS 2022

experienced a knee operate at similarly varied temperatures of cycling, discharge rates and SOC ranges.

Typically knee points occur later in a battery's operational life as accumulated degradation impacts cell performance[3]. This has been correlated to cells

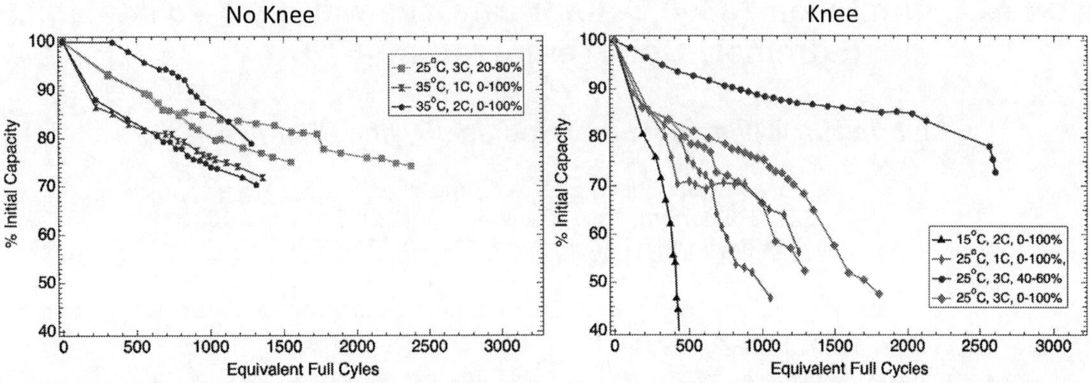

Figure 4: Example of NMC cells that have not experienced a knee (left) and cells that have experienced a knee transition (right). Cells do not show a consistent trend in which form knees or not. This is representative of LFP and NCA cells.

approaching 80% capacity[4, 5]. In NMC cells the knees have been correlated to Li-plating, electrolyte oxidation and SEI formation. It has been suggested that higher upper SOC limits, lower discharge rates and temperatures below of 35°C can accelerate NMC knee point formation[3].

We see in Figure 4 all the no knee cells are below 80% capacity and continue to cycle, which is true for both LFP and NCA cells as well. Knee occurrence in NMC cells only correlates with the literature in cycling below 35°C. The selected knee point cells have ambient temperatures at 15 and 25°C. However, this trend is not universal, as shown by two NMC no-knee cells cycling at 25°C below 80% capacity, suggesting that there is not just one parameter that causes or prevents knee growth. This is true for the NCA and LFP cells as well, where knee formation appears to be condition dependent without a discernible trend. Further work will be done to study knee point formation as our study progresses.

Conclusions:

Our study has shown that Li-ion batteries have significant useful life post 80% capacity. Each of the cell chemistries have discharged over 1kWh of energy and averaged an EFC of 400 or greater. LFP cell capacity fade appears to be slower at all conditions than for the NCA and NMC cells. The NCA cells appear to have a fast capacity fade rate and NMC cells showed the most range in fade rates. Currently 3 NMC and NCA cells have reached 40% capacity. For the LFP cells, none have reached 40% capacity, and half are still above 80% capacity.

Knee points occur inconsistently so far in the study. Cells do not universally form knees at or near 80% as suggested in literature. The formation of knees appears to be condition dependent and can occur at any capacity. There is currently no observable trend in our data to predict knee point formation. Further work is needed to better clarify this occurrence.

Post 80% use of Li-ion batteries is feasible but requires careful consideration of their use before and after 80% capacity. Better state of health diagnostics is needed to monitor cells, which will insure optimal use of batteries throughout their entire operational life.

Acknowledgements

Sandia National Laboratories is a multi-mission laboratory managed and operated by National Technology and Engineering Solutions of Sandia, LLC., a wholly owned subsidiary of Honeywell International, Inc., for the U.S. Department of Energy's National Nuclear Security Administration under contract DE-NA0003525. Funded by the U.S. Department of Energy, Office of Electricity, Energy Storage program. Dr. Imre Gyuk, Program Director. We gratefully acknowledge Dr. Megan Diaz's technical review of this document.

References

1. Y. Preger, H. M. Barkholtz, A. Fresquez, D. L. Campbell, B. W. Juba, J. Romàn-Kustas, S. R. Ferreira, and B. Chalamala, *J. Electrochem. Soc.,* **167**, 120532 (2020).
2. *Battery Archive*, www.batteryarchive.org
3. Peter M. Attia, A. Bills, F. B. Planella, P. Dechent, G. d. Reis, M. Dubarry, P. Gasper, S. Greenbank, D. Howey, O. Liu, Y. Preger, A. Soni, S. Sripad, Richard Gilchrist, E. Khoo, A. G. Stefanopoulou, and V. Sulzer, *J. Electrochem. Soc.,* **169** (2022).
4. M. Johnen, S. Pitzen, U. Kamps, M. Kateri, P. Dechent, and D. U. Sauer, *J. Energy Storage,* **34** (2021).
5. N. Kirkaldy, M. A. Samieian, G. J. Offer, M. Marinescu, and Y. Patel, *ACS Appl Energy Mater,* **5** (2022).

Studies on ALE 4Ah Li-ion 18650 Cylindrical Cells with zero volts stability at Extremely Cold Temperature -57°C

Linhua Hu, William Michael Hadala JR, and Jiang Fan

American Lithium Energy Corporation
2261 Rutherford Road, Carlsbad, CA 92008
lhhu@americanlithiumenergy.com / 1-760-599-7388

Abstract

A high energy and high-power ALE 4Ah Li-ion 18650 cylindrical cell has been studied extensively for space exploration and military applications. The cell showed not only a high specific energy ~330 Wh/kg and high power ~700 W/kg, but also strong stability at zero volts. No loss in the power and capacity was observed after repeatedly discharged to zero volts at C/5 and then held at zero volt at 20 ohms for 7 days. Further, there is no change in the cell self-discharge test for ALE 4Ah 18650 cells with zero voltage design. The self-discharge during rest is negligible after 5 times of zero-volt exposure (ZVE) at 20 ohm resistance discharging for 7 days (total 35 days). For a comparison, the commercial 3.5 Ah 18650 cell showed a significant self-discharge after 4 times of ZVE for 7 days (total 28 days). The cell also showed good cycle life and demonstrated about 500 cycles at 80% DOD and >6000 cycles (about two years and cycle life testing is still ongoing) at 20% DOD with <2% energy loss. Further, the cell performed well at extremely low temperatures. No capacity loss was observed after -65°C storage for 3 hours. The cell can deliver >3Ah capacity at -40°C and C/5 rate, and 1.8Ah at -57°C and C/16 rate, respectively, which is the best among all commercial 18650 cells. The results will be discussed according to the military and NASA applications.

Keywords

Li-ion Batteries; 18650 Cylindrical Cells; Si electrode; Zero-volt Exposure; Zero-volt Stability; Zero-volt tolerance; ZVE; ZVT; High energy; High power; Extremely Cold Temperature; NASA; Low Earth Orbit; LEO; Satellite

Introduction

Cylindrical cells have been well developed and one of the top Li-ion batteries (LIB) products for commercial markets and military applications owing to wide voltage window, high energy, and good cycle life. 18650 cylindrical cells have been reported and produced by renowned manufacturers, including LG, Samsung, and Panasonic, etc. A strategy that has gained popularity since 2010 is the addition of Si into graphite electrodes, forming an anode material combination, to increase the nominal cell capacities from 2.2Ah to 3.5Ah. The reported maximum specific energy is ~250Wh/kg, less than pouch cells/prismatic cells with similar chemistry. On the one hand, the demand of high energy density LIB is increasing in military applications where minimal loss of cell capacity is required when LIBs are subject to different abusive conditions.

Specifically, the performance of cylindrical cells at low temperature is severely degraded due to low conductivity of electrolyte, especially at the simulated temperature of space environment, thus limiting their practical applications in aerospace for satellites.

American Lithium Energy Corporation (ALE) has developed a high energy and high-power 4Ah Si Li-ion cell using negative electrodes by Si chemistry and exclusive zero-volt tolerance (ZVT). The theoretical capacity of pure Si anode is ~4000mAh/g, which is nearly 10 times the capacity of traditional graphite anodes. However, the volume expansion is also high, up to ~300%, thus resulting in electrode delamination and poor cycle life. ALE has combined high Si (>50%) and graphite electrodes to get high capacity and also address the expansion issue with exclusive slurry formulation and electrode fabrication.

The corrosion of negative current collector, i.e., Cu foil is the main challenge when the cell is discharged below 1V. ZVT is a patented ALE technology, the central strategy is to add a sacrificial electrode into negative electrode and can protect Cu foil when the voltage is discharged close to 0V or negative voltage. The benefits of ALE patented ZVT are multiple points: (1) sacrificial materials are low cost and not moisture sensitive or air sensitive, (2) not participate in the normal electrochemical reaction, (3) improvement of cycle life owing to the protection as early as cell wetting before formation, (4) wide application for any cell using Cu foil as current conductor, (5) improvement of cell shelf life and cell safety, (6) low temperature performance cooperated with electrolyte additive.

ALE is currently focusing on the production line of 18650 cylindrical cells. ALE has gained 10 million funding support from California State.

4Ah Si Li-ion Cell Rate and Cycle Life

As shown in Figure 1, the 4Ah Si Li-ion cell discharge rates were tested at 0.2C, 0.5C, 1C, and 2C, respectively. The voltage window is 4.4V-2V. The discharge capacity at 1C is 4.2Ah, very close to 2C. The rate capability is excellent and can fit the high-power cell requirement. Therefore, the 4Ah Si Li-ion cell has a high specific energy ~330Wh/kg, and a high-power ~700W/kg.

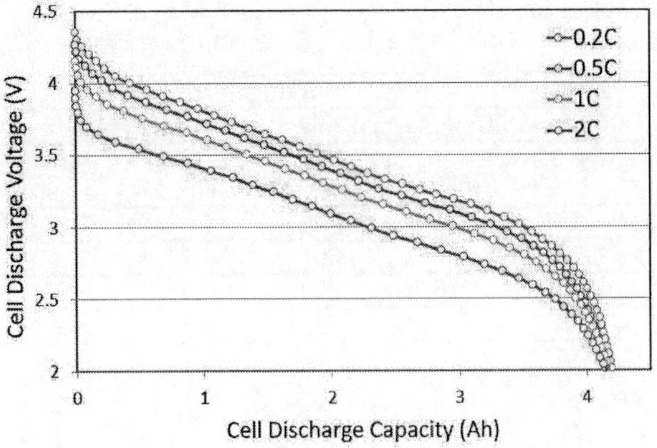

Figure 1. 4Ah Si Li-ion Cell capacity-voltage profiles at different rates

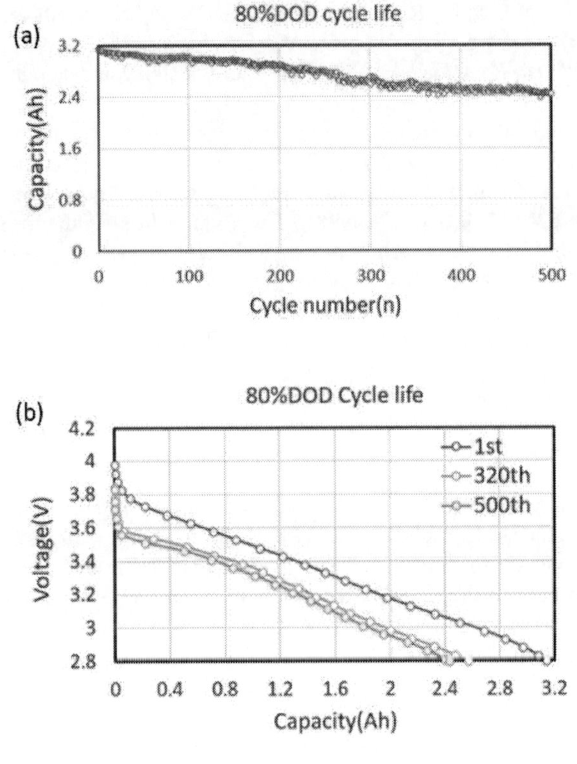

Figure 2. 4Ah Si Li-ion Cell 80%DOD Cycle life (a)Capacity vs cycle number (b) Voltage-capacity profiles at different cycle numbers

The cycle life of 4Ah Si Cell has been tested in 80% DOD and 20% DOD, respectively, per different requirements. Figure 2(a) shows the discharge capacity-cycle number profile of 80%DOD. Figure 2(b) shows the voltage-capacity profile of 80%DOD. The capacity after the 1st cycle is ~3.2Ah, 80% of 4Ah, after the 320th cycle is 2.57Ah, and after the 500th cycle is 2.4Ah. The capacity retention is 80% after 320 cycles, 75% after 500 cycles.

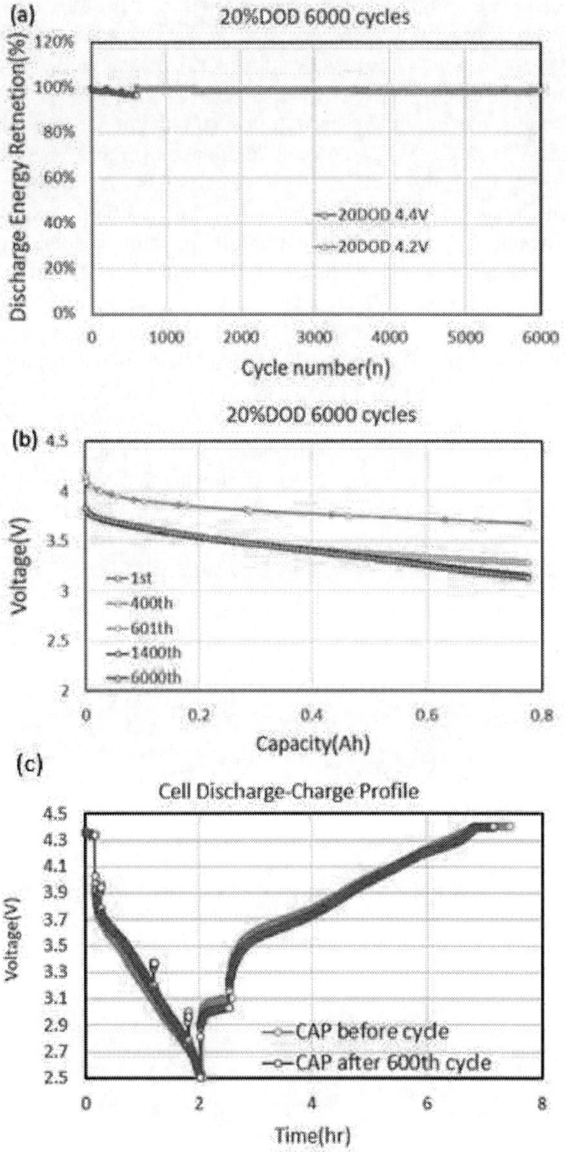

Figure 3. ALE 4Ah Si Li-ion Cell 20%DOD cycle life (a) discharge energy retention vs cycle number (b) Voltage-Capacity profiles at different cycle numbers (c) discharge-charge profile before cycle and after cycles.

Table 1 Capacity and DCR analysis before cycle and after 600 cycles

Parameter	Before Cycle	After 600 cycles	Δ(%)
Ch. Capacity (Ah)	3.692	3.584	-2.92
Dis. Capacity (Ah)	3.684	3.599	-2.30
Ch. Energy (Ah)	14.67	14.06	-4.15
Dis. Energy (Ah)	11.62	11.60	-0.17
C.E. (%)	99.77	100.40	0.63
E.E. (%)	79.18	82.49	4.18

Figure 3 summarizes 20%DOD of 4Ah Si cell. The 1-600 cycles (blue line) were operated at 4.4V, and 601-6000 cycles (orange line) were at 4.2V, respectively. The observed discharge energy loss is 3.3% in this case after 600 cycles is attributed to polarization accumulation, decrease in state of charge (SOC), and cell degradation (Figure 3a). The voltage-capacity between 1st and 400th is identical, indicating no degradation at 4.4V. The voltage-capacity between the 1400th and the 6000th is almost identical, indicating little degradation at 4.1V(Figure 3b). To further verify the real cell degradation, the discharge energy between the 1st cycle and the 600th cycle has been compared with the same procedure (Figure 3c). The real discharge energy loss is 0.17% (Table 1). The total discharge energy loss is ~1.5% after 6000 cycles (~5400 cycles at 4.1V). The projected 20%DOD cycle life is 70000 cycles at 4.1V with ~20% energy loss, which is very promising to fulfill the LEO satellite mission task (25000 cycles, 20%DOD, 5 years shelf life) and close to the requirement of LEO satellite mission task (75000 cycles, 20%DOD, 15 years shelf life).

Zero-Volts Stability

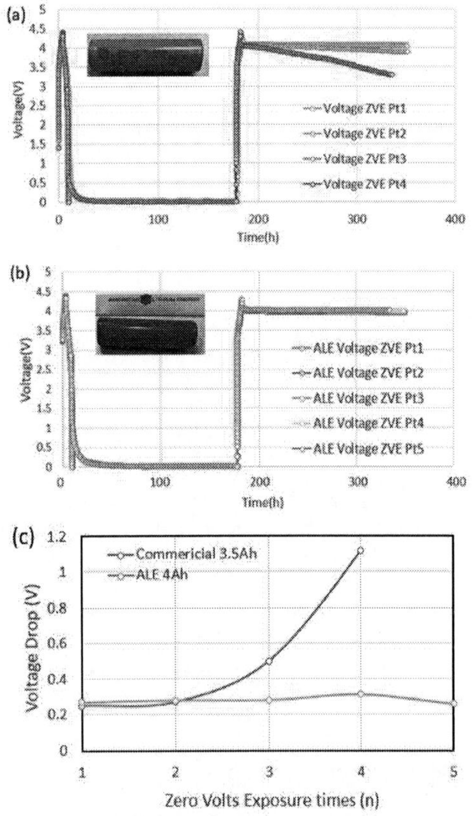

Figure 4. (a) Commercial Graphite 3.5Ah Cell ZVE 20ohm 7days and Rest 7days for 4 times (b) ALE 4Ah Nano Si Li-ion Cell ZVE 20ohm 7days and Rest 7days for 5 times (c) Self-discharge analysis based on voltage drop

Table 2 Self-discharge of commercial 3.5Ah cells and ALE 4Ah Cells after ZVE 20ohm 7days

ZVE	Voltage (V)			
Cell	Commercial 3.5Ah		ALE 4Ah	
Step 8	Before Rest	After Rest	Before Rest	After Rest
1st ZVE	4.28	4.03	4.22	3.95
2nd ZVE	4.34	4.07	4.25	3.97
3rd ZVE	4.40	3.90	4.27	3.99
4th ZVE	4.40	3.28	4.30	3.99
5th ZVE	-	-	4.26	4.00

Zero-volts stability is an important feature of ALE 4Ah Si Li-ion Cell. The self-discharge of the cells have been tested according to the following procedure: (1) CC-CV to 4.4V at C/5, cut off current C/20; (2) Rest 10 minutes; (3) CC DC to 2.5V at C/5; (4) Rest 30 minutes; (5) CC DC to 0V at C/5; (6) Discharge with 20ohm at 0V for 7 days; (7) CC 5hrs at C/5; (8) Rest 7days; (9) Measure OCV at step 7 and step 8.

Figure 4 and Table 2 summarize the zero-volts stability studies after ZVE at 20ohm 7days for up to 5 times. The self-discharge analysis was evaluated based on OCV before rest and after 7 days rest (Step 8). The voltage drops in the first two ZVEs for 3.5Ah is ~ 0.25V, however, the value fast increased larger than 1V after the 4th ZVE. In contrast, the voltage drop for 4Ah Si cell is very stable, ~ 0.26V after the 5th ZVE. This indicates that ALE 4Ah Si cell has excellent zero volts stability. The detailed capacity and DCR studies have been reported in our previous reports.

Cell Abuse Test

Safety is an indispensable feature for all commercial and military cell applications. ALE 4Ah Si Li-ion Cell have subjected to abusive testing including crust, impact, and hotbox per the UN 38.3 requirements.

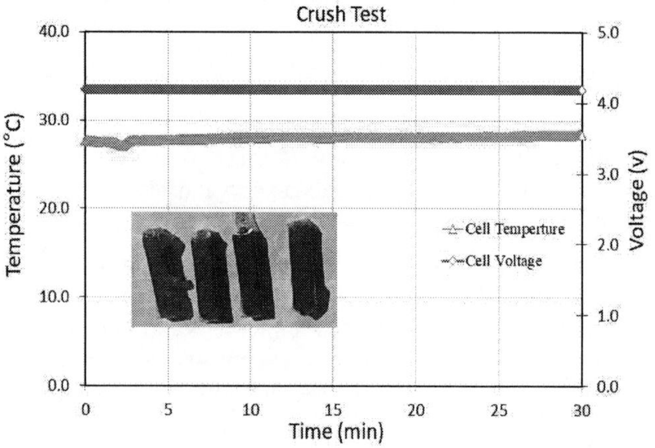

Figure 5. ALE 4Ah Si Li-ion cell crush test at 100% SoC

Figure 5 shows a typical crush test profile at 4.2V under pressure >2500 Psi. The crushed cells are distorted with a flat shape. The initial voltage was 4.2V and doesn't drop after 30 minutes, and the temperature did not significantly change from its initial reading of 28°C during the test. The was repeated several times and has proven reliable.

Figure 6 shows a representative hot box test. The fully charged cell was placed in a temperature-program controlled chamber. The initial temperature was 20°C ramped to 130°C and kept at temperature for 60 minutes, and finally cooling down 60 °C. No leaks, fire, or explosions were observed for all cells subjected to test.

Figure 7 shows a typical impact test at 50% SOC. The voltage was stable during the test at ~3.6V, and temperature was ~25°C. All cells passed the above abuse tests, without fire, explosion, or leakage observed.

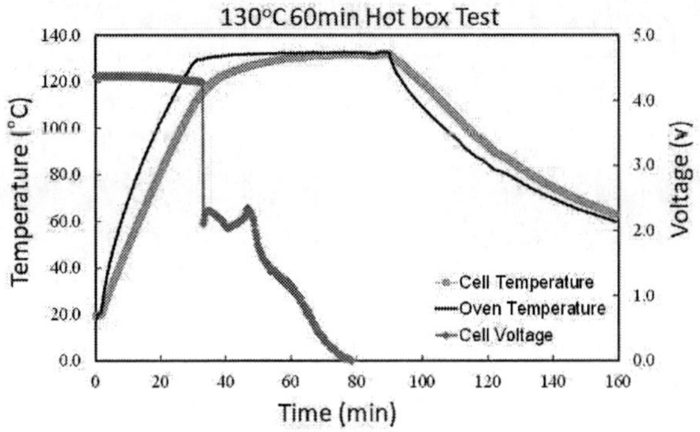

Figure 6. ALE 4Ah Si Li-ion cell hot box test at 100%SOC

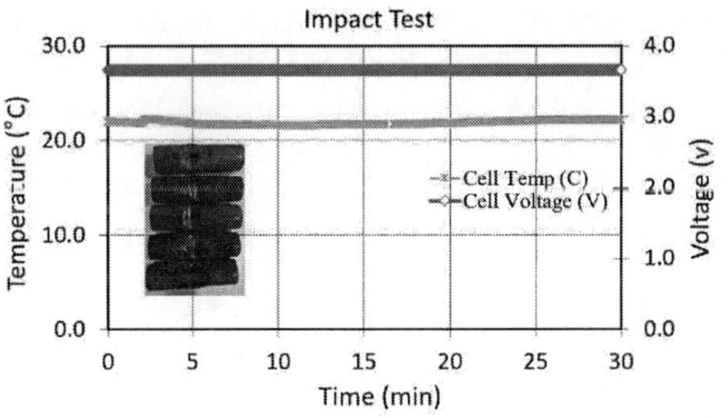

Figure 7. ALE 4Ah Si Li-ion cell impact test at 50% SOC

Low Temperature Performance

The performance of ALE 4Ah Si cells have been tested at various sub-zero temperatures. Figure 8 shows the voltage-capacity profiles at RT, -32°C, -40°C, -51°C, and -57°C. The corresponding capacity is 4.20Ah at C/5, 3.13Ah at C/4, 3.05Ah at C/5, 2.20Ah at C/4, and 1.8Ah at C/16, respectively. Figure 9 shows the cell capacities before and after -65°C storage for 3 hours. No capacity loss was observed for the extremely cold temperature treatment. This is the best result among the current 18650 commercial cells.

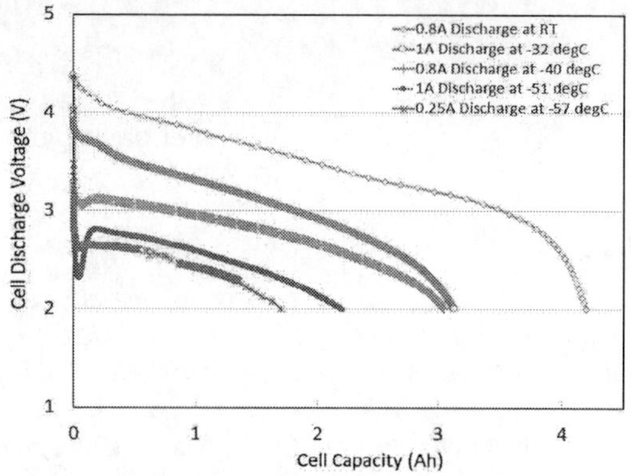

Figure 8. ALE 4Ah Si Li-ion cell capacities at low temperatures down to -57°C

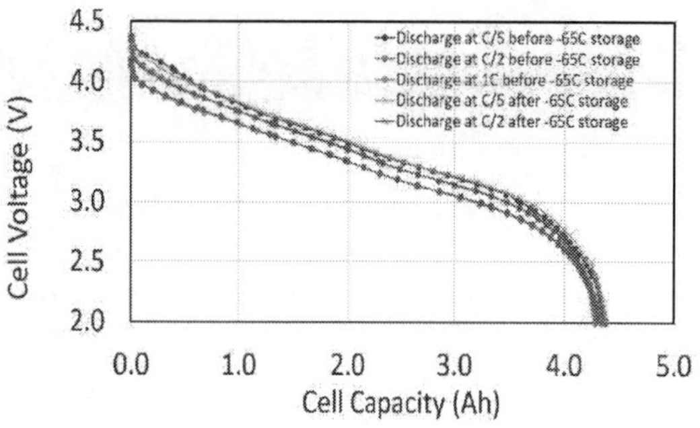

Figure 9. ALE 4Ah Si Li-ion cell capacities before and after -65°C storage for 3 hours.

Acknowledgement

The authors gratefully acknowledge funding from the U.S. Space Force SBIR Phase II program and thank Daniel Romm and Dr. Pinakin Shah for research guidance and helpful discussion.

References

1. Hu L., Fan J., Romm D. Advanced 4Ah 18650 Li-ion Cell Zero-Volt Tolerance for Space Applications. Conference on Advanced Power Systems for Deep Space Exploration, Virtual. Aug. 30, 2022
2. Fan J., L. Hu., Kompella C., Low voltage sacrificial electrodes, PCT/US2021/065097, Dec. 23, 2021.
3. Hu L., Fan J., Romm D. High-Capacity Nano Silicon Li-ion Battery with Zero-Volt Tolerance for Space Applications. 2021 NASA Aerospace Battery Workshop, Virtual. Nov. 16, 2021

Robust, Zero-Volt-Capable, High-Power Lithium-Ion Batteries for Military Platforms

David Ofer, Joseph Bernier, Edward Siegal, Sharon Dalton-Castor, Benjamin Lester and Michael Rutberg

CAMX Power LLC
35 Hartwell Avenue, Lexington, MA 02421
ofer.david@camxpower.com, (781)879-1241

Abstract

CAMX Power has developed and is commercializing a lithium-ion battery technology, trademarked CELX-RC®, with high power and rapid charging capability, long life, exceptional performance and charge acceptance capability at extreme low temperatures (e.g., -60 °C), excellent safety, capability for discharge and storage at 0V, and ability to be implemented in batteries without management electronics. This paper describes CELX-RC technology and its implementation in prototype batteries up to 60Ah size.

Keywords

Lithium ion; LTO; low temperature; rapid charge; 6T, 4HN.

Introduction

Rechargeable batteries needed for military applications face critical challenges including performance at extreme temperatures, compatibility with military logistical processes, phasing out of legacy battery technologies, and poor compatibility of COTS lithium-ion batteries with specialized military operational requirements and legacy platforms. To meet these challenges, CAMX Power has developed and is a commercializing lithium-ion battery technology based on our proprietary GEMX® high-performance cathode materials (licensed to L&F Co., Samsung SDI, LG Energy Solution, and EV Metals Group) implemented opposite commercial lithium titanate (LTO) anode with application-tailored electrolytes. This battery technology, trademarked as CELX-RC®, has high power and rapid charging capability, long life, exceptional performance and charge acceptance capability at extreme low temperatures, excellent safety, capability for discharge and storage at 0V, and can be implemented in batteries without management electronics. CAMX Power is developing CELX-RC for military applications that still rely on legacy chemistries such as lead-acid and nickel-cadmium, and for other applications that will benefit from its unique combination of power, life, safety, and robustness.

CELX-RC Properties

The GEMX materials used in CELX-RC cells offer the highest energy density of any Li-ion cathode material on the market today and has excellent power delivery and low-temperature performance. The LTO anode, although restricting energy density to about half that achievable with conventional graphite Li-ion anodes, nevertheless enables potentially critical performance attributes unattainable for graphite-based cells as described below.

CELX-RC Performance: Figure 1 shows performance capabilities of CELX-RC cells at extreme low temperature, demonstrating that unlike conventional Li-ion, CELX-RC cells can be charged as well as discharged at extreme low temperature.

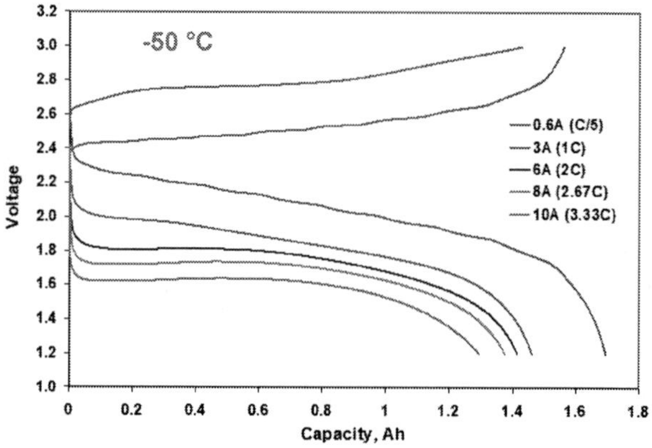

Figure 1. Charge and discharge voltage curves at indicated rates for a 3 Ah CELX-RC pouch cell cycled at -50 °C.

CELX-RC cells exhibit exceptional cycle life and 0V tolerance as demonstrated in Figure 2. Figure 3 shows the benefit of 0V tolerance for storage at elevated temperature.

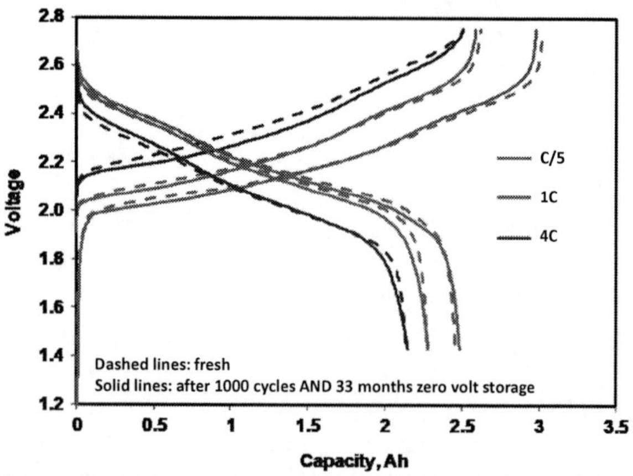

Figure 2. Charge and discharge at indicated rates for a 2.5 Ah CELX-RC pouch cell before and after 1,000 full cycles at 1C/1C rate and almost 3 years storage in the 0V condition.

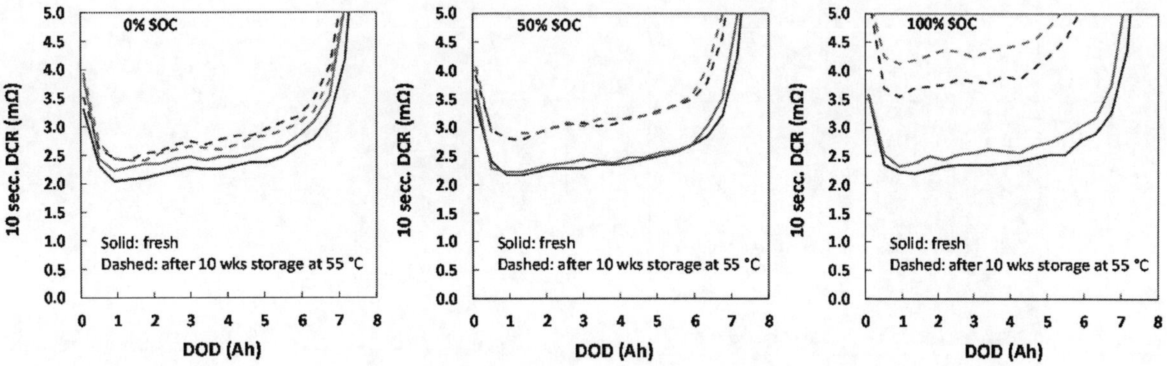

Figure 3. Direct current internal resistance (DCR) measured for 10-second, 5 A pulsing of 8 Ah pouch cells when fresh (solid lines) and after being stored at 55 °C for 10 weeks at 0% (0V), 55%, or 100% SOC (dashed lines).

The enhanced elevated-temperature storage tolerance enabled by 0V discharge capability shown in Figure 3 can greatly facilitate logistical management of batteries.

CELX-RC Safety: The CELX-RC cell technology's safety and exceptional tolerance to severe mechanical abuse have been demonstrated by tests including nail penetration, round bar crush, impact, and cutting with shears of pouch cells up to 6 Ah size and nail penetration and external short circuit testing of 18650 cells. These tests have generally resulted in only mild shorting corresponding to a low-rate discharge at worst. However, even when hard-shorted, the technology is much safer than conventional Li-ion.

Figure 4 shows an 8 Ah, 28 V 11-series pouch cell-based module after it was charged and then fully shorted by a 2 cm diameter steel nail driven through it. The cells vented electrolyte vapor smoke and limited melting of the polycarbonate case occurred (indicating ~300 °C reached), but no flames or sparks were observed, thus demonstrating SAE J2464 hazard severity level ≤ 4 (as is required for a 1-A55 Li-ion 6T battery per MIL-PRF-32565C).

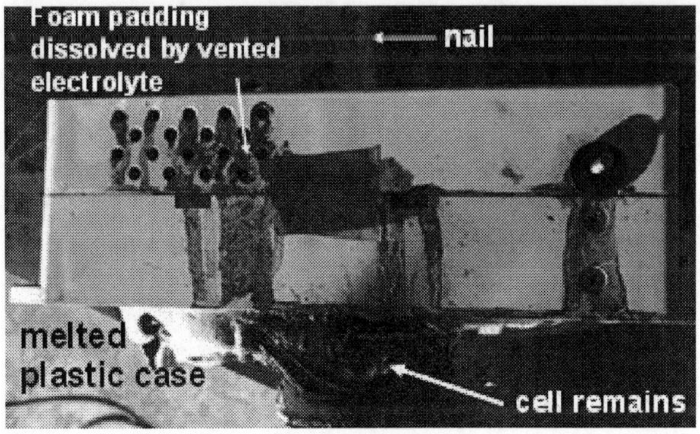

Figure 4. 200 Wh pouch cell module after charged module was penetrated by 2 cm diameter nail.

A post-mortem tear-down of the module revealed that the cells' electrodes and aluminum current collectors were intact as shown in Figure 5, thus indicating that no thermal runaway had taken place.

This level of safety under the most severe abuse conditions cannot be provided by conventional Li-ion batteries.

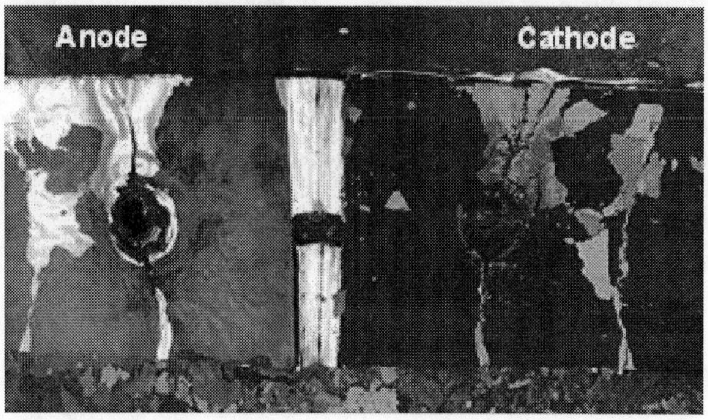

Figure 5. Torn down cell from 200 Wh module following penetration by a 2 cm diameter nail.

CELX-RC Battery Examples

Several different CELX-RC-based military battery prototypes have been or are being developed by CAMX Power in government-sponsored work. Two examples, a 0V-capable 60Ah 6T battery and a high-power buffering module are described below.

0V-Capable 6T Battery:

A CELX-RC-based, 0V-capable 6T battery prototype meeting type 1-A55 battery performance requirements of the MIL-PRF-32565C 6T Lithium-ion battery specification was made at CAMX Power from 6parallel 11-series strings of 10 Ah pouch cells. Figure 6 shows the battery's voltage characteristics. The figure shows that the battery's post-0V room temperature recharge characteristic matches its first charge curve, indicating that discharge to 0V essentially returns the battery to its as-made state. Furthermore, Figure 6 shows that the battery can be fully recharged from the 0V condition at -40 °C (-40 °F).

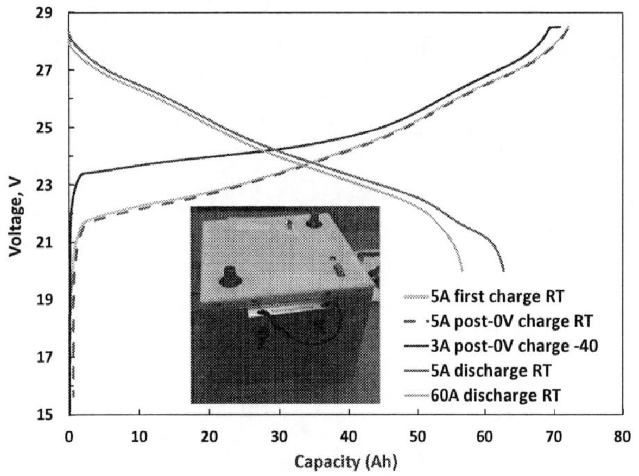

Figure 6. Charge and discharge voltage curves for CELX-RC-based 6T battery prototype (picture inset) at RT and 3A charge curve at -40 °C.

The battery's excellent low-temperature performance was further demonstrated by its cold cranking performance. While meeting the type 1-A55 battery requirement for 30-second 200 A pulse capability above 14.4 V at -40 °C, the battery also met the type 1-B55 requirement for 30-second 400 A pulse capability at -40 °C, as shown in Figure 7.

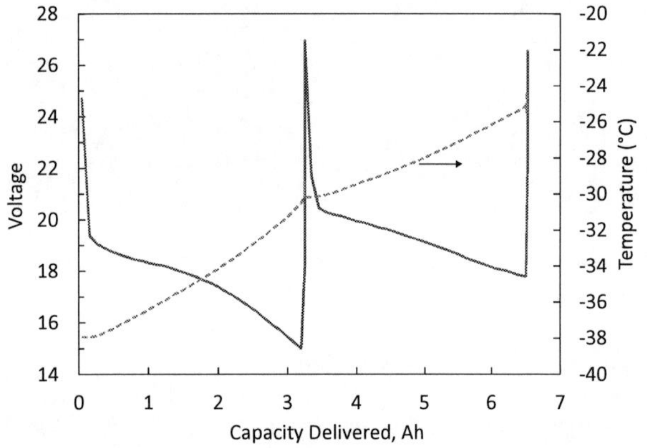

Figure 7. Voltage and internal temperature of CELX-RC-based 6T battery prototype at -40 °C as it was discharged at 400 A in two 30-second pulses with 5 minutes intervening rest.

Figure 7 shows that the battery's ohmic self-heating significantly boosted its low-temperature performance, and this was even more clearly demonstrated by results of discharge testing at -60 °C, shown in Figure 8. Results in Figure 8 show that even at such extremely low temperature, the battery delivered over half of its capacity when discharged at the 1C rate, with voltage reversal starting after about 2 Ah of charge had passed. The -60 °C discharges shown in Figure 8 were performed in sequence without removing the battery from the -60 °C temperature chamber, and with the battery being recharged to 28.5 V at 3 A rate at -60 °C, also demonstrating its exceptional low-temperature charging capabilities.

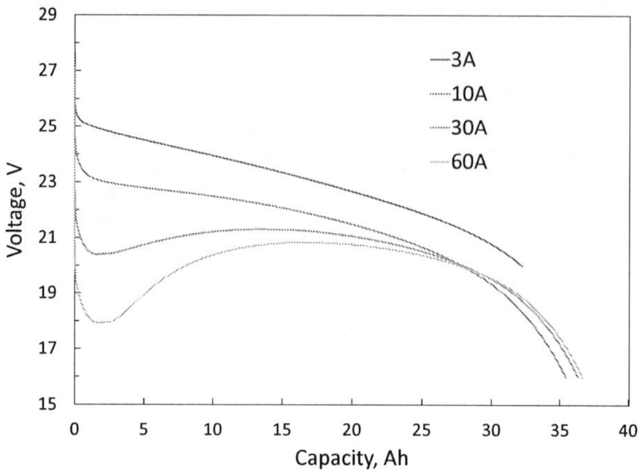

Figure 8. Constant current discharges of CELX-RC-based 6T battery prototype at -60 °C.

A 6T battery of this type could provide several unique advantages. Its 0V capability, robustness, and safety in the fully discharged condition would simplify logistical management. Its exceptional low-temperature performance can be advantageous in the emerging Arctic operational theatre. And its excellent safety in the charged condition can overcome concerns surrounding deployment of Li-ion battery-equipped vehicles by Navy vessels.

High-Power Buffering Module:

An unmanaged CELX-RC-based module built from a 12-series, 2-parallel array of 2 Ah pouch cells was developed to address replacement of the MIL-B-11188/2 4HN flooded lead-acid battery. The 4HN is used in the Bradley Fighting Vehicle to stabilize voltage when electrical load transients occur within the vehicle's turret power bus. Flooded lead-acid batteries are being replaced by AGM types, but these do not tolerate high current charge pulses as well as the older flooded batteries do, prompting interest in alternative technologies.

Figure 9 shows results for pulse charging of the 4.3Ah CELX-RC module when it was already charged to 28.5V and at >90% SOC. Results in Figure 9 show that the module accepted charge power of about 4.5 kW before reaching the 30V limit of the cycler used to run the test, and was projected to accommodate initial pulse current up to 530 A (~17.5 kW) and current up to 370 A (~12 kW) for 1 second within the 33 V operating voltage limit of the MIL-STD-1275 28V DC bus interface standard.

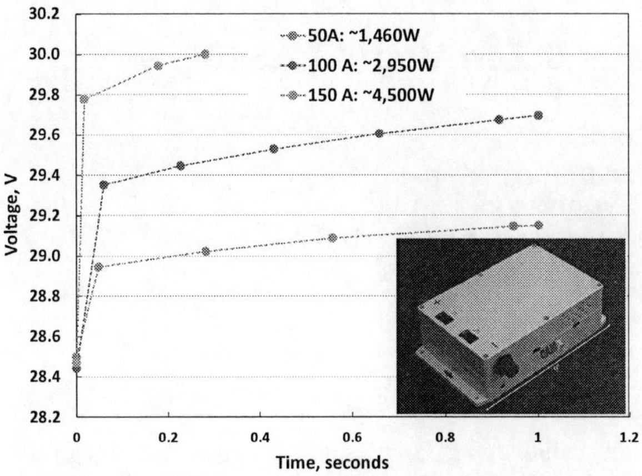

Figure 9. Voltage during constant current charging for 1 second or to 30V of CELX-RC-based 2.7 liter, 4.3 Ah, 100 Wh battery module (picture inset) at indicated currents and corresponding approximate powers, after the module had been charged to 28.5V.

The module also demonstrated exceptional high-power and low-temperature discharge performance as shown by the -18 °C pulse discharge and -40 °C continuous discharge results in Figure 10. Although the module is only one third the volume and less than one fifth the weight of a 4HN battery, it met the MIL-B-11188/2 requirement for the 4HN battery to deliver 75 A above 12V (equivalent to 1 V per cell) at -40 °C for at least 1.75 minutes. In other tests, the module readily performed discharge profiles emulating electrical loads of critical vehicle weapon systems. Other opportunities for high-power CELX-RC technology are being explored, including applications needing the power density of ultracapacitors but with up to 10 times their energy density.

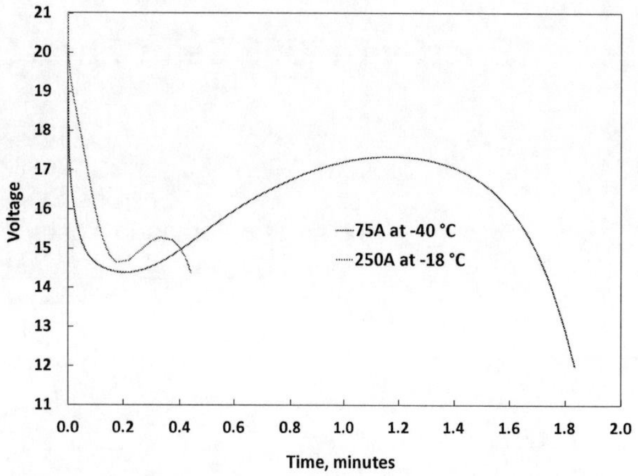

Figure 10. 30-second discharge pulsing at -18 °C and 75 A continuous discharge at -40 °C for CELX-RC-based 4.3 Ah battery module.

Conclusions

CELX-RC Li-ion cell technology offers several unique advantages that conventional Li-ion technology cannot provide for specialized military applications. Specifically, its outstanding safety, low-temperature and rapid charge capabilities, high-power capability, and tolerance for 0V discharge and unmanaged pack cycling can meet military needs that are not shared with the COTS market. CELX-RC batteries can thus provide vital benefits for critical DoD missions.

Acknowledgements

This material is based on work performed under Defense Logistics Agency SBIR contract # SP4701-19-C-0050 and U.S. Army SBIR contract # W56HZV-18-C-001.

EnerSys 18650 Cell Characteristics and ZeroVolt^{TM} Capability

Hiroshi Nakahara
Quallion R&D Group
EnerSys Advanced Systems
12744 San Fernando Road, Suite 03-100, Sylmar, CA 91342, U.S.A.
Hiroshi.nakahara@eas.enersys.com / 818-833-2000

Abstract

Quallion, a subsidiary of EnerSys Advance Systems (EAS) has been developing and manufacturing 18650 secondary lithium-ion cells (QL1500A) with primary focus for aerospace applications. QL1500A (1.5Ah, 3.6V) is expected to last more than 40,000 cycles under low earth orbit (LEO) cycle condition. This cell is EAS's baselined 18650 cell product developed over the past several years. EAS set up the manufacturing line for the QL1500A in Sylmar, CA, U.S.A. in 2013. In this paper, the characteristics of QL1500A is introduced including EAS's 18650 cell manufacturing capability. In addition, EAS added ZeroVolt^{TM} feature [1-3] to QL1500A which enables long-term storage at 0V with no degradation (QL1500A-ZV). The Quallion patented cell provides the unique characteristic of an 18650 cell with ZeroVolt^{TM} capability and is presented in this paper with low cell voltage tolerances of less than 2V. This ZeroVolt^{TM} technology provides low cost and maintenance storage requirements as well as ease of operations. Furthermore, EAS is actively developing the new cell products with higher energy densities of 18650 cells associated with the advanced cell material developments. The status of development in EAS with the methodology to increase energy density on 18650 cell product line is discussed.

Keywords

Lithium secondary battery; Cylindrical cell; 18650; Overdischarge; ZeroVolt; High energy density; Aerospace; Satellite

Introduction

The lithium-ion secondary battery market is growing dramatically in recent years because of its high energy density for a variety of applications. Applications for electric vehicle and mobile devices are accelerating the market-size growth and further technology advancement in energy density. In addition, the supply chains of lithium-ion cells and the raw materials has been challenging domestically, and the major manufacturing locations of lithium-ion cells are localized outside the United States causing geopolitical and logistical concerns. Many automobile manufacturers have been focused on setting up lithium-ion cell mass production and increasing production capacity in the United States to control supply chains of batteries and raw materials.

EAS has been manufacturing lithium-ion secondary cells including 18650 cells for more than two decades, which feature long life and high reliability for medical device and aerospace applications. For those niche applications, EAS developed ZeroVolt^{TM} to enhance long cell life performance. EAS's 18650 cell products include standard type (product code name: QL1500A) and ZeroVolt^{TM}-integrated type (QL1500A-ZV). ZeroVolt^{TM} technology increased the reliability of a power source modules in devices by enabling operation in low cell voltage ranges of less than 2V. This low voltage technology requires little maintenance and is able to use a simplified battery management system, making it ideal for long term storage before a mission, and long periods of dormancy during mission operations. The ZeroVolt^{TM} technology has been validated to preserve the performances of lithium-ion cells after 10-year storage at 0V. EAS is actively improving cell energy density because of the high demand of increasing energy density of EAS's 18650 cell products. As a part of energy density improvement, EAS has developed an 18650 cell with 2.5Ah assembled into power modules for a satellite which was deployed. Furthermore, a 3Ah-class cell was prototyped, which is currently undergoing chemistry and manufacturing optimization.

In this paper, the cell characteristics of QL1500A, QL1500A-ZV, and ZeroVolt^{TM} technology are introduced. Furthermore, improving cell energy density up to 3.4Ah / 270Wh/kg is discussed.

EAS's 18650 Cell Characteristics

QL1500A and QL1500A-ZV cell characteristics baselines are summarized in Table 1. A typical discharge curve of QL1500A-ZV cell is shown in Fig. 1. Cell envelope sizes for QL1500A cell and QL1500A-ZV cell are the same. Cell capacities for both cells at low C-rate discharge are the same as well. AC impedance is for QL1500A-ZV is higher than QL1500A due to the electrode mechanical design. However, QL1500A-ZV has an advantage in its light weight (higher weight energy density) compared with QL1500A (145Wh/kg vs. 120Wh/kg).

Table 1 18650 ZeroVolt cell characteristics

	QL1500A (Standard)	QL1500A-ZV (ZeroVolt-Integrated)
Diameter (mm), max.	18.5	18.5
Length (mm), max.	65.2	65.2
Weight (grams), max.	44	37
AC impedance (Ohms), max.	0.05	0.11
Discharge Capacity (Ah), typical	1.45	1.45
Weight energy density (Wh/kg), typical	120	145

*1 measured at 1kHz, room temperature

*2 measured under the condition of discharging at C/5 after charging under C/5 to 4.1V with tapered current to C/100 at 25°C

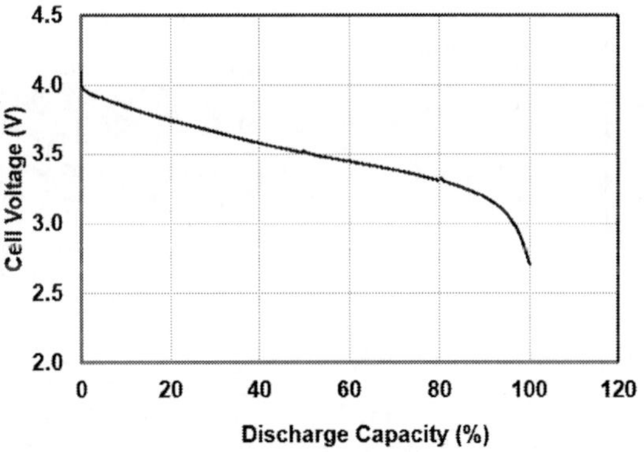

Fig. 1 Discharge curve of EAS 18650 ZeroVolt™ cell under discharging at C/2 after charging under C/5 to 4.1V with tapered current to C/100 at 25°C

ZeroVolt Characterization Results

QL1500A long term characteristic was evaluated under 40% DOD LEO cycling at room temperature. Full discharge capacity to 100% DOD at C/2 and room temperature was measured during 40% LEO cycling every 400 cycles. Fig. 2 shows the measured capacity during 40% LEO cycling at room temperature. Fig. 3 shows the cell voltage at the end of discharge during 40% DOD LEO cycling with QL1500A-ZV. QL1500A cell (R&D test cell) demonstrated more than 98% of capacity retention (measured at 100% DOD at room temperature) after 6,900 LEO cycling. It is expected more than 80% of capacity retention after 40,000 LEO cycles based on this result. In addition, EAS's cell manufacturing capability was evaluated under the same test condition. The cell test results were compared between R&D test cells and production cells manufactured at the cell manufacturing facility in Sylmar, CA. Production cells demonstrated the same capacity retention to R&D cell at 4,000 LEO cycle with the same linear trend on capacity retentions during LEO cycling.

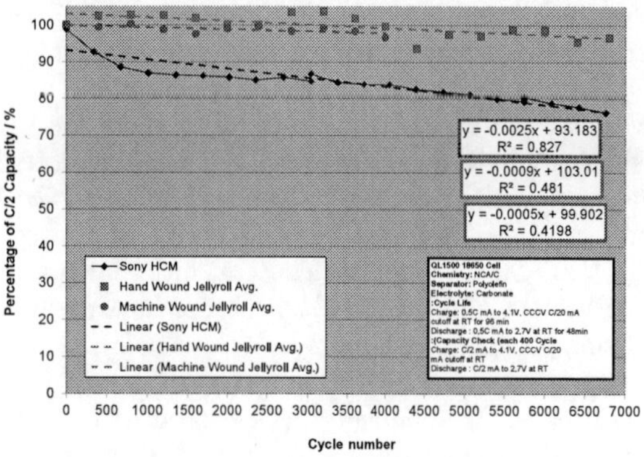

Fig. 2 Capacity retention of QL1500A measured under 100% DOD discharge during 40% DOD LEO cycling at room temperature

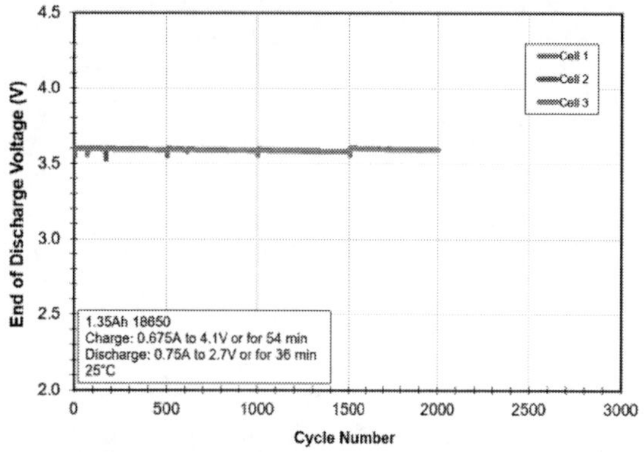

Fig. 3 Capacity retention of QL1500A measured under 100% DOD discharge during 40% DOD LEO cycling at room temperature

ZeroVolt™ technology was integrated to QL1500A-ZV to add more value for aerospace applications. ZeroVolt™ technology was developed by EAS to prevent cell degradations and safety concerns observed in conventional lithium-ion cells in low voltage range (<2V). This technology was originally developed for implantable medical device application cells (0.003 ~ 1.8Ah), and it was applied to QL075KA prismatic cells (72Ah, 3.6V) in the past.

Storage test at 0V was performed with conventional 18650 cells (no ZeroVolt™) and ZeroVolt™ integrated cells by externally shorting with 20-ohm resistor (Fig. 4). Shorted test cells were stored at room temperature for 3 days. After the storage, the test cells were charged to 3V at C/200 at room temperature. The cell discharge capacity was measured under CC-CV charge at C/2 with tapered current cutoff of C/20 followed by discharge at C/2 rate to 2.7V before and after 0V-storage to measure the degrees of cell performance degradation at 0V. Fig. 5 shows discharge curves of 18650 test cells before and after 0V-storage at room temperature. (a) and (b) are the discharge curves for conventional cell and ZeroVolt™ integrated cell, respectively. The conventional 18650 cell lost 77% of discharge capacity during 0V-storage (Fig. 5a). On the other hand, ZeroVolt™ integrated 18650 cells maintained 100% discharge capacity after 0V-storage (Fig. 5b).

ZeroVolt™ technology (QL1500A-ZV) was characterized extensively at lower temperatures between -70°C and -20°C for aerospace applications. The cell was discharged at a rate of C/5 at 20°C and held at zero volts. Cell temperature was ramped to the target storage temperature. Each cell was stored for 7 days at the selected test temperature. Each cell then was returned to 20°C after 0V-storage at the prescribed temperature. Each cell was recharged at a rate of C/20 to 2.7V, then charged at C/5 to 100% SoC with a taper to C/100. Discharge capacity was measured before and after 0V-storage. Each cell was electrically cycled for 100 cycles at a C/2 charge/discharge rate to 100% DoD. After the discharge capacity measurement cycles, 80% DOD cycling test took place at 20°C for the cells.

Fig. 6 shows the discharge capacity retentions of QL1500A-ZV after 0V storage at low temperatures between -70oC ~ -20°C. At first, the discharge capacities measured after storage at 0V for 7 days at respective temperature are plotted. Furthermore, the discharge capacity retentions after 100 cycles under 80% DOD of charge and discharge cycling at 20°C were overlaid on Fig. 6 to evaluate the impact of 0V-storage at low temperatures on cyclability.

Fig. 7 shows the discharge capacities during 80% DOD cycling at 20°C. Discharge capacities of QL1500A-ZV cells after 0V-storage at low temperature were retained fully.

0V-storage did not affect cell cyclability at all. As a result, QL1500A-ZV is suitable for deep space exploration because of 0V-storage capability at wide range of operation temperatures.

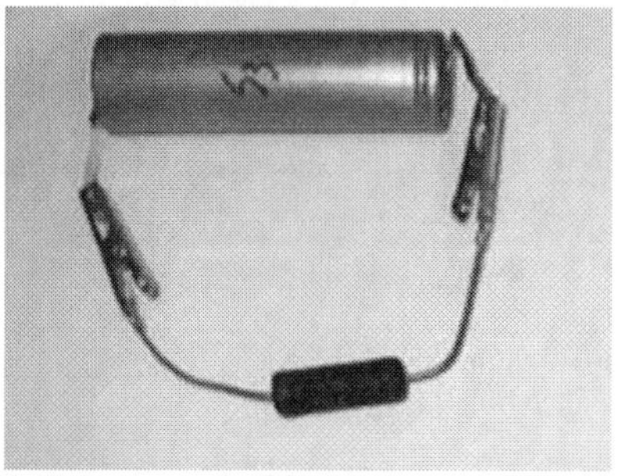

Fig. 4 Photograph of 18650 test cell with a 20-ohm resistor under 0V storage test

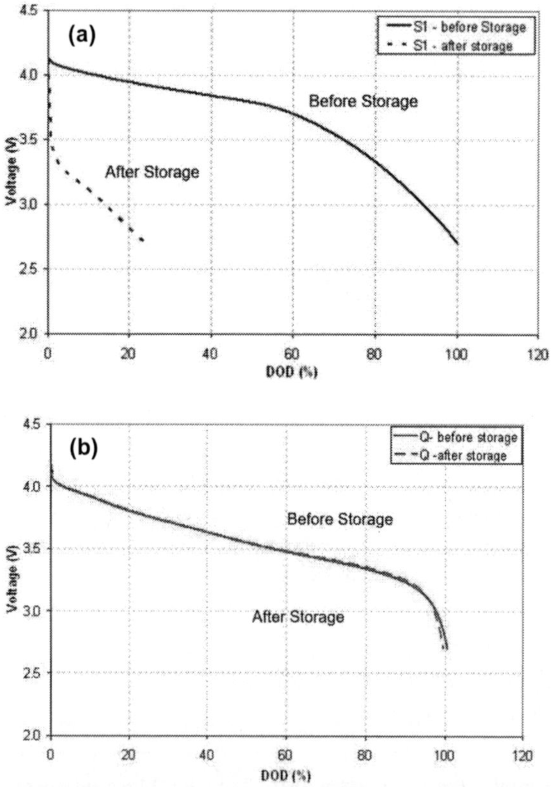

Fig. 5 Discharge curves of 18650 test cells before and after 0V storage at room temperature; (a) conventional cell, (b) ZeroVolt™ integrated cell

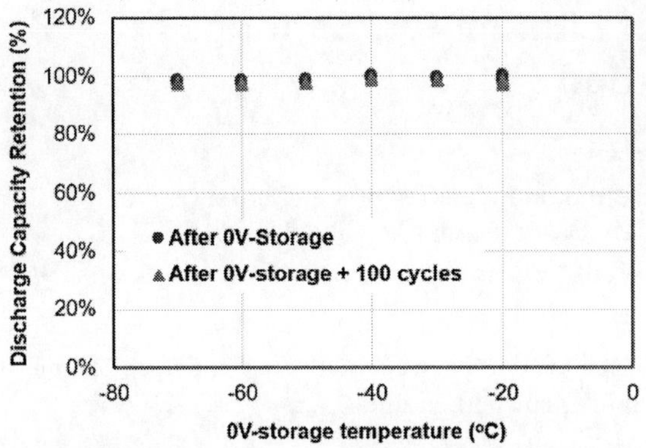

Fig. 6 Discharge capacity retention of QL1500A-ZV after 0V storage at low temperatures between -70°C ~ -20°C. Discharge capacities were measured after storage at 0V for 7 days at respective temperature and were measured one more time after 100 cycles of charge and discharge at 20°C.

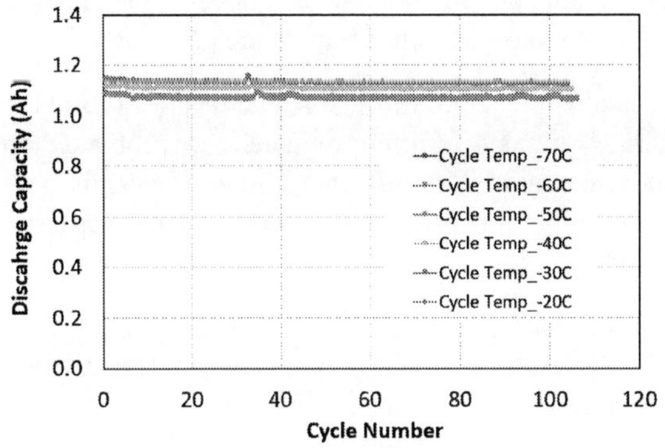

Fig. 7 Discharge capacity retention of QL1500A-ZV during 80% DOD cycling at 20°C

High Energy Density 18650 Cell Development

Improvement on energy density has been carried out in EAS. EAS established a brand name with highly reliable lithium-ion cell manufacturing for critical missions and operations in the medical device and aerospace industries. Because of recent demand for higher energy densities in those applications, EAS has been developing higher energy density 18650 cells. 2.5Ah-class 18650 cells with ZeroVolt^{TM} capability for aerospace application were developed. The new 2.5Ah cell was assembled and has been deployed to a power module for a satellite in operation. This space mission is validating use-case of the cell mechanical design and high energy density chemistry currently day-by-day. Furthermore, EAS is continuing to increase energy density by introducing new chemistries including high nickel NMC cathodes and Si-based anodes. Fig. 8 shows an example of a high energy type 18650 prototype cell (3-Ah class 18650 cell). Discharge capacity was measured under C/10 rate at room temperature. Discharge capacity was 2.95Ah.

Continuous development to increase the energy density of the18650 cell will be done with not only the introduction of new chemistries but also with the improvement of cell manufacturing processes with tighter tolerances and mechanical designs of each component while still balancing the safety characteristics of the cell. Currently, EAS is working towards a 3.4Ah, 270Wh/kg 18650 cell using established ZeroVolt^{TM} technology for an industry leading energy-rich and stable cell.

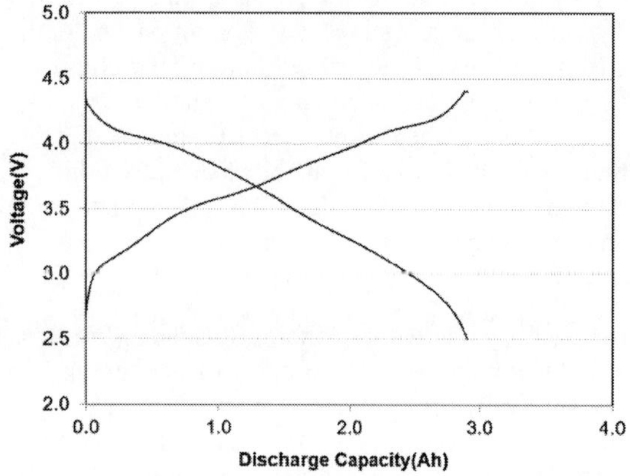

Fig. 8 Charge and discharge curves of 3Ah-class 18650 prototype cell

Summary

EAS 18650 cells (QL1500A and QL1500A-ZV) patented technology have been validated for aerospace applications. ZeroVolt^{TM} technology was characterized extensively at lower temperatures for future deep space explorations. In addition, EAS has developed 2.5Ah cell in these 18650-cell product line which design is also validated in space mission currently. The continuous improvement on increasing energy density will be carried out to respond the high demands from the industries.

Reference

1. USP 6,596,439 and USP 6,553,263 "*Lithium-ion battery capable of being discharged to zero volts*", Hisashi Tsukamoto, Clay Kishiyama, Mikito Nagata, Hiroshi Nakahara, Tiehua Piao (2000)
2. Space Power Workshop, "*Quallion Prismatic Aerospace Batteries*", Hisashi Tsukamoto (2006)
3. NASA Battery Workshop, "*LEO Cycling Performance after Zero Volt Storage of 8 Series Test Module with EnerSys Lithium-Ion Chemistry for the Aerospace Application*" Hiroshi Nakahara (2016)

A Study of the State of Charge of Lithium-ion Batteries in Transportation

Daniel Keslar
Federal Aviation Administration (FAA), William J. Hughes Technical Center
ANG-E212 Fire Test Section, Fire Safety Branch, Atlantic City NJ
Daniel.Keslar@faa.gov

Abstract

The transportation of lithium-ion batteries on aircraft is heavily regulated due to fire hazards associated with these power sources. Domestic and international regulations require lithium-ion cells not packed with or contained in equipment (Lithium-ion batteries, UN3480) to be no greater than 30% state of charge (SOC) when shipped within aircraft. Previous FAA studies have determined that cells that exceed this level are a serious hazard due to risk of thermal runaway and can lead to an unsafe condition on an aircraft.

However, despite these restrictions, isolated fire incidents involving lithium-ion cells have continued to occur at all-cargo sort facilities involving packages previously shipped by aircraft. FAA analyses of these thermal incidents have determined that the cells from these incidents exceeded the 30% SOC limit.

In order to understand the extent of this problem, an analysis was conducted on lithium-ion cells sold on different e-commerce platforms. The SOC of these cells was evaluated using battery analysis equipment. Results indicated that many cells continue to be shipped on aircraft at an unsafe SOC. Furthermore, some shipped packages containing lithium-ion cells were observed to have been inadequately stored and labeled.

Keywords

Lithium-ion; cells; batteries; battery transport; state of charge; SOC; UN3480; thermal runaway

Introduction

Due to the fire hazards associated with lithium-ion batteries, the transportation of lithium-ion cells and batteries on aircraft is heavily regulated. Lithium-ion cells are known to undergo a phenomenon known as thermal runaway, a self-sustaining chemical process in which a sudden uncontrollable increase in temperature occurs, often causing the battery to release toxic gases and flames. Thermal runaway may occur when cells are overheated, overcharged, mishandled or have a manufacturing defect leading to an internal short circuit.

The most well-known plane accident involving lithium-ion cells occurred in 2010 on UPS Airlines Flight 6, a cargo flight in which over 80,000 lithium-ion cells were stored within the aircraft's main cargo deck. A rapidly developing in-flight fire occurred within the cargo deck, which quickly damaged fire protection and critical systems, impeding the pilots' ability to make an emergency landing.

As a direct result of this and similar accidents, bulk cargo shipments of lithium-ion cells are prohibited on passenger aircraft. Shipment of lithium-ion cells are only permitted within cargo aircraft if certain criteria are met.

One of these requirements relates to a cell's SOC. The SOC is a cell's charge level compared to its total capacity.

Previous FAA studies have determined that the thermal energy released by a failure of a lithium-ion cell has a direct relationship between the total electrical cell capacity and SOC (Lyon, Richard, & Walters, 2016). Other studies have shown that cells at high SOCs are more likely to produce higher heat release rates, maximum temperatures, and concentrations of flammable and toxic gases during a thermal runaway event (Maloney, 2016; Wang, et al., 2018; Maloney, 2022). An example of cells undergoing thermal runaway at various SOCs is shown below in Figure 1.

As a consequence of these hazards, domestic and international regulations require that lithium-ion cells not packed with or contained within equipment (UN3480, Lithium-ion Batteries) must have a SOC no greater than 30% when transported on cargo aircraft. Additionally, packages must have specific labeling, signifying the specific UN hazardous material classification and/or forbidding the use in passenger aircraft, if required by regulation.

Figure 1. From left to right: Peak reactions of 6 Watt-hour lithium-ion pouch cells undergoing thermal runaway at 30%, 70% and 100% SOC, respectively

However, despite these restrictions, recent incidents at all-cargo sort facilities and on airport runways have continued to occur. Analyses of the cells from these incidents indicate that many of the cells continue to be shipped at a SOC greater than 30% (Keslar, 2022; Keslar, 2023). Although this data indicates that cells were shipped at high SOCs in isolated events, it is unknown if regulations were being adhered to on a wider scale.

Figure 2. Package containing li-ion cells undergoing thermal runaway in an all-cargo sort facility after previously being shipped on aircraft

In order to determine if air shipment regulations were being followed, an analysis was conducted by the FAA to determine if lithium-ion cells sold on various e-commerce platforms adhered to SOC requirements when shipped by aircraft. Cells were shipped to a non-FAA address and then brought to and tested at the FAA's William J. Hughes Technical Center.

Objective

The primary objective of this study was to measure the as-delivered state of charge of lithium-ion cells that were shipped via aircraft.

A secondary objective of this study was to examine the fire hazard of delivered packages, specifically examining the manner in which the cells were stored and the labeling on the exterior of the packaging.

Evaluated Cells

Lithium-ion cells of a variety of different sizes and chemistries were evaluated. Evaluated chemistries included lithium cobalt oxide ($LiCoO_2$), lithium iron phosphate ($LiFePO_4$), lithium manganese cobalt oxide ($LiMnCoO_2$) and unknown chemistries not specified during purchase.

Both cylindrical and lithium-ion polymer (pouch) cells were evaluated. Prismatic cells were not evaluated. Different sizes of the cylindrical cells include; 32650s, 26650s, 18700s, 18650s, 14500s, and 10440s. All evaluated cells ranged from 1 Watt-hour (Wh) to 22 Wh. A small sample of the cells evaluated within this study is shown below in Figure 3.

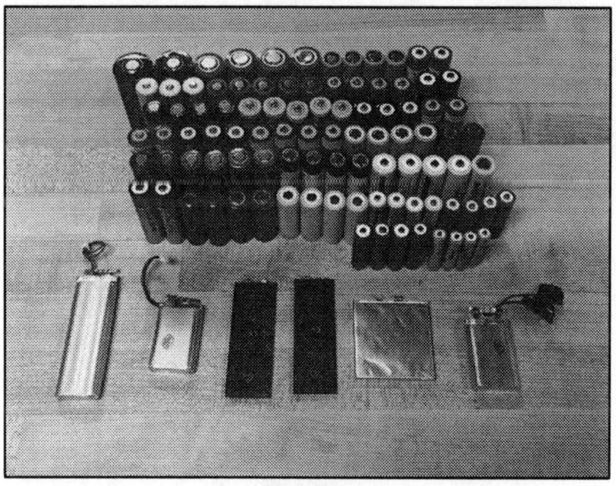

Figure 3. Collection of some of the pouch and cylindrical cells evaluated in this study

Cells that could be delivered within a short time period (1-3 days) from a cross-country business address were targeted. However, it was often noted that packages were delivered without a detailed shipping history. Therefore, cells were categorized based on their suspected mode of transport as follows:

1. Confirmed Air Transport

2. Suspected Air Transport

3. Unknown Transport

4. Land Transport

State of Charge Analysis

The state of charge was measured using an Arbin Instruments battery analyzer, which operates with a measurement accuracy within 0.01% and a control accuracy within 0.02%. Cells were charged to full capacity using a Constant Current – Constant Voltage (CC–CV) charging method and then completely discharged. The current throughout this process was recorded and the initial SOC was calculated using the equation below:

$$SOC_{Initial} = \frac{Capacity_{Total} - Charge\ Capacity}{Capacity_{Total}}$$

The C-rate and temperature are two variables that have been observed to impact SOC measurements. C-rate is the measure of the rate at which a cell is discharged relative to its maximum capacity. Throughout these tests, the ambient temperature was kept constant at room temperature (70°F). Furthermore, a C-rate was used according to manufacturer data sheets. However, if a manufacturer data sheet was unavailable, a 0.2 C-rate of the rated capacity of the cell was used.

Results

Initial test results indicate that many lithium-ion cells continue to be shipped at a SOC greater than the 30% limit. In total, over 100 cells from over 20 different shipments have been evaluated. Figure 4 shows a breakdown of the measured SOC for all cells based on their respective mode of transport.

For cells that were confirmed to have been transported on aircraft, more than 50% of the cells were found to have been shipped at an unsafe SOC. In total, 21 of the evaluated 36 cells were charged greater than the 30% limit.

Cells categorized as "Suspected Air Transport" and "Unknown Transport" had limited shipment information, which prevented confirmation of the shipment method. Overall, similar conclusions were observed for these categorized cells when compared to those shipped by air. The measured SOC for many cells within both of these categories exceeded the required 30% threshold with some observed to exceed 70% SOC.

Cells transported by land do not have to adhere to the 30% SOC requirement. However, data was still collected for the cells categorized in this transport

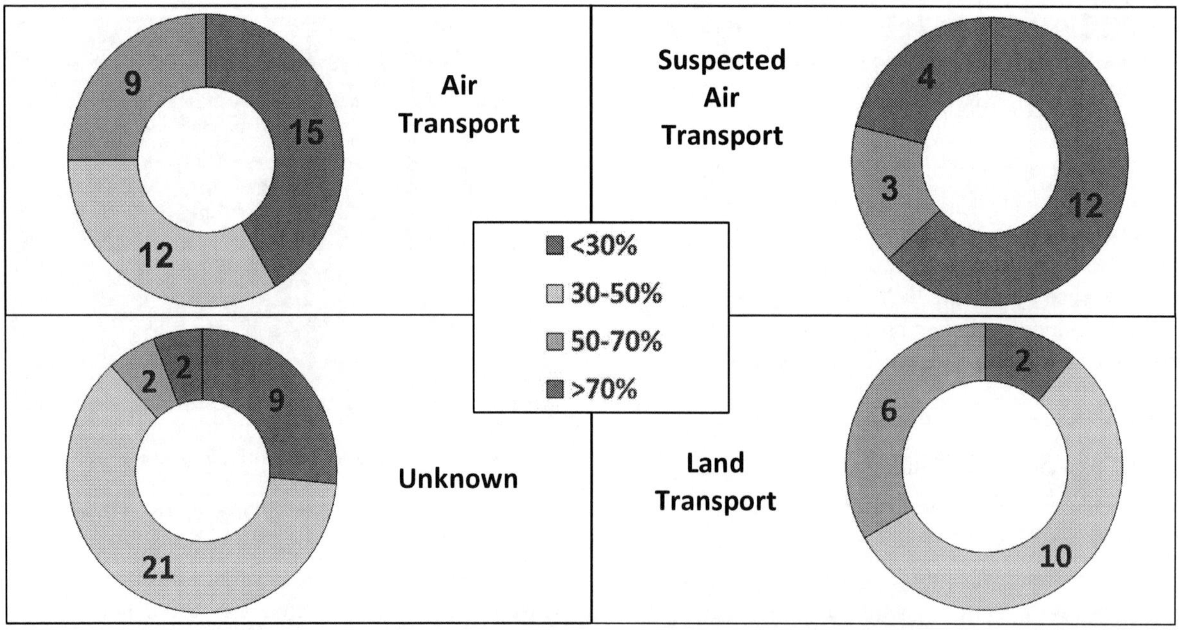

Figure 4. SOC Calculations for all four categorized shipment methods

method because it was noted that multiple sellers and shipment options were available during purchase. Therefore, it is possible that the selected cells could have been shipped via air depending on the selected options.

Packaging and Labeling

In addition to the SOC evaluations, the interior of packages was evaluated for proper storage and labeling. A majority of packages were observed to follow proper storage procedures (i.e., cells placed in non-metallic inner packaging that ensured cells did not make contact with electrically conductive materials or cells of the opposite polarity). However, it was noted that there were some exceptions to this, as shown in Figure 5. This image shows a package ordered from a secondhand seller from one of the evaluated e-commerce platforms.

Figure 5. Untampered package (left) and package with top plastic wrap removed (right)

Within this package, over 60 cells were sporadically stored with little to no protective packaging to prevent cell terminals from making contact with other cells/terminals of the opposite polarity. Furthermore, several of the cells within the package were observed to have significant signs of swelling and corrosion, indicating that a potential fire threat is present amongst secondhand lithium-ion sellers as well.

Besides proper storage, packages were evaluated for proper labeling. A significant number of packages analyzed in this study were found to have incorrect or missing labeling. Cells not packed with or contained in equipment must have UN ID number "3480" and a lithium battery mark on the exterior of the container signifying that lithium-ion cells are contained within. It was observed that a significant number of delivered packages within this analysis did not have this marking.

Conclusions

Regulations require lithium-ion cells not packed with or contained in equipment (UN3480, Lithium-ion Batteries) must have a SOC below 30% when shipped on aircraft. Many of the tested cells were observed to exceed this charge level. Furthermore, some packages confirmed as being shipped by air were determined to be a significant fire risk, as cells were damaged and improperly stored and labeled.

Test results suggest that additional measures may be needed to ensure safe shipment of lithium-ion cells on aircraft. Although regulations have been implemented on SOC to reduce the hazards of lithium-ion cells, enforcement of these regulations is difficult. Measuring the SOC is a difficult value to estimate within the field. Accurate SOC evaluations require expensive equipment and a considerable amount of time. It is not feasible for airlines to measure the SOC of all transported cells prior to air shipment. Therefore, additional safety measures may be needed to ensure safe shipment of lithium-ion batteries on cargo aircraft.

References

1. Keslar, D. (2022). *An Analysis of State of Charge in Lithium-ion Batteries.* FAA.
2. Keslar, D. (2023). *A State of Charge Analysis of Lithium-ion Cells Shipped via Air.* FAA.
3. Lyon, Richard, & Walters, R. (2016, April). *Energy Release by Rechargeable Lithium-Ion Batteries in Thermal Runaway.* FAA. Retrieved from https://www.fire.tc.faa.gov/pdf/TC-TN16-22.pdf
4. Maloney, T. (2016). *Lithium Battery Thermal Runaway Vent Gas Analysis.* FAA.
5. Maloney, T. (2022). *Evaluation of Lithium Battery Thermal Runaway Propagation.* FAA.
6. Wang, Z., Ouyang, D., Chen, M., Wang, X., Zhang, Z., & Wang, J. (2018). *Fire Behavior of Lithium-Ion Battery With Different States of Charge Induced by High Incident Heat Fluxes.*

Discharge in Unactivated Thermal Batteries

Daniel E. Wesolowski*, Brian Perdue, Diane Forbes, Greg Peacock, John Taphouse, Hans Papenguth

Power Sources Technology Group
Sandia National Laboratories
Albuquerque, NM 87185-0614, USA
dewesol@sandia.gov
Contact author: dewesol@sandia.gov / 1-505-845-0614

Abstract:. *Thermal batteries are often kept in a continuous loaded condition for decades. Most modern thermal batteries have a solid-state internal resistance on the order of hundreds of megaohms. Almost any external circuit is a parasitic drain that must be accounted for in estimates of the battery shelf-life. Detailed measurements of battery internal resistance were performed in this study. Temperature was varied at relevant conditions, from room temperature to a maximum short-term storage condition temperature. Battery internal resistance (IR) was estimated from voltage measured across a 2 MOhm external resistor. Leakage current was found to have an excellent fit to an Arrhenius rate relationship for each battery considered. Activation energies (E_a) were measured for CoS_2 and FeS_2 batteries with multiple types of binder (MgO formed by different processes) and multiple electrolytes (eutectic, low melting, and all-lithium). Battery self-discharge rates varied from 0.02%/year to 25%/year at 35°C, meaning for some batteries this mechanism is important for shelf-life estimation. E_a varied linearly in the range of 60 to 100 kJ/mol with the mole fraction of lithium ions in the electrolyte. E_a also varied linearly with the fraction of electrolyte added to the anode. These observations suggest that the charge transfer reaction from the anode to the electrolyte is rate limiting for discharge in the solid state.*

Keywords: molten salt; lithium silicon; iron disulfide and cobalt disulfide; accelerated aging

Introduction

Thermal batteries are used as the power source in many mission-critical applications where an external switch is an unacceptable mission risk. The ignition system for the thermal battery replaces the switch in these applications, enabling the mission circuitry to be brought up as soon as the battery can source sufficient power. Modern thermal batteries (using a lithium or lithium alloy anode, salt mixture electrolyte with a MgO binder, and a metal sulfide cathode) have internal resistances that are on the order of hundreds of megaohms (MOhm) at room temperature. This resistance is so high that batteries have long been considered to be "inert" until activated [1]. Solid-state switches such as field effect transistors (FETs) have leakage currents on the order of 0.1 microamps under similar conditions [2]. 0.1μA at 10V is an internal resistance of 100 MOhm, which is at best on the order of magnitude of the "switch" inside a thermal battery. The relatively low resistance of even the best isolated electrical systems compared to the battery means that any battery connected to a circuit is effectively shorted. This may be through leakage through FETs, reverse current though diodes, capacitor leakage, or the battery might literally be shorted (e.g. through a bridgewire), but any realistic electrical circuit connected to the battery will drop the voltage across the terminals to nearly zero volts. However, the electrochemical couples in the battery stack are still operational, so the battery will discharge during its entire lifetime. This leakage current must be accounted for when designing the thermal battery.

The Li(Si)/FeS_2 thermal battery system was developed in the early 1980's as a long operational life replacement for Ca/$CaCrO_4$ thermal batteries with lower intrinsic hazards [1]. The need for shelf stability is intrinsic to thermal batteries, so several accelerated aging studies were performed prior to the widespread use of this battery technology [3,4]. The studies identified the dominant aging mechanism as lithium oxidation from oxygen leaking through hermetic seals. Follow on work [5,6] has continued to focus on the aging of the chemical reagents within the battery as an isolated system.

This work examines the impact of the external circuit on the shelf-life of the batteries. Primarily, this work consisted of performing precision leakage current measurements at near-ambient conditions. Several anode, cathode, and separator compositions were considered. Electrochemical impedance spectroscopy (EIS) was used to help identify the rate-limiting step in the discharge reaction. Additionally, single-cell testing was performed on cells under accelerated aging conditions to validate that the observed leakage current has relevance to batteries in storage.

Experimental Procedures

Leakage current measurements were performed by measuring the voltage across a 2 MOhm 1/4W resistor using a Keithley 2700 digital multimeter. The input impedance of this meter is greater than 10 GOhm at the 10V range used. The temperature was then raised from room temperature to as high as 75°C by stepping in 10°C increments and holding to equilibrium.

Thermal batteries were constructed from a range of different materials. All were based on a $Li_{13}Si_4$ anode, but electrolyte was mixed with the anode material in the range of 0 to 25wt%. FeS_2 and CoS_2 cathodes were both used. Three electrolytes were considered: eutectic LiCl/KCl, the "all lithium" electrolyte of LiF/LiCl/LiBr, and a low-melting temperature electrolyte with LiCl/LiBr/KBr [8]. MgO binder was used, but several different products were considered. Finally, the batteries were also manufactured at two different battery vendors.

This wide range of changes means many more combinations are possible than were explored in the experimental matrix. The combinations that are available were examined to observe trends, but it is likely other inferences can be made. Accelerated aging studies were also performed in a manner similar to previous reports [5]. Units were held at temperature without any load applied. Single-cell testing was used to determine electrochemical capacity in these units after disassembly. Tests were performed at a constant 0.125 A/cm^2 discharge rate with periodic pulses to assess internal resistance. The key experimental variable in these tests was the use of two different types of MgO binder.

Results

Leakage current in every battery tested obeyed an Arrhenius dependence with temperature. Examples for live batteries are shown in Figure 1. Fit over the temperature range was extremely good, with R^2 values exceeding 0.99 for every test. Measurements of this activation energy were 55 to 82 kJ/mol for manufacturer #1 and about 91 to 107 kJ/mol for manufacturer #2. In addition to having a higher activation energy, the batteries from manufacturer #2 had 2-3 orders of magnitude lower absolute values of leakage current across the entire range of temperatures.

Several MgO types were considered in the study. In Figure 1 the "Traditional" MgO for Sandia batteries is compared to a representative "Alternate" MgO built into batteries by both manufacturers. The Alternate MgO batteries have an order of magnitude higher leakage current than the Traditional MgO, but the temperature dependence was very similar with an activation energy of 68 and 75 kJ/mol for manufacturer #1.

Batteries from Manufacturer #1 had the fraction of electrolyte in the anode varied from 0 to 25%. Batteries were manufactured from both MgOs for the 15% anode electrolyte concentration. Figure 2 shows that the activation energy changes linearly with fraction of electrolyte in the anode in live batteries, regardless of the absolute magnitude of the leakage current. The activation energy for D-tested batteries is also shown in Figure 2. Batteries D-tested in this experiment retain most of their active material (>50% electrochemical margin), so they will behave similarly to live batteries electrochemically. However, the electrolyte will move to its equilibrium location after activation (see Figure 5), and contaminants (such as water) will be consumed.

Batteries from Manufacturer 2 had several MgO types as well as several different electrolytes. Figure 3 shows the dependence of leakage current activation energy on the concentration of lithium ions in the electrolyte. There is a monotonic dependence, with a linear relationship used to guide the eye, but the fit is better against a power law dependence. The MgO used does not affect this relationship.

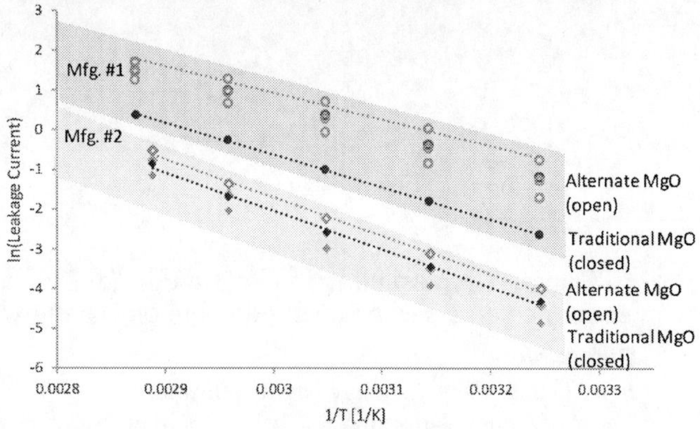

Figure 1. Arrhenius plot of leakage current vs. temperature.

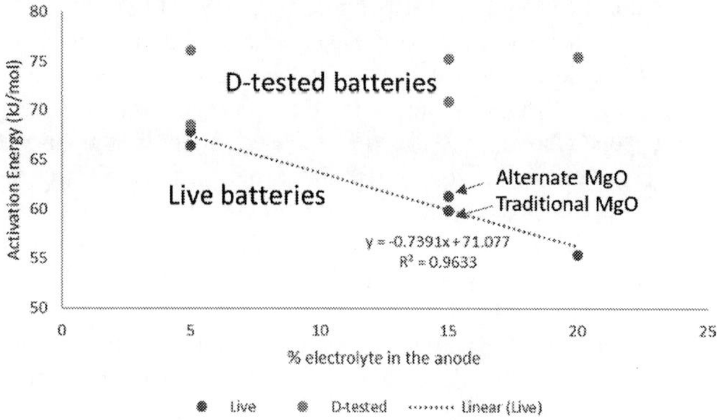

Figure 2. Activation energy vs. %electrolyte in anode (Mfg. #1, Alternate and traditional MgO).

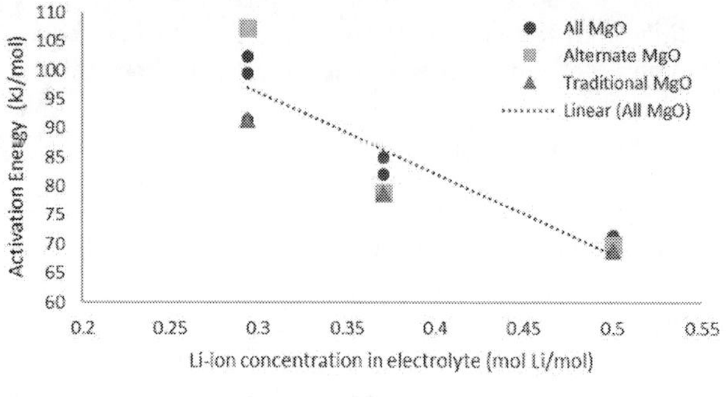

Figure 3. Activation energy vs. concentration of lithium ions in electrolyte (Mfg. 2, FeS_2 and CoS_2)

Electrochemical impedance spectroscopy (EIS) was performed using a Solartron impedance analyzer and analyzed with Scribner ZPlot using an equivalent circuit model. A 100 mV voltage oscillation was used and swept from 1 MHz to 1 mHz after equilibration at the test temperature. The battery tested has a low voltage tap that enables the use of the 10V limited potentiostat. Results for an Alternate MgO battery are in Figure 4.

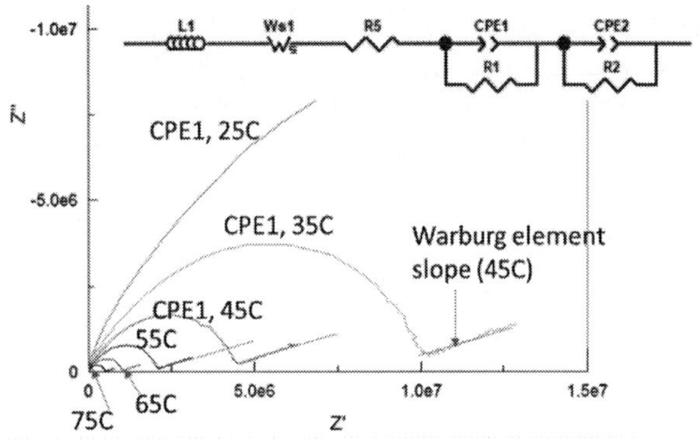

Figure 4. Nyquist plot and circuit model for EIS performed on a section of an Alternate MgO battery.

Discussion

Rate limitation for discharge before activation

The Arrhenius relationship for leakage current (Figure 1) indicates that there is a single activated process for this cathode formulation that controls leakage current over the entire near-ambient temperature range tested (25 to 75°C). This process is most likely the injection of lithium ions from the anode into the electrolyte. This process appears to be rate limiting because the activation energy has a linear dependence on the fraction of electrolyte in the anode (Figure 2). A higher surface area between the electrolyte and anode would only change the activation energy if this interface was related to the process that controls the overall leakage current. There is no dependence of activation energy on fraction of electrolyte in the anode after activation because the electrolyte moves to its equilibrium position, which is likely independent of the amount that is present at the start (Figure 5).

The dependence of activation energy on lithium-ion concentration in the electrolyte (Figure 3) is consistent with an anode-electrolyte interface limited reaction. Higher lithium-ion concentration will create more sites for the mobility of lithium-ions into the solid-state matrix. However, this reduction in activation energy is also consistent with a rate limitation in the separator. The EIS Nyquist plots in Figure 4 show that the electrolyte element of the circuit (the Ws Warburg element) does not have a strong dependence on temperature- it is nearly constant from 35 to 55°C as indicated by the drawn in slope lines. However, the capacitive element does have an exponential dependence on temperature. This corresponds to the electrolyte interface in either the anode or the cathode. The dependence of activation energy on electrolyte concentration in the anode was established in Figure 2. Figure 3 contains data for CoS_2 and FeS_2 batteries; the 37 mol% Li+ electrolyte was paired with CoS_2 cathodes while the other two used FeS_2 cathodes. "All MgO" includes data from two other MgO types, in addition to Traditional and Alternate. The data have been fit to a linear regression with an R^2 of 0.86, despite varying the cathode. This suggests the anode / electrolyte interface limits solid-state discharge.

The activation energy is key to understanding the temperature dependence of leakage current, and therefore calculating an acceleration factor for aging. However, the absolute magnitude of leakage current will drive the total energy lost in storage. There are major differences in the magnitude of leakage current shown in Figure 1 even though the activation energies (slopes) are relatively similar. Within the batteries made by Manufacturer #1, an order of magnitude difference in leakage current exists between batteries made with our Traditional MgO and batteries made with the Alternate MgO. Manufacturer #2 has similar performance for all MgO, but the leakage current is almost two orders of magnitude lower than for Manufacturer #1. These observations suggest that a significant processing difference exists between Manufacturer #1 and #2. It is not clear what this difference is, but a hypothesis is that it is related to the dry room conditions. Water uptake by the salts in the electrolyte will lead to increased leakage current; this phenomenon drives the use of hi-pot testing to check for leakage current in production thermal batteries [6]. The impact of dry room humidity is dramatic, with 4x greater water uptake at -34°C than at -40°C [6]. The Traditional and Alternate MgO have significant structural differences and processing differences in their manufacture that may lead to different levels of residual moisture in the MgO [9]. The processing techniques at Manufacturer #2 may dry both MgO adequately (and prevent rewetting) so the inherent differences between the MgO are less important. Manufacturer #1's processing may not adequately dry the Alternate MgO.

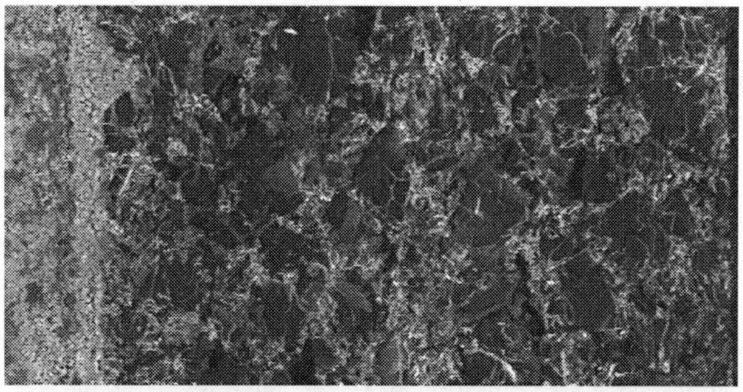

A) Anode, 5% electrolyte (low melting), Alt. MgO

B) Anode, 15% electrolyte (low melting), Alt. MgO

Figure 5. SEM (BSE) showing electrolyte (white) in anode (gray) after battery activation. Equilibrium electrolyte concentration similar in A) and B)

Estimation of capacity loss due to leakage current

The magnitude of leakage current directly impacts the expected lifetime of batteries. For comparison, we will assume a battery with 0.5 Ah capacity and 24V open circuit. Data from the test batteries was normalized to this example, and the resulting capacity loss over a 30 year storage lifetime (at 35°C) is shown in Figure 6. The capacity loss is shown on a log scale to emphasize the dramatic differences in absolute magnitude of leakage current across different manufacturers and electrolyte types. Measured leakage current is proportional to the ionic concentration of lithium in the electrolyte. Note that this is a different statement than Figure 3, which shows the activation energy is inversely proportional; Figure 3 shows the slope of Figure 1 while Figure 6 shows the intercept. High ionic concentration electrolytes both have higher leakage current and are more susceptible to increased leakage at elevated temperature.

The manufacturing differences in leakage current are even more dramatic. The batteries from Manufacturer #1 would lose 25% of their capacity under the storage conditions considered. This compares to about 4.5% capacity loss under identical conditions due to chemical deterioration alone (based on data reported in [5]).

Internal Resistance (IR)

Leakage current can be related to IR by assuming the battery open circuit voltage (OCV) after activation applies (1.92V for Li(Si)/FeS_2 and 1.85V for Li(Si)/CoS_2). The OCV will be different at ambient temperature than active temperature, and the OCV may be primarily driven by contaminants or overpotentials until equilibrium phases have formed. Since this is a lifetime assessment, it is assumed that equilibrium will be achieved before meaningful changes in capacity occur, so the equilibrium OCV is appropriate. The lack of correction for temperature was for convenience, but the free energy change for discharge reactions varies less than 5% from operational to ambient temperature [data from 7], compared to 6 orders of magnitude difference in leakage current depending on conditions. The IR for capacity losses shown in Figure 6 are 49 MOhm for the worst case to as high as 300 GOhm for the best performer. Most batteries were in the 1-10 GOhm range. It is only possible to accurately measure such high resistances by measuring the voltage drop across a reference resistor, since the input impedance of the meter is far lower than the battery itself.

Conclusions

Thermal batteries are batteries even before activation. Parasitic leakage through external circuits connected to the battery may be the dominant source of capacity loss while on mission prior to activation. Leakage current is limited by ionic movement across the anode/electrolyte interface, and the high activation energy (60-100 kJ/mol) means the rate dependence is highly temperature sensitive. Leakage current depends on the electrolyte and processing conditions, not all of which were identified in this study. Expected capacity loss can be easily and quickly measured with non-destructive techniques, such as measuring the voltage across a reference resistor connected to a battery warmed to 35 to 45°C.

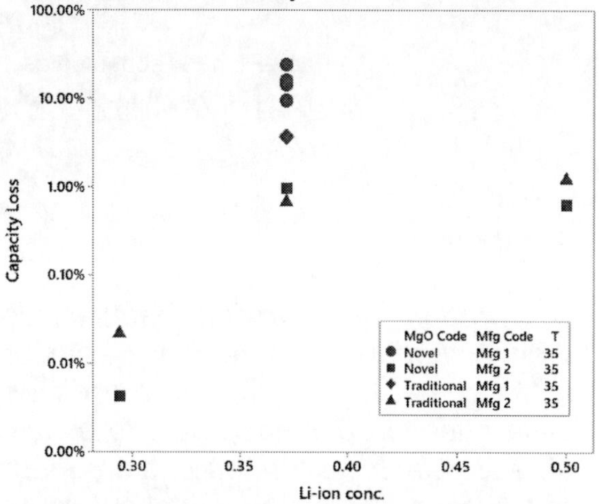

Figure 6. Estimated 30y capacity loss, assuming 24V/0.5Ah battery, vs. electrolyte ionic concentration.

Acknowledgements

Sandia is a multi-mission laboratory managed and operated by National Technology & Engineering Solutions of Sandia, LLC, a wholly owned subsidiary of Honeywell International, Inc., for the U.S. Department of Energy's National Nuclear Security Administration under contract DE-NA0003525.

References

1. R.A. Guidotti, P. Masset. "Thermally activated ("thermal") battery technology Part I: An overview." Journal of Power Sources 161, p. 1443–144 (2006).
2. Survey of parts on Digikey.com (20A N-channel MOSFETs), Feb. 25, 2020.
3. J.Q. Searcy, J.R. Armijo. "Additional Experiments Relative to the Shelf-life of Li(Si)/FeS_2 thermal batteries." Sandia Report SAND84-1510 (1985).
4. J.Q. Searcy, P.A. Neiswander. "Aging Study of Li(Si)/FeS_2 Thermally Activated Batteries." Sandia Report SAND80-0423 (1980).
5. Wesolowski, et al. "Accelerated Aging of Li(Si)/CoS_2 Thermal Batteries," Power Sources Digest, 28-1, p. 472-475, (2018).
6. R.A. Guidotti, F.W. Reinhardt. "Materials-Aging Issues in Thermal Batteries." Sandia Report SAND2006-1903 (2006).
7. A. Roine. (2012). HSC Chemistry for Windows 7.
8. P. Masset, R.A. Guidotti. "Thermal activated (thermal) battery technology Part II. Molten salt electrolytes." Journal of Power Sources 164, p. 397–414 (2007).
9. Papenguth et al. "Historical Production of Maglite S and the Development of a New Magnesium-Oxide Binder for Thermal Batteries," Power Sources Digest, Sandia Report SAND2018-4481C (2018).

Connecting to Thermal Batteries

Nathan V. Moss
EaglePicher Technologies, 1215 West C Street Joplin, MO 64801
Contact Author Email: nathan.moss@eaglepicher.com

Abstract

Through the years the emphasis in thermal battery improvement has been focused on materials and processes. Little attention has been paid to exactly how the electrical connections are made to the battery. Reserve batteries can be particularly difficult to verify installation electrically due to the absence of voltage at the terminals. However, the right mechanical interface can error proof the electrical connections. Certain interconnect methods are prone to damage during handling and may actually compromise battery integrity during installation. In addition to improved reliability, an optimized interconnect design can result in more space for active materials.

This paper will discuss the various interconnect methods EaglePicher has used on thermal batteries and their associated benefits and drawbacks over a range of criteria that includes system installation.

Keywords

Thermal Batteries; D-Subminiature; MIL-DTL-38999; Terminal; Flex Circuit; Error Proofing

The Problem

Power sources require connections. As many changes have come about in thermal battery materials and modeling little attention seems to have been paid to the interface with the rest of the system as little change has been made over the last twenty years.

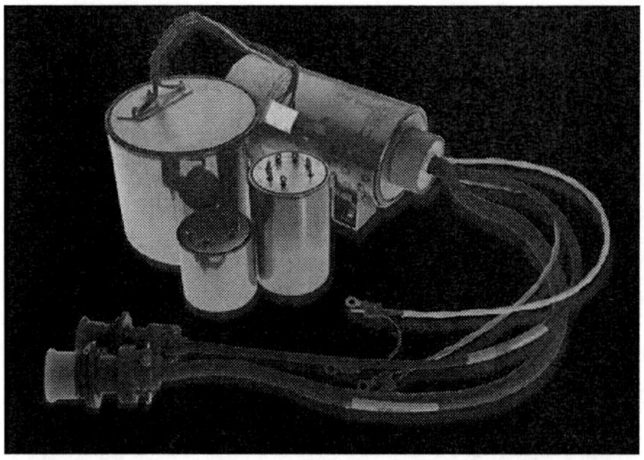

Figure 1: A collection of EaglePicher batteries showing different connection methods.

Connecting to a thermal battery requires a system that is reliable and can endure the heat dissipated by the battery during activation. Another complication, and perhaps the greatest one, is that, unlike other components, the quality of the connection once completed cannot be verified by a simple continuity test. Just as important, is verifying the proper polarity of the connection. Over the years various tests have been attempted to validate thermal battery polarity with mixed results. Without a voltage present at installation, connection validation must be made mechanically as it cannot be validated electrically. At the same time, the connection method needs to protect the adjacent feature that ensures the long shelf life inherent to thermal batteries: the glass to metal seals. There are several options that have been tried;

some with good history, but others that may need to be left behind.

Flattened and Pierced Terminals

Spend any time with thermal batteries and you have most likely experienced flattened and pierced terminals. As perhaps the lowest cost solution, they definitely have an appeal. However, they require a trained technician to install. Unfortunately, mis-wiring can be an incredibly common issue. Verification can be performed via shorts testing. Visual inspection is also an option, especially if unique wire colors are used. However, unique wire colors complicate material procurement. The increased complexity of supplying multiple wire colors can make this option less viable.

Threaded Terminals

The use of threaded terminals has been preferred for some programs. The mating harness will utilize MS25036 or similar terminal lugs installed with the appropriate nut and washer. The popularity of this option has always been a mystery. The most delicate feature of a thermal battery is the glass to metal seal. Threaded terminals call for the terminal lug to be torqued in place to make sure the connection is permanent. If not performed carefully there is the opportunity to twist the terminal in the seal thereby compromising the very seal that is key to a battery's long shelf life. One of the main advantages is that this method does not require certified solder technicians to install. Perhaps it is this very reason the threaded terminals seem to be very popular with first time thermal battery customers. An asymmetrical terminal arrangement and/or different terminal sizes can be an error proofing approach if the mating lugs are constrained in a geometry that can only be installed properly.

Wired Pig Tail

Another approach that has not been incredibly common is the attachment of a short harness that is attached to the battery prior to delivery. An advantage here is for applications where the battery is installed in a difficult to reach area the short harness can move the connection to a location where a positive connection can be made and inspected. A wide range of connection types can be incorporated at the mating end of the harness: D38999, D-subminiature, terminal lugs and possibly even commercial "front release" style connectors. In these designs the battery itself typically uses flattened and pierced terminals. Something to consider is total manufacturing lead time. If a manufacturer is being engaged to fabricate a wiring harness it may be more practical for the harness to terminate at the battery instead of only near it. Depending on the complexity of the interface, it can take many weeks to install small harnesses after battery assembly. Unfortunately, any method that uses discreet terminals is prone to the same unverifiable continuity and polarity issues.

Connector Style Battery Header

A solution that is becoming more popular is the use of integral connector style battery headers. Initially almost exclusively D38999 "round" style connectors were used, but now D-subminiature styles have been incorporated. In contrast to wiring design standards that require socket contacts on power sources these have nearly universally made use of pin style contacts. This is due to the difficulty of obtaining an hermetic seal with sockets as well as the potential for leak test errors. Polarity features in the design of the connectors ensure proper connection at the next assembly. Also, there is no need for time consuming post assembly of attaching the harness either for shipment or for Lot Acceptance Testing as the electrical interface is ready as soon as the battery is completed.

What may dissuade potential customers from connector style headers could be the additional costs. However, a thorough cost analyses could determine the added header costs are offset by reduced labor and lead time. The other disadvantages of connector style headers have more to do with the specifics of the implementation. For instance, it has been the author's experience that the friction fit of the D-subminiature series wears relatively quickly. As the jackposts can be tedious to engage they are not always fully mated. On the other hand, D38999 connectors are relatively simple and mate easily. The required color bands provide yet another error proofing to validate a complete connection.

Use of D38999 style headers is also not without issues. However, this can mainly be overcome by some simple selections. The use of connectors with small (20 awg and 22 awg) contacts can be somewhat delicate with pins getting bent during handling and installation. As the batteries tend to be one of the pricier components in these systems a better choice can be made. Batteries that use larger contacts (16 awg and 12 awg) have proven to be more robust as these designs are rarely, if ever, returned for bent contacts.

Flex Harness

With the primary drawback being the lead time to design and the quantity sensitivity procurement the flex harness has some definite advantages. This is especially pertinent in limited volume next assemblies. Here again, the use of asymmetric layouts provides mechanical error proofing for the electrical continuity and polarity. Also, flex harnesses require skilled technicians to solder the connections. Unfortunately, the most common defect experienced is the overlooking of a solder connection.

Figure 2: Soldered flex harness on a Thermal Battery.

Application Specific Solutions

There are times the existing solutions do not meet the requirements. EaglePicher has at times developed unique solutions. In a D38999 connector the outer shell is either threaded or uses a bayonet pin to engage the inner contacts of the mating connector. An alternate is to have a central threaded feature surrounded by contacts. Engaging the threads mates the contacts. Once again, asymmetric geometry is critical to making the correct connections. To be compatible in the application it was designed for the other end makes use of a common D-Subminiature connector.

Figure 3: Custom solution with threaded stud surrounded by contacts.

Conclusion

As has been presented here there are several options for making connections to thermal batteries. The cost and benefit analysis of these solution may also hinge on the particular program's phase [1]. It has been the author's observation that programs tend to hold to the first solution utilized and may overlook opportunities for improvement.

Acknowledgement

The unique interconnect described in Application Specific Solutions was designed and developed by long-time EaglePicher employee Romeo Saltat.

References

[1] Bhakta, D. *et al. Alternatives to Custom Thermal Batteries* 40th Power Sources Conference, Paper 30.5, 2002.

Design and Implementation of Active Thermal Insulation to Improve Run-Time in Thermal Reserve Batteries

Jahangir Rastegar
Omnitek Partners, LLC
85 Air Park Drive, Unit 3
Ronkonkoma, NY, 11779
j.rastegar@omnitekpartners.com / 1-631-665-4008

Ryan Hightower and Eric Scherzberg
Advanced Thermal Batteries, Inc.
1231 Independence Way
Westminster, MD 21074
Ryan.Hightower@atb-inc.com / 1-443-821-7329

Abstract

In this paper, the development of a novel thermal management method is presented that can be used to significantly increase the run-time of thermal reserve batteries. In this method, the thermal battery core is packaged with a layer of heating "fuse-strips". The relatively thin and slow burning pyrotechnic heating fuse-strips are wrapped between insulation layers around the thermal battery core. The heating fuse-strips burn at a tunable rate, providing a continuous source of heat to the battery core extending the run-time of the battery. Depending on the thermal requirements, the heating fuse-strip geometry, burn time, initiation delay, and initiation location can be varied. The development of the heating fuse components and their incorporation into prototype batteries and results of their testing are presented. The test results, which directly compare the performance of prototypes with active thermal insulation vs. standard thermal batteries, show that the inclusion of heating fuse-strips in small and thermally limited batteries more than doubled their effective run-time. Current research and development efforts and future work are discussed.

Keywords

Thermal Reserve Battery; Molten Salt Battery; Thermal Battery Run-Time; Thermal Battery Thermal Management; Slow-Burning Heating Fuse; Heating Fuse Strips for Reserve Batteries

Introduction

Thermal reserve batteries have many advantages over other reserve power systems. Since all internal components are immobilized solids at ambient temperatures, the units are inherently rugged. They can withstand severe environments of shock, vibration, linear and spin accelerations, high spin rates, and a very wide range of temperatures. Thermal batteries are maintenance free, and can withstand long term storage, retaining the ability to provide immediate power upon activation for well over 20 years. They have been used in production applications for over 70 years and have a proven history of safe operation and high reliability.

Following activation upon ignition of its pyrotechnic heat source and melting of the solid electrolyte, a thermal battery can provide power to an external load so long as its electrolyte is molten. The relatively large surface area to volume ratio in a small thermal battery causes its run-time to be short. To increase the thermal battery run-time, the amount of available heat energy needs to be increased. The initial heat energy that can be provided is limited by the maximum activation temperature that the battery can tolerate without causing a significant performance degradation.

In this paper, a novel thermal management method[1] is presented that can be used to significantly increase the run-time of thermal reserve batteries. The thermal battery core is packaged with a layer of heating "fuse-strips". The relatively thin and slow burning pyrotechnic heating fuse-strips are wrapped between insulation layers around the thermal battery core. The heating fuse-strips burn at a tunable rate, providing a continuous source of heat to the battery core extending the run-time of the battery. Depending on the thermal requirements, the heating fuse-strip geometry, burn time, initiation delay, and initiation location can be varied.

The present technology was developed by Omnitek Partners, LLC, of Ronkonkoma, New York, under a U.S. Navy SBIR project and in collaboration with Advanced Thermal Batteries, Inc. (ATB) of Westminster, MD and Hanley Industries, Inc. of Alton, IL. In this novel thermal

[1] U. S. Patent Number 10,186,713 and 11,031,607 and other pending.

reserve battery technology, the battery core is packaged inside a layer of slow burning and heat generating fuse strip, which is ignited following battery activation to maintain the battery core temperature above the melting point of its electrolyte. The battery run-time is thereby significantly increased. This is particularly the case for smaller batteries used in gun-fired munitions, rockets, and missiles.

The schematic of a typical thermal battery with the integrated slow burning heating fuse strips is shown in Figure 1. The thermal battery may be initiated using inertial igniters or electrical initiators.

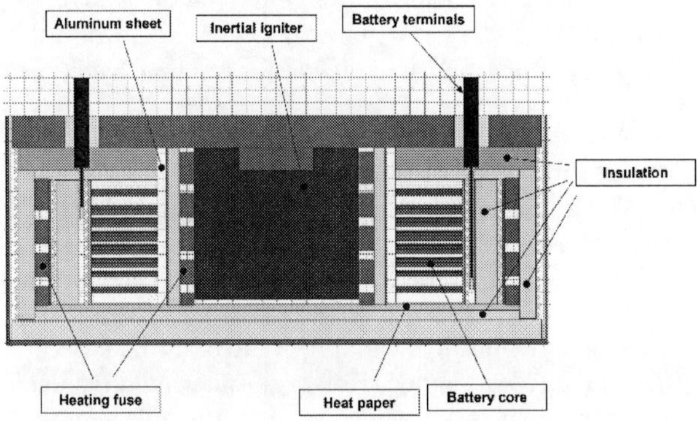

Figure 1: Schematic of a long run-time thermal battery.

Thermal energy at the end of life is often a limiting factor for thermal batteries. The heating fuse is meant to slowly release thermal energy into the battery throughout its life in addition to the heat pellets present in the battery cell stack. This slow release of heat aims to provide the crucial heat needed at the end of life, as the heat pellets begin to lose thermal energy. The purpose of providing slow burning heating fuse coils that are wrapped around the battery core is to keep its electrolyte temperature above its melting point to allow for longer battery life (run-time).

The heating fuses are currently fabricated by Hanley Industries, Inc. of Alton, Illinois, by filling 12 inch long and 0.133" and 0.093" diameter and 0.028" wall thickness annealed stainless-steel tubes with slow burning (5-15 second per inch) pyrotechnic material and compacting the filling, adding a secondary pyrotechnic material to one end, and inserting a flexible fuse element to facilitate its ignition before crimping both ends of the tube. The tubes are annealed prior to filling to assist their crimping, and their coiling and consolidation at Omnitek.

The stainless-steel tubes filled with slow burning pyrotechnic material are then cut to the required length at Omnitek Partners and coiled with extended spiral cap section and flattened to consolidate the pyrotechnic material and to minimize the occupied battery space as can be seen in Figure 2 and fit the intended battery size. In general, two such heating fuse elements are used on a cylindrical battery to also cover its top and bottom section. A thin (around 0.010") layer of aluminum sheet is provided between the heating fuse strips and the battery core to distribute heat and prevent local hot spots. The flexible ignition fuses seen at the bottom end of the heating fuse strip of Figure 2 are thereby positioned at mid-section of the battery for ignition at the time of battery activation.

Figure 2: A coiled and consolidated heating fuse section with integral helical cap section.

Figures 3-7 show the process of fabricating batteries with the slow burning heating fuse strips. Figure 3 shows the battery core as covered with a 0.001" thick aluminum sheet over an insulation layer during the battery assembly. Figures 4 and 5 show the process of assembling the heating fuse strips over thin aluminum foil. Figure 6 shows the process of providing the final insulation layer over the heating fuse strips. Figure 7 shows two assembled thermal battery prototypes, one with (right) and one without (left) heating fuse strips, but with identical battery cores. Figure 8 is an x-ray picture of the two batteries that is commonly made to ensure that the batteries are assembled properly.

Figure 3

Figure 4

Figure 5 Figure 6

Figure 7

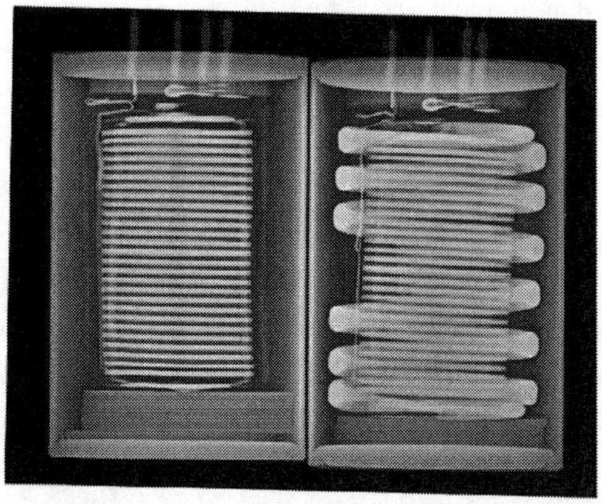

Figure 8

The batteries shown in Figure 7 have a diameter of 1.75" and are 2.9" long and were sized so that a current production battery core could be used for the tests. The run-time of one of the sets of fabricated two prototypes (shown in Figure 7) were tested at -30°C under identical loads. The measured battery run-times are shown in the plots of Figure 9, showing the output voltage of the battery with standard insulation as are commonly manufactured and used in munitions applications and the output voltage of the battery with the heating fuse strip under an identical load as a function of time.

A test of the above size batteries and with the same battery cores with standard insulation material; with Aerogel insulation (best - but costly - available insulation material); and with the heating fuse strips was also performed at -43°C under identical loads. The test results are shown in the plots of Figure 10. As can be seen in Figure 10, at 20.7 Volts, the best available insulation material (Aerogel) increased the battery run time by only 15%, while the heating fuse strips increased the battery run time by around 285%.

Discussion And Conclusions

The developed novel thermal management method is shown to have the potential of significantly increasing the run-time of thermal reserve batteries. The method, as described in this paper, is more effective for use in smaller thermal batteries due to their higher ratio of the battery core surface area to its volume. However, other modifications of the technology, such as the use of multiple heating fuse layers with delayed ignition capability, and/or the provision of generated heat storage capability, should make it possible to achieve similar performances for significantly larger thermal reserve batteries. Furthermore, minimizing the heating fuse volume and finding alternate nonconductive packaging material would be a significant enhancement.

It is noted that the primary goal of the designed and fabricated prototypes and their testing was to demonstrate the potential of the developed technology in significantly increasing thermal reserve battery run-time. To this end, little effort was made for their optimal design to maximize their run-time. It is appreciated that the process of optimally designing thermal reserve batteries with properly sized and distributed heating fuse strips for a prescribed application and its requirements are generally complex and require further efforts.

In addition, the process of fabricating the flattened coiled sections with the spiral caps, Figure 2, such that it would achieve reliable ignition and complete burning along the entire length of the fuse strip requires further development and automation.

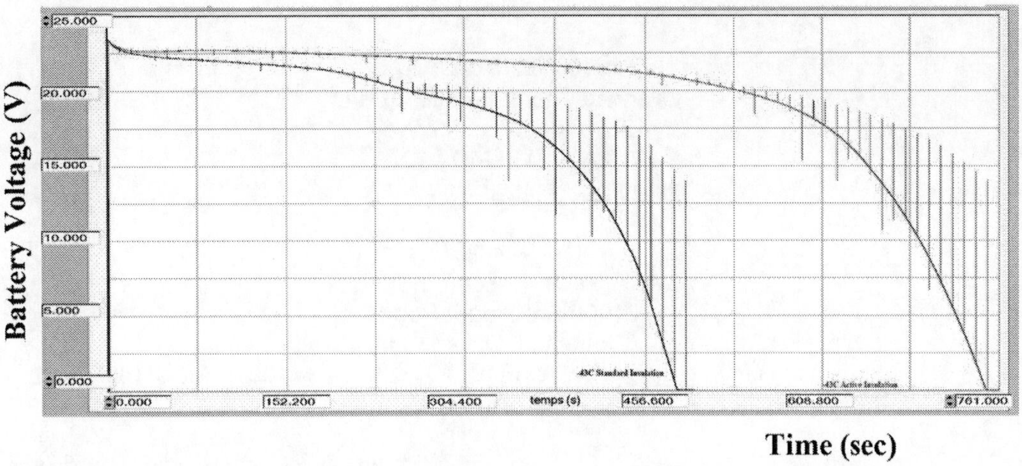

Figure 9: The run-time of the prototype thermal battery with standard insulation and with heating fuse strips demonstrating the increase in the run-time that can be achieved.

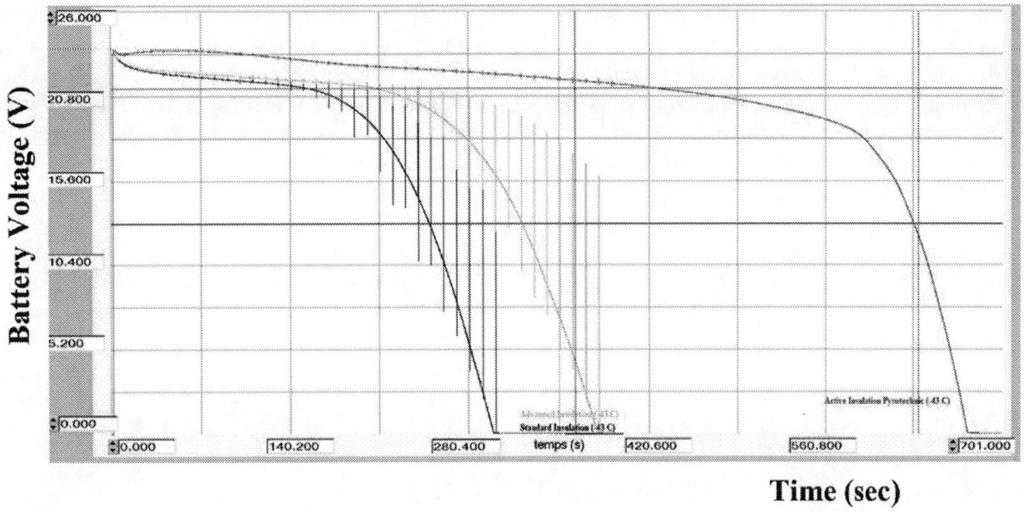

Figure 10: The run-time of the prototype thermal battery with standard insulation (black), Aerogel insulation (green), and with heating fuse strips (red) demonstrating the increase in the run-time that can be achieved.

Long Life Molten Salt Battery for NASA Venus Application

Eric Scherzberg
Advanced Thermal Batteries, Inc.
1231 Independence Way
Westminster, MD 21074
Eric.Scherzberg@atb-inc.com / 1-443-821-7929

Thomas Miller
NASA Glenn Research Center
21000 Brookpark Road
Cleveland, OH 44135
thomas.b.miller@nasa.gov Phone: (216) 433-6300, Fax: (216) 433-6160

Abstract
A development program is being conducted at Advanced Thermal Batteries (ATB) to create a low discharge rate, long life, molten salt battery for a NASA Venus surface probe. Battery goals are 60 days continuous operation at +25V +0/-6 volts and -25V +6/-0 Volts under severe environments of 465°C, 92 atm pressure, and corrosive sulfur dioxide in a super critical carbon dioxide atmosphere. Conveniently, molten salt thermal battery electrochemistry starts to operate efficiently at 330°C. However, a major barrier to direct application of existing thermal battery technology is the high self-discharge rate, resulting in lifetimes in only minutes, not days. The best performance to date, which meets the required voltage regulation, has been a lithium silicon (LiSi) alloy anode discharging through all three voltage plateau versus an iron monosulfide (FeS) cathode. In order to perform reproducibly, additional engineering controls within the battery design are required to limit cell–to–cell parasitic discharge mechanisms. Results of these trials have improved the efficiency and manufacturability of the design.

Keywords
Long Lifetime; Thermal Batteries; Venus; Interplanetary Battery; FeS.

Introduction
A development program is being conducted at Advanced Thermal Batteries (ATB) to create a low discharge rate, long life, molten salt battery for a NASA Venus probe. Battery goals are 60 days continuous operation at +25V +0/-6 volts and -25V +6/-0 Volts under severe environments of 465°C, 92 atm pressure, and corrosive sulfur dioxide in a super critical carbon dioxide atmosphere. Conveniently, molten salt thermal battery electrochemistry starts to operate efficiently at 330°C. However, a major barrier to direct application of existing thermal battery technology is the high self-discharge rate, resulting in lifetimes in only minutes, not days.

Work to date has explored lithium alloy anodes and metal sulfide cathodes in alkali halide molten salt electrolyte. A thick separator employing the use of a non-traditional electrolyte is ATB's strategy to reduce self-discharge while preserving the high temperature performance required for the Venus mission. The best performance to date, which meets the required voltage regulation, has been a lithium silicon (LiSi) alloy anode discharging on the third voltage plateau versus an iron sulfide (FeS) cathode, 1.32V/cell. Operational testing of a 5-cell battery using this electrochemistry has achieved 152 days of continuous discharge to a half-scale load. Also, operational testing of a 17 cell battery was achieved successfully for 117 days before dropping below 19V.

However, it has been determined that in order to perform reproducibly, additional engineering controls within the battery design are required to limit cell–to–cell discharge mechanisms. Destructive physical analysis of the long-life cells has shown that slow migration of lithium-containing material between the cells is the most significant driver for battery failure. Work performed to date has been focused on evaluating new assembly methods to limit interaction between cells using ceramic isolators and containment techniques to limit lithium migration and its effects on the parasitic cell discharge. As these techniques are employed, their functional resistance to dynamic environments will also be considered with the goal of developing a full scale battery capable of handling the dynamic environments of launch, interplanetary space flight, and Venusian atmosphere entry.

The work presented in this paper will be focused on three engineering controls schemes developed to limit the interaction between cells. Previous work on this program at ATB has shown that the most significant driver for accelerated self-discharge in these long life, low load, multicell batteries is migration of electrolyte between cells. Such migration results in an ion-conductive path which bleeds down cell capacity rapidly once formed. Typical migration is increased by materials in contact with the cell stack which may wick the electrolyte between the cells.

To limit such wicking effects, contact to the stack must be limited, an effective barrier must be put in place, or a tortuous path must be created. Minimizing contact with the stack results in an unsupported stack which may be susceptible to both non-operating vibrations and shock which may cause the cells to shift, or slumping during operation which may occur if the battery is tested on its side (the gravity vector lateral to the cell stack).

For this paper, three different designs have been created in order to evaluate each of the proposed controls, each depicted in Figure 1. The bare-cell design was chosen as a baseline and is based on the successful prototypes from the previous work conducted on this project. To pursue the concept of a barrier, the alumina sleeve design was conceptualized to create a tight fit with cell covers to prevent the passage of electrolyte along the length of the battery. Lastly, a stacking ring design was created which is expected to provide both a seal between the cells as well as a tortuous path, resulting in extended operation even in the event that the electrolyte migration begins to occur.

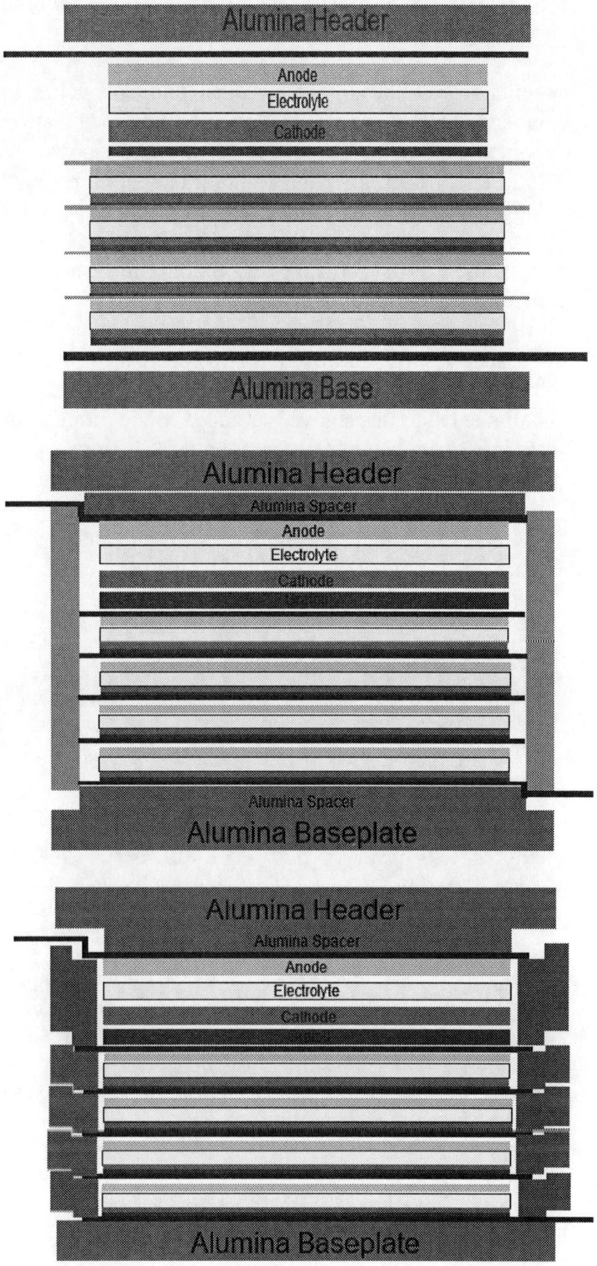

Figure 1. Depiction Of the Three Tested Stack Configurations from top to bottom a) Bare b) Sleeve c) Stacking Ring.

Experimental

Eight 5-cell test units were constructed based on these design concepts utilizing the LiSi/FeS chemistry developed in the previous phase of the work. Serial numbers 1037-1040 were constructed with the bare cell design and overhanging cell covers. SN 1037 and 1038 had larger overhangs from the cells compared to 1039 and 1040. SN 1041 and 1042 were constructed with pure alumina sleeves. SN 1043 and 1044 were constructed using the pure alumina stacking rings.

Units were placed into an oven and connected to independent resistive loads and data acquisition system. Units prepared for testing are shown in Figure 2. Current, voltage and temperature were logged at a rate 1 sample every 10 seconds. A timer circuit and relay switched from "base load" (12 kΩ) to "pulse load" (160 Ω) every 8 hours for 2 minutes to mimic mission parameters.

To start testing, the oven was stepped up to 465°C and held constant during the test. In the event that a unit needed to be removed or added to the furnace for testing, data acquisition was halted, the oven was stepped down to room temperature, and the batteries were added or removed. This process did not appear to impact the other units under test significantly aside from drive a freeze/thaw cycle, which can be seen in the data.

Figure 2. Photograph Of the Units, One Set on the Baseplate and One on the Side, Under Test in the Oven.

Results and Discussion

Initial test units for the SN 1037 and 1038 bare-cell design were constructed based on a scale down in capacity and diameter based on the efficiencies determined from previous testing efforts. In the process of scaling down the cell diameters, the cell covers were left at the original diameter. This characteristic was expected to result in a longer path for the migration of electrolyte between cells. The unintended consequence of this extreme overhang resulted in the deflection of the cells upon heating up and the rapid shorting and discharge of the batteries. An X-ray radiograph of the expended battery in Figure 3 shows the cell cover edge having been significantly deflected to the point of making visible contact.

Repeat tests of the bare-cell designs were realized in SN 1039 (tested on base plate) and 1040 (tested on side). SN 1040 continued to run past the 60-day requirement with margin (~85 days). Voltage data for SN 1040 is shown in in Figure 4. The voltage performance of SN 1040 compared to SN 1039 had a discharge rate which was twice as fast, based on LiSi plateau rundowns, despite demonstrating nominal discharge current. Evaluation of SN 1039 post-test demonstrated an insulation resistance failure between the battery terminals and the case. Further investigation of the glass seals of the feedthrough suggested either dielectric breakdown of the glass at the high temperatures the item was exposed to or contamination from inside the battery condensing on the seals resulting in failure. Such findings suggest that design and procurement of robust electrical feedthroughs are a necessary step in a fully realized battery that is compatible with the Venusian environment. Furthermore, the success of SN 1040 while being tested on its side shows that there are no significant slump characteristics of the cell material.

SN 1041 and 1042 were built to the sleeve design concept. In the construction of SN 1041, the alumina cover insulator bottomed out on the sleeve, and the stack itself was not fully under compression. This resulted in extremely high cell impedance and unusual discharge characteristics. SN 1042 was built with an addition component to compress the cells without losing stack force or bottoming out on the sleeve. Regardless, both 1041 and 1042 showed accelerated self-discharge. Destructive physical analysis (shown in Figure 5) of SN 1041 revealed a large degree of contact between the cell material and the alumina sleeve. Several locations appeared to show clear signs of migration between adjacent cells, likely a prime driver for the observed discharge characteristics.

SN 1043 and 1044 were built with the stacking ring configuration. SN 1043 shows similar discharge characteristic to SN 1040 (bare cell). The stacking ring was significantly simpler to build and more forgiving of misalignment of the cell components. There is expectation also that the more confined cells of the stacking rings will be more resilient against non-operating dynamic environments.

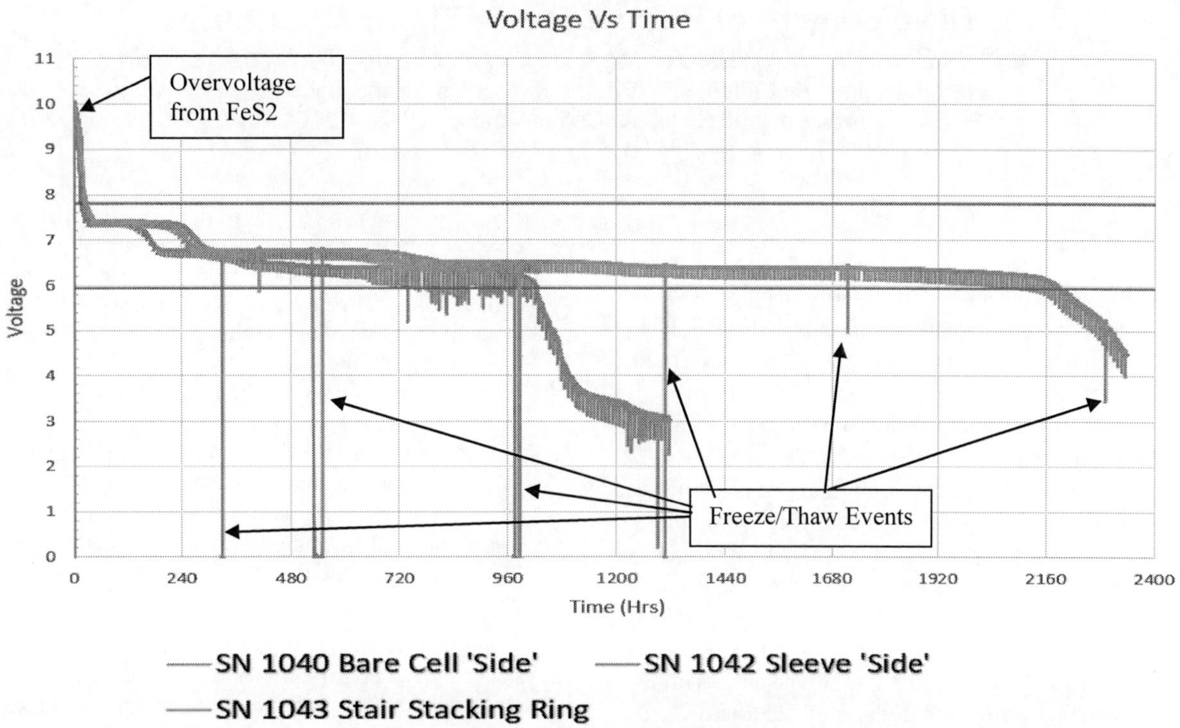

Figure 4. Voltage Data Showing Full Discharge of SN 1040 Bare Cell, and Two Additional Voltage from Additional Designs, with Voltage Regulation Limits and Target Lifetime.

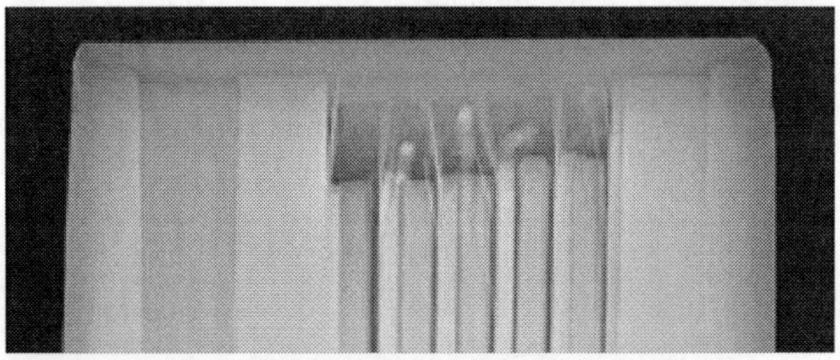

Figure 3. X-ray Radiograph of the SN 1037 Post-Discharged Showing the Deflected Cell Covers.

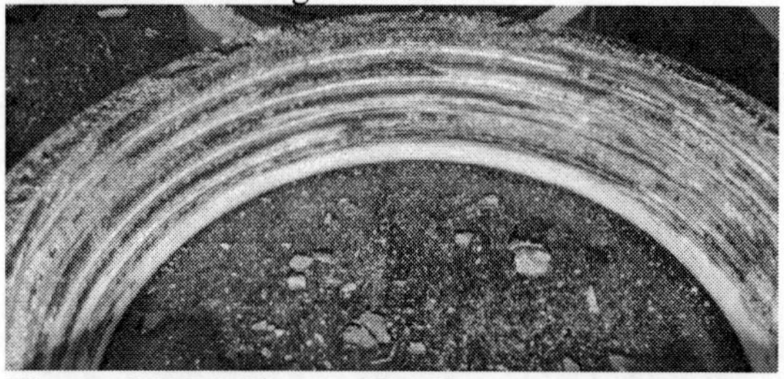

Figure 5. DPA Photo of the Sleeve Contamination.

Conclusion

Based on the results, ATB will be proceeding with 17-cell full scale prototypes based on the stacking ring design. This design style has led to robust performance with relatively little manufacturing complexity. These full-scale prototypes will also be subjected to relevant non-operational dynamics to ensure robust performance. If confirmed as successful, ATB will begin advancing the rest of the required subcomponents need. Future work on this project will begin the process of designing the pressure vessel and electrical feedthroughs required for the harsh Venusian environment.

Development of Rechargeable Thermal Batteries

James Pander, Gabrielle Aversa, Jake Herb, and Christopher Lang
Imperia Batteries, a division of Physical Sciences Inc.,
20 New England Business Center, Andover, MA USA 01810
jpander@psicorp.com / 1-978-738-2257

Abstract

In this work, a rechargeable thermal battery (RTB) system, enabled by a thermally activated electrolyte formulation and a custom integrated heating method, was developed and demonstrated. The RTB was scaled from several mAh cells up to 7 Ah cells and a functional multi-cell battery pack. The cell parameters were optimized for high rate performance, achieving >12.5 kW/L. Cells configured for high energy density operation delivered >840 Wh/L. Over 25 cycles of rechargeable operation was demonstrated. Multiple formulations of a novel, low-melting point solid electrolyte that enables on/off functionality between 80 – 140 °C and enables long-term storage with minimal capacity fade were demonstrated. The developed prototype represents a significant step forward from traditional thermal battery systems which are single-use and require very high operational temperatures (>200°C).

Key Words

rechargeable thermal battery; high power; high energy; battery; directed energy weapons

Introduction

Thermal batteries are primary, reserve-type electrochemical energy sources capable of supplying high power output upon activation with a single-use pyrotechnic heating element, necessitating replacement for multi-use applications.[1,2] Thermal batteries are often employed for military applications (such as missile and torpedo systems), usually as a power source for guidance, propulsion, and safe/arm applications.[3] Directed energy weapons (DEWs) are an evolving class of technology with applications in missile defense and incapacitation of enemy vehicles, among others.[4] DEW devices require a high-power electricity source sustained over several minutes to function and thus are an ideal application for thermal batteries; however, they would benefit from the ability to recharge the battery for subsequent use. Constantly replacing single-use thermal batteries would be costly and generate significant amounts of waste.

Traditional thermal batteries typically utilize a stacked pellet construction and a molten-salt electrolyte that is solid at room temperature (allowing for storage of the battery in an inert state) and liquid after activation (facilitating discharge of the battery).[1,2] The irreversibility of the system stems from both the melting of the electrolyte and the single-use nature of the pyrotechnic heating element. Additionally, due to the fragility of the pellet electrodes, the high operational temperatures, and challenges preventing short-circuiting during shock or vibration, the engineering of the thermal battery system is a challenging technical problem that requires consideration of each component as well as the overall battery pack.[1,2,5-7] Rechargeability would represent a significant advancement over state-of-the-art single-use commercial devices, and a robust, rechargeable solution that addresses each of these technical challenges doubly so.

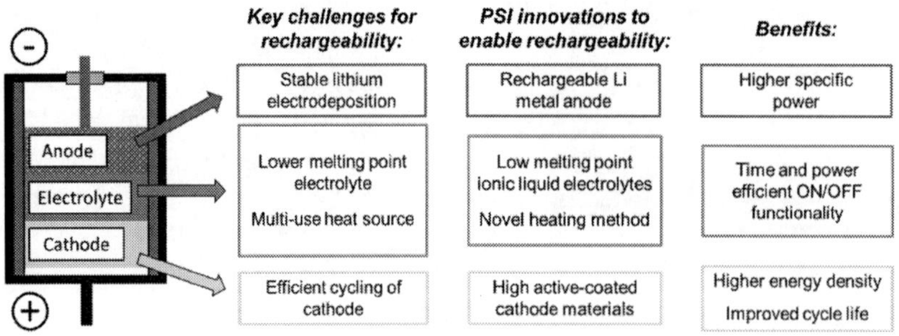

Figure 1. Overview of PSI technologies integrated to create a state-of-the-art rechargeable thermal battery.

Imperia Batteries, a division of Physical Sciences Inc., has successfully demonstrated a rechargeable thermal battery (RTB) with a high energy density (840 Wh/L) that is capable of delivering >12,700 W/L for high power applications with temperature dependent on/off functionality. Imperia's RTB leverages the high energy and power density of lithium metal batteries combined with a novel electrolyte formulation that enables on/off functionality through temperature-modulated conductivity. This technology is well-suited for applications that require intermittent high power pulses over long periods of time. Figure 1 presents a schematic view of Imperia's RTB system highlighting the key innovations and capabilities of the technology.

Results and Discussion

Traditional thermal batteries are activated by melting a solid electrolyte at high temperatures (>200°C) with a single-use pyrotechnic heating element, preventing continued or repeated use. In order to enable a mutli-use thermal battery, the electrolyte needs to have a well-defined temperature at which the mixture becomes conductive. Several approaches have been demonstrated in the literature.[8-12]

The strategy employed in this work utilizes low melting point organic salts combined with traditional lithium salts with a non-flammable, non-carbonate solvent. Lithium bis(trifluoromethanesulfonyl)imide (LiTFSI) is used as the primary electrolyte component, so the TFSI anion was selected as the anion for the low melting point organic salt component. A range of cations were considered and candidates were selected based on literature reports of on/off ionic conduction behavior ca 90°C in mixtures of LiTFSI and the candidate organic salts.[13] This approach enables operation at 100°C instead of 200°C, requiring less startup energy.

By combining this thermally activated electrolyte (TEL) with other lithium ion and lithium metal cell technologies including a patented cathode coating that improves specific power and energy density and an anode-less cell design where lithium metal is deposited from the cathode, Imperia is able to produce high energy density lithium metal batteries with temperature dependent on/off functionality. This on/off functionality is demonstrated at the coin cell scale in Figure 2. At the operating temperature, the system delivers over 690 Wh/L with 97-99% cycle-to-cycle efficiency. When the temperature is reduced to 40 °C, solidification of the electrolyte prevents operation. This inactivity below the operation temperature represents the inert state of the battery and is ideal for long-term storage. Upon reheating to the operating temperature, the system returns to the previous charge/discharge behavior. The resulting RTB benefits from the high specific power, energy density of traditional lithium metal batteries and the inert storage capabilities of a thermal battery while being able to cycle ca. 25 cycles.

Imperia has demonstrated RTB performance in 7 Ah pouch cells, with energy density of 840 Wh/L during a 1C discharge (Figure 3). Additionally, the capacity fade of the full-scale cells during extended cycling was tested. Cells were cycled at 80% depth of discharge. Cells were charged at a 1C nominal rate and discharged at 85°C and a rate of 1C between 4.3 V and 3.55 V (80% DOD as determined by the percentage of the total capacity at the given voltage). The results are summarized in Figure 4.

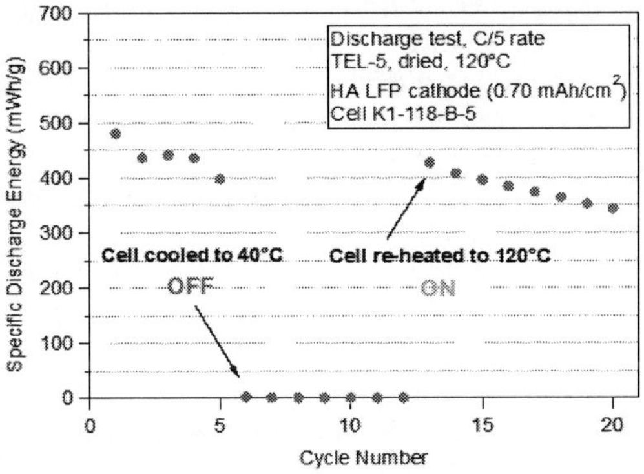

Figure 2. Specific energy delivered in the activated state, cooled to the inert state, and reheated to the operating temperature.

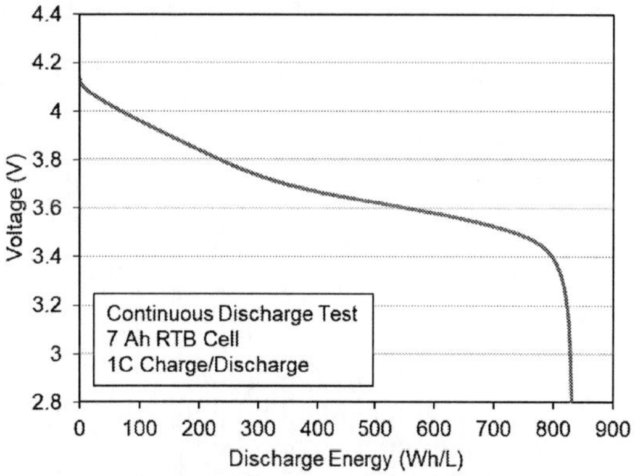

Figure 3. Specific discharge energy of a 7 Ah RTB cell operated using custom PCB heating.

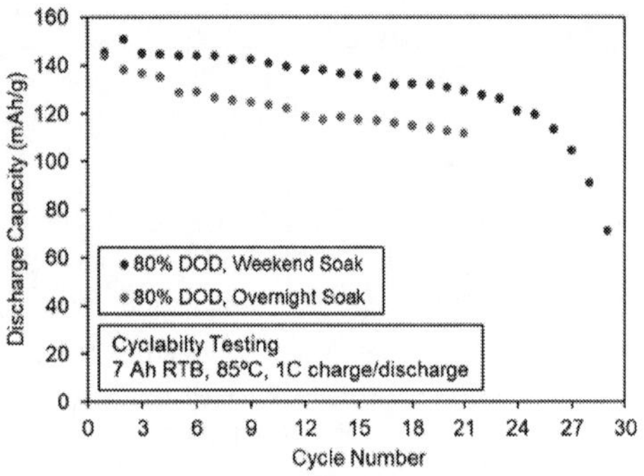

Figure 4. Discharge capacity as a function of cycle number for a cell cycled 80% DOD after soaking overnight (red) and over a weekend (blue).

Imperia has shown that the RTBs can deliver high power discharge pulses up to 54C a (current densities greater than 100 mA/cm2). Figure 5 shows the pulse power density delivered for an RTB discharged with 1 second pulses of increasing current. Imperia's RTB supports high rate discharge pulses up to a power density of 12.7 kW/L. Following the discharge pulse, the system shows rapid recovery of the voltage within milliseconds after the end of the pulse, indicating low internal resistance and the ability to support subsequent high power pulses. The current design can be further modified to achieve a power density as high as 13.5 kW/L.

In order to quickly and efficiently activate the system, Imperia has developed a novel heating technique that can be efficiently integrated into the battery pack design. An integrated circuit and board matching the dimensions of the current battery configuration was fabricated. The custom heater is capable of heating a 7 Ah RTB to operating temperature in under 90 seconds, utilizing 2.84 Wh. Additionally, the activation power efficiency improves as battery pack size and capacity increases.

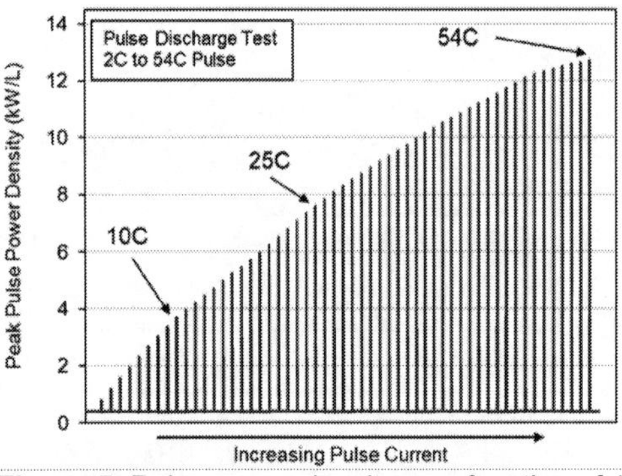

Figure 5. Pulse power density as a function of 1 second pulse rate from 1C to 54C.

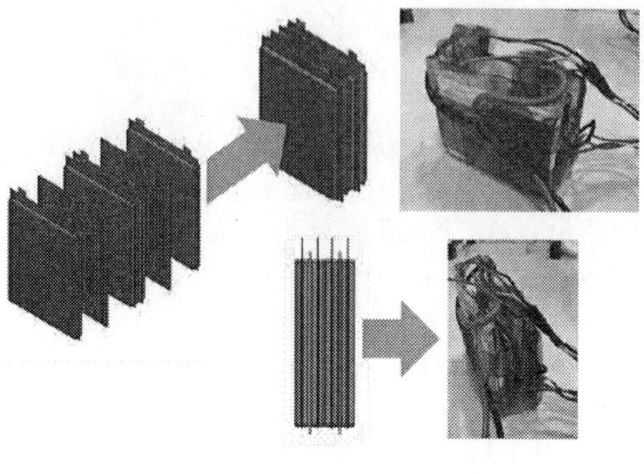

Figure 6. (left) Schematic and **(right)** Photographic depictions of the front (top) and side (bottom) views of 2S2P RTB battery pack with 2 integrated PCB heating boards.

The lithium deposition and discharge profile of a 7 Ah RTB heated with the novel heating method are characteristic of the battery type and indistinguishable from those resulting from a system heated with a conventional oven.

To demonstrate the ability of the cells to be integrated into a rechargeable thermal battery unit, a demonstration unit was produced. To assemble the battery pack, four 7 Ah cells were configured in a 2S2P battery pack, creating a 14 Ah pack with a nominal voltage of 10.8 V. The assembly also integrated two novel heaters after the first and third cells. This battery pack is shown in Figure 7. The battery pack reached operating temperature (as measured on the cell exterior) using the built-in heating system within 110 seconds. After being heated to the activation temperature, the battery pack was successfully charged and discharged using a power source and a programmable load, respectably. This demonstration proves that these technologies can be straightforwardly combined into a prototype rechargeable thermal battery device. By leveraging lithium ion and lithium metal cell designs, high capacity cathode materials, and lithium metal anode technologies, the rechargeable thermal battery is capable of high energy and power densities. By leveraging custom electrolyte blends of lithium salts and low melting point organic salts, temperature dependent on/off behavior was demonstrated. When this electrolyte was paired with a custom heating method, the battery could be quickly and reliably activated and de-activated. Further development work will focus on customization of these technologies towards a specific application – optimizing activation time, total energy density, peak power delivery, and size to match application needs. In the conference talk corresponding with this article, these results as well as potential applications and impacts will be discussed.

References

1 Guidotti, R. A. & Masset, P. Thermally activated ('thermal') battery technology Part I: An overview. *J. Power Sources* **161,** 1443–1449 (2006).

2 P. Masset, R.A. Guidotti, Thermal activated (thermal) battery technology: Part II. Molten salt electrolytes, J. Power Sources 164 (2007) 397–414, https://doi.org/ 10.1016/j.jpowsour.2006.10.080.

3 Davis, P.B.; Winchester, C.S. *Limiting factors to advancing thermal battery technology for naval applications*; NASA STI/Recon Technical Report N; AA(Naval Surface Warfare Center, Silver Spring, MD.), AB (Naval Surface Warfare Center, Silver Spring, MD.), 1991. https://ui.adsabs.harvard.edu/abs/1991STIN...9228568D/abstract (accessed 2022-08-24).

4 Schneider, W. *Defense Science Board Task Force on Directed Energy Weapons*. (2007). doi:10.1080/09700160108455338

5 R.A. Guidotti, W. Reinhardt, Characterization of MgO Powders for Use in Thermal Batteries, Sandia National Labs., Albuquerque, NM (United States), 1996, https:// doi.org/10.2172/380372.

6 P. Masset, S. Schoeffert, J.-Y. Poinso, J.-C. Poignet, Retained molten salt electrolytes in thermal batteries, J. Power Sources 139 (2005) 356–365, https:// doi.org/10.1016/j.jpowsour.2004.07.009.

7 R.A. Guidotti, F.W. Reinhardt, E.V. Thomas, Deformation Study of Separator Pellets for Thermal Batteries, Sandia National Labs., Albuquerque, NM (United States), 1995, https://doi.org/10.2172/86301.

8 Peled, E., Golodnitsky, D., Strauss, E., Lang, J. & Lavi, Y. Li/CPE/FeS2rechargeable battery. *Electrochim. Acta* **43,** 1593–1599 (1998).

9 Lin, X. *et al.* Thermally-responsive, nonflammable phosphonium ionic liquid electrolytes for lithium metal batteries: operating at 100 degrees celsius. *Chem. Sci.* **6,** 6601–6606 (2015).

10 Giwa, C. O. Feasibility study of sulphone-based electrolytes for a medium-temperature reserve cell concept. *J. Power Sources* **42,** 389–397 (1993).

11 Bach, S., Baffier, N., Pereira-Ramos, J. P. & Messina, R. Rechargeable γ-MnO2 for lithium batteries using a sulfone-based electrolyte at 150 °C. *J. Power Sources* **44,** 569-575 (1993).

12 Kubota, K. & Matsumoto, H. Investigation of an Intermediate Temperature Molten Lithium Salt Based on Fluorosulfonyl(trifluoromethylsulfonyl)amide as a Solvent-Free Lithium Battery Electrolyte. *J. Phys. Chem. C* **117,** 18829–18836 (2013).

13 Marczewski, M. J., Stanje, B., Hanzu, I., Wilkening, M. & Johansson, P. 'Ionic Liquids-in-Salt'-a Promising Electrolyte Concept for High-Temperature Lithium Batteries? *Phys. Chem. Chem. Phys.* **16,** 12341–12349 (2014).

Update on NATO Standardisation Efforts For Dismounted Soldier Power

Darren Jonathan Browning[1], Marc Gietter[2], Jasper Groenewegen [3]

[1] Defence Science and Technology Laboratory, Platform Systems Division, Dstl, Salisbury, Wiltshire, UK, SP4 0JQ

[2] US Army CERDEC, Power Division, Command, Power and Integration Directorate, 6631 Cyber Street, Building 5100, Aberdeen Proving Ground, MD 21005-1852

[3] DNV Netherlands B.V. Utrechtseweg, Arnhem, 6812 AR, Netherlands

Abstract: *This paper will provide an update on the latest NATO efforts and standards for power interfaces on the dismounted soldier.*

To improve partner interoperability NATO has the aim to increase standardisation between nations. The NATO Land Capability Group Dismounted Soldier Systems (LCG DSS) is tasked with improving standardisation and interoperability for the dismounted soldier.

The Power Team of Experts (ToE) sub group has written a number of NATO Standardisation Agreements (STANAGs) documents pertaining to dismounted soldier power including defining the battery interface (STANAG 4695), defining a data and power interface (STANAG 4851) and defining requirements for interoperable battery chargers (STANREC 4819).

NATO is now considering whether new future standards are required to allow higher data rates and higher powers for the dismounted soldier.

It is important to socialise such standards to industry and NATO militaries and to discuss opportunities for future standardisation. In particular this paper will describe work on a NATO standard power connector as defined in STANAG 4695 and the associated Allied Engineering Publication, AEP-95, a NATO standard data connector as defined in STANAG 4851 and AEP 4851 and a proposal for a NATO standard battery charging interface as will be defined in STANREC 4819, along with some efforts planned for the future.

The Power Team of Experts is keen to socialize these standards and other efforts around the battery, connector and soldier system community to receive comments on their suitability and to drive wider adoption.

Keywords: standardisation; interoperability; NATO; generic soldier architecture; STANAG 4695, STANAG 4851 STANREC 4819.

Introduction

Many modern conflicts are often undertaken by a coalition of forces consisting of elements from a number of partner nations. NATO war gaming has highlighted the need for greater interoperability between users of dismounted soldier equipment.

In addition, dismounted soldiers are now carrying ever-increasing amounts of electronic capabilities which must be seamlessly integrated within the soldier system, other platforms (vehicle, aviation) and with coalition partners. These trends lead to an increased importance for standardisation (where mechanical and electrical characteristics are specifically defined) and interoperability (allowing different systems to interact). Without standardisation, all solutions become single source which eliminates the ability for a "plug and play" capability. Interoperability is important to assure that the transfer of data between various systems/nations is seamless, as well as the sharing of energy resources. In reality there is no interoperability without some form of standardisation.

Within NATO, the Land Capability Group on Dismounted Soldier Systems (LCG DSS) is responsible for the standardisation and interoperability of everything worn and utilized by the dismounted soldier, from weapons to clothing to tactics. This is accomplished by the creation and acceptance of Standardisation Agreements (STANAGs) and Standardisation Recommendations (STANRECs).

Due to the importance of energy to the success of the dismounted soldier's mission, LCG DSS established the Power Team of Experts as a Sub-Group (SG) The Power Team of Experts is a multinational group of subject matter experts (SMEs) tasked to author STANAGs and STANRECs, and provide technical support for all matters related to power generation and distribution for the dismounted soldier.

Power Interoperability & Connectivity (NATO STANAG 4695)

NATO LCG DSS envisions that in coalition operations soldiers may find their batteries running low and will need to obtain energy from sources other than the system's native battery. These sources may include another nation's battery, some form of portable generator or even a mobile platform such as a vehicle. It assumes that the end item has the ability to use, or condition the energy provided in a safe manner.

To accomplish this will require a standardised connector and definition of expected power source parameters. Ideally coalition partners would standardise on a common set of soldier batteries. However, realistically this is seen as unlikely in the near to medium term. To enable the sharing of energy, the Power Sub-Group authored STANAG 4695; "ELECTRICAL INTERFACE SPECIFICATIONS FOR DISMOUNTED SOLDIER SYSTEMS (DSS) LEVEL 2 POWER CONNECTOR INTEROPERABILITY"[1].

STANAGs tend to be overarching documents and much of the technical detail is provided in the associated Allied Engineering Publication (AEP) AEP 4695[2]. The STANAG 4695 received sufficient votes from NATO members and was approved by the NAAG (NATO Army Armaments Group) for promulgation in 2018. It has subsequently been reviewed and a second edition STANAG 4695 Edition 2 has been written and promulgated in 2022.

The adaptation of this STANAG requires that all power generation equipment designed in the future that might be available to the dismounted soldier have at least one output port that meets the requirements of the STANAG. However, it is expected that legacy equipment will remain for a considerable period of time. This requirement can also be met by the use of adapters.

Definition and implementation of a standard NATO soldier power connector means that even if such a connector is not on every relevant soldier power source, each partner nation will only need to carry a single adapter from their national interface to the common NATO interface, rather than the need to carry adapters to every conceivable partner nation power source.

The NATO STANAG 4695 connector has been based around the US Nett Warrior power connector. It has also been written into the UK Generic Soldier Architecture (GSA) as defined in Defence Standard 23-12. It should however be noted that NATO does not specify a given manufacturer. It does refer to qualified part numbers as tested by the US Army but allows any equivalent connector. The details on how to prove equivalence are not defined and it will be the responsibility of a host nation to provide sponsorship and evidence to the NATO LCG DSS Power Team of Experts to have additional connectors included. The connector cited in the STANAG is already in use on a wide range of military power sources and equipment of a number of nations. This is one of the main reasons it was selected.

The key metrics for the connector are given below.

Table 1. Electrical characteristics of a STANAG 4695 compliant power source

	Level 2 Complaint Power Source
Voltage	8-32 V
Current	0-5 A

Table 2. Pin assignments for a STANAG 4695 compliant connector

Contact location	Description	Terminal markings
1	V+ Battery Voltage	Batt +
2	V- Battery Voltage	Batt -
3	Charge +	Charge +
4	SMBus data	Data
5	SMBus clock	Clock
6	SMBus ID (10K Thermistor to Ground)	SB ID

The only significant revision of the Edition 2 from Edition 1 of STANAG 4695 is the removal of the optional 7th central pin that was allowed to be a second V+ line. Further analysis showed that allowing an optional 7th pin might lead to situations where mating could not be achieved e.g. where one nation had a receptacle with sockets containing only 6 sockets and a filled center pin and another nation had a plug with pins with 7 pins.

It was found that there was a mix of products in the marketplace with both filled and unfilled center sockets. Removal of the optimal 7th pin in Edition 2 removes this risk of non-mating.

Copies of the document can be obtained from your national representative or by contacting one of the authors of this paper.

It is expected that in the first instance this STANAG will allow sharing of batteries but it is also intended to allow alternative power sources such as fuel cells and thermoelectric devices to be shared and ultimately energy harvesting devices such as solar panels and kinetic generators, although some form of power management will be needed to facilitate this.

Data Interoperability & Connectivity (NATO STANAG 4851)

Soldiers also require the ability to share data between body mounted electronic devices such as sensors, an End User Device (EUD), usually a smartphone, and a data enabled radio. NATO also followed the US Army Nett Warrior approach for this connector, using the same physical connector as STANAG 4695 but with different (but coherent) pin assignments. The reasoning for this decision was again the wide use of the connector and the ability to use the same cables for both data and power provision, simplifying logistics and reducing system costs.

The soldier data connector is defined in STANAG 4851, “COMBINED POWER AND DATA ACCESSORY CONNECTOR FOR DISMOUNTED SOLDIER SYSTEMS (DSS)” and the associated AEP 4851. This was promulgated in June 2022. The connector also needs to distribute power to devices since using separate cables for power and data leads to an unacceptable solution for a dismounted soldier. To avoid this problem, the USB 2 data protocol was selected, and the connector also provides a 5 V (up to 2 A) line for low power electronic devices and a 10-20 V 5 A line for higher power devices. It is noted that the input voltage for STANAG 4695 and the distribution voltage of STANG 4851 is different. This was to allow nations to use a wider range of battery inputs from national batteries. Ultimately, the systems could be simplified if all soldier batteries were to be in the 10-20 V range. Table 3 shows the pin assignments. The main difference is the SMBus and charge pins of STANG 4695 have been repurposed as USB voltage and data pins in STANAG 4851. Comparison of the two tables shows that there is a potential risk that if a battery charge pin (pin 3) of STANAG 4695 were to be connected to the V+ pin (Pin 1) and a power source be directly connected to a device expecting the data connector 4851 that a higher voltage could be applied than the 5 V the data device would be expecting, potentially causing harm. For this reason STANAG 4695 recommends a diode, or other protective device, be fitted to the charge pin.

Table 3. Pin assignments for the STANAG 4851 data interface

CONTACT LOCATION	PAN FUNCTION
1	Power (10-20 VDC, 5 A max)
2	Ground – extended pin
3	Power (5 VDC, 250 mA min 2 A max)
4	USB + (data)
5	USB – (data)
6	No connect (or reserved for National Implementation)

Battery Charging Interoperability (NATO STANREC 4819)

For dismounted soldiers fighting side by side, it was identified that there would be operational benefit in being able to charge one another's batteries. NATO War Gaming identified where soldiers from one nation on a joint exercise would end up at the forward operating base of another nation and be unable to recharge their equipment's batteries for the following day's mission.

Originally each new military battery was issued with its own dedicated charger that had the correct charging algorithm preprogrammed. This leads to a proliferation of different, single application chargers which greatly complicates the logistics associated with charging batteries.

Recently such chargers have become more flexible by use of adapter trays. This allows one modular charger to be reconfigured for multiple different types of batteries by using different battery trays. This gives a nation flexibility in that it can buy battery chargers and then upgrade them to charge new batteries when required by buying new battery trays and reprogramming the charger. The charger knows which battery charge profile to use by recognizing the battery tray. This provides a nation some degree of charger standardisation but does little to implement charging interoperability between nations.

The implementation of STANAG 4695 allows for one nation to obtain electrical energy/harvest from another energy source but does not provide sufficient requirements to allow for interoperable battery charging. To enable this a charger must know and apply the correct charging profile for the battery.

STANREC 4819 addresses the need for interoperable charging by defining additional requirements for both military unique batteries and chargers based on commercial standards already established.

Different batteries have different charging requirements. This is because they use different chemistries or have different numbers of cells within them. For safety reasons and to maximize battery lifetimes they must be charged according to their required charging profile. The concept of interoperable charging is further complicated by the actual location of the charging contacts for a specific battery configuration. This makes interoperable charging very difficult.

However, industry has defined a smart battery charging specification which helps with this problem. The Smart Battery Charger (SBC) Specification allows chargers to charge multiple different types of batteries by allowing battery-dependent charge profiles that are dictated by the smart batteries themselves. In effect the battery tells the charger how to charge it.

Therefore, by using the industry standard SBC specification coupled to the STANAG 4695 connector both a standard connector and communication protocol is defined. This should allow one NATO partner nation to recharge their compliant batteries on another nation's compliant charger without any forward planning.

This concept has shown to be successful in limited laboratory testing but has yet to be used operationally. STANREC 4819 was recently (March 2023) submitted to the NATO Standards Organization (NSO) to distribute to NATO member nations for voting.

The NATO LCG DSS Power ToE would welcome comments from battery or battery charger manufacturers as to the viability of this approach and any additional information industry would wish to see in a future STANREC 4819 revision.

Future Effort – Power and Data Connectivity

It is believed that the current connectors defined in STANAGS 4695 and 4851 are sufficient for current needs and this approach has been derisked by their adoption by the US Army and other nations. However, it is recognized that there is likely to be a growth in the demand for more power and more/higher data throughput for dismounted soldier systems in the future.

NATO has also produced STANREC 4845, the NATO Soldier System Reference Architecture (NSSRA). It has been informed by other soldier architecture work including the UK Generic Soldier Architecture and the European Defence Agency's Generic Open Soldier System Reference Architecture (GOSSRA). This is a very large document in seven volumes covering all levels of the NATO Architecture Framework. The most relevant to power sources is volume 5 – Technical view. This recommends a future power standard of USB power delivery (PD) and a future data standard of USB 3. At the time of writing, the STANREC could not recommend a connector since there was not a suitable rugged, open or multiple source connector suitable for soldier systems.

Future Work – Other Endeavors

Other efforts that are planned LCG DSS include:

- Identification of potential connectors for use to connect helmet and weapon mounted peripherals
- Wireless (defined as the lack of cables) power and data transmission
- Including fuel cells into existing and future STANAGs and STANRECs
- Standardisation of a common connector to provide the USB 3 and USB PD functionality recommended by STANREC 4845
-

Conclusions

Future soldier systems are likely to be more integrated than they are today and if they are to remain flexible and upgradable an open architecture is required.

NATO LCG DSS is developing a range of STANAGS which will improve the interoperability of power sources and powered equipment between NATO nations. The first of these, STANAG 4695, defines a power and power related interface to allow batteries to be shared, either directly or via an adaptor and the second STANAG 4851 allows data interoperability. STANREC 4819 adds additional requirements to allow interoperable battery charging.

The ToE welcomes and encourages academia and industry to participate in the development of the various documents. This should be via you national representative to LCG DSS or by contacting the authors of this paper.

Acknowledgements

The author would like to acknowledge all the hard working members of NATO LCG DSS.

References

1. STANAG 4695 "Electrical Interface Specifications For Dismounted Soldier Systems (DSS) Type 2 Power Interoperability" Edition 2
2. AEP 4695 "Electrical Connectivity Standards Between NATO Power Sources And Dismounted Soldier Systems (DSS) - Type 2 Connector To Worn/Carried NATO Power Sources" Edition 2
3. Smart Battery Charger (SBC) Specification, Revision 1.1, December 11, 1998
4. STANAG 4851, Combined Power And Data Accessory Connector For Dismounted Soldier Systems (DSS), Edition 1, June 2022
5. AEP-4851, Combined Power And Data Accessory Connector For Dismounted Soldier Systems (DSS), Edition A version 1, June 2022
6. NATO STANDARD, AEP-4845, VOL. 5, Soldier System Reference Architecture, – Power, Electronics, and Data Infrastructure –Technical View

Advanced Vibration Analysis Techniques for Diagnosing and Repairing Systemic Machine Faults on Tactical Power Sources

David Aebischer
Cintel Inc., Systems Engineering and Integration
Huntsville, AL, USA, 35808
Dave.aebischer@cintel-inc.com/ 1-931-220-8541

Abstract

The PATRIOT Missile Defense System (MDS) Launcher Station (LS) requires an onboard source of precise and reliable electrical power to meet combat mission requirements. The LS uses a 15 kW/400 HZ Advanced Medium Mobile Power Sources (AMMPS) tactical generator, with a customized PATRIOT Applications Kit (PAK), to power its electronic control systems. LS power system failures significantly increase the probability of launch failure. During initial AMMPS fielding in Kuwait, PATRIOT units reported stator weld failures causing catastrophic failure of the AC generator on over 75% of the fleet. Initial weld inspection analysis supported no root cause conclusions. The Cintel Team performed an independent root cause analysis, on behalf of the Integrated Fires Mission Command (IFMC), to characterize the problem, determine the causal chain, analyze all covariates, including the existing PAK, and develop an effective treatment through modification of the existing PAK. Cintel used a set of vibration testing and analysis techniques – to include Cross-channel Phase (CCP), Experimental Modal Analysis (EMA) and Operational Deflection Shapes (ODS) - to determine that the weld fractures were caused by a structural resonance at 3rd harmonic order causing excessive vibration amplitude during operation at normal operating speed. Cintel's work also modeled weldment voids as a moderating effect in the causal path between the resonance and weld fracture and determined that sub-optimal welds are particularly sensitive to the high amplitudes in first bending mode and torsional movements recorded and identified in the ODS. This paper demonstrates the effectiveness of CCP, EMA, and ODS techniques as a comprehensive analytical approach to machine fault diagnoses on combat equipment. This paper also advances the theory that the structural resonance identified during the analysis, if left untreated, is a catalyst for multiple potential failure modes and mechanisms on the AMMPS, to include weld fractures, rotor-stator contact, and rotor bearing degradation.

Keywords

Vibration analysis; Causal Analysis; Experimental Modal Analysis (EMA); Operational Deflection Shapes (ODS); Cross-channel Phase (CCP); Structural Resonance; Natural Frequency (Fn); Bending Mode; Coherence; Bayesian Network (BN); Probabilistic Structural Equation Model (PSEM); Machinery Health Analyzer; Accelerometer; Modal Hammer; Phase; Campbell Diagram; Antinode; Isolators; Durometer; Damping, Magnification Factor.

Introduction

The 15 kW/400 HZ AMMPS LS generators are a direct replacement for the 15 kW/400 HZ Tactical Quiet Generators (TQG), fielded to PATRIOT units in the late 1990s. During initial TQG operational use, PATRIOT units reported several main AC generator failures. Initial inspections of the main AC generator failures showed evidence of rotor-stator contact consistent across all of the population of failed sets. Noting that no such failures were occurring in the 15 kW/60 HZ TQG fleet, analysts focused on the differences between the two 15 kW configurations: turning speed and mass. The 15 kW diesel engine is configured to operate at 2000 RPM; the 60 HZ set engine is configured to operate at 1800 RPM. The 15 kW/400 HZ set is 30 lbs. heavier than the 60 HZ due to the additional stator windings required for 400 HZ. Vibration analyses showed these failures were attributable to a structural resonance occurring just below turning speed of 33 HZ. This was causing bending mode amplitudes sufficient to close the rotor-stator air gap and cause friction between the two surfaces, ultimately leading to short circuit and failure. PATRIOT personnel developed a stiffening and damping treatment to mitigate the problem.

During the initial AMMPS fielding, PATRIOT units reported stator weld fractures causing catastrophic failure of the AC generator. Inspection of the failed AMMPS sets showed a rotor-stator contact, similar to the TQG inspection findings, across the whole population of failed sets. Initial analyses of inspection data suggested the failure mode and mechanism was similar to the TQG problem. These initial data supported no causal conclusions but indicated a high probability of a vibration problem given the similarity between the TQG and AMMPS generators in mass, geometry, and turning speed.

During initial inspection and analysis of failed sets, the Original Equipment Manufacturer (OEM) noted some weld quality issues on distribution of sets in a specific serial number range. During more detailed follow-on analysis, the OEM also performed a set of destructive and non-destructive inspection tests on production welds. Test analyses showed voids in the stator welds between the joined members and the weld fillet. Based on combined data on, and analysis of, weld quality and production process issues, the OEM implemented production weld process improvements to eliminate problems with weld. These data did not suggest a causal connection between the weld quality and the weld fractures, but rather supported that weld quality could be a moderator in the indirect causal connection between a resonance at turning speed, the weld fractures, and rotor-stator contact causing AC generator failure.

Given these combined historical and current TQG and AMMPS data, Cintel initiated a vibration analysis process to determine the root cause, model the exact causal relationships, and identify a treatment. In parallel with the vibration analysis process, Cintel used a knowledge engineering (KE) process to develop a Bayesian Networks (BN)-based causal model of the problem domain using. The KE process is used to combine data and expert knowledge in a Probabilistic Structural Equation Model (PSEM). The PSEM are graphical models that qualify and quantify a specific domain and are then used to facilitate understanding of multivariate relationships in varying conditions. The BN development process was ongoing throughout and was used to update beliefs based on vibration test data and expert analysis.

For all vibration testing and analysis used herein, Cintel used an Emerson AMS 2140 Machinery Health Analyzer, "VibView" and "MeScope" software for the CCP, EMA, and ODS testing and analysis, ICP Triaxial Accelerometers for all measurements, and an Emerson Impulse model force/modal hammer for the EMA testing.

The analytical approach is detailed in six distinct (6) phases.

Phase 1: Initial Cross-channel Phase (CCP) Testing

Based on initial evidence presented from the stator weld fractures, and on historical data from the 15 kW LS generators sets, Cintel identified structural resonance as a potential cause with high probability. Phase testing, in general, is used to determine how two points are moving relative to one another. And in all cases, a structural resonance causes a phase difference, or shift. The CCP test was then indicated for an initial test to reduce entropy in the problem domain and provide decision support for the follow-on test strategy. The CCP leverages the dual channel capability of the Emerson 2140 to provide the test data while the generator is operating at normal operating speed of 2000 RPM (33 HZ). The test was constructed with one accelerometer placed on the main generator at the top center, and a second accelerometer placed 90 degrees from top. The analysis team collected test data for reference/response, response/reference, and coherence values. These data showed an 8:1 ratio between the displacement velocity (in/sec) values at both sensors at a given time in the waveform, with coherence values over 9.0. These data indicated a phase shift with coherence – typical of a structural resonance baseline. This supported the structural resonance hypotheses and a *potential* causal/associative relationship between a resonance at Turning Speed (TS) and/or TS orders, and the weld fractures.

In this phase also began the process of eliminating the LS trailer, the PAK, and weld penetration/quality as covariates for the stator weld failures and subsequent generator failure. The team performed the same CCP tests in all configurations - on/off LS; with/without PAK - and noted no significant difference in values in any combination. This result was not conclusive but suggested that the LS trailer and PAK did not have a direct effect. For the weld quality, the analysis team performed CCP on AMMPS with original stators (pre-production process improvement) and improved stators (post-production process improvement). Data from these tests showed no significant difference between stator types. The team modeled this accordingly in the BN as a structural indirect causal connection from the resonance to the weld to rotor-stator contact to main generator failure. In this model, weld quality values have a moderating effect, wherein suboptimal welds would be more susceptible to failure and optimal/conforming welds would make other vibration-related failure mechanisms more probable, e.g., rotor-stator contact from any of the following individually or in combination: first bending mode action, bearing failure, or winding bond failure.

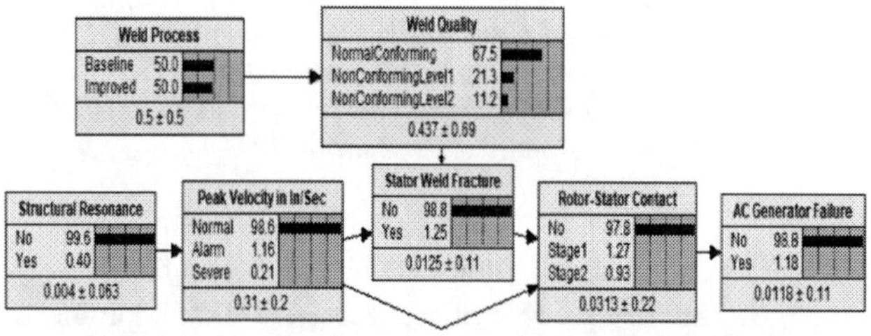

Figure 1. *Bayesian Network (BN) showing the causal relationships between structural resonance, stator weld, and AC generator variables.*

Further testing phases were then specifically designed to confirm the structural resonance hypotheses by characterizing and quantifying it through a set of Experimental Modal Analysis (EMA) and Operational Deflection Shape (ODS) tests. These tests would also provide further characterization of LS trailer, PAK, and weld quality effects.

Phase 2: EMA Baseline

The analysis team constructed an EMA test plan using the Vibration Analyzer, the triaxial accelerometer, and the modal hammer. The test design was to rove the accelerometer at eight (8) points, 45 degrees apart, around the circumference of the main generator – starting at the circumference around the rotor bearing end and moving towards the circumference around the driven end at approximately 4" lateral increments. This design produced five (5) sets of 360 degree test iterations consisting of 40 individual test points. With the accelerometer positioned at a test point, the vibration analyst struck the stator with the modal hammer, one strike at each axis: vertical, radial, and axial. This process produced 120 individual data points covering the entire stator geometry. Cintel used these EMA test data to establish a Natural Frequency (Fn) baseline and to generate a Campbell diagram to show any specific frequencies with major amplification around TS (Figure 2.)

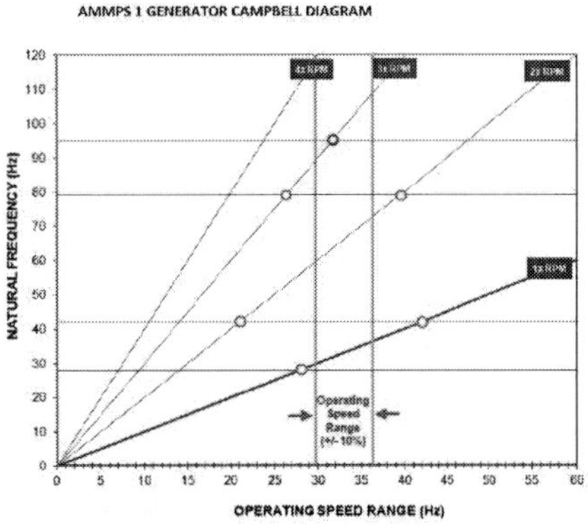

Figure 2. *Campbell Diagram: Representative of Baseline OEM Configuration and OEM with PAK, both on and off LS, Configurations. Fn are relative to Turning Speed (2000 RPM/33.3 HZ) and multiples of Turning Speed (TS). Red, or Bold, circles indicate major amplification points relative to the 10% band around TS*

The 3 x TS peak (~ 96 HZ, in Red), located within the +/- 10% of TS band was indicated for follow-on ODS testing to characterize the movement of the AMMPS at turning speed. To further evaluate the effects of the different AMMPS configurations on the structural dynamics of the AMMPS, the EMA tests were all repeated for the different configurations of on/off LS, PAK/No PAK, and original weld/improved weld. The EMA data from these tested indicated a sharp null of no effect and effectively eliminated the PAK and LS variables from consideration as covariates for the stator weld fractures – further strengthening the arguments underpinning the structural resonance hypothesis. These data did not alter the causal model as regards the potential moderating effect of weld quality.

Phase 3: ODS Baseline

In this phase Cintel focused on building and analyzing a working ODS structural model of the machine using the Analyzer and ODS software. This ODS test was constructed as a process: first building a finite element model of the AMMPS in the ODS software, then collecting ODS data at turning speed, and then interpolating the test data on the ODS structural model. The model development involves creating a grid-like, three-dimensional model of the set and then creating test points as the vertices between grid lines. The test points are then formatted so they are oriented for accelerometer position and location. The end state is comprehensive model of the AMMPS generator and engine geometry with 280 built-in test points. The ODS data were collected by roving a triaxial accelerometer to each test point in sequence and activating an ODS capture at each test point. This process generated 280 data points for each axis (axial, radial, and vertical) for a total of 840 data points. These data were then interpolated on the ODS grid model and then animated at different frequencies – TS and harmonics – to show how the AMMPS set was moving during operation. The initial animations showed a complex movement shape with a first bending mode shape component and a twisting/torsional movement component – both at elevated amplitude levels. The velocity of displacement (in/sec) peaks for these modes and movements were most pronounced at a peak of ~ 99 HZ, or 3 x TS. The ODS data were consistent with the EMA results and confirmed the structural resonance hypothesis. This result indicated for a guided process for developing an initial treatment prototype.

Phase 4: Treatment 1

In this phase Cintel used the combined EMA and ODS results to determine optimum location and geometry of a stiffening bracket designed to move the 3 x TS FN out of the +/- 10% significance band around TS. The existing AMMPS configuration uses two sets of isolators: one set under the engine; one set under the stator. Both sets are affixed to brackets. The engine bracket is part of the engine casting; the generator bracket is welded to the stator frame. Each bracket is fitted with a rubber shock mount to isolate the engine/generator from the frame. The Team determined that the existing engine block boss used to mount the transportation bracket - located at the approximate antinode between the engine and generator - would be a viable location. This effectively created a "middle row" set of brackets (with shock mounts) to stiffen the structural beam created by the engine and generator. After fabricating and installing the prototypes, Cintel repeated the EMA test, and these test data showed the brackets were successful in moving the Fn out of the TS band (Figure 3.)

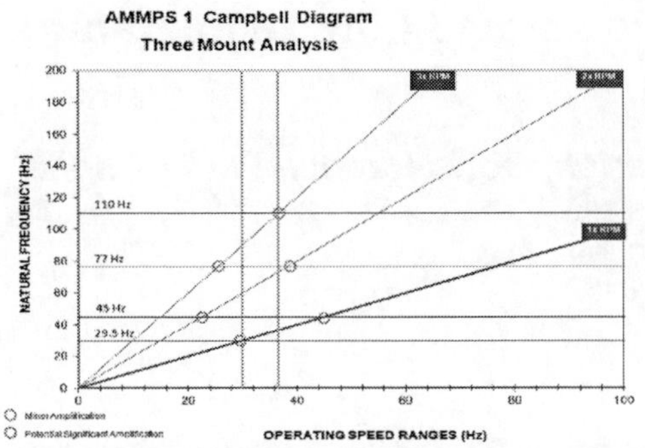

Figure 3. Campbell Diagram: Treatment 1 Fn relative to Turning Speed (2000 RPM/33.3 HZ) and multiples of Turning Speed. Clear circles indicate minor amplification points relative to the 10% band around turning speed. Note absence of any points inside of +/- 10% of TS and absence of red, or bold, circles.

Phase 5: Treatment 1 + 2

In this phase, Cintel first performed another ODS test on the new baseline configuration with stiffening brackets to assess the impact of the brackets on the AMMPS movement at turning speed. These test data showed a significant improvement (decrease in vibration energy) but also showed that further stiffening would not be effective. The ODS showed that a moderate damping treatment- decreasing the isolator shock mount durometer value - could improve performance by reducing the magnification factor, or Q factor, around TS. Figure 4 shows the effectiveness of replacing the existing 70 durometer mounts with 50 durometer mounts.

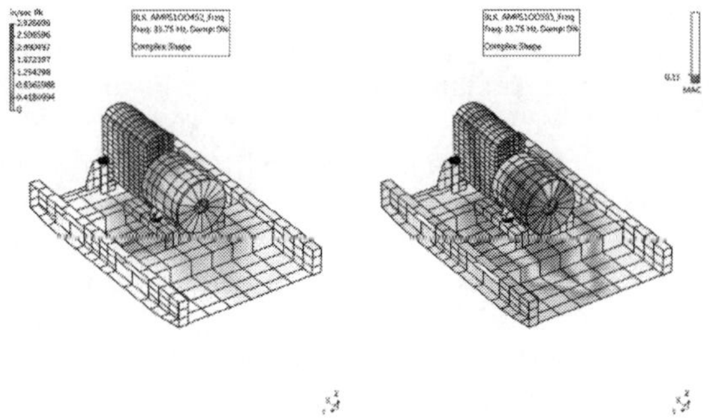

Figure 4. ODS Animation: Snapshot of AMMPS at 33 HZ with amplitude shown on color scale and in inches/sec in Black and White. The snapshot on the right is the Treatment 1 configuration with just the brackets. Note that with only the stiffening bracket there is significant decrease in vibration energy but still some moderate peaks (velocity = ~ 1.6 ips.). The snapshot on the left is the Treatment 1 + 2 configuration with the brackets and 50 durometer isolators. Note the significant decrease in amplitude and vibration energy with the combined treatment (velocity = ~.1 ips)

Testing

In this phase Cintel tested the new prototype treatment against PATRIOT reliability standards. The most critical was the "Shaker Table" test due to the sensitivity of the rubber compound isolators. The original PAK baseline 70 durometer isolators were already proven to pass PATRIOT standards. Cintel's task was to ensure the softer durometer performance would not come at the expense of durability to meet endurance testing requirements. Cintel tested the new 50 durometer isolators in both the original configuration and in the new middle row configuration - using new sets of isolators in each test. These test data showed no significant damage to the isolators or brackets after testing to equivalent of 10000 hours of operation.

Conclusions

Cintel's prototype Treatment 1 + 2 (stiffening and damping) was accepted by IFMC as an approved update to the existing PAK Engineering Change Proposal (ECP) and the vibration mitigation "kit" was fully integrated on all IFMC 15 kW stock. This kit, combined with weld process improvements, provides for a more reliable power source for the PATRIOT MDS. Cintel's work in this problem domain establishes the primacy of CCP, EMA and ODS techniques for testing and analysis of post-design PATRIOT MDS power problems. The versatility of these techniques combined with causal analysis tools provides a potential for much broader applicability to all combat systems as a comprehensive and precise analysis tool.

Acknowledgements
The author wishes to thank Mr. Dan Ambre for his expertise and technical assistance with the critical EMA and ODS analyses.

References

1. Aebischer, D., "Bayesian Networks for Descriptive Analytics in Military Equipment Applications", in Military Applications of Data Analytics, CRC Press, 2018.
2. Aebischer, D., et.al, "Bayesian Networks for Combat Equipment Diagnostics", Interfaces: INFORMS Journal on Applied Analytics, Vol. 47, No. 1. 2017.
3. Crawford, A., "Simplified Handbook of Vibration Analysis, Vol. 2, Computational Systems, 1992.

Lithium-Ion Battery Cells for Ultra High Power and Low Temperature Applications

Chao Lei*, Svetlana Trebukhova, Thomas Barbarich, Boris Ravdel, Frank Puglia
EaglePicher Technologies, LLC
2000 South County Trail
East Greenwich, RI 02818
Chao.Lei@eaglepicher.com

Abstract: *The latest developments in US and global military technologies reinforced the need for a new generation of batteries for the ultra-high-power applications, such as Directed Energy Weapons (DEW), More Electric Aircraft (MEA), and various hybrid systems, etc.*

A successful design must meet greater specific power requirements and often perform at harsher environmental conditions than previous generations. The discharge time for DEW can range from milliseconds up to several minutes, which translates to a rate from 20C to over 300C. There is also a thrust to improve the low temperature performance of the lithium-ion batteries (LIB) and many of the design changes needed to support DEW rates are applicable to low temperature operations.

This paper illustrates the extremely high charge and discharge rates achieved with small pouch cells of the most advanced chemistry and cell design solutions. The projected specific short pulse-power of one 1 Ah cell can reach a breakthrough value of 50 kW/kg! Recharge rates exceeding 100C have also been demonstrated for State of Charge (SOC) changes exceeding 50%. When these cells are combined with EPT's extensive electrolyte development, they demonstrate C/2 discharge performance at temperatures as low as -60 °C.

Keywords: LIB; DEW; MEA; high-rate; ultra-high-power; low temperature;

Introduction

EaglePicher Technologies (EPT) has developed unique battery solutions to fulfill the highly specialized demands of evolving and existing technologies in the defense and aerospace sectors [1]. The demand in power in DEW, MEA and other hybrid systems is consistently increasing. For instance, the military requires more power to operate energy-demanding electronics, radars, and other equipment in MEA. In the case of aircraft applications, battery power requirements can range from 1C to 400C, but more importantly, the operating environment on an aircraft can be very harsh. Typically, battery capable of operating within a wide temperature range of -40 to 70°C is necessary. In this article, we will highlight EPT's recent progress in the design and development of ultra-high-power cells with a rate capability up to 380C discharge and 250C charge, as well as low-temperature electrolyte development with decent cell performance at temperatures as low as -60°C. When combined with EPT's advanced terminal designs and module designs, these cells can provide very high duty cycles to meet current and future extreme requirements.

Ultra-High-Power Pouch Cell

To enhance the rate capability of the cell, it is essential to facilitate the flow of ions and electrons through the cell, particularly through the electrodes and electrode interfaces. EPT has thoroughly selected cell chemistry and each cell component, as well as designed electrode formulation and structure to maximize the power capability. Most of the data presented in this article are based on our single-layer pouch (SLP) or double-layer pouch (DLP) cells with capacity < 0.05Ah. EPT has also manufactured, tested, and delivered to our customers 1.0~2.0Ah prototype cells for use at specific duty cycle profiles with extremely high discharge and charge rates and various temperature conditions.

Discharge rate characterization was performed using the DLP cells at C rate up to 380C and various temperatures. At each temperature, the cells were soaked for at least 6 hours to reach thermal equilibrium. As shown in Figure 1, good discharge rate capability is demonstrated. The cell is able to deliver 72% of 1C room temperature (R.T.) capacity while discharging under 380C at 60°C, and the average voltage during discharge is only reduced from 3.65V at 1C to 3.27V. At a moderate temperature of 40 °C, the cell can deliver >70% of 1C capacity while discharge at 200C, with an average discharge voltage of 3.34V. When the temperature is reduced to 0°C, the cell can still provide >60% of 1C capacity at a 50C rate.

In addition to the cell's exceptional discharge capability across a broad temperature range, the cell also exhibits excellent recharging capability. Figure 2 shows the charge capacity return from 2.5V to 4.1V at various C-rates and temperatures. At 60°C and a constant current of 250C, the cell is recharged from 0%SOC to 60%SOC in just 15 seconds, without a constant voltage (CV) hold. Even at a moderate temperature of 40°C or 20°C, the cell can reach approximately 60%SOC at a rate of 150C or 50C, respectively. This particular cell design is highly suitable for applications such as DEW, where rapid recharge capabilities are essential.

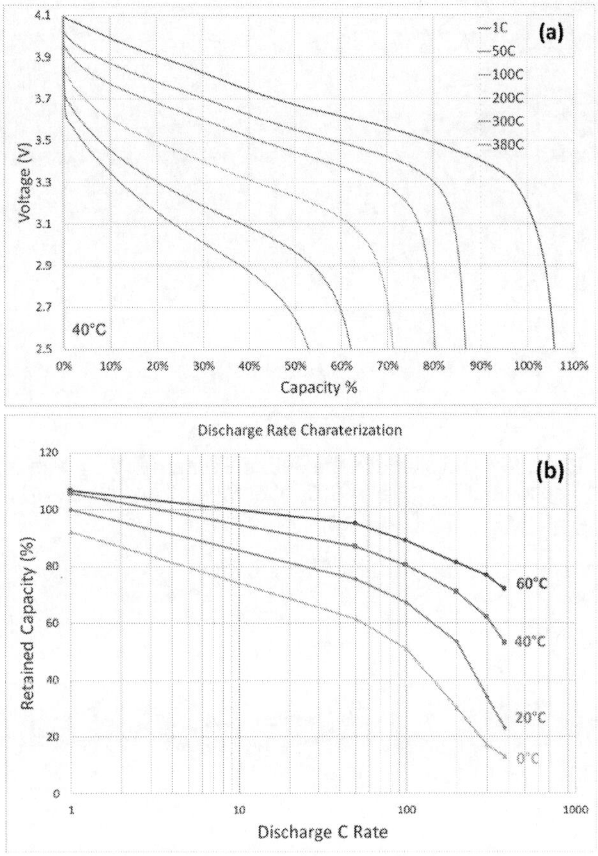

Figure 1. (a) Discharge rate capability at 40°C; (b) Delivered capacity normalized to 1C capacity @20°C, at different C-rates and temperatures.

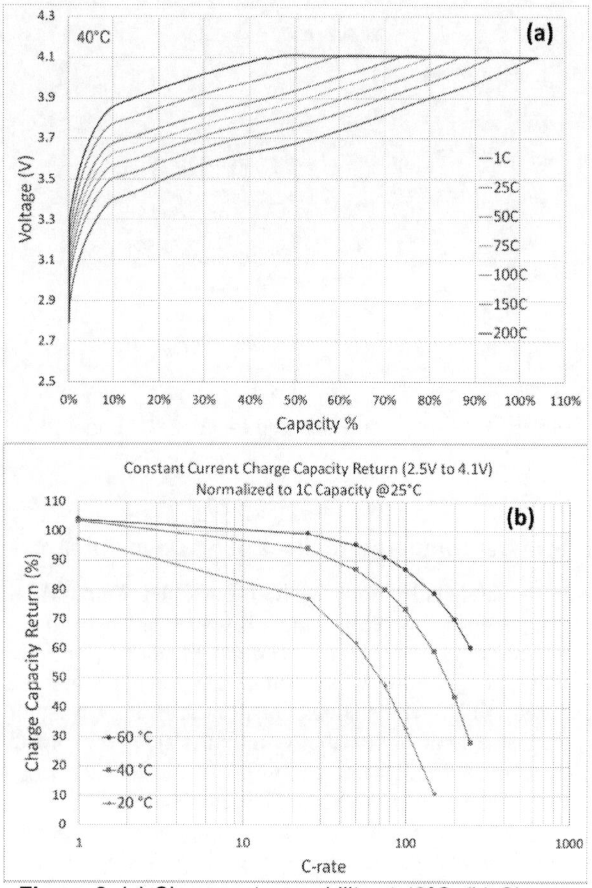

Figure 2. (a) Charge rate capability at 40°C; (b) Charge capacity return at various C-rates charging and temperatures.

To further assess the performance of the DLP cells, they were subjected to cycling at 200C discharge and 150C charge starting at 3.9V, with a 50% depth of discharge (DOD). The results are presented in Figure 3. At 40˚C, the voltage at the end of each discharge (V_{min}) rapidly increased after a few cycles and eventually settled at a relatively constant value of 2.7V. This indicated the cell temperature reached a state of dynamic stability. When the test temperature was elevated to 60˚C, V_{min} was approximately 3.2V and both V_{min} and V_{max} (voltage at the top of charge) remained fairly steady for all cycles. At 40˚C, the energy efficiency (not shown) has risen from 80.4% to a steady state around 82.8%, while at 60˚C, it stayed nearly constant between 88.3% and 89%.

Besides the continuous current tests, the cells were also evaluated for their short pulse capabilities. Figure 4 shows the short pulse discharge test for a SLP cell at 31˚C under a 2V hold. It is found that the current can reach as high as 1288C for milliseconds. For our 1Ah pouch cell, the projected specific short pulse-power density can reach a breakthrough value of 50 kW/kg!

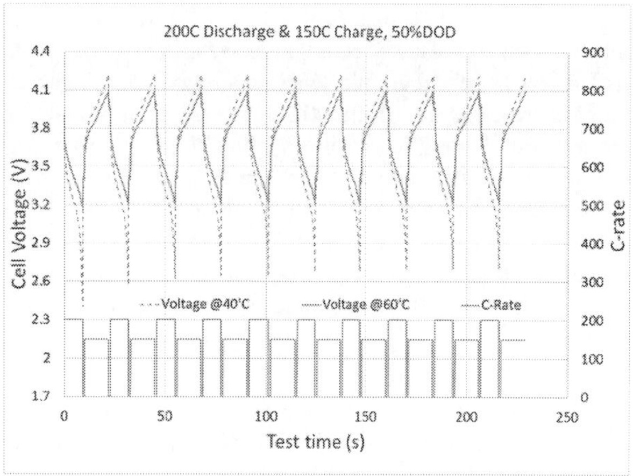

Figure 3. Cell cycling under 200C discharge and 150C charge, 50%DOD

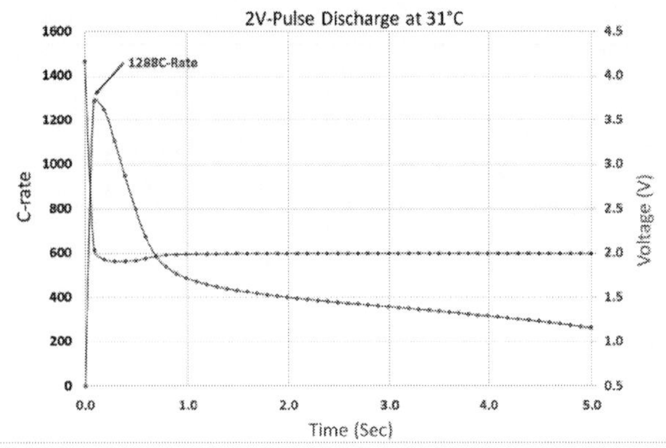

Figure 4. Short pulse discharge test at 31°C under 2V

Ultra-Low Temperature Electrolyte Development

Non-standard applications like high-power DEW and MEA that operate in low temperatures pose a challenge for all components of the LIB. In certain situations, batteries intended for use in low-temperature environments may be exposed to high temperatures. In such cases, the battery or cell must exhibit high stability, minimal side reactions at high temperatures, as well as to maintain excellent energy density and power capability in low-temperature conditions. EPT has developed electrolytes with improved high power at temperatures as low as -40°C with improved stability at elevated temperatures (+70°C).

Various additive and additive packages have been developed to improve the life and high-power performance of batteries in low-temperature environments. Figure 5 displays the voltage at the end of discharge (V_{min}) of a 15-second 5C pulse at -40°C. These cells underwent aging between performance checkpoints by cycling at different temperatures ranging from -40°C to +71°C following a temperature histogram, with a total aging time of approximately one month. Compared with our former baseline, the new electrolytes with both additive package A and additive package B have demonstrated significant reductions in cell overpotential during -40°C discharge, as well as slowed cell degradation resulting from thermal cycling.

Figure 6 displays the voltage at the end of discharge (V_{min}) from a 15-second 5C pulse at -40°C. These cells were subjected to calendar aging at 55°C between performance checkpoints. The large error bars of the data points with former baseline indicates the cell performance varies greatly after high temperature exposure. The electrolytes with new additives show more consistent results, implying better thermal stability. Again, compared with our previous baseline, the new electrolytes have shown substantial reductions in cell overpotential during -40°C discharge and improved calendar life at elevated temperatures.

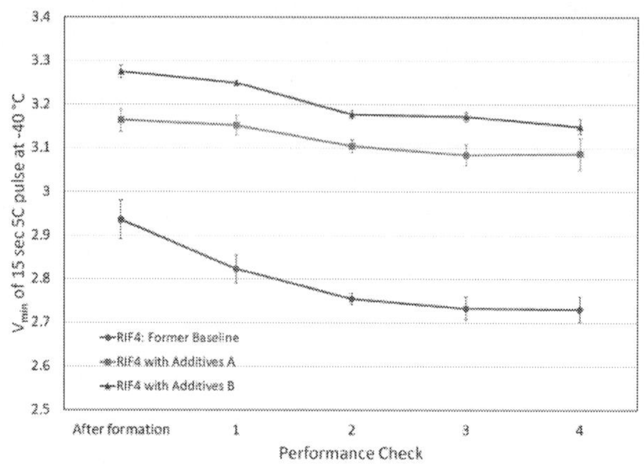

Figure 5. The voltage at the end of discharge (V_{dip}) from a 15 second 5C pulse at -40°C, after thermal aging between each check points

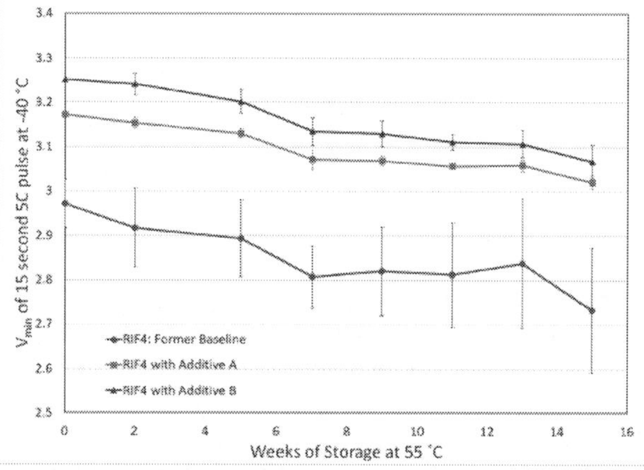

Figure 6. The voltage at the end of discharge (V_{min}) from a 15 second 5C pulse at -40°C, after calendar aging at 55°C between each check points

It is widely believed that ethylene carbonate (EC) is the critical component of the mixed solvent responsible for creating a robust passivation layer on the graphite-based negative electrode, also known as the solid electrolyte interface (SEI) layer. However, the high melting point of EC can result in the solution freezing or phase separation at low temperatures, particularly when the concentration of EC is high.

In response to the challenges posed by extreme-low temperature applications, such as those at -60°C, EPT has developed an "EC-free" electrolyte. As depicted in Figure 7, our baseline EC-based electrolytes can only deliver approximately 40% of the 1C R.T. discharge capacity when discharging at -60°C at C/3. However, with EPT's EC-free electrolytes, the cells can deliver up to 65% capacity at the same rate, representing an improvement of over 60%. Furthermore, after 250 cycles at room temperature, the cells using EC-free electrolyte continue to maintain a relatively high deliverable capacity at -60°C, validating their good cycle life at ambient temperatures.

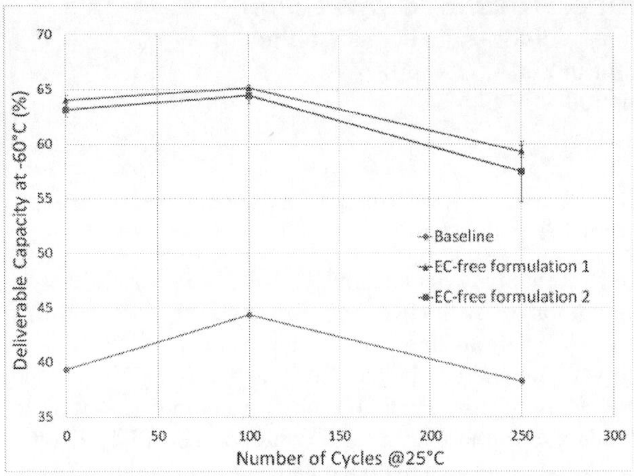

Figure 7. Deliverable capacity percentage at -60°C as a function of cycle numbers

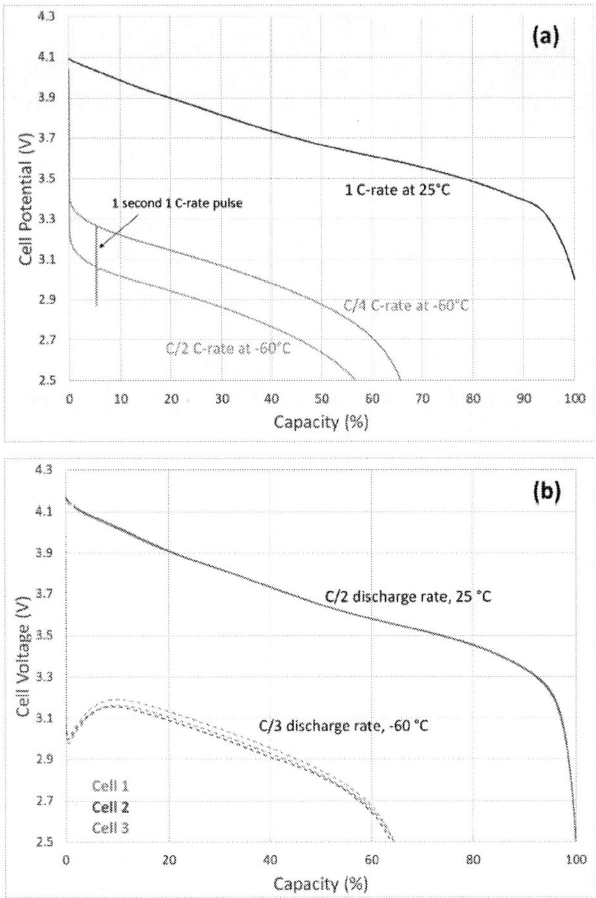

Figure 8. Discharge voltage profile at -60°C for (a) SLP cells and (b) 18650 cylindrical cells

Figure 8 illustrates the discharge voltage profiles of SLP cells and 18650 cylindrical cells at -60°C. At C/4 and C/2 rates, the SLP cells can deliver 66% and 56% of 1C R.T. capacity, respectively. Similarly, the 18650 cells can deliver around 64% of 1C R.T. capacity at C/3. During the discharge, the voltage of the 18650 cells showed a brief recovery at the start, attributed to self-heating. The cell temperature quickly rose by 3-4°C, then stabilized until the end of the discharge. In contrast, due to their small capacity and relatively larger surface area, the SLP cells did not exhibit any significant self-heating.

Conclusions

EPT has developed and demonstrated the impressive charge and discharge capabilities of our small pouch cells, which can deliver continuous power with up to 380C discharge rates. The specific short pulse-power of one 1 Ah cell is projected to reach a groundbreaking 50 kW/kg! These cells can also be recharged from 0%SOC to 60%SOC at a rate exceeding 100C, making them ideal for applications such as DEW and various hybrid systems that require rapid recharge capabilities.

Additionally, EPT has developed electrolytes specifically tailored for non-standard applications such as high-power DEW and MEA that operate in both high and low temperatures. Cells containing the new electrolyte have demonstrated improved high-power performance at temperatures as low as -40°C, with increased stability at elevated temperatures up to +70°C. To address the challenges of extreme-low temperature applications, EPT has also developed an "EC-free" electrolyte that allows the cell to deliver up to 65% of 1C capacity at temperatures as low as -60°C.

Overall, EPT's innovative technologies and solutions are poised to make a significant impact in various fields where high-performance energy storage is essential.

Acknowledgements

The authors would like to acknowledge EaglePicher IRAD supports.

References

1. F. Puglia, S. Trebukhova, B. Ravdel, S. Santee, C. Cook "High Charge and Discharge Power Li-Ion Prismatic Cells", 48th Power Sources Conference 2018 Proceedings, p.228

A Solid Solution-Based Tough Polymer Electrolyte for Structural Energy Storage Applications

Yu-Che Chang, Parya Teymoory, Roger Tessier, Caiwei Shen*
Department of Mechanical Engineering, University of Massachusetts Dartmouth
285 Old Westport Road, North Dartmouth, MA, USA, 02747
* cshen2@umassd.edu / 1-508-999-8449

Abstract

Multifunctional structural energy storage components that can replace existing structural components while providing additional energy storage capability can ease the power demands of various electrically powered systems. The serious trade-offs between the mechanical and electrochemical performance of structural electrolytes are a challenge to realizing practical structural energy storage components. In this research, a solid polymer electrolyte with hydrates was created using polylactic acid and lithium salt. One of the compositions achieved a significant ionic conductivity (3.11 μS/cm) with an excellent toughness (15.4 MJ/m^3) that is one order higher than the base polymer. This study demonstrates the possibility of incorporating electrochemical functionality into structural composites while maintaining or even enhancing mechanical functionality, guiding the design of future structural energy storage components.

Keywords

Structural energy storage; Supercapacitors; Solid polymer electrolyte; Multifunctionality.

Introduction

In electrically powered mobile systems, the heaviest components are energy storage devices and supporting structures. Taking an electric vehicle as an example, about 30% of the weight comes from the battery, and over 35% from structural components including frame, exterior, and interior. To further improve the operation time, travel range, and functionality of such systems, especially when the batteries are approaching their performance limit, one solution is to develop multifunctional structural energy storage components, which can replace existing structural components and provide extra energy storage capability. Researchers have demonstrated structural supercapacitors for this purpose[1]. Most of these devices share the configuration of laminate fiber composites, in which two layers of carbon fiber electrodes are sandwiching a glass fiber separator and filled with an ion-conducting solid electrolyte as the matrix. The energy is stored through the electric double-layer capacitance effect at the carbon fiber-solid electrolyte interface. In almost all previous studies, the solid electrolytes are made of bi-continuous phase electrolytes (BPEs), which are simply the mixtures of liquid electrolytes and epoxy resins[2]. The BPEs, however, have significant trade-offs between mechanical and electrochemical performance and poor electrochemical interfaces with electrode materials.

Our recent study demonstrated a solid polymer electrolyte incorporated with hydrates (denoted as SPE-H) that provides promising multifunctionality[3]. We used polyethylene terephthalate (PET) as the base polymer and melted it together with lithium perchlorate ($LiClO_4$) to produce an amorphous solid solution. The PET- $LiClO_4$ electrolyte was then hydrated under controlled humidity to convert the salt to its trihydrate ($LiClO_4 \cdot 3H_2O$). Unlike previous designs of BPEs, we found that the SPE-H provided significant ionic conductivity while retaining the base polymer's stiffness and toughness. Moreover, such electrolytes showed much better electrochemical interfaces with electrodes.

In this research, we present another SPE-H system made from a different base polymer, polylactic acid (PLA), and another salt, lithium bis(trifluoromethanesulfonyl)imide (LiTFSI). The new material system is easier to process and form desired shapes through various techniques. One of the compositions achieved a significant ionic conductivity (3.11 μS/cm) with an excellent toughness (15.4 MJ/m^3) that is one order higher than the base polymer after proper thermal treatment and controlled hydration. This is the first evidence to show that it is possible to incorporate electrochemical functionality into structural composites while retaining or even enhancing their mechanical functionality. The mechanisms learned in this study can guide the design of better structural energy storage components in the future.

Experiment Details

Sample preparation: In a typical process, 2 grams of PLA and x wt% (x = 10 to 50) of LiTFSI were mixed in 40 ml of dimethylformamide (DMF). The mixture was put on the hot plate and stirred vigorously under 110 °C for 12 hours overnight to ensure the homogeneity of the solution. Then the solution was cast on a Teflon plate at 120 °C for 6 hours. We denote the samples at this stage as "As-cast SE x", where SE stands for structural electrolyte and x reflects the wt% of the salt. The as prepared SE samples had residual DMF, so the cast film was then put into a convection oven at 165 °C for one hour to evaporate the residual solvent as much as possible. The samples are denoted as "Dried SE x" after this step. These dried samples can be melted and shaped through hot press, hot rolling, or injection molding.

The shaped samples were then exposed to air with controlled humidity in an environmental chamber. The samples will absorb water molecules from the air because of the hygroscopic nature of the salt. The amount of water absorbed is self-limiting at fixed temperature (22 °C in our laboratory) and relative humidity, as demonstrated in our previous studies[3,4]. The samples are denoted as "Hydrated SE x" after this step. Although it seems that the hydrated samples are only the results of replacing the DMF in as-cast samples with water, later tests show that the hydrated samples have both higher ionic conductivities and better mechanical properties than the as-cast ones.

Material characterizations: Fourier transform infrared spectroscopy (FTIR) testing was conducted on an Agilent Cary 630 to detect the presence of chemicals. Electrochemical impedance spectroscopy (EIS) was conducted using a Gamry Interface 1010 potentiostat to obtain the impedance of electrolyte samples for ionic conductivity calculation. Tensile tests were conducted using rectangular samples on an Instron 5569 testing machine to obtain their mechanical properties.

Results and Discussions

FTIR results:

The chemical compositions of the electrolyte samples are confirmed by FTIR analysis, which characterizes chemical bonds through the absorbance peaks of infrared light in resonant frequencies. The FTIR spectra of pure chemicals, including PLA, LiTFSI, DMF, and water are first tested and presented in Figure 1a. Pure PLA is featured by an absorption peak near 1749 cm^{-1} caused by C=O stretching, and many peaks in the range of 1500 cm^{-1} to 1250 cm^{-1} due to C-H stretching and 1250 cm^{-1} to 1000 cm^{-1} due to C-O stretching [5]. LiTFSI has strong feature peaks between 1500 cm^{-1} and 1000 cm^{-1}, but it is small peaks around 3600 cm^{-1} that distinguish it from other chemicals. DMF shows the strongest feature peak at 1665 cm^{-1} caused by C=O stretching. Liquid water is featured by a broad peak around 3300 cm^{-1}. The FTIR spectra of representative structural electrolyte samples are plotted in Figure 1b. The as-cast SE 40 sample show two feature peaks at 1749 cm^{-1} and 1665 cm^{-1}, respectively, indicating the existence of both PLA and residual DMF. The DMF can be completely removed after the drying process, as the feature peak of DMF disappears in the dried SE 40 sample. The spectrum of the hydrated SE 40 sample, however, shows little difference from the dried sample. The absence of peaks around 3300 cm^{-1} indicates the absence of liquid water. A small rise of absorbance near 3600 cm^{-1} is caused by the interaction between LiTFSI and water.

Ionic conductivity results:

The ionic conductivities of as-cast SE samples with various compositions are first tested and shown in Figure 2a. The values increase by three orders of magnitude from 4.2×10^{-4} μS/cm to 8.7×10^{-1} μS/cm when the weight ratio of the salt increases from 10% to 50%. The increase of ionic conductivity is partially due to the increased amount of salt ions. More importantly, it is caused by the increased amount of residual DMF that is associated with the salt. When the DMF is completely removed, the ionic conductivity decreases sharply. For example, the ionic conductivity of SE 40 decreases from 4.8×10^{-1} μS/cm (as-cast, Figure 2a) to 1.1×10^{-4} μS/cm (dried, Figure 2b). The hydration process, on the other hand, will restore the ionic conductivity, as shown in Figure 2b. For SE 40, its ionic conductivity increases to 3.11 μS/cm when hydrated at a

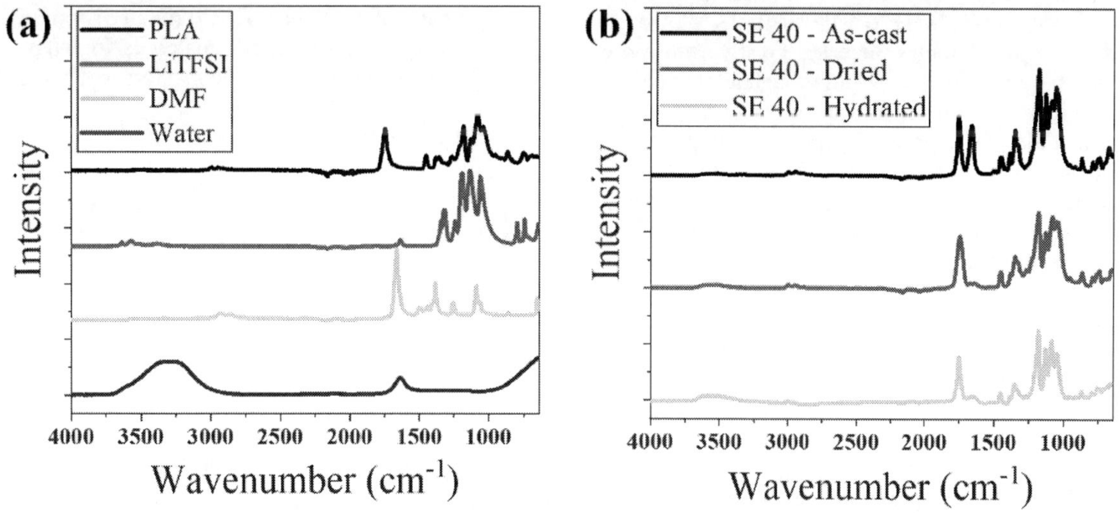

Figure 1. FTIR spectra of (a) pure chemicals used in the preparation of structural electrolyte samples and (b) representative structural electrolyte samples at different stages of processing.

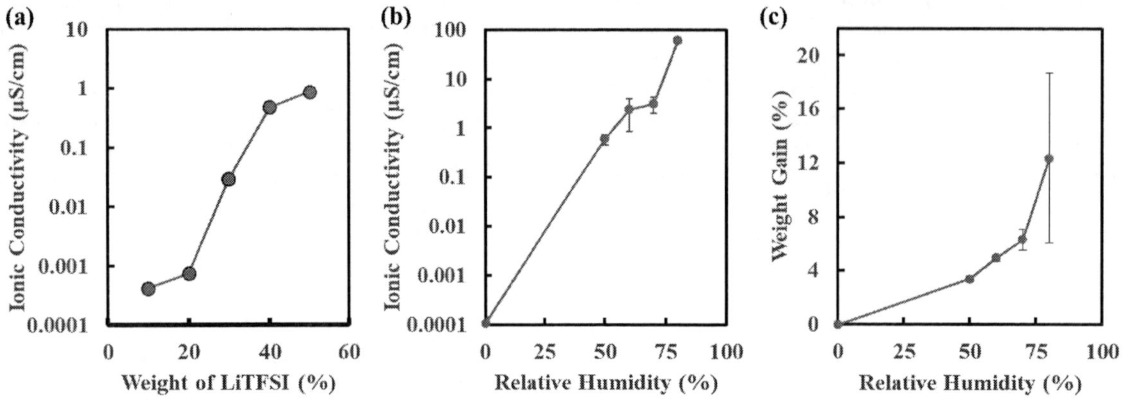

Figure 2. (a) The ionic conductivity of as-cast structural electrolyte samples with various weight ratios of LiTFSI. (b) The ionic conductivity of SE 40 samples hydrated at various relative humidity levels. (c) The weight change of SE 40 samples hydrated at various relative humidity levels.

relative humidity of 70%, and it reaches 59.1 μS/cm when hydrated at 80% humidity. The hydration is self-limiting up to the humidity of 70% as indicated by the controlled weight gain (due to water absorption) measured in Figure 2c. However, the water absorption becomes out of control when the humidity reaches 80%, under which the salt will absorb too much water to form liquid solution. Liquid droplets were detected on samples, and the SE samples became gels with significantly reduced mechanical properties. Therefore, hydration under 70% humidity is considered as the optimized processing condition.

Tensile test results:

The stress-strain curves of as-cast SE samples with various compositions are presented in Figure 3a. As more LiTFSI is added to the polymer matrix, the samples show decreased elastic moduli and tensile strengths. However, the ductility of the samples increases greatly with more salts in them, resulting in very high toughness values as shown in Figure 3b. The significant increase in ductility indicates that the salt, together with the residual DMF, acts as a plasticizer in the material system. The toughness of the base polymer PLA is 1.83 MJ/m^3, which is comparable to the values reported in the literature [6]. The toughness of as-cast SE 40, however, improves by one order of magnitude and achieves 18.5 MJ/m^3. Then the mechanical properties of the SE 40 samples at different stages of processing are tested and shown in Figure 3c. The samples become stiffer and stronger after DMF is removed, while most of the ductility is preserved. As a result, the dried SE 40 presents a toughness of 30.0 MJ/m^3. Hydration of the samples will decrease the elastic modulus and strength again, but they are still stiffer and stronger than the as-cast ones. The hydrated SE 40 (hydrated at 70% humidity) has a toughness of 15.4 MJ/m^3, which is still one order of magnitude higher than that of pure PLA.

Conclusions

We have demonstrated a solid polymer electrolyte incorporated with hydrates (SPE-H) using hydrated PLA-LiTFSI samples for potential structural energy storage applications. We found that the samples prepared by solution casting method have significant solvent residuals that greatly affect the ionic conductivity and mechanical properties of the electrolyte system. The samples can be processed and shaped through various techniques including hot rolling and injection molding after complete removal of the residual solvent. The final electrolyte prepared through proper hydration of the dried samples achieves a significant ionic conductivity (3.11 μS/cm) with an excellent toughness (15.4 MJ/m^3) that is one order higher than the base polymer. Future research will demonstrate the processing of such electrolyte through 3D printing and the combination with electrode materials for high-toughness multifunctional structural energy storage devices.

Acknowledgements

This research work is supported by UMass Dartmouth's Marine and Undersea Technology (MUST) Research Program funded by the Office of Naval Research (ONR) under grant N00014-20-1-2170, and also supported by National Science Foundation grant 2217172.

References

1. Xu, Y., Lu, W., Xu, G. & Chou, T.-W. Structural supercapacitor composites: A review. *Compos. Sci. Technol.* **204**, 108636 (2021).

2. Tu, V. *et al.* Performance of bicontinuous structural electrolytes. *Multifunct. Mater.* **3**, 025001 (2020).

3. Joyal, N., Chang, Y.-C., Shonar, M., Chalivendra,

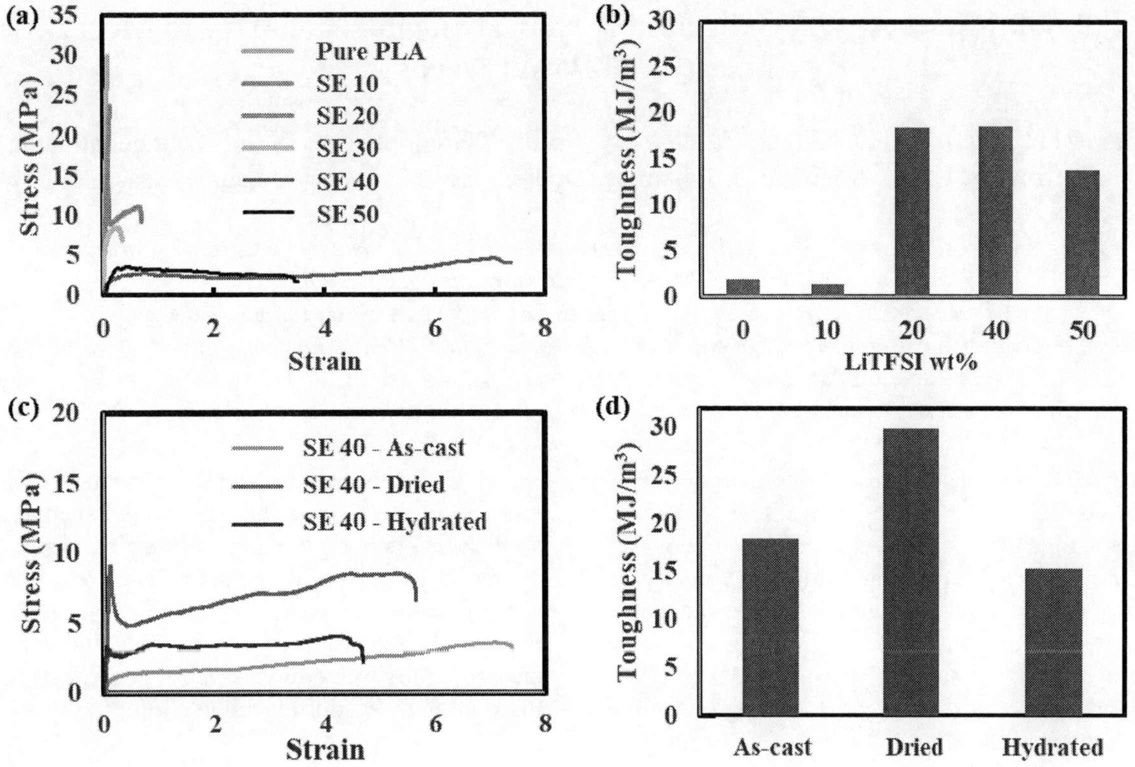

Figure 3. (a) The stress-strain curves of pure PLA and as-cast SE samples with various weight ratios of LiTFSI. (b) The average toughness values of pure PLA and as-cast SE samples with various weight ratios of LiTFSI. (c) The stress-strain curves of SE 40 at different stages of processing. (d) The average toughness values of SE 40 at different stages of processing.

V. & Shen, C. Solid polymer electrolytes with hydrates for structural supercapacitors. *J. Energy Storage* **51**, 104459 (2022).

4. Anjum, N., Joyal, N., Iroegbu, J., Li, D. & Shen, C. Humidity-modulated properties of hydrogel polymer electrolytes for flexible supercapacitors. *J. Power Sources* **499**, 229962 (2021).

5. Li, D. *et al.* Preparation of plasticized poly (lactic acid) and its influence on the properties of composite materials. *PLoS One* **13**, 1–15 (2018).

6. Suttiruengwong, S., Pitak, S., Saedan, M., Wongpornchai, W. & Singho, D. Binary-additives toughened biopolymer for packaging application. *Energy Procedia* **56**, 431–438 (2014).

3D All Solid-State Ag–Zn Batteries: A Non-Strategic Chemistry to Meet DoD Energy and Power Needs

Hunter O. Ford,[1] Brian L. Chaloux,[2] Michael W. Swift,[3] Christopher A. Klug,[2] Youngchan Kim,[4] Jeffrey W. Long,[2] Michelle D. Johannes,[3] Debra R. Rolison,[2] and Megan B. Sassin[2]

[1] *NRL-NRC Postdoctoral Associate in the Chemistry Division, U.S. Naval Research Laboratory, Washington, DC 20375 – hunter.ford.ctr@nrl.navy.mil*

[2] *Chemistry Division, U.S. Naval Research Laboratory, Washington, DC 20375*

[3] *American Society for Engineering Education Postdoctoral Fellow, Center for Computational Materials Science, US Naval Research Laboratory, Washington, DC 20375, USA*

[4] *Materials Science & Technology Division, U.S. Naval Research Laboratory, Washington, DC 20375*

Abstract: Rechargeable silver–zinc batteries, if improved to deliver more than a few tens of cycles, hold promise as next-generation energy-storage devices by offering competitive energy density, inherent safety, supply-chain resilience, and suitability for reconfiguration as a macroscale 3D all solid-state battery (3D SSB). Implementing a 3D SSB design and simultaneously tackling the issue of undesirable Ag migration during battery operation requires developing an anion-conducting solid-state electrolyte (SSE). Here, we assess the ion-transport properties of a series of crosslinked anion-conducting polymeric SSEs based on 4-dimethylaminomethylstyrene (4DMAMS) and divinylbenzene (DVB). By varying the ratio of functional monomer 4DMAMS to crosslinking monomer DVB, an optimal co-polymer SSE composition with high ionic conductivity and mechanical integrity is achieved. The best performing polymer SSE has an ionic conductivity of 43 mS cm^{-1} when fully swelled with water, and 0.02 mS cm^{-1} when equilibrated in 33 % relative humidity (RH).

Keywords: silver–zinc battery, solid-state electrolyte, anion conduction, 3D all solid-state battery

Introduction

Meeting the future energy-storage needs of the civilian market and for defense applications requires battery chemistries that are safer, supply-chain resilient, and more energy dense than lithium-based batteries. A battery chemistry of the past, alkaline silver–zinc (Ag–Zn), is well suited to meet the above requirements.

Silver–zinc batteries are in use as primary cells and as limited secondary batteries, spanning applications across civilian, defense air and naval operations, and NASA systems. The long-term rechargeability of Ag–Zn has been historically prevented by a number of factors, including shape change at the Zn electrode (e.g., Zn dendrites) and dissolution of Ag during cell cycling.[1,2]

With the invention of a three-dimensional (3D) interconnected and electronically wired Zn anode pioneered by the Naval Research Laboratory, the shape-change and subsequent dendritic shorting of the Zn electrode has been abated.[2] Further, the door to an interconnected energy-dense 3D Ag–Zn SSB form factor, in which the 3D NRL-patented Zn sponge serves as both anode and scaffold, has been opened. The remaining challenge is the development of an SSE that supports Ag–Zn redox, is amenable to incorporation into the 3D Zn sponge scaffold, and prevents unwanted Ag dissolution and ion-crossover through the cell.

We use *initiated* chemical vapor deposition (*i*CVD) to generate thin, conformal, and anion-conductive polymers that can uniformly coat 2D and complex 3D substrates. The polymers synthesized via *i*CVD are chemically identical to the same polymers synthesized by conventional bulk polymerization methods.[3] This chemical comparability means that in tandem with the development of thin *i*CVD anion-conducting SSE coatings for 3D Ag–Zn SSBs, traditional bulk polymerization methods can be used to survey the variable space of polymer SSE composition. In doing so, property–performance relationships regarding the influence of polymer composition on ion transport and mechanical properties can be rapidly screened. The findings are then translated back to thin *i*CVD-based polymer SSEs en route to a 3D Ag–Zn SSB.

Here, a series of copolymers consisting of DMAMS (dimethylaminomethylstyrene) and crosslinking agent DVB (divinylbenzene) are synthesized via bulk free-radical polymerization and then converted into charged anion-conducting SSEs via post–synthesis solution-based protocols. The influence of polymer composition (ratio of DVB to DMAMS) and impact of water content on ionic conductivity is quantified with electrochemical impedance spectroscopy (EIS), while the mechanical properties are qualitatively assessed. The more highly crosslinked polymers have lower ionic conductivity (σ_i) and a faster drop-off in σ_i as water content decreases, relative to polymers with lower DVB content. The most conductive co-polymer exhibits a σ_i of 43 mS cm^{-1} when fully swelled with water and 0.02 mS cm^{-1} at 33 % relative humidity.

Experimental

Synthesis of 4-DMAMS monomer: The 4-dimethylaminomethylstyrene (DMAMS) was synthesized according to our recent publication by reacting 1-(chloromethyl)-4-vinylbenze (Oakwood Products, 98 %) with a 5-fold molar excess of dimethylamine (Thermo Fisher, 40% wt/wt aqueous solution) and 1 equivalent K_2CO_3 for 16 hours at 25 °C. The crude product was isolated by aqueous workup (EtOAc/H_2O) and subsequently purified by vacuum distillation (~80 °C, ~200 mTorr). Isolated yields of 75–85% are typical.[4]

Synthesis of DVB-co-DMAMS polymers: As-synthesized DMAMS and commercial DVB (Aldrich, 80% technical grade) were separately passed through short columns of basic alumina to remove inhibitors. For a typical 0.3 g total scale, an appropriate amount of DMAMS was combined with 0.0075 g (2.5 wt%) azobisisobutyronitrile (AIBN, Aldrich, 98 %) in a vial. This mixture was sparged with N_2 for 10 min. After sparging, DVB was added to the solution and mixed, and the entire solution was pipetted onto a 2.5 cm × 3.8 cm section of Whatman glass fiber (GF) filter paper (GF/C 1822-849) on top of a glass slide. Another glass slide was placed on top of the monomer-soaked GF, and the entire sandwich was heated to 75 °C on a hotplate for 1.5 h. The resulting 500 μm thick polymer-GF composite was rinsed with acetone to remove unreacted species.

Conversion to Solid-State Electrolyte (SSE): The polymer-GF composite was entirely submerged in the methylating agent methyl iodide (MeI, Fisher Scientific, 99 %) within a Parafilm-sealed vial for 24 h; the remaining MeI was then allowed to evaporate. The resultant yellow SSE-GF was rinsed three times with acetone, soaked in 1 M KOH aqueous solution for 24 h and then rinsed with deionized water.

Attenuated Total Internal Reflectance (ATR) Fourier-Transform Infrared Spectroscopy: Spectra were collected on a Thermo Scientific Nicolet iS50 with an ATR-IR attachment. Spectra are collected with 32 scans and a resolution of 4 cm^{-1} and baseline corrected with Thermo Fisher Omnic data-processing software.

Hydration of SSEs: For samples that were exposed to different relative humidity (RH), the SSE-GF sample was first fully dehydrated within a N_2 drybox (< 2% RH). Next, the SSE-GF was placed in a sealed vessel containing aqueous saturated salt solutions, such that the sample was not in contact with the solution, only the water vapor. Relative humidity (RH) values of 33, 53, 75, and 97 % were obtained by using saturated solutions of magnesium chloride, magnesium nitrate, sodium chloride, and potassium sulfate, respectively. After 24 h of equilibration, the sample was ready for analysis. Similarly, for samples that were measured in the entirely water-swelled state, the SSE-GF sample was placed in deionized water for 24 h prior to measurement.

Measurement of ionic conductivity: Roughly 1 cm^2 of a SSE-GF sample was sandwiched between stainless-steel electrodes with sufficient force to ensure good contact to the electrodes. Samples were interrogated with electrochemical impedance spectroscopy (EIS) using a Gamry Instruments Reference 620 potentiostat with an AC voltage of 100 mV (RMS) over a range of 4 MHz to 0.1 Hz. The resulting data (plotted in Nyquist form, $-Z''$ vs. Z') were fit with equivalent circuit models to obtain the ionic resistance, from which the ionic conductivity was calculated.

Results and Discussion

In our previous work, *i*CVD was used to prepare thin coatings of pDMAMS which were then converted to SSEs via a reaction with 1-bromo-3-chloropropane.[3] This reaction simultaneously quaternizes and introduces chemical crosslinks into the pDMAMS films, where the quaternary ammonium groups are bridged by a propyl spacer. While this method of crosslinking improved the mechanical stability of the films and introduces tethered positive charge, it suffers from two drawbacks. First, it is difficult to control the degree of crosslinking and therefore difficult to evaluate composition–property–performance relationships. Second, as the quaternary ammonium groups are linked together, the loss of degrees of freedom likely negatively impacts ion dissociation and mobility.

To address both concerns, co-polymers of crosslinking agent DVB and DMAMS are prepared in known ratios: 25:75, 10:90, 5:10, and 2.5:97.5 wt% DVB:wt% DMAMS. Charge is then introduced to the DVB-DMAMS co-polymer by reacting with MeI. In this composition, DVB provides the chemical crosslinking, leaving the quaternary ammonium groups with maximal degrees of freedom, which should improve ionic conductivity.

The final polymer (styrenic quaternized ammonium groups with DVB crosslinking) is not a novel material, but the synthetic route used here is amenable to *i*CVD processing to produce thin (sub-micron) polymer films that are readily converted to SSEs for a 3D Ag–Zn SSB.[5,6] Figure 1 shows ATR-FTIR spectra and chemical structures of the individual monomer components and the 2.5:97.5 DVB-DMAMS SSE-GF co-polymer before and after methylation to introduce positive charge functionality.

The co-polymer is insoluble in solvents that dissolve the respective monomers and contains FTIR peaks associated with both DVB and DMAMS, indicating successful copolymerization and crosslinking. As reported previously, methylation eliminates the amine-tethered C–H peaks at 2770 cm^{-1} and 2810 cm^{-1} with a new peak at 3008 cm^{-1} being formed, assigned to N^+-tethered C–H.[3] A peak at 1613 cm^{-1} is assigned to N^+–C while the broad peaks at 3430 cm^{-1}, 3220 cm^{-1}, and 1660 cm^{-1} are assigned to sorbed water.[7,8] These results confirm the successful methylation of the SSEs.

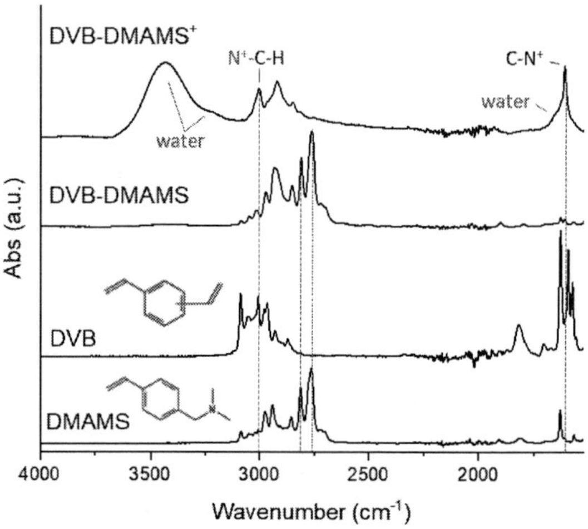

Figure 1. ATR-FTIR spectra of DVB, DMAMS, DVB-DMAMS-GF 2.5:97.5 and DVB-DMAMS$^+$-GF 2.5:97.5.

The ionic conductivity values of the four SSE-GF compositions fully swelled with deionized water are shown in Figure 2. The σ_i of the SSE-GF increases as the content of DVB decreases, even when normalized for the number of ion carriers (intrinsic conductivity). The difference is an order of magnitude at the most extreme, with minor differences between 5:95 and 2.5:97.5 compositions. Higher degrees of crosslinking impede ion mobility, likely by disrupting ion transport pathways and preventing significant water uptake into the polymer.[9,10]

The ionic conductivity of the 5:95 sample is in line with that observed in the literature for a comparable material.[6] Qualitatively, as the DVB content decreases, the membranes are less rigid and glassy, becoming more rubbery in both the swelled and dried states.

The ionic conductivity of the 2.5 wt% DVB SSE-GF sample equilibrated within different RH environments, along with select RH data of the other membranes, is shown in Figure 3. In the driest condition (2% RH), where the SSE-GF

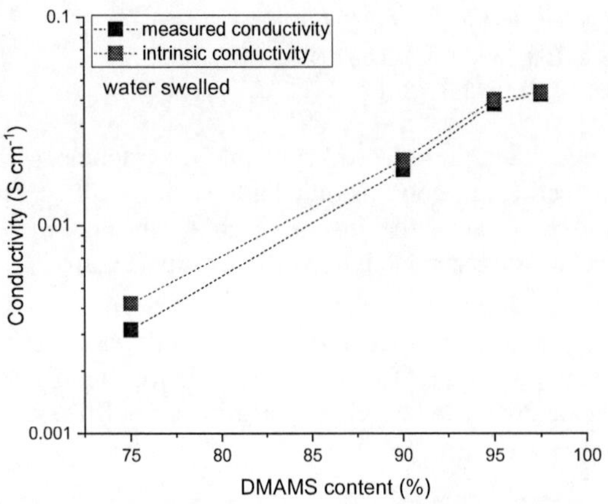

Figure 2. As-measured and intrinsic ionic conductivity of water-swelled SSE-GF samples of varying DMAMS content.

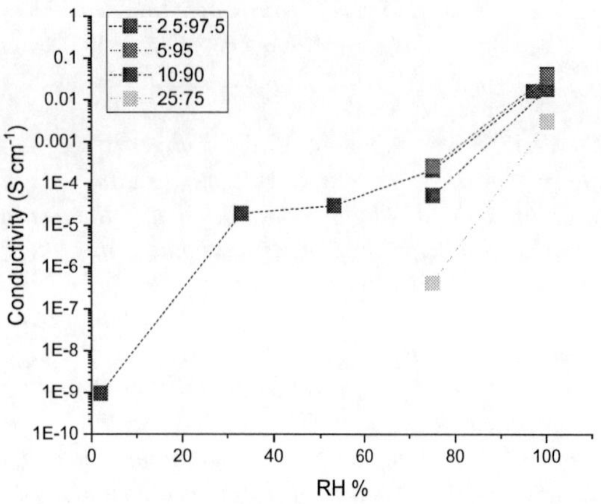

Figure 3. Ionic conductivity of copolymers with varying DMAMS as a function of RH.

sample was dried in the N_2 dry-box, σ_i is almost immeasurable with EIS, indicating little-to-none of the ion conduction within these materials is done through polymer–ion interactions (such as occurs for Li^+ conduction in polyethylene oxide) and instead ion conduction is water mediated.

The 2.5 wt% DVB SSE sample maintains reasonably high σ_i at 33% RH (1×10^{-5} S cm^{-1}). The 5:95 and 2.5:97.5 compositions are similar at both points measured. The additional crosslinking content of the 5:95 sample should lead to improved mechanical stability, indicating this composition may have the optimal blend of high ionic conductivity and mechanical strength to serve as an SSE in a 3D Ag–Zn SSB. The more crosslinked compositions of 10:90 and 25:75 exhibit inferior performance at lower RH, experiencing three and four orders of magnitude drops in σ_i, respectively, compared to the two orders of magnitude decrease of the 2.5:97.5 sample when going from fully swelled to 75% RH.

The trends in σ_i seen in Figures 2 and 3 indicate that compositions containing 2.5–5 wt% DVB should be targeted with *i*CVD to yield crosslinked coatings that are mechanically stable with sufficient ionic conductivity, even in low RH environments. Future work will focus on *i*CVD generation of down-selected copolymer compositions, evaluation of Ag and Zn redox reactions, and Ag crossover in 2D and 3D Ag–Zn cells.

Acknowledgements

H. O. F. gratefully acknowledges the National Research Council Postdoctoral Fellowship Program.

References

1. Parker, J. F.; DeBlock, R. H.; Hopkins, B. J.; Chervin, C. N.; Rolison, D. R.; Long, J. W.; Sassin, M. B. *J. DoD Res. Eng.* **2022**, *5*, 97–106.

2. Parker, J. F.; Chervin, C. N.; Nelson, E. S.; Rolison, D. R.; Long, J. W. *Energy Environ. Sci.* **2014**, *7*(3), 1117–1124.

3. Ford, H. O.; Chaloux, B. L.; Rolison, D. R.; Sassin, M. B. *ACS Appl. Mater. Interfaces* **2023**.

4. Kim, Y. C.; Chaloux, B. L.; Rolison, D. R.; Sassin, M. B.; Johannes, M. D.; Sassin, M. B. *Electrochem. Commun.* **2022**, *140*, 107334.

5. Small, H. *J. Chromatogr. A* **1991**, *546*, 3–15.

6. Maurya, S.; Shin, S. H.; Kim, M. K.; Yun, S. H.; Moon, S. H. *J. Membr. Sci.* **2013**, *443*, 28–35.

7. Ferrari, M. C.; Catalano, J.; Baschetti, M. G.; De Angelis, M. G.; Sarti, G. C. *Macromolecules* **2012**, *45*(4), 1901–1912.

8. Arges, C. G.; Wang, L. H.; Jung, M. S.; Ramani, V. *J. Electrochem. Soc.* **2015**, *162*(7), F686–F693.

9. Tsehaye, M. T.; Choi, N. H.; Fischer, P.; Tubke, J.; Planes, E.; Alloin, F.; Iojoiu, C. *ACS Appl. Energy Mater.* **2022**, *5*(6), 7069–7080.

10. Maurya, S.; Shin, S.-H.; Kim, Y.; Moon, S.-H. *RSC Adv.* **2015**, *5*(47), 37206–37230.

Advanced Electrolyte Solvents to Enable High Ni NMC Lithium Ion Batteries

Tobias O. Johnson, Monica L. Usrey, Peng Du, Sarah Guillot, and Brian Kerber
Koura Global, Inc. 3587 Anderson Street, Suite 108, Madison WI 53704
tobias.johnson@kouraglobal.com 1-608-661-1961

Abstract: *Traditional commercial electrolytes based on carbonate solvents limit the long-term cycling stability, high voltage stability, and thermal stability of lithium-ion batteries (LIB) with high-Nickel NMC cathodes. Thus, there is significant research in the battery field towards developing electrolyte solvents and additives with improved electrochemical and thermal stability. To rationally design next generation electrolytes, a fundamental understanding of how these molecules function in the battery including mechanisms of solvation, surface interaction, and bulk reactivity and how the structure of the molecule contributes to its properties and behavior is required.*

Silatronix has developed a series of organosilicon (OS) materials over several years through molecular design to target specific Li-ion battery performance-related characteristics. This design process included selection of specific ion coordinating functional groups, degree of fluorination, and structure optimization to balance molecular polarity, ionic conductivity, and viscosity. The inclusion of Si in the molecule has proved to be essential for maintaining improved thermal and electrochemical stability.

In addition, Silatronix has developed an optimized suite of tools and best practices that pair a commercially relevant comprehensive performance evaluation with the fundamental electrolyte understanding required to guide additional molecular design and optimization. This process elucidates structure-property relationships to optimize electrolyte formulation for high Ni NMC/graphite Li-ion cells. OS materials applied at only 0.5% to 3% of electrolyte composition have demonstrated improved high-temperature performance, including higher capacity retention, with significantly reduced gas generation and reduced impedance growth. In this paper, we discuss the cell-level performance benefits conferred by OS materials with nitrile-functionality for Li-ion cells with high-nickel cathode materials.

Keywords:

Electrolyte; Lithium Ion; solvent; organosilicon; OS; OS3®; LIB; Li, high nickel; thermal stability; oxidation; reduction; impedance; safety; solvation; $LiPF_6$; SEI; solid electrolyte interphase; energy storage; DSC; ONR; NMC; graphite; gassing; Office of Naval Research; DOD; battery; cell; molecule; electrochemistry; fluorine; Si, Silicon, anode; cathode; NMC811

Introduction

Silatronix® has developed a series of organosilicon (OS) materials using targeted molecular design to provide functional characteristics desirable for LIB applications. Design of unique organosilicon molecules includes selection of specific ion coordinating functional groups, degree of fluorination, and structure optimization to balance molecular polarity, ionic conductivity, and viscosity (Figure 1).

The inclusion of Si in the molecule has proven to be essential for maintaining improved thermal and electrochemical stability. Multiple OS materials developed via this process have demonstrated excellent performance in LIB systems.

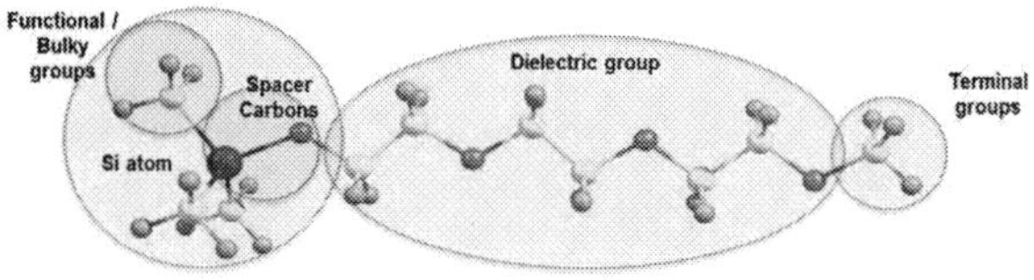

Figure 1. Organosilicon (OS) molecular design

Performance of OS3®

OS3® is an OS-nitrile solvent that is currently used in commercial Silicon-based anode cells. OS3® is also in advanced trials for use in next generation cell designs with partners in the USA, Europe, and Asia. The most comprehensive performance benefits have been observed at < 5 wt % OS3® in the electrolyte which fits comfortably within the additive market space of the LIB industry.

Properties of OS3®: The OS3® structure is balanced to provide excellent high voltage stability, thermal stability, low reactivity, low viscosity, high conductivity, high flash point / boiling point, and low vapor pressure (**Error! Reference source not found.**).

Table 1. Physical Characteristics of OS3®

Dielectric Constant	16.8
Flash Point	82 °C
Boiling Point	202 °C
Freezing Point	-57 °C
Density	0.93 g/cc
Viscosity	2 cP

Stabilizing of $LiPF_6$ salt:
OS3® is a strong coordinator of Li salts in electrolytes and prevents both decomposition of $LiPF_6$ and catalytic production of HF. Figure 2 demonstrates how addition of as little as 2% OS3® to a carbonate electrolyte with $LiPF_6$ results in removal of all initial HF and suppression of additional HF formation. Eliminating $LiPF_6$ decomposition reactions is critical to enabling high energy LIB systems with long calendar life and excellent high temperature performance. This OS3® mechanism protects all components in LIB cells which improves stability and reduces long-term impedance growth.

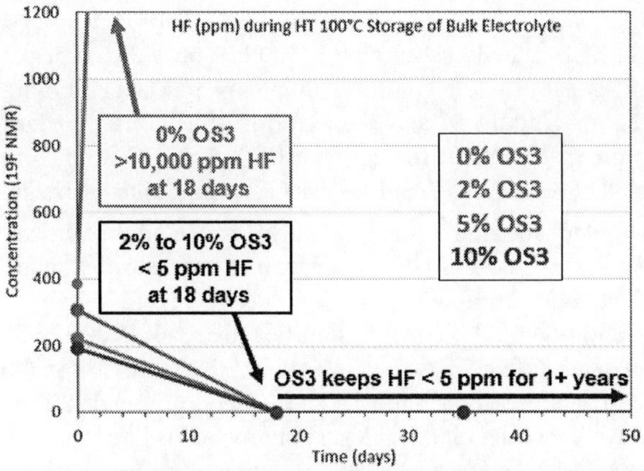

Figure 2. HF concentration in EC/DEC/$LiPF_6$/OS3® electrolytes during HT storage

Thermal stability enhancement:

OS materials have demonstrated the ability to reduce the thermal response of electrodes during differential scanning calorimetry (DSC). DSC testing of the high energy NMC622 cathode found lower peak heating rates and increased onset temperature (Figure 3) with 20% OS3®. In addition, several cell development partners have reported improved safety test results with low concentrations of OS3® (1% to 5%).

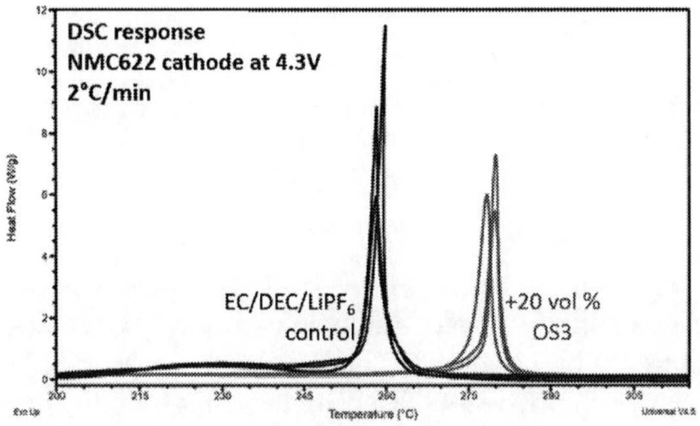

Figure 3. DSC response of OS materials with NMC cathode

Cell-level performance improvements:

Several commercial cell development partners in the US, Asia, and Europe have observed practical improvements to comprehensive battery cell performance; including excellent HT cycling stability, reduced impedance growth, improved calendar life rate capability, reduced gas generation, reduced pouch cell swelling, improved safety / abuse response, and improved low temperature rate capability. Benefits have been observed in various cathode and anode systems.

Full format cell level testing and fundamental research of OS technology has been completed with ONR funding on several programs, including both shipboard and NAVAIR targeted applications. OS3® has demonstrated improved HT stability, reduced gas generation, and reduced impedance growth in multiple cell chemistries, including those utilizing high Ni NMC cathodes.

Molecular Engineering of OS Materials

As discussed above, the OS family of materials is quite versatile by design. As an example, several variations within the OS3® family (nitrile functionality) have been synthesized to target specific physical and electrochemical characteristics. Figure 4 shows the fundamental oxidation stability (on platinum electrodes) for several members of this family. The OS3®-family of materials offers improved oxidative stability compared to an EC/EMC baseline.

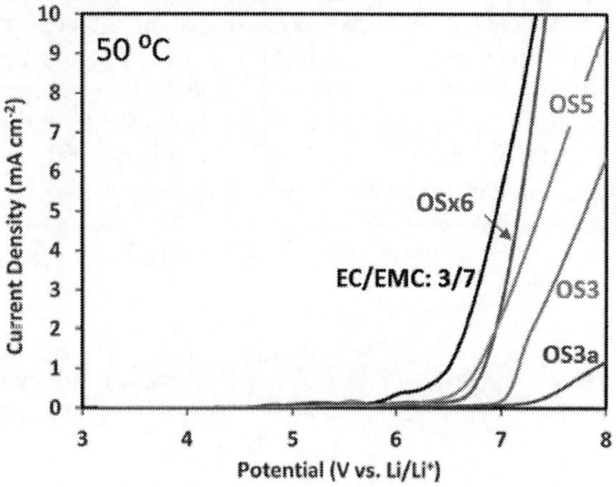

Figure 4. OS-nitrile solvent oxidative stability (Pt)

All members of the OS3® family of solvents share the same fundamental property benefits including strong solvation of Lithium salts, stabilization of Lithium salts, and increased oxidative stability (compared to carbonate control).

In this paper, we highlight and discuss the performance of OS3®, OS5™, OSx6 in LIB cells, including improved capacity retention, reduced impedance growth, and reduced gas generation. Performance of these materials in pouch cells with high-Ni cathodes and graphite anodes is summarized.

Results and Discussion

OS solvents have demonstrated comprehensive performance improvements in several LIB cell systems. The most significant improvements occur in high energy density applications which tend to apply more oxidative stress on the electrolyte on highly reactive active material surfaces. Observed benefits include HT and/or fast charge cycling stability, reduced impedance growth, reduced gas generation, and improved safety / abuse response.

45°C Cycling Performance Improvement

Performance of OS3® and OS5™

The nitrile-family of OS materials significantly improves the 45°C cycling stability of several high Ni NMC chemistries, including 4.35V Gr/NMC622 and 4.3V Gr/NMC811 cells. Addition of 3% OS3® or OS5™ to a carbonate control increased the capacity retention from 75% to 90% after 45°C cycling in ~230 mAh pouch cells with single-crystal NMC811 cathode and graphite anode cycled between 2.75V and 4.3V (Figure 5). The capacity retention benefit was accompanied by a significant reduction in cell gassing (≥ 70%) and impedance growth, especially with OS5™.

XPS surface analysis on the NMC811 cathodes after 45°C cycling (Figure 6) shows the surface layer with OS3® is thicker (lower substrate signal), more inorganic (less C-O, C=O; more LiF and P), and primarily formed from decomposition of the $LiPF_6$ salt, not the carbonate solvents.

The presence of Si and N on the surface demonstrates that OS3® participates in surface layer formation, although its primary function is as a solvent that does not undergo significant consumption during cell operation. Overall, this higher inorganic content cathode layer formed by OS3® results in more stable HT cycling, reduced impedance, and reduced gas generation with high Ni NMC cathodes.

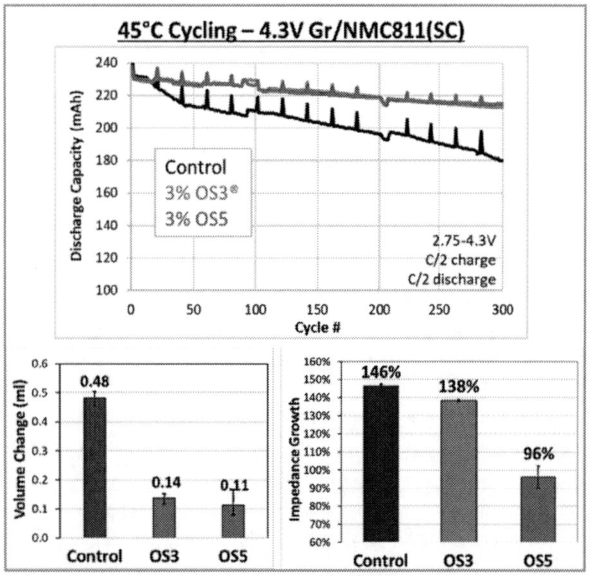

Figure 5. 45°C Cycling in 4.3V Gr/NMC/11(SC) cells.

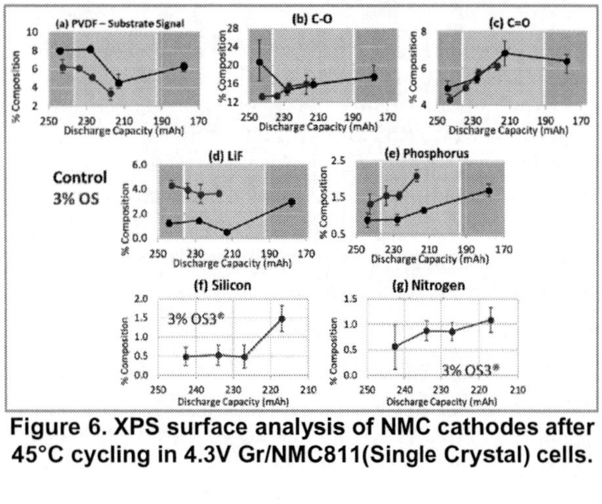

Figure 6. XPS surface analysis of NMC cathodes after 45°C cycling in 4.3V Gr/NMC811(Single Crystal) cells.

Performance of OSx6

Recent 45°C cycling experiments in ~230 mAh 4.3V Gr/NMC811 cells show that 1% OSx6 provides superior cycling stability to a control without any SEI layer forming additives (Figure 8) and outperforms 1% VC, a standard commercial additive for graphite LIB systems. Cells were cycled between 2.75V and 4.3V at C/2 charge and discharge.

To understand the source of performance improvement, modeling of the full cell impedance to estimate the anode and cathode contributions was conducted (Figure 7 – inset). The addition of OSx6 or VC significantly reduces the anode impedance after 45°C cycling with OSx6 providing the lowest anode contribution. The cathode impedance is reduced by both OSx6 and VC similarly and is likely not the source of the performance difference between these additives. This data shows that OSx6 can replace VC and provide a more stable anode/electrolyte interface.

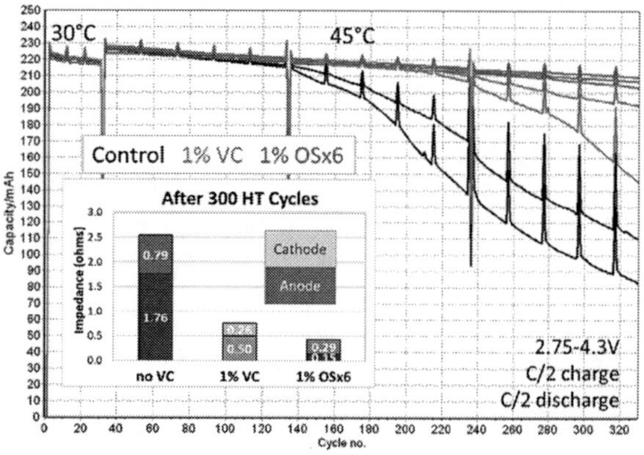

Figure 7. 45°C Cycling in 4.3V Gr/NMC/11(SC) cells.

45°C Fast Charge Cycling Performance Improvement

The comprehensive benefits provided by OS materials can enable operation under multiple extreme operating conditions. For example, both OS3® and OS5™ significantly improve 45°C fast charge cycling stability and reduce cell resistance in ~230 mAh 4.35V Gr/NMC622 cells at low concentration (3%) in a commercial carbonate electrolyte (Figure 8). Cells were cycled between 2.75V and 4.35V at 2C charge C/2 and discharge.

Visual analysis of the graphite anodes after fast charge cycling shows a significant reduction in Li plating with OS addition resulting in a 20-25% improvement in capacity loss depending on the specific OS material.

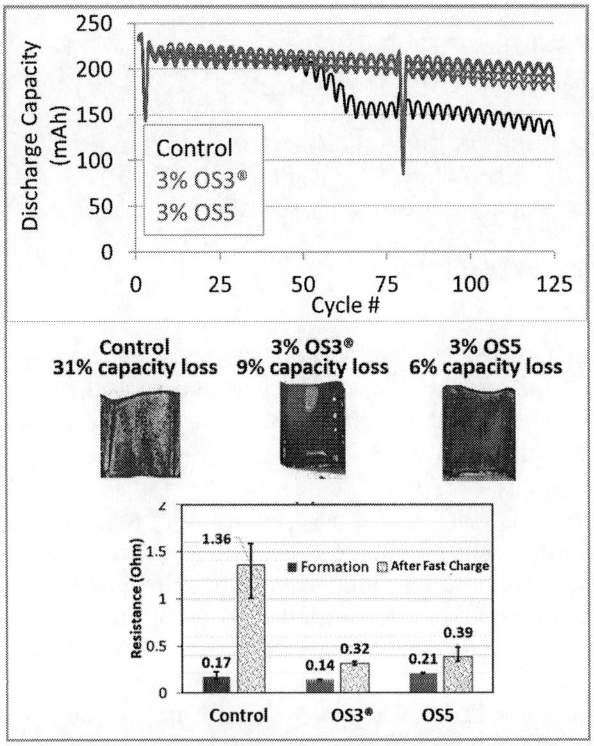

Figure 8. 45°C Fast Charge in 4.35V Gr/NMC622 cells.

60ºC Storage Performance

The OS3® family of solvents also significantly reduce gas generation during HT/HV storage in high Ni NMC cells. Figure 9 shows that increasing gas reduction is observed with increasing OS3® concentration in 4.35V Gr/NMC622 cells. Composition analysis via GC-TCD shows the gas reduction is due to a reduction in all observed gas products, but primarily CO_2. For the control electrolyte, CO_2 is the majority decomposition species attributed to oxidation of carbonate solvents (e.g., EC) at the NMC811 surface.

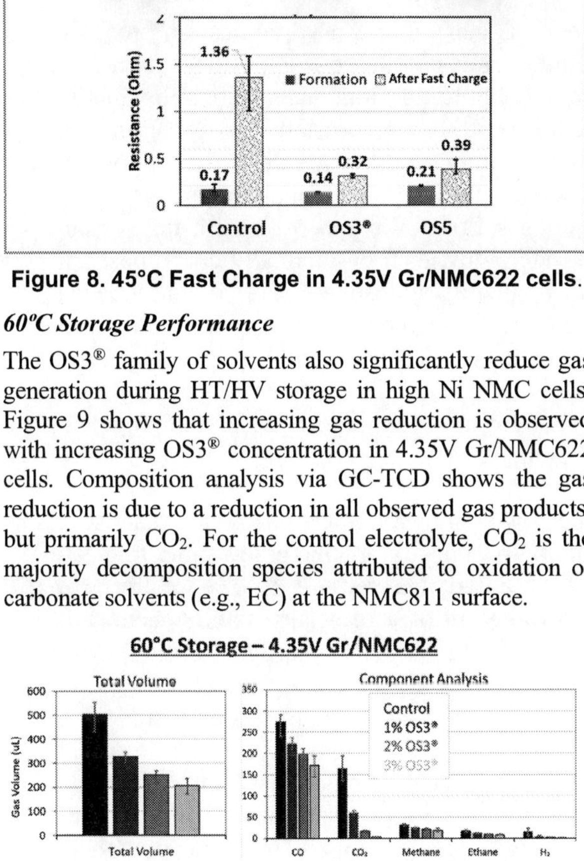

Figure 9: 60°C storage in 4.35V Gr/NMC622 cells.

60°C storage in 4.3V Gr/NMC811 cells with ^{13}C-labeled EC in the electrolyte was conducted to understand the source of the CO_2 generation and elucidate the mechanism of OS3® gas reduction. This data (Figure 10) clearly shows that although EC is a significant source of CO_2, over 60% of the CO_2 generated is from "non-EC" sources. OS materials reduce CO_2 from all sources indicating that the OS gas reduction benefit is not limited to EC protection (Case 1) but is a surface effect (Case 2) or bulk effect (Case 3) or both (Cases 2 and 3) that provides more universal gas reduction.

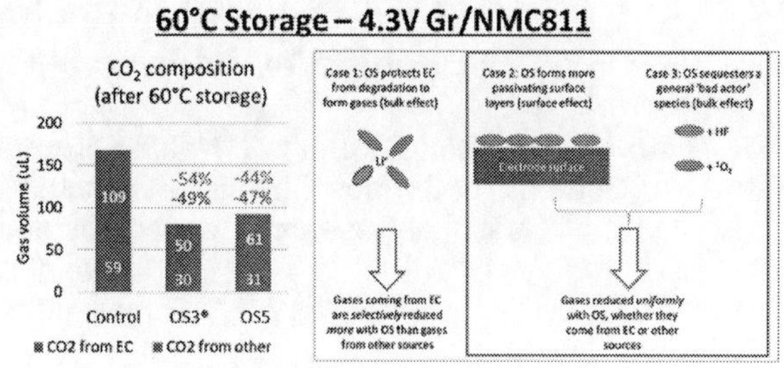

Figure 10: 60°C storage in 4.3V Gr/NMC811 cells with ^{13}C-labeled EC for mechanistic studies.

Conclusions

Organosilicon (OS) solvents have demonstrated excellent performance in high Ni NMC cathode Lithium Ion Battery (LIB) systems. Silatronix® commercial product "OS3®" provides exceptional thermal and electrochemical stability. OS3® is a strong coordinator of Li salts and prevents $LiPF_6$ salt decomposition and catalytic production of HF, which is critical to enablement of high energy LIB systems with long calendar life and excellent high temperature performance.

Comprehensive LIB cell performance benefits have been observed with multiple OS family materials, including excellent HT cycling stability, reduced impedance growth, improved calendar life rate capability, reduced gas generation, reduced pouch cell swelling, and improved safety. Mechanistic studies indicate that the benefits provided by OS family solvents are due to a combination of bulk effects (e.g., $LiPF_6$ salt stabilization and HF removal) and surface effects (e.g., reduced charge transfer resistance, formation of stable surface layers).

Acknowledgements

The authors thank the Office of Naval Research (ONR), and the Department of Energy (DOE) for funding to advance organosilicon technology. These include ONR contracts N00014-15-C-0031, N00014-16-C-2025, N00014-17-C-2031, N00014-19-C-1009, N00014-21-C-1075; and DOE contract DE-EE0007232. Thanks to UW-Madison, Argonne National Lab, Army Research Laboratory, and NSWC Carderock for their collaboration.

References

1. Guillot, S.L.; Usrey, M.; Peña-Hueso, A.; Kerber, B.; Zhou, L.; Du, P.; Johnson, T., Reduced Gassing In Lithium Ion Batteries With Organosilicon Additives. Journal of the Electrochemical Society 2021, 168, 030533.

Next-Generation Rechargeable Silver–Zinc Batteries Enabled by Interfacial Control and Electrode Redesign

Ryan H. DeBlock,[1] Zachary G. Neale,[2] Hunter O. Ford,[2] Debra R. Rolison,[1] and Jeffrey W. Long[*1]*
[1] Code 6170, Surface Chemistry Branch, Naval Research Laboratory, Washington, DC, 20375
[2] National Research Council Postdoctoral Associate, Naval Research Laboratory, Washington, DC, 20375
E-mail: jeffrey.long@nrl.navy.mil

Abstract: Zinc sponge electrodes pioneered at the US Naval Research Laboratory enable a new family of alkaline zinc-based batteries that will serve as energy/power-capable, but safe alternatives to lithium-ion batteries for critical DoD applications. Recent advances in Zn sponge fabrication yield monolithic form factors using a low cost, scalable, and rapidly manufacturable protocol. When incorporated as the anode in lab-scale silver–zinc cells, Zn sponge electrodes facilitate deep-discharge utilization and high-power operation.

Keywords: silver–zinc batteries, aqueous batteries, architected electrodes, zinc batteries, high-power devices

Introduction

Silver–zinc (Ag–Zn) batteries haves served as a mainstay power source for DoD platforms over the past several decades, providing mission-enabling high-power capability in an energy-dense package.[1] Unlike their lithium-ion counterparts, Ag–Zn batteries employ nonstrategic materials and nonflammable aqueous electrolytes. Despite these performance attributes, the broader application of Ag–Zn batteries is hindered by issues of poor-to-moderate cycle life and shelf life. Contraindicating issues arise from multiple deleterious processes at the Ag/Ag_xO cathode, multilayer separator system, and the Zn anode. Recent breakthroughs at the NRL on a 3D Zn "sponge" (Zn_{NRL}) have largely solved the decades-old problem of shape change at the anode, extending cycle life in rechargeable alkaline Ni–Zn cells[2–4] and promoting high-power discharge in Ag–Zn cells.[5,6] The structure of the sponge with three-dimensional, conductive Zn metal pathways and ample open volume for electrolyte access drastically improves power capability over traditional powder-bed composite or foil anodes. We now report protocols that improve scalability and manufacturability with lower input costs.

Previous-generation Zn_{NRL} fabrication protocols require emulsion-based compositions based on organic pore-forming agents (carboxymethyl cellulose (CMC) or cornstarch). After drying and consolidating the particulate zinc–porogen object, followed by thermal processing under inert gas flow (nitrogen or argon), the organic porogen must then be thermally decomposed in an oxidizing atmosphere. As a consequence, metallic Zn in the sponge may be excessively converted to zinc oxide (ZnO). The entire process is conducted in a sealed tube furnace and takes ~10 h for tube purging, thermal ramping, and cooling.

We now employ a fabrication method that uses a thermally stable, inorganic pore-former to create the interconnected Zn architecture.[7] Incorporation of a thermally stable, chemically removable inorganic porogen significantly reduces the time and temperature of thermal processing and allows the use of a simple box furnace and air atmosphere. The resulting monolithic Zn_{NRL} sponge has controllable ZnO content that influences mechanical strength, allowing a greater range of form factors (shape and size). To benchmark electrochemical performance relative to the previous four generations of Zn_{NRL} sponges, we evaluate "Gen 5" sponges in small-scale primary Ag–Zn cells for such metrics as discharge capacity and rate capability.

Results and Discussion

Zinc sponge electrodes are fabricated by mixing Zn powder and calcium carbonate into a 1 wt% aqueous dispersion of high viscosity CMC. The resulting Zn paste is pressed into an acrylic mold and dried overnight at 50–70°C. The ultimate form factor of the monolith is dictated by the shape and dimensions of the mold. Figure 1 shows example Zn monolith shapes, including cylinders and plates at a variety of size scales.

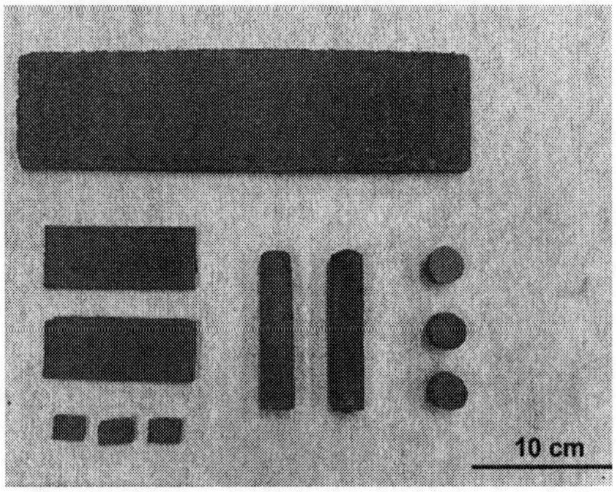

Figure 1. Photograph of Zn_{NRL} sponge monoliths in various sizes and form factors.

To promote Zn particle fusion, the dried monolithic pre-forms are heated at 580°C for 1 h in air. Thermal processing above the melting point of Zn metal (419°C) greatly improves interparticle connectivity (Figure 2), subsequently enhancing mechanical strength and electronic conductivity. After cooling to room temperature, the $CaCO_3$ porogen is removed by submerging the heat-treated, Zn monoliths in 1 M HCl for 5–10 min followed by thorough rinsing with water and then ethanol; the alcohol promotes drying and limits further oxidation of the Zn surfaces. After thermal treatment and acid washing, the Zn architectures comprise ~80% metallic Zn and ~20% ZnO by weight, according to RIR (reference intensity ratio) fitting of the X-ray diffraction pattern (Figure 3). Previous-generation Zn_{NRL} fabrication protocols produce monoliths with 25–40% ZnO,[2-6] which may be undesirable for direct incorporation into some alkaline battery configuration.

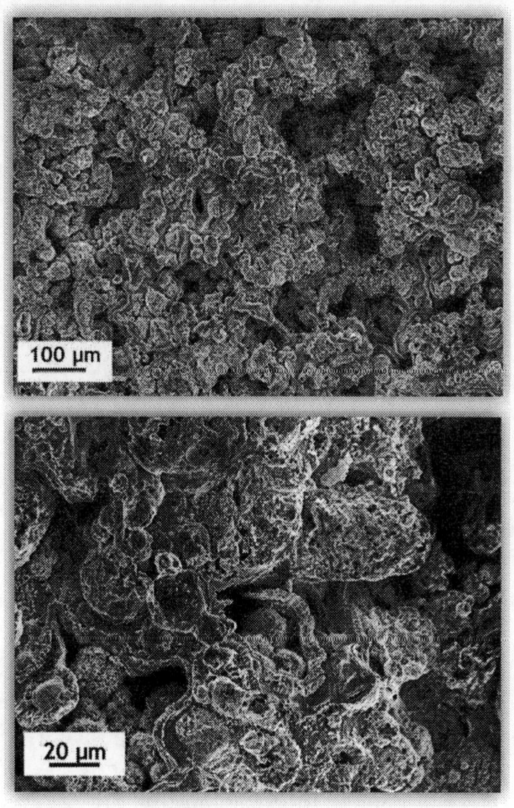

Figure 2. Scanning electron micrographs of Zn_{NRL} sponge monoliths.

A defining capability of Gen-5 fabrication is the use of $CaCO_3$ as an inorganic porogen. The carbonate provides thermal stability and high aqueous acid solubility—the former permits taking Zn above its melting point while the unaffected $CaCO_3$ retains the form factor, and the latter allows facile removal after thermal processing. The organic porogens used to fabricate Zn-sponge generations 1–4 must be removed with high-temperature oxidative treatment. After removal, only air remains to diffuse heat into the Zn structure, which risks inhomogeneous internal heating and increases the degree of thermal oxidation. Because the thermal conductivity of $CaCO_3$ (2.25 W mK^{-1}) is ~100× greater than that of air (0.025 W mK^{-1}), retaining $CaCO_3$ throughout thermal processing disperses heat more quickly and uniformly within the Zn object to enhance fusion of individual Zn particles into a mechanically cohesive network. The resulting Zn sponge has mechanical strength equal to or greater than those derived from organic porogen–based methods.

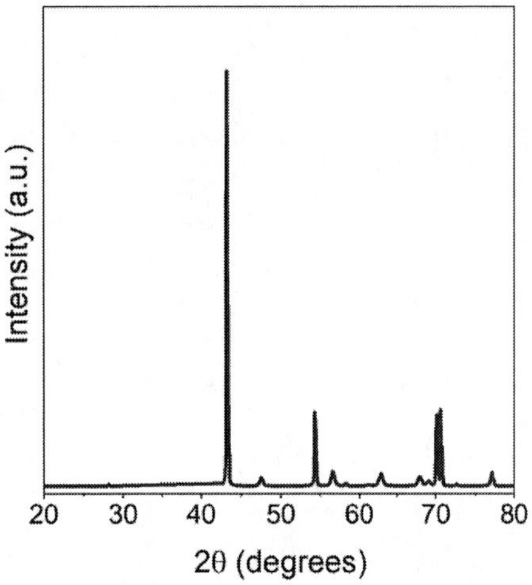

Figure 3. X-ray diffraction (XRD) pattern of Zn_{NRL} monolith after thermal treatment (580 °C, 1 h) and removal of $CaCO_3$ porogen (10 min washing in 1 M HCl).

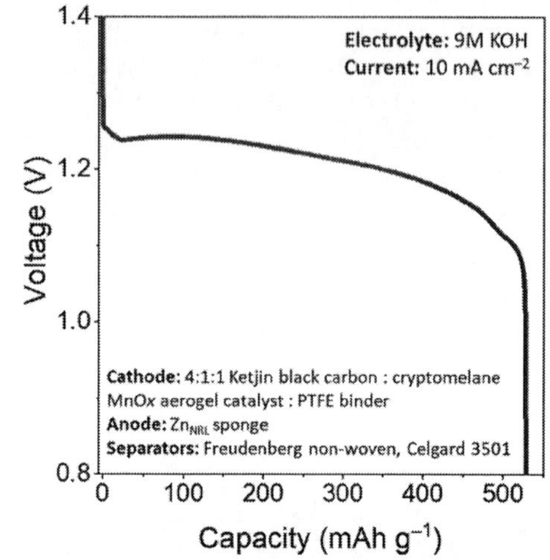

Figure 4. Primary discharge of Zn_{NRL} sponge electrode in a Zn–air cell.

We validate Gen-5 sponges using primary discharge of a Zn–air cell at a modest current density. Unlike Gen-1 and -2 sponges, Gen-5 sponges are not electrochemically pre-reduced before assembling the Zn–air cell. The relatively low ZnO content of Gen-5 enables good physical contact with the current collector of the Zn–air cell, resulting in low ohmic resistance. Primary discharge of these Zn–air cells at 10 mA cm^{-2} shows an expected sloping plateau ~1.2 V, culminating in a specific capacity of 500–550 mAh g_{Zn}^{-1} (Figure 4). Even though the Gen-5 sponges are ~20% ZnO when incorporated into the Zn–air cell, measured capacity is 60–68% of theoretical Zn capacity (819 mAh g^{-1}).

Silver–zinc coin cells are constructed using Gen-5 sponges as the anode and a pellet of silver oxide (Ag_xO) powder pressed at 5 metric tons into Ag mesh as the cathode. Silver and tin foils serve as the positive and negative current collectors, respectively. Even without optimizing the silver oxide cathode, Ag–Zn_{NRL} cells deliver high energy density under extreme current demand (Figure 5). At 0.5 A cm^{-2}, the cell voltage remains above 1 V, resulting in an areal power density >0.5 W cm^{-2}, orders of magnitude more power than Ag–Zn batteries in recent literature.[8,9]

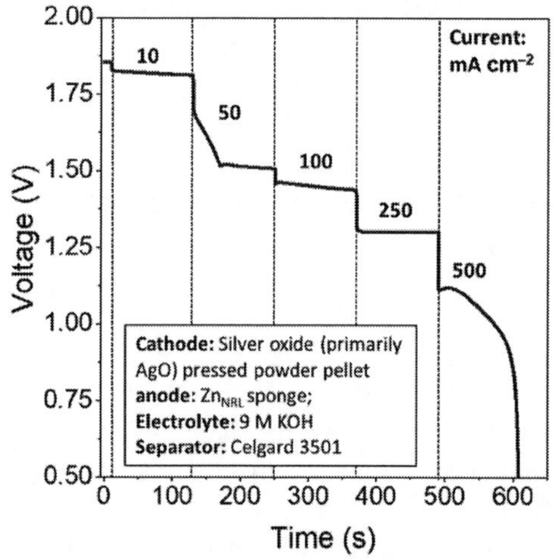

Figure 5. Galvanostatic staircase discharge of Gen-5 Zn_{NRL} sponge configured in a primary Ag–Zn cell. Geometric area of the anode and cathode were identical (1 cm^2). The Zn_{NRL} sponge is 1 mm thick and the cathode:anode capacity ratio is 1.1:1.

Conclusion

Generation-5 Zn sponge electrodes are rapidly fabricated using cheap, scalable components. Thermal processing in air and subsequent treatment in hydrochloric acid produces porous Zn monoliths that discharge >500 mAh g^{-1}, even with ~20% ZnO to improve mechanical integrity.

Silver–zinc batteries utilizing Zn-sponge anodes and pressed-powder Ag_xO cathodes support current densities >100 mA cm^{-2} and >500 mW cm^{-2}. We posit that redesigning the Ag/Ag_xO cathode in a similar sponge-like construct will further elevate the performance of next-generation Ag–Zn batteries in terms of power output and cyclability in rechargeable configurations.

Acknowledgements

This work was supported by the US Office of Naval Research. R.H.D. was an NRL-NRC postdoctoral associate (2020–2023); Z.G.N. and H.O.F. are current NRL-NRC postdoctoral associates.

References

1. J.F. Parker, R.H. DeBlock, B.J. Hopkins, C.N. Chervin, D.R. Rolison, J.W. Long, and M.B. Sassin. Silver–Zinc Batteries for Next-Generation Military and Space Applications. *J. DoD Res. Eng.*, **2022**, *5*, AD1185991.
2. J.F. Parker, C.N. Chervin, E.S. Nelson, D.R. Rolison, and J.W. Long. Wiring Zinc in Three Dimensions Re-writes Battery Performance — Dendrite-Free Cycling. *Energy Env. Sci.*, **2014**, *7*, 1117–1124.
3. J.F. Parker, C.N. Chervin, I.R. Pala, M. Machler, M.F. Burz, J.W. Long, and D.R. Rolison. Rechargeable Nickel–3D Zinc Batteries: An Energy-Dense, Safer Alternative to Lithium-Ion. *Science*, **2017**, *356*, 415–418.
4. B.J. Hopkins, M.B. Sassin, C.N. Chervin, P.A. DeSario, J.F. Parker, J.W. Long, and D.R. Rolison. Fabricating Architected Zinc Electrodes with Unprecedented Volumetric Capacity in Rechargeable Alkaline Cells. *Energy Storage Mater.*, **2020**, *27*, 370–376.
5. B.J. Hopkins, C.N. Chervin, M.B. Sassin, J.W. Long, D.R. Rolison, and J.F. Parker. Low-Cost Green Synthesis of Zinc Sponge for Rechargeable, Sustainable Batteries. *Sustain. Energy Fuels,* **2020**, *4*, 3363–3369.
6. J.S. Ko, A.B. Geltmacher, B.J. Hopkins, D.R. Rolison, J.W. Long, and J.F. Parker. Robust 3D Zn Sponges Enable High-Power, Energy-Dense Alkaline Batteries. *ACS Appl. Energy Mater.,* **2019**, *2*, 212–216.
7. R.H. DeBlock, J.F. Parker, C.N. Chervin, D.R. Rolison, and J.W. Long. Improvements to the Fabrication and Fusion of Zinc Particles in Porous Electrodes. US Patent Application; filed Jan 2023; allowed March 2023 [Navy Case #210,912].
8. Y. Zhu, R. Zhu, F. Chen, S. Zhang, Y.C. Kuo, P. Guan, M. Li, Y. Liu, Z. Han, T. Wan, D. Wang, C. Wang, and D. Chu. High Areal Capacity and Long Cycle Life Flexible Mild Quasi-Solid State Ag–Zn Battery with Dendrite-Free Anode. *Energy Env. Mater.,* **2023**, *0*, e12493.
9. A.R. Mainar, E. Iruin, and J.A. Blázquez. High Performance Secondary Zinc-Air/Silver Hybrid Battery. *J. Energy Storage*, **2021**, *33*, 102103.

High-Rate Performance of Large Format Nickel-Zinc Batteries

Eivind Listerud
Æsir Technologies, Inc.
8125 E 26th Street
Joplin, MO 64804
Contact Author e-mail: eivind.listerud@aesirtec.com

Abstract

This paper presents an overview of the high-rate capability of Nickel-Zinc cells and batteries. New manufacturing techniques and updated electrode design have enabled the manufacturing of cells capable of exceeding 10C continuous rates with relatively high utilization. In addition, large format NiZn batteries are already being manufactured that is capable of delivering 30% more power than a lead-acid battery in an equivalent footprint.

Keywords: Nickel-Zinc; batteries; rechargeable; large format, high power.

Introduction

Nickel-zinc (NiZn) battery technology has advanced considerably in the past several years, both in terms of performance and manufacturability. The historical weakness of poor cycle life has been greatly mitigated to the point where NiZn can readily exceed the cycle performance of lead-acid batteries while offering double the energy density. NiZn is also a potential substitute for lithium-ion batteries in locations and scenarios where safety, cost, and recyclability are of great concern. In addition, recent technical improvements have also been made with regard to high power performance and rechargeability of NiZn. These developments make NiZn batteries a very good fit in high-rate back-up power and standby applications. Suitable areas of use are directed energy, data centers back-up, electric grid augmentation, and EV charging stations.

This paper will discuss some of the developments related to high-rate power performance of NiZn batteries. Specifically, recent efforts to show power characteristics at continuous rates up to 12C in small format cells. Data will also be presented from testing of large format NiZn batteries made for standby and datacenter applications. This will show high wattage voltage profiles conducted while the batteries are on float. Additionally, the paper will discuss advances in manufacturing of NiZn electrodes that has been made by Æsir over the last couple of years.

High-Rate Testing in Small Format Cells

Æsir has in recent years mainly focused on the manufacturing of large format cells and batteries, typically exceeding 120 Ah, for energy and moderate power applications with rate requirement in the continuous 5 to 6C range. There is, however, a large demand for batteries that can perform repeatedly at rates of 10C and higher. In that regard, Æsir has recently made small format cells, ranging in capacity of 6 to 10 Ah, that are designed to perform at continuous 10C rates.

An example of such a cell is shown in Figure 1. The height is 4.09 in, the width is 2.86 in, and the thickness is less than 0.9 in. It is important to note that this prototype is made with a 3D printed case and lid and not truly optimized in terms of volume. The capacity of these cells will vary depending on the different electrode configurations and other design parameters that are being used to achieve the best possible power performance. The key design parameters in the build phase shown in this paper were electrode thicknesses and loadings. The electrodes typically used in larger format NiZn cells are relatively thick and are not optimized for continuous rates up to 10C. Part of the reason for this is the traditional method of manufacturing typically used when making NiZn electrodes. The manufacturing approach has been greatly improved upon, as will be shown later, and it has enabled Æsir to make thinner electrodes with appropriate loading, allowing for a better current distribution in the cell stack and good capacity utilization at 10C rates.

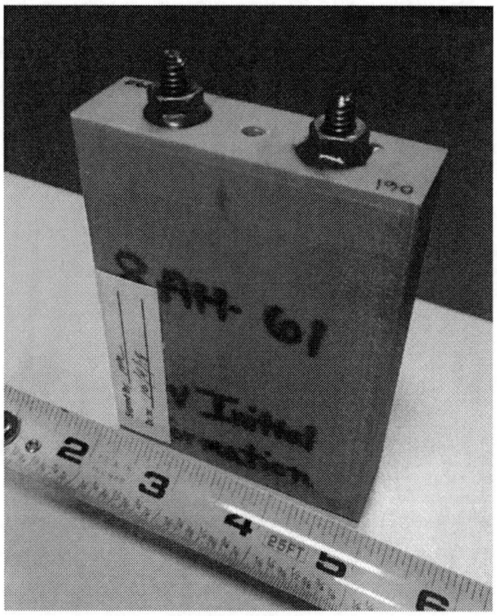

Figure 1: Example of a small prismatic NiZn prototype cell made for high-rate continuous discharge. The case and lid are 3D printed.

Figure 2 shows some of the results from these prototype cell builds. The graph depicts the cell voltage versus time in minutes while the cell is undergoing constant current loads of 8C, 10C, and 12C at a temperature of 21°C. This particular cell design is rated at 7.13Ah. This gives constant current discharge rates of 57A, 71.3A, and 85.6A, respectively. The discharges are cut-off at 1.3V, which is the typical cut-off at lower discharge currents for extracting full capacity. There is insignificant negative impact on NiZn by letting the discharge go down to 1V. Albeit, at some point below 1V there could be gas generation. However, NiZn does not suffer from the same issues as seen with lead-acid and lithium-ion when the cell voltage goes below a certain threshold. In the case shown in Figure 2, it appears to be little benefit letting the voltage go lower. However, this might be worth considering at colder temperatures when the electrolyte impedance will increase, and the overall discharge voltage will decrease.

The voltage curves in Figure 2 show that the cell design is well suited for 8C and 10C continuous loads, running for about 5.5 and 6.8 minutes, respectively. This translates to a capacity of about 6.5Ah, which is about 90% of the nominal nameplate capacity of 7.13Ah at a C/3 rate. The mid-point voltage is above 1.5V and the average power load is 86W and 107W, respectively.

The cell design will also perform reasonably well at the continuous 12C rate of 85.6A. But the duration is just above 3 minutes, and the capacity utilization has dropped to 63.5% with the mid-point voltage below 1.5V. Despite delivering an average power load of 126W, it is clear that this particular design needs further adjustments to deliver a robust 12C run. Æsir believes that this can be accomplished with further electrode design refinement during the ongoing design/build/test phase.

Æsir is also conducting testing with new additives for both electrodes and electrolyte to enhance high power performance. These additives, combined with electrode thickness and loading optimization, will allow for continuous load performance at ranges from 15C to 20C in the near future.

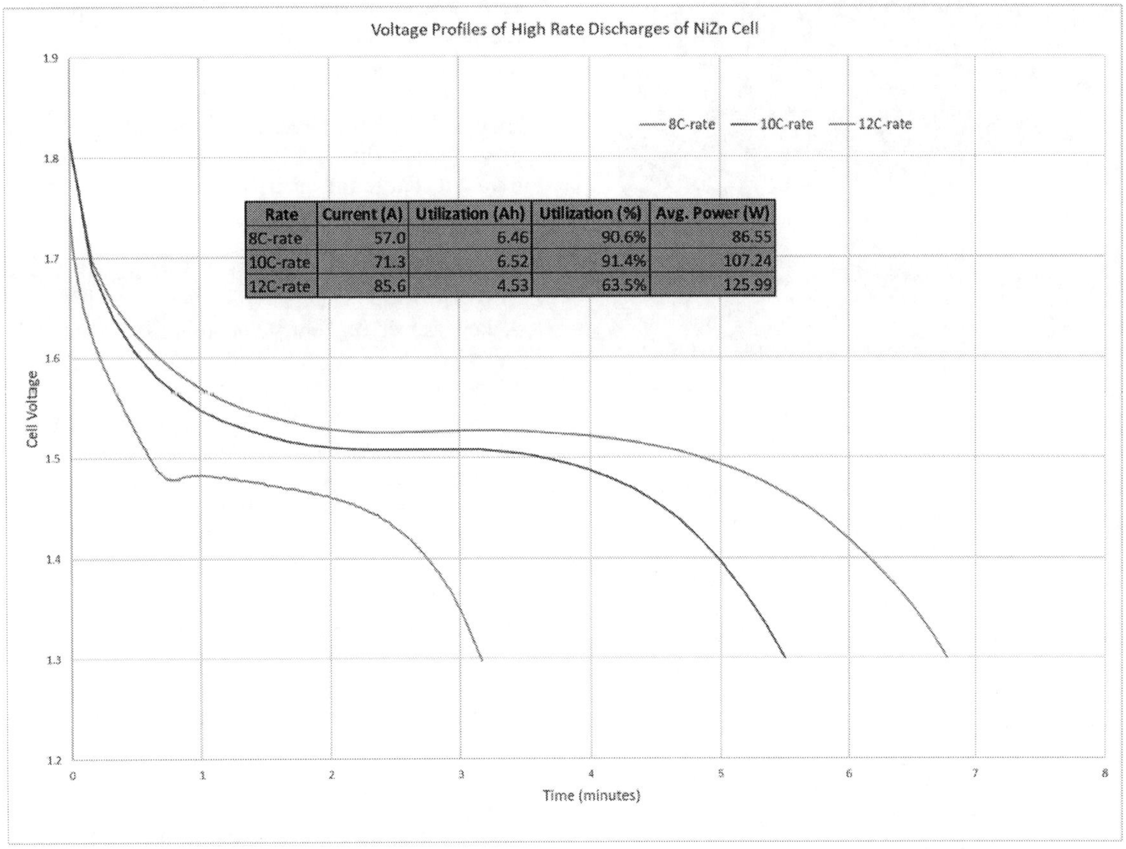

Figure 2: *Voltage versus time characteristics for a 7.31Ah NiZn prototype cell undergoing continuous discharges at 8C, 10C and 12C rates at 21°C.*

Large Format Battery for Standby Applications

On the large format side, Æsir has developed a battery with characteristics that makes it very suitable for standby and backup applications. This is a 12V battery with a capacity of about 150Ah at a C/3-rate. It has eight NiZn cells in series, giving it a nominal voltage of 13.2V. The battery has a length of 23 inches, a width of 4.74 inches, and a height of 12.74 inches. Figure 3 depicts three of these assembled batteries. The geometry is deliberately designed to fit into commercially available battery cabinets used in datacenters. The battery weighs about 105 lbs., which is about 70% of a lead-acid battery in the same volumetric footprint. The cells are designed to be discharged continuously at 5C-rates, or at currents of about 750A. At the battery level this translates to a power load of 8400W for more than 5 minutes when sitting on float charge. This is about 30% more power than a lead-acid battery in similar format.

Figure 3: Three 12V NiZn prototype batteries made for high-rate standby applications. Each battery contains 8 NiZn cells.

Large Format Battery Test Results

An example of the high-power characteristics of this battery is shown in Figure 4, showing the voltage profiles of repeated 8400W constant power discharges performed on a 150Ah 12V battery during an extended float stand. This testing is designed to reflect an accelerated full load event scenario of what would be expected in a datacenter cabinet. For the purpose of testing, it is assumed that a cabinet will house 38 of these 12V batteries in series. The test profile consists of letting the battery sit on float charge at a voltage of 14.72V. This is the equivalent of float charging at 559.4V in a full cabinet. At intervals of about one week, the battery is subjected to a continuous 8400W load until the battery reaches a voltage cut-off of about 10.53V. This voltage cut-off is equivalent to 400.5V in a 38-battery cabinet and a single battery load of 8400W is equivalent to 319.2kW at the cabinet level. Once the battery reaches the cut-off load, it is placed on rest for about 1 hour before it is recharged. The preferred charge profile, after a full discharge, is a constant current – constant voltage (CCCV) profile. For this specific test, Æsir used a constant current of 57A and charged the battery to either 15.52V for about 2.5 hours, or 15.2V for about 24 hours. These battery voltages are equivalent to 589.7V and 577.6V at the cabinet level, respectively. What voltage to be used in the field would be based on a combination of the need to be back to a full state-of-charge in a specific time and the limitations of the charging electronics in the cabinet. It is important to note that this load scenario is very conservative. Typical usage profiles in US based datacenters will run at derated loads and durations of less than 3 minutes.

A sample set of the 8400W load results are shown in Figure 4. The graph shows the battery voltage versus the discharge time in minutes. There are ten discharge curves shown, each representing a weekly load over the span of 2.5 months. Each load is discharged from a float or trickle charge state. Prior to the loads shown in Figure 2, the battery was subjected to seven loads conducted in the same manner and showing a similar outcome. The duration of each load typically lasts for about 7 minutes before reaching the 10.54V cut-off voltage. As the battery ages, this duration will gradually decrease until it no longer can reach the 5-minute mark. Notice that load number 13, shown with the blue line, comes up slightly shorter than the other loads. This is because there was a power outage during recharge and the battery went into this load not fully charged. The battery recovered by the next load.

Electrode Manufacturing and High-Rate Battery Performance

A key aspect of being able to produce good high-rate batteries is to be able to manufacture the electrodes in such a way that they deliver on the intent of the design. Traditionally, NiZn had a very laborious and manual manufacturing method. Not only did this drive cost up and impact reliability of the product, but it also limited some features of the electrode design that is desired for high-rate performance, most notably the thickness and loading. Æsir has made significant improvements to the cathode manufacturing in recent years. The cathode used to be made using a manual tape casting approach that was tedious and it limited what range of slurry density that could be targeted. The implementation of a high-volume automated coater has also enabled Æsir to manufacture better high-rate electrodes when building cells. This new coater can be seen in Figure 5 and compared to the older manual tape caster. Currently an effort is ongoing to improve the anode manufacturing, not just for the benefit of production volume and cost, but also for high-rate performance.

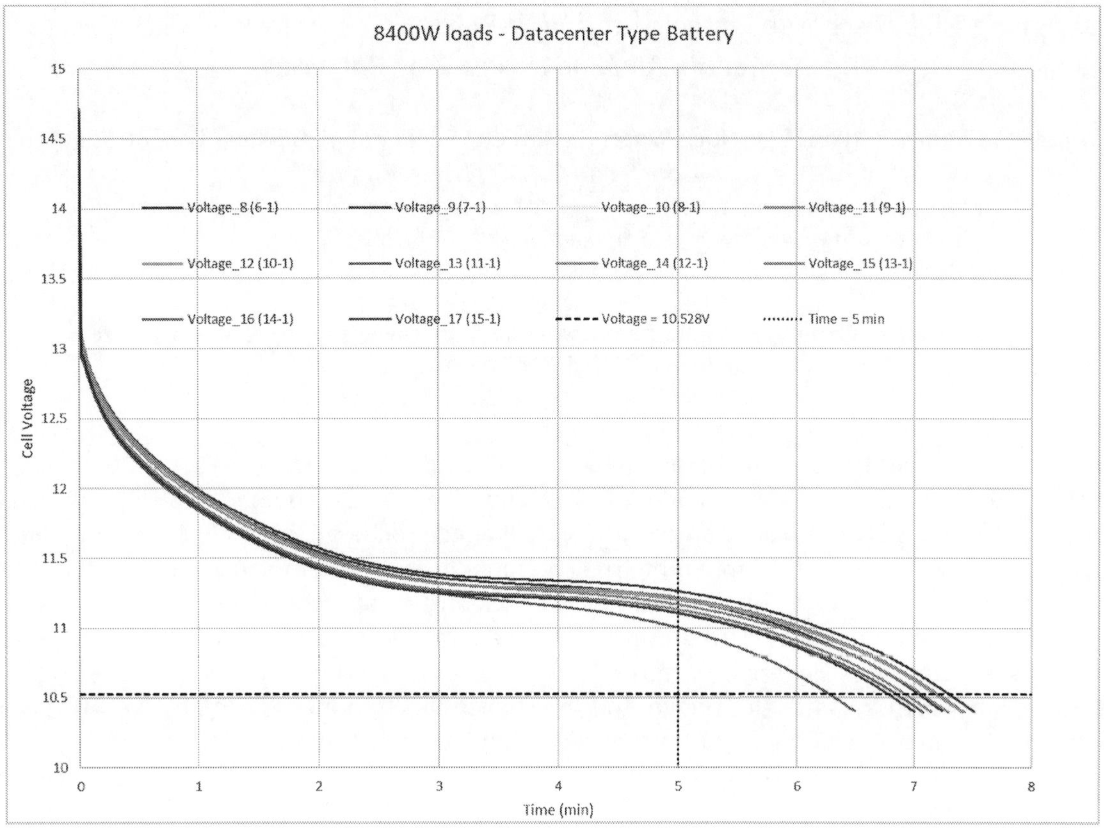

Figure 4: Repeated 8400W continuous power discharge profiles of a 150 Ah 12V Ni-Zn battery while on float charge.

Figure 5: Advancement in the manufacturing process of NiZn cathodes: From manual tape caster to automated coater.

Conclusion

Advancements has been made in producing NiZn cells that can perform at continuous current loads of up to 12C. This phase focused on using thinner electrodes, previously limited my manufacturing, and electrode loading. Future build phases will include evaluation of additives and separator enhancement to raise the power capability. Æsir believe that rates of 15 to 20C are achievable in the near future.

This paper also presented some recent NiZn developments related to high-rate power performance in large format batteries. It was shown that NiZn is capable of delivering about 30% more power than lead-acid batteries in the same geometric footprint with 2/3 of the weight.

Designing High Discharge Capacity and High-Rate Nickel Hydroxide Cathodes for Rechargeable Alkaline Nickel–Zinc Batteries

Samuel W. Kimmel,[1,2] Ryan H. DeBlock,[2] Jaret A. Manley,[3] Benjamin M. Gibson,[3] Cory M. Silguero,[3] Debra R. Rolison,[2]* and Christopher P. Rhodes[1,3]*

[1] Material Science, Engineering, and Commercialization Program, Texas State University
601 University Drive, San Marcos, TX 78666, (512) 245-1839

[2] U.S. Naval Research Laboratory, Surface Chemistry Branch (Code 6170), 4555 Overlook Avenue SW
Washington, D.C. 20375, (202) 767-3617

[3] Department of Chemistry and Biochemistry, Texas State University, 601 University Drive
San Marcos, TX 78666, (512) 245-2156

* Corresponding authors: debra.rolison@nrl.navy.mil; cprhodes@txstate.edu

Abstract: Energy dense, safe, rechargeable batteries are needed for a wide range of applications from portable electronics to electric vehicles. Safety concerns inherent to lithium-ion batteries make them a risk for numerous platforms including airplanes, ships, and undersea vehicles. Nickel–zinc batteries offer an energy dense, safe alternative to lithium-ion, but commercially available nickel cathodes do not match the cyclability of high-performance Zn-sponge anodes. We have developed a process to electron wire $Ni(OH)_2$ active material within a three-dimensional, nonperiodic cathode architecture that enables high rate performance, capacity, and cycle stability of $Ni(OH)_2$ in a Ni–Zn sponge cell.

Keywords: Nickel–zinc batteries, cathodes, three-dimensional architectures

Introduction

Batteries power everything ranging from portable electronics to electric vehicles (EV) and lithium-ion (Li-ion) batteries have been at the vanguard of powering these devices. With an adverse safety record that includes numerous examples of battery-related fires,[1–4] ranging from EV crashes ejecting burning Li-ion batteries into nearby housing, grounding entire fleets of commercial airplanes, or igniting a fire on a cargo ship that burned uncontrollably for days before sinking, the military and consumer need an alternative energy dense, safe, and rechargeable battery chemistry.

Alkaline nickel–zinc (Ni–Zn) batteries use a nonflammable aqueous electrolyte but have limited rechargeability because of the Zn anode; a problem since resolved by staff scientists at the U.S. Naval Research Laboratory (NRL) who reformulated the zinc into a sponge form factor.[5,6] At the single-cell level, Ni–Zn sponge is competitive with Li-ion's lauded energy density.[7] A single Zn-sponge anode can outperform four commercially harvested Ni-cathodes.[8]

Commercially available Ni cathodes are fabricated using β-phase nickel hydroxide ($Ni(OH)_2$), which stores 0.8–0.9 electrons per Ni (relative to two electrons per Zn), limiting the energy density of the Ni–Zn cell. The α-phase of $Ni(OH)_2$ can store more than one electron per Ni but requires crystal-phase stabilization to access its higher theoretical capacity. We previously demonstrated that Al(III)-substituted $Ni(OH)_2$ stabilizes the α-phase and when formulated into a powder-composite cathode, improves the discharge , capacity, discharge voltage, and cycling stability of Ni–Zn sponge cells.[9] We now explore the effects on battery performance of affixing α-Al-$Ni(OH)_2$ onto an architected cathode to enable direct electron wiring of the active material throughout the volume of a freestanding, binder-free cathode structure.

Experimental

Fabrication of Carbon Nanofiber Paper Electrodes. A beaker containing nonionic surfactant (Triton-X 100), 18 MΩ·cm water, and as-received carbon nanofibers (CNF, Sigma) was placed in an ice-water bath and the dispersion mixed using a wand sonicator (Sonics Vibracell VC505, 40% power) for 16 min at 10-s pulse intervals (Figure 1a, step one). Carbon nanofiber paper (CNP) was fabricated by vacuum filtering the CNF dispersion (Figure 1a, step two).

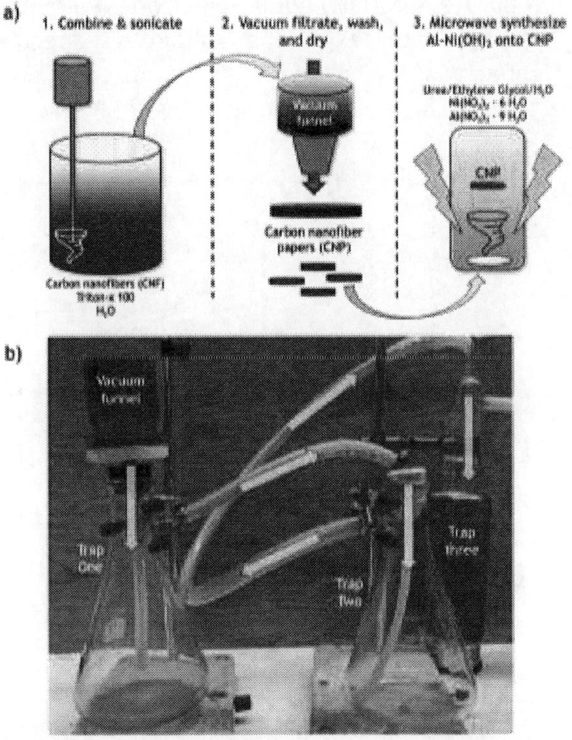

Figure 1. a) The fabrication & synthesis of Al-$Ni(OH)_2$ onto a freestanding carbon nanofiber paper (CNP); b) the vacuum filtration system used to fabricate a freestanding, binder-free carbon nanofiber paper (CNP) with arrows denoting flow direction.

The CNF suspension was vacuum filtered through a three-trap vacuum system: two liquid traps and one liquid nitrogen-cooled vapor trap (Figure 1b). After filtration, the CNP was rinsed with 500 mL of water and dried under vacuum at 120°C for 21 h.

Synthesis of Al-$Ni(OH)_2$@CNP. Alpha-phase Al-$Ni(OH)_2$ nanosheets were affixed onto the fibers within CNPs by adapting our established microwave protocol.[9] A ½" CNP disk and 20 mL of a Ni/Al solution (containing $Ni(NO_3)_2 \cdot 6H_2O$, $Al(NO_3)_2 \cdot 9H_2O$, urea, ethylene glycol, and water; Figure 1a, step three) were placed in a reaction vial within an Anton Parr microwave reactor (Monowave 450). The reaction was conducted using a two-step microwave heating protocol; the solution was heated to 80°C for 60 min, and then the temperature increased to 180°C for 3 min. The CNP was collected, rinsed with water and ethanol, and then dried under vacuum at 120°C for 21 h. The morphology of the Al-$Ni(OH)_2$@CNP was investigated by scanning electron microscopy (FEI-Helios Nanolab 400). The mass of Al-$Ni(OH)_2$ in the CNP was determined by Atomic Absorption (Elmer PinAAcle 900f).

Testing Al-$Ni(OH)_2$@CNP in Nickel–Zinc Cells. Nickel–zinc cells were assembled using alkaline-resistant cells, Zn anodes, and our previously established electrolyte/separator conditions.[8–11] The cells were galvanostatically cycled between 1.30–1.90 V using a constant current, constant-voltage charging protocol at a charging rate of 100 mA/g_{active} and variable-rate discharge at 100, 500, and 3000 mA/g_{active} (Arbin battery cycler).

Results and Discussion

Carbon nanofiber papers (CNP) are fabricated from an aqueous suspension of carbon nanofibers (CNF) and surfactant mixed using a high-energy wand sonicator. The suspension is filtered through a liquid nitrogen (LN_2)-assisted three-trap vacuum system (Figure 1b) producing a CNP with randomly oriented and interwoven strands of CNFs. Vacuum filtration of the suspension generates a significant amount of surfactant bubbles; traps one and two are necessary to capture and contain the liquid bubbles (thereby protecting the vacuum system), and the third LN_2 trap condenses any liquid vapor.

The microwave synthesis of Al-$Ni(OH)_2$ nanosheets onto CNP uses a two-step variable temperature microwave reaction protocol. The temperature is initially set to 80°C for 1 h to equilibrate the Ni and Al at the CNF struts within the CNP; the reaction temperature is then increased to 180°C for 3 min to promote growth of Al-$Ni(OH)_2$ at the fibers. Scanning electron microscopy (SEM) of the CNP after microwave reaction shows two unique Al-$Ni(OH)_2$ nanosheet morphologies: solution-nucleated nanosheet agglomerates and CNF-nucleated nanosheets within the CNP (Figure 2a).

Solution-nucleated nanosheets are large, 0.5–1.0 μm-sized agglomerates that are trapped within the CNP but not directly nucleated or "wired" to the CNP fibers, seen by the cluster of nanosheets in the top right of Figure 2a. By contrast, fiber-nucleated nanosheets emanate from the surface of the CNF struts within the CNP (Figure 2b).

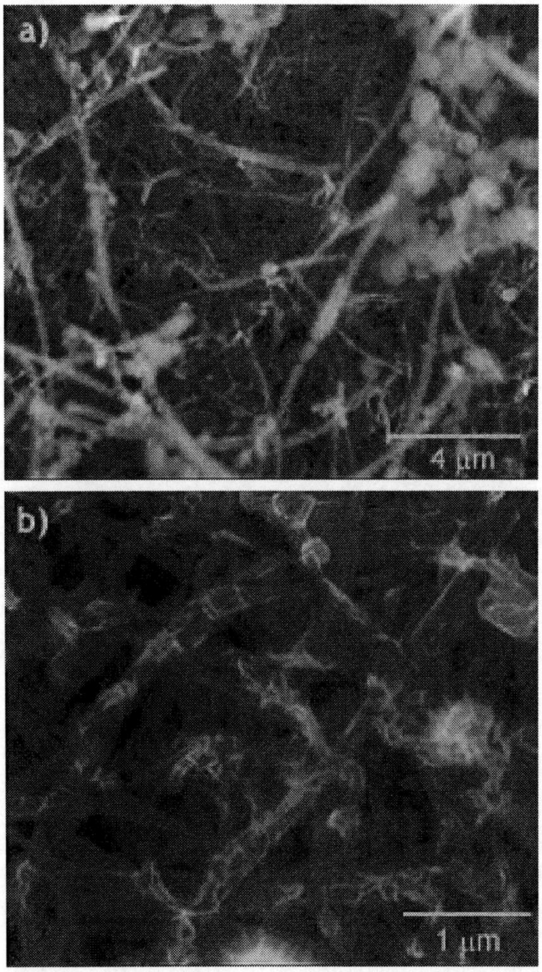

Figure 2. Scanning electron micrographs of Al-$Ni(OH)_2$ deposited within and onto carbon nanofiber paper (CNP).

The Al-$Ni(OH)_2$@CNP is used as the Ni cathode versus the fully rechargeable Zn-sponge anode in a cathode-limiting configuration. The mass of "active" $Ni(OH)_2$ is deposited into the CNP at a loading of 4.0 mg cm^{-2}. The galvanostatic rate capability of the Al-$Ni(OH)_2$@CNP–Zn sponge cell is determined at discharge rates of 100, 250, 500, 1000, 2000, and 3000 mA/g_{active}; five replicate Al-$Ni(OH)_2$@CNP electrodes were run for the rate tests. The voltage vs specific capacity of the cell at 100, 500, 1000, 2000, and 3000 mA/g_{active} is presented in Figure 3.

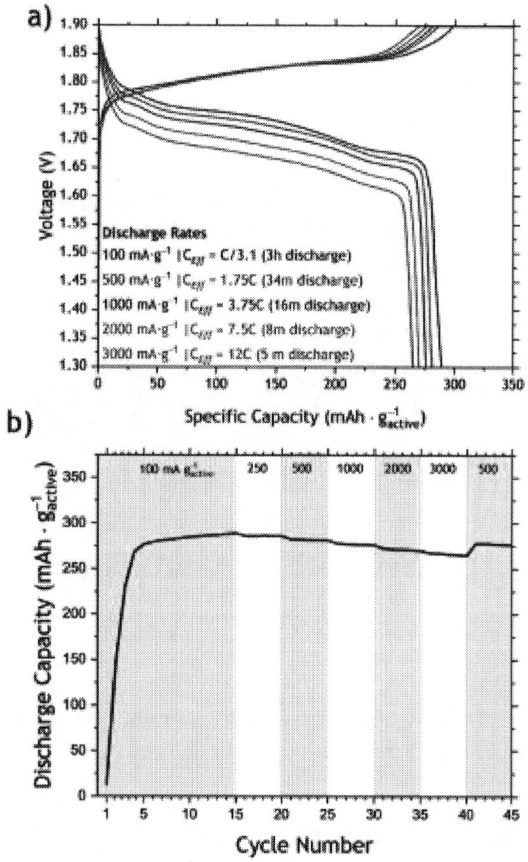

Figure 3. Galvanostatic charge–discharge of an architected Al-$Ni(OH)_2$@CNP–Zn-sponge coin cell: Comparing the effect of a constant rate charge/variable rate discharge on capacity.

The Al-$Ni(OH)_2$@CNP–Zn sponge cell has a discharge capacity of 280 mAh/g_{active} at a discharge rate of 100 mA/g_{active} with an effective C-rate (C_{eff}) of C/3.1 (3.1 h to full discharge). As the discharge rate increases from 100 mA/g_{active} to 3000 mA/g_{active}, discharge capacity decreases by 18 mAh/g_{active} to 262 mA/g_{active} (C_{eff} = 12C or 5-min discharge). As the discharge rate increases, the entire voltage profile decreases (Figure 3a), which we attribute to ohmic loss.

The discharge capacity and cycle stability of the Al-$Ni(OH)_2$@CNP–Zn-sponge cell as a function of cycle number and increasing discharge rate are presented in Figure 3b. The cell is discharged at 100 mA/g_{active} for 15 cycles to accommodate the formation cycles of Al-$Ni(OH)_2$@CNP; after the 15th cycle, the discharge rate is increased every five cycles from 100 to 3000 mA/g_{active} before returning to 500 mA/g_{active} at the 40th cycle (Figure 3b). The capacity fade observed when the discharge rate increases to 3000 mA/g_{active} is reversed when the rate returns to 500 mA/g_{active}.

Conclusions

Using a 3D architected carbon nanofiber paper (CNP) electrode fabricated from commercially available carbon nanofibers (CNF), we developed a synthesis that grows Al-$Ni(OH)_2$ nanosheets onto the CNF struts throughout the CNP. The Al-$Ni(OH)_2$@CNP shows remarkably high rate capabilities and cycle stability as a rechargeable Ni cathode versus the U.S. Naval Research Laboratory's fully rechargeable Zn-sponge anode. This route to an Al-$Ni(OH)_2$@CNP cathode is a practical approach to electron-wiring $Ni(OH)_2$ active material to the electrode architecture.

Acknowledgments

S.W.K., D.R.R., and C.P.R. acknowledge the support of this research from the Office of Naval Research (award no. N00014-21-1-2072), part of the Naval Undersea Research Program (NURP). S.W.K. is an NRL-NREIP (Naval Research Enterprise Internship Program) participant (Summers 2018–2023). R.H.D. was an NRL–NRC Postdoctoral Associate (2020–2023).

References

1. A. Cooper, Dreamliners Grounded Globally Due to Fire Risk, *CNN*, **2013**.
2. P. Lebeau, Electric Car Blaze Raises Questions for Tesla, *NBC NEWS*, **2013**.
3. R. Stumpf, Tesla Model 3 Crash Hurls Burning Battery Cells into Nearby House, Starts Fire, *The Drive*, 2020.
4. J. Knutson, Cargo Ship Carrying Luxury Cars Sinks after Massive Fire, *Axios*, **2022**.
5. J. F. Parker, C. N. Chervin, E. S. Nelson, D. R. Rolison, and J. W. Long, Wiring Zinc in Three Dimensions Re-Writes Battery Performance—Dendrite-Free Cycling, *Energy Environ. Sci.*, 2014, **7**, 1117–1124.
6. D. R. Rolison, J. F. Parker, and J. W. Long, Zinc Electrodes for Batteries, *US Pat.* 9,802,254.
7. J. F. Parker, C. N. Chervin, I. R. Pala, M. Machler, M. F. Burz, J. W. Long, and D. R. Rolison, Rechargeable Nickel–3D Zinc Batteries: An Energy-Dense, Safer Alternative to Lithium-Ion, *Science*, 2017, **356**, 415–418.
8. B. J. Hopkins, M. B. Sassin, C. N. Chervin, P. A. DeSario, J. F. Parker, J. W. Long, and D. R. Rolison, Fabricating Architected Zinc Electrodes with Unprecedented Volumetric Capacity in Rechargeable Alkaline Cells, *Energy Storage Mater.*, 2020, **27**, 370–376.
9. S. W. Kimmel, B. J. Hopkins, C. N. Chervin, N. L. Skeele, J. S. Ko, R. H. DeBlock, J. W. Long, J. F. Parker, B. M. Hudak, R. M. Stroud, D. R. Rolison, and C. P. Rhodes, Capacity and Phase Stability of Metal-Substituted α-$Ni(OH)_2$ Nanosheets in Aqueous Ni–Zn Batteries *Mater. Adv.*, 2021, **2**, 3060–3074.
10. B. J. Hopkins, C. N. Chervin, M. B. Sassin, J. W. Long, D. R. Rolison, and J. F. Parker, Low-Cost Green Synthesis of Zinc Sponge for Rechargeable, Sustainable Batteries, *Sustain. Energy Fuels*, 2020, **4**, 3363–3369.
11. B. J. Hopkins, M. B. Sassin, J. F. Parker, J. W. Long, and D. R. Rolison, Zinc-Sponge Battery Electrodes That Suppress Dendrites, *J. Vis. Exp.*, 2020, **163**, E61770–E61780.

Bipolar Lead Acid – Eliminating the Lead

Michael D. Eskra
Rodney M. LaFollette
Paula K. Ralston
Eskra Technical Products
Saukville, WI 53080-1687
mikeeskra@aol.com / 1-262-707-5855

Abstract:

ETP under an Army Phase II SBIR has developed a bipolar lead acid wafer cell with significantly improved cycle life and specific energy. Typically well suited for high voltage applications, the design was directed towards the 6TAGM battery. Removing the lead grids and intercell connectors, the design increased the specific energy by a factor of two. The design lends itself well to higher power higher voltage designs where further reductions in weight and increased capability naturally occur.

The doubling of specific energy occurred with baseline active material utilization. Further benefits can be obtained as improvements in active materials were incorporated.

Keywords: Battery; Lead-Acid; Pseudobipolar; Titanium; SnO_2; Titanium Silicide, Wafer Cell.

Introduction

High specific energy is a primary objective of designs of secondary batteries to be used in DOD applications. Lithium-ion (Li-ion) batteries are increasingly the choice for such applications due to their superior specific energy with respect to that of existing aqueous batteries. The disadvantages of Li-ion, such as cost and safety, have mandated reexamination of aqueous systems, particularly if increases in specific energy can be achieved.

Lead-acid batteries are still widely used, particularly when low cost and high power are needed, and the relatively low energy density is acceptable. Improvements in energy density of lead-acid batteries would greatly extend their market utility in many applications. Improved energy density can be achieved primarily through three approaches. The first is improvement in the utilization of the solid active materials (Pb and PbO_2). Utilization is typically limited to < 60%. This is caused by reduction in electrode porosity and electronic conductivity during discharge, caused by formation of (voluminous and resistive) $PbSO_4$ crystals. This can be mitigated in part through addition of conductive additives to the electrode masses, or through various means to retain high porosity. A second way to increase energy density is to decrease the mass of various components of the battery structure, such as electrode grids and connectors. Finally, energy density can be improved through more efficient battery geometries (rather than prismatic or spirally-wound cells having lead strap current collectors with welded intercell connections).

Under sponsorship from the U.S. Army (Contract W56HZV-16-C-0059), Eskra Technical Products (ETP) is addressing the need for improved energy density lead-acid batteries. This is being done primarily through the second and third approaches mentioned; i.e. reduction in mass of battery components and improved construction. Improvements in active material have not been the focus of this program. ETP uses a "wafer cell" construction (Figure 1) that reduces the need for most of the supporting lead metal present in traditional lead-acid cells. This highly efficient design can potentially improve upon typical energy density by 100% or greater. The construction is similar to that of a true bipolar cell, except that both electrodes have their own supporting substrates. The individual cells, consisting of electrodes (active material supported on substrates), separator and electrolyte, are packaged in a polymer pouch, with open spaces on the back of both electrode current collectors as shown in Figure 1. Individual cells are stacked next to one another, with external (metal) current collector discs placed in the open circular spaces on the backs of the electrodes. Current flows from one cell to its neighbor, by passing through the external current collector discs, improving on the inherent high power performance of lead-acid batteries by increasing the area of intercell connection and minimizing resistive losses by eliminating grids and providing multiple, high area/short path parallel current paths between adjacent cells. With this design there is significant savings in weight, due to reduction of the mass of intercell connections., with placement of current collector foils external to the outermost cell electrodes of each twelve volt block, connected via current collector discs through openings in the cell package on the outside of the electrodes. The twelve volt, six cell blocks are connected in parallel to copper straps leading directly to the base of the external terminals on top of the battery (Figures 2 and 3). This series-parallel arrangement of cells and blocks lowers the impedance of the battery.

An essential element of the design involves the substrates that support the active material in both electrodes. Lead metal can be used, although it has high specific weight (11.34 g/cm^3). Metals such as copper and titanium have lower specific weight, but are reactive in contact with the sulfuric acid electrolyte, and at the potentials encountered during battery operation. The material chosen for the substrates should be inert with respect to cell materials and environment. This is accomplished through application of various protective coatings to substrate materials. As long as the coatings completely cover the substrates, and are electrochemically stable, lighter weight materials (such as Ti foil) can be used to support the electrodes.

In this paper we present progress in efforts to build very high specific energy lead-acid batteries. The target application has been the 6TAGM battery. Titanium foil is one of the electrode substrates considered for both positive and negative electrodes. Various positive electrode coatings are used, with high conductivity and electrochemical stability being required coating attributes. The literature and our half-cell experiments show SnO_2 and other proprietary materials to be functional as applied to titanium, copper and other metallic substrates. Thin lead coating of substrates or carbon/graphite polymer composite layers are a favored coating for the negative electrode. Projected energy densities are presented to contrast the relative merits of different material choices. The wafer-cell cell and battery construction is used in these calculations.

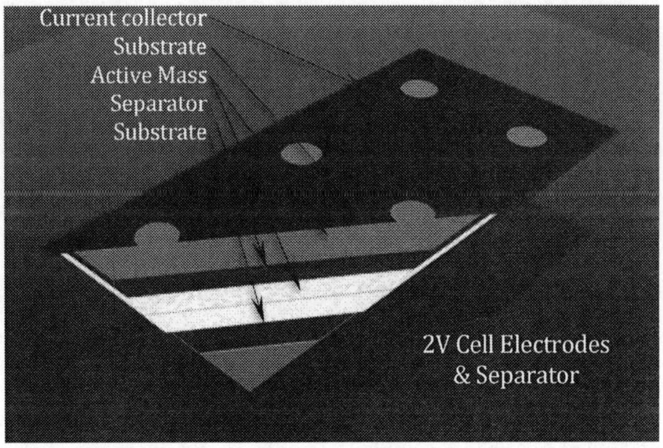

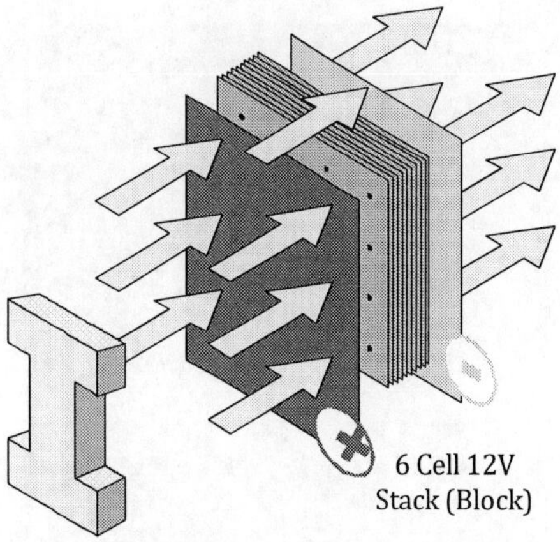

Figure 1. ETP Pseudobipolar "Wafer Cell."

ETP found that forming titanium silicide on the surface of the positive electrode prevented corrosion of the positive current collector. This coating was formed by reacting the surface of the titanium with silicide gas. An alternative method was also to coat the surface of the titanium foil with titanium silicide. The negative electrode will operate when coated with a thin lead, graphite or carbon. Raw copper foil can be used if the cell potentials are carefully monitored.

The cell formation process was performed with open cells and then fully sealed after a charge discharge cycle at the top of charge. Cycling afterward maintained cells operating below 4 psi. Successful formations required that red lead be added to the SLI positive paste mix to allow the formation to initiate.

ETP Battery Design

A battery of particular interest is the 6TAGM. A 12 V battery is constructed through parallel connection of multiple 12 V modules or blocks. Each 12 V block consists of six individual wafer cells, stacked adjacent to one another, and electrically connected in series. Figure 2 shows a 12 V battery schematically, consisting of five individual 12 V blocks/modules. Blocks are connected back-to-back, and are connected to battery posts as shown.

Figure 3 is a photograph of a high power, 450 volt Ni-MH battery, consisting of series-connected 48 volt blocks that contain multiple individual wafer cells. The construction is similar that that of the lead-acid battery described in this paper. Not shown are the current collecting straps that conduct current to the battery posts. This battery was built at Electro Energy, Inc., by one of the authors of this paper. It shows significant improvement in energy density (Wh/l) relative to commercial Ni-MH batteries, particularly in high voltage configurations. It was also capable of extremely high power output, > 1 MW.

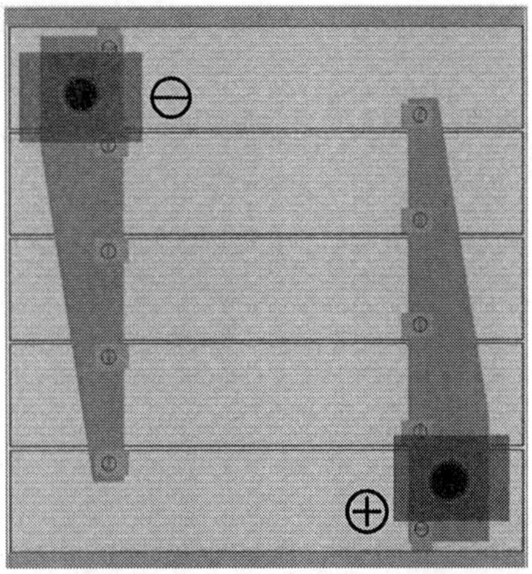

Figure 2. Wafer-Cell 6TAGM Construction Schematic, Top View of Block / Bus Configuration

Figure 3. Wafer-Cell NiMH Battery Construction

Design Calculations

ETP's wafer-cell construction is contrasted with that of traditional 6TAGM batteries through a series of design calculations. These calculations are for batteries such as depicted in Figure 2. Active material utilizations typical of automotive and commercial starting batteries are used. The baseline conditions for calculations are shown in

Table 1.

Table 1. Baseline Conditions for Battery Calculations.

Component	Value
Housing Thickness (inch)	0.375
Capacity (Ah)	154
Voltage (V)	12
Positive Active Material Utilization	0.462
Negative Active Material Utilization	0.600
Acid Specific Mass (g/cm^3)	1.310
Separator Porosity (Compressed)	0.88
Acid Capacity/Solids Capacity	2.0
Compression (kPA)	170
Temperature (Deg C)	25
Width (inch)	10.512
Height (inch) – excluding terminals	8.071
Packaging Thickness (inch)	0.012
Number of Intercell Cu Connectors/Cell	8
Intercell Cu Connector Thickness (in)	0.006
Intercell Cu Connector Diameter (in)	0.92

Figure 4 shows results of calculations done to contrast the traditional 6TAGM design and the ETP wafer cell design. For the calculation, thin Ti foil (12 □m) was used as the positive electrode substrate, with a thin SnO_2 or $TiSi_2$equivalent coating (1.5 □m). For the negative, a 12 □m Cu foil was used, with an 85% graphite filled polyvinylidene fluoride (PVDF) coating (50 □m). The battery consisted of five, 12 volt modules, along with a metal housing, current collector straps, metal (steel) ribbed reinforcing plates at the ends of the battery, and a gas-inflated bladder to maintain pressure on the cells. As shown, the active material fraction is significantly higher in the ETP design. This is due to reduction in the weight of battery containment and conductive/connection components. This savings results in a 61% increase in specific energy (58 Wh/kg vs. 36 Wh/kg of the production 6TAGM).

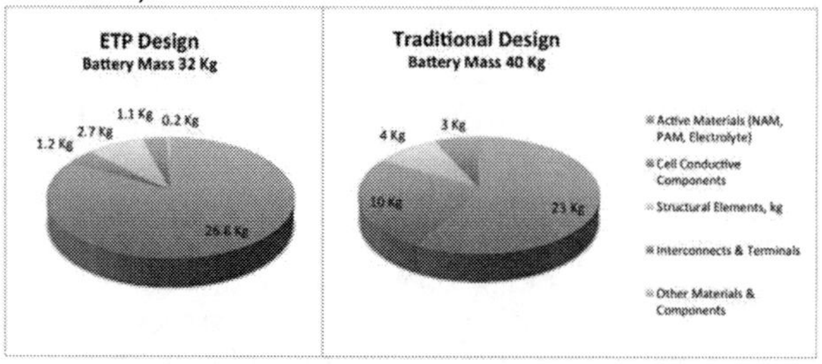

Figure 4. Mass Fractions of Battery Components for 6TAGM Lead-Acid Battery.

Table 2 shows the effects of different supporting (non-active) materials, namely the material used in the housing (Titanium or Steel), and the electrode substrates. As shown, the use of thin titanium or copper for the electrodes improves specific energy by approximately 10-15% over 152 µm lead foil, which in turn offers a 40% increase over a conventional 6TAGM design. The housing material made a smaller difference. The designs use very conservative material utilization values typical of production 6TAGM batteries, and offer opportunities for ongoing, stepwise improvement in energy density, specific energy and specific power with further development of active material utilization strategies described in the literature.

Experimental

Full single pouch cells, such as shown in Figure 5, were built to evaluate substrate performance. Cell construction initially used lead foil as the substrate for both electrodes for concept verification. Electrodes were prepared using standard pasting processes. Typical paste compositions are shown in Table 3.

Table 2. Effects of Substrate Type, Block Count & Housing Material.

12 Volt Blocks	Positive Substrate	Negative Substrate	Housing	Q Wh	Specific Energy Wh/kg	Energy Density Wh/l

5	12 µm Ti / 1.5 µm SnO_2	12 µm Cu/ 50 µm Graphite filled PVDF	Ti	1850	58.0	133
4	12 µm Ti / 1.5 µm SnO_2	12 µm Cu/ 50 µm Graphite filled PVDF	Steel	1830	55.8	132
5	152 µm Pb	152 µm Pb	Steel	1750	50.4	126
Present Production Lead-Acid 6TAGM:				**1440**	**36**	**103**

Figure 5. Single full scale 6TAGM pouch cell electrode, rear face with.

As with the half cell tests, cells were held in compression (Figure 6) and evaluated using Arbin battery testers. After initial formation (C/20 to 2.55 V, 2.55 V for 36 hours), cells were subjected to repeated charge/ discharge cycles. Discharges were typically done at C/20 rate to 1.7 V, and charge was also done at C/20 rate, to 2.55 V, and then 2.55 V to C/30 cutoff current. After testing cells were disassembled and autopsied.

Figure 6. Full Scale 6TAGM Cells Under Test

Summary

A wafer cell construction of lead-acid batteries is proposed that will dramatically improve the specific energy over traditional designs. The pseudobipolar arrangement reduces the amount of support and conduction material (non-energy producing material) needed by 67%. The design approach to lead acid batteries greatly increases energy density and impressively eliminates the principle wearout modes of lead-acid – positive material cycling deterioration and in non-lead substrate implementations, does away with positive grid corrosion. Cycle life is multiplied by the high compression enabled by the design, and the design is ideal for high voltage batteries, which in contrast to conventional designs, result in elimination of interconnect and bus components, further reducing weight and freeing up additional volume for active materials. And experiments have shown the design capable of operating fully sealed, providing submodule and battery charge management capability via inexpensive pressure transducers.

The design is particularly suited to low and high voltage aircraft, heavy duty and tactical vehicles and other high vibration, high voltage and high power applications.

In contrast to other high performance batteries, this design approach is inherently safe, requiring minimal charge and discharge control subsystems and no supplemental containment in safety-critical applications.

Acknowledgements

The authors wish to thank the US Army for its support of this work, under SBIR Phase II Contract W56HZV-16-C-0059.

References

1. D.B. Edwards, C. Schmitz, Journal of Power Sources 85 _2000. 63–71
2. Kurisawaa, K. Fujitaa, M. Shiomib, S. Osumia, K. Matsuia, INTELEC 08, San Diego, CA, 14-18 September 2008, 147-152
3. Fujita, K, Kurisawa

Scalable Production of Electrolytic Manganese dioxide (EMD) and their Electrochemical Energy Storage in Aqueous Electrolyte

Manickam Minakshi and Kethaki Wickramaarachchi
College of Science, Technology, Engineering, and Mathematics, Murdoch University, WA 6150, Australia
minakshi@murdoch.edu.au; lithiumbattery@hotmail.com

Abstract: Among the different forms of MnO_2, electrolytic manganese dioxide (EMD) is well-demanded energy storage material suitable for rechargeable batteries and supercapacitors. However, the limitations such as lower capacitance, irreversibility, and cyclability of EMD in comparison with other metal oxides such as cobalt and nickel oxides, have hindered their application in capacitor energy storage. Therefore, in the current work suitable for power sources conferences, we have synthesized scalable EMD from electrolytic baths with varying biopolymer additive concentrations has been investigated for application as an electrochemical supercapacitor. The presence of alginate influenced both the physical and electrochemical storage properties of the electrodeposited MnO_2. At 0.5 g l^{-1} in the bath, the pristine EMD morphology was rearranged to a cactus-shaped one with flutes. The altered morphology and enhanced particle size are attributed to the ability of the alginate to act as a template for binding the Mn^{2+} ions on the substrate in a relatively ordered and widely distributed manner. The MnO_2 electrowinning plant must consider the effect of electrodeposition parameters that can ensue on the overall impact of electrolytically derived MnO_2 on a larger scale.

Keywords: electrolytic manganese dioxide; aqueous; capacitor; stability; biopolymer, alginate

Introduction

The growing demand for renewable energy sources and the increasing need for grid stability and reliability has led to the development of energy storage technologies. Electrolytic manganese dioxide (EMD) is widely used as a cathode material in batteries and supercapacitors (SC) due to its high electrochemical performance, long cycle life, and low cost. Manganese is also an abundantly available material compared to other transition metal oxides counterparts such as nickel and cobalt oxides which makes it viable. Scalable manganese production is essential for the sustainable development of the global economy, and the efficient use of this critical resource is crucial. The production of manganese by countries must be balanced with the need for environmental protection and social responsibility, ensuring that the benefits of this resource are shared equitably and sustainably. The material MnO_2 exists in different forms of polymorphs which are α-, β-, γ-, λ- and δ- etc. One of the most critical factors affecting EMD's electrochemical performance is its crystal structure. EMD (γ-MnO_2) has a layered structure consisting of MnO_6 octahedra linked together through the edge and corner-sharing, forming tunnels along the c-axis. These tunnels allow for the insertion and removal of lithium ions during charging and discharging cycles. Owing to its excellent electrochemical reactivity compared to other types, γ-MnO_2 has become pre-eminent in energy storage. The higher rate of proton diffusion in the solid phase causes enhanced electrochemical reactivity for delivering high currents at low electrode polarization. The crystal structure and morphology of EMD can be modified through various synthesis methods, such as altering the electrolyte bath concentration while maintaining its pH, to improve its electrochemical performance. Researchers have explored various approaches to synthesize manganese dioxide with varying particle size and morphology, through chemical methods such as template-assisted synthesis, surfactant-assisted synthesis, and microwave-assisted synthesis. The different morphologies with nanostructures show lower diffusion time for electrons and ions compared to the MnO_2 in microstructural morphologies. The EMD has advantages over chemical synthesis due to its low production cost, scalable production, electrochemical activity, and high purity. EMD can be formed from the direct electrolysis of an aqueous electrolytic bath containing manganese sulfate in sulfuric acid. The mode of the electrolysis can be carried out, either way, with potentiostatic or galvanostatic techniques. Galvanostatic synthesis control the reaction rate to provide perfect adherence to the deposit with controlled morphology. Electrodeposition is a simple technique that could be conducted with moderate experimental conditions to tune the material properties such as particle size, density, and morphology, which greatly influence the electrochemical energy storage properties.

Electrolytic manganese dioxide (EMD) analyzed in most of the previous studies were produced as a self-standing electrode for electrochemical energy storage application, particularly for aqueous batteries and supercapacitors. The self-standing method largely retards the scalability of the material utilized to develop commercial applications. EMD material γ-MnO_2 type synthesized in the present study was deposited in bulk on a lead anode (see Figure 1). In our current study, bulk EMD has been deposited at various current densities of 200-600 A m^{-2} and deposition times (4-6 h), and their effects on the microstructure and capacitive behavior were investigated and reported in the presence or absence of additives in the bath. Despite the advantage of producing scalable EMD, the lack of structural stability for the deposited γ-MnO_2 type results in significant energy storage losses over long-term cycling when used as an electrode in SC applications. Therefore, it is a usual practice, to incorporate metal atom dopants in the bath for improving the surface morphology that enhances the cyclability and stability of the deposited EMD material. To date, different composite electrodes of EMD with metal dopants, polymers, and surfactants have been reported by many researchers. In this work, a unique biopolymer (such as Alginate) as an additive has been made to electrodeposit manganese dioxide from manganese sulfate in a sulphuric acid bath containing the additive. Alginate is an anionic biopolymer that naturally originated from brown algae. This has been extensively used for biomedical applications due to its, biocompatibility, low toxicity, and relatively lower cost. The guluronate (G) blocks (shown in Figure 2) in alginate participate in intermolecular crosslinking in the presence of divalent cations. Therefore, the highly reactive carboxylic acid groups can also be reformed by crosslinking by Mn^{2+} cations. When the alginate reacts with the cation, it makes a cross-linked compound that is not soluble in water. The cross-linking is affected by the affinity which depends on alginate properties, pH, ionic strength, ion radius, steric effects, and electronegativity. Thus, the insoluble polymer can migrate towards the anode and the MnO_2 can adsorb onto the polymer resulting in co-precipitation which will alter the surface morphology in terms of particle size reduction and porosity promotion. Hence it is presumed that the alginate will avoid the dissolution of active material and enhance the stability of the pristine EMD electrode. A range of materials with different levels of additives was electro-deposited and tested to find the trade-off between the amount of the biopolymer and the energy storage capability. The electrodeposited dried mass of EMD (Mn^{4+}) scraped from the anode, followed by thorough washing with de-ionized water, and the sulfate-free product was ground and sieved to obtain the final material.

Experimental

The concentrations of Mn^{2+} and H_2SO_4 used in the electrolytic bath were 0.9 and 0.25 M, respectively. The electrolytic bath used for deposition was a 500 ml glass beaker covered by a machined PTFE lid. 99.99 % pure Pb disk was the anode, and the Stainless Steel 304 disk was the cathode. Prior to conducting the electrodeposition, both electrodes were mechanically polished and, rinsed thoroughly with deionized water to remove extra dust attached to the surface and patted with lint-free tissues. The solution was agitated continuously during the experiment with a Teflon-coated magnetic stirring bar. A set of experiments were carried out under a matrix of conditions such as deposition time period and the current density using the galvanostatic electrodeposition technique. The system was left to react and deposit for 4h, 5h, and 6h time periods, and the current supplied was altered as 100 A. m^{-2}, 200 A. m^{-2}, and 300 A. m^{-2}. For convenience those samples will be denoted as $EMD_{(t,I)}$ where 't' represents the time and 'I' represents the current density. Throughout the experiment, bath temperature was maintained in the range of 90 - 95 ^0C. The following reactions (Eqs. 1-3) take place in the electrolytic bath during the process.

$$Mn^{2+} + 2H_2O \rightarrow MnO_2 + 4H^+ + 2e^-$$

$$2H^+ + 2e^- \rightarrow H_2$$

$$Mn^{2+} + 2H_2O \rightarrow MnO_2 + 2H^+ + H_2$$

Soon after the deposition is finished, the Pb electrode was removed from the bath. It was thoroughly rinsed with running deionized water to remove entrained electrolytes. Then it was kept in the oven for drying overnight. The electrodeposited MnO_2 was scraped off the electrode surface cautiously without damaging the electrode to avoid the contamination that occurred by Pb. All pieces were collected and finely ground to get EMD powder. The powdered EMD was rinsed till it completely sweep away the electrolyte attached and dried in the oven at 80 $^\circ C$ overnight. For the Alginate added sample, from a prepared stock solution, the appropriate amount of additive (at different concentrations of Alginate as 0.0, 0.1, 0.25, 0.5, and 1.0 g L^{-1}) was added to the electrolytic bath and stirred constantly. All electrochemical measurements were performed by a potentiostat and EC-Lab software and the battery analyzer. The single electrode cell was constructed with the working electrode, Pt counter electrode, and reference electrode (Hg / HgO) and NaOH 2M aqueous solution was the electrolyte. Manganese dioxide materials were tested within the potential of 0 – 0.6 V for cyclic voltammetry (CV)and charge-discharge (CD) measurements. Various scan rates from 2 to 25 mVs^{-1} were conducted in CV. Current densities from 1 mA to 10 mA were used for CD.

The following equation is used to determine the specific capacitance (F g^{-1}) of MnO_2 by charge-discharge data.

$$C_{sp} = \frac{It}{\Delta V\, m} \qquad \text{Eq. (4)}$$

where, I - current rate (A), t - time for discharge (s), ΔV - potential window (V), m - active mass (g). The specific energy density (Wh kg^{-1}) and the power density (W kg^{-1}) are given by Equation (5) and Equation (6) respectively.

$$E_{sp} = \frac{{}^1\!/_2\, C_{sp}(\Delta E)^2}{3.6} \qquad \text{Eq. (5)}$$

$$P_{sp} = \frac{E_{sp}}{t} \times 3600 \qquad \text{Eq. (6)}$$

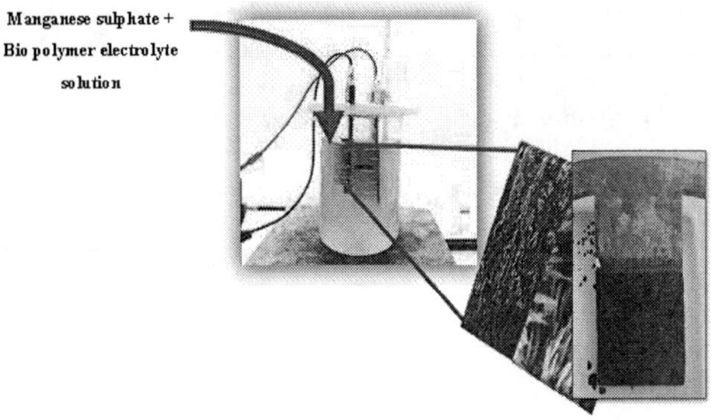

Figure 1 Schematic presentation of the set-up for the electrodeposition of manganese dioxide containing biopolymer additive.

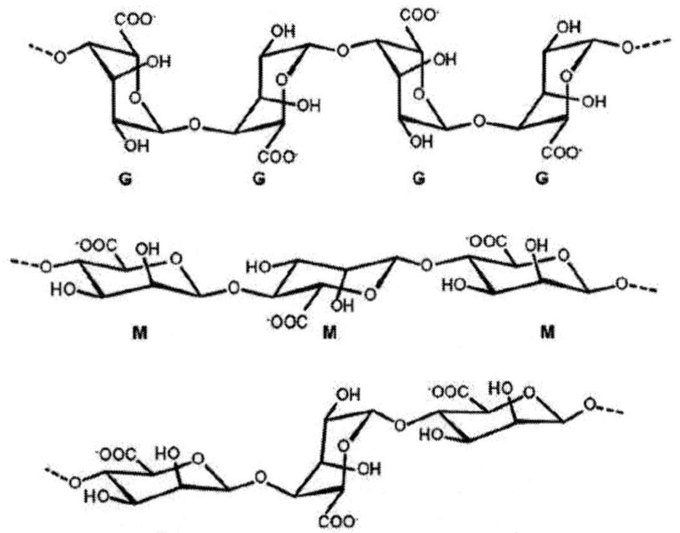

Figure 2 Alginic acid formed by α-L-guluronate (G) and (1,4)-linked β-D mannuronate (M) blocks.

Results and Discussion

Physical Characterization: The X-ray diffraction (in Figure 3) of the EMD material electrodeposited at different conditions shows the presence of well-resolved peaks of crystalline nature. The FESEM image of the final material show (in Figure 4) improved microstructure and a change in morphology that mainly influenced the higher surface area of the biopolymer samples. The XRD patterns on all EMD have the characteristics of γ form MnO_2. The X-ray photoelectron spectroscopy (XPS; not shown) of the Mn 2p was fitted with multiplets, all corresponding to Mn^{4+}

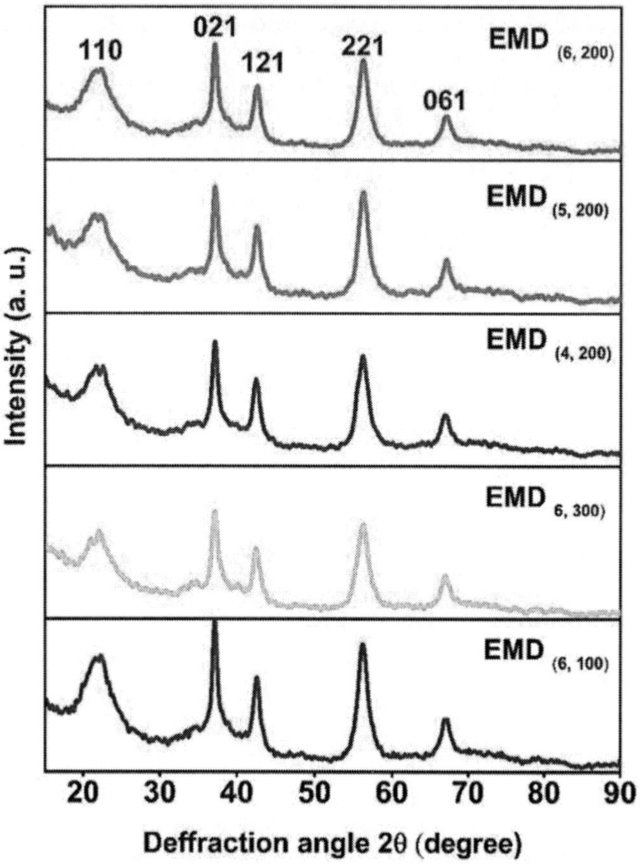

Figure 3 X-ray diffraction patterns of pristine EMD

state. The maximum intensities of the main metal peaks for Mn 2p transitions are found for Mn $2p_{3/2}$ and Mn $2p_{1/2}$ at 641.50 eV and 653.38 eV respectively. The increase in the thickness and elongation of the needle-like spines of the cactus-shaped (Figure 4b) particle indicates that the biopolymer is crosslinked onto the surface layer of electrodeposited MnO_2. The synthesis of EMD through an electrodeposition process within situ addition of a biopolymer in an electrolytic bath is reported here for the first time with an emphasis to enhance the cycling stability of battery and supercapacitor applications.

Electrochemical characterization: For electrochemical single-electrode studies, EMD served as a cathode. The cathode consisted of an active material made of EMD, mixed with acetylene black and binder in the presence of a solvent. The slurry was then coated on a graphite sheet of 1 cm^2 as substrate and dried at 60 °C for 1h. A bio-polymer additive exhibited well-defined quasi-rectangular CV curves (compare Figures 5a & b) and better discharge time (five times larger) upon various current rates corresponding to the pseudocapacitive nature of the biopolymer samples. However, the pristine EMD showed its elliptical CV curves (Fig. 5a) and non-symmetrical charge-discharge curves (compare Figure 5b

&d). At higher scan rates, the shape of the CV curve deviates from quasi-rectangular to elliptical, indicating the deviation from ideal capacitive behavior. Since the EMD described in this work is less crystalline, it tends to follow the surface adsorption/desorption mechanism through the microporous structure allowing the transportation of electrons and ions. The galvanostatic charge–discharge (GCD) tested at a constant current density of 1 mA cm^{-2} delivered enhanced specific capacitance of 487 F g^{-1} for biopolymer-assisted EMD which is about five times that of the pristine EMD. Adding the biopolymer to the electrolytic bath, grafted the EMD molecules onto the anode substrate. The role of biopolymer in the electrolytic bath is shown to be not limited to the material stability but also paving the path for efficient production of EMD. For practical applications, an asymmetric device comprising a two-electrode system has been fabricated (not shown here) using biopolymer-assisted EMD as positive and activated carbon (AC) as negative electrodes delivering a specific capacitance of 52 F g^{-1} having an energy density of 15 Wh kg^{-1}. In terms of Zn-MnO_2 (EMD) battery applications, the obtained initial capacity is 275 mA h g^{-1} and after multiple (50) cycles 75 mA h g^{-1} of the discharge capacity is retained.

Conclusions

The EMD was deposited on the Pb anode via Mn^{2+} oxidation to form Mn^{4+} and its oxide MnO_2. The physicochemical and electrochemical characterization of the obtained EMD powder concluded that the material deposited at 200 A m^{-2} for 5 hours, showing the spindle-like morphology was suitable over others for supercapacitor (SC) application. At 2 mA cm^{-2}, the fabricated hybrid capacitor comprising EMD versus Activated Carbon delivered 52 F g^{-1} specific capacitance, 14 Wh g^{-1} specific energy, 500 W g^{-1} specific power, and 94 % capacitance retention over 5000 cycles. The results highlighted the importance of the functional molecular structure of the biopolymer alginic acid to produce a binary composite of EMD-polymer as a capacitor material. Improving scientific understanding of the anodic electrodeposition of MnO_2 represents an opportunity to guide the electrowinning plant for scalable and economic production.

Figure 4 FESEM images showing the change in morphology of the final material (a) pristine EMD; and (b) biopolymer assisted EMD.

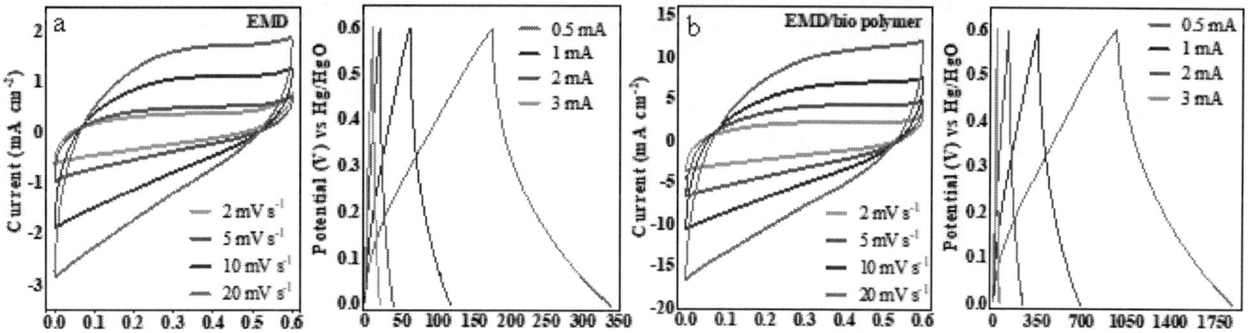

Figure 5 Cyclic voltammogram (CV) and galvanostatic charge-discharge (GCD) curves of a single electrode study (a) pristine EMD materials, (b) biopolymer assisted EMD (0.5 g L–1), respectively conducted in 2M NaOH aqueous electrolyte .

Effect of Misalignment of Inductive Wireless Power Transfer Coils

Christopher Mullen[1, 2], Soobum Lee[2]
[1]U.S. Army Combat Capabilities Development Command (DEVCOM), C5ISR Center, RTI, Power Division
Aberdeen Proving Ground, MD 21005, USA
[2]Department of Mechanical Engineering, University of Maryland, Baltimore County
214 Engineering Building, 1000 Hilltop Circle, Baltimore, MD 21250

Abstract

As inductive wireless power transfer becomes ubiquitous for charging phones and other portable electronics, consumers are less worried about efficiency and more concerned with high charging rates. For a Soldier in the field, less efficiency means they must carry more batteries or fuel, or forgo wireless charging altogether. To determine changes in wireless power transfer efficiency with respect to inductor misalignment, this research develops the equations used to calculate inductance, mutual inductance, and coupling coefficient depending on inductor geometry and distance. The results show that despite inductive coils that are not well coupled, there are strategies to maintain the same power transfer efficiency as perfectly coupled coils.

Keywords

Wireless power transfer; Inductive power transfer; Charging efficiency; Coil misalignment

Introduction

Wireless power transfer (WPT) was introduced by Tesla over one hundred years ago, yet researchers are still peeling back the layers to fully understand the ways we can take advantage of this powerful technology. WPT includes any technology that sends power without being directly connected via wires or cables, from two capacitive plates to an antenna via radio frequency (RF) [1]. Inductive wireless power transfer (IWPT) uses concepts from electrodynamics, specifically Maxwell's equations, whereby an alternating electric current that flows through a wire will produce a magnetic field around the wire. The magnetic field can be described mathematically through the relationship between current density, magnetic field intensity, and material permeability. Current density (J) through the wire is equal to the curl of the magnetic field intensity (H), and the field intensity times material permeability (μ) is equal to the magnetic field (B), sometimes referred to as magnetic flux density [2]. When current flows through a wire, the magnetic field flows around the wire and interacts with its environment. If a second wire is placed within the magnetic field produced by the first wire, that alternating magnetic field will induce an electrical current in the second wire as described by Faraday's Law of electromagnetic induction. The wire is an inductor, and how to optimize the inductor for efficient WPT is the focus of this research.

The quality factor (Q) is the ratio of the reactance to the resistance of the inductor, and as the quality factor increases, so does the power transfer efficiency [3]. For WPT it is important that the wire transmitting power minimizes its resistance and maximizes its inductance, and previous studies have focused on how to create different topologies with the wire that will optimize its quality factor [4]. This paper will focus on circular coil inductors. Quality factor increases proportionately to coil inductance and frequency, and is inversely proportional to coil resistance.

As the secondary coil moves with respect to the primary coil, the change will be reflected in the coupling coefficient (k). As equations have been developed to derive the coupling coefficient, they have customized the Neumann integral to fit coils with rectangular and circular cross-sections. However, only the basic calculation is shown while misalignment of the coils is not generally derived [5]. The coupling coefficient is a measure of how efficiently the primary coil is sending power to the secondary coil, and is calculated by dividing the mutual inductance (M) which is the square root of the product of the two inductors (L1 and L2). When the two coils are perfectly coupled, the coefficient approaches 1.0. Previous papers have manipulated the Neumann integral to show the change in mutual inductance and the coupling coefficient as the secondary coil is displaced with respect to the primary coil [6-7]. This paper will focus on the agreement between the accuracy of the model when compared to experimental results, and will highlight changes in efficiencies with respect to misalignment.

Method of Determining Coupling Coefficient

The Neumann integral is used to calculate the mutual inductance as shown in Equation 1:

$$M_{12} = \frac{\mu 0}{4\pi} \oint \oint \frac{dl1 \cdot dl2}{R_{QN}} \tag{1}$$

The variable μ_0 is the permeability of free space, R_{QN} is the distance between the two differential arc lengths, and defined in Equation 1. R_{QN} can be derived from the Pythagorean Theorem [5].

$$R_{QN} = \sqrt{r_1^2 + r_2^2 + d^2 - 2r_1 r_2 \cos\phi} \tag{2}$$

The variables $r_1, r_2, d,$ and ϕ are defined as the primary coil radius, secondary coil radius, distance between the center of both coils, and the angle defined to indicate the location of the infinitesimal direction vector at each coil: $\boldsymbol{dl_1}$ and $\boldsymbol{dl_2}$, respectively.

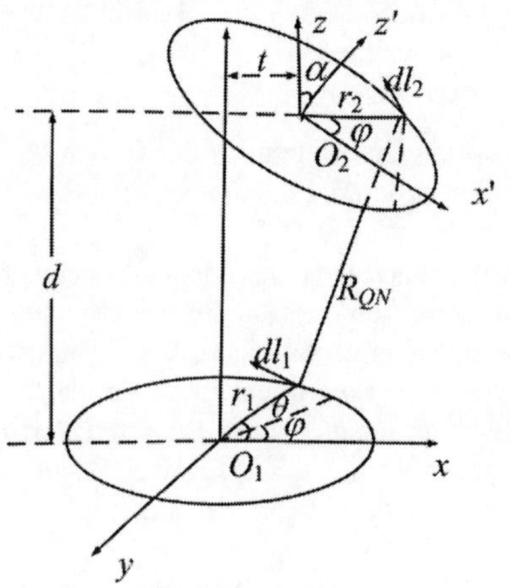

FIG. 1 Two coils separated by distance, *d* [6].

This derivation only takes into consideration a single degree of freedom in the *z*-direction, defined by the distance variable, d. By expanding Equation 1, this paper derives the equations for displacement of the secondary coil in the *x* and *y* direction as well as rotation about the *x* and *y*-axes (φ, α). The dot product between $\boldsymbol{dl_1}$ and $\boldsymbol{dl_2}$ can be rewritten using the radius of each coil along with the angle parameters.

$$dl_1 \cdot dl_2 = r_1 r_2 (\cos\phi_1 \cos\phi_2 \cos\alpha + \sin\phi_1 \sin\phi_2 \quad (3)$$

$$R_{QN} = \sqrt{\begin{aligned}&(x + r_2\cos\phi_2\cos\alpha - r_1\cos\phi_1)^2\\ &+(y + r_2\sin\phi_2 - r_1\sin\phi_1)^2\\ &+(d - r_2\cos\phi_2\sin\alpha)^2\end{aligned}} \quad (4)$$

In Equation 4, the distance (*d*) is simulated by adding the experimental distance between the coils plus half the thickness in the *z*-direction of each coil, so that if both the coils are 1 mm thick, and the experimental distance between the coils is 3 mm, then the simulated distance is 4 mm. When there is no displacement in the *x* and *y* directions and no rotation about the *y*-axis, Equation 4 simplifies to Equation 2. Equation 5 is the result of multiplying out Equation 4, which helps to avoid infinite results when solving the equation.

$$R_{QN} = \sqrt{\begin{aligned}&x^2 + y^2 + d^2 + r_1^2(\cos^2\phi_1 + \sin^2\phi_1)\\ &+r_2^2(\cos^2\phi_2\cos^2\alpha + \sin^2\phi_2 + \cos\phi_2\sin\alpha)\\ &+r_1(2c\cos\phi_1 - 2g\sin\phi_1)\\ &+r_2(2c\cos\phi_2\cos\alpha + 2g\sin\phi_2 - 2d\cos\phi_2\sin\alpha)\\ &-2r_1r_2(\cos\phi_1\cos\phi_2\cos\alpha + \sin\phi_1\sin\phi_2)\end{aligned}} \quad (5)$$

When multi-turn coils are considered (N_1, N_2), Equation 1 can be rewritten as:

$$M_{12} = N_1 N_2 r_1 r_2 \frac{\mu 0}{4\pi} \oint\oint \frac{\cos\phi_1\cos\phi_2\cos\alpha + \sin\phi_1\sin\phi_2}{R_{QN}} \, d\phi_1 d\phi_2 \quad (6)$$

The self-inductance of the coils is derived using the Neumann integral. In this paper, instead of using the distance between two coils, we use the distance between the middle of the coil and the inside diameter of the same coil. For the self-inductance calculation, to take into consideration the interaction of the turns, we are multiplying by N^2 instead of multiplying N_1 and N_2.

$$L_1 = L_2 = \frac{N^2 r(r - r_w)\mu 0}{4\pi} \oint\oint \frac{\cos(\phi_2 - \phi_1)}{R_d} \, d\phi_1 d\phi_2 \quad (7)$$

$$R_d = \sqrt{r^2 + (r - r_w)^2 - 2r(r - r_w)\cos(\phi_2 - \phi_1)} \quad (8)$$

Now that both mutual inductance and self-inductance have been derived. Coupling coefficient is calculated by dividing mutual inductance by the square root of the product of L_1 and L_2.

$$k = \frac{M_{12}}{\sqrt{L_1 L_2}} \quad (9)$$

Method of Experimental Data Collection

The experiments were conducted at the Army Research Center in Adelphi, MD using a network analyzer. The equipment was first calibrated, then the inductors were attached to the network analyzer and placed at intervals ranging from 1mm to 5mm distance for the 10mm diameter multi-turn coils and from 0.25cm to 2cm distance for the 35mm diameter single turn coils. The coils were concentrically placed, and rubber stops were used to hold the inductors in place. Glass microscope slides, 1mm thick, were placed between the 10mm diameter inductors and measurements were taken and saved. For the 35mm diameter coils, glass objects were measured and placed between the inductors. The data was stored in the network analyzer and later transferred for analysis.

Results and Discussion

For the 35mm diameter single turn coils, the results are shown in Table 1 and Table 2 for the experimental and simulation results, respectively, and plotted in Figure 4.

TABLE 1: Experimental results from 35mm diameter single turn coils.

distance	0.25cm	0.5 cm	1 cm	2cm
k	0.3624	0.2956	0.1670	0.0672
L_1 (H)	1.3E-07	1.3E-07	1.3E-07	1.3E-07
L_2 (H)	1.2E-07	1.2E-07	1.2E-07	1.2E-07
M (H)	4.5E-08	3.6E-08	2.1E-08	8.3E-09
f (kHz)	103	103	103	103
R_1 (Ω)	0.0044	0.017	0.0131	0.0038
R_2 (Ω)	0.0159	0.007	0.0105	0.0096

TABLE 2: Simulation results from 35mm diameter single turn coils.

distance	0.25 cm	0.5 cm	1 cm	2cm
k	0.5615	0.3848	0.2226	0.0957
L_1 (H)	8.9E-08	8.9E-08	8.9E-08	8.9E-08
L_2 (H)	8.8E-08	8.8E-08	8.8E-08	8.8E-08
M (H)	5.0E-08	3.4E-08	2.0E-08	8.5E-09
f (kHz)	100	100	100	100

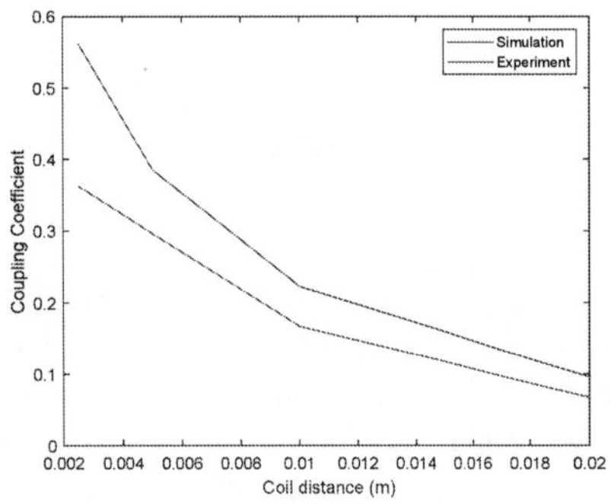

a)

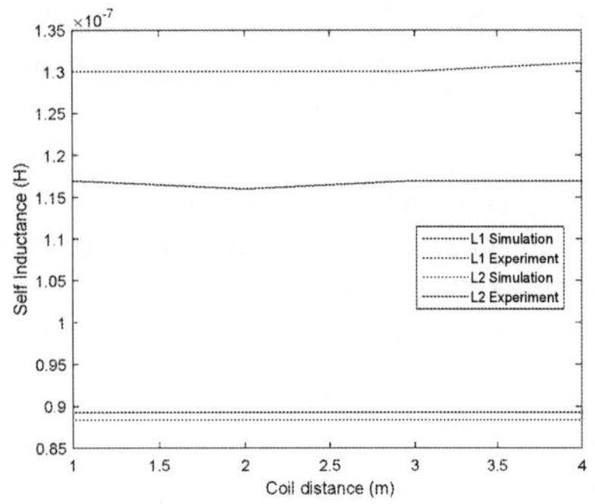

b)

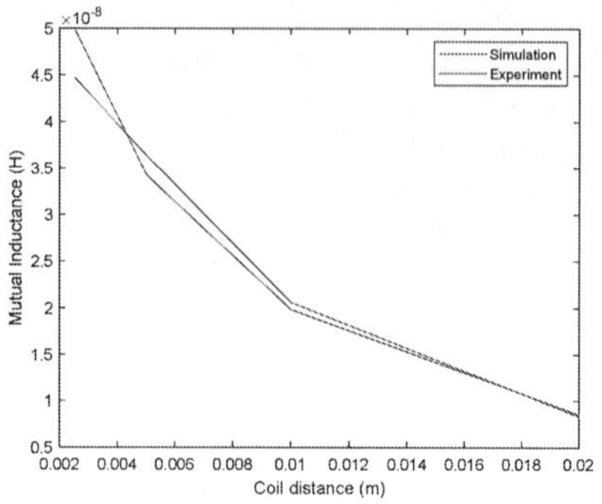

c)

FIG. 3: a) Coupling Coefficient results. b) Self-inductance results. c) Mutual inductance results.

As is typical with inductive power transfer systems, there is an exponential decay in the coupling coefficient as the distance of the concentric coils increases. There is good agreement between the experimental and simulated mutual inductances. The discrepancy in the coupling coefficient calculation comes from the self-inductance results, due to the length of the inductor leads and solder.

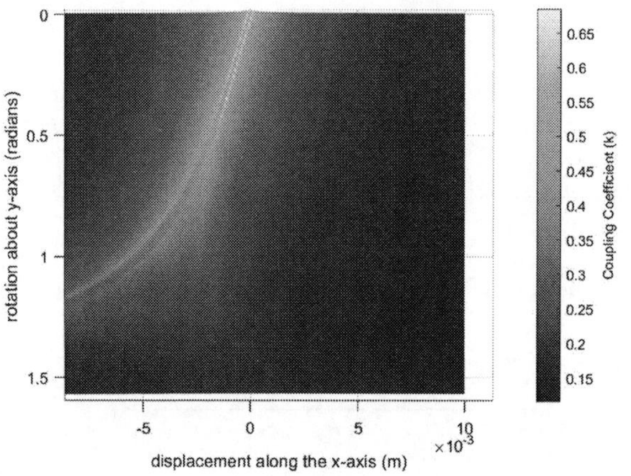

FIG. 4: Coupling coefficient with varying rotation about the y-axis and displacement along the x-axis.

The results of the simulation in Figure 4 show that the most reliable coupling coefficient for the 35 mm diameter coils can be found where the two coils are slightly rotated 0.064 radians when displaced 0.64 mm along the *x*-axis. Intuitively the maximum coupling coefficient is found when zero. The efficiency is well maintained along the path of the magnetic field, diminishing with increasing distance between the coils.

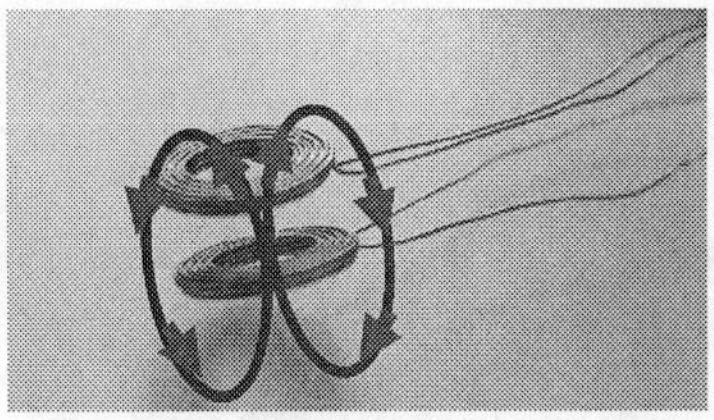

FIG. 5: Shape of the magnetic field from the primary coil.

As the magnetic field moves in a circular direction from "north" to "south", as in Figure 5, the displaced secondary coil can capture more of the field by increasing rotation about the *x* or *y* axes. The secondary coil will be more efficient if it is perpendicular to the direction of the magnetic field. This research quantifies what the angle α and φ of the secondary coil should be with respect to the primary coil given a distance (*d*) between the two coils that will maximize efficiency.

a) 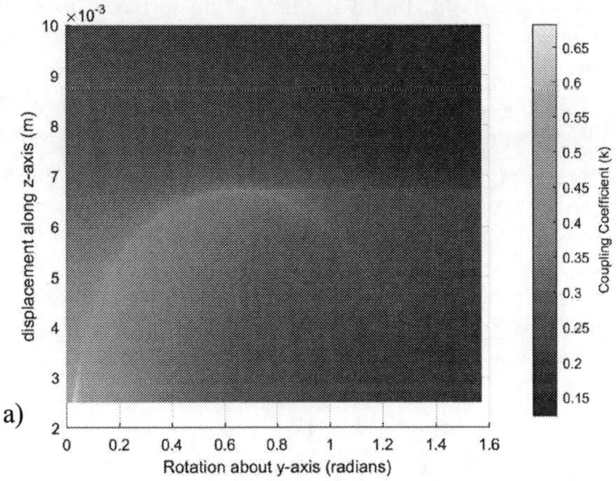

b) 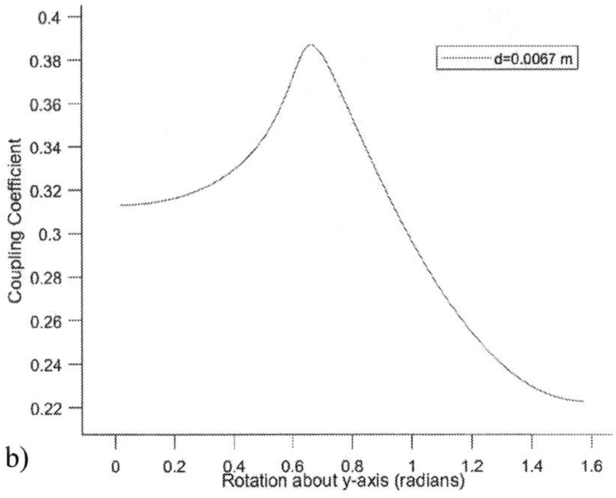

FIG. 6: (a) Coupling coefficient with varying rotation about the y-axis and displacement along the z-axis. (b) Fixed distance (d) with varying rotation about the y-axis.

Looking further at a different combination of alignment variables, Figure 6(a) illustrates the changing coupling coefficient by the change of displacement along the z-axis and rotation about the *y*-axis. The figure shows that as the distance between the coils increases, the optimal rotation of the secondary coil is non-zero due to the shape of the magnetic field. There is no data for a displacement up to 0.0025 m because of the insulation coating the copper inductor. Figure 6(b) holds constant displacement along the *z*-axis (d=0.0067 m) and increases rotation about the *y*-axis, essentially drawing a straight line from the left side of Figure 6(a) to the right side. Given the uncertainty of alignment in applications such as UAVs charging mid-flight and wearable wireless power transfer, this data can be added to a control algorithm for a UAV to maximize efficiency or explain why one set of data is performing better than another.

This research develops the equations used to calculate inductance, mutual inductance, and coupling coefficient depending on inductor geometry and coil misalignment, and uses that information to determine changes in efficiency with greater misalignment. The results show that although inductive coils might not be well coupled, there are strategies to maintain the same power transfer efficiency as perfectly coupled coils.

Acknowledgements

The authors wish to thank the In-House Laboratory Independent Research (ILIR) program for funding this research as part of an effort to optimize wireless power transfer.

References

1. Rim, Chun T., and Chris Mi. *Wireless power transfer for electric vehicles and mobile devices*. John Wiley & Sons, 2017.
2. Griffiths, David J. *Introduction to Electrodynamics Fourth Edition*. Prentice-Hall, 2021.
3. Lazarus, N., and S. S. Bedair. "Improved power transfer to wearable systems through stretchable magnetic composites." *Applied Physics A* 122 (2016): 1-7.
4. Yoo, Byungseok, et al. "Laser Direct Structured 3D Circuits on Silicone." *ACS Applied Materials & Interfaces* 14.16 (2022): 18854-18865.
5. Paul, Clayton R. *Inductance: loop and partial*. John Wiley & Sons, 2011.
6. Gao, Pengfei, et al. "Transmission efficiency analysis and optimization of magnetically coupled resonant wireless power transfer system with misalignments." *AIP Advances* 8.8 (2018): 085016.
7. Fotopoulou, Kyriaki, and Brian W. Flynn. "Wireless power transfer in loosely coupled links: Coil misalignment model." *IEEE Transactions on magnetics* 47.2 (2010): 416-43

Investigations of Multi-Metallic Nanocatalysts for Promoting Plasmon-Augmented Chemical Energy Conversion

Jonathan Boltersdorf,[1] Gregory T. Forcherio,[1,2] Asher C. Leff,[1,3] Amy Chen,[4] Taylor Woehl,[5] Yi-Yu Cai,[6] Behnaz Ostovar,[6] Stephan Link,[6,7,8] Robert J. Dillon,[1] David R. Baker[1]

[1]U.S. Army Combat Capabilities Development Command - Army Research Laboratory, Adelphi, MD 20783 USA
[2]Electro-Optic Technology Division, Naval Surface Warfare Center, Crane, IN 47522 USA
[3]General Technical Services, Adelphi, MD 20783 USA
[4]Department of Materials Science & Engineering, [5]Department of Chemical & Biomolecular Engineering, University of Maryland, College Park, MD, 20742, USA
[6]Department of Electrical & Computer Engineering, [7]Department of Chemistry, & [8]Laboratory for Nanophotonics, Rice University, Houston, TX 77251 USA
jonathan.a.boltersdorf.civ@army.mil / 301-394-0049

Abstract

Plasmonically-sensitized nanocatalysts were investigated for their photocatalytic and photo-electrochemical oxidation of ethanol (EtOH), with an emphasis on breaking the carbon-carbon bond, under solar simulated-light. Material approaches included the (i) surface plasmon resonance (SPR)-functionalization of a traditional metal oxide semiconductor and (ii) bimetallic nanocatalysts composed of noble metals. Results are correlated with nanocatalyst morphology, composition, and homogeneity to maintain plasmon-induced light absorption, enhance the photo-oxidation of EtOH, and mitigate poisoning of the catalyst. Photo-electrochemical measurements were complimented with single-particle spectroscopic measurements to understand the energy conversion pathways for the extraction and utilization of SPR-excited "hot" carriers. EtOH oxidation was achieved, yielding a light-enhanced method for low temperature, complete photo-oxidation of high specific energy hydrocarbon fuels. Further, we have constructed in situ liquid phase transmission electron microscopy (LP-TEM) experiments to study the reduction of a secondary metal onto gold nanorods (AuNRs) under plasmonic excitation to visualize single particle-level processes in solution in real time.

Keywords

Energy conversion; light-matter interactions; plasmon resonance; nanoscale; catalysis; microscopy

Introduction

Light stimulated localized surface plasmon resonance (LSPR) in metallic nanomaterials can promote the excitation of energetic, or "hot", charge carriers that can be locally transferred or thermally dissipated to augment energy conversion processes.[1, 2] Selectively driving energy-intensive industrial scale catalytic reactions at low-temperatures can be enabled at the nanoscale by locally activating adsorbed reactants and accelerating surface kinetics.[1-3] Excitation of surface plasmons further amplifies local electric fields, enhances far-field light scattering, increases the absorption cross section, and produces local thermal gradients.[1, 2] In addition to initiating energy conversion chemical reactions, plasmonic energetic hot carriers can catalyze growth of secondary metals on the surface of plasmonic nanostructures using surface-adsorbed metal salt precursors.[4-8] Plasmonic photodeposition enables targeted nucleation/growth of secondary metals at specific active surface sites, such as the controlled deposition of catalytic metals (e.g., Pd or Pt) on the ends of AuNRs.[5-8] Gold nanoparticles (AuNPs) are excellent model systems as they exhibit highly tunable particle characteristics (i.e., size and morphology) and LSPR-induced optical properties across the electromagnetic spectrum.[1-4, 9] Controlled assembly of multi-metallic plasmonic nanostructures driven by LSPR excitation can couple plasmonic absorbers with co-catalysts. Hybrid plasmonic nanomaterials can be utilized to photosensitize substrates and to provide increased photocatalytic activity *via* hot carriers and localized photothermal heating.[1-3, 5-8, 10, 11]

Plasmonic nanoparticles (NPs) hold promise for several important technological areas, such as information encryption, chemical catalysis, novel manufacturing methods, energy scavenging, theranostics (therapeutics and diagnostics), optical/optoelectronic materials, and uncooled infrared photodetectors. The realization of plasmonics for new technologies necessitates advances in the design and optimization of plasmonic materials, morphologies, synthesis techniques, and spectroscopies with enhanced spatiotemporal resolution to better understand the dynamic behavior of plasmonic hot carriers.[12] Hot carriers and photothermal heating are of significant interest in the catalysis field due to their potential ability to drive chemical reactions, such as catalytic conversion of organic molecules into chemical fuels.[3, 10, 11, 13] Current approaches for measuring these two phenomena utilize ensemble averaged characterization techniques. The relative ratio of the electron decay *via* hot electron generation and thermal dissipation is determined by the NP size, shape, composition, and local environment.[1, 2] There remains a lack of experimental observations of hot electron generation and photothermal heating on single plasmonic NPs. Poor understanding of these two phenomena has limited their application.

Our work has focused on using light to drive energy-intensive photochemical reactions at low temperatures by investigating the ability of plasmonic nanocatalysts to drive the ethanol oxidation reaction (EOR) at plasmonic interfaces. Liquid hydrocarbons are of interest as a fuel source because they have high gravimetric and volumetric energy, are easy to store, and to transport. In our work we utilize EtOH oxidation as the model hydrocarbon reaction. Current challenges associated with using hydrocarbons as fuels are that its energetically unfavorable to cleave the carbon-carbon (C-C) bond, the C-C bond cleavage rate is negligible at ambient conditions, and incomplete oxidation typically yields intermediates, like acetaldehyde (CH_3CHO), with only 4 out of 12 electrons extracted from EtOH.[5, 13, 14] Current materials suffer from low activity and a strong tendency towards adsorbed intermediates, leading to catalyst poisoning. Therefore, high temperatures are typically needed to drive the EOR thermo-electrochemically.

Plasmonic Interfaces for Ethanol Oxidation

The activity for the EOR was compared using plasmonic Au nanospheres and nanorods coupled to titanium dioxide (TiO_2).[3] Plasmonic contributions to the EtOH oxidation process were distinguished by targeting the excitation of high energy interband transitions and low energy intraband transitions. Higher energy interband transitions (<600 nm) correspond to the transverse SPR, which we found enabled the oxidation of formic acid and single-carbon intermediates to carbon dioxide (CO_2). Lower energy intraband transitions (>600 nm) for the longitudinal SPR in the AuNRs facilitated (1) desorbing intermediates and (2) breaking the C-C bond. Plasmon resonance enhanced C-C bond cleavage and complete EtOH oxidation to CO_2 by generating hot carriers and local heating.[3] However, Au alone is not a sufficient catalyst for EtOH oxidation, and a secondary catalytic metal is necessary to efficiently drive EOR.

In a second study, we explored a combination of Au, a plasmonic antenna, with palladium (Pd), an active EOR catalyst that suffers from poisoning effects from carbon monoxide.[10] We systematically varied the composition and structure (alloy vs core-shell) of Au-Pd and studied their ability to improve EtOH oxidation activity and inhibit the poisoning of Pd. The compositional range was developed for colloidal NPs from pure Au to pure Pd for homogenous alloys. Microscopy and elemental mapping showed that the nanospheres maintain their morphology and composition after loading onto TiO_2. Ultraviolet-visible (UV-Vis) spectra (Fig. 1a) show that as the composition was altered from Au-rich to Pd-rich, the SPR was significantly dampened and the maximum absorbance of the SPR peak was shifted to lower wavelengths as more Pd is incorporated. Core-shell NPs were synthesized with a Au core and a thin AuPd or Pd shell, and were embedded on a TiO_2 support. In contrast to the alloys, the AuPd core-shell NPs retained a strong plasmon resonance with little dampening owing to maintaining a sub-2 nm shell.[10]

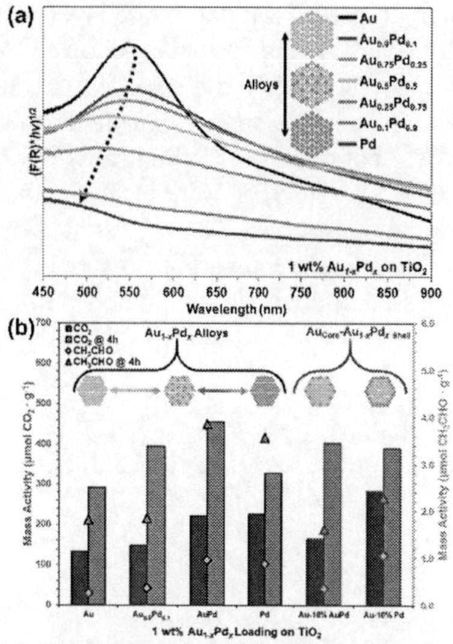

Figure 1. (a) UV–Vis spectra of 1 weight (wt.) % AuPd alloy NPs on TiO_2. (b) Photo-oxidation of EtOH to CO_2 and/or CH_3CHO for AuPd alloy and core-shell NPs on TiO_2 under irradiation. CO_2 is plotted on the left axis with purple (1 h) and blue (4 h) bars. CH_3CHO is plotted on the right axis with orange diamond (1 h) and green triangle (4 h) markers.

A series of AuPd alloy and core-shell NPs loaded on TiO_2 supports were suspended and irradiated in solution with solar simulated light (AM1.5G), the gaseous products were measured by gas chromatography mass spectrometry. Photocatalytic measurements (Fig. 1b) were performed to probe the catalysts' structure and composition to optimize and improve plasmonic enhancement of the EOR. Mass activity for 1h shows that the production of acetaldehyde (orange markers) and CO_2 (purple bars), from complete EtOH oxidation, for AuPd alloys increased with increasing Pd concentration until about 50% Pd, where the activity leveled off. Core-shell NPs with a 10% Pd shell exhibited the highest activity overall. Catalysts that were irradiated for longer periods (4h) showed a linear increase in acetaldehyde (green markers) production over time, while CO_2 (blue bars) production slowed for some compositions. The 1:1 AuPd alloy exhibited the highest overall rate of complete EtOH oxidation to CO_2 and partial oxidation to the acetaldehyde intermediate. Pure Au and Pd showed the lowest rates of long-term oxidation of EtOH to CO_2. Alloy ($Au_{0.9}Pd_{0.1}$) and core-shell NPs with 10% Pd concentration exhibited similar prolonged activity with improved selectivity towards complete EtOH oxidation, as shown by the lower rates of acetaldehyde formation in comparison to AuPd and Pd. Therefore, EtOH photo-oxidation activity was improved by combining a plasmonic antenna and a catalytic metal reactor with the appropriate composition and structure.[10]

Plasmonic AuPd alloys and core-shell NPs were studied using rotating disk electrochemistry (RDE) methods. Working electrodes were 20 wt.% AuPd NPs loaded on conductive carbon supports with a Nafion binder onto a glassy carbon disk. Cyclic voltammetry (CV) measurements (Fig. 2a) generate EOR current by scanning anodically up to

+1.5 V, which coincided with an oxide layer formation on the metal NPs. Peak anodic current is followed by a current drop due to passivation of the electrode. Coverage of the active sites and competition with oxide forming species results in this passivation. Cathodically sweeping the potential from +1.5 V to +0.1 V, reduced the oxide species and EtOH oxidation resumed. The 1:1 AuPd alloy exhibited the highest EOR activity, comparable to pure Pd. In contrast, pure Au, alloyed AuPd with low Pd composition, and core-shell NPs exhibited poor electrochemical EOR activity.[10]

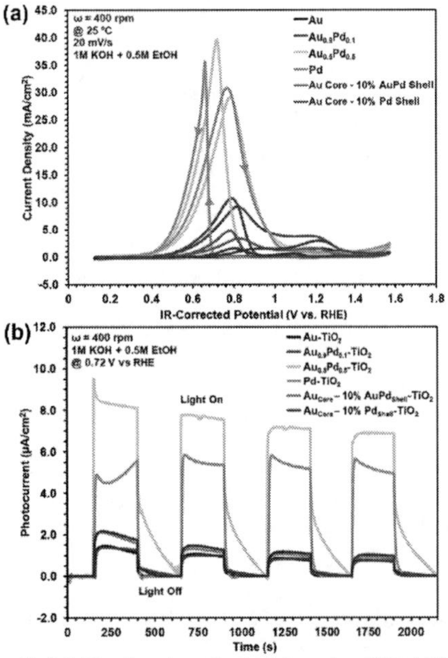

Figure 2. (a) Electrochemical CVs using 20 wt.% AuPd alloy and core-shell NPs on carbon. (b) Photo-electrochemical CAs using 1 wt.% AuPd alloy and core-shell NPs on TiO_2, held at +0.72 V under 250s on/off chopped light, baseline (i.e., 0 μA cm^{-2}) is the dark current. Nanocatalysts deposited onto a rotating disk, glassy carbon working electrode. Reference (Ag/AgCl) and counter (Pt) electrodes used in 0.5 M EtOH with 1 M KOH electrolyte.

Photo-electrochemical studies were performed with 1 wt.% plasmonic NPs on TiO_2 with chronoamperometric (CA) measurements (Fig. 2b) with chopped solar simulated light. Light-induced current (photocurrent) density (mA/cm^2) for each electrode was measured over 2000+ s. Low photocurrent with a 40-53% retention over 2000s was observed for Au-rich compositions. In contrast, Pd is a good EOR catalyst that improves charge separation and transfer, with an 84% photocurrent retention over 2000s. The 1:1 AuPd alloy exhibited the highest prolonged photocurrent activity with 72% retention, which was postulated to be due to injection of hot carriers from Au to Pd active sites, outperforming the EOR activity of pure Au and Pd, as well as other alloy, and core-shell compositions.[10]

Subsequently we investigated using SPR excitation to transfer hot carriers to facilitate the deposition of secondary catalytic metals on anisotropic nanostructures.[13] Gold nanorods (AuNRs) provide a method to target the reductive photodeposition at specific sites at ambient conditions for growth by either interacting with hot carriers or heat dissipated from the metal lattice. We focused on targeting Pd via metal salt reactants due to their well-understood chemistry. The photo-chemical deposition method was tailored to grow a sub-2 nm Pd shell absent of lattice defects via hot carriers generated from longitudinal SPR excitation in the presence of $[PdCl_4]^{-2}$. The growth was accomplished with a 1:5 Pd:Au atomic ratio, resulting in an undampened LSPR response and provided a method to develop bimetallic NPs for plasmonic catalysis.[13]

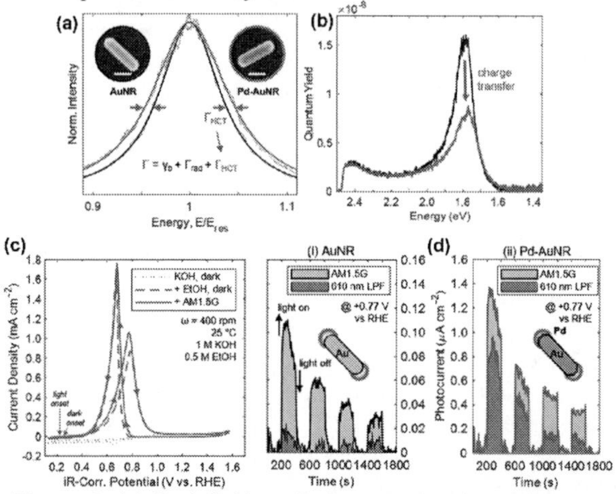

Figure 3. (a) Dark field scattering spectra show plasmon linewidth, **Γ**, expands and (b) luminescence spectra show decrease in quantum yield of AuNRs (black) upon adding Pd (red). Electrochemical EOR used 20 ***μ*g** Pd-AuNRs (red) and AuNRs (black). (b) CVs of Pd-AuNRs without (dotted) and with EtOH under dark and light (solid) conditions. (c) Photoinduced CAs with (i) AuNR and (ii) Pd-AuNR NPs held at +0.77 V under 200s on/off chopped light (gray shaded) and 610 nm long pass filtered (LPF) light (orange shaded).

Single-particle spectroscopic measurements were performed on the AuNRs with Pd end coatings to determine the energy conversion pathway using dark field scattering (Fig. 3a) and photoluminescence (Fig. 3b).[13] Spectra showed quenching (decrease) in the overall radiative quantum yield after depositing Pd on the AuNRs. Measurement results were consistent with separation of intraband hot carriers across the Pd-Au interface, removing excited carriers that could recombine radiatively. Further studies were needed to answer: Are hot carriers the primary driving force for plasmonic energy conversion reactions? The EOR was investigated by CV (Fig. 3c) and CA (Fig. 3d) using the RDE setup and electrochemical conditions previously discussed. CVs showed characteristic redox peaks of EtOH oxidation shown in Fig. 2a for Au and Pd. Light-enhancement was observed for the Pd-AuNRs, with an increase in current density and an anodic shift in the onset potential (~35 mV) under irradiation. CAs showed an increase in the photocurrent density by an order of magnitude after depositing Pd. Plasmonic enhancement was mostly observed at longer wavelengths (>610 nm). Photodeposition of Pd onto AuNRs improved the EOR current in CA 13x under solar-simulated light and 40x for longitudinal SPR-targeted irradiation conditions (>610 nm), revealing 4x more efficient utilization of excited intraband carriers. Corresponding absorbed photon-to-charge carrier efficiency (APCE) was calculated to be 50x improved after Pd photodeposition. The overall low APCE for the plasmonic NPs indicate that most of the excited carriers undergo electron-phonon scattering, resulting in primarily photothermal heating as the dominant mechanism.[13]

In summary, we determined that plasmonic photo-sensitization can enhance the visible-light activity to cleave C-C bonds for EOR. Plasmonic EOR activity can be optimized by modifying AuPd composition and structure. Plasmonic nanocatalysts have had favorable influence on mitigating catalyst poisoning, tuning the selectivity and conversion efficiency. The 1:1 AuPd alloy exhibited optimal mass activity, high electrochemical activity, and prolonged photocurrent for oxidizing EtOH. We developed a method for the targeted plasmonic photodeposition of secondary catalytic metals like Pd on active sites of AuNRs, identified hot carrier transfer from the AuNR to Pd using single particle spectroscopy, and determined the photo-electrochemical methods that photothermal heating may be the primary mechanism for EOR enhancement.

Recently, LP-TEM was utilized to visualize the formation of silver (Ag)-shell on AuNRs in situ in real-time where two distinct Ag shell morphologies, faceted bipyramidal and tip preferential shells, were identified.[15] Electron-beam-induced Ag deposition onto AuNRs observed by aqueous-phase LP-TEM was consistent with radiolysis-induced Ag reduction. Any plasmonic metal deposition via hot electron reduction occurring in aqueous phase LP-TEM imaging was obscured by rapid chemical radical-induced metal deposition as mediated by ligand coverage. An implication of this work is that aqueous-phase LP-TEM imaging is likely not capable of separating plasmon-induced metal reduction from radiolysis-induced processes due to the susceptibility of water to radiolysis and production of aggressive radical species. Instead, this work suggests a potential pathway for investigating plasmonic phenomena with LP-TEM is to utilize radiolysis resistant solvents.[15]

References

(1) Qiu, J.; Wei, W. D. Surface Plasmon-Mediated Photothermal Chemistry. *J. Phys. Chem. C* **2014**, *118*, 20735-20749.

(2) Zhang, Y.; He, S.; Guo, W.; Hu, Y.; Huang, J.; Mulcahy, J. R.; Wei, W. D. Surface-Plasmon-Driven Hot Electron Photochemistry. *Chem. Rev.* **2018**, *118*, 2927-2954.

(3) Boltersdorf, J.; Forcherio, G. T.; McClure, J. P.; Baker, D. R.; Leff, A. C.; Lundgren, C. Visible Light-Promoted Plasmon Resonance to Induce "Hot" Hole Transfer and Photothermal Conversion for Catalytic Oxidation. *J. Phys. Chem. C* **2018**, *122*, 28934-28948.

(4) Boerigter, C.; Aslam, U.; Linic, S. Mechanism of Charge Transfer from Plasmonic Nanostructures to Chemically Attached Materials. *ACS Nano* **2016**, *10*, 6108-6115.

(5) Forcherio, G. T.; Baker, D. R.; Boltersdorf, J.; Leff, A. C.; McClure, J. P.; Grew, K. N.; Lundgren, C. A. Targeted Deposition of Pt onto Gold Nanorods by Plasmonic Hot Electrons. *J. Phys. Chem. C* **2018**, *122*, 28901-28909.

(6) Forcherio, G. T.; Baker, D. R.; Leff, A. C.; Boltersdorf, J.; McClure, J. P.; Grew, K. N.; Lundgren, C. A. Photodeposition of Pd onto Colloidal AuNRs by Surface Plasmon Excitation. *J. Vis. Exp.* **2019**, 150, e60041.

(7) Ortiz, N.; Zoellner, B.; Hong, S. J.; Ji, Y.; Wang, T.; Liu, Y.; Maggard, P. A.; Wang, G. Harnessing Hot Electrons from Near IR Light for Hydrogen Production Using Pt-End-Capped-AuNRs. *ACS Appl. Mater. Interfaces* **2017**, *9*, 25962-25969.

(8) Zheng, Z.; Tachikawa, T.; Majima, T. Plasmon-enhanced formic acid dehydrogenation using anisotropic Pd-Au nanorods studied at the single-particle level. *J. Am. Chem. Soc.* **2015**, *137*, 948-957.

(9) Kim, S. M.; Lee, S. W.; Moon, S. Y.; Park, J. Y. The effect of hot electrons and surface plasmons on heterogeneous catalysis. *J. Phys. Condens. Matter* **2016**, *28*, 254002.

(10) Boltersdorf, J.; Leff, A. C.; Forcherio, G. T.; Baker, D. R. Plasmonic Au–Pd Bimetallic Nanocatalysts for Hot-Carrier-Enhanced Photocatalytic and Electrochemical Ethanol Oxidation. *Crystals* **2021**, *11*, 226.

(11) Boltersdorf, J.; Leff, A. C.; Forcherio, G. T.; McClure, J. P.; Lundgren, C. A. Surface Plasmon Resonant Gold-Palladium Bimetallic Nanoparticles for Promoting Catalytic Oxidation. *MRS Adv.* **2019**, *4*, 1877-1886.

(12) Forcherio, G. T.; Boltersdorf, J. Directed Surface Plasmon Resonance for Hot Carrier Applications. *Crystals* **2021**, *11*, 1497.

(13) Forcherio, G. T.; Ostovar, B.; Boltersdorf, J.; Cai, Y.-Y.; Leff, A. C.; Grew, K. N.; Lundgren, C. A.; Link, S.; Baker, D. R. Single-Particle Insights into Plasmonic Hot Carrier Separation Augmenting Photoelectrochemical Ethanol Oxidation with Photocatalytically Synthesized Pd−Au Bimetallic Nanorods. *ACS Nano* **2022**, *16*, 12377-12389.

(14) Lamy, C.; Belgsir, E. M.; Leger, J. M. Electrocatalytic oxidation of aliphatic alcohols: Application to the direct alcohol fuel cell. *J Appl Electrochem* **2001**, *31*, 799-809.

(15) Chen, A.; Leff, A. C.; Forcherio, G. T.; Boltersdorf, J.; Woehl, T. J. Examining Silver Deposition Pathways onto Gold Nanorods with LP-TEM. *J. Phys. Chem. Lett.* **2023**, *14*, 1379-1388.

Heat Transfer and Cell Failure Analysis for Configuration of a Non-Propagating Li-ion Battery Pack with a Copper Microfibrous Cooling Structure during Extreme-Condition Pulsed Power Operation

Wenhua H. Zhu[a], Jacob Faulkner[a], Kylie W. Minor[b], Paul Dimick[b], and Bruce J. Tatarchuk[a,]*

[a]Center for Microfibrous Materials, Department of Chemical Engineering, Auburn University, 212 Ross Hall, Auburn, AL 36849

[b]IntraMicron, Inc., 368 Industry Drive, Auburn, AL 36831 pdimick@intramicron.com

Abstract

IntraMicron is building a high-power 1000V battery system for NSWC Philadelphia Code 32 to provide additional energy storage capacity for the support of future weapons and other shipboard systems. The modules and system are being designed to mitigate cell-to-cell and module-to-module propagation failure events under harsh operating conditions. This work focuses on the simulated thermal performance of each 50V 12S module under normal operation and cell-failure scenarios. A thermal model for the Li-ion battery pack based on COMSOL Multiphysics has been established to simulate the heat transfer process inside the battery power system for regulating cell temperature during 4C/15C power cycles. Multiple cell configurations of the 12S module were assessed for performance and manufacturability. To fully gauge the capabilities of the cooling structure, it is important to understand the effect of one-cell thermal failure on the nearby Li-ion cells during an unexpected extreme heat generation event. The 2D failure results for 3×4 offset configuration reveal that the maximum cell surface temperature was obtained as ca. 53.1°C for the cells adjacent to the failed cell, indicating that the enhanced cooling structure removes and dissipates sufficient heat to prevent cascade failure. A 3D model structure was also developed to simulate the failure event through coupling of heat transfer, fluid flow, and solid mechanics submodels. To augment the safety assessment of the module during normal operation and single-cell failure, the initial pressure profile inside the cell, the surface temperature at the cell's safety vent, and the total displacement and stress profiles of the cell's top cover were considered through the fluid-structure interaction with the solid mechanics physics package.

Keywords

Metal microfibrous media; hybrid heat transfer modeling; high-power battery pack; Li-ion cell failure and structure safety; energy storage and conversion.

Introduction

A well-designed battery thermal management system (BTMS) is crucial to maintain a Li-ion battery pack's temperature within an acceptable range and uniformity. Initially, passive thermal management (PTM) was achieved using solid-liquid phase-change material (PCM) on the Li-ion battery pack [1]. However, for high peak or pulsed power operating conditions, active thermal management (ATM) is necessary for its higher heat transfer capability and removal rate to dissipate the large amounts of heat generated inside neighboring cells. Liquid cooling enables high-power acceleration in some existing EVs/HEVs such as the Chevrolet and Tesla Model S [2]. Fathabadi used PCM/expanded graphite composite with air duct cooling flow through the battery pack to achieve improved performance [3]. Recently, active cooling tubes were inserted and sintered together with a porous metal microfibrous media structure (MFM) fully embedded with PCM waxes to overcome the low thermal conductivity limitations of paraffin [4]. During load cycling, mechanical cell failure may occur due to cell plasticity deformation caused by compression or tension in the BTMS and cooling structure [5]. Moreover, battery failure or thermal runaway usually occurs when the cell temperature exceeds a certain threshold, resulting in subsequent heat-producing decomposition processes that further increase the cell temperature. This paper establishes a thermal model to evaluate a 12S Li-ion battery pack's performance, comparing the cell surface temperature differences for 2x6 and 3x4 12S configurations. A safety evaluation on the cell structure is also conducted by modeling burst disc stress and displacement with a structural mechanics inclusion.

Model Structure with Structural Mechanics

The COMSOL Multiphysics platform, along with a heat transfer module, was selected for simulating the heat transfer process in a 12S Li-ion battery pack. The 3D simulation was completed by constructing a physical model of the system and coupling it with a heat transfer model in the battery pack including fluid flow in the cooling tubes. A simplified 2D model structure was used to facilitate the module design and module structure evaluation process because of its drastically reduced computational time. The 50 V modules consist of twelve 30 Ah Li-ion cells connected in series, and they were simulated through 4C/15C charge/discharge cycles using previously validated model parameters. The Li-ion cells were assumed to be packed in the actively cooled MFM-PCM cooling structure and operated at an ambient temperature of 60°C. Depending on the specific application, the metal MFM structure can be customized to achieve a specific void volume and heat transfer performance. The enhanced heat transfer of MFM enables nearly instantaneous access to the latent heat capacity of the PCM when responding to temperature changes from dynamic high-power loads. The active cooling tube is an essential component for the MFM-PCM battery thermal management system during extreme-condition high-power cycles. The cooling tube is embedded inside the MFM-PCM matrix and is able to efficiently transfer heat which was absorbed and stored in the MFM-PCM matrix as well as removing cell-generated heat from the surface of the cells. The unique design for the active-cooling structure allows the MFM-PCM matrix to normalize the Li-ion cell surface temperatures in the pack during frequent charge/discharge cycles at high discharge rates. Another advantage is that the specific design enables the battery pack to function at an ambient temperature above the melting point of the paraffin wax.

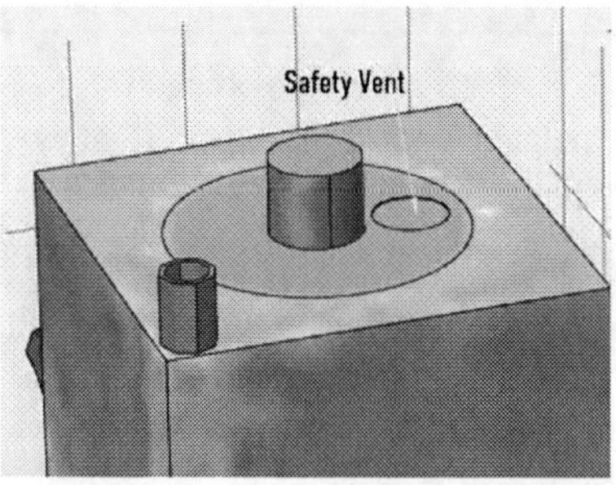

Figure 1. Geometric structure for the Li-ion cell packed inside the MFM-PCM block matrix embedded with the cooling tube.

In this study, the battery pack model and simulation were applied to a group of 30 Ah Li-ion cells with high pulsed power capability. The cells have a diameter of 54 mm, a height of 222 mm, a weight of 1100 g, and a volume of 0.51 dm^3. The battery was cycled between 40°C and 50°C at a 4C charge rate and 15C discharge rate and operated from 91.7% SoC to 100% DoD for testing and evaluation of the structure's thermal performance. The Li-ion cells use a graphite-based anode and nickel oxide-based cathode, and the electrolyte is a blend of LiPF6 and carbonate solvents. To test and evaluate the high-power battery packs, an Arbin battery tester capable of operating at a discharge current up to 600 A was used. The prototypical MFM-PCM matrix structure with active liquid-cooling enhancement was described in previous publications [6]. The structure model parameters for the battery pack were adopted from simulation and validation testing in a similar study with 12 cells in series (12S). Details of this data are not shown because of its proprietary nature. Key parameters were used to determine a practical model and simulation solution. Additionally, theoretical simulation of cascade catastrophic failure for a battery pack can be performed with this model to evaluate extreme condition battery operation.

For the cell failure modeling via the COMSOL-6 platform, the heat transfer and the structural mechanics modules were selected. Two heat transfer submodels (HT1+HT2) were constructed for multiphysics coupling to separate the two fluids in the cell gas and wax fluid. The fluid submodel (Fluid1) was coupled with HT1 to include the cell gas fluid, which was then coupled with the structural mechanics (Mech1) to evaluate the structural interaction between the cell gas fluid, the burst disc, and the cell can. This was especially important at the top cover area. The model evaluated the cell internal pressure, cell surface temperature, and the cell safety vent temperature for a single Cell (number 12) in the MFM-PCM structure near the water outlet after the cell failure via one-second energy release of 511.6 kJ. The coolant temperature was set to 38.18°C, and the ambient temperature was set to 59.04°C. For the MFM-PCM structure, the following parameters were defined: a thermal conductivity correction factor of 0.483, a thin film wrap thermal conductivity 0.15 W/m-K, an inner cooling tube heat transfer coefficient of 3925 W/m^2-K, and an external wall heat transfer coefficient of 5 W/m^2-K. The internal cell pressure can be expressed through the initial gas and DMC saturated vapor pressure [7]. The applied pressure in the cell headspace reached approximately 400 kPa during the initial tests for structure safety evaluation.

The safety vent burst disc was assumed to be a grooved thinner metal foil in the cell top cover for the structural mechanics interaction. The model structure was coupled with two heat transfer submodels, one gas fluid flow submodel, and the solid mechanics submodel. The cell can and the top cover wall were defined as low carbon steel with a shell thickness of 0.04 inches. The groove depth of the vent had a thickness of 0.01 inches. Cell failure was defined to occur with a one-second heat release that started at 7586.74 seconds. The simulation used the time-dependent solver via four segregated solution steps.

Simulation Results

For the 2D cycling tests, it was assumed that a thin thermal resistive layer with a thickness of 0.01 mm exists between the cell and the plastic insulating wrap and the equivalent heat transfer coefficient at the interface was thus obtained as 1775 W/m^2-K. The paraffin wax has with a melting point of 54.8°C. Thus, the estimated thermal conductivity of 58 W/m-K was applied to the cooling structure to evaluate different designs and optimized configurations. The cells connected in series were assumed to be operated at 4C/15C charge/discharge cycles. Four pack-cooling configurations were evaluated with the 2D COMSOL-4.3 thermal model to simulate the high-rate charge/discharge cycles, and the results are shown in Table 1. For each structure, except Type-IV, the 12 cells were arranged in either a 2x6 or 3x4 pattern in the structure. The Type-IV pack contains 14 cells in a 5-4-5 configuration. The results show that the temperatures for the Type-II pack are slightly higher than the other three MFM-PCM cooling structure designs. The highest cell surface temperature is 47.9°C near an adjacent cell using the 2D simulation method. The model results show that there is a small temperature difference on the cell surfaces for the Type-I, III and IV designs. The 2D simulation results show that all four types of battery packs, using the initial MFM-PCM design configurations with active cooling loops, are able to satisfy the BTMS requirement for direct heat removal during short charge/discharge high-power cycles.

Table 1. Simulated steady peak temperature after the 5th cycle at t=4700 s.

Domain Point Probe Location	I. 2x6 OFFSET	II. 3x4 SYMMETRIC	III. 3x4 OFFSET	IV. 545 OVERSIZE
On the block, between 2 cells	46.5°C	47.2°C	46.6°C	46.5°C
On the block, between 4 cells	43.7°C	46.1°C	43.8°C	43.9°C
Between a cell and cooling tube	45.1°C	43.6°C	45.2°C	45.3°C
At cell surface, near another cell	47.0°C	47.9°C	46.8°C	46.7°C
At cell surface, diagonal to another cell	46.9°C	47.1°C	47.0°C	46.1°C
Block edge	44.8°C	44.7°C	44.8°C	43.9°C
Cooling Tube Edge	43.7°C	43.5°C	43.8°C	44.0°C

Failure Analysis

Power system reliability and operating safety are significant challenges for the application of Li-ion battery packs in various fields due to concerns regarding heat generation, overheating, and thermal runaway. This is particularly problematic because the discharge process of a Li-ion cell generates a large amount of heat, particularly during short high-power cycles in cylindrical cells. The use of active cooling loops, however, enables rapid heat removal during high-power short cycles and maintains a cooler and safer operating environment for the MFM-PCM block. As a result, the unique design of the cooling system effectively reduces the risk of overheating in the Li-ion power system. Nevertheless, it is essential to consider the durability of the MFM-PCM cooling block in the event of thermal runaway or unexpected cell failure in the battery pack.

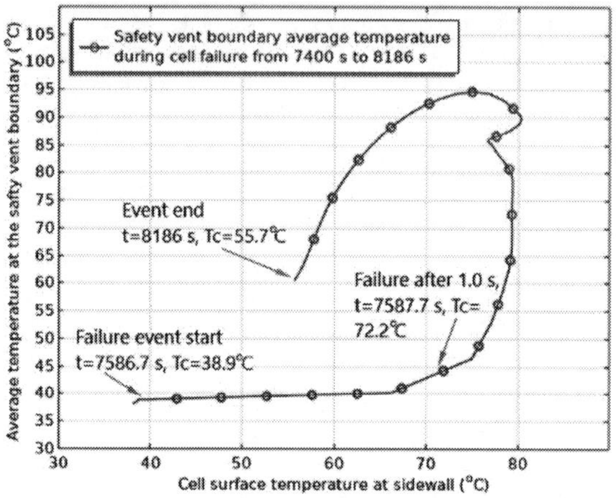

Figure 2. Simulated average temperature at the safety vent as a function of the cell surface temperature at the sidewall.

The ability of the actively cooled MFM-PCM pack to mitigate cascade failure was assessed by evaluating the simulated thermal response in the event of a single-cell failure. The battery pack was assumed to be operating normally from the first to the sixth cycle until it was fully charged during the seventh cycle. At this point, it was assumed that one of the cells, which was in one of the hottest locations, would unexpectedly fail in one second with a maximum energy release of 511.6 kJ after the seventh cycle charge. This was the total energy of a fully charged 30 Ah Li-ion cell with an additional 33% energy generated from related chemical reactions. The battery pack was still operating in a 60°C ambient environment. During the one-second failure period, the other cells continued regular discharge and then turned off 10 minutes after the single-cell failure. Using this assumption, temperature values are obtained at various locations via thermal modeling computation. For the cells adjacent to the failed cell in the Type-II 3x4 battery pack configuration, the maximum cell surface temperature is approximately 53.3°C. After the failure, the block temperatures between two neighboring cells for all four types of cell configurations approach the wax melting point. The temperatures at the failed cell surface exceed the operating limitation of 60°C. The simulation results show that the thermal failure of one cell in the MFM-PCM structure has no destructive effects on the adjacent cells due to latent heat protection from wax liquefaction and rapid heat removal through active cooling circulation inherent to the unique thermal management design for heat transfer enhancement.

To better understand the effect of cell failure on the battery power system, particularly the structural safety of the cell in the MFM-PCM block, a 3D model was developed with the inclusion of the structural mechanics module. The initial simulation results are reported concerning the cell surface temperature, safety vent temperature, total displacement of the safety vent, and von Mises stress on the safety vent of the top cover. The simulation results show visible differences between the cell sidewall surface and the cell safety vent, as shown in Figure 2. The burst disc temperature for the safety vent increases rapidly at 7587.7 s after the cell failure event, reaching a maximum point of 95°C at the burst disc while the cell surface temperature drops from 80°C to 75°C due to the active cooling through tube circulation. The rapid temperature increase is likely caused by the partial pressure increase from the saturated vapor due to the DMC boiling point near 90°C. The vaporization process through the gas fluid flow enhances heat transfer inside the cell. The displacement on the top cover is a function of the cell internal pressure due to cell failure with the assumed extreme heat generation resulting from the cell decomposition and chemical exothermic reactions inside the Li-ion cell. The maximum displacement obtained is approximately 7.9 μm at 308 kPa after the failure event.

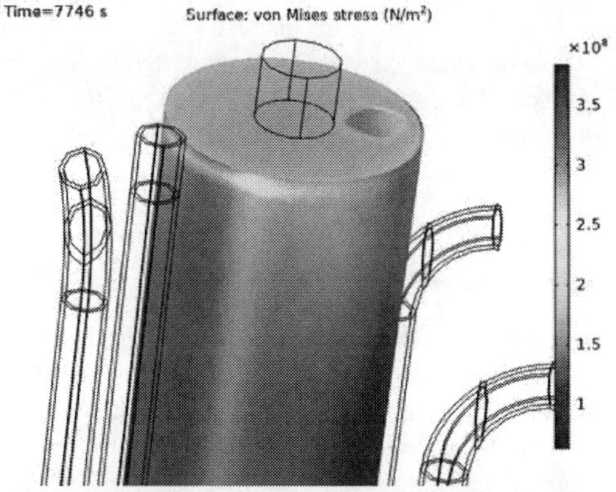

Figure 3. Modeling results for von Mises stress at the safety vent boundary after the cell failure event with extreme heat.

The simulation results for the first principal stress and von Mises stress were obtained to understand the effect of cell failure caused by extreme heat release inside the Li-ion cell on the structural safety of the MFM-PCM block. The first principal stress is the real stress associated with the maximum tensile stress, which is determined by the amount of pressure loading and is normal to the plane where the shear stress is zero. The maximum result for the first principal stress is found to be around 5×10^7 N/m^2 near the cell can edges. The von Mises stress, which predicts the potential failure of a ductile material, was calculated for the top cover with an assumption of fixed constraints for the cell can wall attached to the MFM/PCM block structure. The maximum von Mises stress is found to be around 3.0×10^8 N/m^2 at the cell safety vent boundary, as shown in Figure 3. Although the COMSOL-6 multiphysics platform is capable of coupling different submodels and also can provide better solution routes, the simulation parameters must be refined for changes in pack structure and to provide correlation with actual experimental data. Future work will aim to gain a deeper understanding of Li-ion cell fundamentals during rapid failure events and the performance of the pack structure during these failures with a focus on evaluating for non-propagation. This includes investigating changes in cell gas components and constituents during extreme heat generation within a short period. The results of the future work will enable the proper assessment of cell failure and structure endurance to evaluate the safety of a design prior to real-world failure testing.

Summary

The thermal model developed for the actively cooled MFM-PCM matrix demonstrates the structure can be used to maintain high-power Li-ion cells at an acceptable operating temperature during short charge/discharge cycles under extreme conditions (60°C ambient temperature). The 2D simulation results demonstrate that the neighboring cell surface temperature does not exceed 47.9°C during high-rate normal cycles (4C/15C) for four types of liquid-cooling configuration designs. The single-cell failure models also indicate that the maximum temperature at the cell surface adjacent to the failure cell does not exceed 53.3°C. This suggests that the structure will prevent cell-to-cell propagation due to a thermal excursion. Additionally, the 3D simulation coupled with the structural mechanics module provides valuable information such as cell surface and burst disc temperatures, displacement of the safety vent due to the boundary pressure load and temperature surge, and von Mises stress on the vent structure. Overall, the unique cooling structure of the MFM-PCM matrix enables efficient heat removal from the Li-ion battery pack for high-power operating devices.

Acknowledgements

This work is funded by the Naval Surface Warfare Center Philadelphia (Contract# N6449819D4025). The authors greatly appreciate the financial support.

References

1. S. A. Hallaj and J. R. Selman, *J. Electrochem. Soc.*, vol. 147, no. 9, pp. 3231-3236, 2000.
2. M. Malik, I. Dincer, M. A. Rosen, M. Mathew, and M. Fowler, *Appl. Therm. Eng.*, vol. 129, pp. 472-481, 2018.
3. H. Fathabadi, *Energy*, vol. 70, pp. 529-538, 2014.
4. H. Yang, B. J. Tatarchuk, T. J. Barron, and P. S. Dimick, WO2015123676A1, pp.1-34, 2015.
5. J. Xu, B. H. Liu, L.B. Wang, and S. Shang, *Eng. Fail Anal.*, vol.53, pp.97-110, 2015.
6. W. H. Zhu, H. Y. Yang, K. Webb, T. Barron, P. Dimick, B. J. Tatarchuk, *J Clean Prod*, vol.210, pp.542-551, 2019.
7. P.T. Coman, S. Matefi-Tempfli, C.T. Veje, R. E. White, *J Electrochem Soc*, vol.164, no.9, pp.A1858-A1865, 2017.

Improvement of Low Temperature Performance of Supercapacitors using Ionic Liquid Based Electrolytes

Richard Johnson, III[1]*, Andrew G. Warne[1], Giuseppe L. Di Benedetto[1], Arber Ferati[2], and Peggy A. Sanchez[1]

[1]U.S. Army Combat Capabilities Development Command Armaments Center, Picatinny Arsenal, NJ 07806

[2]SAVIT Corporation, 400 Commons Way, Rockaway, NJ 07866

Contact author email and phone: richard.johnson1097.civ@army.mil / 973.724.9020

Abstract

Supercapacitors (SCs) are energy storage devices that are utilized for fuze setting and pre-flight data hold in weapon systems due to their high-power density. Unfortunately, at low temperatures SCs have shown poor performance due to their electrolyte reaching their freezing point within the operating/storage temperature requirements of the U.S. Army. U.S. Army Combat Capability Development Command Armaments Center (DEVCOM-AC) engineers have identified and characterized the performance of many top-of-the-line commercial off the shelf (COTS) SCs in order to elucidate the lower temperature bounds in which these devices begin to fail. Prototype SCs were fabricated in a coin cell configuration utilizing low freezing point ionic liquid-based electrolytes mixed with solvents to improve low temperature performance. The coin cells were electrochemically tested to decipher the internal series resistance, maximum working voltage, and max current draw these new electrolytes would allow at extreme low temperatures.

Keywords

Ionic Liquid; Low Temperature; Supercapacitor; Ultracapacitor

Introduction

The advancement of electrochemical storage devices is vital to meet the ever-growing energy demands[1]. Electric double-layer capacitors or supercapacitors (SCs) have been highlighted as ideal energy storage devices for high power applications. SCs offer high power density, a long cyclic life, and a faster charge/discharge time when compared to batteries, all while having an extremely long shelf life [1-2]. Despite their high power density and short charge times, SCs show poor and unreliable performance at temperatures below -30ºC (-22ºF). To improve upon the low temperature performance of SCs, the electrolyte that is utilized must change.

The electrolyte utilized within a SCs is prone to freezing at extreme low temperatures based on the physical properties of the electrolyte itself. Typical commercial electrolyte includes acetonitrile (AN) and polypropylene carbonate (PC) which begin to freeze at -40ºC (-40ºF). An ideal candidate to these regularly used solvent are ionic liquid-based electrolytes. Ionic liquids are comprised of large asymmetric organic cations mixed with organic/nonorganic anions, while utilizing solvents with lower freezing points. Since both the cations and anions contribute to the overall conductivity, ionic liquids have a higher operational voltage range of up to 6V. The superior thermal stability of ionic liquids have also led to reliable operation at temperatures as low as -70ºC (-94ºF) [4-6], making them the most attractive option.

There are drawbacks to the utilization of ionic liquids. As temperature begins to fall the viscosity of the liquid increases. This increase in viscosity has been directly correlated to the decrease in overall conductivity. This would result in poor charge times as temperature decreases. Guo et al. [3] and Wong et al. [5] have studied this phenomenon and showed that an optimized molar ratio of AN to 1-ethyl-3-methylimidazolium tetrafluoborate ($EMIMBF_4$) can alleviate these issues at room temperatures.

In order to understand the benefits that a drop-in replacement electrolyte would have on commercial off the shelf (COTS) SCs, these cells will be charged and discharged over a wide temperature range to understand the current state-of-the-art in the commercial market. A solution of $EMIMBF_4$ in AN will then be formulated and utilized with porous carbon-based electrodes in a coin cell configuration to understand the low temperature performance increase these thermally stable electrolytes have compared to standard industry electrolytes.

Experimental

Commercial Off the Shelf Supercapacitors

Supercapacitors (SCs) were purchased from Digikey Electronics. The devices varied in overall capacitance in an effort to characterize SC of various sizes.

Formulation of Electrolyte

Acetonitrile (AN) and 1-ethyl-3-methylimidazolium tetrafluoborate ($EMIMBF_4$) were purchased from Sigma-Aldrich. A solution of $EMIMBF_4$ in AN was measured by volume and mixed at room temperature for 1 hour prior to use. All electrolyte formulation occurred within a dry room.

Preparation of Coin Cells

CR2032 hardware, high surface active carbon, and conductive additive were purchased from MTI Corp. Poly(vinylidene fluoride) and 1-methyl-2-pyrrolidione were purchased from Sigma-Aldrich and were utilized as an electrode binder. A slurry of 80% active carbon to 10% binder and 10% conductive attritive was mixed in a dry room for 24 hours prior to being drop cast onto pre-cut aluminum current collectors. Whatman GF/C glass microfiber filter paper were purchased from Scientific Filers and utilized as the separator. All coin cells were assembled and crimped in a dry room. The coin cell preparation process is depicted in Fig. 1 in which each step of the process is highlighted.

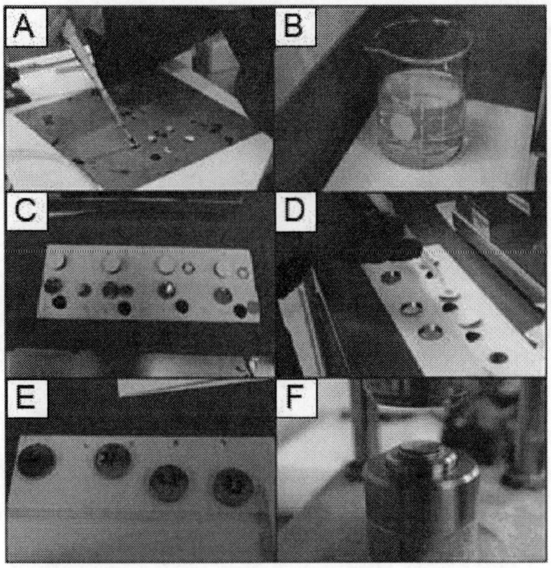

Figure 1. Coin cell preparation: (A) Drop casting of electrode material on aluminum current collector (B) Ionic Liquid Electrolyte (C) All coin cell hardware (D) Addition of electrolyte to coin cells (E) Finalized coin cells (F) Example of coin cell in crimper.

Electrochemical Testing

All electrochemical testing was conducted with a PARSTAT MC multichannel potentiostat loaded with PC100 potentiostats. All electrochemical testing was conducted within an environmental chamber to ensure a constant temperature environment during testing. The test set up can be seen in Fig. 2.

Cyclic voltammograms (CVs) were first conducted on all coin cells and COTS SCs. The voltage limit for the COTS SCs was based on the working voltage outlined in their data sheets and varied from 2.5V to 3V. The voltage limits of the coin cells were 0V to 3.5V. Scan rates varied from 0.1V/s to 1V/s.

Constant current charge and discharge cycling was then conducted on all COTS SCs and coin cells. The applied loads varied from 0.25 A/g to 5 A/g. The mass of the packaged COTS SC was used to determine the load applied, while the mass of the electrode material was used for the load applied to the coin cells.

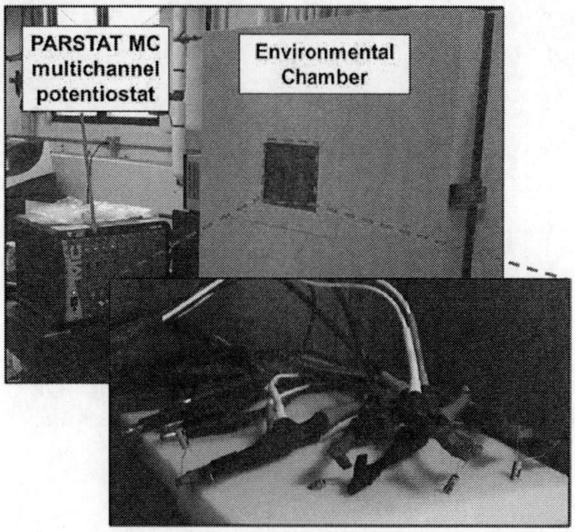

Figure 2. PARSTAT MC potentiostat running into an environmental chamber. An enlarged view of the COTS SCs is shown to display how the SCs were cycled within the chamber.

Testing was conducted from +20°C to -40°C (+68ºF to -40ºF). Increments of 10°C were taken in which a 30-minute dwell time occurred at each temperature to ensure proper soaking.

Discussion

Initial testing of the fabricated coin cells showed a working voltage of 3V with a total capacity of 500μF. To best compare the performance of COTS SCs to the fabricated coin cells, all comparisons in this work were made to the smallest capacity SCs ordered. These COTS SCs have a total capacity of 500mF with a working voltage of 2.5V. From this immediate comparison it is apparent that the utilization of an ionic liquid-based electrolyte allows for a greater operational voltage window which in turn can result in much higher cell capacity due to the direct relation between capacity and working voltage of SCs.

The main electrochemical data compared in this work is the constant current charge and discharge data of both the COTS and ionic liquid-based electrolyte coin cell SC. This data set was chosen based on the low temperature performance of the COTS SC. At -40°C (-40ºF) the COTS SC struggled to cycle and generated mostly noise, which can be seen in Fig. 3. It is important to note that this erratic behavior began at -30°C (-22ºF). The current density of 5A/g was chosen because this rate allowing for fast, yet stable charging of both the COTS and coin cell SCs at all temperature in which the SCs cycled. The coin cells were able to charge at up to 10A/g, while the COTS SC were only able to charge up to 5A/g.

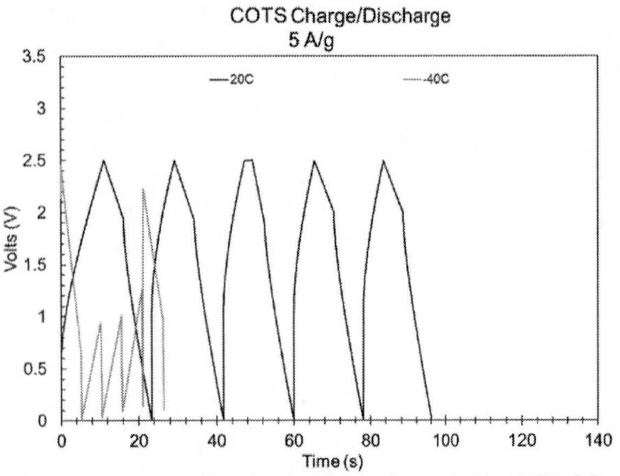

Figure 3. Charge/Discharge data of a 300mF COTS SC. The rate of charging was 5A/g. Data for charging at +20°C (+68°F) (black) and -40°C (-40°F) (orange) is shown.

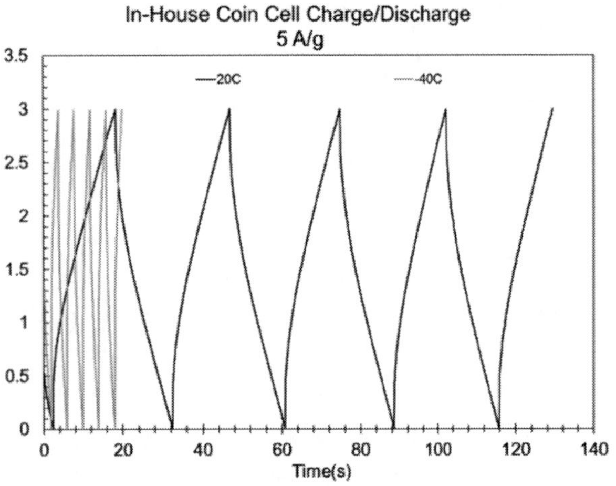

Figure 4. Charge/Discharge data of a 500μF coin cell SC with ionic liquid-based electrolyte. The rate of charging was 5A/g. Data for charging at +20°C (+68°F) (black) and -40°C (-40°F) (orange) is shown.

Fig. 4 shows the charge and discharge data of an in-house ionic liquid-based coin cell. From this data, the charge and discharge time is dramatically reduced when comparing the +20°C (+68°F) data to the -40°C (-40°F). This is due to a loss in capacity of the coin cell as the temperature drops. The capacity loss is shown in Fig. 5 in which the capacity of three cells are displayed. The capacity decreases from 500μF to 100μF between +20°C (+68°F) and -40°C (-40°F). When utilizing the room temperature capacity measurements as a baseline, the capacity loss as a percentage was calculated and shown in Fig. 5. What was observed was a loss of up to 75% the original capacity as temperature reached -40°C (-40°F).

The capacity reduction in attributed to the increase of the equivalent series resistance of the cells as temperature is decreased. The ESR increase is most likely due to the AN beginning to freeze. This conclusion can be made when analyzing Fig.5 and Fig.6. As temperature is reduced from +20°C (+68°F) to -20°C (-4°F) a linear reduction in capacity can be seen. As temperature continues to drop, the reduction of capacity becomes more exponential. The temperature range in which this occurs is also the temperature range the AN begins to freeze. Despite its use as an electrolyte additive for increased conductivity, AN is still not an ideal additive when operating at temperatures below -30°C (-22°F).

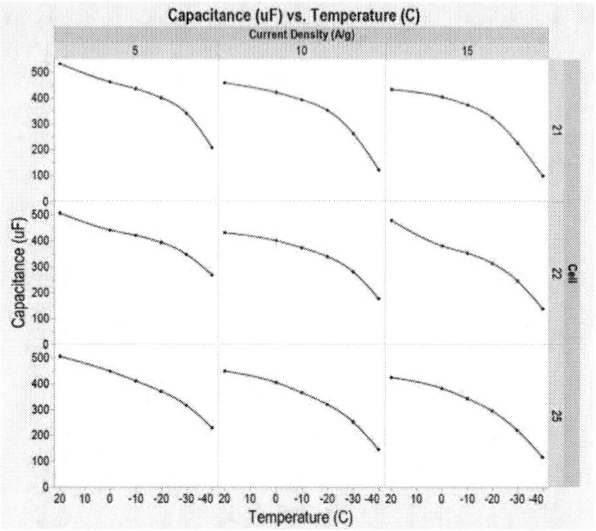

Figure 5. Charge/Discharge data of a 500μF coin cell SC with ionic liquid-based electrolyte. The rate of charging was 5A/g. Data for charging +20°C (+68°F) (black) and -40°C (-40°F) (orange) is shown.

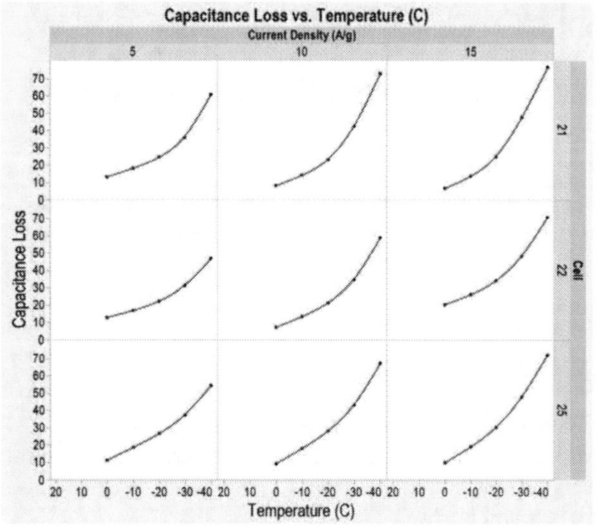

Figure 6. Charge/Discharge data of a 500μF coin cell SC with ionic liquid-based electrolyte. The rate of charging was 5A/g. Data for charging at +20°C (+68°F) (black) and -40°C (-40°F) (orange) is shown.

Conclusion

COTS SCs were cycled from +20°C to -40°C (+68°F to -40°F) to understand their performance stability at extreme low temperatures. From this testing it was observed that they begin to show poor and unreliable performance at temperatures at and below -30°C (-22°F). A solution of $EMIMBF_4$ in AN electrolyte was formulated as a drop-in replacement to the standard AN electrolyte to improve performance. The electrolyte was studied in a coin cell configuration in which improved performance was observed. The working voltage of the coin cells outperformed COTS SCs, while the electrolyte was also able to handle higher current loads. Additionally, the electrolytes allowed for the charging and discharging at temperature up to -40°C (-40°F).

Although the coin cells did cycle, there was still a considerable 75% reduction of capacity at -40°C (-40°F) which can make this electrolyte unreliable when high power applications are vital. This reduction of capacity is due to the freezing of the AN additive. Further optimization of a drop-in replacement electrolyte is needed with a focus on solvents that have freezing points lower than -40°C (-40°F) if low temperature operation is desirable.

Acknowledgements

This work is supported by engineers from DEVCOM-AC's Fuze Division, and Advanced Materials Division

References

1. Winter, M., Brodd, R., "What Are Batteries, Fuel Cells, and Supercapacitors." *Chem Rev.* 2004, 104, 4245-4369
2. Poonam, Sharma, K., Arora, A., & Tripathi, S. (2019, 2 1). Review of supercapacitors: Materials and devices. *Journal of Energy Storage, 21*, 801-825. Elsevier Ltd.
3. Guo, J., Ye, M., Zhao, K., Cui, J., Yang, B., Meng, J., & Yan, X. (2020, 8 5). High voltage supercapacitor based on nonflammable high-concentration-ionic liquid electrolyte. *Colloids and Surfaces A: Physicochemical and Engineering Aspects, 598.*
4. Wang, D., Wang, Y., Liu, H., Xu, W., & Xu, L. (2018, 6 15). Unusual carbon nanomesh constructed by interconnected carbon nanocages for ionic liquid-based supercapacitor with superior rate capability. *Chemical Engineering Journal, 342*, 474-483.
5. Wong, S., Lin, H., Sunarso, J., Wong, B., & Jia, B. (2020, 3 1). Optimization of ionic-liquid based electrolyte concentration for high-energy density graphene supercapacitors. *Applied Materials Today, 18.*
6. Yao, B., Peng, H., Zhnag, H.(2021, 3 10). Printing Porous Carbon Aerogels for Low Temperature Supercapacitors. *Nano Letters, 21, 9, 3731–3737*

Creating Stable Interfaces in Lithium-Metal Batteries via Initiated Chemical Vapor Deposition Nanoscale Coatings

Ramsay B. Nuwayhid[1], Junghoon Yeom[2], Hunter O. Ford[1], Matthew J. Lefler[1], Rachel E. Carter[3], and Corey T. Love[3]

[1]*National Research Council Postdoctoral Associate, U.S. Naval Research Laboratory, Washington, DC, USA*
[2]*Multifunctional Materials Branch (Code 6354), U.S. Naval Research Laboratory, Washington, DC, USA*
[3]*Surface Chemistry Branch (Code 6170), U.S. Naval Research Laboratory, Washington, DC, USA*

ABSTRACT: Anode-Free Li-metal Batteries (AFLBs) are poised to meet the demands required for high-energy power across a broad range of applications. AFLBs offer substantial improvements in energy density compared to conventional anodes, however are hindered by irreversible Li plating/stripping causing rapid capacity loss and buildup of deleterious solid-electrolyte interphase (SEI) layers. To overcome such hurdles, we employ initiated chemical vapor deposition (iCVD) of polymeric coatings as a means to stabilize the Cu-liquid electrolyte interface and mitigate parasitic reactions giving rise to rapid capacity loss in AFLBs. Nanoscale coatings (7-100 nm) of poly(1,3,5-trivinyl-1,3,5-trimethylcyclotrisiloxane) (pV3D3) are applied to Cu current collectors and characterized vs Li metal in coin-cells. Cycling behavior shows a significant improvement with pV3D3 coatings, resulting in a Columbic efficiency >80% for over 100 cycles, more than double that of uncoated Cu. This is attributed to the moderate Li^+ conductivity of pV3D3 (10^{-7} S/cm) promoting homogeneous Li plating/stripping while minimizing SEI formation. This work provides the mechanistic understanding of iCVD polycyclosiloxane layers on Li plating/stripping and demonstrates the capability of conformal interface engineering for enabling next-generation AFLBs.

Keywords: initiated chemical vapor deposition, Li-metal battery, solid-electrolyte interphase, interface engineering

Introduction

Lithium metal is the ideal anode choice for rechargeable batteries due to its maximum theoretical capacity of 3860 mAh/g and light weight compared to conventional graphite anodes (372 mAh/g). The integration of Li metal into batteries comes with its own set of challenges centered upon the extreme reactivity of the metal, inducing significant precautions required for manufacturing due to the extreme H_2O and O_2 sensitivity of Li. A promising approach to alleviate this issue is the construction of anode-free cells, in which the battery is assembled without an anode material and Li is plated from the cathode onto the negative Cu current collector.[1] Nevertheless, the realization of stable anode-free Li-metal batteries (AFLBs) are hindered by low coulombic efficiency (CE) and the formation of unstable solid-electrolyte interphases (SEI) as a result of heterogeneous Li metal plating and stripping at the Cu current collector.

Thin-film coatings have proved the ability to stabilize reactive interfaces in battery systems through the passivation of electrodes and formation of stable interphases between electrodes-electrolytes.[2, 3] Such coatings are typically ceramic metal oxides deposited by atomic layer deposition (ALD) that inherently require high deposition temperatures (>150 °C) and slow deposition rates (0.1-1 nm/min). Initiated chemical vapor deposition (iCVD) is a similar technique to ALD that has more recently demonstrated an enhanced performance with nanoscale electrode passivation in Li-ion batteries.[4-6] The iCVD technique is attractive for applications in battery systems due to its ability to apply nano-to-micro scale coatings with excellent conformality at ambient temperatures (20-50 °C) and high rates (several nm/min). In this work, nanoscale coatings of poly(1,3,5-trivinyl-1,3,5-trimethylcyclotrisiloxane) (pV3D3) are applied to Cu current collectors to promote homogenous and stable Li metal plating and stripping at the Cu current collector. Through nanoscale (7-100 nm) pV3D3 coatings we observe a significant enhancement in the efficiency of Li metal plating and stripping at the Cu electrode, demonstrating the potential of iCVD coatings to offer improvements in AFLBs. We also characterize the role of the pV3D3 layer on Li plating/stripping mechanistically and offer insights towards iCVD interface optimization.

Results and Discussion

The thickness of pV3D3 thin-films on Cu foils were determined from spectroscopic ellipsometry (SE) measurements on Si wafers that were included with the Cu foil for each batch of pV3D3 deposition. Figure 1a shows the corresponding thickness measurements for deposition times ranging from 5 to 42 minutes. A linear increase in film thickness with time is observed from 5-30 minutes with an average growth rate of 1.4 nm/minute. Above 30 minute deposition times, the growth rate nearly doubles to 2.7 nm/minute. This increase in growth rate is attributed to prolonged substrate heating from the hot filament for the longer depositions. However, despite the increase in growth rate of pV3D3 films with deposition times, a strong agreement is observed for the refractive index of each film shown in Figure 1b. The refractive index curve saturates at 1.52 for the 13 nm pV3D3 film and slightly decreases to a value of 1.50 for 53 nm and 100 nm pV3D3 films. The similar optical properties for pV3D3 films with thickness confirms that the film morphology is consistent from a few nm up to 100 nm.

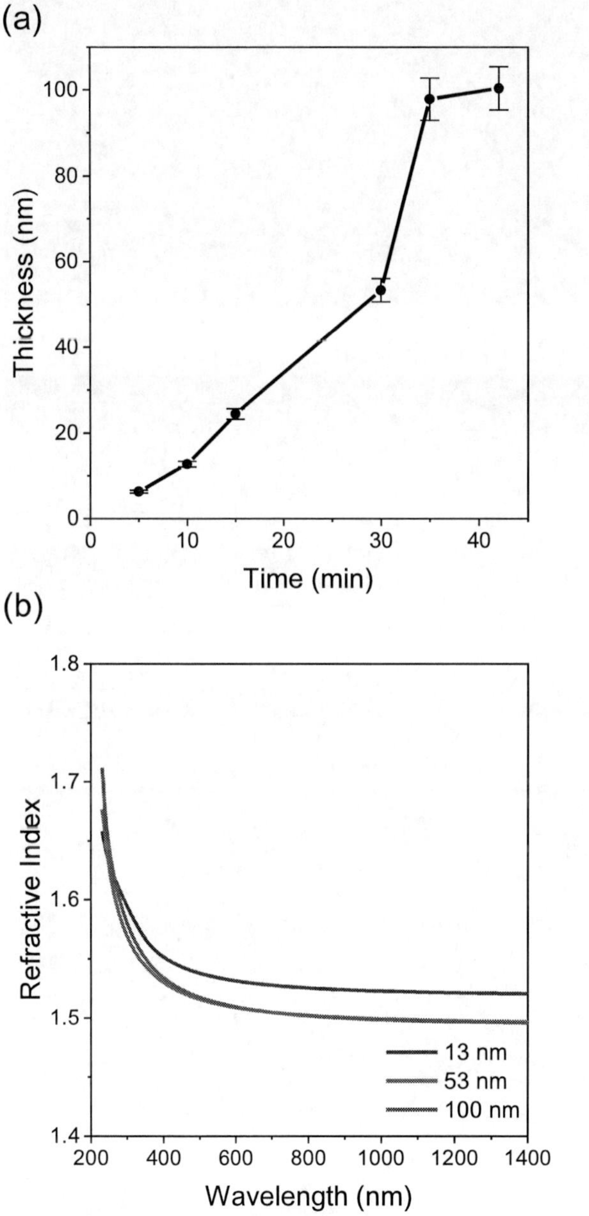

Figure 1. Spectroscopic ellipsometry of pV3D3. (a) Thickness vs. time of pV3D3 depositions. (b) Refractive index as a function of wavelength for 13, 53, and 100 nm pV3D3.

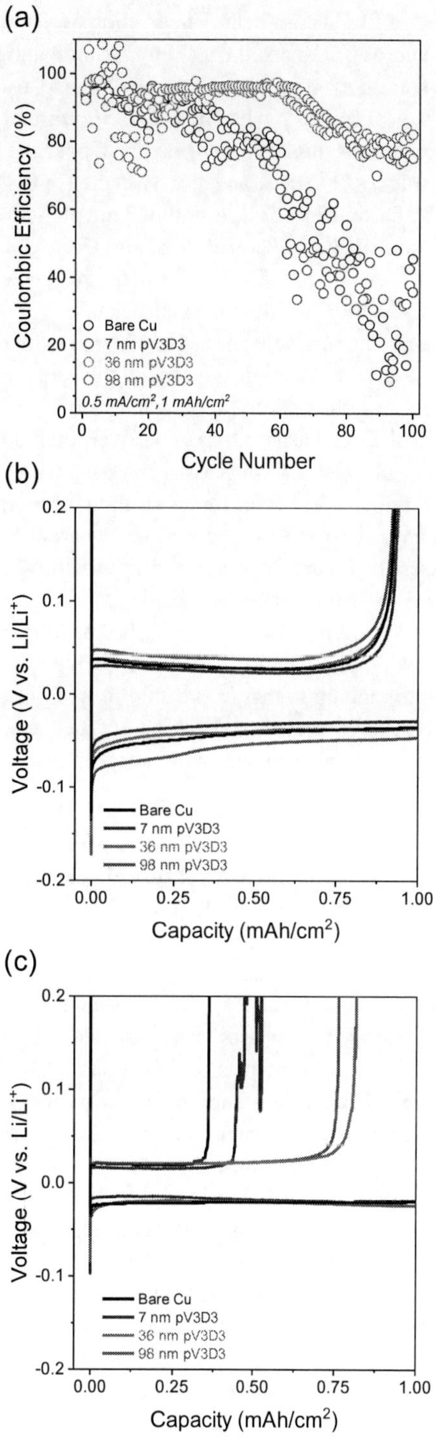

Figure 2. Galvanostatic cycling of bare Cu and pV3D3/Cu electrodes. (a) Coulombic efficiency for 100 cycles. (b) Voltage profiles for cycle 1 and (c) cycle 100. Li metal was plated at a capacity of 1 mAh/cm^2 and charged up to 1 V at 0.5 mA/cm^2 for each cycle.

The effect of pV3D3 on Li metal plating/stripping was evaluated by characterizing the electrochemical cycling efficiency of Li/Cu coin-cells. The cycling performance of bare Cu and pV3D3-coated Cu (7 nm, 36 nm, and 98 nm) cells are summarized in Figure 2. Figure 2a displays the CE of each cell over 100 cycles, in which 36 nm and 97 nm pV3D3 exhibit the highest performance. Both cells retain a CE >90% for ~70 cycles, and slowly decrease to 82% for 36 nm pV3D3 and 75%. The ultrathin 7 nm pV3D3 coating shows minimal improvement to bare Cu, which both electrodes fell below 80% CE after 50 cycles. The individual cycling profiles of each cell are displayed in Figure 2b and 2c for cycle and cycle 100, respectively. The potential for Li nucleation is seen in the large negative voltage spike followed by a plateau region for lithium growth in the discharge curve. The overpotential for Li nucleation in cycle 1 increases linearly with pV3D3 thickness, which is expected for an insulating film in which the dielectric properties become more apparent at higher thicknesses. In Figure 2c, the instability and low capacity of 7 nm pV3D3 is observed displaying heterogeneous voltage spikes during the strip step, whereas 36 nm and 98 nm pV3D3 display stable Li stripping behavior at cycle 100 despite the slight charge capacity drop from cycle 1. These observed phenomena demonstrate the capability of pV3D3 to promote enhanced Li metal plating/stripping.

The surface morphology of electrodeposited Li metal on pV3D3-modified Cu current collectors was characterized with SEM to explain the observed electrochemical phenomena of the Li/Cu cells. Figure 3 shows SEM images of the resulting surface morphology for bare Cu and pV3D3-modified Cu (7 nm and 53 nm). We investigate a 53 nm pV3D3 coating since it is in-between the 36 nm and 98 nm coating thicknesses that resulted in optimum electrochemical performance. In Figure 3a and 3b, bare Cu and 7 nm pV3D3/Cu show similar surface morphologies of Li, in which high surface area Li nucleates are observed in an island-like fashion proceeding towards film growth. This heterogeneous nucleation and growth of Li is known to induces buildup of undesired SEI products leading to the irreversible Li plating/stripping observed in Figure 2.[7] This result implies that the 7 nm pV3D3 has a minimal effect on the interaction of Li with Cu, due to the non-uniform deposition of ultrathin pV3D3 on Cu in such a short deposition time (5 minutes). In Figure 3c, the 53 nm pV3D3 coating is seen to facilitate uniform growth of smooth a smooth Li film, as no exposed areas of the current collector are observed. This supports the evidence for homogeneous and efficient Li plating and stripping for 36 nm and 98 nm pV3D3 coatings observed in Figure 2. The dramatic improvement in surface morphology and electrochemistry with pV3D3 >36 nm is attributed to a uniform and dense pV3D3 passivating the Cu surface, promoting uniform Li^+ transport and preventing buildup of SEI on the Li from the liquid electrolyte. Furthermore, the optical images of the 15 mm diameter electrodes in the insets of Figure 3 clearly demonstrate the stark differences in Li interaction with the substrate dependent on pV3D3 coating.

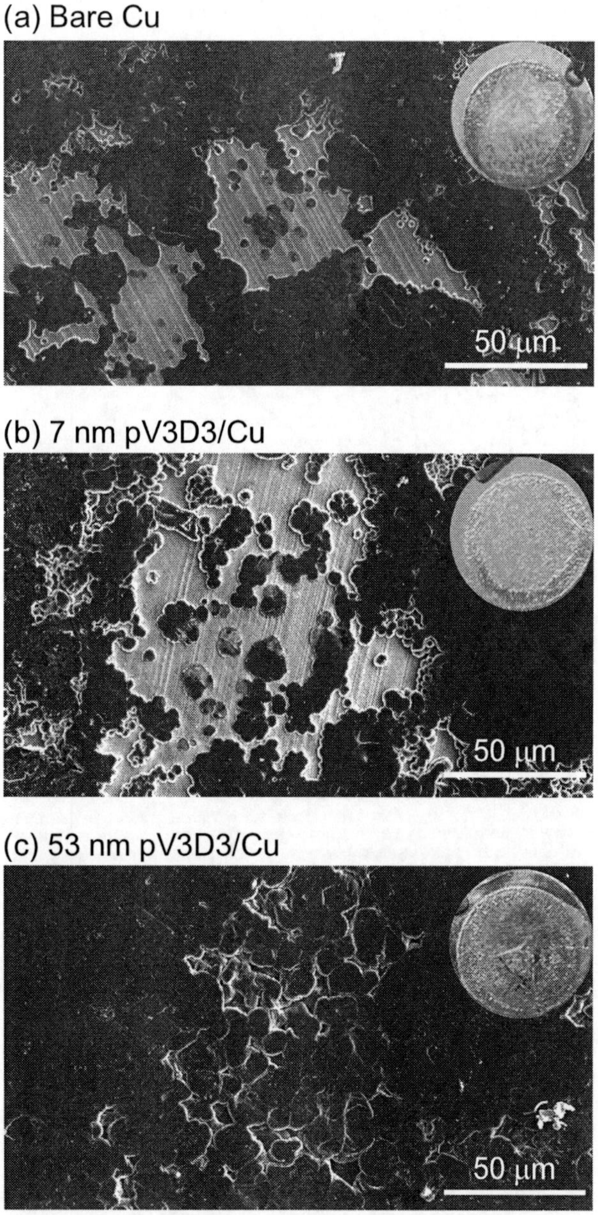

Figure 3. Surface morphology of Li on bare Cu and pV3D3/Cu. SEM image of 1 mAh/cm² Li deposit on (a) bare Cu, (b) 7nm pV3D3/Cu, and (c) 53 nm pV3D3/Cu. Optical image shown of each electrode in the inset.

Conclusions

In this work we demonstrate the importance and capability of nanotechnology in improving battery performance. Thin-film iCVD coatings of pV3D3 are observed to have a dramatic effect on the interaction of Li metal with Cu current collectors. Ultrathin coatings (7 nm) display minimal changes than uncoated current collectors, whereas 36-98 nm pV3D3 coatings display a substantial enhancement in coulombic efficiency and Li plating/stripping stability. This enhancement is explained through the uniform film surface morphology of thicker pV3D3 coatings compared to the heterogeneous high surface area Li deposits for ultrathin pV3D3 and bare Cu. This result demonstrates the promising capability of iCVD pV3D3 films to operate as stable interfaces in Li metal and AFLBs.

Experimental Procedures

Cu foils were prepared for iCVD deposition by rinsing with 0.5 M nitric acid, deionized water, and acetone in a stepwise manner, then blown dry with nitrogen. The iCVD depositions were performed in a GVD Corporation reactor. The V3D3 monomer (>95%, Gelest) was heated to 40 °C and the di-tert-butyl peroxide (TBPO 98%, Aldrich) initiator was kept at room temperature. The lines to the reactor were heated to 70 °C and the reactor substrate was held at 25 °C. Depositions were carried out at 200 mTorr with a flow of 1 SCCM TBPO and monomer flow controlled by a ball hand valve. Thermal excitation was achieved by resistively heating a Nichrome filament to 35 V (~2A, 220 °C).

SE characterization was performed on pV3D3 coated Si wafers using a J.A. Woolam M-2000D ellipsometer. Data was collected at variable angles (55° and 75°) and film thickness was modeled using a general oscillator model consisting of Tauc-Lorentz and Gaussian oscillators. The mean-square error for fittings of pV3D3 films <30 nm was 1.8 and increased slightly to 8 for 100 nm films, confirming a high-quality fit of the model to the experimental data.

Half-cells vs. Li metal were assembled in an Ar glovebox for electrochemical testing. A 1M lithium bis(trifluoromethanesulfonyl)imide (LiTFSI) / 0.2M lithium nitrate ($LiNO_3$) in 1,3-diloxolane (DOL) / 1,2-dimethoxyethane (DME) electrolyte was used with Entek gold separators. Charge/discharge measurements were performed on a Maccor cycler, discharging to 1 mAh/cm^2 and charging to 1 V at a rate of 0.5 mA/cm^2.

For SEM characterization, cells were dissembled in an Ar glovebox, rinsed with DME and dried under vacuum, then transferred to the SEM in an air-tight container. A FEI Nova 600 NanoLab SEM was used for imaging at the following conditions: 5.00 kV, 0.80 nA, 5.00 µs dwell time, and 1000x mag.

Acknowledgements

This research was performed while RBN, HOF, and MJL held National Research Council Postdoctoral Associateship Awards at the U.S. Naval Research Laboratory. The authors thank the program officer, Dr. Michele Anderson of the Office of Naval Research, for funding this work under award number N0001420WX01405.

References

1. Nanda, S.; Gupta, A.; Manthiram, A., Anode-Free Full Cells: A Pathway to High-Energy Density Lithium-Metal Batteries. *Advanced Energy Materials* **2021,** *11* (2), 2000804.
2. Zhao, Y.; Zheng, K.; Sun, X., Addressing Interfacial Issues in Liquid-Based and Solid-State Batteries by Atomic and Molecular Layer Deposition. *Joule* **2018,** *2* (12), 2583-2604.
3. Lin, C.-F.; Qi, Y.; Gregorczyk, K.; Lee, S. B.; Rubloff, G. W., Nanoscale Protection Layers To Mitigate Degradation in High-Energy Electrochemical Energy Storage Systems. *Accounts of Chemical Research* **2018,** *51* (1), 97-106.
4. Carter, R.; Parker, J. F.; Sassin, M. B.; Klein, E. J.; Wolak, M. A.; Love, C. T.; Long, J. W., Initiated Chemical Vapor Deposition of Ultrathin Polymer Coatings at Graphite Electrodes for Enhanced Performance in Li-Ion Batteries. *Journal of The Electrochemical Society* **2020,** *167* (6).
5. Reeja-Jayan, B.; Chen, N.; Lau, J.; Kattirtzi, J. A.; Moni, P.; Liu, A.; Miller, I. G.; Kayser, R.; Willard, A. P.; Dunn, B.; Gleason, K. K., A Group of Cyclic Siloxane and Silazane Polymer Films as Nanoscale Electrolytes for Microbattery Architectures. *Macromolecules* **2015,** *48* (15), 5222-5229.
6. Shen, B. H.; Wang, S.; Tenhaeff, W. E., Ultrathin conformal polycyclosiloxane films to improve silicon cycling stability. *Science Advances* **2019,** *5* (7), eaaw4856.
7. Pei, A.; Zheng, G.; Shi, F.; Li, Y.; Cui, Y., Nanoscale Nucleation and Growth of Electrodeposited Lithium Metal. *Nano Letters* **2017,** *17* (2), 1132-1139.

Fluorinated Battery Electrolytes for High Silicon Anodes and High Voltage Cell Designs

Tobias O. Johnson, Peng Du, Sarah Guillot, Monica Usrey, and *Liu Zhou*
Koura Global, Inc. 3587 Anderson St, Suite 108, Madison WI 53704
tobias.johnson@kouraglobal.com 608-661-1961

Abstract: *Lithium-ion cells with high Si-content anodes encounter myriad challenges in delivering long term cycling stability due to anode pulverization, impedance growth, low efficiency, Lithium loss, and gassing. These factors are compounded when paired with high energy density cathodes (e.g., high-nickel, high-voltage lithium cobalt oxide - LCO). These high energy density designs (>400 Wh/kg) require finely balanced electrolyte formulations which often employ fluorinated solvents, blended Lithium salts, and various anode SEI and cathode CEI additives to stabilize the highly reactive surfaces.*

Although Li-ion technology has advanced significantly over the last decade, traditional electrolytes can rapidly decompose in the high energy density systems at the highly reactive electrode surface interfaces. New advanced electrolytes must be integrated into the cell design to increase energy density, increase charge voltage, improve performance, reliability, and safety of Li-ion batteries.

We have commercialized an advanced organosilane (OS) solvent "OS3®" that prevents $LiPF_6$ decomposition, reduces solvent decomposition, passivates the cathode surface, scavenges HF, and enables fluorinated solvents like FEC to function more effectively. Due to these properties, OS3® has demonstrated performance improvements in high Si cells such as extended cycling stability with reduced cell gassing and impedance growth associated with FEC.

This paper discusses insight into the mechanistic origins of the OS3® material benefits in high energy Si anode cells. XPS surface analysis demonstrated that high temperature (HT) storage and cycling have significant impacts on the anode and cathode surfaces in 4.35V LCO/Si multi-layer pouch cells. The amount of silicon detected on anode surfaces was very low, indicating that a thick surface layer forms that attenuates the underlying silicon signal. SEM images showed reduced surface cracking with OS3® after RT cycling. XPS cathode analysis shows that OS3® affects the cathode surface layer composition (increase in %Si, %S, and %C-H along with decrease in %C-O and %C=O).

Significant portions of this development and analysis work were funded by the Office of Naval Research (ONR) contract N00014-20-C-1053.

Keywords: electrolyte; Lithium Ion; solvent; organosilicon; OS; OS3®; LIB; high voltage; high temperature; thermal stability; oxidation; reduction; impedance; safety; solvation; $LiPF_6$; Lithium; SEI; solid electrolyte interphase; energy storage; ONR; LCO; Silicon; Si; SiO; gassing; ONR; Office of Naval Research; Navy; DOD; battery; cell; molecule; electrochemical; electrochemistry; fluorine; anode; cathode; cycling

Introduction

Silatronix, now operating as the Madison Technology Center within Koura Global, has developed organosilicon (OS) materials using targeted molecular design to provide desirable electrochemical characteristics for Li-ion applications. The design of unique organosilicon molecules includes selection of specific ion coordinating functional groups, degree of fluorination, and structure optimization to balance molecular polarity, ionic conductivity, and viscosity. The inclusion of Si and F in the molecule is critical to the thermal and electrochemical stability. Multiple OS materials have demonstrated excellent performance in Lithium Ion Battery (LIB) systems.

The commercial solvent "OS3®" provides exceptional thermal, and electrochemical stability in LIB systems up to 4.5V with current commercially available electrode materials; and fundamental oxidation stability up to 7V in a platinum reference cell. OS3® has low viscosity, good ionic conductivity, a high flash point (>80°C), and low freezing point (<-55°C) as shown in Table 1. The most comprehensive performance benefits are observed at < 5% OS3®, which fits comfortably within the additive market space of the LIB industry.

Table 1. Physical Characteristics of OS3®

Dielectric	Flash	BP	FP	SG	Visc.
16.8	82°C	202°C	-57°C	0.93	2.0cP

OS3® is a strong coordinator of Li salts in the electrolyte solution preventing both $LiPF_6$ decomposition and catalytic HF production. Elimination of these reactions is critical to enabling high energy LIB systems with long calendar life and stable high temperature performance. OS3 reduces long-term impedance growth. OS3® also significantly reduces gas generation by stabilizing the cathode / electrolyte interface of high energy cathodes that can initiate oxidative decomposition, as illustrated in Figure 1.

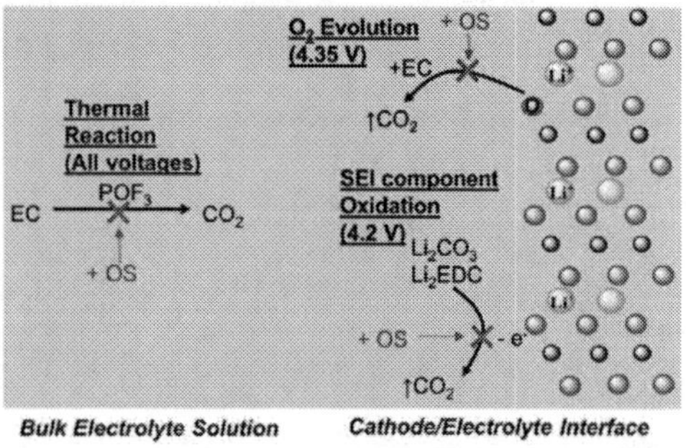

Figure 1. Mechanisms for OS nitrile gas reduction.

Several commercial cell development partners in the US, Asia, and Europe have observed practical improvements to comprehensive cell performance in multiple LIB systems, including excellent HT cycling stability, reduced impedance growth, improved calendar life rate capability, reduced gas generation, improved safety, and improved low temperature rate capability. Benefits have been observed with a variety of cell chemistries but there is a specific synergy between Si anodes and OS3® that improves cycling stability, lowers impedance, and protects the Si anode structure.

This paper summarizes the benefits of OS3® for high-Si content anodes / LCO cathodes. Analysis of the anode and cathode surfaces following cycle life testing provides insights into the mechanism by which OS3® improves cell performance. Full format cell testing and fundamental research of OS technology has been completed with ONR funding, including development efforts on contract N00014-20-C-1053 with collaboration with cell development partner Amprius Technologies. Amprius has developed a 100% Si nanowire anode technology which is paired with a high voltage LCO cathode to produce the highest energy density commercial cell design currently on the market.

Results and Discussion

Reduced gassing in Si nanowire / HV LCO pouch cells

Amprius provided ~ 200 mAh pouch cells with 2-sided Si nanowire anodes sandwiched between 2 single sided LCO cathodes for testing at Silatronix®.

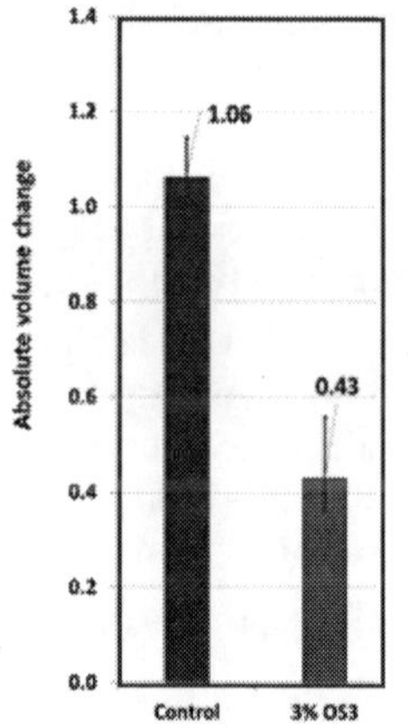

Figure 2: Cell gassing after RT cycling

Electrolyte optimization was conducted to improve the 30°C cycling performance (C/2 rate, 2.75V-4.35V) of a control electrolyte that was a blend of EC, EMC, FEC (<10v%), 1M $LiPF_6$, plus multiple additives at <5% combined concentration (VC, succinonitile, and adiponitrile). Addition of OS3® (3%v) resulted in the significant reduction of gas generation (i.e., 60% lower cell swelling) after 220 cycles at 30°C in the high energy density Amprius cells (Figure 2).

Surface Morphology Analysis using SEM

After 30°C cycling, surface analysis was conducted on Si anodes recovered from the high energy density Si/LCO Amprius cells to investigate the impact of OS3® addition on the morphology and topography of the Si anodes. Cells were disassembled at 50% SOC in an Argon glove box to prevent exposure to oxygen and moisture. Figure 3 shows the images collected for the control (top) and 3% OS3® (bottom) electrolyte formulations.

All anodes showed two distinct areas across the surface of the Si anodes. These are labeled "lighter" and "darker" based on the SEM images. The morphology of the Si anodes in the "darker" areas are very similar for both electrolyte formulations, as the silicon nanowires are clearly visible. However, the SEM images of the "lighter" areas show significant differences. The anode cycled with the OS3® electrolyte displays significantly reduced cracking compared to the control and any observed cracks were significantly smaller than those in the control.

This imaging suggests that the surface layer formed by the OS3® electrolyte is more flexible and stable than that formed by the control electrolyte and results in a more robust surface chemistry that is less prone to cracking during the volume expansion associated with Si anode cycling.

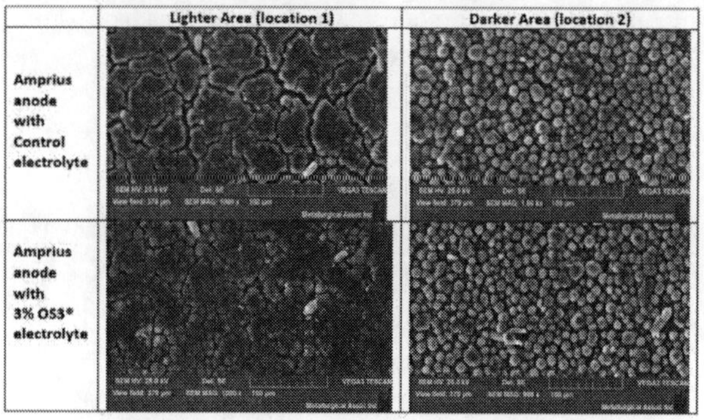

Figure 3: SEM images of Amprius Si anodes after 30°C cycling with control and OS3® electrolytes.

Surface Composition Analysis after Formation (XPS)

After formation of the Amprius 2-layer Si nanowire/LCO pouches, XPS surface analysis was conducted to understand differences in the SEI layer composition depending on electrolyte formulation. Formulations shown Table 2 include additions of OS3® and other OS family molecules with higher degrees of fluorination. OS3®, OS5, and OS6 are all fluorinated organosilicon nitrile molecules. OS3® has the lowest fluorination. OS6 has the greatest fluorination. The concentration of higher fluorinated molecules was adjusted based on previous results that show better performance at lower concentrations.

Table 2: Electrolyte formulations for surface analysis

Formulation Description (vol.%)	Solvents (vol.%)				Additives (vol. %)		
	EC	DEC	EMC	FEC	OS3	OS3-X	VC
Control	30	30	29	10	-	-	1
3% OS3	29	29	28	10	3	-	1
1% OS5	30	29	29	10	-	1	1
0.5% OS6	30	29.5	29	10	-	0.5	1

Figure 4 shows the elemental composition of the Si anode surface layer after formation for the 4 electrolyte formulations shown in Table 2. This data shows that each OS material changes the surface layer in a unique way. While the different concentrations of the added OS may be a factor in the chemical diversity of their anode SEIs, each OS material appears to have a distinct mechanism.

With 3% OS3®, the effect on composition is decreased carbon, oxygen, and cobalt, and increased fluorine and lithium. There is no significant increase in silicon or nitrogen. This suggests that 3% OS3® reduces carbonate decomposition (C, O) and increases salt decomposition (Li, F) while not significantly decomposing itself.

1% OS5 decreases oxygen and increases fluorine (similar to OS3®) but does not impact carbon or lithium. Therefore, OS5 likely affects salt decomposition (F) but not in the exact manner as OS3®. The OS5 surface layer has significant signal from silicon and nitrogen, which indicates that OS5 is forming part of the SEI layer.

Finally, 0.5% OS6 is similar in composition to the control anode for all major elements, while showing increased phosphorus and decreased silicon and cobalt. The lack of silicon and nitrogen signal indicates a lack of direct participation in SEI layer formation.

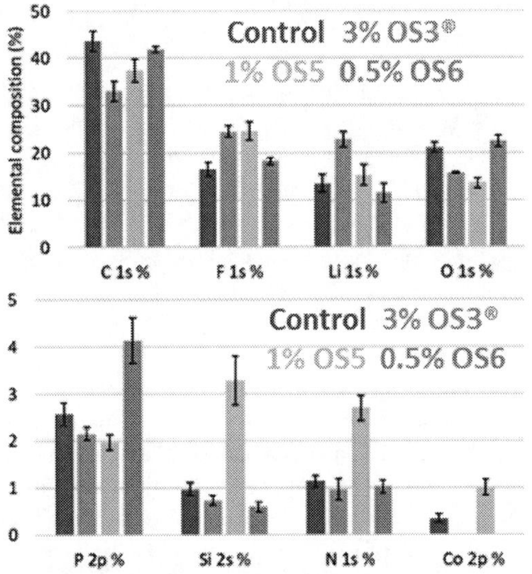

Figure 4: Elemental composition after formation (Si anode).

Examination of the carbon components comprising the overall carbon signal provides more specific information of the impact of OS addition on SEI layer formation (Figure 5). Component analysis shows that all OS materials reduce the most highly oxidized CO_3 component which indicates that OS3®, OS5, and OS6 all impact decomposition of the carbonate solvents. However, 3% OS3® is the only OS that also reduces the C-H and C-O components. This shows that OS3® has the strongest overall impact on carbonate solvent decomposition by impacting multiple mechanisms.

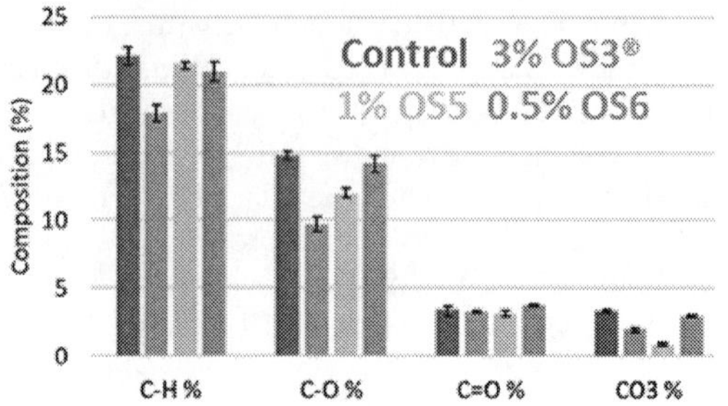

Figure 5: Carbon components after formation (Si anode).

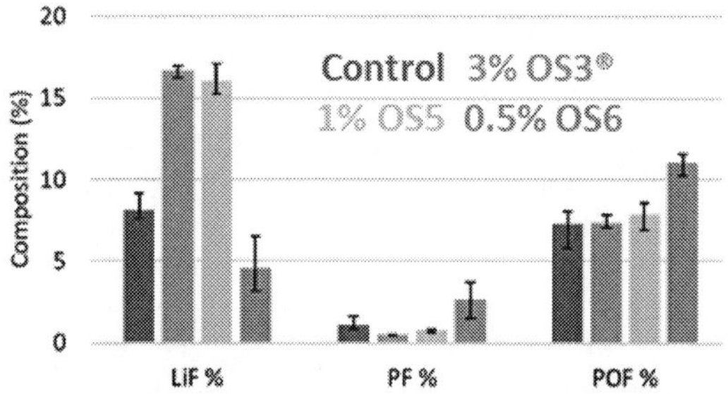

Figure 6: Fluorine components after formation (Si anode).

The impact of OS addition on $LiPF_6$ salt-related SEI layer formation mechanisms was studied by examination of the fluorine components comprising the overall fluorine signal (Figure 5). Similar to the carbon component analysis, different OS molecules show different behavior. Both OS3® and OS5 have significantly increased LiF content compared to the control or OS6. In contrast, OS6 has reduced LiF content compared to the control but higher PF and POF species which is consistent with the higher total phosphorus observed in Figure 4. This indicates that all OS impact $LiPF_6$ salt decomposition; however, there is a significant difference in mechanism with highest OS fluorination (OS6).

Overall, Figures 4, 5, and 6 clearly show that OS addition in the EC/DEC/EMC/FEC control formulation impacts SEI layer formation on the Si anode. While all OS show impacts on both carbonate solvent and $LiPF_6$ salt decomposition mechanisms, each OS demonstrates distinct behavior.

Surface Composition Analysis after HT testing (XPS)

The effect of HT cell testing on the electrode surface layers in the Amprius LCO/Si cells was studied using XPS after formation, after 100 cycles at 50°C, and after storage at 50°C for three weeks. For these tests, the electrolyte used was EC/EMC 3/7 v% + 1M $LiPF_6$ + 10% FEC + 1% ADN + 2% SN + 1% VC + 3% OS3®.

The cathode surface layer thickness can be estimated by the attenuation of the signal from the bulk electrode (typically PVDF binder). After 50°C storage or 50°C cycling, the cathode surface layer thickness increases (+3.5 nm), with no significant difference between storage or cycling (Figure 7). This indicates that decomposition products formed in the electrolyte are building up on the LCO cathode.

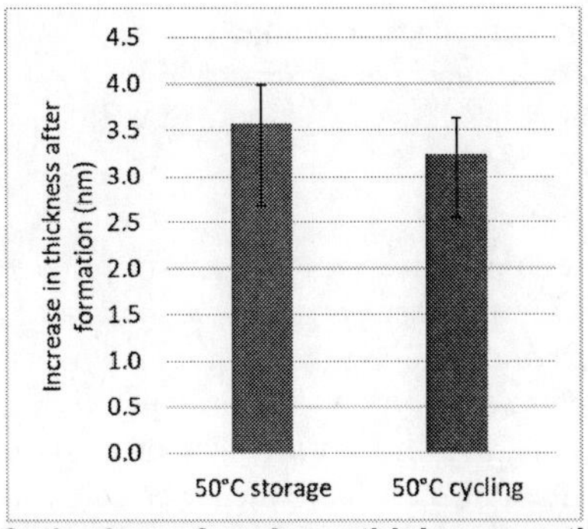

Figure 7: Cathode surface layer thickness estimate after storage or cycling relative to after formation (~1 nm).

The elemental composition of the cathode surface layer after formation, after 50°C storage, and after 50°C cycling is shown in Figure 8.

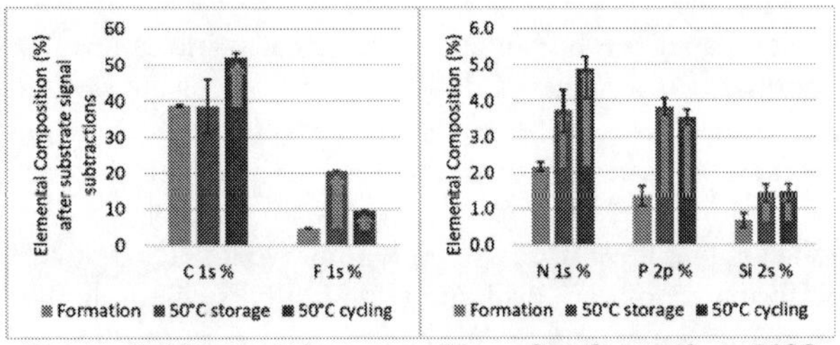

Figure 8: Elemental composition after formation, 50°C storage, and 50°C cycling (LCO cathode).

After 50°C storage, there are significant increases in $LiPF_6$ decomposition (increased fluorine and phosphorus) and evidence of OS3® participation in cathode layer formation (increased silicon and nitrogen). After 50°C cycling, all components increase which shows a similar impact as storage (increased $LiPF_6$ decomposition, OS3® participation) with additional solvent and/or additive decomposition (increased carbon).

The elemental composition of the anode surface layer after formation, after 50°C storage, and after 50°C cycling is shown in Figure 9. The orange line represents the average increase in %Li and is shown directly compared to % differences in other elements and components.

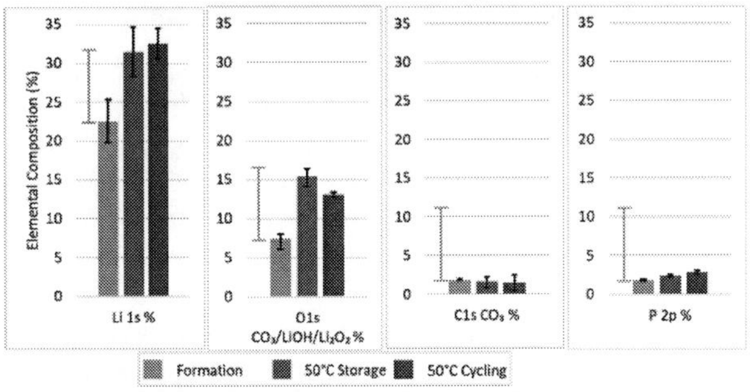

Figure 9: Elemental composition after formation, 50°C storage, and 50°C cycling (Si anode).

The anode surface layer demonstrates increases primarily in lithium and phosphorus after 50°C storage or 50°C cycling relative to after formation. This indicates significant $LiPF_6$ salt decomposition occurs during aging with incorporation of products into the anode SEI throughout cycling and storage. The magnitude of the increase in lithium is significantly greater than that of phosphorus but is matched by the increase in the $CO_3/LiOH/Li_2O_2$ components of the oxygen peak, indicating that on the anode the impact of both cycling and storage is to add lithium oxides to the SEI layer.

Overall, high temperature storage and cycling have significant impacts on both the anode and the cathode surface layers with the EC/EMC 3/7 v% + 1M $LiPF_6$ + 10% FEC + 1% ADN + 2% SN + 1% VC + 3% OS3® electrolyte in Amprius' LCO/Si cells. Visible effects include increasing $LiPF_6$ salt decomposition and increasing solvent and/or additive decomposition (including OS3®).

Conclusions

Organosilicon (OS) solvents have demonstrated excellent performance in Lithium Ion Battery (LIB) systems with Si containing anodes. OS3® functions synergistically with FEC and Si anodes to extend cycling stability while also reducing cell gassing and impedance growth that often accompanies FEC addition. XPS analysis demonstrated that high temperature (HT) storage and cycling have significant impacts on both the anode and the cathode surface in 4.35V LCO/Si multi-layer pouch cells. The amount of silicon detected on anode surfaces was very low, indicating that after formation a thick surface layer has formed that attenuates the underlying silicon signal. Anode SEM images showed less surface cracking with OS3® electrolyte variation after RT cycling. XPS cathode analysis also indicated that OS3® electrolyte affected cathode surface layer composition.

Acknowledgements

The authors wish to thank the Office of Naval Research (ONR) for funding development contract N00014-20-C-1053 to advance organosilicon and Si anode technology, in collaboration with Amprius Technologies and NSWC-Carderock. Additional thanks to The University of Wisconsin – Madison.

References

1. Guillot, S.L.; Usrey, M.; Peña-Hueso, A.; Kerber, B.; Zhou, L.; Du, P.; Johnson, T., Reduced Gassing In Lithium Ion Batteries With Organosilicon Additives. Journal of the Electrochemical Society 2021, 168, 030533.

Fluorinated Battery Electrolytes for Wide Operating Temperature Range

Sarah Guillot[1], Monica Usrey[1], Tobias Johnson[1,] Andy Sharratt[2], Maxine Doran[2],Suresh Sriramulu[2,3]
Koura Global, [1] 3587 Anderson Street, Suite 108, Madison WI 53704, [2] 950 Winter Street, Waltham MA 02451
[3]Suresh.Srirmulu@KouraGlobal.com

Abstract: *Li-ion technology has advanced significantly over the past decade; however, traditional electrolytes based on volatile and flammable organic solvents limit performance under extreme conditions such as high/low temperatures, high voltage, and under fast charge conditions. Koura has developed fluorinated materials for use as solvents / additives in Li-ion battery electrolytes that provide multiple performance advantages. In this paper we highlight the performance of select Koura's fluorinated electrolyte materials in expanding the operating temperature range of graphite-anode/NMC811-cathode pouch cells. Our tests confirm that while conventional ester-based electrolytes can improve low temperature performance of Li-ion cells, the high-temperature stability is quite poor. In contrast, fluorinated solvents not only improve low-temperature performance, but also enable excellent high temperature performance stability.*

Keywords: electrolyte; Lithium Ion; solvent; LIB; low temperature; rate; transport; high temperature; thermal stability; oxidation; reduction; impedance; safety; solvation; $LiPF_6$; Lithium; SEI; solid electrolyte interphase; energy storage; NMC; graphite; gassing; DOE; battery; cell; molecule; electrochemical; electrochemistry; fluorine; anode; cathode; cycling;

Introduction

Li-ion batteries used in Defense applications have to operate under a wide range of operating temperatures. The operating temperature range of Li-ion batteries is dictated by the electrolyte used. In general, electrolytes that enable improved low temperature performance of Li-ion batteries are not stable at higher temperatures or when used with higher voltage cathode materials. For example, methyl acetate, methyl butyrate, and methyl propionate solvents are often used to enhance the low-temperature performance of Li-ion cells. However, these solvents result in poor performance at elevated temperatures. In this paper, we discuss how fluorinated solvents and additives can provide adequate low temperature performance without compromising elevated temperature performance.

Fluorinated Electrolyte Materials

Koura is a fully integrated fluorine technology company with a global footprint that spans mining of fluorine-based minerals to the production of hydrogen fluoride, aluminum fluoride, refrigerants, and medical propellants. We have an emerging business in fluorine-based battery materials. We aim to localize the supply chain for key fluorinated materials used in Li-ion batteries today. In addition, we are developing advanced fluorine-based battery materials.

A focus area for our development is fluorinated solvents and additives for use in Li-ion battery electrolytes. Fluorinated electrolyte components are known to provide multiple benefits to Li-ion battery performance including: improving the safety profile, enabling the use of silicon-based anodes, enabling the use of Mn-rich cathode materials, etc. Koura is leveraging expertise in fluorine chemistry to develop and produce a wide range of fluorinated molecules that have the potential to further enhance Li-ion performance. We have synthesized more than 25 different fluorinated molecules and characterized their physico-chemical properties and electrochemical stability. Rate performance and cycle life were characterized in NMC811/graphite pouch cells across a range of temperatures from -20 °C to 45 °C and charging conditions from C/2 to 4C.

In this paper we highlight two fluorinated molecules – a fluorinated dioxalane (KDC-403) and a fluorinated cyclic carbonate (KDC-301) – that have the potential to expand the operating temperature window of Li-ion cells. We compare the performance of these molecules to commercial ester solvents that have been shown to improve low temperature performance but are also known to not be stable at higher operating temperatures. We present and discuss physico-chemical property as well as electrochemical measurements over a wide temperature range.

Results and Discussion

Bulk Electrolyte Properties: Li^+ Transport: Bulk conductivity and viscosity are commonly cited physical properties in the design of optimized electrolytes for low temperature[1] and fast charge[2] applications. In this study, the low temperature conductivity and viscosity of several electrolytes containing Koura solvents (KDC-301, KDC-403) were compared to a carbonate-only baseline (EC/DEC/EMC – 1/1/1 by volume) and three low temperature optimized electrolytes containing low viscosity ester solvents (methyl acetate – MA, methyl propionate – MP, methyl butyrate – MB). All co-solvents added at 20% by volume. All electrolytes contain 1M $LiPF_6$.

Referring to Figure 1 – top, the ester electrolytes provide the highest bulk conductivity compared to the carbonate control and Koura electrolytes. Overall, methyl propionate (MP) provided the highest conductivity and KDC-301 provided the lowest conductivity. For bulk viscosity (Figure 1 – bottom), a similar trend emerges where the ester-based electrolytes provide the lowest low temperature viscosity while KDC-403 shows lower viscosity compared to the carbonate-only baseline. KDC-301 has the highest viscosity.

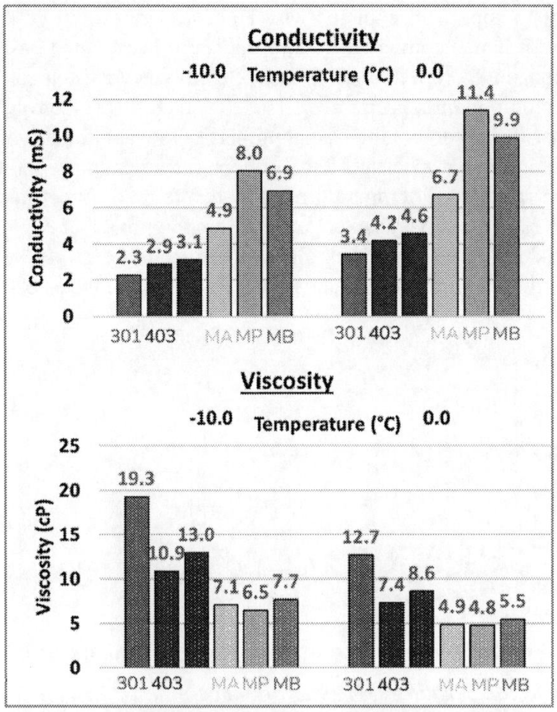

Figure 1. Bulk electrolyte conductivity and viscosity at low temperature (0°C, -10°C).

Li^+ transference number (t_+) is utilized to evaluate Li^+ transport and represents the fraction of the current carried by Li^+ (vs PF_6^-), calculated by comparing the diffusion coefficients of Li^+ and PF_6^-. In general, higher t_+ is better (1 is ideal). The Li^+ conductivity is estimated by multiplying the bulk conductivity by the Li^+ transference number.

Figure 2 summarizes the Li^+ transport parameters for the electrolytes investigated in this study. KDC-403 and methyl butyrate (MB) show the highest Li^+ transference number at 25°C; however, the ester solvents show significantly higher Li^+ conductivity. Overall, methyl propionate (MP) provides the highest Li^+ conductivity.

Based upon the bulk transport data summarized in Figure 1 and Figure 2, we would expect the ester electrolytes should provide the best low temperature performance (specifically methyl propionate), KDC-403 should perform slightly better than the control, and KDC-301 should provide the worst low temperature performance. However, as discussed below, cell performance does not always follow this expectation.

Electrochemical Performance

Low Temperature Performance in Gr/NMC81 pouch cells: Low temperature rate capability performance was evaluated in Gr/NMC811 pouch cells (~ 230 mAh, 4.3V – 2.75V) by measuring the C/2 and 2C discharge capacity at 0°C and -20°C after charging at C/2. Both charge and discharge were conducted at low temperature. All co-solvents were added at 20% by volume to an EC/DEC/EMC (1/1/1, %v) control with 1M $LiPF_6$.

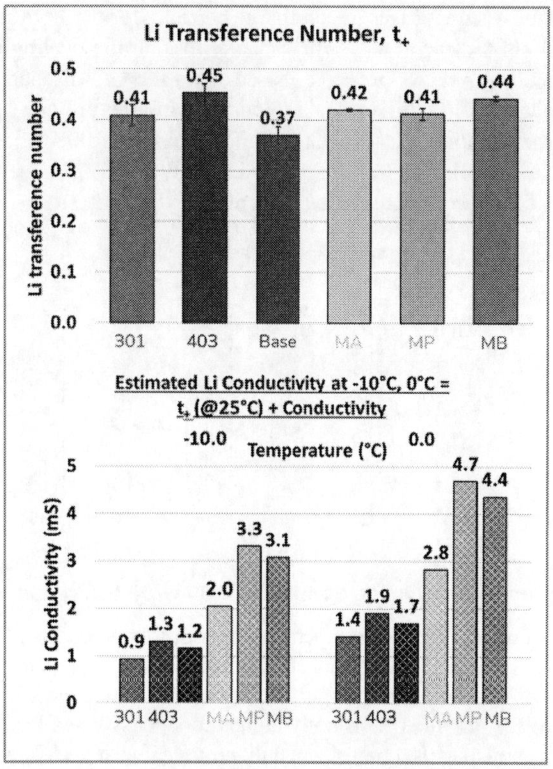

Figure 2. Li^+ Transference number (from NMR) and estimated Li^+ conductivity (at low temperature).

Figure 3 summarizes the discharge capacity at C/2 and 2C measured after 3 cycles at 0°C, and -20°C for the Koura solvent-based electrolytes compared to the carbonate control and ester electrolytes. At C/2, both the Koura electrolytes provide higher discharge capacity compared to the carbonate control while the ester co-solvents do not improve control performance. At 2C, the Koura solvents show distinct behavior. KDC-301 significantly reduces 2C discharge capacity compared to the control at all tested temperatures while KDC-403 provides similar or improved capacity compared to the control at all temperatures. The ester co-solvents provide improved 2C capacity at -10°C and -20°C.

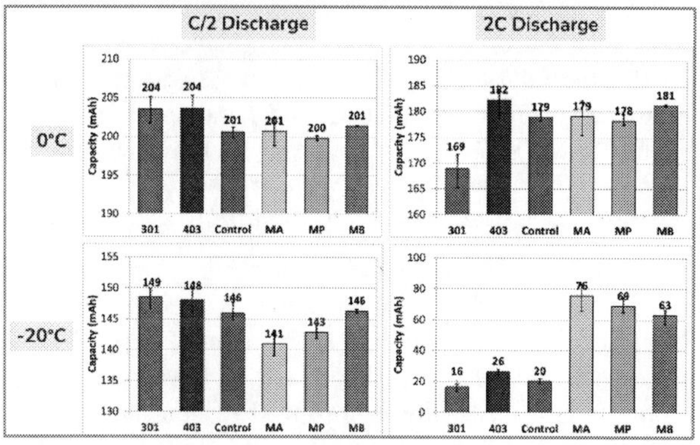

Figure 3. C/2 and 2C Rate Capability at Low Temperature

0°C cycling stability was conducted at C/2 charge and discharge after the low temperature rate capability test.

Figure 4 summarizes the discharge capacity for the 1st cycle and 100th cycle at 0°C. The capacity loss during cycling is shown in red. As expected, based upon the C/2 discharge capacity at 0°C (Figure 3), the Koura electrolytes provide the highest initial 0°C discharge capacity. After 100 cycles, KDC-403 also shows the lowest capacity loss (2.5% vs. ≥ 4% for the control and ester solvents).

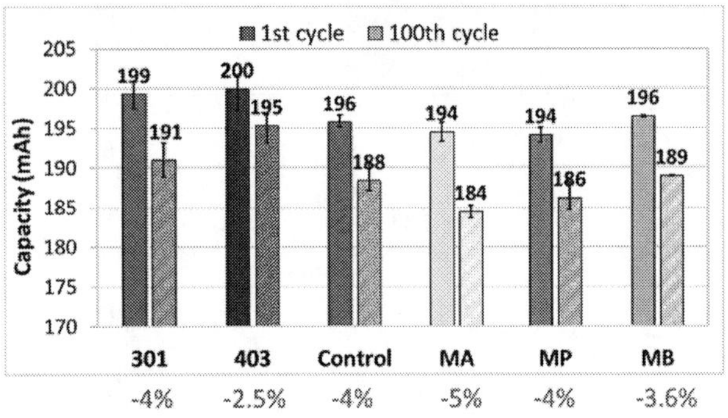

Figure 4. 0°C Cycling Stability in 4.3V Gr/NMC811 cells

In summary, the low temperature testing conducted in 4.3V Gr/NMC811 cells does not strictly follow the trend expected based upon the bulk properties. For example, the ester co-solvents provide consistently higher conductivity and lower viscosity than the control, but only provide improved LT rate capacity at 2C and -20°C. Otherwise, the ester electrolytes are similar to or worse than control. Similarly, while KDC-301 should be consistently worse than the control based upon bulk properties, it provides improved C/2 LT discharge capacity and only significantly underperforms the control at higher rates (2C, 0°C). The KDC-403 solvent shows the best agreement with the expected performance based upon bulk properties as 20% KDC-403 always provides similar or better capacity than the control during the LT rate test (0°C and -20°C) and 0°C cycling. Therefore, despite a significant decrease in 2C capacity at -20°C, the KDC-403 co-solvent provides the most comprehensive low temperature improvement compared to the control for LT rate capability and cycling stability.

Full Cell Impedance as a function of Temperature: To understand the origin of the comprehensive KDC-403 LT benefit, the full cell impedance was measured at multiple temperatures (30°C, 0°C, -20°C) and summarized in Figure 5. The 20% KDC-403 electrolyte has lower impedance at all temperatures while the ester electrolytes show higher impedance, especially at -20°C (+ 50-90%).

Comparison of the impedance, discharge capacity, and conductivity at each temperature allows the identification of the characteristics driving performance, specifically impedance vs. bulk properties. At 0°C, lower impedance results in lower capacity indicating that impedance drives performance. The same is true for C/2 capacity at -20°C. However, at 2C and -20°C, impedance does not clearly correlate with capacity while bulk conductivity does.

This comparison explains why KDC-403 can improve LT performance compared to both the control (expected based upon bulk properties) and ester electrolytes (not expected based upon bulk properties). The 20% KDC-403 electrolyte provides favorable interfacial properties that are key driving factors under specific LT conditions (all rates at moderate temperature, all temperatures at moderate rate). In contrast, the ester co-solvents excel under test conditions that exploit bulk properties and struggle under impedance-driven test conditions (likely due to the known instability of the esters[3]).

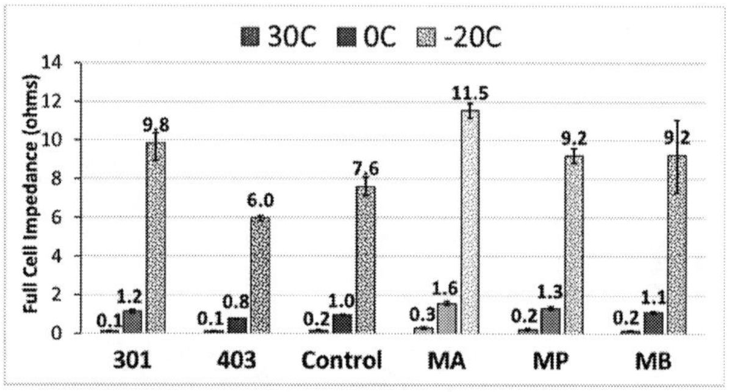

Figure 5: Impedance as a function of temperature.

High Temperature (HT) Performance in 4.3V Gr/NMC81: Cycling Stability at 45°C: To determine the best electrolyte formulation for wide operating range, HT stability was assessed by measuring cycle life at 45°C in Graphite/NMC811 pouch cells (~ 230 mAh, 4.3V – 2.75V). for the fluorinated solvents and compared to the carbonate control and ester-based electrolytes. Figure 6 shows the 45°C cycle life for representative cells and summarizes the discharge capacity for the 1st and 300th cycles.

Overall, both Koura electrolytes provide superior 45°C cycling stability. As expected, the low molecular weight ester solvents (MA, MP) show significantly lower 45°C capacity retention due to their established instability[3]. The highest molecular weight ester (MB) has lower initial 45°C capacity compared to the control with a moderate cycling improvement after 300 cycles.

Comparison of the 45°C capacity retention to the impedance before and after cycling (Figure 7) shows a clear correlation between increased cycling stability and lower impedance. KDC-403 provides the lowest impedance before and after 45°C cycling with significantly less impedance growth compared to the low molecular weight ester electrolytes.

Nyquist impedance plots (Figure 8) for selected electrolytes provide insight into the source of impedance differences. In general, the 1st and 2nd semi-circles are associated with anode and cathode impedance, respectively. KDC-403 shows significantly reduced anode impedance with similar cathode impedance while MA shows similar anode impedance as the control with significantly increased cathode impedance. In separate measurements, we found that the SEI on the graphite anode was thinner with KDC-403-based electrolyte compared to control electrolyte further supporting the impedance measurements in Figure 8.

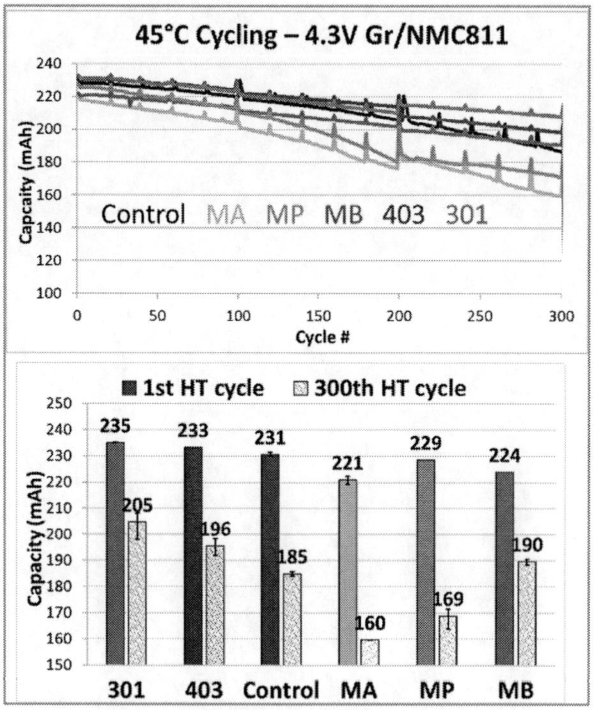

Figure 6: 45°C Cycling Stability in 4.3V Gr/NMC811 cells.

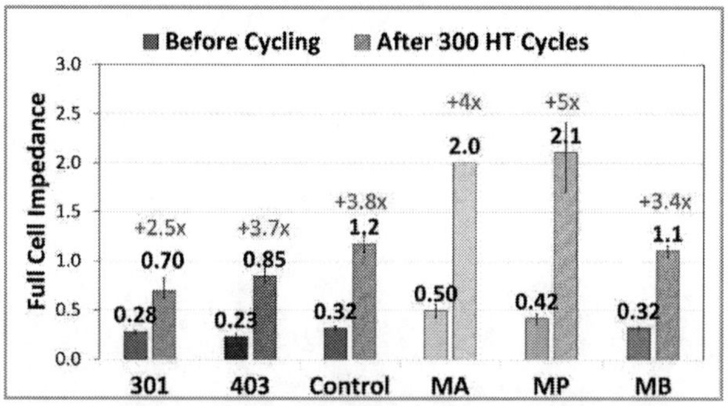

Figure 7: Full cell impedance before and after 45°C cycling.

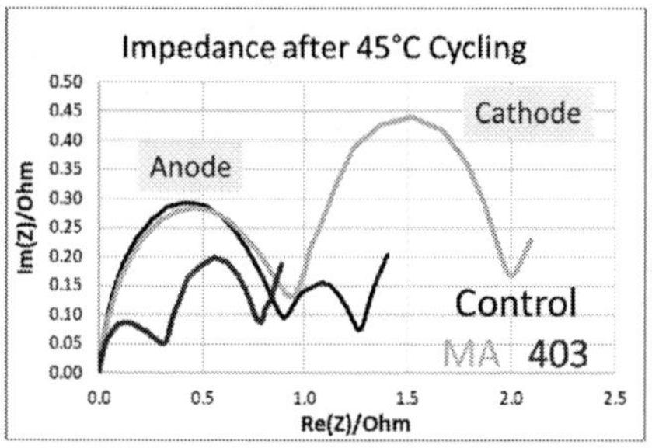

Figure 8: Nyquist plots for select electrolytes after 45°C cycling.

Gas generation during 45°C cycling is another indicator of instability of the electrolyte and/or electrode surface layers. Figure 9 shows the total gas generated during 45°C cycling (cycling data in Figure 7). Like the impedance data, there is a correlation between higher capacity retention and reduced gas generation. Overall, KDC-403 generates the least gas during 45°C cycling although both Koura electrolytes provide a benefit.

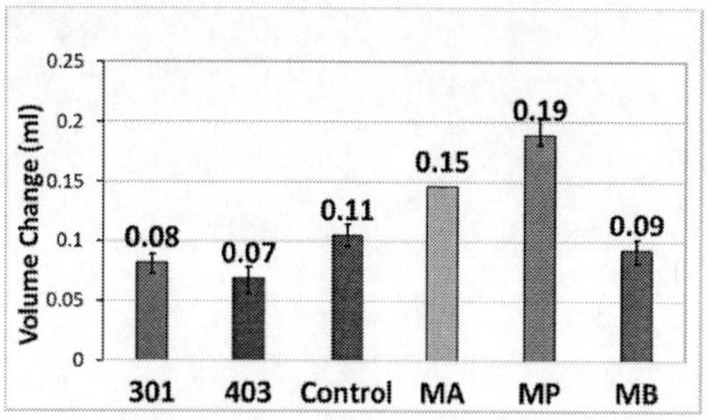

Figure 9: Gas generation during 45°C cycling.

Conclusions

In this study, the wide operating temperature performance of two fluorinated Koura materials was compared to a carbonate control and several low-temperature optimized ester electrolytes. Bulk Li^+ transport properties at low temperature (0°C, -10°C) predict that the ester co-solvents should significantly improve low temperature performance while KDC-403 should be similar to the control. However, full cell impedance measurements at low temperature show that KDC-403 provides the lowest interfacial impedance of all electrolytes tested.

Low temperature rate and cycling stability show that KDC-403 improves performance of the carbonate control when impedance is the primary factor driving capacity (all rates at 0°C, C/2 at -20°C, cycling stability at 0°C) while the ester co-solvents improve control performance where bulk properties drive capacity (2C at -20°C). 45°C cycling stability studies highlight the instability of the low molecular weight ester co-solvents with both Koura electrolytes providing superior 45°C cycling, lower impedance, and lower gas generation.

This study highlights the importance of favorable interfacial properties (i.e., lower full cell impedance, lower impedance growth during cell testing) in addition to bulk Li+ transport properties when optimizing an electrolyte for wide temperature operation.

Acknowledgements

The authors wish to thank the Department of Energy (DOE) for partial support of this work under grant DE- EE0009642.

References

1. Li, Q., et. al, 2021, Chemistry A European Journal (doi.org/10.1002/chem.202101407)
2. Wan, S., et. al, 2022, Batteries and Supercaps (doi.org/10.1002/batt.202200368)
3. Logan, E.R., et. al, *Journal of the Electrochemical Society*, **165** (2) A21-A30 (2018)

Author Index